Visit to the zoo

Written by
Tapasi De

Illustrated by
Suman S. Roy

Last Saturday I went to the zoo.

ZOO

I went with my family.

Dad drove us
to the zoo.

At first, we a
saw a tiger.

It had three
tiny cubs!

Then we saw
an elephant.

After that we went to see a gorilla.

The monkeys
were swinging.

A mamma koala
sat with her
baby!

A bear was playing with her cubs.

There were birds like blue jays, swans and robins.

We ate fruits
and sandwiches
for lunch.

In the evening
we came home
happy.

Let's spell new words

zoo

family

tiger

cubs

elephant

gorilla

lion

lioness

giraffe

monkeys

koalas

bears

sandwiches

drove

tiny

ICOM Committee for Conservation

Preprints 1996, Volume I

ICOM COMMITTEE FOR CONSERVATION

11th Triennial Meeting
Edinburgh, Scotland
1–6 September 1996

Preprints Volume I

JAMES
X
JAMES

EDITOR
Janet Bridgland

ASSOCIATE EDITOR
David Penfold

ASSISTANT EDITOR
Susan Solli

PREPRINTS COMMITTEE
Barbara A. Ramsay-Jolicoeur
National Gallery of Canada
Ottawa, Canada

E. René de la Rie
National Gallery of Art
Washington, DC, USA

Ulrich Schießl
Hochschule für Bildende Künste
Dresden, Germany

François Schweizer
Musée d'art et d'histoire
Geneva, Switzerland

Norman Tennent
Fyne Conservation Services
Argyll, Scotland

Published by James & James (Science Publishers) Ltd, Waterside House, 47 Kentish Town Road, London NW1 8NX, UK

A catalogue record for this book is available from the British Library

ISBN 1 873936 50 8

Printed in the UK by Bell & Bain Ltd, Glasgow

Available from:

James & James (Science Publishers) Ltd.
Waterside House
47 Kentish Town Road
London NW1 8NX
United Kingdom
fax: +44 171 284 3737
email: orders@jxj.com
http://www.jxj.com/

ICOM Committee for Conservation
c/o ICOM Paris
1 rue Miollis
75732 Paris Cedex 15
France
fax: +33 1 43 06 78 62
email: secretariat@icom.org

A NOTE ON THE COVER

St Gile's Church, County Hall and Lawn Market, High St, Edinburgh, from *Modern Athens displayed in a series of views, or, Edinburgh, in the nineteenth century: exhibiting the whole of the new buildings, modern improvements, antiquities & picturesque scenery, of the Scottish metropolis and its environs, from the original drawings by Mr Thomas H. Shepherd, with historical, topographical & critical illustrations.* London. Published by Jones & Co, Temple of the Muses, Finsbury Square 1 January 1829

Contents/Table des matières

Volume I

Working Group A1

Preventive Conservation/Conservation préventive

Working Group A2

Training in Conservation and Restoration/Formation en conservation et restauration

Working Group A3

Theory and History of Restoration/Théorie et histoire de la restauration

Working Group A4

Scientific Examination of Works of Art/Investigation scientifique des oeuvres d'art

Working Group B1

Paintings I: Conservation and Restoration of Paintings/Peinture I: Conservation et restauration des peintures

Working Group B2

Paintings II: Scientific Study of Paintings/Peinture II: Etude scientifique des peintures

Working Group B3

Polychrome Sculpture/Sculpture polychrome

Working Group B4

Mural Paintings and Rock Art/Peintures murales et art rupestre

Volume II

Working Group B5

Graphic Documents/Documents graphiques

Working Group B6

Photographic Records/Documents photographiques

Working Group B7

Ethnographic Collections/Collections ethnographiques

Working Group B16

Resins: Characterization and Evaluation/Résines: Caractérisation et évaluation

Working Group C

Modern Materials/Matériaux modernes

Editor's Note

The preparation of this edition of the Preprints has, once again, been a complex, though rewarding process. Attempts to improve upon past procedures, combined with the implementation of a revised Working Group structure have provided no small challenge to those involved in the production of these volumes. I would like to thank all concerned – authors, Working Group Coordinators, Preprints Committee and publishers – for their collaboration and shared commitment to a professional publication.

Much as I would like to think that we have arrived at an optimum system for producing the Preprints, recent experience suggests that we need to go back to the drawing board one more time.

We aspire to achieve the polished quality of a refereed publication, yet we give authors the latest possible date for submitting their work, on the basis that the Preprints represent the state-of-the-art thinking for the complete Triennial Meeting period. As those involved can attest, this results in nearly impossible deadlines at all other stages of the process. There is insufficient time to consult with Coordinators on the final selection of papers, with authors regarding proposed changes to their manuscripts, or to conduct a thorough review of the papers before going to press.

We also aspire to be representative – geographically as well as by material and discipline covered. More time must be built into the process to ensure that neither of these goals gets overlooked.

I am confident that with our combined experience, we can make the necessary adjustments to arrive at a system that works for us all. Your suggestions are welcomed.

In closing I would like to dedicate my work on these volumes to my Mother, whose support and guidance endure despite her recent passing.

Janet Bridgland
Monitcello, USA
August 1996

These Preprints are dedicated to Dr Harold J. Plenderleith in recognition of his outstanding contribution to the practice of conservation, on the occasion of the Committee's 11th Triennial Meeting in his native Scotland

Working Group A1

Preventive conservation

Lethal Effects of Low Pressure ('Vacuum') on some Museum Pest Insects

J.-E. Bergh,* H. Mourier and K. P. Poulsen
Dalarna University College,
79188 Falun, Sweden

Abstract

The survival after treatment in low pressure (20–100 hPa) of six insect species, known as pests on cultural objects, has been determined. Vacuum as a method for insect control is discussed.

Keywords

Insects, pest control, vaccuum, fumigation

Introduction

As Gilberg and Roach[1] recently discussed, there is an increasing interest in developing non-chemical methods for the control of pest insects in museums, archives and libraries. Since there is an increase in the number of countries where fumigation with ethylene dioxide is becoming illegal, one strategy has been to find harmless methods where fumigation chambers could be used. Principally there are two approaches, either using so-called modified atmosphere (nitrogen or carbon dioxide) or low-pressure (vacuum) treatment. This paper discusses the latter method.

Earlier papers reveal that there is a great difference in response to low pressures between different species, even if they belong to the same genus (see, for example, El Nahal,[2] Xue Yi et al.[3] and Bergh[4]). Several other experiments on the lethal effect of low pressures have been published, e.g. Back and Cotton,[5] Livingstone and Reed,[6] Bhambani,[7] Bergh[8] and Bergh et al.[9]

The variables which are important to study are both biological (species, developmental stage, physiological conditions etc.) and physical (pressure level, time of exposure, temperature). In many papers, figures for relative humidity are given. However, in an environment where the pressure is just a few per cent of the normal atmospheric pressure, the ordinary methods for measuring this variable lose their relevance.

Experimental

The following species have been used in the experiments: *Anthrenus museorum* (L.), *A. verbasci* (L.), *Attagenus woodroffei* (Halstead & Green) (Figure 1), *Ptinus tectus* Boieldieu, *Trogoderma angustum* (Solier) and *Tineola bisselliella* (Hummel).

The investigation was run in two main series:

- Series A, with a fixed pressure of 20 hPa, and three different time-spans of 6, 12 and 24 h.
- Series B, where the time was constant (24 h) and the pressure was 22, 30, 50 or 100 hPa. For details, see Tables 1 and 2.

(Pa = pascal. h=100. Normal atmospheric pressure, 1000 hPa, 100 kPa).

For both series, animals from the cultures of the Danish Pest Infestation Laboratory were used. *T. bisselliella*, *A. woodroffei* and *P. tectus* were kept at about 25°C and 65% RH. *A. museorum*, *A. verbasci* and *T. angustum* were kept at varying room temperature (normally 20 to 24°C) and in fairly dry air (20 to 50% RH).

The diets of the test species were:

- *T. biselliella*, woollen cloth dusted with dried yeast.
- *A.woodroffei*, *A. verbasci* and *A. museorum*, woollen cloth, crushed dog biscuit, fish meal and dried house flies.
- *P. tectus*, wheat bran, rye meal, fish meal and dry yeast.
- *T. angustum*, woollen cloth, crushed dog biscuits and dried house flies.

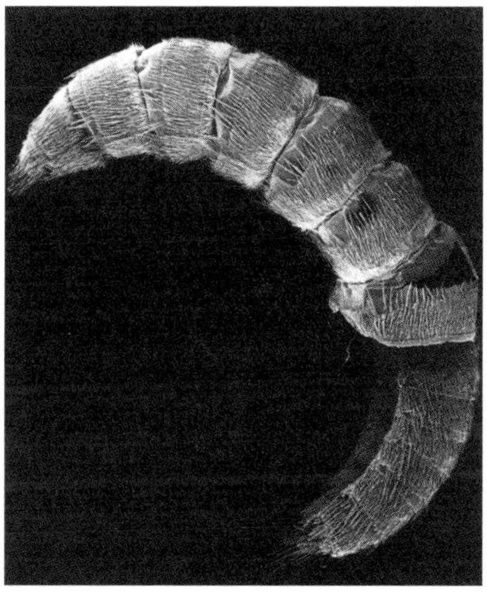

Figure 1. Larvae of Attagenus woodroffei *interrupted during moulting by a vacuum treatment experiment. Magnification × 11 (SEM-photo Gary Wife)*

* Author to whom correspondence should be addressed

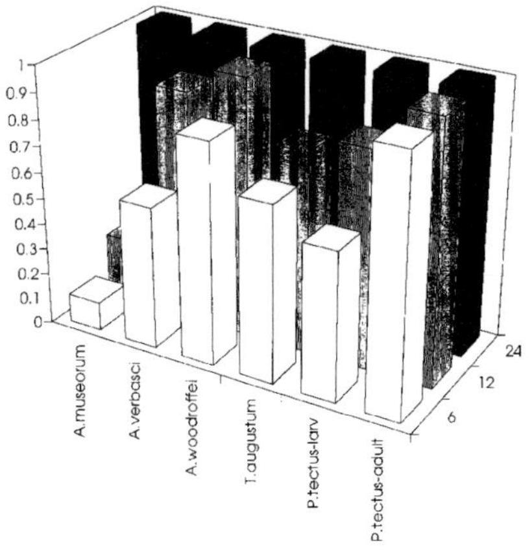

Figure 2. Proportion dead by species and exposure time (h)

Table 1. Effect of vacuum treatment (20 hPa) on pest insects: l larvae; a adults (imagines). *Control conditions showed no, or only negligible, effect on death rate and weight loss*

Species	Exposure (h)	Number	Proportion dead (%)	Weight loss (%)	LT_{50} (h)	Estimated time for 99% dead (h)
Anthrenus	6	100	11.0	11.7	13.5	42.5 (33.6–60.9)
museorum (l)	12	107	25.2	19.9		
	24	80	100.0	32.4		
Anthrenus	6	100	55.0	19.0	5.7	24.7 (18.4–41.6)
verbasci (l)	12	100	89.0	31.8		
	24	99	100.0	42.4		
Attagenus	6	100	85.0	22.9	4.0	11.7 (9.0–39.4)
woodroffei (l)	12	100	99.0	38.2		
	24	101	100.0	47.9		
Trogoderma	6	100	68.0	32.9	4.4	56.4 (33.3–169.9)
angustum (l)	12	100	77.0	41.9		
	24	99	100.0	47.6		
Ptinus	6	100	57.0	36.5	5.5	35.3 (23.1–84.5)
tectus (l)	12	70	82.9	45.4		
	24	61	100.0	50.5		
Ptinus	6	100	98.0	38.3	–	–
tectus (a)	12	100	100.0	46.0		
	24	100	100.0	44.8		
Tineola	12	39	100.0	58.1	–	–
bisselliella (l)						
Tineola	12	29	100.0	–	–	–
bisselliella (a)	24	66	100.0	–		

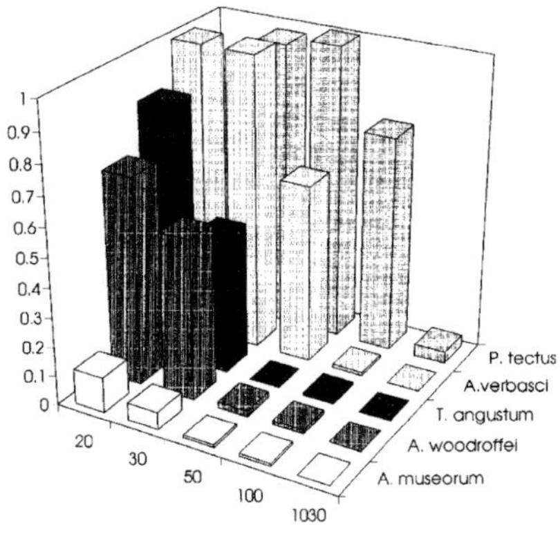

Figure 3. Proportion dead by species and pressure (hPa)

The experimental animals of each species were placed in two (series A) or four (series B) 100 ml plastic tubes. Control animals were moved into one tube and all the tubes were covered with gauze. The controls were stored under normal culturing conditions. The weight of both the experimental and the control animals was recorded. The experimental tubes were then placed in the vacuum chamber at a temperature of 20.5 to 21.5°C, and air was evacuated. Evacuation time was about two minutes. After the treatment, the pressure was raised to normal in the chamber which took one to two minutes. The tubes were immediately put into an desiccator, and the animals were weighed.

Survival of the insects was checked directly after the weighing process and after 24 and 48 h. If an animal showed movement when exposed to tactile stimuli it was regarded as alive. After series A the surviving insects were observed during a 14-day period in order to see whether any long-term damage could be detected.

The vacuum chamber was constructed as a cylinder with a flat bottom and a glass door in front. Inner dimensions are 34 cm in diameter and 52 cm in length, giving a volume of about 45 liters. The chamber is equipped with a thermometer and a shelf where the test tubes are placed.

Pressure was measured by a Leybold DIAVAC DV1000, a mechanical type vacuum meter with a scale from 1000 hPa to 1 hPa. The meter has a logarithmic scale and it is fairly accurate in the low-pressure area, from 100 hPa downwards.

Table 2. Effect of vacuum treatment (24 h) on larvae of pest insects. Control conditions showed no, or only negligible, effect on death rate and weight loss

Species	Exposure (hPa)	Number	Proportion dead (%)	Weight loss (%)
Anthrenus	100	100	1.0	1.7
museorum	50	100	1.0	4.1
	30–26	100	6.0	9.2
	22–19.5	100	12.0	13.3
Anthrenus 100	100	1.0	7.1	
verbasci	50	102	60.8	23.8
	30–26	100	100	34.7
	22–19.5	100	100	40.3
Attagenus	100	75	1.3	1.7
woodroffei	50	51	2.0	7.9
	30–26	75	54.7	31.9
	22–19.5	75	70.7	36.1
Trogoderma	100	99	1.0	1.6
angustum	50	100	0	7.0
	30–26	101	46.5	30.2
	22–19.5	100	86.0	40.5
Ptinus tectus	100	77	74.0	31.1
	50	75	100	38.3
	30–26	75	97.3	41.9
	22–19.5	74	85.1	31.7

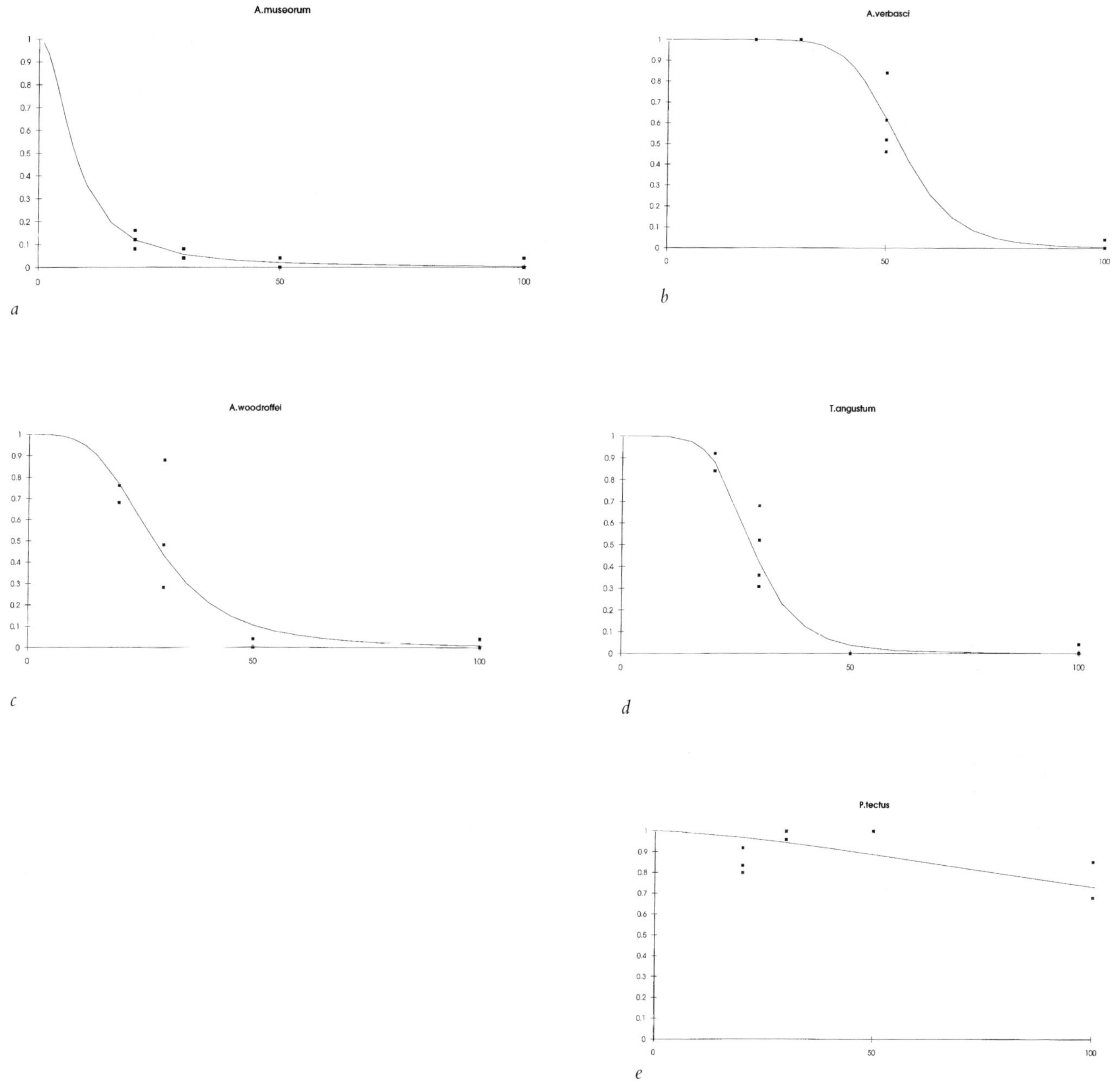

Figure 4. Death rate as a function of pressure (hPa) for the species (a) Anthrenus museorum*; (b)* Anthrenus verbasci*; (c)* Attagenus woodroffei*; (d)* Trogoderma angustum*; (e)* Ptinus tectus

An oil-sealed vacuum pump produced by Leybold was used. The various parts of the vacuum system were connected by solid rubber tubes and equipped with a number of valves so that pressure could be accurately controlled within ±0.5 hPa and the vacuum pump could be protected from oil being sucked up in the vacuum chamber.

Control of pressure was manual, and for some of the more time-consuming experiments deviations occured as a result of lack of close supervision. During series B, it was not possible to keep the pressure constant; during the last hours the pressure fell. Thus 100 hPa actually represents 100–98 hPa, 50 hPa is 50–48 hPa, 30 hPa is 30–26 hPa and 22 hPa, finally, stands for a range of 22–19.5 hPa.

Statistical analysis of the survival data was performed using probit regression,[10] with the Probit procedure of the SAS package.[11] For analysis of the weight loss data, the GLM and REG procedures of the SAS package were used.

Results and discussion

The results for series A are shown in Table 1 and Figures 2, 5, 7 and for series B in Table 2 and Figures 3, 4, 6. A discussion of the results is given below. During observation of the animals surviving the treatments no abnormal behaviour could be seen.

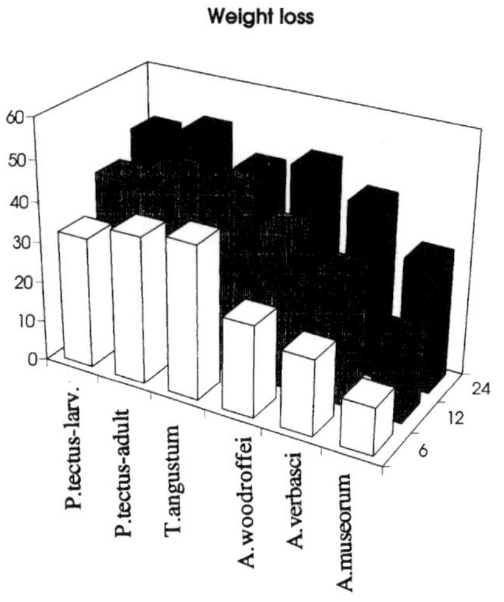

Figure 5. Weight loss (%) by species and time (h)

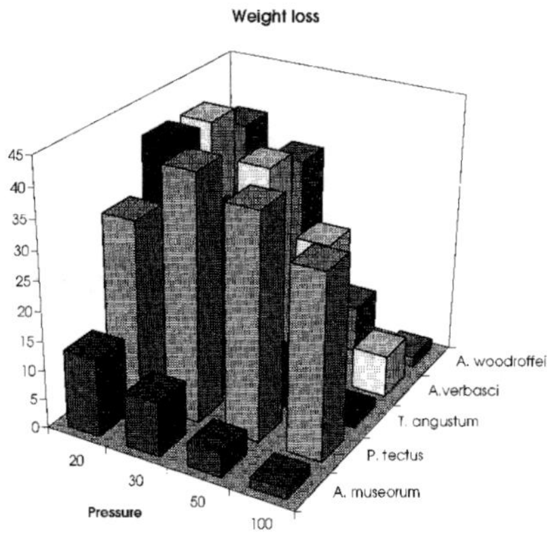

Figure 6. Weight loss (%) by species and pressure (hPa)

Series A

As can be seen in Table 1, none of the animals survived a treatment of 20 hPa for 24 h. After 12 h exposure adult *P. tectus* and larvae and imagines of *T. bisselliella* were dead. Only one out of 100 *A. woodroffei* survived this exposure. During the 6 h exposure *T. bisselliella* was not used because of lack of experimental animals and as a consequence of this the statistical calculations do not include this species. It should be stressed, however, that *T. bisselliella* showed a mortality rate of 100% during the 12 and 24 h tests. When exposed for 6 h, none of the tested species showed 100% mortality. 100% mortality rate must, of course, be the aim of a treatment.

It is of interest to compare the two *Anthrenus* species. *A. museorum* proves to be more resistant to vacuum treatment than *A. verbasci*, which could be seen both from mortality and weight loss (loss of water) figures. This is in agreement with the observations of Bergh.[4] In fact the analysis has shown that *A. verbasci*, *P. tectus* (larvae) and *T. angustum* significantly differ from *A. museorum*, *A. woodroffei* and *P.tectus* (adults).

The differences between species are also obvious when the weight loss factor is taken into account (Figures 5, 7 and Table 1). A two-tailed variance analysis shows a significant difference between species ($p < 0.0001$) as well as a significant effect of time ($p < 0.0001$). In more detail the analysis gives as result that *P. tectus* (larvae and adults) and *T. angustum* have the greatest weight loss without differing significantly from each other. *T. angustum* does not differ significantly from *A.woodroffei*. *A. verbasci* differs significantly from all other species, and this is true also for *A. museorum* which has the smallest weight loss.

Table 1 shows LD_{50} values and and an estimated exposure time for 99% mortality (mean and fiducial limits). For two of the species, *A. museorum* and *T.angustum*, the model's suitability to the behaviour of the species is poorer, e.g. there is no 'linear' correlation between time and mortality. Regression analysis has shown a good level of correlation between weight loss and death rate, and in fact desiccation is a probable cause of death in this treatment as proposed by Livingstone and Reed[6] and Bambhani.[7]

Series B

As a consequence of the results discussed above it was natural to try to find a threshold value for the pressure in a 24 h treatment. The four different pressures tested were chosen so as to get a closer interval in the lowest-pressure region and to investigate the effect of a pressure close to 20 hPa.

As mentioned earlier, this series was characterized by a somewhat falling pressure – from 22 hPa at the beginning to 19.5 hPa at the end of the exposure

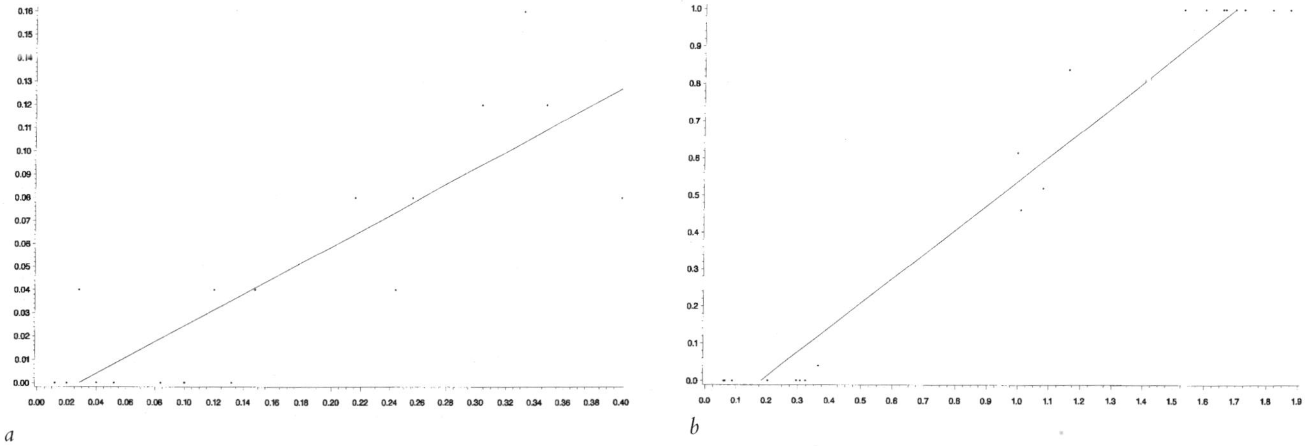

Figure 7. Death rate plotted versus weight loss for (a) Anthrenus museorum *and (b)* A. verbasci

period. Though not planned, this difference between Series A and B turned out to be very interesting, as it indicates that the 24 h threshold value for *A. museorum* is very close to 20 hPa. These results also show that keeping the pressure below the threshold value is extremely important, thus classifying the vacuum method as vulnerable.

The weight loss in relation to the pressure used is shown in Table 2 and Figure 6.

Bergh[4] found that specimen of *A. woodroffei*, *A.museorum* and *T. angustum* could survive 48 h in a pressure of 1–3% of the atmospheric pressure (roughly 10–30 hPa). These experiments were performed with less accurate measuring equipment, but in the light of the results discussed above, there seems not to be a disagreement between the earlier and the later results. The two species of the genus *Anthrenus* showed significantly differing tolerances to low pressures.

Differences in response between related species have been observed and discussed by El Nahal,[2] Bhambani[7] and Xue Yi et al.[3] As the regulation of the water balance is primarily due to the spiracle activity,[12] it is proposed that there is a difference between the species in regulating the closing of the spiracles causing the variation in response.

The museum pest insects also occupy niches in nature, and it should be of interest to look more closely at selection factors in natural breeding areas for the pest species. Such a review lies, however, outside the scope of this study. It is well known that different development stages of insects differ in tolerance to treatment methods. The authors also plan to study eggs, pupae and imagines.

A method for control of museum pest insects must be not only effective in killing the animals but also harmless to the objects. If the vacuum method does turn out to be useful, it will be necessary to check its impact on different types of material.

Acknowledgements

We are grateful to collegues for valuable criticism. Dr Ulf Olsson is thanked for statistical analysis and thanks are also given to Mr Andrew Casson for linguistic revision. The work was financed by a grant from The Swedish Work Environment Fund.

References

1. M. Gilberg and A. Roach, 'The Use of a Commercial Pheromone Trap for Monitoring Lasioderma Serricorne (F.) Infestations in Museum Collections', *Studies in Conservation* 36 (1991): 243–247.
2. A.K.M. El Nahal, 'Responses of Pests to Fumigation. IV – The Responses of *Calandra spp.* to Reduced Pressures', *Bulletin of Entomological Research* 44 (1954): 651–656.
3. Xue Yi, K.-M. Vagn-Jensen, H. Mourier and K.P. Poulsen, 'Laboratory Studies on Vacuum for the Control of Insects in Foodstuffs', *Food and Bioproducts Processing* 70, C (1992): 91–96.
4. J.-E. Bergh, 'Effekten av Vakuum på Larver av Museiskadegörare' *in Nordiskt Symposium om Bekämpning av Skadedjur i Museer*, ed. A. Stenmark and M. Åkerlund, Stockholm, May 1993, (Stockholm: Nordiska kommittén för skadedjur i museer and Naturhistoriska Riksmuseet, 1993), 67–74 (summary in English).
5. E.A. Back and R.T. Cotton, 'The Use of vacuum for Insect Control', *Journal of Agricultural Research* XXXI, no. 11 (1925): 1035–1040.
6. E.M. Livingstone and W.D. Reed, 'Water Vapour as a Factor Affecting the Survival of *Ephestia Elutella* and *Lasioderma Serricorne* at Reduced Pressure', *Entomological Society of America. Annals* Vol.XXXIII (1940): 583–587.
7. H.J. Bhambhani, 'Recent Advances in Vacuum Fumigation', *World Review of Pest Control* 3, no. 1 (1964): 53–56.
8. J.-E. Bergh, 'Vakuumkammare som Insektbekämpningsmedel. I. Vanliga Mjölbaggen, *Tenebrio molitor* L., *Colepotera, Tenebrionidae*', *Meddelelser om Konservering* 1 (1988): 89–93.
9. J.-E. Bergh, K. Karlsson, A. Stenmark and M. Åkerlund, 'Vakuumkammare som Insektbekämpningsmedel. II. *Anobium Rufipes* F.(*Col., Anobiidae*),' *Meddelelser om Konservering* 1 (1988): 93–96.
10. D.J. Finney, *Probit Analysis*, 3rd edn, (London: Cambridge University Press, 1971).
11. SAS Institute, *SAS/STAT User's Guide*, (Cary, NC: SAS Institute Inc., n.d.)
12. V.B. Wigglesworth, *The Principles of Insect Physiology* (London: Chapman and Hall, 7th edn. 1982).

Development of an Environmental Policy for the British Museum

Susan Bradley
Department of Conservation, The British Museum,
London WC1B 3DG

Abstract

The paper discusses the development of an environmental policy for the British Museum. The influence of the way the collection is used, the restrictions of the grade 1 listed building, the stability of the collection, and the results of deterioration studies carried out by the Museum conservation scientists, have been the main factors in defining the policy as a pragmatic document. The environmental factors of most concern are temperature, relative humidity, ultraviolet and visible light, insects, and handling.

Keywords

Museum, environment, policy, humidity, temperature, light, handling

Introduction

The purpose of the British Museum is to hold in trust for the Nation, and in perpetuity, those parts of the National collections in its care; to ensure their accessibility; and to promote knowledge of, and enjoyment in, the subject areas covered by the collection.[1]

In 1992 the Museum Director asked the Department of Conservation to write an environmental policy for the Museum. In the policy document the environmental parameters of concern in the Museum were identified as temperature, relative humidity (RH), atmospheric gases, atmospheric pollutants, particulates, ultraviolet (UV) light, visible light, insects and handling. The policy document represented the first attempt to take a global view of the collection needs.

The main factors informing the policy have been the purpose of the Museum and use of the collection; the constraints of the grade 1 listed building; observation of the stability of the collection in the ambient environments within the Museum; resultant deterioration studies; financial considerations.

Use of the collection

The purpose of the Museum is to hold the collections 'in perpetuity' and to 'ensure their accessibility'. The objects are protected by security and conservation. They are made accessible by curation which includes publishing catalogues, and study of the collection by the Museum's own curators and visiting academics and students; by exhibition within the galleries and on loan to other institutions and to other countries; by the education programme which may include handling of objects in the collection by students, parties of school children and special interest groups.

The British Museum collections are hence seen as working collections; objects are not only handled regularly, they are also sampled for scientific investigations, including deterioration studies. Since the collection contains over six million objects handling of individual objects does not occur every day. The Department of Conservation can make a case for limiting access to an individual object if it can be shown a particular regime for storage would limit deterioration to a substantial extent. But an environmental policy for the collection must be based on accessibility.

The Museum building

The British Museum exhibition galleries are in the main Museum at Bloomsbury and the Museum of Mankind in Piccadilly, where the Ethnography collection is exhibited. The Museum of Mankind is due to close before the end of the century and be relocated to Bloomsbury. The Museum was built between 1823 and 1850 by the architect Sir Robert Smirke. Later additions were the Round Reading Room in the centre of the quadrant and the King Edward Building to the north of the site. The Museum has listed building status, which considerably limits any alterations to those which are not visible from street level around the building, and which do not interfere with the integrity of the internal architecture. Although the present building was built for the Museum, the size of the collection and the number of curatorial and support departments, and associated staff, has grown substantially since 1850. There is also pressure to exhibit more of the collection. The number of visitors each year is now about six million, many more than the building can sustain.

In the 1980s the roof of the King Edward building was raised to create a complex of air-conditioned galleries for the exhibition of the Japanese collection, Oriental scrolls and works of art on paper, and the collection of the Prints and Drawings Department. The decision to build these galleries with full air conditioning was made because of the response of paper and composite organic structures to changes in RH and temperature. The galleries are used for temporary exhibitions of objects from the collections and loans from other institutions. Exhibitions are normally of three to six months duration, although Japanese scrolls are by convention only exhibited for two months.

The Japanese gallery complex and the special exhibitions gallery, built in the development of a bomb-damaged area of the building in the 1970s, are the main galleries which have no natural light. Most galleries in the Museum have windows or skylights. In past gallery refurbishments these were often blocked. Now, as galleries are redeveloped, the original architecture is being revealed. The glass in the skylights is being replaced with double-glazed units containing a UV absorbing layer, an infrared reflecting layer and a light-reducing film. This has the effect of reducing the UV level to less than 50 μwatts per lumen. The visible light level is considerably reduced, but in the summer it is not uncommon for levels of over 5,000 lux to be achieved around midday. Where light sensitive objects are an integral part of an exhibition, they have to be positioned in the shadow of other objects, beneath black glass shelves or in showcases facing away from the skylights to reduce light exposure. Another effect of the skylights is increased temperature in the galleries during the summer.

As so much of the collection presently exhibited at Bloomsbury consists of objects which are stable, see below, the installation of air conditioning in all of the galleries is not necessary. Organic objects that are particularly sensitive to changes in RH can be displayed in showcases which are individually controlled using humidifiers, and actively corroding metals in showcases with dehumidifiers.[2] If a showcase is only humidified, the required maximum is likely to be exceeded during the ambient peak of RH in the summer. Similarly if a showcase is only dehumidified, the required minimum may be exceeded during the winter trough in ambient RH. Even so the RH monitoring within the showcases is for at least 11 months of every year within ±4–5% of the set point. There is no temperature control in the galleries and this affects the absolute moisture content of the air surrounding, and interacting with, the objects. Nevertheless the objects in the 23 showcases controlled in this manner have shown no evidence of deterioration.

The Museum is to undergo a massive development over the next ten years, with the creation of new public areas and new galleries for the Ethnography collection. At present environmental control in Ethnography exhibitions is for the most part achieved through RH control in showcases. There have been no instances of objects on exhibition undergoing damage as a result of the environmental conditions, which on occasions have reached temperatures of over 30°C. Introducing air conditioning for the new Ethnographic galleries would give increased environmental stability and reduce the levels of the pollutant gases and dust. The disadvantages of installing air conditioning are the costs of installation, maintenance, running, and ultimately replacement, as well as the impact of plant and ducting on the architecture of the building. Conditioning the whole gallery and thus introducing temperature control, would benefit both objects and visitors because of the high summer temperatures experienced in recent years.

The stability of the collection

The British Museum has a strong tradition of scientific investigation of the collection to establish the cause and treatment of deterioration. During storage of much of the collection in underground railway tunnels during World War I deterioration of bronze, iron, pottery, stone and paper objects occurred. Dr Alexander Scott was employed to investigate the problems and he later became the first head of the Research Laboratory. By the 1950s the scientists had gained a good understanding of the problems caused by incorrect environments, RH and temperature, particularly with regard to the dimensional stability of organic materials, and these were summarised by Plenderleith.[3]

In the 1950s and 60s Robert Organ carried out research on bronze disease and, in conjunction with Mavis Bimson, on weeping and crizzling glass. Organ measured the length of time that basic copper chloride takes to form on cuprous chloride exposed to different relative humidities, showing that at 35% cuprous chloride ... 'appears to be stable indefinitely'.[4] As a result of Organ's work, mechanically controlled showcases, and later a bronze store, were installed in the Museum to stabilise actively deteriorating bronze (or copper alloy) objects.[5] The control equipment is still functioning and the dehumidified environment has prevented the continuing deterioration of this group of objects. The construction, and the rationale behind, a dehumidified case for storing unstable glass was published in 1957.[6] Although the case described in the article was dismantled in 1993, it was replaced with one of similar design, using a modern drying-wheel type dehumidifier. Again the use of the case has prevented the deterioration of a number of important glass pieces.

Later Alfred Werner introduced air-conditioned storage to 20 ± 2°C and 35 ± 5% RH, to prevent flaking and powdering of a group of sculptures from Amaravati in Andhra Pradesh, India. The rationale for this installation was the difference in climate between the site of the stupa and London. The benefits were proved when the air conditioning failed and the sculptures began to flake. A subsequent investigation of the stone revealed an inherent susceptibility to fluctuations in RH, leading to expansion and contraction of the stone.[7] Werner also introduced humidified storage for the Ethnography collection, when it was moved to a new Museum store in 1971–72. This simple system uses plumbed-in humidifiers to control the RH to 50–60% RH, without controlling temperature.

More recently, a study of sugar objects which were becoming brown has shown that the reaction involved will not proceed if the sugars are kept at 30 ± 5% and 15 ± 2°C,[8] and a study of salt crystallisation on ceramics has identified the movement of objects from an uncontrolled, but stable, store to a damp store in the Museum basement, as the cause. Movement of objects into new stores, without checking that the environment is either the same as, or better than, that of the existing store, has been the cause of a number of deterioration problems investigated during the last ten years.

In the late 1960s and early 1970s investigations into the corrosion of metals by gases evolved from materials used in the storage and display of antiquities were started. A simple corrosion test that could be used to screen materials for potential corrosive effects was devised in the laboratory.[10–12] To date over 3,000 materials have been screened for their suitability for use in the storage and display of the collection. Now the only instances of corrosion of metals caused by outgassing which occur are when the materials for storage and display have never been tested, i.e. they were installed before testing started, or have been used incorrectly, or as a result of outgassing from other objects. Several instances of sulphide-containing gas emissions from objects excavated in waterlogged contexts have been identified. The extent of the problem is currently being assessed. Sulphide gases are also given off by objects made from materials such as wool, leather and parchment, and volatile organic compounds by wood or objects containing wood products.

Even after elimination of additional sources of corrosive gases, the adverse effects of the corrosive gases present in the ambient air in the Museum have to be considered. An absorbent material, zinc oxide pellets, is in the final stages of evaluation for use in the galleries in showcases containing silver. The absorbent reduces the rate of tarnishing of silver by the ambient air by taking up sulphide gases.[13–14] In storage areas charcoal cloth can be used to prevent the corrosion of lead by emissions of the lower carboxylic acids from wood storage cabinets. Fortunately, the Museum has not experienced widespread damage of objects by volatile organic carbonyls as a result of the use of wood in storage areas and in showcases. There is some circumstantial evidence which suggests outgassing from woods is increased during periods of high RH and/or temperature.

Since the 1960s the light level in the Department of Prints and Drawings temporary exhibitions has been 50 lux, with UV reduced to below 75 μwatts per lumen. Only few of the works of art receive more than very occasional exhibition, and none are exposed for the maximum 200 klux-h suggested.[15] The very real difficulties experienced by many visitors in viewing detail at 50 lux was evidenced in the number of complaints received on this subject. In 1989 it was proposed to accept a Japanese recommendation of a visible light level of 80 lux in the new Japanese galleries. The decision was then made to increase the light level in the Prints and Drawings gallery to 80 lux. In both galleries the ambient UV level was below 50 μwatts per lumen. The result is that the objects are more visible, the complaints have disappeared, and there has been no monitorable alteration of the works of art on exhibition.

Insects and biodeterioration problems could pose a substantial threat to the organic objects in the collection, particularly within the Department of Ethnography. Recently, measures have been taken to prevent insects entering the stores and to ensure that any signs of infestation are dealt with immediately. On entering the collection, and on returning from loan, objects are sterilised using a freezing regime. A small nitrogen fumigation chamber is in the process of being installed for objects which it is thought would be unsafe to freeze.

A recent review of storage in the Museum has identified the most important cause of damage as poor handling regimes and overcrowded storage.[16] These issues are both being addressed. The Department of Conservation has put on training courses on handling that cover all aspects of use of the collection, and will continue to do so. The Museum has accepted a new policy on storage, and is in the process of developing a building close to the Bloomsbury site as a central store.

It is notable that documents giving recommendations on environments for collection care rarely agree; and that recommendations overlap to an extent which suggests that a broad band of RH is likely to prove acceptable for a large part of any collection. Recent work by other groups of researchers has supported this view.[17–18] For the Museum collection, which contains every type of material except oil paintings, preserved natural history specimens and large machinery, this proves to be so on visual observation. Clearly visual observation is unlikely to reveal that a very slow chemical or physical change is taking place; only that a major change has occurred. Where groups of objects have shown signs of deterioration, these have been obvious and have continued to appear over long periods of time. Where a controlled environment has been imposed to stabilise objects, loss of the environment has resulted in the visible signs of the deterioration reappearing. This suggests that the major part of the collection, which appears to be stable, actually is stable in the ambient conditions of 35–65% RH and 15–30°C that prevail in the Museum.

The Environmental policy

Considering the evidence available from the collection it was decided that a policy document should not be a list of acceptable ranges of temperature, RH, pollutant and particulate levels. It should be a pragmatic document, putting the emphasis on improving conditions for objects whenever possible, taking into consideration published standards and new research on environments for collection care, but mindful of the constraints imposed by the Museum building and financial resources. The statement of policy is reproduced below. This statement is supported by two appendices. Appendix 1 gives information on the effects of environmental factors on the collections; Appendix 2 gives an overview of environmental requirements of the collection and the methods by which control may be achieved.

Environmental policy for the preservation of the collections in the British Museum[19]

Introduction

The purpose of the British Museum, as stated in its corporate plan 'is to hold in trust for the Nation, and in perpetuity, those parts of the national collections given into its care'. In pursuance of this, the first of the Museum's aims is 'to curate and conserve the collections to the highest possible standards'.

Thus the Museum undertakes to minimise the factors which cause or accelerate deterioration. It cannot prevent deterioration because such reactions are thermodynamically favoured and will inevitably proceed, albeit at a very slow rate in many cases.

There are several factors which contribute to the deterioration of artefacts in the Museum's care; the way the artefacts are stored, displayed and handled and the atmospheric environment in which these activities take place. Damage occurring during poor storage, exhibition and handling is often of a physical nature and can be catastrophic, such as when an artefact is dropped. Damage occurring from poor ambient environment is a mixture of chemical and physical change. It usually occurs slowly, remaining undetected until a physical manifestation occurs, but can be equally catastrophic.

This policy document deals with the prevention of damage to the collection from environmental factors including handling.

The Policy

1 It is the policy of the British Museum that its collections should be stored, exhibited and curated in environments which are conducive to their preservation and that the Department of Conservation should be consulted about these environments.

2 In pursuance of this, the Museum will control, when possible, any of the factors listed below which are shown to be deleterious to any group of objects.
Temperature
Relative humidity
Atmospheric gases
Pollutant gases
Particulates
Ultraviolet light
Visible light
Insects
Handling

3 The Museum will be mindful of national and international guidelines on environmental parameters for the prevention of deterioration, but will consider the history of its own collections, in that this may modify the need for control of environment. This may be particularly so where an object suffered deterioration before being brought into the Museum, but has since come into equilibrium with the environment and is no longer deteriorating.

4 The Museum will consider upgrading environmental control for artefacts when:
(a) artefacts are shown to be deteriorating and the cause is attributable to unsuitable environmental conditions;
(b) storage and exhibition facilities are being upgraded.
In these circumstances, the advice of the Department of Conservation will be sought. The antiquity department concerned, British Museum Works Office, the Design Office and the Department of Conservation will work together to formulate and implement an appropriate strategy.

5 The Museum will consider setting up interdepartmental stores for types of artefacts which would benefit from environmental control

6 The Museum will not normally expose any of its collections to extremes of temperature and relative humidity, other than the summer peak conditions during July and August and winter minimum conditions during January and February each year, except when extremes can be shown to be beneficial to certain objects.

7 The Museum will not expose the collections to sustained high levels of ultraviolet light. Ultraviolet light levels will be reduced to below 75 μwatts per lumen throughout the Museum.

8 The Museum will not expose pigmented and dyed objects to sustained high levels of visible light. For highly light sensitive objects on permanent exhibition the maximum light level will be 50 lux. For such material on temporary exhibition the recommended light level will be 80 lux. For other light sensitive material the Museum will strive to achieve light levels of below 300 lux as appropriate to the objects concerned.

9 The Museum will, where possible, introduce measures to reduce levels of particulates and pollutant gases coming into contact with objects.
10 The Museum will consider the introduction of inert environments for the storage of objects where this can be shown to promote preservation.
11 The Museum will introduce standard procedures for the receipt of, and subsequent storage of, organic artefacts which are capable of harbouring insects and thus infesting other objects.
12 The Museum will strive to improve the handling procedures used by staff for the movement of objects within the departments, and for transport, storage and exhibition of the collection. It will do this by running relevant courses which staff should attend within one year of joining the Museum. All existing staff involved with the handling of the collection will be required to attend refresher courses in these procedures.

Acknowledgements

The author would like to thank the members of the Conservation Research Group, Lorna Green, Vincent Daniels, Yvonne Shashoua, David Thickett and Richard Kibrya, for their part in the collection of environmental data and deterioration studies. She would also like to thank Dr Andrew Oddy, co-author of the environmental policy for his support with the coordination the environmental aspects of conservation.

References

1. British Museum, *Management Plan 1994* (London: British Museum, 1994), 4.
2. Susan Bradley, 'Environmental Monitoring and Control in the Galleries of the British Museum', in *Environmental Monitoring and Control*, ed. Graeme Scott (London: The Museums Association and SSCR, 1989), 68–77.
3. H. J. Plenderleith, *The Conservation of Antiquities and Works of Art* (London: Oxford University Press, 1956), 1–15.
4. R. M. Organ, 'The Examination and Treatment of Bronze Antiquities', in *Recent Advances in Conservation*, ed G. Thomson (London: Butterworths, 1963), 104–110.
5. Hazel Newey, '17 Years of Dehumidified Showcases in the British Museum', (Paper delivered at the Eighth Triennial Meeting of the International Council for Museums Committee for Conservation, Sydney, September 1987), 901–907.
6. R. M. Organ (with Miss M. Bimson), 'The Safe Storage of Unstable Glass', *Museums Journal* 56 (1957): 265–272.
7. S.M. Bradley and I. Freestone, 'A note on the Chemistry and Petrology of the Amaravati Stone, its Suceptibility to Deterioration and the Strategy for its Preservation', in *Catalogue of the Amaravati Sculptures*, ed. R. Knox (London: British Museum Press, 1992), 230–231.
8. V. Daniels and G. Lohneis, 'Deterioration of Sugar Artefacts', *Studies in Conservation*, forthcoming.
9. A.E.A. Werner, 'Conservation and Display: Environmental Control', *Museums Journal* 72 (1972): 58–60.
10. W.A. Oddy, 'An Unsuspected Danger in Display', *Museums Journal* 73 (1973): 27–28.
11. S.M. Blackshaw and V.D. Daniels, 'Selecting Safe Materials for the Storage and Display of Antiquities', (paper delivered at the Fifth Triennial Meeting of the International Council for Museums Committee for Conservation, Zagreb, 1978), 23/2/1–9.
12. L.R. Green and D. Thickett, 'Testing Materials for Use in the Storage and Display of Antiquities – A Revised Methodology', *Studies in Conservation* 40 (1995): 145–152.
13. S.M. Bradley, 'Hydrogen Sulphide Scavengers for the Prevention of Silver Tarnishing', in *Environmental Monitoring and Control*, ed. Graeme Scott (London: The Museums Association and SSCR, 1989), 65–67.
14. L.R. Lee, '1996/10 The Inhibition of Silver Tarnish Using Zinc Oxide Pellets' (British Museum Department of Conservation Internal Report).
15. Garry Thomson, *The Museum Environment*, 2nd edn (London: Butterworths, 1986), 268–269.
16. Susan Bradley, 'A Review of the Storage Strategy in the British Museum' (British Museum Internal Report, 1994).
17. Stefan Michalski, 'Relative Humidity: A Discussion of Correct/Incorrect Values,' (Paper delivered at the Tenth Triennial Meeting of the International Council of Museums Committee for Conservation, Washington, August 1993), 624–629.
18. David Erhardt and Marion Mecklenburg, 'Relative Humidity Re-examined' in *Preventive Conservation Practice, Theory and Research*, (Preprints of the Contributions to the IIC Congress, Ottawa, 12-16 September 1994, ed. Ashok Roy and Perry Smith), 32–37
19. S.M. Bradley and W.A. Oddy, 'Environmental Policy for the Preservation of the Collections in the British Museum', (British Museum Internal Document, 1993).

The Introduction of Preventative Conservation at the Museum of Science and Industry in Manchester

Simon F. Cane
The Museum of Science and Industry in Manchester,
Liverpool Road, Castlefield, Manchester M3 4JP, UK

Abstract

In November 1994 I moved into the newly established post of Collections Services Officer at the Museum of Science and Industry in Manchester. The move represented a personal challenge in the transition from a traditional conservator to a conservator as collections manager. The challenge professionally was to introduce and apply preventative conservation theory and practice into an organisation that had little experience of conservation culture. Management structure, support, flexibility and commitment have been the key to developing an integrated and proactive approach to collections care and management.

Keywords

Collections Services Officer, preventative conservation, collections manager, collections management strategy, collections care

Introduction

I have worked in the field of conservation throughout my professional life. I went through a traditional training that focused on the treatment of objects.

In 1992/4 I was involved with the development and mounting of the *Stop the Rot* exhibition held at York Castle Museum (winner of the IIC Keck award in 1994), probably the most populist exhibition to date on conservation. The exhibition was a turning point for me, both personally and professionally; it had allowed me to step back and think deeply about what conservation was and how we as a profession went about our work. I had always believed in the preventative approach and had been actively involved in the broader issues of collection care. However, a large proportion of my time was still spent dealing with the results of decades of poor collections management. I wanted the opportunity to prove that the proactive management and care of collections was effective, economical and achievable. I was given that opportunity in November 1994 when I was appointed to the post of Collections Services Officer at the Museum of Science and Industry in Manchester.

In this paper I outline the management strategy that has created an integrated and proactive approach to collections care and management and consider the transition from conservator to conservator as collections manager.

Background

To understand my role and its development it is first necessary to understand the development of the Museum. The Museum of Science and Industry in Manchester is on the site of Liverpool Road station, the world's oldest surviving steam railway. The station opened in 1830 and closed in 1975. In 1976 it was taken on by the Liverpool Road Station Society which secured the immediate future of the site. The Greater Manchester Museum of Science and Industry opened on the site in 1983 under local authority control, changing to an independent charitable trust in 1986.

The Museum is 12 years old and its character has developed from its particular connections to railway heritage and working exhibits. The Museum needed to establish itself and create an identity and these factors encouraged the development of a culture of restoration rather than conservation. The emphasis was on the development of the site, exhibits and use of collections. The culture of the organisation had already begun to change prior to my arrival in 1994. This was demonstrated by the sympathetic conversion of the 1830 a Grade 1 listed building, and the construction of the Library and Records Centre containing archival storage conforming to BS 5454 (ISO 11799 presently in draft form) in the basement of the Lower Byrom Street warehouse.

The post of Collections Services Officer had been written into the corporate development plan for 1992-95, demonstrating a commitment to the future care and management of the Museums collections.

The job description was necessarily broad, and demonstrated an awareness of the need for a holistic approach to collections management. My interpretation of the title was that I provide a service to the collections by developing high standards of management and care, thus providing a service to the Museum by ensuring that its prime asset (its collections) are managed efficiently and economically and a service to the public by improving physical, intellectual and sensory access to the collections.

The challenge was to introduce good preventative practices into an organisation that had little practical experience of conservation, preventative or otherwise. In spite of its lack of practical experience the organisation had a commitment to 'best practice' and resources for training and development were available giving the opportunity to develop new skills and achieve high standards without rewriting policy. The management team had the foresight to develop a corporate and collections strategy that provided the management tools to implement an effective programme for the care and management of the Museums collections.

The management tools

The Museum has developed corporate and site strategies that map out the conceptual, organisational and physical development of the Museum. The objectives from the corporate plan are developed into strategic projects within the collections management plan. This allows the collections management plan to become a working document providing a frame of reference for the work of all departments. It is not merely a document that is dusted off and updated when registration comes around. It allows the organisation to focus and co-ordinate its work. It has proved particularly useful in obtaining commitment to and implementing preventative conservation practice.

The corporate objectives as laid out in the collection management plan are:

- **Access:** to provide services that are responsive and good value for all Museum customers;
- **Communication:** to provide a clear, integrated and stimulating experience for Museum customers;
- **Collections:** to care for and manage the collections, including the historic site, and to encourage their use;
- **Resources:** to ensure that all resources available to the Museum are managed effectively and efficiently;
- **Audience Development:** to develop new audiences and increase repeat visits;
- **Developing the Museum:** to enhance public enjoyment of the Museum by the continued development of the collections, historic site, exhibitions and events.

All of these objectives allow scope for the development and implementation of preventative conservation through the collections management plan where strategic objectives are developed into strategic projects that are immediately and directly linked with collections management. Strategic projects are accompanied by:

- Actions (what are we going to do?);
- Performance indicators (what standard do we want to achieve and how do we know we have achieved it?);
- Timetable (when it will be done by?);
- Lead officer (who is responsible?);
- Partners (who else will the project involve?);
- Financial resources (who is paying?).

These are laid out in a tabular format and are reviewed and revised on a quarterly basis. Projects are developed both from the bottom up and the top down.

New ideas and problems are raised and discussed through the collections working group which is attended by the whole department. This system focuses the minds and resources of the department and allows the measurement of performance. Whilst the quarterly review adds flexibility, as well as the revision of ongoing projects and the inclusion of new projects. There is a need for flexibility as plans can change at short notice but this structured approach can accommodate change.

The Museum has published the Citizen's Charter standard statement, which is a commitment to its customers and includes a section stating its commitment to collections care. The Museum has also has a commitment to staff training and development through a system which reviews personal and corporate training needs on an annual basis.

I have used all of these systems to help introduce preventative conservation to the Museum. I have instigated major cleaning programs and introduced minimum standards to a range of practices through the strategic projects. I have been able to deliver training on the basics of preventative conservation, object handling and display through the staff development scheme.

Application

Strategic objectives, corporate objectives, staff development scheme: all sound very plausible, but how do they work in practice?. They all contribute effectively in communicating and applying preventative conservation practices.

Projects are prioritised by the Collection Services Officer, the Curatorial Services Manager, the Senior Curator and the Senior Archivist. Most of the work centres around the Curatorial and Archives departments. Curators and Archivists are expected to commit between 1.5 and 2 days per week to collections management projects. Because the department is relatively small (nine in all) and the collections large in quantity and physical size, we have to tackle projects as a team. This means that curators and archivists must be versatile and prepared to work as non-specialists. In the first year the work has taken two basic forms :

- Rationalisation
- Cleaning and organisation.

It is an anomaly that we may provide better care for collections by disposing of them. Rationalisation is not seen as a solution to any storage problems. It is seen as a method of removing duplicate material and/or material that is not relevant to the policy for developing and managing the collections. This will, in turn, release resources and space in order to improve the care and accommodation of the permanent collections, and to continue to develop them in accordance with the policy and planned developments at the Museum.

We needed to establish basic standards of cleanliness and organisation:

Question: Is this store dirty and disorganised?
Answer: Clean it and reorganise it.

This process involved going through our stores shelf by shelf, object by object and cleaning them. Floors were vacuumed, dust strips fitted to doors and protective sheeting applied to shelving. In one year we have cleaned over 500 m^2 of stores and a good percentage of material on display. The result is stores and collections that are clean and organised to a minimum standard that are accessible.

The processes of rationalisation, cleaning and reorganisation are compatible. You find out what you have, you throw out what you do not want and clean and repack what you keep.

The success of the projects relies on a versatile and enthusiastic staff, prepared to help each other. Curators and archivists cannot hide in professional and subject specialism. The employees of any organisation represent its most expensive resource. We have taken that resource and applied it to the Museums most valuable asset, its collection. The undertaking of major programs of cleaning and reorganisation has positive spin-off's: working in teams encourages good communication; we ensure a high standard of work as we act as our own inspectors; we really get to know what is in the collections, and the department feels a real sense of achievement. Instead of going into stores surveying them and leaving them as found, we have left them improved and could see the evidence of our achievements. It is because we have been prepared to work as a department, with none of the restrictions sometimes attached to professional position hindering us, that we have achieved an acceptable minimum standard of cleanliness and organisation in 65% of our stored collections.

The future

The ongoing challenge is to keep up and improve standards, and to service completed projects. A proactive and integrated approach means that we avoid crisis management; when faced with specific areas of the collection that require special attention, we can assess the problem within the framework of our broader strategy. We may then undertake some remedial work and programme in further work for the future.

The basic minimum standards of organisation and cleanliness form the corner stones of our strategy; once they are in place we can build on them, moving onto more detailed work. New projects are developed directly from curators and archivists, from myself as Collections Services Officer and from the Corporate Plan through the Collections Management Plan. The projects are assessed taking all factors into account, and prioritised.

Training forms an important part of future strategy. The aim of the training is to raise awareness of the issues and standards and develop a feeling of ownership. We hope to provide training to all staff, I believe that all the staff within the Museum should know how to handle an object and be aware of the work that is going on in the collections. All staff receive customer care training, why not object care training? The training will extend to friends of the Museum and volunteers once a format is established.

Conservator to collections manager

More and more museums are creating collections manager positions: as conservators we can see it either as a threat or an opportunity. I obviously view it as an opportunity and my experience has proven to be good so far. I definitely still see myself as a conservator. Though I now deal with objects on a macro level, the training I had as a conservator, to understand objects on a micro level, has proved invaluable. I miss working on objects directly and initially my response to damaged material was to want to treat it directly. My role is to assess the damage, take any immediate remedial action and locate a conservator to treat the material. The position of collections carer/manager is a good one for a conservator and I think it is really a matter of personality and ability as to whether you can adapt to the role. A sound conservation training is an advantage as there is a need to understand the complexities of decay and issues of care. What is essential is to understand that the objects do not represent an end in themselves and, as I outlined above, all the work relates to creating access.

The role of collections care also makes sound economic sense. The emphasis in the UK at present is on managing museums as businesses and we are constantly measured in these terms. The collection represents the prime asset of any museum and allows it to carry out its core functions of care and access, through management, display, interpretation and research. Therefore the care of collections is a primary function, which can be realised through a post such as collections manager/carer.

The role of collections manager/carer is an appropriate role for a conservator. The transition has been easier than I anticipated and has given me a different perspective on conservation. My training has served me well, though I have had to learn a lot of administrative and managerial skills on the job. Perhaps we may see conservation training adapt to produce professional collections managers/ careers whose training is more diverse. I believe that as more conservators become involved with this kind of position, they can only serve to promote the cause of conservators and conservation.

Conclusions

After a year in post I am pleasantly surprised at the progress we have made. That progress has been possible due to a range of factors. My post represents the museum's commitment to collections care and one of my concerns was that introducing conservation in any form can be seen as a new cost and new cost is not welcome in the present economic environment. The work we have carried out has not in effect cost the Museum any more. We have achieved results by redirecting resources and maximising existing ones, such as staff. The management framework is very important I have had good support from departmental managers and the flexible and responsive structure has made the introduction of new practices relatively painless. All of the staff were aware of the problems and many of the solutions. My position has simply provided a focus and acted as a catalyst. The blurring of individual roles and departmental boundaries has been important in achieving results and, as a relatively small department in a large museum, it is absolutely necessary for all staff to acknowledge that our aim must be to care for the collection as a whole. We have been ambitious when setting targets and not achieved everything we set out to in the estimated timetable. Projects can be rescheduled, but this could be problematic in the future as salaries become linked to performance.

As an organisation we have some way to go, but we have made a good start and I am optimistic that we will have a fully integrated system of collections management within five years. I do not advocate that all museums should take on the system outlined; it is a system that works for us in our particular circumstance. We have good policy that enables us, and we are actually putting it into practice. The main message is that an integrated and proactive approach enables effective planning and management of collections and their care. Standards can be improved at relatively low cost, providing there is commitment and versatility. The net result of the programme will be collections that are well cared for, well used and accessible. This is a goal that we can all aspire to.

Daylighting Dosage Prediction for Side-lit Interiors in Museum Galleries and Historic Buildings

Stephen Cannon-Brookes, Malcolm Parry
Welsh School of Architecture, University of Wales, Cardiff, Wales, UK

Abstract

Renewed enthusiasm for daylight in museum galleries and the growing number of conserved historical interiors suggest revisions to current attitudes regarding the daylighting of side-lit interiors. Evaluation of current prediction tools shows that there is a gap between the goal of predictable lighting dosage and the techniques available to achieve them. Long-term monitoring of illuminance levels provides one solution and a strategy for achieving this is reported on. A system for analysing the visual quality of the display of individual exhibits in side-lit interior is also suggested. Comparison of findings shows that there seems to be a relationship between visual quality and illuminance distribution. It is concluded that greater use of side lighting could be made when an awareness of daylighting performance is raised and as daylight is allowed to play a coherent role in visual display.

Keywords

Daylight, illuminance dosage, illuminance prediction, side-lighting, visual quality

Introduction

Since the introduction of conservation guide-lines for lighting exposure, concerns have been raised over the presence of daylight in interiors displaying sensitive materials. Daylight's constant and potentially large variation in intensity led Thomson to conclude that 'side windows should be for views, not for lighting'.[1] As a result, in many museums windows were screened off whilst in historic interiors compromises were sought which attempted to limit object exposure to lighting, while allowing the essential visual character of the space to be maintained. Paradoxically these moves to exclude daylight from interiors resulted in increased awareness of daylight's positive psychological role as well as the quality of lighting that it delivers. Nevertheless, the focus of attention passed from the traditional primary concern of viewing quality to the control of illuminance (light) levels. Today's shift towards preventive conservation has begun to question the rationale for this. Maximising the passive performance of buildings suggests a greater use of daylight and a reduction in the expensive and often unreliable active systems of illuminance level control. In response to this a greater reliance will need to be placed on the use of annual illuminance dosages as opposed to limiting the levels of illuminance for static display lighting.

This paper aims to review the use of daylight in side-lit interiors. It will summarise present methods for predicting illuminance distribution in such interiors and present a system for analysing lighting quality in existing interiors. From this a number of key factors will be drawn which appear to influence both the quantitative and qualitative characteristics of the visual environment of such interiors.

The side-lit interior

Rooms with vertical windows in museums and historic interiors share a common typology and this allows a typical interior to be used for discussion. Figure 1 shows a section through a side-lit interior and its external features as well as a three dimensional view of its partially unfolded plan-isometric. Factors which affect both the distribution and quality of daylight within interior are:

- orientation of the room;
- room proportions;
- daylight control systems;
- surface finishes (reflectances);
- external features (shading);
- the objects and exhibits contained.

The role of these factors will be commented on later.

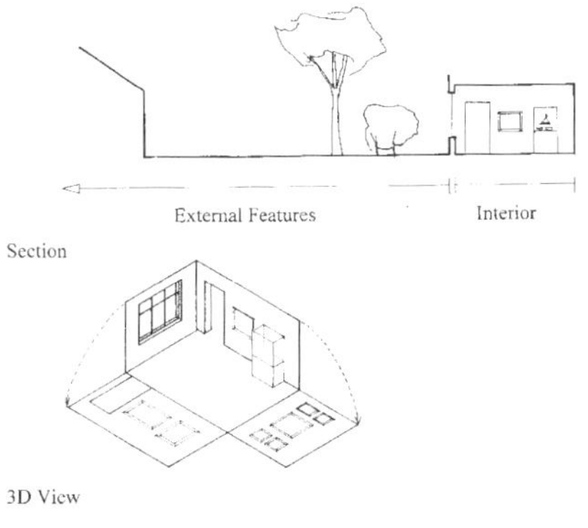

Figure 1. Section and three-dimensional view of a typical side-lit interior

Sky conditions and prediction techniques

Daylight varies constantly in intensity and this variation is determined principally by latitude, location, season and time of day. Further variation within this framework is directly related to sky conditions. In broad terms these can be

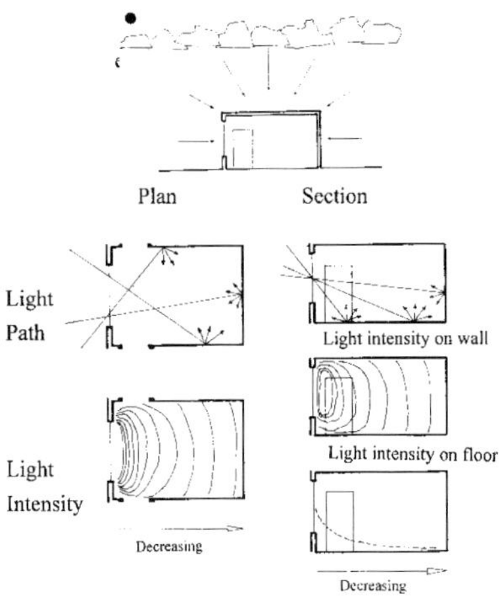

Figure 2. Overcast skies and daylight distribution into side-lit interiors

described as (fully) overcast, clear and variable skies. The latter category encompasses all the sky conditions between the two extremes. Traditionally the prediction of illuminance levels inside buildings has concentrated on clear and overcast skies only, since the physical characteristics of the skies are relatively easy to describe. In this section the interior is used to examine the consequences of each of three conditions along with a summary of the prediction tools associated with them.

Overcast skies

Characteristics of overcast skies (Figure 2) are:

- Diffuse daylight from the whole sky dome;
- Brightness of sky varies over the dome, at the zenith three times brighter than at the horizon;
- Low-intensity light, nearly uniform in all orientations;
- Standard sky condition in temperate climates.

Prediction tools for overcast skies

The stable brightness distribution of overcast skies allows direct comparisons to be made of illuminance levels within an interior. *Daylight factors* are the most widely used tools since they allow illuminance levels to be expressed as a percentage of the illuminance on an horizontal point with an unobstructed of an overcast sky.

Currently daylight protractors, computer simulators and other tabular methods are used to calculate daylight factors and less frequently physical scale exposed to standard sky conditions. Although daylight factors are the primary means of quantitative daylight calculation, they are of limited benefit for determining dosage since they are restricted to fully overcast skies, which occur for a small percentage of sky conditions. Other sky conditions are of greater intensity and are therefore likely to deliver more daylight into a side-lit interior.

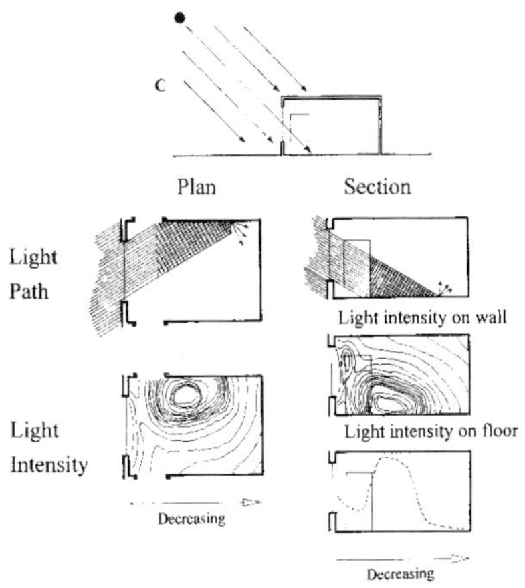

Figure 3. Clear skies and daylight distribution within a side-lit interior

Clear skies

Characteristics of clear skies (Figure 3) are:

- Sun delivers high intensity directional light;
- Sun path is predictable;
- Low intensity diffuse light from blue sky;
- Sky vault brighter at the horizon than at the zenith but distribution of intensity brightness is variable and affected by sun position.

Prediction tools used for clear skies

Movement of the sun prevents a single stable relationship between exterior and interior illuminance levels. Sunlight protractors and computer calculations can be used, but these mostly rely on generalisations of sky brightness or fixed sun positions. Calculation of internal illuminance levels is not straightforward and usually has to be treated on a point-by-point basis with reference to sun position and sky brightness. Non quantitative investigation is routinely carried out to examine sunlight penetration and this is most easily achieved using a physical scale model and sun simulator – a heliodon. Although the elements required for dosage calculations can be defined their size and complexity deter most from attempting them.

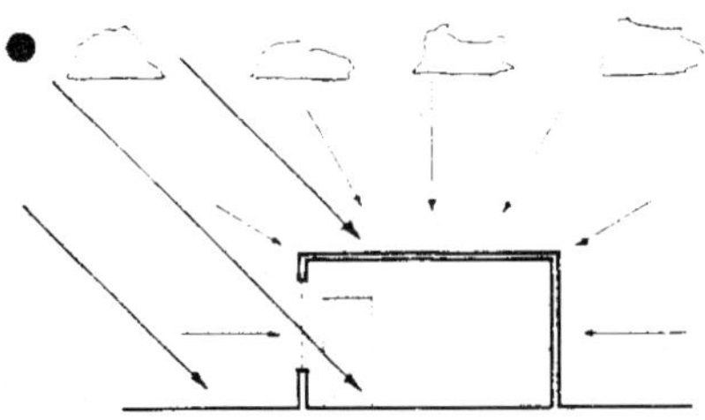

Figure 4. Variable skies

Variable skies

Characteristics of variable skies (Figure 4) are:

- Sky dome of variable brightness;
- Incident light of variable intensity and geometry;
- Interior illuminance levels cannot be predicted absolutely.

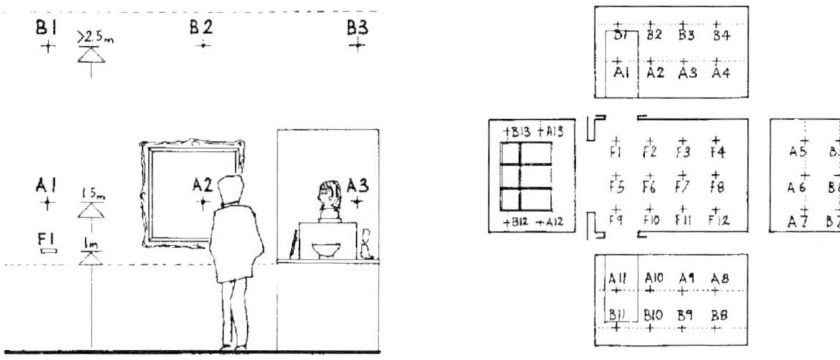

Figure 5. The necklace *of measurement positions used for quantitative and qualitative analysis of side-lit interiors. The section shows the relationship of the* necklace *to the display and a fold down plan with a typical layout of points (same typical plan as in Figure 1)*

Variable skies are the most frequent conditions in temperate climate. However, their unpredictability presents a major barrier to their description and simulation. At present there is little call for illuminance predictions under such conditions since lighting design has evolved to concentrate on the 'extreme' conditions of clear or overcast skies. Although recent surveys of measurements of daylight throughout the world in 1994/95 may give rise to new predictive techniques. However, until then dosage calculation is not possible without the use of real sky data, though some approximation may be made for interiors where sunlight is excluded.

Summary

The current use of 'standard' sky conditions provides no direct method for the prediction of daylighting dosage. Practicable techniques rely either on interpolating between the 'standard' conditions using annual sky data or the long-term monitoring of physical models. Neither are regularly carried out and, as has recently been shown with scale models,[2] substantial margins of error are associated with their results. In this absence of values of direct dosage prediction it is felt that lessons might be drawn from observing the performance of daylight in existing interiors.

Characteristics of side-lit interiors

As indicated in the diagrams of lighting intensity under different sky conditions (Figures 2 to 4) the distribution of daylight within a side-lit interior can vary considerably. This variability precludes the use of one representative position for monitoring illuminance levels. Recent research at the Welsh School of Architecture has sought to formulate a standard system of analysis which allows for both quantitative and qualitative assessments to be made of interiors for display. At its core is a regularly spaced chain of measurement positions, termed a *necklace,* around the walls and across the floor (Figure 5). The height of these positions above the floor was drawn from typical eye-levels and exhibit positions with 1 m for the floor locations and 1.5 m for the primary wall *necklace*. In interiors with high ceilings and more extensive use of the wall surfaces an upper necklace was found to be of benefit. A minimum height of 2.5 m was found to be appropriate for this.

As noted earlier, control of illuminance levels has overtaken viewing quality as the primary concern in daylighting 'sensitive' interiors. One of the aims of a subsequent investigation was to assess the potential relationship between these two concerns. Viewing quality assessment is not a widely covered field. To date most surveys of museum exhibits displays have concentrated on visitor satisfaction with general assessments of the lighting. Lighting research has gone further but experienced problems with semantic scaling of responses to questions and the inarticulacy of those interviewed. Despite these difficulties there remains the opportunity to question any visitor whether in overall terms an individual object is lit well or poorly. It was felt, however, that such a question requires some preparation and as a consequence use was made of *trained observers*, an established technique in lighting studies. This ensured that assessments could be reduced to a

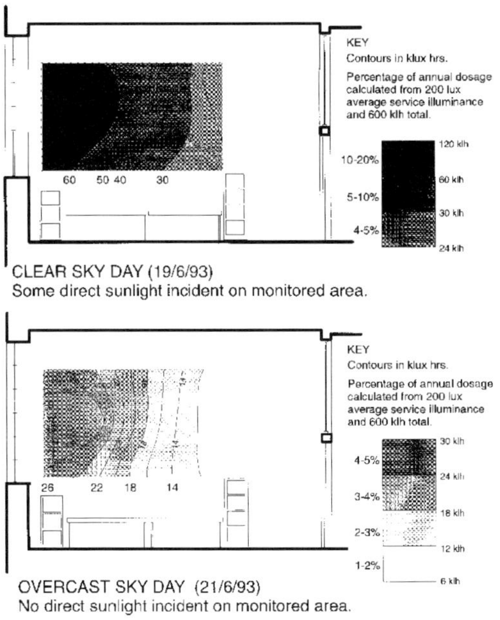

Figure 6. Illuminance dosages for a clear and an overcast day in June. The contoured area indicates where light levels were monitored and the key gives both the dosage and the proportion of annual dosage this represents for a '200 lux' exhibit

numerical score whilst useful comments were also recorded. The data collected were presented graphically making use of the *necklace* distribution since the exhibits usually coincided with measurement positions. This allowed viewing quality to be related both to position with respect to windows and the distribution of daylight.

Dosage

Analysis of dosage and daylight distribution has been carried out in a number of interiors. In this investigation of a side-lit interior in the Welsh School of Architecture in Cardiff (latitude ~52° North), the room has many of the features of side-lit galleries, since it is deeper than it is wide and painted white. Its orientation is north-west which ensures that most sunlight is excluded except during summer afternoons. Monitoring of illuminance levels was carried out during the summer and attention was focused on an area of the westward facing wall adjacent to the window. Illuminance levels were recorded at five-minute intervals using data loggers and 12 mm photo cells. This equipment was assembled for a wider study of gallery daylighting[3] and closely resembled that used by Staniforth in her investigation daylighting dosage in historic houses.[4]

Data from two separate days in June are presented here (Figure 6); one day when clear sky conditions prevailed and the other under an overcast sky. The contoured area in each section represents the dosage of illuminance over the area monitored on the clear-sky day and the fully overcast one. During the clear-sky day sunlight was incident within the monitored area for several hours. The effect of this is apparent when it is compared with dosage on the overcast-sky day, when values of illumination measured were between a half and a third those on the clear sky day. In Figure 6 these findings are put into the context of conservation guide-lines for sensitive materials and the normal recommendation for oil paintings (600 kilolux h). Clearly Thomson's concerns regarding side-lighting are justified.[5] In just one day when incident direct sunlight shone for a short period of time on the area closest to the window, it received between 10 and 20% of the recommended maximum annual dosage! Whereas with an overcast sky the dosage was between 4 and 5% of annual recommendations. If these recommendations were to be observed a normal oil painting placed in such a position would receive its 'allowed' annual dosage within 20 to 25 days.

As expected, dosages declined away from the window, but on neither day did the wall area analysed receive less than the recommended maximum for this category of material. Whilst these results speak for themselves, it is worth noting

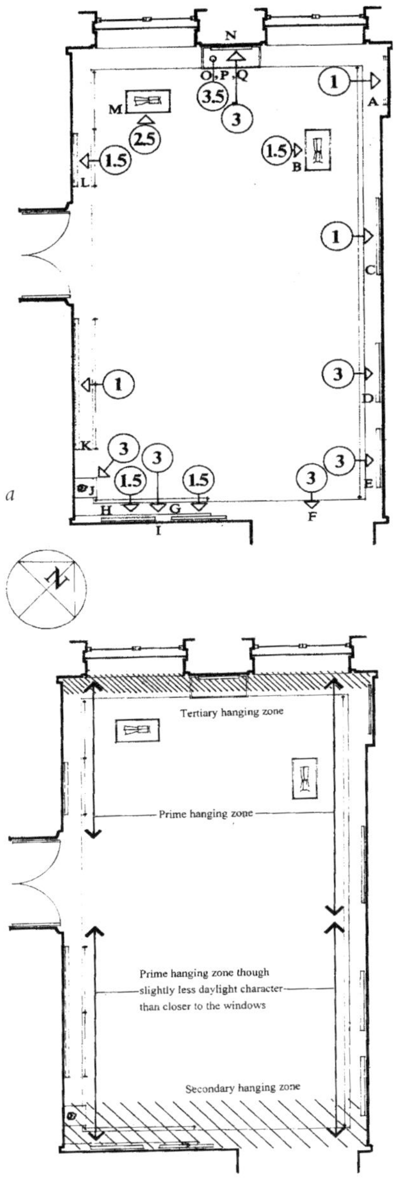

Figure 7. Plan of Gallery 7 in the Musée Picasso, Paris. In (a) each of the exhibits (A–Q) is given a score from 1 (good) to 4 (unsatisfactory) whilst in (b) the individual results are collated to show the distribution of viewing quality in general terms

that these dosages are a 'worst case' scenario. The window has no solar control and values measured are summertime dosages for all daylight hours including those hours in which blackout might have been maintained in a real gallery interior. If the room had been south facing, dosages would have been greater. However, these results indicate a warning to many conservators, since there are numerous examples within current museum and gallery displays where sensitive exhibits are exposed to overly high levels of illuminance such as those measured.

Qualitative evaluation of side-lit interiors

Regular spacing of exhibits around the perimeter of a gallery makes it possible to assess visual quality in roughly the same positions used for monitoring illuminance dosage. In the study carried out a small number of 'observers' were introduced to a wide range of factors that contribute to visual quality. Following this 'training' they were asked to assess each individual exhibit in terms of visual satisfaction using a scale of 1 (good) to 4 (unsatisfactory) . The factors involved were reflections, coherence, modelling, positioning, acuity, light personality (colour appearance, spectral appropriateness) and the display system. Observers were asked to give both an overall score and to comment on the lighting of each piece. The latter measure helped to accommodate the wide variety of lighting geometry and exhibits often found in a single gallery.

This assessment technique was employed in one of the side-lit galleries in the Musée Picasso, Paris. The gallery contained paintings, some but not all glazed, and a number of pieces of sculpture. The display of each exhibit was graded by the observers and their scores were averaged. The plan of the gallery (Figure 7a) shows the average score given to each exhibit (whose position is denoted by a letter between A and Q). Analysis of the distribution of scores indicated some correspondence with the nature of the interior with a hierarchy of positions with respect to visual quality (Figure 7). This was reinforced by the observers comments suggesting the following conclusions:

- The highest scores and therefore the best viewing conditions were experienced along the walls perpendicular to the windows, though the scores dropped with exhibits close to the rear wall.
- The wall facing the windows suffered problems with reflections earning poorer scores.
- The lowest scores, indicating the poorest visual quality, were found in the area directly in front of and between the windows.

A coherent approach to side-lighting

Using the data collected from both quantitative and qualitative analysis an attempt has been made to relate viewing quality to the conservation concerns raised by daylighting. Not surprisingly, greatest viewing satisfaction was recorded in areas where the most intense daylight (directionality and intensity) is experienced (Figure 8). Both viewing quality and vulnerability to over-exposure have been represented by hatching to give an approximate indication of relative values. The areas closest to windows are clearly the most critical for display in a side-lit interior and it is worth noting that this zone was often used for doorways in older domestic and museum buildings.

The zones shown in these diagrams can only provide an indication of likely conditions since these can vary depending on different sky condition and type of exhibit. Analysis of a number of similar interiors has found that, if windows are shielded from direct sunlight, the distribution of daylight entering an interior is relatively consistent, its primary variable being overall intensity. If this type of situation is achieved, then use and design of side-lit interiors breaks down into a number of factors. All of these affect both illuminance levels and the subjective quality of daylight in an interior and must be considered together. Listing them here as primary or subsidiary gives an indication of their relevance and the making of key points provides the basis of a checklist for side-lighting.

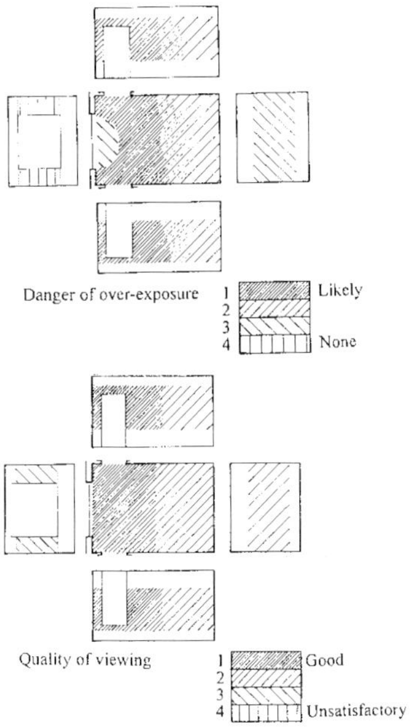

Figure 8. Fold-down plans showing in (a) the relative danger of over-exposure and in (b) the overall quality of viewing on both the walls and across the floor of side-lit interior

Primary factors

Orientation

With sunlight a key factor in causing excess lighting dosage in side-lit interiors, the orientation of windows must be considered. Orientation has long been a consideration in gallery design and north lighting has been commonly used since the beginning of the early 19th century. In both Europe and the USA small side-lit galleries (*cabinets*) were designed specifically to be north facing. Von Klenze's tripartite section of the Alte Pinakothek (1826–36) became a model for subsequent museums with cabinet paintings in small north-lit rooms, larger works in top-lit galleries and sculpture in south facing rooms. This pattern still has relevance today especially as the majority of sculpture is not sensitive to light:

- It is inappropriate for direct sunlight to be incident on the windows of side-lit interiors displaying sensitive materials. Sun shading should be achieved without totally blocking views but this may be difficult when the sun is at low altitudes.
- Care should be taken with south-facing windows in high latitudes and east- and west-facing windows in the tropics.

In existing buildings, especially those of intrinsic merit, control of sunlight usually devolves onto control systems. In all interiors daylight should be excluded outside the hours of opening.

Daylight control systems

Although these are often a remedial measure in many interiors they are usually the only means available to control illuminance levels and potentially glaring sky brightness. Most control systems, whether they are hand-operated shutters or automatic electronically operated blinds or louvres, tend to reduce views out and diffuse the daylight admitted into the interior. The choice of which system to use depends on a number of issues: views, ease of use, maintenance and effect on illuminance distribution and the architectural quality of the display environment.

- Passive control systems such as ultraviolet screening should be considered first.
- Control of daylight is unlikely to be achieved without the use an active system of control if only for blackout – a necessity in controlling dosage.
- Control systems should be evaluated with regard to their suitability to the interior and the overall running of the building, whether an historic structure or museum.

Room proportions

The relationship of interior proportions to window(s) size and orientation are the key to both the quality of daylight as well as its distribution and viewing quality.

- Positions close to windows combine high intensity of daylight with good directional light quality, but are vulnerable to excessive dosage.
- Dependence on reflected light away from windows reduces the risk of overdosage but also reduces the desirable characteristics of daylight incurring the risk of gloominess. For instance, few successful side-lit interiors have a depth more than two and a half times their width or height.

Secondary factors

Surface finishes

Finishes are described in terms of colour, texture and reflectance and all affect the amount of daylight distributed from the window. High-reflectance surfaces, such as white-painted plaster, allow for multiple internal reflections integrating the daylight in an interior and making illuminance levels more uniform than those in interiors with darker surfaces.

- High-reflectance finishes have obvious benefits in terms of making the distribution of light more uniform but this must be balanced against excessive contrasts with low reflectance exhibits.
- Floor and window sills are important reflectors in side-lit interiors and need consideration when evaluating daylight admission.

Contents/exhibits

Rarely are side-lit interiors empty shells and the exhibits and display materials they house tend to reduce the overall reflectance of an interior and the penetration of daylight. Where the contents cover a sizeable percentage of the surfaces, this effect can be significant and may interfere with attempts to maximise the use of internal reflectance to distribute daylight.

- Consideration must be given to the brightness ratio between contents and background. Inappropriate contrasts should be avoided. Appropriate contrasts will help to reduce apparent dullness of the contents, especially as most visitors now expect the 'sparkle' of electrical display lighting that they experience in other contexts.

External features

Landscaping and buildings outside a window can reduce the quantity of daylight admitted. In climates where sunlight predominates, light can be reflected off adjacent buildings and landscape. This may be a preferred measure as it can help to reduce intensity and the avoidance of solar (heat) gains.

- Buildings and vegetation may help to control the amount of daylight reaching windows.
- In hot sunny locations daylight reflected from adjacent external features may be desirable.
- Views out provide both visual relief and psychological contact with the outside.

Conclusions

There still remains a divide between the tools currently available for daylighting prediction and the use of lighting dosages in daylit interiors. Without direct prediction of dosage, then the use of passively controlled daylighting, which is implicitly encouraged by the shift to preventive conservation, will be continue to be impeded. This, however, should not stop a more general re-appraisal of the daylighting in interiors housing light sensitive materials. Thomson's observations[5] on windows are still valid but his conclusions should be revised to take account of both the need to daylight historic interiors for authenticity and the good quality of light which is delivered by vertical windows. The research reported here suggests that there is a close relationship between the distribution of daylight and the level of satisfaction by which exhibits are perceived. Thomson correctly drew attention to the inevitable uneven illuminance levels in daylit interiors and this remains the most serious disincentive to using daylight. However, with actual measured performance data it is perhaps now time to re-evaluate their suitability for display, especially with the growing perception that the quality of 'natural' lighting is desirable to museum and gallery users. Flexibility in display has created the expectation of freedom to place an exhibit anywhere in an interior. This is unreasonable and it militates against displaying collections to take account of illuminance dosage, as well as the lighting quality experienced in different rooms or positions within them. In museum galleries such an approach can be considered, but problems remain with historic interiors where there may be a conflict with the maintenance of an existing ensemble. In these cases the primary objectives must be the careful monitoring of dosage in vulnerable areas and sunlight control.

Current difficulties in predicting dosage are a limitation in new interiors or major refurbishments where reliance on passive performance and control is promoted. Whilst computer-based predictions fail to reach their potential, reliance must be placed on established daylighting prediction tools with knowledge of their limitations. Nonetheless, side-lit interiors will continue to be an important display environment in historic buildings and new interiors. All those involved in the use of these interiors should be aware of daylight's characteristics, limitations and the effect of the factors described here.

References

1. G. Thomson, *The Museum Environment* (London: Butterworths, 1986), 35.
2. S.W.A. Cannon-Brookes, 'Daylight in Museum Galleries: Quantitative Evaluation using Scale Models', (PhD dissertation, University of Wales, 1995).
3. Ibid.
4. S. Staniforth, 'The Logging of Light Levels in National Trust Houses', (Paper delivered at the Ninth Triennial Meeting of the International Council for Museums Committee for Conservation, Dresden, 1990), 602–607.
5. G. Thomson, *The Museum Environment*, 35.

The Effectiveness of Barrier Materials in Reducing Emissions of Organic Gases from Fibreboard: Results of Preliminary Tests

Katherine Eremin,* Paul Wilthew
National Museums of Scotland,
Chambers Street, Edinburgh, EH1 1JF, Scotland, UK

Abstract

Organic gases harmful to museum artifacts are emitted by a wide range of materials used in case construction, including medium density fibreboard (MDF). Several products may provide barriers to the emission of such gases when applied as surface coatings. Fifteen of these were applied to samples of MDF and ZF (zero formaldehyde) MDF. These were placed in sealed inert boxes to replicate a case environment, and levels of emitted formaldehyde, acetaldehyde, acetic and formic acid measured. Levels of emitted gases decreased with most of the sealants tested, the exception being some lacquers. The lowest levels came from samples coated with barrier foils and charcoal cloth, and higher but significantly reduced levels from Dacrylate and polyurethane lacquers. The varnishes and paints tested reduced levels slightly compared to uncoated samples. For barrier foils the application method and quality had a noticeable effect on sealant efficiency.

Keywords

Organic gases, medium density fibreboard, barrier materials, display cases

Introduction

Organic gases

The presence of organic gases, chiefly aldehydes and carboxylic acids, in display and storage cases has been shown to cause corrosion of artifacts in a number of studies, including those in the National Museums of Scotland (NMS).[1–9]

Organic gases can be emitted by a variety of materials commonly used in case manufacture. The most important sources are wood and wood products (e.g. fibreboard), paints, varnishes and lacquers.[10–16] Emissions from these products usually show exponential decay and levels can remain corrosive for years.[10,13–15] Available data suggest that emissions from wood products may occur over a longer time period than those from surface finishes.[10,13-15]

The main corrosive organic gases emitted are formic and acetic acid, formaldehyde and acetaldehyde.[10–15] Most woods release mainly acids (chiefly acetic) although some emit mostly formaldehyde.[10,15] Most paints, lacquers and varnishes release mainly formic acid; others release significant amounts of formaldehyde.[10,14]

Medium density fibreboard

Wood and wood products are favoured for case construction because of their physical properties. One of the most popular construction materials is medium density fibreboard, MDF, which consist of wood chips within a urea formaldehyde resin. This emits low-molecular-weight aldehydes and carboxylic acids, particularly formaldehyde.[11–13] One variety of fibreboard, 'zero formaldehyde' MDF (ZF MDF) is manufactured without adding formaldehyde to the resin. However, organic vapours are still released from the wood fibres.

Formaldehyde within MDF has two sources, residual formaldehyde from incomplete polymerisation during manufacture, and secondary formaldehyde from hydrolytic decomposition of the cured resin.[12] Similarly, acetic acid occurs both as a free acid and from hydrolysis of acetyl groups in the hemicellulose.[15] Other acids may be produced during wood metabolism or through other hydrolysis reactions, e.g. formic acid from the formate ester group.[15]

The problems of sealing MDF have recently been highlighted in the NMS as several new galleries are being prepared and a paint finish was desired in a number of cases. It was decided that a project should be initiated to measure emissions from pieces of MDF coated with a wide range of possible barrier materials, including many suggested by designers. These are considered desirable by the designers and joiners, because of their low cost, ease or speed of application, ability to take a paint finish, etc.

Barrier materials

A range of barrier materials have been proposed for sealing MDF to prevent emission of the corrosive vapours. These include barrier foils, lacquers, paints and varnishes, and their use has been discussed in a number of studies.[8,10,12,14,16, 17]

* Author to whom correspondence should be addressed

Barrier foils

The traditional application method is to iron these onto the MDF to heat seal the foil. Ironing is time consuming and difficult, and the use of such foils increases the time and budget required for construction and installation of new displays. It is not possible to use a paint finish over these products. Hence, foils are unpopular with designers and joiners. More rapid methods of application such as stapling or taping have been suggested. However, the effectiveness of these methods in sealing the MDF is poorly known and the option of using a paint finish is still not available.

Lacquers, varnishes and paints

These can themselves emit harmful vapours.[10,12,14] In general, finishes with oils, nitrocellulose, acrylic and acetate solvents emit corrosive vapours, whilst polyurethane, polyester and epoxide finishes usually do not.[10,12,14] High initial gas levels fall rapidly over a few months, but remain potentially corrosive for years.[12,14] Painted surfaces can develop micro cracks, flake or crack.[12] Corrosion of metal artifacts and high levels of organic gases have been observed in MDF cases coated with polyurethane lacquer[8] and paint.[9] In both instances the finishes are not acting as efficient seals, and the paint appears to emit corrosive vapours.[9] Other studies, however, found that a polyurethane or polyester finish can reduce formaldehyde emission from MDF by a factor of ten.[17] The efficiency of these finishes as sealants for MDF and their emission characteristics are thus open to debate.

Procedure

Introduction

The most common test for emissions harmful to museum artifacts is the Oddy test.[18] This is a simple, standard museum test, and elevated temperature and humidity ensure corrosion rates are accelerated. It was, however, considered unsuitable for this study. Results are qualitative and subjective, and can vary with assessor.[19] Both the fibreboard and the surface finishes may behave differently at the conditions used than at those normally experienced in museum show cases. An alternative method providing quantitative data and simulating conditions experienced in a museum show case was therefore devised.

Experimental conditions

Pieces of MDF and ZF MDF 20 × 15 × 1.5 cm were placed in sealed inert polyethylene boxes commonly used by conservators and other museum staff for object storage. The pieces of MDF and ZF MDF were coated with a range of barrier materials, with an uncoated piece of each included as a comparison in each batch. An empty box was included as a control in all batches.

Temperature and RH were allowed to vary with indoor conditions. Sensors from a Meaco telemetry system were placed in a representative selection of boxes, including the control.

Materials tested

Three batches of samples have been tested to date.

The first batch consisted of six samples of MDF and ZF MDF and two sealant materials, Moistop and a water based lacquer (B). This batch was used to ascertain whether levels and variations in organic gases could be measured.

The second batch included a greater range of barrier materials, applied to ZF MDF and MDF. Two pieces of obechi wood were also submitted.

The third batch was exclusively ZF MDF, with a range of barrier materials applied. Different application methods (ironing, stapling and taping) were used for some foils.

The specific barrier materials tested to date and details of their application are listed in Tables 1 and 2.

Table 1. Products tested

Used as	Type	Product	Batch	Supplier
Substrate	Fibreboard	ZF MDF•	1, 2, 3	Medite of Europe Ltd, Redmondstown, Clommel, Co. Tipperary, Ireland
		MDF ••	1, 2	as above
		MDF 1 •••	2	as above
Substrate	Wood	Obechi	2	
		Moistop 622	1, 2, 3	Rowebb, 208 Bath Street, Glasgow, G2 4H.
		Marvelseal 360	3	Preservation Equipment Ltd, Shelfanger, Diss, Norfolk, IP22 2DG, UK
Barrier	Foils	Pioneer Packaging C315	2	Pioneer Packaging, 328 Cledington Road, Dundee, DD3 8RZ, UK
		Pioneer Packaging C321	2	as above
		Aluminium foil	3	
		Waterbased lacquer 20/EL/30/4; lacquer B	1	Trimite Ltd, Uxbridgde, Middlesex, UK
		Acrylic lacquer (clear); lacquer A	2	Halfords (UK car accessories supplier)
		Dacrylate	3	
Barrier	Liquid finishes	Tor polyurethane coating	3	
		Water based varnish (black ash satan); varnish B	2	Cuprinol Ltd, Adderwell, Frome, Somerset, UK
		Acrylic varnish (rich teak); varnish A	2	as above
		Acrylic paint, Eggshell 10B15	2	Johnstones Paints
		Emulsion paint	2	Dulux
		Water-based stain	2	
		Melinex	3	
Barrier	Other	Type 90 activated charcoal cloth	3	Charcoal Cloth, International Ltd, High Tech House, Commerce way, Arena business park, Houghton-le-Spring, Tyne & Wear, DH 4 5PP, UK

• (contains formaldehyde-free resin)
•• (contains formaldehyde in resin)
••• (Class 1 fire resistance, formaldehyde in resin)

Measurement of emissions

Formaldehyde, acetaldehyde, acetic and formic acid were measured using both passive and active sampling. In order to measure levels within the boxes with minimal disturbance to the interior environment small flaps were cut in each. Detector badges and tubes were posted through these, with passive samplers suspended on thin inert nylon thread. During passive sampling the flaps were closed and sealed with electrical tape. These were then reopened after an appropriate exposure period and the samplers removed with minimum disturbance. For active sampling the flaps were partially closed during sampling but not sealed. After all sampling the flaps were re-sealed with electrical tape.

Active sampling

Levels of formaldehyde, acetaldehyde and acetic acid were initially measured by active monitoring using Gastec detector tubes. A thin length of inert silicon tubing was attached to the end of the tube and extended into the boxes during sampling.

The detector tubes are used for measuring organic gas levels for health and safety of personnel. They provide spot readings and are relatively cheap. However, detection limits are fairly high and results are of limited accuracy (Table 3). Interferences from other related organic gases can affect the reading for a given gas; hence, results may be misleading. Nevertheless the tubes provide a useful tool for screening materials and identifying those with high levels of organic gases. High levels indicate that the materials are not sealing the fibreboard and/or are themselves emitting organic vapours, whilst low levels suggest that the materials are acting as effective sealants. Measurements were taken at intervals over the study period.

Table 2. Details of application of barriers, initiation of tests and sampling times used

Batch	Date barriers applied	Number of days after application of barriers		
		Samples put in boxes	Aldehydes monitored	Acids monitored
1	8 to 9 June 1995	77	131 to 133	133 to 147
2	8 to 9 June 1995	60	14 to 16	104 to 118
			50 to 52 (MDF & MDF1 samples)	104 to 118
3	16 November 1995	8	25 to 27	35 to 49

Table 3. Details of detector tubes and badges used, from Gastec data sheets, BRE and reference 20

Detector	Gas	Detection limit	Measuring range	Accuracy	Reproducibility	T range	RH range
Gastec tube 91L	Formaldehyde	0.05 ppm	0.1–32.5 ppm	±25 %	Not given	Correction	
Gastec tube 81L	Acetic acid		0.125–25 ppm			within error	0–90%
Gastec tube 92M	Acetaldehyde	0.25 ppm	1–100 ppm			from 15–30°C	
GMD 570	Formaldehyde	0.001 mg litre^{-1}	Not given	Not given	0.2–8.7%	10–30°C	10–80%
type badge	Acetaldehyde	0.012 mg litre^{-1}	Not given	Not given	Not given	Not given	Not given

Passive sampling

More accurate measurements were obtained by passive monitoring.

GMD 570 type badges supplied and analysed by the Building Research Establishment (BRE) were used to measure aldehyde levels (Table 3) and Palmes diffusion tubes, supplied and analysed by Strathclyde University, were used for the acids.

The badges were exposed for three days, and the tubes for 14 days. Due to the difference in exposure time the badges were usually exposed first, with subsequent exposure of the tubes.

Results

Environmental conditions

The data collected by the Meaco sensors indicated similar average values of RH and temperature in all boxes. Unfortunately the number of sensors was limited; hence, sensors were only placed in boxes from batch 1. The sensors were removed after four months on the manufacturer's advice as they can be damaged by high levels of formaldehyde.

Fluctuations were greatest in the control and boxes containing samples coated with Moistop, with no significant variation between these. The smallest fluctuations occurred in boxes containing samples with lacquer B (water-based) and uncoated samples, again with little significant variation between these.

This variation is attributed to buffering of environmental conditions by the fibreboard. The reduction in the buffering capacity of samples coated with Moistop compared to uncoated samples indicates reduction of the fibreboard permeability. Hence, it may also be partially sealed to other gases. The high buffering capacity of the lacquered samples suggests that the lacquer does not provide a good seal.

As organic gases are produced within fibreboard by hydrolytic reactions, barrier materials may reduce emission rates by decreasing moisture uptake, hence reducing hydrolysis.[12] The environmental data suggest that hydrolysis will be reduced for samples coated with Moistop, resulting in lower levels of reaction products, chiefly formaldehyde and acetic acid. Initial and primary vapours may still be emitted, depending on the permeability of the sealant to organic vapours relative to water vapour.

Gas levels

For batch 1, five sets of Gastec readings were taken, with subsequent passive sampling in boxes with low levels. For later batches passive sampling occurred after a period of two weeks. Selected measurements are continuing to identify the long-term effectiveness of the barrier materials.

Measurements

Active sampling

In many samples, levels of formaldehyde and acetic acid were high enough to be measurable. In batch 1, levels of acetaldehyde were usually near or below the detection limit. The detection limit for acetaldehyde was therefore considered too high for meaningful results, and acetaldehyde was not measured in batches 2 and 3. Most sealants from batch 3 gave results below the detection limit for all gases.

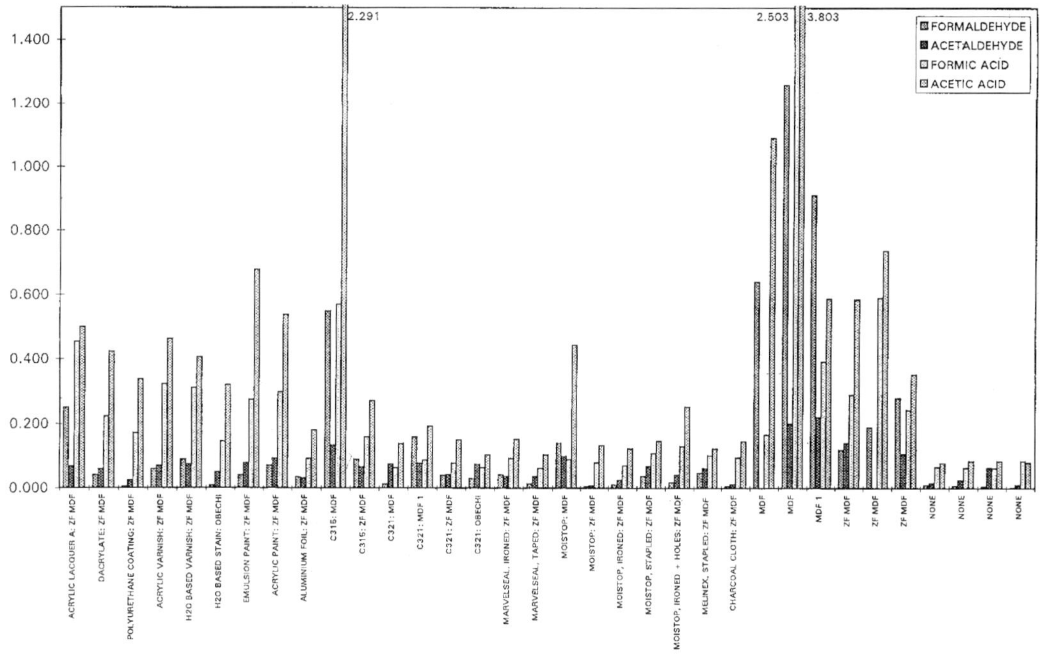

Figure 1. Organic gas levels in the boxes from passive sampling. Values in mg m^{-1}. Coated samples listed as barrier: substrate. Duplicates are shown in batch order. Note the low acetaldehyde from ZF MDF, batch 2, and no acetaldehyde reading for MDF, batch 1

Measurable differences between samples occurred where values were above the detection limit.

Passive sampling

For all samples, levels of organic gases in the boxes were high enough to be measurable, as were differences between samples. Acetaldehyde was anomalously low from ZF MDF in batch 2, and comparison with values from coated samples in this batch was cautious.

Comparison of sampling types

Values from active sampling were higher than those from passive sampling, particularly for acetaldehyde. Passive sampling generally indicated similar levels of both acids, and higher levels of formaldehyde than acetaldehyde, suggesting that interference by related gases will affect active sampling measurements. This interference may explain the discrepancy between active and passive measurements.

The subsequent discussion of results concentrates on those from passive sampling, except in the next section, on equilibration time.

Equilibration time

Although both formaldehyde and acetic acid levels rose slightly over the eight-week period of active sampling of batch 1, all values were within error of each other. This suggests that levels equilibrated within the first week, as far as can be determined with this sampling method.

Substrate

Type

All three types of fibreboard, MDF, MDF1 and ZF MDF, gave high levels of aldehydes and organic acids without barrier materials (Figure 1).

Significant differences occurred between levels from the different types of fibreboard. Aldehyde levels were lowest from ZF MDF, and similar from MDF and MDF1. Organic acid levels were highest from MDF, and similar from MDF 1 and ZF MDF.

The stained sample of obechi wood gave extremely low emissions for all gases, with aldehyde levels less than acid levels. For both, the lower molecular weight gases were lowest.

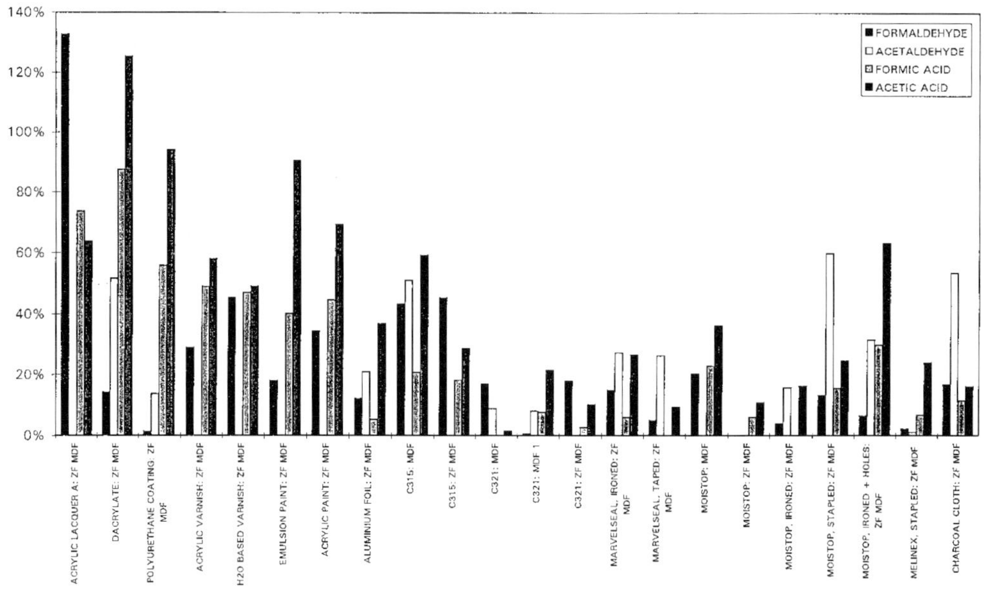

Figure 2. Organic gases from sealed samples as a percantage of the value from the corresponding unsealed substrate. Values are corrected for background using levels in the control boxes. Coated samples listed as barrier: substrate. Duplicates are shown in batch order. Note no acetaldehyde ratios for barriers on ZF MDF, batch 2, or on MDF, batch 1

Batch

Variations occurred in the levels and relative proportions of different organic gases from the same type of fibreboard in different batches (Figure 1). Comparison of absolute values between different batches was avoided because of these variations.

Variations may be due to differences in:

- manufacturing process and/or materials;
- length of time since manufacture.

These factors could affect the proportions of secondary to primary gases, and the relative proportions of different gases.

Barrier foils

These can be divided into two groups on the basis of passive and active sampling:

- **Group I:** reduced levels of all gases – Moistop, Marvelseal, C321, aluminium foil. The relative reduction on different gases varied slightly within this group (Figure 2). In general formaldehyde and/or formic acid were reduced most, and acetaldehyde and/or acetic acid reduced least.
- **Group II:** lesser reductions of formaldehyde and acids, acetaldehyde inconsistent – C315. Formic acid was always reduced most, and acetaldehyde the least, with formaldehyde and acetic acid similar. Reductions were less than for group I (Figure 2).

Variations in both the efficiency of different foils and the efficiency of a foil for different gases are attributed to variations in:

- sealant permeability;
- permeability of a given sealant to different gases.

Substrate and batch

The efficiency of the foils varied when applied to different substrates and between batches for a given foil and substrate (Figure 2). Such discrepancies are hard to explain but may be due to variations in the effectiveness of the seal, possibly from puncturing or imperfect sealing of edges. Increased gas levels may result from puncturing, revealing underlying layers of the surfacing material which emit gases.

APPLICATION METHOD

The efficiency of the foils also varied depending on application method (Figure 2):

- Taping Marvelseal provided a more effective barrier than ironing.
- Ironing Moistop was more effective than stapling. Ironed Moistop with a few small holes behaved similarly to stapled Moistop.

All samples of Moistop and Marvelseal, regardless of application method, gave lower gas levels than most liquid finishes. With taped coatings emitted gases may accumulate at high levels below the sealant layer, resulting in high emission rates if the layer were subsequently pierced. Accumulation of secondary gases may be reduced due to reduction in moisture uptake.

Liquid finishes

The effectiveness of the liquid finishes can be divided into three groups:

- **Group I:** Aldehydes reduced, minimal effect on acids – Polyurethane coating and Dacrylate. Polyurethane was more effective. Both reduced formaldehyde more than acetaldehyde.
- **Group II:** Acetaldehyde increased, other gases reduced – Varnishes A and B, emulsion and acrylic paints. Similar reductions occurred for the acids and formaldehyde, although emulsion paint had little effect on formic acid (Figure 2).
- **Group III:** Aldehydes increased, acids reduced slightly – Acrylic lacquer A. Both acids were similarly reduced, with a greater increase in acetaldehyde than formaldehyde.

A fourth group was indicated by active sampling, lacquer B, with increased aldehyde and acid levels. Environmental data indicated moisture exchange from this sample; hence, hydrolytic production of gases could occur.

Finishes in groups II to IV appear to emit gaseous products themselves. Those in group II appear to be partially sealing the fibreboard, but is doubtful whether lacquers A and B even partially seal the board.

Variation in the relative proportions of different gases may be due to variations in:

- emission characteristics and rates of the finishes;
- permeability of the finishes to different gases;
- production rates of secondary gases.

Other surface finishes

Activated charcoal cloth and Melinex were comparable to Group I foils (Figure 2). The former is the only barrier material that will absorb external pollutants. It has a limited lifetime, and will eventually saturate in organic gases and re-emit these.

Summary

The best sealants were Marvelseal, Moistop, and charcoal cloth. Gas levels were reduced to ≤ 30% of those from the same substrate without a barrier applied, and were often below the detection limit once corrected for the control. C321 and taped aluminium foil also provide good barriers, with similar reductions. The flimsy and fragile nature of the aluminium foil make it unlikely that this is a practical option for a sealant.

The liquid finishes were generally worse than the foils and cloth owing to higher levels of organic acids. The best was polyurethane coating, followed by Dacrylate. For the aldehydes the former gave reductions to ≤ 15% whilst the later gave reductions to ≤ 50%, compared to values from uncoated samples. Both polyurethane coating and Dacrylate gave minimal reductions for the acids (particularly acetic acid) with values from 56 to 125% of those from uncoated samples.

Other liquid finishes did not provide particularly good sealants; values ranged from 40 to 133% of those from samples without barriers.

In general, formaldehyde was the most reduced gas, and acetaldehyde the least. Variations in the effectiveness for different gases may reflect:

- differences in sealant permeability, with the lowest permeability for formaldehyde.
- reduction in moisture uptake preventing formation of formaldehyde by hydrolysis.[17] This suggests that secondary formaldehyde is a major contribution to the overall emitted formaldehyde, and is more important than hydrolytic reactions producing the other gases.
- production of gases by the sealants.

Conclusions

- Levels of formaldehyde, acetaldehyde, acetic and formic acids were measurable and equilibrated rapidly.
- Levels were mostly above the detection limits of the passive samplers but often below those of the Gastec tubes.
- Levels of organic gases emitted by ZF MDF were significantly lower than from MDF but still significantly above levels in the control boxes.
- The majority of the sealants reduced levels of organic gases.
- The effectiveness of a given sealant varied for different gases.
- The most effective sealants were the foils, particularly Marvelseal and Moistop.
- The effectiveness of foil sealants varied depending on the quality and method of sealing.
- Dacrylate and polyurethane coating caused significant reductions for aldehydes.
- The paint and varnishes reduced levels but were far less effective than the foils or inert lacquers.

Further studies

The current study is ongoing and a number of additional tests are planned:

- measurements of levels of organic gases over a period of a year to monitor any changes and assess the long term effectiveness of the sealants;
- testing additional products, particularly Nextel;[21]
- testing other application methods, including piercing taped foils and cloth;
- testing the effect of different numbers of coats of liquid finishes;
- comparison of Oddy test results with the results of this study;
- repetition and duplication of measurements, including setting up new test boxes to check repeatability.

Acknowledgments

The authors wish to acknowledge the collaboration of members of the Design department in the NMS, particularly G. Boyle, G. Nolan and T. Chisholm, in the initiation of the project, and in proposing products and supplying samples. Members of the Conservation and Analytical research department are also thanked for their support, especially J. Tate for valuable suggestions and assistance throughout this project. The University of Strathclyde are thanked for providing the organic acid results.

References

1. N. H. Tennent and T. Baird, 'The Deterioration of Mollusca Collections: Identification of Shell Efflorescence', *Studies in Conservation* 33 (1985): 75–85.
2. N. H. Tennent, J. Tate and L. Cannon, 'The Corrosion of Lead Artifacts in Wooden Storage Cabinets', *SSCR Journal* 4 (1993): 8–11.
3. N. H. Tennent, B.G. Cooksey, D. Littlejohn, B. J. Ottaway, S. E. Tarling and M. Vickers, 'Unusual Corrosion and Efflorescence Products on Bronze and Iron Antiquities Stored

in Wooden Cabinets', *Conservation Science in the UK*, ed. N. H. Tennent (London: James and James, 1993), 60–66.
4. V. Weierter and J. Tate, 'The Corrosion of Lead Communion Tokens', *Conservation Science in the UK*, ed. N. H. Tennent (London: James and James, 1993), 57–59.
5. C. M. Grzywacz and C. D. Stulik, 'Carbonyl Pollutants in the Museum Environment', *SSCR Journal* 4, no. 1 (1993): 16–19.
6. C. M. Grzywacz, 'Using Passive Sampling Devices to Detect Pollutants in Museum Environments' (Paper delivered at the Tenth Triennial Meeting of the International Council of Museums Committee for Conservation, Washington, DC, 1993), 610-615.
7. C. M. Grzywacz, 'European Carbonyl Monitoring Program, Analysis Results and Discussion Report' (Edinburgh: The Royal Museum of Scotland, 1993).
8. M. A. Leveque, 'The Problem of Formaldehyde – a Case Study', (American Institute for Conservation of Historic and Artistic Works, Washington, DC, 1986), 56-65.
9. K. Eremin, P. Wilthew, J. Breeze and M. Mitchell, 'Monitoring Pollutants and Particulates within the National Museums of Scotland', in press.
10. D. Knotkov',a-Cermakova and J. Vlckova, 'Corrosive Effect of Plastics, Rubber and Wood on Metals in Confined Spaces. *British Corrosion Journal* 6 (1971): 17–22.
11. A. Berge and B. Mellegaard, 'Formaldehyde Emission from Particle Board – a New Method for Determination', *Forest Products Journal* (January 1979): 21–25.
12. S. Dombey, 'An Assessment of Surfacing Materials as Barriers to Formaldehyde in Resin-bonded Boards', *Journal of the Oil and Colour Chemists Association* 72 (1989): 108–115.
13. T.W. Zinn, D. Cline and W.F. Lehmann, 'Long Term Study of Formaldehyde Emission Decay from Particle Board', *Forest Products Journal* 4 (1990): 15–18.
14. P. D. Donovan and T. M. Moynehan, 'Corrosion of Metals by Vapours from Oil-drying Paints', *Corrosion Science* 5 (1965): 803–814.
15. P. G. Arni, G. C. Cochrane and J. D. Gray, 'The Emission of Corrosive Vapours by Wood. II*. The Analysis of the Vapours Emitted by Certain Freshly Felled Hardwoods and Softwoods by Gas Chromatography and Spectrophotometry', *Journal of Applied Chemistry* 15 (1965): 463–468.
16. J. Tetreault, 'Display Materials: the Good, the Bad and the Ugly', *Exhibitions and Conservation*, ed. J. Sage, (Scottish Society for Conservation and Restoration, Edinburgh, 1994), 79–89.
17. S. Dombey, 'The Development and Application of a New Small-scale Climate Chamber for Measuring the Rate of Formaldehyde Emission', *Furniture Research Manual* 51 (1988).
18. W.O. Oddy, 'An Unexpected Danger in Display', *Museums Journal* 73, no. 1 (1973): 7–28.
19. L. R. Green and D. Thickett, 'Interlaboratory Comparison of the Oddy Test', *Conservation Science in the UK*, ed. N. Tennent, (London: James and James Scientific Publishers, 1993), 111–116.
20. V. M. Brown, D. R. Crump, M. A. Gavin and D. Gardiner, 'Aldehydes in the Non-industrial Indoor Environment', *Clean Air at Work, Proceedings of the International Symposium, Royal Society of Chemistry Special Publication* 108 (1991): 357–365.
21. M. Cowley, 'Sealed MDF Board', *Museums Journal* (January 1996), 35.

L'usage de la lumière naturelle en muséographie

Jean-Jacques Ezrati
Direction des musées de France
Département de l'architecture, de la muséographie et des équipements
6, rue des Pyramides
75001 Paris, France

Résumé

La lumière naturelle par ces caractéristiques propres représente pour les musées non seulement une lumière parfaite en ce qui concerne le rendu des couleurs mais aussi, malheureusement, une source de danger potentiel pour les collections. Les expérimentations suivantes tendent à démontrer que l'usage réfléchi de la lumière naturelle est possible en muséographie et que l'on peut combattre ses effets néfastes tout en conservant ses qualités au niveau du rendu des couleurs.

Mots-clés

Lumière naturelle, conservation préventive, films autocollants, rendu des couleurs

Introduction

La muséographie représente l'ensemble des techniques nécessaire à la conservation et à la présentation des objets que détiennent les musées, c'est dans ce domaine que l'usage de la lumière naturelle nous interpelle. Les caractéristiques du rayonnement naturel sont connus et nous savons qu'elles représentent un facteur non négligeable de dégradation des collections. Tout comme une source électrique, l'ampoule à filament de tungstène, par exemple, n'est pas utilisée seule mais à travers un luminaire, il en sera de même de la lumière naturelle. Les fenêtres, les baies vitrées, les verrières sont autant de luminaires que l'on équipera de leurs différents accessoires tels les vitrages, les volets, les stores, etc. La réalisation d'un éclairage en lumière naturelle consistera en la maîtrise de ces différents paramètres que sont les sources (soleil et ciel) et les instruments de contrôle (fenêtres, verrières, etc) pour répondre à des objectifs clairement définis (éclairage d'un cabinet des dessins, pourquoi pas!).

Parmi les différents moyens de contrôle existant nous nous proposons de tester les films autocollants tant du point de vue de la conservation que de la présentation.

L'étude des films autocollants

Films autocollants et conservation

Dans de nombreux cas l'usage de films autocollants sur des vitrages existant constitue une excellente solution pour réduire, voire éliminer les effets néfastes du rayonnement naturel dus aux composantes ultraviolette et infrarouge. Une réduction du rayonnement visible est aussi, dans bien des cas, indispensable.

L'étude a constitué à mesurer la décoloration de trois échantillons du test de la laine bleue (#1, 2 et 3) sous différentes protections. La décoloration a été mesurée en utilisant la formule de différence de couleurs de la Commission Internationale de l'Éclairage CIELAB.[1]

Expérimentation

Les 3 échantillons de laine bleue ont été exposé à la lumière du jour, face nord. Une partie de chaque échantillon est restée sous une protection absolue de la lumière, les quatre autres parties sous différentes protections: un film anti-UV (LEE Filters # 226), un film de protection solaire (GLACE CONTRÔLE IR 70 ou MADICO XR 70), un filtre correcteur[2] CTO 3ND (LEE Filters # 207), un filtre neutre (LEE Filter # 209). Une dernière partie des échantillons a été exposée sans aucune protection. La durée d'exposition a été mesurée en continue à l'aide d'un intégrateur de rayonnement équipé d'une sonde photométrique (LI-COR inc: SOLAR MONITOR L-1776). La durée totale d'exposition en fin d'expérimentation été de 4,12 Mluxh. Nous avons effectué 7 mesures sur les 3 échantillons pour les 6 états, en tout 441 mesures (avec 3 prises pour chacune) à l'aide d'un spectrocolorimetre de type "Dataflash 100" de chez datacolor international.[3]

Analyse des résultats

Les mesures ont été organisées en trois séries, une par échantillon de laine bleue, ce qui nous donne les graphiques suivants:

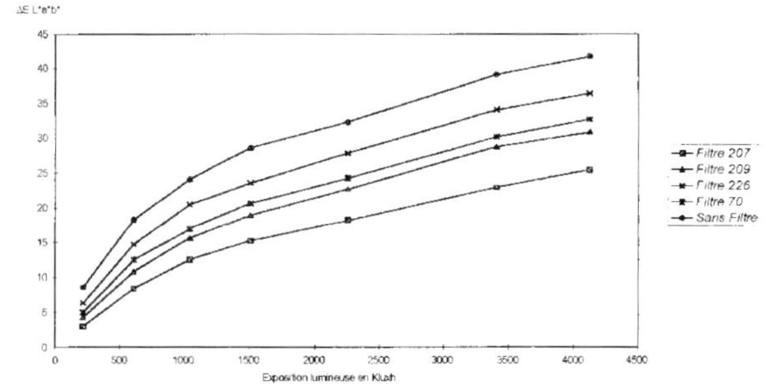

Figure 1. Influence des FILTRES au cours del'exposition lumineuse: laine 1

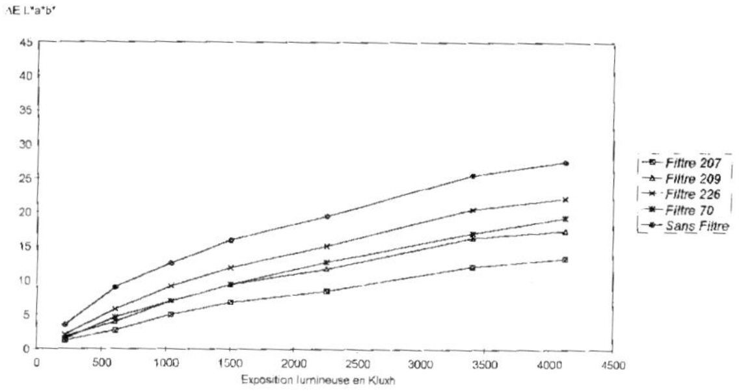

Figure 2. Influence des FILTRES au cours del'exposition lumineuse: laine 2

Les effets des différentes protections sont identiques au cas précédent.

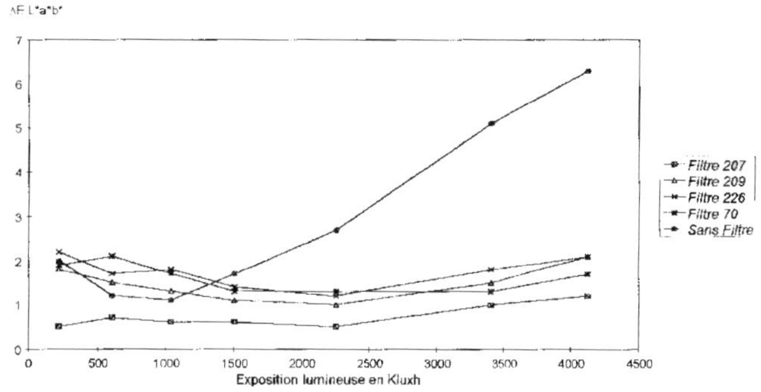

Figure 3. Influence des FILTRES au cours del'exposition lumineuse: laine 3

On note la dégradation extrêmement rapide sur les premiers 1000 Kluxh, ce qui est la confirmation de ce que nous savons déjà sur les réactions photochimiques. Intéressant aussi de noter qu'une protection UV uniquement n'apporte que peu d'amélioration par rapport à des filtres moins performant au niveau de l'absorption des UV mais d'un facteur de transmission de la lumière beaucoup plus faible (XR70), voire de filtres qui transforment le spectre du visible en diminuant encore plus les radiations visibles de faible longueur d'onde (#207). A noter que quelles que soient les protections envisagées, elles améliorent toutes la conservation pour ce niveau de sensibilité.

Conclusion

Les tests effectués confirment la nécessité de non seulement éliminer le rayonnement ultraviolet de la lumière naturelle mais surtout de contrôler, donc souvent de réduire, le rayonnement visible, les filtres teintés étant une des solutions.

Films autocollants et présentation

La proposition d'équiper les vitrages d'une salle d'exposition de films autocollant teintés ne requière pas l'adhésion immédiate de son responsable. L'opposition en est qu'une lumière colorée aura une action pernicieuse au niveau du rendu des couleurs des oeuvres présentées. Ceci est naturellement vrai lorsque nous utilisons une lumière colorée, c'est-à-dire une lumière dont une partie du spectre visible a été éliminé.[4] Mais cela n'est plus vrai si nous diminuons, sans éliminer, une partie du spectre visible par rapport à une autre. Ceci est le cas de la lumière naturelle à différents moments de la journée ou bien tout simplement la lumière d'une lampe à incandescence dont le spectre est très pauvre en radiations visibles de faible longueurs d'ondes (bleu) et très riche en radiations visibles de grandes longueurs d'ondes (rouge). L'expérimentation qui va suivre est de démontrer la justesse de l'hypothèse qui précise que sous une lumière blanche, quelle que soit sa température de couleur, un individu ayant une bonne vision des couleurs, pourra comparer tous les paramètres d'une couleur par rapport à une autre, si naturellement l'éclairement est suffisant.

Expérimentation

Sous une enceinte de vision des couleurs[5] il a été demandé à un certain nombre de sujets d'effectuer un test de vision des couleurs,[6] d'une part sous la lumière de l'enceinte normale, c'est-à-dire une lumière à spectre équilibré à 6500 K, puis d'autre part sous une lumière filtrée par un film autocollant de protection solaire, le XR70. Quelques essais ont même été réalisés avec un filtre bronze dont le facteur de transmission très faible donnait un niveau d'éclairement inférieur à 500 lux incompatible avec le test, augmentant d'autant plus la difficulté.

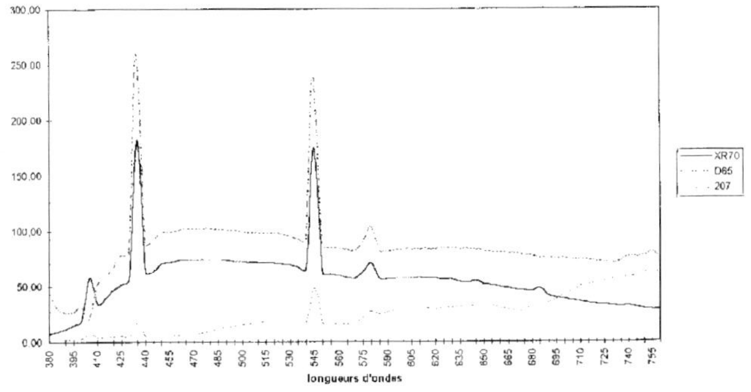

Figure 4. Courbes spectrales d'une enceinte de vision des couleurs sous différentes lumières: D65/XR70/207

Analyse des résultats

Le tableau de mesures ci-dessous résume les résultats obtenus:[7]

n° d'ordre	âge	sexe	points sous D65	points sous D65+XR70	écart	points sous D65+207	écart
1	-30	F	0	4	4	-	-
2	-25	F	20	12	-8	-	-
3	-25	F	12	0	-12	-	-
4	-30	F	20	8	-12	-	-
5	-50	M	20	19	-1	-	-
6	-50	M	4	12	8	-	-
7	-30	F	24	57	33	-	-
8	-30	M	48	59	11	-	-
9	-30	F	8	0	-8	-	-
10	-30	F	20	4	-16	8	-12
11	-30	M	4	4	0	8	4
totaux	-	-	180	179	1	16	-8

D'après les résultats obtenus on peut constater que la pose d'un film de protection solaire légèrement teinté, en dehors d'un cas (le n°7), n'influe pratiquement pas sur la vision des couleurs, le nombre d'erreurs avec ou sans filtre étant du même ordre de grandeur. Même si l'excellent résultat obtenu avec le filtre #207 ne peut donner lieu à une interprétation, le nombre de sujets étant trop faible, il est toutefois intéressant de constater que sur les sujets testés il n'a pas eu d'influence néfaste.

Conclusions

Ces deux expérimentations nous amènent à conseiller l'emploi de films autocollant de protection solaire pour résoudre un nombre important de problèmes posés.

Néanmoins l'installation de tels films requière que nous prenions en compte les recommandations suivantes:

1. Faire le tour de toutes autres possibilités de réduction de la chaleur et de l'éclairement: stores, réduction des ouvertures, parsoleils, etc.
2. Choisir la teinte du film en fonction de l'ambiance lumineuse souhaitée (chaude ou froide).
3. Revêtir du même film toutes les ouvertures des espaces dans lesquels se déplacent les visiteurs (les salles d'expositions adjacentes, les dégagements, les escaliers, etc.).
4. S'assurer de la stabilité du film dans le temps par les références du fabriquant.
5. Choisir l'entreprise de pose sur ses références passées (à vérifier).

Ces recommandations loin d'être éloignées du domaine de la conservation préventive ont tout à fait leur place ici, car la conservation préventive n'est qu'un élément de la muséographie, ne l'oublions pas.

Etude annexe

Nous avons exploité le temps et les moyens de ces deux expérimentations pour nous livrer à une troisième expérimentation dont le but était de vérifier, une fois de plus, la loi de la réciprocité. Deux échantillons de laine bleu n° 2 ont donc été exposés à la lumière du jour, l'un d'une manière continuelle, l'autre d'une manière intermittente. Un troisième échantillon, conservé dans le noir nous a permis de faire les mesures de différence de couleur au fur et à mesure. Les mesures de différences de couleur ont été réalisé directement à l'aide d'un colorimètre (Minolta Chroma Meter II Reflectance). Le graphique ci-dessous visualise les résultats et confirme la loi de la réciprocité.

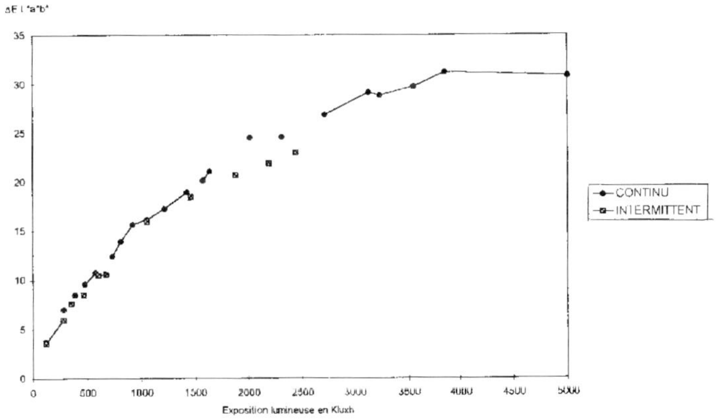

Figure 5. Eclairage continu et intermitent sur un échantillon de laine blue No 2

Remerciements

Je tiens à remercier tout particulièrement Maria Léonor Cuhaonte et Agnes Gandon, stagiaires à la Direction des musées de France, pour leur participation active à la campagne de mesures et la passation des tests, ainsi que les entreprises MICA S.A.(Datacolor international) et GAMAIN, pour le prêt de leurs matériels.

Notes

1. La formule est: $\Delta E^{\star}ab = [(\Delta L^{\star})^2 + (\Delta a^{\star})^2 + (\Delta b^{\star})^2]^{1/2}$
2. Nous avons utilisé un filtre correcteur plutôt qu'un film teinté pour accentuer au maximum le côté bronze et le niveau d'absorption des radiations de faible longueur d'onde. Le taux du visible est de 35%.
3. Caractéristiques principales: géométrie: diffus/8°; monochromateur double barrette de 128 photodiodes et réseau holographique; résolution de 10nm et bande passante de 10 nm.
4. Par exemple une lumière rouge est une lumière blanche dont on a éliminé tous les rayonnements de courte longueur d'onde: du violet au jaune.

5. Enceinte "Gamain ref: 1865".
6. Le test Farnsworth-Munsell 100-hue consiste à ordonner 96 pastilles de teintes différentes.
7. A noter que le test demande une vingtaine de minutes par sujet, demande des conditions physiologiques satisfaisantes et ne peut être répété dans la même séance qu'une ou deux fois, car d'un côté la fatigue visuelle peut intervenir et de l'autre, une certaine accoutumance peut aussi fausser le test.

Bibliographie

Ezrati J.J., "Propriétés anti-UV des films de sécurité", *ICOM Conservation Committee 8th Triennial Meeting Preprints*, 871-874.

Ezrati J.J., "Une méthode pour le choix des films de protection", *La lettre de l'OCIM,* n°11, (Dijon: Ministère de l'Education Nationale, 1991).

Horton D., "Light Transmission Characteristics of Some Window Films", *ICCM Bulletin VIII*, n° 1-2, 1982.

Kowaliski P., *Vision et mesure de la couleur*, (Paris: Masson, 1972).

Sève R., *Physique de la couleur*, (Paris: Masson, 1996).

Preventive Conservation in Swedish Museums: Technical Museum Storage Room Survey 1994–1995

Jan G. Holmberg
Comnord Sweden AB,
Dalagatan 78, 11324 Stockholm, Sweden

Lars-Uno Johansson*
RIK (Conservation Institute of National Antiquities),
Box 5405, 11484 Stockholm, Sweden

Abstract

The Swedish National Council for Cultural Affairs, which wants to see improvements in the preservation of the nation's cultural heritage, has commissioned the Conservation Institute of National Antiquities (RIK) to carry out a survey of the current status of museum storage rooms all over the country. The method used was a physical inventory of a large number of museum storage rooms and use of a relational database with object-oriented tools for storing and processing all the information gathered. The present condition of the collection in every storage room, correlated with its condition when first moved into the storage room, was used as one of the parameters to evaluate the capacity of the storage room to preserve the heritage. The quantity of data gathered is large enough to be representative for the country as a whole. The result of the Swedish Technical Museum Storage Room Survey is that more than 40% of local museums' storage rooms and 20% of regional and central museums' storage rooms are considered to be unacceptable. They do not preserve the collections in storage in an acceptable way.

Keywords

Preventive conservation, museum storage room, storage room, museum warehouse, museum survey, database for museum survey

Objective

This project is a part of the overall aim of the Conservation Institute of National Antiquities (RIK) to preserve the country's material cultural heritage by active and passive measures. Hence, the project title: 'Preventive Conservation in Swedish Museums'. The objective of the technical museum storage inventory is to lay the foundation for improvements where needed.

The initial task was to inventory all the storage rooms in 14 museums, but the number of museums was extended after the project was initiated. The keen interest from the museums affected the decision to increase the number of museums inventoried.

The result was more work for the project group, but this was compensated by the enlarged statistical base and the good relations with the museums. At the present time, more than 350 museum storage rooms have been inventoried.

The work was arranged to give a picture of the technical status of museum storage rooms at central, regional and local levels. Attempts were made within these categories to list how various types of objects and materials are kept. The conditions of the artifacts and objects in museum storage rooms partly constituted the quality of the storage rooms. The risk of damage by handling and the risk of long-term storage damage were also considered here. During the course of the project, the value of a central register of Swedish museum storage rooms and their status became clear. The basis of this register is the database mentioned below.

Methods

Inventory form

The basis for the inventory was the form drawn up by RIK in 1993. It consists of four pages. The first page identified the museum and the storage room and gave some space for a verbal summary of the results. To give the inventory more weight, there was also space for the signatures of the head of the museum and the curator. Many museum heads made use of the opportunity, but not all.

The second page identified the building and the technical systems of note. More than 50 choices are given. During the project, it became clear that even more choices about the building or storage rooms should have been included. The aspects covered were a general identification of the building, the kind of heating and ventilation system installed, its condition, and the security of the museum storage room. An important aspect was to note the storage rooms' accessibility, because many of the staff found this to be inadequate. Finally, the rental costs for each storage room were noted where possible. This information proved to be the hardest to obtain in the whole project.

The third page recorded any damage to the collection. This was done for each individual storage room. The type of object, its material and the volume in % it occupied in the museum storage room were recorded, the risk for handling and storage damage were assessed, and instantaneous measurements were made of the climate and recorded. The museum staff were primed with a short 'instruction

* Author to whom correspondence should be addressed

manual', an explanation of matters regarding the risk for handling and storage damage. A four-point scale was used, ranging from 1 (good) to 4 (unacceptable). The idea was to assess the ability of the storage room to protect objects from handling and storage damage. During the project, it again became clear that more types of material should have been included than the 30 in the Gunnel database.

The last page had space for explanatory diagrams and future plans, and allowed the staff to express the largest single storage problem.

The inventory

The museums that showed an interest and responded to the invitation were visited in order. After the method had been explained, the physical work was carried out. Every storage room now registered in the Gunnel database was inspected in detail: areas were examined, temperature and relative humidity were measured, the volumes occupied by various objects and material types were assessed with the museum staff as an percentage volume figure, and the difficult questions about risk for handling and storage damage were discussed on site in the museum storage room. The inventory fostered a comprehensive dialogue with the museum staff. Most days were long and tiring, and frequently extra days needed to be assigned to a museum.

The value of the dialogues cannot be emphasised enough. Contacts were established between museum staff and RIK conservators. Discussions were often expanded 'on site', and RIK had ample opportunity to point out the significance and value of preventive conservation.

Most importantly, the project initiated further collaboration between museums and RIK, e.g. consultation during the planning and design of new storage room facilities or the improving of old storage rooms.

When the inventory was finished, the original completed forms were handed to the conservator or curator to give him/her time to examine the frequently critical comments and to correct any mistakes. Hopefully, it also gave the conservator or curator time to discuss the situation with the head of the museum, because the latter often confirmed by signature that he/she was aware of the results of the inventory. The information was then inserted into the Gunnel database.

The database

The Gunnel database was specified by RIK and supplied by Energo AB. It is a relational database with object-oriented tools. The software used was Paradox for Windows. The database was installed in a Dell Pentium XPS P60. The hierarchy of the database is:

Database Gunnel
— Museum
—— Storage room
——— Date of inventory
— Fabric, Material, Object etc. etc. etc.

The database can thus have one or more museums; the number is unlimited. Each museum can have several storage rooms. Each storage room can have one or more inventory days and each inventory day can have one or more of the 30 materials or type of object specified by RIK.

If an object, material or category of material exists, it belongs unequivocally to one museum, storage room and inventory day. In the same way, the inventory day and storage room can only belong to one museum. Input is from the top of the hierarchy, i.e. first the museum, then the storage room, then the inventory day, then the description (under the headings Building, Climate, Security, Transport, Rental), then Material and Object. The distinction between Material and Object is not clear. Material means both the kind of material and the kind of object. The form had 20 base variants. At the end of the project, we had 30 variants registered

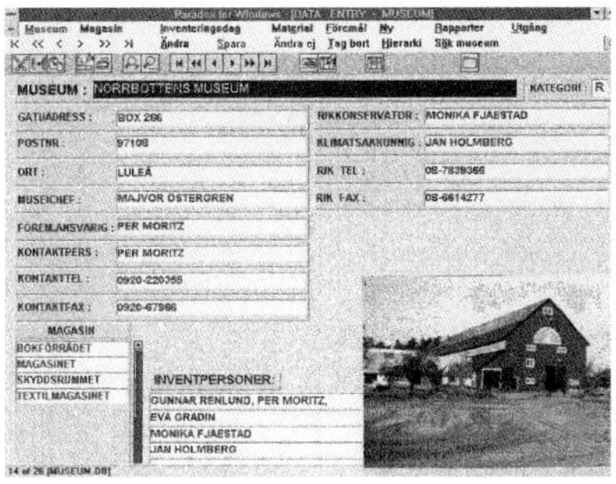

Figure 1. The first screen in Gunnel

in the Gunnel database. The field work required the handling of materials that had not been predicted, e.g. polymers.

The following are the search keys, which cannot be freely moved around:

- The name of the museum
- The name of the storage room
- The date of the inventory
- The name of the material.

An advantage of Gunnel is that the strict hierarchy prevents mixing up inputs by defining the storage room. All information about the building, the objects and the contact addresses is tied in to a specific storage room.

The input data are given in eight screens. Figure 1 (screen 1) shows that Gunnel can handle the installation of graphics, photographs or videos. Many photos were taken during the inventory. Unfortunately, poor conditions were documented more often than good ones.

Because Gunnel has sensitive data, the database is confidential and needs a password for access. Back-up was carried out after input every day. The back-up is protected like other RIK material in locked and fireproof cupboards.

There are currently 27 museums and 354 storage rooms in Gunnel. The database allows museums, storage rooms or materials to be found quickly and easily. There are several reporting routines. The most useful are the damage reports, listed as follows:

1, 2, 3, 4	= No. of m^2 of storage rooms with damage risk levels 1, 2, 3 or 4;
5	= Total No. of m^2 of storage rooms with damage risk.

Damage reports were created for both 'the risk of handling damage' and 'the risk of storage damage'. They were created for every material, i.e. 30 different kinds. Note that the area refers to the floor area, measured or paced out, and the volume is the percentage of the total space (e.g. shelf space, support space or object space) occupied by the material or type of object. The values given in the damage charts are thus specific. On the other hand, when a chart shows temperature or humidity distributions, the number of storage rooms referred to is given.

The Gunnel database is very powerful. The 60-odd building-related variables and the 420-odd material-related variables for each of the 354 storage rooms can be sorted into a large number of combinations. The programme can select and sort out more than 150,000 variables quickly and correctly. It would take too long to list all Gunnel's options in this report.

This paper gives examples of specifications and damage pictures of general interest. Every participating museum will receive a detailed report on all its storage rooms, related to their registered categories, i.e. C for central (national) museums, R for regional (county) museums and L for local (municipal) museums.

Pictures and charts are printed on an HP Deskjet 560C printer.

Statistical relevance

The Gunnel database now contains information on 100,000 m^2 of storage rooms. A questionnaire study indicated that there are 148,000 m^2 of storage rooms in the museums covered by the Museum Survey.[1] What is lacking, therefore, is information on several municipal museums. These museums include native place museums, old homestead museums, school collections, private collections, collections in castles and stately homes, Royal collections etc. Art museums have not been covered at all by this project. Altogether, there is probably a far greater storage room area in the country than the 148,000 suggested by the Museum Survey.[1] The Museum Survey refers to 'the country's 750 museums'.

RIK sent invitations to about 100 museums in the Swedish Museum Federation (SMF) address list to take part in the inventory, i.e. about 200,000 m^2 of storage rooms (the 148,000 m^2 of the Museum Survey, less the area of art museums, plus an estimated 63,800 m^2 of local museums from SMF's address list). The following are now registered:

eight central museums	56,000 m^2
seven regional museums	20,000 m^2
twelve local museums	23,000 m^2
Total	99,000 m^2.

The shortfall is 35% for central museums and 68% for regional museums, based on the figures of the Museum Survey, and about 64% for local museums, based on the SMF address list.

The storage room areas of the local museums have been calculated from the total area according to this inventory, minus the area of the Stockholm and Gothenburg museums, divided by the number of remaining storage rooms (10). The specific storage room area is then 930 m^2 per local museum. According to the SMF register, there are 56 municipal museums. Their estimated storage room area is then 56 ↔ 930 + 11,800 (Stockholm and Gothenburg) = 63,800 m^2. If this figure is at all reasonable, then the relationship between regional and local museums in this inventory is similar to the relationship between the Museum Survey's figure for regional museums and this estimate for local museums. We are comparing m^2.

Therefore the responses of the total population have not been added up. Instead, the properties of the shortfall have been assumed to be the same as those of the regional and local museums of this inventory. Nor has a follow-up selection of the shortfall been made, because of the presumed low-response tendency. Instead, it has been assumed that a suitability assessment is well represented by regional and local museums in the response stratum. By using this as the basis, an estimate has been made of the damage picture in the country as a whole. However, this picture has not been statistically validated.

Discussion

The questionnaire for the Museum Survey shows that 56% of the central and regional museums were satisfactory, but the criteria for 'satisfactory' is not clear. This study shows that about 79% of central and regional storage rooms are acceptable, i.e. 79% have a damage risk of 1 or 2. This assessment has been carried out with the museum conservators and curators. No previous assessment has been found of the quality of local museum storage rooms. This inventory shows that 66% of them are acceptable.

Tables 1 and 2 now give a summary of the damage picture from 27 museums and 354 storage rooms. The summary refers to both material and object damage. The tables are taken from Gunnel and divided up for all museums, central museums, regional museums and local museums.

The assessments of the risk for handling and storage damage were done on site in conjunction with the museum staff. The authors feel that the evaluations have a firm basis, because they have all been preceded by discussions with the various conservators and curators. Where applicable, the museum heads have had the chance to calmly and quietly assess the evaluation and suggest changes. Risk assessments have virtually never been changed after an inventory.

Assessments as to whether a storage room was serviceable or not were likewise based on measurements of temperature and relative humidity, (RH). The measurements were instantaneous and do not give an accurate picture of a storage room's climate over a whole year. But the data give an indication, and in particular the measurements provoked discussions about the climate over a year. Conservators and curators often wanted to discuss their own measurements during the inventory. However, climate measurements in Swedish museums are generally poorly done, even though the staff know that the only way to assess the climate is to measure. A lethargic attitude was noted about the need for continuous climate measurements (monitoring). Only 12% of the 356 storage rooms in the inventory have climate monitoring.

The contacts with the museums studied were seen as positive, and the staff were often keen to resolve the storage room problems in their museums. Unfortunately, in some places it was difficult to get them to shift their major attention from the external to the internal part of the business, despite the staff pointing out this need to both museum managements and boards. During this inventory, the authors tried to point out that it would pay off in the long term, even if the initial costs could be high, to build a new storage room or renovate an old storage. Objects that are a part of the country's cultural heritage would be preserved and a lot of money could be saved on preservation or repair work. By using these inventory results, the conservators and curators have been able to justify their demands for improved museum storage rooms in a more neutral and objective fashion.

The inventory has had a number of consequences. In too many cases the room temperature was too high or, frankly speaking, out of control. That was the main reason for the very low relative humidity levels recorded during the survey. During our visits, climatic adjustments were carried out in storage rooms, work rooms and other rooms. Technicians and operating staff have been informed about how the climate in a room should be related to the activities there. This information has also been given to other senior staff. Several museums have replaced or are going to replace defective air filters in their ventilation system. In several places, it was found that filters had been replaced with ones of lower quality. This was probably due to lack of information, and indicates how inadequate the routines are for climate control. The project showed the need for education in proper preventive conservation, i.e. that *storage conditions affect preservation standards*.

When the security of a storage room was noted, the questions about the lock systems worried the staff. Several conservators and curators were actually hesitant about giving out this kind of information. This indicates the awareness of security matters, which is why the Gunnel database is classified.

Another important matter was to evaluate the accessibility of the storage. Several conservators and curators pointed out deficiencies in this area.

It was difficult to obtain information about rental conditions and costs. The authors believe that this reflects the gap between the managers of the premises and the conservators and curators. Only on rare occasions could the curators assess the premises before they were assigned as storage rooms. Many premises used as storage rooms were so obviously unsuitable that the authors were forced to ask: 'How is this possible?' It seems at times that museum boards believe that any room not suitable for anything else is good enough to preserve the country's cultural heritage.

The last question of the inventory, 'What is the biggest single problem today?', often gave the spontaneous answer, 'the climate'.

Table 1 gives the distribution of the damage levels in 316 storage rooms inventoried in March 1995. Damage levels of 1 and 2 are considered acceptable, 3 and 4 unacceptable (it would be best if the central museums were all in category 1). As mentioned above, the picture given by this inventory of the country's regional and local museums reflects the country's museums as a whole.

Table 2 (overleaf) gives a break-down of the situation in Swedish museum storage rooms by material.

The result of the Swedish Technical Storage Room Survey is that more than 40% of the local museums storage rooms and 20% of the regional and central museums storage rooms are unacceptable.

Finally, a word about the prevailing confusion. What is preventive conservation and what is a museum storage room. The Swedish Museum Survey[1] shows that the museum heads questioned feel that preventive conservation should be given priority. At the same time, more than 60% of them felt that public activities should have the highest priority! The questionnaire given to the museum staff suggests that the museums should concentrate on the preservation of their collections, even

Table 1. Distribution (m²) of damage levels in storage rooms

Inventory of museum storages, m²	Risk of handling damage Grade[a]			Risk of storage damage Grade[a]		
	1 + 2	**3 + 4**	**3 + 4 (%)**	**1 + 2**	**3 + 4**	**3 + 4 (%)**
Central museums, 55,928	44,194	11,733	21.0	44,572	11,355	20.3
Regional museums, 16,677	11,759	4,918	29.4	13,411	3,265	19.5
Suburban museums, 22,871	13,253	9,636	42.1	13,491	9,398	41.0
Total, 95,476	69,207	26,287	27.5	71,475	24,019	25.2

[a] Grade 1 = good; grade 2 = acceptable; Grade 3 = poor; grade 4 = unacceptable. Grades 1 and 2 are considered acceptable, while Grades 3 and 4 are considered unacceptable and are treated as one group.

Table 2. A break-down of the situation in Swedish museum storage rooms by material. Number of museums 26; number of storage rooms 316. Values are given in m^2

Material	Total amount	Risk of handling damage				Risk of storage damage			
		1	2	3	4	1	2	3	4
All materials	95,476	46,454	22,733	11,289	14,998	45,465	25,990	12,686	11,333
Textiles	7,950	4,330	2,744	618	257	2,581	3,045	1,518	805
Furniture	12,577	5,985	3,135	1,511	1,945	7,694	2,012	1,092	1,778
Ceramics	2,001	722	864	236	177	1,513	320	167	0
Glass	873	464	150	73	184	548	100	184	40
Leather	871	309	338	103	120	271	265	285	48
Wood	11,533	5,333	2,108	1,743	2,348	3,699	4,203	1,796	1,834
Wood polychrome	1,405	242	1013	65	84	242	713	324	125
Silver	87	70	0	17	0	87	0	0	0
Tin	9	9	0	0	0	9	0	0	0
Brass/Bronze	645	511	82	34	17	179	408	43	15
Iron	3,992	1,195	755	804	1,237	1,839	924	759	469
Iron, archeological	734	308	308	64	54	75	186	170	303
Composite	18,201	9,976	4,924	663	2,637	10,453	4,857	1,801	1,089
Books/paper	1,260	222	278	541	218	398	371	383	106
Art on paper	480	238	128	110	2	236	167	68	8
Art on canvas	1,943	1,017	235	678	11	635	751	505	51
Nitrate film	43	16	27	0	0	16	0	27	0
Cellulose film	34	0	34	0	0	0	0	34	0
Glass plates	259	220	14	23	0	184	73	1	0
Photos	105	21	81	2	0	31	26	33	15
Carriages	2,578	1,150	634	73	720	800	550	213	1,014
Natural history	11,353	5,725	2,670	2,105	852	5,346	715	1,940	3,352
Electronics	1,337	0	140	1,150	46	0	1,200	73	64
Machinery/ vehicles	10,919	6,360	424	255	3,880	5,945	3,720	1,103	150
Stone	3,677	1,704	1,582	301	90	2,455	1,200	0	22
Fossils	0	0	0	0	0	0	0	0	0
Minerals	6	0	0	6	0	6	0	0	0
Polymer plastics	122	0	0	55	67	0	0	122	0
Other polymer	148	110	0	37	1	0	110	38	0

though 55% felt that the museums should not invest more on the conservation of objects. Confusing! Preventive conservation is more important than the mere custody and registration of object. This is clear from the report of The Association of Nordic Conservators (NFK-S) to the Museum Survey.[2]

What is a museum storage room? The *Föremålssamlingarnas tillväxt*[3] discusses 'the preservation of objects in less costly storage rooms', i.e. those with a low rent. Further on, the argument is that these storage rooms should have the same high standards as 'the storage rooms of the Historical Museum in Stockholm'. Still further on, it says: 'this proposal does not primarily aim to create cheap storage. It is clear that even the cheaper storages, which I mentioned above, ought to be constructed so that objects are not mismanaged. There should be control of the air, humidity and temperature'. We find the situation in Sweden somewhat confusing.

There is an expressed need from many museums in Sweden for access to expert help when designing and planning museum storage rooms. It also seems to be high time to compile a simple handbook or check list that will help conservators and curators and decision-makers to ensure that necessary standards are met for museum storage. Unless this is done, the Swedish Parliament Auditors may have their misgivings justified that moths and rats will determine what remains of the country's cultural heritage.[4] They might also add that mould appears to be actively contributing today.

Conclusions

The survey indicates that the storage room condition affects the preservation of the objects stored. The survey further indicates that if we really want to carry out preventive conservation, then we need to start with the storage room and the management of the storage room. Poor storage conditions have had a devasting effect on several large and important collections in Sweden.

Acknowledgements

This project was initiated by the late Gunnel Werner, conservator and Head of the Department of Conservation of Metals at RIK, Stockholm. Hence the name Gunnel for the large database. The project structure was laid down during long walks and bike rides by Gunnel Werner and Jan Holmberg (head of the Department of Archeological Material at RIK) during time off from the GCI course Preventive Conservation at Marina del Rey 1992. Gunnel, however, was the driving force! Jan G Holmberg is a Chartered Building Services Engineer at present time contracted by RIK.

Monica Fjaestad, successor to Gunnel Werner, and Eva Lundwall, head of the Department of Conservation of Textiles at RIK, have also been active in the project. The survey was financed by the Swedish National Council of Cultural Affairs.

References

1. Government paper. Museiutredningen SOU 1994:51.
2. Report of The Association of Nordic Conservators (NFK-S) to the Museum Survey.
3. *Föremålssamlingarnas tillväxt* ('Growth of Exhibit Collections', Swedish Government paper, Ds U 1982:1).
4. Government Report RR 1993/94:3.

Large-scale Disinfestation of Museum Objects using Nitrogen Anoxia

Shin Maekawa,* Kerstin Elert
The Getty Conservation Institute,
4503 Glencoe Avenue, Marina del Rey, CA 90202, USA

Abstract

Reusable, flexible enclosures and high-volume nitrogen supplies for a large scale insect eradication treatment were investigated. The treatment system consisted of a high-volume nitrogen source, a gas humidification module, an anoxia enclosure or tent, environmental sensors, and a vacuum pump. A 10 m^3 volume reusable tent was fabricated from Filmpak 1193 film with an oxygen leak rate of less than 0.005% (50 ppm) per day. Thus, it could maintain the anoxic condition with no nitrogen flow for several weeks once purged to a 0.1% oxygen level. A commercially available 6 m^3 bubble enclosure from Rentokil had a leak rate low enough to be maintained at 0.3% oxygen by a moderate constant flow of nitrogen. Liquid nitrogen and a nitrogen generator were successfully tested as nitrogen sources for large scale anoxia systems. A humidification module was successfully redesigned for improved accuracy and controllability of relative humidity at both low and high nitrogen flow rates. Safety issues related to large scale applications of nitrogen are discussed.

Keywords

Pest control, disinfestation, nitrogen anoxia, high-volume nitrogen sources, bubble enclosure, anoxia tent

Introduction

The nitrogen anoxia method is being employed by an increasing number of museums for in-house treatment of their collections since the efficacy of the method has been reported by various investigators.[1–4] In a study[5] presented at the meeting of the ICOM Committee for Conservation in 1993, the authors reported on the use of low-oxygen atmospheres for insect eradication of large museum objects using bags. As the procedure has become widely used, conservators have evinced interest in extending it to mass treatment of artifacts in a reusable enclosure.

Recently, the Getty Conservation Institute (GCI) sponsored an extension of the 1990–1991 research project[6] at the University of California, Riverside, involving the mortality of selected museum insects in nitrogen atmospheres.[7] The goal was to determine the lethality of nitrogen containing 0.3% and 0.6% oxygen, in contrast to the original study at a 0.1% oxygen level. Using more than 15,000 life forms in the project, the researchers found that 0.3% oxygen in nitrogen at 25.5°C achieved complete mortality in six days of all life stages of the common museum pests *Anthrenus flavipes* LeConte (furniture carpet beetle) and *Lasioderma serricone* (F.) (cigarette beetle). Thus, the original recommendations of exposure for a minimum of ten days to insure insect elimination at 0.1% oxygen level and 25.5°C are applicable to 0.3% oxygen in nitrogen. Even though nitrogen atmospheres containing 0.6% oxygen did not achieve 100% kill of *Anthrenus flavipes* larvae in 20 days at 25.5°C, increasing the temperature in the test chambers to 30°C produced the 100% kill within six days. The use of 5% of carbon dioxide was marginally effective in increasing the lethality of the 0.6% oxygen in nitrogen atmosphere.

These findings aided the development of large air-tight enclosures and various nitrogen delivery systems in the confidence that maintenance of oxygen levels below 0.3% at 25.5°C would assure lethality to common museum insects within 14 days as a conservative exposure time. The enclosures and types of nitrogen supplies which were tested are described in the following sections.

The use either of a fumigation room or chamber, or of portable fumigation tents and bubbles, is a practical solution for a large-scale fumigation site. A general procedure is to purge the enclosure in which the infested objects are placed with a flow of humidity-controlled nitrogen until the oxygen concentration decreases to less than 0.3%. Then this concentration is maintained for the duration of the anoxic process (approximately 14 days at room temperature) by a flow of gas whose rate depends on the tightness of the enclosure. The method has been successfully used with large plastic bags made from heat-sealed barrier films. However, older fumigation bubbles, which had been designed for methyl bromide fumigation, were found to be too leaky to maintain an anoxic nitrogen environment without continuous purging at high rates of nitrogen flow.[5]

Large anoxia enclosures

The anoxia treatment system for large applications, shown in Figure 1, consists of a high-volume nitrogen source (nitrogen cylinders, a liquid-nitrogen tank or a nitrogen generator), a gas humidification module, the anoxia enclosure, environmental sensors in the enclosure (oxygen, relative humidity (RH), and tempera-

* Author to whom correspondence should be addressed

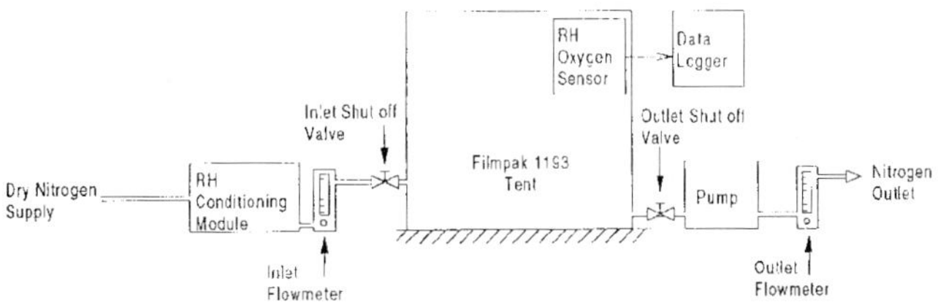

Figure 1. Schematic of anoxia treatment system

ture), and a vacuum pump. The nitrogen entering the enclosure must be at the same RH as the objects being treated and thus RH of the gas must be raised by passing it through a humidification module. The rate of nitrogen in-flow is adjusted to the suction rate of the pump to avoid a pressure build-up in the enclosure. Although such a pressure increase (or a decrease below atmospheric pressure) is easily deduced from the appearance of inflated or deflated enclosures when using a flexible envelope, monitoring of the flow rate at the inlet and outlet is useful to prevent such extremes. Of course, the oxygen concentration, temperature, and RH inside the tent are measured to insure the required anoxic conditions.

Any enclosure can be maintained at the required oxygen concentration of 0.3% by continued purging with high purity nitrogen. The required purging rate depends upon the air-tightness of the enclosure. However, continued purging will mean an additional cost of a large volume of nitrogen gas and increasing complexity of controlling the continual supply and humidification. Failure or drift of the humidification control over a long treatment period can produce disastrous hygroscopic stresses on the objects. For example, if an enclosure requires one complete volume purging of pure nitrogen per day to maintain the anoxia environment, variations of the relative humidity (RH) may result in up to a half of the set RH value if the control fails or if a drift is not repaired for 24 h. The possible RH variation will increase as the purging rate is increased. Therefore, one must select an air-tight enclosure that requires the smallest volume of purging, so that the risk on the object can be minimized.

Custom-made tents for insect anoxia

A reusable tent has been found to be the most versatile enclosure for use in the treatment of relatively large infested objects or mass exposure, such as library books. Any desired size unit can be easily fabricated. Barrier films and their properties, suitable for the method, have been reported by various investigators.[8,9,10]

Previously, we used the Aclar (Bell Fibre: Film-O-Rap 7750) film or Marvelseal 360 to produce heat-sealed, air-tight enclosures. However, both films were found unsuitable for use in large application as the oxygen transmission rate of the Aclar film was too high (51.15 cm^3 m^{-2} day^{-1}) and the Marvelseal 360 film required careful handling because of the possible development of pinhole leaks in the film. Therefore, a 10 m^3 tent for anoxia testing was fabricated using Filmpak 1193 barrier film (a semi-translucent, 0.12 mm thick plastic with an oxygen transmission rate of 0.1 cm^3 m^{-2} day^{-1} and US cost of \$5.50/m^2) at the GCI.

The nearly cubical tent, with a base 2 m on a side and 2.5 m high, had a 30 cm extension or flange on its side to insure wide contact with the base (Figure 2). It was made of heat-sealed 1 m wide strips of Filmpak 1193. Stout loops were made on the top to attach a lifting device and thus provide access to the interior of the tent for easy placement of objects. It was made to fit over an aluminum frame, which acted as internal support and prevented contact with any objects placed therein.

An important consideration in this conveniently raisable tent design is the seal between the flange and the base. The latter can be as simple as a smooth concrete floor coated with several layers of a paint or a large acrylic sheet. A successful seal (shown in Figure 3) between base and flange was produced as follows: Two self-adhesive rubber strips which had been placed in parallel lines on the floor beneath the flange perimeter were lightly greased; then the tent was lowered and its flange adjusted to be wrinkle-free while 1 cm thick and 15 cm wide acrylic plates were placed on the flange perimeter. Finally, the flange was pressed tightly to the

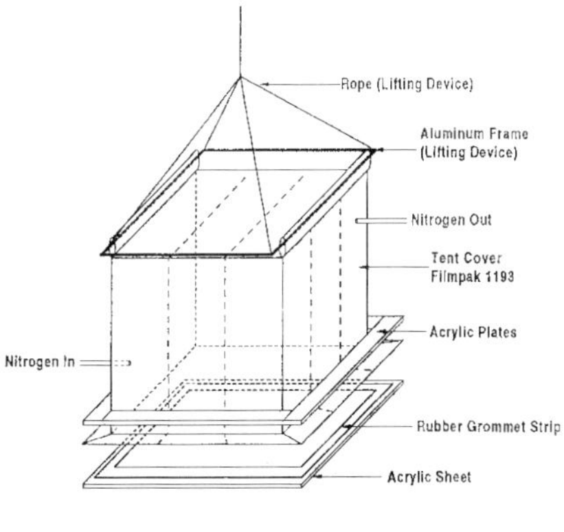

Figure 2. Schematic of anoxia tent

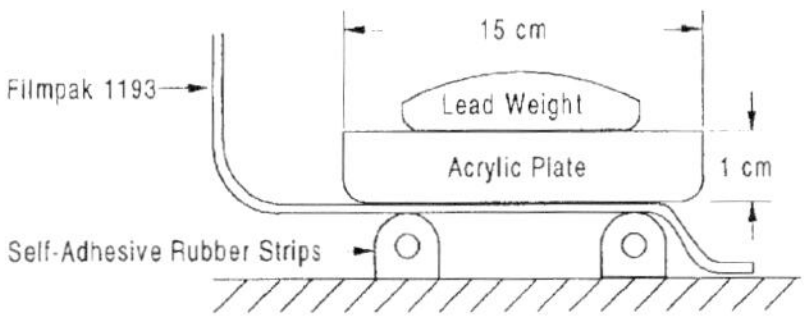

Figure 3. Schematic of hermetic seal

rubber strips by weighting bags filled with lead shot laid on the acrylic plates around the flange. An adequate seal could not be obtained simply by taping the flange to the floor.

Fabrication of the tent required approximately 16 person hours. The total cost of materials for the tent and accessories was approximately $2,500, of which half was for the internal aluminum frame and lead shot weights. The cost could be reduced by at least a third if PVC plastic pipe were used for the frame and sand-filled bags as the weights.

Over the one-month performance test, the anoxia tent showed a consistent oxygen leak rate of 0.005% (50 ppm) per day in a non-air-conditioned warehouse. This air-tightness eliminated the need for continual nitrogen flow after the tent had been purged to 0.1% oxygen concentration, while the required low-oxygen environment of 0.3% was easily maintained for more than a four-week period.

A commercially available fumigation bubble

As part of this investigation, an improved design of the Rentokil Mini Bubble, a 6 m^3 bubble enclosure for a portable CO_2 fumigation system,[11] was examined for its adaptability to nitrogen anoxia treatment. The Bubble produced a leak rate of only 0.04% (400 ppm) per day. This indicates that it can maintain the required oxygen concentration of less than 0.3% by a continual purging with high purity nitrogen at 0.9 m^3 day^{-1} or 0.63 l min^{-1}, an easily attainable requirement. Therefore, the Mini Bubble would be practical as an anoxia enclosure, although there may be some variation in oxygen leak rates from one unit to another.

Nitrogen supplies

In the past, high-pressure nitrogen cylinders containing 8.6 m^3 of gas at atmospheric pressure (designated as T or 1L by US suppliers) were used for anoxia research and development. However, almost ten such cylinders are needed to purge a 10 m^3 tent or similar sized chamber and lower its oxygen content to 0.1%. It is inconvenient and a possible safety hazard to deal with so many bulky and heavy cylinders in conservation work. Therefore, high capacity nitrogen sources rather than high pressure cylinders were tested in order to find the optimal nitrogen supply for use in large-scale anoxia treatment enclosures. (Details of costs of high-pressure cylinders are given below simply for reference for use in smaller volume anoxia applications.)

High-pressure nitrogen gas cylinder

Nitrogen gas comes in various purities (grades) and tank sizes, the most useful size for anoxia in enclosures up to a few thousand liters being T or 1L (depending on the US supplier) containing 8,600 liters at atmospheric pressure. Industrial grade nitrogen, at $24 per T cylinder, has limited use for anoxia because its guaranteed oxygen-free content is only 99.7%. Therefore, it is suitable only during the initial purging stage. High-purity nitrogen with 10 ppm of oxygen or less costs $37 and prepurified nitrogen with 5 ppm of oxygen, $46. Other costs include a regulator at $240 and a tank rental fee of about $6 a month. As already mentioned, it is onerous and a potential hazard to be forced continually to check the status of one cylinder being used to flush a large anoxia chamber, while constantly being ready to replace it with one of a dozen full cylinders. Admittedly, cylinders can be connected in parallel on a manifold to increase the time between multiple cylinder changes, but the net number of cylinders needed is not changed, of course, and the cost of a high-pressure manifold and additional pressure regulators must be considered.

Nitrogen generator

Nitrogen generators, such as those manufactured by Air Products and Chemicals Corporation, are available as a turnkey system in many countries. The Prism nitrogen generator from Air Products and Chemicals Corporation produces purified nitrogen from ambient air by separating the oxygen from the air in a membrane filter system. The unit consists of an air compressor and a series of filters and is equipped with a nitrogen (trace oxygen) analyzer for the output gas. Its operation involves compressing the air between 540kPa and 1290kPa, passing it through pre-filters to remove moisture, dust particulates and any gaseous pollutants before it reaches the multiple tubules which constitute the membrane filter and separate the oxygen in air as a side stream. The system can produce nitrogen of 95 to 99.99% purity, inversely dependent on the flow rate.

We tested Permea Prism Model 1300 in conjunction with the anoxia tent. The unit is in the $18,000 range with a 230 VAC three-phase motor/compressor. Its operational cost, other than power consumption of the compressor, is $200–300 per year for replacement of pre-filter cartridges and the oxygen sensor in the analyzer.

The Prism nitrogen generator was easy to operate and reliable for the two and a half months of non-stop use in our work, although its industrial compressor was somewhat noisy inside a building. It could produce and maintain 41 m^3 per day of 99.99% nitrogen. Of course, this model was oversized for the 10 m^3 tent but would be very satisfactory for a 50–100 m^3 fumigation room. In such a large anoxia installation, a pressurized storage tank for purified nitrogen would utilize the generator fully and thereby increase cost-effectiveness.

Liquid-nitrogen tank

Liquid nitrogen is supplied in tanks containing 100 to 500 liters, one liter of liquid nitrogen being equivalent to 620 liters of gas at atmospheric pressure. Thus, the widely used size of 160 liters, priced at $61 plus $29 a month rental, yields 99,000 liters of gaseous nitrogen – almost the same as 12 T-cylinders. The purity is 99.998% (about 20 ppm of oxygen) and gas can be produced at a flow rate up to nearly 120 liters per minute because of internal heat exchangers which vaporize the cold liquid. Inexpensive, needing no maintenance or mechanical or electrical components, a 160 liter tank of liquid nitrogen easily purged the 10 m^3 GCI anoxia tent to less than 0.1% oxygen. Although somewhat inconvenient rather than dangerous, a large amount of ice formed on the top portion of the tank when a flow rate of 49 m^3 per day (49,000 liters/day or 34 liters/minute) was maintained for a long period. The only constraint on use of the tank was its limited shelf life of only about one month because nitrogen gas must be continuously and automatically released to avoid the excessive pressure increase in the tank at room temperature.

Humidification system

Regardless of the type of nitrogen supply which is used, the gas must be humidified to avoid changes in moisture content of the objects being treated for insect infestation. In our previous work a humidification system consisting of three bottles was used. One contained water, through which a stream of nitrogen was bubbled to yield a nearly saturated gas flow. This was mixed with a dry flow of nitrogen in the second bottle, where any water droplets were removed, and the RH of the mixed stream was measured in the third bottle just prior to passing into the anoxia enclosure. Control of the RH was accomplished by adjusting the flow ratio of the dry and wet streams.[5]

The system had its disadvantages, however: Since the bottles were pressurized, the RH reading in the third bottle was not that at atmospheric pressure; and the system responded slowly in a low-flow condition as a result of the large total volume of the humidification system, making exact control difficult because the RH sensor took about five minutes for an equilibrated response.

The humidification module was improved by inserting flow meters in the wet and dry nitrogen streams to insure more precise and predictable control of the wet and dry streams and by eliminating the third bottle to reduce the system's total volume and thereby to increase the rapidity of RH response (Figure 4). Theoretically, a 1:1 mixture of the two flows should produce nitrogen with a RH of 50%. However, at high flow rates, it was not possible to saturate fully the nitrogen bubbling through water, e.g. nitrogen passed through a four liter bottle had a RH

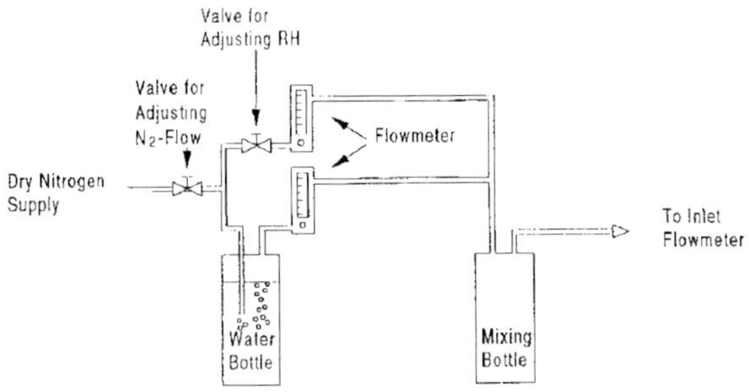

Figure 4. Schematics of new humidification module

of 86% at a flow rate of 17 liter per minute. Thus, it was necessary to calibrate flow ratios for the wide variation of RH and flow conditions desired.

Safety issues

Gaseous nitrogen is inert, colorless, odorless, tasteless, non-corrosive, and non-flammable. However, it could cause produce suffocation if a large volume of the gas flows into an occupied space which is poorly ventilated. Exposure to an oxygen-deficient atmosphere below the oxygen concentration of 19.5% (normal atmosphere is 20.9%) may produce dizziness, nausea, vomiting, loss of consciousness, and even death. Death may also result from errors in judgment, confusion, or loss of consciousness which prevents self-rescue. Unconsciousness may occur in seconds without warning.

Conclusions

High-volume nitrogen supplies and reusable enclosures for the eradication of insects from large cultural objects or large groups of small objects via nitrogen anoxia were investigated. The treatment system consisted of a high-volume nitrogen source, a gas humidification module, the anoxia enclosure or tent, environmental sensors, and a vacuum pump. Simplicity of operation and off-the-shelf or easily fabricated products were major goals of the work.

Reusable tents of Filmpak 1193 film, a heat-sealable, low-oxygen-permeable plastic, can be easily fabricated in desired sizes by conservators at a low cost. We constructed a 10 m^3 tent mounted on a framework which, with the tent's flanges sealed tightly to the painted floor, had a leak rate of less than 0.005% (50 ppm) per day. Thus, it could maintain the anoxic condition with no nitrogen flow for several weeks once it is purged to a 0.1% oxygen level. Clearly, larger tents of this design would be feasible as reusable anoxia enclosures. Simple enclosure shapes are recommended for the application. Complexly shaped enclosures to fit an infested object, intended to reduce nitrogen volume, are not recommended as they could produce leaky seals at their joints. Rentokil's Mini Bubble, a commercially available 6 m^3 bubble enclosure had a low enough leak rate to be maintained at 0.3% oxygen by a constant moderate flow of nitrogen (0.63 l min^{-1}) after initial purging of the air, although there may be some variation in oxygen leak rates from one unit to another.

Liquid nitrogen and a nitrogen generator were tested as nitrogen sources for large scale anoxia systems (nitrogen from high pressure cylinders involves too many cylinders, both a logistic and potential safety hazard, because of the great quantity of nitrogen gas required). Although the nitrogen generator produced better than 99.99% pure nitrogen at a high rate and was found easy and reliable to operate, it is most cost-effective for very large fixed fumigation chambers in major museums. For 3 m^3 and bigger anoxia enclosures, liquid nitrogen is the least expensive. Its ease of use and availability makes the large scale anoxia treatment practical. An improved humidification module allows more accurate control of nitrogen's RH in a large scale operation. Good room ventilation and placement of an oxygen monitor with an alarm is recommended for safety if a large scale anoxia treatment is to be conducted.

Acknowledgment

The authors thank Dr. Frank Lambert for his technical expertise throughout the project. The authors also thank Air Products and Chemicals, Inc. in Allentown, Pennsylvania for their generosity in loaning us a PRISM nitrogen generator for this study.

References

1. M. Gilberg, "Inert Atmosphere Fumigation of Museum Objects," *Studies in Conservation* 34 (1989): 80–84.
2. R.J. Koestler, "Practical Application of Nitrogen and Argon Fumigation Procedures for Insect Control in Museum Objects," (Paper delivered at the 2nd International Conference on Biodeterioration of Cultural Property, Yokohama, Japan, 1992), 96–98.
3. N. Valentin, "Insect Eradication in Museums and Archives by Oxygen Replacement, a Pilot Project," (Paper delivered at the Ninth Triennial Meeting of the International Council of Museums Committee for Conservation, Dresden, August 1990), 821–823.
4. N. Valentin, and F. Preusser, "Insect Control by Inert Gases in Museums, Archives and Museum Collections," *Restaurator* 11 (1990): 22–33.
5. V. Daniel, S. Maekawa and F. Preusser, "Nitrogen Fumigation: A Viable Alternative," (Paper delivered at the Tenth Triennial Meeting of the International Council of Museums Committee for Conservation, Washington, DC, August 1993), 863–867.
6. M. Rust and J. Kennedy, "The Feasibility of Using Modified Atmospheres to Control Insect Pests in Museums," (The Getty Conservation Institute Scientific Program Report, March 1993).
7. M. Rust and J. Kennedy, "Enhancing the Effectiveness of Modified Atmospheres to Control Insect Pests in Museums," (The Getty Conservation Insitute Final Draft, April 1995).
8. J. Burke, "Vapor Barrier Films," *WAAC Newsletter* 14 (1992): 13–17.
9. M. Gilberg and D. Grattan, "Oxygen-free Storage using Ageless Oxygen Absorber," (Paper delivered at the IIC Congress, Ottawa, September 1994), 177–180.
10. Y. Shashoua, "Recent Investigation into Barrier Films for Use in Preventive Conservation at the British Museum," *SSCR Journal* 3 (March 1992): 12–13.
11. C.P. Smith and J. Newton (Rentokil), "Carbon Dioxide: The Fumigant of the Future," (Paper presented at the Seminar on Research in Conservation, Columbia University, New York, 26th May 1991).

Abstract

The Science Museum has on permanent loan some 200,000 objects belonging to the Wellcome Trust. The collection reflects Sir Henry Wellcome's interest in a wide range of archaeological, historical and ethnographic objects relating to the history of medicine. A small percentage of the collection is on display in the Wellcome Galleries at the Science Museum at South Kensington. The remainder is located in the Museum's Reserve Store in West London, where approximately 22,000 objects still remain in the 1,250 boxes in which they were transported to the Museum following cataloguing at the Trust's premises in North London in 1977. Recently a two-year project was initiated by the Museum and funded by the Wellcome Trust to unpack, sort and store the collection. This paper will discuss the planning, organisation and implementation of the project. It will also highlight conservation issues which arose, including allocation of condition grades, treatment selection and storage recommendations.

Keywords

Project organisation, mixed-media, condition grades, infestation, storage furniture

The Wellcome Unpacking Project – Preparing a Multi-Material Collection for Storage

Catherine Nightingale, Helen Kingsley*
Science Museum,
London SW7 2DD, UK

Introduction

Henry Wellcome, of the Burroughs Wellcome Drugs Company, amassed a fortune by introducing tableted medicines into Britain in the 19th Century; this fortune he ploughed into his interest in anthropology, history and the history of medicine. The resulting collection ranges from Egyptian mummies to X-ray machines and from stethoscopes to African carvings. In 1977, the Wellcome Medical Collection was placed on permanent loan to the Science Museum, with the Museum continuing to develop areas of the thirty sub-collections, maintaining their unrivalled interest and scope.

In November 1993, a project bid was presented to the Wellcome Trust to make possible the final unpacking and storage of approximately 22,000 objects. A large proportion of the Collection had previously been unpacked between 1977 and 1989 and put on display or in store. A working party of three Wellcome Collection Assistant Curators, the Stores Manager and a Senior Conservator (Helen Kingsley) was set up with the objective of unpacking and placing the objects on shelves in the store within two years. They needed to:

- Assess the storage requirements in terms of furniture and environment
- Assess the staffing requirements of the project.
- Assess the documentation requirements of the sub-collections.
- Allocate unpacking priorities to the sub-collections.
- Set up the unpacking and conservation recording procedures.

Storage and environment

The small objects store

The building was opened in 1903 as the new Post Office Savings Bank headquarters, which it remained until the late 1970s. It is now shared between three national museums: the British Museum, the Victoria & Albert Museum and the Science Museum, each having approximately one third of the space. As a result of structural limitations, the facility is primarily used for storing the smaller Science Museum objects. These are kept visible as part of the Museum's open storage policy for visitor access. About 85% of the whole of the Museum's collections are stored at this facility, covering a vast range of collections including Textile, Hand and Machine Tools, Astronomy, Electronic Components, Metallurgy, Plastics, Acoustics, Air and Water Transport and the Wellcome Medical Collection.

Since October 1994 the Conservation Section has monitored the relative humidity and temperature fluctuations in locations around the store. The results are being evaluated with a view to producing a more stable environment with simple, low-cost solutions being sought. An extensive pest monitoring and control programme is also in progress in the store.

The building has seen very little structural or internal alteration since changing its function. However, all windows have been covered and sealed using a water-based acrylic filler and plaster board. The majority of the boards have foil-covered

* Author to whom correspondence should be addressed

Figure 1. Storage of the Classical and Medieval sub-collection

Figure 2. Cupboard used for the storage of small objects.

outer surfaces to provide a vapour barrier and a reflecting surface for IR radiation. Dust seals have been added to all perimeter doors.

Working party recommendations

Storage

A plan of each of the 43 rooms was produced depicting the storage requirements and furniture locations. The majority of the smaller Wellcome objects were stored in British Standard racking with doors (Dexion type) or Gratnell cupboards with Perspex doors and drawers. The larger objects were stored on longspan racking or pallets or were free standing. Most of the existing furniture was inadequate and much did not meet conservation standards. For example several of the cupboards were distorted and would not open without causing a great deal of vibration. It was decided to purchase new furniture where needed and renew inadequate furniture where possible. The furniture to be purchased fell into three types:

- longspan racking (Apex), for large heavy objects;
- open bay shelving (Welconstruct), for medium-sized heavy to light objects (Figure 1);
- cupboards with drawers (TLM Engineering), for small and/or delicate objects, (Figures 1 and 2).

The cupboards were to be powder-coated metal, which is a more inert system of surface coating needing fewer chemicals. The doors were to have a Plastazote® dust seal rather than a rubber seal which would create a micro environment within the cupboard. Plastazote® was also used around the windows rather than the suggested rubber seal. The windows were to be glass, rather than Perspex which is a softer material and more easily scratched.

The furniture shelves and drawers were to be covered with Plastazote® sheets. Plastazote®, crystal boxes, acid-free boxes and tissue paper could be used with objects where extra support was needed.

Environment recommendations

During the winter months the monitoring devices revealed an increase in temperature levels in many of the rooms, even when the radiators were switched off. This was due to hot water pipes running along the walls. The higher temperatures were causing a decrease in the relative humidity to below the minimum desired. Therefore, a list of priority areas was drawn up, and lagging of the pipes in these areas was to be carried out before the installation of the furniture.

Pest traps had identified a problem area where a number of dried plant materials were stored. Since all the material from this room was to be transferred to another, it had to be frozen or fumigated before this could be carried out. Once the room had been emptied of objects it was recommended that it be fumigated before housing another collection.

Health hazards

Some of the boxes included objects which could present health and safety hazards. i.e. human/animal remains, mercury, asbestos, formalin, corroded lead, poisons/controlled drugs, chemicals and radioactive isotopes. A computer search was carried out to assess the extent of the problem and lists of hazardous or potentially hazardous objects were compiled to identify the problem collections. It was recommended that inert tags should be tied on to objects stating the hazard. Risk assessments were to be compiled for certain tasks. Protective equipment would be available to staff, e.g. face respirators, goggles, latex gloves, mercury spill kit etc., to be used when necessary.

Staffing and project management

Staffing requirements were restricted by financial constraints. It was decided that two Curatorial Assistants would be employed on a fixed-term two-year contract. There would also be input from the three existing Wellcome Collection Assistant Curators, one of whom was to be selected as the Project Leader, ensuring that the objects would be unpacked in the time allotted, i.e. two years. When the initial project bid was compiled, conservation time was not included. The working party recommended the addition of a full-time conservator on the team, but funds were not available. Therefore, the Collections Management Group agreed to fund a full-time post jointly with the Project Grant.

Prioritise unpacking and documentation requirements

Collections were to be unpacked systematically, collection by collection. Priorities were drawn up to assess the order in which the collections were to be unpacked:

- sub-collections with the highest proportion of Wellcome objects;
- importance to research activities;
- level of current acquisition activity;
- size of sub-collection;
- quantity of objects remaining to be unpacked;
- conservation considerations;
- quantity of objects unlocated;
- loan/enquiry activities.

Other unpacking and storage considerations were taken into account, e.g. delivery and installation of new furniture, maximising the use of space, facilitating access to the Collection and grouping the objects in a meaningful and practical fashion.

The Wellcome Collection was comprehensively catalogued before its transfer to the Museum in 1977. Documentation needs, therefore, would only entail the input of new locations.

Unpacking and conservation recording procedures

The project was allocated a room within the store for the unpacking process. This meant that the boxes could be emptied and the objects sorted into various pre-determined categories and unwrapped, before being delivered to their final location.

After unwrapping, each object would be examined for possible conservation problems. Any active deterioration, along with a condition grade, would be noted on a specially devised conservation form. In order to make this as straightforward as possible, the form would simply require a tick in the relevant damage category box and an overall condition grade. Types of damage category would include: 'major structural', such as breakages; 'chemical', under which would be recorded chemical deterioration such as corrosion or red rot; and 'biological', which would be ticked if the object had insect infestation or mould, for example. A separate reference sheet would describe these categories in more detail, material by material. The condition grades would run from one to four, although, on the whole, only those objects considered a grade three or four would be recorded, three being any object felt to be in poor condition and probably unstable, and four being those objects thought to be actively deteriorating and highly unstable.

The project in progress

Problems encountered so far are wide-ranging, reflecting both the variety of objects and materials in the Collection, as well as the different levels of packing and subsequent storage. Initially, the project conservator was directly involved in supervising the unpacking staff and curators, but as they became more familiar with the various categories of problem and aware of what would be considered active deterioration, they were left to record problems with occasional advice from the conservator where necessary. The original idea behind the conservation form was for the conservator then to be able to retrieve the objects and work on them; in fact, it soon became clear that the number of actively deteriorating objects was well beyond the capacity of one conservator to treat in two years. In the first nine months of the project, approximately 20,000 objects were put into their final locations (7,900 newly unpacked, the rest already elsewhere in store), 3,069 of which were considered to be grade three or four.

The main concern of the project is to store all objects in the Collection to a satisfactory level, rather than actively conserve all objects. Thus the more immediate challenge for the conservator is to advise on storage methods for particular problem objects, or groups of objects, and then to begin to tackle more pressing deterioration issues. With a strict deadline for completion of the project, there is constant pressure on the unpacking team to put away as many objects as possible. The weekly target of (at the time of writing), 800 objects a week, has to be taken into consideration when attempting to find solutions to problems.

Conservation issues

Physical damage

One of the most common problems is physical damage as a result of inadequate packing and/or subsequent inappropriate handling of the fibre boxes. Although most of the objects retrieved from the fibre boxes are wrapped in bubble-wrap, and fairly well protected in polystyrene chips, many are simply in plastic bags, with the inevitable result that breakages have occurred. In addition, some objects were recorded as broken even before packing. Since most of the broken objects are thought to be relatively stable, unless edges are crumbling or flaking, they are allocated a grade two. They are recorded on the conservation form for future reference and, since they will not be treated as a priority, it is important that they are stored in a way which will not further damage vulnerable parts.

Pest infestation

Of the grade three and four objects noted on the conservation form, a large proportion are suffering from insect infestation. A variety of pests have been found, often depending on the collection and the type of material found within it. Some of the objects were obviously infested before packing up. Others may have been affected by objects stored in the same fibre box: we found that certain groups of wooden herb boxes in the Pharmacy-ware Collection, for example, were infested with woodworm (*Anobium punctatum*). Problems have also been found with sub-collections already unpacked and inadequately stored; the Orthopaedics Collection, for example, which consists of a large number of felt-lined false legs, had a fairly serious problem of moth infestation, no doubt made worse by the fact that many of the objects had been piled on top of each other in a cupboard for many years. One of the worst affected areas of the Collection is *Materia Medica*, mentioned above, which is particularly vulnerable, as much of it consists of dried plant material. The part of the sub-collection previously stored was known to be quite badly infested with both carpet beetle (*Anthrenus verbasci*) and biscuit beetle (*Stegobium paniceum*) at the start of the project.

Active corrosion

The other major contributor to the grade four category is the active corrosion of metals, mainly copper and iron alloys. There are a large number of surgical instruments throughout the various sub-collections, many of which have been stored in the sealed polyethylene bags they have been packed in since arriving at the museum. In addition, many have non-acid-free paper labels in the bag with them, and this appears to have contributed to the corrosion; we found that the side of the object resting on the label seemed, in many cases, to be more corroded than the other side. Of the objects previously unpacked, a large collection of pestles and mortars shows signs of active corrosion, probably due to the fact that they have been stored stacked one inside the other in a rather damp basement room.

Previous conservation

There have also been a few problems caused by previous conservation/restoration attempts, such as failed joins on ceramic objects. A group of oriental masks unpacked at the start of the project appears to have been repainted and varnished and then packed up before being properly dry, or possibly subjected to conditions which have caused the varnish to soften. This has resulted in the polyethylene bags in which the masks were packed becoming stuck to the surface of the objects, in some cases smudging the paint beneath.

Modern materials

Of the more modern materials, we have found very deteriorated rubber, completely brittle and crumbling, such as that on the First World War gas masks in the Public Health Collection, as well as plastic objects which are no more than a pile of fragments in a bag, where once there was a beautiful colostomy cup. It is possible that the objects were already undergoing chemical and physical changes before being packed up, but we suspect that being in a sealed plastic bag for several years has speeded up these reactions.

Hazardous materials

Owing to the nature of the Collection, many of the objects we have been dealing with present hazards on health and safety grounds, as mentioned above. The lists of potentially hazardous objects with their relevant box numbers are used so that adequate steps can be taken before removing and unwrapping them. Those objects considered to be hazardous or containing hazardous materials are clearly labelled with a standard inert red plastic tag with the relevant warning sticker attached. They are listed along with their location and hazard and, depending on the nature of the hazard, are often placed in a Stewart® box. Lead objects, such as a collection of Roman lead pipes that were slightly corroded, have been covered with a lid made of Correx® in order to minimize corrosion dust levels. Added to this is the problem of leaking contents from jars, bottles etc. which were not always placed in the fibre boxes in an upright position, and which, often being obscured by bubble wrap, are easy to tip upside down when unpacking.

Treatment of infested material

Treatment of objects found to be infested is considered a priority, not only to prevent insects spreading to other objects, but also to minimise the time that the infested items remain in sealed bags (any objects thought to be infested are placed in polyethylene bags and stored in their proper locations until treatment). We have been dealing with the problem in one of two ways: either by freezing or by exposing the object to an atmosphere of methyl bromide.

Where possible, objects are sealed in polyethylene bags with the minimum amount of air possible and placed in a pre-cooled freezer at –38°C for 72 hours. They are returned to room temperature gradually, to avoid condensation forming, by leaving in the freezer after it has been turned off. In this way we have treated large numbers of textile objects as well as plant materials and objects made of vegetable fibres. Larger objects and those made of wood are fumigated using methyl bromide, and clearly labelled after treatment using the inert tags with hazard stickers.

A significant amount of time has been spent dealing with the infestation problem in the *Materia Medica* Collection. All areas in the room have been affected, including wooden medicine chests and their contents, with the vast majority of infested material consisting of dried plant remains in glass jars, with either cork or glass stoppers. Since the collection was being moved to a different room, it was vital that the affected objects were treated before relocation. Initially, the infested contents were removed, put into polyethylene bags and frozen before being returned to the cleaned jars, and sealed with Parafilm®. It soon became apparent, however, that this would involve an enormous number of man hours (there are some 8,000 objects), so it was decided to treat the objects with methyl bromide.

Fibre boxes were used to hold the jars, and the lids of the jars were removed at the last minute. In this way we have treated all objects, which are now on shelves clearly marked with hazard labels.

Storage methods

Implementation of storage recommendations

In general, the Collection presents problems for storage in terms of its diversity; many objects are of an awkward size and shape as well as being heavy and often weakened through deterioration. Space within the storage areas has to be used as efficiently as possible, and, with limited materials available, there have been many challenges involved in devising safe and practical storage for these objects. The extremely wide range of material and type of object means that the staff involved in assessing the conservation needs of each object are constantly being faced with unfamiliar problems. Thus, much of the project conservator's time is taken up with discussing these problems.

Each collection is stored in a specific room or rooms with categories of objects grouped together as far as possible in numerical order. Thus objects are stored according to type rather than material and any one cupboard will have a wide range of materials within it. The smaller objects are stored in Perspex drawers lined with Plastazote® (Figure 2) and are usually laid out in the drawers while still in the unpacking room. The larger objects are placed on Welconstruct shelves, or Apex racking, also lined with Plastazote®, except where this is felt to be harmful, for example, under wooden medicine chests, which have delicate felt bases likely to be damaged by friction if pulled across Plastazote®. The inventory number of each object is written on an acid-free label, which is placed in front of it.

Figure 3. Cupboard drawer lined with wide channelled Plastazote®

In general, because of the museum's policy on storage, the objects are not wrapped or covered, although as far as possible they are in cupboards with closing doors. Exceptions to this include textiles, which are usually stored padded and covered with acid-free tissue paper in acid-free archive storage boxes, and flat paper items which are placed in Melinex® sleeves.

Object-supporting materials

We have devised various methods of supporting delicate or unstable objects to prevent movement or collapse, all with the premise that they should involve the minimum amount of staff time. One of the most useful support materials for small objects is the channelled or grooved Plastazote® specifically designed in two sizes for the project. It can be used to line a Perspex drawer, or cut for support of individual items within a drawer. The wider type has proved particularly adaptable for the type of objects in the Wellcome Collection. We have employed the narrow grooved Plastazote® for the storage of surgical instruments as it prevents the objects rolling around within the drawer as it is opened, whilst still enabling a large number of instruments to be placed in one drawer. The wider type has been used to support empty narrow glass vessels (laid on their sides), delicate ivory statues, sets of small copper alloy weights, etc., as well as any other object which is likely to roll (Figure 3). We have also used it to line the fixed shelves on which the large collection of copper alloy and stone pestles is stored, enabling large numbers of objects to be placed on one shelf without movement, or contact between them.

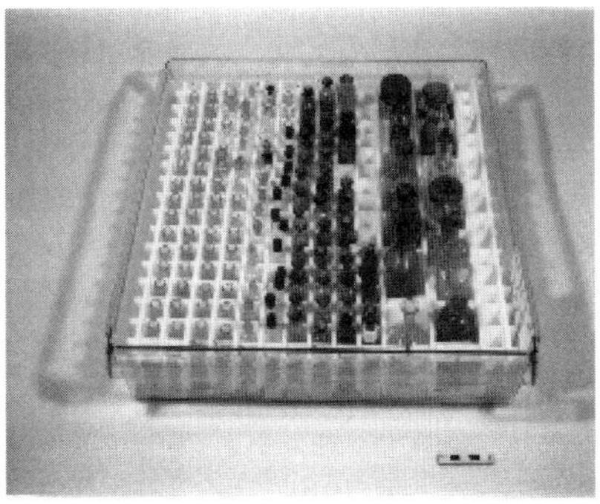

Figure 4. Cupboard drawer lined with interlocking Plastazote®

The large number of small bottles in the Medical Glassware Collection meant that a method of storage was required which would maximise the use of the limited space available, whilst providing protection for the objects, and still allow easy access to them. It was decided to store the objects in Perspex drawers lined with Plastazote® and use specially manufactured strips of interlocking Plastazote® to create separate cells for each object (Figure 4). This has proved very successful for groups of bottles of particular sizes, i.e. those of the same width as the cells and tall enough to be easily removed. It becomes far more time consuming when this is not the case, as it is then necessary to pad out the space around the object.

Several groups of the larger objects have required special consideration when storing owing to their awkward shapes and/or poor preservation. Often this has simply meant using blocks of Plastazote®, cut to fit around the object, to support it in the best position.

Crystal boxes are often used for the more fragile smaller objects, after lining with Plastazote® and acid-free tissue paper. In this way, objects with fragile surfaces, leaking contents, etc. can be placed on the shelf or drawer and can be handled without causing further damage until conservation treatment can be carried out. Crystal boxes are also used to store pieces from broken objects, laid on the shelf or drawer next to the object. Larger broken pieces have been laid out on Plastazote®-lined Perspex drawers.

Conclusion

At the time of writing, the project is half way towards completion, and so far has proved very successful from a conservation point of view. The staff involved are considering conservation issues at all stages of the unpacking process, which is a particularly noteworthy achievement considering the limited time available. As a result, all objects processed so far have been stored to a satisfactory level, records have been kept of all deteriorating objects, and the profile of conservation has been raised throughout the store. The importance of having a full-time conservator on such a project cannot be over-emphasised as it has enabled training and supervision of non-conservation staff from the outset.

The environmental conditions in the storage areas have been improved; lagging of hot water pipes has reduced temperature levels, and monitoring for pests in the new store room for the *Materia Medica* Collection has revealed no reinfestation

Acknowledgement

The authors would like to acknowledge the help and support given by Hazel Newey (Head of Conservation), Emma Hedderwick (Stores Manager) and Stewart Emmens (Project Leader).

Product suppliers

- Acid-free card labels and Melinex® sleeves (polyester): Conservation By Design Ltd, Timecare Works, 60 Park Road West, Bedford MK41 7SL. Tel: 01234 217258.
- Acid-free tissue paper and archival boxes: Atlantis European Ltd, 146 Brick Lane, London E1 6RU. Tel: 0171 377 8855.
- Bay shelving: Welconstruct, 127 Hagley Road, Edgbaston, Birmingham B16 8XU. Tel: 0121 455 9798.
- Correx® (polypropylene/polyethylene copolymer): Wey Display, Pollock & Searby Ltd, 9/10 Mill Lane, Alton, Hampshire GU34 2QU. Tel: 01420 86924.
- Crystal Boxes (polystyrene) and Stewart® boxes (polypropylene): The Stewart Company, Stewart House, Waddon Marsh Way, Purley Way, Croydon CR9 4HS. Tel: 0181 760 0007.
- Cupboards: TLM Engineering: 39, Mincing Lane, Chobham, Surrey GU24 8RS. Tel: 01276 856663.
- Fumigation treatment (Methyl bromide): Rentokil Ltd, 187 Romford Road, Stratford, London E15 4JF. Tel: 0181 519 0030,
- Hazard tags (polypropylene): Seton Limited, Department P, PO Box 77, Banbury, Oxon OX16 7LS. Tel: 0800 585501.
- Longspan racking: Apex Storage Systems Ltd, Apex House, Garamonde Drive, Wymbush, Milton Keynes MK8 8ND. Tel: 01908 56122.
- Mercury spill kit and Parafilm® (polyolefines and paraffine wax): Fisher Scientific UK, Bishop Meadow Road, Loughborough, Leicestershire LE11 0RG. Tel: 01509 231166.
- Perspex drawers: Gratnell's Ltd, 258 Church Road, London E10 7JQ. Tel 0181 556 9021.
- Plastazote® (polyethylene foam): Polyformes Ltd, Cherrycourt Way, Stanbridge Road, Leighton Buzzard, Bedfordshire LU7 8UN. Tel: 01525 852444.
- Safety equipment (Latex gloves, face respirators, goggles): Man-Equip Ltd, Unit 2, Corium House, Douglas Drive, Catteshall Lane, Godalming, Surrey GU7 1JX. Tel: 01483 4261000.

A Case History of Managing Outbreaks of Webbing Clothes Moth (*Tineola bisselliella*)

Ruth E. Norton
Heritage Conservation,
PO Box 363, Cuttingsville, Vermont 05738, USA

Abstract

Factors promoting infestations of the webbing clothes moth (*Tineola bisselliella*) were found to be storage of soiled protein materials and poor housekeeping. Procedures for monitoring, containing and cleaning up infestations are outlined. Monitoring is done using inspection, sticky traps and pheromone lures. Annual resources required to monitor a collection of one million objects in 7830 m^2 of storage and work space comprise 112 person-hours and US 1300. Containing and cleaning up infestations in collection areas is based on freezing objects, vacuuming and washing storage facilities, and removing insect residue from objects. Resources required for an area 16 m^2 holding 400 objects comprise 515 person hours and 300 of materials. Most staff hours were used in removing insect residue from objects. Containing and cleaning up infestations in non-collection areas was based on vacuuming and washing, with material being discarded or frozen. Average required resources comprise 35 person hours.

Keywords

Anthropology, natural history, *Tineola bisselliella*, webbing clothes moth, pest management, non-toxic pest control

Introduction

The Field Museum of Natural History Chicago, holds Botany, Zoology, Geology and Anthropology collections of 23 million objects and specimens. The Education Department also has substantial holdings of materials. A spring sighting of the webbing clothes moth (*Tineola bisselliella*) in an Anthropology storeroom was of great concern to all of us responsible for these collections. The Conservation Department, within Anthropology, was immediately responsible.

We all knew a fair amount in theory and casual practice about pest management. However, when faced with an infestation of such great potential magnitude, there seemed to be too many gaps in our experience and in the literature when it came to specific procedures. The solution finally adopted made such obvious common sense – it was based on the life and habits of the insect, involved minimum handling of objects, involved optional use of pesticides – that we now look at it and wonder what the fuss was about. But it makes common sense in hindsight: considerable examination, reading and discussion were required to reach it.

This paper outlines the procedures used and summarises the resources required to monitor a collection and contain and clean up an infestation. It is intended to offer specific and practical information which could be applied to other collections for managing and budgeting.

The case

In late March 1995, a severe infestation of *T. bisselliella* was found in Anthropology Store Room 3. An object with concentrated activity was located. It and adjacent objects were bagged and frozen. As a number of moths were sighted throughout Room 3, it was not known how widespread the infestation was in that room. Also, other storerooms were felt to be at risk because objects from the infested room had been moved into three adjacent storerooms over the past several months. A large number of objects were involved: 4,700 in the infested room and 38,000 in the adjacent rooms. All were on open shelving. The immediate and potential danger to the Anthropology collection was high.

Initial inquiry[1,2] confirmed that isolating the infestation and slowing down the moth activity until a method of management could be established were first priorities. Luckily, Room 3 was on an individually controlled thermostat, so the temperature could be lowered to 16°C to reduce activity of all stages of the moth. The room was sealed off with plastic sheet and tape over doors and vents. Access to Room 3 and adjacent storerooms was restricted.

Given the large number of objects immediately involved, the danger to the collection if the extent of the infestation was not determined and contained, and the small number of staff available (2° people in Conservation), professional pest management expertise was clearly required. Seven pest control companies and advisers were invited to submit advice and bids to set up a monitoring program to determine the extent of the infestation in Anthropology, and bring the infestation in Room 3 under control.

The size of the infested area, the number and nature of the objects, the location and construction of the room, and public and staff safety issues placed constraints on means of combating the problem. The storeroom is in an interior space which cannot be sealed from staff and public areas, eliminating the use of toxic gas. Water-based pyrethrin spray could have been safe for staff and public, but could not be used on objects. The room is constructed of masonry and concrete, which had proved in past to be too permeable to utilise gaseous N_2 or CO_2 for oxygen deprivation.

Monitoring Anthropology storerooms, workrooms, offices and labs to determine the extent of the infestation appeared to be fairly straightforward, However, several very different approaches were proposed for eradicating the current infestation in Room 3. Evaluating these took considerable time and discussion with entomologists.

Evaluation of proposed approaches

Two proposals relied on trapping to reduce the population to a manageable level. One suggested low voltage ultraviolet (UV) light traps to attract adults. The adult is attracted by the light, is stunned and fails into a sticky trap below. The cost of light traps for 2575 m^2 of storage space (Room 3 and adjacent store rooms) was under 5,000. The proposal had two immediate disadvantages. We were not comfortable with introducing UV lights into object storerooms and work areas, and references[3–5] indicated that the adult *T. bisselliella* is not particularly attracted to light. [T. Parker (personal communication) has since indicated that all males and those females not heavy with eggs are attracted to daylight and UV light. They tend to fly at the couple of hours at dusk.]

The other trapping proposal used intensive pheromone trapping to reduce the male adult population. Sticky traps baited with the pheromone lures would be hung in the 2575 m^2 of storage space and monitored biweekly. The cost for traps and monitoring was under 3000.

Both of the trapping proposals relied on reducing the flying adult population. As only the male does extensive flying, both methods relied on male mortality with subsequent low rate of fertilisation in the population. Entomologists consulted[6,7] had found that in practice this approach has not been effective. A few untrapped males can easily fertilise a substantial next generation. Both methods had the advantages of little investment in staff time and no handling of objects, but there was little evidence that they would effectively control the outbreak.

Other proposals comprised killing all stages of the insects on objects by freezing or fumigation. A large freezer facility was available an hour's drive from the museum: however, we preferred to avoid subjecting the objects to the rigors of packing and road transport, The cost of on-site rental of a large freezer or fumigation van was fairly reasonable, about 600 per load. In each case, the cost in materials and staff time to pack and move 4,700 objects was prohibitive. As the operation would be done in large quantities in a short space of time, extra staff would have to be contracted. Risk of damage to the collection in movement and increased security costs were also factors. These approaches would however, clear out the room, making thorough cleaning easier.

The approach finally adopted[8] was one which was based directly on the known behaviour of the insect, necessitated only minimal movement of objects, and could be implemented solely by museum staff.

Particular aspects of the life cycle and habits of *T. bisselliella* were important to the final program implemented.[9–11] The larval stage of the insect is the only one which has mouthparts and can cause loss in objects. Because of their preference for dark, hidden spots, and the complex structure of many of the objects they feed on, their presence may be undetected for years, and a population may reach considerable size. The larvae can lie dormant in their feeding webs and the eggs and pupae are securely attached to their substrates: so all are easily transported on material to new sites. As the larva incorporates surrounding fragments in its pupal cocoon, the pupa is very well camouflaged. While the eggs are usually deposited on a food source, the pupae are found on any material, including paper, plastic and metal. Thus thorough cleaning or freezing of all materials and structures around the infestation is demanding and necessary.

On the positive side, if a population is detected soon after emergence, the actual area of concern is limited, *T. bisselliella* has a tendency to aggregate and remain for generations in a dense core, not moving until food is depleted, at which time the population emerges and swarms. Although both male and female adult can fly, the female is heavily laden with eggs and does not usually fly or walk far, she is more likely to tumble to a lower shelf. As the females and larvae do not travel far, the eggs and pupae from which the next generation will emerge are found within 2–3 meters of the infestation core. This considerably reduces the area and number or objects requiring treatment. Although the male adults fly readily, they are not inherently a problem. In fact their movement provides an important clue that a population is emerging, and their concentration can be used to pinpoint the infestation core.

The rate of development varies greatly with environmental conditions. Warm, humid environments encourage growth, 22°C and 75% RH is perfect. The lower the humidity and temperature. The slower the activity. There is seasonal variation in growth spurts as well. In temperate climates, early spring and late autumn seem to be times when a population emergence is most likely to occur, and when inspection may be required more frequently.

Procedure implemented to determine extent of infestation

Our primary concern was to determine whether the infestation was confined to Room 3, or whether it had been carried to the adjacent storerooms. We also hoped to determine whether it had spread throughout Room 3, or was confined to the area of the infestation core, and whether moths were a significant problem elsewhere in Anthropology.

The procedure used consisted of establishing and maintaining a long-term monitoring program for *T. bisselliella*. Suspended sticky traps containing its pheromone lure were used. The lure is the chemical equivalent of the female sex hormone to which adult males are attracted. Each lure is effective over a 6 m radius. After three months its effectiveness decreases and a new lure must be added to the trap. The pheromone is prone to oxidation. So unopened lures have a refrigerated shelf life of one year.[12]

Traps and lures were placed in all Anthropology storerooms, offices, workrooms and labs. Each trap was inspected once a month. During spring and autumn when outbreaks are most likely to occur, traps may be inspected more frequently. Those adjacent to the infestation were checked every week for the first month. Species and number of any insects found in the traps are recorded on a database.

After nine months of monitoring, no significant number of insects have been found in the infested and adjacent storerooms. Out of the 20 traps covering the area, only four moths have been found. These occur in different locations and are probably strays. It appears that the infestation had not spread beyond the core and that removal of the core objects and cleanup of the immediate area effectively removed the infestation. However, a moth is consistently found in a couple curatorial offices every month. This probably results from the regular traffic in coats and outside objects in these offices. It is not a cause of major concern, but points to the need for more active awareness of pests by all staff and the need to continually monitor for any sudden increase in population.

The above outlines the aspects of the monitoring program directly related to the infestation of *T. bisselliella*. The monitoring program actually implemented was much broader and included window and floor traps and lures for dermestids and cigarette beetle. It was based on information gained during a detailed site inspection by an entomologist with pest management experience (Dave Mueller. Insects Limited Inc). The site inspection was extremely beneficial and is recommended to any institution establishing a pest monitoring program.

The total monitoring program covered 20 Anthropology offices. Labs and workrooms and nine object storerooms comprising a total floor area of 7830 m^2. About 100 floor, window and hanging sticky traps and 70 lures were used. Sticky traps need changing about once a year and lures need to be added four times a year. The type and location of trap is flexible and may be modified in response to visible clues arising during inspections.

The annual cost of the monitoring program is about 1300 for traps and lures. Total staff time for inspecting, recording data and adding lures is 112 person hours.

Setting out the traps and the database required an initial investment of 25 person hours.

Procedure for controlling and cleaning up after a major infestation in a collection storeroom

The principle is to remove and freeze all material in the infested area, clean the infested area, and clean all objects before replacement in storage. If the outbreak is caught shortly after emergence from the core, the actual area of infestation is fairly restricted, and the population can be eliminated. The effectiveness of this approach was evidenced by our monitoring program.

1. Locate infestation core by visual inspection or by using traps to triangulate greatest population density.
2. Identify the species of insect, and its life cycle and habits. The procedure used will be based on this information.
3. Lower temperature if possible to 15–16°C to slow down activity during isolation and cleanup.
4. Bag, seal and remove all infested material and all material surrounding the core. Bagging keeps individual insects from being spread around while moving objects and prevents condensation on objects when they are removed from the freezer. The size or the area to be cleared may vary depending on the insect and the extent of human activity. For *T. bisselliella* in an area with little human activity, we were primarily concerned with the area within a 2–3 meter radius of the core.
5. Freeze all bagged material. We used −20°C for seven days.[13,14]
6. Dispose of or freeze all shelving and support padding, plastic, paper and boxes. Eggs and pupae can be firmly attached to them. Don't just carry them out. Bag or box them first so eggs, larvae, pupae and adults are not dropped and distributed.
7. Thoroughly vacuum the cleared area. Thoroughly means tops, bottoms, and sides of all surfaces, cracks, crevices, every place you can reach. A vacuum cleaner that is dedicated to pest cleanup is best, but any vacuum cleaner will do as long as it uses disposable vacuum bags. After vacuuming the area, seal the vacuum bag in a plastic bag and dispose of it immediately in a dumpster outside the museum building. Remember, you have vacuumed up eggs, larvae, pupae and adults into a warm dark vacuum bag: perfect for hatching and growth. Freeze the vacuum cleaner to kill any insect stages caught in hoses and nozzles.
8. Thoroughly wipe and mop down the cleared area with warm water and disinfectant soap or with alcohol. Rinse if necessary. Again, you are trying to get rid of any eggs, larvae, pupae which have settled or fallen on surfaces and in cracks.
9. A pyrethrin spray can be applied to cracks and crevasses to kill off anything you have not been able to remove. Pyrethrins are contact insecticides with little or no residual power: their application is not likely to do anything that you have not already done with vacuuming and wiping. But if there are hard to get crevasses, it might help. We found the pyrethrin spray more useful in reducing activity in initial cleanup of outbreaks in non-collection areas of the museum.
10. After freezing, remove all insect residue from objects before replacing them in storage. This makes future inspection workable as you will know that any insect residue found is a new problem and not just a leftover from a previous problem. This was by far the most time consuming part of the cleanup, but one which should not be skimped.

    In our case, we freshly bagged and sealed all objects before returning them to storage. This was partially because of dust problems in storage, and partially so that these objects would not require retreatment should the infestation prove to have spread beyond the treated area.
11. Mark all objects frozen and cleaned with the procedure and date. We used contact labels attached to object bags, boxes or labels. Although this information is in the object files, inspections are easier if the information is in storage.

Resources used to contain and clean up a *T. bisselliella* infestation in an Anthropology storeroom (an area 16 m^2 holding 400 objects) included 515 person hours, 300 of materials, and 18 weeks of freezer space. In addition, access to the infested storeroom was severely restricted for three months, and access to adjacent storerooms was restricted for one month:

1. Conservator (inspection, monitoring, consultation, evaluation and supervision; this would be shorter in future as not as much groundwork would need to be covered) – 110 hours.
2. Cleanup of infested area:
   Conservator (moving objects, bagging, freezing, cleaning, rebagging, labelling) – 335 person hours.
   Collection Manager (moving objects) – 35 person hours.
   Housekeeper with experience in collection areas (cleaning storeroom) – 35 person hours
3. Materials for bagging and rehousing (polyethylene sheet and foam, polyester sheet, acid-free board) – 300.
4. Freezer time:
   Walk-in freezer (18.6 cubic meters) – 3 weeks.
   Chest freezer (2.2 cubic meters) – 15 weeks.

Occurrence and clean-up of *T. bisselliella* in non-collection areas of the museum

Infestations in non-collection areas of the museum help maintain a resident population for reinfesting collection areas. Three examples are briefly related, followed by general comments.

Moths were sighted in an Education Department school learning center. Examination revealed dense populations growing behind carpeted benches, which had clearly not been pulled out for cleaning in quite some time (budget cuts had resulted in reduced housekeeping staff). The wool carpet was a food source for the moths: but there were nearby areas of wool carpet which were not supporting moths. The difference seemed to be that the carpet in the resource center was dirty and undisturbed.

Infestations were found in two Education closets housing materials for school group activities. The open closets fit into spaces behind display cases full of collection obiects. Over the years, materials such as feathers, raw wool, and birds' nests had been brought in by staff and volunteers. No-one was responsible for cleaning the closets or disposing of material left with changes of programs and staff.

A swarming infestation core was found on carpeted bases which had been abandoned in a crowded bay in Shipping. The carpet was wool, heavily soiled from years on display. Supplies and discarded equipment were stacked over the bases. No particular department was responsible for the storage bay. Again, dirt and neglect created an ideal environment for insect growth. A potential food source, wool, was made into a great food source, soiled wool, and was left undisturbed in a dark, enclosed area.

Some common factors clearly emerged as jointly responsible for creating problems. First, there is an ideal food source. The source is not just the presence of a protein material. In all cases it is a used, soiled protein material. Second are enclosed, dark, undisturbed spaces. These not only provide ideal breeding arounds, but are very difficult to monitor by visual inspection. Third is neglect. Either no-one was designated to be responsible for an area, or the area was used by a number of departments, or cleaning was not a high enough priority to survive funding cuts, or people were not aware of the danger.

Much of the problem could be averted with basic knowledge about pest habits and with generous application of good, old-fashioned housekeeping. Most pest management strategies recommend that a specific department or staff member be appointed responsible for monitoring for pests and ensuring that good housekeeping is maintained. Although the Field Museum does not have a designated pest management officer, those departments which have undertaken pest management in their own areas have a good record. This works well where there are members of staff who are willing to take on the responsibility. Unfortunately, there will always be some "unclaimed" spaces, and some sections without the expertise or staff time to maintain good housekeeping.

The procedures for containing and cleaning up non-collection infestations are similar to those in collections, but, because one is often dealing with disposable material, the resource of staff time is considerably reduced. Refer to the previous section for details of the following steps:

1. Identify the species of insect, and its lifecycle and habits.
2. Lower temperature to reduce activity. Also, pyrethrin spray can be used to kill adults and larvae, making them easier to contain and handle.
3. Thoroughly vacuum and wipe down all structures and materials to be saved within a 2–3 m radius of the infestation core. Materials which can not be vacuumed should be bagged and frozen.
4. All infested material to be discarded should be bagged or laid on plastic sheet to contain eggs, larvae, pupae or adults and immediately moved to a dumpster outside the museum building.

Resources required for containing and cleaning up infestations of *T. bisselliella* in non-collection areas varied, but generally required little material and an average staff time of 35 hours.

Conclusion

Dealing with webbing clothes moth *T. bisselliella* infestations in Anthropology storage and throughout the museum highlighted several practical and management issues.

Factors promoting infestations of *T. bisselliella* were found to be storage of soiled protein materials and poor housekeeping. Good housekeeping practices – regular and thorough cleaning of all areas of the museum, and regular inspection and inventory of stored and incoming materials – could considerably reduce the risk of infestations.

A detailed and practical understanding of the lifecycle and habits of the specific pest is critical to effective pest management. Monitoring and cleanup procedures are based on this.

Monitoring and inspection indicate that the procedures used to contain and clean up infestations of *T. bisselliella* (freezing objects, vacuuming and washing storage facilities within 3 meters of the infestation core, and removing insect residue from objects before returning them to storage) have been effective.

Annual resources required to monitor a collection of one million objects in 7830 m^2 of storage and work space comprise 112 person hours and 1300. Resources required to contain and clean up an infestation in a storeroom comprised 515 person hours, 300 and 18 weeks of freezer space. In addition, access to the storeroom was severely restricted for three months, Cleanup of non-collection areas required only 35 person hours on average, as infested material was often disposable. Using local salaries, the annual cost of monitoring all of Anthropology was 1680, while the cost of containing and cleaning up infestations in Anthropology storage and in non-collection areas of the museum was 8585 and 1630, respectively.

Acknowledgments

The following staff of the Field Museum were an integral part of the pest monitoring and managing program: Catherine Sease – Head of Conservation, Catherine Anderson – Conservator, Tony Valentino – Housekeeper, Wil Grewe-Mullins – Assistant Collection Manager, Norm Radke – Facilities Manager, and Phil Parrillo and Dan Summers, Curator and Collection Manager respectively of Entomology. Catherine Sease kindly reviewed this paper.

References

1. D. Mueller. Personal communication (Insects Limited Inc,. 10540 Jessup Blvd. Indianapolis, Indiana 46280-1451, USA, 1995).
2. D. Pinniger. *Insect Pests in Museums* (London: Archtype, 1994).
3. A. Mallis, revised T. Parker, "Clothes Moths," in *Handbook of Pest Control.* (Cleveland: Franzak and Foster,1990), 350–357.
4. Mueller. Personal communication.
5. T. Parker. Personal communication (Pest Control Services Inc., Landsdowne, Pennsylvania, USA, 1995).
6. Ibid.
7. Mueller. Personal communication.
8. Procedures were based in large part on advise by D. Mueller, Personal communication.
9. Mallis. "Clothes Moths".
10. Mueller, Personal communication.
11. L.A. Zycherman and J.R. Schrock,. eds, *A Guide to Museum Pest Control* (Washington DC: Foundation of the American Institute for Conservation and the Association of Systematics Collections, 1988).
12. Mueller. Personal communication.
13. T. Strang, "A Review of Published Temperatures for the Control of Insect Pests in Museums," *Collection Forum* 8, no. 2 (1992): 41–67.
14. M-L. Florian, "The effect on artifact materials of the fumigant ethylene oxide and freezing used in insect control," in Eighth Triennial Meeting, Sydney, Australia, of the International Council of Museums Committee for Conservation) Marina del Rey: Getty Conservation Institute. 1987), 199-208.

Materials and suppliers

NoSurvivor® Diamond trap (hanging sticky trap), Webbing clothes moth Bullet® lure, Cigarette beetle Bullet® lure, Trogoderma spp. Bullet® lure: Produced and supplied by Insects Limited Inc, 10540 Jessup Blvd, Indianapolis, Indiana 48280-1451, USA. Tel. 1-800-992-1991.

Mr. Sticky® (floor and window sticky trap): Manufactured by Mr. Sticky South, 819 Main St., Greenville. Mississippi 38701, USA. Tel. 1-601-335-6390.

PT® 565 Pyrethrin Insect Fogger (0.5% pyrethrins, 1% piperonyl butoxide, 1% n-octyl bicycloheptene dicarboximide. 97.5% inert ingredients): Manufactured by Whitmire Research Laboratories Inc. 3568 Tree Court Industrial Blvd., St. Louis, Missouri 63122, USA. Tel. 1-800-325-3668.

Low-energy Climate Control in Museum Stores: A Postscript

Tim Padfield
Conservation Department,
The National Museum of Denmark,
Brede, DK-2800 Lyngby,
Denmark

Abstract

A large museum storage building whose relative humidity was controlled by warming to reduce relative humidity showed a violently oscillating temperature with a period of about a week, as predicted by a computer model. The principle of humidity control by heating a building when the RH drops below the set point does not work in buildings that have a small air exchange rate and are filled with water absorbent materials. Such buildings must be controlled by dehumidification or by heating at constant energy input.

Keywords

Climate control, conservation heating

Introduction

At the ICOM-CC meeting in Dresden in 1990 Poul Jensen and I presented a paper[1] in which we analysed various methods of relative humidity control for museum stores. The unusual feature of this analysis was the inclusion of the stored objects in the calculation of heat and moisture variation. The analysis was a contribution to the planning of new storage rooms for the National Museum. It was done entirely on a computer, without the possibility of experimental verification on the real buildings at that time.

Two of the methods described in that paper, warming to constant relative humidity (RH) and dehumidification to constant RH, have now been tested in one of these storage buildings. This building (Figure 1) has an average height of 7.5 m and a ground plan of 1700 m^2, divided into three halls of equal size. Its walls are of lightweight concrete, 250 mm thick, clad with tongue-and-groove timber painted black. The space between concrete and wood is filled with 50 mm of insulation. The roof is black tar paper on insulating panels. The stored collection is very varied but includes many large wooden objects. The ventilation system gives one air change per hour. It is provided with heaters to control the relative humidity.

One prediction of the computer analysis was that a room filled with moisture-absorbant materials, such as paper, wood, leather and textiles, cannot reliably be controlled by heating to constant relative humidity, because raising the temperature to counteract a RH rising above the set point will lead to a further rise in RH, through moisture release from the stored objects. The process runs out of control because of this 'positive feedback'. The relative humidity remains only slightly above the set point but the absolute humidity of the air rises with the temperature, fed by the drying objects. The runaway heating eventually stops because there is always some infiltration of outside air. This air will have a much lower moisture content than the inside air, even if it is raining, because its temperature is lower.

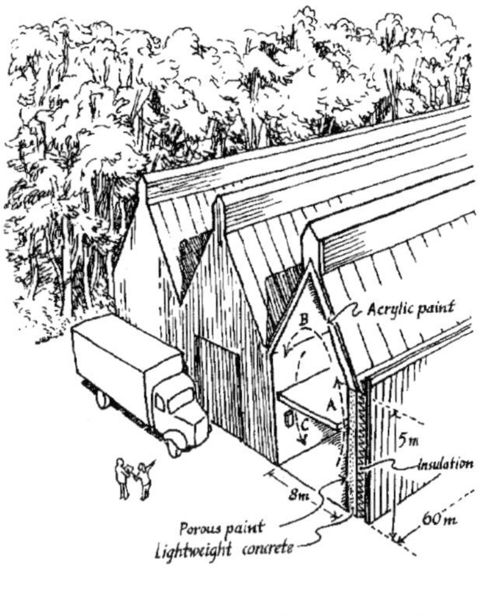

Figure 1. A view from the south of the National Museum's storage building for large objects, in Ørholm, north of Copenhagen. The building is 60 m long and 24 m across the gable end. The wall is 5 m high. The walls are of expanded concrete blocks clad with wooden boarding painted black. The roof is of tar paper on insulating panels. The sectioned south aisle shows the pattern of air circulation which transfers moisture evaporated from the heated south wall and causes a high relative humidity at the RH sensor shown on the north wall. The process is described in detail in the text.

The RH will first fall below the set point when the low moisture content of the air coming in from outside compensates for the water contributed by the objects, which must draw water from ever deeper layers. Then the whole process goes into reverse: the temperature falls, the objects absorb water, further reducing the RH. The cooling eventually stops when the outside air, now entering a cooler building, contains more water vapour than the inside air. The cycle then repeats.

Several conservators have expressed scepticism over the possibility that this process can occur outside a computer's memory, pointing out that RH control by a humidistat that calls for warmth when the RH increases over a set point, is used successfully in many places, particularly in historic buildings.

The National Museum's storage building in Ørholm

This scepticism was shared by the building committee. It decided to continue with the planned climate control method: warming to constant relative humidity, using outside air for cooling. Our advice was, however, partly heeded in later buildings, which have full air conditioning, scaled down to take advantage of the stabilising influence of the stored objects.

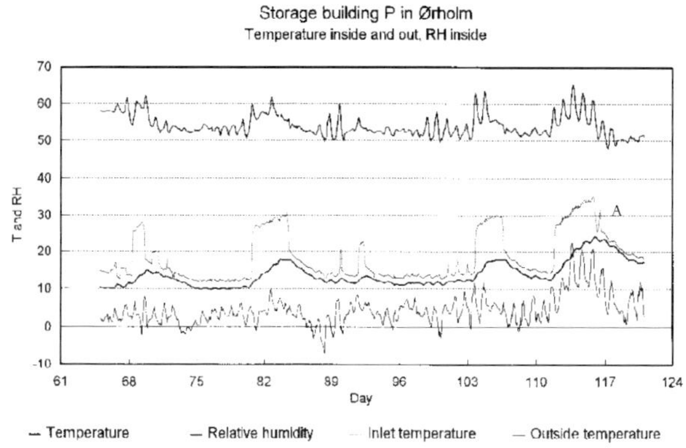

Figure 2. The climate in the building during April and May 1995. The dotted line A is the temperature of the air blown in from the climate control equipment. The lower dotted line is the outside temperature.

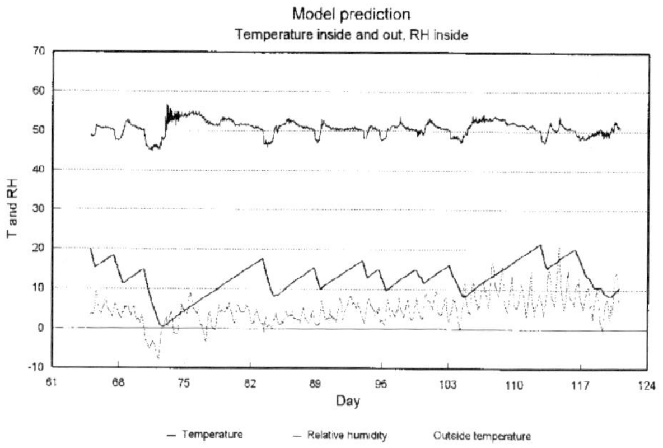

Figure 3. Corresponding data from the computer model.[1] The chaotic cycling of the inside temperature shows a similar pattern to Figure 2, but the steepness of the cooling part of the cycle is different, because in the computer model the air was forcibly cooled. In the real building the heating is simply switched off and outside air let in.

It seems that the heating to constant RH soon proved unstable, even though there were few objects in the vast interior. A dehumidifier was installed but the authors of the computer simulation were not told and were therefore denied an opportunity to check the detailed predictions of their model against reality as the building was steadily filled with objects.

Fortunately, for us, an opportunity came two years later when the dehumidifier broke down. The original control program had been left in the silicon memory that controls the air-conditioning equipment. The heating system again took over the job of relative humidity control. The result for a two-month period is shown in Figure 2. The room temperature shows cycles of heating and cooling over a period of about a week. The steeply rising and falling dotted line is the temperature of the air blown in from the air-conditioning unit. Notice that the rise in temperature does not cause a fall in RH.

Figure 3 shows the computer model results for the same period in the 'Test Reference Year', using exactly the same data and calculations as in the 1990 paper. The pattern of episodes of heating for about five days, accompanied by a relative humidity stubbornly above the set point, followed by rapid cooling, is strikingly similar in the two graphs. The cooling periods are more abrupt in the model because the temperature was actively driven down, whereas in the real building the heating was simply shut off and fresh air let in, if its temperature and dew point were suitable. The cooling pattern is therefore not identical between model and reality.

Notice that in both graphs the trigger that starts a cycle of instability is a rise in the outside temperature. This temperature rise penetrates the insulation and slightly heats the objects, which then desorb moisture to send the inside RH over the set point.

The predicted good climate regulation by dehumidification resumed as soon as the dehumidifer was repaired. This is shown in Figure 4 in the data for June and July. The dramatic temperature cycling has stopped but now we see a daily cycle in RH in the building, out of phase with the daily fall in outside RH during the morning and much too large to attribute to the reaction of the stored objects to the rising temperature.

I attribute this phenomenon to warming of the concrete block wall by heat transmission from the black timber cladding, which is fully exposed to the south. Water evaporates into the building from the porous concrete, which is coated on the inside with porous lime wash. Such a wall is a very efficient humidity buffer, *at its surface temperature*, as shown by a recent study of a church with a similarly porous wall surface.[2] This warm air, with a higher moisture content than the air in the centre of the room, rises convectively to the roof and convects down again past the sensor, which is on the inner wall forming the north side of the south aisle. The mezzanine floor does not meet the walls and serves to keep the convective circulation close to the wall surface. The roof is coated on the inside with relatively

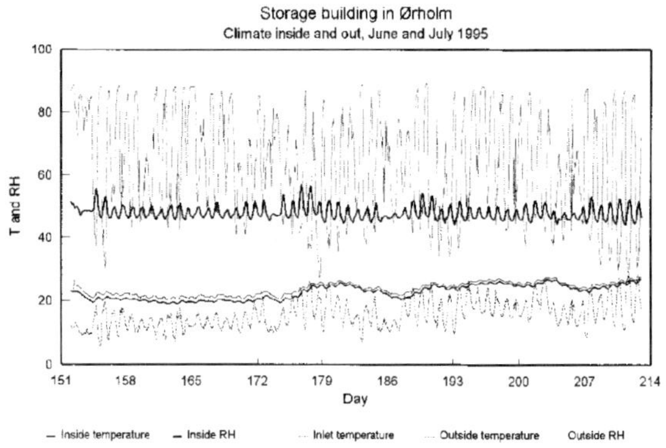

Figure 4. The climate in the building during June and July 1995, after the dehumidifier had been repaired. Notice the less dramatic variation in inside temperature, which follows the outside temperature. The outside RH is superimposed on the inside RH to show that they vary out of phase. The inside RH follows the outside temperature, probably because of evaporation of water into the interior from the cellular concrete wall as it is warmed by solar radiation absorbed by the black wooden cladding (see text and Figure 1)

impermeable acrylic paint, so the air retains its high water content as it descends past the cooler north side of the pitched roof. On the downward part of the cycle the air reaches temperature equilibrium with the room but not moisture equilibrium, so the sensor sees a high RH in the air streaming past it. The process is sketched in Figure 1. Indirect support for this explanation is provided by the much more stable environment in the north aisle, which shares the same ventilation system but receives no solar radiation on its walls.

Radiant heating was not included in the computer model. I had not anticipated that the entire building would be painted black!

Why does heating to constant humidity often work?

The short answer is that it works when the air exchange in the building is fast and when there is little humidity buffering from the building structure and furniture.

The RH in a sealed container rises with temperature if there is more than about 100 g of small pieces of unvarnished wood per cubic meter of air. In a leaking case, such as a large building, a larger quantity of moisture absorbent material is needed to ensure that the RH rises with temperature. Furthermore, the moisture in the material must be readily available.

In the building described here there is an abundance of bare wood and cardboard containers, the walls are lightweight concrete with a significant buffer capacity, coated with a porous paint. There are no windows and the air conditioning is designed to stop outside air being sucked in above a certain inside temperature, thus worsening the situation. In the historic houses that are warmed to constant relative humidity there is a much greater natural ventilation, through windows, doors and chimneys. The availability of moisture from furnishing and panelling is usually surprisingly small. Wood panelling and walls coated with oil paint or plastic paint have negligible buffer effect. In such houses the RH falls as the temperature rises and humidistatic control by heating is possible.

One should not, however, be complacent about extending this humidity control principle to storage rooms in buildings designed specially, or adapted for storage. In these buildings the natural air exchange is generally smaller and the risk of a rising RH with heating is significant. It is not practical to assume a constant or predictable air exchange in a building, because the air exchange is dependent on wind and on temperature gradient.

Conclusion

A computer model predicting an unstable climate in store rooms designed to be heated to attain constant humidity has been confirmed by the behaviour of a real, large building. Dehumidification is a better method for relative humidity control in store rooms, particularly those with a small natural air exchange rate. Dehumidification also results in a lower average temperature, which is good for the collection.

If relative humidity control by heating is preferred, there are several ways of preventing runaway heating. The feedback loop, in which the RH sensor relays ambiguous information to the control electronics, cannot be used. The temperature can be adjusted according to the time of year, to hold the temperature about 5øC above the expected temperature, taken from averages over many years. The same average excess temperature can be achieved by heating with constant energy, after establishing by trial and error how many watts are needed. If the building is well insulated, well sealed and massive, with a very slow response to changes in the outdoor temperature and humidity, the problem can be avoided by installing a very low powered heating system, so that the temperature can only rise very slowly, ensuring that even a slow air exchange is enough to prevent a rise in RH.[1]

References

1. T. Padfield and P. Jensen, "Low Energy Climate Control in Museum Stores", (Paper delivered at the Triennial meeting of the International Commission of Museums Committee for Conservation, Dresden, 1990), 596–601.
2. B. Eshøj and T. Padfield, "The use of porous building materials to provide a stable relative humidity", (Paper delivered at the Triennial meeting of the International Commission of Museums Committee for Conservation, Washington, 1993), 605–609.
3. This suggestion is based on climate data from the building housing the State Archive of Schleswig-Holstein, Germany, collected by Lars Christoffersen, Birch & Krogboe K/S, Virum, Denmark.

The Climate behind Pictures Mounted against the Outer Walls of the Chapel of Ledreborg, Denmark

Tim Padfield*
Conservation Department,
The National Museum of Denmark,
Brede, DK-2800 Lyngby,
Denmark

Annabel Robinson
The Clock Tower, off Barnes Lane,
Milford-on-Sea, Lymington,
Hampshire SO41 0JH, UK

Abstract

The climate behind oil paintings on canvas, mounted in shallow recesses in the outer walls of the baroque chapel of a country house, Ledreborg, near Roskilde in Denmark, is rather more stable and scarcely more humid than the climate in the room. The climate in the chapel is typical of a building which is seldom heated. The average relative humidity, about 70%, is higher than would be considered acceptable in a museum but is similar to the climate in many churches and historic houses in which paintings and woodwork survive in reasonable condition. An experimental painting was protected with polyester foil stretched over the back of the stretcher. This provided an even more stable microclimate with a hygrometric half life of about a month. There is no real need for special protection of the paintings against damp but the screening is effective against large insects and nesting bats. If permanent heating were installed, the climate behind the pictures would be quite different, because of the permanent temperature difference that would be established between the painting and the wall surface behind it.

Keywords

Microclimate, relative humidity buffering

Figure 1. The chapel of Ledreborg, looking north west. Notice the outside door opening directly into the chapel and another outside door on the balcony. The windows are large and single-glazed; there is relatively free air circulation to the loft through the holes made for the oval ceiling windows. The furniture is varnished wood, the floor is stone. The room is poorly sealed against air exchange, uninsulated and poorly buffered against RH variation.

Introduction

Conservators are generally rather anxious about the welfare of pictures that hang on the outer walls of houses. Various strategies have been proposed, and used, for securing a gentle climate at the back of the picture: boards mounted across the back of the frame made of some material that buffers RH or that is inert to moisture, air gaps, thermal insulation. This article is a quantitative contribution to the debate. We present no general solution: just an analysis of the microclimate in a particular place, which suggests that an analysis of the microclimate in each particular place is a reasonable, though time consuming, route to choosing a rational action, or inaction.

The climate measurements

Ledreborg house has hardly altered since the eighteenth century. The chapel (Figure 1) is a baroque room with stone floor and painted wooden panelling covering the walls. The room occupies the full width and height of the west end of the main house. The construction is massive brick, cement-rendered on the outside and lime-plastered on the inside. The main rooms are wood-panelled.

The chapel has oil paintings set in shallow recesses in the outer walls (Figure 2). The conservators who have responsibility for the paintings were worried about the development of a damaging microclimate behind the pictures. The urgency of a climate study was reinforced when a large fruiting body of the dry rot fungus, *Serpula lacrymans*, was found clinging to the back of a canvas that was removed for conservation. We used this stimulus, and the availability of the wall niche, to measure the climate in the room and behind two paintings which were used to replace the original while it was under restoration.

The two pictures were set side by side in the recess, as shown in Figure 2. One of the paintings had polyester foil stretched across the back of the stretcher to prevent water vapour transfer (but not heat transfer) from the wall. Temperature and humidity sensors were placed in front of these pictures and in the air space between the canvas and the wall. The outside climate was measured in a shaded spot on the flat roof of the west wing, just outside the chapel.

The microclimate around the pictures

The climate measurements are summarised in three graphs. Figure 3 shows the outside (dotted) and inside temperature and relative humidity (RH) for a 15 week period starting on 14 March 1994. The inside relative humidity is generally a moderated version of the outside RH. The daily cycles of RH are caused mainly by the daily temperature cycle acting upon room air that is rapidly exchanging with outside air. The outer door has no lobby, the door at the balcony level is poorly fitting and the windows are not particularly airtight. The room is high and open, encouraging convective air exchange (the 'stack effect').

The temperature and humidity cycling is not effectively damped out by the room. The abundant wood panelling is a fairly good thermal insulator, reducing

* Author to whom correspondence should be addressed

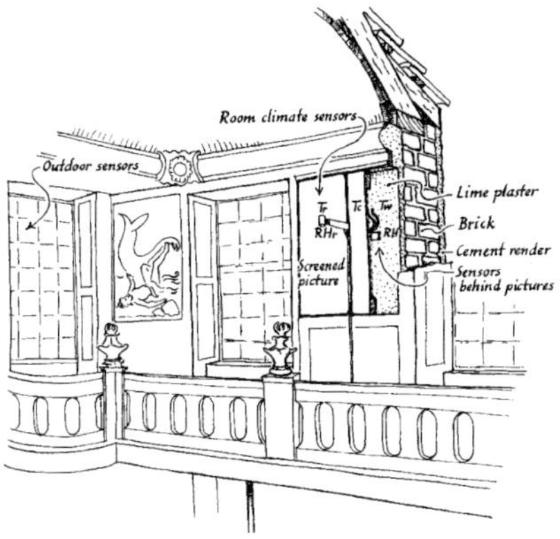

Figure 2. A diagram showing a section of the wall and the positions of the climate sensors. The room temperature and relative humidity are measured at the end of a post sticking 200 mm out in front of the paintings. Behind each painting are two temperature sensors (thermocouples) touching the surface of the canvas and the surface of the wall respectively. Temperature and relative humidity sensors are enclosed in a radiation shield in the middle of the air space behind each picture.

the stabilising influence of the thermal inertia of the wall. The paint on the wood prevents moisture movement which would stabilise the relative humidity.

Figure 4 shows the microclimate around the paintings. The upper curves show the RH in the room (dotted) and at the back of each of the two experimental paintings. Both the polyester-protected canvas (bold line) and the unprotected canvas (thin line) had been stored for several weeks in a room at about 40% RH. The unprotected canvas came rapidly to equilibrium close to the running average of the RH in the chapel, while the protected canvas came slowly to equilibrium with its new surroundings over a period of about two months. At the end of the measuring period the two RH traces have converged. The RH behind both canvases is more stable than that in the room.

A detailed study of Figures 3 and 4, with a close up of a shorter period, shown in Figure 5, suggests that the canvas of the screened picture is stabilising the RH of the air trapped behind it, but that the wall is actively stabilising the RH behind the unprotected picture, and therefore behind all the other pictures in the room.

The lowest line in Figure 5 is the temperature difference between the pictures and the wall surface (the two pictures have identical thermal environments). Notice that the RH behind the unprotected canvas (thin line) is cycling up and down with minimum values that coincide with maximum values of the temperature difference between the picture and the wall (the picture surface is warmer than the wall surface). At first glance this could be attributed to air exchange with the room, because the RH in the room goes up and down in the same pattern. However, a closer look at Figure 3 shows that the relationship between RH in the room and behind the painting is not easily explained by this theory. Around day 130 the RH behind the picture is varying more than that in the room, but the peaks in room RH on days 105, 137 and 145, when the temperature was rather stable, do not penetrate behind the canvas.

These observations can be explained by assuming that the wall is controlling the RH to a constant value *at the wall surface.* This air then convects away from the wall to the back surface of the painting, keeping the exact water content it acquired when it came to equilibrium with the wall surface. Because the picture canvas is at a higher temperature than the wall, the air warms up and therefore drops in relative humidity.

This explanation may seem very indirect and speculative, but it is supported by a consideration of what happens at the back of the protected painting (thick line in Figure 5). Here the wall plays no part in the moisture transfer, because of the impermeable polyester sheet which separates the wall from the air space behind the picture. The air trapped behind this picture exchanges water vapour only with the

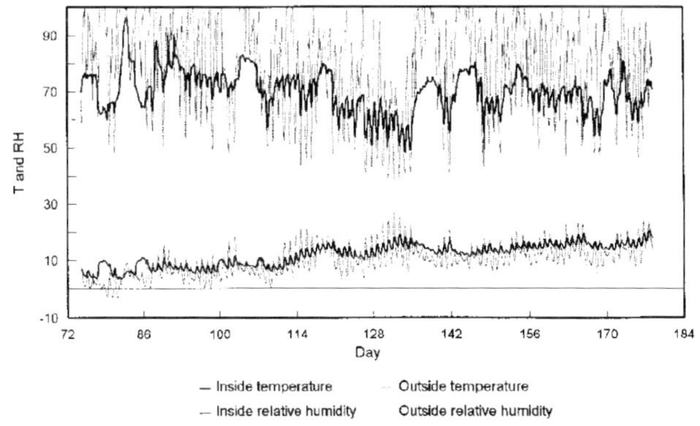

Figure 3. Temperature and relative humidity inside the chapel (bold line) and outside (dotted line). Notice the relatively poor relative humidity buffering of the room air, due to rapid air exchange through windows and doors, combined with varnish on the woodwork, which prevents humidity buffering.

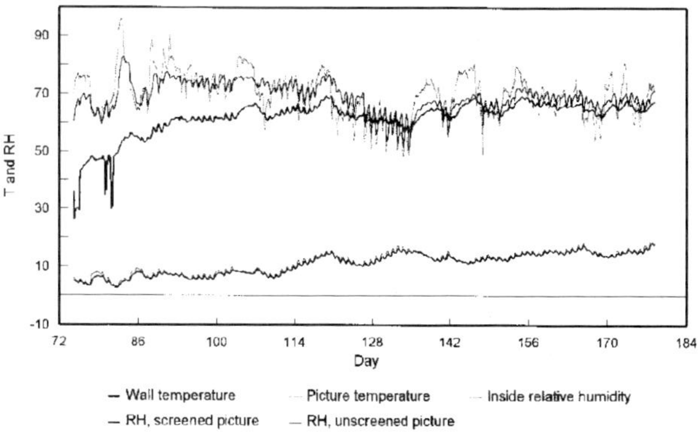

Figure 4. Relative humidity in the chapel (dotted line) and behind the two pictures. The bold line is the RH calculated for the canvas back surface of the picture screened from the wall by polyester foil. Notice the slow climb in RH from the value in the conservation laboratory, about 40%, to equilibrium with the chapel after about two months. The dips at the beginning of the record are instrument failures. The thin continuous line is the RH calculated for the canvas of the unscreened picture. It follows the running average of the room RH, with a noticeable buffering, caused not by the canvas itself but by the wall, as shown in Figure 5.

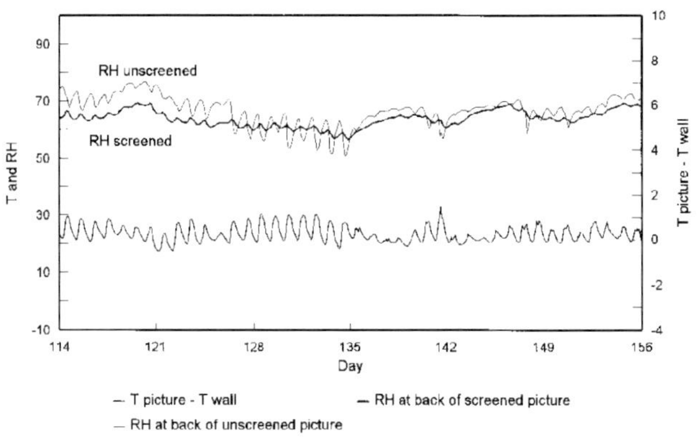

Figure 5. The two traces at the top are the RH behind the two pictures. At the bottom is the temperature difference between picture and wall. The screened picture (bold line) has small RH peaks that approximately coincide with temperature peaks at the canvas. This RH pattern is characteristic of a closed container filled with abundant buffer, in this case the canvas. The unscreened RH (thin line) has larger RH peaks when the temperature difference is at a minimum. This can be attributed to buffering of RH by the wall at the wall temperature. This buffered air warms up to the canvas temperature with consequent fall in RH.

canvas of the picture itself, so the RH at the back of the screened picture is much more constant. There is just a slight increase of RH as the temperature rises, which is a known property of cellulosic fibres in a confined, nearly airtight space.

The opposite pattern of the RH cycle behind the unscreened painting confirms that the reasonable RH stability cannot be due to poor air circulation, because this would allow the canvas to buffer the RH just as it does for the screened picture. The wall is actually such a powerful stabiliser of RH that it overrides the influence of the canvas.

We have used many words to describe this apparently minor phenomenon because it is not generally appreciated by architects and building engineers (maybe not even by conservators) that porous walls confer considerable climatic stability on the rooms which they enclose.[1] The modern practice of sealing porous walls with plastic paint prevents them from exerting this beneficial influence on house interiors. The painted and varnished baroque panelling of Ledreborg unfortunately has the same effect of screening the wall from the air in the room. The wall can therefore only influence the climate behind the panels and the paintings.

Conclusions

The climate measurements are unexpectedly reassuring: the climate behind the pictures is actually more stable than the climate in the room and is not significantly moister. The fungus which formed such a dramatic, baroque embellishment to the back of the original painting had not significantly attacked the painting or its frame: the observed damage can be attributed to the moisture oozing from the fruiting body. The dried residue on the back of the picture was the fruiting body of mycelium that was probably digesting the lower part of the roof construction, which is not far above the level of the top of the picture. There is no evidence that the wall is unusually damp at the level of the paintings and panelling in the chapel, but there are constructional details at the edge of the roof which have caused dry rot within the roof timbers.

The climate in the chapel can be described as far from ideal for preservation of the splendid interior, but not acutely dangerous. In particular there is no ground for special anxiety over the microclimate around the pictures mounted on the outside walls. They have the best climate in the room!

The best way to secure the stability of the paintings is to improve the climate in the chapel by reducing air leakage and heat flow. The sealing around doors and windows can be improved. The daily temperature cycle can be reduced by minimising heat flow through the windows, by the use of heat-reflecting curtains or, more controversially and expensively, by adding a layer of coated, though colourless, glass to reflect radiant energy.

Biological deterioration is a more urgent problem. The danger from dry rot in the roof timbers migrating to the back of the picture while trying to disperse its spores in free air will continue as long as damp conditions prevail where the roof springs from the walls. This matter is at present being attended to. There remains one other biological threat: The protected bats of Ledreborg should be dissuaded from setting up home behind the pictures. A permeable but tightly woven polyester cloth stretched over the back of the paintings' frames should serve this purpose without causing unexpected side effects.

Technical details

The temperatures were measured with type K thermocouples. These are better than the more usual type T, recommended for climate measurements, because of the lower thermal conductivity of type K. The surface temperature measurements were made with the thin thermocouple wires lying on the surface for about 20 mm from the metal junction. The relative humidity was measured with resistive polymer sensors from the General Eastern Company. The pulsed excitation was provided by a Campbell Scientific CR10 data logger, which collected all the data. The calibration of the RH sensors was done with saturated salt solutions, before and after the investigation. Sensors were screened against radiant heat by polished stainless steel shields. The outdoor sensors were in a double-shielded enclosure with convective air circulation. The indoor room measurements were made at a point 200 mm in front of the experimental paintings. This position has the same climate as in the centre of the room, within experimental error and natural variation.

Acknowledgements

We thank the Holstein Ledreborg family and their staff for their help in this investigation.

Reference

1. B. Eshøj and T. Padfield, "The use of porous building materials to provide a stable relative humidity", (Paper presented at the Triennial meeting of the International Commission of Museums Committee for Conservation, Washington, 1993), 605–609.

Quantifying the Conservation Backlog: The Trøndelag Project

Elizabeth E. Peacock and Roar Sæterhaug
Vitenskapsmuseet, The Norwegian University of Technology and Science, N-7004 Trondheim, Norway

Abstract

An assessment of the registration and conservation needs of museum collections in the Trøndelag region of Norway was carried out. A comprehensive questionnaire was developed which is multiple choice, easy to complete, and suitable for both an electronic database and statistical anlaysis. The questionnaire maps both the status of the collections and the localities and buildings which contain them, and the investment needed to remedy the situation. The results have been extrapolated to represent the whole of Norway, and correspond well with the results of a similar independent survey conducted in Sweden.

Keywords

Norway, Trøndelag, condition survey, preventive conservation

Introduction

Norway with a population of 4 million has 1,000 museums spread over the entire country. The relatively large number of museums reflects the interest which Norwegians have in preserving local and regional social history. Of the 15 million museum objects in Norwegian museums, 12 million are in the collections of the four university museums, which together function as a national museum. The 81 conservation posts are to be found at the largest museums, concentrated in Oslo in the southernmost part of a geographically very long and narrow country. Regional Norway is more or less without any type of conservation service. Preserving these collections has not been given priority, and Norway lacks a comprehensive overview of the current status of its museum collections.

All aspects of the museum system in Norway are currently under review. The Ministry of Culture's Museum Committee, which submits its report in spring 1996, is addressing the conservation needs of collections, among other issues. However, without an overview of the status of museum collections it is difficult to develop a strategy for solutions. Norsk Museumsutvikling (NMU)/Norwegian Museums Development took the initiative in 1994 to survey the museums in the two-county Trøndelag region of Mid-Norway to assess their registration and conservation needs. Trøndelag was seen as being representative for the country, and the survey could be used to determine the situation for the entire country.

The assessment

The goal of the survey was to map the current status of museum collections in Trøndelag with regard to the registration and condition of the artefacts, environmental conditions of storage and displays, and conservation service. The survey was to provide the objective basis for quantifying the registration, preventive conservation, and active conservation needs, both for the accumulated backlog and to maintain the collection. It was hoped that the Trøndelag project could serve as a model with methods, comparable analyses and results applicable to other areas of the country.

Trøndelag was selected because it is a region with a varied museum community with art, social history, and natural history museums. Geographically and climatically it is also a representative cross section of the country with an extensive coastline and remote inland mountain regions. Vitenskapsmuseet (VM), which is the university museum of the Norwegian University of Technology and Science, with an established conservation laboratory, had carried out a similar storage survey of one of its regional museums and had already expressed concern about the lack of conservation services in Trøndelag. The two central partners in the Trøndelag Project were NMU and VM. The Conservation Section (VM) planned and carried out the data collection, while NMU analysed the raw data. The data was to be in a form that could be statistically analysed.

The method

Selection of museums

Half of the museums in Trøndelag were selected for inclusion in the survey. These 29 museums were a representative cross section of all types of museums and classes

Table 1. Number of museum objects in Trøndelag

	Total number of objects	Objects surveyed
University Museum	1,967,000	1,967,000
Sør-Trøndelag County	206,000	164,000
Nord-Trøndelag County	102,000	85,000
Total	2,275,000	2,216,000
National total	14,902,000	

of museum objects, as well as a balanced geographical distribution within the region. All the large regional museums and the one university museum were included. 97% of museum objects in the two-county region were surveyed (Table 1).

Collecting the data

Approach

Several previous attempts in Norway to assess conservation needs relied upon museum's own descriptions and estimates of their needs. Many museums have no staff and are the responsibility of local historical societies or local municipal authorities. It was decided the Trøndelag mapping would use a questionnaire which would be completed by a team of professional conservators through a visit to the museum and interview with local people involved with the museum.

Survey questionnaire

A comprehensive questionnaire was designed (Figure 1) modelled after that developed for the survey of industrial collections in the UK.[1] A pilot collections storage survey carried out at a local regional museum formed the basis for the questionnaire's format and content. The questionnaire was developed on the principle of multiple choice, with standard choices, and numerical answers (e.g. number of objects). Possible free text was reduced to a minimum. This approach resulted in a form that had standard answers, was quick to complete, and gave data in a form that could be analysed statistically. In addition, it was developed as an electronic database which could be entered and analysed directly. The database was programmed in Superbase® and data analysis was carried out in Excel®.

Trøndelag Survey
Field Questionnaire

Museum:	Museum No.:
Building:	Building No.:
Store/Display:	Floor Area: m2

Part I

01. Total number of objects registered at institution ______
02. Number of objects not registered ______
03. Existing conservation service
04. Preventive conservation work from outside institution
05. Preventive conservation work for other institutions (bought/sold)
06. Interventive conservation work from outside institution
07. Interventive conservation work for other institutions (bought/sold)
08. Does the institution share a conservation service with other institutions?
09. Staff responsible for stores/displays
10. Survey team's assessment of institution's conservation needs
11. Institution's list for conservation assistance
12. Distance to nearest fire / police station :______km
13. Comments:

Part II

01. Building Type
02. Store/Display
03. Construction Materials
04. Insulated Building
05. Roofing Material
06. Building Maintenance
07. Electricity
08. Security Risk
09. Fire Risk
10. Fire Extinguishing
11. Risk of Water Damage
12. Access for Objects
13. Flooring
14. Temperature Conditions
15. Relative Humidity
16. Lighting Conditions
17. Biological Infestation
18. Organisation of Storage Area / Display
19. Inspection
20. Type of Collection
21. Number of objects in store/display: ______
22. Number satisfactorily registered: ______
23. Backlog registration : ______mos.
24. Percent organic material: ______%
25. Percent inorganic material: ______%
26. Mixed material: ______%
27. Percent polychrome material: (percent of No.21) ______%
28. Status for preventive conservation
29. Status for active conservation
30. How much is conserved: ______%
31. How much is conserved by a professional conservator: ______%
32. Backlog prevent. conservation: ______mos.
33. On-going prevent. conservation: ______mos.
34. Backlog active conservation: ______mos.
35. On-going active conservation: ______mos.
36. Need for reorganising store/display
37. Other problems
38. Comments:

Figure 1. Field questionaire

The questionnaire is in two parts. The first section maps general information about a museum, such as the size of the collection, whether it is recorded, conservation service, staff responsible for the collections, and comments. The second section maps the physical and environmental state of each building and locality within containing artefacts, the type of collection, number of objects, material type, and registration and conservation needs.

Field work

Each museum selected for inclusion in the survey was sent a description of the project, a suggested date for site visit by the survey team, and a copy of the questionnaire. The letter also stressed the importance of a representative of the museum assisting in the mapping. A visiting timetable was established, providing a half day for most museums and a full day for the largest museums. Field work took three months and was carried out from October to December 1994, during which time the team covered 2,500 km.

A team of three full-time professional conservators, each with different academic training and work experience, collected the data. Each museum was visited by the entire team. The first section of the questionnaire was completed together with the museum's representative. This section was filled out once for each museum. A second section was filled out for each storage and display area in each building. In cases where several areas in one building had similar environmental conditions, these were treated as one unit. For the 29 museums surveyed 264 store/display questionnaires were completed.

In most cases the museum representative accompanied the team around the museum while the store/display sections were filled out. This provided an excellent opportunity for the team to explain about preventive conservation and advise concerning remedies directly applicable to the museum, many of which the museum could undertake with minimum resources. In the majority of instances it was the first time museums has been visited by a conservator, and the first time those responsible had contact with a professional conservator.

At the outset it was intended to fill out the questionnaire by directly entering the information into a portable computer. This proved impractical simply because it was not flexible enough. The questionnaire needed to be a fluid working document able to accommodate comments, notes and question marks in the first instance, i.e. an old-fashioned paper questionnaire worked best. Each evening the completed forms were discussed and assessed and adjustments made. The team of three had to be in agreement on all points. Data entry of all the completed forms was carried out once the field work was complete.

A site diary was kept, in which impressions, notes and other information of a descriptive nature were noted. Buildings and display and storage areas were photographed, initially to assist the team in its later analysis; but this material now forms a valuable visual archive of the status of collections in Trøndelag.

Quantifying the situation

In cases where a museum had accurate registration records of its collection, these were used to determine how many objects were in each storage and display area. In most instances, however, such records did not exist, and these collections were tallied on the spot. At the same time each group of objects was broken down into percentages of organic, inorganic, mixed and polychrome materials.

The status for preventive and active conservation was registered as falling within one of four categories (0–25%, 26–50%, 51–75% or 76–100%) ranging from "everything needs attention" to "under control". Objects were not assessed individually. The team operated with a strict definition of conservation. The majority of institutions visited were rural open-air museums with social history collections. Preventive conservation was prioritised, and defined as action necessary to stabilise an object's environment, e.g. environmental conditions such as a leaky roof. Active conservation of entire collections of this nature was seen as unrealistic.

The number of months' work required within both preventive and active conservation to deal with the backlog and with on-going need was calculated, based upon the size and type of collection and condition. The team had no factor

Table 2. The Swedish and Norwegian surveys

	Number of objects	Years work (Backlog)	Years work (1994)
Sweden	38,000,000	5700	200
Norway	15,000,000	3400	80
Trøndelag	2,200,000	467	8

on which to base this calculation other than the experience of the individual members, and this could be considered the most subjective aspect of the assessment.

The number of months' work required to register the backlog of artefacts was calculated based upon a factor of 300 objects/month for social history and 400 objects/month for natural history collections. This is a factor arrived at by the team. Interestingly one of the museums surveyed operated with such a factor arrived at independently. Their registration procedure was estimated at 240 objects/month, but included photodocumentation. Allowing for this addition, the two factors were considered comparable.

Evaluation of the method and results

The questionnaire served the survey team well. Based upon standard answers to standard questions, it was relatively quick and easy to fill out. It was perhaps too detailed regarding the technical aspects of the buildings housing museum objects. Statistical analysis of the vast majority of items was successful in quantifying the situation.

The fact that the same persons collected the data from all the museums visited meant that the calculations and results are comparable both within each institution surveyed and among the institutions surveyed. It was especially through discussions with those responsible for the museums that information and conditions not otherwise "mapable" came to light, i.e. information museums would not have included had they been sent the questionnaire to complete.

Those responsible for the museums and the conservation team often had different ideas about preservation of the museum collections. Museums were more interested in using their collections, whereas, the conservation team was more concerned about storage and display conditions and collections management. Exhibition and outreach overshadowed the unseen tasks of collection maintenance. With few exceptions, museums generally had no particular strategy for solving the registration and conservation problem. Many expected the government to provide answers.

At several institutions the actual number of objects in the museum did not correspond with the museum's records. Some museums did not know what they had, others had collections they did not consider as part of the museum. This was especially true for collections which originated as gifts.

The Trøndelag survey team did not carry out the statistical analysis of the data nor extrapolation of the results to represent the situation in Norway as a whole.[2] This was carried out by Norwegian Museums Development. A similar independent assessment of the conservation needs of collections has recently been carried out in Sweden.[3] It is interesting to compare Sweden's results with the "national" results for Norway (Table 2). The results of these two surveys correspond well, giving support to the criteria evaluated in each.

Conclusion

The Trøndelag collections condition survey is not unique, and simply one of many that the conservation community has undertaken throughout the world over the past 20 years. It is the first of its kind in Norway, a predominantly rural, geographically isolated country with no regional conservation service. The survey was undertaken by a team of three professional conservators, and information was gathered on a comprehensive questionnaire consisting of predetermined choices to predetermined questions. This method has enabled not simply identification but also quantification of the conservation needs in Norway.

References

1. J.D. Storer, *The Conservation of Industrial Collections* (London: The Science Museum and The Museum and Galleries Commission, 1989).
2. E. Hernes, E.E. Peacock, A. Sommer-Larsen and R. Sæterhaug, "Trøndelags Undersøkerlsen 1994-95", *Skriftserie* 4/95, (Norsk Museumsutvikling, Oslo, 1995).
3. "Minne och Bildning", (Museumsutredning, Stockholm, 1995).

Torpid Larvae of the Webbing Clothes Moth, *Tineola bisselliella* (Lepidoptera:Tineidae), and Moth Control Success in Museums

Irene N. Provorova
Biological Laboratory, State Research Institute for Restoration (GosNIIR), Gastello Street 44, Moscow 107014, Russia

Abstract

It is shown that the ecological hardiness of the webbing clothes moth, *Tineola bisselliella*, is due in part to the fact that a majority (85 to 100%) of middle-aged larvae do not perish under unfavourable conditions (lack of suitable food, anti-feedant or weak biocidal properties of food substrate, lowered oxygen content). They convert instead to a physiologically inactive state that is a kind of torpidness or facultative diapause. These larvae can stay in closed silk cocoons without food and movement for 2–3 months. This inactive state is reversed when limiting conditions return to normal values. Thus the greater part of larvae in moth populations can outlive prolonged extreme but sub-lethal conditions in a state of physiological rest. Such a fact must be considered during moth control. It essential that all controlling conditions reach their lethal value.

Keywords

Museum pest control, webbing clothes moth, torpid larvae, physiological rest, facultative diapause, ecological hardiness

Introduction

It is now generally accepted that insect control in museums has to be founded on the in-depth study of pest species biology. This paper deals with a dangerous fabric pest, the webbing clothes moth, *Tineola bisselliella* (Humm.) (Lepidoptera: Tineidae), and with a new aspect of hardiness in this species. As a household keratin-eating insect, it is found in human dwellings where temperature and humidity have no sudden fluctuations and where there is a lot of food. That is why *T. bisselliella* has lost the ability to endure a wide a range of changes in habitat conditions, and appears to be vulnerable to them.

Successful development and reproduction of insects, including museum pests, are possible only with a favourable combination of external conditions, such as temperature, humidity, and lighting, as well as sufficient stores of suitable food. In the course of evolution, insects have developed an ability to withstand changes of habitat that are out of their normal range of endurance by entering a state of physiological resting. The different forms of this state are torpidness, hibernation, and diapause.

It is not yet clear whether there is true diapause in the contemporary understanding of the meaning of that word within the development cycle of the webbing clothes moth. Diapause is considered to be the most developed and prevailing form of resting among insects. It is characterized by the suppression of development or reproduction, and arises as an obligatory stage of individual development, or as a reaction to external factors.[1]

For each species diapause corresponds to a definite stage of ontogeny and occurs well before a difficult period for survival. The main feature of the diapause state is some physiological preparation which enables the insect to withstand, for a long period of time, conditions lethal to the developing stages. Thus, true diapause differs fundamentally from a stage of non-adaptive torpidness which can occur at any moment under the influence of sublethal factors.[2] Lastly, the state of diapause is characterised by high non-specific resistance to external factors.[3]

Titschack[4] considered that the webbing clothes moth had no diapause in any stage of development. Zagulajev[5] noted that newly emerged larvae of *T. bisselliella* are very mobile and begin to feed at once, but after 4–10 days they stop moving and stay in that position for 30–35 days. After that, they begin to feed and then cast their coats normally. Zaguleyev made some conclusions about the essence of this phenomenon.[6] Saphonova[7] mentioned optional diapause in *T. bisselliella* larval stages under some unfavourable conditions. Griswold[8] also notes that *T. bisselliella* larvae may remain without feeding within 'resting cocoons' for as long as four months, but nothing is known of the factors that initiate diapause, or whether the species does indeed diapause.

Experimental procedure

In the present article we have tried to elucidate how food quality influenced the course of development of *T. bisselliella* larvae. Making observations on middle-aged larvae (not younger than fourth instar) of *T. bisselliella* from laboratory culture, we discovered that in the case of compelled breeding on an unsuitable food substrate (for example, manufactured leather) a fraction of the larvae perished as the result of cannibalism and the others (up to 80%) became torpid. They built closed silk cocoons, cast in them, and remained without food and movement for several months. In another group kept without any food, larvae also became torpid. All the larvae of a group on woollen flannel were actively feeding, having built friable webbing cases, open at both ends.

After two weeks, the cocoons of torpid larvae were placed on woollen flannel. Fourteen days later, 80% of these larvae had lengthened their cocoons with webbing and began to feed. In comparison, the larvae of torpid larvae left without suitable food did not change their state (six months observations). Thus the appearance of normal food reactivates the torpid larvae.

In further experiments we studied the influence of inedible food on larval development in detail. We placed five larvae on each sample of woollen fabric (1.5 × 1.5 cm) saturated with solutions of (poly)hexamethylene guanydine (PHMG, MW = 10,000) in three different concentrations. This substance has a pronounced antifeedant action and only feeble biocidal action. The samples were incubated 14 days at 24 ± 1°C and 60 ± 7% RH. The test group of larvae was bred on the woollen flannel. Each condition was repeated four times. The results are given in Table 1.

Table 1. The influence of feeding conditions on development of webbing clothes moth larvae

Concentration of PHMG, g l^{-1}	Average quantity of torpid larvae after two weeks	Average quantity of torpid larvae after 2.5 months	Adult emergence after 2.5 months	Larval mortality after 2.5 months
0 (control)	33%	33%	8%	8%
5	100%	67%	17%	16%
15	100%	58%	8%	34%
30	100%	75%	8%	17%

As we can see in Table 1, after two weeks no larvae were feeding, since all were torpid in silk cocoons. After two months the quantity of such larvae had decreased a little, partly due to pupation and emerging of adults and partly due to death. The majority of larvae in the course of that two months stayed inside the cocoons as before.

Some of the larvae moulted twice with decreased dimensions of the head capsule and entire body. A fraction left their cocoons and built new ones in other places without starting to feed on a sample. All the adults which appeared in this experiment were of small size (3 to 6 mm in length in comparison with 10 mm in the culture), which suggests premature pupation of the larvae.

Approximately a third of the control group larvae also became torpid. This may have been caused by the change of the feeding substrate from breeding colony to the substrate used in the experiments. This change may be an unfavourable factor. It is known that the change of food from more to less nourishing can cause an unexpectedly high mortality of larvae.[9]

Thus, as a result of this experiment, we have found that the middle-aged larvae of *T. bisselliella* became non-active if they were placed on a substrate which was unsuitable for development. This state can last for at least 2–3 months and it is reversible. The same phenomenon is observed when the food lacks full value, or during other unfavourable conditions, such as lowered oxygen content in the atmosphere.

This state of physiological resting differs from diapause as it is not an obligatory stage of the individual development of a larva, but occurs as a result of rapid influence by unfavourable external factors on a larva and ends after quick return of those factors to normal values. At the same time the torpid larvae show some elevated non-specific resistance to unfavourable external factors. For example, other experiments with inert gas mixtures showed that these larvae could withstand the lowered oxygen content in the atmosphere for a longer time.

Apparently it would be premature to consider the described resting state of *T. bisselliella* larvae to be a diapause without additional study of physiological mechanisms. Perhaps it should be defined as a facultative diapause similar to that of some dermestid larvae.[10,11]

Conclusions

Insect control in museums can be successful only if it takes into consideration peculiarities of pest biology. If we know how a species depends on external conditions, we can handle its abundance by changing these conditions. Experimental confirmation of the inactive state demonstrated by *T. bisselliella* larvae has important meaning for the practice of moth control in museums. We showed that the majority (85 to 100%) of middle-aged larvae of the webbing clothes moth did not perish under conditions which were unfavourable for development (e.g. lack of suitable food, antifeedant or weak biocidal properties of feeding substrate, lowered oxygen atmosphere content). The larvae convert to a physiologically inactive state that is a kind of torpidness or facultative diapause. Such ability raises considerably the ecological hardiness of the webbing clothes moth, as the greater part of larvae in pest populations can outlive rather prolonged (greater than 2–3 months) sublethal deviation of external factors while in the state of physiological rest.

Insufficient effectiveness of some measures of moth control may be explained by the appearance of that state. Thus in the course of physical or chemical control of the webbing clothes moth one must pay special attention to reaching lethal levels of extreme factors or insecticide doses.

It is also necessary to note that after removing moth infested articles from a room, the larvae remaining in the resting state can wait until food reappears. Thus it is important to clean carefully the inner surfaces of receptacles where infested things were kept, and also to treat those surfaces with antimoth contact insecticides.

Understanding the inactive torpid state of the webbing clothes moth larvae will improve considerably the effectiveness of moth control in museums.

Acknowledgements

This research was undertaken within the bounds of dissertational work required by the Department of Entomology of the Moscow State University and the State Research Institute for Restoration. The author would like to thank Professor G.A.Mazochin-Porshnyakov of MSU Department of Entomology for support and critical reading of the manuscript.

References

1. V.A. Zaslavskii, 'Photoperiodical and Temperature Control of Insects Development', *Transactions of the Zoological Institute of the USSR Academy of Sciences* 120 (1984): 184 (in Russian).
2. G.Ya. Bei-Bienko, *General Entomology* (Moscow: Vysshaya Shkola Publ., 1971), 480 (in Russian).
3. S.I. Chernysh, Ph.K. Girphanova and V.P. Tyshchenko, 'The State of Nonspecific Resistance during Insects Diapause', *General Entomology, Transactions of the All-Union Entomological Society* 68 (1986): 92–95 (in Russian).
4. E. Titschack, 'Beitrage zu einer Monographie der Kleidermotte *Tineola bisselliella* Humm.', *Zeitschrift für technische Biologie* 10 (1922), 1–168.
5. A.K. Zagulajev, 'The True Moths (Tineidae)', *Fauna of the USSR* 4, no. 33 (1960): 38 (in Russian).
6. Ibid.
7. R.A. Saphonova, 'Influence of Temperature on the Life Cycles of the Webbing Clothes Moth', *Transactions of VNII Hunting Economics & Fur Farming* 26 (1976): 366–376 (in Russian).
8. G. Griswold, 'Studies on the Biology of the Webbing Clothes Moth, *Tineola bisselliella* Hum.', *Memoranda of the Cornell Agricultural Experimental Station*, vol.262 (1944), p.1-59.
9. C.S. Whewell, 'Moths and Mothproofing', *The Dyer* 80 (1938): 537–538.
10. H.D. Burges, 'Diapause, Pest Status and Control of the Khapra Beetle, *Trogoderma granarium* Everts.', *Annals of Applied Biology*, (1961), p.55.
11. R.D. Zhantiev, *Dermestid Beetles of the USSR Fauna* (Moscow: Moscow State University Publ., 1976), 22 (in Russian).

Maintenance of Microbiological Safety of Artifacts in Different Conditions of Storage: From Show-case to Open Air

N.L.Rebrikova*
State Scientific Research Institute for Restoration,
Gastello str.44, Moscow 107014, Russia

N.V.Manturovskaya
Russian State Library,
Vozdvijenka str. 3, Moscow Russia

Abstract

Although the general rule is that relative humidity (RH) below 60% provides microbiological safety, in real museum situations micro-organisms do not always develop on sensitive materials, despite high RH. Conversely, they may develop on materials that are not particularly sensitive, and when the RH in the room is relatively low. Rooms with average conditions below those needed for fungal growth may contain microzones that do allow growth. These can arise in closed volumes as a result of differences in temperature, or near external walls of buildings and overloaded storage rooms. Air circulation can eliminate such conditions. Low temperature slows down the growth of micro-organisms at any humidity level. The freezing of wet objects controls growth (wet by accident, or wet at excavation). Limited winter heating of architectural monuments of stone, plinth and brick, in central and northern Russia, has been found to provide effective control of micro-organisms on plaster, wall paintings and iconostasis carving.

Keywords

Microscopic fungi, environment, relative humidity, temperature, show-cases, closed volumes, architectural monuments

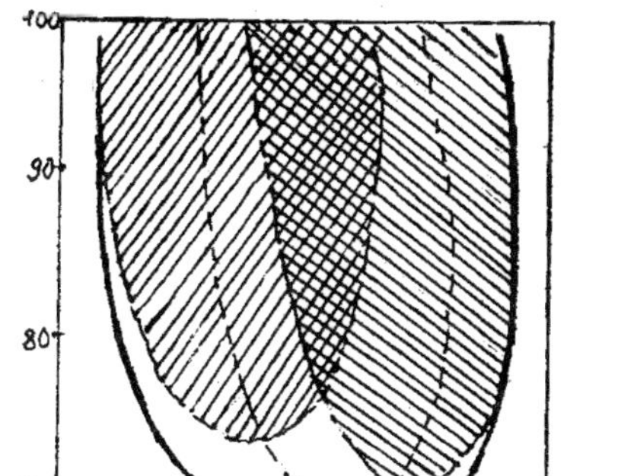

Figure 1. The influence of relative humidity and temperature on growth of micro-organisms. The development of micro-organisms is possible only within the boundary lines shown. The unshaded area shows mesophylic species, /// shows psychrophylic species, \\\ shows thermophylic species.

Introduction

The control of growth of micro-organisms through regulation of the environment, primarily of humidity and temperature, is one of the most ancient and important ways of preventing material damage. These actions are of particular significance for museum collections.

The rate of achievement of equilibrium moisture content in masses of hygroscopic materials

Relative humidities above 65% at temperatures higher than 10°C damage vulnerable materials such as graphic arts materials, photographs, watercolors, pastels, and books, by microscopic fungi, if their moisture content reaches equilibrium with these elevated humidities. It can take a long time for such an equilibrium to be established. It also depends on the properties of the materials, initial moisture content, and the relationship of material mass to volume where the humidity changes occur. Figure 1 shows the borders of humidity and temperature limiting the development of micro-organisms.

In the department of rare books of the museum-farmstead 'Yasnaia polyana' during the period June–September RH was predominantly about 70%. It increased to 80% on individual days. Much the same environment had been observed in this depository in previous years. After the onset of heating at the end of September the RH was reduced to 50–60%. No signs of fungal development were revealed during the mycological inspection of books in February 1995. The lack of fungal growth on books despite brief periods of high RH in summer was due to the fact that they were packed closely together on the shelves, occupied large volumes of the room, and thus did not reach the RH equilibrium parameters necessary for growth.

Drying during the heating period and moistening during the summer bring about the deformation of books. These conditions are unfavourable for the preservation of collections.

It is well known that hygroscopic materials absorb moisture slowly, and give it back slowly. Special methods that accelerate drying are necessary to prevent the development of micro-organisms following very damp conditions in collection storage.

Climatic microareas in collection storage

For storage of mixed museum collections the following parameters of microclimate are recommended: RH of about 50–60% and temperature of 18–20°C . These conditions are unfavourable for the development of micro-organisms. Nevertheless, in storage areas as well as display areas, microzones may exist with microclimates that support fungi.

These microclimates arise in overloaded depositories, in show-cases, and cabinets during wide fluctuations of temperature. The fungi grow slowly in these conditions. They have non-typical morphological characteristics: reduced

* Author for correspondence

conidiophores, suppressed sporogenesis, an increasing ability to form extracellular pigments etc. The RH difference between a cabinet and the room can be more than 10%.

Recommended levels of air exchange and air motion can eliminate microclimates. Cabinets and show-cases should not be located on the external walls of the building. Dramatic changes of temperature and humidity should be prevented in the storage room. Cabinets and vaults where graphic materials, manuscripts, books, textiles and leather are stored should be ventilated no less than once a week.

In the A.S. Pushkin Museum of Fine Arts evidence of fungal growth has been observed on elephant's ivory of two miniatures in medallions with glass covers. Other paintings, stored in the same facility with the miniatures, did not show any traces of fungal development. In this room, the RH during the year did not exceed 60%, and in winter it did not rise higher than 40-45%. Microscopic analysis revealed brown mycelium and yellow cleistothecia, characteristic of ascospore formation of the genus *Aspergillus* on the coloured area of one of the miniatures. Only greyish-brown distorted mycelium was observed on the other one. *Aspergillus repens* was isolated from the first miniature, and *Mycelia sterilia* from the second. *A. repens* belongs to an extreme xerophylic fungi which can develop on solid substrates at low humidity when the development of other micro-organisms is not possible. In an experiment under conditions of moisture desorption, xerophylic species from the group of *A. glaucus: A. chevalieri, A. repens,* and *A. ruber* isolated from museum subjects, grew slowly on materials from natural fibres. They did not form spores at RH of about 70% and temperatures around 22°C. Ecological peculiarities of the isolated strain and the character of fungal growth (ascospore formation or only a mycelium, mycelium deformation) allowed us to assume that the fungi had grown under conditions of moisture deficiency and in a short time. Microclimate analysis before the investigation had shown that an abrupt temperature drop occurred daily in winter due to switching-off of the heating. This caused condensate formation in the miniature case. The relatively small amount of condensate limited fungal growth.

Fluctuations of temperature can provoke the growth of microscopic fungi on hygroscopic materials in show-cases, especially on archaeological leather and textiles which are frequently softened by glycerol. The mummy of Ramses II in the show-case of the Cairo museum was damaged by fungi owing to fluctuations of temperature.[1] We observed the development of fungi on clothes of a skiff nomad in a show-case of the Historical Museum in Moscow. The clothes were in a hall where temperature fluctuations took place, although the RH in this hall did not exceed the museum norms.

The examples described demonstrate the danger for museum collections of abrupt temperature fluctuations. For temporary exhibitions, transportation, etc., where temperature fluctuations cannot be excluded, it is necessary to stabilise RH in show-cases and containers with hygroscopic materials such as silica gel, Kaken gel or saturated salt solutions. Alternatively, air exchange between show-cases, cabinets, vaults, and the building promotes RH equalisation.

The experience of storage shows that good preservation against mould is provided by stable microclimates. These depend on show-cases and cabinets made of hygroscopic materials, humidity buffers, and air exchange between the internal volume and the environment.

Controlled gas environments

Show-cases are available now in Russia which pass the internal air through polymeric membranes. They protect the museum subjects from air pollution and decrease oxidative destruction. The membranes both sorb gases and filter particulates. They arrest the cells of micro-organisms and deplete oxygen. The optimal composition of the obtained gas mixture contains about 95–98% of nitrogen and about 2–5 % of oxygen. A special humidity regulator creates the RH required for the specific exhibit.[2]

Curators ask whether the transfer of exhibits to standard atmosphere after storage in low-oxygen atmosphere will cause any changes. Conditions of oxygen

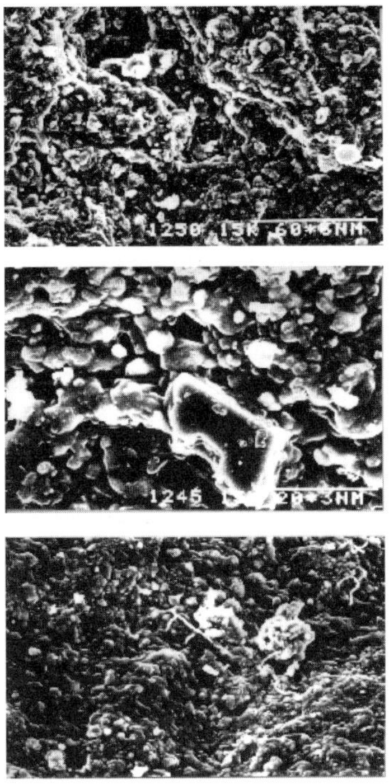

Figure 2. SEM micrographs of samples from the surface of paint layers in a building with controlled, limited heating (the Mirozjski monastery in Pskov, the Cathedral of the Saviour's transfiguration, 12th century) In (a) and (b) the cells of micro-organisms are absent; (a) × 1,000, (b) × 3,000. In (c) (× 1,000) there is some restricted growth of micro-organisms on the paint layer.

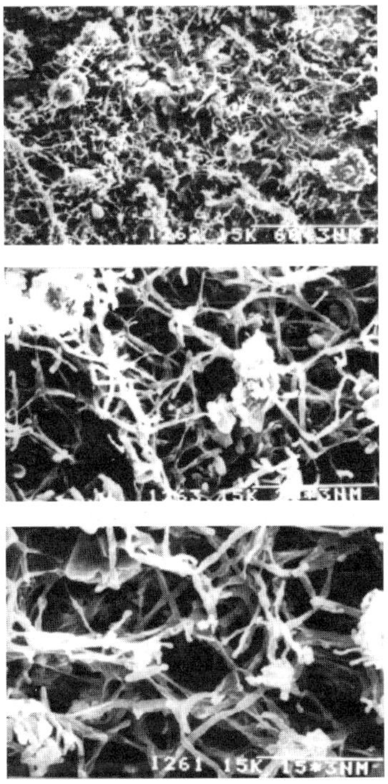

Figure 3. SEM micrographs of samples from the surface of paint layers in a building with no heating (the Cathedral of the Assumption of the Virgin in Meletovo, 14th century).(a), (b) and (c) all show intensive growth of micro-organisms on the painting layer; (a) × 1,000, (b) × 3,000, (c) × 4,000

depletion seem to be preferable for archaeological materials, since during burial they were often depleted of oxygen.

Although the polymer membrane blocks microbes, both fungal cells and other micro-organisms can exist on exhibits in show-cases. How does the reduced oxygen content affect the cells of micro-organisms? To answer this question, the viability of fungal spores put on samples of material was tested in containers with a certain gas mixture for one year. In comparison with the spores stored in standard atmosphere, no loss of viability was revealed for dormant spores existing in a gas mixture with about 2% of oxygen.

Oxygen depletion and low temperature

The examples described above were in normal non-wet situations. Wet materials may occur as a result of emergencies, or naturally as part of archaeological excavations.

Oxygen depletion can be used to control the growth of aerobic micro-organisms on wet materials. When oxygen content is reduced to 1%, inhibition of fungal metabolic activity is initiated. Further reduction of oxygen concentration amplifies the effect.[3] For complete inhibition of growth, oxygen concentration should not exceed 0.1%. Oxygen depletion has been used to prevent fungal damage on wet archaeological and ethnographic materials during periods of temporary storage.[4]

Growth of micro-organisms is inhibited by low temperatures at any moisture content. Transfer of museum objects damaged by water to refrigerators (–18°C), with subsequent drying in vacuum chambers, prevents the initiation of fungal growth or inhibits it. These precautions minimize the need for antimicrobial agents. Freeze-drying is successful on wet wood, textiles, and leathers found in archaeological excavations.

The control of micro-organisms in Old Russian architectural monuments

Most Old Russian architectural monuments have no heating. A high level of natural air infiltration, insufficient protection from all kinds of external moisture, and slow warming up in spring are peculiar to them. In addition to these factors, destruction of old drainage, variation of hydrological conditions, and old restoration work have all resulted in the deterioration of the microclimate. This has promoted growth of micro-organisms on building materials, on wall paintings, on carving, and on icons in the lower circles of iconostases.

Maintenance of temperature and humidity in monuments by mechanical systems has its problems. Architectural monuments have complex internal volumes, non-uniform wall thickness, deep niches, and other peculiarities, all of which require non-standard design in the system. The maintenance of temperatures only slightly above ambient in winter (about +5°C at the lowest) avoids spring condensation. This kind of setting leads to unfavourable conditions for the growth of micro-organisms (Figures 2 and 3). The two examples of such treatment are the Old Russian monuments of the 12th and 13th centuries in Pskov and another is a monument of the 15th century in Zvenigorod. Other work on waterproofing bases, sealing door and window openings and tambour arrangements was carried out before introduction of limited heating.

The control of micro-organisms and algae on outdoor monuments

Monuments are affected by algae, lichens, moss and micro-organisms outdoors. Algal and microbial damage to stone sculpture and monuments is limited to the most moistened and darkened areas. The nature and intensity of destruction depend on the type of stone, its composition, porosity and structure. Carbonate stones are heavily damaged, especially the limestones. Sandstone with high amounts of carbonate cement is also severely affected.

Biological deterioration of sculptures in parks and cemeteries is promoted by the expansion of tree crowns. Architectural arches and niches, which do not protect the sculpture completely from rain and snow, prevent rapid evaporation. On the other hand, roofing held up on posts above the sculpture will protect against rain and snow, without preventing air movement. This prevents biological impairments. Unfortunately, such roofing arrangements cannot be widely applied for aesthetic reasons.

Preventive conservation of stone in the open air includes winter cover of sculptures, consideration of surrounding bushes and trees, the removal of pollution from surfaces, and protective applications to the face of historical buildings such as whitewash with biocide properties or local hydrophobic protection of the wettest areas.

Conclusions

Nature gives us examples of unique preservation of ancient materials at certain combinations of external conditions. In alternative environments they would not be preserved, as e result of biological destruction, among other factors. The remains of people and animals are very well preserved in permafrost. Low temperature and deficiency of oxygen promote preservation of organic materials in marshes and under water. The constant microclimate of caves, caverns and funeral chambers provides unique preservation of subjects in certain cases. The use of these conditions for preservations of museum collections brings a series of problems. Low-temperature and low-oxygen conditions mean restricted access for research and exhibition of the objects.

In the majority of cases the maintenance of a stable optimal microclimate provides fair preservation. Microclimates that change gradually seasonally are favourable for ancient architectural monuments. This regime provides a relatively constant moisture content of the plaster layer of the interior of ancient monuments. The maintenance of conditions unsuitable for growth of micro-organisms and alga outdoors also promotes their safety. All these preventive measures reduce the dependence on biocides.

References

1. J. Mouchacca, 'Les Champignons de la Momie de Ramses II', *'Contes Rendues Académie des Sciences, Paris* 285, sér. D (19 September 1977), 515–517.
2. L.I. Dushkina et al., 'The Creation of a Gas Environment of Given Structure and Controllable Relative Humidity in Museum Show-cases' (Paper delivered at the 3rd seminar 'The problems of preventive conservation and storage of cultural values ',24–25 January 1994, St Petersburg), 11–14.
3. M. Valentin, M. Lidstrom and F. Preusser, 'Microbial Control by Low Oxygen and Low Relative Humidity Environment', *Studies in Conservation* 35, no. 4 (1980), 222–230.
4. H. Arai and H. Mori, 'Studies on the Long-term Conservation of Cultural Properties (Part 1) (1) Using Biaxially Oriented Polyvinyl–Alcohol Film to Prevent the Biodeterioration of Cultural Properties', *Scientific Papers of Japanese Antiques and Art Crafts* 25 (1980), 83–102.

Light-Induced Damage: Investigating the Reciprocity Principle

David Saunders, Jo Kirby
Scientific Department, The National Gallery,
Trafalgar Square, London WC2N 5DN, UK

Abstract

The changes in colour in five identical sets of 25 light-sensitive pigments and other materials, exposed to light under selected neutral density filters, were measured. It was found that in the majority of cases the amount of damage, measured as colour change, caused by a given light exposure in lux-hours was independent of the level of illumination. These findings demonstrate that, for many light-sensitive materials, the reciprocity principle is followed and that limiting the overall dose of light to which an object is exposed during a period on display can be an appropriate method of controlling deterioration.

Keywords

Reciprocity, colour change, light exposure, deterioration, cumulative exposure

Introduction

For several years, many museums and galleries have operated a policy of controlling the total annual light exposure for objects containing materials sensitive to light deterioration. This approach can provide a convenient alternative to maintaining constant, or near constant, levels of light during museum opening hours; it is also less demanding on electrical and mechanical systems controlling the illumination. The reasoning behind the control of annual exposure is that the amount of damage suffered by an object is determined by the total light exposure received, that is the product of time and light level. Thus, the same amount of damage should result from exposure to an illuminance of 100 lux for 10 h as from exposure to light at a level of 200 lux for 5 h; the total, or cumulative, exposure in either case is 1000 lux-hours (lux.h). This relationship between time and light level is known as the reciprocity principle.

Although the reciprocity principle is well-established and much used, there is little experimental evidence for its applicability to the light-sensitive materials found in museum objects.[1] A recent study of the effects of electronic flash on artists pigments concluded that the deterioration caused by a number of 'flashes' was equal to that caused by an equivalent exposure to ambient light in two galleries,[2] that is the reciprocity law was followed. Here, we present the results of a further experiment designed to test the reciprocity principle over a range of rates of exposure.

Experimental

Six identical sets of pigments and certain other materials that are known to fade, darken or otherwise change colour at different rates were prepared. Each set included ISO Blue Wool Standards Nos 1 to 3 as a reference.[3] The appendix gives details of the 25 samples included in each set. The first set was used as a dark control; it was placed within an opaque enclosure in the fading chamber at the same temperature and relative humidity as the other samples (30 ± 1°C and 45 ± 5% RH). The remaining five sets were exposed to light, but at different levels of illumination. To allow these sample sets to be exposed simultaneously, four were placed beneath neutral density filters, constructed by sandwiching 100 ´ 100mm gelatin filters with nominal transmittances of 50, 25, 10 and 1% between two pieces of 1 mm glass; the glass was used to avoid contact between the gelatin filter and the samples. An ultraviolet-absorbing filter was included in each sandwich to exclude radiation of wavelengths less than c. 380nm. The fifth filter consisted of two pieces of 1 mm glass and the ultraviolet filter. The transmittance of this clear filter was used to normalize the transmittances of the other four. The resulting filters show a fairly constant absorbance across the visible region of the spectrum, particularly between 400 and 700 nm, with transmittances roughly in the ratio 1:0.5:0.25:0.1:0.01; see Figure 1.

The samples were exposed to light from a bank of Thorn Artificial Daylight fluorescent lamps, providing an illumination on the neutral density filters of c. 8,000 lux. The colour of each sample was measured before exposure and periodically during the experiment using a Minolta CR200 chroma meter. The results were stored on a computer as CIE (Commission International de l'Eclairage)

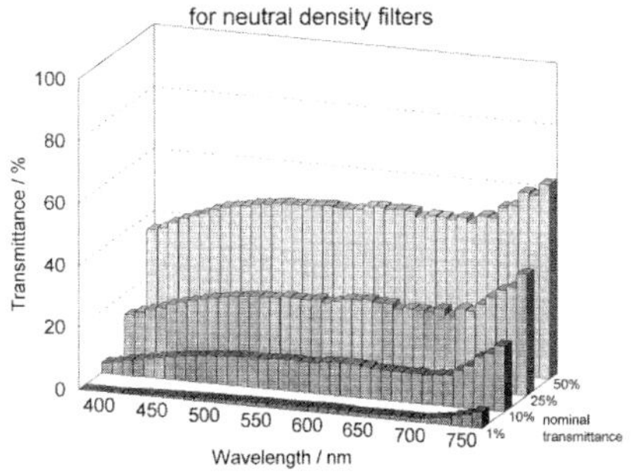

Figure 1. Transmittance curves for the neutral density filters. The transmittances are normalized with respect to the 'clear filter'

$L^\star$, $a^\star$ and $b^\star$ coordinates under the CIE standard illuminant D65.[4] For each sample, the difference (ΔE) between the colour before light exposure and at each measurement during the experiment was calculated according to British Standard 6923:1988;[5] the error in colour measurement was of the order of $\Delta E \pm 0.5$. The procedures for light exposure and colour measurement have been described in more detail previously.[6]

Results and discussion

Colour measurements made before exposure indicated that the six samples of each material had comparable colour coordinates. No colour changes were observed in the samples that had not been exposed to light, except for the low-quality paper (newsprint) and vermilion, which showed slight changes in colour as the experiment proceeded. In these cases, however, the colour change in the dark was small compared to the light-induced alteration.

Assuming that the spectral power distribution of the illuminant does not change with time, the total light exposure (H) will be proportional to the product of the level of illumination (E_v) and the transmittance of the filter (τ) integrated over the exposure time (t):

$$H \propto \int_0^t E_v . \tau \; dt$$

The fluorescent lamps were run for 100 h before use and replaced after 3,000 h of operation to ensure that the spectral characteristics were reasonably consistent.[7] At 550 nm, the centre of the visible region, the measured transmittances (t) for the five filter combinations were 100, 48.8, 23.8, 9.83 and 1.22% respectively. There was a reduction in the level of illumination of around 5% during the course of the experiment (400 days), hence the use of the integral in the equation above rather than the simple product of illumination, filter transmittance and time.

For each light-sensitive material, plots of colour change (ΔE) against total exposure (H) under the five different filters were produced on the same axes. Figure 2 shows a typical plot, for buckthorn lake. It is clear that the five traces are coincident, confirming that, regardless of the level of illumination, damage (measured as colour change in this case) is determined by the total exposure.

Similar plots were obtained for the majority of the samples examined, including the three ISO blue wool standards, low grade paper and most of the lake pigment samples. Colour difference data for these samples are summarized in Table 1. In one case, that of massicot–lead(II) oxide, the colour change was so rapid that it was difficult to assess the relationship between colour change and exposure.

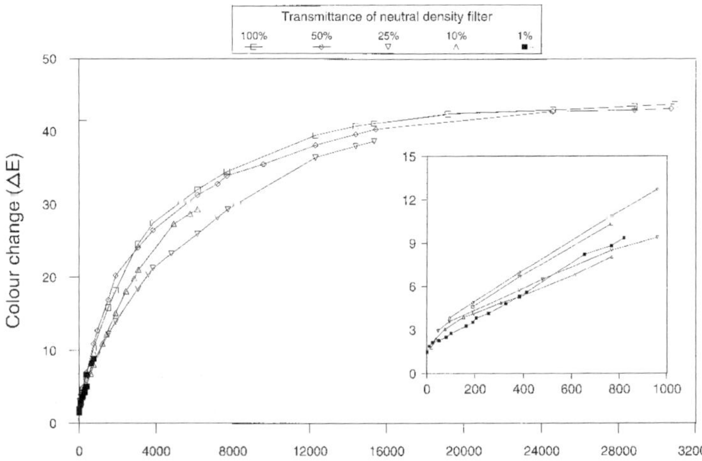

Figure 2. Plot of colour change (DE) against exposure (klux.h) for a sample of buckthorn lake.
The inset shows the changes in colour during the first 1000 klux.h on an expanded scale

Table 1. Colour change (DE) for a selection of samples at two different levels of exposure (400 and 6000 klux.h). During the course of this experiment, an exposure of 6000 klux.h was not reached for samples under the filter with 1% transmittance

Sample	Exposure (klux.h)	Colour change (ΔE) under filter of transmittance 100%	50%	25%	10%	1%
ISO blue wool	400	9.90	10.49	8.97	8.87	8.86
standard No 1	6000	37.15	37.46	35.45	38.83	-
ISO blue wool	400	5.58	6.23	4.98	4.74	4.84
standard No 2	6000	26.11	25.34	23.24	26.54	–
ISO blue wool	400	1.33	1.14	1.26	1.16	1.06
standard No 3	6000	11.31	9.42	10.84	12.89	–
Low grade paper	400	10.96	11.63	10.29	10.46	11.61
	6000	22.57	22.12	21.90	23.99	–
Orpiment	400	5.35	6.29	7.26	6.96	5.68
	6000	8.37	9.13	10.71	10.67	–
Lead tetroxide (Pb_3O_4)	400	6.18	5.86	5.63	4.74	5.23
	6000	8.19	7.32	6.88	6.81	–
Lead(II) oxide	400	26.34	24.80	22.55	20.29	13.72
	6000	31.12	30.44	23.39	24.18	–
Gamboge	400	0.51	0.32	0.45	0.56	0.81
	6000	8.51	7.76	7.81	8.43	–
Quercitron lake	400	3.13	3.01	3.36	3.21	2.83
	6000	23.68	21.78	21.50	23.88	–
Buckthorn lake	400	6.66	6.16	5.73	5.27	6.78
	6000	32.06	31.35	29.94	29.36	–
Brasilwood lake	400	8.31	6.56	6.25	6.14	7.48
	6000	57.21	55.91	53.71	59.80	–
Madder lake	400	1.26	1.28	1.03	0.93	0.97
	6000	7.27	6.66	7.20	6.84	–
Kermes lake	400	4.66	4.20	3.76	3.03	3.36
	6000	17.05	18.78	17.69	17.35	–
Cochineal lake	400	6.66	5.55	5.17	4.29	5.19
	6000	22.50	22.71	22.11	23.63	–
Lac lake	400	3.27	3.83	3.38	2.70	3.43
	6000	16.55	15.54	15.22	17.08	–
Litmus	400	16.88	17.64	15.86	15.61	16.79
	6000	44.28	44.77	46.39	45.07	–
Sap green	400	4.61	4.03	4.04	3.82	3.95
	6000	9.83	9.08	9.39	9.83	–
Weld lake	400	3.35	2.87	3.47	2.88	2.89
	6000	15.35	13.52	14.41	16.52	–

A number of the samples did not show a clear relationship between colour change and exposure. These fell into two groups. The first group comprised Prussian blue, indigo, rose madder and alizarin crimson. Although these pigments have been demonstrated to be light-sensitive, they change colour very much more slowly than the materials listed in Table 1. Over a longer exposure period errors in colour measurement would be less apparent, and it seems likely that these pigments will show behaviour similar to that illustrated in Figure 2.

The second group contained the two samples of vermilion studied. Here, it is clear that the darkening of the pigment is not related simply to the light exposure: indeed, the colour change shown by the samples not exposed to light is indicative of this.

Conclusions

For the majority of the 25 materials included in this study, the amount of damage caused by a given light exposure is independent of the time over which that dose is delivered; that is, reciprocity is followed. For vermilion, slight differences between the individual samples are likely to be partly responsible for the variability in the colour change observed under the five filters.

Although this study reinforces the existing evidence that a given exposure causes the same damage regardless of the light level, it should be remembered that, because the relationship between damage and exposure is not simply linear, twice as much exposure does not necessarily result in twice the damage.

It seems reasonable therefore to control the overall dose of light to which an object is exposed. Such a cumulative approach allows a greater variation in natural light levels to be tolerated than would be possible if the illuminance had to be maintained at a constant value. The choice of an appropriate maximum annual dose must take account of the materials within the work of art and what is deemed to be an acceptable rate of deterioration.

Appendix: Samples used in the experiment

Sample	Source	Reference
ISO blue wool standard No 1	British Standards Institution, Milton Keynes (UK)	3
ISO blue wool standard No 2	British Standards Institution, Milton Keynes (UK)	3
ISO blue wool standard No 3	British Standards Institution, Milton Keynes (UK)	3
Low grade paper	Daily newspaper	–
Zinc white	Amalgamated oxides, Dartford (UK)	–
Vermilion	BDH chemicals, Poole (UK)	–
Vermilion	Kremer pigmente, Aichstetten (D)	–
Orpiment	Kremer pigmente, Aichstetten (D)	–
Indigo	Ashill colour studio, Bedford (UK)	8
Prussian blue	Prepared at the National Gallery	9
Lead tetroxide (Pb_3O_4)	BDH chemicals, Poole (UK)	–
Lead(II) oxide (PbO)	BDH chemicals, Poole (UK)	–
Gamboge	Kremer pigmente, Aichstetten (D	–
Quercitron lake	Prepared at the National Gallery	6
Buckthorn lake (3)	Prepared at the National Gallery	6
Brasilwood lake (BrBrm)	Prepared at the National Gallery	6
Madder lake (MM1)	Prepared at the National Gallery	6
Kermes lake (KD1)	Prepared at the National Gallery	6
Cochineal lake (4)	Prepared at the National Gallery	6
Lac lake (LL1)	Prepared at the National Gallery	6
Weld lake (WW1)	Prepared at the National Gallery	6
Alizarin crimson	C. Roberson & Co., London (UK)	6
Rose madder	Winsor & Newton, London (UK)	–
Litmus	Prepared at the National Gallery	8
Sap green	Prepared at the National Gallery	8

References

1. J. L. Down, 'The Yellowing of Epoxy Resin Adhesives: Report on High-intensity Light Aging', *Studies in Conservation* 31 (1986): 159–170.
2. D. Saunders, 'Photographic Flash: Threat or Nuisance?', *National Gallery Technical Bulletin* 16 (1995): 66–72.
3. British Standard 1006:1990 (issue 2, October 1992*), British Standard Methods of Test for Colourfastness of Textiles and Leather* (Milton Keynes: British Standards Institution, 1992), B01/1–7.
4. Commission Internationale de l Eclairage, 'Recommendations on uniform color spaces, color difference equations, psychometric color terms', Supplement No.2 to *CIE Publication* No.15 (E-2.3.1), 1971/(TC-1.3) (1978).
5. F.J.J. Clarke, R. McDonald and B. Rigg, 'Modification to the JCP79 Colour-difference Formula', *Journal of the Society of Dyers and Colourists* 100 (1984): 128–132.
6. D. Saunders and J. Kirby, 'Light-induced Colour Changes in Red and Yellow Lake Pigments', *National Gallery Technical Bulletin* 15 (1994): 79–97.
7. B.J. Cannell, 'Fluorescent Lamps', in *Lamps and Lighting*, 3rd edn, ed. M. A. Cayless and A. M. Marsden, (London: Edward Arnold, 1983), 183–201, particularly page 195.
8. D. Saunders and J. Kirby, 'Wavelength-dependent Fading of Artists Pigments', in *Preventive Conservation: Practice, Theory and Research*, ed. A. Roy and P. Smith, (London: IIC, 1994), 190–194.
9. J.S. Remington and W. Francis, *Pigments: Their Manufacture, Properties and Use*, (London, 1954), 94–98.

Mould Growth in Tropical Environments: A Discussion

Graeme Scott
Materials Conservation Division, The Australian Museum, Sydney

Abstract

Since mould grows on the surface of materials, surface conditions of susceptible materials should be examined in order to determine the likelihood of growth in any circumstance. In uncontrolled museum environments moisture content in surface layers is the only factor that is likely to be influenced by atmospheric conditions and that is known to be critical to growth. Experimental data are presented which demonstrate the influence of variable atmospheric RH on thin sections of balsa wood. Variable RH is unlikely to be the only determinant of mould growth, however, and other possibilities are discussed.

Keywords

Mould, biodeterioration, tropics, ventilation

Introduction

Mould feeds and grows on the surface of organic material. So, if risks of growth are being assessed, surface conditions are the ones which should be monitored – and not those in the atmosphere, which conservators are accustomed to monitoring. The ubiquitous nature of mould spores means that they are always likely to be present in an unfiltered atmosphere and are therefore always likely to have been deposited on surfaces – so if surface conditions are favourable, growth will occur. Of all the factors necessary for germination and growth of mould spores – appropriate pH, nutrient and oxygen/carbon dioxide levels etc. – it is the availability of moisture in sufficient quantities adjacent to where the spores settle that will finally determine their germination and growth.[1] Aerial spore counts will only indicate the likely concentration of spores on surfaces, not the likelihood of their growth.

Ventilation is often believed to prevent mould growth but to do so it must be able to influence the factors determining growth of spores – and in uncontrolled museum environments this can only mean by affecting moisture content next to surfaces. Since ventilation and air circulation changes the air next to surfaces, variations in atmospheric RH have the potential to alter the surface condition of materials.[2] To assess the impact of these variations on materials commonly found in collections in the tropics a number of experiments have been conducted.

Experimental

The following experiments were designed to establish how long it takes for atmospheric changes to be reflected in surface layers and whether the pattern, duration or repetition of those changes has any significance for the way surface layers respond.

The hypotheses being tested were that moisture content of surface layers of a substrate changes in response to variable atmospheric conditions and that changes in that moisture content can influence germination and growth of mould spores.

Terms used

Mycologists use the term 'water activity' (a_w) to describe the moisture condition of a substrate material. It is quantified by measuring RH of air above a sample of the material, inside a closed container and once equilibrium conditions have been established. The substrate moisture content providing that condition will be specific to each particular material. Water activity can therefore be considered equivalent to equilibrium relative humidity (ERH). In the experiments described below moisture content was used as the measure of condition since only one substrate material was investigated, and 'water activity' is referred to since this is the term used in the microbiological literature to describe limiting and optimum conditions of growth.[3]

Table 1. Descriptive statistics. Number of samples in each case = 12

RH range	Weight gain (g) (unsoaked)				Weight gain (g) (soaked)			
	Mean	**Range**	**Var**	**St.dev.**	**Mean**	**Range**	**Var**	**St.dev.**
0–20%	0.0024	0.0018	0.0000	0.0006	0.0071	0.0014	0.0000	0.0005
20–50%	0.0073	0.0027	0.0000	0.0008	0.0211	0.0027	0.0000	0.0010
50–80%	0.0098	0.0036	0.0000	0.0046	0.0500	0.0161	0.0000	0.0046
0–80% in steps	0.0196	0.0078	0.0000	0.0023	0.0780	0.0200	0.0000	0.0059
0–80% direct	0.0204	0.0075	0.0000	0.0025	0.0603	0.0249	0.0000	0.0068

Table 2. Results of t-tests

RH range	**t-value**	**Degrees of freedom**	**Two-tailed significance of t-value**
0–20% soaked/unsoaked	−22.42	22	0.000
20–50% soaked/unsoaked	−36.83	22	0.000
50–80%[a] soaked/unsoaked	−38.22	22	0.000
0–80% in steps – both groups	−0.12	2	0.913
0–80% direct – both groups	−0.86	22	0.398

[a] Since the data for the two groups in this range did not have equal variance the weight gain figures were transformed using the natural logarithm. The results shown relate to the transformed data

Table 3. Analysis-of-variance results

Source	**Degrees of freedom**	**Sum of squares**	**Mean squares**	***F* Ratio**	**Probability of *F***
Between groups	3	0.0482	0.0161	136.8660	0.0000
Within groups	32	0.0038	0.0001		
Total	35	0.0519			

Samples and experimental procedure

50 mm square samples of 0.8 mm thick balsa wood were cut from sheets selected at random from those on sale at a craft shop. Balsa itself is not commonly used to make artefacts but it is similar to some of the porous woods commonly found in museum collections in the tropical Pacific region. It was considered that if atmospheric conditions do influence the samples significantly, then other types of wood would also respond but to a greater or lesser extent.

A proportion of samples was soaked in 10% w/v solution of D-glucose in distilled water to provide an excess of nutrient. The rate of moisture take-up or loss after an atmospheric change is significant in determining the substrate's response to change, so the effect of soaking samples in sugar solution was examined before proceeding with experiments on different RH cycles.

This set of samples was soaked until weights stopped increasing rapidly – around 60 h. Both soaked and a set of unsoaked samples were placed in an environmental chamber running at 0% RH, 22°C, until their weights did not significantly decrease.

RH in the chamber was raised in stages to 20%, 50% then 80% once sample weights had stabilised. RH was then set to 0% to dry the samples for a second time, before being increased directly to 80%. This was to check for differences in weight gain between a direct change from 0% to 80% and a stepped change from 0% to 20% to 50% to 80%.

Experimental results[4]

The acceptance level for significance/probability of all of the following results was set at 0.05.

Comparison between experimental procedures

From the results in Tables 1 and 2 it can be seen that there were no statistically significant differences between weight gains within soaked and unsoaked sample groups, but there were differences between the groups, i.e. stepped or direct changes in RH produced no difference in weight gain but soaking did.

Table 4. Descriptive statistics

Group	Count	Mean	Std.dev.	Min.	Max.
1 (unsoaked)	12	0.0764	0.0077	0.0949	0.0886
1 (soaked)	12	0.1502	0.0159	0.1092	0.1742
2 (unsoaked)	6	0.0851	0.0059	0.0801	0.0928
2 (soaked)	6	0.1561	0.0055	0.1510	0.1652
Total	36	0.1157	0.0385	0.0646	0.1742

Comparison between response of soaked and unsoaked samples

An analysis of variance was carried out to compare samples taken from two separate balsa sheets. Samples were grouped according to their origin and whether they were soaked. The results in Table 3 represent the difference between each sample's 'dry' weight and that measured after 72 h at 80% RH, divided by the 'dry' weight (i.e. the increase related to the initial weight of the sample).

The probability of F in Table 3 indicates that there are significant differences between groups which had been soaked and those not soaked.

From Table 4 it can be seen that the mean weight gains for the soaked samples were greater, so moisture must have been absorbed by the sugar in addition to that absorbed by the wood. Soaking in sugar solution must therefore add to the amount of moisture absorbed in response to an increase in atmospheric humidity.

Samples used for later experiments were not soaked in sugar solution.

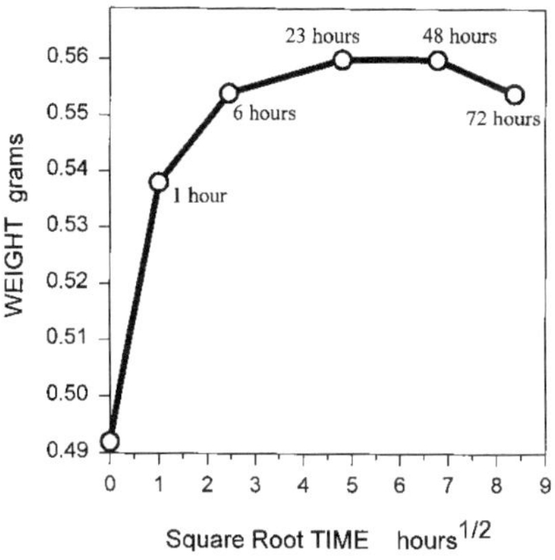

Figure 1. Example of weight gain data, for a change from 0 to 80%RH. (The square root time axis is conventional for sorption data on sheet samples, since it gives an initial straight-line climb whose slope is proportional to the sample's diffusion coefficient)

Speed of response to atmospheric RH change

In order to examine how long it took for the samples to respond to atmospheric RH changes, data were examined from samples exposed to changes in RH from 0–80%, 20–50% and 50–80%.

Figure 1 represents, for clarity, data from only one set of samples. These had equilibrated to 0% RH and were then exposed to constant conditions of 80% RH. Figure 1 shows that the equilibrium weight reached after 72 h was first reached after about 6 h and that most of the increase occurred within the first hour.

In Table 5, data from two sets of samples were used. The figures represent the increase from the 'dry' weight at each interval divided by the 'dry' weight. The symbols in Table 5 indicate where the tests found significant differences between the mean weight measured at each stage. The results indicate that equilibration occurred, effectively, within 3–6 h.

Comparison between different patterns of RH change

In order to establish whether rates of mould growth could be influenced by particularly 'dry' daytime conditions or whether the samples tend, as a result of 'lag' in response, to approximate a 'mean' condition over time, another experiment was conducted.

Samples were exposed to two sets of cycles of RH – one of 8 h spent at 50% and 16 h at 90%, the other of 8 h at 72% and 16 h at 90% – i.e. each being a 24 h cycle, repeated five times. They were weighed near the end of each exposure period. No statistically significant differences were found between the weights of

Table 5. Analysis-of-variance post hoc *test results*

Change in RH	Mean weight	No. of 1 hours	3	6	24	48	72
0–80%	0.0163	1					
	0.0672	3	#				
	0.0725	6	#*+	#			
	0.0764	24	#*+	#*+			
	0.0797	48	#*+	#*+	#		
20–50%	0.0204	1					
	0.0215	3					
	0.0257	6	#*+	#*+			
	0.0241	24	#*+	#			
	0.0271	48	#*+	#*+	#		
50–80%	0.0331	3	n/a		#		
	0.0298	6	n/a				
	0.0371	24	n/a	#	#*+		
	0.0355	48	n/a		#*+		

Least-square difference test; * Bonferroni test; + Scheffe test

Table 6. Analysis of variance – repeated cycles with different minimum RH. 120 cases were processed

Source of variation	Sum of squares	Degrees of freedom	Mean square	F	Significance of F
Main effects	0.000	5	0.000	2.578	0.030
(1) End of 90% periods	0.000	4	0.000	2.772	0.031
(2) End of 50% and 72% periods	0.000	1	0.000	1.805	0.182
Two-way interactions	0.000	4	0.000	1.461	0.219
(1) and (2) above	0.000	4	0.000	1.461	0.219
Explained	0.000	9	0.000	2.082	0.037
Residual	0.000	110	0.000		
Total	0.000	119	0.000		

samples measured after any 8 h period and those measured after equilibration to the respective RH levels.

The figures in Table 6 for the significance of *F* indicate that differences were found between the weights measured after one or more of the 16 h periods at 90% (variable 1), but that no differences were found in relation to whether the minimum RH in the cycle was 50% or 72% (variable 2).

Further analysis indicated that one cycle produced a higher than usual weight gain at the end of the period at 90% RH, but that only one of the associated *post hoc* tests (least-square difference) found the figure to be statistically significant. There appeared to be no trend in the weight gains for each cycle, so this high figure was considered to be a chance result.

In summary, irrespective of whether the minima of the cycles were 50 or 72% RH, moisture contents of the samples had equilibrated at the end of the 8 h period. This is consistent with results of the previous experiments, which indicate that effective equilibration to any changed conditions occurs within 3–6 h. Repeated cycles of changing RH did not alter the pattern of response.

Conclusions from experimental results

The addition of soluble materials to a substrate increases the amount of moisture absorbed in response to rises in atmospheric humidity.

Thin sections – and by extension, surface layers – of materials respond to relatively short-term variations in atmospheric RH. The pattern of variations which can occur during a 24 hour period and which may result from movement of air into and around buildings, can therefore cause significant changes in the moisture content of surface layers. Since repeated cycles of change do not appear to alter the response of the samples, mould growth rates can be expected to be determined by conditions prevailing at any particular point in time near surfaces.

Is variability the answer?

In November 1995 conservators from the Australian Museum went to the Cultural Centre in Port Vila, Vanuatu to help move the collections to a new building. The collections – of mostly organic materials – had been brought in from outlying islands to the museum over a period of about 30 years and had therefore never been kept in controlled conditions.

The new building had copious ventilation in the main exhibition room. Rooms in the centre of the building had no windows, low roofs and unsealed concrete floors. Unlike the rest of the building, which felt much 'better' than the old museum, these areas felt very humid and uncomfortable.

RH measurements taken in these rooms and in the main exhibition space showed steady conditions of between 95 and 100% in both areas, whereas the old building showed a steady 70%. Thus, though free ventilation made some spaces feel more comfortable, the conditions were actually 'worse' than in the old building. Human perceptions are therefore unreliable indicators of potential RH problems. However, variations in RH were not a noticeable feature of conditions inside either building during our visit.

Despite this, mould was only seen on barkcloth inside a well-sealed case that had become wet when rain leaked in from a damaged roof, and on glass shelving in a display case containing plant fibre and feather masks. Thus, instances of mould growth were confined to localised, prolonged dampness of organic materials and to the surface of materials with negligible moisture capacity.

There appears to be little published data on actual environmental conditions inside tropical buildings and on the occurrence of mould growth. However, several other conservators who have visited museum collections in the tropics also report only isolated cases – usually associated with water ingress or artificially cooled surfaces.[5]

Other factors influencing surface conditions

From these observations it appears that ventilation and variable RH are not the only factors influencing surface moisture content and therefore mould growth. Other influences may include temperature of surfaces, moisture capacity and surface permeability, and air movement.

Temperature of surfaces

If a material is cool relative to the adjacent air, RH in that air will increase. In permeable or hydrophilic materials vapour will tend to move from the air into and through surface layers as a result of the difference in vapour pressure, increasing moisture content at the surface. Absorption can continue until capacity is reached or until the pressure gradient disappears. If the material is relatively warm, then RH in adjacent air will be reduced and moisture will move out from the surface.

Radiant heating by the sun, for example, is one way that some materials might have a lower moisture content and water activity than may be expected from atmospheric measurements.[6] Water leaks from roofs, gutters or plumbing and rising damp can increase moisture content of materials, independently of what happens in surrounding or enclosed air.

Moisture capacity and surface permeability

If an atmospheric change, such as a diurnal temperature cycle or a change in the weather, causes a 'pulse' of higher atmospheric vapour pressure, water vapour will move into permeable surfaces – more rapidly if the pressure gradient is steep, more deeply the longer the gradient is maintained.[7] However, the actual amount of moisture passing into a material may be tiny in comparison to its overall content and capacity.

The permeability and high moisture capacity of a material such as wood means that vapour or condensed water can be absorbed throughout the mass of the material – moisture will not necessarily remain in high concentrations in surface layers but can spread throughout.

However, impermeable or hydrophobic materials such as metal or glass and fatty or waxy coatings can only adsorb moisture on surfaces and cannot dissipate it within their mass. Dust or contaminants adhering to these materials may, however, be able to absorb moisture – behaving as a very thin and responsive surface layer – providing potential growth sites for mould spores.

An example of this occurred at the Australian Museum when some mammal and reptile mounts were left for a couple of weeks in a closed room served by cooled but non-humidity-controlled air. Since it was summer in Sydney, the incoming air was consistently warm and humid and the cooling raised the room RH to over 90%. Luxuriant mould growth was found on the animal specimens when the door was finally opened, but it was confined to lips, eyelids, toenails etc. What may distinguish these surfaces from others is that they are relatively waxy, fatty or impermeable.

Some materials or coatings may therefore be more likely than others to provide conditions suitable for mould growth but these may not be the ones normally associated with such damage.

Air movement

Ventilation and air movement will dissipate stable boundary layers[8] and air pockets and introduce 'new' air. When moisture evaporates from surfaces moisture content of the adjacent air will increase. In still air this will result in a decreasing pressure gradient, slowing evaporation until it finally ceases. However, if the adjacent air moves and replacement air is at lower RH then evaporation can continue. The amount of air in effective contact with the surface is therefore increased and the total moisture capacity of air in contact with the surface will also be increased.

With air circulation allowing evaporation to continue longer than would be possible in still air, moisture content and water activity of materials may be lower than would be expected in still conditions.

Further work

It is apparent from data such as those collected by the Australian Museum in Vanuatu and from some of the meteorological data which are available for tropical areas, that variations in atmospheric RH cannot be the only factor preventing mould growth in hot, humid climates. In Vanuatu RH remained high and stable but there were only isolated incidences of growth. To monitor what actually happens in buildings in the tropics, a remote environmental monitoring unit is being set up, with the assistance of a grant from the Australian Research Council, which will be used to collect a range of temperature, RH and climatic data inside and outside a variety of building types. The first installations will be in tropical Australia.

It seems that the capacity of different materials to absorb moisture and to buffer humidity in adjacent air could also be influential in determining where mould growth is likely to occur. Experiments will have to be designed to compare rates of mould growth on a range of absorbent and non-absorbent materials.

The experiments detailed above were on one substrate material only. Rates of mould growth on that substrate under similar conditions are currently being investigated. Growth rates on other substrate materials will also have to be studied.

Notes and references

1. J.I. Pitt and A.D. Hocking, *Fungi and Food Spoilage* (Sydney: Academic Press, 1985).
2. G. Scott, 'Moisture, Ventilation and Mould Growth', in *Preventive Conservation: Practice, Theory and Research* – Preprints of the Ottawa Congress (London: IIC, 1994).
3. Pitt and Hocking.
4. All results were analysed using 'SPSS for Windows' version 6.1 statistical software. Student's t-tests were used for comparisons between individual groups of data and analysis of variance procedures used (in conjunction with 'least-square difference', 'Bonferroni' and 'Scheffe' *post hoc* tests) to compare several groups of data simultaneously.
5. Report by Vinod Daniel on a survey visit to museums in India (unpublished), and reports presented verbally at the Australian Museum by Colin Pearson, Margaret McCord and others on survey and other visits to museums in Australia, Indonesia, Asia and the Pacific region.
6. A. Thorn, 'Direct Measurements to Determine Sandstone Deterioration', in *Preventive Conservation: Practice, Theory and Research* – Preprints of the Ottawa Congress (London: IIC, 1994).
7. M.J. Cunningham, 'Effective Penetration Depth and Effective Resistance in Moisture Transfer', *Building and Environment* 27 (1992): 379–386.
8. For details about the formation and depth of boundary layers see S. Michalski, 'Leakage Prediction for Buildings, Cases, Bags and Bottles', *Studies in Conservation* 39 (1994): 169–186.

"Interactive" Didactic Material in Conservation

B. de Tapol
Museum of Catalonia,
08038 Barcelona, Spain

Abstract

A "Criterion Referenced Instruction" (CRI) kit has been developed by ICCROM on the subject of climate control in museums. It has been used for several years, in several countries, and evaluated by professionals in the field. Its strengths and inappropriate applications are discussed.

Keywords

Climate control, relative humidity, training, CRI, ICCROM

Introduction

ICCROM, in its commitment to rapid and satisfactory distribution of knowledge in conservation, started ten years ago to create "interactive" didactic material, the purpose of which was to improve the quality of teaching and teachers in the museum field. Gaël de Guichen promoted the use of the Mager[1] method of training, Criterion Referenced Instruction (CRI), for the study of climate in museums. After four years' work under extreme financial difficulties, the CRI climate training set was born.

This article will describe:

1. What the CRI climate training set looks like.
2. How the Mager method can solve problems common to traditional teaching methods.
3. How professionals in museums can use this new training set as educational support for teachers at universities and conservation schools.

The CRI climate training set includes:

- A map of the pyramid of items and objectives so that participants may reach the final objective at their own pace.
- 650 pages of text grouped in interactive modules with theoretical parts, practical exercises, experiments, and evaluations of the learning process.
- 140 kg of equipment (objects, instruments) for practice and experimentation.
- A small bilingual library of 130 selected articles dealing with environmental control.
- 150 slides describing real or simulated situations.
- A course manager for individual orientation, tests, answers, and equipment organization.

In addition, each training manager receives a manual with test answers,practical information on how to evaluate the entry level and behaviour of the group, and instructions for the final test, both for a simulated and for a real situation.

Each participant starts the course individually, by following the instructions found in the module for reading, carrying out experiments, and discussions. The objectives and competencies are clearly defined at the beginning of the course. Each participant controls their own training. They are free to choose the course of study, and decide their own timetable, all within a defined framework. The 52 modules created for the topic "Climate control in museums" contain 60% of the necessary knowledge. The remainder is acquired through experiments and discussions with managers and colleagues, as well as from slides and analysis of selected literature. The acquisition of knowledge is progressive. Participants check their competence at each module to ensure that they are able to continue. The training is intensive. For non-specialists in climate, three weeks (100 hours) is necessary.

The manager has multiple roles: to guide, encourage, share personal experiences, create teams of participants for difficult exercises, answer questions, check tests, manage equipment and time, etc.

Strengths of the CRI method

In traditional training, participants must follow the teacher's pace. With the CRI method, participants learn at their own pace; there is no established working hours. At any time they can return to any part of the course and some parts of the course can be done at home.

In traditional training, the objectives of the course are fuzzy, or described in an abstract way. With the CRI method, participants are aware of their goals from the beginning of the training. Final objectives, sub-objectives, resources and limitations are all described.

In traditional training, course notes are very short, usually just some photocopies with an abstract of the course. The CRI has involved a tremendous effort to collect the right information and references.

In traditional training, there is usually a single test of the acquired knowledge. This test is generally taken at the end of the course, and its contents are often arbitrary and selective.

With the CRI, participants with experience in climate control do not have to repeat parts of the course already known. If they can pass the test on a module, then they can continue their progress without delay.

After the CRI course, participants are able to plan and implement because theory and practice are intimately linked.

Weaknesses of the CRI method

We evaluated the course by questionnaires during its first use in 1989. The results were extremely positive.[2] Response to three of the ten questions merit consideration here:

Question 1: If we compare this type of course to a traditional one, do you think the method requires more personal effort?

much more	55%
more	45%
same	15%
less	0%

Obviously, in this case participants are much more responsible for their own training. They have to read quite a lot. Some participants are not used to it and find this method time consuming.

Question 2: If we compare this type of course to a traditional one, do you think the method creates intellectual stimulation?

much more	73%
more	27%
same	0%
less	0%

As with all interactive methods, the intellectual stimulation of the CRI is high, but it can result in stress if working conditions are not adequate. Facilities need a peaceful atmosphere, comfortable space and furniture. Stress can also appear if participants do not understand that the course is not a race. The first one to finish is not the necessarily the best. Competition is the greatest enemy of the CRI method.

Question 3: If we compare this type of course to a traditional one, do you think, the course manager is

much more available	27%
more available	73%
same	0%
less available	0%

In general, most of the criticism on self-teaching focuses on the impersonal, dehumanised aspects. Obviously, a traditional, and very good, teacher will be able to catch the interest of the class and transmit his own experience in a short time. But for each good teacher, how many are boring and unprepared!

With the CRI, there is no "one man show". The relationship of participant to trainer is less formal, more adapted to adult training.

We estimate that the participant spends an average of 15 h with the training manager and 12 h in discussions with other participants.

The last five years and the future

In 1991, Intercultura asked ICCROM to train Colombian conservators, chemists and curators in environmental control. The course length was too short (ten days) to allow use of the full CRI material. We decided to mix traditional and module training. From the CRI we selected:

- 15 tests,
- six written exercises,
- five instructions on using instruments,
- 25 drawings for overhead transparencies,
- one shortened bibliography,
- 150 pages of course notes.

We thus proved that the CRI set could also be used as a background resource for conventional lectures.

Between 1989 and 1992, the CRI climate set was used routinely for the PREMA course (Preventive Conservation in Museums in Africa). Some modules and instructions were modified to fit the African context: museums built in the 1960s, specific sub-Saharan collections, poor maintenance, extreme contrast between wet and dry season or constant hot and humid climate, etc. This demonstrated that the CRI can be adapted and updated easily.

CRI used as a didactic tool for teachers

In 1993, the CRI was evaluated by a group of professionals, conservators and chemists dealing with training in climate in different countries. In order to have a representative group, we selected participants from four different continents. Participants came from Belgium, the USA, Botswana, Chile, France, Colombia, and Denmark.

Participants recognised three main advantages:

- The pyramid of objectives is built in a very pragmatic way. For the first time a book presents the problem as a whole. This is particularly helpful for teaching.
- A whole package is available: a condensed manual, exercises, experiments, graphics, references to all types of objects (archeological materials to photographs), and different case studies with an international overview.
- Systematic pedagogic tools are used throughout the CRI, such as written objectives, criterion tests, feed-back.

Two main aspects were discussed:

- Entry level: two participants felt that some of the modules at the beginning of the course were too junior in content. (However, if participants find a module too easy, they should proceed immediately to the test, thereby passing quickly to modules that engage them).
- How many hours are dedicated to climate control in universities and conservation programs? Very few, obviously. If teachers used the CRI method, they would need about 100 h of class time. Everyone agreed that this is not feasible in existing programs. On the other hand, everyone agreed that lectures on climate are undervalued, especially since climate is widely recognised as one of the essential factors for the safe-guarding our heritage.

In conclusion, we can be very optimistic. Most professionals are aware of the climate control package. There have been suggestions for improvements, and many requests for use.

References

1. R. Maser and P. Pipe, *CRI Criterion-Referenced Instruction in Analysis, Design, and Implementation*, 2nd edn, (Asfordis Conseil, 16 rue de Londres, 75009-Paris, France,1980)
2. B. de Tapol, 'Une Nouvelle Méthode d'Enseignement par Objectifs', *Conservation Restauration des Biens Culturels revue ARAAFU*, no. 2 (1990).

Working Group A2

Training in conservation and restoration

Training in Conservation and Restoration

Coordinators: Janey Cronyn, Kate Foley
Assistant Coordinator: Colin Pearson

Our major task for the 1993–1996 Triennium was to agree on the development of standards and levels of practice for conservators in relation to education and training. To help us better address current issues, as a group we agreed to move on from the conventional approach of measuring standards from conservation schools by inputs – lengths of course, details of curriculum, type of qualification obtained – by looking at measuring outputs. Could we all agree on what qualities and competences a conservator needs, irrespective of where in the world s/he practices? Could this approach safeguard standards whilst respecting the plurality of our global needs?

At the Interim Meeting of the Working Group (now published as: Cronyn, J.M. & Foley, K. (eds.) (1996) *A qualified community: towards internationally agreed standards of qualification for conservation*, Proceedings of the ICOM-CC Training Working Group Interim Meeting April 1995, London: English Heritage/MGC) we discovered that we had only just begun to address this complex problem. But the encouraging result was a commitment from the Group to go on exploring the true meaning of professional standards in different contexts. The next task might well be to look again at the *ICOM Definition of the conservator-restorer* (1984) and at other guidelines such as those for the teaching of conservation proposed at the Interim Meeting by Colin Pearson and Robert Ferguson with a view to defining more precisely how conservation schools can best discharge their responsibilites in the forming of conservators in conjunction with the profession itself.

The papers for the 1996 Triennial Meeting continue to reflect this preoccupation with standards. Joyce Hill Stoner, for example, analyses different educational approaches and suggests how the vital but often neglected "soft" skills may be reinforced. Chris Caple and David Watkinson with Siobhan Stevenson both look in critical detail at specific learning and assessment methodologies whilst Bethania Reis Veloso refers us back to the vital problem of specific local needs through a description of a Brazilian course, a theme which is much amplified by the training providers of ICCROM: Neal Putt, Terry Little *et al.* They describe the attempt to match training provision with need and resources in the Pacific and in Africa respectively. Colin Pearson discusses some of the problems that providers may find when required to deliver longer courses to meet local needs. The Group's contribution is rounded off by a paper by Emmanuel Caillé who stresses the growing need for continuous professional development for conservators who can no longer consider themselves fit to answer every professional demand by completing one initial course of study.

Another task, begun but not completed following the Interim Meeting, was an attempt to bring together representatives of many of the international organisations involved in relevant aspects of conservation to discuss the possibility of sharing policy papers on education and standards at an early stage. We are discussing with ICCROM the creation of a framework for distributing such information. We hope by this means to engender a sharing of ideas and to counteract a tendency to reinvent the wheel. A third task underway is the update of the Bibliography of theses, dissertations and research reports in conservation (ICCROM 1991).

Finally, our newsletters as well as the papers described above reflect the tendency of the Group to wrestle with the very difficult issue of finding non-formulaic standards that address the depth and complexity of our global task of conservation education.

La formation professionnelle. Une affaire à suivre

Emmanuel Caillé
ICCROM
13 via di San Michele
00153 Rome, Italie

Résumé

L'efficacité de la formation professionnelle en conservation-restauration est difficile à évaluer essentiellement par manque de suivi. Dans le cadre de PREMA (PREvention dans les Musées Africain), l'ICCROM a tenté une autre approche afin de "rentabiliser" la formation. Sur le thème du contrôle du climat muséal, trois semaines de formation ont été intégrées à un projet d'étude climatique comparée qui sera mené pendant un an par chaque participant dans son musée et aboutira à une publication collective. L'auteur expose ici la méthodologie mise en place pour ce projet et les résultats déjà obtenus quant à la réalisation effective des études, la formation dans le domaine climatique des participants mais aussi l'évaluation des moyens de formation et des outils didactiques utilisés, qui ont permis un suivi régulier et le dialogue constant durant plus d'une année avec les participants.

Mots-clés

Assistance technique, conservation préventive, climat, formation

Introduction

Depuis sa création l'ICCROM (Centre International d'études pour la Conservation et la restauration des biens culturels) organise des cours de formation professionnelle. Ces cours internationaux sont des événements ponctuels. Ils rassemblent un public d'horizon professionnel et culturel extrêmement diversifié. C'est un moment de rencontre privilégié ou les échanges avec un spécialiste nourrissent l'activité des participants.

Ces événements créent une très grande effervescence dans le groupe enseignants-participants, mais ces derniers gardent généralement une attitude relativement passive de réception. D'autre part, il est rare qu'un enseignant puisse garder un contact régulier avec ses anciens participants. Il est donc difficile d'évaluer les conséquences de la formation à long terme et en particulier ses points forts ou faibles et la réalité de son application sur le terrain.

Le programme PREMA 1990–2000[1] (PREvention dans les Musées Africains) de l'ICCROM a essayé de résoudre ces difficultés en mettant à la disposition de ses anciens participants du matériel technique pour encourager l'application de leurs connaissances. D'autre part, PREMA souhaitait conserver des contacts avec ses anciens participants en développant et animant un réseau de professionnels. Les résultats de ces tentatives se sont révélés insuffisants quant à une évaluation systématique de la formation.Nous avons alors tenté une nouvelle approche dans laquelle le cours n'est plus le moment culminant mais seulement une étape du processus de formation. La mise en application du cours in-situ, dans ce cas particulier, la mise en place, la réalisation et le bilan d'une étude climatique dans un Musée pendant un an devient l'étape fondamentale du processus de formation. L'enseignant en assurant un suivi est alors un soutien et un guide pour chaque participant, mais aussi une courroie de transmission entre eux pour leur permettre petit à petit de construire ensemble leur expérience.

Le suivi est le pivot de l'opération et permet aussi:

- de contrôler les réalisations effectives et d'évaluer la facilité de mise en application du cours et donc la relation entre la théorie et la pratique
- d'identifier les problèmes sur lesquels les participants butent et donc les failles de l'enseignement
- d'évaluer le coût financier, humain et en matériel du travail réalisé et de l'enseignement.

Mais cette expérience n'est valide que si l'on donne aux participants les moyens de mener à bien un tel travail. Ceci signifie: 1) non seulement de leur donner les connaissances et le soutien scientifique nécessaires pour réaliser ce travail, 2) mais aussi de leur donner le matériel indispensable, et 3) surtout de permettre à chacun d'eux de développer une démarche scientifique, rigoureuse et systématique malgré l'éloignement et l'isolement des personnes.

Méthode utilisée

Soutien scientifique: l'atelier CRI

Un atelier de spécialisation sur le climat fut organisé en collaboration avec le Musée d'Art Africain de Dakar pendant quatre semaines. L'atelier exploitait un outil pédagogique crée à l'ICCROM: le CRI-Climat2. Le CRI3, Criterion-Referenced Instruction (Instruction référencée par critère) est une méthode d'enseignement développée aux Etats-Unis par R. Mager et P. Pipe qui a été appliquée au thème du climat dans les musées par Gaël de Guichen et Benoît de Tapol. Cet outil développe des méthodesd'inspection des collections et du bâtiment afin de pouvoir évaluer les conséquences du climat sur l'ensemble du Musée (contenu et contenant). Il expose aussi l'ensemble des solutions de modification des conditions climatiques qui existent sur le marché. Il est structuré pour être directement applicable sur le terrain.

Toutes les connaissances nécessaires sont contenues dans le matériel pédagogique que chaque participant peut absorber à son rythme et presque dans l'ordre qu'il souhaite. Les enseignants orientent et encouragent l'étude, et valident leurs examens. Une relation individuelle s'instaure entre les participants et les enseignants. Ce type de relation établit un contact direct qui sera très utile après la fin du cours. En chiffres le CRI-Climat c'est 650 pages de texte richement illustrées, plus de 150 exercices corrigés, 150 kilos de matériel de démonstration et d'expérimentation, 120 références bibliographiques et 49 examens. Cet atelier a fourni à tous les participants un outil de travail et les moyens de l'utiliser, une méthodologie et un vocabulaire communs.

Soutien matériel

Le besoin d'un soutien en matériel permet d'engager les premiers travaux avec une motivation supplémentaire. Chaque participant, une fois retourné dans son musée, réalise les rapports préparatoires que sont les inspections des collections et des bâtiments. Des conclusions de ceux-ci il peut déduire ses besoins et rédiger sa requête de matériel. Ces rapports sont les premiers résultats tangibles de l'application du cours par les participants et la reprise de contact avec PREMA est laissée à leur initiative. Ainsi nous sommes assurés d'une réelle implication et d'un engagement de fait pour continuer l'investissement entrepris.

Développement de la démarche scientifique

L'étude climatique est un travail long, astreignant et dont les résultats immédiats ne sont pas très encourageants. De plus, l'isolement de chacun, qui est particulièrement fort en Afrique où le personnel formé à la conservation est rare et où les coûts et les délais de communication sont très élevés, est un facteur très démotivant pour ce type de travail. Nous avons essayé de créer plusieurs outils pour permettre une confrontation régulière de l'ensemble des travaux et faciliter leur évolution rigoureuse et scientifique.

La sélection

La sélection devient un élément fondamental pour une bonne poursuite du projet. Nous avons préféré nous adresser à des personnes connues: d'anciens participants des cours PREMA. Ensuite nous avons essayé d'évaluer l'intérêt et l'expérience dans ce domaine en nous concentrant sur les réalisations déjà exécutées et sur l'utilisation du matériel à disposition. Douze personnes de 11 musées différents de 10 pays de l'Afrique sub-saharienne ont été ainsi choisies pour participer à ce projet appelé PREMA-Climat 95.

Le travail d'équipe

Cette méthode de confrontation requiert des contacts constants, c'est un véritable travail d'équipe. Il s'agissait de matérialiser cette notion malgré la séparation et l'isolement des personnes. Nous avons alors impliqué l'ensemble des participants dans l'organisation pratique, proposé un produit final commun et la mise en place d'un bulletin de liaison.

Implication dans l'organisation pratique

Il nous a paru important d'engager les participants dans l'organisation de l'étude pour essayer de créer une équipe dont le coordinateur est membre au même titre que tous les autres participants et ceci afin d'encourager les initiatives. A la fin du cours l'ensemble des participants (ICCROM et représentants des musées) se sont donc réunis pour mettre au point l'étude climatique. Les attentes des uns et des autres ont pu s'exprimer et l'organisation pratique a été clarifiée, en particulier, la procédure pour l'obtention d'une assistance technique. Les participants ont souhaité dans la mesure du possible que toutes les études commencent en même temps. Ils ont aussi insisté pour fixer la date de lancement de l'étude approfondie durant la réunion. Sur la base de cette date, PREMA a établi un calendrier écrit qui leur a été envoyé et qui a été approuvé par l'ensemble d'entre eux. Ces dates sont devenues, lors des travaux de suivi, de véritables "leitmotiv", des sous-objectifs à respecter absolument pour nombre d'entre eux.

Un objectif stimulant

Pour créer un esprit d'équipe il fallait transformer le travail individuel de chacun en élément d'un travail commun. Le but de ce travail commun devait être motivant et intéressant pour tous. Nous avons alors choisi de proposer la publication d'un ouvrage collectif: "Etudes Climatiques Comparées dans les musées de l'Afrique sub-saharienne". Ce but a l'avantage de porter en lui une exigence de sérieux et de rigueur dans la réalisation du travail.

Un élément fédérateur sur le long terme.

Pour maintenir vivante la notion d'équipe et entretenir une implication réelle de chacun, le soutien individuel a été doublé par un soutien collectif, un bulletin de liaison: "Quelques nouvelles du front ... Hygrométrique".

Sa diffusion régulière (mensuel pendant les travaux de préparation, trimestriels après le lancement de la majorité des études) et l'introduction de nouvelles un peu personnelles dans les *Brèves* ont contribué à familiariser les participants avec le bulletin. Il est considéré avant tout comme une tribune ouverte pour tous où nous incitons à une participation directe et à l'expression de chacun. La rubrique *Proposition* permet de régler l'ensemble des problèmes pratiques qui peuvent apparaître au cours de l'étude. Par exemple comment rattraper le retard que nous avons pris? Que faire si des instruments reçus sont endommagés? Comment gérer le petit matériel pour ne pas se trouver à court de stock? Des suggestions, issues des participants ou de PREMA qui modifient l'organisation comme accepter un nouveau musée dans l'équipe ou demander à chaque participant de se fixer la fréquence de ses correspondances avec nous, peuvent aussi figurer sous cette rubrique. Les participants sont ainsi incités à se prononcer sur l'organisation de l'étude.

Pour encourager les participants dans leurs travaux nous leur communiquons les résultats des autres sous la rubrique *Le point sur les études*. Ils peuvent ainsi se situer dans l'ensemble du travail et le caractère global de ces tâches individuelles est constamment souligné. Le souhait de voir des résultats diffusés dans le bulletin incite nombre d'entre eux à nous communiquer leurs travaux régulièrement et facilite le suivi individuel.

Enfin sous la rubrique *La question du front*, nous avons soumis des questions plus "scientifiques" à la réflexion de tous. Un problème issu d'un travail d'un des participants, a été diffusé. Les réponses que nous avons reçues ont été incluses dans les numéros suivants pour essayer de stimuler l'ensemble du groupe. Ces réponses ont amené d'autres questions et ont fait évoluer la discussion.

Résultats

Dans l'état actuel de nos travaux tous les participants ont gardé un premier contact avec le projet. Dix musées nous informent régulièrement de l'état de leurs travaux. Huit assistances techniques ont été envoyées et sept musées ont commencé leur étude climatique approfondie. Ces résultats sont très satisfaisants.

Par contre nous avons accumulé un important retard dans le calendrier. Les ralentissements dus aux petits ajustements pratiques pour les envois de matériels (corrections des requêtes, manques d'information pour l'expédition, délais de livraison de matériel) ont été fortement amplifiés par les problèmes de communication en Afrique. Un échange de courrier supplémentaire peut signifier trois mois de plus.

Nous n'avions pas non plus accordé une très grande importance aux échéances. Comme signalé auparavant, elles ont fonctionné comme de véritables "leitmotiv" pour de nombreux participants. Lorsque, malgré leurs efforts et pour des raisons indépendantes de leur volonté, ces échéances n'ont pas été respectées, ils ont parfois senti une certaine démotivation, particulièrement sensible dans les musées qui n'avaient pas du tout de matériel. Pour limiter l'effet des lenteurs de communication nous avons décidé d'attribuer un stock relativement large de matériel de consommation (feutres ...) à chaque musée. Celui-ci doit nous prévenir dès qu'il utilise un élément pour nous permettre de le remplacer immédiatement. Cela nous permettra d'éviter des ruptures de stock qui peuvent perturber l'étude et d'évaluer la durée de vie de certains éléments (feutres) et le coût de fonctionnement d'une étude.

Le développement du bulletin de liaison reste un signe du réel succès de PREMA-Climat 95. Son volume a été multiplié par quatre entre le premier et le cinquième numéro. Surtout la participation de l'ICCROM qui était de 100% dans le n°1 n'est plus que de 60% et a changé de nature. Elle se nourrit maintenant des interventions des autres participants qui sont de plus en plus nombreuses et de plus en plus riches. Les participants s'encouragent mutuellement, préviennent s'ils auront du retard ce qui montre la construction petit à petit d'un esprit de collaboration et de solidarité.

Conclusion

Le succès de ce suivi intégré ne doit pas nous faire sous-estimer l'importance du cours. C'est certainement les trois semaines d'atelier qui se sont très bien déroulées, qui ont donné un corps à l'idée d'équipe. A cette occasion des liens personnels se sont développés et ont doublé les relations professionnelles. L'autre apport fondamental de l'atelier a été la dotation de chaque participant d'un instrument de référence commun qu'est le texte du CRI-Climat et surtout des moyens pratiques et linguistiques de son exploitation. La référence au texte a été constante dans nos relations, les corrections et les observations qui ont été faites lors de l'analyse des rapports ou des résultats qui m'ont été communiqués, sont systématiquement complétés par des renvois au texte du CRI. D'autre part, la question du vocabulaire s'est révélée ici essentielle. Sans cette maîtrise commune, les échanges directs par courrier auraient été fortement compliqués par des problèmes de communication et surtout de définition de certains termes techniques. Quand nous parlons de rapport d'inspection, d'étude préliminaire, d'étude approfondie, de zone climatique, de charte d'enregistrement ou de synthèse graphique, nous entendons tous la même chose. Enfin les différents développements dans les bulletins n'auraient certainement pas pu avoir cet écho parmi les participants et n'auraient pas été aussi riches. Ainsi les "Quelques nouvelles du front ... Hygrométrique" auraient perdu une grande part de leur intérêt.

D'autre part, un suivi organisé, surtout quand il dure deux ans rend ce type de formation beaucoup plus coûteuse. Ici le projet multiplie l'investissement du cours par 1.8 sans compter la persévérance nécessaire que nous y avons consacrée.

En contrepartie, nous avons un retour en qualité. Nous avons pu aborder des problèmes que le temps restreint du cours et la somme d'informations qu'il contenait ne nous avaient pas permis d'approfondir. Nous avons aussi touché du doigt la limite de l'application de la théorie face à la pratique. Comment doit-on traiter les conclusions que nous pouvons tirer des données collectées sur le bâtiment par rapport aux résultats d'une étude préliminaire? Comment exploiter ces conclusions pour expliquer certains résultats pratiques? Ou encore, quelle réalité a une zone climatique? Quelle est sa fonction? Quels peuvent être ses critères de définition? Quelle en sera la précision? sont quelques exemples des questions qui se développent dans Quelques nouvelles du front ...Hygrométrique". Le fait que ces questions s'appuient sur des expériences précises issues du travail de l'équipe facilite la discussion qui ne se développe plus sur des concepts mais sur des données réelles.

Enfin pour comparer vraiment les coûts de ces deux types de formation, il faudrait avoir les résultats tangibles des fruits que donne une opération ponctuelle comme un cours. L'intégration du suivi au processus de formation nous a permis d'une part, de favoriser l'application pratique de l'enseignement et ainsi d'assurer et d'augmenter son assimilation; mais aussi de revenir sur les éléments qui étaient restés flous. L'enseignement a rendu l'expérience possible qui vient à son tour enrichir la formation. D'autre part, elle met en place un système où le participant prend une part active et est responsabilisé dans sa formation, où il apprend à communiquer régulièrement avec ses pairs, où il se confronte avec des problèmes réels et construit son expérience. Il pourra devenir demain un animateur potentiel d'un autre groupe et rediffuser ainsi sa connaissance et son expérience. Cette responsabilisation et ces échanges sont certainement à l'origine de l'investissement des participants qui est la clé de réussite du projet. Cette démarche de confrontation et de communication est fondamentale pour le développement et l'enrichissement de notre profession, mais elle reste rare en Afrique où le personnel de musée formé est peu nombreux. Elle doit être encouragée si nous souhaitons que ce continent puisse prendre en charge la formation de son personnel. (Une affaire a suivre...)

Remerciements

Ce projet n'aurait pas été possible sans le soutien financier de l'Agence de Coopération Culturelle et Technique (ACCT), le Ministère de la coopération, (France), la Direction pour la coopération et de l'aide humanitaire (Suisse), et la Fondation Elf, qu'ils en soient remerciés.

Mes remerciements vont aussi à Gaël de Guichen et à l'ensemble de l'équipe du programme PREMA et tout particulièrement à Catherine Antomarchi qui n'a pas ménagé son aide et ses conseils avisés lors de la rédaction de cet article.

Notes

[1] PREMA 1990–2000 est un programme de formation de professionnel de musée de l'Afrique sub-saharienne à la conservation des biens culturels. PREMA a développé plusieurs types d'activités depuis sa création, dont l'organisation de cours de 9 mois, de cours de 3 mois et de séminaire de sensibilisation.
C. Antomarchi, "PREMA une nouvelle conception de la formation en conservation préventive", *Conservation restauration des biens culturels* n°1, (1989): 49–50.
R.L. Barclay, "Le programme PREMA 1990–2000", *Bulletin de l'Institut Canadien de Conservation*, n°14 (1994): 11–12.
Bob Barclay, "PREMA Zambie", *Bulletin de L'Institut canadien de conservation*, n°9 (1992): 11–12.
A. Godonou et C. Laroque, "Cours de conservation dans les musées nationaux du Bénin", *Conservation restauration des biens culturels* n°5, (1993): 10–14.

Références

1. Benoît de Tapol, "Une nouvelle méthode didactique appliquée à l'enseignement en conservation-restauration", *Conservation restauration des biens culturels* n°1, (1989): 51–53.
2. R. F. Marger, P. Pipe, *C.R.I: Criterion-Referenced Instruction, Analysis, Design and Implementation*, third edition, (The center for Effective Performances, Inc.).

The Creation of Self-development Learning Packages (SDLP) and Formalised Object Construction and Use Sequences (FOCUS)

Chris Caple
Department of Archaeology,
46 Saddler Street, Durham DH1 3NU, UK

Abstract

The pressures of student number on current UK university-based conservation courses is promoting the creation of open-learning or self-study material. The MA Conservation of Historic Objects (Archaeology) course at the University of Durham has created 22 self-development learning packages (SDLP) which support the student in learning materials identification and object recording and analysis skills. The development of skills in analysing the construction and use of an object are promoted using a formal methodology entitled: formalised object construction and use sequence (FOCUS). This methodology is effective in efficiently describing the construction and use history of objects, and may have wider application than use on training courses.

Keywords

SDLP, FOCUS, training, open learning, materials identification, recording, object construction

Introduction

All conservation courses in the UK currently face the dilemma of teaching a fast expanding subject, which demands high levels of knowledge and competence from its practitioners, to a rising number of students with diminishing financial resources and an increasingly high ratio of students to staff. Thus there is a requirement to teach more with less. This is hardly a new phenomenon and is the present norm in almost all subjects taught in UK universities. The responses to this phenomenon are numerous and varied. These include: students contributing to course funding; finding additional sources of funding; extending teaching hours of tutors; cutting down on expensive aspects of the training, e.g. materials and visits; further involving the conservation industry in teaching; and using self-study/open-learning methods.

Conservation courses in the UK are engaged in virtually all these activities. The effects of these developments and pressures on the courses in the UK have been described elsewhere[1,2] and on courses internationally by Pearson.[3] There has, as yet, been relatively little discussion of the extent to which self-study/open-learning materials are increasingly being developed to support the present generation of teaching courses.[4] Although there has been a marked increase in the number of textbooks such as the Butterworths series and others[5,6] available since the early 1980s, and aids such as videos are becoming increasingly available, there are relatively few examples of commercially available self-study or open-learning materials that are specifically designed for conservation students . In this paper I will briefly describe the self-learning packages that we are currently developing to support the teaching of conservation at Durham and an object recording system (FOCUS) that developed from this work, and which may have much wider application in conservation.

Open-learning materials

Anyone who, tired of contact with an inquisitive child and has given them something to 'go away and play with', can claim to have provided self-study or open-learning materials. The development of simple play materials into carefully designed information packages, planned to initiate a specific learning response in the youngster, triggered the development of this ancient form of play-learning into a major industry for teaching both children and adults. Open-learning or self-study materials became part of the education of children during the 1960s and 1970s as the educational culture increasingly concentrated on the learning experience and moved away from the traditional 'chalk and talk' teaching experience. These materials have become part of the culture of UK university education of the 1980s and 1990s, since the rising numbers of students have made the effort involved in creating such materials 'cost and time effective.'

It should be emphasised that there are a wide variety of names and forms for materials designed for the student to learn from, at their own pace. Terms used include: open learning, self study, distance learning, self-directed learning, self instruction, independent learning and many others. Most materials go beyond the oldest and simplest, the basic book, in requiring the reader to perform certain actions, such as an experiment, or undertake some form of calculation or activity which usually concludes with some form or testing of what has been learnt.[7,8] Conservation has, until recently, not found it worth while to make extensive investment in creating self-learning materials. The reasons that have mitigated against such an investment have included: the small number of students; the large input of staff time involved; the quickly evolving nature of the subject; the need to deal with real objects and thus very few situations which are standardised or predictable; the small number of tutors with little available time; and the historical preference for contact with a tutor. The advent of larger student numbers is now causing many course tutors to spend more time creating such materials.[4] At the simplest level they are making greater use of handouts and photocopies. Exercises such as tests in the use of libraries, using psychrometric charts, light meters, titrations or other simple chemical reactions are being more fully and formally documented to allow easier repetition in future years. Far more time and effort, however, is required to create self-study/open-learning packages using objects. Most conservation course tutors have, over the course of their professional careers, acquired a range of objects which they use to demonstrate to students: ancient materials; decay processes; failures of conservation; and successful pieces of conservation. These can be made more freely available for teaching through a self-study/open-learning package. However, problems of value and ownership complicate this process greatly.

Although most conservation course tutors are now busy producing their own open-learning/self-study materials, there has, as yet, been little public discussion about such materials and I am aware of relatively few examples of sharing such materials. Given the pressure on all courses, it would appear to be an area where increased communication and some further funding would be beneficial.

Given the rising student numbers and associated administration burden with the consequent reduction in the number of hours that any individual student spends with his or her course tutor, it is necessary to have some form of self-study or open-learning material in order to replace the contact with the tutor. By carefully designing self-learning materials, we can raise the quality of the education and avoid the inevitable feeling of rejection consequent upon simply giving a student an unprepared book or object and saying 'I'm busy, just go away and look at this'.

Self-development learning packages (SDLP)

The self-development learning packages (SDLP) are a series of 22 exercises being developed for the purpose of helping students to recognise materials and analyse objects. The topics are designed to be those activities, such as learning to identify materials from hand specimens or microscopic samples, which are clearly best learnt at a students own pace and which would not be so well adsorbed when taken at the speed of a lecture.

The working list of topics is:

A: *Microscopic identification*
1. Vegetable fibres
2. Animal fibres
3. Archaeological wood
4. Metallographic sections: ferrous
5. Metallographic sections: non-ferrous
6. Paint cross-sections

B: *Hand specimens*
7. Historic wood
8. Historic plastics
9. Historic metals and metals with coatings
10. Historic textiles
11. Leather
12. Bone, antler, horn, ivory
13. Vitreous materials: glass and ceramics
14. Vitreous materials: slags and industrial wastes
15. Stone

C: *Study of objects*
16. Pair of upholstered chairs
17. Rifle
18. Ethnographic arrows
19. Ethnographic spear
20. Copper alloy vessel

D: *Problem solving*
21. Interpreting radiographs
22. Designing a storage system

The SDLPs are in the form of boxes of material that can be worked on independently by each student, without the need for staff supervision. It should take the student from one to three hours to complete each exercise, which can thus be done in a single afternoon.

The boxes for groups A and B contain:

1. A workbook which directs the student through this learning package.
2. A series of numbered specimens which are described and identified in the workbook. The student works through these known specimens, making his or her own notes and diagrams, so learning to identify this type of material.
3. A relevant textbook that provides further background information and a bibliography. Thus the student is able to take the study of this topic as far as they wish.

The students test themselves by identifying a number of unknown lettered samples. The students record their identification, together with the reasoning behind the identification, and hand this work into the supervising tutor at the end of the afternoon. This is then checked. Where a student has failed to grasp the identification process, he or she can then be advised by the tutor and can retake the SDLP at a later date. This process can be repeated until the students successfully learn to identify all the material. The importance of the knowledge testing phase is emphasised in almost all self-learning materials.[7,8] It provides students with confidence that they are learning correctly and prevents any gross misunderstandings developing.

The boxes for group C contain a workbook with instructions on how students are to proceed and an object. The students examine the object and attempt to work out what materials it was made of, how it was created and how it has been used. They present this information as a written report. This mimics the written report that every conservator would expect to write before starting any form of conservation work on an object. In order to help students develop a rigorous approach to the examination of the object, we have devised a system named FOCUS (formalised object construction and use sequences) which is outlined below.

An initial group of these packages has already been created and the packages were tested on the 1995/96 student intake onto the Durham conservation course. There has been a great deal of positive feedback from students about this experience. Almost all the SDLPs should be in use for the academic year 1996/97. Funding is essential for such a project, both to employ authors whilst they create the workbooks and prepare the learning materials and to purchase objects and textbooks. The SDLP project has been financially supported by: the University of Durham; the Conservation Unit of the Museums and Galleries Commission; and the Department of Archaeology itself.

Together with the conservation course tutor, the principal authors and creators of the initial SDLP were recently graduated students Jo Dillon and Ida Hovmand. Recently graduated students were deliberately used since they were highly aware of the level of knowledge of the student consumer and were keen to develop their own expertise in these areas. Many of us have suffered with instruction manuals written by experts, particularly those supporting computer software. They invariably fail to tell you, simply enough, about the obvious things you need to get started; thus it would appear that training materials are often most useful when written by those who are still fully aware of the potential ignorance of the intended user. In certain areas, however, expertise was required that was not available in Durham; thus, the textiles SDLP is being created for us by Mary Brooks (Textile

Conservation Centre) and the SDLP on bone, antler, horn and ivory by Sonia O'Connor (until recently of the York Archaeological Trust).

In order to ensure that the packages are short and at a basic level, since the students on the Durham postgraduate conservation course only have a limited time available, the costs were deliberately kept low. We also obtained almost all specimens as gifts; otherwise they have been purchased cheaply from local markets or auctions. These specimens form a handling collection and after years of student use, even conservation students, the objects will fall to pieces. Thus we cannot have valuable artefacts, or those which we do not own, in the packages. It was also desired to create these packages quickly, thus multiple authors and objects promised for the future were deliberately avoided.

It has been important for all authors, funding authorities and students using the packages to be aware that the student using the package will not learn all they need to know about identifying hand specimens of fabric, metal, wood and polymers in the three hours of a single afternoon. All students and their future employers retain the responsibility for engaging in further training to develop these basic skills to a higher level. Higher education has the function of making students aware and giving them the tools to learn, not ensuring that they all possess the full range of technical skills which every future employer could require.

Formalised object construction and use sequences (FOCUS)

Part of the training of any conservator involves fully recording an object. This activity is a prerequisite to any conservation treatment and is enshrined in the AIC, UKIC and ICOM-CC codes of ethics.[9–11] It may take many forms, but invariably involves a pictorial record such as a photograph or drawing and a written description. The written description will normally include identification of all the materials of which any object is composed, details of the order and way in which they were assembled and evidence of subsequent use and repair of the object. Considerable effort is made in training courses to acquaint students with materials-identification skills and information about the use of materials in the historic and archaeological past as well as the constructional techniques used. Though students are enthusiastic and readily learn materials-identification skills, it has proved more difficult for students to acquire an understanding about the sequence in which materials were assembled into objects and particularly to observe and document accurately evidence of the use of the object. This is particularly acute in the case of evidence of use such as wear, repair, reattachment etc. and appears, in part, due to lack of textbooks and published examples on this subject.

In the published work of many conservators, the sequence of an object's construction and use is often referred to, but it is virtually never specifically described or fully reproduced. In many cases this may be because it is a simple sequence, or the conservator does not consider it necessary for the purposes of the article. Thus the information is often only present in the records of the object's conservation treatment. Even when in this form it is usually present as a rambling discourse without any formal structure and there is often no easy digest or summary of it.

In recent years at Durham University, we have been evolving a more formalised system for recording the construction and use the objects, in order to help students appreciate all the steps involved in this process. This alerts students to look for evidence of construction and use present in any object, and helps them record this information in a coherent manner.

FOCUS theory

The need for systems to encourage rigorous thinking are present in a wide range of academic disciplines. Such systems both simplify complex problems and assist in communication between practitioners, even if it does often develop into jargon. An example of one such system is the Harris Matrix used in archaeology.[12] In this system every archaeological feature or context such a layer of soil, wall, pit or posthole is given a unique number. The numbers, usually enclosed in boxes, are arranged vertically one above the other matching the stratigraphy of the site. If two features overlapped in the ground then a line is drawn between the two boxes, so indicating a definite stratigraphic relationship. The matrix for the whole site is built

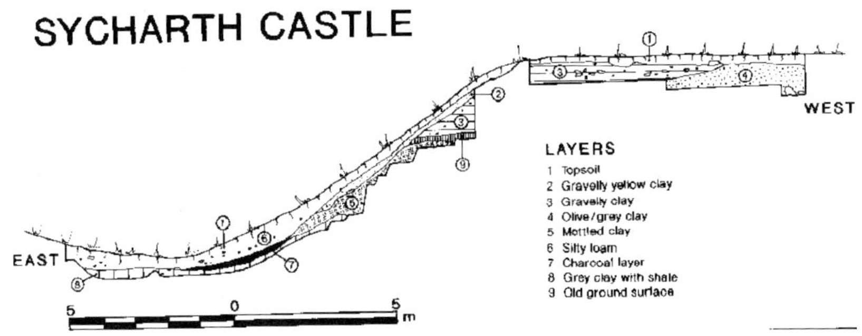

Figure 1. A drawing of the section cut through the archaeological layers of the castle of Owen Glyndwr

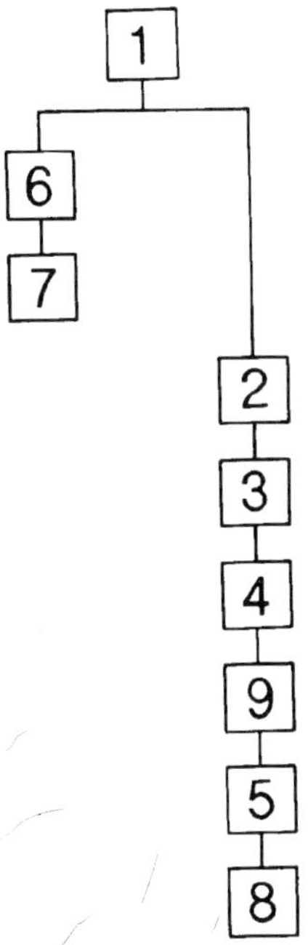

Figure 2: The section of Figure 1 expressed as a Harris Matrix

up in this manner, often involving many hundreds or thousands of layers. The purpose of the system is to enable the archaeologist to derive a clear sequence of relative order and thus dating of the layer or features across the whole of their site. No indication about the nature of the feature, whether a wall or soil layer, is depicted in the matrix nor any indication of the layer's contents or even any absolute dating evidence, such as a coin; only a unique number and its relationship to the surrounding layers is recorded in the Harris matrix. If the lines between the boxes are reduced to the minimum in order to establish the simplest matrix, the archaeologist is left with a 'skeleton matrix' that is an absolutely logical depiction of the relative order in which layers were deposited or features were constructed on that site. This makes it easy to look at the development of the whole site and see what was constructed there initially, what was built next and so on. Thus the cross section through the construction and occupation of the motte and bailey castle of Sycharth[13] (Figure 1) can be reduced to a simple Harris matrix sequence (Figure 2).

A system of this nature could be applied to the examination and recording of artefacts. However, since most objects have relatively short sequences of activity there would be very little information about the nature of the object provided by such a system. The FOCUS system uses and conveys a wider range of information than the Harris Matrix, but it contains the basic tenet of stripping down the information displayed and presenting it in a specific order so that a clear picture of the overall history of the object is discernible.

FOCUS

The elements recorded in a simple FOCUS are:

1. The relative chronology of construction and use;
2(a) The physical evidence of activity, both as part of the object which was assembled and evidence of subsequent use and repair;
2(b) The materials used in construction or applied subsequently;
3. Deductions drawn from the physical evidence and materials of construction.

The aim is to record these facts and deductions so as to present a complete picture of the history of construction and use of the object. If full statements were recorded in the sequence on each of these topics, then the resulting outpouring of words would be so lengthy and complex as to obscure the overall picture of the object. Thus short phrases must suffice. Where it is desired to communicate further information, numbers can be incorporated into the sequence which relate to a series of footnotes. The information is arranged in sequence, latest at the top of the page, earliest at the bottom of the page. Thus the chronological sequence of activities which have befallen the object are arranged in order. This ordering presents the information as a deconstruction sequence. All the information is arranged in two columns, the left-hand column being a sequence of major events in the objects life, the right-hand column the evidence, materials and deductions, which are distinguished by being placed in square brackets.

FOCUS can be used on virtually any object and can be extended to any level of detail required. The basic sequences used to illustrate this article are taken from initial learning material, but far greater levels of detail are possible, and in some instances expected. The format described here is not the only means of recording this information, but having experimented with several other formats, we feel that the one presented here is the most simple and rigorous that we have yet devised. The terms used are often simplistic in order to achieve brevity, the main emphasis remains on deriving the sequence of events, not worrying about the minutia of the composition and exact extent of one particular paint coating. Thus FOCUS descriptions are a tool, to be adapted to each job as required. It is the object, and the information about it, that remain important, not the exact specifications of the tool used to recover it.

FOCUS in practice

To enact FOCUS it is advisable to proceed in two stages:

1. All the parts of the object are listed; this is usually most effectively achieved using a labelled diagram. This will include all parts of the object, e.g. legs, arms and stretchers of a chair, all the fastenings, e.g.. nails, screws, and coverings, e.g. coats of paint or varnish. All the materials used in the construction of the object are then listed. This will include the materials of which the screws and coatings are made, as well as descriptions of the colour and texture, e.g. the colour of the wood stain. All the signs of wear or use, e.g. scratches, abrasion and traces of earlier paint coatings, are then also listed. These three lists are created with the sole objective of detecting all the information that is readily visible on the object. This activity will not only challenge students' ability to observe, but also encourage them to confront the problem of how they describe the evidence they see and, finally, force them to learn the correct names for the various parts of an object.

2a The evidence from the three lists is then placed in chronological order in a single column, with the latest action at the top of the page and, at the base of the page, the earliest shaping of the initial materials used to construct the object. The placing in order will present challenges to the students to try and find reasons as to why one event happened before another. Each event that can be separated in time from another has a blank line between events. Where events cannot be separated, they are recorded one above the other in the most sensible order, but without any blank lines, so signifying continuity. Every piece of physical evidence and every material mentioned in the initial lists should be present in the chronologically ordered sequence or in the footnotes.

2b Beneath the physical evidence, and in square brackets, students describe the deductions that they make from the list of physical evidence. This is an important step since students are often very ready simply to accept the existence of a scratch or nailhole without questioning why it is there, for example the probability that a hinge or other attachment device was originally present. This has created a deconstruction sequence for the history of the object.

2c A second column to the left of the first is created in which groups of pieces of evidence, which we might refer to as 'phases of activity' in the object's history, are given a descriptive name. Where descriptive names are repeated, they are numbered up from the base of the sequence, e.g. Use 1, Use 2. This process is designed to clarify the history of the object, so giving a label to the separate phases of repair and use.
It is essential to try and make the written comments in these two columns as brief as possible but still be communicative.

2d Wherever a longer description or explanation is required, a number is entered in the right-hand evidence and deduction column. The numbered footnotes appear at the base of the FOCUS listing and are an integral part of that sequence. Information such as material identification details, deductions about the previous history of materials added to the object, or details about the shaping or fashioning of a part of the object are typical footnotes.

Two examples are presented as Tables 1 and 2 to illustrate the application of the FOCUS system.

Table 1. FOCUS Example 1: Medieval arrowhead from Dryslwyn Castle

Object Sequence	*Evidence* *[Deduction]*
Buried	recovered from excavation[1] object composed of iron oxides [originally iron arrowhead now corroded] fibrous structure in corroded base of object [mineral replaced wood from arrow shaft the original wood having rotted]
Used	tip bent [arrow fired at hard surface in Dryslwyn castle in 13th century[2]]
Edge Sharpened	point and edge are sharp [sharpened on a hone stone]
Shafted	fibrous structure in corroded base of object [wooden shaft, ash? hafted into arrow feather flights give effective arrow form]
Arrowhead Forged	forge lines and object shape of diamond shaped cross-section pointed head tapering to circular cross section flaring to form circular socket below[3] [a single piece of metal forged to form the arrowhead]
Wrought Iron	iron minerals form corrosion products object is magnetic [iron metal blank forged from bloom or from recycled objects with particles of slag and charcoal entrapped in the metal [3]]

(1) Excavation revealed castle occupation AD 1220–1420. This arrowhead with others coming from a deposit of siege material dated 1287.
(2) Evidence from X-ray and cleaning object
(3) Evidence from X-ray

The FOCUS system has aided students to become more aware of the antiquity and the detail of the past history of the objects with which they are dealing. In previous years the emphasis on the preservation of evidence has led to an unhealthy interest by students in preserving museum and saleroom numbers and the other easily observed marks of an objects recent past. This manifested itself in the preciousness they ascribed to preserving the marks of damage gained by an object during its recovery or during its storage within the museum. The FOCUS exercises have allowed them to put this evidence in the larger context of the object's whole life.

Conclusion

The use of open-learning materials represents an opportunity to improve the quality of teaching, even if the need to develop such materials has been precipitated by the pressure of increasing student numbers as much as by developing theories on improving the learning of students. The self development learning projects (SDLP) created by the MA Conservation course at Durham are an example of open-learning materials that are successful in improving the learning abilities of students in the areas of material identification and object construction. The use of a methodology such as the formalised object construction and use sequence (FOCUS) has proved an important development in raising the awareness of students to the sequence of construction of objects and the evidence that remains on many objects with a long lifetime of use. The FOCUS system may have a far wider application for analysing and recording objects.

References

1. C. Caple, "Teaching Postgraduate Conservation; Past, Present and Future," in *Archaeological Conservation: Training and Employment,* UKIC Occasional Paper, ed. R. White (1992), 11–15
2. C. Caple, "The Development of Managerial and Communication Skills in Conservation Trainees; The Durham Experience," (Paper presented at the ICOM-CC Tenth Triennial Conference, Washington, 1993), 715–720
3. C. Pearson, "Crisis Facing the Conservation Teaching Profession," *Conservation News* 52, (November 1993): 12–14

Table 2. FOCUS Example 2: Edwardian bedroom chair

Object Sequence	*Evidence* [*Deduction*]
Sold 2	Self adhesive label with number. [Lot number from auction sale] [Previous sale].
Sold I	Traces of self -adhesive label [Previous sale]
Use 2	Emulsion paint spots. [Painting undertaking near chair.] Green fabric heavily worn[1]. Varnish chipped.
Seat recovered	Brass domed-headed studs nailed in place. Green pile velour[2]. Padding[3] Ply-wood base board cut to shape and nailed to seat frame[4].
Use I	Cane seat worn through or rendered unserviceable. [The seat was subsequently recovered.]
Cane seat	Cane woven through holes in frame to create seat. [Rattan normally used]
Varnished Stained	Golden varnish. Yellow-brown colour; probably stain.
Assembled	Nails used to attach seat to the back legs and top back rail to back legs. [To increase rigidity and stability] Wooden pieces assembled joints glued Front stretcher cut down to fit pre-drilled holes.
Wood decorated/finished	Legs and upper part of seat sanded. Wooden elements cut with tenons and holes drilled to form mortices Front legs and stretcher turned, spindle marks and regular incised ring decoration applied[5]. Top back rail cut to curve[6] , and machine carved. [The machine carving and standard design of the chair suggest mass production.]
Wood shaped	Back legs and lower back rail shaped; clamped and steamed. Pieces for seat shaped. Wooden pieces of various sizes sawn to shape. [From planks.]
Wood obtained	Beech [Timber felled, seasoned and cut into planks.]

(1) This fabric is a machine-woven textile comprising a blue grey, possibly cotton cloth, with a bright bottle green raised pile of man made fibre. A bow and orb pattern shadow is visible in the blue fabric. The lack of any other coloured pile fibre suggests that the pattern was created by cutting into the pile.
(2) Two seams are visible, this suggests recycling, as one width of fabric is too narrow to cover the seat.
(3) Padding includes cut up scraps of cloth, felt and earlier upholstery stuffing
(4) (DTMS-MS)The presence of nail holes and shadows of battens indicates previous use
(5) Bobbin spindle legs, lathe turned possessing dimples on centre of the leg ends.
(6) Distinguishable from the grain pattern.

4. S. Thomas, and J. Greenwood "Crisis Facing the Conservation Teaching Profession: A Response," *Conservation News* 53, (March 1994): 8–9.
5. J.M. Cronyn, *The Elements of Archaeological Conservation* (London: Routledge, 1990)
6. C.V. Horie *Materials for Conservation* (London: Butterworths, 1987)
7. R. Lewis, *Open Learning in Action* (London: Council for Educational Technology in the UK, 1984)
8. D. Rowntree *Teaching Through Self-Instruction: How to Develop Open Learning Materials* (London: Kogan Page, 1990)
9. AIC, "Code of Ethics and Guidelines for Practice," *AIC News* (May 1994), 17–20
10. UKIC, *Guidance for Conservation Practice* (London: UKIC, 1983)
11. ICOM-CC, *The Conservator-Restorer; A Definition of the Profession* (Copenhagen: ICOM, 1984)
12. E.C. Harris, *Principles of Archaeological Stratigraphy* (London: Academic Press, 1989)
13. D.B. Hague, and C. Warhurst, "Excavations at Sycharth Castle, Denbighshire," *Archaeologia Cambrensis* 115 (1966): 108–127.

PREMA: A Training Strategy for a Change or 'Let's Stop Building Castles in the Sand'

Terry Little, Catherine Antomarchi,* Gaël de Guichen,
Alain Godonou
ICCROM
via di San Michele 13
00153 Rome
Italy

Abstract

Training schemes aimed at heritage professionals in the developing world encounter considerable challenges and obstacles – sometimes successfully, but more often with ambiguous, if not negative results. When faced with the enormous task of addressing conservation training needs in sub-Saharan Africa, ICCROM decided to get off the beaten track by producing a long-term strategy. Ten years after launching PREMA, the prospects of autonomous training and heritage preservation in Africa are no longer elusive. The paper highlights the program's philosophy, strategy and achievements in hopes of improving training programs in developing countries and ... why not elsewhere?

Keywords

Training, strategy, sustainability, sub-Saharan Africa, trainees, preventive conservation, museums

What is successful training?

What constitutes successful training? The quantity of applications for a course? The participants' level of satisfaction? Positive evaluations from lecturers? If the scope is to assess the training activity itself, one could certainly measure some type of success from these criteria. However, if your training aim is to have widespread, regional or institutional impact, these criteria would result in some very empty figures.

When the developed world reaches out to help the developing world, training is increasingly synonymous with assistance. There are a great number of training schemes and initiatives in place in the developing world. They all have worthy and noble aims: developing human resources, creating networks and cultivating skills and knowledge in a wide variety of fields. However, when the training product is conceived and implemented as a single course or short-term experience, it might have some immediate positive impact, but only by chance will it have institutional or sustainable impact in developing countries.

ICCROM declares war

Such common training activities, lacking both vision and a long-term strategy, are destined to flounder, leaving both trainees and trainers frustrated and sometimes bitter. This is what ICCROM experienced after having organized dozens of short and targeted training sessions in museums in Latin America, the Middle East, Asia and especially after completing two one-month courses at the request of an African institute in 1985. In spite of the very positive, immediate results, it was obvious that the skills and enthusiasm would dissipate just as quickly as they had been developed after each participant returned to face the inevitable material, financial and human difficulties in his or her museum – alone. At the moment of recognizing this absurd, costly, and ethically unacceptable reality, PREMA was conceived.

Responding to the situation required more than a course or a project. Borrowing military terminology, ICCROM devised a strategy: 'the art of war; the management of an army or armies in a campaign or; the planning and direction of the larger military movements and overall operations of a campaign'.[1] Since it is not too difficult to think of conservation of cultural heritage as a struggle, ICCROM's response was to plan and direct a campaign ... 'a series of military operations in a definite area or to achieve a particular objective.'[2]

When one is dealing with problems as broad and complex as those in sub-Saharan Africa, a strategy must be conceived in a large, all-encompassing framework that looks beyond single battles. It is essential to develop a strategy in terms of training programs as opposed to simply training projects. It is essential to map such a strategy with *objectives which are quantifiable and with fixed dates*. After all, you are going to want to know when you have achieved your objectives ... and so will your funders.

Attacking the problems

How would we deal with these complex problems? There was no conservation training in Africa, and so we were going to create courses with the universities of

* Author to whom correspondence should be addressed

the Sorbonne and London to defend the profession. There were no conservators to train and so we were going to involve all the existing museum categories to create the vocation. There was no communication between the museums and so we were going to create multinational groups and establish newsletters to ensure follow-up and exchange. There was no guarantee that the trained professionals would stay in the field and so we were going to cultivate patiently the human resources for 14 years to make up for losses and promotions.

There were 'unaware' directors and we were going to involve them in the training and in the development of their personnel and we were to motivate them in safeguarding their collections. There were museums ignored by their communities and we were going to appeal to the media and community leaders to recognize and appreciate them. There were situations that were much more complicated and difficult than academic case studies and we were going to activate and inspire all the teachers and participants from all the involved countries to attack and overcome the real difficulties on-site. We were going to give the collections the care, documentation and environment they needed so that the museums could provide educational and cultural services to the public.

To achieve all this would require abundant expertise and we would look for the collaboration of colleagues in institutions and museums around the globe. It would require the time and effort of at least one generation to prepare the future leaders and actors from that moment. It would require millions of dollars to work all this out but we would find it. It would require a great measure of idealism. We had plenty of that.

It would need a *nom de guerre* and we called it PREMA – *PRE*vention in *M*useums of *A*frica. It would need objectives and we established two:

1. By the year 2000 create a network of African professionals who can assume the responsibility for conservation of movable property and future training; and
2. Ensure the conservation of sub-Saharan African museum collections.

It would need a series of well designed and co-ordinated operations and we defined five annual activities:

1. International University Courses
2. National Courses
3. Regional Seminars for Directors
4. Staff Development Activities
5. Technical Assistance.

Long-term, low-tech, high-sensitivity

Preventive conservation has taught us to think and work comprehensively: collections instead of objects, long-term instead of day-to-day. In that same spirit, PREMA encourages thinking globally instead of individually. While it may be true that the world changes one person at a time, you need to consider all the factors which affect that change or are affected by that change to ensure that it is an enduring change with the greatest possible positive impact. This is especially true in the developing world where training needs are so acute and resources for addressing them are so limited.

PREMA's strategy, in fact, includes courses only as a part of the formula to respond to the assessed needs. Considering what can and does influence the outcome of training, PREMA fashioned a program that integrates five different activities and looks beyond the technical results. PREMA's methodology might be described as long-term, low-tech and high-sensitivity.

PREMA grew with flaws and handicaps. There have been mistakes ranging from selection of participants and training methods to fund-raising and follow-up. From the pilot course in 1986, the program has been in a state of evolution. Continuous evaluation and review, mostly in the form of regular meetings with former participants, teachers, sponsors and collaborators, have consistently contributed ideas and improvements.

Preventing envy

We have learned more from preventive conservation which endeavours to improve the environment, to ensure the welfare of the object. In that same spirit PREMA seeks to ensure the efficiency of the trainee by buffering and reducing the difficulties of her/his environment. What is the working environment which PREMA trainees come from and return to? What motivates them? What type of relationships do they have with their superiors and colleagues? What tools do they have to perform their duties? These questions are relevant to any museum professional. All too often, however, institutes responsible for developing training have not given these questions, or more importantly the answers to these questions, the consideration they deserve. In the case of PREMA, we were compelled to consider the answers as they would heavily condition our approach to training.

Take, for instance, the PREMA participants who successfully completed the first three university-level courses at the ICCROM headquarters in Rome in 1987, 1988 and 1989. Not surprisingly, they were proud of the fact that they had attended a course at a prestigious international organization in Europe which resulted in a university diploma from Paris or London. They had the chance to make contacts with professionals from dozens of other countries. They had acquired skills and knowledge. They felt motivated and empowered. What could possibly impede them from implementing their training? 'Envy: a feeling of discontented or resentful longing aroused by another's better fortune etc.'[3]

We came up with one option to deal with this problem: integrate communications training in the activities. The solution was swiftly, if belatedly, introduced into the university-level course. It now has the same weight as the technical aspects of the course: approximately 60 hours of theory and practicals. The communication course is aimed at easing the re-entry of participants into their environments. Topics such as public speaking, intercultural communications and self-perception are aimed at encouraging teamwork and developing positive attitudes. Subjects like task analysis, writing objectives, visual design and use of teaching aids are meant to develop skills in the participants so that they can share and develop their training with others.

Preventing isolation

Other difficulties that trainees face upon returning to their museums include isolation and a feeling of helplessness. Where do they begin? How can they quickly and effectively demonstrate the benefits of their training? What material tools do they have to complement and support their cognitive skills? One way of dealing with this was by incorporating a program of technical assistance as part of the follow-up. Through the development of conservation projects, trainees and former University Course participants are motivated to maintain continuous contact for at least a full year after the course.

During that time, each participant proposes, develops, plans, budgets (to up to US $1,000), and implements a preventive conservation project in his/her museum. They are encouraged to use local resources and sustainable approaches to solve conservation problems. ICCROM sends the necessary funds or, in exceptional cases, equipment, as soon as the project is formally endorsed by the participant's museum director. Recently completed projects include storage reorganization in Kenya, a staff education workshop on handling and transport in Uganda, construction of storage units and storage space improvement in Nigeria, renewal of infested exhibition structures in Tanzania, and a conservation survey of all national museums in Zimbabwe.

Flexible approach to motivation

Perhaps the most acute barrier to long-term conservation development is the lack of professional recognition and the meagre possibilities for career development which the museum world can offer in Africa. In order to counter such frustration and to contribute to networking, personal opportunities are offered to the most motivated individuals as part of the PREMA 'staff development' component.

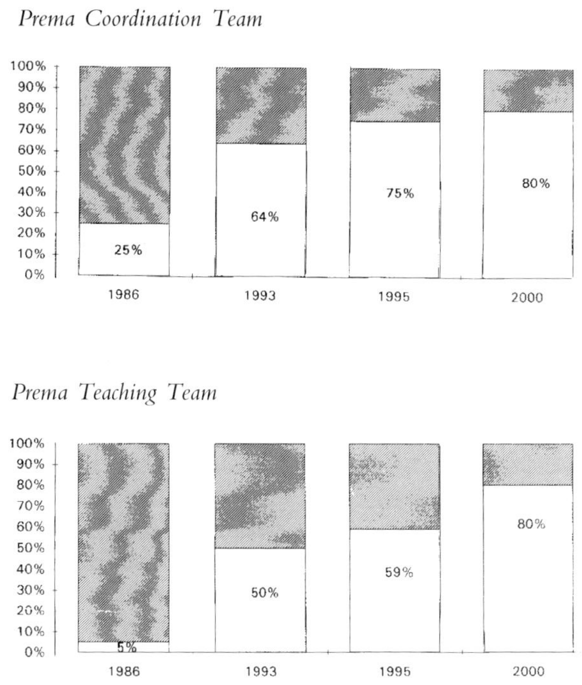

Figure 1. PREMA teams: percentage of African professionals

This component offers possibilities of being re-integrated in the PREMA training activities as assistants, associate teachers, teachers, tutors and co-ordinators. It provides scholarships for participating in international conferences such as ICOM, ICOM-CC and IIC. It encourages specialization through grants for further studies (ranging from language to pest management courses and even post-graduate studies) or, occasionally, internships.[4] As a general rule, a participant can apply or be proposed for these projects only once she or he has spent a full year in her or his museum after completing a PREMA course.

The fact that the staff development component is not too formalized has allowed us to promote individual initiative in a program directed towards institutions. This flexibility has enabled us to create and establish a group of professionals who are gaining the necessary expertise to take over and manage future activities.

In 1986, there was only one African on the PREMA team. In 1994–95 alone, 33 of the African professionals who had completed the University Course took part in the growing number of PREMA activities in teaching or co-ordinating roles in Gabon, Ghana, Madagascar, Senegal and Zimbabwe (Figure 1).

To sustain or not to sustain

Over 300 museum directors, professionals and technicians have now participated in PREMA activities (Table 1). An impressive 90% of the 87 participants on the University Course are still working in the field. How can we ensure that there will be continuity and sustainable improvements after the ten years which ICCROM has engaged to fight the battle? What type of network will be in place? What role can other institutions play? What are the prospects after the year 2000?

One of PREMA's aims is to activate and promote relations between local, regional, and international institutes to ensure continuity. This continuity can only be secured by true collaboration between all partners and beneficiaries. This depends on abundant goodwill on everyone's part but there are also some very practical aspects to be considered:

1. Institutional agreements. PREMA has developed a model agreement for all activities. It sets out the main aspects (management, logistics, education, media, fund-raising) which clearly designates responsibilities for each partner. After

Table 1. PREMA facts and figures.
Ten years of fund-raising efforts and 20 sponsors have resulted in $5,000,000 to develop a network of professionals working in museums in Africa. $1,600,000 are needed to complete the program. The following activities have made it possible to create an active network of more than 300 colleagues working in 46 African Countries.

Seven International Courses (Italy, Nigeria, Ghana)[a]
Six National Courses (Ghana, Côte d'Ivoire, Zambia, Benin, Madagascar, Zimbabwe)[b]
Seven Directors' Seminars (Niger, Zambia, Mali, Nigeria, Madagascar, Gabon, Ghana)
Two Workshops (Italy, Senegal)
Five Newsletters

[a] 95% of the participants have received the diploma; 90% still work in the field.
[b] Nine storage facilities reorganized and one new 200 m^2 storage built.

signing an agreement, regular meetings between partners make it possible to verify the involvement of the partners and to make modifications if necessary.

2. Task definitions for each team member. The responsibilities of each person, whether an ICCROM staff member or a member of a local co-ordination team, must be clearly assigned and written to ensure a sound base for review and modification.
3. Equitable compensation that takes into consideration local circumstances and cost of living. This delicate aspect cannot be ignored. It is all too common for co-operative projects and activities to calculate remuneration without considering the local context (some payments amount to 10–50 times an average salary). This can destroy the sustainability of local projects. On the other hand, it is a mistake to assume that the local partner should be satisfied with only his or her own means for work which exceeds his or her daily work and responsibilities. This may imply a lack of recognition and respect.
4. Open decision-making process. It is important to involve collaborators in planning or at least explain clearly to them the reasons for all major decisions dealing with program content, selection of participants and teachers, calendar, budget evaluation and fund-raising.
5. Division of key responsibilities. Rather than hoarding responsibilities, it is important to share them. The first on-site PREMA activity in 1989 had one non-African co-ordinator. The activities in the following years had one non-African and one African co-ordinator. Since 1994, all on-site co-ordination teams have been entirely made of professionals from the region although outside collaborators may participate briefly. ICCROM supports local teams to analyse problems, find solutions and intervenes directly only when requested.

Past experience shows that, when the transfer of responsibility and activities occurred too brusquely, projects and programs became candidates for failure. It became clear that progressive and planned transfer of responsibilities would empower and motivate a network like PREMA's to develop local capabilities and confidence. Former PREMA participants are steadily taking over a large part of the training and co-ordination. Gradually, they are managing budget planning, accounting and fund raising responsibilities. There are four years left for the program to achieve its objective of having 80% of teaching and co-ordination teams from Africa. This will be one of the key elements to ensure that a sustainable conservation strategy be decided and implemented in Africa.

PREMA beneficiary: the profession as a whole

Through PREMA, ICCROM has been obliged to modify drastically its approach to training in conservation. The problems to solve in Africa were so great and the museums' situations were such that, on one hand, working from scratch made it possible to apprehend the holistic concept of preventive conservation and the range of its practical applications. Consequently, prevention, which was only one topic among many others, has become a fundamental one. On the other hand, this situation forced us to develop and implement a *training strategy*.

PREMA has been beneficial to the participants and African institutes involved. But it has also been beneficial to ICCROM and we hope to the profession as a whole. That is one of the reasons why we think it is important that 20% of the teaching and co-ordination teams continue to be non-African. While electronic communications revolutionize the developed world, human contact will continue to be the main source of exchange of ideas and stimulation both in sub-Saharan Africa and in other parts of the world. For everyone's benefit, let us avoid the creation of a localized professional ghetto in any region of the world.

We would like to recognize our African colleagues because what we initially thought of as a technical battle has turned out to be an extraordinary professional and human experience.

Acknowledgements

Since the launching of PREMA in 1986, nearly US $5,000,000 has been awarded by 20 funding partners. We wish to recognize the important contribution of these partners to the program and to the protection of Africa's cultural heritage:

- International agencies:
  UNESCO, European Union, ACCT (Agence de Coopération Culturelle et Technique)
- Ministries and co-operation agencies:
  Denmark, Finland, France, Italy, Germany, Norway, Netherlands, Sweden, Switzerland, UK, USA
- Foundations:
  Dapper, Elf, Ford, Getty Grant Program, Leventis, Skaggs
- Technical partners:
  Université de Paris – Panthéon-Sorbonne, University of London – External Programme, Canadian Conservation Institute, Museo L. Pigorini, Rome

Notes and References

1. J. Pearsall, B Trumble, *The Oxford English Reference Dictionary* (Oxford: Oxford University Press, 1995), 1428.
2. Ibid., 1428.
3. Ibid., 210.
4. Museum internships are not included in the regular PREMA program as we do not have much faith in their impact. It is only when they are carefully prepared with the hosting institution and only as a complement to a previous education program, that we feel they can be of value.

Conservation Training for Developing Countries: The Hopes and Realities

Colin Pearson
National Centre for Cultural Heritage Science Studies,
University of Canberra, PO Box 1, Belconnen
ACT 2616, Australia

Abstract

The majority of conservators from developing countries are trained overseas. A few conservators are able to get funding to attend a university-level course but most have to rely on short courses. Although trainees are usually enthusiastic and motivated at the completion of their course, in reality very little may have been achieved in the long term. They return home to no conservation support infrastructure, no funds to purchase conservation equipment, materials and books, and within a short time are probably doing very little more that is new than before the course. The strengths and weaknesses of providing conservation training for developing countries are discussed, followed by proposals to make such training more effective in the long term.

Keywords

Conservation, training, developing countries, university, courses

Introduction

Few countries outside of the Western world have their own conservation training courses. This means that conservators in developing countries, such as those in South East Asia and the Pacific, are trained either by attending courses overseas from one to four weeks duration up to a three-year university degree program, or through courses run in their own country. None of these processes is ideal, but understanding the problems can hopefully help conservators get the most out of these courses.

The Conservation of Cultural Materials Training Program at the University of Canberra has been involved with conservation training in South East Asia and the Pacific for over 12 years, and has carried out surveys and run courses in a number of countries in the region. Projects are currently being carried out in Laos, Vietnam, Pohnepei (Federated States of Micronesia) and Malaysia, and the Program is a partner with the International Centre for Conservation in Rome (ICCROM) in the Preventive Conservation in Museums of Oceania project (PREMO).[1] In addition, conservators from Malaysia, Brunei, Fiji, Solomon Islands, New Zealand, South Africa, Canada and the USA have been trained through the University of Canberra regular conservation undergraduate and postgraduate courses. It is hoped that the intake for 1996 will include two students from Africa.

From experience with teaching conservators from a wide range of countries and at different levels, we are aware of some of the problems faced in training conservators in developing countries, and suggest how some of these can be overcome to make the best out of limited resources.

Conservation career-entry level training

It is essential for the development of the conservation profession in any country that conservators are trained through a university level academic course. Unfortunately, many conservators have been trained on short courses, most of which provide relatively little benefit to the conservator (see later). Only by obtaining a recognised university degree will conservators gain employment in a cultural institution, in a government agency or in private practice, at the level necessary for them to have status, responsibility and a salary to perform as professional conservators. In the museum industry conservators are often seen as technicians, not professionals, merely providing a service to curators with little professional input into decisions, policy making and their implementation. Of interest is that the majority of conservators in the USA and Canada are trained through a three-year postgraduate Master's degree on top of a Bachelor's degree with a double major in arts and science. On the other hand, many curators have been employed having only a basic bachelor's degree with no specific training in museum studies. In addition, the majority of postgraduate courses in museum studies are a one-year postgraduate diploma. Therefore, conservators are invariably more highly trained than curators when entering the work force, yet often do not have equivalent status and salary, a situation which is to be deplored.

It is also important that the qualification gained by conservators is recognised by their institution when they return home, and that they are employed at a level and salary commensurate with a university degree. If not, there is danger that the graduate will seek employment elsewhere at a higher salary level. This is unfortunately quite common in developing countries where the museum cannot afford to pay the comparatively high salaries offered in, say, government departments and industry and a person with an overseas degree often has a wide choice of alternative career opportunities.

The "Guidelines for Conservation Teaching",[2] recently proposed at the Interim Meeting of the ICOM Committee for Conservation (ICOM-CC) Working Group on Training in Conservation and Restoration, are to assist teachers in developing, managing and implementing training courses and, although directed specifically at courses which produce a competent, appropriately qualified conservator, the principles can also be applied to short introductory or specialised courses. The Guidelines detail a typical course content to provide the knowledge and skills required of a qualified conservator, some or all of which will be required for the different levels of training offered: introductory; entry to conservation career; mid-career; and specialised. Any course offered should provide a foundation on which the conservator can develop further. These are only guidelines and do not necessarily overcome the problems discussed below.

There are a number of specific problems experienced by overseas students attending university level conservation training courses in other countries.

Duration of the course

Most degree courses require at least three years of full-time study. This is a long time for students from developing countries to be away from home. There is also the cultural shock of living in a different culture and climate, and this is exacerbated if the student has to leave his/her family back at home. If already employed in the conservation field, will there be funds provided for a temporary replacement while the student is away? There are courses shorter than three years, but, if these do not provide a university qualification, then their value will be limited.

Funding

Most overseas students now have to pay tuition fees (in Australia ranging from AUD $10,000–15,000 per annum depending on the course). This is in addition to funds required for travel, accommodation and a living allowance. It may be possible to obtain financial assistance through funding agencies; in Australia this is the Australian Agency for International Development (AusAID). However, there are quota restrictions and, more important, each country will determine its own priorities for overseas training, and cultural heritage is invariably low on this list. Therefore, although each year the University of Canberra offers places to students from developing countries, often they do not turn up.

A special system of funding which does exist in Australia (through AusAID) is the Equity Merit Scheme. Here applicants are judged solely on their own merits, that is, educational background, experience and potential to complete the chosen course, and this does not depend on government priorities. Unfortunately, this is not available in every country in the region.

There are also the international funding bodies such as UNESCO and UNDP, but because of the heavy demand on their funds there is never enough to go round.

Another problem is that if students are not adequately funded then they may have to resort to part-time work to survive. This means that they cannot give all their time to their studies, and this is very important for overseas students who often have language and other study difficulties.

Academic background of the student

Students who apply to enter a degree course must have achieved university-entrance-level standard in their secondary education; otherwise they will probably have many problems coping with the academic level of the course. This can be difficult as academic standards can vary so much from country to country. There is sometimes the temptation to turn a blind eye to these academic requirements and take in overseas students by making a special case for them. In the long term, this may be causing a lot of problems for the students as they can find the course very difficult, sometimes even failing to complete the course and having to return home a failure.

English language

Every overseas student wishing to train in Australia must satisfy English requirements before being allowed to enrol in a course. For students from South East Asia and the Pacific, this test, which is carried out through the Australian Embassy, High Commission or Consulate in each country, is not easy, especially as English will be a second language for students. However, this barrier is essential to ensure that students can cope with lectures and carry out written work etc.. Similar language requirements will apply for entrance to all overseas training courses.

Relevance of conservation training to student's home country

This is probably the most important aspect of training overseas students – the relevance to their own country of conservation training received in another country. It can be argued, and rightly so, that it is better if overseas conservators are trained in their own country, with their own collections, with their own special problems, and using their own facilities. Unfortunately this is not possible for most of the developing countries.

In order to offer training that is relevant to overseas students, the course will need to be carefully planned taking into account the cultural diversity of their backgrounds. For example, the region of South East Asia contains a vast array of religions, beliefs and cultural values, and a thorough understanding of these cultures will be fundamental to producing a course that is both comprehensible and comprehensive. The ethics and philosophy of conservation can also vary from country to country and must be discussed in detail.[3] To be of lasting value to the students, the course will also need a substantive practical component that must be relevant to local experience and values. Only then can it be considered a useful course. The question is, do we have the knowledge, expertise and facilities to offer this form of training? ICCROM is now providing training courses for teachers and is addressing the above concerns in particular.

On a related issue, at the University of Canberra we have found problems simply with our approach to teaching. Some students will have come from countries in the region where culturally you just do not question the statements/teachings of your elders, especially your teachers. University professors are seen as being infallible – all they say must be true. The same applies to the written word. If the author is a world authority in a conservation discipline, who are students to question his or her words? This makes it very difficult for such students to evaluate critically the conservation literature, for example. Plagiarism is not seen as being wrong, in that quoting a source word for word is in fact a compliment to the writer. One also cannot criticise an authority. These problems have to be overcome if we are to produce well-trained, lateral-thinking and questioning conservators.

Conservation techniques used for treating a wide range of works of art and artefacts do not vary significantly according to the country of origin of the object. Obviously materials and techniques of fabrication of the object may be different, but the subsequent deterioration and conservation processes, being basically chemical or physical in nature, can often apply across a wide range of objects from different countries and cultures. However, as mentioned earlier, it is necessary to understand the ethical and philosophical approach to conservation in each country and these must be discussed. It is also important to look at the cultural use and context of objects and collections.[4]

In Australia we encourage overseas students to bring with them objects from their own country, or we provide such objects from Australian museums. We can then train students to work on their own material, and at the same time this becomes an educational process for fellow students. Also, in the third year of the degree program, students carry out a conservation project, and overseas students are encouraged to study a problem relevant to their country. For example, a student from Malaysia studied the effectiveness of Malaysian fungicides (i.e. those available in Malaysia) in the treatment of mould growth on Malaysian wooden artefacts.

Another problem arises when the student returns home after completing their course. What is the availability in the student's home country of equipment, materials, chemicals and conservation literature, used in the overseas conservation training course? The purchase from overseas of such supplies, as well as books and journals, can be difficult owing to currency exchange problems. There may also be high import duties. What alternative materials/chemicals are there? Are they good substitutes or poor substitutes? So, if materials and facilities are not available, will graduates be able to do any conservation work when they get back home? In Australia our universities and conservation laboratories are large and well staffed and equipped, and are on a completely different scale to those elsewhere in South East Asia and the Pacific. Should we therefore be running courses, teaching techniques and processes which are directed according to the availability of equipment and materials etc., in the student's home country? It is not easy to train conservators from other countries so that they are capable of performing at a professional level on returning home. Close contact needs to be kept with students over the first two years to help them get established. Follow-up surveys need to be carried out to determine the effectiveness of training received by overseas students graduating from university courses. If these have been carried out it would be useful to publish the results and, in particular, the processes being used to rectify any problems.

Short courses

It will be found that the majority of training received by conservators from South East Asia and the Pacific is through short courses, particularly from countries such as Italy (ICCROM), India (NRLC, Lucknow) and Thailand (SEAMEO Project in Archaeology and Fine Arts). These courses can be up to six months in duration (apart from the year-long PREMA course run by ICCROM), but are normally only two to four weeks long. They are obviously very limited in what they can achieve, particularly as they probably have 15–20 participants from six or more different countries. Such courses usually only provide training at a very basic level, although there is now a move to offer professional development workshops at an advanced level.

Some of the problems with short courses are as follows.

Relevance of the course

A person trained, for example, in stone conservation in a course overseas, returns home, and is then the "expert" on stone conservation. This is irrespective of the fact that the course was probably only of four weeks duration and the training they received was in the conservation of marble when their own problems are with sandstone. In some instances the "trained conservator" is then also expected to be an authority in other fields of conservation.

Concentration on practice rather than theory

"A little learning is a dangerous thing" is particularly applicable to conservation. Short courses tend to concentrate on the practice rather than the theory of conservation. So the emphasis is how to do it rather than on why, and on what is actually happening during the doing. On returning home, the conservator is very limited in what he or she can do. Some (probably fortunately) do nothing, whereas others may be over-confident and have the potential to do a lot of harm to collections.

Certificates of attendance

For short courses it is usual to award certificates of attendance. This can be required by the participant's employer or sponsor. Unfortunately, these certificates of attendance are often used for much more than they were intended, to infer that a certain standard of conservation has been achieved. This is not only dangerous but unethical.[3] A participant may not have understood what was being taught, or may have hardly participated in, say, practical work, but they still receive the certificate of attendance. This in fact means nothing. If a certificate is to be awarded, it should be only following formal assessment of the participant at the end of the course. This certificate will then have some meaning. If certificates of attendance are required by employers, then the certificates should detail the content and level of the course, any form of assessment carried out and whether the participant attended all sessions of the course.

Follow-up

A major problem with short courses is: what happens at the end of the course? Students are usually enthusiastic and motivated, but then go back home and invariably nothing changes. As mentioned earlier, they may not have the equipment and materials to carry out the conservation work learnt in the course. What happens if they come across a problem? Who do they turn to? There is the important need for follow-up to each training course to determine its effectiveness and to assist the participants in using the skills acquired in the course. Unfortunately, follow-ups rarely take place because of the costs and the logistics of visiting all the participants of the course.

Most short courses are only at a basic level – if not, they should be, because of the problems raised above. There is the need, however, for professional development workshops to provide advanced training in a specific field of conservation. Here it is essential that the participants have already reached an acceptable professional standard before being admitted into the course.

An alternative means of training by short courses is for a consultant to be appointed to run a course for a particular cultural institution, government agency or educational institution in that country. By this means a number of local conservators can be trained at the same time. This will remove the problems of producing the single "expert", and also conservators will normally be trained using local facilities and equipment and locally available supplies, and, most importantly, on local collections and their problems. It does mean, however, that the consultant must be well prepared and also knowledgeable about the collections and conservation problems of that country. There are also language difficulties and, from experience in Indonesia and Vietnam, it is very trying to have to lecture for two weeks through a translator. The level of effectiveness is about one third of that if the teacher and students speak the same language. This is compounded by the lack of conservation literature in the languages of developing countries and, although efforts are being made through organisations such as ICCROM, UNESCO and ICOM, only the major languages of the world are being covered.

Collaboration in conservation training

There are developments nationally and internationally to improve the level of conservation training, especially in developing countries. ICCROM in particular is a leader in this field. There are, however, problems with the co-ordination of training activities, avoidance of duplication and the maximisation of scarce resources of finance and expertise.

There are too many instances of, for example, a course on the conservation of textiles being provided for a developing country by one agency, only for a different agency to offer a similar course just a few weeks later. In one case, only by chance was it found out that two training courses for conservators in Cambodia were being held at the same time, one at the National Museum and the other across the road at the University. Why was this? Rarely will the host country complain as they will be receiving free training, and the more the better.

At the international level it is necessary for organisations such as UNESCO and ICCROM to communicate and co-ordinate conservation training programs, not only with each other but also with those institutions/countries providing aid in the region, and these are well documented. The problem is that there is no formal process, so everything is done on an *ad hoc* basis. How can this be improved?

In Australia, in order to provide the best preservation and conservation assistance to developing countries in the South East Asia and Pacific regions, an informal group has been established called "Australian Preservation and Conservation Abroad" (APACA). It is managed through the National Preservation Office of the National Library of Australia in Canberra. It holds regular meetings – basically an exchange of information – and is linked through its membership with organisations such as ICOM, ICOMOS, UNESCO, ICCROM and relevant Australian Government Departments. An important publication from APACA is the *Survey of Australian Heritage Preservation & Conservation Assistance & Related Activities in the Asia-Pacific Region 1984–94*.[5] This provides details of over 80 conservation projects, the majority of which have taken place over the past four years.

An important Australian Government initiative was launched in 1995 by the Department of Communications and the Arts. Known as AusHeritage, it is a national network to develop opportunities for earning export income from the international application of Australian expertise in caring for heritage. Although set up primarily to provide a fee for service, and still in its development stage, it is anticipated that AusHeritage will play a co-ordinating role in heritage preservation activities in the South East Asia and Pacific regions. It has just funded a series of pilot projects to demonstrate the potential for the export of Australia's cultural heritage industry.

Conclusions

Conservation of cultural material is a small profession, and, being part of the wider cultural heritage field which invariably has low government priority, it will be many years, if ever, before conservation training programs are established in many of the developing countries. In the meantime it will be necessary to use existing overseas training courses or bring in overseas experts to provide education and training in each country. It is also necessary to communicate and co-ordinate such activities in order to maximise the use of the scarce resources available. This is not an ideal situation, but if the problems involved are understood and remedial action taken, it should be possible to organise courses and select participants so that the best possible results can be achieved. The goal in the long term should be to raise the standard of conservation world-wide to an acceptable professional level.

References

1. N. Putt, "PREMO 1994–1998: Heritage Preservation in the Pacific Island States, Programme and Budget" (ICCROM, January 1995).
2. C. Pearson, R. Ferguson, "A Proposal for Guidelines for Conservation Teaching", in J.M. Cronyn, K. Foley (eds), *A Qualified Community: Towards Internationally Agreed Standards of Qualification for Conservation* (Proceedings of the ICOM-CC Training Working Group Interim Meeting, April 1995) (London: English Heritage/MGC, 1996).
3. C. Pearson, "Codes of Ethics for Conservation Practice", *in Study Series, Committee for Conservation (ICOM-CC)* (ICOM, 1995), 18–20.
4. M. Clavir, "An Examination of the Conservation Codes of Ethics in Relation to Collections of First Peoples", in *First Peoples Art and Artefacts: Heritage and Conservation Issues* (Art Conservation Training Programs 18th Annual Conference, Kingston, Ontario, 1992), 1–9.
5. P. Petherbridge, P. Wilson, *Survey of Australian Heritage Preservation & Conservation Assistance & Related Activities in the Asia-Pacific Region, 1984–94* (APACA, National Library of Australia, 1995).

Conservation Training: The Pacific Islands' Priorities

Neal Putt
ICCROM,
13 Via di San Michele, 00153 Rome, Italy

Abstract

In 1993, conservators from ICCROM and the University of Canberra met with Pacific museum directors to plan a conservation program for the Pacific island states. The PREMO 1994–1998 program is unique compared to ICCROM's experience in other world regions, because it is designed to adapt to the unique geographical, cultural and museological context of the region. In adapting to the context, training programs have been produced that are unfamiliar to funding agencies and colleagues. This is also likely to occur in other world regions, in the future. It is necessary for conservators to make a strong case linking their training programs to the local context.

Keywords

Ethics, Pacific island states, preventive conservation, public awareness, training

Introduction

The geographic, cultural, and economic context of each nation requires that the practice of conservation differs from place to place. This is not just a question of adapting to changes in climate or supplies, but includes adapting to differences in ethics and goals of museums. To suit the practice of conservation, training must also vary from place to place.

Museum directors and conservators have prepared a conservation development program, including training, for the Pacific islands region. Conservators must be able to explain how the Pacific context justifies the "unusual" aspects of the conservation training program, in order to succeed in gaining professional support and funding. The same would be true of any changes in conservation training to suit a local context.

The Pacific – isolated museums in isolated states

The 22 Pacific island states are scattered over a sea area of 60 million km^2, roughly the size of North and South America combined, with islands forming only 1% of the total area. The government structures and economies of these states are still developing – 16 states have become self-governing since 1962. The typical museum is a relatively new institution, with a very small population to call on for support – all but four of the 22 states have under 250,000 citizens, ranging down to the smallest self-governing state of 2,500 citizens.

Each island state usually has one museum, so museum professionals are extremely isolated. A typical island state museum is 1,000 km from the nearest museum in the next state. The average airfare to attend an international event in the region is US $2,000, and a museum worker could require one week for all the flights to get there. There is not yet a museums association for the region.

The government ministry responsible for a museum may not offer much support, since it usually does not include heritage professionals on its staff. A museum is invariably a small part of a ministry responsible for education, tourism, women's affairs or even aviation. Government attitude to the museum can be ambivalent, as a result of needs for expenditures in health care, education, and economic development.

Social role of museums, mixed roles of professionals

Part of the role of museums is helping to define the identity of the 22 complex island states. This is difficult, since each state includes many subcultures, ranging from very traditional to highly modern. For example, the Republic of Vanuatu counts 105 languages among its population of 170,000.[1] As many as four colonial powers may have dominated each state, and new community members continue to arrive from all parts of the world.

The weakness of the island economies has required some of the highest foreign aid rates in the world. Economic growth in forestry, mining, tourism and fisheries is rapid. The results include environmental damage, urbanization, loss of historic sites, sacred sites, languages and traditions. Some cultures are at risk of disappearance. In this context, the first priority of museums is to offer services which preserve and strengthen living cultures.

To suit the priority of preserving living culture, the concept of "museum" is changing dramatically from the original model provided by colonial museums. In many cases the museum staff are responsible for a complex of services under one roof, including a library, archives, cultural centre, art gallery, crafts shop or audio/video service. Programs to preserve songs, dance, ceremonies, and oral traditions are common. Some museums and cultural centres put great emphasis on promoting tourism and craft sales, sometimes acting as a buffer between traditional cultures and tourists. Many museums include programs to preserve traditional skills, such as canoe building, and many others put great emphasis on organizing national constitutional celebrations and cultural competitions.[2] Still others advocate broad social objectives, such as combatting racial conflict, rural–urban disharmony, or environmental damage.

In some cases there is no acceptance of the idea of a museum among citizens, and no support from government. Some island states instead continue traditional methods of heritage preservation.

Unique collections and causes of damage

To support their services for living cultures, each museum or cultural centre is slowly building its collections and displays. The average collection has about 3,500 artifacts.[3] Museum staff and the communities place especially high significance on collections of ethnographic materials and documentation of disappearing cultures. Museums report that new collections of photographs, films and videotapes, used to record living cultures, are the largest part of their collection. The huge majority of collections of artifacts from the Pacific islands are found not in the island museums, but in those of Europe and the Pacific rim. Should these collections ever be repatriated, the types and volume of conservation problems will change drastically.

Pacific islands museum directors are aware of the damaged caused to their collections by the hot humid climates of the region, and they want to do something about it. Sixty per cent of museum directors report that their collections are being damaged by high temperature and mold, 80% report damage by high humidity, and 95% report damage from insects. Directors report that wood, bark and photographs are the collections suffering the most damage. Directors are also keenly aware that the Pacific is the genesis of cyclones, and virtually every museum will be subject to a cyclone once every ten years. Some museums have been severely damaged on more than one occasion.

The care of the collection competes with other tasks for attention. In the 22 island states only one museum has a trained conservator. Apart from cleaning and security staff, the average museum has five professionals, who share and overlap many duties. It is rare to find a staff member whose main duty is collections care.

Planning a conservation program for the Pacific

In 1991–92, conservators from ICCROM and the University of Canberra completed a conservation needs assessment of the museums, cultural centres and responsible ministries in the Pacific islands.[4] This was followed up by a meeting in 1993 of two conservators from the needs assessment team with seven museum directors from the island states to plan a conservation program for the region. The meeting was hosted by the Belau National Museum and the Government of Palau.

In spite of their interest in preserving their collections, the museum directors maintained their priority for preserving and strengthening living cultures. Directors also felt pressure to strengthen community and political support for their museums. They wanted a program which would publicly validate investments in the conservation of collections, with the incidental benefit of increasing support for growth of collections and the entire museum.

In programs in other regions, ICCROM had found a number of professionals who had responsibility for conservation as primary job duty. The usual response of ICCROM had been to train the conservation professionals and provide back-up advisory and information services. But in the Pacific the "conservators" could also be the curators, the museum directors, the site managers, as well as several other "staff positions".

Conservation training had to complement the other duties that are part of every museum staff member's job, and help overcome the isolation of professionals in the region. Without adjusting to the context and developing long-term support for conservation, conservation training would be irrelevant, or would waste away.

A framework for training and supporting development

The Palau meeting worked out a framework for a conservation program, called PREMO 1994–1998: Heritage Preservation in the Pacific Island States.[5]

In view of the context, the fundamental objective of PREMO 1994–1998 is to establish a sustainable network of professionals, able to lead the conservation of cultural property in the Pacific island states. The second objective is to improve the conservation of museum collections. The activities to achieve these objectives have training at their core, but around the core of training courses there are two other groups of activities which develop a network of professionals, and create awareness and support for conservation. The activities include:

Network development

- Fax network
- Newsletter
- Electronic mail
- Database of heritage professionals
- Development of a Pacific islands museums association
- Fund-raising

Practical courses

- 1994 – Preservation of Heritage Records in the Pacific Island States, New Caledonia
- 1996 – Preservation of Pacific Heritage Sites, Federated States of Micronesia
- 1997 – Introduction to Preventive Conservation
- 1998 – Preventive Conservation Management

Awareness

- Children's poster competition (in conjunction with UNESCO Office for the Pacific States)
- Radio, press, TV coverage of PREMO events
- Public events, living culture events
- Government advocacy

To start up co-ordination of all activities, the Palau meeting recommended the creation of a Regional Board of six key museum professionals in the region. The Board would also give overall guidance and direction. ICCROM and the University of Canberra have been the two leading "outside" institutions supporting the co-ordination of PREMO 1994–1998.[6] UNESCO, especially through its "Vaka Moana" program for Pacific heritage preservation and development, is also providing strong support.

Training at the core of the conservation development program

At the world-wide level, more and more training programs focus on conservation as a specialty, culminating in multi-year university-level specialist programs. Even ICCROM would rarely have a course as short as one month, most courses lasting three to nine months. The training planned by the PREMO participants and conservators is different, and it has been challenging to explain it to other conservators and funding agencies.

To begin, conservation training is limited to preventive conservation. Solutions to treatment problems must come later, after establishing a sound regional network and a strong foothold in preventive conservation at specific museums.

Given the budgets and priorities of museums, there is little likelihood of adding conservators in the region at present. Training, therefore, is for heritage professionals who are now at work – those who have multiple responsibilities. To suit the non-specialist audience, the Palau meeting recommended short courses of about two weeks. The short length also ensures that each museum staff corps is not depleted by the long absence of a key staff member; the length also adjusts to the needs of staff who find it difficult to be away from their community and culture for long periods. Each course includes participants from previous courses, as each course builds on the previous one.

Topics are chosen for conservation motives, and to complement other museum programs and aims. From the point of view of ICCROM, this sometimes leads us into unusual topics. The first PREMO course, which was also the first ever conservation course planned for all museums in the region, was on preserving photographs, audio-tapes and video-tapes (the course was held in Noumea, New Caledonia in 1994).[7] The topic, rather than a "general introduction to preventive conservation", demonstrated immediately the relevance of preventive conservation. Since recording media are often the largest parts of museum collections and there is public recognition of their value for documenting disappearing cultures, the course attracted wide professional and public attention. It conveyed the value of museum collections, the threats to their existence, and the principles of preventive conservation. It was highly successful in leading to plans for further courses in preventive conservation. The course evaluations also indicated that participants planned significant improvements in preventive conservation of recording media as a result of the course.

The training curricula of the short courses include basic preventive conservation principles and methods, adapted slightly to the islands' climatic and economic context. Training also touches on a number of aspects supporting each topic. A wide variety of professionals find conservation as a common ground and develop support skills necessary to successfully implement preventive conservation and even other museum objectives. The supporting topics include collections management, public awareness of conservation, fund-raising and development of government legislation. Disaster preparedness is included in every conservation course. Teaching techniques include participants' preparation of point-by-point plans to improve preventive conservation of their collections.

The short PREMO training events allow regular and relatively frequent scheduling, gradually moving from nation to nation among the three major subregions of the Pacific (Micronesia, Melanesia and Polynesia).

Training as a focus for network-building

Training events are at the core of the PREMO activities, but they would fail to achieve preventive conservation without awareness and network-building activities to support the museum staff members.

The training events themselves are one of the most important network-building tools. The repetition of events in many different nations allows vital face-to-face meetings, exploration of new museums, and exchange of ideas. It also ensures that a number of nations develop the skills of planning, funding, and co-ordinating training events, which will serve conservation development in the future. National hosts for training courses raise funds, handle most logistics, and take an active role in defining course objectives and selecting instructors. ICCROM provides advice and co-ordinating assistance.

Course participants are selected not only on professional criteria, but also for their commitment to developing the regional network. The aim for each course is to have at least one participant from each of ten different nations to distribute the network-building effect as much as possible.

Conservation instructors are chosen for their professional expertise, but are also chosen from those institutions which favor ongoing networking between the instructors and participants.

Since there is no regional museums association, the Palau meeting recommended that PREMO 1994–1998 work towards one. There are not enough conservation specialists to form a "conservation association". In 1994, the UNESCO

Office for the Pacific States organized a regional museums meeting which created a Committee for The Pacific Islands Museums Association (PIMA). The committee is now drafting a constitution and proposals for membership.[8,9] PIMA may be a future co-ordinator for basic conservation training and will certainly be the most important networking organization for conservation workers, after PREMO 1994–1998. The membership of the Committee for PIMA and the PREMO Regional Coordinating Board overlap.

PREMO 1994–1998, supported by the Committee for PIMA, is already using a newsletter to activate the network of heritage professionals responsible for preventive conservation. The Fiji Museum has agreed to publish the next two issues of the newsletter. ICCROM has meanwhile published a PREMO directory of 250 heritage professionals and institutions active in the Pacific islands region.

Since mail can take two to three months between museums, PREMO 1994–1998 also includes the PEPPERLEAF VINE fax network. This is a system of fax numbers in which nine key individuals join in sending faxes to all island states and key professionals elsewhere, to give news reports, co-ordinate events and make announcements. ICCROM is also promoting the potential and exploring possibilities of e-mail in the region.

Training as the core of awareness activities

The PREMO awareness activities are based on training events as "hooks" to attract public and government support for conservation. The 1994 course held in Noumea, the capital of the French territory of New Caledonia, is a good example.[10]

The Kanak community and the Government of France in New Caledonia combined to open the course. Observers from all New Caledonia heritage institutions and departments attended. News releases stressed the gathering of highly qualified professionals, the value of audio-visual collections, the threats to their preservation, and preventive conservation. The result was a total of 18 news stories, in various media, in three nations.

The Musée Territorial de Nouvelle Calédonie also linked the PREMO course to an additional public event to increase knowledge of the role of the museum. At the closing of the conservation course, Kanak elders led a ceremony to celebrate the chiefly lineage of the traditional residents of the capital city area of New Caledonia. Some of the musical instruments used had been revived by reconstruction from archives and museum evidence. This truly remarkable event managed to link preservation of living cultures with preventive conservation, while at the same time increasing public use and support of the museum. The ceremony had not been conducted in the capital city in living memory, and 200 people attended.

Conclusion

Because of the interdisciplinary work of museum professionals in the Pacific region, the borders between conservation and other museum disciplines are blurred. When training the staff member who implements preventive conservation, we could also be dealing with the fund-raising officer and cultural events co-ordinator, all in one person. The mixture of staff responsibilities is a reality to which conservation training can be suitably adjusted. The museum can then benefit from conservation training not just for conservation objectives, but for other priorities. Planning, public awareness and other topics included in conservation training provide skills useful in other museum tasks. The networking and awareness activities of PREMO 1994–1998, which are essential for the implementation of conservation, support the entire museum and its role in the community. The museums which participate in training build both knowledge and support for this implementation.

The entire package is a sensible approach to the context of the Pacific, but it is one that may look unfamiliar to conservators and funding agencies not used to this region. The training methods necessary for the Pacific need to be explained carefully, making it clear that conservation remains the focus and that supporting topics are both necessary and appropriately handled.

Conservation training for every region has to be adjusted to geographic, cultural and economic variation. The Pacific islands example of this is very clear. It also shows how conservation trainers can use imaginative methods to support museums as a whole, without sacrificing conservation objectives.

Acknowledgements

I would like to thank the directors and staff of the Pacific island museums, who have provided guidance and direction for PREMO 1994–1998. I would also like to acknowledge Margaret McCord and Colin Pearson, the two conservators who attended the Palau planning meeting for PREMO 1994–1998. The L.J. and Mary C. Skaggs Foundation, The Getty Grant Program, UNESCO (Cultural Heritage Division and World Heritage Committee), and the Government of France have provided financial support towards PREMO 1994–1998.

References

1. Anon. "Keeping the language alive," *Pacific Islands Monthly* 58, no. 5 (1988): 14–15.
2. *PREMO 1994–1998 An Informal Newsletter* 1, no. 1 (1994).
3. C. Antomarchi, M. McCord, B. Johnson, C. Pearson, "PREMO Evaluation Mission November 1991–January 1992 Interim Report" (Unpublished report, ICCROM and the University of Canberra, 1992).
4. Antomarchi *et al.* "PREMO evaluation."
5. "PREMO 1993" (Unpublished report, ICCROM and the University of Canberra, 1994).
6. "PREMO 1994–1998: Heritage Preservation in the Pacific Island States, Programme and Budget" (Unpublished report, Regional Coordinating Board of PREMO 1994–1998 and ICCROM, 1995).
7. *PREMO 1994–1998 An Informal Newsletter* 1, no. 1 (1994).
8. "Resolutions of the Pacific Islands Museum Directors Meeting, 'Living Museums with Grassroots Support', Suva, Fiji, November 30, 1994" (Unpublished report, UNESCO Office for the Pacific States, Apia, Western Samoa).
9. "Draft Minutes of PIMA/PREMO Meeting in Vanuatu Coinciding with the Unesco Museum Curators' Workshop from 26-28 July, 1995" (Unpublished report, Regional Coordinating Board of PREMO).
10. *PREMO 1994–1998 An Informal Newsletter* 1, no. 1 (1994).

The Education and Training of Art Conservators: Teaching the Triptych of Practice, History and Science

Joyce Hill Stoner
Winterthur/University of Delaware Program in Art Conservation,
303 Old College, University of Delaware, Newark,
DE 19716-2515, USA

Abstract

Surveys approaches to the teaching of studio skills, connoisseurship, and science based on published literature, a questionnaire received from 24 conservation programs internationally, and observations made on site at the Winterthur/University of Delaware program. Some skills can be taught, and other attributes, such as commitment, enthusiasm, honesty, a sense of respect and responsibility, a compatible temperament, problem-solving skills, intelligence, and academic ability, must be inherent. A combination of a one-on-one apprenticeship and study in an academic environment is considered ideal.

Keywords

Conservation education, apprenticeship, international training, studio skills, connoisseurship

In 1994, I was asked to prepare a chapter on international conservation training for a book on the restoration of paintings and sculpture. To counter my North American bias in preparing this chapter, I sent a questionnaire on educational concerns to 42 programs in Europe, South America, and North America listed in the 1990 ICCROM *Bibliography: Theses, Dissertations, Research Reports in Conservation*;[1] I received detailed responses from 24 programs representing 15 countries. Most respondents reinforced the idea of the triptych approach to conservation – studio skills, art history and material culture, and scientific ability – in both the attributes of the applicants and the approach of the teaching. My chapter was concerned primarily with the training of paintings conservators, but I received thoughtful responses from a spectrum of conservation disciplines. This paper will therefore discuss concerns related to all specialties.

Selecting among the applicants

What are the ideal characteristics of conservators? In my opinion, model conservators are visibly engaged in front of works of art or cultural heritage, possibly because of an effective passage of brushwork or carving (an aesthetic observation) or possibly because of the window opened onto a past society through the discovery of the meaning of a small detail in a tapestry or bookplate (a historical clue). They are never cavalier or indifferent regarding delicate procedures, as they are aware that the life of the work is potentially at risk while in their hands. Aware of this responsibility, they will be life-long learners who constantly challenge past methods, albeit politely and with loyalty to their mentors even as they may surpass them. They collaborate. One may have a scientific bent, but has learned to share observations with a colleague who has a photographic visual memory or a scholarly background in art history. They are humble enough to ask for assistance when needed but brave enough to express conviction and shoulder responsibility. They know they can never know all that should be known in order to design a treatment for every work they will encounter in the future, so they must build sturdy and lasting bridges to scientists and art historians or anthropologists. They are aware of their responsibilities to the community, including the conservation profession, partner disciplines, and the public. They are culturally omniverous and rarely bored; they are interested in music, theatre, literature, cooking, gardening, or movies, as well as the latest museum exhibition or new ways to take a sample or texture a fill. And it should go almost without saying that they are intelligent, patient, dedicated, careful, and very, very good with their hands.

Figure 1. Dr Joyce Hill Stoner and Wendy Samet discuss comparative visual material with student Mark Lewis during his treatment

Some skills can be taught in a training program, but certain abilities must be innate. One senior conservator told me, only partly in jest, that our program accepts excellent people and then doesn't hurt them very much. Our faculty realizes that the admissions procedures are crucial. We are lucky in the USA to have an excellent pool of applicants and stringent prerequisites. Our Delaware program receives almost 500 inquiries annually regarding the requirements and about 100 formal, paid applications from which we interview 24 and accept ten. All four current North American graduate fine arts programs require essentially a "triple major" of precisely specified coursework in general and organic chemistry, studio arts and crafts, and art history or anthropology. Graduate Record Examinations

(GRE) or Tests of English as a Foreign Language (TOEFL) are required by most US universities and provide a standard academic performance measure that cuts across varying baccalaureate grading systems. I have found our students with high GRE scores to be unphased by academic challenges, to be rapid learners of connoisseurship principles, eager for additional problem-solving challenges, and likely to go on to leadership positions.

In my questionnaire to international conservation training programs, I inquired what others considered to be key traits for successful conservation students. Many felt that most conservation skills could be taught, but that commitment, enthusiasm, honesty, a sense of respect and responsibility, a compatible temperament, problem-solving skills, "taste for perfection," artistic talent, an eye for color, an ability to record observations accurately, intelligence, and academic ability must be inborn. Opinion was divided regarding patience, an open mind, hand–eye skills, inpainting, and connoisseurship; some thought these abilities must be inherent, others felt they could be taught in the conservation courses. Special mention was also made of the importance of speaking and writing abilities, foreign languages, maturity, structured thinking, and a realistic outlook. Caroline Keck, a pioneer educator involved with founding or advising all three US programs, believes that anything can be taught to malleable students; she focused instead on building up a diverse "team" of students with balanced genders, ages, and specialties to facilitate the teaching.[2]

How are the innate abilities judged? Some European programs require applicants to pass entrance examinations in painting, sculpture, history of art, chemistry, and physics. Some North American programs use color matching, color blindness, and dexterity tests. We have a still-life drawing test which serves as our standardized test for hand-eye-coordination; some students who have earned high grades in studio coursework are not actually able to draw well. Being able to see drawings of precisely the same subject by each applicant is helpful for the admissions committee deliberations. However, poor results in a drawing test may be outweighed by other positive attributes. Helmut Ruhemann described his test for the "flair and intelligence" he felt were prerequisites for a conservator:

> I have 32 x-ray photographs, 16 of them from original Van Goghs and 16 from the forgeries made after these. I shuffle them together like a pack of cards and the candidate has to put the originals in one row and the imitations in another.[3]

Several North American educators note judging applicants by the respect with which they handle their own works of art in addition to how they demonstrate respect for works by known artists. Some conservation programs require previous conservation treatment experience and letters of recommendation from the supervising conservators; the tradition of volunteering in museum conservation departments goes back to the early days of this century. Our program formally requires 400 hours of supervised conservation experience before we will interview a candidate. The requirement has a two-fold purpose aiding both the applicant and the program. First, by working for many hours scraping glue or inpainting, the applicants have probably discovered whether they have the appropriate patience and powers of concentration to spend a lifetime career at the easel or bench. Second, the letters from the supervising conservators tell our admissions committee members information that could never be apparent in an academic transcript or a GRE score – that the candidate is suited to the field and has many of the personality characteristics listed above including the eye, the hand, the mind, and the heart with the potential for fine tuning.

Methods of teaching the conservation triptych

The traditionally accepted triptych of conservation – practice, art or cultural history, and science, also called the "three-legged stool" by George L. Stout,[4] one of the Fogg Art Museum pioneers – survives as a foundation for most international conservation programs. Each of the three areas represents branches of knowledge normally kept distinct in most universities: the applied arts, the humanities, and the natural sciences. Each of the three areas has a significant academic tradition which must be taught and can be assessed by tests, papers, and practical activities, as has been traditional in the academic world. Yet each of the three areas also has more illusive components involving judgment, taste, talent, attitude, integrity, Ruhemann's "flair," sensitivity, intuition, and problem-solving abilities which must also be taught or at least refined, and are more difficult to assess with traditional academic methods.

The international programs vary with regard to academic level, content, and duration. There are now about at least 100 programs a year in duration in over 30 countries to train practicing conservators of moveable works of art or cultural heritage. Most last between two and six years, and many award a Master's degree, although some programs are carried out on the baccalaureate level. The Repin Art Institute of the Russian Academy of Fine Arts admits 19-year-old students, and our program admits applicants in their twenties, thirties, and even forties. Time spent on practical work reported by 24 questionnaire respondents varied from 20 to 75%; most at about 40–50%. Some respondents divided their response by years; in the first years there are generally more lecture presentations regarding theory and in the final years more supervised practical work. Time spent carrying out library or scientific research ranged from 12 to 35% and time spent writing reports or papers ranged from 1 to 20% of the allotted program time. Programs in Russia and Poland reported that 25 to 40% of their students' time was spent in drawing, painting, and copying classes. In contrast, one North American program director noted the importance of training conservators who are not "hands on."

How do you learn or teach artistic sensitivity? The Hamilton Kerr Institute, according to articles by Norman Brommelle, Herbert Lank, and Ian McClure,[5] incorporates constant looking at high-quality paintings into a formal training program that combines the strengths of practical apprenticeship to an established restorer with more formally organized academic training. Over three years, the content of this Certificate Course is approximately 75% practical work. Connoisseurship is conscientiously taught through discussing aspects of the painting at the easel, encouraging appropriate art historians and curators to visit and comment, and requiring comparative evaluations (*e.g.* looking at other versions of a painting and examining pictures by the same artist in better or worse condition). In the third year, each student makes a copy of a painting from the Fitzwilliam Museum.

> In making the copy the student must examine the condition and technique of the original work, carry out necessary conservation work and undertake, where possible, sufficient scientific analysis to determine the artists' materials. The copy is, therefore, a reconstruction of the original rather than an imitation of the present surface appearance, and gives insight into the artists' working methods and materials and often demonstrates the degree of change that occurs both through changes to the original materials and as a result of restoration treatment in the past.[6]

Ideally, each applicant to any program has gone to art galleries since childhood and has a passion for the visual arts. Ian McClure, Director of the Hamilton Kerr Institute, notes:

> I had a father who was very interested in paintings and I visited many galleries with him as a child (not always willingly). I have always been interested in painting and was lucky when taught art history to be taught by someone who encouraged examination of real objects rather than photographs. I also developed a strong sense of the structure of things, again helped by a conservation and techniques course in the art history program of Edinburgh.[7]

Constant looking should be accompanied by a background in academic art history or anthropology to ensure wide knowledge of periods, cultures, history, and styles.

Conservators need to know basic general and organic chemistry, and they must be problem solvers. They must understand the materials of art objects and their alteration. They must understand the products and techniques they choose to use during a treatment. Gilbert Delcroix of the Institute Français de Restauration des Oeuvres d'Art notes that scientific reasoning "is a way to exercise a logical, objective, analytical and critical thought which will lead the restorer to a minimal treatment." He wrote that use of a scientific approach teaches the student how "to observe, to find out the parameters, to make conclusions and to check them out (this does not mean that the art object should be experimented with)," and also "how to explain, how to describe a problem with accurate language."[8] The North American programs require independent research projects to further problem-solving skills. Paintings conservation students in Dresden must carry out "research and development work." A student who has successfully completed his or her own research is on the way to becoming a wiser consumer of published research by others.

There are varying theories on the most successful approach to the teaching of the practical third of the triptych: conservation studio skills. Theory and practice are ideally interwoven. Ingo Sandner of Dresden noted: "only the simultaneous development of artistic intuition and ability with the study of restoration methods leads to an integral view."[9] According to my experience, fine skills in retouching or "inpainting" can be taught. Some students enter the field with outstanding painting skills that simply need to be guided toward the reversible materials acceptable for restoration work and the ethics and diverse means of applying compensation. However, I have also worked with bright, motivated, sympathetic students with strong backgrounds in art history and connoisseurship who initially could not match color, texture, gloss, or form but went on to become superb inpainters. Their moment of change generally occurred with sympathetic mentors during their internships (the apprenticeship phases of graduate training). In one case the hurdle was cleared after months of frustration when the supervising conservator inpainted half of a large loss, and the student first imitated her imitation and then was able to turn and imitate thereafter the brushwork and technique of the original artist.

Graduates of the six-year Master's-degree programs in Eastern Europe are known for outstanding inpainting and other craft skills. As mentioned earlier, more time is spent in these programs on atelier work in drawing, painting, and copying than in other programs, and much additional time is allotted to supervised practical treatment. Respondents to my questionnaire from three Polish programs and one Russian program all listed studio art talent as a high-priority prerequisite. Applicants must pass rigorous practical examinations in drawing, painting, and copying. The students' innate artistic abilities then receive extensive advanced training. The writing of reports or papers is allotted only from 1 to 10% of program time. Dr Alyushin notes:

> the main task is to acquire skill in artistic and restoration work, employing both theoretical and practical training. The future specialist is not supposed to be limited by the narrow bounds of scientific analysis, but to be able to interpret the works of art and the restoration processes from the standpoint of an artist-aesthete. . . . From the first to the fifth year, the student restorers have the same curriculum in painting and drawing as those in the painting faculty. . . . the restorers have a complete course of both plastic anatomy and of the technique and technology of artists' materials ... constant work at copying during six years of learning trains the future restorer not only to study the paintings of different schools and epochs but also to show respect to them, treating the works with care.[10]

Apprenticeship vs academic training

Discussion continues among conservation professionals regarding the strengths and drawbacks of both types of training. Norman Brommelle, for many years the secretary-general of the International Institute for Conservation, remarked, "I think that almost every conservator when asked how conservation training should be organized cites his own training as the ideal,"[11] and I have found that also to be the case with many conservators interviewed for our Foundation of the American Institute for Conservation oral history project.[12] Since there was an international growth spurt in the number of conservation programs in the 1970s, by the 1990s we are now seeing an increase in the number of available teachers who were themselves trained in academic programs. Most educators note that the current systems in schools combine both modes of instruction; apprenticeship experience may be expected before entry into a program, and most schools require internships with a senior conservator during the summer months or as an integral part of the multi-year coursework. Colin Pearson and Robert Ferguson note in their proposed international Code of Practice for Conservation Education and Training, "It is recognized that an internship of at least twelve months duration is an essential component of any career entry course."[13]

An apprenticeship is often a one-on-one experience; its value is dependent on the skills, abilities, attitude, scholarship, and character of the supervisor. Norman Brommelle documented his own studio life in the 1950s which

> was a matter of the student, or rather apprentice, sitting in the same room as the master and sharing in the life of the studio. The master usually only had two or three assistants. The master in this particular case was Helmut Ruhemann. He would be working at his important painting and would occasionally call us over to his easel to give a running commentary on the things that he was doing. We worked on paintings of lesser importance and he would come over and make often scathing criticisms of our work. We occasionally worked on minor parts of his picture. At the time when I first arrived in the National Gallery, he had cleaned and was restoring Leonardo's *Virgin of the Rocks* and, as a colleague of mine pointed out later, he restored the Virgin and we restored the rocks.[14]

Thomas Brachert, a supporter of apprenticeship and opponent of classroom instruction, wrote as recently as 1987 that "the loss of practical training in favour of ever increasing organized classroom instruction within the framework of curriculum and semester hours", which involves the "over-estimating of cognitive learning processes, in particular in the area of the natural sciences at the expense of artistic training," promotes "schizophrenia and favours rampant professional nihilism."[15] On the other hand, Chris Caple of the University of Durham comments, "Though often effective training, apprenticeships contained little education, and were often 'rights of passage' for the apprentices, serving principally to re-enforce the status of the master."[16] Respondents to my questionnaire note that apprenticeships are generally more personal and that the learning outcomes are more likely to vary and be difficult to assess. However the practical experience gained in working closely with an experienced conservator is considered invaluable.

The strengths of an academic environment noted by questionnaire respondents include the broad surveys of techniques and approaches, the exchange of ideas, inculcating the habit of teamwork, the learning of problem-solving methodology and the theoretical underpinnings for treatment decisions, the academic coursework in science and art history, the availability of libraries and scientific research facilities, awareness of safety regulations, and training in connoisseurship and museum management. Drawbacks may include the lack of both routine and repetition of similar tasks, and the shortage of time for extensive practical work. If one is lucky, an excellent apprenticeship may have many of the same strengths as an academic setting, including the learning of theory, connoisseurship, ethics, and a variety of techniques, but the situation is less predictable. Leaders in the field continue to emerge who have been trained by apprenticeship, but job-seekers say that degrees have increasingly become mandatory for many positions. Most respondents to the questionnaire agree that a combination of the two approaches is ideal.

After a student has mastered theory, ethics, and history of current and past conservation practice and is one-on-one with a painting on the easel, it is – in the end – as John Brealey has written:

> the quality of the individual's judgment that matters. Every teacher knows that although he or she can present an argument no one can supply understanding. The heart of the matter lies in the quality of the understanding which springs from a natural intuitive response, the right exposure and informed guidance.[17]

Conclusion

A wide variety of approaches exists internationally regarding the emphasis placed by conservation educators on studio skills, research abilities, and priorities for time spent during academic training. Most academic programs now seek to combine the strengths of apprenticeship and classroom coursework. Conservation educators worldwide seek to provide what they consider to be the right exposure and informed guidance in history, connoisseurship, vision, and intuition; scientific literacy and problem-solving abilities; and to create finely honed eyes, hands, and judgment.

Acknowledgements

The author would like to thank all the international training program coordinators who answered her questionnaire and Mitchell Bishop, Janey Cronyn, Colin Pearson, and the librarians of the Canadian Conservation Institute who assisted with bibliographic sources.

References

1. G. Krist, et al. (eds.), *Bibliography: Theses, Dissertations, Research Reports in Conservation* (Rome: ICCROM, 1990).
2. C. K. Keck, letter to the author, 16 January 1996.
3. H. Ruhemann, "The Training of Restorers," *Recent Advances in Conservation* (London: Butterworths, 1963), 203.
4. C. H. Smyth, "The Conservation Center: Origins and Early Years,"*Training in Conservation.* (New York: Institute of Fine Arts, New York University, 1989), 10.
5. N. S. Brommelle; H. Lank, "Aims and Achievements" and I. McClure, "The Training Programme" in *The First Ten Years: The Examination and Conservation of Paintings 1977–1987; The Bulletin of the Hamilton Kerr Institute*, no. 1 (1988).
6. I. McClure, "The Training Programme," 10.
7. I. McClure, letter to the author, 24 May 1995.
8. G. Delcroix, "Teaching Science in Conservation: Why? What? How?" *Proceedings of the Interim Meeting of the ICOM Committee for Conservation Working Group on Training in Conservation and Restoration, London* (1986), 32.
9. I. Sander, "Artistic Restorer or Restoration Engineer?"(Paper delivered at the Triennial meeting of the International Commission of Museums Committee for Conservation, Dresden, 1990), 696.
10. A. B. Alyushin, "Training Paintings Restorers at the Repin Institute, St. Petersburg," *The Picture Restorer*, no 3 (Spring 1993), 16.
11. N. S. Brommelle, "Training in Conservation, the Appropriate Context", *Training in Conservation*, (New York: Institute of Fine Arts, New York University, 1989), 67.
12. Archive of the Foundation of the American Institute for Conservation oral history project, Winterthur Museum, Winterthur, Delaware, USA.
13. C. Pearson, R. Ferguson, "Code of Practice for Conservation Education and Training" (Paper delivered at the Triennial meeting of the International Commission of Museums Committee for Conservation, Washington, 1993), 734.
14. N. S. Brommelle, 68.
15. T. Brachert, "Die Bildung schwindet, die Unterrichtung wächst," *Maltechnik-restauro*, 93, no. 4 (1987), 28-35.
16. C. Caple, "The Development of Managerial and Communications Skills in Conservation Trainees: The Durham Experience," Paper delivered at the Triennial meeting of the International Commission of Museums Committee for Conservation, Washington, 1993), 715.
17. J. Brealey, "Who Needs a Conservator?" *Training in Conservation* (New York: Institute of Fine Arts, New York University, 1989), 35.

Education of the Conservator-Restorer at the Fine Arts School of the Federal University of Minas Gerais, Brazil

Bethania Reis Veloso
Centro de Conservação e Restauração de Bens Culturais Móveis – CECOR,
Escola de Belas Artes, Universidade Federal de Minas Gerais,
Avenida Antônio Carlos nº 6627, Belo Horizonte, MG Brasil

Abstract

The education of the Conservator-Restorer of Movable Cultural Heritage has, since 1978, been accomplished at the Centre for Conservation and Restoration of Movable Cultural Heritage – CECOR, of the Fine Arts School of the Federal University of Minas Gerais. This has been achieved through a postgraduate course in paintings and polychromed sculpture at a specialized level, which currently takes two years. The course and CECOR work closely together in the area of heritage preservation and they are bringing about a new conception of this profession in Brazil.

Keywords

Training, education, course, Brazil.

Introduction

The specialist level postgraduate course in Conservation/Restoration of Movable Cultural Heritage is held at the building of the Centre for Conservation and Restoration of Movable Cultural Heritage – CECOR, which is a Complementary Unit of the Fine Arts School of the Federal University of Minas Gerais – UFMG – Brazil.

Officially created in 1980, CECOR has been acting in the heritage preservation area since 1976, when several canvases belonging to the Music School of UFMG were brought to the Fine Arts School to be restored. That experience revealed the need for a course to educate in restoration, a deficient area in our country. Coincidentally, there was an Inter-ministerial Administrative Directive (Ministry of Planning, Ministry of Education and Culture, and Ministry of Interior Affairs) stimulating the preservation of the heritage and offering incentives for the education of restorers. With this support, the course was initiated in 1978.

In 1980, the Centre's building was finished and CECOR was inaugurated. In 1988 its physical space was enlarged with the building of the second floor. Today, CECOR's building has an area of 760 m^2, containing classrooms, a conservation science laboratory, a restoration atelier for the students, ateliers for restoration work on paper, paintings and sculptures, a laboratory for development and enlargement of photographs, a photography and X-ray studio, a technical storage room, together with rooms for the secretariat, directorate, professors and other staff, a documentation section, and a meeting room.

Essentially multi-disciplinary, the restoration work finds at the University an ideal environment in which to be developed. CECOR is supported by various sections of the University community, both in terms of equipment and human expertise (physicists, biologists, and art historians), fulfilling the requirements of its field of work.

Research, studies and work on easel paintings, polychromed sculpture, and work on paper are carried out at CECOR.

The goals of CECOR are:

- To educate human expertise and contribute to enlarging the consciousness of cultural preservation in Brazil by means of courses, internships, lectures, seminars, exhibitions, publications, and other promotional activities.
- To devise and develop research on the technology of works of art, the causes of deterioration, the preventive conservation of cultural heritage, the improvement of techniques and the methodology of work.
- To establish and maintain interchange with university sections and institutions that work in the field of preserving the national and international heritage.
- To be helpful in doing specialized technical work, answering the requests of public, private, and religious institutions, as well as of individuals.

At CECOR, when we perform conservation and/or restoration work, we evaluate the problems of each piece, collecting and analyzing evidence such as: authorship, style, period, context, possible previous interventions, state of conservation, bibliography, features, and constitutive or accreted materials; then we record the collected information.

This evaluation is the basis of any additional intervention undertaken. Besides the treatment applied to a particular object, the work includes working proposals concerning the environmental conditions of the place where the object belongs, aiming at preventive conservation.

The objects belong to public or private institutions, given that CECOR does not have its own collection. We have to guarantee the durability of the treatment applied, and we advise the owners on better conservation of their collections, since the objects are returned to their original places, where the environmental conditions are not controlled.

The Specialist Level Postgraduate Course in Conservation/ Restoration of Movable Cultural Heritage

The Specialist Level Course in Conservation/Restoration of Movable Cultural Heritage is co-ordinated by a council and it is associated with the Plastic Arts Department, one of the three Departments of the Fine Arts School. The Course has the aim of educating professionals to work in the conservation and restoration of movable cultural heritage (paintings and polychrome sculpture), advising them so that they will be able to identify, discuss and solve problems in this field of work, helping them develop their critical sense and initiative so that they will be able to look for appropriate solutions to real problems, and stimulating them towards the aspects of research in the field.

Background

The Specialist Level courses in Conservation/Restoration have been offered for 18 years, and have taken place eleven times. The first course was in 1978.

Initially, the courses were maintained by the resources offered by the UFMG, and by means of associations with the Planning Secretariat of the Presidency of the Republic and the Institute of Historical and Artistic Heritage – IPHAN. Similarly, the Coordination for the Improvement of Higher Level Personnel – CAPES – and the National Council for the Scientific and Technological Development – CNPq – have been providing study grants to the students attending the course, in view of the exclusive dedication the latter are required to give.

The three first courses were offered exclusively to candidates who worked at heritage preservation institutions, and they were run under the following conditions:

- The places offered were filled by candidates with or without a university degree.
- Students with a university degree received the final certificate as specialists.
- Students without a university degree received the final certificate of an academic extension course.

After the third course, only candidates with a university degree were accepted.

The first six courses lasted for one school year, with an average of 15 students per course. Since 1984, for each course, three vacancies have been offered to Latin-American and Caribbean candidates with the support of the UNESCO-UNDP United Nations Development Program. In 1988, the course acquired the format that lasted until the tenth course: two years of duration, 1,050 hours of classwork, 12 places offered to Brazilian candidates and three places to foreign candidates. Since 1994, the number of places offered has been reduced to ten, including foreign students, in a proportion of 80% Brazilians and 20% foreigners.

The applications for the course have been growing every year, and only one abandonment has been registered in its 18 years of existence. Approximately 85% of the professionals who have attended the course are working today in different areas of heritage preservation in several States of Brazil. So far, 119 Brazilian and seven foreign professionals have completed the course.

Different national and foreign experts have participated in the courses as invited professors, both for compulsory disciplines and for programs of Special Topics on Conservation/Restoration.

To be accepted, the candidates from different Brazilian States and from varying graduation areas (plastic arts, architecture, history, industrial design, chemistry, etc.) are evaluated with respect to their *Curriculum Vitae* (presenting their commitment to the area of heritage preservation), interviews, foreign language tests (English or French), manual ability, color reproduction, and history of art. The acceptance of foreign candidates based on a detailed analysis of their *Curriculum Vitae* to evaluate their education and work in the field of heritage preservation in their home countries.

Conservation/restoration as currently conceived, with a scientific basis and carried out by professionals with specialized education, has a short history in our country. In its early stages it was performed by artists who did not know the criteria and the concepts which guide the true philosophy of conservation/restoration.

The Specialist Level Course, created in 1978 when the preservation of the heritage in Brazil was moving slowly, has today, in 1996, a tradition in educating conservation/restoration professionals. This tradition has come about gradually as recognition by the public and professionals in the field has confirmed the course's importance, so that it has been able to consolidate an outstanding position of leadership in the preservation of the national heritage.

The Specialist Level Course in Restoration/Conservation of Movable Cultural Heritage of the UFMG is the only one in Brazil (we accept participants from all over the country), and one of few in Latin America, with a staff of university-level professors dedicated to the various academic activities of education, research, and extension. Since it is offered as part of the University structure, the course may be considered one of the Latin American courses that has the greatest availability of personnel resources, scientific, technical, and supporting substructure, e.g. library, as well as other services.

The current situation

The 12th course will have study hours increased to 1,425 per class. This change is due to the accumulation of practical activities which require the teacher's advice and a better training of the student, so that there is less risk to the pieces that are being restored. Only applicants who have an undergraduate degree are accepted.

The disciplines are imparted in three ways: theoretical/practical, theoretical, and practical.

The theoretical/practical disciplines are taught in the classroom, in the ateliers for sculpture, painting, and paper of CECOR, and in the photography laboratory of the Fine Arts School. In each atelier, practical activities of restoration of works of art of historical and/or artistic value, kept under the responsibility of CECOR, are performed. These activities are always supervised and advised by the professors who are responsible for the discipline, and they are of extreme importance, since the students have to participate practically, using the theory they have learned during the theoretical classes. The students are always stimulated to develop research work, which is presented at national congresses in the field. In the photography laboratory the students learn to perform specific photographic documentation for restoration purposes. These disciplines amount to 930 class hours and they are as follows:

- Restoration of easel paintings I – 165 hours per class
- Restoration of easel paintings II – 165 hours per class
- Restoration of polychromed sculpture I – 165 hours per class
- Restoration of polychromed sculpture II – 165 hours per class
- Paper conservation – 120 hours per class
- Paper restoration – 120 hours per class
- Oriented visits – 15 hours per class

The theoretical disciplines are taught by presentation of the subject and by use of slides and overhead projection. The classes always refer to practical conservation/restoration examples of analysis and to investigation related to the subject. These disciplines, which amount to 360 class hours, are as follows:

- Theory of restoration – 15 hours per class
- Plastic arts in Brazil I – 30 hours per class
- Plastic arts in Brazil II – 30 hours per class
- Plastic arts in Brazil III – 15 hours per class
- Critical analysis of the work of art – 45 hours per class
- Semiotics – 15 hours per class
- Religious iconography – 15 hours per class
- Scientific fundamentals of restoration – 75 hours per class
- Preventive conservation – 60 hours per class
- Special topics in conservation/restoration – 30 hours per class (national and foreign professors are invited to give lectures on subjects of interest to the course).

With respect to the practical disciplines, activities are developed in the ateliers and in the conservation science laboratory of CECOR as practical work and/or research under the advice and supervision of the professors. The student must attend at least two disciplines of the following, amounting to 180 hours/class. Special studies in conservation/restoration include:

- Practical work in the painting atelier – 90 hours per class
- Practical work in the sculpture atelier – 90 hours per class
- Laboratory work – 90 hours per class
- Introduction to the conservation of works on paper – 90 hours per class

During the course the students are obliged to accomplish an internship of 160 hours in institutions that work directly on heritage preservation or at private ateliers. At the end of the internship period they have to present evidential documentation, a technical report, and a seminar, which must be approved by their supervisor.

At the end of the course, the students have to present their final project, orally and with a written dissertation, before an examining board. This project must be the restoration of a work of art, and its content has to include a thorough study of the piece, and the criteria, techniques and procedures adopted for the interventions. The works of art restored by the students come from important collections of the State of Minas Gerais that are under the responsibility of IPHAN or other institutions. Eventually, depending on the course co-ordination criteria, these pieces may also come from private collections.

An ongoing concern about the organization of these courses has been, as well as giving priority to conservation and restoration techniques, to impart a theoretical and scientific basis to these activities and to stimulate research in the field.

Since 1988 the course has been subject to the Postgraduate Council and Pro-rectory of the UFMG. Successful students receive a certificate of specialization–postgraduate level at the end of the course.

This course, the only one in Brazil with these features and one of only a few in Latin America, is held within the university and educates, at the specialization level, experts in the preservation of historical and artistic heritage. Its value is evident in the large number of applications, both at national and international level, in the outstanding performance of the professionals who have attended it, in institutions, meetings, and congresses of the field, and by the support and acknowledgment of national and international institutions.

Many students from previous courses are today heads of conservation/restoration in ateliers, museum directors, and restorers working at important official institutions for heritage preservation in the country.

Outlook and conclusions

After the 11th course and with the 12th course at the planning stage, we feel the need to review the course, also a requirement of the Brazilian university system.

The possibility of changing the course to undergraduate level is not feasible, given the following points:

- The expensive budget of a four-year course.
- The need for a greater number of professors to offer semestral disciplines.
- Semestral acceptance of students, according to the general system of Brazilian universities.
- Maintenance of eight semestral student groups working simultaneously.
- Works of art to be studied and treated during the course.
- Materials to be used in the conservation and restoration processes, many of them imported.
- The lack of maturity of undergraduate candidates with respect to the conception of the profession of conservator/restorer.

To offer a master's degree in conservation/restoration is not a practical possibility today either, considering that the professors in the specific area of restoration do not have a doctorate degree, which is an essential step to upgrade from specialization to master's level. Another point that should be considered is the need we have in Brazil for experts who work directly with collections of our heritage and not for those whose major interest is academic.

Therefore, the Postgraduate Course at the Specialist Level in Conservation/ Restoration of Movable Cultural Heritage, given the Brazilian reality, fulfils the expectation of the heritage preservation policy.

There is a huge and extremely rich collection in our country that must be preserved. The State of Minas Gerais, as well as the others, has the need for specialized and capable professionals to work in the rescue of the national heritage.

Acknowledgments

The author would like to thank Professor Beatriz Ramos de Vasconcellos Coelho for her fruitful comments on the manuscript.

Assessing Student Practical Work

David Watkinson* and Siobhan Stevenson
Conservation Section, School of History and Archaeology,
University of Wales Cardiff, PO Box 909, Cardiff, CF1 3XU, Wales, UK

Abstract

Differences between assessing written and practical work are examined. Problems associated with assessment of practical work are discussed. A scheme for subdividing practical into a range of performance factors and recording marks on a proforma mark sheet is suggested. Advantages include time saving, accountable records, uniform assessment for each student and clarity of interpretation for both staff and students.

Keywords

Teaching, practical, assessment, proforma mark sheet.

Introduction

Many conservators receive their primary academic and practical training within a university degree scheme. By definition, all university teaching has an educational goal which, in this instance, is also vocational. Like students of medicine, zoology, chemistry and many other university degrees, conservation students must fully integrate theory and practice in order to gain a qualification.

The balance and quantity of theory and practice within a degree scheme is, to a large extent, determined by expectations of graduate competence within the conservation profession. Structure also relates to the level of conservation professional that a course aims to produce and its mission statement. Until recently the definition of a trained conservator was broadly defined by ICOM-CC,[1] with no reference to levels of competence, other than those which could be extrapolated from examples of core syllabi.[2] Lately the situation has changed, owing to the advent of National Vocational Qualifications.[3] Their production relied on input from a large number of conservators to the extent that, in effect, these qualifications define standards of competence for practising conservators. This will benefit academic institutions when structuring their conservation courses.

Once the strategic exercise of producing a balanced and relevant course structure is complete, there remains the tactical challenge of assessing student performance. Most teachers prefer an uncomplicated assessment system that can be applied to a variety of work. Grading quality of work is normally mathematical and is often based on percentages, which equate to levels of achievement, ranging from excellent to inadequate [fail].

Such schemes are easy to apply to written work, where all the factors that one may wish to assess, such as rational discussion, interpretation, reference sources, research potential, clarity of expression, lateral thought and overall understanding, are all presented on paper. Even tutorial discussion with the student tends to evolve from what he or she has written and an overall mark is easy to allocate. The situation is entirely different with practical work.

The first obvious difference is that the tangible end result, in the form of a conserved object, does not provide the teacher with any real insight as to how the conservation process evolved or was carried out. Even though there may be informative written work to accompany the object, detailing thought and decision making processes, it cannot provide insight into laboratory practice or practical touch, in the same way that a well or poorly written essay tends to expose ability to synthesise and present data. Assessing practical work requires a different approach.

This begins by defining good practice within conservation practical and then deciding how and what to assess within this definition.. Whatever the outcome of the defining process, good practice dictates that assessment should involve verbal communication with the student, at formative periods of the conservation process.[4] Retrospective vocal recovery of data, which the end product fails to reveal about the processes that produced it, will always remain secondary to students demonstrating and discussing their practical work as is occurs.

Whilst the grading system employed can be the same as that used for written work, the introduction of manual skills and extensive vocal discussion introduces more subjective methods of marking. Although this must be guarded against,

* Author to whom correspondence should be addressed

informal discussion is recognised as being essential to the assessment process because 'education as most people conceive it, cannot be measured solely by formal assessment'.[5]

As a result of examining the marking system used for practical work within the Cardiff Archaeological Conservation BSc, some of the difficulties associated with assessing practical work are discussed and possible solutions are suggested.

Aims of practical work assessment

The assessment of practical work is a time consuming exercise which conservation teachers must place in perspective against their many other commitments, such as other forms of teaching, research, administration and course development, if overall quality is to be maintained.[6] However, whether it is taught in house with vacation placements (University of Wales Cardiff, University College London[7]), predominantly via placements (Durham University[8]) or is a museum-based course [Royal College of Art/Victoria and Albert Museum[9]), practical work invariably occupies a large percentage of teaching time and normally has considerable influence on the final degree mark. Its importance means that its assessment must be rigorous, efficient and directly comparable between students.

Before determining variety and mode of assessment, it is essential to decide the purpose and objectives of assessment. Practical work is the most common reason why students want to become conservators. It is therefore essential that they understand that practical is the embodiment of conservation theory, and that ultimately they are aiming for a seamless integration between theory and practice. This is expected to be evident within all they say, write and do within practical sessions. Therefore any marking system should be designed to determine whether the student is developing an integrated approach to practical work. Quantifying overall performance requires an all-encompassing assessment scheme, which may create an environment that breeds feelings of fear and pressure within students. To prevent this, the range of factors being assessed must be seen to be sufficiently integrated and mutually supporting, to create a single unit which students recognise as being assessable only as a whole. All their actions and thoughts within practical classes are then part of this whole, rather than a collection of separate activities. This form of assessment is to their benefit, as it is vocationally oriented towards professional proficiency and lessens their desire to see assessment as an end in itself – which it is not.

Assessing conservation practical work requires a cognitive and constructionalist approach. Learning objectives focused on discrete skills must not be taught out of context and should be seen as part of a network with connections in many directions. Gipps[10] describes this as 'an organic process of reorganising and restructuring as the learning process moves forward'. The system required to assess this should aim at detecting what mental representations students hold of important ideas and what facility they have for bringing these understandings to bear in solving their problems.[11] Assessing conservation practical work is performance testing of higher-order skills.

Developing assessment and marking systems

Twenty years ago, assessing practical work at Cardiff was an informal process which was based on a high degree of trust and interaction between staff and students. Staff discussed practical work with students, noted progress and examined laboratory records. Students were awarded a practical mark at an interview called to discuss their progress. Although this was a successful exercise, it has since been replaced by more accountable methods, with increased feedback to students.

Recently, all Cardiff University degrees became modular. After first year matriculation, students study a total of 24 modules in years two and three, upon which their overall degree grade is decided. Within this scheme, practical occupies four modules per academic year, at the end of which students are awarded an overall practical mark, although interim marks are provided midway through the academic year. The importance of practical work is reflected in that it constitutes one third of the overall degree grade.

The overall grade provided for a four module block of practical work is obtained by assessing specific performance factors, designed to locate strong and weak points in student performance. This also provides a fixed number of points for assessing each student, thereby introducing a degree of uniformity to the exercise.

Assessment focuses on formal material factors, such as written records and execution of practical work, as well as on less formal verbal exchanges. To an extent, this can be seen as tangible and intangible marking methods, both of which are often used to assess the same performance factor.

It is not unreasonable to suggest that conservation practical can intimidate students, producing a lack of direction and feeling of insecurity. Unlike other sciences such as chemistry, where teaching experiments are predictable, expendable and supported by clear written instructions, each conservation student is presented with unique cultural objects each with their own individual problems. To solve these requires a clear decision making process on the part of the student and consultation with teaching staff. There is no room for error, as failure could mean the loss of the object. To minimise these feelings, practical work must be seen as a coherent unit and introduction to it must be incremental and supported by underpinning knowledge.

Whilst most students wish to begin conserving artifacts from day one of their study, this is not necessarily the best approach in terms of either their academic progress or efficient use of teaching time. The first year at Cardiff is spent in providing a base line of knowledge and good practice, in preparation for the intensive practical work of years two and three. An outline of the structure, performance and decay of artifactual and conservation materials is supported by an understanding of ethics and museum environment. In turn, this is underpinned by a range of exercises designed to develop various practical and investigative skills, in areas such as mechanical and solvent cleaning, adhesion and infrared spectrophotometry. These are supported by detailed instruction sheets and take place on expendable or simulated objects/surfaces/samples, with assessment being more objective-based than in years two and three. Importantly, one artifact or artifact group is conserved during this time to show the theory and practice of conservation from inception to completion.

At the beginning of year two, students are provided with a general structure and direction for their practical work, centred on what staff consider to be good conservation practice, and they are encouraged to develop this in their own way. They enter their objects into the laboratory documentation system, examine and research their objects' history and technology. Assessment of condition follows, accompanied by initial thoughts on conservation needs and possible conservation procedures. All this information is recorded in a Project Note Book, which aims to provide an insight into the thought patterns of the student, whereas the treatment is recorded on the concise and regimented laboratory record. Whilst guidelines on the structure of Project Note Books is provided, their final form is the decision of individual students. In addition, interviews with staff allow the student to reveal the breadth and depth of their thinking and to show the standard of their communication skills – essential for any successful conservator. A joint conservation plan is agreed with staff. Pro-forma forms are used to aid this process, on which material resources, projected treatment times etc. are recorded. The dual approach of discussion and Project Note Book helps prevent discrimination against the more laconic student.

The individuality of each artifact means that there can be no egalitarian policy of asking each student the same questions or even providing the same amount of time for each interview. However, each student can be asked the same type of question, thereby providing equal opportunity for them to develop discussion. Of course, students are free to ask staff whatever questions they may choose. The most talkative student is not necessarily the most lucid or informative, as economic use of words, incisiveness and quality of delivery are all important factors. In this way, it becomes a reasonably straightforward task to grade students according to the quality of their thought processes. This is an ongoing process throughout the treatment of an object and is accompanied by regular observation of the quantity and quality of practical work.

At the end of each semester students present a short written report on one aspect of their practical work, such as a set of guidelines to a client for care of a completed object. This is expected to be produced to a professional standard.

Structured assessment and marking

Grading falls into the standard degree bands found in British universities. In general terms these relate to specific educational goals and are allocated mark bands which could be summarised as:

- 1. First class degree. Excellent all round performance. Outstanding communication skills, lateral thought and research potential shown in all areas of activity – 70% and above.
- 2.1. Second class degree upper division. A good all round performance to a high standard. Considerable lateral thought and initiative with research potential – 60% to 69%.
- 2.2. Second class degree lower division. A solid performance showing a high degree of competence in most areas of activity – 50% to 59%.
- 3. Third class degree. Overall acceptable levels of performance – 45% to 49%.
- Pass degree : Minimum requirements met – 40% to 44%.
- Fail : Failure to meet required standard in several areas – 39% and less.

Final degree grade depends on performance in all courses taken by the student and produces an overall performance profile, evident on their transcript.

Assessment categories

The practical work is assessed under a number of general headings.

Core skills

These are the basic academic building blocks required to produce good-quality practical work. Assessment is focused on investigative powers, background research, treatment rationale, ethical context, innovation and research potential. To perform well here, students must have a broad understanding of theory, which they are able to translate into working solutions for the problems confronting them. They also have to show initiative and good communication skills with other specialists.

Practical skills

These include all factors relating to the physical aspects of practical work. In effect, they are a measure of how well the core skills can be translated into practice. Assessment headings include: ability to translate theory into practice; quality of practical work, as evidenced by the overall outcome on the object; manual skills and outcomes with a wide range of tools and techniques, as well as innovative use of equipment; aesthetic appreciation; handling and care of objects.

Project book

This is assessed as a separate item because, along with the outcomes on the object itself, it provides a tangible focus for student progress. The quality of presentation, clarity of expression, extent of research and justification of treatment procedure, are typical of the factors looked for in this work. Performance here is clearly linked to Core skills.

Organisational skills

These relate to general efficiency in carrying out practical work. Is the student wasting time by choosing an inefficient route to the end result? Is the student able to efficiently allocate his or her time to a range of tasks or is he or she a one task

Table 1. Proforma mark sheet for conservation practical : hypothetical student profile (L, M and U refer to lower, middle and upper bands)

Name : *Tom Simpson*			SEMESTER : *Winter 1995*									
	Fail	Pass	Third	Lower 2nd			Upper 2nd			First Class		
				L	M	U	L	M	U	L	M	U
Core Skills												
Ivestigative powers							✓					
Background Research						✓						
Treatment Rationale							✓					
Ethics								✓				
Insight & New Ideas						✓						
Practical Skills												
Theory into Practice						✓						
Quality of Prac.Work								✓				
Manual Skills								✓				
Aesthetics								✓				
Handling Objects									✓			
Project Book												
Presentation						✓						
Structure						✓						
Clarity of Expression				✓								
Treatment Procedure				✓								
Organisational Skills												
Work Structure			✓									
Work Temprament						✓						
Rate of Work			✓									
Punctuality									✓			
Good Practice												
Safety & COSHH									✓			
Tidyness & Lab Duty									✓			
Equipment Care								✓				
Security								✓				
Seminars												
1. Placement presentation.						✓						
2. Laboratory design									✓			
3. Iron stabilisation and storage.							✓					

NOTES: *Student is keen, conscientious and well organised, with good practical skills and a sound understanding of ethics which, in turn allows for a good aesthetic appreciation. Whilst written work is well presented, expression and content requires considerable development. Core skills are sound but require a more consistent overall performance to become a 2.1 grade.*

person? Is the student working at what would be considered to be a cost-efficient rate? Is the student's temperament suited to the work he or she is doing? Is the student punctual? These are typical of the many questions posed here.

General good practice

This is seen to be integral with the conduct of a qualified conservator, and is important to the overall performance of a student. It relates to common sense and diligence on the part of the student, rather than intrinsic intelligence. Within this category would be safety within the laboratory and COSHH regulations, general tidiness and efficient execution of duties allocated on the laboratory rota, efficient use and care of equipment and laboratory security.

Seminars

There are various seminars such as 'Reporting Vacation Work' and 'Discussing Treatment Regimes'. These are marked individually. Quality and quantity of contribution is assessed for each student as appropriate to the seminar title. The essential factors sought for here are communication skills, rapid response and overall understanding.

To make it easy for students to view their performance and for staff to offer advice, a proforma mark sheet is used to provide a profile of performance strength and weakness (see Table 1 above). Even though the focus of each topic is different, they tend to be interdependent with similar methods of assessment. Marking takes into account expected rates of student development from years two to three.

Performance in one category can influence the mark in another. For instance, a student may show a good ability to translate theory into practice, but the depth and range of this ability would be influenced by his or her understanding of core skills. Similarly a student with excellent organisational and practical skills, may have a painfully unrealistic work rate.

It is important that students are able to equate what they are doing in the teaching institution with what occurs in the workplace. Placements during the vacation provide a perspective for their in course practical work. Reports from supervisors are received on a simple proforma, which is compared to their collegiate practical work and influences their overall mark.

Conclusion

Assessing practical work is quite different to assessing written work, although the same arithmetical marking system can be used. Subdivision of assessment into categories helps the students to understand what they are seeking to achieve and to view their progress, as well as providing quality accountable records for audit, all with limited expenditure of time. However, the simplicity of forms should not obscure the intensive tuition and structured rigorous vocal and written assessment that makes them possible. Importantly, students must not see assessment as an end in itself, rather as a personal guide to their progress towards being practical conservators.

References

1. ICOM Committee for Conservation. Working Group for Training in Conservation and Restoration, *The Conservator-Restorer : A Definition of the Profession.* (1984)
2. *UKIC Past Present and Future* Report by a Steering Committee to the UKIC Executive Committee (UKIC, London, 1985).
3. Museums Training Institute, *Standards and qualifications for submission to NCVQ* (1994).
4. C. Pearson, R. Ferguson, "Code of Practice for Conservation Education and Training" (Paper presented at the Tenth Triennial International Council of Museums Committee for Conservation Meeting, Washington,, 1993), 731–737.
5. D. S. Frith, H. G. Mackintosh, *A Teachers Guide to Assessment.* (Cheltenam: Stanley Thornes, 1984).
6. D. E. Watkinson, "Teaching Conservation: Educational Changes and Syllabus Congestion" in *Quelle Restauration; Table Ronde sur la Formation Professionelle du Conservateur–Restaurateur d'Oeuvres d'Art en Europe* (Udine, 1994), 63–73.
7. Personal communication, Elizabeth Pye, Institute of Archaeology, University College, London.
8. Personal communication, Chris Caple, University of Durham, Durham.
9. Personal communication, Alan Cummings, RCA/V & A Course, Victoria and Albert Museum, London.
10. C. V. Gipps, *Beyond Testing : Towards a Theory of Educational Assessment.* (London: Falmer Press, 1994).
11. L. Sheppard, "Psychometricians beliefs about learning," in *Educational Researcher* 20, no. 7 (1991).

Working Group A3

Theory and history of restoration

Theory and History of Restoration

Cornelia Weyer, Coordinator
Restaurierungszentrum der Landeshauptstadt Düsseldorf/Schenkung Henkel
Ehrenhof 3a
D-40479 Düsseldorf, Germany

Koos Levy-van Halm, Assistant Coordinator
Sarphatipark 29
NL-1073 CP Amsterdam, The Netherlands

36 members

In the 1993–1996 triennium, the Working Group on Theory and History of Restoration focussed on two central points: professionalization and ethics. The individual studies proposed for the ICOM-CC meeting at Edinburgh in September 1996 therefore not only reflect their authors' immediate research interest, but also a common concern in the development of the profession of restorer as such from its beginnings to the present.

The process of professionalization can be described by various means. Kornelius Götz makes use of sociological tools when he takes a close look at conservators' associations and institutes of higher education in post-war Germany. Michael von der Goltz on the other hand approaches the German situation before World War II with methods used by the humanities, analyzing written source material. As shown by Mireille Maria te Marvelde's research on the 18th-century picture cleaner Jan van Dijk, the characterization of personalities also serves to elucidate the degree of professionalism that had been reached at a certain period of time. A striking parameter of professionalization is to be found in the relationship between the conservator's claim to self-determination and the various kinds of dependencies that actually influence his work. Under this aspect Johannes Röd analyzes the conflict between the Norwegian conservator Harald Brun and his superior, museum director Jens Tiis, at the beginning of the 20th century. In addition, his study provides a remarkable insight into that generation's professional ethics. The necessity of gaining autonomy in discussing theories of restoration is stated by Erling S. Skaug in his review of the cleaning controversy; whereas Françoise Hanssen-Bauer deals with the self-given code of restoration ethics when she questions the traditional understanding of the principle of stability.

There still remains much to do before the international restoration community will share a distinct notion of "who we are and where we came from". Cornelia Weyer and Rebecca Anne Rushfield are working in this respect on a bibliography on restoration ethics, with assistance from some other members of the Working Group. A draft of the bibliography, which is intended to serve for later research work in the field of professionalization and restoration theory, will be presented in Edinburgh.

Abstract

The Canadian Association of Professional Conservators (CAPC) is a professional accreditation body incorporated in 1971 under the Canada Corporations Act. This paper discusses the structure of CAPC's peer-review accreditation mechanism and how the association operates.

Keywords

Accreditation, certification, professional, association, eligibility, Canada, Canadian Association of Professional Conservators (CAPC)

Accreditation in Conservation: the Canadian Experience

Karen Colby-Stothart, Carole Dignard,* and Michaela Keyserlingk
Canadian Association of Professional Conservators,
280 Metcalfe Street, suite 400,
Ottawa, Ontario K2P 1R7, Canada

Introduction

While there are very few countries with established conservation accreditation schemes in place, many are now exploring ways of setting up professional accreditation systems. Canada has had a professional accreditation programme for conservators in effect since 1971 and the authors of this paper hope to contribute to the dialogue now taking place in the international community by describing our context and how the Canadian Association of Professional Conservators (CAPC) operates.

The Canadian context

Although a small conservation community has existed in Canada since the 1930s, the field expanded tremendously beginning in the early 1970s when unprecedented financial support was directed at the conservation and museum community by the federal government. At the time there was a lack of existing organizational infrastructure in the field and a large scale search for conservators, to fill newly created positions and government funded laboratories, was ongoing. This unique early environment resulted in widespread community concern for the establishment of definitions and standards and was instrumental in the evolution of an association dedicated to accreditation in Canada at that time.

The Canadian Association of Professional Art Conservators (CAPAC, whose name was later changed to the Canadian Association of Professional Conservators or CAPC) was established in 1971. Its aims were to define and maintain standards of professional practice, to promote an understanding of these standards among conservators, clients, and custodians, and to provide a voice for Canadian conservators on conservation issues. Membership was restricted to those who successfully completed an examination through peer review. CAPAC was instrumental in, among other things, the establishment of the first Canadian university training programme at Queen's University in 1974.

Another cornerstone of the Canadian conservation community, established in these early years, was the International Institute for Conservation – Canadian Group (IIC-CG). Unlike CAPC which has professional entrance requirements, this association is open to any individuals or organizations interested in conservation. Its role is to promote communication within the field and to disseminate information through conferences, training workshops, a scholarly journal, a newsletter and *ad hoc* committees on relevant issues.

CAPC and IIC-CG were established with mutually supportive roles and have collaborated closely on a number of important projects, including the publication of the *Code of Ethics and Guidance for Practice for Those Involved in the Conservation of Cultural Property in Canada* (1986, 1989) and the establishment of conservation internship grants through federally funded programmes. Discussions regarding the possible amalgamation of the two organizations have taken place in the past, but careful consideration has, to date, favoured the benefits of two independent organizations serving complementary functions. It is always possible that this question will be discussed again in the future and that a new structure might evolve.

*Author to whom correspondence should be addressed.

Today the conservation community consists of approximately 400 individuals, including educators, students, technicians, conservators and conservation scientists. It is estimated that the IIC-CG membership represents about 75% of those active in conservation in Canada. The CAPC membership represents approximately 20 to 25% of conservators who meet CAPC eligibility requirements.

CAPC structure

CAPC is a non-profit corporation administered by a Board of Directors consisting of a President, Vice-President, Secretary, Treasurer, Member-at-large and, since 1995, a Membership Chair, all of whom are elected and serve two-year terms. In addition, since 1995 the Past-President is an ex-officio voting member of the Board of Directors, a change intended to enhance continuity of experience at the Board of Directors level. All Directors serve without remuneration. Although successful in the past in obtaining grants from the federal government, notably through the federal Museums Assistance Programme, CAPC is self-supporting and depends on revenues generated through membership fees to support the costs associated with processing applications.

Following is a summary of CAPC's membership categories and accreditation mechanism. The CAPC Membership Directory describes these in greater detail and is available on request.

Categories of membership and areas of specialization

There is one membership category, that of the "Professional Member", and two sub-categories, namely, the "Conservator" and the "Conservation Scientist". Professional members are accredited in one or more area(s) of specialization. These include the traditional specialities such as paintings, textiles, objects, etc, as well as management, education, mixed collections, preventive conservation and others. The applicant specifies his/her area(s) of specialization in his/her application.

Prerequisites for membership

An applicant must satisfy the following basic eligibility requirements:

- He/she must have received training in conservation through an academic training programme, apprenticeship or some other form of training (including self-training).
- He/she must have a minimum of six full years of experience in conservation including training and practice, or at least three years of conservation practice after graduation from a college or university conservation training programme.
- He/she must have demonstrated an active involvement in the conservation field during at least four years (e.g. through professional interaction with other conservators or through membership in conservation associations).
- He/she must be currently active in the field of conservation and either a Canadian citizen, a landed immigrant, or a practitioner working principally in Canada.

Submission of an application

The candidate must submit a formal application which includes a completed CAPC membership application form, supporting documents to confirm training (such as transcripts of formal conservation training, if applicable) and experience (such as letters of reference or letters of confirmation of work experience), and an application fee (currently CAN$50). A further examination fee of $100 is required if the applicant successfully passes the examination, which also covers the fee for the first year of membership.

Applications received by the association are processed in strict confidence by the Membership Committee, following the association's Rules and Regulations Governing Membership. The Membership Committee's role is largely administrative and, among other duties, serves to pre-screen applicants for basic eligibility requirements. The committee is also responsible for assembling a suitable Board of Examiners for each applicant (subject to the approval by the Board of Directors), and, in general, facilitating the processing of applications.

Examination by a Board of Examiners

The examination is a peer review evaluation in which a Board of Examiners assesses the application and portfolio, and interviews the applicant. The process is fully described in CAPC's Rules and Regulations Governing Membership and is provided to anyone who expresses interest in joining CAPC. The Board of Examiners consists of at least four peers, two of whom are experienced in performing these examinations, and at least two who are specialists in the applicant's field (see *Constitution and duties of the Board of Examiners* below). The aim of the examination is to establish the applicant's professional competence and ability to take full responsibility for the initiation and execution of conservation projects of a practical, scientific or managerial nature. It is designed to assess the applicant's knowledge, abilities and ethical principles.

There are two major areas covered in the assessment. The first concerns general knowledge and principles common to all professionals in the field of conservation, such as: effects and control of the environment; basic care, handling, storage and transportation of cultural property; ethical principles, including the relationship of the conservation profession to society, the cultural object, the custodian or owner of the object, the originator of the objects and the conservation profession itself. The second area covered in the assessment concerns knowledge, ability and standards of practice specific to the applicant's area/s of specialization, and normally includes: cultural and historical significance of the object; examination techniques; documentation procedures; materials of the object; technology and fabrication of the object; conservation materials and processes; possible effects of treatments on objects; relevant literature; organization and design of appropriate workspace; health hazards, safety and precautions; insurance responsibilities; and security.

The assessment is done through the following methods:

- Examination of a portfolio of five to ten conservation projects or case histories for which the applicant has been responsible. The actual number of projects included in the portfolio may vary depending on the magnitude and complexity of the projects submitted. The applicant is asked to submit projects that are recent, that are representative of his or her range of conservation experience and that illustrate the level of documentation maintained.
- Consideration of three letters of reference attesting to the quality of work, methods of practice, and work experience, where applicable.
- Assessment of publications, where relevant.
- Assessment of the applicant's conservation facilities, described in the applicant's application. If the applicant does not have a laboratory, he/she must demonstrate knowledge of laboratory related issues, including basic facilities, equipment, tools and supplies for the applicant's field of specialization, adequate equipment for the types of work undertaken, acceptable level of security for objects, health and safety concerns, and so on.
- A one and a half-hour interview with the Board of Examiners, where all of the above information is discussed and reviewed.

The Board of Examiners may request additional information during the application process including: additional documentation on projects; additional letters of reference; or the holding of an *in situ* examination of laboratory facilities and work in progress.

Laboratory visit

Until 1995, the examination process required a visit to the applicant's laboratory or studio facilities, in order to assess the work environment and work in progress. This was done by two persons, at least one of whom was a member of the Board of Examiners and one who was experienced in the applicant's area of specialization. However, the cost of continuing this practice as a matter of routine has become prohibitive. As of February 1996, the laboratory visit has become an optional component of the examination. The applicant is now asked to describe his facilities and work in progress in the application form, portfolio and interview, and if, after the interview, a member of the Board of Examiners feels that a laboratory visit would be of further use in assessing the applicant, then a visit is arranged.

Constitution and duties of the Board of Examiners

The Board of Examiners consists of at least four experienced members of the conservation profession, as follows:

- Two Standing Members. These examiners are responsible for ensuring that the examination follows CAPC Rules and Regulations Governing Membership and that it is carried out in a consistent manner. All Standing Members are designated annually by the Board of Directors from among CAPC members who have experience with other CAPC Boards of Examiners. The Chairperson of the Board of Examiners must be one of the Standing Members, and must have served on a minimum of three previous Boards of Examiners.
- A minimum of two other *ad hoc* members. These examiners need not be members of CAPC. They are appointed on the basis of expertise to ensure that the applicant's area of specialization is adequately represented.

Members of a Board of Examiners are proposed by the Membership Committee and approved by the Board of Directors. They must sign an oath of confidentiality upon appointment. Their duties involve assessing the applicant's eligibility for membership as demonstrated through the application and portfolio; conducting the examination interview; determining if a laboratory visit is necessary and, if so, how it will be conducted; providing the Board of Directors with a written report of the examination; providing a list of recommendations regarding possible areas of improvement; recommending if the applicant should be admitted to the Association, and in which category and area/s of specialization.

The number of examiners on Boards was reduced in 1996 from "at least five members", to "at least four". The main reason for this was to make the process less costly and to improve efficiency. After a review of CAPC's Boards of Examiners, it was felt that a minimum of four examiners were necessary to ensure fairness to each applicant. It is now possible, under exceptional circumstances, for teleconferencing of one member of the Board of Examiners. Another major change, implemented in September 1995, is that the President or Vice-President need not be a member of each Board. In the past, this was viewed as necessary to ensure a uniform level of assessment on all Boards. However this obligation was extremely demanding on the President's time and decreased the efficiency of the processing of applications. The association now relies on the two experienced Standing Members per Board of Examiners, for continuity in the examination process.

Admission of applicants and appeals

The Board of Examiners submits its report and recommendations to the Board of Directors of CAPC. Only under exceptional circumstances would the decision of a Board of Examiners not be ratified. The applicant is informed by letter and receives a membership certificate. If the Board of Examiners recommends against the admission of an applicant, and the applicant is dissatisfied with the explanation given, he or she can request a meeting with one of the Standing Members of the Board of Examiners to review the findings and recommendations. If the applicant is still dissatisfied after this meeting, he or she may appeal directly to the Board of Directors.

Benefits to clients, to the community and to members

Membership in CAPC demonstrates that a practitioner has achieved a recognized level of competence, as acknowledged by the peer review process. This can be useful for employers, clients and the museum community, who may rely on the professional association to provide a means of recognizing qualified conservation professionals. CAPC produces a Directory of Members which it distributes widely to those enquiring about conservation services in Canada and has produced a brochure promoting the understanding of the CAPC professional designation, aimed at collectors and custodians. CAPC does, however, recognize that there are many qualified practitioners in Canada who are not members of CAPC and has collaborated with IIC-CG in the joint production of the brochure entitled *Selecting and Employing a Conservator in Canada* aimed at guiding custodians of cultural property in selecting a conservator. Other joint CAPC/IIC-CG outreach brochures are in the process of being produced. CAPC also regularly responds with comments and suggestions to government initiatives, task forces and other policy papers regarding government museum and cultural issues, when required.

CAPC has a formal complaint mechanism in place. If a client (or other) is dissatisfied with the work carried out by a CAPC member, he/she may appeal to the association for a review of the member's competence and ethical judgment. There are clear procedures in the association's Bylaws which may be found in the Membership Directory. If the complaint is found to be without justification, the member is exonerated; if the complaint is found to be minor, the member is notified of the perceived deficiency and advised to upgrade his/her standards; if the complaint is more serious, in addition to the previous, the member is censured and warned that future violations could lead to revocation of membership; and finally, if the complaint is a major violation of the Code of Ethics or a repeated violation, then membership is terminated.

Individual members may benefit in different ways from their association with CAPC. Those in private practice or regularly seeking new contracts may benefit from a professional designation that employers and clients in Canada increasingly recognize as important. Conservators without formal academic training may benefit from the endorsement that CAPC accreditation can provide for them. And finally, all conservators and conservation scientists, in all situations, benefit from the increased professionalization of the conservation field in Canada. Some work is ongoing to provide group insurance and other practical member benefits, and collaboration with IIC-CG on internship training programmes and other projects of direct relevance to the conservation community will continue.

The most important beneficiary, however, is the Canadian museum community and the cultural heritage in question. In maintaining a membership dedicated to high standards of practice and the promotion of the understanding of the need for the use of skilled professionals by all custodians or owners of cultural property, CAPC is first and foremost committed to safeguarding our cultural heritage for the future.

Conclusion

CAPC has been accrediting professional conservators for 25 years. New pressures for efficiency and cost effectiveness in our structure and procedures have led to the most recent refinements of the original peer review process first established in 1971. All procedures are fully described in the CAPC literature and can be made available upon request.

Bibliography

Note: all CAPC publications are published in English and French.

Canadian Association of Professional Conservators, *Canadian Association of Professional Conservators – Information for Collectors and Custodians* (Ottawa, 1995), 5 pp.

Canadian Association of Professional Conservators, *Canadian Association of Professional Conservators Membership Directory* (Ottawa, 1996), 71 pp. (Includes CAPC's Bylaws and Rules and Regulations Governing Membership.)

International Institute for Conservation – Canadian Group and Canadian Association of Professional Conservators, *Code of Ethics and Guidance for Practice for Those Involved in the Conservation of Cultural Property in Canada*, 2nd edition (Ottawa, 1989), 20 pp.

B.A., Ramsay-Jolicoeur, "Accreditation in Conservation: Towards Professional Status", *Journal of the IIC-Canadian Group* 19 (1994): 24–30.

International Institute for Conservation – Canadian Group and Canadian Association of Professional Conservators, *Selecting and Employing a Conservator in Canada* (Ottawa, 1989), 7 pp.

Abstract

The process of professionalization of conservators in Germany is investigated in terms of two features: the organization into professional bodies and the turning of vocational training into a graduate profession. With respect to the association system for conservators, the process of professionalization has been concluded; with regard to turning vocational training into a graduate profession, it has reached approximately a fifth of the way. In addition, the recruiting practice of colleges in appointing their academic staff is examined: only half of the staff at institutes of higher education presently have a doctorate. Finally, two further features of professionalization are briefly considered: the dissociation from incompetent competitors and the codification of professional standards. Closer examination of all four features shows that the professionalization of conservators in Germany has not yet been completed. Deficiencies persist in the disassociation from incompetent competitors and with regard to the extent of turning the vocation into a graduate profession.

Keywords

Professionalization, professional bodies, vocational training, graduate profession, Germany

The State of the Professionalization of Conservators in Germany. Existing Data for Conservators' Associations and Institutes of Higher Education

Kornelius Götz
Landesmuseum für Technik und Arbeit,
Museumsstrasse 1, 68165 Mannheim, Germany

"A conservator is an advanced tradesman with brains"

This quotation comes from 1993 and was said at a conference of archaeologists, who were discussing the latest developments in the training of conservators in Germany. The quotation was, of course, dismissed as purely polemical by the conservators. Nevertheless: where does the profession of conservator actually stand in Germany today?

In the following investigation, I would like to go into this question in more detail. I thereby allowed myself to be guided by the theory that "professionalization" of a vocation needs a certain amount of time,[1] and that various features contribute to professionalization. Research into professionalization can, for example, view its research subject as a process, which is only concluded when the following features have been made available:

- Academic nature and specialization: from this follows the tendency to disassociate from incompetent competitors under the formation of a monopoly, the setting up of a self-regulatory system for practising professionals and the achievement of a high social status;
- The codification of professional standards;
- The organization of members of the profession into professional bodies;
- The turning of vocational training into a graduate profession; this includes offering vocational education at technical colleges, art colleges and universities, together with the recruitment of academic staff from the profession itself.[2]

The justification for taking these features as a gauge of the professionalization of conservators is given by Corfield in his article about the past and the future of conservators in Great Britain.[3]

My investigation tries to determine the degree of professionalization of conservators in Germany by taking the third and fourth features above. I chose these two since they are open to quantitative definition: for one, the organization of conservators into associations was investigated; for the other, the level of academic education was ascertained. In 1995 data for both features, in the form of a national survey, were collected. Since each of the groups questioned was relatively small, I have collected an absolute cross-section, that is, without having acquired a sample survey from all of the associations and institutes of higher education in Germany.

Towards the end of this paper, I will also briefly go into the first two features. I have not taken any further features into account, for example, "Social Attitudes to Conservation" and "The Role of the Individual", as named by Watkinson.[4]

At this point, it should be mentioned that the "theoretical approach" to the features that I used is not directly condoned on the sociological side: above all, establishing a degree of professionalization by stringing together outward features can be criticised.[5] Nevertheless, I decided on this approach since I am of the opinion that the critics should provide some proof of a conclusive alternative concept. However, criticism is justified where it warns against spontaneous belief in an apparently precise interpretation of statistical data.

The organization of conservators in professional bodies

Since the 1950s, various conservators' associations have been founded in Germany. Their professional policy became outwardly apparent in 1968 with the drawing up of a pay agreement for conservators within the civil service,[6] and with the establishing of college education in the 1980s. Since 1994 they have had an umbrella association and have published a bill for the protection of the job title "Conservator".

I would like to take the following (specialist) association definitions as a basis for the investigation into the organization of conservators. Conservators' associations:

- are independent amalgamations of conservators over a lengthy period of time;
- are formally organized as legally recognized associations, and thus have democratic minimum standards;
- represent specialist interests externally;
- deal predominantly with economic issues and those concerning employment law externally; cultural maintenance and scientific matters are dealt with internally.

On the basis of these proposed definitions, all German conservators' associations could simply be referred to as professional bodies:

> professional bodies are formed when persons practising the same profession merge together to form independent amalgamations under civil law.[7]

Membership details of German conservators' associations for 1995 are recorded in the tables below.[8] In each case, only members who pay subscriptions were taken as the standard. The total number of members is useful as a criterion of the census because the financial strength of an association determines its internal and external activities.

The following features of the organization of conservators' associations can be summarized from Table 1 as follows:

- Conservators are formally organized into legally registered associations, i.e. the conservators' associations have written rules and are subject to the regulations of the Civil Code.
- As a rule, their level of organization is national, even if individual associations, such as the *Arbeitsgemeinschaft der Restauratoren* (AdR) have a considerable number of international members. On the basis of its name, the *Internationale Arbeitsgemeinschaft der Archiv-, Bibliotheks- und Grafikrestauratoren* (IADA) apparently constitutes an exception; nevertheless, it is counted as one of the German associations since it was founded in Germany, has its administrative offices here and over 60% of its 756 members work in Germany.
- There are no reliable details about the degree of the organization of conservators in Germany. Only the total number of approximately 4,000 subscription-paying members in all of the conservators' associations in Germany is certain,

Table 1. Membership details from conservators' associations in Germany – general information – (for 1995)

Association	Year established	Total no. of members 1995
Arbeitsgemeinschaft der Restauratoren (AdR)	1956	1767
Berufsverband d. staatl. geprüft. RestauratorInnen (BdsgR)	1989	79
Bundesverband Deutscher DiplomrestauratorInnen (bdr)	1992	113
Berufsverband der Restauratoren Sachsens (BdRS)	1990	62
Deutscher Restauratorenverband (DRV)	1958	839
Deutscher Verband freiberuflicher Restauratoren (DVfR)	1980	140
Internationale Arbeitsgemeinschaft der Archiv-, Bibliotheks- u. Graphikrestauratoren (IADA)	1957	756
Restauratoren Fachverband (RFV)	1991	165
Sächsischer Restauratorenverband (SRV)	1990	74
Total:		3995

as shown in column 3 of Table 1. Dual membership[9] and institutional members (juristic persons, e.g. museums, departments for the preservation of historical monuments, companies etc.) must be subtracted from this figure. An unknown remaining number represents the conservators not organized within an association. The associations themselves estimate that 3,000–3,500 conservators work in Germany, which, based on the available data, seems realistic. It is obvious that this number does not constitute any "potential political force" within society as a whole.

It is clear from Table 2 that 56% of conservators in organizations are employees and 22% are self-employed. Those remaining are divided into institutional members (7%) and those still in training (15%).

However, a rising number of self-employed members is to be reckoned with, since the lack of positions in the civil service will increasingly force graduates with a relevant college education onto the labour market for the self-employed.

A typology of conservators' associations in Germany, based on Tables 1 and 2, can be developed. Three types of associations can be distinguished:

- The three associations with the largest membership AdR, DRV and IADA, all founded between 1956 and 1958. This epoch could also be referred to as the "Formation phase" of the profession in Germany. At that time, the concept of "specialist self help" was to the fore, although, interestingly, the AdR, DRV and IADA do not have any structured data with regard to the formal qualifications of their members. In 1994, 83% of registered conservators were members of the AdR, DRV and IADA.
- The founding of associations in West Germany for the representation of "particular professional interests"; such as the DVfR for self-employed conservators, the BdsgR for state-certified conservators and the bdr for qualified conservators. Nine per cent of conservators in an organization in 1994 belonged to one of these. This epoch between 1980 and 1992 could be defined as the "Distinction phase".
- The founding of the BdRS, RFV and SRV in East Germany (GDR), directly before and after the Reunification; 8% of the recorded number of conservators in organizations are here. The epoch of 1990/91 could be viewed as the "Regionalization phase". The motive for founding these organizations was, among other things, to retain the "Protection of the Job Title", (in existence in the GDR), even after Reunification, which, just like a similar attempt in West Germany in the 1980s, did not succeed.

The conservators' associations in Germany particularly took this last situation into account when founding an umbrella association in 1994: the umbrella association is called the *Vereinigung Deutscher Restauratorenverbände* (VDR). Members are the

Table 2. Status and qualifications of members in conservators' associations in Germany (for 1995). The figures in parentheses are the percentage of the total membership.

Association	Total membership	Employed	Self employed	In training	College education in conservation	Other college qualifications	Other education
AdR	1767	1234 (70)	169 (10)	231 (13)	–[a]	–[a]	–[d]
BdsgR	79	13 (16)	62 (78)	4 (5)	0	4 (4)	75 (95)
bdr	113	44 (39)	33 (29)	26 (23)	86 (76)	1 (1)	–
BdRS	62	47 (76)	15 (24)	–[c]	36 (58)	3 (5)	23 (37)
DRV	839	157 (19)	209 (25)	301 (36)	–[a]	–[a]	–[a]
DVfR	140	20 (14)	120 (86)	–[c]	–[b]	–[b]	–[b]
IADA	756	671 (89)	85 (11)	40 (5)	–[a]	–[a]	–[a]
RFV	165	39 (24)	122 (74)	–[c]	88 (53)	15 (9)	58 (35)
SRV	74	19 (26)	55 (74)	–[c]	44 (59)	9 (12)	21 (28)
Total[d]		2244 (56)	870 (22)	602 (15)			

Key:
a Association has no reliable data
b Association does not publish this data
c Owing to regulations, members still in training not permitted
d The total of the first three categories does not add up to 3995 (100%) since the institutional members (7%) are not included.

German conservators' associations; personal membership by individuals is not possible. Its strategy is to mobilize public opinion through various media on the one hand (pressure) and, on the other hand, to influence political decision-makers, or rather, to supply the administration with ammunition (lobbying).

The purpose of the rules of the VDR up until now is exclusively to protect the job title "Conservator".[10] For this purpose, in 1994 the umbrella association formulated a bill for the "Protection of the Job Title Conservator". This bill has not yet passed into law, however (1995).

Turning vocational training into a graduate profession

Conservators

In 1981, the West German conservators' associations published the so called "Rosa Papier" (pink paper).[11] It called for conservators to be educated at technical colleges. Technical colleges were decided on because the education there is practice-orientated and the research is orientated towards application. Strictly speaking, this initiative aims to extend college education for painting and sculpture conservators at art colleges – in existence since 1978 – to all remaining subject areas of conservation. The associations were thoroughly successful in their endeavours, as Table 3 shows.

Table 3. The number of higher education diplomas granted to conservators in Germany in 1995 (Source: *oral information from the respective college examination offices)*

College	Recorded period of time	No. of courses offered	No. of graduates (%)
Berlin (Fachschulfernstudium)	1977–1994	9	approx. 300 (45)[a]
Dresden (Hochsch. f. Bild. Kunst)	since 1978	3	149 (23)[b]
Hildesheim (Fachhochschule)	since 1990	2	32 (5)[c]
Köln (Fachhochschule)	since 1990	5	86 (13)[d]
Stuttgart (Staatl. Akad. d. Bild. Künste)	since 1978	2	92 (14)[e]
Total:			659 (100)

Key:

a This form of training only existed in the GDR. It was discontinued by the Unification Agreement with the consequence that no new correspondence degree courses have been offered by technical colleges since 1991. Furthermore, the Unification Agreement specified that holders of correspondence degrees could apply to have their certificates equated with diplomas from West German technical colleges. From the total number of degree certificates awarded, about 30–40 final year graduates had to be withdrawn since they were exempt from the equality clause in the Unification Agreement. Nine specialist subjects were offered in total: "Wood", "Metal", "Pre- and Early History", "Excavation", "Book/Paper","Textiles", "Ceramics/Glass", "Stone" and "Musical Instruments". Subjects are listed in decreasing order of graduate numbers.

b The distribution between "Painting", "Sculpture" and "Mural Painting/Stone Masonry" is approximately equal.

c Of these, 17 diplomas are in "Mural Painting and Stone Masonry" and 15 in "Painted Wooden Objects".

d 27 diplomas are in "Painting/Sculpture", 27 in "Mural Painting and Stone Masonry", 21 in "Painted Wooden Objects", 6 in "Textile Objects" and 5 in "Paper".

e 86 diplomas in "Painting/ Sculpture" and 6 in "Archaeological, Craft, Folkloristic, Ethnological and Technical Objects" (since 1993).

Since academic education for conservators began, 659 diplomas have been granted in East and West Germany. How high, therefore, is the degree of professionalization in Germany with regard to the education of conservators?

In order to answer this question, the total number of diplomas must be compared with the total number of working conservators, that is, the total number of conservators in organizations. As shown, it amounts to 3,000–3,500 practising professionals, of whom, according to Table 3, 659 (19–20%) are qualified conservators with college diplomas. The level of academic professionalization of conservators stands accordingly at a fifth of the total number of conservators in organizations.

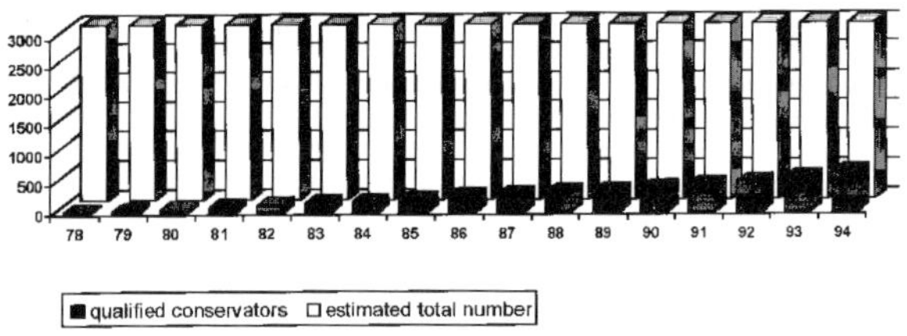

Figure 1. The number of qualified conservators compared with the estimated total number of conservators in organizations

Figure 1 shows the number of qualified conservators compared with the estimated total number of conservators presently working, which can be taken as 3,000. The figure 3,000 comes from the total number of conservators in organizations (see Table 1: 3,995=100%) minus the number of dual members (2%)[9] and institutional members (see Table 2: 7%). A figure of 3,641 conservators in organizations can be calculated from this. The figure of 3,000 is thus the lower limit.

Besides the total number of diplomas awarded up to 1995, it is also interesting to establish the number of diplomas awarded per year and per course. Table 4 gives some information on this. These average values can be used to draw up a projection of future academic professionalization of conservators.

Table 4. Average number of diplomas awarded per year and course, 1978–1994. The table illustrates the annual figure of diplomas awarded using examples from: Staatliche Akademie der Bildenden Künste in Stuttgart, in "Painting/Sculpture"; Fachhochschule Köln, in "Painting/Sculpture"; Fachhochschule Hildesheim, in "Mural Painting and Stone Masonry"; Hochschule für Bildende Kunst in Dresden; only the total number of graduates in all three courses was available

	78–80	81–83	84–86	87–89	90	91	92	93	94	average per year
Stuttgart	4.6	4.6	6.3	3.3	5	8	7	5	4	5.30
Köln					5	3	7	4	7	5.20
Hildesheim						2	3	7	5	4.25
Dresden										3.00
Average of all colleges per year:										4.40

The projection (Figure 2) is based on the following assumptions:

1. An estimated total number of 3,000 conservators belong to associations (Figure 1). It has been assumed that, on account of age, retiring unqualified conservators will gradually be replaced by qualified ones.
2. In 1994, 55 diplomas were awarded. This will increase to 61 in 1996, as the first students graduate from the "Paper" course in Stuttgart.
3. Further diplomas will be added from 1997 onwards, since, in addition to the existing colleges, the first leavers will graduate from the new education courses at technical colleges in Berlin, Erfurt and Potsdam. This figure of 30 is based on two courses offered at three colleges with an average of five graduates per course.
4. In addition, five further graduates have been assumed for the time period 1998–2000, since, by then, the first graduates will have graduated from a further course in "Excavation" in Berlin.

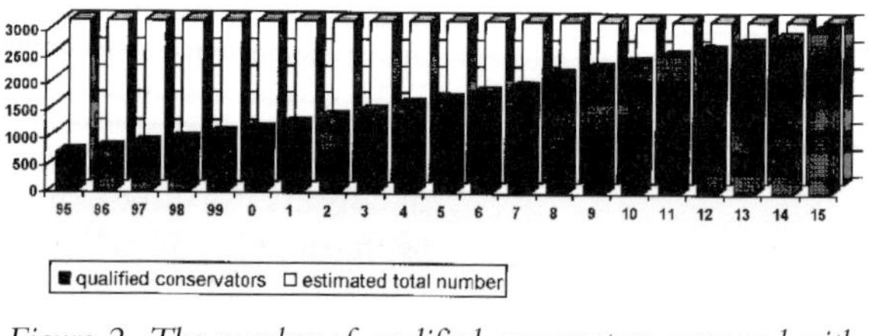

Figure 2. The number of qualified conservators compared with the total number of conservators in organizations – projection for the time period 1995–2015

Table 5. The number of professors with and without doctorates

Professors with doctorates	18 (52%)
Professors without doctorates	16 (48%)
Total:	34 (100%)

Table 6. Educational background of professors teaching conservators

Background	Number
Conservator (with or without diploma)	11 (32%)
Other college degree	10 (30%)
Conservator with a different college degree	13 (38%)
Total:	34 (100%)

5. From the year 2002 onwards, the total number of graduates has been calculated at 115 per year; this assumes a final increase of nine additional graduates from two further courses at two colleges (Berlin and Hildesheim).

If these conditions are accepted, academic professionalization of the occupation could be said to be complete by 2015 at the earliest. With academic education for conservators having begun in Germany in 1978, the academic process of professionalization would, according to this prognosis, last 37 years or, to put it in other words, almost exactly as long as a working generation.

Teaching staff

Within the framework of turning a vocational training into an academic one, an interesting question arises as to what extent conservators in Germany are in a position to provide up-and-coming academics with academically educated teachers from within their own ranks. One of the wide-spread opinions concerning the education of conservators in Germany is that it is dominated by teaching staff "foreign" to the subject.[12] This opinion seems to be supported by the fact that German colleges always demand a formal doctoral qualification when advertising a vacancy. However, at present, if conservators want to "finish off" their conservator's qualification by gaining a doctorate, it is impossible for them to obtain one that is directly relevant.

Keeping this in mind, I examined the recruitment of teaching staff. The results are summarized in Tables 5 and 6. Table 5 shows that the number of professors with or without doctorates, who undertake the academic teaching of conservators, balance one another. If the results from Table 6 are taken in addition to these figures, the picture shifts even more clearly in favour of self-recruitment from the panels of professors who teach conservators:

If the figures from backgrounds 1 and 3 in Table 6 are added together, it can be seen that 70% of the present teaching staff have an education in conservation. There can therefore be no question of a heteronomy within the academic education of conservators in Germany by teaching staff foreign to the subject. Besides, Table 6 seems to confirm that the definition for teachers who educate conservators, suggested by Pearson and Ferguson ("... may or may not have formal qualifications ..."),[13] is complied with in many German colleges, probably without the definition even being known.

Further features of professionalization

To conclude, I would like to go briefly into two further features of professionalization, the tendency to disassociate from incompetent competitors and the codification of professional standards.

The tendency to disassociate from incompetent competitors undoubtedly exists in the field of conservation in Germany. This was verified in the case, won at the last appeal in 1990, in which the Federal Administrative Court confirmed, among other things, that conservation is neither a craft nor an artistic occupation.[14] Furthermore, disassociation tendencies can vehemently be illustrated by the draft bill submitted in 1994 concerning the Protection of the Job Title Conservator.[15] Other affected lobbying groups have taken further action on this point. However, German conservators are still not in a position to be able to specify exactly when this bill will pass into law. Thus, in this respect, their professionalization has not yet been concluded.

In comparison, the codification of professional standards has made great progress nationally and internationally within the last few years; increasingly, its publication has been spreading from the closed circle of specialist associations to the more readily available trade magazines.[16] In addition, this development is becoming apparent in Germany as new members are obliged to comply with the regulations of the associations which, in turn, are based on the published papers. Using this as a basis, a separate body of literature is also beginning to take shape, which examines the existing codification and interprets the daily work of conservators.[17] With regard to this "codification", the professionalization of conservators in Germany can be viewed as having been concluded.

Conclusion

What is the professional standing of conservators in Germany today?

With the organization of persons belonging to this profession into professional bodies, it can clearly be seen that Germany has a highly diversified system of conservators' associations. There is an association for almost every particular interest! There are many in Germany who see this particular diversity as a cause for the failure of the overriding issue of the past: the protection of the profession.[18] The founding of the umbrella association, VDR, ought, however, to give new impetus to a previously unresolved issue. Because, like the establishment of an academic level of education in the 1980s, the key to success here seems to lie in common action by all the associations. And why should this example not be repeated? With regard to the organization into professional bodies, conservators in Germany can be described, in any case, as professionalized.

Concerning turning the training of conservators into a graduate profession, there is, similarly, a definite opinion: the degree of professionalization stands presently at a fifth, with reference to the total of at least 3,000 conservators in organizations in Germany. "Full academic status" is likely to be reached in 20 years at the earliest. Although the possibility of obtaining a doctorate in conservation does not exist, this does not seem to have had a negative effect on the recruitment of teaching staff up until now. This is an unexpected result of my investigation. It must, however, be said that, in comparison with other professions, there is one thing missing for conservators in Germany in turning their training into a graduate profession: the offer of a university course.

By discussing these four features which characterize the degree of professionalization, I have outlined the present state of our profession in Germany: no longer simply "advanced tradesmen with brains", but also not yet completely professionalized. We have deficiencies in our disassociation from incompetent competitors and in completely turning the vocational training into a graduate profession. The reduction of both deficiencies is now more a question of time; a considerable part of the way appears to be behind us!

References:

1. H.-U. Wehler (ed.), "Professionalisierung in historischer Perspektive," *Geschichte und Gesellschaft*, no.3, (1980).
2. H.-W. Schloz, "Professionalisierung im Verbandsmanagement" (Diplomarbeit, Universität Konstanz, 1991), 33. Nearly same information is given in K. Levy-van Halm, "Professionalization" (quoted in: *Newsletter of Working Group 11, International Council of Museums Committee for Conservation*, 29 June 1994), 1.
3. M. Corfield, "Towards a Conservation Profession", in *Conservation Today*, papers presented at the UKIC 30th Anniversary Conference, compiler V. Todd (1988), 4–7.
4. D. E. Watkinson, "Conservators and Conservation Technicians: Definitions and Differences", (Paper delivered at the Tenth Triennial Meeting of the International Council of Museums Committee for Conservation, Washington, 1993), 75.
5. H. U. Otto, B. Drewe, *Professionalisierung in der Sozialarbeit / Sozialpädagogik* (Course 3164, FernUniversität, Hagen 1984), Vol. 3, 26 ff.
6. "Gewerkschaft Öffentlicher Dienst, Transport und Verkehr ÖTV (ed.)," *Vergütungsordnung zum Bundesangestellten Tarifvertrag BAT (Tätigkeitsmerkmale)*, Anlage 1a und 1b zum BAT, Stand 1. Mai 1991; (Stuttgart 1991), 199 ff.
7. U. Battis and I. Felkl, *Öffentliches Dienstrecht* (Course 5371, FernUniversität, Hagen 1993), 16.
8. Data collected by the author from March to May 1995; the ensuing fusion of BdRS and SRM in the meantime was disregarded, since no exact data were available.
9. Data collected by the author from the member registers of the AdR and DRV (1992) which resulted in 57 dual members (2%); because of the traditional differences between the two associations, it is assumed that there are, in total, relatively few dual members.
10. § 2, Paragraphs 1 and 2 of the rules for the VDR, registered at the district court in Cologne.
11. "Rosa Papier" Arbeitsgemeinschaft des technischen Museumspersonals (AtM), Deutscher Restauratorenverband (DRV), Deutscher Verband freiberuflicher Restauratoren (DVfR), "Berufsbild und Ausbildung des Restaurators in der Bundesrepublik Deutschland", in *Der Restaurator-Heute, Beiträge zur Definition eines Berufes*, ed. Arbeitsgemeinschaft der Restauratoren (Bamberg, 1982), 55–59.
12. Th. Brachert, "Verschulung: ein Thema ohne Ende", *Restauro*, no. 2 (1991), 137.

13. C. Pearson, R. Ferguson, "Code of Practice for Conservation Education and Training (Paper delivered at the Tenth Triennial Meeting of the International Council of Museums Committee for Conservation, Washington, 1993), 731.
14. Arbeitsgemeinschaft der Restauratoren (ed.) AdR-aktuell, Sonderheft Urteile, (Freiburg, 1991).
15. Vereinigung Deutscher Restauratorenverbände (VDR), "Entwurf eines Gesetzes über die Führung der Berufsbezeichnung Restaurator", *AdR-aktuell*, no.3 (1994), 8ff.
16. U. Besch (ed.), *Restauratoren-Taschenbuch*, Callwey, (München, 1995), 38–51.
17. C. Weyer, "Restaurierungsethik, Die Argumente der aktuellen Debatte", *Zeitschrift für Kunsttechnologie und Konservierung*, no.2 (1994), 345–355.
18. C. F. Lange von Stocmeier, "Berufsschutz - aus Sicht der Hochschule", *DRV-Mitteilungen*, no.2 (1994), 32–39.

Stability as a Technical and an Ethical Requirement in Conservation

Françoise Hanssen-Bauer
Nasjonalgalleriet,
Postboks 8159 Dep,
N-0033 Oslo, Norway

Abstract

The purpose of this paper is to deconstruct the concept of stability and explore the technical and ethical problems raised by the conventional formulation of the principle of stability.

Keywords

Ethics in conservation, principle of stability

The main purpose of conservation is to preserve art and other cultural artefacts in such a condition that coming generations may experience and study their value. This value may be historical, aesthetic, social, economic, and religious. Therefore, in deciding on if, and eventually how, a given object shall be preserved, it is the duty of the conservator to assess not only the technical condition, but all the various qualities of the object. Over the past two hundred years, our profession has formed ethical guidelines for designing treatments that optimise a range of different requirements and that take the aesthetic and the technical considerations into a balanced account.

Three chief principles to guide any intervention have been formulated, namely that any treatment should be minimalist, reversible and stable:[1]

- The *minimalist principle* tells the conservator to constrain interventions to those that can be justified as needed. Both the justification and the treatment itself must be documented, and the intervention should be restrained to a minimum to cover the need.
- The *principle of reversibility* constrains the conservator to employ means and remedies that may be removed without destroying the object, either now or in the future. At least, the intervention should not reduce the possibilities for future treatment of the object.
- According to our common understanding of the *principle of stability*, the conservator must use means of high stability, in order to ensure that the artefact remains unaltered for a long time after the completion of the treatment.

These standards of professionalism in performing conservation are clear and sound in theory and as principles.[2] In reality, however, the difficulties we encounter in observing them in practice have led to serious questioning of the formulation of the principles. The principle of reversibility is one that is much debated .[3–6] It has been argued that the principle cannot imply an absolute claim that any product used should be and remain soluble or completely removable over time. That is a too unrealistic and ambitious goal. Instead, it is more common to consider the conserving treatment in the context of the total process of preserving the artefact over the years. In such a holistic perspective, the predominant requirement is neither to be able to remove every product that has been added nor to reverse any intervention made. Rather, the imperative goal is to ensure that no individual preservation step reduces the potential for other interventions and treatments at a later stage. Similar reformulations and distinctions are also being put forward concerning the two other principles.

The principle of stability

The purpose of this paper is to deconstruct the concept of stability and to explore the technical and ethical problems raised by the conventional formulation of the principle of stability. In practical terms, when we are concerned with stability we consider treatments like surface consolidation, impregnating, gluing, filling in, puttying, retouching, fixing and varnishing. This means that the principle of stability applies for any intervention that implies that new material is added to the artefact under preservation. The products added may be glues, binders, and varnishes – in other words, natural and synthetic polymer compounds. These polymers can be in the form of solutions, dispersions or emulsions. In the following, I will argue that a consideration of the time perspective and of various aspects of the ageing process of the materials is needed to reformulate the principle of stability.

In everyday speech we normally understand the concept of stability as synonymous for steadiness, firmness, durability and something that changes very little. Something that is stable is permanent, durable, unchangeable, steady, lasting, eternal. In chemistry, stability is used for compounds or substances that resist destruction.[7,8] Both these understandings of the concept allude to a condition that is ambiguous when it comes to time. The everyday usage refers to a condition unaffected by time, wherein the artefact remains unaltered during an indefinite, or at least an undefined, period of time. The professional chemical definition opens up the concept that the resistance against destruction may not last for ever. We are induced to think that the opposite, an unstable composition, is prone to change relatively rapidly towards a more stable form.

The usage of the concept in conservation literature builds on the chemical notion of stability and has the same inherent ambiguity about time. To a certain extent, we have come to terms with this and we concede that the properties of the products we use are changing over time. Stability, therefore, cannot be a measure of durability and permanence within an undefined time perspective, but rather a *measure of resistance over time to ageing*. This concept raises four challenging issues which will be treated in turn below:

- The time aspect: how fast can we accept that a product/material is broken down?
- The ageing aspect: how are the properties changing, and which alterations can be tolerated and which of them are depreciating the artefact's expression or statement in an unacceptable way?
- Standardisation: do we possess the measures to evaluate and to fulfil the demands for stability?
- Approach: Can our intervention strategy be changed to ensure that our treatments better approximate both technical and ethical requirements defined in our codes of professionalism?

The time aspect

The purpose of conservation is to preserve the object's material constitution, as well as its documentary value, for the benefit of future generations. Therefore, the materials used for conservation should ideally stay unaltered for ever. However, both conservators and the professional literature hold more realistic expectations about durability of the materials. The anticipated stability in time is often defined in terms that are rather general or relative. We see expressions like "the means of conservation used should remain stable for as long as possible", or "the material utilised must deteriorate more rapidly than the original matter", or "among possible materials, one should choose the one that after testing proves to be the most stable". Sometimes, the time perspective may be expressed in absolute measures. Horie, in his book on materials in conservation, mentions that materials used for conservation should be stable for at least 20 years, and, preferably, for more than a century, in order to minimise the total number of interventions required.[9]

Robert Feller, in his paper on standardisation of testing methods, refers to different time measures depending on what a given material is to be used for.[10] He distinguishes between materials for temporary use and materials that should be of more lasting stability. He then proceeds to classify the materials according to their expected stability based on tests. Materials for temporary use comprise those that are supposed to be stable for a period ranging from 6 months to 20 years. These materials can be further subdivided into a Class T, those of expected stability of around 6 months, and all the rest in a Class C. Feller groups the materials that are expected to be stable for more than 20, but less than 100, years into a Class B. Where the requirements for resistance against disintegration are high, the materials should remain stable longer and at least for a century. These latter products are further divided by Feller into two classes. Class A2 products have an expected stability of more than 100 years, but less than the class A1 products, that are expected to resist ageing for 500 years. At that time, the name of the conservator, if not everything else, will probably already have been lost from memory.

The question was posed above as to how fast it can be tolerated that a material used for conservation is disintegrating. The classes defined by Feller are often cited and they are used as standards in classifying materials according to their stability. This must imply that the profession agrees to a century as a reasonable and rational time frame for stability requirements. In the professional literature we find other examples of nuances of duration, expressed in years or in more general terms. Most such evaluations agree on reducing the requirements for stability from eternity to a more achievable goal of a couple of centuries. The problem, however, is that such time indications — as useful as they may be – do not provide *sufficient* guidance for choosing materials. The pertinent question is whether the material with the highest stability should always be preferred.

Technical vs aesthetic properties of ageing

First, let us consider the issue of *when* a given material is considered by conservators as disintegrated. In general terms, disintegration may be defined as an alteration of the material resulting in it being no longer able to fulfil its function. When a glue is changed to a degree where it no longer holds two parts together, we would consider it to be disintegrated.

However, the functional requirements of the conservator are normally more comprehensive and we need a deeper understanding of the processes of disintegration. It is not sufficient that the glue sticks the two parts together. In addition, the joining must satisfy aesthetic requirements and, by way of an example, should not change in colour. The conservator will consider that the varnish on a painting or the protective layer on a metal item are disintegrated when they show signs of yellowing or cracking. The conservator aims at satisfying both technical and aesthetic requirements. The object must be preserved in a good technical condition and with its aesthetic expression intact. The material of conservation, therefore, must fulfil both technical and aesthetic requirements at the time it is applied and for a long time thereafter.

Alterations at this level of complexity are difficult to measure and we even lack the standardised terminology to describe the process of ageing. How can we draw distinctions between yellow, a little yellow, very much yellow – between the acceptable yellowing and the unacceptable one? Well, it may be measured with a colorimeter. No colorimeter, however, can substitute for the complex aesthetic evaluations implied when the conservator draws a line between acceptable yellowing and the repudiating discolouring that is faking the artistic expression. On the two artefacts the colorimeter may show identical measures and, nevertheless, the adept conservator may accept the one and judge the other to be inadmissible.

Therefore, it is impossible to answer in general terms the question of when a change is beyond the limits of the acceptable. Such evaluations belong to the realm of subjectivity, where even the exact specifications needed to perform objective tests are lacking. Standards derived from testing must be based on results from assessable and reproducible phenomena, and subjective interpretation of a change can neither be measured nor reproduced. If not everything is forgotten after 100 years, at least there will be a different conservator who will impose his or her personal assessment. And, we must admit, the stability of aesthetic senses and exigencies, at least, can hardly be guaranteed.

Standardisation: properties and profile of disintegration

The aesthetic appraisal is complex and based on personal distinction. Primarily, the materials we use must satisfy our functional requirements. In addition, they should not modify the appearance of the artefact or its documentary value, either at the time of application or after a long time. Even this is not exhaustive. A full series of additional functional conditions of the various materials must normally be met, and this fact makes us review a comprehensive register of their properties. Every one of these properties changes over time and disintegrates, they being, for example, flexibility, stiffness, mechanical strength, pH neutrality, evaporation and formation of derivatives, solubility etc. – and, again, colour stability. The conservator must separately take into account all the ageing properties, as well as how they interfere and interact with other materials within the environment wherein they are introduced.

Few of the materials in use for conservation are produced specifically for the purpose of preserving damaged artefacts. Since the turn of this century, the conservators have been utilising materials produced mainly for industrial needs. Their composition has changed over time, in terms of recipes, of additives and of production processes in order to suit their industrial purposes better. As these changes are beyond any control of the conservators, we often confront traditional and recent materials for which we ignore the exact composition and the production process in detail. All of them may have desired properties, but at the same time they often have a documented stability that is much lower than any standard of use in conservation. Some of the materials may operate under the same name, but nevertheless be different and react differently along disintegration determinants like light, changes in relative humidity and temperature. It is pertinent to ask whether the conservator uses means that are appropriate to guide him or her, such as testing methods, standards and procedures.

The answer to this question is that we have these means only to a limited degree. Ageing of traditional and synthetic materials used in conservation has been analysed and tested over the last 50 years.[10–13] Research has been dedicated to improving their ageing properties by means of additives that can increase their resistance to disintegration. Such testing has provided important knowledge about ageing processes, even if in the literature the descriptions of results are accompanied by reservations about the value of comparative tests for generalisations. The procedures are not standardised and we lack standards for assessing the properties under study. For example, there are no standards in physics to depict the degree of brittleness, or even less to decide what is acceptable. The tests are conducted under conditions that cannot be directly compared to those under which the artefacts are placed. Nor are the tests conducted directly on the artefacts concerned. Therefore, the tests are unable to catch effects from interaction with other products. Furthermore, most studies focus on a limited set of materials that are tested against one single variable, like testing yellowing affected by light without taking into account the interaction with other affecting variables (such as light and temperature together).

All things may improve in the future. Then, we may have established standards for each of the properties of importance for our use of materials. Testing procedures will be improved and we will have comparable results to guide us. All in all, this will enable us to describe a *profile of destruction* for all the products we are utilising. Such a profile will sum up our knowledge about the various properties of ageing for a given product. It will inform us about how the ageing process will unfold for the various properties, as well as at what speed the ageing process is likely to run. At this time, we will probably be able to influence the industry to provide us with materials with ageing properties according to our requirements.

However, even in this situation we are not likely to be satisfied. We can still but dream about the possibility of getting materials with properties that are perfectly adapted to the artefact's original materials, its condition and environment – and, in addition, which are respecting the artefact's cultural and aesthetic values. Even if we should be able to define and describe better the stability of our products, the number of variables to include in the analytical model if all interaction effects are to be explored will be so high as to make quantification and measures beyond any realism. So, what can we do? We cannot but continue to search for materials that resist ageing. In addition, we probably have to search for alternative roads, through discussing the very approach in conservation to choice of treatment in a view of changing our strategy of intervention.

Approach to stability and strategy of treatment

The last point to explore in this paper is whether we can adapt our strategy of intervention with a view to administering treatments that are closer to the technical and aesthetic requirements defined in our professional codes. The normal approach so far has been to utilise the material that after testing has been given the best recommendations regarding its stability. In other words, referring to the classes defined by Feller, we prefer to work with Class A materials.

However, as pointed out above, this approach is not always followed in practice, nor is it necessarily respecting the challenges of transforming our theoretical notions into a fuller understanding of stability under realistic conditions. We simply cannot adapt quality requirements and performance indicators for materials in conservation to each artefact under every kind of treatment, simply by always choosing the material with the best results on stability. "The best" is a relative measure. The material with the highest stability, taken in isolation, will not necessarily yield the optimal solution when we take into account the complexity of properties and the variety of environments into which the product will be introduced.

A better approach is to make a two-stage assessment. First, we should evaluate the profile of disintegration of the potential materials for conservation and choose the one with the optimal combination of ageing properties in relation to what the material will be used for and where it will be introduced. We must choose according to what we here can call the *product stability*. The second stage consists of an appraisal of the interaction effects with other materials and variables and an evaluation of how all factors combined may affect the total disintegration process. Here, we should choose materials that cause the least stress on other original materials when they all disintegrate together. Furthermore, we should assess the stability of the environment with a view to safeguarding the possibilities for new treatments. This is what we could call the interaction stability.

Approximately ten years ago, G. Torracca introduced a principle for the technology of conservation that he called the principle of compatibility.[14] His main claim was that materials used for conservation should disintegrate without destroying the artefact itself. Compatibility can be defined as a relationship between the profile of disintegration of the materials of conservation and the disintegration of the original materials of the artefact. Compatibility is the degree to which the original materials are able to endure the chemical, physical, and mechanical changes in the added materials over time. In practical terms, within this approach, we require that the products used for conservation should disintegrate more rapidly than the original materials and without damaging the latter.

Torraca was concerned with the profile of disintegration of materials for conservation with a focus on the physical, mechanical and chemical aspects, and explored the compatibility with original materials. His purely technical approach to compatibility may be expanded by introducing an aesthetic dimension to the compatibility issue. This additional approach, then, would focus on the aesthetic compatibility of the materials of conservation in relation to the artefact's expression and appearance. Within such a view, the problem is not any longer to estimate the time it will take before a given material yellows, but rather to weigh the propensity to yellowing against how other worthwhile properties will change over time in a total assessment of the effect on the artefact's expression and appearance. The task of the conservator is to consider how both yellowing and other forms of disintegration may be accommodated to the artefact without impairing aesthetic, documentary or technical qualities. The conservator may then, within a given environment, influence the ageing processes by speeding up certain aspects or by seeking to contain others. The choice is not one between the evil and the good, between the stable and the perishable, but rather to pick, among many alternative materials, the one that is best suited for the unique artefact at hand in its given context. This way, the principle of product stability is reformulated to become a principle of compatibility or fit between the properties of disintegration of the materials used for preservation and the same properties of the original materials, as well as with the aesthetic expression of the artefact.

This principle of *compatible stability* opens new approaches to formulating strategies for treatment and for choosing materials. Among all materials that are perishable in the perspective of eternity, we choose those that, within a total assessment, have the properties of ageing that best fit the ones of the original materials of the artefact, its condition, its expression and appearance – taking into consideration the environmental conditions surrounding the artefact.

We have now departed radically from the traditional way of defining stability. Stability is no longer a measure for resistance against disintegration, but rather a comparative assessment of the materials' properties in relation to the distinctiveness of the artefact and the singularity of its environment. This way, we reintroduce relativism into the heart of the principle of stability, and, doing this, we tend to shift our focus from the material of conservation to the artefact itself.

References

1. F. Hanssen-Bauer, "Naturlige og Syntetiske Harpikser. En Forskningshistorisk og Bibliografisk Oversikt," Ferniss-seminar 1990, Nordic Association of Conservators – Norwegian Section (1990): 24–53
2. H. Jedrzejewska, *Ethics in Conservation,* Kungl. Konsthögskolan, Institutet för materialkunsap, Skeppholmen, Stockholm (1976), 16pp.
3. B. Appelbaum, "Criteria for Treatment: Reversibility," *Journal of the American Institute of Conservation* 26 (1987): 65-73
4. C.V. Horie, "Reversibility of Polymer Treatments," in Resins in Conservation, Proceedings of the symposium, Edinburgh 1982, University of Edinburgh Extra Mural Department (1982) 3-1–3-6.
5. H. Jedrzejewska, "The Concept of Reversibility as an Ethical Problem in Conservation," Third International Restorer Seminar, Veszprém, Hungary, *Problems of Completion, Ethics and Scientifical Investigation in the Restoration* (Budapest 1982), 27–32.
6. R.D. Smith, "Reversibility: A Questionable Philosophy," (Paper given at the 15th Annual AIC meeting, Vancouver, British Colombia, Canada, 1987), 132–137.
7. *Adhesives and coatings*, Science for Conservators: Book 3, (Craft Council Conservation Science Teaching Series, 1983).
8. J.S. Crighton, "Degradation of Polymeric Materials", in Modern Organic Materials, Preprints of the Meeting, Edinburgh, 1988), 11–19.
9. C.V. Horie, *Materials for Conservation: Organic Consolidants, Adhesives and Coatings* (London: Butterworths, 1987).
10. R.L. Feller, "Standards in the Evaluation of Thermoplastic Resins," (Paper given at the Fifth Triennal meeting of the International Council of Museums ICOM Committee for Conservation, Zagreb, 1978), 1–11.
11. G.A. Berger, H. Zeliger, "Procédure de Mise au Point d'Adhésifs pour Peintures: Importance des Tests de Validité," (Paper given at the Xe Congrès International, Adhésifs et Consolidants, Paris, 1984), 9–13.
12. J.L. Down, "Un Programme d'Essai d'Adhésifs à l'Institut Canadien de Conservation," (Paper given at the Xe Congrès International, Adhésifs et Consolidants, Paris, 1984), 14–17.
13. J.L. Down, M.A. Macdonald, J. Tétreault, R. Scott Williams, "Adhesives Testing at the Canadian Conservation Institute – An Evaluation of Selected Poly(vinylactate) and Acrylic Adhesives, Environment and Deterioration"Report No 1603, *Conservation Research Services*, (1992): 1–37.
14. G. Torraca, "Processes and Materials used in Conservation, Paper distributed at SPC-course, ICCROM, (1987), 4 pages.

The Cleaning Controversy and the Keeping of Secrets at the National Gallery in Oslo 1917–1921

Johannes Rød
National Gallery,
Universitetsgaten 13, P.O. Box 8157 Dep.
0033 Oslo, Norway

Abstract

In 1905 the painter Harald Brun received a permanent position as a conservator at the National Gallery, three years prior to the appointment of the museum's first director, Jens Thiis. In 1917, Brun accused Thiis of letting the caretaker clean the paintings in the collection, and thereby destroying several of them. Thiis accused Brun of the destruction of several other paintings by overcleaning. This cleaning controversy lasted for four years. Thiis claimed complete control in the matter of conservation and, unless he was successful in this, he would resign his position as a director. Brun pleaded not guilty and stated that he had taken an oath not to reveal any information about his materials and method. With written statements from colleagues in Germany, Denmark and Sweden, we get an insight into the phenomenon of "keeping secrets" in the field of conservation.

Keywords

Conservation history, cleaning controversy, keeping of secrets

The National Gallery in Oslo was established as an institution in 1837. During the first few decades the collection led a rootless existence before the oldest part of the current building was completed in 1882 and the collection could be moved in. In 1870, the painter Christen Brun was employed as a conservator, and since that time a conservation department has been a part of the museum.

Harald Brun was appointed conservator after Christen Brun's death in 1905. Like his predecessor with the same family name, but who was no relation, he too was a painter. After being employed as a conservator at the National Gallery, he studied painting conservation with Alois Hauser at the Kaiser Friedrich Museum in Berlin and with Sven Rønne at Statens Museum for Kunst in Copenhagen. Brun worked for about three years in the museum before its first director, Jens Thiis, was appointed in 1908. The director and Brun co-operated, apparently without any major problems, until 1917.

The cleaning controversy

The conflict with Director Thiis started when the director himself ordered the caretaker to clean all the paintings in the collection during Harald Brun's summer vacation in 1917. Brun wrote:

> After returning from my vacation, I learned that, during my absence, Director Thiis – without conferring with me at all – had permitted the currently acting caretaker and one of his assistants to clean the paintings then hanging in the gallery (with very few exceptions). . . . A director who has no competence in this field must not have any immediate right or authority to damage through his ignorance of treatment methods the finest art in the country. This being the joint property of artists and the general public".[1]

Brun listed around 20 paintings which he believed had been damaged by this cleaning.[2]

The letter with Harald Brun's complaints was sent directly to the Ministry of Church Affairs without his directly confronting the director. In Thiis's response to Brun's letter, we get a clear picture of how strained their relationship actually was.[3] Thiis described the action of Brun as disloyal and he put forward demands and contentions that can be listed, in condensed form, as follows:

1. The director claimed total control of all conservation activity.
2. Brun did not fulfil his duties as to keeping the paintings clean. As the director and the person responsible for the exhibition, he did not hesitate in ordering the caretaker to clean the paintings with pure water.
3. Taking into account the National Gallery's reputation, he had for many years hesitated in expressing his opinion that Brun had destroyed several of the paintings in the museum.
4. Brun had removed glazes and over-cleaned two portraits by Barthel Beham.[4] As experts, he introduced the painter Eilif Peterssen and the director of Statens Museum for Kunst in Copenhagen, Karl Madsen.
5. Brun had removed glazes from Miervelt's "Portrait of a Man"[5] and Abraham Wuchter's "Portrait of a Woman".[6]

6. Brun had destroyed essential areas in Pieter van der Plas's "The Falconers". Among other things, he had overcleaned several areas in the painting. In a newspaper article he accused Brun of having completely cleaned away one of the legs on a donkey.[7]
7. In many ways, Brun is a skilful conservator. He is capable of cleaning modern paintings, relining paintings and regenerating old varnish. On the other hand, Thiis is doubtful as to his skills in the field of cleaning old varnish and retouching.
8. As long as Brun maintains his principles of keeping his conservation methods secret without any access and control, he can be left no paintings for treatment.

Brun made a remark concerning Thiis's assertion that he did not fulfil his duties:

> . . . this proves how little interest Thiis is putting into the treatment of the paintings in the gallery... I have tried to explain to the director the necessity of not cleaning the paintings so often. I have told him that a majority of the museums abroad do not clean their paintings often than once every four or five years. Cleaning often damages the varnish, making it "cloudy" and matte. On the contrary, there are other means of avoiding too frequent cleaning of the surfaces; the protection against dust and grime. Sometimes the surface developed a whitish film that the director interpreted as being dust. This is, in fact, a phenomenon that occurs with a change in weather conditions and the varnish gets a bluish hue. This was often the case with newly varnished pictures. The director was of the opinion – in spite of the fact that I have told him the truth of the matter – that this was my fault and that I used a varnish of not very good quality. I was told that in Paris they used much better varnish, and that I probably was not acquainted with this fact. During an exhibition of French Master paintings in the museum, the paintings on loan also got the same blue/whitish film on the surfaces. Thiis then had to admit the truth in my statement, and his accusations were put to rest.[8,9]

Figure 1. Barthel Beham "Portrait of a Man"

Of the several accusations against Brun, the one that intimated the overcleaning, and thereby the destruction, of several pictures in the ownership of the National Gallery was the most serious. However, he maintained his innocence. Many years had passed since the actual cleaning of the paintings, and he wrote:

> . . . And for how long would the Director have kept this destructive secret for the sake of the museum's reputation, if I hadn't disturbed this perfect idyll with my complaints to the ministry? I regret the fact that the director, during the past 10 years, has not been familiar with the thought that he could not, under any circumstances, get the knowledge of the different methods of picture conservation from me – and because of this fact, his behaviour towards me has resulted in such unfair and improper accusations. A few words from Mr. Thiis to the ministry would have been sufficient to stop the destruction that I have been accused of.[8,9]

Concerning the two portraits by Barthel Beham (see Figures 1 and 2), Brun gave the following statement:

Figure 2. Barthel Beham "Portrait of a Woman"

> . . . The decision to clean the paintings was taken by the director after consulting me. The director was present during the start of the work, but found it too tiresome to be present until the cleaning was finished. The decision of removing old discoloured overpaint was also taken by the director after a discussion with me. The need for this overpaint was occasioned by the fact that the paintings had been destroyed by previous restorations. The previous damages in the paint layer were also hidden. This was unfortunately, and still is, the practice, in a lot of public collections today. With the removal of the overpaint, we got to know the true fact that the paint layer in several areas had been damaged down to the white ground. Thiis wanted me to overpaint in order to hide the damages, so that the pictures should look undamaged. In this matter, the director and I disagreed, and we still do.[8,9]

As mentioned before, Thiis pleaded the support of the painter Eilif Peterssen and the director of Statens Museum for Kunst in Copenhagen as to the fact that Brun had overcleaned and damaged the Beham paintings. Brun wrote:

> . . . A short time ago, when I was passing through Copenhagen, I visited Mr. Madsen and asked him if he had made any comments concerning my cleaning of the actual

Figure 3. Pieter van der Plas "The Falconers"

paintings as Mr. Thiis had stated. Mr. Madsen answered me then that he had never made such a statement. He had not seen the paintings before cleaning them and concluded as much.[8,9]

Upon request, Brun got a statement from Peterssen that said:

> . . . The paintings by Barthel Beham have always been of great interest to me. I cannot deny that I was rather surprised after the cleaning, and I told several persons, among them Mr. Thiis, that I thought them too clean. I have never discussed if this was due to the loss in the final glazes or the patina, that all old paintings develop after some years.[8,9]

It was the director's word against the conservator's. But the pronouncements of those possessing expert knowledge had no value whatsoever as to the question of guilt. About seventy years later, in 1994, the two portraits by Barthel Beham were examined and restored in the conservation department at the National Gallery. This examination revealed that both paintings have been over-cleaned and over-painted extensively. There are traces of at least three previous restorations before the treatment by Brun. It is likely that the condition of the paintings came to view after Brun had removed the strongly tinted varnish. His cleaning had nothing to do with the picture's present condition.

The controversy between the director and the conservator about the treatment of the Beham portraits was kept as an internal affair between the museum and the ministry. A different view of the matter was the accusations that Brun had removed (by cleaning) essential parts of the composition in Pieter van der Plas painting: "The Falconers"[11] (see Figure 3). As an answer to two articles Brun wrote in the newspaper *Dagbladet* with the title: "The reason for my dismissal",[12] Thiis wrote:

> . . . Once, after he had removed one leg of a donkey by over-cleaning, I told him that he had to give one leg back. A three-legged donkey is an absurdity."[13]

Brun answered as follows:

> . . . I don't understand the inference in Director Thiis' article concerning the one leg of the donkey that I should have removed. The donkey has never had more than two visible legs, a fact that anyone can be assured of by looking at the painting. This remark must be considered as an attempt to be funny, and I give him credit for this joke.[14]

If Jens Thiis had studied the painting properly, he would have seen that the donkey had only got two visible legs. The director's accusations against the conservator were in this case truly false.

The keeping of secrets

Thiis described Brun's letter of 1917[1] as an act of disloyalty, and he claimed total control over all conservation activity. He wanted this to be a written paragraph in the conservator's employment instructions.[3] Brun reacted to this with anger, and wrote:

> . . . however, I have a reason not to let anyone gain access to the conservation studio during my work, and as an indispensible condition for me to learn the secrets in the field of conservation, I had to take an oath, that I would never show or teach the methods to anyone but my children or the person that I trust as my successor in the museum. Persons that have knowledge in the field of conservation have to make this vow, because this knowledge is something which is handed down and practically never passed on in other ways.[15]

Thiis's opinion in this matter was crystal clear. As long as Brun maintained his principles of keeping the different methods and materials used in the conservation process secret, without giving any access to control, he would not be given paintings for conservation treatment. Brun wrote a commentary on this:

> Because of the promise to keep my methods and materials secret, I do not have to state the reason for not accepting control by the director. I am, of course, willing to have

the director in the studio, both to look at and discuss the pictures I am working on, as long as it does not interfere with my promise to keep certain parts of the conservation process a secret. If such a paragraph should be adopted by the ministry, I have to withdraw from my position as conservator at this museum, and the director must get hold of another person willing to submit to the director's control."[15]

Director Thiis did not believe that Brun had taken an oath to keep the "conservation secrets" and he characterized this as nonsense. Individually, both Thiis and Brun got in touch with conservators and museum directors in Sweden, Denmark and Germany to have this documented. The occasion for Thiis to react like this had two reasons: primarily, once and for all to prove that Brun was not a trustworthy person, and, secondly, that he could use this in his arguments with the Ministry in order to claim complete control over the conservation work.

Thiis asked for a statement from Director Karl Madsen and Chief Conservator Sven Rønne of the Statens Museum for Kunst in Copenhagen, from Director Erik G. Folcher and Chief Conservator C.W. Jaensson of the Nasjonalmuseet in Stockholm, and from Director Bode of the Kaiser Friedrich Museum in Berlin.[16] The written statements are phrased in a very general manner, underlining the importance of co-operation between the conservator and the director in matters concerning conservation. The statements also stress the fact that the director must have the possibility of being present during conservation work and, if he is interested, to be able to obtain the knowledge of the actual methods in use. The question concerning Brun having taken an oath on keeping his knowledge secret was not mentioned in these statements.

The statements Brun got from Alois Hauser and O. Knobloch of the Kaiser Friedrich Museum in Berlin, from Theodor Krause of the Staatliche Gemäldegalerie in Dresden and Sven Rønne of the Statens Museum for Kunst in Copenhagen contained quite a different opinion. Knobloch wrote:

> . . . To this day, I have never been in a position where someone has insisted that I should reveal my methods. Knowledge of this "art" and my methods have only been given to former conservator Richter in Leipzig and yourself [Brun]. This knowledge is partly based on my own experience and partly on my own inventions, and I will not under any circumstances reveal my methods to anyone else.[17]

Alois Hauser was of the opinion that the studio should be open to everyone working in the museum, and underlined the fact that the director, Mr Bode, was often present during the conservation process. He answered Brun:

> . . . But the director has never been in the relining room in the basement. The director may be present during my work cleaning the paintings, but he has never asked what kind of mixture I am using. A short time ago, I finished my invention of a new formula for the cleaning of modern paintings. The director said at once, that I must keep the recipe to myself and only pass it on to colleagues I trust. This is the formula I have effected to you, dear colleague, and I wish you luck with it.[17]

Theodor Krause in Dresden answered Brun:

> . . . not even towards the director or other superiors does the conservator have any obligation to reveal his own accumulated knowledge.[17]

Brun was thought to have obtained much knowledge from the German conservators during his studies in Germany. Some of this knowledge he passed on to other colleagues after they had taken an oath. Sven Rønne wrote:

> . . . We have an obligation not under any circumstances to reveal or, in any other way, to publish the knowledge from Professor Hauser in Berlin given to us by Harald Brun. This knowledge, concerning formulas and methods in the field of conservation of paintings, can be passed on to the conservators and the assistants within the museum, as long as they make the same obligation not to reveal this knowledge.[17]

However, to be employed as a conservator associated with a museum was not sufficient grounds for receiving this knowledge from other fellow conservators. Thiis had got a letter from the Swedish conservator C.W. Jaensson. He wrote:

"Not under any circumstances would it be appropriate to keep formulas and methods secret."[17]

Thiis adopted this statement in order to justify his own opinion in this matter, and he wrote to the ministry: ". . . as long as Brun upholds his absurd and dangerous principles about the keeping of secrets, I am not willing to give him the responsibility for treating valuable paintings in the collection."[18]

Sven Rønne and Harald Brun were of quite the opposite opinion to Thiis concerning the statement from Jaensson. Rønne said that "...it is a fact that Mr. Jaensson is an elderly man who does not know anything about the new methods in conservation." Brun underlined that Jaensson was not a person one could trust in the matter of formulas and methods in conservation, and "he was not familiar with the new methods and thereby had no obligation to keep any secrets."

Conclusion

The existing written sources point to the fact that both the manner of keeping secrets and the revelation of the secrets were connected to individuals. When actual information and knowledge was confided to someone, the same person was also authorized to decide to whom he was going to pass this knowledge on.

Thiis was willing to give up his position as director of the National Gallery if he was refused complete control in the matter of conservation.[8,9] Brun, however, because of his oath, could not accept the new instructions for the conservation department. The Ministry gave Thiis the authority to formulate the new instructions and Brun was dismissed from his duties in 1921. It seems that the oath taken in Berlin in 1906/07 was more important to him than his position as a conservator at the National Gallery.

References

1. National Archives of Norway, Ministry of Church Affairs, D.J.No.0309, 22 September 1917.
2. National Archives of Norway, Ministry of Church Affairs, D.J.No.3423, 5 June 1918, pp. 10-11.
3. National Archives of Norway, Ministry of Church Affairs,D.J.No.0309, 23 January 1918.
4. NG.M. 71 and NG.M. 72.
5. NG.M. 110.
6. NG.M. 321.
7. *Dagbladet*, 12 may 1921.
8. National Archives of Norway, Ministry of Church Affairs, D.J.No.3423, 5 June 1918. Letter from Mr Brun to the Ministry, June 1, 1918.
9. National Gallery Archives, NG.J.No. 27/1921. Letter from Mr Thiis to the ministry, September 15, 1921.
10. National Archives of Norway, Ministry of Church Affairs Archives, D.J.No.7580, 22. Dec. 1919.
11. N.G.M. 150.
12. *Dagbladet*, 9 and 11 May 1921.
13. *Dagbladet*, 12 May 1921.
14. *Dagbladet*, 19 May 1921.
15. National Archives of Norway, Ministry of Church Affairs Archives, D.J.No.6220, 22 December 1917.
16. National Archives of Norway, Ministry of Church Affairs Archives, D.J.No.7365, 9 December 1919.
17. National Archives of Norway, Ministry of Church Affairs Archives, D.J.No.4891, 18 October 1920.
18. National Gallery Archives. NG.J.No.27/1921.

Cleaning Controversies and "the Two Cultures": Steps towards Professional Autonomy

Erling S. Skaug
Universitetets Oldsaksamling,
Frederiks gt. 3, N-0164 Oslo, Norway

Abstract

The paper reviews a limited aspect of the discussion of cleaning of paintings. Statements made in the 1950s by the art historians Ernst Gombrich and René Huyge are examined, and found to be extreme expressions of the "humanist" culture. Conservation and restoration requires a balance between the "scientific" and "humanist" approaches, and the visual and aesthetic aspects of cleaning in particular call for an analysis of empirical observations. The recent analysis of cleaning practices by Gerry Hedley is drawn directly from professional activity. As a contribution to the theoretical basis for restoration it also means a significant step in the development of our profession's autonomy. When principles are confronted with the variables of reality there is no end to the considerations to be made: the paper finally addresses a possible argument in favour of so-called "total cleaning".

Keywords

Cleaning of paintings, history, ethics

The complexity of the cleaning controversies over the past two centuries remains to be comprehensively reviewed and analysed. In recent years valuable studies have been made by the late Gerry Hedley[1] and Bettina Wechsler,[2] both trained restorers. Hedley's analysis of the three main approaches to cleaning has greatly improved our understanding of the problem and gives, in retrospect, a clearer perspective on the controversies. Hedley's work will be returned to below. The limited purpose of the present paper is to examine statements by two influential art historians, Sir Ernst Gombrich and René Huyghe, expressed in the 1950s during the London controversy. A study of these statements will demonstrate the extreme nature of a conventional – though deceptive – type of "humanist approach" exposed at the time. They serve to show that valid concepts in conservation and restoration are not necessarily formulated by the humanist scholar, based upon metaphors or drawn from the "world of ideas". Restoration theory must relate to phenomena actually observed during the practical work.

Interdisciplinary perspective

From a historical point of view, conflicts between art historians and restorers are of considerable interest. Art historians are usually our superiors in the administrative sense, as curators and museum directors. They have also been, and occasionally still are, our superiors in strictly professional matters, supplying some of the more rigid principles in restoration (for example retouching systems by *astrazione* and *selezione cromatica*, involving a disputable non-empirical colour theory). Inevitably, they have strong views on cleaning. It is agreed today that problems in the field should be resolved by interdisciplinary collaboration and shared responsibility, but conditional to this is a common understanding of the phenomena and processes involved. Some problems of the past owe to failure on this point, based upon incongruous ideas which may still be with us. Disagreements between art historians and restorers, moreover, have been interpreted as disagreement about the painting either as an aesthetic expression or merely as a material document. Such an interpretation may not be correct. It does, however, reflect an important point – the essentially dualistic nature of the work of art itself.

The visual work of art is both a spiritual testimony and a physical object – both idea and matter. It has a life in the crossroads between what C. P. Snow called "the two cultures", in simplified terms the humanist and scientific points of view, respectively.[3] In the following we will not try and list "pros" and "cons" on both sides, but simply show how the humanist culture alone can go astray when intervening in a discussion that requires a balance between the two. More precisely, we will *not* deal with "humanism" vs "science" in a broad sense, but rather with problems arising from merely verbal constructions vs. empirical observations.

For the humanist/art historian – and for everyone else enjoying its aesthetic and spiritual qualities – the work of art may form a basis for immaterial visions, for metaphors, and in fact for any association whatsoever. The verbal communication of such experiences can take us quite far away from the thing itself, and yet these associations are perfectly legitimate and relevant to the work of art as an expression of human creativity and imagination. Verbal discourse, moreover, is perfectly harmless to the work of art itself. It leaves the work open to any other interpretation or experience by other persons now and in the future. Along the same lines, even wrong datings and attributions on stylistic criteria leave the painting untouched and unchanged for further study and investigation. In this sense, the art historian's treatment of the work of art is not comparable to the responsibility of a surgeon, a pilot, or a restorer, for example. However, where the professional interests of art historians and restorers meet, the possibility exists that concepts and mental conventions within the literary/humanist tradition may be applied uncritically to phenomena and processes of the physical world. The statements to be examined here will show that this possibility is not just a hypothetical one.

To clean or not to clean?

In the present discussion we will deal with the problem of cleaning exclusively from a visual point of view, not with its technical strategies and safety precautions. Briefly recapitulated, cleaning is necessary for two reasons – dirt and varnish. Surface dirt makes light areas of the picture darker and dark areas lighter, and will gradually reduce contrasts until the picture is concealed beneath a uniform greyish layer. Varnish yellows, distorting the relationships between "cold" and "warm" colours, will gradually tend to transform the picture into a monochrome. Sooner or later the dirt and varnish must be removed in order to see the picture at all. The painting itself, however, is no longer as it was originally – pigments have faded or changed with time, paint layers have become more transparent, and so on. This is the so-called "actual state": at any point of time the painting is as close to the original as it can be, *the authentic object with its own, constitutional changes* – no more and no less. This situation faces us with a classic problem of presentation. What do we do?

One option – although it was not stated explicitly – during the London controversy was to do nothing at all. In a remarkable chain of reasoning, Sir Ernst Gombrich began by stating that the purpose of cleaning was

> not to restore the individual pigments to their pristine colour, but something infinitely more tricky and delicate – to preserve relationships.[4]

Relationships in a painting, Gombrich maintains a few pages before, are comparable to intervals in music. This refers to the fact that the tone intervals (in the tempered system) are exactly the same when a tune is played in the keys of E major and in C major, for example – in the latter case the whole piece sounds only a little lower. In Gombrich's words:

> Just as a tune remains the same whatever the key it is played in, so we respond to light intervals, to what have been called "gradients", rather than to the measurable quantity of light reflected from any given object.[5]

After referring to Köhler's experiments with chickens and shades of grey paper, he continues:

> Whenever [the restorer] starts the process of cleaning, he will produce a . . . difference of brightness . which will look as if light were streaming into the picture. It is a psychological effect ... This seductive impression of daylight's dispelling the gloom is created within the picture; [but] will disappear when the cleaning is finished. As soon as we are then attuned to the new key of brightness, the constancies come into their own and the mind returns to its proper business of assessing gradients and relationships. We adapt ourselves to different varnishes as we adapt ourselves to different conditions of light in the gallery, provided, of course, that visibility is not completely obscured. The added brilliance ... sinks back as soon as the shock wears off.[6]

It is a trivial fact that the contrast between the cleaned and the uncleaned parts disappears when the cleaning is finished. From this correct observation Gombrich changes subject and turns to the relationships between the pictorial elements. He implies that, since we can adapt ourselves to varying conditions of light, we actually see the same colours and values before and after cleaning. The "gradients and relationships" are, according to Gombrich, "constancies", which we perceive regardless of light levels or amount of surface accumulations. As we know, however, this is not so. Relationships between colours and values become distorted and contrasts become reduced. They do anything but remain constant. The musical analogy is absurd – white cannot be whiter and black cannot be blacker: the "intervals" in a painting cannot undergo parallel transpositions like those of a tune played in different keys. "Intervals" in a painting are not the same before and after cleaning. Gombrich makes the reservation that visibility must not be "completely obscured", but deals with this as if the light is either turned on or off. He overlooks the fact that the transition from full daylight to total darkness is a gradual one, with a corresponding gradual loss of visibility. Or, as a musical analogy: the "intervals" become reduced, and converge towards one single note in the middle register. The argument as a whole, with its blend of incongruous phenomena, is disconnected from reality.

Some of the (lack of) substance in the cleaning controversy is here apparent, and it becomes excessively clear when Sir Ernst – who cannot have realized the irony of his book-title at this point – concludes:

> I fear it is in the nature of things that the art historian will always be distrustful of the man of action [i.e. the restorer] in these difficult and delicate matters.

The cleaning options

Whatever Gombrich meant, a picture must be cleaned. The three main approaches, as identified by Hedley, are "total cleaning", "semi-(or partial) cleaning", and "selective cleaning". Semi-cleaning leaves some dirt and varnish on the surface. There are several arguments for it. Quite generally, it stresses the age of the object. The passage of time, represented by dirt and discoloured varnish, is given a higher rank than in the case of total cleaning. One idea associated with semi-cleaning is that the historical object should be seen through a kind of fine fog or haze: the distance *in time* is symbolized indirectly by the effect of distance *in space*. Another idea is the compromise, the meeting half-way, as a compensation for disharmony and imbalance caused with time. Both of these contributions from "the world of ideas" have been combined in defence of semi-cleaning by the eloquent art historian:

"A thin covering of more or less light patina will restore the balance", said René Huyghe, chief curator of the Louvre and responsible for its cleaning policy in the post-war period. In a poetic metaphor he compared a picture to a woman,

> . . . a beauty, originally famous and admired, but upon whom the years have left their devastating mark. What we prize in her is the memory of her past splendour, not her present state of decay; our interest is in what she was, not in what she is. Should we, therefore, reasoning somewhat crudely and seeking for the plain "truth", expose her to a glaring light that will accentuate her wrinkles rather than the features they deform, or should we rather adopt a softened light that, by veiling only the changes she has undergone, restores to her face that former beauty which is all we seek in her?[7]

One problem here is "memory" as the operative factor. Taken literally, it is valid only for a woman (or a painting) more or less of René Huyghe's (or any visitor's) own age, whom he would be able to remember as young and beautiful. It excludes paintings (or women) one, two or five hundred years old. Another problem is whether semi-cleaning (disguised under the metaphor "softened light") actually works like cosmetics (e.g., filling in cracks and wrinkles) and thus "restores . . . that former beauty", i.e. brings us closer to an illusion of (or "the memory of") the object's original appearance. Actually, we all know that women and paintings age in different ways, and that any attempt to understand these passages literally, or to apply them directly to the actual situation, is irrelevant: metaphors, by their very nature, work by analogies only. Huyghe's rhetoric, in brief, does not concern the actual issue.

These quotations are not necessarily typical for art historians' way of thinking. They do belong, however, to the realm of purely verbal exercises. Ernst Gombrich's argument seems to be that of a brilliant humanist reasoning at his writing desk, unhampered by empirical facts. René Huyghe's metaphor avoids the phenomena under discussion and directs attention to something else. This kind of activity, as already said, may well stimulate an interest in the immaterial aspects of art and enhance imagination in general. It is hard to see, though, how it applies to visual aesthetics in a constructive way, increasing our understanding of a given painting's actual appearance to the human eye. A meta-debate may be entertaining, but in a context with physical implications it must be ethically questionable.[8]

There are more reasons for semi-cleaning than those referred to above, but we are concerned here with the more specific "humanist" arguments. Symptoms of inter-disciplinary contagion are also to be found behind the third approach, selective cleaning. This system consists in cleaning more in some areas and less in others. It attempts to re-establish the original tonal and spatial relationships in the picture, its unity and balance, or – as formulated by John Brealey, former chief restorer at the Metropolitan Museum of Art – "to bring back some semblance of the picture's original cohesion".[9] The problem with this approach is that there are an endless number of changes in an aged painting, in degrees virtually impossible to assess with certainty. In principle, selective cleaning presupposes, like Huyghe's metaphor, a reincarnated memory of the picture's original state. Its emphasis on interpretation, in any case, inevitably leaves the result very much to the restorer's personal judgement and taste.

Hedley's analysis

Thus, no cleaning system as such will guarantee a fully satisfactory result. Total cleaning does not give us back the work of art as it was originally. Semi-cleaning, with the purpose of masking the changes, will give us new changes without correcting the old ones. Selective cleaning, with the purpose of restoring the balance, will give us personal interpretations. We realize this situation clearly today thanks to the too early deceased Gerry Hedley, former restorer and teacher at the Courtauld Institute of Art. In his critical essay of 1990, he points out that the controversies reflect

> an unwillingness to accept the relativistic aspects of cleaning . . . Everyone wishes to have God, or at least an Old Master, on his or her side . . . Much of the vehemence of the debates stems from this search for an impossible absolute.[10]

Hedley underlines that the original relationships between the elements in a picture disappeared a long time ago – they are "long lost relations". Cleaning offers new relationships: the three main approaches give either the original substance in its actual state or the same plus its marks of time, or various attitudes to other, additional marks of time. All of these approaches are relative – they are "new found relativities". Every one of them establishes "a definably coherent relationship to aspects of the artist's intentions and the passage of time." Thus they all have a parallel validity. Hedley introduced no definitive solution to the problem of cleaning. He sketched a first rational basis for the evaluation of cleaning systems.[11] In principle, however, he put a definitive end to cleaning controversies as we know them, in which fundamentalists have been fighting for the one and only valid solution.

There is little reason for restorers, as a profession, to look back on the cleaning controversies with pride, as a comprehensive review of viewpoints in the past will show. However, it must be valid to point out that the fighting has occasionally taken place in a fog of incongruous metaphors – imposed from outside the profession.

Progress in the field depends on improved methods, but must also relate to a professional code of ethics. Gerry Hedley's analysis means a progress in ethics in the sense that it makes a complex field conceptually easier to handle. By listing advantages and weaknesses for each of the three main approaches, he emphasized that further critical work with the problems of cleaning may provide leeway for choices. Each approach may be preferred with good reason.[12] The rest of this paper is intended merely as a modest supplement to the number of continuous considerations to be made, without necessarily providing a final answer or including any rigid set of ethical rules.

A supplementary view

As already mentioned, so-called total cleaning radically concerns our general attitude *to the authentic, constitutional changes of the object with time*. The implications are far-reaching. For example, in contemporary art, colour changes and other alterations may occur long before the picture needs cleaning. The work of art reaches a state that, visually speaking, corresponds to the result of total cleaning – before the restorer's cotton swab is needed at all. Contemporary works often go quickly into museums, and if mounted in glass – instead of being varnished, which modern artists often dislike[13] – this situation may theoretically develop for centuries. Should, then, the parallel validity of the three main approaches be questioned? In other words, is it ethically valid to suggest an intervention of "balancing" or "harmonizing" of this state of affairs, for example by painted glazes? If not, should we then accept the "actual state" – the authentic state at any point of time – as the optimal result of presentation, and indeed as a preferred ideal for cleaning?

Admittedly, there is a hypothetical – some may even say unrealistic – element involved in the comparison of cleaned and uncleaned paintings. However, since the changes with time as such are an important part of the aesthetic argument in favour of semi- and partial cleaning, the problem is worth addressing.

Notes and references

1. G. Hedley developed his analysis in two main papers, "On humanism, aesthetics and the cleaning controversy", delivered as lectures at the Canadian Conservation Institute, 1985 (mimeograph), reprinted in *Measured Opinions* (London: UK Institute of Conservation, 1993), 156–166; and "Long lost relations and new found relativities: issues in the cleaning of paintings", in *Appearance, Opinion, Change: Evaluating the Look of Paintings* (London: UK Institute of Conservation, 1990), 8–13.
2. B. Wechsler, "Cleaning Controversy. Zur Diskussion der Gemäldereinigung in England von 1946–1963", *Zeitschrift für Kunsttechnologie und Konservierung* 1, Heft 2 (1987): 88–132. The article is an abridged version of the author's MA thesis and gives an account of some of the issues at stake during the London controversy.
3. C. P. Snow, The Two Cultures and the Scientific Revolution (Cambridge University Press, 1959).
4. E. Gombrich, *Art and Illusion* (London, 1959), 56.
5. Ibid., 49–50.
6. Ibid., 56–57.
7. R. Huyghe, "The Louvre Museum and the problem of the cleaning of old pictures", The Weaver Report, Part Two, Museum (1950), 190.
8. I am not aware of the present criticism of Gombrich and Huyghe in print elsewhere. Wechsler, "Cleaning Controversy", refers to other passages in Gombrich's book (pp. 73–77), but not to the one above. Hedley, "On humanism", 156, quotes Gombrich's opinion on colour relationships in connection with psychology of perception as such; idem, "Long lost relations" 10, notes 18–19, refers to the same with regard to recent theories on border contrasts. Thirty years ago, my teacher Leif E. Plahter orally pointed out to me Gombrich's false musical analogy. For a comment on Huyge see also E. Skaug, *Punch Marks from Giotto to Fra Angelico* (Oslo, 1994), I, 18, note 10.
9. J. H. Stoner, "John Brealey's Trained and Sympathetic Eye," *Museum News* 59, No. 7 (1981): 26.
10. Hedley, "Long lost relations", 9–10.
11. In practical work the three main approaches are not always a matter of free choice: for example, if one colour or surface area is more difficult to clean than the rest we may have to employ semi-cleaning, bordering perhaps on selective cleaning, in order to maintain a "balance" in the amounts of dirt left. Hedley's thesis of the coherent relationship, and the points at which it may be jeopardised, covers such situations.
12. Hedley, "Long lost relations", 11–12.
13. Cf. Hedley, "On humanism", 164.

Jan van Dijk, an 18th-century Restorer of Paintings*

Mireille Maria te Marvelde
Koninklijk Kabinet van Schilderijen Mauritshuis,
Korte Vijverberg 8, 2513 AB Den Haag, The Netherlands

Abstract

In 1971, a unique 18th-century portrait of a restorer surfaced. The man was shown to be Jan van Dijk (c. 1690–1769), who worked as a restorer for the City of Amsterdam and the Court of the Stadholder. The question is raised as to the identity of this man, who had himself depicted as a picture cleaner, an activity that had very little social status. Extensive biographical research revealed that Jan van Dijk was primarily engaged in picture cleaning during the last 23 years of his life. He criticized his colleagues for overcleaning paintings. Although Jan van Dijk was a painter as well, the large scale of his restoration activities and his true love and care for works of art explain his choice to be portrayed as a cleaner of paintings.

Keywords

Jan van Dijk, history of restoration, 18th-century restoration, cleaning of paintings, overcleaning

Figure 1. Jan ten Compe, "Portrait of the restorer Jan van Dijk" (1754)

Introduction

In 1971, a small-sized 18th-century painting (Figure 1) surfaced,[1] which was at first sight believed to be a portrait of a painter at his easel. Since the coat of arms of the City of Amsterdam was depicted in the painting, it was purchased by the Amsterdam Historical Museum. At the time, neither the authorship of the painting nor the identity of the person portrayed was known.

In the course of a restoration preceding the purchase of the painting from a private collection, it had already been noticed that the upper right-hand corner of the picture on the easel showed a remarkably light contrast with the rest of the painting. Since the patch was clearly delimited, it was believed to be the result of a cleaning test. Further research proved that this was indeed the case, though not in the sense that a portion of the painting itself had been cleaned. The cleaned area on the picture on the easel had been executed in a lighter shade of paint. This is how it became evident that the man had not been portrayed as a painter but as a paintings restorer.

The sitter is looking at the spectator and with his right hand he points at the landscape painting on his easel. Next to the easel is a small table with a porcelain bowl, two glass jars, a brush and a piece of cloth hanging over the edge of the table. A second brush has been stuck in one of the holes in the left leg of the easel. In his left hand the man is holding another piece of cloth. Evidently, these are the attributes needed by a restorer to carry out his work.

Behind the chair on which he is sitting, an open door can be seen, revealing a room in which a painting is leaning against a wall.

Microscopic examination showed that the work is signed by the painter Jan ten Compe, who was chiefly known as a painter of topographical representations, and that it is dated 1754.

After it had been established that the painting depicted a restorer at work, the sitter was identified – with a high degree of probability – as the painter/restorer Jan van Dijk.[2] The emphatic presence of the city arms of Amsterdam played an important role in his identification, as did the date of 1754, since it was known from the account books of the City of Amsterdam that between 1746 and 1766 Jan van Dijk was the only one to have been commissioned to carry out conservation and restoration work on paintings in the possession of the city.[3] Jan van Dijk had close contacts with the Amsterdam Town Hall, because he was the supervisor of the *Kunstkamer*, the art collection in the Town Hall, where he staged a permanent exhibition, according to a nineteenth-century lexicon.[4] Furthermore, in 1756, Van Dijk published a booklet describing all the paintings kept in the Town Hall.[5] To these descriptions he added several critical remarks on previous restorations of the paintings. This criticism shows that van Dijk was convinced that works of art should be preserved in a responsible manner (whatever that may have meant in those times).

* This paper is based on a thesis in the History of Art, University of Amsterdam, 1989: Mireille te Marvelde, "*Jan van Dijk een achttiende eeuws kunstschilder en schilderijenrestaurator*". The paper has been translated into English by Mandy Sikkens, Amsterdam.

Several years later, in 1767, he published another booklet, describing the paintings in the Oranjezaal – the extensively decorated central Hall of the palace Huis Ten Bosch – which he had recently cleaned, as appears from the booklet's introduction and afterword.[6]

In the international world of restoration, the portrait of Jan van Dijk has become a well-known and cherished picture,[7] without it being known what sort of person he really was.

The above-mentioned documents were initially the only sources providing information on the person of Jan van Dijk.[8] These documents and the existence of the portrait, which – as far as we know – is the only 18th-century portrait (and perhaps even the only portrait, irrespective of period) of a paintings restorer at work, inspired me to carry out extensive biographical research. It proved possible to retrieve much information, enabling me to trace Van Dijk's many-sided activities, and revealing his extraordinary role as a restorer.

The research also showed that the reconstruction of the life of a restorer can be a very fruitful method for research on the history of restoration. In this case, biographical research proved to be the only way to gain access to documents containing historical information concerning restoration, which otherwise would have remained hidden in the large mass of archival documents.

The research revealed that Jan Van Dijk's work as a picture cleaner was the most important aspect of his career. It became evident that he had clear reasons for having himself portrayed as such.

The social status of a cleaner of paintings

As is generally known, the profession of restorer did not exist as early as the 18th century. Depending on the different types of damage, restoration activities were carried out by different craftsmen. Problems with panels, for instance, were dealt with by cabinetmakers, while the touching up of the painted image was, logically, part of the work of painters. The cleaning of paintings was also often carried out by painters. Research into the documented payments made by the City of Amsterdam for the restoration of paintings shows that these activities were often carried out by unknown or minor painters. Painters with a greater reputation did not need to bother themselves with restoration, as they received enough important commissions. If they accepted the restoration work, it was most likely carried out by others under their supervision.

This is shown by a document from 1780 of the Amsterdam Guild of Surgeons, in which it is mentioned that the painter Jacobus Buys (who had a good reputation as a painter) refused a restoration commission because he was offended

> ... that the board had taken him for a picture cleaner, a work which he occasionally had others carry out under his supervision, and that he was an artist...(*...voor een schilderij-schoonmaker bij het collegie aangemerkt te worden, 't welk hij wel door andere onder zijn opsigt liet doen, maar dat hij een konstschilder is...*)[9]

Regrettably, the materials and methods used to remove discoloured varnish in the second part of the 18th century in the Netherlands are not mentioned in the sources known so far (including Van Dijk's own publications). Although a few recipes are known from 18th-century texts, the practice of cleaning must have been carried out in a secretive atmosphere, which applied to the entire practice of restoration. It is evident that the exclusive possession of such professional secrets had an economic background, but the fact that restorers often worked experimentally and carelessly, causing damage which then had to be repaired without it being noticed, no doubt also played a role.

Jan van Dijk, a cleaner of paintings

Although Jan van Dijk was a painter – on his death certificate he is still referred to as such – he did not have himself portrayed in this role, which had a higher social status. Apparently, he was more proud of being a cleaner of paintings.

This pride must have come from his keen interest in the art of painting and the ensuing feeling of responsibility for the preservation of old masterpieces. In his description of the paintings of the City of Amsterdam kept in the then Town Hall (the present Royal Palace on the Dam), both aspects are emphasized.

In this publication, Van Dijk acts as a connoisseur, explaining the meaning of the paintings and telling something about the lives of the painters in question. He was motivated to do this by, as he said himself, the "love of art, like the love of truth..." ("*Liefde tot de kunst, als tot de waarheid...*").[10] Between the lines he criticizes the way in which paintings had been (and still were) treated by what he calls "malicious people" ("*kwaadaardige mensen*").[11] In a poem of his hand, printed under the allegorical title print of his booklet, he distinguishes two major enemies of art: "Time and Ignorance" ("*Tijd en Domheid*").[12] He is particularly incensed at the ignorance of people who restore paintings. At the beginning of his description, he draws attention to the poor condition of the paintings in the Town Hall and he also remarks with indignation that this situation is mainly due to people who have worked carelessly and without knowing what they were doing:

> ... the great many old Jewels of Art, ruined by bunglers' hands, not to say incapable claws, [...] which have been overcleaned in such a way that the panels show through the lit part as well as through the dark parts... (*...wat is er niet een meenigte van oude Juweelen der Kunst, door broddelaarshanden, men mag wel zeggen onkundige klaauwen bedorven, [...] die zodanig veschuurt zyn, dat men de Paneelen zo wel door de daging als door de schaduwe ziet doorschynen...*)[13]

Remarkably, Van Dijk's indignation is particularly aimed at badly performed cleaning. In one case he explicitly mentions two damaged paintings: two frescoes in the Town Hall, which, according to him, could have been saved, had not one of those "Nitwits of Art" ("*Weetnieten der Kunst*") scrubbed them with "water and Brussels sand" ("*Water en Brusselssant*") (a finely ground, abrasive powder).[14]

In the introduction to his booklet, Jan van Dijk expresses his gratitude for the confidence placed in him concerning the reparation of "maltreated remnants of the Art of Painting" (*"zo mishandelde overblyfzelen der Schilderkunst*").[15] He considered it an honour to be allowed to do this work and one can be certain that he was aware of the dangers involved and carried out his own cleaning as carefully as possible.

Apart from his exceptional attitude towards the cleaning of paintings, the reconstruction of his life also revealed that cleaning was the most frequently performed treatment within his restoration practice.

On practically all the payments made to him by the City of Amsterdam, it is explicitly mentioned that – apart from some payments for "reparation" ("*repareren*") or, in isolated cases, the "lining" ("*verdubbelen*") of paintings – the payments were "for the cleaning" ("*voort schoonmaken*") of paintings.[16]

Between 1766 and his death in 1769, Van Dijk received several major commissions from Stadholder Prince Willem V, which again included the large-scale cleaning of paintings. The commissions concerned the collection of paintings in palace Het Loo, the paintings in the Oranjezaal in Huis Ten Bosch mentioned earlier (on which he published his second booklet) and the collection of paintings in Huis Honselaarsdijk, one of the other palaces of the Stadholder.[17]

The fact that Van Dijk, in addition to his work for the Stadholder and the City of Amsterdam, removed layers of varnish for private customers as well, is evident from a note found in a notebook from around 1750 belonging to Cornelia Maria Bors van Waveren of Amsterdam, which happened to have been preserved: "Jan van Dijk, residing at Spiegelstraat, has cleaned the paintings in the alcove" ("*Jan van Dijk woont in de Spiegelstraat, heeft de schilderijen in de alkoof schoongemaakt*").[18]

Jan Van Dijk must have enjoyed a good reputation in the field of restoration and particularly in the field of cleaning. During that entire period, from the moment the City of Amsterdam paid him for the first time, in 1746, until his death in 1769, he was the only person to have been mentioned in the sources regarding the activities carried out for the two most important patrons in the Netherlands: the City of Amsterdam and the Court of the Stadholder.

The beginning of Jan van Dijk's career as a painter, connoisseur and restorer

Although Jan van Dijk, in this period of his life, appears to have practically only carried out restorations, his activities during the previous period had been extremely varied. In the early 18th century, he came to Oranienstein Castle in Diez (near Limburg an der Lahn), the Court of the widow of the Frisian Stadholder Casimir II of Nassau-Diez, as the young assistant of a carpenter. Documents kept in the local archives show that, in the course of the years, Jan van Dijk acted as a court painter and restorer, connoisseur/appraiser, art teacher, gilder and even as a building supervisor of all the palaces and public buildings in the counties of Diez and Beilstein.[19]

Between 1710 and 1716, as a court painter at Oranienstein, he executed 11 ceiling paintings and eight small medallions flanking the paintings. These ceiling paintings, one of them showing a Christian theme (in the chapel) and the others depicting subjects from classical mythology, have been preserved.[20] As far as we know, these are the only paintings by Jan van Dijk to have survived and, on the basis of these paintings, unfortunately, it cannot be said that he was a great master. They lead one to suspect that he had not enjoyed a thorough training as a painter.

The paintings betray his limited knowledge of anatomy and the often poorly executed perspective, the inconsistent handling of light and shade, and the application of heavy contours prove his incompetence as a painter. His switching completely to restoration is quite understandable, in the light of the above.

Van Dijk's love of art, so obvious in his later years, was also apparent in this earlier period of his life. Despite the fact that he does not appear to have enjoyed any training in art, in 1726, in connection with the death of queen Amalia van Anhalt, he was capable of evaluating the paintings at Oranienstein Castle.[21] (This is how we know now what paintings were kept there.)

Two years later, he did the same at Dillenburg, another castle belonging to the Orange-Nassau family.[22] At that time, therefore, he must already have acquired the relevant expertise in the field of art. His knowledgeability is also evident from a letter dated 1735 to the Dutch Prince Willem IV, in which he advises the prince to purchase a specific painting.[23]

Being a court painter, the conservation of the collection at the court must have been one of his tasks, and his activities in the field of restoration presumably originated there. In a letter to Prince Willem IV, Van Dijk mentions that he had offered the "princess" (in all probability one of Amalia's six daughters who had remained at Oranienstein Castle after her death) to repair four paintings, which had been damaged by moisture from the walls, because otherwise they would certainly be lost. The princess, however, answered that she was no longer able to afford this. Because he saw that the paintings were deteriorating further from day to day, he could not refrain from informing Prince Willem of this.[24]

Conclusion

Jan van Dijk appears to have been more a restorer than a painter. The fact that he almost entirely devoted himself to restoration during the last 23 years of his life, was, as said above, probably a result of his incompetence as a painter. However, this will not have been the only reason. Everything points towards his true and intense love for the art of painting and of his great interest in the preservation of art. As far as can be concluded from the sources, this attitude can be regarded as exceptional in comparison with his contemporaries. This grants him an important place in the history of restoration in the Netherlands as an early prototype of the professional restorer. Even though we know nothing about Van Dijk's restoration methods, we may conclude from his statements that he probably treated the paintings more carefully than many of his colleagues. Jan van Dijk, who cleaned Rembrandt's "Nightwatch" and many other important Dutch paintings, possibly saved these paintings from disaster. Ironically, his own portrait has been severely damaged by overcleaning. One can only hope that it will be preserved from a new generation of "... malicious people with incapable claws".

References

1. Technique: oilpaint on elmwood; Measurements: 35.5 ´ 30.5 cm; Signed and dated: "(J. t)en Co(mp)e f 1754" (very much abraded); Owner: City of Amsterdam, acquired 10 June 1971; Place: Amsterdam Historical Museum, Inventory number: A 33842. For more technical information, see the report of the Seminar "Technical Aspects of Painting",

given by E. van de Wetering, Art-historical Institute of the University of Amsterdam, 1978.

2. S. H. Levie, "Een Uniek Gevalletje: het Portret van Amsterdams Stadsrestaurateur Jan van Dijk door Jan ten Compe:", in *Album Amicorum J.G. van Gelder* (Martinus Nyhoff: Den Haag, 1973), 219–222.
3. W.F.H. Oldewelt, "Eenige Posten uit de Thesauriersmemorialen van Amsterdam van 1664 tot 1764", *Oud Holland* 51 (J.H. de Bussy: Amsterdam 1934), 69–72, 140–142, 162–165, 237–239, 267–270; "Eenige Posten uit de Thesauriersmemorialen van Amsterdam van 1764 tot 1811", *Oud Holland* 52 (1935), 87–88, 179, 258–260.
4. C. Kramm, *De Levens en Werken der Hollandsche en Vlaamsche Kunstschilders, Beeldhouwers, Graveurs en Bouwmeesters van den Vroegsten tot op Onzen Tijd* (Amsterdam, 1857–64), part 2, 408–409.
5. J. van Dijk, *Kunst- en Historie-kundige Beschrijving van alle Schilderijen op het Stadhuis van Amsterdam, met Beoordelingen en Aanmerkingen over de Stukken en Korte Levensbeschrijvingen van Derzelver Schilders* (Diedericks: Amsterdam, 1758), second edition.
6. J. van Dijk, *Beschrijving der schilderijen in de Oranjezaal van het Vorstelijke Huys in 't Bosch* (Den Haag, 1767).
7. The portrait has been shown in several lectures by Ernst van de Wetering since its surfacing in 1971 and by Koos Levy-van Halm ("Zur Geschichte der Restaurierung in Holland, eine Skizze" *Proceedings of the International Congress on the History of Restoration, Interlaken* (1989), 97–112).
8. All this information was obtained from Levie, "Een uniek gevalletje", 219–222.
9. A.B. de Vries, *Rembrandt in the Mauritshuis*, (Sythoff and Noordhoff 1978), 220.
10. Van Dijk "Kunst-", 3.
11. Ibid., 19.
12. Ibid., title page.
13. Ibid., 19.
14. Ibid., 81.
15. Ibid., 6-7.
16. Oldewelt, "Eenige posten".
17. D. F. Slothouwer, *De paleizen van Frederik Hendrik* (A.W. Sythoff: Leiden, 1945), 86–87, 212, 261, 278, 288.
18. I.H van Eeghen, "De leveranciers van Mevrouw Deutz van Assendelft", *Maandblad Amselodamum* 48 (J.H. de Bussy: Amsterdam 1961): 142–143.
19. Archives Hessisches Hauptstaatarchiv Wiesbaden, Germany. F. Storto, "Jan van Dijck, Hofmaler und Bauinspector", *Diezer Heimatblätter* 9 Heft 3/4 (1962): 40–44.
20. F. Storto, *Oranienstein, Barockschloss an der Lahn, Geschichte eines Stammschlosses des Niederländischen Königshauses*, (Görres: Koblenz, 1986).
21. R. Heck, *Die fürstlich nassau-diezische Gemäldesammlung in Schloss Oranienstein zu Diez an der Lahn*, (Diez an der Lahn, 1927), 14.
22. HStAW (Hessisches Hauptstaatarchiv) Abt. 171, D 749 Bd. 1.
23. S.W.A. Drossaers, Th.W. Lunsingh Scheurleer, *Inventarissen van de inboedels in de verblijven van de Oranjes 1567–1795* (Martinus Nyhoff: Den Haag, 1974), part 2, 368.
24. Koninklijk Huisarchief (KHA) Den Haag: A17–173(14) (516).

The State of Professionalism in Restoration in the 1930s in Germany

Michael von der Goltz
Niedersächsisches Landesmuseum,
Am Maschpark 5, 30169 Hannover, Germany

Abstract

The purpose of this research, based on inquiries, literature and archives, was to find out how far professionalism in restoration progressed in prewar Germany. With training, references and ethics used as criteria, national professionalism had not come far, while it developed quite fast at the international level. German activities at an international level ended when the National Socialists assumed power in 1933. They tried to support national professionalism by law but finally did not succeed.

Keywords

Professionalism, history of restoration, Germany, the 1930s, restoration of paintings

Introduction

Research into the state of professionalism in Germany during the thirties[1] is based on the following criteria defining "profession":

> An occupation based on scientific studies and leading to practice. Members of the profession adhere to specific ethics and believe in their colleagues as their main reference group. Strong attraction to their work is combined with the consciousness of fulfilling important tasks for society and these need freedom of decision and autonomy. External criteria are public appreciation and esteem, which should result in an appropriate fee.[2]

Background situation and the autonomy of decision

In Germany restoration took place in three main areas: museum, preservation of historical monuments and private enterprise. These differed in their specific situations, which will be described first.

Museums[3]

Half the museums had their own employed or official restorers. 10% had employees such as porters, electricians or joiners, who carried out restoration under the supervision of curators. A third did not have their own restorers and, depending on their financial positions, gave commissions to freelances. In 10% of cases private restorers worked in the workshops of the museums, some of them with guaranteed payments up to a certain level.

The differences in the salaries of employed or civil servant restorers were based on the hierarchy. The official titles were: head of conservation and conservator, technical custodian and technical assistant, restorer, assistant restorer and museum technician. The title "conservator" was used to describe a functionary in a museum or the offices for the preservation of historical monuments,[4] but some restorers tried to reserve the title for restoration and conservation to express the central activity of their work.[5]

Usually officials or employees did not discuss their work in public. In a rigid system of hierarchy they worked under the control and the supervision, but also under the protection, of the curators or directors, who presented the restoration to the public and published important results and methods.

In museum restoration there was the following division of labour: directors and their restoration committees, as well as curators, were permitted to issue directives, as well as to supervise the work and handle publicity. Where available, chemists analysed materials and colours and gave advice on restoration. The restorers finally had to convert the directives into practice. So the "freedom of decision and autonomy", mentioned above, existed only within narrow limitations for the museum restorer.

Of course, there were exceptions like the restorer of the municipal art collection of Freiburg/Breisgau, Paul H. Hübner, who had excellent connections with the press,[6] or Helmut Ruhemann, until 1933 chief restorer and conservator at the Kaiser-Friedrich-Museum in Berlin, who was famous for his international activities.

Preservation of historical monuments

Here the percentage of employees and civil servants was lower – only a few curators of historical monuments had their own restorers (for example the Bavarian office for the preservation of historical monuments in Munich[7]), but sometimes the workshops of the provincial museums also worked on the preservation of historical monuments. Most curators had to commission private restorers.

In this field we find the following titles: head of conservation, conservator, restorer, foreman and preparator.[8]

Usually the directives, supervision and publicity were also the responsibility of the curator, who was normally an art historian or an architect.

Private enterprise

Freelances least deserved the title "restorer", as they usually also worked in other professions. They called themselves, for example, painters and only sometimes added "and restorer". This group of freelance artist- and craftman-restorers often included those who had professorships for the technical side of painting at the academies, like Max Doerner in Munich. These men also taught the art of restoration on the side.

Of the restorers in all three fields (museum, preservation of historical monuments, private restoration), it was the freelance who had the greatest "freedom of decision and autonomy" and the best possibility of publishing (see below).

Training

In 1926 the director of the municipal gallery and the *Staedelsche* art institute in Frankfurt, A. Wolters, described the disaster of restoration in the museums caused by unregulated training:

> The museums without restorers were forced to take freelances, who used quick restorations to try to achieve aesthetic results because they were corrupted by art dealers. The museum restorers, whose guarded knowledge was based only on amateurish experience, were secretive. The controlling ignorant curators were dependent on the knowledge of the restorers.

Wolters pleaded for a restoration school based on science and craftmanship, which should be attended not only by restorers but also by future curators before getting their first responsible job in a museum.[9]

What was the training situation like?

As far as we can reconstruct from biographies, museum restorers had formerly been painters, graphic artists or joiners. The restoring jurist Jakob von Danzas was an exception.[10]

If the aspirant had already been working in a museum, he usually was sent on a practical course with a restorer in a museum. Most of the others gained experience in a private restorer's workshop.

There was an interesting arrangement for the successor of Friedrich Koch, a freelance restorer in the workshop of the Provincial museum in Hannover: in 1927, the provincial government arranged by contract that Koch should give systematic training in restoring to the graphic artist of the museum and would therefore get a lifetime pension on retiring. When in 1936 the 77-year-old Koch retired, he had already trained his successor for nine years, and received 100 Reichmarks per month for life.[11]

The restorers in the preservation of historical monuments also mainly seemed to be painters. Their knowledge was sometimes based on practical courses in museums but sometimes only on their art studies.

The training situation of the freelances is difficult to reconstruct. Usually they seemed to be artists, house painters or sculptors.[12]

So we see that the training of restorers was not normally based on scientific studies. If there was training at all, it was a practical course in a workshop.

A not very well known exception was the academy in Karlsruhe, where the restorer of the art museum, Marga Eschenbach, taught painting restoration from 1927 to 1937.[13]

Ethics

The slogan "conservation instead of restoration" had been one of the few so-called ethical positions. Already popular at the end of the 19th century, it became a slogan in the Weimar Republic, often being used to discredit others by imputing them the opposite view. This slogan had been widespread, but there existed other ethical points of view, as well, which will not be described here. The interpretation of such a slogan must take into consideration that the meaning of the terms may have changed today.

Groups of reference

Until 1933 colleagues in other fields were not regarded as a reference group. For example, if a museum restorer ever got in contact with a colleague, it was usually with a fellow museum restorer. In particular, the relationship between the freelances and the museum restorers was often very tense. Many of the conflicts between them occurred in the same way: at first a freelance accused a director or restorer of a museum of having destroyed something by a bad restoration. This accusation produced much paperwork, often involving the ministries, followed by waves of solidarity and finally by court proceedings. Often the accusations seemed to involve reasons outside the field of restoration; some of them seemed to have a political background.

The possibility of having a committee of colleagues as a reference group would imply some kind of organization. The *Deutsche Museumsbund* (German Federation of Museums), founded in 1917, was the representative of interests of the higher civil servants[14] and therefore could not represent most of the restorers. However, one of the goals of the *Deutsche Gesellschaft für rationelle Malverfahren* (DG) (German Society for Rational Painting Methods), founded in 1884, was to develop methods for the conservation and restoration of painting by experience and science.[15] As, traditionally, the members of this society had been house-painters and artists etc. the restorers who were members also came from that field and had usually been freelances. Though a member of the State Museum and the office of preservation of historical monuments should have sat in the technical committee of that society,[16] very few museum restorers were involved.

Though at the national level colleagues had not been accepted as a reference group, the situation at the international level was quite different. However, the group of people active in international contacts and professionalism was not exactly the same as those acting at the national level.

The interest in the situation in foreign countries was based on two different intentions. First, as a comparison with the national situation, reports with chauvinistic tendencies came out in newspapers as the following examples of the organ of the DG, *Technische Mitteilungen für Malerei* (*TM*) (Technical news on painting) show:

- In 1929 a report on the exemplary development of the Russian Soviet government gave an account of the founding of Igor Grabars's "Central workshops for restoration" after the revolution, where restorers were trained in the techniques of the old masters. The report, ending with the demand to develop something similar in Germany,[17] gave rise to protests that in Germany and Austria there had been possibilities of training restorers much earlier than in Russia. In 1936 the friendly attitude towards Russia had already changed, when it was reported that in Russian museums art decayed in cellars and sheds.[18]
- In 1931, the proposal of the American Roerich Museum for a convention on the protection of artificial and natural monuments was critically commented on, in that the authorship of this idea was not American but German, as Gustav Eberlein had already suggested it in 1913.[19]

- The German situation of research into painting techniques and care of paintings was declared to be better than in England, where until 1920 no organization had cared about it and, after that, all attempts suffered from a chronic lack of money.[20]

More important than those reports had been the attempts to form a partnership with foreign countries in order to reach a common standard. In quite a short time the development of international professionalism had been much more successful than the attempts at a national level.

Before 1930 only a few had contacts with foreign countries. One of them was Alexander Eibner, chief of the *Versuchsanstalt und Auskunftsstelle für Maltechnik* (Experimental Station and Inquiry office for Painting Technique) in Munich, who was a friend of A.P.Laurie and a corresponding member of the Royal Academy of Arts in London.[21] The international contact intensified when in 1930 the International Committee on Intellectual Co-operation, an organisation of the League of Nations, and its suborganisation of 1926, the International Museums Office, organized the first "International Conference for the Study of Scientific Methods for the Examination and Preservation of Works of Art" in Rome. As this was an arrangement of the Museums Office, some of the more combative artist-restorers like Max Doerner had not been invited.[22]

In spite of only being a few days long (13 to 17 October), this first international conference succeeded in making an important step forward towards professionalism. The "Conclusions by the Committee on Restoration of Paintings and the Use of Varnish"[23] may have been the first international attempt at "ethics". The following were members of this Committee: W.G. Constable (National Gallery, London), P. Glanz (University of Basle), D. Boud-Bovy (Commission of Fine Arts, Switzerland), A. Eibner (Technical University Munich), I.G. Goulinat (Commission for the Restoration at the National Museums, Paris), W. Graeff (Pinakothek Munich), S. Kennedy-North (Great Britain), A.P. Laurie (Royal Academy of Arts), A.M. de Wild (La Haye), H. Ruhemann (State Museum, Berlin), D. Silvestri (Italy) and P. Tudor-Hart (Great Britain).[24]

A committee made up of almost the same people (instead of A. Eibner, W. Graeff, S. Kennedy-North, O. Silvestry and P. Tudor-Hart, there were Folch y Torres, Barcelona, H.J. Plenderleith, London, E. Lavanino, Rome, G.L. Stout, Cambridge, USA, and J. Maroger, Paris) had been commissioned to elaborate rules for the restoration of paintings, which, edited in a handbook, could be sent to museums, owners of paintings and other interested persons. When the committee met for the first time in May 1933 it fixed the table of contents of the book and decided to ask for further cooperating specialists. As the members of the committee agreed on the main principles very quickly, they were sure about finishing the book soon.[25] But when it was finally completed in 1939, it was already without official German participation.

After the conference of 1930 the participants and the Committee on Intellectual Co-operation stayed active in promoting training, occupational protection, reference groups, ethics and internationalism:

- Walter Graeff demanded the founding of an international institute for scientific examination of paintings.[26]
- Justus Koch, syndic of the "Reichsverband der bildenden Künste", elaborated legal principles for restoration.[27]
- To reach some kind of federation of restorers who had participated in Rome, negotiations with restorers and governments had been started.[28]
- The head of the institute for the examination of paintings and sculptures at the academy of fine arts in Vienna, Robert Maurer, had been asked by the International Committee to explain his view of restoration and protection of the profession.[29] He wanted every country to form a commission of historians of art, artists, collectors and restorers (2:1:1:4), which could test the knowledge of restorers and nominate "authorized restorers". The qualifications for the examination were an artistic preparatory training at an academy and a practical course of at least three years at a restoration school or the workshop of a recognized master. The test consisted of a practical work of restoration, a copy

of an old-master painting and questions on technique and modern methods of examination. Those restorers who had been chosen by an unanimous vote of the commission should constitute group "A" and become heads of restoration schools or restorers in museums. Those who had been chosen by a bare majority should belong to group "B" and become private restorers. Those who did not pass would not be allowed to restore.
Maurer divided the work of restoration into three processes of different risks which should be done by restorers of different qualifications:
1. The restoration of the support, the ground and the paint layer;
2. Removal of the varnish, the retouchings and the overpaintings;
3. Completion of losses.
The risky work, processes 1 and 2, should be strictly supervised.

- With regard to the next conference in Athens in 1933 Helmut Rinnebach and the director of the museum of Altona, Lehmann, aspired to a bill for the international preservation of all historical monuments, regardless of their kind. The International Office of Museums in Paris was to ask the competent authority of the League of Nations to work out the statute.[30]

During this conference in Athens important decisions for international co-operation between states and their technicians had again been made. It was agreed that all monuments should be protected and that a climate of tolerance should be developed for those monuments which were not in fashion at a given moment in time.[31]

What changed after 1933?

German activities in international professionalism ended in 1933 when it left the League of Nations. Though reports of the newspaper *Mouseion* were translated and reprinted in the *Technische Mitteilungen für Malerei* until 1939, the international conference of museums in Madrid on 28 October 1934 had already taken place without German participation.[32] One of the most active German participants, Helmut Ruhemann, had already emigrated to England in 1933. Finally, the production of the English edition of the *Manuel de la Conservation et Restauration des Tableaux*[24] became risky for Monsieur Foundukidis under German occupation.[33]

At the national level there had been an attempt to form a kind of professionalism by law, which had been awaited with great expectation by important parts of the DG.[34]

The corporate trend of national socialist ideology furthered the degree of organization of the restorers. A precondition for staying in the occupation became the membership of the *Reichskammer der bildenden Künste*, which divided its subordinate branches into four sections. One of them was "reproduction, conservation and care for cultural heritage: copyists and restorers".[35] So there was some kind of protection for the profession, because membership of a section could only be achieved by application.[36]

Moreover, a reference institution was founded, the *Reichsinstitut für Maltechnik - Doernerinstitut* (Institute of the Reich for Painting Technique). Max Doerner, Professor for the Technique of Painting at the Academy in Munich, had many students who were becoming famous and influential under the National Socialists. One of those was the painter Adolf Ziegler who, in 1933, had been nominated for a professorship at the Academy in Munich and, in 1936, as President of the *Reichskammer der bildenden Künste*.[37] He was one of the most important supporters of Max Doerner. After the head of *the Versuchsanstalt und Auskunftsstelle für Maltechnik*, Alexander Eibner, had retired, Doerner was asked, in 1934, by the Ministry of School and Cultural Affairs for his opinion on the future of this institute. As he and Eibner had been rivals for many years, Doerner gave a bad report on the Institute and suggested that it become a part of the Academy with new staff and under his own supervision. The Institute should be a place where "apart from the science of the materials (. . .), the composition of paintings, the techniques of the old and new masters, should be examined more deeply than before, and care for tradition come into its own, according to the words of the

Führer".[38] Furthermore, Doerner wanted to build a school for restorers in co-operation with the workshops of the Institute for Preservation of Historic Monuments and the Pinakothek,[39] with which he had been in disagreement for many years.

Doerner's wishes were willingly accepted and in May 1937, the *Reichsinstitut für Maltechnik* was already in existence. One of its main functions was "the inquiry into the care and conservation of paintings".[40] The solemn inauguration was celebrated by Adolf Ziegler one year later on 9 July 1938, the "*Tag der Deutschen Kunst*" (Day of German Art). Again it was emphasized that "the question of the method of preservation or conservation of old masterworks and monuments (. . .) would be an important function of the Institute" and that "the results of the work should be put down in legal directives".[41]

Conclusion

After Germany had left the very promising international co-operation which was leading towards a profession on the basis of social need, a kind of state professionalism was attempted in Germany with forced corporations and reference institutes having legal powers. However, besides the appropriate fee, the freedom of decision and autonomy were not granted, largely due to the political system and the wartime situation inGermany. So the mark of professionalism was not attained.

Notes and references

1. The restriction to Germany results from the theme of my dissertation and the consideration that, in spite of all common points, the European or global situation varied too much and has not been investigated enough to show a common view of the profession of restoration. Early attempts tend to a positivistic view of history, which does no justice to the individual case.
   Many thanks to Bettina von der Goltz and Michael Wolfson for their helpful support.
2. H. Kahlert, "Auf dem Weg zur Profession – Ein Rückblick 1830–1939," *Museumskunde* 56, no. 1 (1991): 15.
3. The information on 36 larger museums is based on two inquiries by Ferdinand Stuttmann from 1940 and 1942, allowing conclusions on the 1930s, and my own inquiry from 1994/95, as well as information from different archives and from the literature.
4. J. Jahn, *Wörterbuch der Kunst* (Stuttgart: A.Kröner Verlag, 1940), 301.
5. R. Lischka, "Restaurieren oder Konservieren ?" *Technische Mitteilungen für Malerei* 49, no. 17 (1933): 137; G.Hurst, "Gemäldekonservierung und Bilderfirnis", ibid., no 22 (1933): 177. Many thanks to the Schweizerisches Institut für Kunstwissenschaft, Zürich, Christian Marty and especially to Anna Stoll for their friendly support in making literature available to me.
6. Thanks to Christoph Müller, Augustinermuseum Freiburg, for making important information available to me.
7. G. Lill, "Wiederhergestellte süddeutsche Bildwerke", *Pantheon* XVI (1935): 406, note 1.
8. Ibid.
9. A. Wolters, "Die Ausbildung von Restauratoren für die Museen", *Kunstchronik und Kunstmarkt* 46/47 (1926): 697–698.
10. K. Wehlte, "Konservator Jakob von Danzas gestorben", *Deutsche Zeitschrift für Maltechnik* 60 (1944): 15–16.
11. A. Dorner, "Ausführliche Bemerkung zur Stellung des Restaurators am Landesmuseum, Hannover, (July 8, 1936): 2; Letter of the provincial president to the director of the art department (27 April 1935), Niedersächsisches Hauptstaatsarchiv Hannover.
12. Christian Buhmann, *100 Jahre Bildhauer- und Restaurierungswerkstatt Baenke – Buhmann* (Hannover, 1989/90).
13. Anon., *Technische Mitteilungen für Malerei* 55, no.14 (1939): 112; Letter of Dr. Noack (1 January 1938), Sammlungsbetrieb/Restaurierung, Städt. Museen Freiburg; thanks to Thomas Heidenreich, Staatliche Kunsthalle Karlsruhe, for helpful information.
14. Kahlert, "Auf dem Weg zur Profession," 18–19.
15. Copy of the new articles, point 7, *Deutsche Gesellschaft für rationelle Malverfahren e.V. (Adolf Wilhelm Keim Gesellschaft), Einladung zur ordentlichen Generalversammlung für das Jahr 1926 und 1927*, (Munich, 24 May 1928): 2.
16. Ibid., 3.
17. H. Rinnebach, "Über moderne Maltechnik," *Technische Mitteilungen für Malerei* 45, no. 15 (1929): 187.
18. Anon., *Technische Mitteilungen für Malerei* 52, no. 13 (1936): 106–107.
19. H. Rinnebach, "Amerikanische Vorschläge für eine internationale Konvention zum Schutze der Kunst- und Naturdenkmäler im Kriegsfalle," *Technische Mitteilungen für Malerei* 47, no. 17 (1931): 200.

20. Anon., translated by L. Trillich, "Organisation der Forschung über Maltechnik und Gemäldepflege in England," *Technische Mitteilungen für Malerei* 47, no. 16 (1931): 187–188.
21. Anon., *Technische Mitteilungen für Malerei* 42, no. 1 (1926): 12.
22. K. Wehlte, "Wissenschaftliche Methoden zur Prüfung und Erhaltung von Kunstwerken," *Technische Mitteilungen für Malerei* 46, no. 24 (1930): 282.
23. "Conclusions de la Commission spéciale pour la Restauration des Peintures et l'Application des Vernis," *Mouseion* 5, no. 13–14 (1931): 129.
24. Ibid., note 1.
25. H. Ruhemann, "Organisation der wissenschaftlichen Untersuchungs- und Konservierungsmethoden für Kunstwerke," *Technische Mitteilungen für Malerei* 49, no. 12 (1933): 94–95; for the English edition of "Manuel de la conservation et de la restauration des peintures" see H. Ruhemann, *The Cleaning of Paintings* (London: Faber and Faber, 1968), 55; J. Plesters, "Bibliography", H. Ruhemann, *The Cleaning of Paintings*, 402, no. 28.
26. H.Rinnebach, *Technische Mitteilungen für Malerei* 47, no. 9 (1931): 103–104.
27. J. Koch, "Rechtsgrundsätze zur Restaurierungsfrage," Zentralarchiv der Staatlichen Museen zu Berlin/Preussischer Kulturbesitz.
28. Letter of R. Graul to H. Ruhemann (13 May 1931), ibid.
29. R. Maurer, "Schutz den Kunstwerken", *Technische Mitteilungen für Malerei* 48, no. 2 (1932): 11 13.
30. Letter of H. Rinnebach to H. Ruhemann (13 October 1931), Zentralarchiv der Staatlichen Museen zu Berlin/Preussischer Kulturbesitz.
31. "Auszug aus dem Bericht des internationalen Büros der Museen," *Technische Mitteilungen für Malerei* 49, no. 8 (1933): 59–60.
32. Anon., translated by L. Trillich, "Bilderpflege in Museen," *Technische Mitteilungen für Malerei* 49, no. 8 (1933): 59–60; K. Wehlte, "Probleme der Gemäldeerhaltung", *Zeitschrift für Kunstgeschichte*, no. 12 (1949): 90.
33. Ruhemann, "The Cleaning of paintings," 55.
34. The editor, "Zum Geleit," *Technische Mitteilungen für Malerei* 50, no. 1 (1934): 3–4.
35. G. Menz, "Der Aufbau des Kulturstandes," (Munich/Berlin, 1938) cited in J. Wulf, *Die Bildenden Künste im Dritten Reich*, (Gütersloh: Siegbert Mohn Verlag, 1963): 102.
36. Letter of the provincial leader of the *Reichskammer der bildenden Künste*, Weser-Ems, Fricke, to the Provincialmuseum Hannover (21 July 1936), Niedersächsisches Hauptstaatsarchiv Hannover.
37. *Mitteilungsblatt der RKdbK* (7 December 1936): 3, in Wulf, *Die Bildenden Künste*, 140; *Technische Mitteilungen für Malerei* 52, no. 24 (1936): 196.
38. M. Doerner, "Gutachten über die Frage der Weiterführung der Versuchsanstalt und Auskunftsstelle für Maltechnik," (1934): 1–2, Bayerisches Hauptstaatsarchiv.
39. Ibid.
40. Anon., "Reichsinstitut für Maltechnik," *Münchner Neueste Nachrichten*, no. 125 (9 May 1937); O. Liskowsky, "Ein Reichsinstitut für Maltechnik," *Technische Mitteilungen für Malerei* 53, no. 9 (1937): 99–100.
41. Anon., "Einweihung der Werkprüfungs- und Forschungsanstalt für Maltechnik München," *Völkischer Beobachter*, Berlin edition (10 July 1938); Anon., "Die andere Seite der Malerei," *Münchner Neueste Nachrichten/Münchner Stadtanzeiger* (8 September 1938); O. Thomae, *Die Propaganda-Maschine/Bildende Kunst und Öffentlichkeitsarbeit im Dritten Reich* (Berlin: Gebr. Mann Verlag, 1978): 538.

Working Group A4

Scientific examination of works of art

A Mass Spectrometric Study of the Effect of Varnish Removal from a 19th Century Solvent-sensitive Wax Oil Painting

Jaap J.Boon*
MOLART-project for Painted Art,
FOM Institute for Atomic and Molecular Physics, Kruislaan 407,
1098 SJ Amsterdam, The Netherlands
Jos van Och
MOLART-project for Painted Art,
SRAL, Daems Lunet 1C, 6221KZ Maastricht, The Netherlands

Abstract

Preliminary cleaning tests of a non-relined painting by the Dutch impressionist painter W. Maris (1844–1910) revealed that the paint softened considerably upon exposure to solvents. Multicomponent sensitive direct mass spectrometric (MS) techniques were used to identify organic components in microgram-sized samples taken from selected paint layers. The unknown yellow tinted varnish was identified as a slightly aged methylcyclohexanone resin of the AW2 type. Residues from a previously removed oxidised Dammar varnish were also identified. The impasto paints were oil with beeswax which makes these paints sensitive to all solvents. The effect of a fast solvent-based varnish removal technique (maximum contact time 2 s) was investigated by mass spectrometric analysis of the paint layers. The isooctane/ethanol (1:1) removed the varnish and fatty acids from the top layers of the paint but did not affect the wax esters and alkanes from the beeswax. The organic composition of the deeper paint layers was not changed. MS studies of the ground layer suggests that during a previous cleaning, fatty acids, diacids, diacylglycerols and a small amount of the beeswax have migrated to the highly absorbent chalk ground which has a yellowed somewhat transparent fatty appearance.

Keywords

Methylcyclohexanone resin, AW2, wax oil paint, beeswax, solvent cleaning effects, direct temperature mass spectrometry (DTMS), thermally assisted transmethylation, Gas chromatography mass spectrometry (GCMS), fatty acids, W.Maris

Introduction

The 19th century is a period in the history of painting technique in which major changes occur in the production of painting materials as well in their use in paintings. It is likely therefore that 19th century paintings are much more complex in their chemistry than paintings from previous centuries. Innovations in chemical synthesis led to new pigments which were readily used by painters with an experimental mind such as Turner.[1] Beliefs in the techniques of the Old Masters led to the use of additives such as oil/resin gels (megilps) or wax.[1,2] In fact, a relatively large body of handbooks, manuals and technical literature was written in this century to "analyse" painting technique of earlier masters and to assist the aspiring new artist.[3,4] New production methods and the desire for prolonged shelf life of the paint by the color man/manufacturer led to paint formulations which may not always have been in the interest of the ill-informed oil painter. Materials were not always what they were supposed to be. The painter Holman Hunt got so frustrated about adulteration of pigments that he set up his own laboratory to investigate the properties and ageing behavior of his painting materials.[5,6]

On the molecular level we still know very little about how mixtures of various paint materials affect each other in the long term. How is the polymer network of dried oil paint affected by additives, the various metals of the pigments and anionic species? What is the precise effect of addition of resins and other materials on the properties of the resulting oil film? Questions like these, are worded in the language of the practicing artist in the booklet by Roelofs.[7] Roelofs, a painter himself and acquainted with many painters in the late 19th century, wrote a treatise on proper oil painting technique in which he discusses "many do's and don'ts". Of relevance for our study, one topic discussed in this book is the photograph of a palette of J. Maris (1837–1899) dating from 1884. According to Roelofs the paint on this palette could still be used by simple mixing with some turpentine many years after the death of the painter. The secret, as explained by Roelofs, was the addition of wax to these paints. Apparently, the wax prevents the drying of oils beyond the formation of prepolymers of a relatively small size. The practice may have been widespread because the idea that "dried" paints could be revitalised on the palette was apparently popular. Hence, it is important to investigate the painting technique of A. Mauve (1838–1888), W. Maris (1844–1910), G.H. Breitner (1857–1923) and others in that period, not only because of curiosity about their painting methods, but also because such additions would seriously affect the restoration methodology.

In this paper, we have used mass spectrometric analytical techniques to investigate the materials in a painting by W. Maris, an important Dutch Impressionist (The Hague School).[8] The painting is still on its original support (unrelined canvas), but had been varnished with an unknown yellow (saffron?) tinted resin, which is now considered undesirable because it changes the colors of the painting. The softening of the paint after the preliminary varnish removal tests by the restorer suggested that the painting could be extremely solvent sensitive. Some of the concerns were the weakening and deformation of the paint layers upon varnish removal, paint loss at the surface and the fear of penetration of the varnish into the paint during solvent contact.

* Author to whom correspondence should be addressed

The analytical investigation concentrated on:

- a detailed analysis of the varnish and its ageing condition;
- the molecular level analysis of the organic constituents of the paint layers in order to get a better understanding of the vulnerability of the paints for solvents;
- compositional studies of the paint after solvent removal of the varnish to evaluate leaching and migration of solvent sensitive compounds.

Direct temperature resolved mass spectrometry (DTMS) was chosen as the main analytical technique because of its sensitivity and ability to investigate the distribution of a wide range of compound classes in one analytical run.[9] This technique has been developed in our group for direct analysis without wet chemical workup of paint samples and has been applied to paintings by Rembrandt, Steen, Bol, Turner, Sargent, Whistler and others.[10–12] Additional experiments with PyGCMS techniques were also performed to investigate specific compound classes. Microscopy and SEM-EDAX (scanning electron microscopy/energy-dispersive X-ray analysis) helped in the characterization of inorganic components.

Experimental

The painting "De Eendenfamilie" was painted by W. Maris (1844–1910) in 1868 and is presently the property of the Van Abbemuseum, Eindhoven, The Netherlands (inventory number 83). The painting is not lined and is covered with an unknown yellow tinted varnish. No restoration report is known to exist. The painting is in good condition and shows very little paint loss. The size of the painting is 65 ↔ 93 cm. Minute paint samples from the painting were taken, before and after cleaning, with steel needles with special edges suitable for unidirectional cutting. Coordinates of samples reported in this paper were:

(a) marbled olive green paint on the rim LH (left) and 45 mm up (code WM1);
(b) cross section of chocolate brown paint on top of olive green paint and white ground taken 5 mm LH and 48 mm up (code WM2).

The latter area was also used for the investigation of effects of the varnish removal. Varnish samples for analysis were removed with a cotton swab or with a specially designed suction device which acts like a solvent vacuum cleaner. The solvent for varnish removal was isooctane/ethanol (v/v =1/1).

Sample preparation

Samples were examined in the MS laboratory under a binocular microscope, dissected and transferred to mini glass mortars for homogenisation in about 25 μl of ethanol. Aliquots of the ethanol suspension were applied to the tip of the filament probe (sample load of solid paint materials less than 10 μm) and dried in vacuum. The probe was then transferred to the vacuum lock of the MS system and inserted into the ionisation chamber. The sample-coated filament is placed almost in the center of the ion source, to avoid losses by condensation and to insure a short time interval between generation of neutral molecules and production of ions.

Direct temperature resolved mass spectrometry (DTMS)

The mass spectrometric experiments were performed on a JEOL SX-102A double focusing mass spectrometer (B/E) using a direct insertion probe equipped with a resistively heatable platinum/rhodium (9/1) filament (diameter 100 μm). The probe filament was temperature programmed to heat at a rate of 1A min^{-1} corresponding to about 16°C s^{-1}. Ions were generated by electron impact ionisation, extracted at 10 kV and mass separated and post-accelerated to 20 kV. The mass spectrometer was scanned from m/z 20 to 1000 at a cycle time of 1 scan s^{-1} at a resolution of 3000. Data acquisition was performed on-line on a JEOL MP-7000 system.

Gas chromatography mass spectrometry (GCMS)

Capillary GCMS was performed on a Carlo Erba MEGA2 (Fisons series 8565 HRGC) coupled directly to a JEOL DX-303 double focusing mass spectrometer (E/B). A FOM-4LX pyrolysis unit suitable for Curie-point pyrolysis was used for thermally assisted analytical studies. A temperature programmable FOM built RF power supply was used for the generation of the high-frequency field. A ferromagnetic probe with a Curie-point temperature of 610°C was used. TMAH spiking took place by addition of 10 μl of a 2.5% aqueous solution of Tetramethylammoniumhydroxide (TMAH) to the dried paint particles. The GC was equipped with a 25 m fused silica column (i.d. 0.32 mm) coated with SGE BPX5 (0.25 mm film) with helium as carrier gas. The mass spectrometry was performed under electron impact conditions at 70 eV, ions were extracted at 3 kV, separated by scanning of the magnet and ESA from m/z 40 to 700 with a cycle time of 1 s, and post-accelerated to 10 kV. A JEOL MP-7000 was used for data acquisition and processing.

Paint composition in cross section

The painting "De Eendenfamilie" pictures ducks near a pond surrounded by trees. Most of the lower part of the painting is covered with a marbled green paint, which on microscopic examination of the painting at high magnification consists of brown, yellow and green streaks. This characteristic marbling painting technique is most likely responsible for the freshness of the color and the lush appearance of the meadow around the pond on the painting. The same technique was also observed in other paintings by W. Maris and may be his trademark. These paints were found to be rather solvent sensitive and softened considerably upon solvent contact. DTMS studies were performed on a larger number of samples from the painting, but here we can only present data on a representative cross section of the paints and ground layer of the WM2 sample. Prior to dissection and subsampling for DTMS study, a separate painting cross section was examined by light microscopy and SEM-EDAX. Paint layers observed were a thin (8 μm) upper layer of a chocolate brown paint with vermilion and Prussian blue, on top of a thick (40 μm) olive green paint with Naples yellow, lead chrome yellow, Prussian blue and zinc white. These paint layers are isolated from a thick priming ground by a thin partly cracked layer of lead white (15 μm). The SEM-EDAX data on the priming ground shows Ca as the main component with a minor amount of Zn. In the absence of sulfur, this mineral phase is identified as chalk. Chalk grounds with zinc white as additive were not uncommon in the 19th century.[13] Such chalk grounds are usually bound with protein binders. The ground layer in the Maris painting is yellowed, has a very fatty consistency and is rather transparent upon examination in reflection microscopy. A substantial absorption of oil-derived fatty substances could explain the apparent match in refractive index because oily material in chalk is rather transparent.[14] A thermally assisted transmethylation GCMS study of the ground was undertaken to investigate this phenomenon.

Organic components in the paint layers

Figure 1(A–C) presents the DTMS data of the upper layer of WM2 before (A) and after varnish removal (A^1), and data on the green paint (B) and priming ground layer (C) as far as they could be separated manually. The chalk ground could be separated easily from the lead white layer, but the latter was strongly attached to the olive green paint. The olive green paint sample (from WM1) free of the lead white layer was investigated for comparison and gave similar MS data. The MS data before varnish removal of the upper chocolate-brown paint with very little green paint (see Figure 1(A)) shows a large number of characteristic ions over a wide mass range. Most of these peaks disappear upon varnish removal with isoctane/ethanol (1:1) as is evident from Figure 1(A^1). The latter sample could not be prepared free of small amounts of the lower lying green paint. Prominent ions in the spectra in Figures 1(A^1) and 1(B) are m/z 206, 207, 208 of the isotopes of lead and an ion series at m/z 592, 620, 648, 676, 704 and 732. The lead is released at high temperature

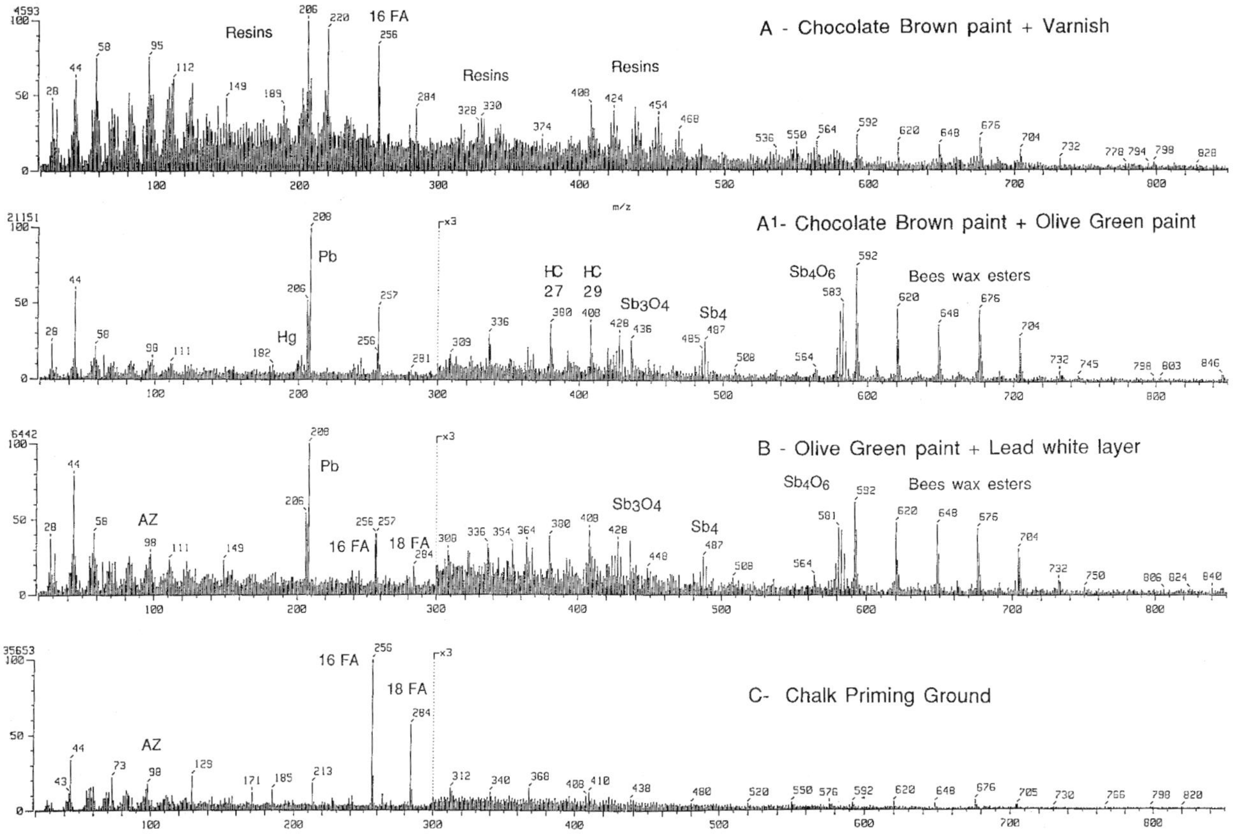

Figure 1. DTMS data of the chocolate-brown paint top layer before (A) and after varnish removal (A¹), the lower olive green paint layer including a lead white layer of the priming (B), and the chalk ground (C)

and corresponds to the decomposition of the lead chrome yellow and the Naples yellow (lead antimonate). The ion series at *m/z* 592, 620, 648, 676, 704 and 732 in combination with the relatively intense ion *m/z* 257 is indicative of esters of beeswax[11] and corresponds closely to the MS data of beeswax reference material. This ion series is most prominent in the MS data in the scan range indicative of volatile components. The m/z 257 is the main EI fragment ion the fatty acid moiety of the beeswax esters series C16 fatty acid/C24 alcohol (molecular ion 592) to C16 fatty acid /C34 alcohol (molecular ion 732). This ion series is often seen in wax/resin-lined paintings as a result of impregnation of the paint in the lining process.[10] This painting is not lined however, so the wax is present as a paint additive. The presence of beeswax is probably the main cause of the solvent sensitivity of the paint, but it is not clear how to explain this on the molecular level. We speculate that beeswax interferes with the polymerisation process and reduces the size of the polymer network. This will be investigated further.

Interesting clusters of isotopes appear at *m/z* 579, 581, 583 and 585 which are assigned to Sb_4O_6 [reference 15] from the antimonate in the Naples yellow. Antimonate also decomposes under the analysis conditions which is evident from the isotopic cluster of Sb_3O_4 (main peak at *m/z* 428) and the appearance of the fully reduced Sb_4 and Sb_2. Prussian blue (ferriferrocyanide), which is another important color determining pigment in the paint, is evident from *m/z* 27 (HCN) a thermal decomposition product, which occurs in the same analytical temperature window as the Prussian blue reference material. The vermilion in the top layer decomposes under DTMS to mercury which is observed by its isotope pattern at *m/z* 199, 200 201, 202 and 203 (marked as Hg in Figure 1(A¹)). Fatty acid information from saturated fatty acids is present in the DTMS data as *m/z* 256 (16FA-palmitic acid) and *m/z* 284 (18FA-stearic acid). These fatty acids are mainly present as free fatty acids. Their relative intensity is low in comparison to the ground layer and compared to other oil paints. The *m/z* 98 and 152 (marked as AZ) are indicative of azelaic acid. Much of the small "chemical noise" in the spectrum of Figure 1(B) is from the oil-paint network in this layer.

As the beeswax can potentially contribute substantially to the palmitic acid content of the sample, a ratio of C16/C18 is not trustworthy as an indicator of the oil medium used. If we assume that beeswax has contributed some palmitic acid, the ratio approaches the typical value for linseed oil (between 1 and 2).[16] There are no indications for diterpenoid or triterpenoid resins used as additives in the paint. The DTMS data of the priming ground shown in Figure. 1(C) is mainly from free fatty acids with C16 (*m/z* 256) and C18 (*m/z* 284) saturated fatty acid as the main components. There are minor amounts of the C20 (*m/z* 312), C22 (*m/z* 340) and C24 (*m/z* 368) fatty acids. The *m/z* 98 and 152 are indicative of C9 diacid (AZ). The *m/z* 550 (C16/C16) and 576 (C16/C18) are from diacylglycerols. Very small peaks of beeswax esters are visible in the spectrum of the ground. Temperature-resolved data indicate that all these lipids are present in mobile phases because there were no indications for the presence of an oil network in the high-temperature analytical window.

Identification of the varnish

The mass spectrum of the resin on the painting and on a cotton swab (Figure 2(A)) used in a removal test did not resemble any previous MS data which we had obtained on aged dammar and mastic resins.[10,11,17] These natural resins age on the paintings forming various oxidised dammarane and oleanane skeletal compounds with strong signals in the DTMS data at *m/z* 143 (loss of a tetrahydrofuran side chain in ocotillone like dammar derivatives) and parent ions in the *m/z* 400–470 range. Instead, the mass spectrum of the resin on the Maris painting showed an ion series over a wide mass range up to *m/z* 800 with a certain regularity in mass increment of about 110 mass units. This suggested a regularity in molecular structure which is usually observed in synthetic resins. Comparative studies with ketone resins (Laropal K80 or Ketone N) showed comparable regularities, but with the wrong mass numbers. The increments were smaller and the main ions were *m/z* 98, 192, 206, 304, etc. (Figure 2(B)). Examination of the ions of the unknown varnish showed strong ions at *m/z* 95, 112, 206, 220 and mass clusters around *m/z* 330, 440, 550 and 670. This suggests that methylketone resins had been used as the varnish. Indeed, comparison with Figures 1(C) and 1(D) from the reference materials MS2 (Laporte) and AW2 (BASF) supported this idea. The presence of a relatively strong *m/z* 95, *m/z* 112, a *m/z* 206 > 220 and cluster ions around *m/z* 330, 440 and 550 strongly suggest that the varnish has originally been the AW2 BASF product. This identification was further supported by the results of pyrolysis GCMS experiments. Evidence for residual Dammar could also be derived from these PYGCMS data because ocotillone was found as a component, which is an indicator for oxidised Dammar[17] and seen as evidence for a previous natural varnish. The distribution of ions in Figure 1(A) is not exactly the same as the fresh reference material (Figure 1(D)), which suggests that ageing of the varnish on the painting has left its traces. An indication for such changes is the general tendency for some of the heavier ion series to have two or four hydrogen atoms less than the reference material, which we interpret as an indication for oxidative hydrogen abstraction. This phenomenon will be studied in more detail by high resolution mass spectrometry and reported elsewhere.

The AW2 is assumed to be the basis of many proprietary picture varnishes. The methylated ketone resins were one of the earliest ketone resins introduced (about 1950).[16] The use of ketone resins in museums in the Netherlands appears to be discontinued at the beginning of the 1970s.[18] The chemical condition of the synthetic varnish is still quite good when judged on the basis of the resemblance between the unknown and the reference material. The conditions on the painting are apparently milder than those in artificial ageing devices which test the resistance to failing of the varnish.[19] The composition of the paint dictates a polar solvent to avoid dissolution and migration of the apolar constituents (alkanes and beeswax) in the paint.

Effect of ultra-fast varnish removal

A new method of varnish removal was attempted in which the varnish was wetted with solvent [isooctane–ethanol (1/1)] and the soluble material was immediately removed by a high-power solvent suction device allowing a maximum exposure time of 2 s. The effect of this ultra-fast varnish removal was tested by examination of the composition of the paint and ground layers before and after cleaning using

Table 1. Fatty acids and diacids identified as methyl esters by thermally assisted transmethylation GCMS in the chalk ground layer of the Maris painting "De Eendenfamilie" (Eindhoven, van Abbemuseum inventory no. 83)

Identification	Relative intensity (%)
C5 diacid	1.4
C6 diacid	2.2
C7 diacid	5.6
C8 diacid	7.1
C9 diacid	27.5
C10 diacid	2.3
C11 diacid	1.2
C14:0 fatty acid	1.8
C15:0 fatty acid	1.0
C16:0 fatty acid	100.0
C17:0 fatty acid	1.1
C18:0 fatty acid	39.3
C20:0 fatty acid	2.0
C22:0 fatty acid	1.2
C24:0 fatty acid	2.1
C26:0 fatty acid	trace
C28:0 fatty acid	trace
C18:1 fatty acid	1.7
epoxy C18 fatty acid	1.3
OH-C18:1 fatty acid	7.8
9,10-diOH-C18 fatty acid	11.2

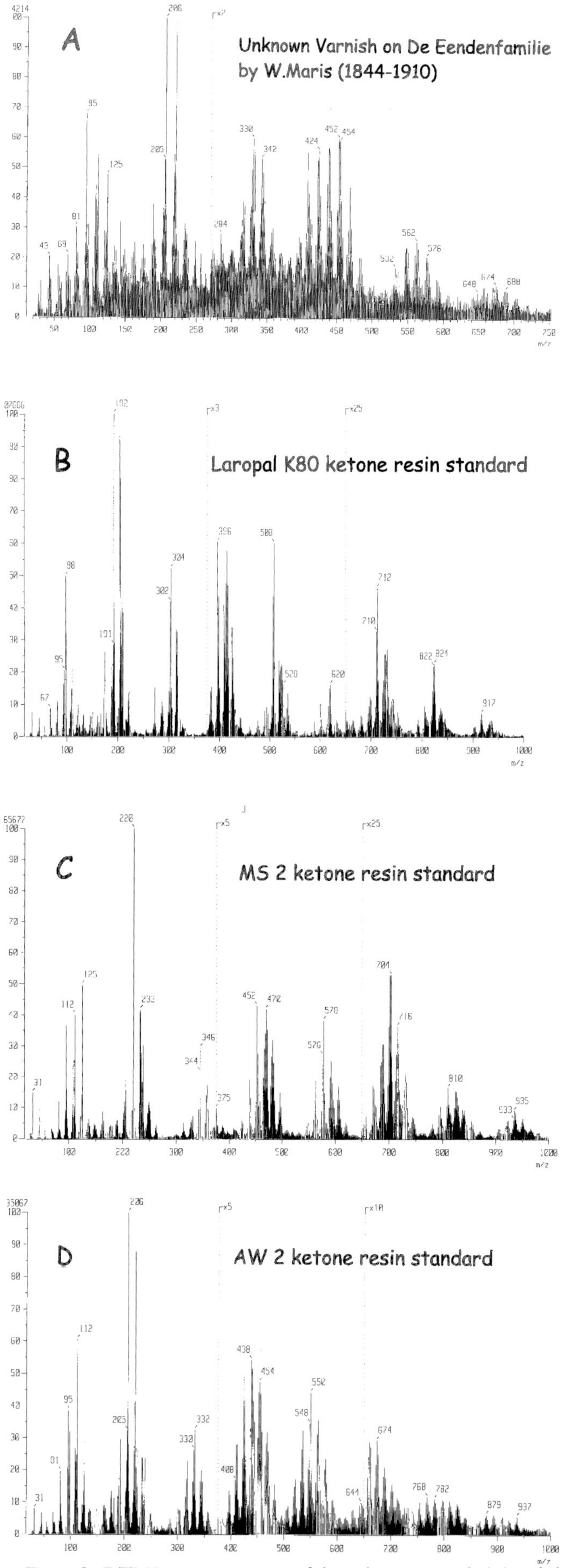

Figure 2. DTMS summary spectra of the unknown varnish (A) and the ketone resin reference materials Laropal K-80 (B), MS2 (Laporte) (C) and AW2 BASF (D). The unknown is identified as a slightly aged AW2 methylketone resin

DTMS. Experimental studies at AMOLF have demonstrated that this approach is a good way to determine the extent of migration of mobile phases in paintings.[10] Although analysis of a swab used for varnish removal – an undesirable technique in the case of this solvent sensitive painting – would give information on what is removed from the surface of the painting, it will not give information on the effects of solvents and migration of soluble compounds in the paint layers of the painting.

The DTMS data of WM2 in Figure 1(A) prior to solvent contact shows the MS pattern of the methyl ketone resin AW2 of the varnish, the beeswax MS pattern as well as relatively high intensity peaks for the palmitic (m/z 256) and stearic acid (m/z 284). The observed ratio of the fatty acids indicates that some non-drying oil may have been a component of the ketone resin. This practice is not uncommon in factory-made ketone resins products.[19] DTMS of the paint after the short exposure to the solvent (Figure 1(A^1)) demonstrates that the beeswax esters are still present but the resin is completely removed. Even the alkanes of the beeswax in the paint (m/z 380 (C27H56), 408 (C29H60) and 436 (C31H64) are preserved. The high intensity peaks of the free fatty acids present in Figure 1(A) have decreased strongly in relative intensity however. DTMS data of the green paint and ground layer after varnish removal are very similar to the spectrum before the solvent treatment. In the deeper layers of the paint, the fatty acid signature is not changed by the short solvent contact at the surface. The short exposure and fast varnish removal process in combination with the polarity choice of the cleaning solvent preserves the hydrocarbon-soluble components (alkanes and beeswax) but affects the fatty acids in the top layer.

Fatty acids in the ground layer

The appearance of the ground layer and the relatively low intensity of the fatty acid signature in the wax oil paint suggests that fatty acids had accumulated in the chalk. DTMS data indicates that only mobile fatty acids were present. Earlier we have proposed that the paint layers could have been losing oil by absorption of binding oil by the ground during construction of the painting.[21] To test this hypothesis, evidence was obtained for polymerisation of this oil in the chalk. A sample of the priming ground was analysed with temperature-resolved thermally assisted trans-methylation Curie-point pyrolysis GCMS. The TMAH-treated sample was first analysed at a Curie-point temperature of 250°C and analysed by GCMS. Then, the GCMS was prepared for another analytical run and the residue of the sample remaining was analysed at a temperature of 600°C. Table 1 lists the identified compounds. The main peak of the transmethylated compounds is from palmitic acid. The ratio of palmitic to stearic acid is 2.5, which is too high for linseed oil as such according to Mills and White.[16] An addition of some poppyseed oil cannot be excluded considering its wider usage in the 19th century.[13] The various smaller diacids are indicative for isomerisation of double bonds of the oil (prepolymerisation?). The epoxy and hydroxy C18 fatty acids are presumably from oxidised monounsaturated C18 fatty acids. Apart from the C20, C22 and C24 saturated fatty acids, the data do contain C26 and C28 fatty acids in smaller relative amounts. We have seen the C20 and C22 more often in modern linseed oils, but the C24, C26 and C28 are more likely derived from beeswax. The amount seems to small to have any effect on the P/S ratio. The odd fatty acids (C15:0 and C17:0) are very unusual for plants but very common in bacteria.[22] There are even some minor peaks indicative of bacterial iso-branched odd fatty acids (not mentioned in the table). It is possible that bacteria have colonised the fatty ground layer. All compounds were found to be volatilised at low temperature. Compared to polymerised oil reference material,[23] no evidence was found for an oil network polymer. An oil ground in chalk without any dryer would have been strange in the light of what is known about priming grounds.[7,13] It therefore seems likely that the fatty acids have been imported as mobile phase into the ground layer at a later stage after drying of the paint. We now believe that the migration of fatty acids most likely must have taken place when a Dammar varnish was replaced by the synthetic resin varnish in the middle of this century. Another indication for migration is the small amount of intact beeswax in the ground layer. This indicates that relatively polar solvents were used in the past for the cleaning process. Apolar solvents would have severely extracted and mobilised the wax and hydrocarbon components in the paint layers, leading to higher relative amounts in the ground and severe damage to the impasto of the painting. A polar solvent and prolonged contact with such a solvent would mostly have affected the more polar free fatty acids and the diacylglycerols in the paint, of which a certain fraction ended up in the highly absorbent chalk of the primer of the canvas.

Main points and concluding remarks

Why did Willem Maris use wax oil paint? Perhaps archival studies may reveal his motivation. Maris wanted to paint with light and he did not choose his subject matter to represent cows or ducks as such.[24] His method seems to be painting with marbled pure paints as fine streaks on a submacroscopic level to maintain optical clarity and brightness. Our speculation is that addition of more viscous materials such as wax prevented extensive mixing of the paint on the palette and canvas thus maintaining the special marbling effect. If he also tried to increase the viscosity by lowering of the oil content of the paint on an absorbing material, the drying process of the paint itself could have been affected. It is not known whether Maris could buy paints of the right consistency for his technique in his time. It is quite possible that he prepared his paints himself. Comparative studies are under way on paintings by the Maris brothers, Mauve and Breitner. Experiments to reconstruct these paints will be undertaken in the context of the MOLART project.

There are implications for restorative treatment. The composition of the painting is sensitive to solvents and heat treatment. As wax/resin lining has been common practice in the Netherlands – also for 19th century paintings – it is certain that other paintings of W. Maris have undergone this treatment. Comparative studies on the effects of lining and varnish removal on related paintings by W. Maris are planned and hopefully will shed light on the potential damage and longer-term effects.

Can the synthetic varnish be safely removed? Hydrocarbon solvents are forbidden. A mildly polar solvent does the job but also removes fatty acids from the top layers. The ultra-fast removal technique invented by Van Och at SRAL, with its very short exposure time, seems to do the least amount of damage and is worth further exploration. The fraction of free fatty acids from the paints which are presently in the ground layer indicates that the previous cleaning of an aged Dammar varnish may have soaked the painting with solvent and displaced mobile fractions to the ground and the canvas.

DTMS proved to be powerful as an identification method, despite the limitations of dissecting paint layers manually. An innovative technique for varnishes, paint media and pigments developed in our laboratory will make it possible to use the same mass spectrometric identification method but coupled with microscopy and laser assisted spot heating (spot size 10 μm) [25]. This should provide us with more detailed knowledge on the composition and spatial distribution of complex paint media mixtures which seem to have been so common in the 19th century.

Acknowledgments

Research on paintings and other art objects in the Unit for Mass Spectrometry of Macromolecular Systems is part of the research program of the NWO Priority program of MOLART – a project on the Ageing of Painted Art – and FOM (Foundation for Fundamental Research on Matter), a subsidiary of the Dutch Organisation for Scientific Research (NWO). The author acknowledges support from the European Committee within the Program for Human Capital and Mobility (SCICULT grant; nr. ERBCHGCT920135) and the Environment Program Phase II (ERA project EV5VCT94-0548). The authors thank the Stichting Restauration Atelier Limburg (SRAL) and Anne van Grevenstein for the opportunity to perform this research. The assistance of Karin Groen (CL), Rene Huigen (MOLART), Jos Pureveen (FOM), KlaasJan van den Berg and Leo Spetter (MOLART) is gratefully acknowledged. Tom Learner (Tate Gallery, London) and Elisabeth Bracht (Stedelijk Museum, Amsterdam) are thanked for providing ketone resin reference samples. Professor Dr J. van Asperen de Boer, Professor Dr R. de la Rie and an unknown reviewer are thanked for constructive remarks on the manuscript.

Notes and references

1. J.H. Townsend. *Turner's Painting Techniques* (London: Tate Gallery, 1993).
2. L.A. Carlyle and A. Southall, "No Short Mechanic Road to Fame. The Implications of Certain Artist Materials for the Durability of British Painting: 1770–1840". *Robert Vernon's Gift*, ed. Robin Hamlyn (London: Tate Gallery, 1993).
3. L.A. Carlyle, "Varnish Preparation and Practice 1750–1850", in *Turner's Painting Techniques in Context*, ed. J.H.Townsend (London: UKIC, 1995), 21–29.
4. L.A. Carlyle, "A Critical Analysis of Artists' Handbooks Manuals and Treatises on Oil Painting Published in Britain from 1800 to 1900: With References to Selected Eighteenth Century Sources" (Doctoral thesis, Courtauld Institute of Art, University of London, 1991).
5. M.R. Katz, "William Holman Hunt and the "Pre-Raphaelite Technique", in *Historical Painting Techniques, Materials and Studio Practice*, ed. A.Wallert, E.Hermens and M.Peek (Marina del Rey, CA: The Getty Conservation Institute, 1995), 158–166.
6. L.A. Carlyle, "Beyond the Collection of Data: What Can We Learn from Documentary Sources on Artists' Materials and Techniques", in *Historical Painting Techniques, Materials and Studio Practice*, ed. A.Wallert, E.Hermens and M.Peek (Marina del Rey, CA: The Getty Conservation Institute, 1995), 1–5.
7. W.E. Roelofs Jr, *DePpraktijk van het Schilderen*. (Amsterdam: Maatschappij voor goede en goedkope lectuur, 1919).
8. I. Chilvers, H. Osborne and D. Farr, *The Oxford Dictionary of Art* (Oxford: Oxford University Press, 1988), 313.
9. J.J. Boon, "Analytical Pyrolysis Mass Spectrometry: New Vistas Opened by Temperature Resolved In-source PYMS". *International Journal of Mass spectrometry and Ion Processes* 118/119 (1992): 755–787.
10. J.J. Boon, J. Pureveen, D. Rainford and K. Groen, "Direct Temperature Resolved Mass Spectrometry of the Mobile and Chemically Bound Organic Constituents in Rembrandt's Jewish Bride", *Restauratie Jaarboek*, vol. 1. *De Acht Rembrandts* (Amsterdam: Rijksmusem, 1994), in press. Part of this information was reported at the Rembrandt Technical Symposium, held at the National Gallery in London (May 1992).
11. J.J. Boon, J. Pureveen, D. Rainford and J.H.Townsend, "The Opening of the Walhalla, 1842: Studies on the Molecular Signature of Turner's Paint by Direct Temperature Resolved Mass Spectrometry (DTMS)". In *Turner's Painting Techniques in Context*, ed. J.H.Townsend (London, UKIC, 1995), 21–29.
12. J.J. Boon, Unpublished results.
13. M. Koller, "Das Staffeleibild der Neuzeit". in *Reclams Handbuch der Kuenstlerischen Techniken* 1 (Stuttgart: Philipp Reclam jr., 1984), 389–392 and 402–405.
14. H. Kuehn, "Farbmaterialien. Pigmente und Bindemittel" in *Reclams Handbuch der Kuenstlerischen Techniken* 1 (Stuttgart: Philipp Reclam jr., 1984), 12–14.
15. R.M.A. Heeren, C.G. de Koster and J.J. Boon, "Direct Temperature Resolved HRMS of Fire Retarded Polymers by In-Source PYMS on an External Source Fourier Transform Ion Cyclotron Resonance Mass Spectrometer". *Analytical Chemistry* 67 (1995): 3965–3970.
16. J.S. Mills and R. White, *The Chemistry of Museum Objects*, 2nd edn (Oxford: Butterworth-Heinemann, 1994).
17. G.A. van der Doelen and J.J. Boon, "Mass Spectrometry of Resinous Compounds from Paintings: Characterisation of Dammar and Naturally Aged Dammar Varnish by DTMS and HPLC/GCMS", in *Resins. Ancient and Modern*, ed. M.M.Wright and J.H.Townsend (Edinburgh, SSCR, 1995), 70–76 and errata.
18. E. Bracht (Stedelijk Museum, Amsterdam), personal communication.
19. J.R.J.van Asperen de Boer, personal communication.
20. E.R. de la Rie, "Stable Varnishes for Old Master Paintings" (PhD Dissertation, University of Amsterdam, 1988), 134.
21. J.J. Boon, K-J van den Berg, J. Pureveen, G. van der Doelen, K. Groen, J. van Och and A. van Grevenstein. "Direct Temperature Resolved Mass Spectrometry (DTMS) as a Tool to Study Painted Art: A Case Study of the "Eendenfamilie" by W.Maris, a 19th Century Dutch Impressionist Painter". Extended abstract 745 of a poster in *Proceedings of the 43rd ASMS Conference on Mass Spectrometry and Allied Topics*, Atlanta, (1995), 745.
22. N. Shaw. "Lipid Composition as a Guide to Classification of Bacteria", in *Advances in Applied Microbiology* 17, ed. D. Perlman (New York: Academic Press, 1973), 63-109.
23. O. Van der Brink and J.J. Boon, Unpublished observations from MS studies on polymerised unsaturated fatty acid standards. Manuscript in preparation.
24. J. Kiers, W. Loos, H. van Os, F. Tissink and A. Vels Heijn. *Een eeuw apart*. (Amsterdam: Rijksmuseum Stichting, 1993), 124,125.
25. This instrument was designed by Dr R.M.A. Heeren (AMOLF) and is based on an external ion source ion trap mass spectrometer (ITMS). At the time of writing, the instrument is operational for DTMS studies. The microscopy laser desorption unit will be implemented later this year.

Apport de l'analyse PIXE à l'étude de la technique picturale d'un thang-ka peint du musée Guimet de Paris

Sylvie Colinart*
Laboratoire de recherche des musées de France
6 rue des Pyramides, 75041 Paris, France

Duncan Mac Arthur
Queen's University
Kingston ON 3N6
Canada

Gilles Béguin
Musée Cernuschi
7 Av. Vélasquez
75008 Paris, France

Résumé

Cet article décrit l'apport de l'analyse PIXE (Particle Induced X-ray Emission) en faisceau extrait, réalisée avec le système d'analyse AGLAE du Laboratoire de Recherche des Musées de France basé sur un accélérateur de particules, à l'examen d'un thang-ka du XIVè siècle appartenant aux collections du Musée Guimet de Paris. Cette oeuvre fait partie d'une série de peintures portatives rattachées à la tradition de *sTag-lung*, monastère fondé au Tibet central, en 1180. Son exécution éblouissante rappelle l'art du manuscrit. A partir d'une première approche de la technique picturale effectuée par les méthodes d'examens traditionnelles, l'identification des pigments minéraux et des décors métalliques est principalement menée par analyse PIXE. Sur ce thang-ka en bon état de conservation, les constituants de la palette chromatique sont ainsi appréhendés; en particulier, un pigment blanc à base d'oxyde d'arsenic est décelé. L'examen de ce thang-ka met en valeur la maîtrise de l'artiste pour préparer et utiliser les différentes substances dont il disposait.

Mots-clés

Thang-ka, peinture, Tibet central, PIXE, pigments, liant

Figure 1. Le lama *(Inv.: MA 6083), thang-ka peint vers 1300, appartenant aux collections du musée national des Arts asiatiques - Guimet.*

Introduction

Entre 1989 et 1994, le Laboratoire de recherche des musées de France (LRMF) a étudié dix thang-ka anciens du musée Guimet de Paris, allant du XIIIe au XVIIe siècle, en vue de leur expertise avant achat ou restauration. Dans ce contexte, nous avons pu définir leur état de conservation par des examens préliminaires et nous avons identifié les constituants du support et de la matière picturale à partir de microprélèvements.[1] La technique de fabrication de ces peintures, qui surprennent souvent l'oeil occidental par leur iconographie complexe et par leurs couleurs, a ainsi pu être précisée, mettant en évidence les différentes étapes de la création, de la mise en place du dessin préparatoire à l'application des couleurs.[2] La technique picturale paraît, par ailleurs, très proche de celle d'aujourd'hui.[3]

En juin 1994, la nouvelle acquisition, par le musée Guimet de Paris, d'un thang-ka ancien en parfait état de conservation, a amené à envisager une approche différente de l'analyse de la matière picturale afin de restreindre au strict nécessaire le nombre de prélèvements. L'analyse PIXE (Particle Induced X-ray Emission) en faisceau extrait, mise en oeuvre grâce à un accélérateur de particules, nous a paru répondre à cette contrainte, le LRMF disposant d'un tel système.[4] Installé en 1987, dans l'enceinte du musée du Louvre à Paris, AGLAE (Accélérateur Grand Louvre d'Analyse Elémentaire) est dédié aux techniques d'analyse par faisceaux d'ions, plus connues sous leur acronyme anglo-saxon IBA pour Ion Beam Analysis, appliquées à l'étude des oeuvres d'art et d'archéologie.[5]

Présentation de l'oeuvre

Le thang-ka (Inv.: MA 6083), acquis en juin 1994 par le musée Guimet est une pièce de taille modeste, 0,50 mètre de hauteur sur 0,38 mètre de large. Datée vers 1300, il est répertorié comme faisant partie d'une série de peintures portatives rattachées à la tradition de *sTag-lung*, monastère fondé au Tibet central, en 1180.[6] Il représente un *lama* exécutant le geste de tourner la roue de la loi (Figure 1). Malgré les inscriptions figurant sur la peinture, le nom du lama reste inconnu. Ce lama est entouré de deux bodhisattva. Celui situé à sa droite a pu être identifié comme étant Mañjuçrî jaune. Des personnages correspondant aux maîtres de la filiation spirituelle du lama sont répartis dans de petites cavernes aux rochers stylisés. Sur un registre supplémentaire, juste au dessous du trône, des arhat[7] de la tradition chinoise, au nombre de dix-sept constituent l'une des curiosités de ce thang-ka ainsi que la présence anecdotique de petits animaux au dessus de l'auréole du personnage principal et sur la crête de la montagne supérieure.

Ce thang-ka d'une exécution éblouissante possède, par la précision du dessin, la minutie d'une enluminure. La palette chromatique très subtile est principalement constituée de pigments minéraux où le rouge domine. De nombreuses autres couleurs sont présentes: du blanc, comme pour les carnations du lama, un jaune vif, des nuances orange, deux tons de bleu et de vert, du noir, une laque rouge et de la dorure en poudre. Il faut remarquer également un gris, appliqué sur les deux éléphants près du lama et sur les carnations de quelques buddha, couleur que nous n'avons jamais observée sur les thang-ka anciens examinés au laboratoire. La surface de la peinture a un aspect brillant dû à l'application d'une fine couche de vernis.

*Auteur à qui la correspondance doit être adressée

Figure 2. Le revers du lama *(Inv.: MA 6083)* .

Figure 3. Radiographie du thang-ka mettant en évidence le bon état général de conservation de l'oeuvre à l'exception du côté droit.

Le revers est orné d'un texte en lettres dorées et d'un stûpa aux contours tracés avec une encre dont la couleur s'est affadie au cours du temps (Figure 2).

Résultats des examens classiques

Dans un premier temps, des examens photographiques et radiographiques ainsi que des observations de la peinture en lumière transmise et sous loupe binoculaire ont été menés afin de préciser l'état de conservation du thang-ka et de faire une première estimation visuelle de la composition des couleurs. Deux prélèvements ont également pu être effectués et analysés. Cette première étape apporte les informations suivantes:

Il existe peu de lacunes de matière picturale et de toile, et l'image obtenue en lumière transmise est en accord avec le cliché radiographique (Figure 3). La toile originale est faite d'une seule pièce au tissage peu serré, environ 12 fils verticaux par centimètre et 19 horizontaux. La coupe transversale d'un prélèvement de quelques fibres montre qu'il s'agit de coton. Quelques manques sont rebouchés avec une toile de texture plus serrée que la toile de coton originale et ils sont masqués par un enduit de couleur proche de celle de la préparation. L'analyse par diffraction X[8] et par tests microchimiques[9] d'un prélèvement de préparation, pris sur le revers du thang-ka, caractérise un mélange de calcite et de liant protéinique. Seul le côté droit a subi une restauration. Quelques interventions ponctuelles sont également observées. Ces examens confirment le bon état général de conservation de l'oeuvre.

Sur cette peinture très élaborée, aucun dessin préparatoire ni repère de couleur ne sont mis en évidence par réflectographie infrarouge ou par photographie infrarouge comme, par exemple, sur un détail du thang-ka du *buddha Vajrasattva*, daté de la première moitié du XIII siècle (MA 1089, musée Guimet), (Figures 4, 5). En revanche, la photographie infrarouge, offre une lecture différente des couleurs dont la restitution en noir et blanc épure l'image et permet de mieux localiser l'alternance de certaines nuances. En particulier, sur le côté gauche de la photographie (Figure 6) sont mis en évidence des éléments d'architecture peints en alternance avec des couleurs bleues de composition différente. L'observation sous loupe binoculaire montre que l'un est un bleu sombre à la texture très homogène correspondant probablement à de l'indigo, transparent dans l'infrarouge, et l'autre est à base d'azurite, pigment opaque dans ces longueurs d'ondes.[10] Il en est de même pour des plages vertes sur le nimbe du lama et sur quelques pétales du lotus. L'analyse par diffraction X d'un prélèvement de ce vert indique qu'il s'agit de malachite.

Sous lumière ultraviolette, les lacunes et les restaurations sont accentuées. Au revers, le texte doré est plus facilement lisible (Figure 7). Des zones sombres apparaissent également. Sur la face, elles correspondent aux éléments peints avec de l'azurite et de la malachite. Leur présence pourrait s'expliquer par une migration du liant de la couleur à travers la préparation et la toile. Ce phénomène semble être en liaison avec le broyage de ces pigments dont la taille des grains plus importante que pour les autres couleurs aurait nécessité un excès de liant.

Analyse PIXE

Figure 4. Détail en lumière direct du thang-ka du buddha Vajrasattva, *(Inv.: MA 1089).*

AGLAE est un système d'analyse basé sur un accélérateur de particules Pelletron 6-SDH2, d'une tension d'accélération maximale de 2000 kvolts. C'est une machine éléctrostatique à deux étages d'accélération, de type tandem construite par la société américaine NEC (Figure 8). Elle fut mise au point par une équipe regroupant des physiciens, des électroniciens et des informaticiens du LRMF associés à des chercheurs du monde universitaire, du CNRS et d'autres organismes de recherche étrangers. AGLAE produit des ions de tous les éléments légers jusqu'à l'azote, les plus couramment employés à ce jour étant l'hydrogène, le deutérium et l'hélium. Le faisceau d'ions est distribué par un aimant d'analyse sur l'une des trois lignes expérimentales:

1. Une chambre sous vide pour la mise en oeuvre de l'ensemble des techniques IBA.[11, 12]
2. Une microsonde nucléaire à balayage avec un faisceau focalisé sur un spot de 2 à 3 micromètres de diamètre.

Figure 5. Même détail en photographie infrarouge du buddha Vajrasattva, *(Inv.: MA 1089) révélant les lignes de construction.*

Figure 6. Photographie infrarouge du lama *permettant de localiser les zones peintes avec les couleurs bleues de compositions différentes et montrant les restaurations du côté droit de l'oeuvre ainsi que quelques retouches ponctuelles dans le bas.*

Figure 7. Revers du lama, *sous lumière ultraviolette. Les lettres dorées deviennent plus visibles. Certains éléments de la face apparaissent en sombre. Le côté restauré se caractérise par une fluorescence différente.*

3. Un dispositif de faisceau extrait à l'air qui fut particulièrement perfectionné par l'équipe AGLAE, car totalement adapté à l'analyse des oeuvres précieuses et délicates des musées.[13, 14]

Parmi les différentes techniques IBA, l'analyse PIXE a été développée, depuis les années 1970 environ, pour l'analyse élémentaire de matériaux de toute sorte. C'est une méthode d'analyse multiélémentaire rapide et sensible avec des limites de détection de l'ordre du microgramme par gramme. Sa mise en oeuvre s'effectue, aujourd'hui, surtout à l'air,[15] en extrayant le faisceau de particules à travers une fenêtre de kapton de 10 micromètres d'épaisseur. Le faisceau extrait peut être collimé à des diamètres de quelques dixièmes de millimètre. Ceci constitue l'un des avantages majeurs du PIXE par rapport à la fluorescence X pour étudier des détails d'une oeuvre.

Pour le thang-ka présenté, ici, la faible épaisseur de sa matière picturale appliquée sur un fin support de coton en faisait un objet "idéal" pour l'analyse en mode PIXE car il peut être assimilé à une "cible semi-mince". La rapidité de l'analyse offre aussi la possibilité de multiplier le nombre de points examinés. Enfin, cette technique d'analyse permet de quantifier les éléments traces qui pourraient révéler la provenance de certains pigments.

Dans le cas du thang-ka du musée Guimet, quarante cinq points d'analyse ont été réalisés sur les différentes couleurs avec un faisceau de protons d'énergie 2,8 MeV sur la cible et une intensité de courant de l'ordre de 100 pA pour un diamètre de faisceau d'environ 300 micromètres (Figure 9). Le choix de l'énergie est toujours un compromis entre une valeur minimale pour induire l'émission X d'une gamme suffisante d'éléments chimiques et une valeur maximale pour éviter d'endommager la matière picturale. Deux détecteurs silicium - lithium sont montés sur la ligne d'analyse. L'un, sans filtre et sous flux d'hélium afin que les rayons X mous ne soient pas absorbés par l'atmosphère, détecte les éléments légers comme le sodium, jusqu'au fer. Le second, avec un film de kapton de 200 micromètres d'épaisseur, possède un grand angle solide et mesure les rayons X plus durs des éléments en traces. Les spectres sont enregistrés sur un analyseur multicanal puis interprétés grâce à un logiciel mis au point par Duncan MacArthur.

Résultats des analyses PIXE

Les résultats semi-quantitatifs de l'analyse PIXE nous confirment que la palette est principalement à base de pigments minéraux. Il y a cependant quelques couleurs organiques qui tiennent une place importante dans l'étape de finition de la peinture: laque rouge, noir organique et bleu organique, probablement de l'indigo.

Le rouge, ton dominant de cette peinture renferme principalement du soufre et du mercure. Il s'agit d'un vermillon finement broyé pour lequel, il est impossible de préciser si cette couleur a été obtenue à partir de cinabre, pigment d'origine naturelle, ou de vermillon synthétique dont la fabrication était déjà connue en Chine au IIe siècle a.p. JC, ces deux substances ayant la même composition chimique et une structure cristalline identique.[16]

Les jaunes sont à base d'orpiment caractérisé par la présence de soufre et d'arsenic. La couleur orange, comme celle du vêtement du lama rehaussé de dorure, est un mélange d'orpiment et de vermillon. Pour la dorure, il s'agit d'or additionné d'argent et d'une faible quantité de cuivre. Pour l'azurite des éléments de décors entourant le lama, l'analyse par PIXE est en accord avec la présence d'un pigment bleu au cuivre. Il en est de même pour la malachite à gros broyage visible sur le nimbe du lama et sur les pétales de lotus du trône. L'autre nuance de vert visible, par exemple, sur le boddhisatva à la gauche du lama, est un mélange d'orpiment et de bleu organique.

Les blancs, comme la carnation du lama, sont peints avec un pigment finement broyé pour lequel l'analyse PIXE décèle de l'arsenic associé à un peu d'aluminium et de calcium mais sans présence de soufre. Il pourrait s'agir d'un oxyde d'arsenic d'origine naturelle comme l'arsenolite (As_2O_3) ou la claudetite (As_4O_6). A ce jour, nous n'avons jamais rencontré un minéral de ce type, utilisé volontairement comme pigment sur les diverses oeuvres peintes étudiées par le LRMF. En

Figure 8. AGLAE: le système d'analyse basé sur l'accélérateur de particules du LRMF.

Figure 9. Le thang-ka en position d'analyse sur la ligne de faisceau extrait.

particulier, sur les dix thang-ka anciens du musée Guimet, les blancs, en général, de même nature que la préparation de leur toile, sont à base de terres blanches, de kaolinite ou de calcite. Dans la littérature, à l'exception de l'altération de l'orpiment en oxyde d'arsenic, il n'est nullement fait mention d'un pigment à base d'oxyde d'arsenic.[17] Ce pigment rentre également dans la composition des couleurs grises obtenues probablement par ajout d'un noir organique non détectable dans les conditions d'analyse PIXE choisies.

Sur tous les spectres apparaissent, en plus des éléments appartement à une couleur donnée, ceux provenant de la préparation; en particulier la présence de fer et de silice probablement associée à la calcite de la préparation sous forme d'ocre ou d'oxyde de fer (Figure 10). Les couleurs restaurées se distinguent également lors de l'analyse élémentaire. En particulier, du rouge de cadmium avec une charge de blanc de plomb est identifié sur le côté droit du thang-ka. La présence de ce pigment rouge est caractéristique d'une restauration du XXème siècle.

Conclusion

Pour l'analyse par faisceaux d'ions, ce thang-ka représente une cible semi-mince. Malgré l'interprétation complexe des résultats due à la superposition des différentes couches de matière picturale, il a été possible d'identifier la majorité des constituants minéraux de la matière picturale grâce à l'analyse. La rapidité d'analyse a favorisé la multiplication des points examinés.

Grâce au couplage des résultats d'examens plus classiques et de ceux de l'analyse par faisceaux d'ions, nous avons pu restreindre le nombre de prélèvements au strict nécessaire. Seuls, deux prélèvements ont été effectués afin de préciser par diffraction X la nature de la préparation et du pigment minéral vert. La palette chromatique est ainsi appréhendée et révèle la maîtrise de l'artiste pour la fabrication de ses couleurs, appliquées pures ou en mélanges, étendues en large plage, en fins glacis ou en traits pour l'étape de finition. Les pigments minéraux et les couleurs organiques identifiés sur cette oeuvre sont en accord avec ceux cités dans la littérature et avec les matériaux déjà identifiés sur les dix thang-ka anciens du musée Guimet, à l'exception du pigment blanc à base probablement d'oxyde d'arsenic que nous observons pour la première fois.

En conclusion, l'analyse PIXE en faisceau extrait répond aux contraintes liées au bon état de conservation de ce thang-ka et paraît bien adaptée à l'examen de ce

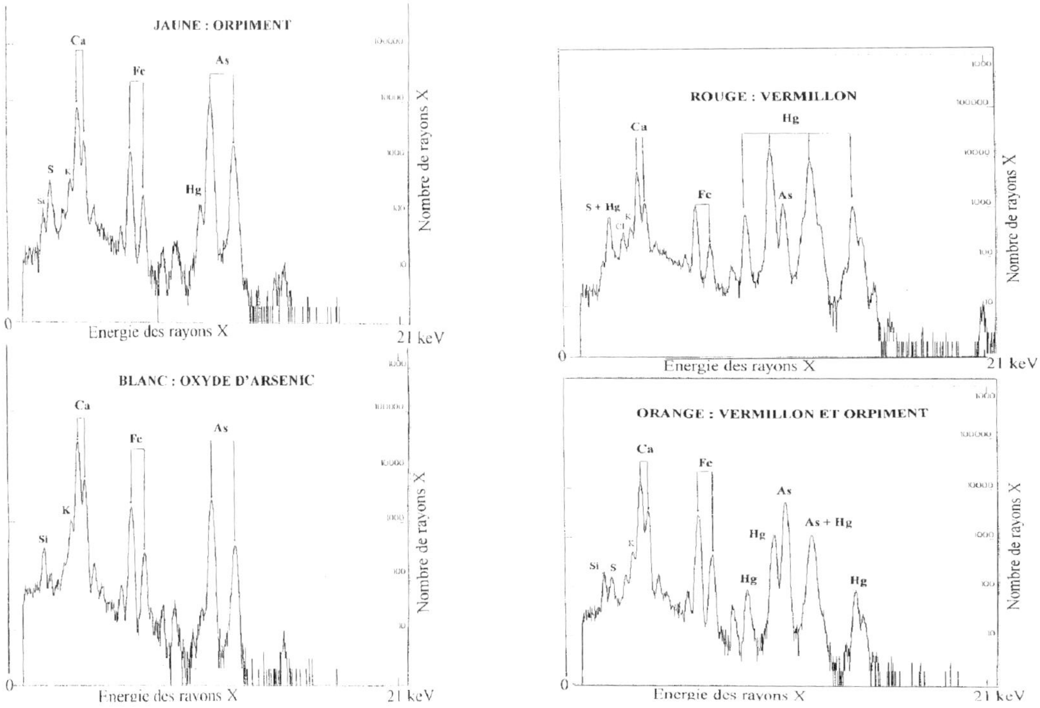

Figure 10. Spectres de quatre couleurs identifiées sur le lama. *Rouge: sulfure de mercure, vermillon. Jaune: sulfure d'arsenic, orpiment. Orange: mélange de vermillon et d'orpiment. Blanc: un oxyde d'arsenic.*

type d'oeuvres dont l'épaisseur de la matière picturale est à mi-chemin entre celle d'un parchemin et celle d'une peinture de chevalet.

Remerciements

A toute l'équipe AGLAE. Aux photographes du LRMF pour les documents de cet article. A Michel Menu pour son aide et ces précieux conseils.

Notes et Références

1. S. Colinart, "Un pas vers le Tibet ou dix thang-ka peints du musée Guimet", *Techne*, Edition Réunion des musées nationaux (Paris 1995), 2, 93–104.
2. G. Béguin et S. Colinart, "Techniques", *Les peintures du bouddhisme tibétain*, musée national des Arts asiatiques - Guimet, Edition Réunion des musées nationaux (Paris 1995), 20–31.
3. D. et J. Jackson, "La peinture tibétaine", Edition française Peuple du monde, (Paris 1990).
4. J.M. Dupouy, "AGLAE, l'accélérateur de particules du laboratoire de recherche des musées de France", *Techne*, Edition Réunion des musées nationaux (Paris 1995), 2, 39–49.
5. M. Menu et al., "The dedicated accelerator based IBA facility AGLAE at the Louvre", *Nuclear Instruments and Methods*, (1990), B45, 610–614.
6. G. Béguin, "Peinture récemment acquise", *Les peintures du bouddhisme tibétain*, musée national des Arts asiatiques - Guimet, Edition Réunion des musées nationaux (Paris 1995), 482–483.
7. cf note 5, G. Béguin, "Arhat", 333–336. Le terme sanskrit "arhat" signifie "méritant". Il désigne, selon l'usage courant éloigné des considérations philosophiques, les moines qui ont reçu directement l'enseignement du Bouddha Çâkyamuni dont l'excellence leur a permis d'atteindre l'éveil.
8. La technique en chambre Debye Sherrer a été choisie pour la diffraction de rayons X et réalisée par M. Eveno, LRMF.
9. E. Martin, "Application des tests sur coupes minces à l'identification des émulsions dans les liants de peinture", *Annales du laboratoire de recherche des musées de France* (1977), 23–29.
10. P. Le Chanu, "Dessin sous-jacent et histoire de l'art", *Techne*, Edition Réunion des musées nationaux (Paris 1995), 2, 165–177. La photographie infrarouge est utilisée vers 0,8 micromètres tandis qu'en réflectographie, la caméra a un pouvoir de pénétration se situant entre 1,8 à 2,5 micromètres.
11. J.R. Bird, "Total Analysis by IBA", *Nuclear Instruments and Methods*, (1990), B45, 516–518.
12. C. Lahanier et al, "Ion beam analysis in the Art and Archaeology", *Nuclear Instruments and Methods*, (1986), B14 n°1, 1–168.
13. D. MacArthur, "AGLAE et l'étude des encres et des colorants des manuscrits", *Techne*, Edition Réunion des musées nationaux (Paris 1995), 2, 68–75.
14. T. Calligaro et al, "An improved experimental setup for the simultaneous PIXE analysis of heavy and light elements with a 3 MeV proton external beam", *Nuclear Instruments and Methods*, à paraître.
15. M. Menu, "External beam application to painting materials", *Nuclear Instruments and Methods*, (1993), B75, 469–475.
16. cf. note 1, S. Colinart, p 102.
17. L. Green, "Recent analysis of pigments from Ancient Egyptian artefacts", *Conservation of Ancient Egyptian materials II*, Londres (1995), à paraître.

Gas Chromatographic Analysis of Amino Acids as Ethyl Chloroformate Derivatives.
III. Identification of Proteinaceous Binding Media by Interpretation of Amino Acid Composition Data

Michael R. Schilling,* Herant P. Khanjian
The Getty Conservation Institute,
4503 Glencoe Avenue, Marina del Rey, CA 90292-7913, USA

Abstract

Proteins, plant gums, and other substances that contain amino acids were identified in paints and gesso samples by a mathematical procedure for evaluating amino acid composition data. Correlation coefficient calculations were suitable for samples containing one amino acid-containing substance. For samples suspected of containing a mixture of two substances composed of amino acids, algebraic equations were used to identify the substances and to estimate the composition. Samples from the wall paintings of the St Juda church in Prague, tested by gas chromatographic analysis of amino acid-ethyl chloroformate derivatives, were found to contain casein, or admixtures of animal glue and egg tempera. Using the procedure, data from two published high-performance liquid chromatography studies of paint and gessoes were re-evaluated. Although many of the original findings were supported, there was reason to suspect that some samples, originally believed to contain a single proteinaceous material, may also contain a second.

Keywords

Gas chromatography, protein, amino acid, tempera paint, gesso, correlation coefficient

Introduction

There has been considerable interest, of late, in the analysis and identification of proteins used as binding media and adhesives. The proteins most often used by artists include animal and fish glue, casein, glair and egg yolk.[1] Other proteins may be present on objects, monuments and artifacts that can interfere with protein identification. Sources for these proteins include contamination from microbes,[2] the use of saliva for cleaning painted surfaces,[3] skin from the handling of objects,[4] and others.[5] Additionally, some non-proteinaceous natural products that contain traces of amino acids may be mistaken for protein in an analysis. For instance, plant gums are composed of glycoproteins, substances in which amino acids are bonded to carbohydrate groups.[5–7]

The intent of this paper is to describe a new mathematical procedure for evaluating amino acid composition data that permits the identification of proteins (and other substances that contain amino acids) in samples from art objects. Data from gas chromatography and high-performance liquid chromatography analyses of paint and gesso were evaluated in order to illustrate the utility of the procedure. For the sake of simplicity, any substance that contains amino acids will be referred to in this article, henceforth, as a protein. It should be remembered that this term may include gums or other non-proteinaceous materials that are composed, in part, of amino acids.

Analytical methods for protein identification

Proteins may be differentiated by their relative proportions of amino acids. Twenty natural amino acids are commonly found in proteins, although many others have been identified. A number of analytical techniques for identifying proteins measure the concentrations of amino acids present in acid hydrolysates, such as ion chromatography,[8–11] high-performance liquid chromatography,[2,12–14] and gas chromatography.[5,7,15–19]

One derivatization procedure reported recently in the literature has proven to be highly effective for preparing amino acid hydrolysates for gas chromatographic analysis. Ethyl chloroformate (ECF) forms N(O,S)-ethoxycarbonyl ethyl ester derivatives of most amino acids rapidly and quantitatively.[18,19] In a comprehensive study of the effects of pigments and physical aging on the procedure,[5,7] it was discovered that the concentrations of amino acids substituted with alkyl groups (alanine, valine, isoleucine, leucine and glycine) and imino groups (proline, hydroxyproline) were relatively unaffected by pigment interferences and aging. Accordingly, they were termed "stable" amino acids. It was found that unknown proteins could be identified reliably in samples from art objects on the basis of stable amino acid mole percentages (moles of stable amino acid per 100 moles of all stable amino acids detected), as discussed below.

* Author to whom correspondence should be addressed

Evaluation of amino acid composition data using correlation coefficients

In order to identify proteins that are present in samples, test results for the samples are compared to the corresponding results for proteinaceous reference materials. In order to eliminate tedious quantitative analysis, peak area ratios have been used for protein identification, using flowcharts[14,16] or a graphical form of data presentation.[17] However, the best methods rely on amino acid composition data. In most published studies, the amino acid composition of the sample is compared to data for a set of proteinaceous reference materials, in order to find a material whose composition most closely resembles the unknown.[2,9,10,13] Because the identification is based on inspection only, a certain amount of precision is lacking.

Another technique to aid in the identification of unknown proteins is the calculation of correlation coefficients. This technique was used to identify proteins in adhesives based on high performance liquid chromatography (HPLC) analysis data[12]. The equation for calculating the correlation coefficient is as follows[20]:

$$r = \{\Sigma XY - [(\Sigma X \Sigma Y)/n]\}/\{[\Sigma X^2 - ([\Sigma X]^2/n)][\Sigma Y^2 - ([\Sigma Y]^2/n)]\}^{1/2} \quad (1)$$

where X and Y are the molar compositions for each amino acid, n is the number of amino acids measured, and r is the correlation coefficient. By definition, sample data are represented by X, and reference data by Y.

The technique provides an easy means for comparing large data sets: a correlation coefficient of 1.00 indicates a perfect match between the sample data and reference data, and a coefficient of 0 indicates that no relationship exists. Excel, a spreadsheet program from Microsoft, is a convenient tool for calculating correlation coefficients, and also for data storage.

Attempts were made to identify proteins present in samples from tempera paintings and grounds, by using correlation coefficient calculations with the analytical data obtained by the ECF method. Because pigments and aging affect the concentrations of amino acids with reactive functional groups, it was discovered that the data from samples from art objects correlated poorly to data for fresh, unpigmented protein reference samples. Greatly improved correlation matrix results could be obtained from the relative molar percentages of "stable" amino acids.[7] The Appendix lists the "stable" amino acid compositions for a large number of proteinaceous reference materials that can be used with equation (1).

Provided that suitable reference data exist, correlation coefficients are the simplest means for identifying proteins in paint samples that contain a single proteinaceous material. However, a sample that contains two proteinaceous substances will not correlate well to a single reference material, because the composition represents a mixture of two substances. Also, samples from painted objects often contain particles originating from each paint and ground layer, and the binding medium from each layer contributes to the final composition.

In instances where protein mixtures are suspected, one relies on intuition, old recipes, test results from other analytical techniques, or common sense to ascertain which materials may be present in the sample, based on the amino acid composition data. In the past, there has been no means to demonstrate that a mixture of the two suspected materials could, in fact, produce the actual amino acid composition of the sample.

Estimating the composition of binary mixtures of proteins

A procedure that is based on simple algebraic equations has now been developed for estimating the proportions of a hypothetical binary protein mixture that closely matches the amino acid composition of a paint sample. The first step in the procedure is selection of two proteinaceous reference materials that are likely to be present in the sample. Next, the equations are applied to the "stable" amino acid molar percentage data for the sample and the two references materials suspected of being present. If the two reference proteins are, in fact, present in the sample, the percentage differences between the compositions of the hypothetical mixture and the sample should be relatively small. Otherwise, the calculations should be

Table 1. Determination of the binary mixture composition for a paint made from lead white mixed with whole egg and rabbit skin glue

	Ala	Val	Ile	Leu	Gly	Pro	OHP
Composition of sample (X_i)	19.7	10.9	7.5	13.9	29.1	13.0	6.0
Composition of Protein #1: Whole egg (Y_i)	22.0	17.4	13.2	22.0	14.5	10.9	0.0
Composition of Protein #2: Collagen/gelatin (Z_i)	15.7	3.0	1.8	3.7	46.7	16.7	12.4
Weight fraction of Protein #1 based on each amino acid (F_i	0.63	0.54	0.51	0.56	0.55	0.64	0.52
Average of F_i values ($\bar{F}$) = 0.56							
Composition of hypothetical mixture (M_i) based on $\bar{F}$ = 0.56	19.2	11.1	8.2	14.0	28.6	13.5	5.4
Percentage difference between sample and mixture compositions	2	-2	-9	-1	2	-4	9

repeated on data for another pair of reference protein materials until good agreement is achieved.

The authors used Excel to perform these calculations, because of the ease in copying sets of reference data into the formulae until a good match was found. The procedure is outlined below, and is illustrated in Table 1 for a paint made from lead white and a mixture of rabbit skin glue and whole egg with a known proportion.

1. Use equation (2) to calculate the proportions of a hypothetical mixture of Protein #1 and Protein #2 that would have a "stable" amino acid molar percentage equivalent to that of the sample:

$$F_i = (X_i - Y_i)/(Y_i - Z_i) \qquad (2)$$

   where X_i, Y_i and Z_i are the molar percentages for one of the "stable" amino acids present in the sample, Protein #1 and Protein #2, respectively. F_i is the weight fraction of Protein #1 (in the mixture with Protein #2) that is based on the molar percentage X_i. The calculation is performed for each of the seven "stable" amino acids, giving seven F_i values (one for alanine, one for valine, and so forth).
2. Calculate the average weight fraction, $\bar{F}$ from the seven F_i values.
3. Use $\bar{F}$ and equation (3) to determine the proportions of the final hypothetical mixture of Proteins #1 and #2 that has a total "stable" amino acid composition approximating that of the sample:

$$M_i = \bar{F}Y_i + (1 - \bar{F})Z_i \qquad (3)$$

   where M_i is the molar percentage of one of the seven "stable" amino acids present in the final hypothetical mixture of Protein #1 and Protein #2. This

Table 2. Amino acid composition of samples from art objects

Sample description	Mole % of all ECF-derivatized amino acids														
	Ala	Val	Ile	Leu	Gly	Pro	Asp	Thr	Met	Ser	Glu	Phe	OHP	Lys	% Protein
Ronca: gesso SG 1 "gelatin"	12.8	4.1	3.1	5.8	26.8	12.2	5.4	3.0	0.8	4.8	8.9	2.4	9.2	0.7	3
Ronca: polychrome BC 2 "egg emulsion"	12.5	6.5	5.3	7.2	14.5	7.1	6.5	8.4	1.8	9.5	12.7	3.7	0.0	4.3	0.5
Halpine: Tura #5 – green – "egg + glue"	13.6	7.7	4.9	7.6	19.8	11.0	5.5	7.0	0.3	9.5	4.4	2.6	6.3	0.0	–
Halpine: Tura #3 – brown – "egg + glue"	10.6	5.8	5.0	7.6	16.7	7.1	10.8	5.1	1.4	8.9	10.4	3.5	4.0	3.2	–
Halpine: Tura #6 – red – "yolk"	8.1	6.8	3.9	8.5	13.4	5.7	12.8	7.6	1.3	11.8	13.2	3.7	0.33	2.7	–
ECF: St Juda church – yellow	5.9	5.5	6.9	12.0	6.2	18.0	10.2	0.0	0.0	1.6	20.9	4.7	0.0	8.7	3.5
ECF: St Juda church – light brown	10.5	5.4	4.8	8.4	14.2	8.0	10.7	5.7	0.0	4.8	16.2	2.8	4.7	4.0	1.3
ECF: St Juda church – yellow with glaze	11.6	5.5	3.8	5.3	18.4	8.7	7.9	5.6	0.3	4.8	18.4	1.9	3.7	3.9	1.7

Note: Published HPLC analysis results were taken from Ronca[2] and Halpine[13]

ECF refers to data obtained by the authors using GC analysis of amino acid–ethyl chloroformate derivatives

Legend: Ala – alanine; Val – valine; Ile – isoleucine; Leu – leucine; Gly – glycine; Pro – proline; OHP – hydroxyproline; Asp – aspartic acid; Thr – threonine; Met – methionine; Ser – serine; Glu – glutamic acid; Phe – phenylalanine; Lys – lysine

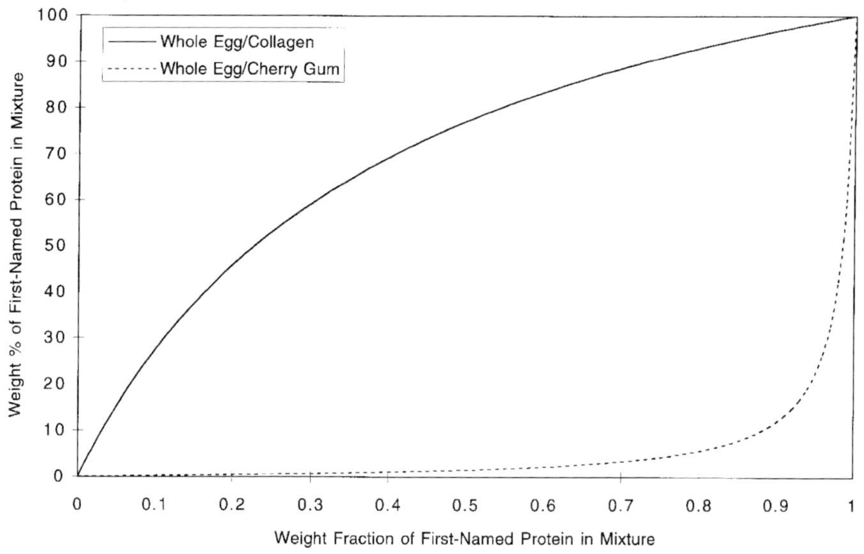

Figure 1. Weight percent versus weight fraction for binary mixture of two proteins, based on equation (4) and data in the Appendix

calculation is repeated for each "stable" amino acid to give the composition of the hypothetical mixture that approximates the sample composition.

4. For each of the seven "stable" amino acids, determine the percentage difference between the sample and the hypothetical mixture. In the example shown in Table 1, the hypothetical weight fraction result of 0.56 agrees well with the actual composition of the paint, which has a weight fraction of 0.57.
5. If desired, equation (4) may be used to calculate the weight percentage composition of the hypothetical mixture:

$$\%P_1 = W_{S2} / \{ W_{S2} + W_{S1}[(1/F) - 1] \} \quad (4)$$

where $\%P_1$ is the weight percentage of Protein #1 present in the hypothetical mixture, and W_{S1} and W_{S2} are the "stable" amino acid weight percentages for pure Protein #1 and Protein #2 that are listed in the Appendix.

The accuracy of equation (4) depends on the specific combination of two proteinaceous reference materials, and is affected by the standard deviation of the weight fraction data. In general, when weight fraction data are converted to weight percentages, the highest accuracy can be obtained for regions of the graph of equation (4) at which the slope is near zero (Figure 1). For example, the accuracy is high for egg/glue mixtures which have weight fractions of egg exceeding 0.75, and for egg/gum mixtures with less than 0.8 weight fraction of egg.

Thus, amino acid composition data are evaluated first by correlation coefficients in order to determine if a single proteinaceous material is present. If a good match cannot be found, the mixture equations are applied until a reasonable combination

Table 3. Correlation coefficients relating sample data to reference data

Reference description	Ronca: gesso SG I "gelatin"	Ronca: polychrome BC 2 "egg emulsion"	Halpine: Tura #5 – green – "egg+glue"	Halpine: Tura #3 – brown – "egg+glue"	Halpine: Tura #6 – red – "yolk"	ECF: St Juda church – yellow	ECF: St Juda church – light brown	ECF: St Juda church – yellow with glaze
Whole egg – mean	–0.035	0.673	0.254	0.384	0.670	0.341	0.421	0.269
Egg white – mean	–0.025	0.680	0.268	0.394	0.681	0.306	0.423	0.282
Egg yolk – mean	–0.061	0.638	0.218	0.354	0.656	0.417	0.404	0.232
Rice starch – Kremer	0.677	0.991	0.852	0.897	0.926	0.342	0.900	0.873
Casein – mean	–0.219	0.159	–0.061	–0.077	0.223	0.943	0.020	–0.073
Wheat flour	0.215	0.367	0.316	0.242	0.391	0.956	0.340	0.298
Apricot gum – Glendale	0.848	0.954	0.961	0.978	0.893	0.045	0.956	0.970
Cherry gum – Glendale	0.799	0.937	0.938	0.908	0.805	0.042	0.890	0.942
Cherry gum – Kremer	0.886	0.868	0.949	0.966	0.848	0.052	0.986	0.940
Collagen/gelatine – mean	0.994	0.649	0.925	0.880	0.640	–0.037	0.846	0.925

Note: Sample data listed in Table 4, and reference data appears in the Appendix
Correlation coefficients calculated using equation (1)

Table 4. Identification of proteins present in samples from art objects, based on amino acid composition data published by Ronca[2]

Name (weight fraction Protein #1)	Ala	Val	Ile	Leu	Gly	Pro	OHP
Ronca SG 1	17.3	5.5	4.2	7.8	36.2	16.5	12.4
Collagen	15.7	3.0	1.8	3.7	46.7	16.7	12.4
Percentage difference	9	45	57	52	−29	−1	0
Ronca SG 1	17.3	5.5	4.2	7.8	36.2	16.5	12.4
Whole egg/collagen (0.18)	16.8	5.6	3.8	6.9	41.0	15.7	10.2
Percentage difference	3	−2	9	12	−13	5	18
Ronca BC 2	23.6	12.2	10.0	13.6	27.3	13.3	0.0
Whole egg/cherry gum (0.40)	24.9	14.7	9.2	13.4	23.8	12.7	1.1
Percentage difference	−6	−21	7	1	13	4	–

of two materials is identified. The materials should be within the realm of possibility for the object in question.

Interestingly, it was discovered that this procedure, originally developed for the ECF-derivatization method, was also applicable to amino acid concentration data obtained from HPLC analysis of phenylthiocarbamyl derivatives. Although a thorough study of pigment interferences in this HPLC procedure has not been published, it is reasonable to assume that "stable" amino acids are least likely to be affected by pigments in this analytical procedure also.

Interpretation of amino acid data for samples from art and artifacts

In order to illustrate the utility of the data evaluation method, the amino acid composition data of a number of samples from art and artifacts were evaluated. The data include results obtained from application of the ECF method, and from two published HPLC studies in which the identifications were based solely upon simple inspection of data. All amino acid data were expressed as relative molar percentages of all ECF-derivatizable amino acids (Table 2) and "stable" amino acids (Tables 4 to 6) prior to evaluation. When available, the content of protein in the samples are also listed. The correlation matrix data are listed in Table 3. For samples that did not correlate well to a pure reference material, the calculations for identifying hypothetical binary mixtures are given in Tables 4 to 6.

In the first HPLC study, Ronca[2] identified the proteinaceous substances present in samples from a number of objects. Sample SG 1 is a sample that contains the gesso ground and black paint from a 15th century wooden statue from Pisa, Italy. Based on the high levels of hydroxyproline, Ronca identified animal glue as the binding medium. In Table 3, this identification was confirmed by a high correlation coefficient (0.994) to collagen. However, the compositional differences between the sample and collagen were of sufficient magnitude that a mixture was suspected. Table 4 shows a good agreement between the sample and a mixture of egg (0.18 weight fraction) with glue. It is interesting to note that a simple inspection of the data was inadequate to detect egg in the sample.

The paint on an outdoor polychromed stone sculpture at a Gothic cathedral of St Etienne in Bourges, France (sample BC 2), was also analyzed by Ronca. Because no hydroxyproline was detected, animal glue was excluded as a possible medium. Considering that the composition did not exactly match egg protein, Ronca cited old recipes to support the conclusion that an emulsion of egg yolk with a plant gum (possibly gum arabic) might actually be present.

Oddly enough, rice starch gives a good correlation to BC 2 (Table 3). However, rice starch could not have been used as medium and, furthermore, the amino acid content of the sample (0.5%) exceeds the amount present in pure rice starch (0.4%). Hence, by using the binary mixture equations (Table 4), good agreement was found between a mixture of whole egg (weight fraction 0.40) with cherry gum. Considering that the hypothetical mixture should contain hydroxyproline (OHP), whereas the sample does not, it is possible that hydroxyproline was below the HPLC detection limit. Given the low level of OHP normally present in cherry gum, and the small amount of protein detected in the sample, this explanation appears reasonable. Thus, the identification of gum and egg is entirely consistent with Ronca's assessment based on old recipes, and supports her explanation.

Table 5. Identification of proteins present in samples from Tura painting, based on amino acid composition data published by Halpine[13]

Name (weight fraction Protein #1)	Ala	Val	Ile	Leu	Gly	Pro	OHP
Halpine #5 – green	19.2	10.8	6.9	10.7	28.0	15.5	8.9
Whole egg/collagen (0.43)	18.4	9.2	6.7	11.6	32.8	14.2	7.0
% Difference	4	15	3	−9	−17	8	21
Halpine #3 – brown	18.6	10.2	8.8	13.4	29.4	12.5	7.1
Whole egg/collagen (0.54)	19.1	10.8	8.0	13.6	29.2	13.6	5.6
Percentage difference	−3	−6	9	−2	1	−9	20
Halpine #6 – red	17.3	14.5	8.4	18.2	28.7	12.1	0.7
Whole egg/collagen (0.67)	19.9	12.7	9.5	16.0	25.0	12.8	4.0
Percentage difference	−15	12	−12	12	13	−6	−476
Halpine C2 – control red	19.2	14.7	9.6	18.9	24.3	12.0	1.3
Whole egg/collagen (0.79)	19.8	13.7	10.9	19.1	21.0	12.9	2.6
Percentage difference	−4	7	−14	−1	14	−7	−95

In the second HPLC study, Halpine analyzed a set of paint samples removed from 15th century panel paintings by Cosimo Tura.[13] For comparison, samples of tempera test paints applied over glue-based gesso were also analyzed. Halpine identified the media present in the green paint (Tura sample 5) and the brown paint (Tura sample 3) as animal glue and egg, although it was postulated that the glue may have originated from the ground layer. Not surprisingly, correlation of the compositions to pure materials was poor (Table 3). Fortunately, there was good agreement between the samples and mixtures of egg and collagen with weight fractions of 0.43 and 0.54, respectively (Table 5). As in the previous example, the re-evaluation of the data supports the author's interpretation based on knowledge of the samples and old recipes.

The major component in the binding medium of the organic red paint (Tura sample 6) was identified by Halpine as egg, although the low level of hydroxyproline indicated that the sample was contaminated with particles of ground. Not surprisingly, Table 3 shows a poor correlation between the red paint and pure egg. Interestingly, the composition of a hypothetical mixture of whole egg and glue closely approximated the composition of the red for all "stable" amino acids except hydroxyproline (which had a difference of nearly 500%). However, this trend was also observed for the egg tempera paint made with an organic red colorant (sample C2). Thus, there is an indication that the organic red colorant interferes with the phenylthiocarbamyl derivatization method, a supposition which could be tested in a thorough study of pigment interferences in the HPLC procedure.

The ECF procedure[5] was used to analyze samples from the wall paintings of the St Juda church in Prague. The church was constructed in the 17th and 18th centuries, and decorated in the Baroque style. A number of restorations and repaintings occurred, beginning in the 19th century and continuing into the 20th century. Samples of yellow, light brown, and a yellow with a glaze layer were removed for testing during the most recent conservation treatments.

The yellow paint sample matched reasonably well to casein (Table 6). Although the correlation coefficient was not quite as high as one would expect (Table 3), the composition of casein is quite unlike that of any other material. This is evidenced in Table 3 by the very low correlation coefficients between casein and the other samples from objects. The low recovery for valine in the sample is due to a partial overlap with a peak present in a blank analysis, which causes some difficulty in blank subtraction, and is further exacerbated by a low total protein content in the

Table 6. Identification of proteins present in samples from St Juda Church, based on amino acid molar percentages. Obtained by GC analysis of ECF derivatives

Name (weight fraction Protein #1)	Ala	Val	Ile	Leu	Gly	Pro	OHP
ECF – St Juda – yellow	10.9	10.0	12.6	22.0	11.4	33.1	0.0
Casein	10.9	16.9	12.8	22.0	8.6	28.8	0.0
Percentage difference	0	−69	−2	0	24	13	0
ECF – St Juda – light brown	18.8	9.6	8.5	15.0	25.3	14.3	8.4
Whole egg/collagen (0.51)	18.9	10.4	7.6	13.0	30.3	13.8	6.1
Percentage difference	−1	−8	11	13	−19	3	28
ECF – St Juda – yellow & glaze	20.3	9.7	6.7	9.3	32.3	15.2	6.5
Whole egg/collagen (0.44)	18.5	9.4	6.8	11.8	32.4	14.2	6.9
Percentage difference	9	3	−2	−27	0	7	−5

sample. Yet, it is clear from the absence of hydroxyproline in the sample that animal glue and plant gums cannot be present. Furthermore, only trace amounts of palmitic and stearic acid were found, and no azelaic acid was detected. Therefore, the identification of casein appears quite reasonable.

Based on the low correlation coefficients (Table 3), and the calculations in Table 6, the light brown paint and yellow paint with glaze most probably contain both egg and glue. Because it is extremely unlikely that mixed egg and glue media were applied, the compositions are entirely consistent with techniques in which egg tempera paint is applied over a glue-based ground layer.

Conclusions

Until now, no systematic procedure has been available for reliable identification of proteins and other materials that contain amino acids in samples of paint from art objects. The procedure described in this paper, founded on research presented in the two previous papers of the series, utilizes mathematical evaluation of amino acid molar composition data. In addition to being simple to use, it can be applied to samples that contain one or two binding media composed of amino acids. The procedure appears not to be limited to amino acid composition data obtained from gas chromatographic analysis of amino acid–ECF derivatives, but may also be applied to results from HPLC analysis of phenylthiocarbamyl derivatives. Furthermore, because protein identifications were based solely on the molar composition of "stable" amino acids, pigment interferences and aging of proteins had little or no apparent effect on the results.

Some concerns about the validity of the procedure will, no doubt, remain even after reviewing this work. One may argue that regional variations in the compositions of eggs, casein, animal glue, plant gums, and other materials may make it impossible to identify a particular binding medium with any degree of confidence based solely on amino acid composition. Furthermore, it may be thought that estimates of mixture compositions are over-interpretations of analytical results; perhaps more than one hypothetical mixture of proteins could be found that has an amino acid composition identical to the sample. And lastly, there are concerns that the effects of physical aging may alter the compositions of proteins to such an extent that a positive identification would be impossible.

However, experience with the data evaluation procedure has shown that these concerns may be unfounded. Based on extensive testing of organic binding media from the collection of the Getty Conservation Institute, compiled with amino acid compositions from published sources, little variation is, in fact, observed in the compositions of proteinaceous binding media that originate from different geographic sources. This reduces the possibility that an art object may contain a common proteinaceous material that has a composition radically different from those tabulated in the Appendix.

To address the issue of over-interpretation of data, most fears of over-interpretation stem from insufficient testing of the methodology in question. In the case of protein identification by gas chromatographic analysis of ECF derivatives, much of the groundwork has already been done, so that reliable identifications can now be made. Furthermore, only a limited number of materials that contain amino acids are likely to be present in most objects of art. Because of the simplicity of the data evaluation procedure, it is easy to perform the calculations on many different combinations of proteinaceous materials until the best match to the sample composition is obtained. For nearly every sample that has been tested by the authors, only one combination of materials has been found to match the *entire* stable amino acid composition reasonably well. As a point of comparison, it is interesting to note that drying oils have been reliably identified for nearly 30 years on the basis of only *two* fatty acid ratios.

To minimize misinterpretation, other analytical techniques can, and should, be used to verify the findings from protein identification. For example, it would be interesting if the paint from the stone sculpture could be analyzed by FTIR, or by gas chromatography of carbohydrates, in order to determine if a plant gum is indeed present with egg.

It is our hope that others will adapt this procedure to their work and find that it does, indeed, provide reliable results.

Acknowledgments

The authors wish to thank the following members of the Scientific Program of the Getty Conservation Institute (GCI): Alberto Tagle, Director, Scientific Program, who supported this work; Dusan Stulik, head, Analytical Section, who initiated the organic binding medium analysis project; James Druzik, who discussed many aspects of this research and encouraged the authors. Special thanks go to: Milena Necaskova, a private paintings conservator in Prague, who obtained the samples from the St Juda church; Luiz A. C. Souza, a former research fellow at The GCI and presently at CECOR, EBA, Universidade Federal de Minas Gerais, Belo Horizonte, MG, Brazil, who helped to develop the ECF procedure with the authors.

Appendix (see Table below)

Weight percentage and "stable" amino acid composition data for fresh, unpigmented reference materials. Data taken from reference 5. Mean values reported for

	Mole % Stable Amino Acid								Weight % of AAs	
Sample description	Ala	Val	Ile	Leu	Gly	Pro	OHP	Mole % stable AAs	All ECF	Stable
Silk (fibroin)	37.8	2.8	0.8	0.7	57.4	0.4	0.0	83	–	–
Human epidermis	15.5	11.2	10.1	22.7	34.4	6.2	0.0	52	76	35
Hempseed (edestin)	18.3	17.4	13.4	19.2	21.2	10.5	0.0	44	–	–
Animal blood – US Customs	26.9	18.3	2.1	27.1	16.7	8.9	0.0	53	62	29
Whole egg – mean	22.0	17.4	13.2	22.0	14.5	10.9	0.0	45	46	18
Egg white – mean	22.0	18.3	12.8	21.6	14.8	10.5	0.0	48	64	26
Egg yolk – mean	20.9	16.6	13.3	23.2	14.1	11.9	0.0	45	27	11
Human blood	26.4	20.4	1.3	26.9	14.4	10.6	0.0	58	82	43
Rice starch – Kremer	21.6	11.6	10.9	14.2	26.3	15.3	0.0	48	0.37	0.15
Bovine horn	13.5	16.2	10.8	21.6	18.9	18.9	0.0	47	–	–
Wool (keratin)	13.8	14.8	9.1	18.9	25.1	18.3	0.0	50	–	–
Chitin – Polysciences	26.0	16.2	7.2	9.4	24.5	16.8	0.0	56	6.1	3.0
Feather (keratin)	14.3	17.7	10.8	14.3	22.6	20.4	0.0	55	–	–
Casein – mean	10.9	16.9	12.8	22.0	8.6	28.8	0.0	47	87	33
Wheat flour	11.3	12.3	8.8	17.9	15.9	33.8	0.0	43	–	–
Human saliva	10.7	7.9	5.5	12.2	27.6	35.5	0.7	51	24	11
Moth	23.5	12.8	10.1	18.4	19.7	14.8	0.7	51	12	5.4
Apricot gum – Glendale	25.2	10.7	5.2	10.5	35.5	11.5	1.5	39	1.5	0.48
Cherry gum – Glendale	26.3	12.7	6.5	7.6	29.4	13.8	3.7	39	0.86	0.28
Bird guano	20.0	10.5	8.9	16.8	24.7	16.3	2.8	51	3.2	1.4
Gum guar – A.F. Suter	16.3	8.3	6.2	11.8	45.6	8.6	3.1	52	3.0	1.3
Cherry gum – Kremer	22.6	7.6	3.6	15.3	31.4	12.1	7.6	48	0.45	0.18
Gum arabic – Luxor Egypt	18.1	4.9	7.6	17.2	29.5	14.0	8.7	52	0.44	0.19
Almond gum – Pomona	16.9	10.6	7.8	15.2	20.9	18.2	10.4	46	0.48	0.19
Karaya gum – CCI	13.6	12.9	6.9	16.7	22.2	14.8	12.7	52	0.44	0.21
Collagen/ gelatine – mean	15.7	3.0	1.8	3.7	46.7	16.7	12.4	77	90	61
Gum ghatti – A.F. Suter	13.1	7.2	5.6	7.2	16.7	13.0	37.2	54	2.3	1.2
Gum arabic – mean	6.6	5.6	2.2	11.3	12.4	13.4	48.5	58	2.7	1.5
Gum tragacanth – mean	8.1	12.9	4.8	7.3	8.1	12.7	46.1	63	2.0	1.2

Legend: Ala – alanine; Val – valine; Ile – isoleucine; Leu – leucine; Gly – glycine; Pro – proline; OHP – hydroxyproline.

materials from multiple sources. Weight % protein estimated from sum of weight percentages for all ECF-derivatized amino acids detected.

References

1. H. Kühn, *Conservation and Restoration of Works of Art and Antiquities*, Vol. 1 (London: Butterworths, 1986), 157–167.
2. F. Ronca, "Protein Determination in Polychromed Stone Sculptures, Stuccoes and Gesso Grounds," *Studies in Conservation* 39 (1994): 107–120.
3. P. M. S. Romão, A. M. Alarcão and C. A. N. Viana, "Human Saliva as a Cleaning Agent for Dirty Surfaces," *Studies in Conservation* 35 (1990): 153–155.
4. P. B. Hamilton, "Amino-acids on Hands," *Nature* 205 (1965): 284–285.
5. M. R. Schilling, H. P. Khanjian and L. A. C. Souza, "Gas Chromatographic Analysis of Amino Acids as Ethyl Chloroformate Derivatives I. Composition of Proteins Associated with Objects of Art and Monuments," *Journal of the American Institute for Conservation*, 35 (1996): 45–59.
6. N. Sharon, *Complex Carbohydrates: Their Chemistry, Biosynthesis, and Functions* (Reading, MA: Addison-Wesley, 1975), 48–98.
7. M. R. Schilling and H. P. Khanjian, "Gas Chromatographic Analysis of Amino Acids as Ethyl Chloroformate Derivatives II. Effects of Pigments and Accelerated Aging on the Identification of Proteinaceous Binding Media," accepted by *Journal of the American Institute for Conservation* (to appear in Summer 1996).
8. M. V. Pickering and P. Newton, "Amino Acid Hydrolysis: Old Problems, New Solutions," *LC/GC* 8, no. 10 (1990): 778–781.
9. S. Keck and T. Peters Jr, "Identification of Protein-Containing Paint Media by Quantitative Amino Acid Analysis," *Studies in Conservation* 14 (1969): 75–82.
10. S. P. Sack, F. C. Tahk and T. Peters, "A Technical Examination of an Ancient Egyptian Painting on Canvas," *Studies in Conservation* 26 (1981): 15–23.
11. M. V. Pickering, "Ion-exchange Chromatography of Free Amino Acids," *LC/GC* 7, no. 6 (1989): 484–490.
12. T. Sinkai and R. Sugisita, "Identification of Protein-containing Binding Media and Adhesives in Works of Art by Amino Acid Analysis," *Journal of Archaeological Science of Japan* 35 (1990): 1–12.
13. S. Halpine, "Amino Acid Analysis of Proteinaceous Media from Cosimo Tura's *The Annunciation with Saint Francis and Saint Louis of Toulouse*," *Studies in Conservation* 37 (1992): 22–38.
14. C. M. Grzywacz, "Identification of Proteinaceous Binding Media in Paintings by Amino Acid Analysis using 9-Fluorenylmethyl Chloroformate Derivatization and Reversed-phase High-performance Liquid Chromatography," *Journal of Chromatography A* 676, no. 1 (1994): 177–183.
15. L. Masschelein-Kleiner, "Contribution to the Study of Aged Proteinaceous Media," in *Conservation and Restoration of Pictorial Art*, ed. N. Brommelle and P. Smith (London: IIC-Butterworths, 1976), 84–88.
16. R. White, "The Characterization of Proteinaceous Binders in Art Objects," *National Gallery Technical Bulletin* 8 (1984): 5–14.
17. R. Pancella and R. Bart, "Identification des Liants Organiques dans les Couches Picturales par Chromatographie en Phase Gazeuse," *Zeitschrift fur Kunsttechnologie* 3, no. 3 (1989): 101–111.
18. P. Hu√ek, "Rapid Derivatization and Gas Chromatographic Determination of Amino Acids," *Journal of Chromatography* 552 (1991): 289–299.
19. W. Nowik, "Acides Amines et Acides Gras sur un Meme Chromatogramme – Un Autre Regard sur l'Analyse des Liants en Peinture," *Studies in Conservation* 40 (1995): 120–126.
20. R. L. Anderson, *Practical Statistics for Analytical Chemists* (New York: Van Nostrand Reinhold, 1987).

Gas Chromatographic Determination of the Fatty Acid and Glycerol Content of Lipids. I. The Effects of Pigments and Aging on the Composition of Oil Paints

Michael R. Schilling,* Herant P. Khanjian
The Getty Conservation Institute,
4503 Glencoe Avenue, Marina del Rey, CA 90292-7913, USA

Abstract

A gas chromatographic procedure for the analysis of fatty acids (as methyl esters) and glycerol (as isopropylidene glycerol) in oil paints is described. Molar ratios of selected fatty acids to the glycerol content were useful for characterizing lipids used in conservation. Evaluation of pigment interferences revealed that, of the pigments tested, only Paris blue, azurite and red lead had any measurable effect on the analytical results. Exposure of oil paint specimens to heat and light significantly increased the concentrations of most dicarboxylic fatty acids, whereas the amount of azelaic acid increased only slightly. Surprisingly, exposure to heat and light reduced the concentrations of saturated fatty acids in oil paints. Test results of samples from oil paintings were consistent with the trends established by the exposed oil paint specimens.

Keywords

Gas chromatography, drying oils, fatty acids, glycerol, lipids, oil paints

Introduction

Perhaps the most widespread and successful application of gas chromatography (GC) in conservation science is the analysis and identification of oils and fats in paintings. Beginning with the pioneering work of Mills[1] and Stolow,[2] there have been numerous studies of oil paintings in which GC has played a major role in characterizing the medium. Considering the importance of oil media and the availability of GC instrumentation, this trend is likely to continue.

Although the chemistry of lipids and their behavior in oil and tempera paints have been adequately described elsewhere,[1,3] it is necessary to discuss a few essential concepts. Fats and oils belong to the class of chemical compounds known as lipids, and are composed of triglycerides. Triglycerides are esters of one molecule of glycerol with three molecules of fatty acids. Fatty acids present in lipids may be saturated or unsaturated (that is, possess double bonds). Most common vegetable oils contain approximately 10% by weight of glycerol.

Oils and other lipids differ primarily in the fatty acid distribution. So-called drying oils (linseed, walnut and poppyseed) have a high proportion of 18-carbon unsaturated fatty acids (such as oleic, linoleic and linolenic acids, which have one, two or three double bonds, respectively). Fats, such as those present in animal and fish glues,[4] casein,[5] and egg yolk[6] contain large amounts of saturated fatty acids (palmitic acid has 16 carbons, stearic acid has 18).

During drying and aging of oil films, cross-linking and photo-oxidation reactions occur which alter the original fatty acid composition. The amounts of unsaturated fatty acids are reduced to such an extent that they cannot be detected in aged oil films. Saturated fatty acids, being less reactive, remain in the film. Due to their relative stability, saturated fatty acids have been utilized as internal standards in studies of oil paint degradation,[1,2] although this practice may not be entirely sound, as shall be shown later. It should also be noted that the weight of oil films change during drying. For instance, uptake of oxygen causes an increase in film weight, whereas loss of volatile products (such as water, aldehydes, ketones) leads to a decrease in weight.

Furthermore, aged oil films contain chain scission products. Azelaic acid (a nine-carbon dicarboxylic acid) is the most abundant product, and other dicarboxylic acids (with two to ten carbons) may also be present. High levels of azelaic acid are present in aged drying oil films, whereas the amount present in non-drying media (such as animal glue) may be orders of magnitude lower.

Gas chromatography has been employed for analysis of lipids in paintings and archaeological specimens. In most procedures, fatty acids are first converted to methyl esters (FAMEs) prior to analysis, and glycerol is not detected.[1,2,7–10] Traditionally, oils are identified on the basis of peak area ratios of FAMEs.[1] If a sample has an azelaic to palmitic (A/P) ratio greater than 1, this indicates that a drying oil is present in the sample, whereas an A/P ratio near 0.1 suggests that egg tempera may be present. Linseed oil has a nominal palmitic to stearic (P/S) ratio of 1.5, whereas the ratio is 5 for poppy oil, 2.5 for walnut oil, and 3 for egg. Because the ratio for walnut oil falls between the ratios for linseed and poppy, it is not possible to differentiate between pure walnut oil, and mixtures of linseed and poppy oil, based solely on P/S.

* Author to whom correspondence should be addressed.

A major shortcoming of the existing procedures is that glycerol cannot be determined. Because glycerol is present in each triglyceride molecule, it would be possible to determine the oil content of a paint sample if the glycerol concentration was known. Thin-layer chromatography[11] and modern biochemical reagents[12] rely on glycerol detection as the basis of lipid identification, yet these methods cannot be used for quantitative analysis on paint microsamples.

In 1964 a GC procedure was developed for determining the fatty acid and glycerol composition of food oils,[13] yet it was never tried on oil paints. In this procedure, FAMEs and isopropylidene glycerol (IPG, a volatile glycerol derivative) were produced quantitatively from oil samples, and analyzed in a single chromatogram. However, quantitative conversion of free fatty acids (such as azelaic acid) to methyl esters could not be achieved by following the literature procedure. In addition, the extent to which pigments interfere with the procedure had not been studied. Also, it was uncertain what effect physical aging would have on the analytical results.

Scope of research

The procedure for the analysis of food oils was modified in order to permit the analysis of free fatty acids and triglycerides in oil paints (see Appendix 1 for details). The derivative concentrations were converted to molar composition ratios for meaningful comparisons. The procedure was used to test a large number of fresh, unpigmented oils and lipids from the binding media collection of the Getty Conservation Institute.[14] The collection included products distributed by many different suppliers worldwide. A brief summary of those materials tested is: casein (2 samples); animal glue (2); egg yolk (1); linseed oil (27); poppyseed oil (14); safflower oil (1); sunflower oil (1); tung oil (1); walnut oil (7). A complete list of suppliers for all products that were tested is available on request.

Next, a study of the effects of pigment interferences on the procedure was conducted. To 4 ml glass vials were added 300 μg of alkali-refined linseed oil, 200 μg of azelaic acid, and 500 μg of one of 29 different pigments. The samples were tested using the modified procedure, and the results were compared to the data for the unpigmented mixture. The pigments included Paris blue, orpiment, green earth, burnt umber, hematite, vermilion, titanium white, lithopone, zinc white, gypseous spar, kaolin, pyrite, marble dust, manganese black, vine black, bone black, cadmium red, red lead, yellow ochre, Naples yellow, lead white, viridian, verdigris, chrome oxide green, iron oxide, mars red, cobalt blue, azurite, and ultramarine.

To ascertain the effects of light and heat aging on oil paint media, paints were prepared from selected pigments and oil media with known pigment-to-binder composition following traditional procedures.[15] The oils included blown linseed oil, cold-pressed walnut oil and poppyseed oil; the pigments included lead white, vine black and yellow ochre. Paints and samples of the unpigmented oils were applied to glass plates and allowed to dry at room temperature for at least six months. Afterwards, one set of all paint samples was aged at 80°C for six weeks, an identical set was placed in a Weather-O-Meter exposure chamber at 50°C and 50% RH for 500 h, and a third set was stored at ambient conditions of lighting, humidity, and temperature. After aging, 500 μg samples of the paints were prepared and tested in one ml of reagents.

Paints made with cold-pressed linseed, stand linseed and egg yolk were also prepared but, at the time of writing, the oven and Weather-O-Meter exposure periods had not been completed. Results for the testing of these paints will be included in a subsequent publication. In place of these paints, four month-old films of various drying oils, egg yolk, and triglyceride standards were exposed to light in a Suntest chamber for four days.

Samples from three paintings, tested in order to determine if the procedure was suitable for use with art objects, included: brown paint from "Beggars Brawl" by Georges de la Tour, from the collections of the J. Paul Getty Museum; dark greenish brown paint from "Venus and Adonis" by Titian, from the J. Paul Getty Museum; pink, light blue and green paints from "Waterlilies" by Claude Monet, from the collections of the Museum of Modern Art, New York. The analytical results were compared to the data for the Suntest-aged oil samples.

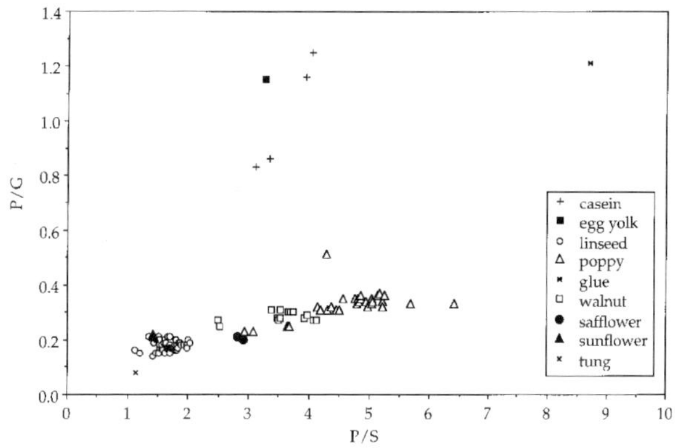

Figure 1. P/G versus P/S for fresh lipid materials

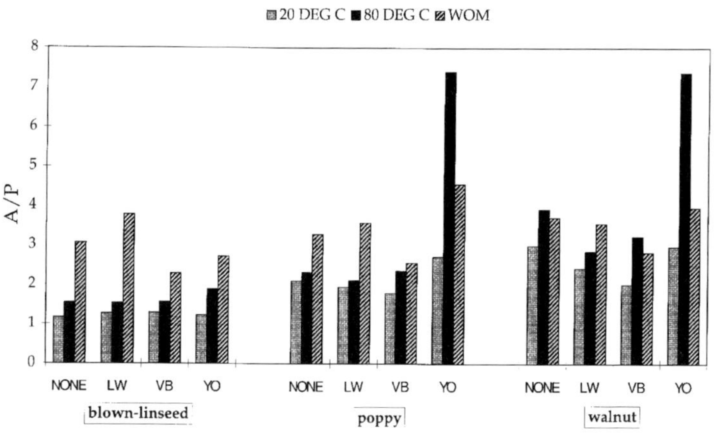

Figure 2. A/P molar ratio data for aged oil paints: NONE = no pigment; LW = lead white; VB = vine black; YO = yellow ochre; WOM = paints exposed in a Weather-O-Meter

Results and discussion

The test results for the GCI binding media library lipid samples are presented in Figure 1, a graph of the molar ratios of P/G (palmitic acid to glycerol) versus P/S (palmitic acid to stearic acid). It is apparent that the non-drying lipids in casein, egg yolk, and animal glue exhibit very high P/G values, whereas the P/G data for drying oils is much less than 0.5. It should be noted that the molar ratios for sunflower oil and safflower oil overlap with the data for linseed oil and walnut oil, respectively. When testing paint samples from objects, this should be kept in mind to avoid misidentification.

Figure 1 also shows that the test results for linseed, walnut and poppyseed oils separate into clusters. Linseed oil data form a separate group that is easily differentiated from walnut oil and poppy oil. Because the groups for walnut oil and poppyseed oil overlap slightly, positive identification of these oils is difficult, at best. Equally unfortunate is the fact that the group for walnut oil lies between the groups for linseed and poppyseed. Therefore, the new procedure fails to differentiate between pure walnut oil, and mixtures of linseed with poppyseed, as does the traditional method of Mills.[1]

The pigment interference study revealed that most pigments had no measurable effect on the experimentally-determined composition of the linseed oil/azelaic acid test mixture. Overall, the P/S data averaged 1.62 ± 0.06 (1σ). The average yield for azelaic acid was 101 ± 5% (1σ), and for glycerol the average yield was 96 ± 4% (1σ). Pigments that gave glycerol yields outside the error range were Paris blue (21% yield), red lead (64%), and azurite (66%). Possibly these pigments interfered with IPG formation through complexation. Care should, therefore, be taken when interpreting results from paints made with these pigments.

Very interesting results were obtained from the study of aged oil paints. For the entire set of samples, the glycerol recovery averaged 89 ± 11% (1σ). Greater variability in the glycerol recovery for the aged paints is a direct result of changes in film weight that occur during drying, which affect the actual percentage of glycerol in the film. As described earlier, most drying oil films increase in weight because of oxygen uptake, which *decreases* the weight percentage of glycerol. This was evident for the aged oil paints. On the contrary, films that have lost total mass through evaporation of volatile molecules[16] experience an *increase* in the weight percentage of glycerol. This would most likely be evident in highly degraded oil paints.

Regardless of exposure condition, the P/S molar ratio data did not vary beyond the error limits determined from the pigment interference study, which is in agreement with other studies.[1,9] Conversely, the A/P molar ratios varied widely, being affected by heat and light exposure, and also the nature of the pigment present (Figure 2).

The A/P ratio findings were consistent with an earlier study,[2] in which linseed oil paints exposed to UV light were periodically analyzed by GC. Marked increases over time were observed in the weight percent of azelaic acid present in the paints,

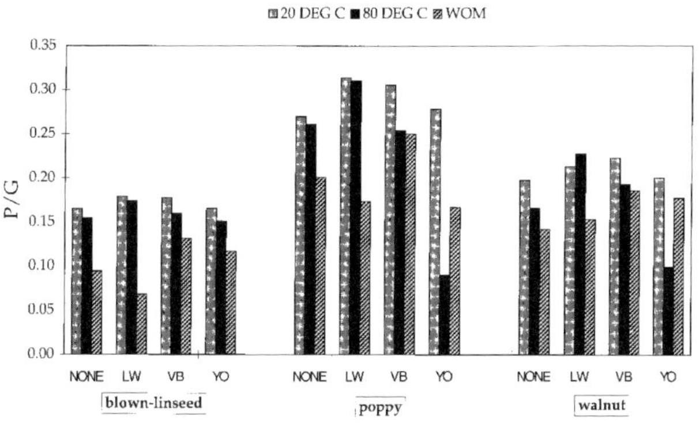

Figure 3. P/G molar ratio data for aged oil paints: NONE = no pigment; LW = lead white; VB = vine black; YO = yellow ochre; WOM = paints exposed in a Weather-O-Meter

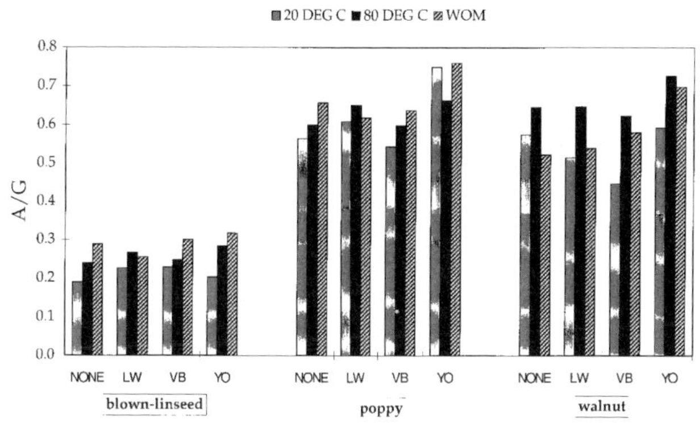

Figure 4. A/G molar ratio data for aged oil paints: NONE = no pigment; LW = lead white; VB = vine black; YO = yellow ochre; WOM = paints exposed in a Weather-O-Meter

relative to the total saturated fatty acid content. This result is based on the assumption that the saturated fatty acid content of the paint is stable over the exposure period.

In a surprising new discovery, it was found that variations in the A/P ratio for the aged paints are not due solely to increases in the azelaic acid content, but rather are mainly due to reductions in the amount of saturated fatty acids. A graph of P/G for the aged oil paints (Figure 3) shows that the extent of reduction in palmitic acid content may exceed 50%. In contrast, for a given drying oil the molar ratio of A/G was largely unaffected by physical aging and pigmentation (Figure 4). The A/G ratio was approximately 0.6 for paints made with poppyseed oil or walnut oil, and 0.25 for paints made with blown linseed oil.

Thus, Figures 3 and 4 show that the levels of saturated fatty acids may be reduced markedly in aged oil paints by heat and light exposure, whereas the azelaic acid content remains relatively unaffected. Ultimately, these findings may lead to a clearer understanding of the aging and decomposition of oil paints.

Whereas the amount of azelaic acid (relative to the glycerol content) was largely unaffected by physical aging, the formation of the other dicarboxylic acids was greatly enhanced. The sum of the (C3 to C8 plus C10) dicarboxylic acids, expressed as a molar ratio to the glycerol content, increased after exposure to heat or light (Figure 5). This fact, combined with the data in Figure 4, seems to indicate that azelaic acid is formed by a different mechanism than the other dicarboxylic fatty acids, since its concentration increases only slightly with aging. It is possible that azelaic acid is formed during the drying process, whereas the other dicarboxylic acids are formed during film degradation.

The effects of heat and light aging on the test paints are most clearly seen in the molar ratio graph of (C3 to C8 plus C10 dicarboxylic fatty acids)/G versus P/G (Figure 6). All of the paints stored at ambient conditions have the highest levels of

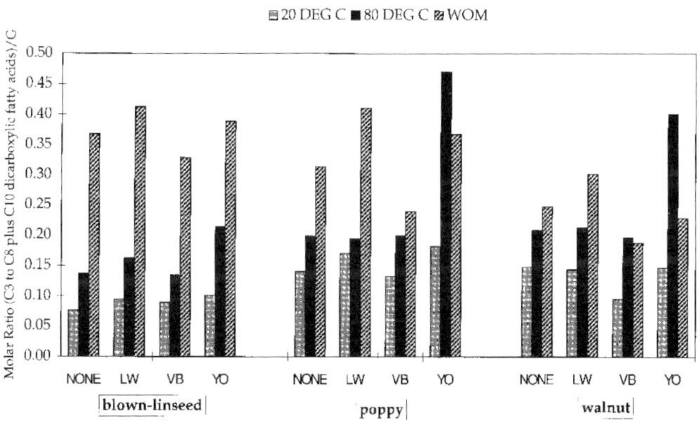

Figure 5. (C3 to C8 plus C10 dicarboxylic fatty acids)/G molar ratio data for aged oil paints: NONE = no pigment; LW = lead white; VB = vine black; YO = yellow ochre; WOM = paints exposed in a Weather-O-Meter

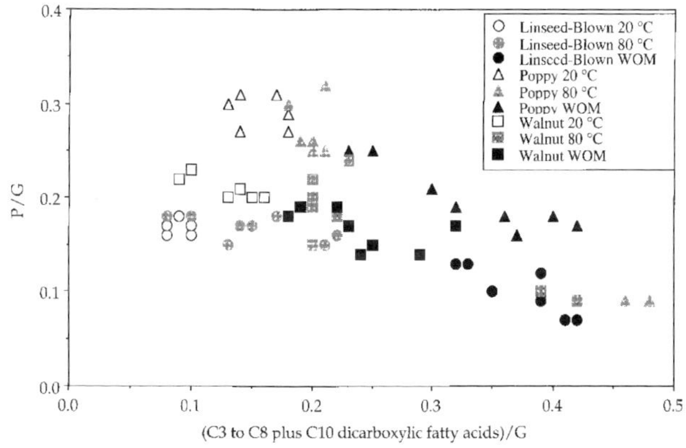

Figure 6. Molar ratios of P/G Versus (C3 to C8 plus C10 dicarboxylic fatty acids)/G for aged oil paints

Table I: Summary Of Testing For Samples From Art Objects And Reference Lipids. Reference lipids were one mil films drawn onto glass slides, dried for at least four months in the laboratory, and exposed for four days in a Suntest chamber

Sample[b]	Weight, μg	Volume, μl	% Oil[a]	P + S	Weight percent of oil content[a] Azelaic	Dicarboxylic acids	Oleic	Glycerol
Cold-pressed (a) linseed	1110	1016	93.2	5.6	8.8	11.7	0.9	9.6
Stand linseed (b)	1610	1016	88.1	4.5	4.6	10.0	0.1	9.1
Poppyseed (c)	1620	1016	106	7.5	13.9	19.7	0.1	11.0
Cold-pressed walnut (a)	980	1016	103	6.1	13.9	19.8	0.1	10.7
Trilinolenin (d)	1530	1016	84.9	0	5	5.3	0.1	8.7
Trilinolein (d)	1330	1016	106	0	16	20.8	0.1	10.9
Triolein (d)	610	1016	123	0	17	27.1	0.7	12.7
Egg yolk	1040	1016	49.3	15.0	3.3	7.5	0.2	5.1
de la Tour – brown paint	32.2	22.7	1.7	5.7	3.8	12.8	3.6	10.3
Titian – dark green and brown paint	17.5	11.3	3.9	14.2	7.9	9.6	3.6	10.3
Monet – green paint	71	56.7	12.1	14.0	11.5	14.2	1.9	10.3
Monet – pink paint	126.8	113.5	11.7	6.2	6.7	8.8	0.9	10.3
Monet – light blue paint	320.4	226.9	12.5	10.4	13.7	18.6	1.1	10.3

[a] Based on a glycerol content of 10.3% for linseed oil.
[b] Sources of Lipids: (a) Zecchi; (b) Schebiningen; (c) Le Franc and Bourgeois; (d) Sigma Chemical

palmitic acid, and the lowest levels of dicarboxylic fatty acids. Exposure to heat causes a slight reduction in palmitic acid, and an increase in dicarboxylic fatty acid products. After exposure to light, large amounts of dicarboxylic fatty acids are formed, and the palmitic acid content is reduced significantly.

The question of how the chemical composition of dried oil paints is affected by aging and solvent leaching[10,17] is the subject of on-going research, and will be reported in the second paper of this series.

Tables 1 and 2 list the analytical results for the samples from objects of art, and the test lipids exposed in the Suntest chamber. The oil content of the samples from objects, estimated from the glycerol content, was found to be on the order of 10% in the Monet, and much lower in the Titian and the de la Tour. Several explanations may be postulated for the variability in the oil content data. It is likely that the extent of solvent cleaning each painting has received will affect the residual oil of the samples. Another possible explanation is that a substance may be present which contributes to sample weight (such as varnish or relining adhesive), thereby diluting the samples. It is also possible that the artists may have prepared the paints with somewhat less oil originally. As more samples from objects are tested with the procedure, increasing the size of the information database, the results for these paintings may be clarified.

The P/S, P/G and A/G molar ratio data for the green and pink from the Monet correlate well to aged walnut oil paints, whereas somewhat higher P/S and P/G results obtained for the light blue paint are a closer match to poppy oil. Low values

Table 2. Molar ratios for samples from art objects and reference lipids

Sample	Molar ratios P/S	A/P	A/G	P/G	(C3 to C8 plus C10 dicarboxylic fatty acids)/G
Cold-pressed linseed	1.42	3.85	0.45	0.12	0.16
Stand linseed	1.62	2.35	0.25	0.11	0.33
Poppyseed	5.61	3.02	0.62	0.21	0.29
Cold-pressed walnut	3.57	4.07	0.64	0.16	0.30
Trilinolenin	n.d.	n.a.	0.25	0.0	0.05
Trilinolein	n.d.	n.a.	0.70	0.0	0.27
Triolein	n.d.	n.a.	0.64	0.0	0.46
Egg yolk	3.29	0.40	0.32	0.79	0.47
de la Tour – brown paint	1.31	1.68	0.18	0.11	0.56
Titian – dark green and brown paint	1.14	1.50	0.38	0.25	0.08
Monet – green paint	2.45	1.62	0.55	0.34	0.14
Monet – pink paint	2.89	2.01	0.32	0.16	0.11
Monet – light blue paint	3.72	2.32	0.65	0.28	0.25

for P/S and A/G indicate that linseed oil is present in the Titian and the de la Tour samples.

As shown by the molar ratio of (C3 to C8 plus C10 dicarboxylic fatty acids)/G, the data for the three Monet samples lie near the results for test paints stored in ambient conditions. Undoubtedly this is because the painting is fairly young (only 90 years old) compared to the other samples.

The ratios of (C3 to C8 plus C10 dicarboxylic fatty acids)/G and A/G for the Titian sample are similar to the data for aged cold-pressed linseed oil, whereas the ratios for the de la Tour indicate that stand linseed oil is likely to be present. It has been shown previously that the amount of azelaic acid, relative to the other dicarboxylic acids, is high for films of cold-pressed linseed oil, and low for heat-bodied linseed oil films,[18] and the present results support these findings. The difference in dicarboxylic acid composition may be related to the formation of azelaic acid rather early in the drying period, compared to the formation of the other diacids only after exposure to heat or light. This will be the subject of future studies.

Conclusions

The ability to detect glycerol and FAMEs, the ease of the procedure, and the use of a standard polar GC column are all attractive features of the new procedure for identifying lipids in samples from art objects. The present study shows how the detection of glycerol and fatty acids leads to a more complete knowledge of the chemical composition of dried oil paints. Exposure to light and, to a lesser extent heat, caused the formation large amounts of all dicarboxylic fatty acids except azelaic acid, and the loss of saturated fatty acids.

Acknowledgments

The authors wish to thank the following members of the Scientific Program of The Getty Conservation Institute (GCI): Alberto Tagle, Director, Scientific Program, who supported this research with much enthusiasm; Dusan Stulik, Head, Analytical Section, who developed the binding medium research project and provided encouragement; James Druzik, William Ginell, David Scott, and Charles Selwitz, who reviewed this manuscript; Arie Wallert, Associate Scientist, who provided the sample of the Titian. Special thanks go to: Andrew E. Parker, former research assistant at the GCI, presently at Perkin-Elmer Corp., who prepared paint samples and who worked on the initial phases of the oil identification research; Antoinette King, Head, Paintings Conservation, Museum of Modern Art, New York, who provided the samples from the Monet painting; Elisabeth Mention, Associate Conservator, Paintings Conservation, The J. Paul Getty Museum, who provided the samples of the de la Tour painting.

Appendix 1

Experimental procedure

All volumetric glassware and 1 ml glass conical vials (Pierce Chemical Co.) were washed with PCC54 cleaner (Pierce Chemical Co.) and baked at 500°C prior to use. Variable volumetric pipettors (Rainin Instrument Co.) were used for all liquid transfers.

Methanolic base (approximately 0.5M sodium methoxide in methanol) and methanolic HCl (approximately 1.5M HCl in methanol) were obtained from Supelco Corporation. Prior to use, the methanolic base strength was checked by titration against potassium hydrogen phthalate (Aldrich) to a red phenolphthalein endpoint. Methanolic acid strength was checked by back-titrating a known amount of excess base with acid to a colorless endpoint. Dilutions of acid and base for use in titrations were made with HPLC-grade water (Burdick and Jackson).

A derivatizing solution consisting of a 5:2:3 ratio by volume of benzene (residue grade, J. T. Baker), 2,2-dimethoxypropane (Supelco), and methanolic base was prepared in a 100 ml volumetric flask. Hexachlorobenzene (Aldrich) was added to give a final concentration of approximately 100 ppm. A solid neutralizing mixture was prepared from a 2:1:2 ratio by weight of sodium bicarbonate, sodium carbonate, and anhydrous sodium sulfate (all from E. Merck).

Paint and unpigmented oil test samples were weighed into a 4 ml screw-top glass vial (Waters Associates). Sufficient derivatizing solution was added to each vial in order to maintain the analyte concentrations within the calibration ranges (typically 1 ml of reagents per 0.5 mg of oil). Samples from art objects were weighed onto aluminum pans to the nearest 0.1 μg using a Cahn ultramicrobalance, transferred to 1 ml conical vials, and approximately 1 μl of reagents was added per μg of paint.

The vials were shaken to promote extraction of the lipid materials, and afterwards were allowed to stand overnight. The following morning sufficient methanolic acid was added to the sample vials in order to neutralize the base and provide exactly 60.0 μmoles of excess acid per ml of reagents. The vials were shaken thoroughly, and the contents were allowed to react for exactly 60 minutes. Afterwards, approximately 75 mg of solid neutralizer per ml of reagents was added to the vials, and after 30 minutes the solutions were ready for GC-FID analysis. Duplicate samples were prepared for all test samples.

Appendix 2

Gas chromatograph instrumental parameters

A Hewlett Packard 5890A gas chromatograph equipped with a flame ionization detector, split/splitless inlet and Pascal ChemStation was used for the analysis. FAMEs and IPG were separated on a 15 M × 0.25 mm fused silica capillary column coated with a 0.25 μm film of HP-INNOWAX. Helium was used as carrier gas at a nominal linear velocity of 95 cm s^{-1} (measured at 70°C and an inlet pressure of 17 psig); the split vent flow rate was 50 ml min^{-1} and the septum purge flow rate was 0.4 ml min^{-1}. The inlet temperature was set to 250°C, and the splitless purge delay was 90 s. The oven, maintained at 65°C for 5 min, was heated at a rate of 27°C min^{-1} to 260°C, and held at that temperature for 0.78 min. The detector, set to 250°C, was adjusted to detect peaks with widths greater than 0.01 min.

Fatty acid methyl esters (from Sigma Chemical Co. and Aldrich Chemical Co.) and isopropylidene glycerol (Solketal, from Aldrich Chemical Co.) were used without further purification. Calibration standards were prepared by serial dilution of a FAME and IPG stock solution; nominal concentrations ranged from 1 to 100 ppm. Hexachlorobenzene was added as an internal standard at a concentration of 100 ppm. Calibration curves for all analytes exhibited correlation coefficients of 0.998 or better.

References

1. J. S. Mills, "The Gas Chromatographic Examination of Paint Media. Part I. Fatty Acid Composition and Identification of Dried Oil Films," *Studies in Conservation* 11 (1966): 92–107.
2. N. Stolow and G. De W. Rogers, "Gas Chromatography and Pyrolysis Techniques to Establish Ageing Characteristics of Works of Art," in *Application of Science in Examination of Works of Art;* Proceeding of the Seminar, June 15 19, 1970 , ed. W. J. Young (Boston: Museum of Fine Arts, 1973), 213–228.
3. H. Kühn, *Conservation and Restoration of Works of Art and Antiquities*, Vol. 1 (London: Butterworths, 1986), 157–167.
4. B. Skans and P. Michelsen, "Die Bedeutung von Fett in Tierleim fuer Malzwecke," *Maltechnik* 96, no. 2 (1986): 63–71.
5. C. W. Hall, "Milk and Milk Products," in *Kirk-Othmer Encyclopedia of Chemical Technology* 3rd edn, vol. 15 (New York: John Wiley and Sons, 1981), 522–570.
6. D. Bergquist, "Eggs," in *Kirk-Othmer Encyclopedia of Chemical Technology* 3rd edn, vol. 8 (New York: John Wiley and Sons, 1981), 429–445.
7. L. Masschelein-Kleiner, J. Heylen and F. Tricot-Marckx, "Contribution à l'Analyse des Liants, Adhésifs et Vernis Anciens," *Studies in Conservation* 13 (1968): 105–121.
8. E. W. Hammond, "Analysis of Lipids: A Personal Approach to an Analytical Service," *Chemistry and Industry* 20 (1981): 710–715.
9. R. Stevanato, S. Mazzocchin, S. Calogero and L. Lazzarini, "A Simplified Procedure for Gas Chromatographic Identification of Dried Oils in Painting Media and its

Application to Some Venetian Masterpieces," *Science and Technology for Cultural Heritage* 2 (1993): 75–80.

10. D. Erhardt and J. Tsang, "The Extractable Components of Oil Paint Films," in *Cleaning, Retouching and coatings: Technology and Practice for Easel Paintings and Polychrome Sculpture,* Preprints of the Contributions to the Brussels Congress, 3–7 September 1990 , ed. J. S. Mills and P. Smith (London: IIC, 1990), 93–97.
11. M. Johnson and E. Packard, "Methods used for the Identification of Binding Media in Italian Paintings of the Fifteenth and Sixteenth Centuries," *Studies in Conservation* 16 (1971): 145–164.
12. D. Stulik and H. Florsheim, "Binding Media Identification in Painted Ethnographic Objects," *Journal of the American Institute for Conservation* 31 (1992): 275–288.
13. M. E. Mason, Mary E. Eager and George R. Waller, "A Procedure for the Simultaneous Quantitative Determination of Glycerol and Fatty Acid Contents of Fats and Oils," *Analytical Chemistry* 36, no. 3 (1964): 587–590.
14. D. C. Stulik, C. M. G. Druzik, M. R. Derrick and J. M. Landry, "Standard Materials for Analysis of Binding Media and GCI Binding Media Library," American Institute for Conservation 19th Annual Meeting Preprints, Albuquerque, 1991.
15. R. Kay, *The Painter's Guide to Studio Methods and Materials* (Englewood Cliffs, NJ: Prentice-Hall, 1983).
16. R. S. Yamasaki, "Chemical Kinetics of Photo-oxidative Degradation of Dried Trilinolein Film," *Journal of Paint Technology* 39, no. 506 (1967): 134–143.
17. N. Stolow, "Solvent Action," in *On Picture Varnishes and Their Solvents* , 2nd edn (Cleveland, OH: Case Western Reserve University, 1971), 45–116.
18. J. S. Mills and R. White, "Organic Mass Spectrometry of Art Materials: Work in Progress," *National Gallery Technical Bulletin* 6 (1982): 3–16.

Working Group B1

Paintings I: Conservation and restoration of paintings

Glue-Paste Lining of Paintings: An Evaluation of Some Additive Materials

Paul Ackroyd
Conservation Department, National Gallery,
Trafalgar Square, London WC2N 5DN, UK

Abstract

A number of prepared glue-paste samples, containing commonly used additives in glue-paste recipes have been examined. Peel strength tests were conducted on the samples to give measurements of the bond performance, and uniaxial load/extension tests were carried out to give indications of the relative stiffness of the lining supports. The majority of the additives tested – plasticisers, (Venice turpentine, linseed oil and molasses), wetting agents, (vinegar), and a bulking agent, (rye flour) – reduced the bond strength and had no appreciable effect in reducing the stiffness of the lining materials. Ox gall was the only additive tested that increased the flexibility of the lining without lowering the bond strength. Hydrogen peroxide, mixed with glue-paste as a non-toxic preservative, prevented mould growth in the wet paste but further examination is required to ensure that this does not degrade the canvas.

Keywords

Glue-paste lining, plasticiser, wetting agent, bulking agent, preservative, additive, bond performance, relative stiffness, paintings

Introduction

Glue-paste lining[1] is rooted in a manual craft-based tradition, where the individual skill of the liner is seen to be crucial to the successful outcome of a glue lining. The empirical wisdom that paste liners rely upon has run contrary to the more scientific and technical advances that have tended to dominate the professional literature over the last 50 years. Consequently, there has been little published interest in glue-paste lining and a lack of technical information on the actual adhesives. This is surprising considering their long and continual use throughout much of Europe.

This study is a further part of a continuing technical examination of glue-paste adhesives. The initial research in this project looked at a number of simple formulations of flour or starch mixed with animal, or fish glues.[2] The purpose here is to expand this work to include an evaluation of the effects that a number of commonly used additive materials have on the bond performance and the relative stiffness of the lining materials.

In addition, several preservatives were examined. The formulation of adhesives becomes increasingly complex when more than two components are added. The majority of glue-paste formulations incorporate several additive materials.[3–6] These mixtures, not unlike some culinary recipes, have evolved through an oral tradition, one generation has inherited the practice of the previous generation, often over a period of centuries. As a result, there has been little enquiry into the function of the various ingredients and the effects they have on the adhesive as they age.

The additives used in glue-paste adhesives

Only a few formulations of glue-paste involve simple mixtures of just flour and glue. Some mixtures include as many as four or five additives, sometimes in significant quantities. The function of these materials is varied and includes plasticisers, wetting and bulking agents, and preservatives. Table 1 shows the materials that were examined and the proportions by which they were added to one particular glue-paste adhesive. The proportions were added by ratio of weight to weight and are representative of the quantities found in many recipes.

Table 1. The proportions of additives examined

Additive		Proportions by ratio of wt/wt	
Plasticisers	Venice turpentine	1/2 part	1 part
	Linseed oil	1/2 part	1 part
Wetting agents	Ox gall	1/2 part	1 1/2 parts
	Vinegar	1/2 part	1 part
Bulking agent	Rye flour	2 parts rye flour:2 parts wheat flour:1 part bone glue	
		4 parts rye flour:4 parts wheat flour:1 part bone glue	
		6 parts rye flour:6 parts wheat flour:1 part bone glue	
Preservatives	Phenol (2% solution in water)	2% v/v	5% v/v.
	Cetyl trimethyl ammonium bromide	1% w/v.	2% w/v.

Hydrogen peroxide 27.5% by wt of 100 Vol. hydrogen peroxide was mixed with 100 ml water. 1% and 2.5% by volume of this solution was added to the cold glue-paste.

Plasticisers

Plasticisers are added to the adhesive with the purpose of increasing the long-term flexibility of the lining. Many practitioners try to avoid the stiff, board-like appearance sometimes produced by glue linings. It is significant that the recipes which require large proportions of glue attempt to compensate for this additional rigidity with additions of plasticising agents. Plasticisers may also be used to improve the working properties of the wet adhesive.

Venice turpentine

Venice turpentine is often used as a plasticising agent in glue-paste mixtures. It is a viscous exudation product from the European larch tree, mainly consisting of diturpenoid resins and essential oils. When mixed with glue-paste the Venice turpentine forms a colloidal suspension, where aggregates of the resins and essential oils are suspended within the aqueous adhesive. These hydrophobic substances repel the more hydrophilic polysaccharides and proteins in the paste. This repulsion has a lubricating effect and may give the adhesive better handling properties, whilst in its wet state. However, as the adhesive dries and the colloidal suspension collapses the plasticising effect of the Venice turpentine is likely to be short-lived. The essential oils eventually evaporate leaving the diturpenoid resins to oxidise and form micro crystalline structures. This may result in an increase in the stiffness or brittleness of the adhesive – the opposite effect of what was originally intended. Venice turpentine may also increase the acidity and promote the degradation of the canvas. The essential oils, before they evaporate, have anti-biotic properties that inhibit mould growth.

Linseed oil

This is another well-used additive, also employed as a plasticising ingredient. The oil is expressed by crushing flax seeds. The better oils, those used by artists, are extracted cold and further refined with alkalis. In glue-paste mixtures the oil forms a colloidal suspension and, like Venice turpentine, it may improve the working properties of the wet paste. The aging of linseed oil has been well researched[7] and involves the oxidation and cross-linking of the polymer chains. If used in sufficient quantities the oil produces a hard and stiff adhesive film on aging which may compromise the future reversibility of the lining; again, the reverse effect of what was intended. Contained within the adhesive, the linseed oil is protected from direct exposure to light and oxygen and the aging processes are likely to progress at a relatively slow rate.

Some recipes require the use of crushed linseed/flax seeds. These were not tested, but apart from the oil the seeds contain polysaccharides and proteins. Lecithin is also present and acts as an emulsifying agent which may ensure the stability of the wet glue-paste mixture.

Molasses

Molasses, another frequently employed plasticising agent, is often used in significant quantities. Like honey, it is a mixture of sugars in water and is known as humectant. These substances in glue-paste act indirectly as plasticisers by attracting and retaining moisture from the surrounding atmosphere. This in turn reduces the stiffness of the glue component. Some practitioners claim that humectants prevent the desiccation of paste linings in dry environments. But, in very dry conditions the moisture content may be reduced to such an extent that the molasses or honey crystallises, most probably resulting in an increase in the stiffness of the lining. Furthermore, the risk of mould growth may be greater when these materials are incorporated

Wetting agents

Wetting agents lower the surface tension between liquids and solids. In glue-paste recipes they are used to maintain the stability of the wet mixture and improve the surface contact between the adhesive and the canvases. Consequently they may increase the uniformity of the bond.

Ox gall

This is produced from gall stones in ox bladders and largely consists of cholesterol related compounds. In watercolour painting it is used as a wetting agent, but in glue-paste mixtures it may also function as a plasticiser. Ox gall may oxidise to some degree but its molecular weight is likely to change little. It is a relatively stable material.

Vinegar

Vinegar or acetic acid is frequently referred to in glue-paste recipes and as a constituent of aqueous facing adhesives. The acid lowers the viscosity of the animal glue and may improve the penetration of the adhesive, enhancing the uniformity of the bond. However, the presence of acids in the paste contribute to increases in the degradation of both the original and lining canvases.

Bulking agents

Bulking agents or fillers are sometimes added to glue-paste to improve the bond performance when the original or lining canvas is coarsely woven. Rye flour, on account of its coarse, granular texture, is often used for this purpose and may be added in large quantities. Like wheat flour it mainly consists of polysaccharides and proteins.

Preservatives

Preservatives are added in small quantities to glue-paste in order to prevent mould growth. Moulds are species of fungi which secrete enzymes in order to digest the substrate material, in this instance, causing the decay of canvas and glue.

Phenol

Phenol is well used in glue-paste and acts as a preservative by interfering with the metabolism of the mould. The acidic properties of phenol also inhibit mould formation but, at the same time, promote the degradation of the canvas. Phenol also has the disadvantage of being toxic, and contact with the skin is to be avoided.[8] Although fairly volatile, the phenol remains in the adhesive for some time after the lining has been carried out, offering some prolonged protection against mould.

Cetyl trimethyl ammonium bromide (CTAB)

CTAB[9] and hydrogen peroxide have not been used in glue-paste formulations, but were examined to find a non-toxic alternative to the phenol. CTAB is a bacteriocide and is used in low concentrations in commercial antiseptic creams. It acts by killing the bacteria that promote the growth of fungi. CTAB decomposes when heated and needs to be added to the paste once it has cooled. It is unlikely to offer prolonged protection as it is likely to decompose when heated during the lining process.

Hydrogen peroxide

Hydrogen peroxide is used in small quantities as a bleach and preservative in the food industry. It has been used in conservation as a preservative for solutions of sturgeons glue.[10] Peroxides are known to destroy both algae and fungal organisms. Hydrogen peroxide is a powerful oxidising agent and may promote the oxidation of the canvas, particularly when trace amounts of metal catalysts are present. However, its activity as an oxidising agent will be short lived as it decomposes rapidly, forming water and oxygen.

Sample preparation

Sample linings were prepared in exactly the same manner as those used in the previously published research on the plain flour and glue mixtures.[11] Commercially prepared linen canvases, used to simulate the original painting, and the linen lining canvas were identical to those used in the first part of this project. The proportions of additives were mixed by ratios of weight to weight with just one glue-paste adhesive, consisting of 8:1 wheat flour and bone glue. Although this was not the optimum glue-paste formulation, it was representative of some commonly used paste adhesives.[12]

Each additive was mixed and cooked on its own to each batch of glue-paste. The CTAB and hydrogen peroxide were added after the paste had cooled. A small amount of phenol, 3% by volume, was added to each mixture except in the tests with the other preservatives. A fine, commercially primed, linen canvas was used in all the samples. In addition, a coarse, primed linen canvas was employed in the linings containing the rye flour in order to gain some indication of the effects of the canvas topography on bond strength.

Lining procedure

The linings were carried out by hand according to current practice at the National Gallery, London. A description of the lining process is given in the publication on the initial part of this research.[13] The samples were given two separate ironings, with approximately three hours drying allowed between each pressing. The first ironing was carried out at 70°C and the second at 80°C. These temperatures represent the upper end of the range of those normally employed.

The samples were left for three months before testing by the methods described below.

Testing procedure

Peel strength tests

Peel strength tests were carried out to give a reliable indication of bond strength and uniformity of adhesion. The conditions of these tests were identical to those used in the previous research.[14] The ambient conditions during these and the load/extension tests were 30–40% RH and 17–19°C.

Load/extension tests

These tests were carried out on samples of the lining canvas alone with just the application of each adhesive. They did not include the primed canvas simulating the painting. The tests were designed to give a measurement of force experienced by the lining support at given amounts of uniaxial extension. From these measurements the relative stiffness of the samples could be ascertained.[15] The test conditions were the same as those in the previously published research.[16]

Testing of the preservatives

The preservatives were tested simply by monitoring the lengths of time the adhesive containing each preservative remained free of mould. The adhesives were left uncovered, open to room conditions, monitored at 50–56% RH, 20–22°C.

Results of the peel strength tests

Figure 1 shows the average peel strengths for the 8:1 wheat flour/bone glue linings containing the plasticising and wetting agents. These results were compared with those of the plain 8:1 wheat flour/bone glue sample. Table 2 summarises the results of all the peel strength tests.

All the additives in Figure 1, except for one, significantly reduced the bond strength. In comparison with the plain 8:1 flour/glue lining the plasticisers and wetting agents reduced the average peel strengths from 1080 g to approximately 700–800 g. There does not appear to be any ready explanation for these decreases in peel strength. Although these bonds may be considered to be acceptable and in some circumstances could provide adequate linings, they may not be able to offer sufficient support to paintings with more serious structural problems, such as large tears or joins.[17]

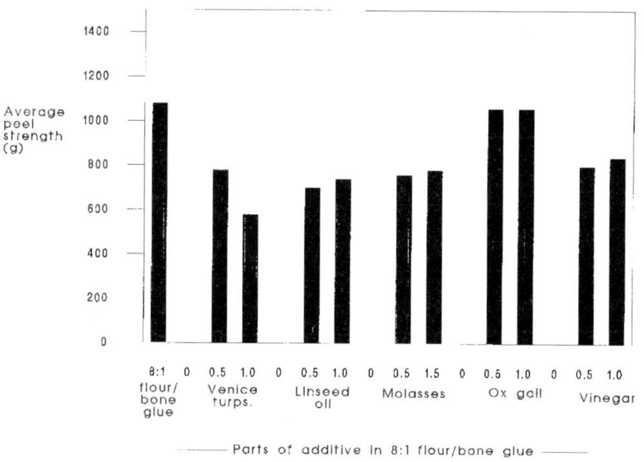

Figure 1. Average peel strength data for the formulations containing additives

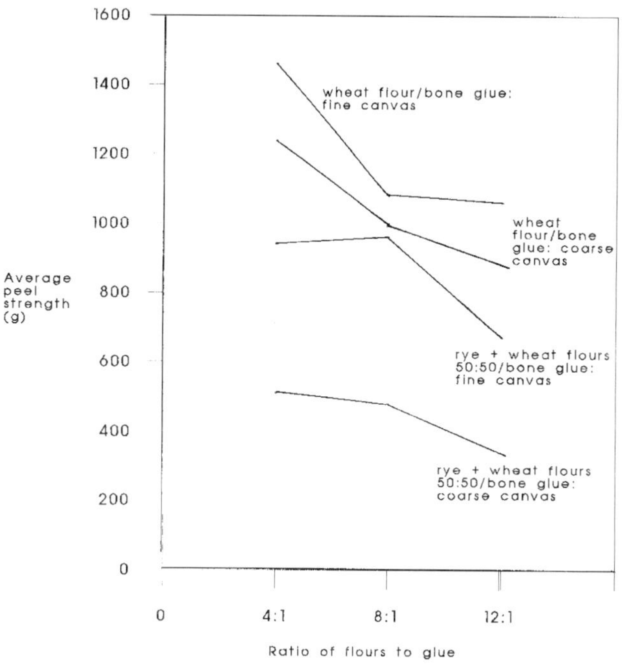

Figure 2. Average peel strength data for the formulations containing rye flour

The larger quantities of plasticising or wetting agents in the paste had little additional effect on the bond performance, with the exception of the greater amount of Venice turpentine, which further reduced the peel strength considerably. There appeared to be little advantage in adding more than half a part by weight of any of these materials.

The samples with the larger proportions of Venice turpentine, linseed oil and molasses, however, did improve the uniformity of adhesion.

The addition of vinegar did not improve the bond performance at all.

Ox gall, unlike the other materials, had little effect on the peel strength and improved the uniformity of the bond. The sample containing half a part by weight of ox gall appeared to produce the optimum result.

Figure 2 shows the average peel strengths for the linings containing the 50:50 mixtures of rye and wheat flours in varying proportions to bone glue. Comparisons were drawn with the equivalent plain wheat flour/bone glue linings. Figure 2 also illustrates the effects that the coarse primed linen had on the bond strength.

The addition of the rye flour decreased the average peel strengths and uniformity of adhesion in each case. The bonds became weaker as more rye flour was added – the peel strengths continued to fall between the 4:4:1 rye flour/wheat

Table 2. Results of the peel strength tests

Peel strengths (g)	Additives	Avrge	Min.	Max.
8 parts wheat flour: 1 part bone glue:		1080	660	1350
8 parts wheat flour: 1 part bone glue:	½ part Ven. turps.	780	550	1060
8 parts wheat flour: 1 part bone glue:	1 part Ven. turps.	580	400	740
8 parts wheat flour: 1 part bone glue:	½ part linseed oil	700	420	870
8 parts wheat flour: 1 part bone glue:	1 part linseed oil	740	490	920
8 parts wheat flour: 1 part bone glue:	½ part molasses	760	500	940
8 parts wheat flour: 1 part bone glue:	1½ parts molasses	780	610	1000
8 parts wheat flour: 1 part bone glue:	½ part ox gall	1060	660	1250
8 parts wheat flour: 1 part bone glue:	1 part ox gall	1060	740	1280
8 parts wheat flour: 1 part bone glue:	½ part vinegar	800	600	960
8 parts wheat flour: 1 part bone glue:	1 part vinegar	840	650	1100
Mixtures of rye and wheat and bone glue with the fine primed linen				
4:1 – 2 rye flour: 2 wheat flour: 1 bone glue		940	550	1160
8:1 – 4 rye flour: 4 wheat flour: 1 bone glue		960	580	1200
12:1 – 6 rye flour: 6 wheat flour: 1 bone glue		670	440	820
Mixtures of rye and wheat and bone with the coarse primed linen				
4:1 – 2 rye flour: 2 wheat flour: 1 bone glue		510	290	820
8:1 – 4 rye flour: 4 wheat flour: 1 bone glue		480	300	780
12:1 – 6 rye flour: 6 wheat flour: 1 bone glue		340	200	480

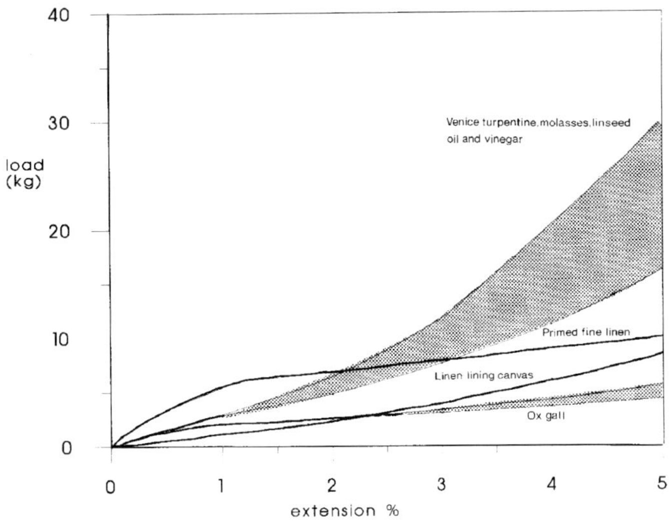

Figure 3. Load/extension data for the formulations containing additives

flour/bone glue, (8:1 flours/glue), to the 6:6:1 rye flour/wheat flour/bone glue, (12:1 flours/glue). In contrast, the losses between the 8:1 and 12:1 wheat flour/bone glue linings had stabilised.

The linings made with the coarser canvas and the glue-paste formulations containing rye flour showed particularly weak bonds. The peel strengths fell below what might be considered to be a minimum working requirement.[18] The large particles in the rye flour appeared to act as localised sites for poor adhesion and consequently impaired the performance of the glue-paste.

Results of the load/extension tests

Figure 3 shows the results of the uniaxial load/extension tests which gave indications of the relative stiffness of the linings containing the plasticising and wetting agents. Similar measurements from a plain 8:1 wheat flour/bone glue sample are included here for comparison. Figure 4 illustrates the load/extension measurements from the linings containing the additions of rye flour. In these graphs the extension, expressed as a percentage increase on original length, is plotted against load. Addition of most of the plasticisers, Venice turpentine, linseed oil and molasses, did not increase the flexibility of the lining support. On the contrary, they showed slight but insignificant, increases in the stiffness of the lining supports. The differences in relative stiffness between most of the additives are small and are within experimental error. Therefore, they are shown in Figure 3 as a shaded band.

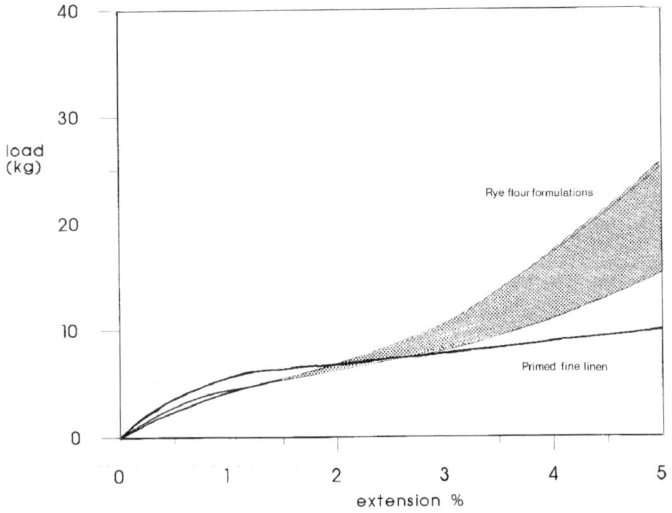

Figure 4. Load/extension data for the formulations containing rye flour

Both ox gall samples, on the other hand, demonstrated noticeable increases in the flexibility of the lining materials. The results of the lining supports containing the additions of rye flour, in Figure 4, again displayed slight but insignificant increases in the stiffness.

Preservative performance

The additions of CTAB did not prevent the formation of mould which appeared after two days. The mixture containing 2% by volume of phenol showed signs of mould growth after three to four days, but the 5% addition of phenol remained unaffected throughout the two month duration of these trials.

Similarly, even the smaller quantity of hydrogen peroxide was effective in preventing mould growth over the two month period.

During these trials it was found that the purity of the materials made a considerable difference. Mould grew less rapidly in adhesives containing the purer wheat starch and refined gelatin than equivalent formulations composed of flour and unrefined bone glue.

Conclusion

All the glue-paste additives examined here, except for the ox gall, reduced the bond strength and are likely to be unstable on aging. The plasticising agents only improved the working properties of the wet paste and had no appreciable plasticising effect once the adhesive had dried. Further increases in the stiffness of these materials are expected as they change on aging. Furthermore, the acidity of Venice turpentine and vinegar promote the degradation of both the original and lining canvases.

Additions of rye flour rather than improving the adhesion with coarser canvases tended to weaken the bonds, to such an extent that these linings were probably unable to offer adequate support to more serious structural problems. The hydrogen peroxide preservative gave good results as a non-toxic alternative to phenol but further work is necessary to ensure that it does not damage the canvas. Ox gall differed from the other materials examined here – it is likely to be relatively stable on aging and improved the uniformity of the bond without affecting the peel strength. Even in small quantities ox gall was an effective plasticiser significantly reducing the stiffness of the lining materials.

It is debatable whether a plasticiser serves any useful purpose in glue-paste linings. Aesthetically, a less rigid lining is obviously more desirable. However, lowering the stiffness of the lining materials may impair the function of the lining support. It is generally accepted that the greatest tensile stress in a stretched painting is experienced in the layers with the highest modulus of elasticity (stiffness). Research into the mechanical properties of paint and canvas has indicated the potential for reducing the physical degradation of canvas paintings by transferring tensile stresses in a stretched canvas to a stiffer lining support.[19–21] It is to be expected, at least at ambient humidities and below, that glue-paste linings might perform well in this respect on account of the comparatively high modulus of animal glues. Therefore, lowering the stiffness of the adhesive by using a plasticiser reduces the stress carried by the lining and its ability to function as a support to the painting.

Increasing the flexibility of the lining support with a plasticiser, on the other hand, may be beneficial in dry conditions, by reducing stress and decreasing the rate at which mechanical failure occurs due to fatigue cycling. However, this hypothetical benefit requires further investigation.

This study has demonstrated that the performance of glue-paste adhesives, in most instances, is reduced by the inclusion of just one additive. This suggests that the performance may be further impaired as more than one additive is incorporated into the adhesive. There seems to be little added benefit in combining more than the two basic components – flour and glue – with a little preservative.

Acknowledgements

I am grateful to the Technology Department, Courtauld Institute of Art, for the use of their tensile testing machine. I would also like to thank Raymond White from the National Gallery, London, Scientific Department, and Alan Phenix of the Technology Department, Courtauld Institute of Art, for their advice.

Notes and References

1. Glue-paste generally refers to the mixture of animal or fish glues with various kinds of flour paste. Glue-paste lining is also referred to as glue lining, paste lining or compo lining.
2. P. Ackroyd, "Glue-Paste Lining: An Evaluation of the Bond Performance and Relative Stiffness of Some Glue-Paste Linings" (Paper delivered at the UKIC Lining and Backing Conference, 1995), 83–91.
3. E. Motta, Jr, "A Survey of Hand Lining Techniques Based on Animal Glue/Starch Paste Adhesives", (Final Year Project, Technology Department, Courtauld Institute of Art, London, 1988).
4. E. Rostain, *Rentoilage et Transposition des Tableaux* (Paris: L'EREC, 1981).
5. P. Newman, "A Method for Lining Canvas Paintings with Glue-Composition", Report on the Conference on Comparative Lining Techniques, Greenwich Maritime Museum, Greenwich (1974).
6. J.M. Reifsnyder, "The Florentine Paste Technique: What Makes It Different from Other Glue-Paste Linings for Paintings" (Paper delivered at the UKIC Lining and Backing Conference, 1995), 77–82.
7. S.O. Crecelus, R.E. Kaganse, and A.L. Alexander, "Drying Oil Oxidation. Mechanism, Film Formation, and Degradation", *Industrial and Engineering Chemistry* 47 (1955): 1643–49.
8. Phenol is a suspected carcinogen. Readily absorbed through skin causing instant dermatitis and severe burns. TLV5ppm, STEL 10ppm.
9. M.R. Porter, *Handbook of Surfactants* (London and Glasgow: Blackie, 1991), 180.
10. V. Routledge, "Hydrogen Peroxide Used as a Preservative in Solutions of Sturgeon Glue", private correspondence (1995).
11. Ackroyd, "Glue-Paste Lining", 84.
12. Ibid., 89.
13. Ibid., 84.
14. Ibid., 85.
15. G. Hedley and C. Villers, "Polyester Sailcloth: A High Stiffness Lining Support", Science and Technology in the Service of Conservation (Paper delivered at the IIC Congress, Washington, 1982).
16. Ackroyd, "Glue-Paste Lining", 86.
17 Ibid., 85.
18. Ibid., 85.
19. M. Mecklenburg, "Some Aspects of the Mechanical Behaviour of Fabric Supported Paintings", (Report to the Smithsonian Institution, Washington DC, 1982).
20. M. Mecklenburg and J.E. Colville, "The Deterioration of Fabric Supported Paint Films", (Report to the Smithsonian Institution, Washington DC, 1978).
21. G. Hedley, "The Stiffness of Lining Fabrics: Theoretical and Practical Considerations" (Paper delivered at the Sixth Triennial Meeting of the International Council of Museums Committee for Conservation, 1981), 1–13.

Materials

- Bone glue, Pearl glue, (good quality bone glue), from Brodie and Middleton Ltd, 68 Drury Lane, London, WC2B 5SP. Tel. 0171 836 3289.
- Wheat flour, McDougalls, plain, refined flour obtainable from most UK supermarkets.
- Rye flour, Doves Farm Mill, Marlborough, Wiltshire. Available from Waitrose supermarkets, UK.
- Molasses - from Holland and Barrett Health Food Stores, Hinckley, Leicester. Tel. 01455 251 900.
- Vinegar, Sarsons clear vinegar obtainable from most UK supermarkets.
- Phenol and hydrogen peroxide, from Merck B.D.H. Ltd, Hunter Boulevard, Magna Park, Littleworth, Leicester, LE17 4XN. Tel. 0800 223344/01455 558600.
- Venice turpentine, from A.F. Suter and Co. Ltd, Swan Wharf, 60 Dace Road, Bow, London, E3 2NQ. Tel. 0181 986 8218.
- Artists linseed oil and ox gall, from Winsor and Newton, 51 Rathbone Place, London, W1P 1AB. Tel. 0171 636 4231.
- Fine primed linen and coarse primed linen canvas, commercially prepared Belgian canvas. Trade name 'Berge', obtainable from Winsor and Newton, 51 Rathbone Place, London W1P 1AB. Tel. 0171 636 4231.
- Fine Linen lining canvas, from Ulster Weavers, 47 Linfield Road, Belfast, BT12 5GL, Northern Ireland. Tel: 01232 32494.
- Cetyl trimethyl ammonium bromide, from Sigma Chemical Company Ltd, Ferry Road, Poole, Dorset, BH17 7BR. Tel. 01202 733114.#

Transparent Lining of Paintings

Gustav A. Berger
Art Conservation Research Foundation, Ltd.,
115 West 73rd Street, apt.4D,
New York, NY 10023-2914, USA

Abstract

Some artists like to sign their paintings on the reverse of the canvas, adding the date, size, remarks, dedications, and sometimes sketches. To preserve such important details, the author has utilized a variety of modern materials to develop his technique of transparent linings. The original system is described, and more recent materials and methods were added. A shortened version of an actual Conservation Report is given.

Keywords

Double-sided paintings, transparent linings, BEVA, PeCap

Figure 1. Inscription on the reverse of a self-portrait by Oskar Kokoschka: "Looking out of the picture am I, Looking at me are you" 24 December 1914.

Introduction

Canvas paintings often carry on their reverse the artists' signatures, dates, dedications and remarks, sketches, and sometimes even complete paintings. These details are of considerable interest and documentary value because they add to the understanding and dating of the artist's work. Usually, the remarks and sketches on the reverse of the canvas have been left by the artist himself, intentionally (Figure 1). Therefore, they form an integral part of his work, and should not be obscured.

Some of these paintings, however, were done on flimsy or damaged materials or in the case of Rouault, for instance, on old, torn paper.[1,2] Such paintings cannot be displayed unless mounted on a stronger support. Until the 1960s, the available supports would obscure the entire reverse, and nothing but a photographic record would remain. Alain G. Boissonnas was the first one to use a fiberglass fabric to reline paintings transparently, using wax resin in 1961.[3]

Since then, many modern synthetic fabrics (such as nylon, polyester, etc.), made of fully transparent materials became available. In addition, there exist a number of synthetic films and plates, some almost unbreakable, which are fully transparent, as well as stable adhesives which stay glass-clear (Figure 2).

Problems connected with transparent linings

A solid transparent support is often unacceptable for paintings done on both sides of a canvas because the painting on the reverse contains impasto or irregularities which make a successful, transparent attachment to any solid support impossible. Not only could impasto be squashed during lining, but still more disturbing is the fact that the irregularities of the reverse create enclosures in which air is trapped (Figure 3). We will call them "air-bubbles", although they do not have the form of a bubble but usually follow the outlines of the paint or texture of the mounted surface instead. The "air bubbles" sparkle because they deflect the light falling on the surfaces of the canvas and the solid support, both of which are coated with the adhesive. Thus, they defeat the purpose of the transparent lining which is to reinforce the painting in an almost invisible, or at least unobtrusive enough manner so as not to destroy all of the effect of the original.

These bubbles can teach us an important lesson: two surfaces joined by adhesives are connected only at the points where the adhesive joins them together. Any trapped air must interfere with the adhesion between the surfaces, thus creating an uneven, interrupted bond. The implications, however, are even more important because they indicate a failure of the vacuum pressure system. Clearly, the vacuum system can generate pressure only if the air is evacuated. The presence of "air bubbles" in the laminate attests that in this particular arrangement of layers of the laminate *the vacuum system has failed*: it did not generate effective, overall pressure that would produce a good bond between the two layers since it did not eliminate these air bubbles. In order to achieve a good vacuum lining porous layers have to be sandwiched between the materials to be bonded, i.e. all parts of the materials must connect to the air intake of the vacuum pump. That this can be done without damage to the surface of the painting was demonstrated by this author during the International Symposium on Comparative Lining Techniques in Greenwich,

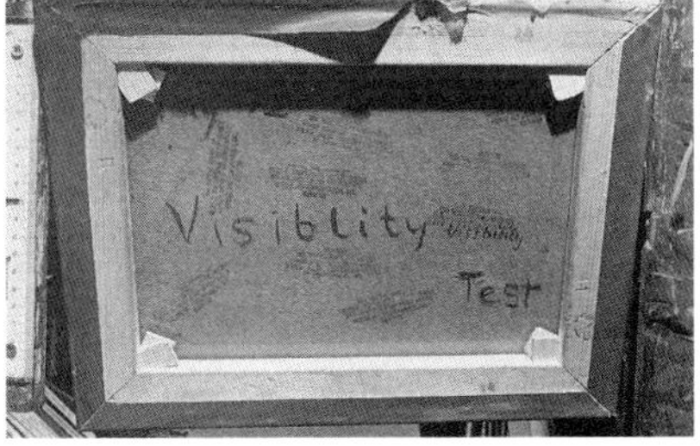

Figure 2. Visibility test. Sample lined transparently with BEVA 371 on Teflon in 1971. Teflon is not *recommended for lining because it is too soft.*

Figure 3. "Sentry and Bull" (recto) and "Bull" (verso), by Eugene Berman (1899–1972), oil on paper, 12¼ ′ 16¼ (31 ′ 41.5 cm). Transparently mounted on Lexan in 1980. Verso shows trapped air (bubbles) because the primed paper was impervious.

Figure 4. Visibility test. Sample lined transparently with BEVA on PeCap (polyester monofilament screen). PeCap produces no bubbles. On white cotton duck the transparent PeCap would not show at all, but small details are hard to read because of reflections in the filament.

when he lined a freshly painted collage containing a dry butterfly on a vacuum hot table. This was described in detail in a paper presented to ICOM-CC.[4]

Preparation of the painting for a transparent lining

The same treatments which are required prior to a regular, effective lining must also precede a transparent lining:

1. All loose paint has to be reattached and, if necessary, protected by facing.
2. Tears, breaks and perforations must be closed.
3. The reverse of the canvas to be lined should be smooth. If this cannot be achieved because of the condition of the paint which it carries (impasto), then a vacuum envelope, or a cast of the face of the painting might be considered, in order to create at least one plane surface.[5]
4. Severe cupping and other distortions of the canvas must be softened and treated.

Transparent lining of unprimed cotton duck carrying an inscription

The porosity of the cotton duck is utilized to provide a homogeneous evacuation of the air. Since penetration of the adhesive into the cotton duck has to be avoided to insure safe reversibility of the lining, it is advisable to spray the reverse of the canvas with high molecular polyvinylacetate, such as BEVA Isolating Varnish, or diluted BEVA D-8 emulsion, to serve as a barrier.

A sheet of BEVA® Film (2.5 mil), is put on the cold vacuum table (with the Silicone-coated, white release sheet face up), and cut to the size of the painting. BEVA Film is now available in 135 cm wide rolls and, if necessary, can be easily "butt-joined" to achieve larger widths. The Silicone release sheet is then removed (rolled off), and the prepared painting placed on it, face up. The painting is covered with a thin, flexible membrane, such as Silicone-coated 0.5 mil Mylar (Melinex), or Dartek, and heat-sealed to the BEVA Film at minimal pressure.

Since the air is exhausted through the porous cotton duck covering the entire reverse of the painting, uniform pressure is created at all points of the laminate. Paper thermometers are placed on top of the membrane at distances of no more than 50 cm from each other, to make sure that the activation temperature of the BEVA is reached at every point, and the film sealed to the reverse of the painting. When the table has cooled, the painting is removed from it together with the attached film and its Mylar backing.

A piece of PeCap SP 7-33S, or other screen, of a similar thread count and weave as the original canvas or cotton is cut to be slightly larger than the painting and its tacking margins, and placed on the hot table. PeCap is extremely permeable and strong. Indeed, the resistance of such screens to tension and creep is equal to or larger than that of steel, and some 50 times the resistance of canvas. The hot table is carefully cleaned and the piece of PeCap put on it (Figure 4).

The painting is turned face down on the work table. The Mylar backing is removed from the BEVA Film to which it was attached exposing the film. The painting is placed carefully on the PeCap and heat-sealed to it. The PeCap screen assures a uniform vacuum under the painting, and presses the monofilament threads into the BEVA Film. The screen remains uncoated, but the BEVA Film behind it is open to the hazards of air pollution and dust. It is, therefore, advisable to keep it protected, either by a transparent cover or by a light spray of B-72, or both.

To get the maximum benefit of the PeCap lining support it is best to mount the lined painting on an aluminum stretcher. To be put on a stretcher, PeCap can be bent easily by heating with an electric spatula to 50–70°C, or a hot air blower. PeCap which is white works well for cotton duck and other light-color fabrics with contrasting inscriptions and similar weave. However, for dark fabrics, or in cases where large areas of dark paint cover the canvas, we have used Stabiltex 4, a very fine polyester fabric which comes in seven colors. The use of brown Stabiltex for a transparent lining of a painting by Klee on burlap, was described elsewhere.[6]

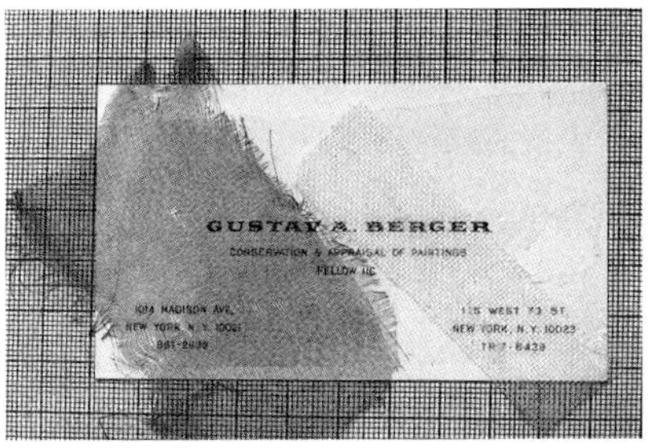

Figure 5. Stabiltex and PeCap compared. Any dark-color Stabiltex has considerably fewer reflections than white PeCap. Therefore, the black lettering is more readable through the Stabiltex (on the left) than through the PeCap (on the right). The brown Stabiltext becomes almost invisible when used on an old, darkened canvas.

Figure 6. "Circus Trio", by Rouault, oil on paper mounted on canvas by the artist, 74 ′ 104 cm.

Figure 7. Same painting as in Figure 6. Sketch of Christ, found on the reverse of the painting, shows patches made by the artist while mounting it on canvas (a and b).

However, using Stabiltex is more complicated than using PeCap because it is very delicate and has to be lightly stretched before use. In most cases this can be accomplished on the hot table, with the help of tape. A piece of fairly stiff Mylar (at least 2 mil) is lightly coated with BEVA (and allowed to dry) or with BEVA Film (1 mil), on one side, and cut slightly smaller (2–3mm) than the painting, all around. The Stabiltex is stretched on the vacuum table, and the prepared Mylar slid under it, with the coated side up. Usually, the Stabiltex will need additional straightening. When all is adjusted, the Stabiltex is heat-sealed to the Mylar.

Prior to lining, the back of the painting is sprayed with BEVA D-8 or BEVA Isolating Varnish. The Mylar, covered with Stabiltex, is then heat-sealed to the reverse of the painting, fabric-to-fabric. This is done to assure reversibility, should removal of the lining ever become necessary. If it were attached to the back of the painting directly, the Mylar interleaf would make complete removal of the BEVA lining with solvents very difficult.

For a truly elegant look, the back of the Mylar is lightly coated with BEVA 371 and covered with Stabiltex, which makes the lining almost invisible because it covers the reflexions of the Mylar. The Mylar interleaf makes the lining stiff enough to keep the painting straight even if it has high impasto or severe cupping.

In the cases described so far, only an approximation of the color of the painting has to be preserved to render the signature or inscription legible (Figures 4 and 5). The porosity of the screen eliminates air bubbles and the slight "filter" effects of darker or lighter screens are usually acceptable. However, if the reverse carries another painting, a greater degree of transparency is required. This can be achieved by submerging the screen in a transparent material, a kind of "varnish" of resins of similar refractive index as that of the screen. This gives even a strong lining the look of a heavy coat of varnish. In such a case, it is essential to avoid the creation of air bubbles. An example of how to achieve it is described below.

Conservation Report on a fully transparent lining (shortened)[7]

"Circus Trio"

Oil and gouache on old, torn paper, mounted on canvas with glue paste, 74x104cm, signed G. Rouault. Painted ca. 1924 (see Figure 6). Owner: The Phillips Collection, Washington, DC.

Condition

When brought to our studio, the paper was delaminating over most of its surface causing scattered paint losses. There were several large tears. Interruption of the brush strokes over the tears indicates that they existed before the paper was painted. This was proven when the lining canvas was removed.

If a paper is mounted onto a canvas with glue paste it must lead to the destruction of the paper and any paint layer it may carry, because canvas shrinks while paper expands when the RH rises. Every change in temperature and RH causes new stresses in the laminate. Therefore, relining "Circus Trio" onto a solid support, such as acid-free cardboard, honeycomb, etc. was recommended.

Treatment

The painting was "faced" with wet-strength tissue, using BEVA 371 as the adhesive. Removal of the lining canvas revealed an oil sketch of Christ on the reverse of the original paper, in the vertical position (Figure 7).[8] Rouault seemed to have liked the roughness of old sketches and, having worked some years as a restorer, he frequently lined the old papers onto canvas himself.

The Phillips Collection wanted to preserve the sketch, and it was decided to line the painting transparently.

We had to make sure that the tears would not open during treatment and would remain joined should removal of the lining become necessary. Stabiltex (App.), a thin, strong polyester monofilament screen was, therefore, selected for the new support.

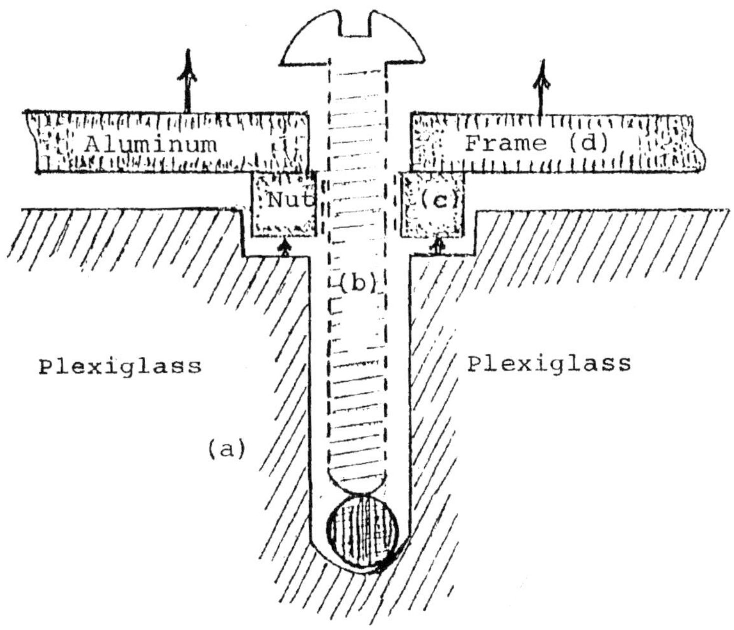

Figure 8. The special stretcher built for the Rouault to make both sides of the painting visible. A ready-made aluminum frame, slightly larger than the painting, was mounted on a plexiglass plate, 1 cm thick. Holes were drilled into the edge of the the plexiglass at 15 cm intervals. The purpose of these holes was to guide the bolts (b) loosely. The bolts turned in nuts (c), for which notches were cut in the edge of the plexiglass. When turned, the bolts press against tiny steel balls previously inserted into the drill holes (a). Further turning of the bolts causes the nuts to ride up on the bolts, pushing the sides of the aluminum frame (d) outwards, simultaneously stretching the painting.

Since the old stretcher would have covered a 6 cm wide area of the sketch all around, the painting had to be enlarged. New margins were added, and a larger stretcher built with an inner opening the size of the sketch. A sheet of acid-free drawing paper of similar weight and texture as the original, was cut 12 cm larger than the painting all around. The center of this sheet was cut out following the outline of the painting to create a homogenous continuation of the laminate. The new edges and the sketch on the reverse received a heavy coat of BEVA 371. After drying, a piece of white Stabiltex, which was to hold all the parts together, was "stretched" on a strainer and tacked over it. A piece of Promatco Lining (App.) was put on the hot table to serve as a cushion. It was covered with a sheet of fine Silicone-coated Mylar (0.5 mil). The stretched Stabiltex, with the painting attached to it, was placed on top of the Mylar. The painting was covered with a membrane of the same fine, Silicone-coated Mylar, and heat sealed at 65°C an a vacuum pressure of 100 mm at the gage.

The "facing" was removed with naphtha and the face of the painting coated with a Ketone varnish for protection. Since the Stabiltex, tacked to the back of the painting, carried no adhesive, it formed a porous layer which allowed the evacuation of air from between painting and table. After heat sealing, the new laminate was cut from the strainer. The many different pieces of paper with their tears, as well as the new edges, all coated with BEVA, were connected and held securely by the Stabiltex. Because of the many breaks in the original support, and the strong expansions and contractions of paper in response to changes in RH, it was decided to add stiffness to the laminate by mounting it onto a heavy, clear Mylar (2 mil). To avoid the creation of air bubbles, the Stabiltex screen on the back had to be filled completely, to form a smooth surface. To achieve this goal, we alternated coats of BEVA D-8 and BEVA 371, with BEVA 371 as the final coat. The painting was heated on the Silicone-coated Mylar. This procedure was repeated several times until the back of the painting showed a completely clear and smooth surface. Note that we placed the porous Promatco Lining and the porous Stabiltex between the hot table and the coated painting.

A similar method was described by Søren Bernsted to achieve a transparent lining of a transparent painting using Plextol B-500.[7] Like all high-molecular materials, Plextol B-500 is slow and difficult to dissolve and reverse.

To facilitate the removal (reversibility) of such coatings it is always recommended to use a coat of BEVA 371 on the back of the painting and as alternate layers between high-molecular coatings, such as Plextol B-500, BEVA D-8 and BEVA Gel.

A 2 mil Mylar sheet, 10–15 cm larger than the laminate, was placed on the hot table. The laminate was covered with the Silicone-coated Mylar membrane, thus forming a vacuum envelope. The vacuum pressure was turned to 100–150 mm at the gage. To "massage" the membrane, slight pressure was exerted by hand from the center of the painting to the outside, in order to evacuate any unnoticed air bubbles. This kept the Mylar lightly attached, and the laminate could be inverted, inspected, and all the air bubbles removed. When all was found to be satisfactory, the painting was then heat-sealed to the Mylar backing at 65°C.

The special stretcher

For the painting to be displayed from both sides, a special stretcher had to be designed. It had to be strong, yet thin, so as not to take too much space in the frame. Thus, a ready-made, modular aluminum frame was mounted onto a 1 cm thick plate of plexiglass. Holes were drilled into the edges of the plexiglass for bolts which would allow for movements of the laminate.[8] The frame was cut to have an inner opening the size of the sketch to be displayed (Figures 7 and 8). Thus, the plexiglass made it possible to view the entire sketch undisturbed by cross-bars. It also provided a solid backing for the lined painting (loose lining), and carried the mechanism for additional tensioning ("keying out") of the painting should this become necessary (Today, we would replace the plexiglass with Lexane (Du Pont), an almost indestructible, glass-clear, polycarbonate.)

Reversibility

To remove this lining, the following steps are to be taken:

1. Remove painting from stretcher.
2. Staple margins to a board covered with Silicone-coated paper.
3. Heat board lightly on the hot table (to 40–50°C).
4. Coat edges with naphtha. Cover entire assembly with a membrane (to reduce evaporation of the naphtha into the surrounding air).
5. Lift Mylar edges leaving the Stabiltex in place.
6. Cut Mylar loose leaving the staples and Stabiltex in place.
7. Free Mylar from the Stabiltex by using a small, flat brush dipped in naphtha. Start from the corner leaving the Stabiltex intact. The Stabiltex protects the painting and keeps the torn parts of the original paper joined together.

Conclusions

In the past 30 years, adhesives, fabrics, and films have been developed which are exceptionally stable, strong, and glass-clear. These new materials enable conservators to reinforce and protect aged, weakened paintings without obscuring their reverse. Even double-sided paintings can now be transparently lined without significant loss of legibility or color values. The process, however, requires a perfectly uniform laminate, without entrapped air or inner reflections.

In addition to preserving the visibility of historical data, transparent lining gives us an insight into the quality of the adhesion of our reinforcements, the workings of the vacuum hot table and our capability to control them. Following are the resulting observations:

- A vacuum can only be generated when the air is extracted.
- To assure that an area is compressed by vacuum pressure it must be connected to the air exhaust by a porous layer (breather). Conversely, if an area is covered by a viscous adhesive layer which prevents the air from being exhausted, there can be no vacuum pressure even if the painting is placed on a suction table.

- Vacuum pressure, heat treatments and adhesives are tools. As with every other tool, their proper use must be learned, understood, and practiced before results of good quality can be expected.

Acknowledgement

The author wishes to thank the Samuel H. Kress Foundation and its President, Dr Marilyn Perry, for continuous financial and moral support of his various research projects.

Materials and suppliers

Monofilament polyester screens, PeCap SP 7-33S, and a variety of others are produced in Switzerland and available through their representative in the USA, TETKO, Inc, 420 Sawmill River Road, Elmsford, NY 01523. Smaller quantities are available from TALAS, 568 Broadway, New York, NY 10012-9989. Tel.:(212) 219-0770.

Stabiltex 4, a plain weave, very fine, silk-like, polyester fabric which is produced in seven colors, available from Schweizerische Seidegazenfabrik AG, Gruetlistrasse 68, CH-8027 Zurich 2, Switzerland.

BEVA® 371, BEVA FILM, BEVA D-8 Dispersion, BEVA Isolating Varnish, other *BEVA* products for conservation, as well as *Silicone-coated, 0.5 mil Mylar* (Melinex) are produced by Conservator's Products Company, P.O.Box 411, Chatham, NJ 07928, USA, Tel. (201) 927-4855. In Europe, the name of this adhesive was changed to *Gustav Berger's Original Formula 371* to protect the genuine formula, because Lascaux has used the name Beva for a product manufactured beyond the author's control. *C.T.S. S.R.L.* Via Piave 20/22, 36077 Altavilla Vicentina (VI), Italy, Tel. (0444) 349088, is the sole producer of *G. Berger's Original Formula 371,* as well as of other *BEVA* products. The author continues to test every batch of formulations produced by C.T.S.

Promatco Lining has since been discontinued. A good replacement would be *Gortex,* available from TALAS. Their distributor in the UK is: W.L.Gore & Associates, Kirkcon South Road, Kirkcon Campus West Lothian, Livingston EH54 7BT, Scotland.

Dartek, a flexible nylon film produced by DuPont, 0.75 mil thick, available in 2.235 meter-wide and 61 meter-long rolls from Conservation Materials Ltd, Box 2884, 1395 Greg Street, S-te 110, Sparks, NV 89431, Tel.:(702) 331-0582, or (800) 733-5283.

Paper thermometers, produced by Paper Thermometer Co.,P.O.Box 129, Greenfield, NH 03047,Tel. (603) 547-2034.

Notes and references

1. G.A. Berger, "Formulating Adhesives for the Conservation of Paintings," in *Conservation and Restoration of Pictorial Art,* eds N.S. Brommelle and P. Smith (London: Butterworths, 1976), 169–181.
2. O.H. Riley, G.A. Berger, "New Solutions for Modern Problems," *Museum News,* January (1973), 31–36.
3. A.G. Boissonnas, "Relining with Glass-Fiber Fabric", *Studies in Conservation* 6 (1961): 26–29.
4. G.A. Berger, W.H. Russell, "Changes in the Resistance of Canvas to Deformation and Cracking (Modulus of Elasticity "E") as Caused by Sizing and Lining," (Paper delivered at the Ninth Triennial Meeting of the International Council of Museums Committee for Conservation, Dresden, 1990), Vol.I, 107–112.
5. G.A. Berger, "A Vacuum Envelope for Treating Panel Paintings," *Studies in Conservation* 10, no.1 (1965): 18–22.
6. G.A. Berger, "More Unconventional Treatments for Unconventional Art", Ibid., 35, no.1 (1990): 1–14.
7. S. Bernsted, "Transparent Cold Lining of a Transparent Painting," (Paper delivered at the Tenth Triennial Meeting of the International Council of Museums Committee for Conservation, Washington, DC, 1993), Vol.I, 118–121.
8. G.A. Berger, "Moderne Konservierung zeitgenoessischer Kunst," *Maltechnik/Restauro* 8, no.1 (1980), 155–161.
9. A mirror image of the same sketch was published in the book *George Rouault - The Graphic Work,* by Alan Wofsy, San Francisco, 1976. It is a cancelled plate of the Miserere et Guerre Series, #174, p. 58, titled: L'Enseignement.

Canvas Shrinkage: A Preliminary Investigation into the Response of a Woven Structure

Thomas Bilson
Courtauld Institute of Art
Somerset House, Strand, London WC2 0RN, UK

Abstract

This paper presents preliminary research into the shrinkage of canvas supports at high levels of humidity. The three-dimensional response of canvas as a woven material is discussed, including the actions of longitudinal and transverse yarn swelling as the precursors of shrinkage. A technological context for shrinkage in 19th-century canvases is given, along with directions for further research into the influence of preparation and conservation techniques. An experimental section compares the response of a new unprepared canvas to a 19th-century primed loose lining using a non-contact, non-destructive technique of analysing images of the weave obtained with a CCD camera at varying levels of RH. An appendix discusses the usefulness of this technique in overcoming the inherent variability of woven material.

Keywords

Canvas, painting, textile, linen, humidity, shrinkage, image processing/analysis

Introduction

One of the most serious problems facing conservators of canvas-supported paintings or painted textiles lies in the unpredictable capacity of the support to shrink or buckle in the presence of moisture.[1] These potentially destructive phenomena may be induced by anything from slight changes in environmental humidity to accidental contact with water, and may result in textural change, compression and, ultimately, loss of the overlying paint (Figures 1 to 3).

The aims of the research described here are twofold: to develop a non-contact, non-destructive method for the measurement of humidity-induced shrinkage within canvas paintings or painted textiles, and to relate the mechanism, degree and point of onset of shrinkage to the weave structure of the underlying support. It is hoped that this work will contribute towards an appreciation and understanding of the distinctly three-dimensional nature and behaviour of canvas as a support material, particularly in the context of conservation treatments which use water or changes in the moisture content of the surrounding air.

Background

It is seldom recognised that the water-induced shrinkage of unrestrained textiles, or the generation of stresses within restrained textiles, occurs because the yarns themselves swell across their widths and displace each other, rather than reducing individually in length. In other words, canvas shrinkage is a phenomenon associated with the response of a *woven* structure. This topic has been discussed empirically in the context of conservation treatments by Hedley,[2] and in developing his theme we may consider the translation of yarn swelling into canvas shrinkage from the work of Collins,[3] Morehead[4] and Abbott et al.[5]

If a cellulosic yarn is immersed in water, the constituent fibres swell longitudinally along their lengths and transversely across their widths. Typical ratios for longitudinal versus transverse swelling in different cellulosic fibres through an increase in RH from approximately 45% to saturation have been given as: cotton 1%:14%,[6] viscose rayon 5%:40%,[7] and ramie (flax) 5%:>>40%.[8] Although it is clear

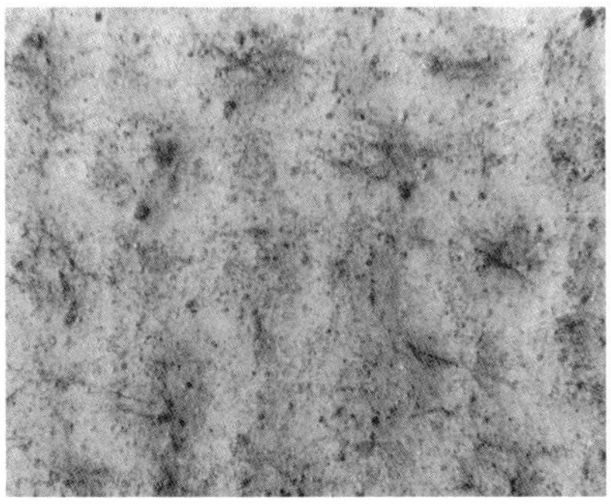

Figure 1. Nineteenth-century primed canvas showing a detail of the paint at 25 × magnification. The warp direction runs from top to bottom. Photographed at 30% RH

Figure 2. As Figure 1, photographed after exposure to 94% RH for three hours

Figure 3. As Figure 1, photographed after exposure to 100% RH (saturation) for three hours

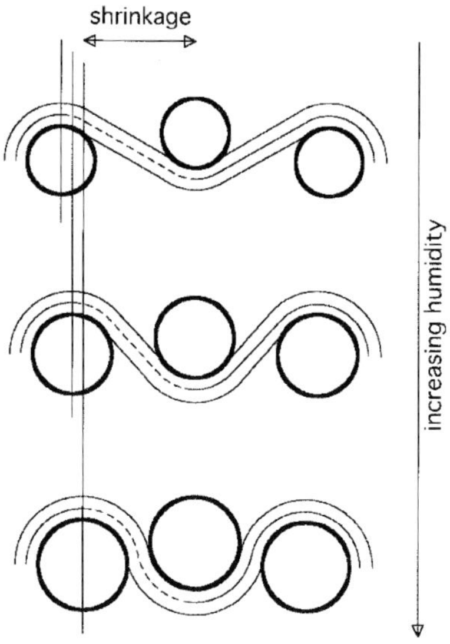

Figure 4. The mechanism of canvas shrinkage adapted from Collins[3]

that the translation of fibre swelling into yarn swelling is mediated by the tension, angle of twist and lateral compression of the fibres, in addition to the internal structure of the yarn as determined by the method of spinning,[9] a very compact yarn may itself show increases in length and width of a magnitude almost equal to that of its constituent fibres.[10] In other words, increasing the RH from ambient to saturation may cause a tightly spun flax yarn to increase in length by 5%, while increasing in cross-sectional area by over 40%. So how does this behaviour of the yarns induce shrinkage within the canvas?

The process is illustrated by the diagram adapted from Collins which shows a cross-section through a plain-woven canvas (Figure 4).[11] Assuming that the yarns are inelastic, and that friction is sufficient to stop them sliding past each other, the length marked with the dotted line – the central axis of the yarn between each cross-over – must remain constant. Whilst wetting would in reality be accompanied both by a fall in elastic modulus of the yarns and by a slight increase in yarn length, in the case of a shrinking canvas these effects are offset by the far greater increase in yarn diameter. Since the yarns are trapped by the weave and unable to slide past each other, they are deformed into following paths of increasingly greater curvature. As the only means to maintain distance between adjacent cross-overs is for the yarns themselves to move closer together, the weave thickens and closes up, and the canvas shrinks.

The data for swelling given above imply that one of the primary factors influencing shrinkage is fibre type. Most conservators, however, are familiar with the huge differences in shrinkage behaviour exhibited by a single material – the ubiquitous linen canvas. Whilst species variability, ecological factors, and selective processing of the fibres prior to spinning will all influence the swelling characteristics of an individual single flax yarn, to gain an understanding of why some linen canvases remain dimensionally stable through changes in RH whilst others shrink (or in some cases expand) we must turn our attention to the morphology and position of yarns within the weave – factors often termed the *geometry* of the canvas.[12]

Shrinkage and canvas geometry

Canvas shrinkage is thus the nett result of two separate processes: a loss of crimp and tension as a consequence of longitudinal yarn swelling together with a fall in elastic modulus, being outweighed by a re-introduction of crimp and regain in tension as a consequence of transverse yarn swelling. However, whilst swelling in both longitudinal and transverse directions occurs simultaneously, the initial stages of shrinkage may, in certain circumstances, be observed as discrete events. By measuring the behaviour of uniaxially strained samples of viscose to sudden wetting, Abbott et al.[13] showed the response to be divided into two phases: an immediate fall in tension, offset several seconds later by a regain in tension to a higher degree. Put simply, sudden wetting may cause a canvas to expand briefly before it shrinks.

These results may be explained by considering the critical influence of weave structure over the magnitude and direction of the response. As the fall in canvas tension as a consequence of longitudinal swelling is influenced neither by the intersection of warp and weft nor by the geometry of the canvas, i.e. it is a *yarn*-based rather than a *weave*-based phenomenon, there is no obstacle to prevent it occurring immediately upon wetting. However, as the translation of transverse swelling into shrinkage (or the generation of shrinkage forces) requires the yarns to displace each other at points of intersection, it can only take place after free spaces within the weave have begun to be filled. The effects of transverse swelling are thus delayed, resulting in the two-stage response of tension fall and tension re-gain shown by the dotted line (Figure 5).

As may be expected, any increase in the proportion of free space diminishes the proportion of transverse swelling available to induce shrinkage, and may result ultimately in a canvas that shows a nett expansion upon contact with water rather than shrinking. In a conservation context this free space may be divided into two categories: that created initially by the method of canvas manufacture, and that determined through subsequent modification of the canvas, either as part of its

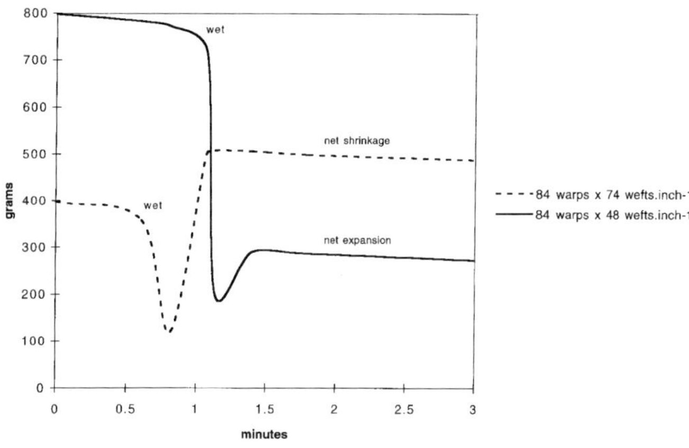

Figure 5. The influence of yarn spacing on longitudinal/transverse swelling in viscose. Adapted from Abbott et al.[5]

preparation as an artists' material, or during the course of a conservation treatment. Instances of free space include gaps between individual fibres within yarns and spaces separating adjacent yarns, as well as intermittent contact between intersecting yarns. The importance of yarn spacing in determining shrinkage was demonstrated by Abbott et al.,[14] who also tested the wetting response of an otherwise identical sample of viscose, but woven with half the number of yarns perpendicular to the direction of stress measurement. As expected, most of the transverse swelling was absorbed, filling the increased free space within the sample, and the proportion available to induce shrinkage was not sufficient to outweigh the initial loss in tension. This resulted in a nett loss of tension (or increase in canvas area) shown in Figure 5 by the continuous line.

A context for shrinkage

Relating these factors to the historical development of artists' canvases gives a basic explanation of their shrinkage responses. The degree to which a canvas may be qualitatively described as loose or tight is determined initially by the processes through which the yarns are spun or woven into cloth. Since the rapid industrialisation of the linen industry during the 19th century centred upon two innovations – wet spinning and the development of the power loom – it is not surprising that their effects contribute to the observed tendency for canvases of this period to shrink unpredictably at elevated levels of RH.[15] The immersion of flax fibres in often boiling water to ease their passage and drawing out between the rollers of the spinning frame tended to produce yarns which were both compact and tightly spun. Their conversion into cloth on the early power loom, especially through the operations of *shedding* (opening the warp to create a passage for the shuttle), *beating up* (in which the reed pushes each succeeding weft against its predecessor) and *letting off* (the mechanism by which the cloth is wound on, thereby controlling the force with which the reed drives succeeding wefts into position) would have resulted in canvases with far tighter weaves and fewer free spaces than their hand-woven counterparts.[16]

Other factors influencing this response include the frequency and position of cross-overs, and the degree to which crimp may have been set in either a dry or swollen state. As the translation of transverse yarn swelling into shrinkage can only occur at points in the canvas where warp and weft intersect, a weave characterised by a high proportion of floating yarns and few interlacings, e.g. certain types of twill, satin or damask, will be less prone to shrinkage in wet or humid conditions than a plain-weave of the same yarn count. Other types of weave in which the yarns are locked into position or *jammed*, e.g. a warp or weft-faced poplin or canalé, will also exhibit less shrinkage. Although changing the initial yarn spacing or weave structure is obviously not an option open to restorers, the manipulation of crimp – a process most often associated with wetting and stretching of lining canvases is a practised widely. Although this is justified usually in terms of crimp removal, any stretching of a canvas whilst wet will tend to both reduce free space between fibres in the yarns, and pack intersecting yarns closer together. Whether or not this procedure predisposes the canvas to shrink will be investigated during the further course of this research, along with the influence of fibre type, weave geometry, artists' preparation techniques and the calendering effects associated with the deformation of a weave on a vacuum table.[17]

Experimental

Most of our understanding of canvas behaviour in response to changes in RH has been based upon measuring uniaxial or biaxial stress/strain relationships. Although this 'engineering' approach has characterised the majority of research undertaken in both painting conservation and textile science, it tends to reduce the structure and properties of the support to those of a two-dimensional plane. These methods also require the canvas to be placed under an initial strain, and are thus unsuited to measuring shrinkage in unrestrained conditions. Movement towards a more realistic understanding of canvas behaviour requires this work to be interpreted alongside an approach integrating the three-dimensional properties and behaviour of the fibres, yarns and cloth at the level of the weave. The research described below shows how both shrinkage and, more importantly, its precursor of yarn swelling may be measured, and how these results may be used to map the onset and progression of shrinkage at low levels of humidity before dimensional change takes place.

Measurement of shrinkage

This preliminary study compares the response of a new, unprepared linen canvas to a glue-sized and oil-primed mid-19th century loose lining canvas which was known to shrink in the presence of moisture. Both were plain-woven from single, Z-spun yarns: the approximate counts being 15 warps and 16 wefts per centimetre for the new sample, and 14 warps and 15 wefts per centimetre for the primed sample. Despite forces exerted at cross-overs causing the yarns to assume an elliptical section within the cloth, a qualitative assessment of cross-sectional area based on the major diameter showed the wefts in each case to be generally 20 to 30% thicker than the warps. A qualitative assessment of twist showed the warps to be medium spun, whilst the wefts were loosely spun.[18]

As the capacity for greatest movement within the canvas occurs when a painting hangs loose (a condition which may exist either across the whole surface, or in discrete areas), the samples were allowed to shrink restrained only by friction between the underside of the canvas and a supporting surface. To accomplish this, 6 × 10 cm pieces of the two canvases were placed on a stretched membrane of Reemay 2006 – a spun-bonded polyester chosen for its porosity, smoothness and relative insensitivity to moisture. The whole assembly was then placed in a humidity chamber with space allowed for air to circulate above and below the samples. Humidity levels were maintained with a portable ultrasonic humidifier in combination with a fan, and recorded with a KM004 combined temperature and humidity probe (accuracy ± 2% RH, ±1°C). Temperature within the chamber was maintained at ambient levels of around 18 to 22°C.

Measurements of yarn swelling and shrinkage within the samples were taken using a Sony three-chip CCD camera linked to a Power Macintosh computer running Optilab image analysis software.[19,20] Problems of illumination associated with resolving yarn boundaries amidst other areas of shadow were overcome by placing the humidity chamber above a source of diffuse light and recording the shape of the yarns from above – sufficient light being transmitted through the primed sample to enable measurements to be taken. Images from the two samples at 10 × magnification showing areas of canvas approximately 21 × 16 mm were taken at RH levels of 30, 47, 65, 72, 86, 94 and 100% (saturation achieved by spraying) – the samples being maintained at each level for three hours. All images were captured and stored on the computer before analysis and measurement were undertaken.

As part of the capture process the images had already been digitised into 8-bit greyscale (i.e. drawn from a maximum palette of 256 levels of grey) at a size of 768 × 576 pixels. Although the lens system introduced very little distortion, the outermost edges of each image were clipped, thereby reducing their sizes to

740 × 575 pixels (413 kbytes). Each image was then re-sampled to give a final physical size of 1484×1114 pixels (1.617 Mbytes). Although re-sampling produced images containing nearly four times as much data, it should be noted that there was no corresponding increase in the resolution of detail. Re-sampling was used solely to improve the accuracy with which the edges of the yarns could be marked. All images were then calibrated against the same reference image of a graduated scale. Dividing the area of canvas under investigation by the resolution of the CCD array showed the smallest resolvable unit of measurement within each image (discounting the spurious increase in image size through re-sampling) to be 0.02743 mm. Three separate sets of measurements were taken from each image: those of changes in free space between each individual pair of intersecting and adjacent yarns, changes in yarn diameter and spacing along the length of each warp between intersections, and dimensional changes in an area bounded by four marked yarns. The following description outlines the methodology by which the first set of measurements was taken, and from which the other sets of data were derived.

Whilst the detection and measurement of particles (in this case yarns) required the software to perceive them as separate objects, the intersection of warps and wefts presented difficulties in that the computer perceived the whole canvas as a single, grid-like structure. Although this could have been overcome through either the use of complex lighting and filtering, or canvases woven specially with different coloured warps and wefts, a simple solution was found in measuring changes in the area and dimensions of those parts of images which were *not* canvas – the discrete spaces *between* every pair of intersecting and adjacent yarns.[21] Although deciding on a level of contrast between black (0) and white (255) at which to divide the spaces from the surrounding canvas was an arbitrary decision, the levels of 101 and 23 were chosen for the raw and primed samples respectively (the lower figure reflecting the reduced levels of contrast in the primed sample due to light being transmitted through the paint). Algorithms within the software were then used to measure the dimensions and area of each individual space within the canvas, and from these calculations were made of mean free area between each pair of adjacent and intersecting yarns, and mean yarn widths in warp and weft. Although each image yielded data from over 500 separate spaces, some numerical filtering was carried out to reject instances where thresholding had inadvertently joined adjacent spaces or yarns together. Spaces with an impossibly large area exceeding 0.18 mm^2, together with horizontal and vertical yarn diameters greater than 0.56 mm were therefore eliminated from the calculations, as were spaces of area less than 0.01 mm^2 resulting from pinpoints of light shining through cracks in the paint or yarns. This filtering process reduced the number of measurements in each image by approximately 2%. Data from these measurements, including changes in surface area, are summarised in the graphs (Figures 6, 7 and 8), whilst a note on the statistical techniques used to verify the work is given in the Appendix.

Results and discussion

Despite the results being based on the behaviour of a very limited range of material, several important observations can be made. Although obtained using a non-contact method, the changes in surface area shown in Figure 6 reflect the trends

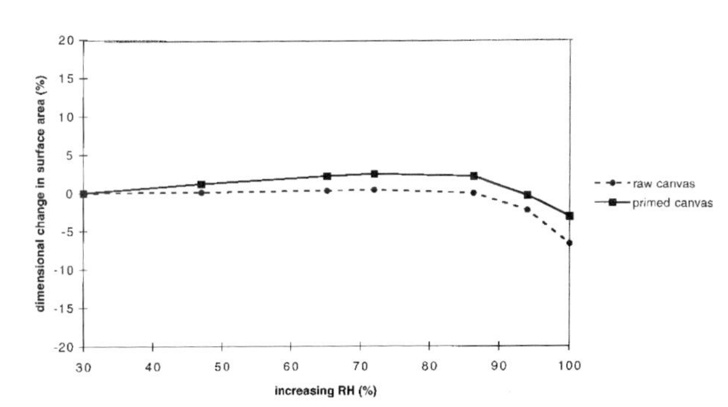

Figure 6. Change in surface area with increasing RH in raw and primed samples

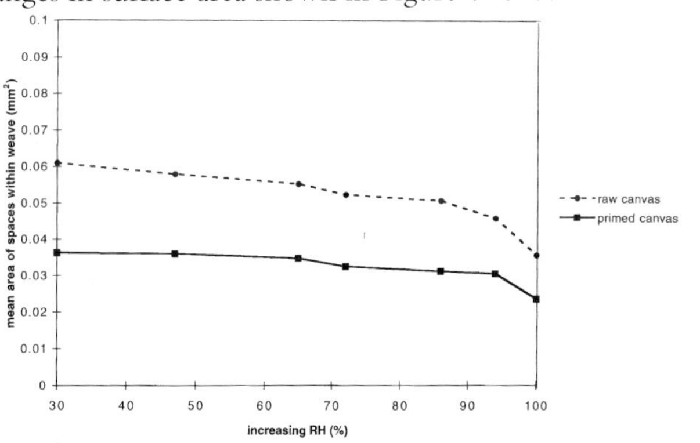

Figure 7. Change in mean area of spaces within the weave with increasing RH in raw and primed samples

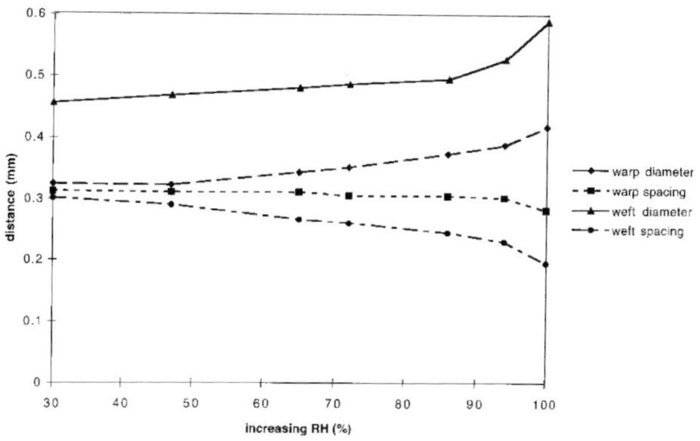

Figure 8. Change in yarn spacing and diameter with increasing RH in raw and primed samples

shown by Mecklenburg[22] and Hedley[23] in measuring the effects of humidity on the stress/strain response of canvas painting composites. The response of the primed sample is characterised by the familiar (although upside-down) tick-shaped curve – the canvas taking over from the size as the dominant stress-generating layer at high levels of RH. The raw sample remained dimensionally stable at low RH, only to tighten up at levels above 60%. Yet these examples illustrate one of the most critical problems associated with measuring and predicting the onset of shrinkage. Whilst an ideal approach would track the development and magnitude of shrinkage within the canvas at all levels of humidity, the early stages of the canvas response tend to be masked by the opposing responses of the size and ground layers. When the canvas finally emerges and takes over as the most moisture sensitive component, only a relatively small increase in humidity separates safe conditions of low stress from the adverse and possibly de-laminating conditions of 90% and above.

Figure 7 shows changes in area of free space between intersecting and adjacent yarns. From this it is clear that transverse yarn swelling can be detected at even low RH, and that its progression as the precursor of shrinkage can be followed, despite the opposing action of the size and the balancing action of longitudinal swelling. Figure 8 shows the differences in transverse swelling between the weft (loose spun/ larger diameter) and that of the warp (medium spun/small diameter). The predominance of transverse swelling in the weft is related to its diameter being larger than that of the warp, a condition which would induce greater dimensional shrinkage in the warp direction (see Figure 4). However most of the damage to the paint at 94 and 100% RH has been caused by the local effects of transverse weft swelling (see Figures 2 and 3) – the losses corresponding exactly with the position of weft, rather than warp crowns. Although damage to the paint through the generation of compression forces is clearly the most significant action of canvas shrinkage, we must also consider damage caused by the local swelling of underlying yarns – a phenomenon which may occur in both loosely and tightly woven canvases irrespective of whether they remain stable dimensionally through changes in RH.

Conclusions

Image processing has thus been shown to be a useful technique for measuring yarn swelling in canvases at both high and low levels of RH. Further work will now be undertaken on the influence of weave type and method of preparation, together with conservation techniques which may purposefully or inadvertently bring about a modification to the structure of the canvas. Existing mathematical theories of cloth structure will also be used as a basis for generating three-dimensional graphical models showing the development and magnitude of shrinkage within canvas supports as part of the painting composite. Although the computer is well-suited to the integration and manipulation of data, it is hoped that this work will prompt anyone working with canvas supports on a practical level to gain some useful insight for their complex and seemingly unpredictable behaviour.

Acknowledgements

I would like to acknowledge the generous support of the Leverhulme Trust for funding this research as part of a three year fellowship, the Clothworkers'

Foundation for funding computer equipment and Sony Broadcast and Professional UK for supporting the acquisition of a camera and lens.

Special thanks are extended to Spike Bucklow and Christopher Hurst of the Hamilton Kerr Institute, University of Cambridge who kindly provided samples of primed canvases and assisted with the photomacrographs.

Appendix

Although textiles appear to be regular, repeating structures, anyone taking measurements at the level of the weave will be familiar with huge variability in yarn spacing and diameter. These are particularly evident in canvases made from natural fibres which have been spun and/or woven by hand. As the standard deviations of data based on small samples frequently approach the mean, the level at which any real meaning can be attached to measurements is called to question. At some point, however, a sample size becomes sufficiently large as to reflect adequately the population from which it has been drawn. The analysis of variance (ANOVA) usually shows whether two or more sample means differ from each other significantly, thus allowing the inference to be made that they come from different populations. In this case the ANOVA was used to show whether ten different images of the *same* primed canvas taken at random – each yielding a sample of around 500 discrete yarn measurements – did *not* differ significantly from each other. If this was true, it could then be assumed with some confidence that the images were sufficiently large and contained enough information to reflect the composition of the canvas from which they were drawn. Although the ANOVA is designed around rejecting rather than accepting a null hypothesis, the sensitivity of this technique has been demonstrated on similar material.[24]

Ten images were taken of the surface of the primed canvas under the same lighting conditions and magnification as used to measure changes in geometry with increases in RH. Care was taken to maintain humidity throughout at a constant level of 34% RH. The images were calibrated and thresholded as described earlier, and measurements were taken of free space between each pair of intersecting and adjacent yarns. The data sets for each image comprised approximately 500 individual measurements which were grouped between 50 equally spaced classes to produce ten different frequency distributions.

In keeping with convention null (H_0) and alternative (H_1) hypotheses were expressed:

H_0 There is little or no difference between the distributions of free spaces within the ten images and they therefore represent adequately the canvas from which they are taken.

H_1 There is a significant difference between the distributions of free spaces within the ten images and they therefore do not represent adequately the canvas from which they are taken.

The F ratio in each case was insignificant:

Degrees of freedom = (9,490)
F ratio = 0.4674
Probability of the samples being drawn from the same population = 89.6%

and the null hypothesis was accepted.

Notes and references

1. Throughout this paper the word canvas is used to describe the woven textile support of a painting. As there is little consensus as to the precise stage in manufacture at which flax becomes linen, flax is used to describe the fibres and yarns, and linen is used to describe the woven cloth.

2. G. Hedley, 'The Practicalities of the Interaction of Moisture with Oil Paintings on Canvas', *Measured Opinion* (London:United Kingdom Institute for Conservation, 1993), 112–122.
3. G.E. Collins, 'Fundamental Principles that Govern the Shrinkage of Cotton Goods by Washing', *Journal of the Textile Institute* 30 (1939): 46–61.

4. F.F. Morehead, 'A Method for Studying the Effect of Humidity on the Cross-Sectional Swelling of Some Common Fibres', *Textile Research Journal* (1952): 535–539.
5. N.J. Abbott, F. Khoury and L. Barish, 'The Mechanism of Fabric Shrinkage: The Role of Fibre Swelling', *Journal of the Textile Institute* 55 (1964): T111–T127.
6. G.E. Collins, 'Fundamental Principles'.
7. F.F. Morehead, 'Some Comparative Data on the Cross-sectional Swelling of Textile Fabrics', *Textile Research Journal* 17 (1947): 96.
8. H.J. Woods, 'The Structure of textile fibres: III – Fibre Properties and Molecular Arrangement', *Journal of the Textile Institute* 40 (1949): 367. In the absence of data for flax figures are given for ramie, a coarser although anatomically related bast fibre that demonstrates a similar swelling response to water.
9. See J.W.S. Hearle, P. Grossberg and S. Backer, *Structural Mechanics of Fibres, Yarns and Fabrics*, vol. 1 (New York: Wiley Interscience, 1969), 148–165.
10. G.E. Collins, 'Fundamental Principles'.
11. Ibid.
12. A term associated with the work of Frederick Peirce and used in the title of his seminal paper: F.T. Peirce, 'The Geometry of Cloth Structure', *Journal of the Textile Institute* 28 (1937): T45–T96.
13. Abbott, Khoury and Barish, 'The Mechanism of Fabric Shrinkage'.
14. Ibid.
15. Over the 33 year period from 1835 to 1868 the number of water- or steam-driven looms in Ireland increased from 12 to 12,969. C. Gill, *The Rise of the Irish Linen Industry* (Oxford: Clarendon Press, 1925).
16. The development and effects of mechanisation within the linen industry are given in: T. Woodhouse and P. Kilgour, *Spinning, Weaving and Finishing of Flax and Jute* (London: Pitman, 1929).
17. The setting of crimp at high levels of humidity is discussed in: F.T. Peirce, 'The Geometry of Cloth Structure' and F.T. Peirce, 'Geometrical Principles Applicable to the Design o Functional Fabrics', *Textile Research Journal*, 17 (1947): 123.
18. All textile nomenclature is based upon: I. Emery, *The Primary Structures of Fabrics*, 3rd edn (Washington, DC: The Textile Museum; London: Thames and Hudson, 1994). Definitions of yarn twist are given as *loose* up to 10°, *medium* 10° to 25° and *tight* 25° to 45°.
19. Images were acquired directly from the surface of the canvas using a Sony DXC 930-P three-chip colour CCD camera fitted with a Canon PH12.5x7.5, 7.5–90 mm macro zoom lens, The images were digitised using a Neotech IG24 board installed in a Macintosh Power PC 8100/80 running 64 Mbytes of RAM with graphics acceleration. They were stored initially on one of two one Gbyte hard drives and later archived onto 230 Mbyte optical discs. For the purposes of this work and to reduce file size the images were converted from 24-bit colour into 8-bit greyscale. All aspects of image processing and measurement were carried out using Graftek Optilab software.
20. For an account of image processing techniques and technology used in this research see: J. C. Russ, *The Image Processing Handbook* (Boca Ranton: CRC Press, 1992). For an account of image acquisition with particular reference to the resolution of detail see: P. Robinson, *The Digitization of Primary Textual Source* (Oxford: Oxford University Office for Humanities Communication, 1993).
21. In the course of his teaching Gerry Hedley demonstrated shrinkage by shining a light through a canvas during wetting. This may be expanded by using a light meter to obtain a useful correlation between changes in transmitted light as a result of yarn swelling and changes in RH.
22. M.F. Mecklenburg, 'Some Aspects of the Mechanical Behavior of Fabric Supported Paintings' (Report to the Smithsonian Institution, 1982).
23. G. Hedley, 'Relative Humidity and the Stress/Strain Responses of Canvas Paintings: Uniaxial Measurements of Naturally Aged Samples', *Studies in Conservation* 33 (1988): 133–148.
24. T.W. Bilson, 'The Characterisation and Conservation of a Roman Egyptian Painted Shroud Fragment' (Unpublished diploma report, Textile Conservation Centre, Courtauld Institute of Art, University of London, 1991).

Materials and equipment

- Reemay 2006: DHJ, Etherow House, Woolley Bridge, Hollingworth, Cheshire SK14 8NS.
- KM004 Temperature and Humidity Probe: Comark Ltd., Swallowfields, Welwyn Garden City, Hertfordshire AL7 1JP.
- Optilab: Graftek, le Moulin de l'Image, 26270 Mirmande, France. (distributed and supported in the UK by: ME Electronics, 4 Weighbridge Row, Cardiff Road, Reading, Berkshire RG1 8LX).
- Sony DXC 930-P three chip colour CCD camera: Sony Broadcast and Professional UK Ltd., The Heights, Brooklands, Weybridge, Surrey KT13 OXW.

A Study of the Clearance of Solvent Gels Used for Varnish Removal from Paintings

Aviva Burnstock,* Tanya Kieslich
Department of Conservation and Technology,
Courtauld Institute of Art, Somerset House, The Strand
London WC2R ORN, England

Abstract

A range of clearance procedures were tested for solvent gel formulations containing Ethomeen (a non-volatile surfactant) that were designed to remove varnish from a simulated canvas painting aged naturally for 12 years and an 18th century painting fragment. The experiment followed typical procedures used by conservators for varnish removal from paintings. Qualitative analysis of samples of paint using gas chromatography–mass spectrometry (GC-MS) indicated the presence of residual Ethomeen after all the clearance procedures tested. Specific clearance procedures removed components of the Ethomeen formulation differentially. Clearance using the solvent mixture in the gel removed more surfactant than other procedures tested. Surfactant residues were more effectively removed from the simulated canvas painting than the 18th century paint film. Examination of the surface of paint and varnish using scanning electron microscopy (SEM) suggested that the solvents used for clearance influenced the surface appearance of the painting. Similar surface changes in the simulated canvas painting were observed after treatment with gels followed by clearance with solvent mixtures and using solvents alone for varnish removal. Recommendation for future study include the long term effects of residual components of Ethomeen formulations on oil paint.

Keywords

Cleaning, easel paintings, solvent gels, aged paint, clearance, GC-MS, SEM, Ethomeen

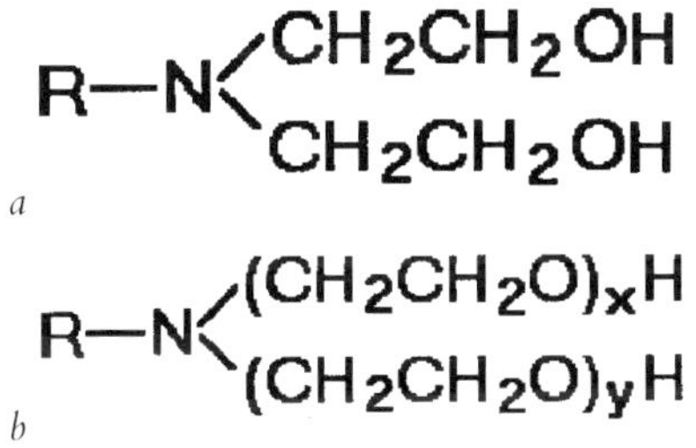

Figure 1. (a) The structure of Ethomeen C12: R= alkyl chain length of 8 to 20 carbon atoms, molecular weight range 217–385. (b) The structure of Ethomeen C25: R= alkyl chain length of 8 to 20 carbons; the sum of x *and* y *is 15, molecular weight range 789–957*

Introduction

Following Wolbers's introduction of a range of gel formulations for removal of surface coatings from paintings in the 1980s, many conservators have recognised the usefulness of gels as an addition to the traditional methods using free solvents for removal of varnish and repaints. Several published studies describe the treatment of paintings using solvent containing gels[1,2] and recipes are given in professional newsletters.[3,4]

Apart from the advantages of greater control of layer removal by precision formulation of gels and ease of use, solvent gels may reduce risks associated with solvent cleaning, such as leaching of polar material from oil paint. Gelled solvents of lower polarity may remove a layer as effectively as a more polar free solvent or solvent mixture. Gelling may also reduce the rate of evaporation of solvents.

Concerns about the use of gelled formulations have been raised in a number of studies of resin soap gels.[5–11] Perhaps the most important issue is the clearance of non-volatile compounds from the painting after treatment and the long term effects of residues of the cleaning agent on the painting. Findings from studies of soap gels suggested that traces of non-ionic surfactant Triton X-100 present in the gel formulations may initiate degradation reactions in residual varnish.[12]

Surfactants are integral to the formulation of solvent gels. It is therefore likely that similar concerns for effective clearance should apply to their use on paintings.

Solvent gel formulation

The following introduction discusses the issue of clearance of a non-volatile surfactant in solvent gel formulations described by Wolbers[13] and examined in the present study. Formulations contain solvent, Carbopol(954, a polyacrylic acid resin used for gelling, and a surfactant, Ethomeen((C12 or C25). Specific formulations are described below.

Ethomeen

The molecular structure of Ethomeen C12 (hydrophyl/lipophile balance number (HLB) = 10), or cocobis (2-hydroxyethyl) amine and Ethomeen C25 (HLB 19), or polyoxyethylene(15)cocoamine are shown in Figure 1.

Both C12 and C25 are weakly basic, have a long chain alkyl group and, through the amine group, form a salt with Carbopol. The properties of the surfactant, including solubility, depend on the chain length of the ethoxy group. Ethomeen C12 has one hydroxyl group, while Ethomeen C25 has a polyethoxy chain. Manufacturer's data states that both formulations contain additions of approximately 3% which include primary and secondary amines. Ethomeen C12 has been recommended for formulations of gels which contain aromatic hydrocarbon solvents and C25 is more suitable for gels which include polar solvents including water.

Previous studies using solvent gels

Only two published studies have examined aspects of the activity of solvent gels. Tsang and Erhardt found that comparable amounts of palmitic acid were leached from young oil paint films immersed in ethanol and ethanol gel.[14] A preliminary

* Author for correspondence

study of the activity of solvent gels on paint and varnish showed qualitative differences between residual varnish cleaned with solvent gels and resin soap gels.[15] An unpublished study by Curteis, employing solvent gels to remove wax coatings from the surface of a wall painting, contains some useful observations about the activity of selected solvent gels on porous substrates.[16]

The main concern identified for resin soap gels, of the clearance of residual surfactant in the gel formulations from the painting after treatment has not yet been studied in a practical context, where solvent gels are used for cleaning varnish from a painting. Studies of a painting after treatment with surfactant solutions showed that surfactant concentration and the extent of swelling of the paint film influenced the retention of surfactant.[17] Solvent gels that contain a relatively high proportion of surfactant and solvents that swell the paint film present potential risks which require investigation.

Review of clearance procedures for solvent gels

Effective clearance of solvent gels involves the removal of all non-volatile compounds in the formulation, including the bulk gel (Carbopol matrix) and the surfactant Ethomeen C12 or C25. Practitioners using solvent gels have employed a range of clearance procedures. Wolbers suggested Shellsol A[18] for removal of a gel containing solvents of low polarity or, alternatively, a mixture of solvents used in the formulation.[19] Stringari used 5% aromatic hydrocarbon solvent for clearance of a gel containing propan-2-ol, water and Ethomeen C12.[20] Personal communication with conservators provided alternative clearance procedures, including combinations of saliva or water followed by aromatic hydrocarbon solvent.[21] Studies of the clearance of other classes of gel suggest that generous swabbing of the surface with water or solvent was necessary for effective clearance[22] and this was taken into consideration in the present study.

The aims of the present study

The aim of the present study was to compare the effectiveness of a range of clearance procedures for solvent gels used in a practical context, for varnish removal from paintings. Removal of the bulk gel and clearance of the non-volatile surfactants Ethomeen C12 and C25 used in the gel formulations was studied using gas chromatography–mass spectrometry (GCMS) for detection of organic materials and scanning electron microscopy (SEM) for surface examination.

Experimental

The paintings treated

- **An 18th century painting.** A large painting was donated to the Courtauld Institute for research purposes. An area for study was selected which offered some uniformity in application of pigment and layers of superficial varnish. The layer structure of paint and varnish was examined using a standard cross-section technique. The area selected for study consisted of a single layer of paint, containing lead white with a few particles of smalt, carbon black and earth pigments, over a double red-brown ground.
  The painting had two layers of oxidised varnish. Staining tests using Rhodamine B were carried out on cross-sections of paint and varnish to examine the distribution of drying oil, as recommended by Wolbers.[23] Results suggested that an oil binding medium was used for the paint film. This was confirmed by GCMS, which indicated the presence of linseed oil (palmitate:stearate ratio P:S of 1.2). Oil was not present in either layer of varnish. GCMS analysis indicated the presence of mastic and pine resins and a small amount of wax that may have originated from an earlier lining.
- **A simulated canvas painting.** The simulated canvas painting described by Burnstock and White, and now aged for about 12 years in museum conditions, was re-examined. The canvas was primed with a mixture of titanium and lead

Table 1. Solubility of varnish in free solvents

Painting	varnish layer	low polarity solvents[a]	propan-2-ol	IMS	acetone	mix 1	mix 2	mix 3	mix 4
18thC painting	upper	insol	sol	sol 1min	sol 30s	insol	under cut		
	lower	insol	sol 1.5 min	sol	sol	insol	sol 2 min		
SCP	upper	insol	sol	sol 30s	sol			insol	insol
	lower two layers	insol	insol	insol	sol uneven			insol	insol

[a] Including Stoddard solvent, Shellsol A, xylene and toluene

white pigment, bound in linseed oil. Three layers of varnish had been applied: two of dammar resin and a final coat of oil and mastic.[24]

The two paintings tested were selected because they offered the opportunity to examine paint of different age and condition. The aged painting surface was porous and cracked compared with the relatively smooth paint layer presented by the simulated canvas painting and therefore may require different clearance procedures. Both paintings were coated with layers of significantly oxidised varnish, which could be removed separately, allowing aspects of the specificity of formulations of gels to be examined.

Solvent gels and their preparation

Gels were formulated according to the following rationale. The solubility of the varnish layers was assessed using free solvents (Table 1). Solvent solubility parameters for the individual layers of varnish in each painting were established. Both paintings contained upper layers of varnish which were more oxidised than the layers beneath. In all cases, solvent mixtures in gelled form were more active than the free solvent mixture. The aim was to select a solvent mixture of the lowest possible polarity which when gelled, would remove the desired layer. Table 2 lists the solvent formulations used.

Gels were formulated according to the manufacturers technical handbook.[25] Carbopol was dispersed in the principal solvent, using a motor-driven safety mixer. Ethomeen and secondary solvent were then added and the water was added dropwise until thickening occurred. Attempts were made to produce gels of equal viscosity.

Cleaning procedure: application of solvent gels

The cleaning procedure employed was typical of the method used by conservators for removal of varnish from easel paintings using solvent gels. A small paintbrush

Table 2. Formulations of solvent gels

Gel 1	1 g	Carbopol 954	Formulated to remove
	6 ml	Ethomeen C25	all layers of varnish
	120 ml	Propan-2-ol	from the 18th century painting.
	40 ml	Toluene	
	40ml	Deionised Water	
Gel 2	1 g	Carbopol 954	Formulated to remove
	6 ml	Ethomeen C12	the upper layer of varnish
	50 ml	Xylene	from the 18th century painting.
	10 ml	Propan-2-ol	
	10 ml	Deionised Water	
Gel 3	1 g	Carbopol 954	Formulated to remove
	6 ml	Ethomeen C12	the upper layer of
	60 ml	Xylene	varnish from the
	20 ml	Propan-2-ol	simulated canvas painting.
	5 ml	Deionised Water	
Gel 4	1 g	Carbopol 954	Formulated to remove
	6 ml	Ethomeen C12	all layers of varnish from
	40 ml	Xylene	the simulated canvas painting.
	15 ml	Propan-2-ol	
	15 ml	Stoddard solvent	
	5 ml	Deionised Water	

was used to apply the gel to the surface. Gel was applied to an area about 1.5 cm square. After 30 s, the gel was picked up with a dry cottonwool swab. Care was taken to avoid mechanical abrasion of the surface. Following surface treatment, four separate clearance procedures were applied for evaluation:

- dry swab only;
- saliva followed by 25% aromatic hydrocarbon solvent mixture (1:3, xylene in Stoddard solvent, white spirit, shortened in the text to "25%aro-HC");
- Shellsol A (a C9 aromatic hydrocarbon);
- the same solvent mixture present in the gel (e.g. for clearance of gel 2, a solvent mixture of xylene:propan-2-ol (5:1) was used).

Solvents used for clearance were applied in generous amounts on cottonwool swabs rolled over the area for 5 s without exerting downward force. The procedure followed was estimated to be sufficient for effective clearance in a practical context, so that all visible traces of gel had been removed.

Analytical techniques and sample preparation

Gas chromatography–mass spectrometry (GCMS)

GCMS was used to characterise the Ethomeen formulations and to identify any residues of surfactants in samples of paint after treatment. The method chosen for sample preparation in this study was recommended by White[26] and uses trifluoro-methyl-phenyl-trimethyl ammonium hydroxide (TFTMTH) for methylation.

Samples, taken by lightly scraping the surface of the paint (and in some cases, residual varnish), were transferred to pre-washed reaction vials capped with Teflon coated septa. Using a Pasteur pipette, one drop of TFTMTH (1% in methanol) was added. The vials were heated at 60°C for 3 h and shaken by hand every hour. Samples were allowed to cool to room temperature for at least 2 h before injection into the column.

Analysis was carried out using a Hewlett Packard Series II Gas Chromatograph coupled to a JEOL JMS-AX505W Mass Spectrometer. Data was collected on a JEOL complement data system. The temperature of the injector was set at 300(C and 1.5 *m*litre aliquots of sample were injected. A 25 mm long capillary column of bore 0.22 mm was set initially at 100°C, held for one minute; then the temperature was increased by 10°C min^{-1} to 330°C . A scan rate of 0.9 s/decade was employed.

The molecular fragmentation of Ethomeen was examined by direct insertion of less than one *m*litre of material, drawn into a quartz capillary tube, into the mass spectrometer. The temperature was increased from room temperature to 350°C at a rate of 65°C min^{-1}.

Scanning electron microscopy (SEM) and environmental scanning electron microscopy (ESEM)

A combination of SEM and empirical visual observation was used to examine the surface of paint samples. Samples treated with solvent were examined using a JEOL JSM35C SEM. Micrographs were recorded using Ilford FP4 120 black-and-white film. Preparation of samples and coating procedures were the same as those used previously.[27]

Samples treated with gels were examined using an ISI ABT-55 environmental scanning electron microscope (ESEM), which allows samples containing volatile materials to be examined at high magnification with good resolution in a low-vacuum environment; samples were uncoated. Back-scattered electron images were recorded under comparable conditions of acceleration voltage (keV), working distance and magnification to those used for conventional SEM to assist comparison of the micrographs.

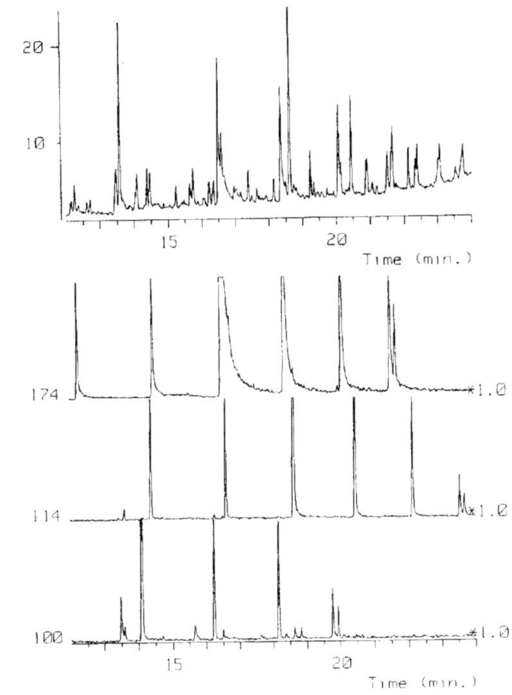

Figure 2. Total ion chromatogram of Gel 2 (containing Ethomeen C12), compared with mass chromatograms for M/Z *=174, 114 and 100. Fragmentograms are truncated for display only: peak areas were calculated accurately from corrected data*

Results

Characterisation of Ethomeen C12 and C25

Using GCMS, it was possible to characterise components of manufacturers formulations of Ethomeen C12 and Ethomeen C25 and to design a criteria for qualitative detection of the surfactant in treated paint samples.

ETHOMEEN C12

Gel formulations containing Ethomeen C12 were prepared for analysis using the reagents described above. Three series of molecular ions were identified which characterised components of the surfactant formulation. Figure 2 illustrates mass chromatograms of the series. Peaks which reached a maximum of 1500 counts were truncated and accommodated for in peak width. A series with a base peak of *M/Z* =174 atomic mass units could be derived from the molecular ion of Ethomeen C12 with an alkyl chain containing 12–20 carbon atoms. A second series with *M/Z* = 114 characterised homologues of primary amine and a third series of fragment ions with *M/Z* = 100 was identified and attributed to secondary amine present in the formulation.

The same fragmentation patterns were observed in samples of surfactant analysed without preparation using the methylating reagent and by direct insertion into the mass spectrometer.

The three series of fragment ions were thus defined as indicators of the presence of the surfactant in samples of paint analysed after treatment. The fragments were distinct from peaks which indicated oils or resins in the samples and an assessment could be made of the relative amounts of oil, resin and surfactant present.

ETHOMEEN C25

The molecular ion representing Ethomeen C25 was of too high molecular weight to be detected using the chosen method for preparation of samples in this study.

A total ion chromatogram from the analysis of Gel 1 (containing Ethomeen C25: see Table 2 for formulation) contained peaks indicative of the presence of ion fragments of the same three series present in the C12 formulation in different relative proportions. Gel 1 (formulated with Ethomeen C25) contained a significantly greater proportion of M/Z = 100 relative to M/Z = 114 and 174. Gel 2 (formulated with Ethomeen C12) contained relatively less series M/Z = 100 and a greater proportion of M/Z = 114 and 174.

Figure 3. ESEM micrograph of surface of varnish from the 18th century painting before treatment (170×)

GCMS analysis of samples after treatment

The relative amounts of ion fragment series M/Z = 174, 114 and 100 present after the range of treatments was calculated by measuring the peak areas from chromatograms. Calculation of the amount of surfactant relative to the proportion of oil and resin in the sample was estimated to give a qualitative indication of the effectiveness of the clearance procedures.

Clearance of the bulk of the gel from both the 18th century (18thC) painting and the simulated canvas painting (SCP) – and a significant proportion of the surfactant therein – was effected using a dry swab. Dry swabbing significantly reduced the proportion of fragment ion series M/Z = 114 and 174 in samples treated with Gel 2. Swab clearance of Gel 3 from the SCP was more effective; series M/Z = 114 and 174 contributed less than 10% of the sample volume. Clearance of both Gels 2 and 3 using Shellsol A further reduced the proportion of fragment ion series with base peak M/Z = 174 while clearance using saliva and 25% aro-HC was still more effective. The most effective clearance procedure was the solvent mixture, which reduced series M/Z = 174 and 114 combined to less than 1% of the sample. The percentages given indicate the relative amounts present; quantitative values were not calculated.

Figure 4. SEM micrograph of the paint surface from the tacking edge of the simulated canvas painting before treatment (440×)

The components of the surfactants associated with fragment series M/Z = 114 and 100 were cleared differentially. While, in general, all clearance procedures reduced the relative proportion of series M/Z = 114 in the residual surfactant, the proportion of fragment series M/Z = 100 was comparatively less affected after treatment using gels containing both Ethomeen C12 and C25.

Fragment ion series M/Z = 174 and 114 were not detected in any of the samples treated with Gel 1 (containing Ethomeen C25) after clearance. Residual surfactant was indicated only by ion series M/Z = 100, which was present in minor proportions in samples after clearance.

There were notable differences between the relative proportions of characteristic fragment series in samples of gels containing Ethomeen C25 and samples of paint containing uncleared gel. Analysis of Gel 1 alone contained series M/Z = 174 in relatively low proportion to series M/Z = 100, while samples of Gel applied to paint but not cleared contained a relatively significant amount of series M/Z = 100 and no fragments of the M/Z = 174 series. These results require further investigation: differences may be due to inhomogeneity of the gel formulations or the samples examined or possibly to selective absorption of some components in the surfactant into the paint layers.

Figure 5. ESEM micrograph of surface of the 18thC painting with Gel 1 applied but not cleared (110×). Gel appears smooth and dark on the right of the paint surface

Surface examination

Characterisation of the surfaces of paint and varnish before treatment

Figure 3 illustrates the surface of the varnish from the 18thC painting before treatment using SEM (magnified 170×). The surface undulations which were not evident on visual inspection contributed to the matt appearance characteristic of the aged resin varnish. The relatively smooth varnish has been etched by the action of cotton wool and saliva swabbing during a superficial surface cleaning: Horizontal marks follow the movement of the swab, redepositing residual surface dirt into fine cracks in the varnish. Bright particles of charged loose surface dirt are also evident on the surface.

An electron micrograph was taken of the surface of a sample of the paint from the tacking margin of the simulated canvas painting to characterise the surface before treatment (Figure 4, 440×). The paint film is relatively smooth with an even coating

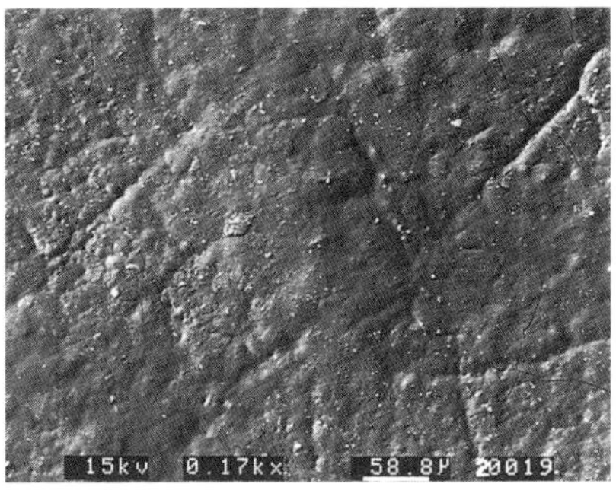

Figure 6. ESEM micrograph of surface of the 18thC painting treated with Gel 2 and cleared with a dry swab (170×). Deposits of smooth gel cover fine cracks in the varnish layer beneath

of pigment particles leanly bound with oil medium. The paint retains a fine craquelure and is coated with a thin layer of superficial dirt. The paint layer has been characterised in a previous study, which included a micrograph of the paint surface at 1960×, showing the relationship between pigment and binding medium at the paint surface.[28]

The appearance of solvent gels on paint and varnish

Using ESEM it was possible to examine the relationship between the gel and the painting surface in samples where the gel was applied without subsequent clearance and where gel was cleared with a dry swab alone. Figure 5 (110×) shows the surface of the 18thC painting after treatment with Gel 1 where gel was not cleared. The gel forms a smooth film which covers the paint and varnish on the right of the image. Charged particles of dust (which appear white on the micrograph) adhere to the gel.

An ESEM micrograph of the surface of the 18thC painting after removal of a layer of varnish and subsequent clearance using a dry swab alone showed thin patches of residual gel on the remaining varnish layer (Figure 6, 170×). The residual gel covers fine cracks in varnish beneath. Fine particles of dirt evident in this micrograph were a feature of all the surfaces that retained gel detectable using ESEM. Residual gel was not identified with surety using SEM or ESEM on the surface of samples after any of the clearance procedures involving solvents.

Figure 7. ESEM micrograph of surface of the 18thC painting treated with Gel 2 and cleared with solvent mixture (220×). A thin film of residual varnish remains over a rough underlying layer of varnish

Selective removal of varnish

The surface characteristics of samples were examined and compared after varnish removal and clearance. The effectiveness of gels formulated to selectively remove the upper layer of varnish and the effects of the gel and clearance procedure on the varnish layer beneath were assessed.

Gel 2 was effective in selective removal of the upper varnish layer from the 18thC painting. The surface of a sample treated with Gel 2 and cleared with saliva and 25% aro-HC revealed a layer of remaining varnish that was significantly smoother than the upper varnish layer removed by the gel and exhibited a glossy, saturated appearance. Figure 7 (220×) illustrates the surface after treatment using the same gel, followed by clearance using the solvent mixture in the gel. In this case the surface was characterised by a thin, smooth layer of residual varnish over a rough and porous lower layer of varnish.

The duration of application of Gel 3 was found to be crucial for selective removal of the uppermost layer of varnish from the SCP. While application of the gel for a maximum of 30 seconds thinned the upper layer, longer application of the gel resulted in undercutting of the layer and preferential removal of the less polar varnish layers beneath. An electron micrograph (Figure 8, 2200×) illustrates a detail of the surface of a sample after treatment with Gel 3 and clearance with Shellsol A. Characteristic clumps of fractured varnish remained in the interstices of the paint film.

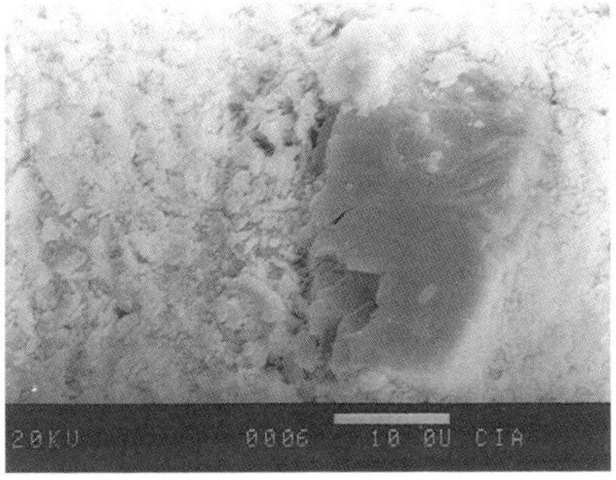

Figure 8. SEM micrograph of surface of SCP treated with Gel 3 for 1 minute and cleared with Shellsol A (2200×). A fractured fragment of the lower layer of varnish remains in the interstices of the paint film

Complete varnish removal and the effects of clearance procedures

Application of Gel 4 for removal of the lower varnish layers from the simulated canvas painting followed by clearance using solvent mixtures removed all but a trace of varnish (Figure 9, 940×). Similar smooth deposits of varnish were observed in 11 samples which were subjected to clearance using solvent mixtures, or had undergone varnish removal using free solvents. Particles of underbound pigment are evident in the micrograph (Figure 9), which suggests that some abrasion of the surface, or disturbance of the binding medium, has occurred. Similar abrasion and underbound pigment was evident in micrographs of samples where varnish was removed using free solvents. This suggests that the solvent clearance, rather than the gel, produced the surface change.

Removal of all the varnish layers from the 18thC painting using Gel 1 was dependent on the clearance procedure which followed gel application. While clearance using the solvent mixture removed all but patches of thin residual varnish, clearance using saliva/25% aro-HC left a thicker layer of varnish. After clearance with Shellsol A, the surface retained a layer of pitted varnish (Figure 10, 320×). The surface shows the contrast between the relatively light particulate paint layer beneath a dark contrasting discontinuous layer of varnish.

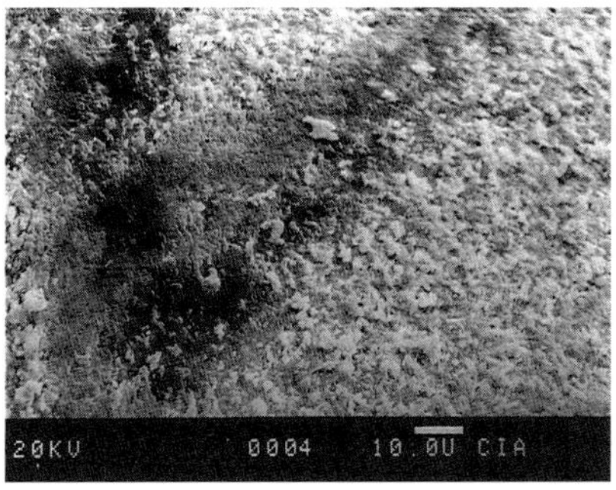

Figure 9. SEM micrograph of surface of SCP treated with Gel 4 and cleared with the solvent mixture in the gel (940×). A thin patch of residual varnish (dark area) redepositied by solvent remains on the paint surface

Discussion

Comparative effectiveness of the clearance procedures

Using GCMS, traces of components of formulations of both Ethomeen C12 and C25 were found after all clearance procedures used. Clearance using the solvent mixture in the gel formulations removed the surfactant most effectively, while greater proportions of residual surfactant were detected in samples after the other procedures tested. In general, clearance of the SCP was more effective than the 18thC paint film, probably because of the relative ease of removing gel from a smooth surface.

Clearance methods involving solvents reduced the proportions of components differentially. The fragment series with base peak of $M/Z = 174$, representing the molecular ion of Ethomeen C12, was reduced more after clearance using polar solvents. The fragment series representing the primary amine in the formulation (base peak $M/Z = 114$) was more effectively reduced after clearance with saliva and 25% aromatic hydrocarbon solvent or the mixture of solvents used in the gel than after treatment with Shellsol A. The series of fragments ions indicative of the secondary amine (base peak $M/Z = 100$) was relatively unaffected by any of the clearance procedures.

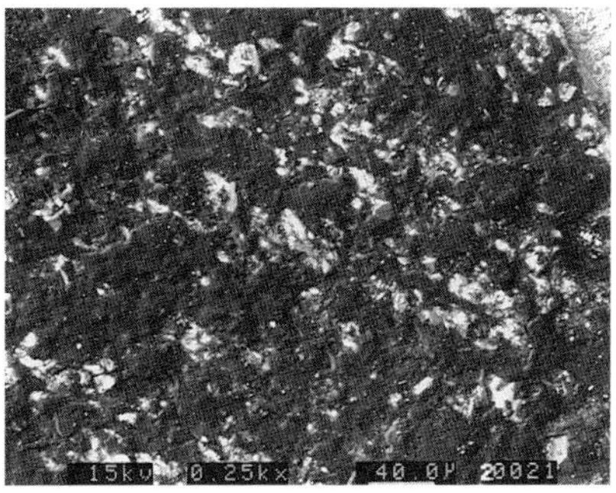

Figure 10. ESEM micrograph of the 18thC painting treated with Gel 1 and cleared with Shellsol A (320×). A layer of abraded, discontinuous varnish remains over the contrastingly light particulate paint film

Clearance of larger molecular ions present in surfactant formulations of Ethomeen C25 was not examined in this study. The series of fragment ions that were indicative of lower homologues of Ethomeen and the primary amine were entirely absent from the cleared samples, which may suggest that clearance of the larger molecules is more efficient than that of the lower molecular weight components.

SEM and ESEM microscopy used for surface examination of samples from treated areas suggested that the bulk of the gel is removed using a dry swab. Residual gel was not identified on the surface of samples after clearance using any of the other clearance procedures. This finding, together with the results from GCMS, points to the possibility that components of the surfactant may separate. Lower molecular weight components may remain on the painting that are less accessible to clearance by solvents or mechanical methods of clearance, such as dry swabbing of the surface. While these components are not visible on the surface using SEM, residues were detectable using a sensitive technique of organic analysis. The possibility of migration of low molecular weight components of residual surfactant into the paint film needs further study.

Formulations that contain surfactant which does not react with carboxylate ions in the Carbopol resin are retained as "free" Ethomeen within the gel matrix. Reacted and free Ethomeen may require different clearance procedures. Assay of the volume of free and bound Ethomeen and the related issues of clearance could be studied, for example using radio isotropic markers, as in a previous study of soap gel clearance.[29]

The mechanism of varnish removal

Evidence provided by SEM microscopic examination suggested that the gels remove varnish by a combination of solvation and mechanical action, in concurrence with previous studies.[30] Solvation predominated over mechanical fracture of varnish where gels were better formulated for removal of the upper varnish layer. The method used for clearance had an effect on the appearance of the residual varnish. Solvents of low polarity (Shellsol A) left a rough residual layer of varnish, while clearance with more polar solvent mixtures swelled and redeposited residual varnish in a smooth film. Previous studies have reported similar trends in the activity of gels containing polar solvents independent of the clearance procedure.[31] Therefore it may be reasonable to conclude that solvents have similar effects, whether they are applied in gel or as free solvent for clearance.

Whether the solvent gel formulations used in this study reduced the risk of leaching of oil paint films that is implicit in the use of free solvents is arguable. Study of the relative rate of swelling of oil films imparted by gelled and free solvents could inform the relative risks. Previous studies which found roughly equal potential for fatty acid extraction by ethanol gelled and free ethanol suggest similar potential for leaching.[32] Clearance procedures involving solvents may increase the risk of leaching, by further prolonging the contact time of the solvent with the paint surface.

The leaching of paint after treatment was not examined quantitatively in this study. Signs of abrasion, including the presence of unbound pigment particles, and possible erosion of the binding medium was observed (using SEM) on the surface of the paint film after treatment using solvent gels followed by clearance with solvent mixtures. Similar surface effects were observed after varnish removal using free solvents. These findings may indicate that solvent gels may not significantly reduce the risk of swelling and concomitant leaching of oil paint films.

The possibility of residual deposition of Carbopol resins present in solvent gel formulations was not examined in the present study, nor the long-term effects of residual deposits of secondary amine and ethoxylate homologues of Ethomeen assessed.

Conclusion

Ethomeen surfactant present in formulations of solvent gels was detected in samples of paint after all the clearance procedures tested. Qualitative assessment of the amount of residual surfactant present suggested that the most effective clearance procedure was the use of the solvent mixture used for the gel formulation, while other clearance procedures were less effective.

There was evidence that different clearance procedures selectively removed components of the Ethomeen formulations.

Clearance procedures influenced the nature of the surface of residual varnish and in some cases, the paint layer. Clearance using solvent mixtures used in the gels swelled residual varnish, while non-polar solvents used for clearance left a roughened, discontinuous varnish film. Similar signs of surface abrasion of the paint film were observed following varnish removal using free solvents and samples treated with gel followed by clearance with solvent mixtures.

The consequences of residual deposition of components of Ethomeen formulations, on oil paint, in particular, secondary amine and lower homologues of the Ethomeen formulation requires examination before solvent gels can be used with confidence where they may remain in contact with the paint layer.

Acknowledgements

The authors would like to thank: Professor Frank Hibbert and Andy Cakebread at Kings College London (KCL), Department of Chemistry, for organising space and running the GCMS. Dr. Chris Jones at the Natural History Museum EM unit for access to, and operation of, the ESEM. Thanks in particular to Raymond White at the National Gallery for his advice and guidance, which was essential to this study.

Materials and suppliers

- *GPR Propan-2-ol, GPR Acetone, GPR Toluene, GPR Industrial Methylated Spirits, GPR Xylene, Methanol 'HiPerSolv' for HPLC*, 99.8% purity, and *Stoddard Solvent*. BDH Laboratory Supplies, Poole, BH15 1TD, England Tel: 01212 669700.
- *Shellsol A*. Alcohols Ltd., Charringtons House, The Causeway, Bishop's Stortford, Hertfordshire, CM23 2EW, England Tel: 01279 658464:
- *Trifluoro-methyl-phenyl-trimethyl-ammonium-hydroxide* (1% in methanol). Chrompak (UK) Ltd., Unit 4, Indescon Court, Millharbour, London, E14 9TN, England, Tel: 0171 515-8080.
- *Carbopol 954*, manufactured by B.F. Goodrich, and *Ethomeen C12* and *Ethomeen C25*, manufactured by Armak Chemicals.Fine Chemicals for Conservation, Newmans Lane, Surbiton, Surrey, KT6 4QQ, England, Tel: 0181 390-6420:
- *Wheaton V-vials*, 1.0 ml, graduated with open top screw cap. Aldrich Chemical Company, The Old Brickyard, New Road, Gillingham, Dorset, SP8 4JL, England, Tel: 0800 717-181/01747 822211.
- *Tuf Bond Discs* 12mm. Pierce & Warringer, 44 Upper Northgate St., Chester, CH1 4EF, England, Tel: (0800) 252185/01244 382525.
- *HT8 quartz capillary column*. Scientific Glass Engineering (UK) Ltd., 1 Potters Lane, Kiln Farm, Milton Keynes, MK11 3LA, England, Tel: 01908 568844.

References

1. C. Stringari, "Vincent Van Gogh's Triptych of Trees in Blossom, Arles (1888) Part I. Examination and Treatment of the Altered Surface Coatings." *Cleaning, Retouching and Coatings*, (Paper delivered at the IIC Congress, Brussels, 3–7 September 1990), 126–130.
2. R. Wolbers, "Notes for the Workshop on New Methods in the Cleaning of Paintings," The Getty Conservation Institute, August 1989.
3. A. Southall, "New Approach to Cleaning Painted Surfaces" *Conservation News* (UKIC) no. 37 (1988): 43–44.
4. S. Blank and C. Stavroudis, "Solvents and Sensibility," *WAAC Newsletter* 11, no. 2 (1989): 2–10.
5. J. S. Tsang and D. Erhardt, "Current Research on the Effects of Solvents and Gelled and Aqueous Cleaning Systems on Oil Paint Films" *Journal of the American Institute of Conservation* 31, no. 1 (1992): 87–94.
6. A. Burnstock and R. White, "The Effects of Selected Solvents and Soaps on a Simulated Canvas Painting," *Cleaning, Retouching and Coatings* (Paper delivered at the IIC Congress, Brussels, 3–7 September 1990), 111–118.
7. J. Koller, "Cleaning of a Nineteenth-Century Painting with Deoxycholate Soap: Mechanism and Residue Studies," *Cleaning, Retouching and Coatings* (Paper delivered at the IIC Congress, Brussels, 3–7 September 1990), 106–110.
8. R. Wolbers, "A Radio-Isotopic Assay for the Direct Measurement of Residual Cleaning Materials on Paint Films," *Cleaning, Retouching and Coatings* (Paper delivered at the IIC Congress, Brussels, 3–7 September 1990), 119–125.
9. D. Erhardt and J. Bischoff, "The Roles of Various Components of Resin Soaps, Bile Acid Soaps and Gels, and Their Effects on Oil Paint Films," *Studies in Conservation* 39, no. 1 (1994): 3–27.
10. B. Ford and A. Byrne, "The Lipid Stripping Potential of Resin Soap Gels Used for Cleaning Paintings," *AICCM Bulletin* 17, no. 1 (1991): 51–60.
11. J. Dimond, "Resin Soap Experiments," *Conservation News* no.41 (1990): 8–10.
12. Burnstock and White, "The Effects of Selected Solvents," 114–117.
13. R. Wolbers, "Resin Soap Formulas, Solvent Gels and Current Formulations," compiled July 1986 (handout given in Workshop on New Methods in the Cleaning of Paintings, The Getty Conservation Institute, August 1989).
14. Tsang and Erhardt, "Current Research," 92.
15. A. Burnstock and R. White, "Cleaning Gels: Further Studies," (Paper delivered at the meeting, Conservation Science in the UK, Glasgow, May 1993), 36–39.
16. T. Curteis, " An Investigation of the Use of Solvent Gels for the Removal of Wax-Based Coatings from Wall Paintings," (Final year project, Wall Paintings Department, Courtauld Institute of Art, 1991), 19–20.
17. Wolbers, "A Radio-Isotopic Assay," 121–125.
18. Wolbers, "Notes for the Workshop," B5.
19. Ibid., 14.
20. Stringari, "Vincent Van Gogh's Triptych," 129.
21. A. Southall, Personal communication, September 1995.
22. Burnstock and White, "The Effects of Selected Solvents," 117.
23. Wolbers, "Notes for the Workshop," A31.
24. Burnstock and White "The Effects of Selected Solvents," 117.
25. B. F. Goodrich *Carbopol Resins Handbook*. Technical Data (Carbopol: Cleveland, USA, 1991).
26. R. White and J. Pilc, "Analysis of Paint Media, " *National Gallery Technical Bulletin* 17 (1996): 101 (note 32).
27. Burnstock and White "The Effects of Selected Solvents," 117.
28. Ibid.," 112–113.
29. Wolbers, "A Radio-Isotopic Assay," 119–125.
30. A. Burnstock and T. Learner., "Changes in the Surface Characteristics of Artificially Aged Mastic Varnishes After Cleaning Using Alkaline Reagents," *Studies in Conservation* 37, no.3 (1992): 165–184.
31. Burnstock and White, "Cleaning Gels," 36–39.
32. Tsang and Erhardt, "Current Research," 92.

La restauration d'une Vièrge hodigitria attribuée à l'Ecole d'Onuphre XVIème siècle: Exemple de coopération internationale dans le domaine de la conservation

Nicole S. Delsaux*
Service de Restauration des Musées de France
Petites Ecuries du Roy
78000 Versailles, France

Abrégé

C'est à l'occasion du programme "Courant d'Est" réalisé par le Ministère de la Culture et le Ministère des Affaires Etrangères que cette icône a été confiée en février 1993 au Service de Restauration des Musées de France (SRMN). Par un accord bilatéral entre les ministères de la Culture de France et d'Albanie il a été convenu que la restauration de cette icône serait effectuée au sein du SRMN par un restaurateur spécialiste français et servirait de base à la formation de deux restaurateurs albanais, ce travail en commun étant un cas exemplaire d'échange entre les deux pays. Le premier stage a été effectué sous la direction de Nicole Delsaux par Kristofor Naslazi, restaurateur au Musée de Korçë, Albanie pendant le mois de février 1993 et le second par Edouard Soppi, restaurateur à l'Institut des Monuments à Tirana, Albanie pendant le mois de juin 1993. Durant ces deux périodes, la première partie de l'intervention: l'élimination d'un surpeint récent couvrant l'ensemble de l'oeuvre, a été mise au point et commencée en étroite collaboration. La restauration a été terminée par Nicole Delsaux de juillet 1994 à mai 1996.

Mots-clés

Icône, Albanie, Onuphre, surpeint, dégagement, lacunes, réintégration

Introduction

Il s'agit d'une Vierge à l'Enfant de type hodigitria qui provient de l'église Saint Constantin et Hélène à Berat, Albanie (Figures 1 and 2). Elle mesure 79 cm de haut par 63 cm de large. L'attribution exacte de cette oeuvre n'avait pas été déterminée avant son départ par les historiens d'art albanais, l'icône ancienne étant totalement dissimulée par le surpeint moderne. Néanmoins la radiographie et l'examen de la portion de couche picturale découverte par un sondage laissaient espérer qu'il pouvait s'agir d'une oeuvre de l'Ecole d'Onuphre de Néokastra qui fut au XVIème siècle en Albanie un maître réputé tant en peinture murale qu'en peinture d'icônes. Issu de la tradition byzantine, il fut le premier à fonder une école typiquement albanaise. Autour de lui on connaît Nicolas, son fils et Jean, collaborateur de Nicolas. Son style a exercé une forte influence, il a été suivi par de nombreux peintres apparus plus tard.[1]

Technologie de l'icône originale

Le panneau est formé d'une seule planche d'orme,[2] le fil du bois est vertical. Sa face est plane, il n'est pas creusé en son centre pour former un cadre attenant. L'épaisseur du panneau est irrégulière, la tranche inférieure est par endroits de plus faible épaisseur que la tranche supérieure. Au revers un enduit blanchâtre est visible, il est réparti de façon irrégulière, le panneau est légèrement creusé en sa partie

Figure 1. Ensemble avant restauration, après sondage 1973 dans le manteau du Christ et essais 1993 dans la partie inférieure du cadre et la main du Christ. D'après diapositive SRMF/J. Réquilé N°46909.

Figure 2. Ensemble après restauration

*Adresse de correspondance: 6 bis bd Pereire,75017 Paris, France

centrale. Deux traverses à contre-fil sont maintenus au revers par des clous. La traverse supérieure mesure 14 × 3,5 cm et la traverse inférieure 21,5 × 3 cm. Elles sont biseautées sur le côté du bord latéral gauche et coupées à 6 cm du bord latéral droit (peut-être pour permettre l'intégration de l'icône dans une iconostase). Un cadre rapporté formé de quatre lattes de bois de 4,5 cm de large et de 1 cm d'épaisseur taillées en biseau du côté interne, est cloué sur la face du panneau par de nombreux clous métalliques. Un prélèvement a été effectué sur la latte inférieure, l'essence identifiée est le peuplier.[2]

La toile est visible par observation directe. Elle recouvre probablement la totalité du panneau mais on ne peut affirmer qu'elle recouvre la totalité du cadre. Elle a été observée sur la partie inférieure mais pas sur les bords latéraux. Il s'agit de lin.[3]

La préparation originale est constituée de sulfate de calcium, plus précisément de gypse.[4] Elle peut atteindre 700 µm ou plus. Le liant est la colle protéinique. Des incisions circulaires délimitent les auréoles mais aucune incision n'a été décelée dans la composition picturale. En revanche le dessin sous-jacent est bien visible par observation directe et sur la photo prise en lumière infrarouge. Il est de couleur noire et probablement posé au pinceau.

Le fond de l'icône a originellement été couvert d'une feuille d'argent posée sur un bolus orangé. Les prélèvements effectués montrent que ce fond est extrêmement lacunaire. Les auréoles sont recouvertes de feuilles d'or posées sur un fin bolus orangé. Le caractère cruciforme de celle du Christ et les inscriptions traditionnelles sont définis par un décor vermillon peint sur l'or. Le cadre est recouvert de feuilles d'or sur bolus orangé. Il comporte des motifs poinçonnés et est bordé d'un liseré vermillon. La dorure a été reprise et c'est la latte supérieure qui est la plus ancienne. L'auréole de la Vierge empiète sur le cadre et se prolonge jusqu'à son bord supérieur.

Une chrysographie a été réalisée sur mixtion orangée, on la trouve sur le manteau du Christ, sur la manche gauche de sa tunique et sur les franges du maphorion de la Vierge.

Le liant de la couche picturale est l'oeuf. Son épaisseur est environ de 20 à 60 µm.

- **Carnations**. L'observation et l'étude des coupes stratigraphiques montrent qu'elles ont été réalisées en trois couches:
  La première (proplasmos) est composée d'une terre (terre verte probablement) en mélange avec du vermillon et avec la présence d'inclusions riches en calcium.
  La deuxième est composée d'une majorité de blanc de plomb avec la présence de rares inclusions rouges (vermillon probablement).
  La troisième correspond aux lumières finales. Elle est composée de blanc de plomb.
- **Maphorion de la Vierge**. Réalisé avec de l'hématite majoritaire et probablement un peu de vermillon.
- **Tunique et bonnet de la Vierge**. La couche de base est réalisée avec un mélange de bleu organique et de blanc de plomb et les lumières avec un mélange d'azurite et de blanc de plomb.
- **Manteau du Christ**. Réalisé en une couche de minium.
- **Couche protectrice**. Un vernis oléorésineux fortement oxydé recouvre l'icône originale. Son épaisseur est très variable selon les zones. On le trouve surtout sur les vêtements et les carnations. Il est lacunaire ou absent sur les feuilles métalliques.

Constat d'état

A son arrivée dans le Service de Restauration des Musées de France l'icône était entièrement recouverte d'un surpeint récent, à l'exeption d'un sondage réalisé sur place en 1973 par un restaurateur italien. C'est ce sondage qui a révélé la qualité de l'oeuvre et incité les autorités albanaises à confier sa restauration au Service de Restauration des Musées de France.

- **Support**. Une fente verticale, légèrement oblique, affecte le panneau dans toute son épaisseur et est bien visible au revers. Elle part d'une large lacune située dans l'ovale du visage de la Vierge au niveau du bas de la joue gauche et du menton et se prolonge jusqu'au bord inférieur, à l'extrémité du pied gauche du Christ. On pourrait la qualifier de fissure du bois car il est probable qu'elle est consécutive à la présence d'un noeud situé à l'emplacement de la lacune ainsi qu'aux tensions internes du bois. La présence des éléments cloués à contre-fil tels que les traverses et les lattes supérieure et inférieure du cadre rapporté ne semble pas avoir provoqué cette altération.

- **Préparation et couche colorée**. L'ensemble de l'icône est recouverte d'un surpeint épais et grossier, probablement exécuté à la fin du XIXème siècle ou au début du XXème. Le liant du surpeint est l'oeuf. Les pigments inclus dans les prélèvements analysés sont l'outremer (probablement artificiel), le blanc de zinc, le jaune de chrome et le sulfate de baryum. Entre le surpeint et l'original on trouve sur certaines zones une nouvelle préparation alors que sur d'autres on trouve une ancienne couche protectrice oléo-résineuse épaisse et oxydée.

Sur les zones qui sont (ou furent) recouvertes de feuilles d'argent ou d'or: le fond, les auréoles ainsi que sur certaines parties du maphorion, on trouve entre le surpeint et l'original la préparation récente composée de sulfate de calcium (gypse + anhydrite) liée à la colle et posée directement sur l'original. Dans ces zones la préparation originale sous jacente est affectée de pulvérulence, de soulèvements et d'importants réseaux de craquelures. On ne peut savoir avec certitude si cette altération était antérieure au surpeint, la seconde préparation étant destinée à la masquer, ou bien si la pose d'une matière liquide et chaude sur les feuilles métalliques non protégées a provoqué les altérations. Celles-ci sont très importantes dans le fond ou l'argent semble avoir presque totalement disparu. L'or, sur les auréoles, a moins souffert. Sur d'autres zones le surpeint repose sur la couche protectrice oléo-résineuse plus ou moins épaisse qui a protégé l'original.

Deux grandes lacunes défigurent l'icône, la plus importante se trouve dans le visage de la Vierge et se prolonge le long de la fente oblique en passant par sa main droite jusqu'au bord inférieur. La seconde, beaucoup plus petite dans le cou du Christ. Elles sont actuellement plus ou moins comblées par un repeint ancien sur mastic craquelé et fragile. Deux autres se trouvent sur la pommette droite de la Vierge, empiétant sur le bonnet, elles conservent un mastic plus récent et ne sont pas comblées par un repeint ancien. De nombreuses petites lacunes consécutives à d'anciens soulèvements ou à des chocs parsèment l'icône.

Le fond d'argent a presque totalement disparu. Il a été recouvert d'une nouvelle préparation et d'un épais surpeint ocre rouge. Certaines zones du maphorion ont été usées et recouvertes d'un surpeint en glacis. Les trois étoiles du maphorion de la Vierge ont été grattées, celle de l'épaule droite plus largement que les deux autres. Le fond a été recouvert, par dessus le surpeint, de plaques de métal ciselées et décorées d'émaux, fixées par des clous. Elles semblent anciennes. Deux auréoles métalliques de facture plus récente ont été clouées autour de la tête de la Vierge et du Christ ainsi qu'une main sur le poignet droit de la Vierge.

Elimination du surpeint

L'opération essentielle de la restauration de cette icône étant l'élimination du surpeint recouvrant l'ensemble de l'oeuvre, il fallait en premier lieu prendre les décisions de principe et déterminer la méthode qui serait utilisée.

Les icônes, tout comme les sculptures polychromes d'Occident ont une fonction culturelle et liturgique. Elles sont fréquemment surpeintes et il n'est pas rare de trouver plusieurs couches successives sur les icônes très anciennes. C'est alors qu'il importe d'établir un plan d'intervention mûrement réfléchi en se basant sur des critères bien définis et une méthodologie de restauration plus proche de celle des sculptures polychromes que de celle des peintures.

L'icône confiée par l'Albanie présentait un cas relativement simple: le dernier surpeint étant incontestablement de qualité très médiocre et d'exécution récente, le dilemme habituellement posé entre la préservation du surpeint et le dégagement de l'original semblait donc pouvoir se résoudre aisément sur le plan esthétique.

Sur le plan de la conservation, le sondage opéré en 1973 démontrait qu'on pouvait espérer trouver en dessous une oeuvre en état convenable (Figure 3). Le dossier scientifique établi par le Laboratoire de Recherche des Musées de France : radiographies, photographies en lumière directe et rasante, sous fluorescence d'ultraviolets et rayonnement infrarouge confirmait cette hypothèse.

En 1993 le Service de Restauration des Musées de France a décidé, sur proposition de Nicole Delsaux avec l'accord de Kristofor Naslazi de procéder à de nouveaux sondages en employant une méthode de travail différente de celle utilisée en 1973. A l'heure actuelle plusieurs types de méthode sont pratiqués pour éliminer un surpeint:

Figure 3. Détail sondage dans l'oeil droit de la Vierge. D'après diapositive SRMF/J. Réquilé N°47257.

1) **en employant des solvants organiques**. Cette méthode nécessite l'emploi de solvants pénétrants et puissants, généralement appliqués par compresses laissées en place assez longtemps. Pour séparer deux couches de tempéra il faut en effet solubiliser la couche oléorésineuse, généralement oxydée, qui les sépare. Cette méthode, encore largement pratiquée, est remise en cause par un certain nombre de restaurateurs et d'instituts qui ont constaté les dégâts causés dans les préparations poreuses par les solvants et les solutés oxydés. Dans certains cas les restaurateurs tiennent à dégager l'original tout en sauvegardant le ou les surpeints qu'ils transposent ensuite sur un nouveau support. Leur méthode est dérivée de la première mais elle est actuellement fortement contestée.
2) **en travaillant à sec** en clivant les couches entre elles au moyen de fines lames de métal dur ou de lames chirurgicales. Cette méthode est beaucoup plus longue et doit impérativement être pratiquée sous microscope binoculaire.

Figure 4. Détail en cours de dégagement du surpeint avec témoin. D'après diapositive SRMF/J. Réquilé N°58131.

C'est la méthode à sec, sous microscope binoculaire qui a été choisie d'un commun accord pour procéder aux nouveaux sondages qui ont révélé que l'icône est en bon état de conservation, compte tenu de l'ancienneté de l'oeuvre, à l'exception du fond, de la grande lacune et de la fissure.

Le second stage, effectué par Edouard Soppi en juin, a permis de poursuivre les sondages en employant la même méthode. Commencé par les deux restaurateurs albanais en étroite collaboration avec la restauratrice française, ce traitement a été l'occasion pour Kristofor Naslazi puis pour Edouard Soppi de pratiquer ce type de méthode et de s'y entraîner.

Le Service de Restauration des Musées de France sur proposition des deux restaurateurs a pris la décision de procéder au dégagement du surpeint (Figure 4). Il a également été convenu que, jusqu'à nouvelle décision prise en commun, on conserverait le surpeint récent du fond et les surpeints anciens de la joue de la Vierge et du cou du Christ. Les ornements métalliques ayant été déposés, l'élimination du surpeint le plus récent a été poursuivie par Nicole Delsaux à partir de juillet 1994. La méthode au scalpel sous microscope binoculaire permettant de sélectionner les repeints et surpeints à préserver, le dégagement a été fait progressivement. Le surpeint récent a été éliminé sur l'ensemble des zones où l'original présentait un état satisfaisant. Sur celles où un repeint sous-jacent plus ancien existait et était susceptible d'être utilisé pour la présentation esthétique de l'oeuvre, la grande lacune dans la joue de la Vierge et la petite dans le cou du Christ, le surpeint récent a été éliminé mais le surpeint ancien préservé (Figure 5). Dans le maphorion de la Vierge, un large surpeint ancien en glacis assez transparent masquant certaines usures a été préservé en raison de sa qualité, de son ancienneté et de son intégration harmonieuse.

Figure 5. Ensemble après dégagement du surpeint récent. D'après diapositive SRMF/J. Réquilé N°58551.

Refixage

Sur les zones très altérées et recouvertes d'un nouvel enduit il a fallu procéder à de multiples refixages et infiltrations d'adhésif. Une colle protéinique (colle Totin) a été choisie parce qu'elle est analogue au matériau constitutif de l'oeuvre et que son processus de vieillissement est bien connu.

Réintégration

Après la première partie de sa restauration, consolidation et élimination du surpeint, se pose le problème de la présentation esthétique de l'oeuvre. Selon les tendances culturelles de chaque pays, selon son ancienneté, sa valeur esthétique et le contexte de son lieu de conservation ultérieur, chaque icône pose un problème spécifique.

L'icône de l'Ecole d'Onuphre confiée pour sa restauration par l'Albanie à la France était après son nettoyage dans un état de présentation ne permettant pas d'apprécier pleinement sa valeur esthétique car deux problèmes importants restaient posés:

1) Le problème de la grande lacune dans la joue de la Vierge. Le mastic ancien etait en mauvais état de conservation, son réseau de craquelures etait hétérogène, le repeint ancien était esthétiquement impossible à intégrer car sa tonalité etait beaucoup plus sombre que l'original.
2) Le problème du repeint du fond. Il fallait signaler qu'en l'éliminant, on ne trouverait probablement que la préparation originale, les feuilles d'argent sur bolus ayant presque totalement disparu lors d'un nettoyage ancien; il fallait aussi considérer que l'accès à cette préparation permettrait de la consolider.

Les options devant être prises par les responsables juridiques de l'oeuvre ainsi que par le SRMN, il était important d'interroger le Ministère de la Culture d'Albanie avant de poursuivre et d'aborder la deuxième partie de la restauration.

La décision s'est orientée vers l'élimination complète des repeints et mastics, le rétablissement des éléments métalliques émaillés sur le fond et la réintégration des lacunes profondes. D'un commun accord l'option systématiquement "archéologique" a été rejetée à cause de la situation des lacunes, estimant qu'elle aurait sacrifié la dimension esthétique de l'oeuvre : en exposant des icônes mutilées par des lacunes situées dans les visages, on méconnaît son principe essentiel qui doit être la représentation du monde transfiguré et non un témoignage historique, un document chirurgical vidé de son message. Nous avons choisi ensemble une retouche rétablissant la continuité formelle, exécutée dans le technique de l'icône, sans interprétation et en laissant un fin liseré autour des lacunes pour établir une solution de continuité entre l'adjonction et l'original. Ce choix permet lecture et contemplation de l'oeuvre sans apporter de trouble tout en respectant les principes de la restauration moderne puisque la topographie des lacunes reste parfaitement discernable.

Conclusion

Cette collaboration a été l'occasion d'une réflexion commune entre restaurateurs de l'Est et de l'Ouest autour d'une icône de grande valeur artistique. Sur le plan du dégagement du surpeint elle a permis d'expérimenter ensemble le travail à sec, sous microscope binoculaire, à l'aide d'un scalpel et d'en comparer le résultat avec celui du sondage effectué sur la même icône avec des solvants.[5] Aucun de ces deux restaurateurs albanais ne connaissaient ce type de traitement. Ils ont été convaincus de sa supériorité incontestable.[6] Cette collaboration a également permis de constater une fois encore que le traitement des lacunes d'une icône est subtil et que chaque cas doit être attentivement étudié.

Notes et Références

1. T. Popa, «Icônes et miniatures du Moyen Age en Albanie-Tirana» (1974).
2. Analyses par le Centre Technique du Bois.
3. Analyses par l'Institut Textile de France.
4. Analyses des pigments et liants effectuées au Laboratoire de Recherche des Musées de France par E. de Brevern Joukoff.
5. O. Lélékova, "Problème de restauration des icônes russes," *ICOM Committee for Conservation 11th Triennial Meeting Preprints, Dresden* (1990): 772–776.
6. Cette méthode est pratiquée au State Research Institute For Restoration à Moscou sous la direction de O. Lélékova qui l'a transmise à N. Delsaux.

Investigation into the Deformations of Panel Paintings

K. Dreiner,* P. Klein, I. Zillich
Universität Hamburg, Ordinariat für Holzbiologie,
21027 Hamburg, Germany

Abstract

The influence of environmental variations on dimensional stability and conservation of panel paintings is an important and not sufficiently known subject. Changes of wood moisture content may cause significant dimensional variations and deformations in panel paintings, and induce deformations and stresses due to differential shrinkage or swelling. Often shrinkage/swelling behaviour seriously damages the colour layers as well. Such developments have not yet been sufficiently applied in the field of panel paintings, where phenomena connected to moisture and energy transfer, rheology and hygromechanical behaviour are of the greatest significance. An approach to this subject was taken by recording the surface form of historical panel paintings with a self developed measuring device. The results show characteristic deformation patterns for wood species, growth ring orientation, and colour layer.

Keywords

Panel paintings, dimensional stability, warping, deformation, environmental stresses

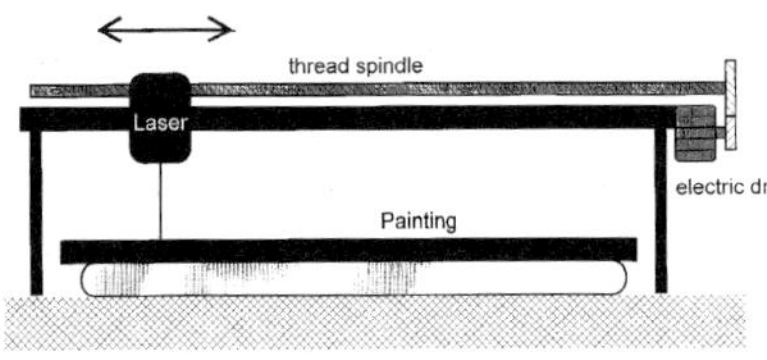

Figure 1. General layout of the measuring unit

Introduction

It is well known that environmental stresses like temperature and moisture variations cause significant dimensional variations and deformations in panel paintings. Shrinking and swelling induce stresses in the wood as well as between the wooden support and the colour layers. During the long lifetime of panel paintings these stresses often result in permanent plastic deformations. Many authors have described damage to panel paintings caused by these factors.[1–3]

Some common deformation patterns like convex warping have been identified, but up to now there has been no systematic investigation of the form and amount of the deformation of panel paintings. For that reason a two-year research project in this field was begun, supported by DFG (Deutsche Forschungsgemeinschaft), by monitoring and identifying the actual deformations of ancient painted panels.

The measurement system

The surface form of a painting is described by the x, y and z coordinates of a set of surface spots. Coordinate data is obtained by moving a measuring sensor along the x and y axes in a plane. The z coordinate of each observed surface spot is then determined by measuring the distance between the measuring plane and the surface of the painting. Essentially the deformations are influenced by structural properties of the wooden support, which has to be considered when deciding on the measuring grid. Since the surface profiles of a painting perpendicular to the grain are very similar, but differ distinctively along the grain a measuring grid was chosen with a step of 1 mm across the grain (x-axis) and 100 mm along the grain. The measuring device consists of an optical distance sensor attached to a linear runner (Figure 1). A thread spindle moves the sensor in the x direction. After each

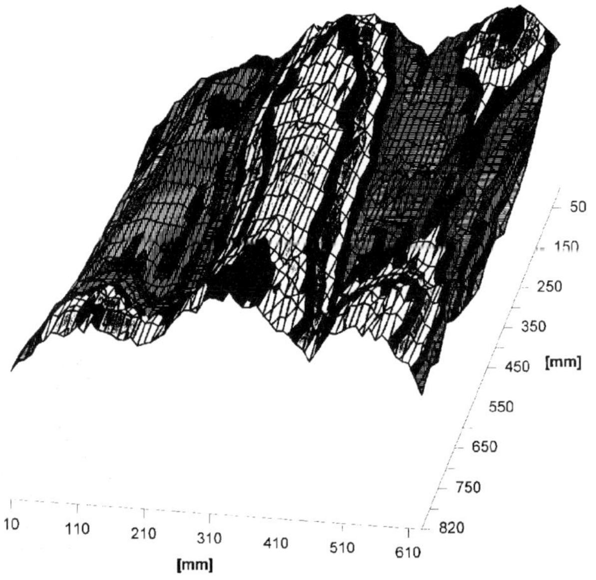

Figure 2. Three-dimensional plot of the surface deformations of a panel painting

*Author to whom correspondence should be addressed

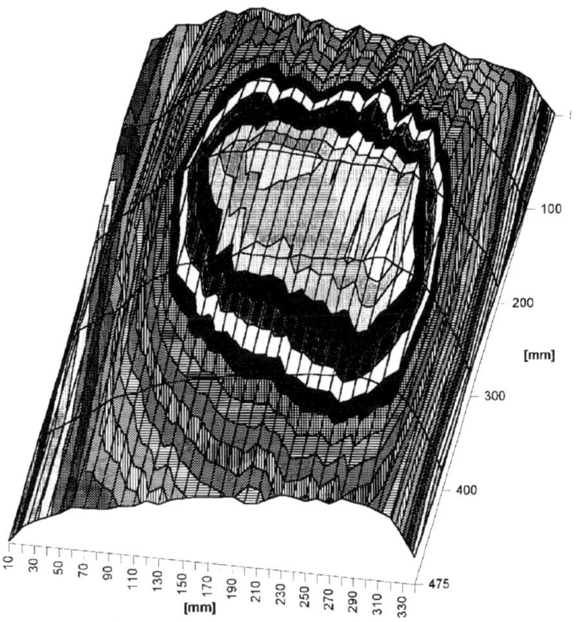

Figure 3. Different amounts of warping caused by permeability variations in the colour layers

1 mm step a reading is taken. Positioning in the *y* direction is done manually. Tests with different painting materials have proved that the low-energy beam of this sensor-type does not affect the colour layers at all.

Measurements were taken in Munich (Bayerisches Nationalmuseum) and Frankfurt (Städelsches Kunstinstitut). The data allow visualisation of the surface form (Figure 2) as well as computations of deformation ratio.

The deviations are plotted on a large scale so that the plots even show deformations not visible to the naked eye. It was found that specific deformation patterns coincide with wood species, panel thickness, growth ring orientation, different cradle systems, and characteristics of the colour layers. So, for example, the pronounced warping in the middle area of one painting (Figure 3) is likely caused by less permeable colour coating.

Frequently restorers have to decide whether a cradle system attached to the back may affect a painting. Paintings with back-side cradle often show typical, pronounced deformation patterns (Figure 4). While paintings without a cradle show regular warping over the total surface, this painting shows several single deformations in the spaces between the cradle ledges. The deformation ratio, which is a good indication of possible damage to the colour layers, is much bigger than in panels without a supporting cradle. Actually, detached colour layers were often found, especially near the cradle ledges. In this special case two cradle ledges

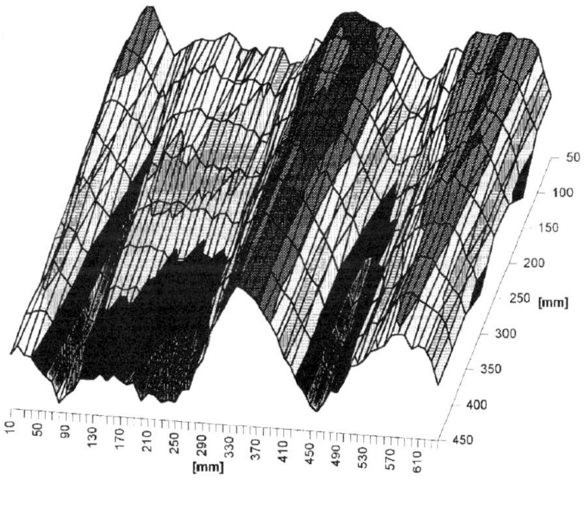

Figure 4. Deformatio patterns caused by the cradle system

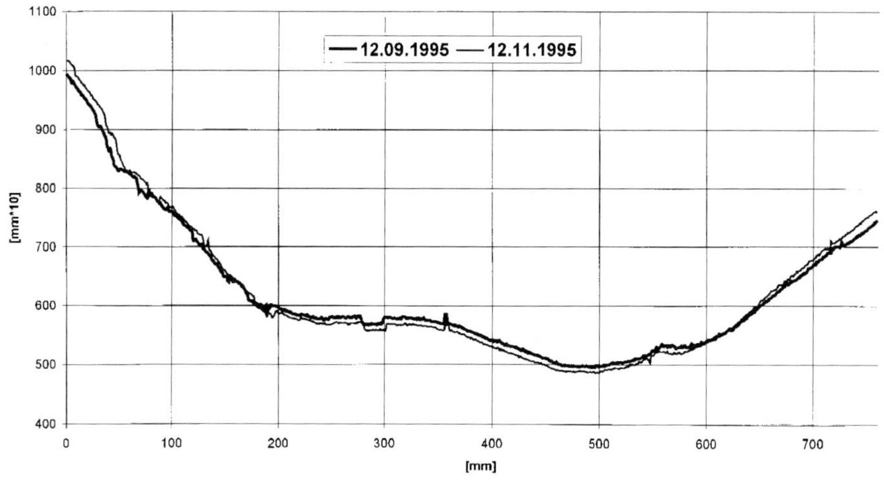

Figure 5. Deformations due to climate changes

are situated exactly under the two pronounced warpings on the right-hand side, which means that they have become loosened from the back of the panel. So if there is a question of whether a cradle system can be removed or not, this measuring method can give a good indications of the effects of doing so.

Monitoring panel movements

Scanning the surface form is not only useful for identifying the actual deformation, but can also be used to measure panel movements induced by climate changes or transport. The comparison of two readings taken before and after climate changes (Figure 5) show exactly the deformations that appear in the mean time. For example, the thick and the thin lines in Figure 5 show the surface profiles of a painting taken before and after a two-month interval. The later reading indicates shrinking of the panel, as well as stronger warping. In this special case the painting was treated with water soluble materials that had moistened the wood before the first measurement. Although the increase of moisture content is supposed to have been very small, the movements were probably caused by later drying. Since permanent movements may lead to damage to the colour layers, in some cases it may be necessary to observe the bending, stretching or compression in the panel surface. The described scanning system provides an accurate and reliable method to record these movements

Conclusions

Scanning of panel painting surfaces gives an overview of characteristic deformation patterns and allows conclusions regarding the origin of panel deformations. It also gives an additional chance to predict the effects of restoration or other intervention. If, for example, the readings show loosened glue edges or cradle detatchment, it is more likely that removal of the cradle system is possible without damage. Additionally scanning can be used to monitor deformations due to climate change or transport.

References

1. Buck, R.D. "Some applications of mechanics to the treatment of panelpaintings" in *Recent Advantages in Conservation, Contributions to the IIC Rome Conference, 1961*, ed. G. Thompson, (London: Butterworths, 1963), 156–162.
2. L. Uzielli and O. Casazza, *Conservazione dei Dipinti su Tavola* (Firenze: Ministero dell'Universita e della Ricerca Scientifica e Tecnologica-Universita di Firenze, 1992), 120–142.
3. Bünsche, B. "Schäden an der Grundier- und Malschicht an Holztafelbildern", *Restauro* 4 (July–August 1993), 246–249.

Studies on the Deacidification of Canvas Supports with Magnesium Methoxy Methyl Carbonate (MMC)

Stephen Hackney,* Joyce Townsend, Nicolas Wyplosz
Conservation Department, Tate Gallery, Millbank,
London SW1P 4RG, UK

Abstract

Scanning electron microscopy–energy-dispersive X-ray analysis (SEM-EDX), Fourier transform Infrared (FTIR), Raman microscopy and X-ray photo-electron spectroscopy (XPS) methods were used to assess the penetration of deacidification solutions of magnesium methoxymethylcarbonate (MMC) in methanol and trifluorochloroethane applied to new and aged primed linen canvases. Differences in penetration were observed by the distribution of magnesium (Mg) and these were related to methods of application in order to devise better procedures and understand the likely protection provided. Conditions varied from excessive accumulation of Mg on the reverse to salts being deposited on the front by passage through cracks in the priming.

Keywords

Canvas, deacidification, Mg, MMC, painting, SEM-EDX, XPS, FTIR

Introduction

The application of weakly alkaline material has been proposed as a means of protecting from acidic degradation linen or cotton canvas used in oil painting supports.[1] This is proposed not only as a treatment for severely degraded canvas before lining but also as a treatment for canvas which substantially retains its original strength.[2] Such a preventive treatment has the potential for extending considerably the useful lifetime of a canvas and for deferring the need to line a painting for a significant time. Artificial ageing of paper and textiles and experience of natural ageing of paper suggest that deacidification which leaves an alkaline reserve or buffer can reduce the rate of hydrolysis by an order of magnitude.

Alkali reacts with acidic breakdown products from the oxidation of cellulose and with deposited pollutants from external sources or from the immediate environment of a canvas. It thereby prevents acid hydrolysis which would otherwise cause scission of long-chain cellulose molecules, leading to embrittlement and loss of strength. If an excess of alkaline material is applied it will remain to prevent future acidity. Provided the pH of the canvas is not made too high, the conditions for alkaline hydrolysis are not created.

Despite considerable study of the physical and mechanical problems associated with oil painting supports, effective lining treatments remain elusive. Indeed, an increased understanding of the forces within the painting composite and their changes with environmental conditions and time suggest that lining may never be an effective solution. For many modern paintings future treatments will be even more problematic. Preservation of the original support is therefore a worthwhile aim.

A limited number of deacidification treatments has been carried out over several years to gain experience[3] and to detect any possible side-effects[4]. Long-term effects are best assessed by artificially accelerating any mechanism of change. Absolute certainty is therefore not possible, but so far no serious consequences have been identified. Short-term effects such as the problems of application can be studied more directly. The present study is to discover how well alkaline material is distributed throughout a canvas painting using our currently favoured methods of application of magnesium methoxymethylcarbonate (MMC).[5,6]

The main concerns during application are the need to use organic solvents such as methanol and Freon (trifluorochloroethane). Methanol can swell oil primings and paint films and if it comes into contact with the varnish will swell and dissolve it. It is also toxic. Freon is very volatile and has less opportunity to swell paint media. However, because fluorinated and chlorinated hydrocarbons accumulate in the Earth's upper atmosphere and contribute to damage of the ozone layer, its future use cannot be guaranteed. The dangers that solvent and magnesium salts might reach the paint and varnish layers or conversely fail to penetrate sufficiently to protect the canvas fibres from internally generated acidity were investigated.

The aims of this experimental study were:

*Author to whom correspondence should be addressed.

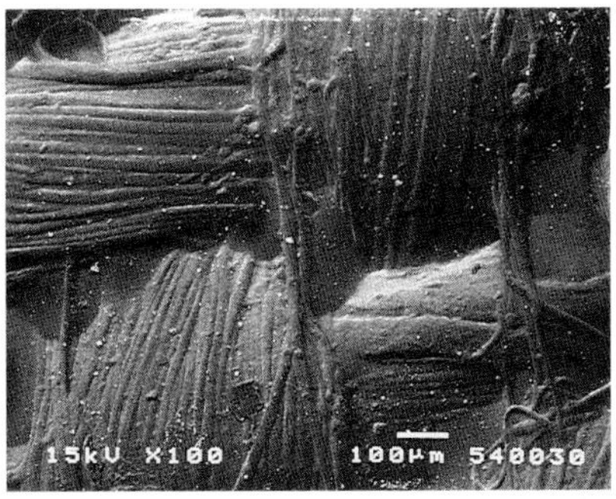

Figure 1. LVSEM image of modern glue-sized linen canvas, showing coatings of fibres by the size film, and bridging of the interstices by the glue film.

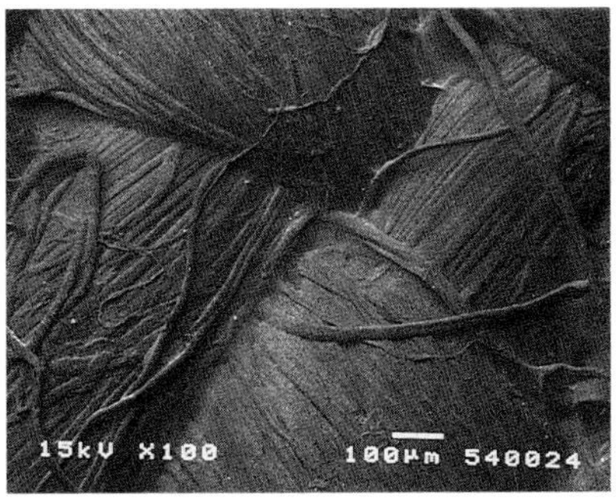

Figure 2. LVSEM image of the same canvas, submitted to 5 successive weeks of thermal and UV-free light ageing, alternating each week. The fibres are still coated and bridged by the size film, and no surface fissuring is evident.

- to seek ways of mapping the distribution of magnesium carbonate within a canvas;
- to compare the efficiency of different application methods, such as brushing and spraying;
- to compare the effect of a single treatment versus several, with different intervals between treatment;
- to see whether partly-reacted MMC from a previously-opened bottle was still effective;
- to check whether, and in what circumstances, Mg compounds penetrate to the surface of the paint (a white surface powder on varnished, deacidified canvases has been noted previously[2]).

Methods of application of MMC

MMC reacts with water to form magnesium hydroxide, which then converts to magnesium carbonate, volatile ethanol and carbon dioxide gas. Because MMC reacts with moisture in the atmosphere as well as moisture in canvas fibres, the one-litre bottles normally supplied begin to deteriorate as soon as they are opened. Bubbling through dry argon or nitrogen gas, to fill the dead volume, prevents this. It was our normal practice to decant the MMC into 100 ml bottles and fill each dead space with argon, repeating this after each opening. This ensures that most of the initial (somewhat expensive) supply can ultimately be used. Dry nitrogen, when available, is a cheaper gas to use for more extensive work.

MMC was applied in a realistic manner to canvases kept in typical museum environments, which is to say at room temperature (16–22°C) and an RH of 50%. It is therefore to be expected that the fibres will have a significant moisture content.

Brushing of canvas samples was done, for simplicity, with the samples face-down on a table. The solvent soon evaporates, and the second brushstroke is applied to an already dry-looking canvas, which makes it impossible to coat a large surface without double-brushing some areas and missing others.

Spraying was carried out with a hand-pumped sprayer chosen because it can be used with only 20 ml of liquid in the chamber. (The excess in the chamber must be discarded, since it has reacted with moisture. Sometimes it reacts quickly enough to block the sprayer, which is unblocked by opening the chamber first, not the aperture, and clearing out the aperture.) The sprayer works best when the samples are near-vertical, and masked if they are small, to prevent the solution running under them.

Transport of solvents within yarns

Canvas is a woven fabric, which is generally coated on both sides with glue or other size. A heavily-sized canvas may in effect have the yarns immersed in size. Scanning electron microscopy (SEM) imaging of the surface of both modern and 19th century canvases shows a fairly continuous film of low-MW material bridging intersecting yarns, and coating the highest fibres (Figures 1 and 2). It is much harder to obtain images that distinguish between coated and immersed canvases. In older canvases, this size layer is assumed to be cracked, since it responds rapidly to variations in relative humidity, but is constrained by stiffer materials which react more slowly to such changes. The size layer, when aged, may be cracked internally, or on the interfacial side to the paint: no fissures were seen on the reverse side during SEM examination of 100- and 150-year-old stretched canvases.

A liquid applied to the reverse of the canvas has to pass through the film of size to reach the fibres. It is likely to be transported along the length of the outermost fibres, ie across, rather than into, the canvas. Drops of dyed methanol illustrate this: they spread instantly, then penetrate the canvas. If the fibres are twisted, a fast means of transport in the canvas plane is provided. But penetration from one fibre to the next one in is slower, probably weave-dependent, and may in practice be negated by evaporation of the delivery solvent and drawing out of the MMC before it has reacted with moisture in the fibre. The MMC probably takes some minutes to form hydroxide, and then a longer period, perhaps hours, to form carbonate, whereas methanol transport and evaporation takes place in seconds.

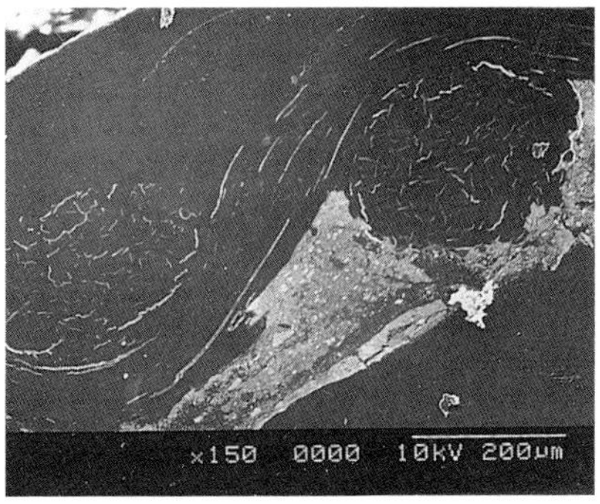

Figure 3. SEM image of primed, modern glue-sized canvas after MMC treatment, embedded in Spurr resin and microtomed.

An inefficient method of application of MMC might result in a surface-accumulation of a film of magnesium hydroxide, converting to magnesium carbonate, which would impede the penetration into the canvas of subsequent applications of MMC. If it happened immediately after application, there might be a period during which further applications are especially ineffective at penetrating the canvas.

Very open-weave canvases may allow methanol and MMC to reach the priming layer directly, through gaps in the weave, which are not completely bridged by the size layer. Aged ones may also have cracked and damaged size-layers.

Cracks in paint and priming provide a means for methanol which has penetrated the canvas to travel through to the paint surface and spread onto it, by capillary transport through the cracks.

Methods of examination and analysis

Samples (either free or embedded canvas) were coated with carbon, and examined in a Hitachi S-2400 SEM. Both the reverse of canvas samples, i.e. the treated side, and the front were imaged. Energy-dispersive X-ray analysis (EDX) was carried out on small areas, including those near to cracks in the paint or priming on the front of the canvas, using a Link ISIS detector for secondary electrons, and Link ISIS and software. This detector is more sensitive to elements of low atomic number, e.g. Mg, than the detectors used with earlier Link packages. With the latter, Mg in treated canvas was barely detectable. A limited number of uncoated samples were examined in a JEOL JSM-5400-LV low vacuum SEM with an air pressure of $5–7 \times 10^{-2}$ torr in the sample chamber.

Cross-sections of canvas were prepared and embedded in the typical manner for paint cross-sections, by embedding in Metset FT polyester resin, grinding with water and silicon carbide paper, and then polishing dry with Micromesh cushioned silicon carbide paper. But Mg applied by a typical MMC process proved to be only just detectable, and it was feared that polishing was removing it selectively from the surface. Another concern that could not be discounted was that the embedding resin, while liquid, might mobilise Mg compounds and re-distribute them in the threads, by capillary transport along the cut ends of fibres. Further samples were embedded in Spurr low-viscosity epoxy resin and cut dry at room temperature with a diamond knife, the last 20–30 passes being set to cut 5 nm only, so as not to spread out sample material, and thus to eliminate this problem with semi-quantitative spot analyses of Mg, or elemental mapping of Mg. These samples were also coated with carbon, and provided good images of the layer structure (e.g. Figure 3).

(Attempts to microtome polyester-embedded sections of aged canvas and brittle lead/oil primings were unsuccessful at room temperature, both with glass and diamond knives. FTIR microscopy and mapping in transmission had been planned for the thin sections, as a means of visualising the Mg carbonate deposited in the yarns. Fourier transform infrared (FTIR) microscopy in reflectance mode was noise-limited to such an extent that the carbonate peak could not be distinguished from cellulose peaks from the canvas fibres. Raman microscopy and FT Raman of the reverse of treated samples also failed to detect Mg carbonate, perhaps because it has poor crystallinity, and this technique too might have been more successful in transmission, on thin sections.)

Treated and untreated samples of canvas of diameter 50mm were examined with a VG Escalab 220 I XL system for X-ray photoelectron spectroscopy (XPS). This can give quantitative results on surface elemental concentrations within a narrow depth, typically a few nanometres. Comparison of the quantitation at different Auger energies for the same element can reveal if it is regularly distributed through the first 2-8nm of the depth of the sample. (In principle, destructive ion-beam etching of the surface would allow greater depths to be examined.)

Results

Raman spectroscopic techniques failed to reveal any Mg compounds on the reverse of a treated canvas, though EDX showed Mg to be present even where it had not formed a crystalline deposit (Figure 4). This suggests that the Mg on the

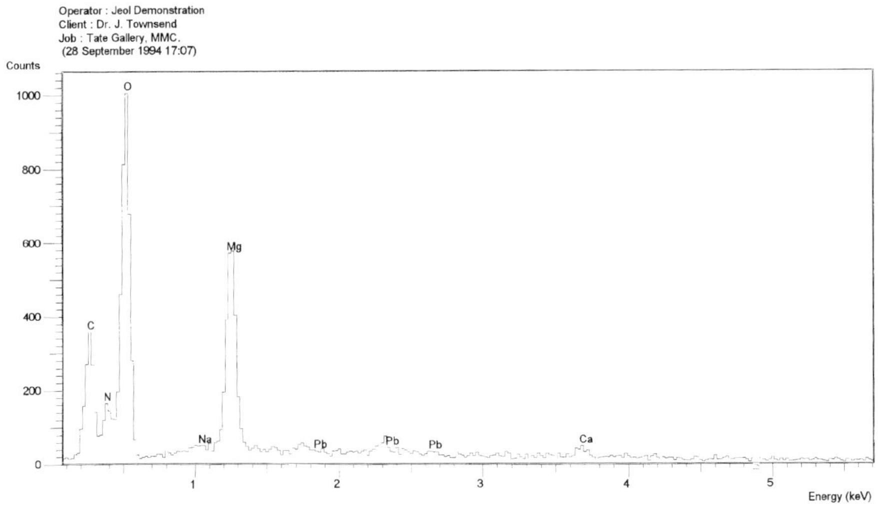

Figure 4. EDX spot analysis of modern glue-sized canvas after MMC treatment, an area with a filmed appearance but no crystals. Magnesium (Mg) is readily detectable. Traces of lead are due to fragments of lead white priming scattered over the sample during cutting. Calcium (Ca, presumed to be chalk) is found in most modern and all 19th century size layers examined thus far. Sodium (Na) contamination, from handling of the canvas, is nearly always picked up by this detector.

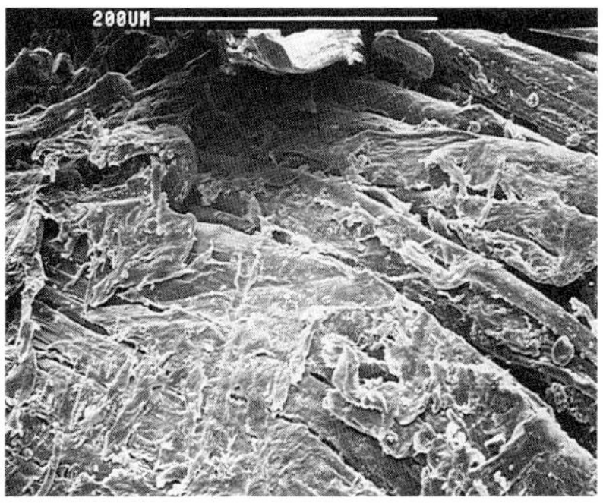

Figure 5. SEM image of canvas after MMC treatments. The Mg-rich film is thicker than glue size films.

surface is fine-grained and poorly crystallised. The former is advantageous for a film intended to remain present in the long term: fine grains may bond more firmly to the canvas fibres than would coarse ones.

SEM studies of cross-sections of primed canvases and qualitative interpretation of EDX spectra gave the most useful results.

Surface uptake is similar for brushing and spraying (Figure 5). However, brushing leads to improved penetration of the whole thickness of the yarn.

Treating two or three times with a few hours drying between applications improves uptake by three and five times respectively, compared to successive treatments at intervals of only a few minutes.

Treatment more than three or four times leaves on the surface of the canvas a friable, rough magnesium-rich film (presumed to be the carbonate), which has a poor chance of survival, and consequently reduced potential as a long-term alkaline reserve, or as a physical protection against the ingress of pollutant gases.

Samples treated with a large amount of MMC, for example by immersion, or brushed/sprayed several times with only minutes between applications, had a thicker film on the reverse side than glue size alone could account for, and no improved penetration through the thread (Figure 6).

Slightly cloudy, previously opened samples of MMC are just as effective as newly-opened ones, although there is risk of leaving white deposits on the canvas reverse surface.

Already-aged canvases (100 and 150 years) may have a slightly poorer uptake of MMC than new ones, but the effect is small.

Mg could be detected on the priming/paint side near cracks, i.e. cracks did allow penetration of MMC to the front (and aged canvases are more likely to have cracked primings).

The limited XPS study showed that the Mg concentration was higher on the immediate surface than at a depth of just a few nanometres, i.e. it confirmed that there is a very thin crust of it on the surface, hindering penetration by later applications of MMC.

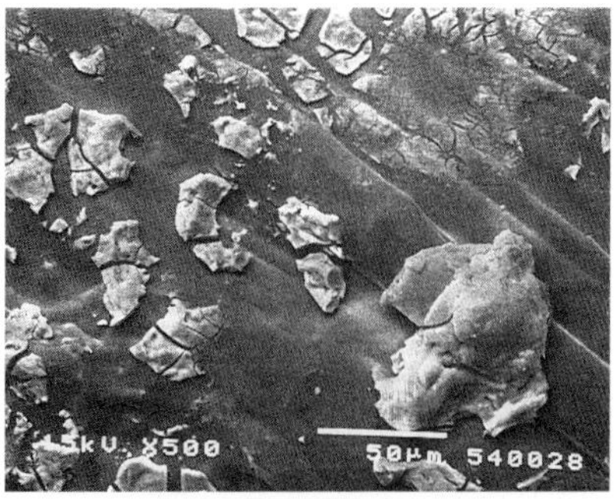

Figure 6. SEM image of modern glue-sized linen canvas, 'over-treated' with MMC, showing Mg-rich friable flakes on the surface.

Conclusions

Methanol solvent (5% in Freon) can be applied safely to the reverse of a canvas of an oil painting provided suitable precautions are taken, such as ensuring that the solvent is free to evaporate and is not trapped at the front of the work. However, methanol and Freon are readily drawn through by capillary forces in the canvas yarns and any cracks in the priming and paint layers. For this reason it is advisable to deacidify cracked and varnished paintings only after varnish removal or during treatment of the support (when access to the reverse is better). MMC solution also spreads laterally ensuring an even application across a canvas. Because of these capillary effects Mg can be deposited effectively within the woven structure. Most thorough application is obtained by brushing two coats separated by adequate drying time. Spraying produces more even results, less risk to the paint/varnish surface but less penetration. Accumulation of Mg on the reverse should be avoided since this forms a barrier to further application.

Work is continuing in order to assess deacidification methods and their side effects and to devise optimum procedures. MMC appears to be the best choice of deacidification if moisture cannot be employed. Alternatives used in paper conservation have not been investigated thoroughly but most have some drawbacks, such as requiring unacceptably dry conditions. At present the aim of treating relatively unaged canvases is not yet feasible since the risks are not sufficiently assessed and various practicalities restrict the employment of effective procedures. The value of thorough penetration of MMC has not been established. Future studies will involve artificial ageing of treated samples to assess the protection provided by different types of application and also attempt to identify MMC penetration within the yarns.

Acknowledgements

The authors are grateful to the following people who provided analytical equipment and training in its use to NW: Andrew Beard, Birkbeck College, London and Mike Faulkner, Royal Holloway, London (EDX), Marcus Daniels, University College London (Raman spectrocopy); John Forsdyke, Oxford Microscopy Services, UK (microtomy); Geoff Henshaw, University College, London (XPS); Kristine Moore, Birkbeck College, London and Matthew Murray of the Building Research Establishment, UK (FTIR); Marianne Odlyha, Birkbeck College, London (TMA); Andrew Yarwood and Roger Hockham, JEOL (UK) Ltd (LVSEM).

References

1. S.J. Hackney, G.A. Hedley, "Linen Canvas Artificially Aged" (Paper delivered at the Seventh Triennial Meeting of the International Council of Museums Committee for Conservation, Copenhagen, 1984), Vol. 2.16–21.
2. Stephen Hackney, Torben Ernst, "The Applicability of Alkaline Reserves To Painting Canvases", *Preventive Conservation*, IIC, Ottawa (1994), 223–227.
3. N. Ryder, "Acidity in Canvas Painting Supports: Deacidification of Two 20th Century Paintings", *The Conservator* 10 (1986): 31–36.
4. N. Ryder, "Deacidification of the Canvas Supports of Paintings", Student Research Project, Courtauld Institute of Art, University of London (1984).
5. G.B. Kelly et al., US Patent No: 3,939,091 (February 17, 1976).
6. R.D. Smith, US Patent No: 4,318,963 (March 9, 1982).

Materials

- MMC 60:40 ethyl:methyl Mg carbonate (4.7% methanol vol/vol) Conservation Resources (UK) Ltd, Unit 1,2 &4 Pony Road, Horspath Industrial Estate, Cowley, Oxford OX4 2RD.

The Consolidation of Paintings on Copper Supports

Isabel Horovitz
The Painting Conservation Studio,
Unit 208B Belgravia Workshops, 157-163 Marlborough Road
London N19 4NP, UK

Abstract

Flaking paintings on copper supports can be extremely difficult to treat. This paper discusses some possible causes of delamination of the paint layer, includes observations on the presence of copper oleate beneath the paint film, and certain aspects of preparatory techniques. A range of conventional treatments and materials used for consolidation of these paintings is reviewed. Some effects of the copper support that may influence the choice of consolidant and method of application are considered, such as lack of diffusion of solvents through the support, reactions of consolidants with copper, and use of heat. Different types of flaking are identified, and broad suggestions for their treatment given. Fillers are mentioned briefly. The fundamental principle is that paintings on copper require specifically appropriate attention.

Keywords

Paintings, copper supports, delamination, consolidants, fillers, treatment methods

Introduction

Painting on copper became popular in Europe from the latter half of the 16th century until the mid-18th century, and by this time, began to flourish in Spain's American colonies. Paintings on copper are often found to be in extraordinarily good state of preservation, or in appalling condition, with widespread delamination and loss of the paint film.

Delamination of the paint film

It is not clear why some paintings survive well and others fare so badly, as little systematic evidence has been gathered. There are a number of possible factors which play their part in the delamination processes; some will be similar to cleavage in paintings on canvas or wood, others relate particularly to copper supports. Some aspects of the latter will be outlined briefly, but it is not intended to discuss either corrosion mechanisms or deformation of sheet metals, studies of which are extensively covered in scientific and archaeological literature.

The rigidity of heavily beaten plates and the durability of copper under normal indoor conditions provide good reasons for the excellent, sometimes pristine condition of these paintings. Mechanical damage, by poor handling and flexing, and often brutal fitting into frames must account for much of the delamination of paint films, which can be dramatic in appearance.

The extent to which corrosion may be responsible for delamination is unknown, but it is not frequently encountered. Environmental factors may affect adhesion of the paint film to the support, but is less likely to be the primary cause in many cases. If active corrosion of the copper has occurred, as distinct from reactions between paint or ground media and the support, crusty corrosion products will protrude from beneath the paint film or emerge through crackle systems. This is highly unusual and its discussion is outside the scope of this paper.

It is important to highlight the distinction between reactions occurring as a result of contact between the copper and the media, and visibly active or destructive corrosion of the support. A film of copper oleate is formed when linseed, poppy and nut oils (and others) are applied to the surface of copper. This is due to the reaction of copper ions with the fatty acid content of the oils and should not be regarded negatively as corrosion. Indeed, it is sometimes thought that this layer, which can be seen in cross-section samples or under magnification at the edges of damages, can help to bond the ground and paint film to the copper.[1] Typically thin, vividly transparent green, and non-particulate, copper oleate has been observed on a number of finely preserved paintings. A well-known example is Guercino's "Angels Weeping over the Dead Christ" (National Gallery, London).

Comparatively few paintings on copper have undergone extensive analytical investigation (particularly of media), which would increase understanding of the part played by the formation of copper oleate in respect of adhesion to the support. There are paintings with a history of flaking, which on examination, also have a layer of copper oleate. Interestingly, though perhaps not surprisingly, it is found on the underside of detached flakes, and is clearly part of the paint film – its bond with the copper substrate has failed. Factors such as whether oil was applied as a separate preparatory layer, or whether it sank to the bottom of the ground layer

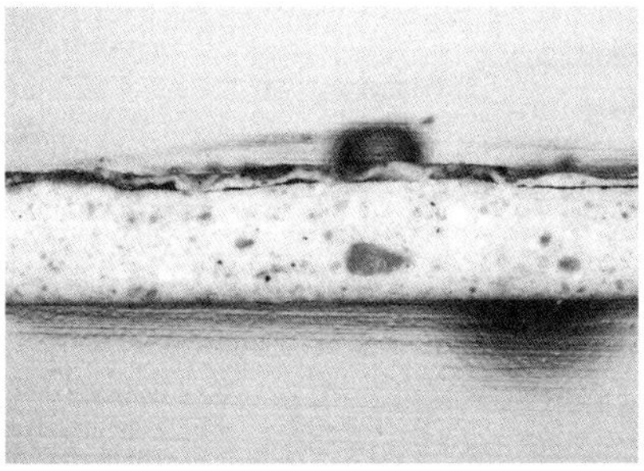

Figure 1. Cross-section, 100× magnification, from oil on copper by George Brookshaw, early eighteenth century, Private collection

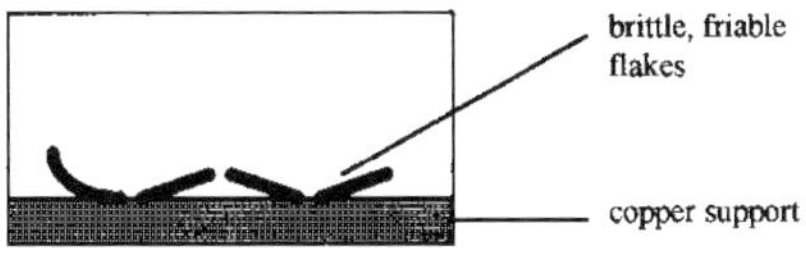

Figure 2. Raised brittle flakes

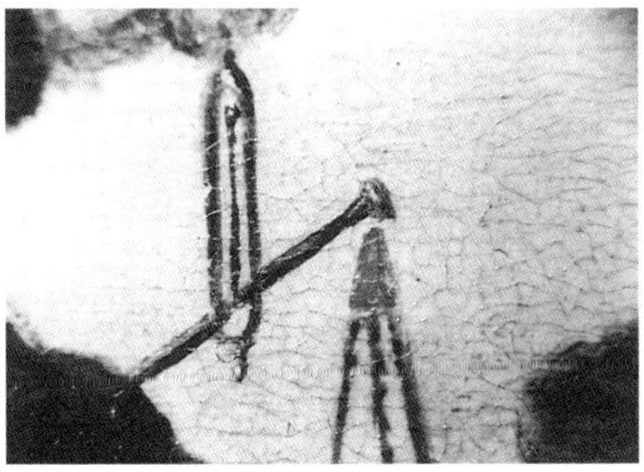

Figure 3. Detail, Avercamp, "Winter Landscape with a Frozen River and Figures", c.1620, The Harold Samuel Collection, Corporation of London

Figure 4. Thin curled flakes

or paint film and then reacted with the copper, the thickness of the ground and paint layers, and the ratio of medium to lead white or other constituents of the ground, must be relevant.

In one example of severe delamination, an unusually thick ground layer was present, the underside of which was pale green, and opaque (Figure 1). The complete lack of adhesion to the support beneath, despite the presence of some copper oleate,[2] may have been due to inadequate medium-to-pigment ratio. More saturation of a thinner ground layer might have provided a stronger bond. Palomino, writing in 1715–24, on "Why many Excellent Pictures Flake", observes that it is an "infallible rule that the thinner the imprimación... the more secure, solid, and durable the painting will be".[3]

Clearly the preparatory techniques, whether used deliberately or coincidentally, due to plates having been obtained or used previously for engraving or etching,[4] could affect the subsequent adhesion of the paint layers.

Copper plates were undoubtedly easier and quicker to prepare than wooden panels, but still required roughening, degreasing or cleaning, to provide a fresh surface to accept the paint film. There are references in the literature to garlic, ashes, pumice and linseed oil having been used either to roughen the plate or to remove etching acids and waxes.[5] Any of these substances and practices which may have been in current use, particularly as etching plates are described as sold "ready polished",[6] could in some way alter the adhesive properties of copper oleate or paint layers.

The extent to which surface roughening itself may also play a part is inconclusive. Lack of it is usually cited as a cause of delamination, with good reason.[7] However, examples of surface roughening have been seen, yet delamination has occurred, perhaps due to mechanical damage.[8]

Coatings, such as lead–tin alloys, lead, tin or zinc, were sometimes applied to copper plate and some of these have been analysed or reported.[9] Occasional instances of gold or other metal leaf having been applied, either over a ground or directly oil gilded onto the copper, have been observed.[10] It is suggested that artists may have been experimenting with coatings in order to ensure good adhesion of the paint film to the support, or that such experiments were conceived for aesthetic reasons. The incredible luminosity achieved in the work of Elsheimer, who often used tinned copper, and in Reni's "The Coronation of the Virgin" (National Gallery, London), coated with a lead–tin alloy, analysed spectrographically, would seem to bear this out. Effects on subsequent adhesion for coated plates are not possible to assess, because insufficient examples have been examined.

Types of flaking

Inevitably, variations on the types and extent of flaking will be such that each case will present individual problems. However, some broad categories which have been observed will be described.

The commonest form of flaking is illustrated in Figure 2, and the brittle, raised flakes can be tiny or quite large. The cracks may be filled with degenerated varnish and bulky old consolidating material. A painting illustrating this is shown in Figure 3.

Thin, curled flakes of the type shown in Figure 4 may detach if the painting is not kept flat in a completely draught-free environment. An added complication is that such paintings are often covered in surface dirt. The handling problems presented by these paintings prior to and during conservation are obviously considerable. A painting with this type of flaking is illustrated in Figure 5.[11]

The is the most difficult category of flaking to assess and to treat is that associated with blind blisters and cleavage (Figure 6). On initial examination, it may appear that the problem is localised; however, once treatment begins it can become apparent that delamination is widespread. In these cases especially, the lack of diffusion of the solvent into the support presents major practical problems. A dramatic example of blind blistering is illustrated in Figure 7.

Past and current treatments

Generally, paintings on copper have been treated in much the same way as wooden panels and canvas paintings, and the choice of consolidants used has followed the normal customs of the studio concerned. There has been little attempt to look at the specific needs of paintings on copper.

It is not surprising, therefore, to find that virtually the entire range of consolidants from beeswax, wax–resin mixtures,[12] mastic and stand oil, gelatine, other animal or fish glues, to BEVA 371®, poly(vinyl acetate), and acrylic solutions and dispersions have all been used to consolidate paintings on copper. The rates and indeed the definition of "successful" treatments are impossible to assess, but it is clear that some paintings on copper have a continuous history of flaking despite repeated treatments, that many are only superficially consolidated, and that, sometimes, deterioration can occur as a result of unsatisfactory consolidants.

Figure 5. Detail, Austrian School, "Albert Archduke of Austria (1559-1621)", 17th century. The Royal Collection[l] Her Majesty The Queen

Considerations affecting choice of consolidants specifically for paintings on copper

The main considerations and differences between consolidating a painting on copper as opposed to one on canvas or panel are:

- The consolidant must be capable of adhering paint to metal.
- The solvent can only evaporate through cracks or gaps in the paint film – it cannot penetrate or impregnate the support.
- Some consolidants will react with copper.
- The reliability of a consolidation treatment is unpredictable, and although reversibility is inherently impractical, the consolidant used must not hinder future treatment.

These factors implicitly govern the choice of consolidants, and the methods of their application.

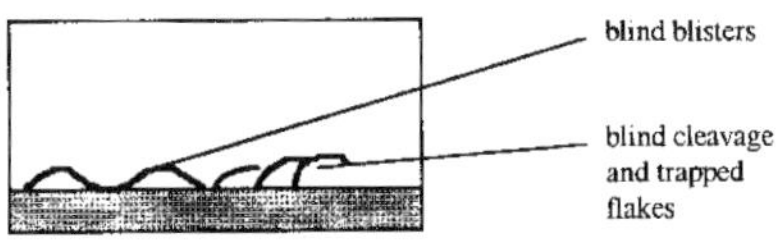

Figure 6. Blind blisters and cleavage

Evaluation of consolidants

The aim of this evaluation was to re-examine samples of consolidants applied to sheet copper in 1981,[13] and to supplement these with more examples, since some have been discontinued, and to comment on handling properties which are of particular concern when used with copper supports. The consolidants were selected on the basis that they are or have been used for consolidating flaking paint film on copper, and not necessarily that they are suitable. Various consolidants were applied to sheet copper, degreased with acetone. These assessments, not intended as a formal study, were based simply on practical observations concerning reactions, adhesion and handling, after one month, and where relevant after 14 years (see Table 1).

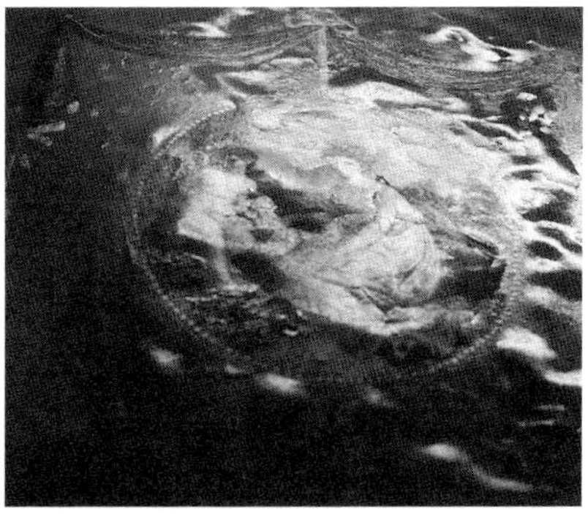

Figure 7. Detail, George Brookshaw, oil on copper, 61 × 51cm, early eighteenth century, Private collection

Methods of application

It will be apparent that there are a number of consolidants which satisfy the basic criteria of stability and good adhesion to copper. However the handling of the consolidants with respect to the various types of delamination encountered is by no means easy, owing mainly to the problems created by slow evaporation and lack of diffusion into the support of the solvent.

The viscosity of the consolidant used in solution will vary according to individual preference, but it is important to consider the amount of solvent being introduced under a paint film, particularly in the case of a painting with large blind blisters or cleavage (see Figures 6 and 7) If the solids-to-liquid ratio is low, good penetration will be achieved, but evaporation of the solvent will be too slow and adhesion may never take place. Since the solvent will obviously be in prolonged contact with the ground and/or paint layers, it may cause swelling and tests should be carried out. This would be particularly important if Paraloid B48 is used dissolved partly in acetone.[14] (Also, there is a risk in cases of totally unattached flakes, that the flakes will simply float into surrounding areas.) However, if the consolidant is too thick, there is a danger that excessive bulk may be introduced, the removal of which may be difficult, or that adhesion will be uneven beneath the blisters. A solution between 10% and 20% (of B72, or B72 + B48S in toluene, for example) may prove useful, and it may be necessary to inject the consolidant with a syringe.

Table 1. Observations on consolidants applied to sheet copper

Consolidant	Visible reaction	Adhesion	Handling
Gelatine	No discoloration of film but slight change in colour of copper beneath	None	Cools quickly on contact with copper
Isinglass	As gelatine	Negligible	As gelatine
Sturgeon glue + 50% honey	No change noted but glue is yellow	Good initially but detached after three weeks	As gelatine
Mowilith DMC2	Green/black	Good	Strong surface tension, poor flow on copper
Vinamul 3252	Green tinge	Very good	Satisfactory
Plextol B500	Green tinge Aged sample: green tinge	Good Aged sample: peeled up	Film shrinkage occurred
Mastic + 10% stand oil	No change Aged mastic sample: greeny yellow	Good	Good flow due to turpentine dilution
Lascaux® wax	Mildly yellow	Good	Tacky, poor flow
Wax–resin	Turning yellow	Good	Bulky
Beeswax	Aged sample: vividly green, crusty corrosion beneath	Lifting	Bulky
BEVA® 371	Whitish, opaque Aged sample: unchanged	Very good Aged sample unchanged	Relatively bulky, tacky, solvent and heat required
Bedacryl 122X	Aged sample clear	Aged sample: very good	Solvent concentration difficult to determine
Plexisol P550	No change Aged sample: unchanged	Good Aged sample: still soft (low T_g)	As above
Mowilith 20 AYAB	No change Aged sample: unchanged	Good Aged sample: unchanged	As above
Paraloid B72	No change Aged sample: unchanged	Excellent Aged sample unchanged	As above
Paraloid B48S	No change	Excellent	As above. Stringy when viscous

Heat, which is normally one of the most useful aids to successful consolidation of canvas or panel paintings, is another aspect that becomes unpredictable when used on copper paintings. Since copper is a good conductor of heat, a large area of the support can be heated extremely quickly. In some cases, it is possible that the use of heat could further disturb the already vulnerable bond between the paint and the support. Its use should be restricted to essential cases when it is felt that adhesion is compromised without it. Furthermore, provided adhesion is satisfactory, the return of flakes entirely to plane should not always be considered a top priority, because in the case of extremely brittle flakes (see Figure 2), there is a real risk of damaging the edges of the flakes by even the most gentle pressure, since the support beneath is so rigid.

When heat is considered necessary, and a solvent based consolidant is used, it may be helpful to allow at least 24–48 hours for solvent evaporation to occur. If Melinex has been used to hold flakes in place (tissue is not recommended), it should be applied in very small sections, allowing gaps for solvent evaporation; this also facilitates its removal. If a heated spatula is used while there is still too much solvent in the structure, adhesion will only be temporary. Provided good and thorough access beneath flakes is available, it may be possible to insert small strips of BEVA® Film, and to heat-seal, thus avoiding the use of solvents. A hot air "pen" may occasionally be a useful alternative to a heated spatula.

On contact with a cold copper painting, warmed consolidants, such as animal glues, waxes and BEVA® 371, will cool extremely quickly, with the effect, on their working properties, of restricting flow. This may in some cases effectively rule out their use, if the additional problems created by lower solution concentration and risks of applying widespread heat are taken into consideration.

Manoeuvring displaced flakes individually into position requires the aid of a vacuum tweezer unit, and it is often possible to use tiny quantities of more viscous consolidant, applied precisely to the base of the flake and/or to the copper in the appropriate area of loss, to secure the flake.

It may be feasible in some cases which exhibit very thin, curled up flakes (see Figure 4), but which still retain some basic attachment, to remove surface dirt with a small sable brush, flake by flake, and then to apply a solution of consolidant (such as B72 in toluene) of 10%, by small sable brush, in limited areas at a time. The flakes, as a result of their extreme thinness and light weight, should simply return to plane, and will be secure as they are virtually encapsulated by the consolidant.

The copper support obviously impedes any form of impregnation from the reverse. Attempts to impregnate an entire painting from the front are unsatisfactory, unless it is absolutely clear that the consolidant will penetrate beneath each flake of paint. This is only possible if thick old varnish films are absent and surface dirt removed.

A note on fillers

Inasmuch as the choice of consolidant is affected by the copper support, so too is the choice of filler.[15] As with the consolidants, the range of fillers used has been conventional – oil putties, chalk and glue, and synthetic ready-made proprietary brands. Chalk and Paraloid B72 fills have been used, but are unsatisfactory to apply, and may be disrupted by a B72 isolating varnish, which is advised in order to seal the copper.

Some fillers were applied to sheet copper, and were observed, scratched and the copper beneath deformed when dry. They varied considerably. Rowney Acrylic Texture Paste® was rubbery and difficult to carve, but suitable for small deep losses. Liquitex Acrylic Gesso® was very spreadable and suitable for large flat areas of thin paint loss. Fine Surface Polyfilla® could be useful when coarse texture is required. Plextol B500 could be used with chalk, but adhesion was not as satisfactory, the addition of filler affecting the mechanical properties of the polymer. Chalk added to B48S produced an extremely hard filler, and the advantages of using B48 directly on metal (the inclusion of acrylic acid in the copolymer promoting adhesion to metal), would be outweighed by it being stringy to handle and, like B72, complicate the application of isolating varnish. BEVA® 371 mixed with chalk spontaneously peeled off on drying.

It is assumed that fillers would be applied over a B72 isolating varnish, so that the use of water-based fillers would not pose any corrosion threat. The acrylic fillers would obviously be highly compatible with B72, and they are extremely flexible. Liquitex Gesso®, in particular, appeared to have useful qualities for copper painting fills, being extremely smooth, and easy to carve.

Conclusions

It is clear that not only the consolidant itself needs to be intrinsically effective, but also that the methods of application must be suitable for a copper support and the type of delamination which is present. The successful handling of materials and equipment is, as always, dependent on an individual familiarity, but the specific considerations that these paintings require may call for some adaptation of habitual practice.

While it is generally advisable to use consolidants that are classed as suitable in archaeological conservation for metals, such as Paraloid B72 and B48, or BEVA® 371, the solvent presence needed to ensure penetration may prove difficult to handle in practice. The use of aqueous consolidants is not recommended, not only because of the risk of inducing corrosion, but also because the adhesion to metal is much less satisfactory – non-existent in the case of gelatine, although the good adhesion of sturgeon glue initially was interesting. Of the consolidants requiring heat, BEVA Film® has uses, but materials containing beeswax are not advised, with initial green discoloration eventually leading to corrosion, causing the wax to lift.

Notwithstanding the many practical problems to which attention has been drawn, it is still possible to improve greatly the stability of many flaking paintings on copper. However, despite the most carefully considered and painstakingly applied consolidation treatments, some paintings on copper will continue to be unstable. This must be due to the fact that only localised treatments are feasible, and whilst this may involve treating the entire surface of the painting, it does not necessarily mean that a truly overall consolidation has taken place.

Acknowledgements

I am grateful to many conservators who have shared information with me. In particular, Karen Ashworth, Ruth Bubb, Aviva Burnstock, Jill Dunkerton, Nicholas Eastaugh, Peter Holmes, Gillian Keay, Viola Pemberton-Pigott, Anna Sanden, Nonie Tasker, Jørgen Wadum, Valentine Walsh, Carol Willoughby, and Martin Wyld. Sue Pratt kindly arranged use of the Courtauld Institute of Art Conservation Library. I should also like to thank Michael Komanecky, of the Phoenix Art Museum, Arizona, as project director of a major exhibition of "Old Master Paintings on Copper, 1525–1775", scheduled to open in the USA in 1998, which has provided a focus for research into this field.

Notes and references

1. J.A. van der Graaf, "Development of Oil Paint and the Use of Metal Plates as a Support," (Paper delivered at the IIC Lisbon Congress, 1972) ,139ff. and in *Conservation and Restoration of Pictorial Art,* ed. N.S. Brommelle and P. Smith, (London: Butterworths, 1976), 48–51.
2. Analysis of the sample was carried out by UCL Painting Analysis Ltd.
3. A. Palomino, "El museo pictórico y la escala óptica," in *Artists' Techniques in Golden Age Spain – Six Treatises in Translation*, ed. and translated by Z. Veliz (Cambridge University Press, 1986).
4. E.P. Bowron, " 'Full of Details and Very Subtly and Carefully Executed': Oil Paintings on Copper around 1600," *The International Fine Art Fair* (New York, 1995). Other authors cite rare examples. I have seen or know of eleven examples at present.
5. E.S. Lumsden, *The Art of Etching* (New York: Dover Publications, 1962).
6. M.R.S Beal, *A Study of Richard Symonds: His Italian Notebooks and Their Relevance to Seventeenth Century Painting Techniques* (New York: Garland Publishing Inc., 1984), 291; J.G. Hidalgo, "Principles for Studying the Sovereign and most noble Art of Painting," (1693) in Palamino/Veliz, *Artists' Techniques in Golden Age Spain*, 137–138.
7. A. Scott-Moncrieff, "Conservation and Reconstruction of Two Landscapes on Copper Attributed to F P Ferg at Southampton Art Gallery," *The Picture Restorer*, no.3 (1993): 18–19.
8. I have examined paintings in public and private collections, where surface roughening is evident but the paint film is vulnerable to flaking.
9. K. Andrews, *Adam Elsheimer* , (Oxford University Press 1977), 169–170; R.D. Buck, "Domenichino's Copper Plate" *Bulletin of the American Group, IIC* 2, no.1.(1970); D. Scrase, "Paintings on Copper at Apsley House," *The Victoria and Albert Album* 5 (1986): 40–48.
10. A.B. De Vries, M. Toth-Ubens, and W. Froentjes, *Rembrandt in the Mauritshuis* (Netherlands: Fijthoft and Nordhoff, 1978), 16, 48–55. I am grateful to Charlotte Hale and Katherine Eirk for information on other instances.
11. I am grateful to Karen Ashworth for this example.
12. Musée Magnin, Musée des Beaux Arts Dijon, "Conservation et Restauration", *Peintures des Musées de Dijon: Les Dossiers du Département des Peintures* 27 (Paris: Réunion des Musées Nationaux, 1983)
13. I. Horovitz, "Paintings on copper supports: Techniques, Deterioration and Conservation," *The Conservator* 10 (1986): 44–48.
14. D. Kushel, "Varnish Resins for Conservation - Useful Working Data" (Art Conservation Department, Buffalo State College, April 1988), 6.
15. I am grateful to Nonie Tasker for useful discussions.

Materials

- *Vinamul 3252* (eva dispersion): Vinamul Ltd, Carshalton, Surrey, SM5 2JU, UK. Tel. 0181 669 4422.
- *Mowilith DMC2* (pva emulsion): discontinued.
- *Isinglass, gelatine, beeswax, mastic, stand oil* etc.: Cornelissen & Son, 105 Gt. Russell Street, London WC1 B 3RY, UK.Tel. 0171 636 1045.
- *Sturgeon glue*: I am grateful to Christian Scheidemann for a ready prepared sample, not supplied in connection with copper paintings.
- *Plextol B500* (acrylic dispersion), Paraloid B72, Paraloid B48S: Rohm and Haas (UK)Ltd, Lennig House, 2 Mason's Avenue, Croydon CR9 3NB, UK. Tel. 0181 686 8844.
- *Synacryl 9122X* (acrylic resin, similar to Bedacryl 122X): Cray Valley Ltd, Waterloo Works, Machen, Newport, Gwent NP1 8YN, UK. Tel. 01633 440 356.
- *Mowilith 20 AYAB* (pva): Hoechst Aktiengellschaft, D6230, Frankfurt (Main) 80, Germany.
- *BEVA® 371* and *BEVA Film®*: Conservation Resources (UK) Ltd, Unit 1, Pony Road, Horspath Industrial Estate, Cowley, Oxford OX4 2RD, UK. Tel. 01865 747 755.
- *Liquitex® Acrylic Gesso*: Binney & Smith Inc., Easton, PA 18044-0431 USA.
- *Rowney Acrylic Texture Paste®*: Daler-Rowney, Bracknell, Berkshire, UK. Tel. 01344 424 621
- *Fine Surface Polyfilla®*: Polycell Products Ltd, Broadwater Road, Welwyn Garden City, Herts. AL7 3AZ, UK. Tel. 01707 328 131.

The Discovery of Oil Sketches on the Reverse of "Le Bassin De Jas De Bouffan"

Gillian McMillan
Conservation Department, Guggenheim Museum,
1071 Fifth Avenue, New York, NY 10128, USA

Abstract

The treatment of a landscape painting long accepted but recently questioned as being a painting by Cézanne is described. An X-radiograph made at the Swiss Institute for Art Research revealed what appeared to be a still-life painting on the reverse of the double-lined original canvas. At the Solomon R. Guggenheim Museum, the landscape was cleaned. Cleaning revealed insufficient new information to confirm the attribution to Cézanne. After serious consideration, a decision was made to remove two linings to reveal the image on the reverse. Four small oil sketches were uncovered: a still life, a single bather, a faint landscape and a plant study. The double-sided painting was then re-stretched onto a newly designed double-sided stretcher. While there are many examples of composite sketches in pencil by Cezanne, to our knowledge this would be the only known example of a composite oil painting sketch by the artist.

Keywords

Paul Cezanne, X-radiograph, infrared reflectography, lining removal, double-sided painting, oil sketches, double-sided stretcher design

Figure 1. "Le Bassin du Jas de Bouffan" 1878?

Introduction

This painting entitled "Le Bassin du Jas de Bouffan" 1878?, (Figure 1) belongs to the Silva-Casa Foundation in Bern, Switzerland, the Estate of the late Hilde Thannhauser. The Guggenheim has a close working relationship with the Foundation, having received the Justin K. Thannhauser Bequest in 1976 and 1992. The Thannhauser Bequest is primarily a collection of French paintings from the Impressionist and Post-Impressionist eras.[1] The Guggenheim's conservation department had recently cleaned five paintings by Cézanne from the Museum's collection, three of which were part of the Thannhauser Bequest.

"Le Bassin du Jas de Bouffan" was brought to the conservation department at the Guggenheim Museum in 1993 for examination. The examination was requested because John Rewald, a leading Cézanne scholar, did not plan to include this painting in his Cézanne *catalogue raisonné*. John Rewald largely completed this publication before his death in January 1994. He gave no explanation for his rejection of the painting. He never saw the sketches on the reverse.

Historical background

The Thannhauser painting is one of nine works by Cézanne of which photographs mounted together on a single panel were exhibited at the Salon d'Automne in 1904. The other photographs shown in this exhibition were all of known paintings by Cézanne. 18 other undisputed paintings were also shown in photographs on two additional panels according to Cézanne's dealer Ambroise Vollard. These photographs were exhibited along with some 28 equally undisputed paintings. This was during Cézanne's lifetime and the exhibition was a retrospective intended to honor him. The Thannhauser painting represents a recognizable motif from the grounds of Cézanne's family home, but not one that corresponds exactly to any of his other paintings or watercolors.[2] The painting was included in Lionello Venturi's *catalogue raisonné* in 1936 (Venturi 484).[3]

Provenance

The provenance of the painting is reported to be the following: Paul Cézanne *fils*, Paris; Ambroise Vollard, Paris (to 1939); heirs of Ambroise Vollard, France (to 1951); Planque, Paris; Amante Paris; Galerie Beyeler, Basel (to 1959); Justin K. Thannhauser, New York and Bern; Mrs. Justin K. Thannhauser, Bern.[4]

Previous examination

The painting had previously been examined at The Swiss Institute for Art Research, Zurich in 1992. The aim of their investigation was to verify with scientific methods that the painting could have been executed after 1878 and before 1904. Pigment identification was carried out using a microscope (6–80 magnification) and X-ray fluorescence analysis. The pigments identified were cobalt blue, emerald green, chrome yellow, yellow ocher, carbon black, zinc white, lead white, cinnabar and red ocher. The conclusion was that the presence

Figure 2. The still-life, as seen in the X-radiograph

of these pigments did not contradict a date for the painting of between 1878 and 1904. The Institute also compared their results with those of ten major works by Cézanne from the last three decades of the 19th century examined at the Philadelphia Museum of Art. This comparison shows that the pigments correspond to the ones observed in Philadelphia.[5] The Swiss Institute also produced an X-radiograph of the painting. Their report said the following, "The X-radiographs show that in the upper right half of the painting, two images are overlapping. The visible forms can be interpreted as fruit still life. This is found not on the front under the visible paint layer but most likely on the back of the original canvas." (Figure 2).[6]

Examination

The dimensions of the painting are 74.0 × 60.7 cm. The condition of the work when it arrived in the Guggenheim conservation studio was as follows.

Support

The stretcher did not appear to be the original.[7] It was patinated on the back side with a medium brown stain. The original canvas, which is quite fine with an open weave, had two linings. These had clearly been applied at different times. The lining fabrics were different but both were closely woven linen. The lining adhesives were both aqueous glue/paste. Under magnification, one could observe an off-white material in the interstices of the original canvas weave, apparently applied to the reverse of the canvas. This off-white material looked more like paint than lining glue. This observation would support the Swiss Institute's statement that there is another painting on the reverse of the canvas. The painting had rather a lumpy surface texture and there was quite dramatic weave impression caused by the lining processes. Some of the lumpiness may be caused by the presence of the painting on the reverse or by a thick uneven lining adhesive application. There were two small tears in the painting, both in the upper left quadrant of the painting. These tears may be the reason for the application of the first lining.

Ground and paint layers

There is no continuous ground layer on the painting on the front. The paint appears to be applied directly to the canvas.[8] There are areas of darkened exposed canvas visible in places. There were several explanations for this. It is possible that the darkening of the canvas is a result of

- varnishing;
- absorption of oil from the paint into the linen;
- oxidation of the linen; or
- possibly even an application of a tone by the artist –Cézanne is known to have made use of toned grounds.[9]

The paint layers are of variable thicknesses, ranging from fairly thin to medium thick with some areas of low impasto. There were deposits of the lining glue and/or facing adhesive on the front surface between the paint and the varnish. Under magnification the tops of the canvas threads could be seen in many places. The exposed thread tops may be a result of abrasion to the paint layer which occurred during the lining process or a previous cleaning.

Varnish

There was a thick varnish layer which exhibited a yellow milky fluorescence in ultraviolet light and was therefore estimated to be a natural resin. In natural light the varnish layer was thick, glossy and very yellowed. Large quantities of glue residue remained on the front surface of the painting between the paint and the varnish. These may be residues from the lining and/or the facing processes. The glue residues had also discolored and could be seen with the naked eye in several locations over the painting's surface. These glue residues were especially noticeable in the troughs of the impasto and in the valleys of the canvas weave and were causing disruption between the paint and varnish, resulting in a somewhat cloudy appearance to the surface of the painting.

Treatment proposal

The possible merits of cleaning the painting were discussed. The discolored glossy varnish and the cloudy glue were compromising the palette and the paint texture considerably. Unfortunately, no reasons had been given for the rejection of the work by John Rewald and so it was not known whether removing the varnish and correcting these anomalies would be sufficient to re-establish the attribution to Cézanne. Some cursory tests were carried out which seemed to indicate that the outer lining would be rather simple to remove while the inner lining could prove much more complicated. The decision was made to clean the painting and assess the results before deciding upon the lining removal.

Treatment

Cleaning

The varnish was removed from the front of the painting with acetone. It had been hoped that the areas of darkened exposed canvas would become lighter in tone once the varnish was removed. However, these areas did not lighten up significantly. The glue remnants on the surface of the painting were removed with saliva.[10] After cleaning the painting was assessed and the removal of the linings was deemed crucial to the painting's attribution. This was only to be attempted if there was absolutely no risk to the painting on the front. It was necessary to conduct further tests from the reverse.

Strip-lining

The painting was prepared for the testing of the lining removal. A strip-lining of fine linen was prepared and attached to the edges of the front of the painting with Beva 371® using a heated spatula. The painting was then removed from its stretcher and attached to a loom in preparation for testing of the removal of the linings. The use of moisture during the poultice application could potentially structurally affect the work on the front. This loom allowed access to the front of the painting at all times during the treatment.

Tests

A wheat starch paste poultice was applied to a small area on the reverse and carefully monitored. This small section of the outer lining could be peeled back easily after about 20 min with little effect on the inner lining. The poultice was then applied to the inner lining canvas and carefully monitored every few minutes to establish the optimal time for peeling the inner lining. Approximately the same amount of time was required. During testing the presence of a cheesecloth interleaf between the inner lining and the reverse of the original canvas was discovered. It was extremely fortunate that this interleaf of cheesecloth had been used, as its presence was to prove invaluable for the removal of both the inner lining fabric and the old glue/paste. The painting was examined from the reverse with an infrared vidicon camera,[11] but no image could seen.

Removal of the linings

The reverse of the painting was cleaned in three stages. The outer lining was removed by applying the starch paste poultice to the reverse of the painting in small sections. These were covered with a piece of Mylar® and left for approximately 20–30 min, after which the lining was carefully peeled back and cut, in areas of about 2–5 cm^2 at a time. During this lining removal two inscriptions and canvas stamp

Figure 3. The reverse during lining removal

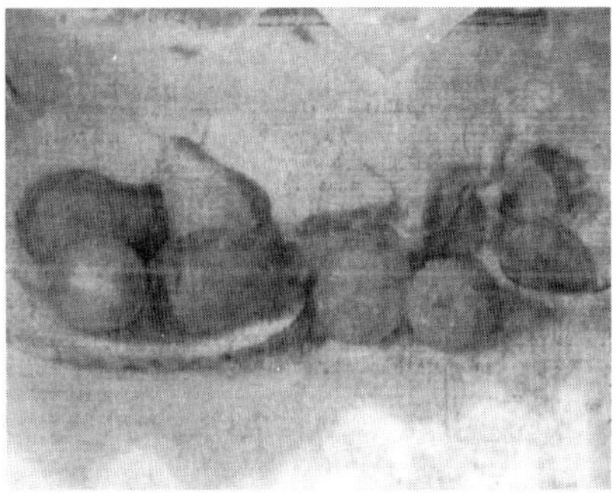

Figure 4. The infrared image of the fruit

Figure 5. The reverse of the painting. showing that the sketches overlap

on the inner lining canvas were found. The number 571 written in blue ink, and another, 666, written in pencil. No interpretation for these numbers has been found yet. However the canvas stamp appeared to be a French customs stamp, as the word "Douane" was legible. The inner lining was removed in a similar way using starch paste poultices (Figure 3).

After the removal of the inner lining the painting was still mostly covered with a thick opaque layer of brown lining glue and the cheesecloth interleaf. No complete images were visible at this stage. The painting was examined again with the infrared vidicon camera, and a striking image of the still-life could be seen in the top right hand corner of the reverse. Photographs were taken of the infrared image on the screen (Figure 4). It was unclear at this stage whether any other images existed on the reverse.

A third starch poultice cleaning was necessary to uncover the images. Over the course of many weeks sketches of a bather, a plant study, a faint landscape and finally the still life were uncovered. The poultice described above was used to swell and soften the glue. The bulk of the soft glue was then removed from the surface leaving the cheesecloth in place. The remainder of the glue was then removed under magnification. Cleaning through the cheesecloth greatly assisted in protecting the ground and paint layers. The unpainted ground was fragile,[12] though in general the sketches were remarkably intact.

The sketches of the faint landscape and that of the figure are almost like watercolor in their delicacy. The still life is more thickly painted and the background is blocked in to create a complete little composition which measures 19.9 × 43.4 cm. The plant study is also painted with a fairly thick paint application and it slightly overlaps the small still-life. The order in which the sketches appear to have been painted is; first the landscape; second the bather, his head seems to overlap the landscape and sky; third, the still life; and fourth the plant study parts of which overlap the still life and the landscape (Figure 5).

On the reverse side of the painting there was some cupping of the ground and paint layers under the glue, particularly in the area of the still-life where the paint is most thickly applied. This cupping relaxed during the poultice application and then with gentle pressure the cupping could be coaxed flat. The whole surface was cleaned in this way with the cheesecloth in place. The cheesecloth was then gently moistened with water using a brush and was carefully removed from the surface. During the lining and glue removal, the front surface of the painting remained remarkably stable and it was carefully monitored during the whole procedure.

Consolidation

The painting on the reverse was still fragile at this stage. It was consolidated with an 8% w/w in water gelatin solution. After consolidation the surface was cleaned again with distilled water to remove any excess consolidant and the last traces of the discolored glue that remained on the surface.

Mending the tears

The edges of the two small tears were very slightly overlapping in places, however they were very flat and the decision was made not to disturb them by trying to manipulate them into exact alignment. This would almost certainly have resulted in a bulge which may then have been stubborn to flatten and to keep flat. A 24-hour setting Epo-Tek® epoxy was sparingly applied at the tear edges with a needle and placed under weights until set.

In-painting

In-painting was intentionally kept to a minimum, as the sketches were to be studied by Cézanne scholars. A simple approach was employed, reducing the distracting tiny dark losses in the ground so that the forms could be seen more clearly. All in-painting was carried out in gouache and watercolor. A neutral brown was used to in-paint the small areas of abrasion (which were light in appearance) along the cracks in the darkly painted areas of the still-life image. A

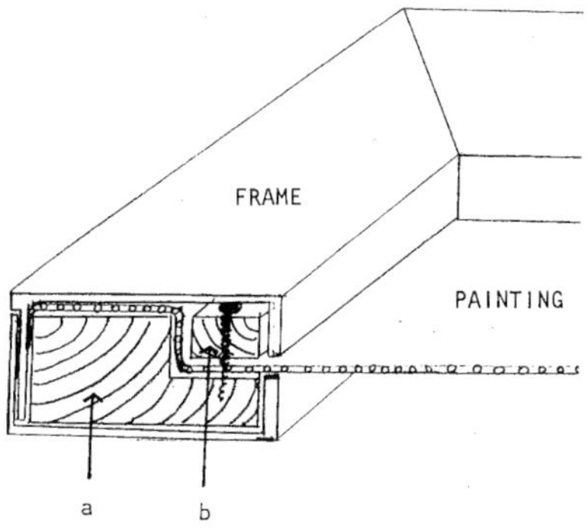

Figure 6. Attaching the stretcher to the frame

reasonable color match was sought for the in-painting of the two small tears on both the front and on the reverse.

Re-stretching

A custom-designed and quite compact stretcher and frame for this double-sided painting was made in cherry wood. The approach was to design an expansion-bolt stretcher that held both sides of the painting equidistant from the frame surfaces. This was achieved by constructing the stretcher in two sections. The painting was stretched and attached to the main component of the stretcher. This main component holds the painting in the middle of the cross-section of the stretcher (see a on Figure 6). Then the small component of the stretcher (see b on Figure 6) was fitted into place and screwed into the main component. The frame was designed so that it encases the stretcher, like a clam-shell, see Figure 6. This particular frame was left undecorated, but it could easily act as a base for molding or gilding or whatever decoration might be desired. Another option would be to place plexiglas or reflection-free glass for protection between the stretcher and frame if the frame is made slightly deeper,

Conclusion

The result of this treatment is an enigmatic, two-sided painting. The landscape on the front, though not in pristine condition, can now be viewed in an honest state, the palette and texture of the artist's brushwork are no longer congested by the thick glossy discolored varnish and old glue residues. The composite sketches on the reverse, which were so carefully revealed, present the work in close to its original manifestation. The sketches are doubtless of a high quality.

The decision to remove the linings was not made easily. However, given the historical importance of the work on the reverse, it was considered to be a reasonable course of action. It is recognized that this painting is now in a more fragile state than before treatment, as a two-sided painting on a fairly thin support. Prior to seeing the sketches it had been suggested that, depending on its structural integrity, the work might require a transparent support after the lining removal. However, once the images were revealed, it became clear that re-lining this delicate surface would not be desirable. After assessing the actual strength of the canvas a strip-lining was considered sufficient. The newly designed double-sided stretcher enhances the presentation of both faces of the painting.

During the treatment a number of interesting comparisons were noted. There are numerous examples of composite pencil sketches by Cézanne.[13] Some of them have one particular sketch delineated in a similar way to the still-life in this painting.[14] Some of the pencil sketches show a similar indifference to the overlapping of images.[15] In the Thannhauser painting the sketches are all oriented in the same direction. This is not always the case with the pencil sketches.[16] There are other small still-life paintings[17] by Cézanne which are similar in scale to the sketches on the reverse of the Thannhauser painting. Some are cropped in slightly awkward ways, which may indicate that perhaps they could have been cut from larger canvases. Until further laboratory examination is carried out this is only conjecture. However, Cézanne's son is reported to have engaged in the practice of cutting up and selling individually the drawings on his father's sheets of studies. Perhaps this composite sketch survived because of the larger, more marketable landscape on the other side of the canvas.[18]

During the course of future examinations of other works by Cézanne these findings could be borne in mind and details such as cropping of edges, evidence of overlapping sketches or evidence of work on the reverse of paintings could ultimately provide important comparisons for this work. If indeed this work is by Cézanne it would reveal a whole new aspect of the artist's working method in oil.

Acknowledgements

I extend my thanks to Janet Briner, Curator of the Silva-Casa Foundation and to Paul Schwartzbaun, Chief Conservator, Guggenheim Museum for their help and enthusiastic support during this project. My thanks also to Thomas Krens, Director of the Guggenheim Museum for making my time available to work this interesting project. I gratefully acknowledge Professor Theodore Reff of Columbia University, for so much of the art historical information contained in this paper. Thank you to Christian Marty, of the Swiss Institute for Art Research for allowing me to include the results of the pigment analysis and for making the first X-ray showing that there was something on the reverse of this painting. My thanks also to Simon Liu, Simon Liu Inc., New York, for collaborating on the design of the double-sided stretcher.

Notes and References

1. V. E. Barnett, *The Guggenheim Museum: Justin K. Thannhauser Collection* (New York: 1978).
2. T. Reff, "A Study on the Authenticity of Cézanne's painting Le Bassin du Jas de Bouffan," (Unpublished paper written for the Silva-Casa Foundation, Bern, November 1994, revised January 1996).
3. L. Venturi *Cézanne, son art, son oeuvre* (Paris: Paul Rosenberg editeur, 1936). Future references to V numbers refer to these Venturi *catalogue raisonné* numbers.
4. Information from Janet Briner, curator of the Silva-Casa Foundation's collection.
5. M. Butler, "An Investigation of the Materials and Technique Used by Paul Cézanne," (Preprints of papers presented at the twelfth annual meeting of the American Institute for conservation of Historic and Artistic Works, Los Angeles, California, 1984).
6. Unpublished report written in German by Swiss Institute for Art Research, Zurich. Translated by Katherine Katz.
7. The stretcher had only very few tackholes in addition to those housing the tacks used to attach the painting to the stretcher.
8. To date we have not been able to identify with certainty another painting by Cézanne with no ground.
9. R.W. Ratcliffe, "Cézanne's Working Methods and Their Theoretical Background" (PhD thesis, University of London, 1960).
10. Cleaning tests were conducted with cold water, warm water, saliva and enzymes to determine best method of removal. Details available upon request.
11. Infrared equipment: Hamamatsu vidicon camera control and head Model C1000, Tektronix 634 video monitor: Hamamatsu Systems Inc, 40 Bear Hill Road, Waltham, MA 02154, USA.
12. The ground application on the reverse was found to be similar to the ground application on "Bibemus" and "Madame Cézanne," two other works in the Guggenheim collection. They have a similar color, texture and thickness;samples are presently being analyzed.
13. Venturi, V.1224. V.1218, V.1449, V.1479, V.1294.
14. Venturi, V.1448, V1217, V.1251, V.1576.
15. Venturi, V.1484, V.1579, V.1578.
16. There are at least two earlier works in oil which contain more than one visible image but in these two cases the later image seems to have been layered over the work beneath with no attempt to preserve the legibility of the underlying images, V.17, V.68.
17. Venturi, V.352, V.508t V.506, V.509, V.614
18. Reff, "A study on the Authenticity."

Materials

- Beva 371®: ethylene/vinyl acetate copolymer (major ingredient): Conservation Materials, 1165 Marietta Way, Sparks, NV 8943l, USA.
- Epoxy resin: Epo-Tek Epoxy Technology Inc., Box 567, 14 Fortune Drive, Billerica, MA 01821, USA.
- Wheat starch paste recipe: Wheat starch powder mixed with cold water 1 part starch to 3 parts water. Brought to boil while constantly stirring. Allowed to thicken and constantly stirred for a further 30 min until semi-translucent. Mixture placed under a trickling tap for 1 h until set into a thick paste, Mixture pressed through a horse-hair sieve prior to use each day.
- Stretcher made by Simon Liu Inc. , 51 Pearl Street, Brooklyn, NY 11201, USA.

CCI Lining Project: Preliminary Testing of Lined Model Paintings

Stefan Michalski,* Debra Daly Hartin†
Canadian Conservation Institute,
1030 Innes Rd., Ottawa, Ontario, Canada, K1A 0M5

Abstract

The third phase of the CCI Lining Project involves investigating the performance of some lining systems in order to assess their ability to minimize defects in a painting. Uniaxial samples of lining supports and lined-model paintings (model oil painting and chalk ground painting) have been exposed to 50% RH, strained, then exposed to 12% RH and left for several months. Tension is monitored continuously. Models used for data analysis have been taken from viscoelastic/plastic polymer mechanics. Preliminary results of the testing of lined model paintings emphasize the importance of stress relaxation as a performance criterion of a lining support. Linings onto linen and a multifilament polyester fabric were observed to stress relax at a similar rate to that of an unlined model oil painting, thus offering no support to the painting. A lining with unimpregnated polyester sailcloth showed high initial tension and much slower relaxation than the model oil painting, so significant support is maintained. Samples of linen alone, with an Acryloid B72 size or wax-resin impregnation, show high initial tension, but stress relax relatively fast. The wax-resin lining onto linen showed great effectiveness in slowing down the response to RH change.

Keywords

Lining, paintings, tension, stress relaxation, linen, sailcloth, polyester

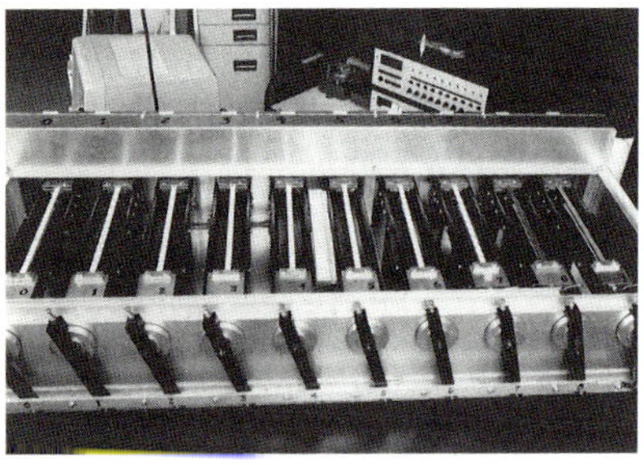

Figure 1. Samples installed in testing apparatus

Figure 2. Detail of end of sample in clamp

Introduction

The behaviour of lined paintings has been studied at the Canadian Conservation Institute (CCI) in the CCI Lining Project. The project has entered its third phase: the testing of selected lining systems in terms of their ability to reduce cracking, delamination, cupping, and sagging; due to stretching, stress relaxation, humidity fluctuations, or temperature fluctuations. Tension is being monitored in the samples to assist in the interpretation of their performance.

The first phase of the Lining Project, reported on at the 1987 ICOM-CC meeting in Sydney, was the measurement of tension[1] and its relaxation (unpublished) in various model paintings as humidity changed. The second phase, reported on at the 1993 ICOM-CC meeting in Washington, DC, was the measurement of the peel strength of selected lining systems.[2] This peel strength data will help the interpretation of any delamination or slippage observed in phase three.

Reported here are some preliminary data from phase three: tests of lined model paintings. Since the tension measuring equipment was completely renovated subsequent to phase one, some unlined paintings were included in phase three to replicate, as well as extend, the earlier data on the model paintings.

The 1980s work of Hedley, Mecklenburg, and others established that the lining applied to a painting on canvas must be significantly stiffer than the painting itself in order to offer support. These models used single values of stiffness or elasticity, measured by industry over a few minutes, or by conservation researchers over several days.

This study takes this concept the next step by adding the parameter of time. Linings must dominate stiffness during millisecond strains (against transit shocks, keying out) during month-long strains (against RH- and T-driven cupping, cracking) and during many years (against deformation memories, long-term cupping and cracking, ageing and creep of materials).

Materials and measurement device

Eleven uniaxial samples are being tested at a time. (Sample preparations are described in Appendix 1.) Ten samples are placed in uniaxial restraining jigs which can be monitored for tension on an ongoing basis (Figure 1). The tension is logged by computer every five seconds during rapid phenomena and proportionally less often for slower phenomena. In addition, one marouflaged sample has been included for observation.

The samples are clamped such that at one end the jaw holds both the lining support and the painting, and at the other end the jaw holds the lining fabric only where the painting ends 1 mm short of the clamp (Figure 2). This represents a tear or edge of a painting, and is observed for delamination or cupping. A mark on the end of the painting is monitored with a travelling microscope to measure any slippage of the painting relative to the clamp holding the lining (Figure 3).

Uniaxial samples provide valuable information with a minimum of sample area, a critical factor given the fixed number of naturally aged model oil paintings

* Author to whom experimental/analytical-related inquiries should be addressed
† Author to whom lining/treatment-related inquiries should be addressed

Figure 3. Travelling microscope used to monitor slippage of painting

prepared (now ten years old). On the other hand, uniaxial samples can be misleading in studies of painting and lining mechanics. Therefore, a limited number of biaxial samples were also prepared. Biaxial samples consist of a model painting (20 × 20 cm in size) lined onto a lining support (23 × 23 cm in size). Prior to lining, a T-shaped "tear" was cut at the centre of each model painting. These biaxial samples have been set aside for future testing, pending the studies with more numerous uniaxial samples.

Relaxation of viscoelastic polymers

Relaxation of tension (stress) can be seen as a change in the effective modulus of elasticity over time. It follows four regimes: glassy for short time periods, leathery over longer time periods, and rubbery over the longest time periods; rubbery elasticity gives way to rubbery flow if the polymer is uncrosslinked.

Thus the behaviour of some paint layer or lining fibre may be said to change from glassy to leathery to rubbery as time passes. This does not mean that a glassy polymer turns into a material that feels rubbery to our hands. It means that the tension in a material that feels glassy to our hands will have relaxed, after many years, to a level similar to that which would have occurred in a few seconds in a material that feels rubbery to our hands.

As shown in Figure 4, when the horizontal axis is plotted as log time and the vertical axis as log tension, the glassy, leathery, rubbery, rubbery flow regimes give distinctive slopes as indicated. The tension relaxation data of the samples will be interpreted in terms of these regions, on axes of identical proportion, along with the known data on painting materials.[3]

Relaxation results at 50% RH: from minutes to years

Model oil painting

Figure 5 shows the tension in the model oil painting (linen, 7% rabbit-skin glue size, lead white oil ground, lead white oil paint) as a result of its initial elongation and subsequent stress relaxation. The climb at the beginning of the curve represents the gradual application of one millistrain (0.001, 1 mm in a metre) over the course of four minutes. The spikes in the middle of the data, and the slight waviness at the

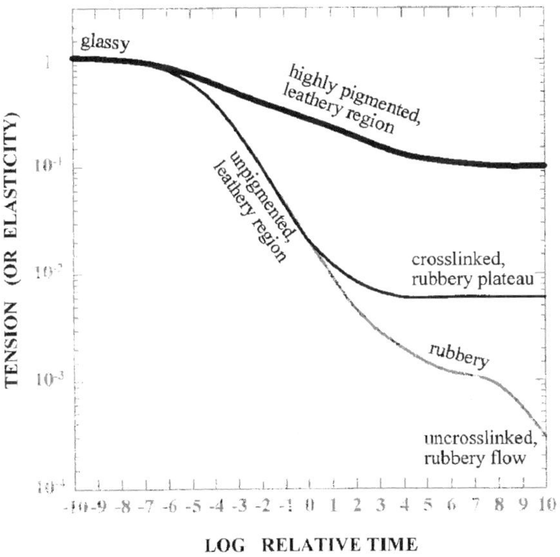

Figure 4. Relaxation of viscoelastic polymers. Time axis indicates very fast events to the left (fractions of a second for a shock event) and extremely slow events (years) to the right

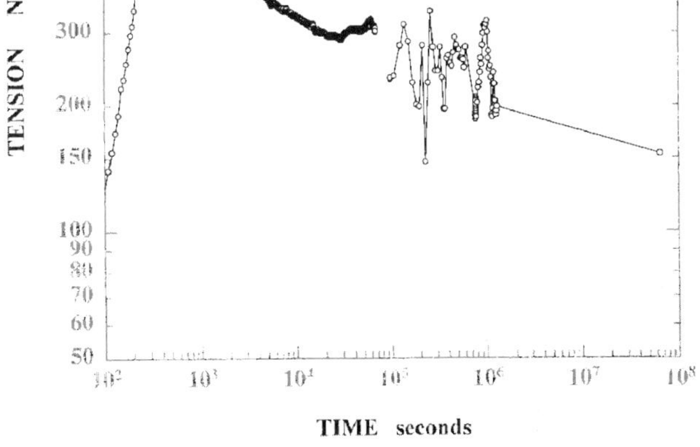

Figure 5. Tension, over time, at 50% RH for sample 8 (see Table 4)

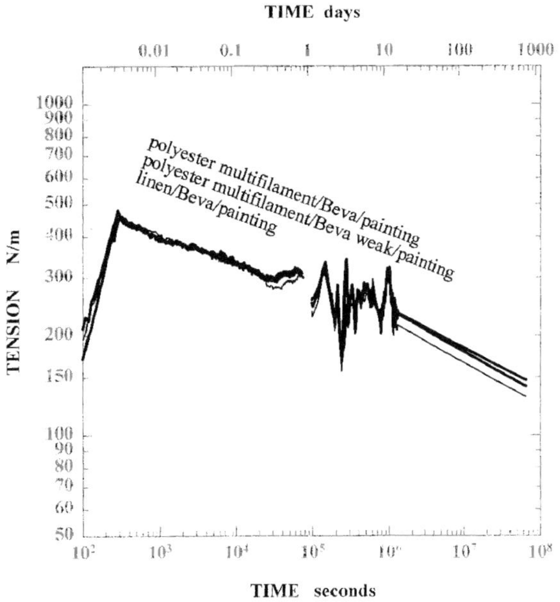

Figure 6. Tension, over time, at 50% RH for samples 3, 4 and 6 (see Table 4)

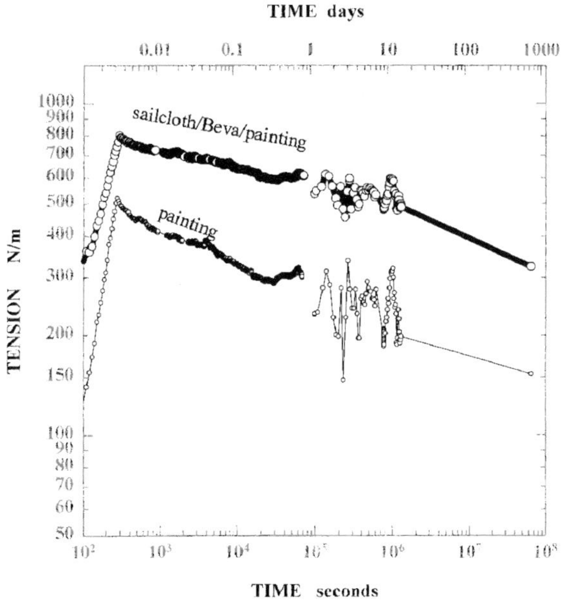

Figure 7. Tension, over time, at 50% RH for samples 5 and 8 (see Table 4)

beginning, are due to moderate daily humidity fluctuations in the lab, since the sample chamber was not closed during this preliminary 15-day test. The last data point was taken 20 October 1995. The blank in the data points during the last third of the graph, (approximately two years represented by a straight line) represents one year of tests at 12% RH, followed by a return to 50% RH (closed chamber) for most of the last year.

The curve is as expected for a system dominated by the lead white oil ground:

- Since it is oil media, leathery behaviour is already in place by the beginning of the test.
- Since it has high pigment concentration, this leathery slope is only gradual.
- Since it is well crosslinked by the lead white, it will approach a rubbery plateau, though this would not show clearly for several decades.

Multifilament yarn fabrics: linings that never carried significant tension

The three lined samples shown in Figure 6 gave curves identical to those of the unlined painting alone. This means the linings carried no significant tension, except between the end of the painting and the metal clamp. This is not surprising, since the multifilament yarn fabrics used as lining supports have low stiffness at small elongations due to yarn compression and decrimping, despite fibres of high stiffness. Biaxial samples will show better stiffness than these uniaxial samples, but it is doubtful whether they will change the results significantly.

These data show that after stretching of these lining/painting systems, the paintings with lead white ground (or paints of similar stiffness) will carry most of the tension, not just immediately, but indefinitely. Thus, the formation of new cracks due to overstretching will not be prevented. Also, the tendency toward cupping, caused by stress alignment in a cracked painting, will not be prevented by these linings. By stress alignment is meant the tendency, in a taut painting, for the fabric hinges that bridge each crack to try to align themselves with the average plane of the paint fragments. This forces a bending, or cupping, of the edges of these paint fragments.

Polyester sailcloth: a lining that carries significant tension at 50% RH

The polyester sailcloth lining carries significant tension, as Mecklenburg, Hedley and others suggested, based on short-term measures of tension. The present data demonstrate the even greater proportional benefit of sailcloth over long time periods (Figure 7). Immediately after stretching, the lining/painting composite carried 810 N m^{-1} tension, the painting alone 510 N m^{-1}, so the lining carried the

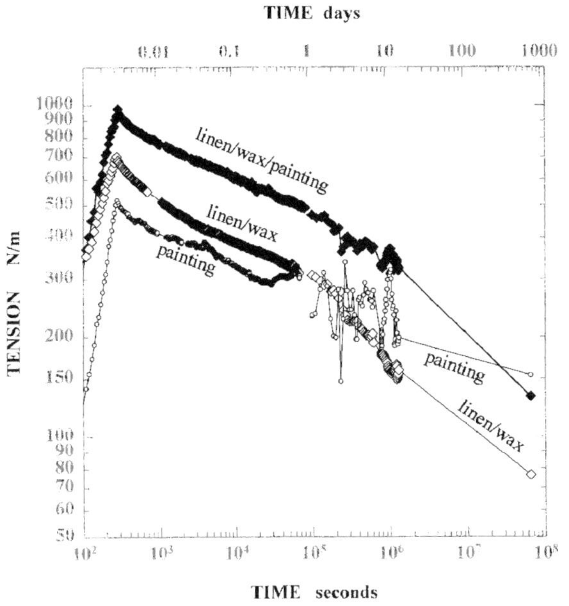

Figure 8. Tension, over time, at 50% RH for samples 1, 8 and 9 (see Table 4)

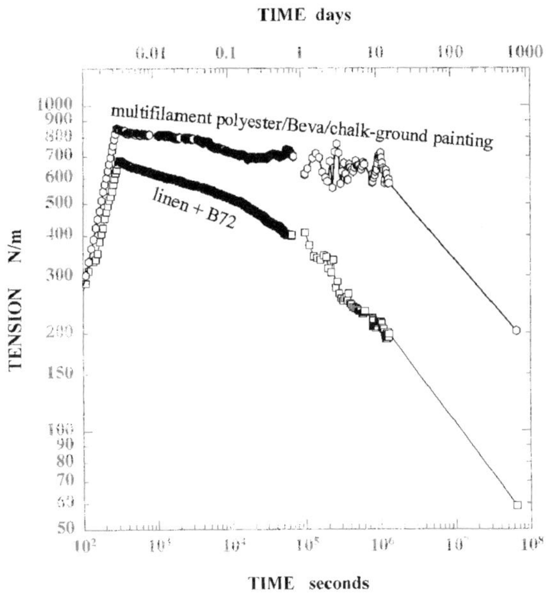

Figure 9. Tension, over time, at 50% RH for samples 7 and 10 (see Table 4)

difference: 300 N m^{-1}. The ratio of lining to painting tension is therefore L:P = 300:510 = 0.6:1. By the end of two years, the ratio L:P = 160:150 = 1.1:1.

This means the sailcloth can reduce cupping of the type caused by stress alignment, both at the time of stretching and for years after, because it carries much of the tension. On the other hand, as the sailcloth does not dominate the painting, it cannot eliminate cupping. It simply comes closer than any other single fabric to matching the stiffness of an oil-ground painting. As such, it can also reduce cracking due to overstretching (assuming that this is judged by tension).

Wax-resin impregnated linen

The wax-resin impregnated linen alone shows a complex curve, probably showing different leathery or even rubbery flow transitions of various constituents in the wax-resin (Figure 8).

Initially, the wax-impregnated linen contributes even more support than the sailcloth, and this support lasts for weeks. However, at about 100 days, the supporting tension has relaxed away to nothing significant. (The fact that the tension in the lined painting sample relaxes to less than that of the painting alone, as did all the ineffective linings, indicates the painting is slipping at the adhesive bond, or that the 1 mm tab of bare lining is stretching.)

The impressive performance of the wax-resin impregnated linen for up to a 100 days does show the importance of impregnation in fabric stiffness. It locks the fibres in a solid matrix, so that yarn compression and decrimping cannot take place until the matrix relaxes a great deal. The matrix polymer essentially obtains leverage through the stiff fibres, so that the relaxation of the composite is much slower than that of the polymer alone. Any adequate impregnant could do this in a multifilament fabric.

Two initially glassy, uncrosslinked systems: Acryloid B72 and chalk ground

The effect of a sizing of 10% Acryloid B72 on the behaviour of linen was studied (Figure 9). It provides a nice example of a transition from glassy to leathery behaviour at about one day, as expected for Acryloid B72 alone. The drop in the leathery region is fast, typical of unpigmented acrylics. Unlike the full impregnation achieved with molten wax-resin, this 10% sizing would not saturate the fabric, so the result is more of a fibre-filled foam than a fibre-reinforced solid.

The system of lining/chalk ground painting is dominated by the chalk ground. It shows behaviour already demonstrated for glue and gelatin[4] and for blue gessos,[5]

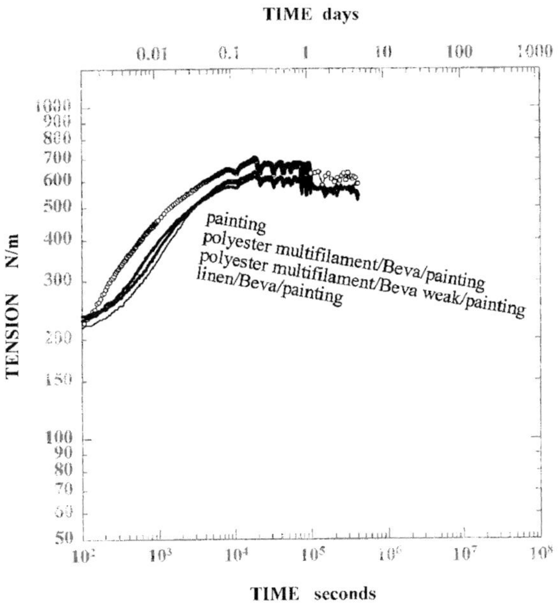

Figure 10. Tension as a result of a drop from 50 to 12% RH and subsequent relaxation for samples 3, 4, 6 and 8 (see Table 4)

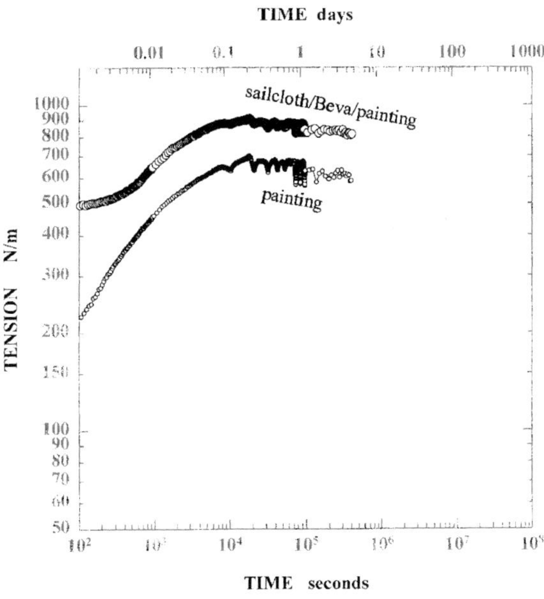

Figure 11. Tension as a result of a drop from 50 to 12% RH and subsequent relaxation for samples 5 and 8 (see Table 4)

i.e. glassy behaviour for weeks, followed by the drop to leathery behaviour somewhere between 20 and 100 days. If the RH were 80%, this drop would occur in seconds, if it were 10%, it would not occur for years.[4]

Response to low humidity

Model painting and linings that contribute no tension at 12% RH

The sample chamber was taken to 12% from 50% RH within about 100 se by a recirculating desiccant dehumidifier. Some data are shown in Figure 10, on the same axes as before, so that comparison of slopes is possible. (RH fluctuations from the dehumidifier yield the spikes in the curve, a problem to be corrected.)

The painting tension climbed at a rate determined by moisture diffusion and peaked at about 5 h (0.2 days), then relaxation took over. The leathery relaxation at 12% RH is much less steep than at 50% RH, since moisture, a plasticizer for oil and glue, has been reduced. Plasticizer removal shifts transitions to longer times. Stress relaxation in general, and the transition from one regime to the next, occurs more slowly as a result of removal of the plasticizer. In addition, the materials shrink because of volume loss.

The linings that provided inadequate support at 50% RH, continue to provide inadequate support at 12% RH, other than to slow the loss of moisture.

Sailcloth: a lining that contributes some tension at 12% RH

Figure 11 shows the tension in the sailcloth-lined sample and the model oil painting as a result of a drop in RH from 50 to 12% and the subsequent relaxation.

Before the drop to 12% RH, the sailcloth/painting system carries about 500 N m^{-1} tension, the painting about 200 N m^{-1}. Thus the lining is carrying 300 N m^{-2}. By the time the response to 12% RH peaks, the painting has climbed to 700 N m^{-1}, a rise of 500 N m^{-1} (consistent with the phase one studies). The lining, which is not responsive to humidity, can only contribute the same 300 N m^{-1},[6] so the tension ratio L:P drops to 300:700 = 0.4:1. The sailcloth is now carrying less than half the total tension in the painting; it is therefore providing much less support at low RH.

Extrapolation of the 50% RH data to ten years shows the sailcloth and oil painting will relax to tensions of about 150 N m^{-1} each. Unfortunately, every new event of low RH will see the painting tension climb by 500 N m^{-1}, so in ten years a day of low RH would see the painting tension rise to 150 + 500 = 650 N m^{-7}. There will be no change in the sailcloth value since it is not moisture sensitive: just 150 N m^{-1} in ten years. Thus in ten years, the tension ratio of L:P after a cycle of low

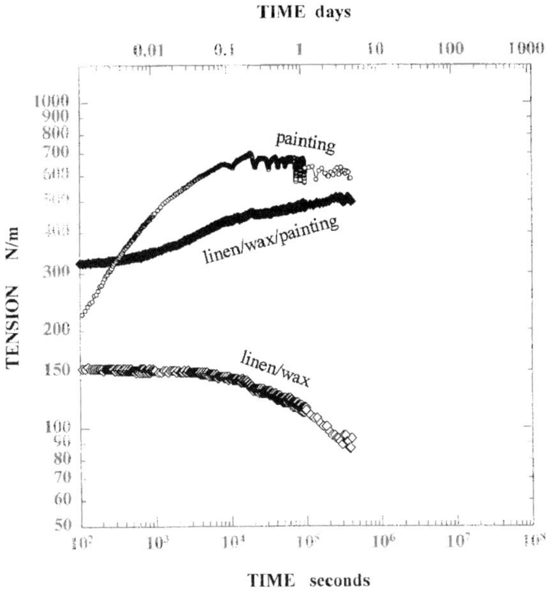

Figure 12. Tension as a result of a drop from 50 to 12% RH and subsequent relaxation for samples 1, 8 and 9 (see Table 4)

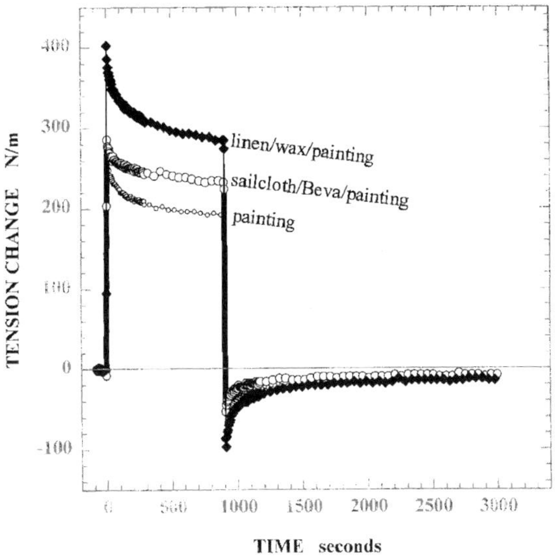

Figure 13. Tension and relaxation after small, fast strain; linear time for samples 1, 5 and 8 (see Table 4)

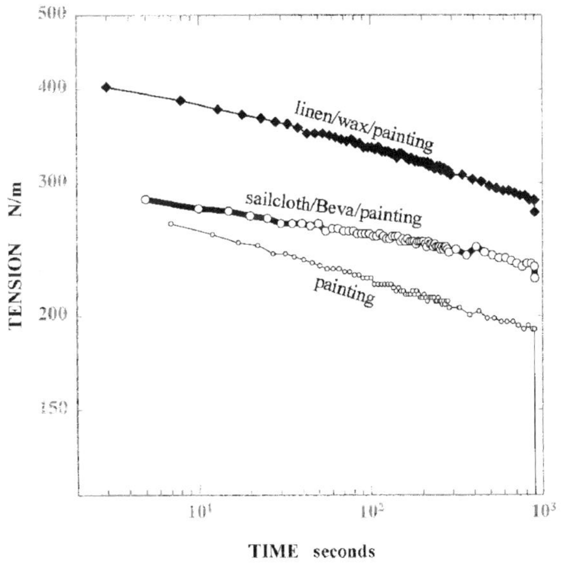

Figure 14. Tension and relaxation after small, fast strain; log time for samples 1, 5 and 8 (see Table 4)

RH will be 150:650 = 0.2:1. The single layer of sailcloth will do little to prevent cupping due to stress alignment. It will also do little to prevent cracking due to low RH.

Linen impregnated with wax-resin at 12% RH

Figure 12 shows the tension in the wax-resin impregnated linen and linen/wax-resin lined model painting samples in comparison with the model oil painting alone.

The tension in the wax-impregnated linen sample drops dramatically. The linen fibres shrink and decrimping drops the tension. Loss of tension does, however, take many days, and is still not complete when this data stops.

The lined painting takes a similarly long time to respond, and it has not responded completely in these data. It takes so long that the painting will peak at only 550 N m^{-1} in about ten days, compared to the bare painting which peaks at 700 N m^{-1} in five hours. This will reduce cracking. The painting completely dominates tension as it heads for this 550 N m^{-1}, however, so cupping will be a problem.

Relaxation results after faster events: between one second and minutes

The initial elongation of one millistrain was added to the samples slowly (over the course of four minutes). To study faster events, a device was made to add a small increment in elongation (0.3 mm in a metre) to each sample over the course of about one second, and then accurately subtract it some time later.

Three curves have been selected here for interest: the oil painting, the sailcloth lined painting, and the linen wax-lined painting, all at 50% RH (Figure 13). These are shown here plotted against linear time, to remind one of the typical decay appearance when plotted this way, and to show the spring-back curves when the incremental elongation is removed.

The fact that recovery is virtually complete[7] indicates that there is no significant slippage of the lining in the short term.

In log time (Figure 14), the curves straighten out. They appear as virtually straight lines since they span only three decades of time. In terms of the full viscoelastic curve shown in Figure 4, which covers 20 decades of time, these are only short segments.

The sailcloth lining plot shows the same glassy behaviour already established at longer times. It cannot get much glassier at shorter times as it is near its glassy plateau. The painting, however, can still climb steeply, since it is still in its leathery range, and shows an imminent crossover for events faster than one second, from sailcloth dominance to painting dominance. This test is still not fast enough to show this cross-over, just the approach. A faster motor drive could be used, to approach the time scale of shock from transit or vandalism (0.01 s). Extrapolation to shock times indicates that the lead white ground will totally dominate tension, despite a single sailcloth lining.

The wax-resin/linen lining dominates tension as it approaches its own glassy behaviour simply because it is thick.[8] An equivalent weight of sailcloth would do as well during shock, and much better during longer events.

Conclusions

The following are the observations made on the performance of the linings and a summary of the tension data.

- None of the linings tested in this preliminary group "failed" in any noticeable way, despite severe low RH. No delamination and no cracks were observed. The linings that contributed little tension did show slight cupping, especially of the chalk ground at low RH. It was discovered that these phenomena are too subtle for informal visual techniques, so a change will be made to photographic recording. Also, some model oil paintings will be aged to the point of severe surface embrittlement, by exposure to intense UV.
- Tension in paintings and linings relaxes continuously over time. Viscoelastic polymer mechanics explains the different rates of various layers.
- Lead white oil ground is a formidable material to match in stiffness. Unimpregnated multifilament polyester linings offer no significant support.
- Wax-resin/linen offers support during rapid events (shock) but not over the long term.
- Polyester sailcloth comes closest to matching oil ground stiffness. It can reduce cupping by stress alignment and can reduce cracking due to some overstretching; but, at the fastest events (shock) and after periods of low RH the painting will carry most of the tension and will be vulnerable to defects. Several layers of sailcloth bonded together, or a heavier weight cloth, could extend support to these events as well.
- Impregnation is very important in any fabric's performance. It increases initial tension, slows subsequent relaxation and can slow the rate of response to change

in RH. On the other hand, a size which does not saturate the fabric will only influence the short term tension (a few days) after an applied strain.

Acknowledgement

The authors would like to acknowledge and thank Tom Strang at CCI, who developed our data collection program.

Materials

- Linen #9803: Ulster Weaving Co. Ltd, 148 Madison Ave., New York, NY 10016, USA. Tel. (212) 684-5534.
- Polyester-multifilament #2324: B. Henr. Lampe. B.V., Julianstraat - Sophiastraat, Postbus 202, 8600 AE Sneek, Holland. Tel. 05150-1 25 41.
- Polyester sailcloth: Picture Restoration Fabric; 00169/Z; Richard Hayward & Co., Tiverton, Devon EX16 5LL, England. tel 01884 257867; Fax 01884 252866.
- Acryloid B72: Rohm and Haas Canada, Inc., 2 Manse Rd., West Hill, Ontario, Canada M1E 3T9. Tel. (416) 284-4711.
- Rabbit Skin Glue: Grumbacher, M. Canada, Inc., 460 Rinchdene Square, Scarborough, Canada M1X 1C4. Tel. (416) 299-7000.
- Fredrix Lead White Ground; Universal Air, 90 Minuk Acres, Scarborough, Ontario, Canada M1E 4Y6. Tel. (416) 284-4188.
- Grumbacher Lead White Oil Paint; Grumbacher, M. Canada, Inc., 460 Rinchdene Square, Scarborough, Canada M1X 1C4. Tel. (416) 299-7000.
- BEVA 371 – ethylene/vinyl acetate copolymer (major ingredient): Conservator's Products Co. of Canada, 23 Morrow Ave., Toronto, Ontario, Canada M6R 2H9. Tel. (416) 539-8069.
- Multiwax W445: Witco Chemical Co., S1200-2 Lansing Square, Willowdale, Ontario, Canada M2J 4Z4. Tel. (416) 497-9991
- Laropal K 80: BASF, P.O. Box 430, Stat. St. Laurent, Montreal, Quebec, Canada H4L 4V8.Tel. (514) 341-5411.

Appendix I: Sample preparation and descriptions

Table 1 gives details of the model paintings, Table 2 describes the lining adhesives and size used, Table 3 describes the lining supports and Table 4 gives the sample descriptions.

Table 1. Model paintings

Oil	Linen (unwashed) 7% Rabbit-skin glue size (one brush coat) Fredrix lead white ground, two brush coats Grumbacher lead white oil paint, one brush coat Ten years old, kept at 21–23°C, 40–50% RH, under indirect north daylight through glass, and UV filtered fluorescent lamps
Chalk	(to simulate a Linen (unwashed) brittle painting) 7 % RSG size, (brush coat)
calcium	Chalk ground, two brush coats (equal parts by volume of: zinc white, carbonate, 7% RSG) Prepared one month before lining; three months old when installed in jigs

Table 2. Lining adhesives and size

Nap-bond adhesive: Flocked Beva 371	Beva 371 / VM&P Naptha (1:1) 11 flocked spray coats; Lined at 15 inches of water column pressure, at 69°C for bond of "moderate" strength and at 59°C for a "weak" bond
Wax resin impregnation	Eight parts refined Beeswax/one part Multiwax W445 / 2 parts Laropal K 80 (Model painting and lining support impregnated separately, then lined at approximately 65°C)
Acryloid B72 Size	Brushed both sides of stretched, washed, restretched linen with 10% Acryloid B72/toluene

Table 3. Lining supports

Fabric	Preparation
Linen	Stretched, washed, restretched
Linen sized with Acryloid B72	Brushed both sides of stretched, washed, restretched linen with 10% Acryloid B72 in toluene
Polyester – Multifilament	Stretched
Sailcloth – Unimpregnated monofilament polyester	Tacked to board

Table 4. Sample descriptions (uniaxial samples: 30 cm between clamps; 1 cm wide: lining supports cut along weft direction unless noted otherwise; model paintings cut along the warp direction)

1.	Model oil painting lined onto linen with wax-resin impregnating adhesive
2.	Model oil painting lined onto linen with flocked Beva 371 (nap-bond)
3.	Model oil painting lined onto linen (warp direction) with flocked Beva 371 (nap-bond)
4.	Model oil painting lined onto polyester multifilament with flocked Beva 371 (nap-bond)
5.	Model oil painting lined onto polyester sailcloth with flocked Beva 371 (nap-bond)
6.	Model oil painting lined onto polyester multifilament with flocked Beva 371 (to produce a weak nap-bond)
7.	Model chalk-ground painting lined onto polyester multifilament with a flocked Beva 371 (nap-bond)
8.	Model oil painting
9.	Linen lining fabric impregnated with wax-resin
10.	Linen lining fabric sized with Acryloid B72
11.	Model chalk-ground painting marouflaged with flocked Beva 371 (nap-bond) to an aluminum sheet covered with a polyester multifilament interleaf

Notes and references

1. D. Daly and S. Michalski, "Methodology and Status of the Lining Project, CCI," (Paper delivered at the Eighth Triennial Meeting of the International Council of Museums Committee for Conservation, Sydney, 1987), 145–152.
2. D. Daly Hartin, S. Michalski and C. Pacquet, "Ongoing Research in the CCI Lining Project: Peel Testing of BEVA 371 and Wax-Resin Adhesives with Different Lining Supports," (Paper delivered at the Tenth Triennial Meeting of the International Council of Museums Committee for Conservation, Washington, 1993), 128–134.
3. S. Michalski, "Paintings: Their Response to Temperature, Relative Humidity, Shock and Vibration," *Art in Transit*, ed. M. Mecklenburg (Washington: National Gallery of Art, 1991), 223–248.
4. Ibid., 223–248.
5. S. Michalski, "Crack Mechanisms in Gilding," *Gilded Wood; Conservation and History*, ed. D. Bigelow, (Madison CT: Sound View Press, 1991), 171–181.

6. The actual data at 12% RH indicate an even lower contribution by the sailcloth, only 200 N m^{-1}, a drop from the 300 N m^{-1} it has at 50% RH. This may be due to unrestrained shrinkage of the painting across the uniaxial sample, which compresses the sailcloth, and releases tension along its length. This is the type of artifact that would not occur in a biaxial sample.
7. The residual unrecovered tension may represent backlash in the mechanical device, since only 2 mm backlash in the 90 mm incremental movement of each clamp would cause the observed –5 N m^{-1} residual.
8. In an analogous situation, a stiff backing board attached to the stretcher can be stiffer than the oil ground, and thus prevent cracking during corner drops, not by virtue of amazing material properties, but by virtue of its much greater thickness. This would just leave the risk of spiderweb cracking due to direct blows from the front. A board directly behind the painting canvas would reduce, if not eliminate, this risk.

Non-Invasive Evaluation of Moisture Sorption and Desorption Processes in Canvases

M.Odlyha*, G.Foster
Birkbeck College, University of London, 29 Gordon Square, London WC1H OPP, UK
M. Scharff
Danish Royal Academy of Fine Arts, Esplanaden 34, DK 1263 Copenhagen K, Denmark

Abstract

Dielectric analysis using the open-ended coaxial probe technique was applied to the non-invasive monitoring of moisture sorption and desorption processes in three different samples. Results are reported for the humidification and dehumidification studies in naturally aged unprimed canvas containing remnants of aged lining adhesive, the response of artificially aged primed canvas sample to atmospheres of relative humidities corresponding to 60%, 80% and 95%, and the effect of temperature variation on moisture sorption processes in naturally aged primed canvas from Landseer's 'Study of a Lion'.

Keywords

Canvas, non-invasive dielectric analysis, open-ended coaxial probe, moisture sorption and desorption

Introduction

This paper describes the application of dielectric analysis using the open-ended coaxial probe technique[1,2] to evaluate non-invasively the moisture sorption and desorption processes. These occur, for example, during humidification procedures using suction table techniques on canvas paintings. The conservation of canvas paintings by means of suction table (low pressure) techniques was developed in the sixties in Denmark, and other suction table techniques were developed in the seventies in the Netherlands.[3] Since that time these techniques have enjoyed wide recognition and their use is rapidly spreading.[4] In general, it has been recognised that a combination of heat, moisture, aqueous glues and minimal pressure has for a long time proved useful in the relaxation, regeneration and consolidation of paintings on canvas.[5,6] A major advantage of suction table techniques is the possibility of controlled use of humidity as part of conservation procedures, as in the regeneration of aged and partially deteriorated animal glue in canvas paintings, and in flattening of deformed painted structures and cupped paint layers. An additional advantage is that part of the treatment can be carried out without covering the painting under treatment with a facing or with membranes; this makes it possible to gain access to the paint surface during treatment for local intervention. This would allow a small dielectric probe, such as the one used in this experiment , to be placed onto the surface being treated to monitor moisture uptake through the material.

In this paper preliminary measurements are described where a small coaxial probe is placed on the surface of a sample contained in a glass cell. The glass cell is attached to a humidification system so that air at a controlled humidity passes from the bottom of the cell and flows through the sample for defined periods of time. The first example to be discussed in this paper is the effect of humidification treatment at room temperature on aged lining adhesive on a sample of 19th century lining canvas from an unknown painting. The second example considers the effect of humidification on an artificially aged sample of primed glue-sized canvas where the priming consists of a layer of cremnitz white in oil. And the third example demonstrates the effect of temperature on moisture uptake in the case of a naturally aged sample (19th century Landseer's 'Study of a Lion'). This sample was chosen since a large amount of information already exists on its behaviour with respect to relative humidity. Originally its mechanical behaviour during relative humidity cycling was studied.[7] The sample is on closely woven linen and is primed with a lean mixture of lead white and calcium carbonate. Its response to variations in relative humidity and temperature has also been studied by thermomechanical and dielectric techniques.[8,9] Information therefore exists on the value of its softening temperature (in the region of 50°C at relative humidity values of 50% RH), and how this varies with exposure to different values of relative humidity (nearly room temperature at relative humidity values above 90%).[10]

The technique of dielectric analysis involves the application of an alternating electric field to a sample. If the sample is polar the dipoles within that material will orientate in order to reduce their free energy to a minimum. The rate at which these relaxation processes occur provides information on the structure and

*Author to whom correspondence should be addressed.

behaviour of a given sample. In previous studies low-frequency dielectric analysis has been used to measure the degree to which water is bound within the system.[6] This is of considerable interest in connection with both conservation treatment involving humidification and the effect of environmental variations on the painting. In this paper the dielectric analysis measurements have been made in the microwave region. In the frequency region between 2.45 and 20 GHz the dielectric constant (ε') and the dielectric loss factor (ε'') are highly correlated with moisture content since the permittivity of water greatly exceeds that of the dry sample. The relaxation processes of the dipoles associated with the sample are not observed. What are observed, however, are the relaxation processes of water molecules and other small molecules such as methanol.

Since the behaviour of the dielectric constant is more regular than that of the loss factor with respect to changes in moisture content and the frequency of the applied fields,[11] it is this parameter that has been monitored in this experiment.

The objectives of this experimental study were:

1. to set up a system for the humidification of canvas samples;
2. to use the small coaxial probe (0.86 mm o.d.) to monitor changes in the sample during humidification and dehumidification processes and to atmospheres of defined relative humidities;
3. to evaluate the effect of temperature variation (in the range 20 to 60°C) on moisture sorption; and
4. to provide information on the actual moisture content of the samples during these processes.

Evaluation of the effects of 2 and 3 is of importance since both the equilibrium moisture content of the sample and the rate at which it absorbs moisture are controlled by the relative humidity of the environment and temperature of the sample. In studies of composite materials,[12] several routes by which water is absorbed into a composite have been identified:

- absorption by the matrix;
- penetration through surface crazes and cracks;
- absorption along fibres through capillary action;
- moisture absorption by the reinforcement.

These processes can also be considered as occurring in the primed canvas samples. Such intrusion by moisture, which may also be caused by environmental exposure for extended periods, is known to have an adverse effect on the structural integrity of polymer matrix composite materials.[13] Diffusion through the organic matrix may lead to degradation of the polymer structure and moisture migration along the fibre–matrix interface which weakens the interfacial bond.

Experimental procedure

Measuring system

The equipment used in this study consisted of an 8720C Hewlett-Packard Network Analyser system with a semi-rigid coaxial probe. The open end of a coaxial probe (0.86 mm o.d.) was placed in contact with the sample and the reflection characteristics at the interface were measured using the network analyser. The methodology and measurement technique have been reported elsewhere.[1] In this paper further developments in the software have made it possible to record permittivity values of the samples in a continuous manner as a function of time and hence to directly monitor changes in the samples during their exposure to different environments.

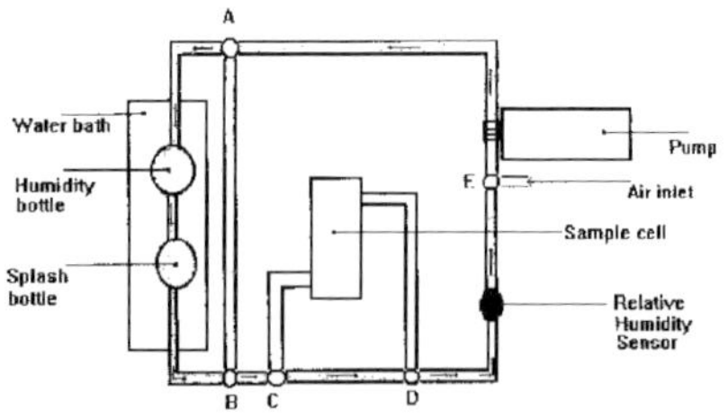

Figure 1. Experimental humidification system used for aged lining adhesive. This shows initial circulation of humid air in closed system excluding the sample cell

Humidification of naturally aged canvas containing remnants of aged lining adhesive

A glass sample cell was connected to a system which included a peristaltic pump and two Dreschel bottles placed in a water bath at 25°C (Figure 1). A humidity

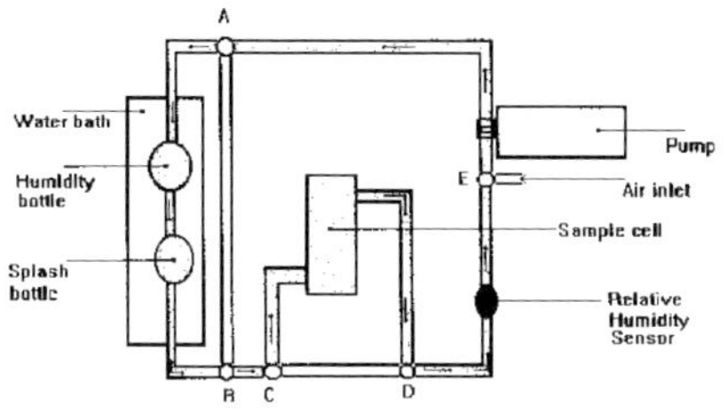

Figure 2. Experimental humidification system used for aged lining adhesive. This shows circulation of humid air in closed system including the sample cell

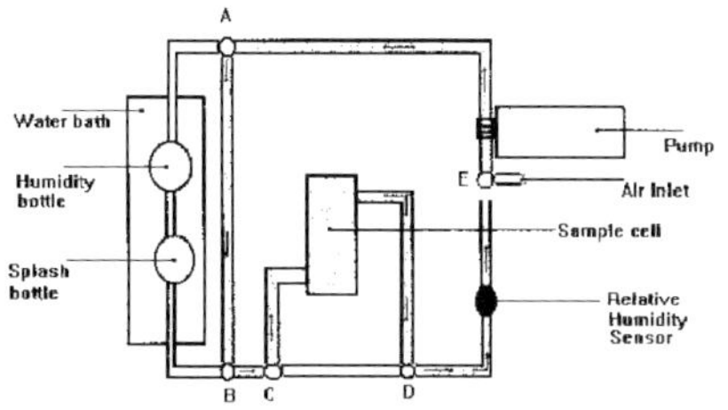

Figure 3. Experimental system used for aged lining adhesive. This shows circulation of air in closed system excluding the humidification system in the water bath

sensor was placed in line to measure the relative humidity and temperature of the system. Humidified air was initially circulated in the closed system to establish equilibrium conditions (Figure 1). After about 30 min taps A, C and D were opened to include the sample cell (Figure 2). Taps A and B were then turned to a position to close the circulation of humid air and to allow drying out of the system and dehumidification (Figure 3).

Readings of permittivity were made against frequency (2.45 to 20 GHz) before introduction of the humid air (Figure 4a) and then after the introduction of air saturated with water vapour (corresponding to 100% RH) at room temperature(Figure 4b). The sample was then dehumidified and readings were taken after about an hour of drying the sample and when there were no further changes to the values recorded (Figure 4c). The sample was then rehumidified (Figure 4d).

Permittivity data were also recorded continuously as a function of time at a selected frequency (2.45 GHz) for a period of 200 min. The results are shown in Figure 5 (a, c, e humidification and b, d, f dehumidification processes).

Humidification of the artificially aged primed canvas sample

The system was modified as shown in Figure 6 to provide temperature control in the sample chamber. Water was pumped from the water bath and circulated around the chamber. The shape of the cell was also modified to provide a small lower compartment to hold H_2SO_4/H_2O mixtures for generating environments of specified RH.

Prior to exposure of the samples to humid air, values of the glass transition temperature (T_g) and initial moisture content of the samples were determined by dynamic mechanical thermal analysis (DMTA) and thermogravimetric analysis (TGA) respectively. After this evaluation samples were placed on the wire gauze in the sample cell, the dielectric probe positioned on the sample with optimum contact (determined by the level of noise obtained in the response). The whole system was thoroughly dried, starting sample permittivity values were recorded, and the measuring system was activated to read continuously as a function of time. Solutions containing known amounts of H_2SO_4/H_2O were introduced through the side arm with a teat pipette. Air was bubbled through these solutions via a peristaltic pump to assist in the circulation of the required humidity.

After humidification, samples were rapidly removed and sealed into aluminium crucibles. A small hole was pierced in the crucible and the sample was promptly heated in a thermogravimetry system (Shimadzu TG-50 thermogravimetric

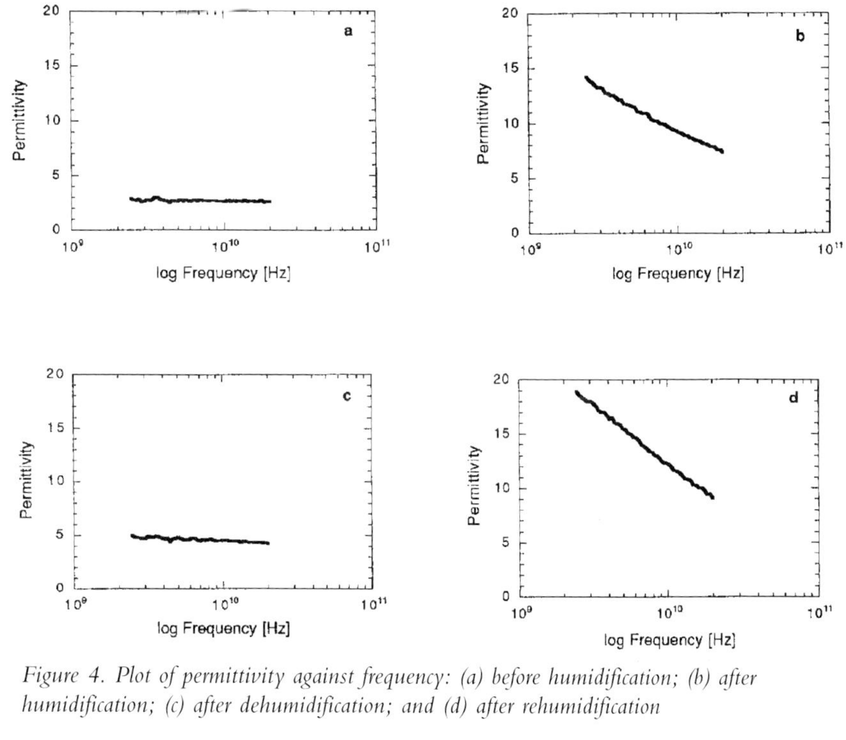

Figure 4. Plot of permittivity against frequency: (a) before humidification; (b) after humidification; (c) after dehumidification; and (d) after rehumidification

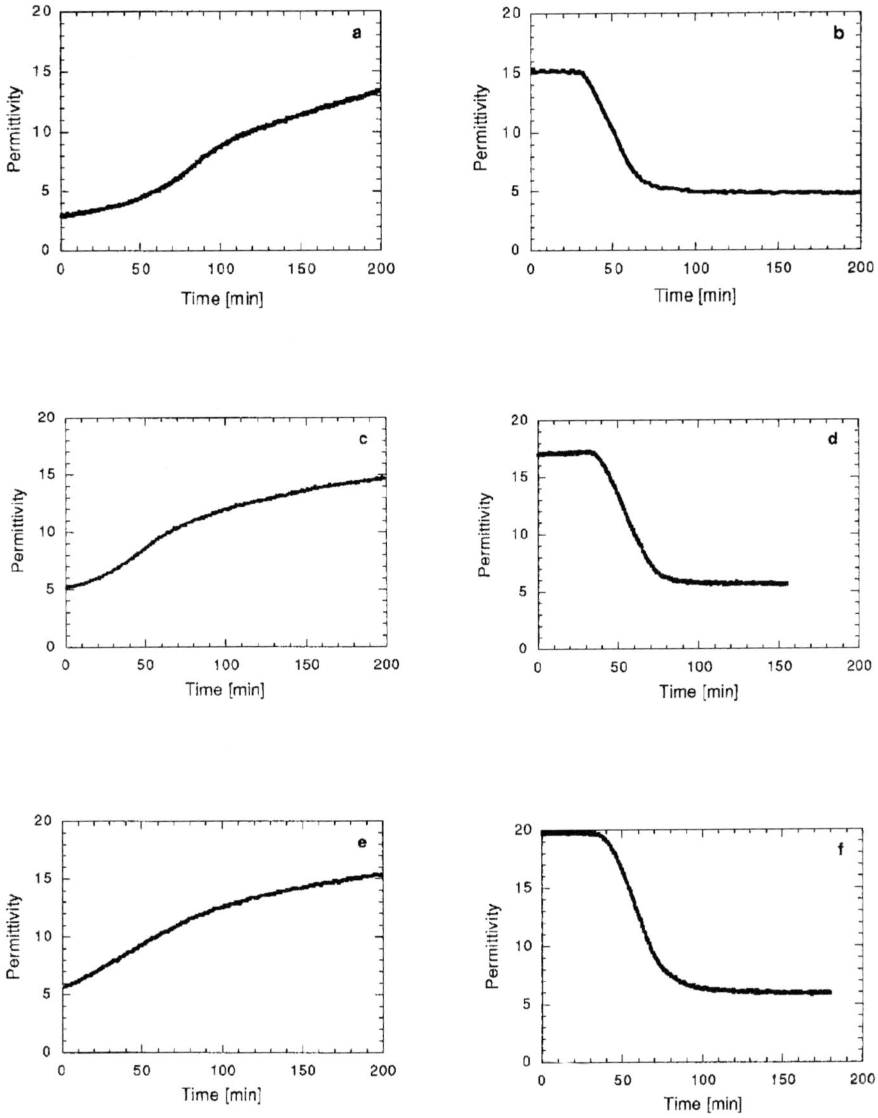

Figure 5. Plot of permittivity against time (a, c, e humidification and b, d, f dehumidification) at 2.45 GHz

analyser) to 200°C to determine the weight loss due to moisture uptake and to provide a means of correlating measured weight with permittivity values.

Humidification of Landseer's 'Study of a Lion' at varying temperatures

A similar experimental procedure was followed to that described already for the previous primed sample. Differences can be summarized as follows: the lower compartment of the sample chamber was replaced by water (temperature variation provides variation in RH and so it was decided to work at saturated water vapour conditions); there was no bubbling of air through the lower compartment as with increase in temperature this led to problems of wetting of the sample.

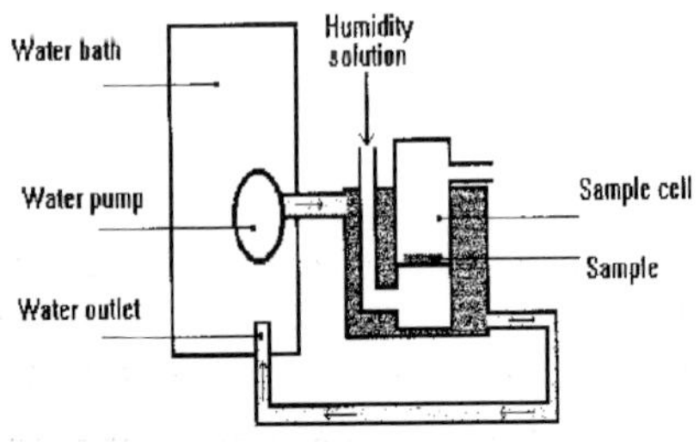

Figure 6. Modification of experimental system for humidification studies of primed canvas samples

Results and discussion

Humidification of naturally aged canvas containing remnants of aged lining adhesive

Figure 5a shows the increase in permittivity with time during humidification with air saturated with water vapour at 25°C. The first 50 min shows a slow increase in permittivity. This is then followed by a more pronounced increase over the next 40 min, which again changes to a slower rate after 100 min. The changes in slope at the different times indicate different rates of sorption and are indicative of different mechanisms that may be occurring in the composite sample. The humid

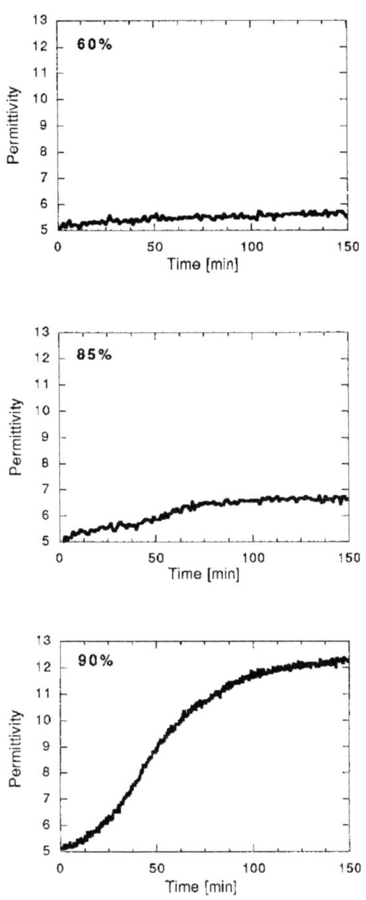

Figure 7. Plot of permittivity against time for response of artificially aged primed sample to 60%, 85% and 90% RH

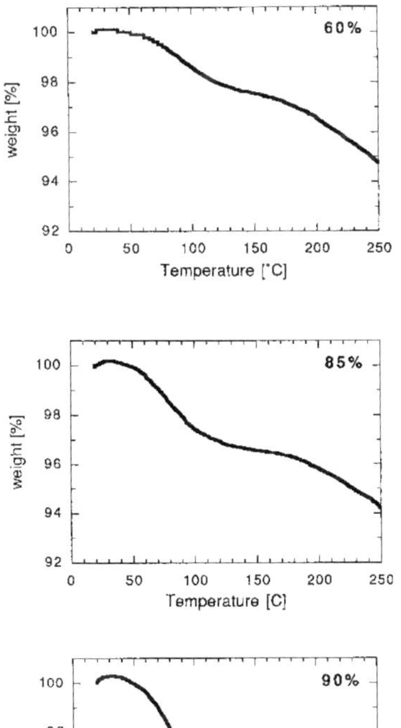

Figure 8. Thermogravimetry curves for artificially aged primed canvas sample after exposure to 60%, 85% and 90% RH

air passes through the canvas side and then migrates through the composite. Figure 5b shows the dehumidification of the sample. Moisture is lost after 30 min and the moisture loss extends over a period of 40 min. Dehumidification or drying of the material was continued for a period of 200 min and to a stage where the permittivity value had reached a definite plateau.

Figure 5c shows re-humidification of the same sample. The starting value of the permittivity is higher than the original value. This indicates that the material exhibits a memory effect in its response to moisture. The response to initial uptake is faster than in the original case and the overall increase in permittivity is higher. The dehumidification starts at a higher value of permittivity (Figure 5d), but the overall shape of the curve is similar to that of the curve in Figure 5b.

Figure 5e shows the second re-humidification of the sample. These processes have been recorded without removing the probe from the sample. The curve shows no initial delay like that in the curves in Figure 5 (a) and (c) and the starting value of permittivity is once again higher than in the previous two cases. Figure 5f shows the third de-humidification process. The starting value is higher than in the previous two cases. The loss occurs after the first 30 min and continues until 90 min.

Humidification of the artificially aged primed canvas sample

The sample exposed to 60% RH showed a small increase in permittivity over the period of 150 min. The increase appeared almost in a linear manner as a function of time (Figure 7).

The sample exposed to 85% RH (Figure 7) showed a slightly faster rate in moisture uptake than the 60%. At the end of the first 40 min there is an increase in the rate of uptake for the next 30 min and this is followed by a levelling off to a higher value than that obtained for the 60% RH.

The sample exposed to 90% RH(Figure 7) shows immediately a more rapid rate of uptake and the final value is considerably higher than in the other two cases.

The corresponding weight uptakes for the three samples (measured as a mass loss by TGA) were found to be 2.7%, 3.7% and 5.3% (Figure 8). The weight loss for an untreated sample under normal laboratory conditions was 2.2%. The difference then corresponds to the amount of moisture present in the sample after humidification for 150 min and there is a definite increase in weight with increasing RH. An increase in relative humidity is known to increase the moisture content of samples and it can be measured in this experiment in terms of increasing values of permittivity. Thus values of permittivity can be directly related to increasing values obtained for the weight losses.

Explanation of the enhanced moisture uptake at higher values of relative humidity can be made in terms of the glass transition temperature. It is well established in polymer science that water sorption below the T_g of materials is lower than at temperatures above the T_g. Measurement of the T_g of the sample studied was found to be about 40°C. This is obtained from the dynamic mechanical thermal analysis (DMTA) curve (Figure 9) at the temperature where the storage modulus starts to fall in value or from the temperature of the tan δ peak. A discussion of the DMTA technique and the meaning of parameters storage modulus and tan δ have been described elsewhere.[8] At higher values of relative humidity the T_g of materials is lowered. Therefore at 90% RH the T_g value of the sample will be shifted to temperatures at which the measurements are being made (25°C) and so moisture sorption will be in the region of the T_g and will increase.

Humidification of Landseer's 'Study of a Lion' at varying temperatures

Figure10 shows the results for the humidification (100% RH) of the 19th century primed canvas sample at 25°C. There are three distinct regions of response : in the first 20 min a slow uptake followed by a sharp increase of over 4 permittivity units and a levelling off in its value. At 40°C there is an immediate linear increase in the first 10 min, which then continues until it levels off to a higher value of 14 at the end of 50 min. At 60°C there is an increase of about 8 permittivity units over a period of 5 min, followed by a slower increase of 4 units over the next 20 min.

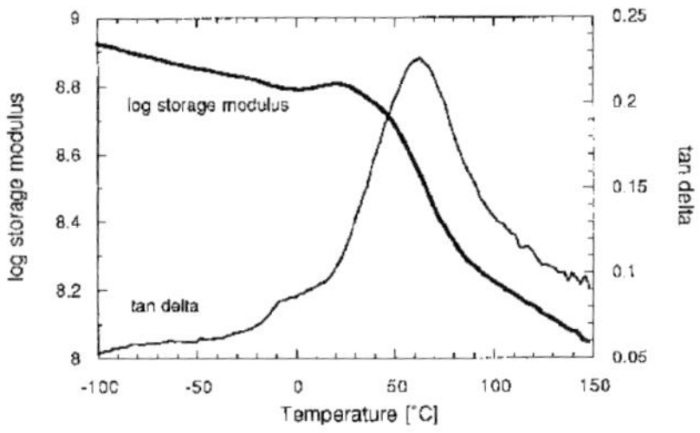

Figure 9. Dynamic mechanical thermal analysis curve for artificially aged primed canvas sample

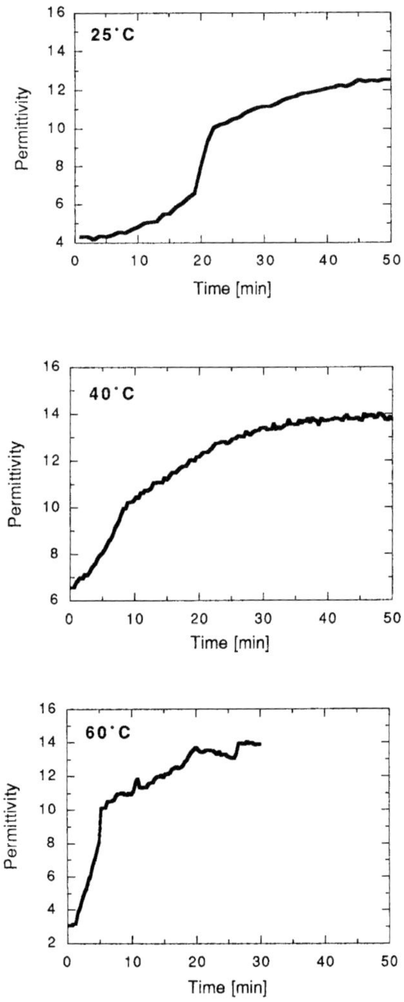

Figure 10. Plot of permittivity against time for humidification of naturally aged Landseer primed canvas at 25°C, 40°C and 60°C

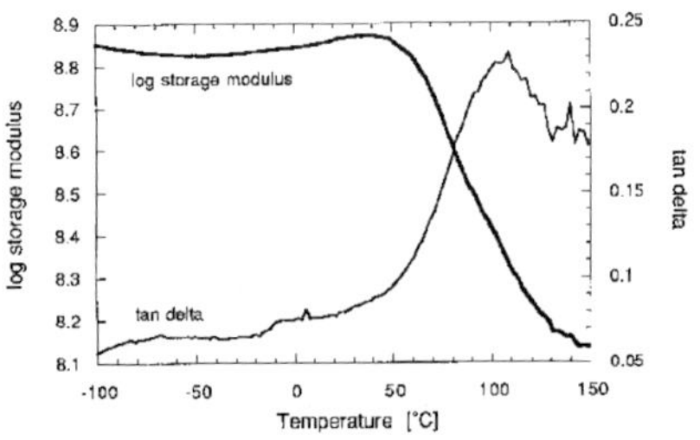

Figure 11. Dynamic mechanical thermal analysis curve for naturally aged Landseer primed canvas

The T_g of this sample is shown in Figure 11 and the softening of the modulus value occurs in the region of 50°C. As temperature increases the shift occurs closer to the T_g of the sample and increase in moisture sorption occurs.

Conclusions

The dielectric probe is sensitive to changes in the moisture content of the sample. The ability to monitor continuously as a function of time provides the facility for understanding the response of the composite whether moisture uptake occurs in a linear fashion or whether it occurs in a number of steps at differing rates.

Acknowledgements

The authors are most grateful and would like to sincerely thank Dr Scott Conrad of Hewlett Packard in providing the measuring system. Without his sympathetic attitude and practical assistance this paper would not have been possible. The authors would like to thank Dr A.Chan for the use of the software for operating the measuring system, Stephen Hackney and Dr J. Townsend for providing the artificially aged sample and the Landseer primed sample, and Dr Stella Casagrande in Felder for assistance in the preparation of the figures.

References

1. T.Y.AS. Chan, M. Odlyha and M. Scharff, "In situ Non-invasive Spectroscopy for Monitoring Conservation Treatment of Canvas Paintings" *Deutsche Gesellschaft für Zerstörungsfreie Prüfung*, (Berlin, 1994), 510–520.
2. T.Y.AS. Chan, M.Odlyha and M.Scharff, "In situ Dielectric Analysis for Canvas Paintings", *Conservator* 19 (1995): 10–19.
3. B. Hacke, "En Utraditonel Metode til Vacuumtoilering af Temperamalei på Lærred", *Meddelelser om Konservering* (1963–1964); V.R Mehra, "A Low Pressure Cold Lining Table", (Paper delivered at Conference on Comparative Lining Techniques, National Maritime Museum, Greenwich, 1974); V.R Mehra, "Further Developments in Cold Lining (Nap-bond System)", (Paper delivered at the fourth Triennal Meeting of the International Council for Museums Committee for Conservation, Venice, 1975).
4. A. Reeve, P. Ackroyd and A. Stephenson-Wright, "The Multi-Purpose Low Pressure Conservation Table", *National Gallery Technical Bulletin* 12 (1988): 4–15.
5. G. Hedley, "The Practicalities of the Interaction of Moisture with Oil Paintings on Canvas" *Measured Opinions* (London: United Kingdom Institute for Conservation, 1993): 112–123.
6. G. Hedley and M. Odlyha, "The Moisture Softening of Paint Films and its Implications for the Treatment of Fabric-supported Paintings" *Measured Opinions* (London: United Kingdom Institute for Conservation, 1993): 99–102.
7. G. Hedley, "Relative Humidity and the Stress Strain Response of Canvas Paintings: Uniaxial Measurements of Naturally Aged Samples" *Measured Opinions* (London: United Kingdom Institute for Conservation, 1993): 86–96.
8. M. Odlyha, T.Y.A. Chan, and O. Pages, "Evaluation of Relative Humidity Effects on Fabric-Supported Paintings by Dynamic Mechanical and Dielectric Analysis" *Thermochimica Acta* 263 (1995): 7–21.
9. M. Odlyha, D.Q.M. Craig, and R.M.Hill, "Dielectric Analysis of Relative Humidity Variations in Canvas Paintings" *Journal of Thermal Analysis* 39 (1993): 1181–1192.
10. R. MacBeth, M. Odlyha, A. Burnstock, C. Villers, and R. Bruce-Gardner, "Evaluation of Moisture Treatment of Fabric-Supported Paintings", (Paperdelivered at the Tenth Triennial Meeting of the International Council for Museums Committee for Conservation, Washington, DC, 1993), 150–156.
11. S. Nelson, W.Forbus Jr, and K. Lawrence "Permittivities of Fresh Fruits and Vegetables at 0.2 to 20 GHz" *Journal of Microwave Power nd Electromagnetic Energy* 29 (1994): 82–92.
12. K.B. Armstrong "Repairing the Damage" in *Proceedimgs of the Seminar 'Bonding and Repair of Composites'* (London: Butterworths, 1989), 93–99.
13. J. Summerscales, "Non-destructive Measurement of the Moisture Content in Fibre Reinforced Plastics" *British Journal of Non-Destructive Testing* 36 (1994): 66–71.

Use of KrF Excimer Laser for Cleaning Fragile and Problematic Paint Surfaces

William A. Real*
The Carnegie Museum of Art, 4400 Forbes Avenue, Pittsburgh, PA 15213, USA

Ioanna Zergioti, Yota Spetsidou, Demetrios Anglos
Foundation for Research and Technology–Hellas (FORTH), PO Box 1527, 711 10 Heraklion, Crete, Greece

Abstract

Preliminary tests were conducted to evaluate the potential for using KrF excimer lasers for removing unwanted material from fragile, damaged, or otherwise problematic paint surfaces where conventional cleaning methods might not be satisfactory. Some examples: removal of adhesive tape from unbound pigment; removal of surface coatings from underbound matte paint of similar solubility parameter; removal of spray paint from unvarnished acrylic, marker, and pastel; removal of soot and other stains from a fresh acrylic film; and removal of surface coatings from poorly adhered, flaking substrates. Results of the tests are evaluated and described, including details of the laser irradiation parameters, visual observation, microscopic observation, and reflectance spectrophotometry. Preliminary conclusions are proposed.

Keywords

Paintings, contemporary, laser, test, cleaning, stain removal, reflectance spectrophotometry

Introduction

The use of laser technology for treatment of works of art has a brief history. Neodymium-YAG lasers have been studied since the 1970s, primarily for stone cleaning[1–6,15–18] and more recently for removal of mold stains from paper.[7] The potential applicability of excimer lasers for removing foreign material from painted surfaces has been proposed only recently, primarily for removing aged natural resin varnishes and/or overpaint from traditional tempera or oil paintings.[8–12] Based on this research, and on reported success using lasers to remove encrustation from badly deteriorated stone surfaces with no observed damage to the original porous and friable material,[15] the concept of using similar laser techniques to remove unwanted material from fragile, modern paint surfaces appears to be worthy of investigation.

To this end, the first author collaborated with researchers at The Foundation for Research and Technology-Hellas (FORTH) in Heraklion, Crete, Greece, who first reported the methodology to the conservation community in the USA.[11] Samples were prepared to simulate conditions sometimes found particularly in modern and contemporary paintings that would be vexing or impossible to resolve with the existing conservation repertoire. The problems posed included:

- removal of adhesive tape from unbound pigment;
- removal of surface coatings from underbound matte paint of similar solubility parameter;
- removal of spray paint from unvarnished acrylic, marker, and pastel;
- removal of soot and other stains from a fresh acrylic film;
- removal of surface coatings from poorly adhered, flaking substrates.

We hoped that the results would suggest whether the laser offered a potentially practical alternative to resolve such problems, which applications showed the most promise, and what further improvements might be indicated. Prior experience using excimer laser for paintings conservation had been to clean aged natural resin varnishes and overpaint from older paint films, for which the appropriate irradiation parameters had to be worked out through extensive experimentation. Thus, the tests that form the subject of this paper represent a new line of application, and though preliminary, the results do indicate some conclusions.

Sample preparation and laser irradiation conditions

Primary sample materials are described under each test below; others are listed in the Materials section. After preparation, all samples were oven-dried at 65°C for five days.

The cleaning was performed on an experimental work station constructed at the laser laboratories at FORTH. Samples were irradiated using a krypton fluoride (KrF) excimer laser (LPX-205 Lambda Physik) emitting 15 ns pulses at a wavelength (λ) of 248 nm. The laser beam typically covered an area about 1 cm^2; however, the size of the beam could be modified with an intervening mask or

*Author to whom correspondence should be addressed.

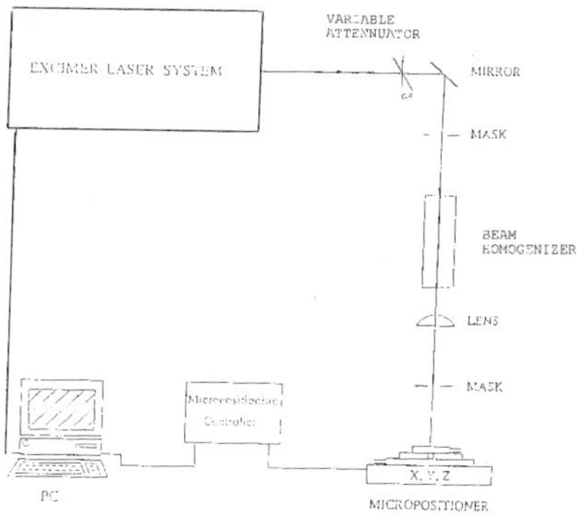

Figure 1. Schematic diagram of KrF excimer laser cleaning system

modulated with a focusing lens (Figure 1). The irradiation parameters were recorded, including the energy fluence of the laser pulse in joules per square centimeter (J cm^{-2}); whether the beam was focused or unfocused; the number of pulses; the repetition rate of the pulses (Hz); and whether the pulses were applied ("scanned") in an overlapping sequence to cover a wider area, using an *X/Y/Z* micropositioning easel.

Two laser physicists operated the equipment[20] – one entering coordinates for the micropositioning easel and one entering the laser exposure parameters based largely upon prior experimentation with traditional paintings. These tests were thus meant more to gain preliminary insight into the laser's potential applicability in these situations than to measure and compare the results of various laser irradiation parameters on various materials.

The "scanning" technique developed in prior laser cleaning work at FORTH was used in some tests to simulate the way in which the laser might actually be applied. Comparisons between static exposure tests and "scanning" tests must take into account that since scanned exposures overlap, the total laser energy input in any given sample area is greater than it would be with the identical irradiation conditions in a static exposure.[21]

Test results were evaluated with visual and microscopic observation, and visible-light reflectance spectrophotometry. Samples were photographed before and after treatment.

Test results

Test 1. Removal of spray paint from unvarnished acrylic, marker, and pastel

This series of tests was designed to simulate troublesome graffiti-removal problems. Krylon® #1601 Glossy Black Interior/Exterior Enamel was applied to the white acrylic ground of a proprietary canvas panel, and also over the same surface with lines made with a black Pilot® Fineliner marker and white Eberhard-Faber NuPastel®.

To remove the black paint directly from the white ground, an area was irradiated with a focused beam with 22 pulses at 1.3 J cm^{-2} and a repetition rate of 10 Hz, scanned across 35 mm. The laser removed the black paint, but also removed some of the original acrylic paint and induced a grayish discoloration. Under the microscope a pattern caused by the scanned overlapping exposures was clearly visible, especially at the edges of the irradiated area.

In another area, the black overpaint was irradiated (40 pulses, unfocused, at 0.21 J cm^{-2} and 5 Hz) with much better results: only tiny islands of black paint remained in the valleys of the surface; the white ground appeared undamaged under microscopic inspection.

To remove the black spray paint from the marker, we employed 40 pulses, unfocused, 0.21 J cm^{-2} and 10 Hz were applied. Before the laser could remove all of the black spray paint, it began to remove (or fade) the marker ink.

The black overpaint was "thinned" in an area containing the marker and pastel lines, using 54 pulses, unfocused, beam at 0.19–0.21 J cm^{-2}, at 10 Hz, scanned over 35 mm. Though some material was removed, visual improvement was minimal. As before, the scanned pattern was evident under the microscope at the edges of the irradiated area.

Test 2. Removal of soot and stains from a fresh unvarnished acrylic film

This series of tests was designed to simulate stain removal problems in modern and contemporary paintings. Typically stains and accretions are difficult to remove because of solubility problems and the risk of burnishing or dulling the original surface from contact with the cleaning swab.

A proprietary acrylic-primed canvas panel was soiled with blue ball point pen ink, chocolate, machine oil, linseed oil, beeswax, and soot from a butane cigarette lighter. In addition, the panel was randomly handled to create fingermarkings of unknown substances on the acrylic surface.

In one soot-removal test (three pulses, focused, at 1.3 J cm^{-2} and 10 Hz) paint at the center of the exposed area showed a pronounced grayish discoloration while at the sides it was free of soot and apparently undamaged. Apparently the more appropriate exposure occurred at the perimeter of the beam, while the more focused and intense center part of the beam damaged the paint. A simple adjustment of the beam size relative to the focal distance of the lens from the irradiated surface would have produced more homogenous results, but was not attempted.

In another test (five pulses, unfocused, at a lower fluence of 0.23 J cm^{-2} and 10 Hz) the soot layer was substantially and evenly thinned, leaving the underlying paint apparently undamaged.

Tests on other stains generally resulted in minimal removal of material, accompanied by a grayish discoloration of the acrylic paint.[22]

Test 3. Removal of surface coatings from underbound matte paint and/or paint of similar solubility parameter

This series of tests was designed to simulate an inappropriately varnished modern or contemporary painting with a particularly sensitive surface. Attempts to clean such a painting with solvents could drive the solubilized coating into the porous substrate, causing staining or tidelining. Direct contact with the surface during treatment might also cause removal of original material or permanent alteration of the reflective qualities of the original surface by abrasion or burnishing.

Maimeri® Restauro Colore a Vernice, Cadmium Red Medium (#723) diluted in xylene to a very lean mixture was applied to a proprietary acrylic-primed panel and then sprayed with Krylon® Crystal-Clear Acrylic Spray Coating #1303. The lean Maimeri varnish medium was chosen to approximate the unusual artist-formulated paints sometimes found on contemporary paintings. Three different exposures resulted in partial ablation of the coating. The best results were obtained with one pulse, unfocused, at 0.15 J cm^{-2} followed by careful brushing away of disrupted material. The central 70–80% of the area was mostly free of coating; microscopic examination revealed small remaining islands. Comparison of the uncoated, coated, and irradiated areas was made using visible light reflectance spectrophotometry; the results are discussed below.

In another test, an extremely lean mixture of dry pigment in Acryloid® B-72 was coated with a brushcoat of Soluvar® Gloss varnish. Irradiation (12 pulses, unfocused, at 0.12–0.15 J cm^{-2} and 1 Hz) ablated some of the relatively thick Soluvar layer, leaving behind a layer of variable thickness. The results of this test and others in this series suggest that the excimer laser can remove coatings incrementally given the correct irradiation parameters.

Test 4. Removal of surface coatings from poorly adhered, flaking substrates

These samples were prepared by applying Schminke® carmine red gouache to a nonabsorbent acrylic ground and coating by spray (Acryloid® B-72 10% in xylene) or brush (Liquitex® Soluvar Gloss varnish). After oven drying, some of the gouache was precariously flaking; paint that appeared adhered to the ground could also be disrupted by direct touch or friction. Typically a conservator in this situation would consolidate the fragile paint before removing any foreign material, introducing complications of solubility, staining, and removal of the foreign material after consolidation. We wondered if the laser could safely remove the coating first, allowing straightforward resolution of the consolidation problem after cleaning.

An area of pronounced flaking was irradiated with eight pulses, unfocused, at 0.15 J cm^{-2} and 1 Hz. The B-72 was removed, exposing the apparently undamaged paint, although there was a slight but visible movement of the lifting paint during irradiation. Later, during reflectance spectral analysis, the paint flaked away either by gravity or inadvertent handling. Microscopic observation of the remaining paint revealed that the varnish had not been completely removed; small islands remained, and tiny flakes of dislodged varnish were gently brushed away.

Similar results occurred in an adjacent area irradiated with similar conditions (unfocused, seven pulses at 0.14–0.15 J cm^{-2}, 1 Hz), and in an area of gouache covered by Soluvar® (unfocused, nine pulses at 0.15–0.19 J cm^{-2}, 1 Hz). Disrupted coating that remained tenuously adhered to the surface was carefully brushed away. Visually, in terms of color, saturation, and reflectance characteristics these areas appeared similar to adjacent uncoated areas of gouache; comparison of the uncoated, coated, and laser-irradiated areas by visible light reflectance spectrophotometry is discussed below.

In the B-72/gouache test, the unfocused beam left a pronounced pattern: at either side of the irradiated area, the B-72 was not ablated, but appeared blanched in a narrow band. In the Soluvar/gouache test, the unfocused beam left a similar whitish banding at the edges of the irradiated area, and removed the coating discontinuously over about three-quarters of the beam's center. As in test #2, a simple adjustment of the optical parameters might well have corrected these heterogeneous results.

Test 5. Removal of Scotch® Magic Transparent tape from unbound pigment

This test was designed to create a situation that, though unlikely, would be virtually impossible to resolve with conventional conservation techniques.

The sample was prepared by brushing Cadmium Red pigment (Conservation Materials #4065) suspended in turpentine onto a proprietary acrylic canvas board and allowing the solvent to evaporate. The tape was pressed in place directly over the pigment. One test (60 pulses, unfocused, at 0.12 J cm^{-2} and 10 Hz) successfully removed the carrier and the adhesive in the center of the test with no observable damage to the substrate. To either side of the beam center, the tape acquired a whitish appearance either from increased scattering from a disrupted carrier surface, or from partial detachment of the carrier from the substrate. By contrast, a test conducted over a scanned area with a focused beam at higher energy fluence (0.79 J cm^{-2}) and fewer pulses (30) yielded discontinuous removal and charring of tape material and removal of original pigment substrate.

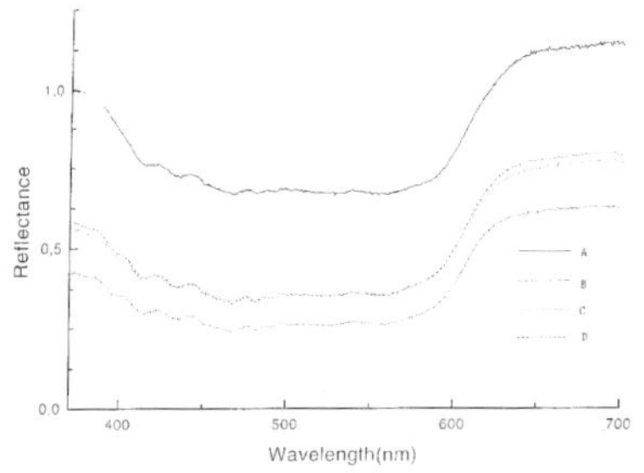

Figure 2. Reflectance spectra from Krylon/ Maimeri test: A: Maimeri Colori a Restauro Cadmium Red Medium spray-coated with Krylon Crystal Clear Acrylic varnish. B: Uncoated Maimeri Colori a Restauro and C and D: Two partially laser-cleaned areas

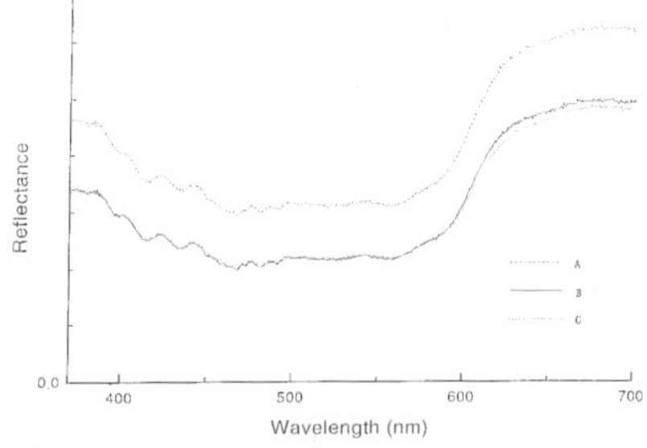

Figure 3. Reflectance spectra from B-72/ Gouache test: A: Schminke Carmine Red Gouache spray coated with Acryloid B-72. B: Uncoated Gouache. C: Gouache cleaned with laser

Test 6. Removal of masking tape from acrylic ground

Tests made with various parameters succeeded in removing the tape carrier, but only partially removed the adhesive, in some cases charring the adhesive and damaging the acrylic ground.

Comparison of reflectance spectra

Tests 3 and 4 were evaluated using visible light reflectance spectrophotometry, to confirm or modify our visual impressions that the treated areas appeared very similar to the original, uncoated areas. Spectra were taken of the original uncoated areas, the untreated coated areas, and one or more of the laser-treated areas. In the case of the Krylon/Maimeri, the spectra of the irradiated areas – which had significant residues of coating – predictably showed a higher reflectance than the original uncoated paint surface, with no apparent associated color shift (Figure 2).

In the B-72/gouache samples, the spectra of the original uncoated and laser-treated areas very nearly conformed, with some slight but measurable loss of reflectance in the 600–700 nm range in the laser-treated area (Figure 3). These spectra confirm the very successful results of this test – perhaps the most promising results of this study. It would be instructive to compare these results with those of more traditional cleaning methods..

Discussion

The mechanism of excimer cleaning is complex and not yet perfectly understood.[12–19] In simple terms, the intense photon energy of the laser, absorbed by the irradiated material, initiates a variety of processes, collectively described by the term "photoablation," including electronic excitation, selective heating, evaporation, plasma and shock wave formation.

What actually happens in any given exposure is the result of a complex interaction of light with matter, depending on the particular laser exposure parameters (wavelength, peak power, fluence, pulse duration and shape, repetition rate, and irradiation geometry) and the material parameters of the irradiated structure (absorption coefficient, reflectivity, thermal diffusivity, enthalpy of evaporation and heat capacity).[12] The filtering effects of plasma plumes during "scanning" or repetitive pulses may be another factor. Ultimately the irradiation may produce only photoablation of a thin layer of material (as little as 0.5 to 1 m), or it may also disrupt material by shock and/or rapid oxidation by thermal effects. The challenge in laser cleaning of paintings is to match the laser parameters to the material parameters to achieve a controllable material removal with no damage to the underlying structure. Some initial investigation in this area has been reported.[7,13,14]

In theory, the results of laser cleaning should be predictable based upon the known absorption spectra of various materials at the emitted laser wavelength and under a limited range of quantifiable exposure parameters. At the very least, theoretical calculations might suggest the types of structures that are not promising candidates for laser cleaning.

In our tests, we observed a range of laser–material interactions, from what we speculate to be simple photoablation (for example, tests 2 and 3), to disruption of material from shock wave (for example, test 4), to damage to original material from thermal charring (for example, tests 1, 5 and 6).

We also observed what may have been photochemical fading of the black marker ink in test 1, suggesting that the ultraviolet energy in an exposure is significant despite the brief pulse duration of 15 ns. Even when color changes or photochemical damage are not observed to the naked eye, it is possible that changes occur invisibly at the molecular level, becoming visibly manifest only after further aging. These questions require further inquiry.

The results suggest that when shock is involved, the adhesion of the coating to the substrate and the brittleness of the coating have a pronounced effect on the result of laser irradiation and its shock component. For example, the relatively brittle tape carrier was more easily removed than the adhesive. By contrast, the Acryloid B-72, comparatively poorly adhered to the gouache, almost cleanly shattered away, apparently as much by shock as by actual photoablation. In the case of the Krylon Crystal Clear on the lean Maimeri paint – a predictably more tightly bound layer interface – the shock effect of irradiation yielded far more discontinuous removal of the coating.

The scanning method used in some of these tests left an evident pattern in the irradiated surface. This pattern may not be important if the residual material, as in previous applications, is to be further removed with solvents,[8–12] but it certainly is in situations, such as those simulated in the test panels, where the laser might be the primary or only method of removal. In applications such as these, the scanning parameters would have to be modified to eliminate uneven overlapping exposure patterns.

Conclusions

Although the test design did not permit a thorough optimization of exposure parameters for each sample, the results do suggest some preliminary conclusions.

The laser appears to have the potential to successfully remove accretions from badly flaking substrates, with the caveat that more brittle substrates than those tested might become dislodged by the movement generated upon laser irradiation. The laser also appears capable of removing varnish from less friable, potentially soluble matte surfaces, with very nearly complete retrieval of the original surface characteristics, as confirmed by spectrophotometry.

The laser also succeeded in removing tape from an unbound paint film, a remarkable achievement in an admittedly unlikely conservation scenario that may nonetheless suggest other promising practical applications. Even if some superficial grains of pigment were also removed along with the tape, the result is still far better than one might hope for with traditional methods.

Some successes were achieved in removing coatings similar in solubility to the substrate, though sometimes with uneven or discontinuous results. Residues had to be brushed away, involving direct contact with the surface, somewhat diminishing the advantage of the laser over traditional methods.

The use of the laser may be less promising in cases where the substrate is not particularly lightfast, such as the Pilot marker, which began to disappear before the overlying black spray paint could be removed. This would apply to any situation in which the amount of energy required to remove the overlying material is greater than the energy the underlying material can withstand, since the laser also acts beneath the surface being irradiated. The use of lasers in the visible range, rather than the UV, might be more successful.

The tests were also less successful for the removal of stains from unvarnished acrylic surfaces, which tended to discolor before stain removal was complete. The more promising exceptions, based on these tests, appear to be stains of a superficial and/or particulate nature, such as soot and overpaint. In these more successful cases, the contrast between the color of the removed material (black) and the substrate (white) is probably a critical factor.

Test 2, in which black paint residues were left in the interstices of the paint texture despite an otherwise successful cleaning, suggests that generally it may be challenging for the laser to cope with the widely variable thicknesses of real paint and coating layers.

Overall, the results indicate that in some situations simulated by the tests, the KrF laser could provide an alternative tool, with some limitations, for cleaning problematic paint surfaces for which traditional methods would prove inadequate.

Acknowledgements

This research was conducted with bilateral support from FORTH and The Carnegie Museum of Art. The excimer laser was kindly provided by Lambda Physik, Germany. The first author also acknowledges Paul Whitmore, Karen Trentleman, and Costas Fotakis.

Notes and references

1. J. F. Asmus, " Properties of Laser-Cleaned Carrara Marble Surfaces," *Geological Society of America* (1978): 81–88.
2. L. Lazzarini, *La Pulitura dei Materiali Lapidei da Construzione e Scultura: Metodi Industriali e di Restauro* (Padua: Casa Editrice Dott. Antonio Milani, 1981).
3. K. Lal Gauri, "Stone Conservation Planning: Analysis of Intricate Systems," *Science and Technology in the Service of Conservation* (IIC Preprints, 1982): 46–50.
4. J. Asmus, "More Light for Art Conservation," *Circuits and Devices Magazine* 2, No. 2 (March 1986): 6–15.
5. J.F. Asmus, G. Guattari, L. Lazzarini, G. Musumeci, and R.F. Wuerker, "Holography in the Conservation of Statuary," *Studies in Conservation* 18 (1973): 49–63.
6. J.R. Vitkus and J.F. Asmus, "Treatment of Leather and Vellum with Transient Heating," *AIC Preprints*, 4th Annual Meeting (Washington, DC: American Institute for Conservation, 1976): 111–117.
7. H.M. Szchepanowska and W.R. Moomaw, "Laser Stain Removal of Fungus-Induced Stains from Paper," *Journal of the American Institute for Conservation* 33, no. 1 (Spring 1994): 25–34. Very recently T. R. Friberg has investigated KrF excimer laser for removing mold on paper: T. R. Friberg et al., "Laser Removal of Fungi and Stains from Paper Substrates: Recent Studies" (Paper delivered at LACONA, Workshop on Lasers in the Conservation of Artworks, 4–6 October 1995, Heraklion, Crete, Greece), 21.
8. E. Hontzopoulos, C. Fotakis, and M. Doulgeridis, "Excimer Laser in Art Restoration," *SPIE Gas Flow and Chemical Lasers* 1810 (1992): 748–751.
9. N. Morgan, "Excimer Lasers Restore 14th Century Icons," *Opto & Laser Europe* 7 (September 1993): 36.
10. E. Hontzopoulos, C. Fotakis, and M. Doulgeridis, "Art Conservation Studies By Excimer Laser," *1994 Conference on Lasers and Electro Optics Europe: Technical Digest*. (Paper delivered at the conference, Amsterdam, 28 August–2 September 1994), 7–8.
11. C. Fotakis et al., "Laser Applications in Painting Conservation." (Paper delivered at the 23rd Annual Meeting of the American Institute for Conservation, St. Paul, MN, 10 June 1995). In *Postprints of Papers Presented at the Paintings Specialty Group, 1995 AIC Meeting, 1996*, 36–42.
12. C. Fotakis, "Lasers for Art's Sake," *Optics and Photonics News* 6, (May 1995): 30–35.
13. Ibid., 32–33.

14. E. Matthias et al., "In-situ investigation of laser ablation of thin films," *Thin Solid Films* 254 (1995): 139.
15. M.I. Cooper and J.H. Larson, "Laser Cleaning of Marble Sculpture," (Paper delivered at LACONA, Workshop on Lasers in the Conservation of Artworks, 4–6 October 1995, Heraklion, Crete, Greece), 6.
16. Th. Skoulikidis, P. Vassiliou, P. Papakonstantinou, A. Moraitou, V. Zafiropulos, M. Kalaitzati, P. Spetsidou, V. Perdikatsis and P. Maravelaki, "Some Remarks on Nd:YAG and Excimer UV Lasers for Cleaning of Soiled Sulfated Monument Surfaces," (Paper delivered at LACONA, Workshop on Lasers in the Conservation of Artworks, 4–6 October 1995, Heraklion, Crete, Greece), 7.
17. K.G. Watkins, "A Review of Materials Interaction During Laser Cleaning in Art Restoration," (Paper delivered at LACONA, Workshop on Lasers in the Conservation of Artworks, 4–6 October 1995, Heraklion, Crete, Greece), 3.
18. G. Calcagno, A. Raspa, and J.F. Asmus, "Cleaning of Sandstone, Carbonic Stone, Microcrystalline Marble, Through Nd:YAG Laser 1064–532 nm in Normal Mode Q-Switch," (Paper delivered at LACONA, Workshop on Lasers in the Conservation of Artworks, 4–6 October 1995, Heraklion, Crete, Greece), 5.
19. G. Brassard et al. "Effects of the Q-Switched YAG Laser on Binders and Pigments for Mural Painting." (Paper presented at LACONA, Workshop on Lasers in the Conservation of Artworks, 4–6 October 1995, Heraklion, Crete, Greece), 9.
20. With proper training, the equipment could be operated by a conservator as well.
21. The scanning includes the relative stepwise translation of the sample with respect to the irradiating beam and is performed in a way which takes into account the Gaussian profile of the laser beam along the axis of the scanning. This is done by controlling the degree of overlap between sequential exposures so that as nearly as possible the delivered energy at any given area of the substrate is uniform and within a value predetermined by the user. Therefore, in practice, in going from static exposures to "scanning" one must take into account the exposure overlap factor in order to achieve optimum results.
22. Other tests using the 1,064 nm output of a nanosecond Q-switched Nd:YAG laser imparted a brownish discoloration to the substrate. This difference in discoloration between the Nd:YAG and KrF laser exposures most likely indicates a different type of physical interaction between the material and the laser.

Further reading

A.D. Karoutis and E. Helidonis, "A New Method of Cleaning Skulls By Means of ArF Excimer Laser," (Unpublished manuscript, University of Crete, Faculty of Medicine, Heraklion, Crete), 1–4.

A.C. Engelsberg, "Removal of Surface Contamination Using Dry, Laser-assisted Process." (Paper delivered at "Microcontamination 93", San Jose, CA, 23 September 1993).

R. Salimbeni, et. al., "Excimer Laser Cleaning of Stained Glass." (Paper presented at LACONA, Workshop on Lasers in the Conservation of Artworks, 4–6 October, 1995, Heraklion, Crete, Greece), 11.

L. Shekede, "Lasers: A Preliminary Study of Their Potential for the Cleaning and Uncovering of Wall Paintings." (Paper presented at LACONA, Workshop on Lasers in the Conservation of Artworks, 4–6 October 1995, Heraklion, Crete, Greece), 18.

Materials not identified in the text

Primary support panels:

- Wolsey® Canvas acrylic-primed Panel
- Houston Art and Frame® Gessoed Masonite Panel

Kinetics of Cellulose Fiber Degradation and Correlation with Some Tensile Properties to Plan Consolidation or Lining Interventions

Giovanna C. Scicolone*
Scuola per la Valorizzazione dei Beni Culturali,
Ex Monastero della Trinità, Enaip Lombardia, via Panoramica 42,
25082 Botticino Sera (Brescia), Italy

Elena Rossi, Antonio Sardella, Alberto Seves, Giovanni Testa
Stazione Sperimentale per la Cellulosa,
Carta e Fibre Tessili Vegetali ed Artficiali,
Piazza Leonardo da Vinci 24, Milano, Italy

Abstract

In its native state, cellulose is characterized by a high degree of polymerization (DP) and, like most fibrous materials, good tensile properties. However, these characteristics are influenced by several chemical and physico-chemical processes. Some heterogenous degradation phenomena have been investigated in this study by evaluating the effect of light, temperature and acid hydrolysis on two cellulosic materials: flax and cotton. Both separate and combined effects were studied. The degradation reactions, which were evaluated by determining intrinsic viscosity values ($\Delta l/\Delta P$), develop in two steps at different rates. The possible relation between kinetics and yarn tensile properties were also investigated and are of importance in extrapolating useful indications on the future life time of the art object and on the use of consolidation which is an appropriate conservative intervention before lining becomes really necessary.

Keywords

Flexible supports, linen, cotton, kinetics of cellulose degradation, tensile properties, consolidation, lining

Preamble

To project preservation interventions correctly on canvas painting supports, the restorer must first carry out the necessary cognitive investigations on the fibers. The most common investigations[1] do not only offer indications on the type of fiber and the state of conservation (degree of polymerization, biological attack and chemicophysical degradation),[2] but also give essential correlations from which to evaluate the behavioral data of the material (tenacity and ultimate tensile strength) and can also furnish indications on the future life probabilities of the art object; the latter is an aspect of even more relevance to the restorer.

Knowing the type of fiber – and therefore its behavioral characteristics determined from its constituent elements, knowing the cause and the level of degradation, and, finally, knowing the environment in which the work will be kept, one can forecast a reasonable approximation of the future life of the object.

In other words, the restorer is able to hypothesize on the amount of time the work will survive after an intervention which, in the specific case of cellulosic supports, would be consolidation or lining.

The degree of polymerization of the fiber gives some conventional values (it will be recalled that this refers to a small portion of material; the sampling may involve only a few fibers of a single strand from a significant area of the support), but a given value on its own does not automatically justify the necessity of a specific operation;[3] the restorer must evaluate, in the case of each specific work being examined, whether, for example, a degree of polymerization (DP) of 300 warrants a lining or simply a suitable consolidation. In this case the correlation with the tensile properties becomes the determining factor to study.

It is significant to know the environment with which the work has been interacting and with which it will again be interacting, both to obtain a possible dating of the work and, in the planning stage of any possible operation, to forecast how much additional life the restoration will give to the painting.

If consolidation is not carried out, for how much longer can the present behavioral characteristics of the support be counted on? And if carried out? Do the tensile characteristics of the support justify the execution of a lining?

These questions are answered by the present research into the kinetics of degradation.

Introduction

Thermal, hydrolytic, photolytic, photochemical and enzymatic degradation of cellulosic fibers is essentially due to the scission of cellulosic chains, which can be regarded as a number of bonds being broken.

The degradative scission can be followed by measuring the change of the intrinsic fluidity $1/[\eta]$,[4–6] expressed as the inverse of the average degree of polymerization (l/DP). In the literature[7–9] it has been demonstrated that no decrease occurs in the rate at which the chains are being broken.

The random scission of bonds in a linear chain polymer follows a first-order kinetics rate law:

*Author to whom correspondence should be addressed

$$dN/dt = KN \qquad (1)$$

where N is the total number of bonds between monomer units, t is the time and K is the observed rate constant. This relationship may also be expressed in terms of the fraction of the total number of available bonds, $1 - 1/DP_n$, where DP_n is the number-average degree of polymerization:

$$d[1 - (1/DP_n)]/dt = K[1 - (1/DP_n)]. \qquad (2)$$

This equation can be simplified when only a small fraction of the bonds have been broken:

$$\{[(1/(DP_n)_t] - [1/(DP_n)_0]\} = \alpha K' t \qquad (3)$$

where α is a measure of the bonds' accessibility and K' is the rate constant for the rate of bonds being broken in the anydroglucose chains. The chain breaking rate follows simple zero-order kinetics.

In zero-order chemical kinetics, an equal number of bonds are broken in a given length of time. Moreover, for a randomly degraded polymer, the number-average degree of polymerization, DP_n, is approximately half of the weight-average degree of polymerization, DP_w, which can be correctly measured by viscosimetry. Therefore, replacing DP_n with $DP_w/2$ in equation (3) and multiplying by a factor of 100, we obtain the expression:

$$100[(2/DP_w)_f - (2/DP_w)_0 = \alpha K'' t. \qquad (4)$$

The left-hand side gives the percentage of the initial bonds that have been broken.

In this paper we consider the kinetics of cellulose fiber degradation caused by light, heat and acid-catalyzed hydrolysis (heterogeneous hydrolysis).

As we know well, degradation also causes changes in a wide range of macroscopic properties,[10] e.g. in tensile strength. The decrease of yarn tensile strengths (mainly load breaking and specific stress or tenacity) compared to the $2/DP_w$ changes has been studied.

Experimental

Materials

Raw and bleached cotton and raw flax fabrics were examined. The removal of impurities was carried out by Soxhlet treatments with warm water and petroleum ether for 1 h for each treatment. The fibrous materials were washed several times in distilled water and finally stored in the dark at 20°C, 65% relative humidity (RH).

Heterogeneous acid hydrolysis

Bleached cotton fabric was treated in 1*N* hydrochloric acid at 20°C for different lengths of time. The pH of the solution and the relationship between the weight of cotton and the hydrolytic agent were kept constant . The samples, removed at different times, were washed repeatedly in distilled water at 20°C until free from acid and then conditioned at 20°C, 65% RH.

Exposure to artificial light

10 × 4.5 cm fabric samples were put in standard specimen holders and exposed in a high-pressure xenon arc apparatus (Xenotest Hanau 150 S). The instrument was operated at 45°C, 65% RH, and equipped with Pyrex-glass filters that eliminate UV radiation below 290 nm. These filters simulate the ozone-layer filtering effect of the radiation from the sun.

Thermal degradation

Fabric samples were thermally treated in a laboratory oven at 70°C with 10% RH in dark conditions.

Viscosity determinations

Viscosity was measured in 0.5 M cupriethylenediammine (CuEn) at 25°C with a Sappet viscosimeter. The intrinsic viscosity [η] was determined according to UNI 8282, which partially agrees with ISO 5351/1. Values for the viscosity-average degree of polymerization were obtained by multiplying the intrinsic viscosity by a factor of 1.5.

Tensile properties

Tensile properties (breaking strength, tenacity) were determined on warp yarns extracted from the fabrics and conditioned at 20°C, 65% RH. Their breaking loads were determined at a gauge length of 8.0 cm and a rate of extension of 20 mm min^{-2} on an Instron mod.1122 apparatus. The reported values of the retained breaking strength were based on the breaking load of yarns extracted from untreated fabrics.

Results

If equation (4) is used to follow the overall course of the heterogeneous degradation of cellulosic polymer, it is possible to recognize more distinct stages.[4] The rapid initial stage, not revealed in these experimental conditions, is considered to represent the breaking of a limited quantity of 1,4-β-glucosidic bonds that are particularly sensitive.[11–13]

The second stage proceeds at a slower rate and was attributed to the breaking of 1,4-β-glucosidic bonds located in the amorphous region.[14] The third one indicates that the degradation proceeds at an extremely slow rate, while DP values are approaching the levelling off degree of polymerization (LODP).[15]

In this paper the change in the number of bonds broken in cotton and flax is first examined, under degradation caused by photolysis, heterogeneous acid hydrolysis and thermal aging. DP_w values of the different starting materials at time 0 are reported in Table 1.

Table 1. DP_w and percentage of bonds broken N_t (%)at the break time (t) of degradative actions, photolysis and acid hydrolysis; $N_t = 100[(2/DP_w)_t - (2/DP_w)_0]$

Materials	Degradative action				
	None	Photolysis		Acid hydrolysis	
	$(DP_w)_0$	$(DP_w)_t$	N_t (%)	$(DP_w)_t$	N_t (%)
Raw flax	3,060	340	0.52	–	–
Raw cotton	2,610	380	0.45	–	–
Bleached cotton	2,405	–	–	330	0.52

The degradative scission of cellulosic chains can be considered in terms of two sets of zero-order kinetics: the initial stage (first kinetics) is always the fastest. As is well known, in zero-order kinetics the number of bonds broken is constant in time. In Figure 1 the data are plotted in terms of percentage of the initial number

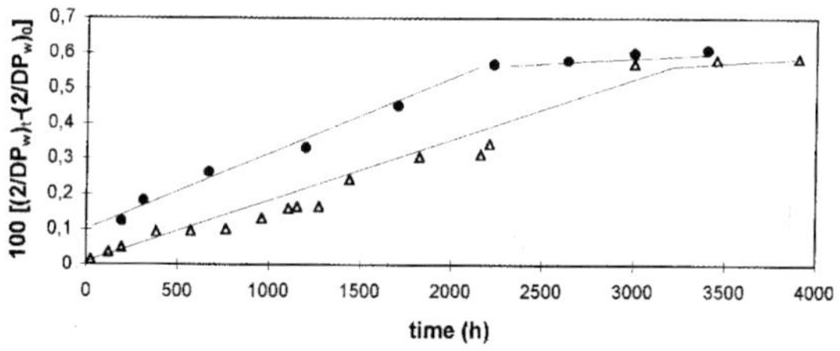

Figure 1. Percentage of bonds broken as a function of time of exposure to xenon arc lamp: ● raw cotton; Δ raw flax

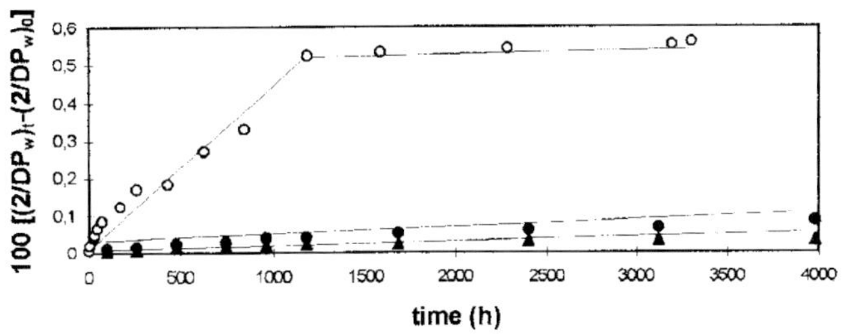

Figure 2. Percentage of bonds broken as a function of time of heterogeneous acid hydrolysis (open symbols) or thermal aging (70°C) (filled symbols): ○ bleached cotton; ● raw cotton; △ raw flax

of bonds that have been broken, $100[(2/DP_w)_t - (2/DP_w)_0]$, versus time of exposure to xenon arc lamp of raw flax and cotton. The first kinetics for raw cotton is faster than that of raw flax, while the second slower stage is characterized by a similar rate for both.

Further, the apparent break occurs when about 0.45–0.52% of bonds have been broken for both cellulosic materials (Table l). The heterogeneous acid hydrolysis (1*N* HCl at 20°C) of bleached cotton exhibits analogous behaviour, with two rates of reaction (Figure 2). These results indicate that the degradation rate of normal 1,4-β-glucosidic bonds is influenced by the accessibility of fibrous material during the different stages of hydrolysis.

As shown in Figure 2, only one rate of degradation is present when raw flax and cotton are thermally treated at 70°C. During the exposure time considered, the thermal aging causes only a small percentage of bonds to be broken (0.03–0.08%); as with photodegradation carried out by exposure to xenon arc lamp, the degradation rate is faster for cotton than for flax. As shown in Figures 3 and 4, a linear correlation between the decrease of the yarn's tenacity, the breaking strength retained and the DP_w changes was found, independently of the degradative action considered. It is interesting to note that these tensile properties also seem to follow two distinct stages, with a break at a value of about 0.35% of bonds broken. This value corresponds to $400 \leq DP_w \leq 450$.

As is well known, the tensile properties of a textile structure such as a fiber depend on the nature and arrangement of the component macromolecules. Tie molecules, linking the microfibrils, are more involved in the mechanical strength of fibers, while "*ciglia*" and folded end chains have less significance. During degradation, the breaking of chains can statistically involve all kinds of macromolecules; when about 0.35% of bonds have been broken, the degradative process has already compromised the action of the tie molecules. Further attack, however,

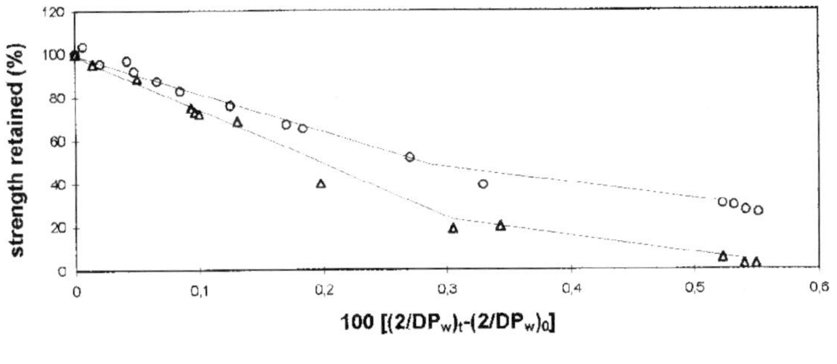

Figure 3. Breaking strength retained by warp yarns as a function of percentage of bonds broken: ○ heterogeneous acid hydrolysis of bleached cotton; Δ photolysis of raw flax

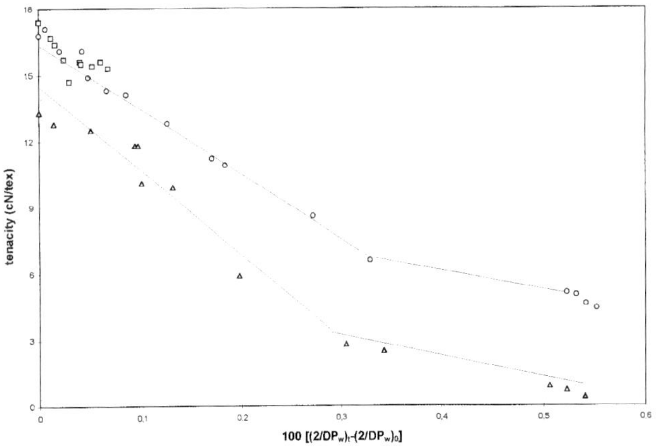

Figure 4. Tenacity of warp yarns as a function of percentage of bonds broken: □ heterogeneous acid hydrolysis of bleached cotton; △ photolysis of raw flax

included in the first step of degradation processes, will affect macromolecules that are less important for the tenacity of the fiber.

Conclusions

These results confirm the data already reported in the literature for the kinetics of degradation of cellulose fibers.[4,11] It was confirmed that degradation carried out by photolysis and heterogeneous acid hydrolysis followed two steps, each represented by zero-order kinetics. During the second step the value of LODP (level of degree of polymerization) is slowly reached. The kinetic rate of cellulosic degradation was slower for flax than for cotton. The main aim of this work was to check the relation between the changes in intrinsic fluidity ($1/[\eta]$) and some macroscopic properties such as yarn tensile strength and tenacity. The data obtained confirm this relation, which could be useful in predicting the durability of cellulose fibers manufactured under known degradative conditions.

Obviously the different values of strength retained in the transition zone between the two rates of decrease in strength shown in Figures 3 and 4 were influenced by the degradation mechanism (photolysis, hydrolysis) and by morphological and structural parameters of cellulosic materials.

On the basis of these results some comments can be made that determine different possible attitudes and operating choices. First of all, the further speed of degradation in supports that have already suffered a loss of tensile property characteristics is such as to ensure a better outcome by applying alternative methods to lining, i.e. consolidation; we know, in fact, that the results obtained are not limited to being positive immediately but the influence on the behavioral characteristics of the painting system go on with aging.

With regard to antique paintings, as we know that the level of degradation will be maintained near to the present value for a very long time, a less problematic intervention project is faced. Much more maintenance and preventive care is foreseen as being needed for contemporary works, with very careful checks on the microenvironment and with preventive intervention on paint films.

The presence of ground and paint films constitutes an element of protection for the canvas, a type of plastering of the support that is shown to be a great help.

A preparation with chalk and bonding agents blocks the macrodeformability of the canvas support and impedes the reciprocal movements between the warp and the weft of the yarn. Therefore only small dimensional variations are permitted and it is from this perspective that the importance of the effects of the consolidating agents on the mechanical properties of the work must be seen. With the right use of consolidation, an improvement in the compactness of the yarn can be anticipated. The material's resistance to lacerations diminishes drastically when reciprocal slip of the yarn warp and weft is impeded. In this way, in a material in which the yarn is not able to slip, the lacerations lead to subsequent breakage of various yarns, while if the same material were to maintain its mobility, the lacerations would be obstructed by the co-operative action of the strick of yarn that is formed perpendicularly to the propagation of the laceration.

Consolidating agents are not able to revive the integrity of the cellulose chain and consequently the degree of polymerization of cellulose. Their action is expressed only at the macroscopic level, anchoring the fiber material, which is reduced to fragments by the degradation, to the yarn.

Moreover, the consolidating agent can be considered suitable if:

- it increases the difficulty of initial elastic deformation of the support, that is if the elastic modulus of the yarn making up the support is increased (by elastic modulus we mean the physical mechanical property that expresses the load-stretch ratio);
- it reduces the deformability that can be caused by the absorption of the relative humidity (synthetic consolidating agents are, for example, generally not very hygroscopic);
- it obstructs the propagation of lacerations in painting supports, so that a not excessively rigid support is preferable.

Therefore, it is of particular importance to select support consolidation interventions using materials that really give to the fiber a protection from stress and suitable behavioral characteristics.

In short, consolidation is an intervention which can prolong the life of a canvas and which limits subsequent degradation. This method must therefore be carefully considered.

References

1. E. Rossi, "Misure del Grado di Polimerizzazione per la Valutazione dello Stato di Deterioramento di un Materiale Fibroso Cellulosico", in *Dipinti su Tela* (Firenze: Nardini, 1993), 25; V. Richter, "Indagine Condotta con Microscopia Elettronica a Scansione su Materiali Fibrosi Cellulosici", in *Dipinti su Tela* (Firenze: Nardini, 1993), 31; G.C. Scicolone, A. Seves,"Il Restauro dei Supporti Cellulosici Tessili in Dipinti Monocromi: Alcune Indagini Comparative", in *Il Restauro dell'Arte Contemporanea* (Firenze: Nardini, 1992), 113.
2. A. Seves, G. Testa, G. Bozzi, A. Sardella, "Degradazione di Supporti Tessili Cellulosici di Dipinti", in *Dipinti su Tela* (Firenze: Nardini 1993), 15; G. Testa, "Il Problema della Conservazione dei Dipinti su Tela in Ambienti Contaminati da Inquinanti: Effetto degli Ossidi di Azoto (NO_x)", in *Dipinti su tela* (Firenze: Nardini, 1993), 77; G. C. Scicolone, A. Seves, M. Bonfatti, G. Testa, E. Rossi, "Invecchiamento di Supporti Cellulosici di Dipinti su Tela: Simulazione in Laboratorio del Fenomeno di Invecchiamento", *Kermes*, no. 27 (1996).
3. G.C. Scicolone, "Qualcosa che è Forse Oggi Necessario Riconsiderare: L'opportunità della Foderatura e la Validità delle Metodologie Tradizionali", in *Il Restauro dei Dipinti Contemporanei: Soluzioni per Evitare la Foderatura o per Limitare i Danni che Essa Comporta*, (Botticino: Enaip, 1990); G.C. Scicolone, "La Foderatura e Gli Interventi Sostitutivi nelle Opere Contemporanee", in *OPD* (Firenze: Opus Libri, 1993).
4. R.L. Fellers, S.B. Lee, J. Bogard, "The Kinetics of Cellulose Deterioration", in *Historic Textile and Paper Materials*, eds H.L.Needles, S. Haig Zeronian , *Adv. Chem.Ser.*, no. 212 (1986): 329–347.
5. A.F. Ekenstam, *Ber. dtsch. Chem. Ges. A* 69 (1936): 553.
6. G.V.Schulz, H.J. Lohmann: *J.Prakt. Chem.*, 157 (l941): 238.
7. A. Sharples, *J.Polym.Sci.* 13(1954): 95.
8. W.A.J. Bryce, C.T. Greenwood, *J.Polym Sci.* 25, no. 111 (1957): 480.
9. A. Sharples, *J.Polym.Sci.* 13 (1954): 393.
10. J.M. Cardamone, P. Brown, "Evaluation of Degradation in Museum Textiles Using Properly Kinetics", in *Historic Textile and Paper Materials*, eds H.L.Needles, S. Haig Zeronian , *Adv. Chem.Ser.*, no. 212 (1986):.41–75.
11. E.H. Daruwalla, A.P. D'Silva, A.C. Mehta. *Text. Res. J.* 37, no. 3 (1967): 147.
12. M. Marx-Figini, M. Coun-Matus, *Makromol. Chem.* 182 (1981): 3603.
13. A. Sharples, in *Cellulose and Cellulose Derivates*, eds N.M. Bikales, L. Segal. Vol.V, 2nd ed., (NewYork, 1971), 991–1006.
14. A. Sharples, *J.Polym. Sci.* 14 (1954): 95.
15. M.M.Y. Chang, *J. Polym. Sci.* 12 (1974): 1349.
16. G.C. Scicolone, A.M. Bonfatti, E. Rossi, A .Sardella, A. Seves, G. Testa, "Indagine sugli Effetti del Consolidamento di Supporti Cellulosici Tessili a Diversi Stadi di Degradazione", *Kermes*, no. 22 (1995): 11.

The Silver-framed Icons in Old Russian Art

Anna Nikolaievna Trifonova
Pskovskaya ul. 38–92, Novgorod, Russia 173009

Abstract

The issues concerning the old Russian icons framed with gilt silver mountings, and the principles of their storage and their restoration are among the most controversial in modern museum and restoration practice. Two major approaches to these problems exist. The first consists of removing the mounting from the icon during the process of restoration and keeping it separately after the restoration is finished. This approach allows detailed examination of the icon, its panel, textiles, and paint layers. However, because of its removal, the mounting loses its status as the attribute of the icon and as a work of art. The second approach recognises the icon's integrity to be dependent upon the existence of its mounting. This derives from the fact that the tradition of adorning the icons with gold and silver was one of the oldest in Christian art and played an important role in the way people perceived the holy images and regarded the icon's beauty and sacred strength. The author of this paper favours the second approach and stresses the importance of regarding the icon mountings as historic monuments and pieces of the artistic culture of their time. The paper considers the icons in silver mountings of the 16th century – the time when the tradition of decorating icons with silver was at its peak in Russia. Most of the high-quality icon mountings preserved today date back to that period.

Keywords

Icons, basma, silver-framed icons, Russia, religious art

Icon silver mounting – basma, Novgorod, 16th century

The museums of Russia own a vast number of icons in silver mountings. The majority of these icons date back to the 16th to 19th centuries and only a few to earlier times. Obviously, this has led to the belief that the icon mountings are a product of the later epoch only. Within the framework of this theory, most clearly defined by Nikolay Sichev in 1916,[1] the popularity of the silver-adorned icons is associated with the decline of the art of icon painting, which must have led to the decadence in artistic tastes, with the dictatorship of Maecenases who aimed at replacing the ideological and esthetic value of the icons with the lavishness of their mountings. As a result of such attitudes towards icon mountings, they were often neglected and destroyed as works of art. They were removed from the icons as unnecessary additions distorting the icon's original appearance.

However, studies of icon decoration, begun a century ago by Nikodim Kondakov and resumed in recent decades,[2] show that such an utterly negative look at this phenomenon of Christian art is unhistorical. Such a negative approach seems to ignore the system of mediaeval aesthetic views. Precious metals, gold especially, were regarded in the Byzantine world as sacred materials: it was thought then that holy images made of precious metals contained no less of the divine energy than religious painting. The tradition of decorating icons with mountings has its roots in the early history of Christianity. It was brought to the Balkans and then to Russia from Byzantium after the new religion had been adopted and the cult of icons established. Icons that were originally intended to be, to a great extent, enclosed by a cover made of precious metal, had already began to appear in Russian art during the pre-Mongol time. Throughout the 13th to 15th centuries precious icons, i.e. icons framed with gold or silver settings, were owned by royal and boyar families, and were being placed in monasteries with the family relics. They served as the altar and altar screen images in cathedrals and monastery churches. They prepared the way for the golden age of the tradition of decorating icons with silver, which came about in the 16th century. This period saw the development of the type of high iconostasis on which all the icons had precious decoration: the margins, backgrounds and the saints' haloes were adorned with gilt silver.

Icons in silver mountings should therefore be looked at as complex pieces of art, composed of many elements. Their examination, storage and restoration require the solution of several specific problems, working with basma-framed icons being an especially difficult task.

Basma is thin gold, silver or bronze sheets or strips with images impressed upon them. The printing, or impression, was done with matrices, caste from copper alloys with the use of stone moulds, or, in exceptional cases, with matrices carved out of wood. During this process not only was the image that the matrix bore imprinted, but also the edges of the matrix itself. It is possible to see those edges among the basma mounting designs. Sometimes ready-made casts or articles were used as matrices. Because the sheets or stripes of basma were small, the whole setting was pieced together from several parts. They were fastened with nails to the icon background and edges, on which a thin layer of waxen mastic was put before hand. Under the basma on the saints' haloes strips of mastic were put.

The oldest examples of basma icon mountings date back to the late 12th or early 13th century, but until the end of the 15th century not many Russian icons were

Figure 1. A sample of silver basma. Second half of the 16th century. Novgorod State Museum

Figure 2. "Boris and Gleb". The icon from the Boris and Gleb church in Novgorod. The icon was created in about 1377 and the silver mounting in 1536–1537. Novgorod State Museum

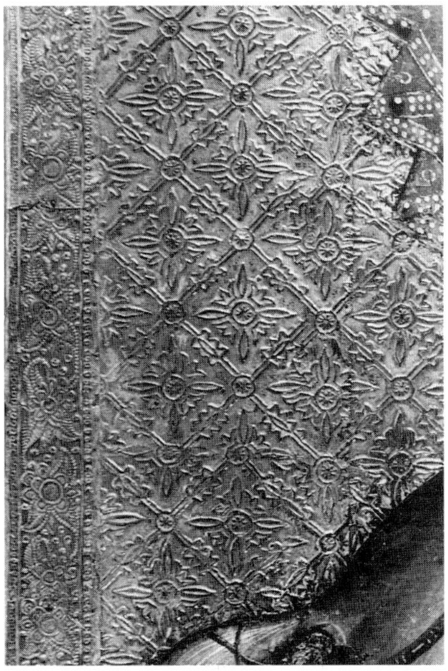

Figure 3. Detail of "Boris and Gleb". Novgorod State Museum

decorated with basma. It is the 16th century that is known as the golden age of the basma technique in Russian art. The 17th century also saw basma icon mountings being produced in large numbers, but in many cases their quality was poor. Some samples of basma also appeared during the 18th and 19th centuries, but as a rule these were basma pieces made for restoration purposes and that is why, with a different level of skill and precision, they imitate the ornaments of the basma mountings of the 14th to 16th centuries.

During the 16th and 17th centuries not only new, but also old icons and iconostases were decorated with basma mountings. The wide spread of the tradition at that time is the cause of many complicated problems for museum restorers and art experts. A significant number of early Russian icons have lost their 16th- and 17th-century mountings in the process of museum restoration. The autonomous existence of basma mountings is, however, impossible – after the mounting is removed from the icon it basically becomes silver scrap. A sad memory of it remains only in the pattern of numerous nail punctures left on the icon painting.

In our opinion, there is a need for a careful approach to the question of removing the mounting from the icon. One has to consider numerous factors, such as the circumstances under which the mounting was created, its artistic value and the role it plays in the way the icon image is perceived, as well as the condition of the painting under the basma. It is also necessary to remember that decorating the icons with gold and silver was often related to the activity of outstanding people, and to important events in church and state history. That is why the loss of the mounting always ruins pieces of spiritual culture, destroys historical evidence and, maybe unconsciously for us today, breaks the links with the past. Let us give a few examples from the history of the icon collection owned by the Novgorod Museum.

"The Descent into the Hell", created in the early 14th century in Novgorod, was until 1911 in the Vedensky monastery in Tichvin. The icon's mounting was decorated with the designs that were common for basma mountings of the second half of the 16th century. The origination date of one of these ornaments, consisting of heart-shaped tendrils of grass stalks (Figure 1), can be determined very precisely. A similar ornament first appeared on the head-piece of the New Testament that was published in Russia in 1555. In 1572 Novgorod Archbishop Leonid presented the "Predsta Tsaritsa" icon, in a basma mounting showing a similar grass ornament, to Prince Ivan, Tsar Ivan the Terrible's son (the icon is in the Russian Museum, St Petersburg). The mounting of "The Descent into the Hell" dates to approximately the same period of time. We may guess that its creation is connected with the events of 1560. According to the Chronicles, this was the year when Novgorod Archbishop Pimen went to Tichvin and founded a new monastery. Usually when going on such trips, the church officials carried with them from their treasury the mounting-framed icons specially reserved for the blessings and gifts. Most probably the ancient icon, decorated with basma by the Archbishop's silversmith, was among the gifts Pimen gave to the Tichvin monastery.

The basma was removed from the icon during its restoration in 1926–1930. We think that the decision to do so was a mistake. First, the mounting was known for its quality of craftsmanship and it had been related to a very important stage of the icon's history. Second, by the time the mounting was created, "The Descent into the Hell" painting already had suffered significant losses. For example, almost all the original gilt on the icon's background and margins was absent. The gilt silver basma, whose ornaments symbolised Eden's eternal blossom, was intended to compensate the losses. It spoiled the ancient image no more than the solid spots of the bare ground with numerous additions of a later time and with the nail punctures that we observe nowadays.

The testimony to the excellence of Russian silver craftsmanship is the mounting on the 14th century "Boris and Gleb" icon. This icon was painted for the Boris and Gleb church, built in Novgorod in 1377. In 1536–1537 the church had undergone reconstruction. Before the church had been blessed after the renewal, the old icon was decorated with silver basma (Figures 2 and 3). When creating the mounting, the silversmith followed the rich decoration that could be traced on the icon. The spiral interweaving of grass that we see on the basma saints' haloes

Figure 4. "Theodor Stratilat with the Scenes from His Life". The icon from the Theodor Stratilat church in Novgorod, 1530–1540. Novgorod State Museum

Figure 5. The silver mounting on "John the Forerunner", the icon of the iconostasis at St Sophia Cathedral in Novgorod, 1537

Figure 6. Detail from "John the Forerunner"

Figure 7. "The Transfiguration", the icon of the iconostasis at the St Sophia Cathedral in Novgorod. The icon (copy) is from the 14th century, the silver mounting from 1537–1558

resembles the design that decorates the Boris horse's saddle. The large rosettes with long thin leaves and the stars on the silver cover's background, as well as the flower designs on the basma margins, have a lot in common with the flowers and stars scattered over the saints' clothes. The exquisite ornamental decoration of the mounting corresponds to the aristocratic style in which the images of the prince-warriors are painted on the Novgorod icons.

The metal printing technology determined the close connection between basma and bronze casting, stone and wood carving, leather printing and the decoration of the first books printed in Russia. The peculiarities of the printing technique explain why basma was mass-produced and we are aware of different types of basma which have survived until now in more than one copy. However, on the "Boris and Gleb" background there is a unique basma. Its decoration resembles only the leather book-covers, in the so-called "gothic" style, that were being made in Novgorod in the 15th and the first half of the 16th centuries; these book-covers also have the diamond-shaped designs with the rosettes.

The ornaments of the other parts of the "Boris and Gleb" mounting have, on the other hand, many analogues in Russian applied art. The interwoven grass on the saints' silver haloes can be associated with the decoration of the following wooden carved pieces: the Ambo of 1533 from the Novgorod St Sophia (Russian Museum); the 16th-century Holy Door from the iconostasis of the Mjachino church near Novgorod (Novgorod State Museum); and the Tsar's throne of 1551 from the Domition Cathedral in Moscow. There is also a similar ornament on the bottom frame of the bronze Romanesque door of 1152–1154 owned by the Novgorod St Sophia Cathedral (this frame is a restoration addition of 1530). The upper and low basma margins on the "Boris and Gleb" icon have the diamond-shaped design with flowers, the simplified variants of which decorate the Ambo of 1533 and the Holy Doors of the 1550–1560s from the Peter and Paul church and the Sirkov monastery in Novgorod (Novgorod State Museum). But the closest analogues to the silver margins and haloes of the "Boris and Gleb" icon are to be found in the basma mountings of 1537–1558 arches of the St Sophia icons. The spiral grass interweaving enriches the saint's haloes in the deesis and the backgrounds in the feast tier from the Domition (Big) iconostasis of the Cathedral (Figure 7). The flower designs of the "Boris and Gleb" margins are repeated on the margins of the prophet icons located in the Domition iconostasis and in the chapel (Small) iconostasis of St Sophia.

The mountings of the Cathedral's icons represent the vast collection of the basma ornaments. These are different kinds of interweaving, motifs imitating filigree, and designs composed of palmettes, cones, grass and flowers (Figures 4 to 10). Flowers of different shapes (from the simplest rosette to the rich fantastic plant) prevail. They are inserted in the segments, rhombohedra, and heart-shaped figures that form the borders or the "carpet"-like compositions. The ornaments are beautiful and expressive. Their excellence shows up in the contrast of the lavish thin lines. In contrast to the earlier examples of the Novgorod basma (of the 12th to 14th centuries), the St Sophia icon mountings were not chased during the final stage of their production. The preciseness of the images was achieved by the thorough work on the matrices, by the plasticity of the high-quality thin silver strips and by the accurate following of the basma technology guidelines.

The ornaments of the basma mountings executed from 1500 to 1550 are deeply traditional. They bear the ancient mark of schematism and symbolism. This can be observed especially in the basma that covers the backgrounds of the deesis icons from St Sophia. The design of this basma consists of segments placed in chessboard order with rosettes within the segments (Figure 5). The segmented designs were widespread in the Russian basma of the 16th century. In this case, however, we see an extremely rare variant, which is a peculiar, non-standard example of the ornament with segments and rosettes larger in size than usual. Such an ornament was easily seen from the distance and thus it perfectly fitted the iconistasis mountings. The early 1540s saw the appearance of an analogous basma on the deesis and feast icons of the Domition Cathedral at the Kirillo–Belozersky monastery. This type of basma decorates "Theodor Stratilat" – large altar screen icon, created in 1530s and 1540s for the Theodor Stratilat church in Novgorod (Novgorod State Museum) (Figure 4).

Figure 8. The silver mounting on "Prophet Samuel", the icon of the iconostasis at St Sophia Cathedral in Novgorod, 1537–1558

Figure 9. "Our Savior Enthroned", the icon of the chapel iconostasis at St Sophia Cathedral in Novgorod, 1558

The traditional ornaments are treated rather differently by the silversmiths of the 16th century, as is testified by the basma decoration of "Our Savior Enthroned" from the chapel iconostasis of St Sophia Cathedral (Figures 9 and 10). The design on the icon's margins is composed of flowers with horn-like petals, whose curve is underlined by the longitudinal corrugation. In the Novgorod basma this motif goes back to earlier times. A similar design decorates the plate of a bronze icon mounting of the late 12th/13th century and a 14th-century altar cross from the Novgorod State Museum. The analogous, but simpler, flowers appear on the basma mounting of "Virgin of Don" made in the late 14th/early 15th century (Tretjakovskaja Gallery in Moscow) and on the silver engraved Panagia from the Spas–Kamenny monastery, most probably executed in Novgorod at the same time (Vologda State Museum). Almost without any change this ornament is reproduced on the printing of Novgorod leather book-covers up to the mid 16th century. A corresponding design with the large five-petal flowers is also present on the margins of the "Theodor Stratilat" icon mentioned above.

It is interesting that, among the wooden Holy Doors from the iconostases of the mid 16th century, there are those on which the carving almost completely imitates the flower-ornamented basma of "Our Savior Enthroned" and "Theodor Stratilat". These are the Holy Doors from the Nativity of the Virgin church on the Kulikovo field (History Museum in Moscow), from the Iljinkoje settlement near Kaluga (about 1550) and the Krasny Cholm settlement near Tver (1558–1564) ("Kolomenskoje" Museum in Moscow). It should not be overlooked that these wooden carved pieces were made by the Novgorod masters who participated in the creation of the basma printing matrixes.

The Domition iconostasis of St Sophia has 54 deesis, feast and prophet icons of the 14th–early 16th centuries covered with basma. The adorning of the Cathedral's icons with silver was begun in 1537 with the creation of the "Big deesis" mountings and had been carried on for many years. The initiator of these works was an outstanding leader of the Russian church, Novgorod Archbishop Makary, who in 1542 ascended the Metropolitan throne. In 1558 the chapel iconostasis was made. Its mountings were printed on the basma matrices of the feast and prophet ranges of the Domition iconostasis. Already, before Makary, whole iconostases, and not only separate icons, had been covered with silver (for example, the Annunciation iconostasis in the Moscow Kremlin, 1508). But this was the first time that a multi-tier iconostasis of one of the most important Russian Cathedrals had been decorated with gilt silver mountings. This act required the raising of large amounts of money, which were received not only from the Archbishop, but also from private contributors and the city budget. The decoration of the icons with the mountings and the presentation of the precious gifts to the holy images was a way for people to show their respect to the icons and to perform a spiritual duty. However, because they were considered as the fruit of hard human labour and the long fund-raising process, the icon mountings were considered to be treasures of importance to the state and, therefore, were subject to strict regulation by the state officials, as, for example, can be seen from the Novgorod distraint of 1617.

The adorning of the iconostasis with the precious decorations was possible only during a situation of economic stability. Such a situation existed in Novgorod in the first half and middle of the 16th century – the time when most probably the mountings of the two other large Novgorod iconostases were created. These iconotases were located in the Cathedrals of the Yriev and Khutin monasteries. Their silver covers were scraped off by the Swedes during the 1611–1617 period of Novgorod's occupation.

It is commonly known that Russian 16th century culture was under retrospective influences. The ideologues of the Russian centralized state, Makary among them, had underlined the special role of being the spiritual heiress to the Byzantine and Kiev state that Moscow Russia had assumed. Iconostases fully covered with the gilt silver were intended to revive in people's minds the memories of the precious altar screens of the early-Christian and pre-Mongol churches. Not surprisingly, among the first iconostases to be covered with silver was the high iconostasis of St Sophia, built in 1045–1052, as well as perhaps the iconostasis in the Cathedral of the Yriev monastery, erected in 1119. Famous icons, originating from the altar screens of those Cathedrals – "Our Savior with the Golden Robe"

Figure 10. Detail of "Our Savior Enthroned"

and "Peter and Paul" of the mid 11th century, "St George" and "The Annunciation" of the 12th century – were mounted with silver when they were created.

"Peter and Paul" and its mounting are stored in the Novgorod Museum. We know about the way "Our Savior with Golden Robe" looked from the Chronicles. On both of the icons the chased gilt silver mountings covered the whole painting, except the faces, hands and legs of the saints. In other words, the most ancient altar screen of Novgorod, constituted by these icons, was a magnificent piece of the jewelry art. By the adorning the Cathedral's iconostasis with silver, Archbishop Makary went back to that tradition. That is why it is so important today to preserve the integrity of the iconostases covered with basma settings. Few of them still exist. A vast number of such iconostases have been destroyed or lost during the turmoils of the Russian history, from the "Troubled Time" (1600s) up to World War II. The aim of the religious officials in the 18th and 19th centuries to "renew" church interiors, as well as the aspirations of the museum restorers and art experts to make discoveries in the field of Old Russian painting, also led to the vanishing of basma pieces.

Worth mention in this context is the destiny of the Domition Cathedral's iconostasis of the Kirillo–Belozersky monastery.[3] The iconostasis, composed of the local, deesis, feast and prophet ranges, was created in 1497. In the 1540s, i.e. practically simultaneously with the Novgorod St Sophia iconostasis, it was enriched with beautiful gilt silver basma. After the reconstruction of the iconostasis in the 1760–1770s, some of the 15th century icons were transferred to the Domition Cathedral's altar and to different monastery churches. In 1864 the basma was taken off those icons, probably for the making of new church vessels or for commercial purposes.

In 1918 the story of the restoration of the Kirillo–Belozersky icons began. The restoration lasted for decades and was finally completed in the 1980s by the experts of the Restoration Institute in Moscow under the leadership of Dr Olga Lelekova. They carried out complex investigations of the icons, providing unique information about the materials and techniques of the panels, textiles, paint layers, and mountings, which made possible the restoration of the composition of the original iconostasis. This was very important because the icons, taken from the iconostasis in the 18th century and for a long time the object of interest to collectors, art historians and restorers, were eventually placed in different museum collections. However, the research undertaken showed the need to remove the basma from the icons located in the iconostasis as well. With a specially invented technique the basma was transferred onto canvas and is now stored separately. Only on a few icons do the mountings remain untouched.

The composition of the deesis, feast and prophet tiers of the Novgorod St Sophia iconostasis has not changed for centuries. Neither, up to now, has the iconostasis been closely examined by restorers. As a result, the majority of the basma mountings are still in their original places, except for the 14th century feast icons. Their old painting was cleaned in the 1960–1970s.[4] After that the icons were handed over to the Novgorod Museum for exhibition. In the process of the restoration the mountings were removed in order to be placed on the replicas of the icon that were to be installed in the iconostasis. This project, however, was not completed.

We hope that when the decision is made about the future restoration of the St Sophia, an historic approach to the monument will be taken. Its destiny is closely connected with the history of the St Sophia, which in 1991 was returned to the Russian Orthodox church, gaining the status of a Cathedral–Museum. Already this single fact excludes a purely analytical approach to the works of art kept in St Sophia, the kind of the approach that very often was transferred from science to museum and restoration practice.

It is important to take into consideration one more thing, regarding the creation of replicas of respected icons and using scientific methods to make copies of the paintings and preserving the material, technological and stylistic peculiarities of the original. One can obtain a high-quality replica of the icon, but attempts to copy the mounting-framed icons, which have been undertaken recently, are, to our mind, bound to fail from the start. The mounting replicas, made of plain metal from casts of the ancient basma, do indeed reproduce the relief and the ornamental motifs of its decoration, but they fail to express the beauty and power that the mounting's materials – gold and gilt silver – possess; they fail to reproduce the quality of the substance that has the "divine light" in it. Almost the whole meaning of the existence of the mountings is contained in this substance.

We think that it is time to bridge the gap between the understanding of a few historians that the silver-framed icon is a natural step in the development of Christian art and the mass mentality, which underestimates the importance of this step, the mentality that usually determines the storage and restoration practice of dealing with the mountings. The "discovery" of the icon does not mean releasing it from the mounting. It means realising the spiritual interdependence of all the icon's elements and understanding the fact that the divine strength of the icon, and the secret of its impact on people, is in its integrity.

Acknowledgements

The paper was translated into English by Denis Trifonov.

References

1. N.P.Sichev, *Izbrannie trudi* (Moscow: Sovetsky khudoznik, 1976), 184–185.
2. Selected bibliography: S.Radojcic, "Zur Geschichte der silbergetriebenen Reliefs in der byzantinischen Kunst", *Tortulae. Romische Quartalschrift*, no.30. Supplement Heft (1966): 229–242; A. Grabar, *Les revêtements en or et en argent des icones byzantines du Moyen Age* (Venice, 1978); A.N. Trifonova, "Serebrjanije okladi novgorodskih ikon X11 – XV11 vekov" (PhD dissertation, Leningrad University, 1985) (with a detailed bibliography); E.A. Gordienko and A.N. Trifonova, "Katalog serebrjanih okladov Novgorodskogo Museja-Zapovednika", *Muzej*, no.6 (Moscow: Sovetsky khudoznik, 1986): 209–261; I.A. Sterligova, "Dragozenny ubor russkih ikon X1-X111 vekov", in *EX ORIENTE LUX. Mélanges offerts en hommage au professeur Jean Blankoff*, vol.1 (Brussels, 1991), 331–346.
3. O.V.Lelekova. *The Iconostasis of 1497 from the Domition Cathedral of the Cirillo-Belozersky Monastery (Investigations and restoration)* (Moscow: VNIIR, 1988).
4. V.V.Filatov, *Church Feast Range at St Sophia's Cathedral* (Leningrad: Avrora, 1974).

Biaxial Properties of Sized Cotton-Duck

Christina R.T. Young
Department of Mechanical Engineering,
Imperial College of Science, Technology and Medicine,
Exhibition Road, London SW7 2BX, UK

Abstract

A painting on canvas can be treated as a composite of inhomogeneous polymer layers. The key to understanding the deterioration processes is understanding how these layers interact. The first step is a knowledge of the fundamental mechanical properties and a working theoretical framework, verifiable by experiment, which can predict easel painting behaviour. A biaxial tensile tester has been built to investigate easel painting mechanics. A series of experiments have been conducted which demonstrate how each process, in constructing an easel painting, modifies its uniaxial and biaxial mechanical properties. Initial results reported here, concentrate on plain weave cotton-duck as the support, and the application and effect of the size layers. These results are used to test the conventional description of an easel painting as a deformable solid. It is suggested that alternative mechanical models might be more suitable when considering the painting as a whole.

Keywords

Biaxial , tensile testing, canvas, anisotropic, strain

Introduction

Direct determination of the mechanical properties of canvas is difficult to achieve because of:

- the non-linear, visco-elastic and frictional effects at the fibre, yarn and fabric level;
- variability in the yarns and across the weave;
- variations in spacing and density of fabric; and
- the geometrical changes of the weave due to external forces.

The addition of size and subsequent paint layers, with their own variations and interactions, add further difficulties, especially when combined with the differing response to environmental factors such as temperature and relative humidity. The behaviour of woven fabrics has been reported in various contexts.[1–5] The characteristics, which are seen as most relevant to the behaviour of canvas supports are:

1. anisotropy;
2. non-linear stress-strain behaviour;
3. time dependent stress-strain response (creep);
4. previous loading history affecting stress-strain response;
5. the stress-strain response in one yarn direction can be strongly dependent on the stress applied in the orthogonal direction;
6. the strain maybe load-path dependent.

Hedley[6] and Mikalski[7] have noted the occurrence of the first three and Hedley considered that the 4 and 5 would have an effect. Further research is required to ascertain which factors have a significant effect on the behaviour of canvas and how they are altered by the addition of size, oil paint or acrylic. The uniaxial and biaxial tests reported in this paper concentrate on the canvas and size layer. These results, and earlier preliminary tests on linen and cotton-duck,[8] indicate that all the above characteristics are observed in a canvas support, that they are modified slightly by the wetting process and greatly altered by the application of size.

Hedley[9] has shown the need and relevance of biaxial tensile testing, proving that two-dimensional strain distribution of a stretched canvas is heterogeneous, with some areas of the canvas in compression. Berger[10] has identified many important trends in the biaxial tension response of real canvases to varying environmental conditions. He states that the factors which influence the tension in canvas "cannot be considered in isolation because many of them interact and affect each other". A different approach has been taken in this research. Experiments, where one parameter at a time is varied over a realistic range, make the identification of critical parameters easier and provide a sound platform for further analysis. The Finite Element Analysis work of Mecklenburg,[11] using uniaxial data to model biaxial behaviour provides an important point of reference. The uniaxial and biaxial investigations of Hedley[12] and Berger,[13] respectively, have partially verified Mecklenburg's approach, as well as highlighted the complex interactions which occur. The thrust of this new research project is both to consolidate some of this

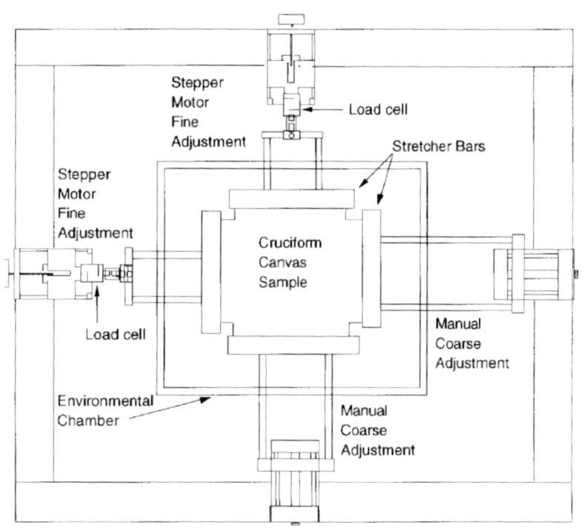

Figure 1. Biaxial tensile tester

earlier work, and to investigate the processes causing deterioration of easel paintings, taking into account their anisotropic nature.

Design of the biaxial tensile tester

A biaxial tensile tester, with integral environmental chamber, has been designed and built specifically for the research, in collaboration with the Tate Gallery, London. An electronic speckle pattern interferometer (ESPI)[14] has also been designed to operate in conjunction with the biaxial tensile tester; this provides a non-destructive method of mapping non-linear strain. The design and calibration of the biaxial tester is reported separately.[15] A paper giving a detailed description of the instrument, integrated with the ESPI system, is in preparation.

The rig is designed to mimic a typical wooden stretcher with some features simplified to avoid ambiguities in the interpretation of the data. It is designed to stretch canvas from its raw state, through the wetting, re-stretching and sizing processes.

The rig consists of a rigid steel frame, onto which four independent stretcher bars are coupled via translation stages (Figure 1). The stretcher bars grip the canvas and apply uniform load to the sides of the sample. In each axis there is a fine translation stage, with computer controlled stepper motor, and a manual coarse translation stage. The fine stage moves the stretcher bars in 0.01 mm increments over a range of 50 mm. Extensions are measured from the motor steps, whilst load cells in each axis measure the applied loads. Table 1 gives the operating parameters and calibration for the tester.

Time, temperature and relative humidity, inside and outside the environmental chamber, stretcher bar position and tension in each axis are logged continuously and downloaded to a PC for analysis. Feedback control enables the tensile tester to operate in constant-extension or constant-load mode.

The environmental chamber consists of a Perspex box, enclosing the central area of the tensile tester. The duration of the present load-extension tests means that the enclosed box is sufficient to keep the temperature and humidity constant (see Table 3). An actively controlled environmental chamber for cycling temperature and humidity is under design.

The canvas is directly gripped by the stretcher bars. This is a consistent and reliable way to set up each sample. It also reduces erroneous extension measurements resulting from insufficient stiffness in any interconnections . The sample is gripped by wrapping the edges around 6 mm diameter studding, which is then clamped between two aluminium plates. The front edges of the clamp are relieved to ensure that the canvas is only held by the studding and that no stress concentrations occur along the edges. The sample shape is cruciform with the crossarms aligned in the warp and weft directions. The sample has a 260× 260 mm central area and a length from grip to grip of 360 mm. As a result of edge effects, only the area within the central square of the cruciform is subjected to a uniform biaxial tension. This configuration cannot give useful information about stress

Table 1. Biaxial tensile tester specification and calibration

Extension	50mm/ stage
Displacement resolution	0.01mm
Maximum tension	500N/axis
Tension resolution	0.1% of full scale
Load cell linearity	0.001% of full scale
Load cell repeatability	± 0.03% of full scale
Load cell accuracy	± 0.05N
Load cell hysteresis	none measured within the resolution of the system
Translation stage linearity	0.01% over 1mm
Translation stage repeatability	±1.0% over 1mm
Translation stage accuracy	±0.5% over 1mm

Table 2. Cotton-duck material properties

Supplied by Russell and Chappell, Monmouth Street, London	Samples stored between silica gel sheets at 20°C and 35% relative humidity
Weight 12oz cotton-duck	Gauge length 360mm
Weave – plain weave	Width of material in grip 260 mm
Weft yarns/m 1450	Warp yarns/m 2083
Weft yarn diameter 0.42 mm (average of 50 readings)	Warp yarn diameter 0.33 mm (average of 50 readings)
Weft area/m 200×10^{-6} m^2	Warp Area/m 178 ´ 10^{-6} m^2

states at the corners of a painting on a stretcher. However, it is felt that overall material properties need to be established before looking at specific problems, e.g. the effects of keying out. A separate clamping arrangement is being designed to investigate the corner stress distribution; this aspect and edge effects are best investigated using the ESPI system.

Experimental procedures

The uniaxial and biaxial tests described below were designed to investigate:

- the theoretical framework described below;
- the effect of cyclic loading;
- the mechanical role of the size layer.

Samples were prepared from a single roll of modern raw cotton-duck (see Table 2). A new sample was used for each test, to ensure that any pre-loading history could not affect the stress–strain response. The loading area for the canvas was calculated from measurements of the number of yarns/m and average yarn diameter, made using a Shadowgraph. Load-extension tests were performed at constant temperature and humidity. The complete testing schedule is shown in Table 3.

Table 3. Testing schedule

Material	Type of loading	Direction of loading	Pre-conditioning	External temperature °C/Relative humidity I%	Test measured parameters
Cotton-duck	Uniaxial	Weft	Raw	18.0/32.5	Load/extension
Cotton-duck	Uniaxial	Warp	Raw	18.0/32.5	Load/extension
Cotton-duck	Biaxial		Raw	19.8/33.5	Load/extension
Cotton-duck	Uniaxial	Weft	Biaxial load/extension	19.8/33.5	Load/extension
Cotton-duck	Uniaxial	Warp	Raw	18.6/33.0	Wetting
			Wetted	18.0/32.5	Load/extension
Cotton-duck	Uniaxial	Weft	Raw	18.6/33.0	Wetting
			Wetted	18.4/37.5	Load/extension
Cotton-duck	Biaxial		Raw	18.4/37.5	Wetting
			Wetted		Load/time
				17.8/36.0	Load/extension
Cotton-duck	Biaxial		Raw	18/37.0	Wetting
			Wetted		Load/time
			1st sized	18.8/38.5	Sizing
					Load/time
				19.8/38.5	Load/extension
Cotton-duck	Biaxial		Raw		Wetting
			Wetted	18.8/39.5	Load/time
			1st sized	20.2/39.5	Sizing
			2nd sized		Load/time
					Sizing
					Load/time
				18.4/35.5	Load/extension
Cotton-duck	Uniaxial	Warp	Biaxial load/extension	19.4/37.5	Load/extension
Cotton-duck	Biaxial		Uniaxial load/extension	19.2/36.5	Load/extension
Cotton-duck	Uniaxial	Weft			Wetting
				18.4/32.5	Load/time
				19.2/38.0	Sizing
					Load/time
					Sizing
					Load/time
				19.2/50.5	Load/extension
Cotton-duck	Biaxial		Uniaxial load/extension	19.2/50.5	Load/extension

Load/time tests

Stretching, wetting and sizing are performed with the canvas on the rig. The change and redistribution of the tension in weft and warp can be monitored continuously as a function of time. When stretching, the grips were moved to produce a biaxial tension of 50N and then held at that position. Therefore, the canvas is restrained at a constant extension during wetting and sizing. Natural drying occurs at ambient room temperature and relative humidity. Each size layer consists of rabbit skin glue in a 1:20 water-based solution, applied warm.

Uniaxial tests

It is important, when uniaxial measurements are performed on large flexible specimens, that a very small constant load is kept in the non-loading direction; this prevents the tendency of the fabric to ruck-up and pucker leading to uneven loading distribution and erroneous measurements. The load should just keep the specimen flat without introducing biaxial stress states. This is achieved by moving the stretcher bar to maintain a constant load of 5 N. This movement gives the change in dimension in the non-loading direction. In the loading direction, the stretcher bar is driven in 0.01 mm steps until a load of 75 N (equivalent to a stress of 1.5 MPa) is reached and then reversed to unload (1 MPa is a typical stress for newly stretched supports or linings). This loading pattern is repeated for ten cycles.

Biaxial tests

The canvas is set up in the rig with the same initial conditions as the uniaxial tests. The stretcher bars in each axis are driven out together in 0.01mm steps until a maximum of 75 N is reached. They then move in the opposite direction down to the initial loading. During the cycle the loads are maintained equal, to within 3 N, under closed loop control. This loading pattern is repeated for ten cycles.

Theoretical background

A consistent integrated theory to describe easel painting mechanics has not, as yet, been developed. It is usual, within conservation literature, for a painting and its constituents to be treated as three-dimensional deformable solids. Often "stiffness" values, the modulus of elasticity and Poisson's ratio are calculated based on this assumption. It is important to establish whether this is valid and a useful theoretical framework, when a painting is considered as a composite under biaxial tension. The crucial assumptions to test are:

- Does it behave as a deformable solid under uniaxial and biaxial tension?
- Is there a Poisson effect?
- Is it valid to use uniaxial measurements to model biaxial properties?
- How does each layer change the overall mechanical properties?
- How do environmental conditions alter overall mechanical properties?

Within the elastic region and under biaxial loading, the following equations apply, if the canvas, in raw, wetted and sized states, can be assumed to be a deformable solid, which has different properties in the axes corresponding to the warp and weft directions:

$$E_{warp} = 1/\varepsilon_{warp}\,[\sigma_{warp} - \gamma_{warp}\sigma_{weft}] \qquad (1)$$

$$E_{weft} = (1/\varepsilon_{weft})[\sigma_{weft} - \gamma_{weft}\sigma_{warp}] \qquad (2)$$

where the uniaxial properties are:

$$\varepsilon_{warp} = \Delta L_{warp}/L_{warp} \qquad \varepsilon_{weft} = \Delta L_{weft}/L_{weft}$$

$$\sigma_{warp} = F_{warp}/A_{warp} \qquad \sigma_{weft} = F_{weft}/A_{weft}$$

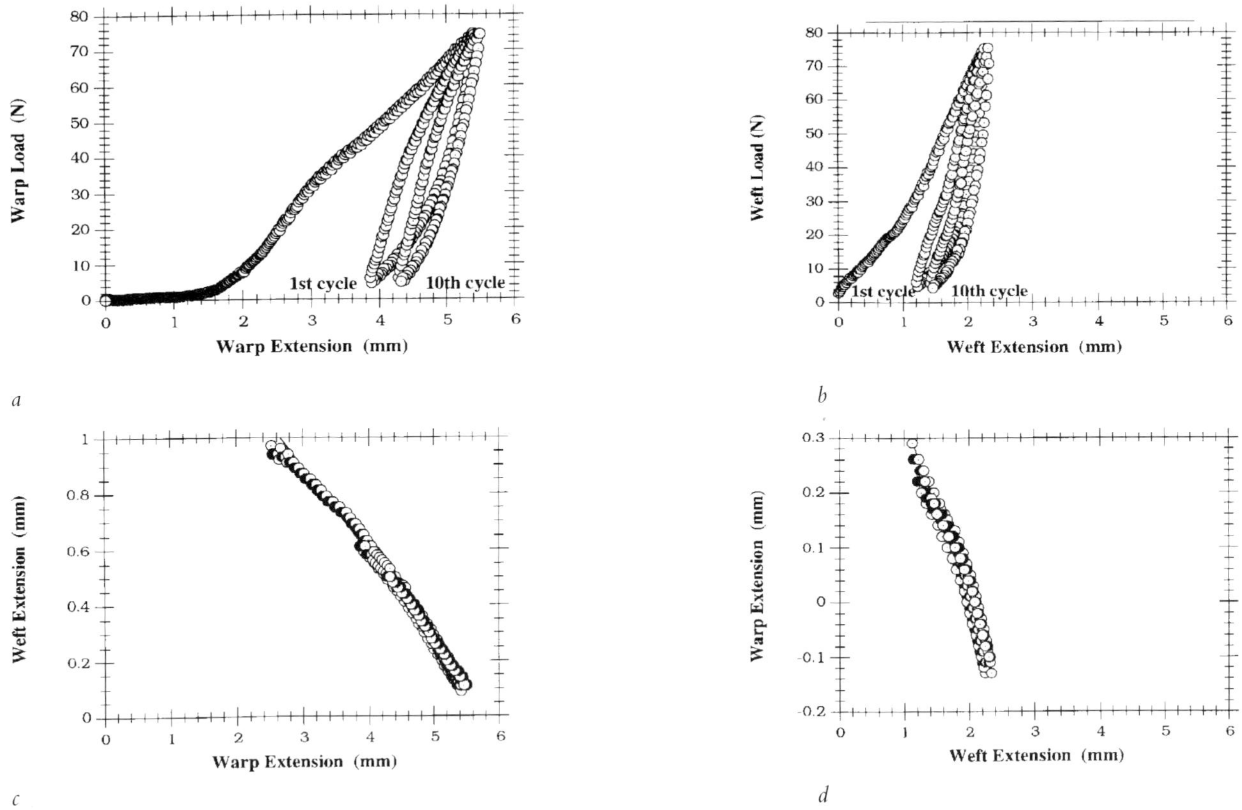

Figure 2 Uniaxial load–extension in the warp (a) and weft (b). Uniaxial extension ratio in the warp (c) and weft (d)

$$\gamma_{warp} = \Delta L_{weft}/\Delta L_{warp\ warp} \qquad \gamma_{weft} = \Delta L_{warp}/\Delta L_{weft}$$

where E is the modulus of elasticity, γ is Poisson's Ratio, L is the original sample length, ΔL is the change in length (extension), F is the applied force and A is the area over which the force is applied.

By measuring uniaxial properties in weft and warp one can calculate the biaxial extensions for a given biaxial tension. If this theoretical framework is a good description of the under-layers of a painting, then the calculations should agree with the biaxial measurements. A stiffness modulus, **S** and extension ratio, **e**, are defined as the elastic modulus and Poisson's ratio at a specified tension. The stiffness ratio, $\mathbf{r}_s$, is defined as the ratio of warp stiffness to weft stiffness.

Uniaxial and biaxial load–extension results

The following assumptions have been made in the data analysis:

- Measurement of stress and strain are integrated values taking no account of local non-linearity.
- Errors resulting from crossarm extensions are minimal when performing biaxial tests.
- Constant initial dimensions and uniformity in the bulk properties of all samples

.

The uniaxial load–extension curves for raw cotton-duck in both weft and warp are shown in Figure 2. In both cases, on initial loading, a "bedding down" of the fabric occurs as yarns, in the loading direction, straighten out. Comparison of Figure 2a with Figure 2c over the extension region, 2.0 to 4.0mm, demonstrates that in the non-loading direction the overall dimension decreases, suggesting that a crimp interchange has occurred. If a geometrical description of woven fabric is assumed,[16] yarns in the loading direction straighten out and the yarns in the orthogonal direction therefore have a longer geometrical path. Since there is no force to restrain them, their crimp increases and the "apparent" overall dimension decreases. When the weft is the loading direction, this initial region is much shorter because the weft yarns have much less initial crimp. The cotton-duck becomes stiffer with each loading cycle; by the tenth cycle the change in stiffness is small,

Table 4. Uniaxial and biaxial load–extension results

Preconditioning of cotton-duck	Load direction	Stiffness S(MPa) at 50 N	Ratio warp stiffness to weft stiffness at 50 N	Extension ratio, e at 50 N	Calculated biaxial extension *DL* (mm) at 50 N	Measured biaxial extension ΔL (mm) @ 50N
Raw uniaxial	Warp	375		0.40		
	Weft	680	0.55	0.30		
Raw biaxial	Warp	603			0.66	0.63
	Weft	1315	0.45		0.34	0.37
Wetted uniaxial	Warp	282		0.29		
	Weft	504	0.56	0.40		
Wetted biaxial	Warp	362			1.03	0.80
	Weft	777	0.46		0.41	0.40
1st sized Biaxial	Warp	688				
	Weft	973	0.71			
2nd sized uniaxial	Warp	612		0.096		
	Weft	915	0.56	0.11		
2nd sized biaxial	Warp	812			0.58	0.55
	Weft	1138	0.70		0.33	0.31

as most of the crimp has been removed in the loading direction. Both weft and warp exhibit creep on loading and hysteresis on unloading, the weft having a higher degree of non-linearity and stiffness.

Over the cyclic region in Figure 2c the relative changes in dimension between weft and warp can be thought of in two ways, either as a continual crimp interchange, as the yarns in the loading direction straighten under loading and regain some of their crimp on unloading, or as the Poisson effect, which occurs in deformed solids. With uniaxial data the stiffness modulus, **S**, can be calculated (Table 4). If an orthotropic deformed solid description is assumed, the biaxial extensions, for a given biaxial load, can be calculated using equations (1) and (2). From the values in Table 4, the biaxial extension in the weft direction is calculated as 0.34 mm at 50 N. The measured values from Figures 2a and 2b were found to be 0.36 mm at 50 N (0.1% strain). Similarly in the warp the biaxial extension calculated from uniaxial measurements is 0.66 mm at 50N, whilst the measured value is 0.63 mm at 50 N. The above calculations and measurements were repeated for wetted and wetted/sized cotton-duck (Table 4). The largest error in the

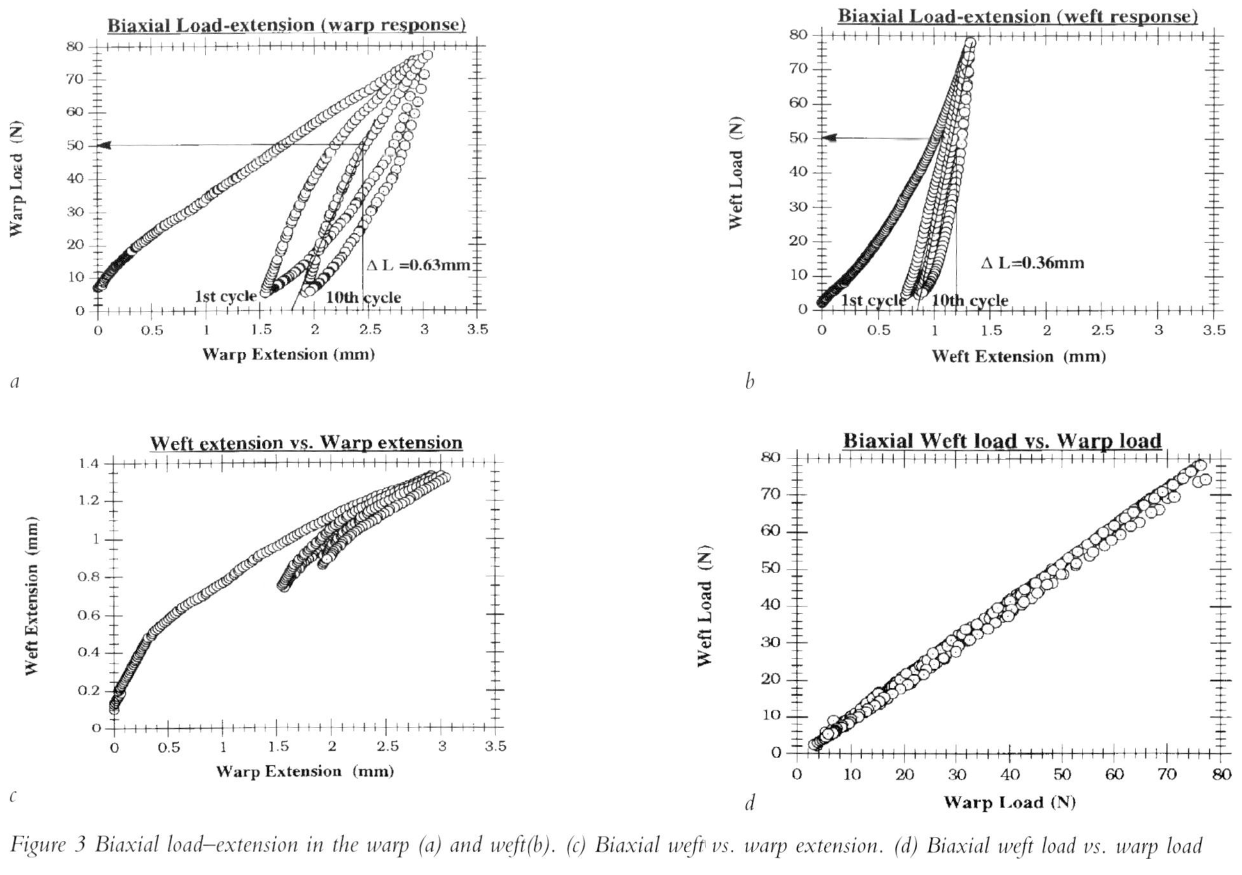

Figure 3 Biaxial load–extension in the warp (a) and weft(b). (c) Biaxial weft vs. warp extension. (d) Biaxial weft load vs. warp load

predicted extensions is for wetted biaxial warp (19% error); all other values are within 6%.

With reference to Table 4 and Figure 7 some interesting features can be identified:

- In all cases measured values of stiffness are higher under biaxial tension.
- Stiffness values for wetted cotton-duck are lower than unconditioned cotton-duck and the hysteresis curves show greater linearity. This reduction in hysteresis is associated with a decrease in the inter-yarn frictional forces, suggesting that local stresses imposed on the yarns during weaving are released by the wetting process.
- Sizing has the largest effect on the mechanical properties. Compared to wetted cotton-duck, the biaxial stiffness increases in the warp by a factor of two and the stiffness ratio, $\mathbf{r}_s$, between warp and weft increases to 0.7 from 0.46.
- Sized cotton-duck exhibits a linear stress–strain behaviour on loading in the stress region 0.5 to 1.5 MPa. (typical of the internal stresses set up prior to applying the ground layer) and hysteresis on unloading.
- For the sized samples, creep is not discernible over the period of the tests, and the increase in stiffness with successive loading is less than in unsized samples.
- The most significant change is the decrease in the weft extension ratio, **e** , from 0.4 to 0.11, which occurs between wetted and second-sized samples.
- The second sizing increases the stiffness in both weft and warp, but does not alter the stiffness ratio.

Biaxial load–time results

A continuous load–time curve is shown in Figure 4. On the same time scale, Figure 5 shows the environmental conditions during the test. The internal relative humidity sensor was situated below the canvas. The raw cotton-duck was stretched to an initial biaxial tension 50 N (1 MPa stress) in both weft and warp. While moving the stretcher bars to obtain the biaxial tension the material creeps as it does when stretching on a wooden stretcher. In all the tests presented, the weft creeps more than the warp when stretching the raw fabric. When the creep slows down to 0.002 MPa s^{-1}, the canvas is then wetted.

At point A, just after wetting, the stress reduces to 0.5 MPa (25 N). This initial decrease in tension is associated with a release of fibre strains locked into the fabric during manufacture.[17] The water reduces the friction at intersection points allowing yarn slippage and stress relaxation. This initial reduction in tension is not usually observed in tests. After two minutes the biaxial tension starts to rise, reaching a maximum, B, where the weft stress is 3.3 MPa and 3.0 MPa in the warp. This is the point where the yarn fibres have swelled because of water absorption, and crimp increases.[18] The weft and warp yarns now have longer geometrical paths resulting from increased yarn diameter. Assuming that any elongation of the yarn itself is small, compared to the increased crimp, the complete fabric matrix tries to contract. Because it is restrained by the stretcher bars the tension increases. The

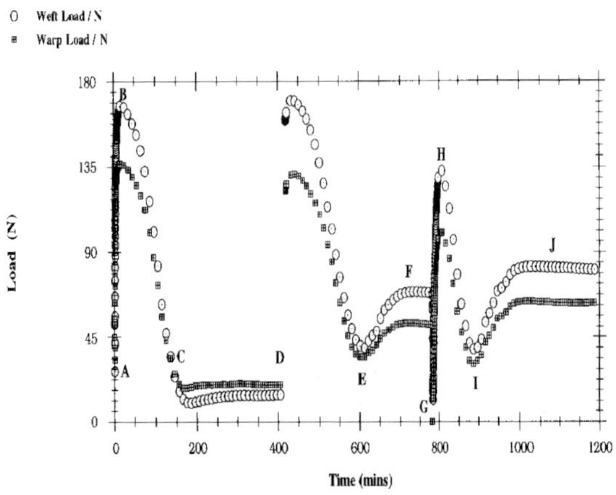

Figure 4. Load–time raw to 2nd Sized

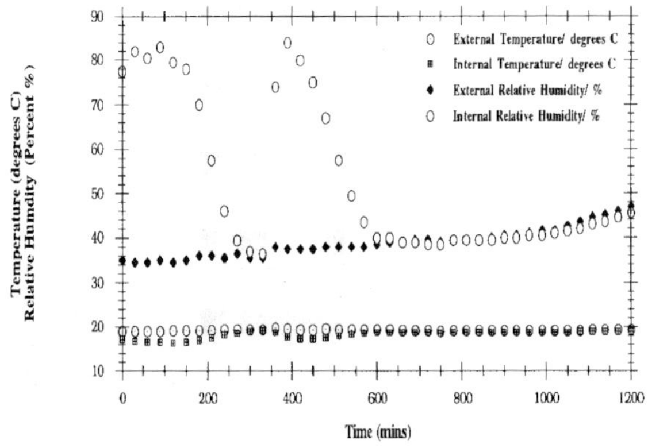

Figure 5. Environmental conditions for the wetting

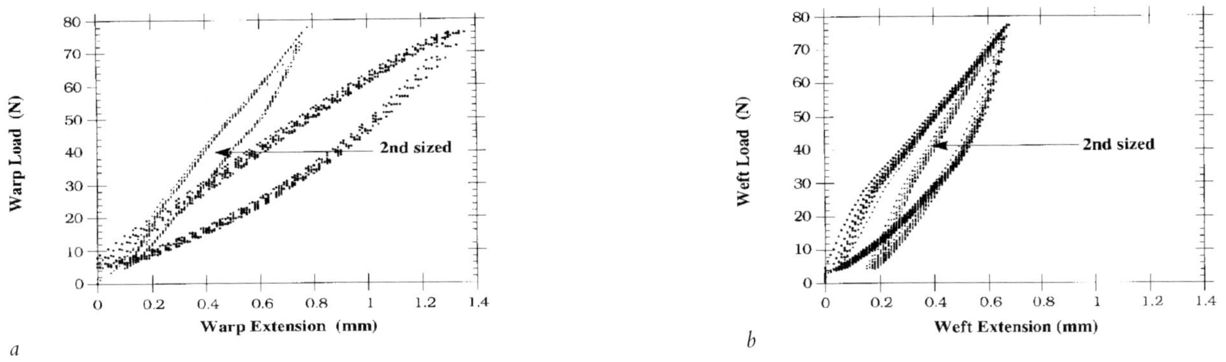

Figure 6 a & b Biaxial wetted/Biaxial 2nd sized weft (a) and warp (b) load–extension response

canvas then dries and, as a result of stress relaxation, drops to a tension below its original value. At the crossover point C, the warp load rises above the weft load, implying that crimp redistribution occurs on stress relaxation. The form of the curve from A to D has been observed in plain weave, cotton-duck and linen.

After re-tensioning to 1 MPa the canvas is warm sized. Initially, the behaviour is the same as before, owing to the absorption of water from the size. The biaxial tension reaches a minimum at E where, presumably, all the water in the canvas has evaporated (a crossover point does not occur). The tension then starts to rise to a point F where it stabilises at 1 MPa in the warp and 1.4 MPa in the weft. This results from the size layer contacting the canvas, as it contracts on desiccation. A second application of size causes an immediate and complete loss of tension in both weft and warp, at G. This is due to the size layer losing its strength on absorption of water.[19] The general form of the curve is the same as in the first sizing, except that the biaxial tensions at H are lower than at B, because the size layer forms a gelatinous film over the yarns which prevents them from absorbing as much water. This is consistent with the almost constant internal relative humidity (Figure 5) at that point. The tensions at J are higher than at F because there is more size present; as demonstrated earlier, the second size layer slightly stiffens the canvas. The ratio of stresses at F and J is 0.7; this appears to correlate with the load–extension results for sized canvas where the stiffness ratio, $\mathbf{r}_s$, is also 0.7.

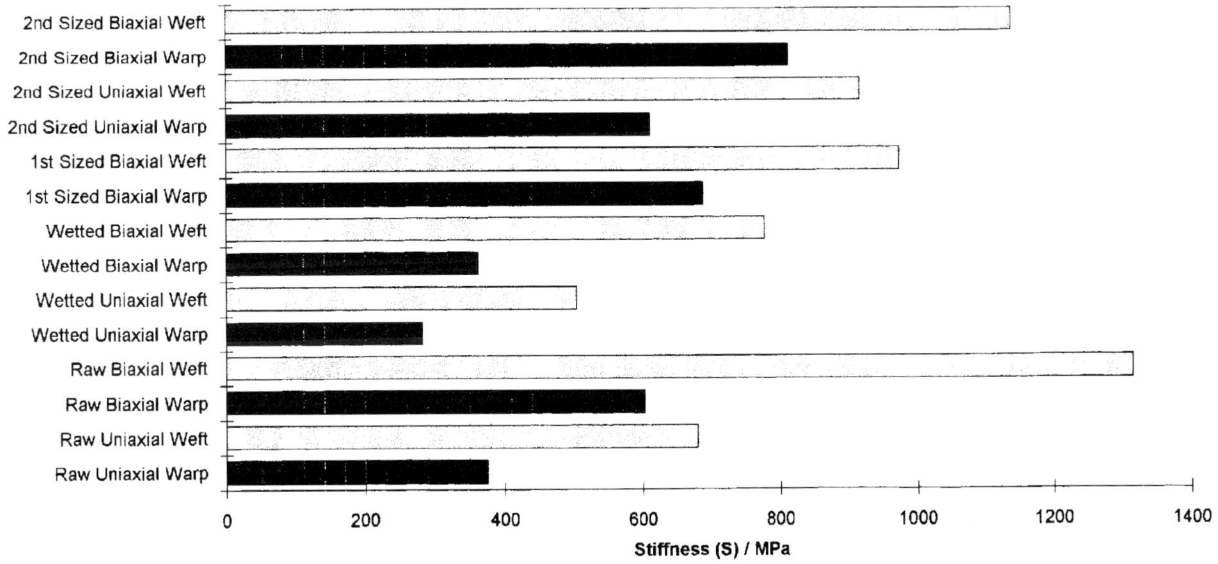

Figure 7. Comparison of stiffness values

Conclusions

The geometrical approach, first formulated by Pierce[20] for describing weave geometry, still provides the most useful working description of raw canvas, which behaves more like individual yarns moving in a matrix.

Size stiffens the canvas, partially equalises the weft and warp stiffnesses and prevents short-term creep (Figures 6a and 6b). The overall effect is that sized canvas behaves more like an isotropic material, although the low extension ratio, **e**, suggests other physical mechanisms may occur. At high relative humidity the size loses strength as a result of hydration; subsequently some moisture is absorbed into the yarns and the canvas tension rises; the anisotropic behaviour of the canvas itself becomes a more dominant factor in the overall response. As the size desiccates it produces higher overall stress in the canvas because it locks the yarns together and contracts. These results are consistent with Hedley's uniaxial measurements[21] on naturally aged samples. Mecklenburg has suggested that it is the size layer which is responsible for most of the humidity-related damage[22] and the data reported here tend to confirm this.

To a first approximation, sized canvas can be described as a deformable solid. Although it is heterogeneous, the "integrated" biaxial behaviour can be predicted from uniaxial measurements. It is a useful starting point for understanding more complex representations needed for realistic descriptions of composite structures. The basic mechanical framework needs to be extended to include non-linear elasticity and visco-elastic and inelastic behaviour, involving both time and history dependence.[23] A possible alternative theoretical framework for examining the mechanics of easel paintings is "membrane theory".[24] This approach does not require the assumption of homogeneity and allows for the addition of non-linear and time-dependent behaviour.

The results are for one type of cotton-duck using the warm sizing technique. However, the trends are consistent with the empirical knowledge of practising conservators. Even with a minimum number of variables, the data is difficult to interpret, highlighting the requirement for methodical testing. Measurements of different weave, weights of canvas and material, at different temperatures and relative humidity are in progress. This should lay the foundations for studying the interaction with the paint layers for new and aged samples.

Because of the difficulties of performing reliable biaxial measurements and the complexity of analysing the data, the ability to measure non-linear heterogeneous strain is essential in gaining a detailed understanding of the mechanical processes occurring within a painting. It is hoped that by combining the experimental methodology adopted in the paper, with the optical ESPI system, the origin and effect of some of the complex mechanical properties can be identified and quantified in terms of their contribution to easel painting deterioration.

Acknowledgements

The author wishes to thank: the Trustees of the Gerry Hedley Research Scholarship for the award which enabled this research to be carried out, the Tate Gallery for funding the Biaxial Tensile Tester and the Courtauld Institute of Art for encouragement and support.

References

1. S. Kawabata et al., "The Finite-deformation Theory of Plain Weave Fabrics. Part 1. The Biaxial Deformation Theory", *Journal of the Textile Institute* 64, no. 1 (1973): 137–149.
2. R. Haas et al., "The Stretching of the Fabric and Deformation of the Envelope in Non Rigid Balloons", National Advisory Committee for Aeronautics, Report No. 16, 3rd Annual Report (1977), 144–271.
3. M.F. Culpin, "The Shearing of Fabrics: A Novel Approach", *Journal of the Textile Institute* 70, no. 3 (1979): 81–88.
4. E.E. Clulow and H.M. Taylor, "An Experimental and Theoretical Investigation of Biaxial Stress–Strain Relations in a Plain-weave Cloth", *Journal of the Textile Institute* (1963): 323–347.
5. G. Hedley, "Relative Humidity and the Stress/Strain Response of Canvas Paintings: Uniaxial Measurements of Naturally Aged Samples", *Studies in Conservation* 33 (1988): 133–148.

6. G. Hedley, "The Effect of Beeswax Impregnation on the Tensile Properties of Canvas" in *Measured Opinions*, ed. C. Villers. (London: UKIC, 1993), 17–20.
7. S. Mickalski, "Paintings – Their Response to Temperature, Relative Humidity, Shock and Vibration", *Art in Transit: Studies in the Packing and Transportation of Paintings*, ed. J. Gruver, (National Gallery of Washington, 1991), 223–248.
8. C.R.T. Young, "Preliminary Biaxial Tests on Cotton-duck and Linen", Third Seminar to the Conservation Department, Courtauld Institute, London, November 1995.
9. G. Hedley, "Some Empirical Determinations of the Strain Distibution of Stretched Canvas" in *Measured Opinions*, ed. C. Villers (London: UKIC, 1993), 21–26.
10. G.A. Berger and W.H. Russell, "An Evaluation of the Preparation on Canvas Paintings Using Stress Measurements", *Studies in Conservation* 33 (1988): 187–204.
11. M.F. Mecklenburg and C.S. Tumosa, "Mechanical Behaviour of Paintings Subjected To Changes in Temperature and Relative Humidity", ", *Art in Transit: Studies in the Packing and Transportation of Paintings*, ed. J. Gruver, (National Gallery of Washington, 1991), 173–216.
12. Hedley, "Relative Humidity".
13. Berger and Russell, "An Evaluation".
14. C.R.T. Young, "Measurement of Biaxial Strain of Paintings on Canvas Using ESPI", Internal Report No.1 for the Courtauld Institute of Art, July 1995, 78–81.
15. Ibid., 87–109.
16. F.T. Pierce, "The Geometry of Cloth Structure", *Journal of the Textile Institute, Transactions* 28, no.3 (March 1937): 45–96.
17. S. de Jong, and R. Postle, "An Introduction to the Study of Fabric Mechanics Using Energy Methods", *Textile Institute and Industry* (November 1977): 376–379.
18. A.S. Wagh and D.C. Snowden, "The Mechanism of Fabric Shrinkage", *The Textile Manufacturer* (October 1968): 422–427.
19. Mecklenburg and Tumosa, "Mechanical Behaviour".
20. Pierce, "The Geometry".
21. Hedley, "Relative Humidity".
22. Mecklenburg and Tumosa, "Mechanical Behaviour".
23. D.W. Lloyd, "The Analysis of Complex Fabric Deformations " in *Mechanics of Flexible Fibre Assemblies*, ed. J.W. Hearle et al. (Alphen aan den Rijn: Sijthoff and Noordhoff, 1980), 311–341.
24. Ibid.

Working Group B2

Paintings II: Scientific study of paintings

Interpretation as an Inevitable Risk in Conservation of Icons

Yuri Bobrov
The Repin Institute of the Russian Academy of Art, 197101,
Kamennoostrovsky pr.-2-21, Saint Petersburg, Russia

Abstract

Conservation and restoration of medieval Russian icons deals with specific objects that cannot be recognized merely as works of art or as part of the cultural museum heritage. They contain polysemantic values in the same material substance. In general, the approaches taken and the methods of treating the icons are determined by mechanisms of perception, forming the basis of the conservator's decisions. The image-conceptual model of every work of art results from psychological directives, in which both aesthetic and intellectual notions of a subject are concentrated. This model can be understood by considering it as an interpretation of the material substance, which is the inevitable outcome of every conservation treatment. Therefore, conservation brings with it the risk of aesthetic interpretation of an icon, just as for every other work of art.

Keywords

Icons, works of art, psychological directives, image-conceptual model, aesthetic, interpretation, recognition, mutilation, perception

International experience in the conservation of icons, medieval or modern, faces the specific problem of interpretation. There are scientific, theological and artistic points of view on icons in general. There is also the question of conservation methodology, because icons cannot be treated merely as cultural objects or as works of art. Leonid Uspenskij wrote that "what the icon contains, what it bears does not depend on culture, even on ecclesiastical culture."[1] These polysemantic values of an icon determine the variability of conservation approaches. For decades, the Russian experience of icon conservation has followed archeological principles, the main idea of which is the recognition of an icon as an object of cultural heritage. Now, we are witnessing a revival of Orthodox Christian values in Russian society. This makes it necessary to observe the basic mechanisms that cause inevitable variations in conservation approaches, although we do not want to be deeply involved in a discussion concerning theological aspects.

A professional attitude that can be extended to icons was set out in the Venice Charter, which is still the fundamental international document interpreting principles of restoration, proclaiming that the basic aim of restoration work is to preserve an object both as a work of art and as a historical document. One of its main paragraphs runs as follows:

> Restoration should be carried out in exceptional cases – if it is necessitated by the need to protect a monument and also by the aspiration to emphasize its aesthetic and historical value. Moreover, restoration work must not violate original materials and should be based on authentic documents. Restoration should stop where hypothesis begins; any new, completely indispensable details should depend on architectural composition and bear the character of our epoch.[2]

Although architectural monuments are being referred to here, the theses of the Charter express the modern attitude towards cultural values as a whole. Thus, both the object and the subject of restoration activity are involved in a contradiction between historical and cultural approaches. On the one hand, respect for the historical appearance of a work of art requires a kind of minimal intervention that would to the greatest possible extent guarantee the preservation of its actual condition. This supposes the treatment of an object conceived as a documentary illustration, regardless of loss of artistic meaning. On the other hand, aesthetic reactions, which are aroused by any objects accessible to perception, make us aspire to compensate for the damaged semantic and formal structure of a work of art that is going to be restored. All operations involving the removal of some supplementary elements, the preservation of others or the reconstruction of missing parts are dictated by those conceptions of human consciousness that express a particular approach to a subject. We should remember that the idea that the aesthetic applies to the sphere of relationships, i.e. the aesthetic does not have a specific object, was universally recognized a long time ago. This judgement is a matter of principle for understanding or conforming to the laws of the nature of conservation procedures on works of art. However, at the same time, there are "technocratic" attitudes in conservation, which try not to take this into consideration.

The psychology of aesthetic feelings

Aesthetic feelings arise in close connection with psychological directives, orienting the process of perception to the search for a defined inner order of form. Aesthetic satisfaction is aroused when this order is felt.[3] Not every perception has an aesthetic aspect, but every perception strives for order. This means that our brain and eye organize incoming visible information,[4] while satisfaction, in its turn, leads to preference, which would be impossible without comparison. This was proved by experiments in 1920s on chickens, whose perception is also based on the comparison of forms and qualities.[5] A human being, like a chicken, expresses a feeling of preference in everything, choosing the best "grains". Can a restorer be free of the "unfreedom" of choice? The answer is obvious – he or she cannot, because all the conservation operations executed on an object by a restorer are based on two factors: a personal psychological directive and the needs of society. Cesare Brandi was right when he defined restoration as an instance of recognition of a work of art.[6] We would add to this that restoration is an instance of recognition on the part of a person, as well as on the part of society, or some circle of it. Icons give a remarkable example of that. The same icon should be recognized and treated in a different way if it is intended for a museum, for an exhibition or for a church.

On the other hand, "rules" of recognition and the appropriate methodology of treatment are determined by a certain conception of conservation, of which there is no shortage in the course of history. These rules work as a part of psychological directives. In psychology the theory of "Uznadze directives" means "the definite openness of a subject to any (operational–psychological, epistemological, aesthetic or other) form of activity."[7] The essence of the theory is that at the particular moment when a subject is influenced by some object, some psychological state arises in the consciousness, which consists of sensible phenomena and qualities of form of the object. This state is not complete until "recognition" of the image comes as a result of comprehending of the certain significance of the image by the subject. Let us remember that it is just at this moment that a chicken selects a grain and picks it up. This very significance of the image from the beginning considerably changes indefinite feelings of form in full accord with the law of Gestalt psychology.[8] Characteristics of psychological direction are indissolubly linked with the inner psychological state of the personality and with activities realizing that direction in behaviour. Then, actions of the subject are not determined in a strict way, but probably as a "manner" or "style" of action.[9] It is essential to bear in mind that the theory of directive has a fundamental character and its mechanisms appear in all kinds of activities, but most obviously in connection with artistic objects. It is no mere chance that, in aesthetics, the most primitive aesthetic image is built up from the end, that is from the sense of the whole. To understand mechanisms forming "conservational" approaches, it is important to bear in mind that a psychological directive arises under conditions of both objective and subjective systems. A directive requires both general and individual necessity as a "general state of an individual".[10] In formulating his or her position, establishing the aims of the work to be carried out on an object and consequently the methods of his or her work, the conservator, if we are not to see him or her as a robot, bases everything on certain motives. A motive, from the psychological point of view, is an understanding of the advantages of a value "for me"; it is an emotional justification of one of the forms of behaviour in which a certain idea, significance and values are realized. Unlike aims, motives are not concretely understood by the subject: "Behind the comprehended motivation an uncomprehended motive can be hidden; motives are not disconnected from the consciousness".[11] Embodied in an aim, a subjective motive becomes a perception and, as a result, is corrected by an object.[12] At this point it is essential to understand the interaction between the motive and the object.

The essence of this interaction is that content of perception is not predetermined by a stimulus (the object) once and for all. According to D. Uznadze's idea, "it is caused first and foremost by the significance which the observer puts into an exhibited object."[13] This means that the motive and the aim do not fully arise from perceiving the quality (degree of preservation) of an object, but partly precede this moment. In other words, an approach in conservation in one sense precedes the perception of an object. A personal direction, in full accord with the laws of psychology, participates in the comprehension of a perceived object and, moreover, influences its condition after conservation. This happens because the conservation treatment is a consequence of judgement based on an "image-conceptual model" of an object.[14] The paradox is that, while the substance of the object does exist objectively and independently of the human being like any part of nature, it also exists as the thing for the human being, and as a social thing it exists only in the guise of the "image-conceptual model", which is not the same as the matter of the object. The purpose of an act of conservation is to protect the authenticity of the material thing from the variety of interventions provided by the "image-conceptual model". By definition, it is impossible to provide complete protection, but the option of minimizing the effects of the possible interpretation remains.

The dilemma of intervention

It thus appears that the dilemma of defining what exactly is on the receiving end of conservational intervention, a material substance or an image, can in practice have no resolution. This is because conservation treatment is directed at material, which is perceived as an image. Optical apparatus and other advanced technical aids can improve the quality of treatment, but cannot change its essence.

The directives of the Venice Charter, what we might call "generalized directives", distinguish two meanings in the material of the object: historical meaning and aesthetic meaning. This immediately puts the object into a position of inevitable contradiction if it is to undergo intervention. This is not a fault of the internationally recognized Charter, but is a natural effect of the process of subjectivization of the image at the moment of its recognition: when we perceive something, we look for and find its meaning. In other words, we recognize an object "for ourselves".

A question arises: is it realistic to separate the values of a work of art in its material substance, or at least in its "model" in our consciousness ? Psychology gives only one answer: division of the aesthetic and rational is groundless, because in human thought verbal and figurative thinking are unified.

Consequently, conservation, while keeping the balance between the historical and aesthetic positions, and confining treatment to the material sphere, although at the same time inevitably affecting the image-bearing sphere of the work of art, cannot fail to bear signs of interpretation. Since conservation procedures are always carried out at a certain historical distance, which separates the time of creation of a work of art from the time of restoration treatment, we can only be talking about critical interpretation.

The problem of interpretation was initially discussed by Cesare Brandi and then by Paul Phillipot, but only with regard to the question of "the treatment of losses on damaged areas in painting."[15]

It is here that the problem of inevitable risk created by conservation procedures on works of art of the past arises. It cannot be resolved just by saying: "we are treating only matter, not an image", or by exchanging the definition of "a work of art" for "an object". The preference shown to the principle of conservation that supposedly gives us an opportunity to avoid problems of interpretation is also ineffective. There are two reasons for this: first, an object created as a form with meanings cannot lose them: it can only take on other, so called latent, meanings. Second, psychological directives motivate all actions, including those which are strictly conservational. It is important to realize that interpretation appears not only as a problem of retouching of losses or of a restorer's ambitions to reconstruct, but also as a conformity to natural laws of every action carried out on a work of art; be it removal of added elements, strengthening of substances or altering presentation. Interpretation is a moment of understanding an object and, as such, it motivates actions as far back as the unconscious level.

Figure 1. Saint George. Novgorod icon, 12th century, Tretiakov Gallery, Moscow. Photograph taken in 1927 during restoration (painting contains remains of later additions: highlights on the face etc.)

An example

The experience of restoration in the 1930s of a 12th century icon of Saint George in the Tretiakov gallery, Moscow (Figure 1) can be seen as an example of "critical" interpretation. For this purpose we shall quote from the minutes of a discussion relating to this icon:

> Completion of restoration of the monument directly depends on the purpose of the monument and aims to construct a system of correlation of parts belonging to different times. If a monument is restored in this way as a museum exhibit it will provide the maximum amount of material to the observer . . . Remove the paint applied to the left hand in the 16th century leaving the 14th century layer; where paint has been lost, retain the repair, changing its dark brown colour to match the lighter 14th century parts . . . The existing dark green colour of the ground makes a negative impression. It breaks up the general impression of the item, creating dissonance in it.[16]

U. Olsufjev remarks that "this is why the dark green paint should be removed from the gesso." The other supervisor of the work, N. Sichov, considers that "the hilt of the sword and the sheath should be retained in their present form so that observers can see all the layers from different centuries

The cited document is a classic example of the polemic regarding the restoration of not only icons but other works of art, which is nowadays only carried on in exceptional cases.

Two types of interpretation

The concept of interpretation (Latin *Interpretatio* – explanation, commentary) embraces interpreting, disclosing the meaning of something, in one sense, and, in another sense, execution that is, in the given context, bringing into the existing work of art something based on one's own interpretation. Such a conception of the term, originating from its basic sense, makes us affirm that interpretation is always present in any act of conservation as a characteristic of perception over a certain historical interval.

It is necessary to distinguish clearly two types of interpretation. One, merely theoretical, is the intentional type, meaning orientation of consciousness of an object, that is, holding the object in one's mind. The result of this is an image – a conceptual model of an object. Acts of consciousness themselves do not change anything in the material world. At the same time, a physical subject, like a work of art, takes on some intentional characteristics and becomes a physical basis for a new subject existing in the mind. Undoubtedly, interpretation arising as a consequence of intentionality of consciousness is an ontological characteristic of any action connected with conservation intervention. However, a specific feature of this kind of activity is that it leads to a real action, the intervention into the material substance of a work of art. So, interpretation can also assume the character of a practical action, what we might call manipulation or restorational interpretation, because it would be neither intentional (creating images) nor creative (embodying forms as in music) interpretation. However, in any sense a treatment means manipulation.

Restorational interpretation is not the creation of a new product on the basis of an original one, but it provides an inevitable moment of recognition of a work of art. It is contained in every presentation or even in environmental circumstances. Allocating value sense to an object is already a moment of recognition because in this way we distinguish it from the commonness of previous existence. The "new life" of a work of art and the new attitude towards it begins from the moment of recognition. Even in a case when presentation does not affect the physical substance of work of art directly, if we disregard the influence of light, temperature, humidity etc., it involves a considerable amount of interpretation. That is why artists always worry about the organization of exhibitions of their works. Eduard Manet once complained to A. Proust:

> Your portrait has already been hanging in the Salon, dear friend, for three weeks. It is badly located between a window and the door, and the criticism has been even worse. But it is my destiny – to be badly hung up, – and I regard this philosophically.[17]

As the sphere of treatment moves from conservation to cleaning and then to restitution of losses, the extent of possible interpretation may either grow or

Figure 2. Apostle Peter and Paul. Novgorod icon, 13th century, Russian Museum, St Petersburg. Fragment: Saint Paul. Photograph taken in the 1920s during restoration (insertion of 16th century painting)

Figure 3. Lot with his daughters. Unknown italian painter, 17th century, Pavlovsk Museum, St Petersburg. Under cleaning (fragment of later overpainting representing Lot with daughters combined within original composition. Original figures had been cut out during a previous treatment)

Figure 4. Lot with his daughters (Figure 3). Later inpainting

decrease depending on the initial condition. Restorational interpretation in this practical, operational sense can be understood as any action that provides an opportunity to realize an object differently (emotionally or intellectually) from before intervention. Let us take a simple example: providing a painting with new varnish. This operation contains two complicated aspects, chemical and artistic, both of which have been discussed for decades.[18,19] Both the patina of the aged varnish film and the lifeless lustre of synthetic resins play a remarkable role in the appearance of a painting and, as a result, in its meaning.

The distinction between "work of art" and "historical document", in which the two poles in the same substance are designated "author's" and "historical" must to a certain extent be relative, because the two are inseparable, and the object will sometimes include later additions (see Figure 2). The actual form of a mutilated object must be interpreted in the course of treatment in compliance with one or another direction. It is possible to say: less intervention into object – more intentional interpretation, on one hand, or, on the other, more intervention especially with the goal of reintegration – more artistic creative interpretation. It is possible to say that conservation cannot contain less interpretation than restoration. So, in any situation, a conservator faces the risk of projection, according to Martin Heidegger's words, of his or her own sense onto the "text" (see Figures 3 and 4). Even in the situation where an object is only treated as having "historical value", one can see "projection" of a new sense, as happened with romantic images of ruins of ancient temples, which inspired architectural-type "ruins" in European gardens of the 18th century.

Conclusion

Consideration of interpretation as a natural property of human activity, predetermined by consciousness, allows us to say that, if it is impossible to avoid this risk, we can try to reduce it by accepting "for ourselves" that every intervention in a work of art has an aesthetic effect. This means that conservation is a kind of aesthetic activity, but not in that vulgar sense where aesthetic is recognized as the same as artistic reconstruction, from which every conservator tries to be distanced. Moreover, in connection with icons it is absolutely necessary to respect spiritual values as well as aesthetic values.

References

1. L. Uspenskij, *Bogoslovie ikoni pravoslavnoj tcerkvi* (*Theology of Orthodox Icons*), (Moscow: Western-European Ecsarchat,1989), 405.
2. Venice Charter, article 9.
3. D.G. Berlyne, " Measures of Aesthetic Preference ", in *Psychology and The Visual Arts*, ed. James Hogg (London: 1970).
4. R. Arnheim, *Art and Visual Perception. New Versions* (Berkeley and Los Angeles: University of California Press, 1974).
5. L.S. Vigotskij, *Psykhologia Iskusstv* (*Psychology of Art*) (Moscow: Iskusstvo,1986), 78–79.
6. C. Brandi, *Teoria del Restauro* (Rome: Edizioni di Storia e Letteratura,1963), 34.
7. A.E. Sherozia, "Soznanie, Bessoznatel'noe Psykhicheskoe i Sistema Fundamental``nych Otnoshenij Lichnosty" ("Consciousness, the Psychology of the Unconscious and a System of Fundamental Relations in Human Personality"), in *Bessoznatel'noe* ("*The Unconscious*") Vol.1, (Tbilisi, 1978), 69–70.
8. D.N. Uznadze, *Psykhologicheskie issledovanija* (*Psychological Researches*), (Moscow: Nauka, 1966), 41–47.
9. *Bessoznatel'noe* (*The Unconscious*), Vol.3, 344.
10. D.N. Uznadze, (*Psykhologicheskie issledovanija*, 168.
11. *Bessoznatel'noe* (*The Unconscious*), Vol.3, 342.
12. A.N. Leontiev, *Myshlenie, Soznanie, Lichnost* (*Thinking, Consciousness, Personality*), (Moscow: Nauka, 1975), 109.
13. D.N. Uznadze, *Psykhologicheskie issledovanija*, 35.
14. V.P. Zinchenko, V.M. Muninov, V.M. Gordon, "Issledovanije Vizual`nogo Myshlenija" ("Researches in Visual Thinking"), *Voprosi Psykhologiji* (*Problems of Psychology*), no. 2 (1973): 4.
15. P. Philippot, "Restoration: Philosophy, criteria, guidelines, " in *Preservation and Conservation: principles and practices, North American International Regional Conference, Williamsburg and Philadelphia* (10-16 Sept. 1972), 367–382.

16. Yu. Bobrov, *Istoria restavraciji drevnerusskoj zivopisi* (*The History of Restoration of Old Russian Icon Painting*), (Leningrad: Khudoshnik RSFSR, 1987), 106–109.
17. *Eduard Manet. Szizn, Pis'ma. Vospominania. Kritika sovremennikov* (*Edouard Manet. Life. Letters. Memoires. Critiques of contemporaries*), (Moscow: Iskusstvo,1965), 175.
18. R. Feller, N.Stolow, E.Jones, *On Picture Varnishes and Their Solvents*, (Washington: National Gallery of Art, 1985).
19. E.H. Gombrich, "Dark varnishes", *Burlington Magazine* 54, no. 707 (1962): 51–55; O.Kurz, "Time the Painter", *Burlington Magazine* 55, no. 720 (1963): 94–97.

Formal Connoisseurship and the Study of Paintings Techniques

Spike L. Bucklow
Hamilton Kerr Institute,
Mill Lane, Whittlesford,
Cambridgeshire CB2 4NE, UK

Abstract

The relationship between formal connoisseurship and the study of paintings techniques is described. The paper focuses on craquelure and its attributional significance to connoisseurs. A selected literature of craquelure is outlined and the potential scope of craquelure as a non-invasive means of investigating the material composition of a painting is determined. The general validity of connoisseurial assertions is demonstrated and some basic features of craquelure are identified which allow conclusions to be drawn about a painting's support and ground.

Keywords

Connoisseurship, attribution, craquelure, support, ground

Introduction

The scientific study of paintings techniques includes invasive activities such as pigment identification and media analysis. Indeed, in general, the scientific method has proven itself most successful when examining material objects and describing them in abstract terms. Whilst unambiguous, these abstract terms – particular elements, molecules, etc. – may provide insights into particular, narrowly defined, aspects of the painting.

However, if we are willing to sacrifice a degree of certitude in the results of a scientific examination, then insights may be acquired simultaneously into several aspects of the painting's rich and complex structure. Advances in computational methods, such as image processing and statistical analysis, enable us to take visual information as our data and provide tools to help interpret the results we obtain.

The visual aspect of a painting is arguably its *raison d'être* and, as well as being enjoyed, it has long been methodically exploited by connoisseurs. One of the primary functions of connoisseurship is the establishment of an artist's *oeuvre*. Formal connoisseurship, which can discriminate between autograph and copyist's works, depends largely upon reference to the painter's technique. It is this aspect of connoisseurship which may contribute novel and non-invasive methods of studying paintings techniques to the conservation profession.

The history of formal connoisseurship is long and is interwoven with other disciplines involving systematic observation, such as medicine.[1] Much of formal connoisseurship rests upon the morphological analysis of painted details. Thus, in trying to determine an artist's hand, the connoisseur selects a detail and mentally compares its shape with his or her understanding of how the artist would be expected to execute that shape.[2] This is where the uncertainty of the method arises – it is assumed that types of shapes remain predictable across an artist's *oeuvre* and that the same type of shape is perceptually different when executed by another hand.

Those connoisseurs who have written about the task of attributing paintings to hands have attempted to minimise the risks associated with these two assumptions by carefully choosing which detail to analyse. Thus the physician to Urbano VIII (Pope from 1623 to 1644), a Sienese called Giulio Mancini (1558–1630), chose to exercise his diagnostic skills on those painted details which were swiftly executed and somewhat stylised. He noted that:

> Curls and waves of hair, if they are to be reproduced exactly, are very laborious to do; this will show in the painting, and if the copyist fails to get them right they will lack the perfection of the master's version. And these parts of a painting are like strokes of the pen and flourishes in handwriting, which need the master's sure and resolute touch.[3,4]

Some two and a half centuries later, Giovanni Morelli (1816–1891) made similar observations about the ways in which artists worked:

> As most men, both speakers and writers, make use of habitual modes of expression, favourite words and sayings, which they often employ involuntarily ... so almost every painter has his own peculiarities which escape him without his being aware of it.[5]

He established a system of attribution which enjoyed some degree of acceptance, for example by Berenson,[6] and which was based upon the identification of an artist from his habitual modes of expression. Morelli, who studied comparative anatomy in his youth,[7] drew particularly upon the formulaic depiction of those parts of the body that had a minor contribution to the painting's composition. For him, the shapes of ears and hands were symptomatic of particular artists.[8]

The theoretical significance of the "flourishes" recognised by Mancini and the "habitual" details noted by Morelli found support in the work of Mauritz van Dantzig (1903–1960), an amateur with a keen interest in psychology.[9] Van Dantzig's systematic visual examination of paintings, which started with the comparison of paintings by Vermeer and van Meegeren, has not enjoyed widespread acceptance; indeed it has been described as "the over zealous application of positivist objectivity".[10]

It is, however, worthy of note in this context as it physiologically rationalised the difference between the master's "spontaneous" and the copyist's "inhibited" brushstrokes.[11] The method also explicitly used information (derived from purely visual examination) about the sequence in which an artist worked.[12]

A recent study of paintings by Lely and studio of Lely[13] demonstrates that paint layer structures as well as complex brushstrokes and the outlines of pictorial fragments are amenable to the morphological analysis of formal connoisseurship. In the study, a correlation of attributions with technical evidence of working methods concluded that clear differences could be determined between the Lely's paintings and those of his assistants. Broadly, in the case of Lely's studio, it appeared that studio assistants copied particular visual effects but not the means whereby the master achieved those effects.

The examples cited above illustrate the connoisseurial utilisation of individual differences in the process of creating a painting. In all cases the visual forms studied are the record the mechanical actions of the artist captured in the paint film. However, the attributional significance of ageing has also been noted for paintings, as Pietro Edwards wrote in the 1770s, "consist of heterogeneous elements artificially held together contrary to their natural affinities".[14] In the case of ageing, the visible forms studied are the record of the inherent chemical and mechanical actions of the object.

Craquelure

One example of an ageing process which can assist the connoisseur in his or her attribution of a painting is provided by the craquelure pattern. Max Friedländer noted the importance of craquelure as a clue to the date of a painting[15] and Marijnissen stated that: "Crack formation has always been a very important element in judging authenticity. The bibliography should be long and detailed. Curiously enough, literature on the subject is sparse".[16] Most descriptions of craquelure that exist in the literature are evocative and have been written to draw attention to the significance of the pattern rather than to enable its exploitation. For example, Sarah Walden writes :

> The infinite variety and intricacy of craquelure can reflect the biography of a painting, as of a face. A history of a canvas or a panel can often be traced by this suggestive network, since different periods and techniques leave a different tracery.[17]

Indeed, where the exact nature of the craquelure pattern is the subject of a paper in the literature, it is usually illustrated and description is not attempted.[18,19] The apparently random nature of the craquelure pattern helps it elude formal description. Consequently, those systems for explicitly describing cracks which have been proposed have not been widely adopted.[20]

Notwithstanding the difficulties presented by the description of craquelure patterns, conservation scientists and restorers have continued to refer to them. Laurie suggested that: "Flemish oil paintings have a regular crackle, while Italian tempera paintings are more likely to possess an irregular crackle".[21] But these assertions cannot always be taken at face value. For example, Major Roller incorrectly stated that: "tempera always shows minute rectangular cracking which is quite characteristic and different from the curvilinear cracking of oil pictures".[22]

So, craquelure's inscrutability has deterred our description of it in terms of appearance and description in terms of its causation is complex. The difficulties historically associated with describing craquelure in terms of paint media are due to the conflation of painting materials.

The morphological analysis of the product of an ageing process may have liberated us from some assumptions about the creative act, but it does rest upon assumptions about the behaviour of painting materials. This is because the craquelure pattern is the visible record of the way in which tensions have accumulated, and been dissipated, within the structure of the painting. The accumulation and dissipation of tension depends on the particular materials used and the methods of construction employed by the artist. If the craquelure pattern is to be used as an indicator of these materials and methods, then we must assume that details about the external agents which cause tensions within paintings can be ignored. In other words, we must assume that changes in humidity and temperature will effect the degree to which, but not the way in which, craquelure develops.

For the craquelure pattern to offer clues to the origins of a painting to a connoisseur, it must vary in a predictable way both chronologically and geographically. Thus particular craft traditions and workshop practices may produce particular craquelure patterns. The significance of craquelure as an indicator of painting materials and methods is therefore restricted to periods and regions that are associated with a constrained set of materials and a strong craft tradition.

Research[23] has sought a statistical correlation of craquelure pattern features with materials, methods and art historic categories. The art historic categories which were felt to satisfy the above conditions included; 14th and 15th century Italian paintings on panel; 15th and 16th century Flemish paintings on panel; 17th century Dutch paintings on canvas and 18th century French paintings on canvas. These categories were chosen because they were well represented in public galleries in England, France and the Netherlands. More than 500 black-and-white close-up photographs were taken of craquelure patterns on paintings in these categories. The craquelure patterns photographed were areas of painting which did not display cracks that could be directly attributable to some specific source. Thus, "whirls" or "spirals" due to impact, "herring-bones" due to scraping, cracks due to stretcher bars, tacking and keying-out of paintings on canvas were avoided, as were joints, splits and framing tensions on panel paintings. By removing these local sources of tension from the survey of craquelure, the patterns due to the inherent tensions associated with the support, ground, media and pigments could be studied.

Particle size, shape and pigment identity have been shown to influence the mechanical properties of paint layers[24] and it can be seen that crack patterns may change significantly between adjacent paint passages. Since pigment identification and particle data were not available on the wide range of paintings surveyed, the paint passages chosen for the craquelure study were those where the pigment content was most predictable. Lead white particles are usually small and the use of lead white is a constant factor in all the categories of painting included in the study. The survey therefore concentrated on paint passages rich in lead white, which is the predominant pigment in the depiction of much flesh, many architectural elements and some sky. These paint passages are also associated with little use of impasto and the gradual modulation of pigments, two other factors which encourage the uniform development of craquelure. Lead-white-rich paint passages have the further advantage of providing a good contrast with the craquelure pattern.

Data about paint media are also not available for many paintings on public display. Although the distinction between oil and tempera paintings is the one most frequently encountered in the literature of craquelure, observations are usually based upon assumptions about, rather than knowledge of, media. A provisional conclusion from the survey is that media is probably one of the less influential factors in the development of the craquelure pattern in the categories of paintings studied.

The nature of the ground layer, however, appears to be very influential in the development of the craquelure pattern. Again, exact data were not always available for all the paintings photographed, although, in the art historic categories in question broad generalisations can be made about the composition of ground layers. It is not just the composition of the ground layer which affects the craquelure pattern but also its thickness, a fact noted by Renders:

> The cracks produced in (Flemish paintings with) a thin or medium priming faithfully follow the grain of the wood. Those in a thick priming form more independently and at double or treble the distance between lines formed by the grain of the wood.[25]

As this quotation suggests, the support is also crucial to the development of the craquelure pattern. This is because it is the environmentally responsive nature of the support that generates the tensions which are released in the relatively unresponsive and embrittled paint layers.[26] Different canvases and woods have characteristically different responses to environmental fluctuations and therefore create different stresses within the painting when subjected to the same external stresses.

Thus the support, ground and paint layers of the painting generate, transmit and release tensions in different manners creating visibly different patterns. Craquelure is the summation of interactions between these components and the attributional assertions of connoisseurs imply that the patterns are characteristic of certain traditional combinations of components. The present research has found this to be so.

The final pattern of a crack network is the result of a number of competing mechanical processes. Competition in the release of tension is controlled by the relative ease of propagating existing cracks compared to the ease of nucleating new cracks in the paint layer. Competition in the transmission of tension is controlled by the nature of the support and ground layers. Cracks in the paint layer may either be closely related to the structure of the support or may be locally isolated from it by the ground layer.

Competition between rates of nucleation and rates of propagation of cracks results in many short cracks if nucleation is easier than propagation, or fewer longer cracks if propagation is easier than nucleation. Equally, the close relationship between the support and paint layers, allowed by a thin or brittle ground layer, leads to cracks which follow the grain of wood or weave of canvas. On the other hand, if the ground is thicker or less brittle, it will reduce the local influence of the support on the paint layer and lead to cracks, the form of which is largely determined by the mechanical properties of the ground layer. In practice, the outcome is not clear-cut and the influence of the various processes will vary within any given painting.

The connoisseur cannot perceive these competing processes, and he or she need not even be aware of them, yet their formal consequences can be recognised as symptomatic of the painting's sub-structure. The cracks – few or many, long or short, determined by the support or mediated by the ground – combine together into a network which exposes some aspect of the painting's structure whilst obscuring others. The connoisseur looks therefore not at cracks, but crack networks; the rhythms of cracks and the textures they create.

It has been observed that: "European languages discriminate very finely in some areas (e.g. underlying Euclidean form) and very coarsely in others (e.g. seen surface texture)".[27] This characteristic of European languages may account for the "sparse" craquelure literature noted by Marijnissen. Stout, possibly influenced by the imprecise nature European texture vocabularies, asserted that: "Patterns are linear".[28] Whilst it is certainly true that individual cracks can be described as linear, craquelure, as the combination of cracks, has undeniable rhythmic and network qualities and is also "spatial".

In the absence of a linguistically natural way of describing craquelure directly as the visual texture it appears to be, it must be described in terms of characteristics isolated from the pattern. It is beyond the scope of this paper to outline the means (derived from clinical psychology and statistics) whereby the crack pattern characteristics were isolated and interpreted. However, research has shown that, collectively, eight simple characteristics are sufficient to describe craquelure patterns for attributional purposes.

The characteristics used to describe craquelure in this research are both linear and spatial. They are:

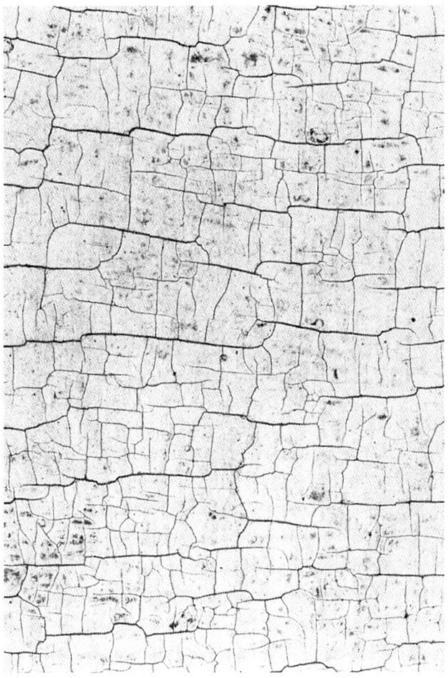

Figure 1. Typical craquelure on an early Italian panel painting (maximum dimension c. 5 cm, parallel with wood grain)

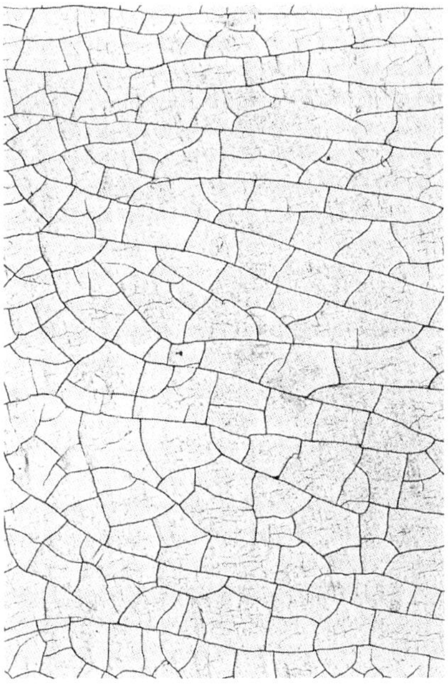

Figure 2. Typical craquelure on an early Flemish panel painting (maximum dimension c. 5 cm, perpendicular to wood grain)

- continuity of the network (do cracks form junctions or do they terminate?);
- degree of organisation in the network (is the network relatively ordered or relatively random?);
- predominant direction of the cracks (is there an overall direction, and if so, what is its orientation?);
- shape of "islands" between cracks (are they square or not?);
- fine detail of the cracks (are they smooth or jagged?);
- shape of the cracks (are they straight or do they curve?);
- thickness of the cracks (are all cracks the same thickness or is there a significant pattern to their variation?);
- spatial frequency (approximately how far apart are the cracks?).

With these eight characteristics describing craquelure from the four categories of paintings under study, it has been found that the school of a painting may be predicted with approximately 90% accuracy.

The reduction of the craquelure pattern to these characteristics is artificially analytical and rules which govern their recombination are complex.[29] In contrast, the connoisseur's naturally synthetic approach to the task is the fruit of experience. The following examples give a broad indication of the significance of a few important pattern characteristics.

A characteristic of early Flemish oak panels is that the cracks run parallel to the grain of the wood (Figure 1). Figure 1 also shows that the cracks are relatively smooth, a characteristic of chalk grounds on panel. A characteristic of early Italian poplar panels is that cracks run perpendicular to the grain of the wood (Figure 2). Figure 2 also show that individual cracks are jagged, a characteristic of gypsum grounds. These two features (predominantly parallel vs. perpendicular and smooth vs. jagged) cannot be viewed in isolation and many early Flemish and Italian panels do not exhibit them.

A detail from a Dutch 17th century painting shows jagged cracks with a square (strictly speaking, orthogonal) relationship (Figure 3). These features are associated with characteristically thin brittle grounds which allow cracks to faithfully follow the (plain) canvas weave. A detail from a French 18th century painting shows smooth, curved cracks (Figure 4). These features are associated with thick (possibly double) grounds, which allow the complete liberation of the crack pattern from the underlying structure of the canvas. As with the features noted on the two panel paintings above, caution must be exercised in interpreting these features. A continuum exists between being strongly influenced by the weave and being insulated from the weave by the ground.

Conclusion

Although disputed by some, it is probable that connoisseurs do not use the details of a painting to draw conclusions about its attribution.[30] Rather, they use details to provide evidence to confirm or refute conclusions made with reference to the whole painting.[31] As such, craquelure probably provides as accurate an attributional clue as any other detail – formal or chemical – taken in isolation. This work does not imply that connoisseurs analytically search for features such as the ones listed above when looking at craquelure. It merely confirms many of their assertions and acknowledges their rôle in raising awareness of craquelure's significance.

The study of craquelure indicates that the broad connoisseurial overview of art historic categories can be translated into specific observations which focus on particular aspects of paintings techniques. A statistically significant survey of craquelure demonstrates that correlations can be found that relate the craquelure pattern to the use of certain painting materials and techniques.

The complexity of the visual information provided by the craquelure has hitherto restricted its utilisation as a means of confirmation or prediction about a painting's origins to the experienced connoisseur. However, statistical techniques enable the identification of simple features which allow conclusions to be drawn from the craquelure pattern with varying degrees of certainty. Thus, from the non-invasive visual inspection of the craquelure pattern in the paint layer, one is able to determine an understanding of the nature of the support and the ground layer.

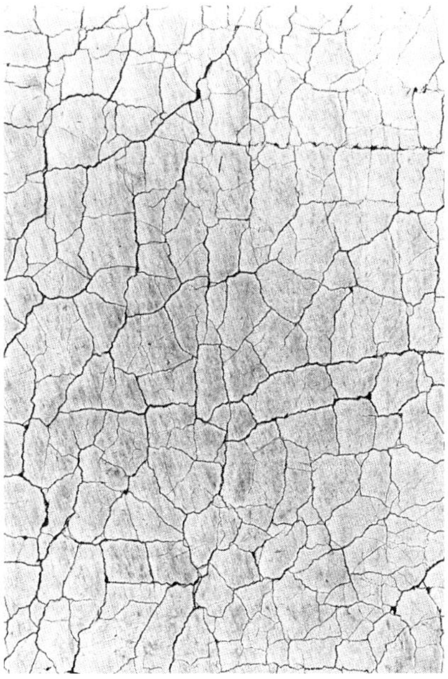

Figure 3. Typical craquelure on a 17th century Dutch painting on canvas (maximum dimension c. 6 cm, aligned with canvas weave)

The ability to interpret the craquelure pattern derives from the traditional usages and predictable behaviours of certain combinations of materials. This ability has significance to the study of paintings techniques in three distinct ways. First, one can visually confirm the degree of adherence to a particular workshop or craft tradition and thereby determine the extent of that tradition's chronological or geographic influence, for example, gauging the relative influence of Flemish techniques across German paintings panel of the same period. Second, one can trace the transmission of techniques associated with one tradition in the works of another tradition, for example, the rather "Flemish" quality of craquelure on "The Agony in the Garden", by Giovanni Bellini (no. 726, National Gallery, London).

Finally, one can be alerted to changes in the supply of materials such as may occur when an artist works abroad and buys his supplies locally, for example, the very "French" quality of craquelure on topographic paintings of Paris by the Dutch artist Johannes Augustus Knip (a 1357 & c 1456, Rijksmuseum, Amsterdam).

Thus, the formal analysis of craquelure offers us a method which complements the detailed study of supports and ground layers by broadly assigning identity to these normally hidden components at a glance.

Acknowledgements

The author gratefully acknowledges the support of The Queen Elizabeth Scholarship Trust and Harold Wingate Foundation. He would also like to thank the staff of the Fitzwilliam Museum, Cambridge, Courtauld Institute, Wallace Collection, Tate Gallery and National Gallery, London, the Rijksmuseum and the Louvre.

Notes

1. C. Ginzburg, "Morelli, Freud and Sherlock Holmes: Clues and the Scientific Method," *History Workshop* 9 (1980): 5–36.
2. R. Offner, *Studies in Florentine Painting* (New York: Julius Press, 1972), 135.
3. G. Mancini, *Considerazioi Sulla Pittura*, ed. A. Marucchi, 2 vols., (Rome, 1956-7), cited in Ginzburg, "Morelli, Freud and Sherlock Holmes," 18.
4. D. Mahon, *Studies in Seicento Art and Theory* (London, Warburg Institute, 1947), 277–331.
5. G. Morelli, *Italian Painters: Critical Studies of their Works*, 2 vols., trans. C. J. Ffoulkes (London, 1892–1893), vol. 1, 75.
6. B. Berenson, *Three Essays in Method* (Oxford: University Press, 1926), 52.
7. R. Wollheim, *On Art and the Mind* (London: Allen Lane, 1977), 177.
8. G. Morelli, *Italian Painters*, vol. 2, 3.
9. M. M. van Dantzig, *Pictology*, ed. The van Dantzig Foundation (Leiden: E. J. Brill, 1973).
10. P. Cannon-Brookes, "Art History, Connoisseurship and Scientific Literacy," *The International Journal of Museum Management and Curatorship*, 7 (1988): 6.
11. J. Storm van Leeuwen, "The Concept of Pictology and its Application to works by Frans Hals," in *Authentication in the Visual Arts*, ed. H. L. C. Jaffe et al., (Amsterdam: B. M. Israel B. V., 1979), 59.
12. M. M. van Dantzig, *Pictology*, 17.
13. E. Hendriks and K. Groen, "Lely's Studio Practice", in *Bulletin Number 2*, ed. I. McClure (Cambridge: Hamilton Kerr Institute, 1994), 21–37.
14. B. Raphael, "The Edwards Manuscripts", (Cooperstown, 1971), quoted in C. Keck, "Lining Adhesives: their History, Uses and Abuses," *Journal of the American Institute of Conservation* 17 (1977): 47.
15. M. J. Friedländer, *On Art and Connoisseurship*, trans. T. Borenius (London: Bruno Cassirer, 1942), 193.
16. R. H. Marijnissen, *Paintings*, (Brussels: Elsevier, 1985), 114.
17. S. Walden, *The Ravished Image*, (London: Weidenfeld and Nicolson, 1985), 125.
18. A. de Pereira, *Aurons-nous encore une Renaissance en Peinture? Du procédé de la Peinture en Détrempe Chez les Anciens Maîtres de la Renaissance de son Emploi pour Peindre d'après leur Manière*, L'Ecole Royale des Beaux-Arts, Stuttgart, 1842.
19. M. N. M. Boers, "Reference Standards for the Description of Various Types and Degrees of Cracking and Similar Faults in Paint Coats," (Paper delivered at the Fifth F.A.T.I.P.E.C. Congress, Milan, 1959), 821–833.
20. G. Stout, "A Trial Index of Laminal Disruption," *Journal of the American Institute for Conservation* 17, (1977): 17–26.
21. A. P. Laurie, "Crackle and Forgeries of Primitives," *The Connoisseur*, 81 (1928): 157.
22. N. Heaton, (Report to the Committee on the Preservation of Pictures, Royal Academy of Arts, London, 25 June 1925), 2.

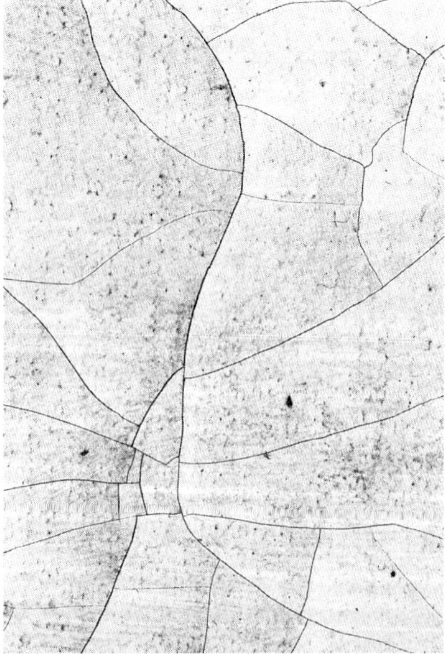

Figure 4. Typical craquelure on a 18th century French painting on canvas (maximum dimension c. 6 cm, aligned with canvas weave)

23. S. Bucklow, "Craquelure and the Formal Analysis of Paintings" (Ph.D. dissertation, University of Cambridge, 1996).
24. A Toussaint, "Influence of Pigmentation on the Mechanical Properties of Paint Films," *Progress in Organic Coatings* 2, (1973/4): 237–267.
25. E. Renders, "Cracks in Flemish Primitives," *The Connoisseur* (1928): 59.
26. J. Colville, W. Kilpatrick and M. Mecklenburg, "A Finite Element Analysis of Multilayered Orthotropic Membranes with application to Oil Paintings on Canvas," IIC Conference Preprints, Washington, (1982), 146–150.
27. M. Baxandall, "The Language of Art Critism", in *The Language of Art History*, ed. S. Kemall and I. Gaskell, (Cambridge University Press, 1991), 68.
28. G. Stout, "A Trial Index", 18.
29. Manuscript in preparation.
30. E. Wind, *Art and Anarchy*, (London: Faber and Faber, 1963), 38.
31. M. J. Friedländer, *On Art and Connoisseurship*, 173.

The Technical Examination of Joachim Beuckelaer's 'The Miraculous Draught of Fishes'

Joris Dik
Institute for Art History, University of Amsterdam,
Herengracht 286, 1016 BX Amsterdam, The Netherlands
Arie Wallert*, Yvonne Szafran
GCI/Museum Services Laboratory, J. Paul Getty Museum,
17985 Pacific Coast Highway, Malibu CA 90265, USA
H.J.M. Meijers, K.A.N. Abelskamp, R. Leenheer, H. Kars
Rijksdienst voor het Oudheidkundig Bodemonderzoek (ROB)
Kerkstraat 1, 3811 CV Amersfoort,
The Netherlands

Abstract

The technical examination of Joachim Beuckelaer's 'Miraculous Draught of the Fishes' is discussed. Various analytical methods were used in order to study Beuckelaer's painting technique and his materials. The study aims to gain a better understanding of technical aspects in the artistic relationships in the Antwerp school.

Keywords

Dutch painting, the Netherlands, infrared reflectography, X-ray fluorescence, microscopy, cross-sections, gas chromatography, photo-luminescence spectroscopy

Introduction

This study was undertaken in the context of the research project on technical aspects of paintings in the group of Antwerp painters, Pieter Aertsen and Joachim Beuckelaer, carried out by Peter van den Brink, Margreet Wolters, and J.R.J. van Asperen de Boer of Groningen University. Most of the examinations of paintings by the Groningen team have been done almost exclusively with the use of infrared reflectography, occasionally supported by observations with a stereo microscope. The Groningen researchers have occasionally had the chance to take paint samples in order to examine the paint stratigraphy and to identify pigments, colourants and binding media of the paintings. Our study may contribute to the technical studies in this context. Joachim Beuckelaer's 'The Miraculous Draught of Fishes', previously in the English collection of Lord Macdonald since 1821, was acquired by the Getty Museum in 1971.[1] The painting was first shown publicly in 1951 and has been generally accepted as one of Beuckelaer's largest and most important works.[2]

The 'Miraculous Draught of Fishes', painted in 1563 by Joachim Beuckelaer, has a special position within the group of Antwerp paintings. It represents a stage in the gradual transition from traditional religious painting to a more secular type of representation. The painting shows, from the biblical narrative (John 21:6–13), the scene where Peter recognizes Christ after the miraculous draught of fishes. In the panoramic scene the landing of the boats and the counting and distributing of the fish takes place in the foreground, whereas the actual religious narrative is depicted at a greatly reduced scale in the background (Figure 1). This disparity in scale of the subject matter is carried to extremes in later painting, eventually leading to completely secularized 'genre' painting.[3] The 'Miraculous draught of fishes' is

Figure 1. Joachim Beuckelaer, 'The Miraculous Draught of Fishes', 1563. Oil on panel, 110.5 x 221 cm. J. Paul Getty Museum, Malibu

* Author to whom correspondence should be addressed.

one of the few 'small figure' paintings where traces of colour notations in the underdrawing could be found. We had the chance to study the painting with a number of analytical methods.

The painting was examined with the use of energy-dispersive X-ray fluorescence (XRF),[4] polarized light microscopy (PLM),[5] X-ray diffraction (XRD),[6] and various microchemical tests for the identification of the inorganic pigments. The structure of the different paint layers was studied through the examination of microscopic paint cross sections. Cross sections were also examined in the environmental scanning electron microscope (ESEM). The organic colourants were identified by the use of photo-luminescence spectroscopy (PLS),[7] and high-performance liquid chromatography (HPLC).[8] The binding media were estimated by the staining of the paint cross sections, and analysed, with the use of gas chromatography/mass spectrometry (GCMS).

The underdrawing was examined with the use of infrared reflectography.[9]

The carrier

The signed and dated (monogram JB, 1563 Julia 6) painting, measuring 110 x 221 cm was executed on an oak panel. The panel was constructed of four different planks. As a result of thinning and other interventions on the panel, much information on the original carrier has been lost. The use of such large panels, rather than canvas, does not seem to be uncommon in the works from the Aertsen–Beuckelaer group.

The ground layer

The ground consists mainly of calcium carbonate, as was shown in the examination by PLM of a dispersion of a microsample. It showed nice hexagonal particles with twinning planes parallel to the long axis. The particles were highly birefringent, and had refractive indices lower than that of the mounting medium of 1.66. They had symmetrical extinction.

A (calcium sulphate) microchemical test showed that Ca was present. Presence of the carbonate radical was indicated by strong effervescence in dilute hydrochloric acid. An XRD analysis of the ground confirmed the identification of the material as calcite. The presence of lead-white in the ground could not be detected by staining the cross-section with a Lugol's stain.

The ground could be seen in several cross sections, and seems to be evenly applied and have an average thickness of 25 μm. In all sections the ground has a whitish colour, turning yellow-brownish towards the top.

A paint layer of lead-white was put on top of this ground and the binding medium of the paint layers was apparently absorbed by the material of the ground. This discoloured oil gives the ground a yellowish appearance, as can be seen with the naked eye on several transparent areas of the paint film, for instance on the beach of the lower left corner. On a few spots the ground has been left uncovered by the painter, as was revealed by microscopic examination. These areas of uncovered ground give a good impression of the discolouring of the oil.

In a technical examination of an altar picture by Beuckelaer, signed and dated 1565, Ehmke concluded that *'das Bild is auf einer gelb eingetönten Grundierung gemalt'*.[10] It seems probable that in that painting a similar discoloured oil layer has led the author to this conclusion. However, some of the toning on our panel may be due to a thin film of ochre on the lead white layer. This film would be too thin to be discernable in a cross section.

A good example can be found in the tonal modulation of the trousers of the horseman on the right of the painting, which shows clearly that the light parts have been heightened with lead white. The ground shines here through the paint as a transitional tone between the lighted and shaded parts. This indicates that the ground with the insulation layer on top has not had a plain white colour. It seems that the original ground had a slightly warmer tone than that pure white alone, which then has darkened even more in time.

The layer of lead-white prevented the oil of the actual paint layers from being absorbed by the ground. In Dutch paintings the use of this kind of insulation of

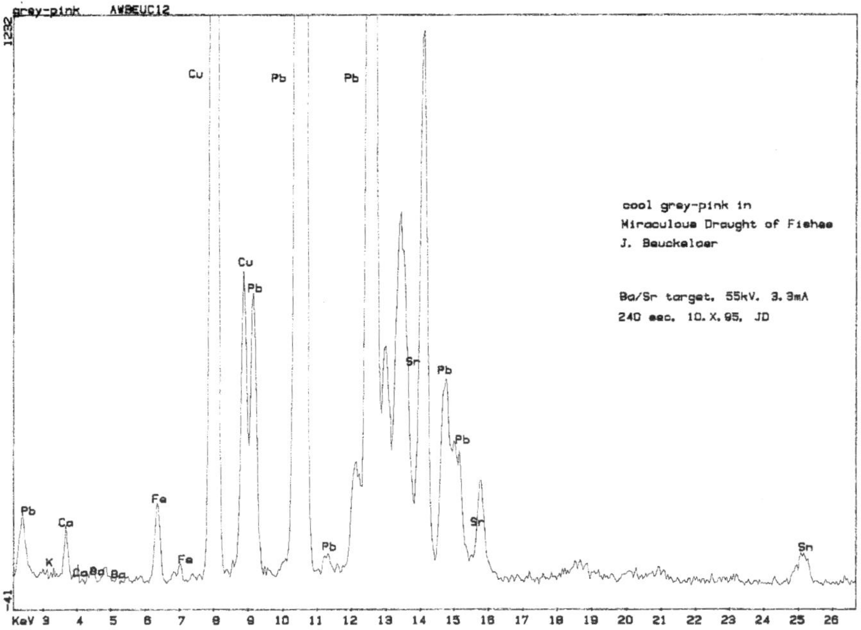

Figure 2. XRF spectrum showing a peak for tin (Sn)

Figure 3. IR reflectograms of the centred group on the foreground

the ground dates back to the second quarter of the 15th century and lasted until the first half of the 16th century.[11] While south of the Alps many Cinquecento painters started to experiment with coloured grounds, known as '*imprimatura*', in the Netherlands the use of the traditional lead-white insulation layer was still maintained. Lead-white layers on top of the ground have been identified in works by Hans Memling,[12] Pieter Bruegel,[13] Jan van Scorel[14] and Jan II van Conincxloo,[15] in the 16th century *drapeniers altaar*[16] and appears to have been the common practice of the time. Our painting from 1563 is one of the more recent paintings on which the use of such a white insulation layer has been shown.

On all spots that were examined by XRF, but in particular in areas where large amounts of lead white were applied, substantial amounts of tin could be seen (Figure 2). Since no tin-based pigments, such as lead tin yellow, were found on these areas, the most likely explanation for the presence of this element would be as an impurity in the raw material used to make the lead-white. It would be interesting to investigate the consistency of the presence of such trace elements in other paintings from the 'Antwerp group'.

The underdrawing

In several cross sections black particles could be seen between the lead-white layer and the next layer of paint. These black chunks probably consist of black carbon. IRR examination revealed an extensive underdrawing over the whole of the painting (Figure 3). The underdrawing in the foreground seems to have been executed in black chalk, while the background underdrawing has much more fluid lines, suggesting the use of a liquid medium. Traces of colour notations were found on the clothes of the centred group of people in the foreground (Figure 4). These colour notations, *pur* for purple, *vv* for white, *root* for red and *bl* for blue, in one case (*bl* under the red skirt of the lady with the hat) did not correspond to the final result. These colour notations showed a very close correspondence to the notations found on Pieter Pietersz's altarpiece in Gouda.[17] Similar notations have also been found in the works of Lucas van Leiden,[18] Jan van Scorel,[19] and Pieter Aertsen.[20] The underdrawing was thus executed on top of the insulation layer, instead of directly on the calcite ground. This can also be seen in the works of Jan van Scorel[21] and Jan II. van Coninxloo.[22]

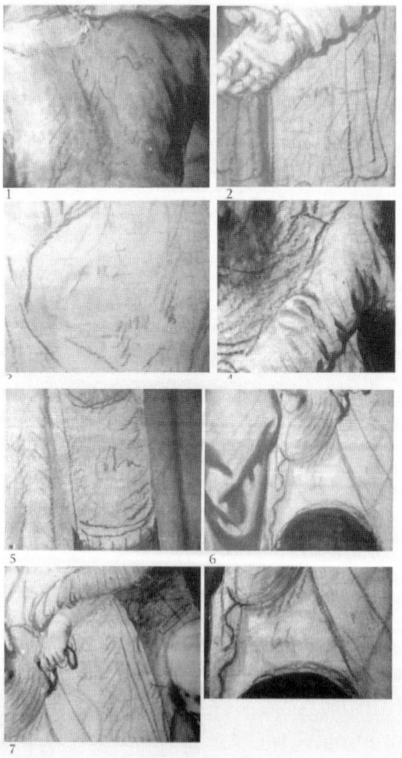

Figure 4. IR reflectograms of colour notations

The paint layers

In the scheme of colours in the 'Miraculous Draught of Fishes', Beuckelaer does not show significant deviation from the practice of his former master Pieter

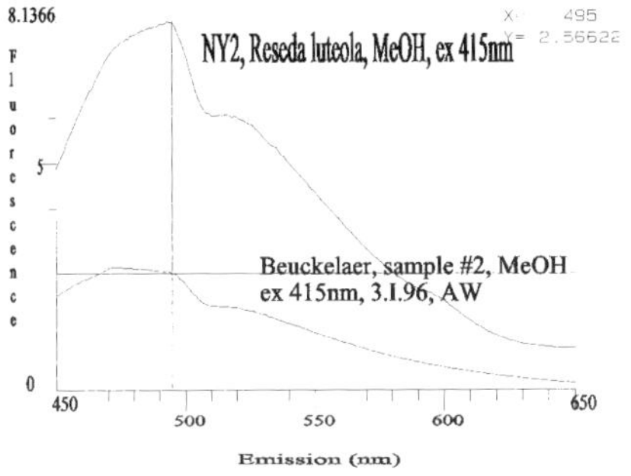

Figure 5. Luminescence emission spectrum of yellow colourant

Aertsen. The use of colours is characterized by a rather monochrome, almost grisaille-like, palette for the background, with stronger colours in the figures on the foreground. But even in these foreground figures, rather dull black, grey, and reddish brown mixed tones dominate over brighter primary colours. In general, there appears to be a greater emphasis on tonal values rather than a contrast in colours. In some areas the paint appears rather thinly applied, so that a brownish tone on the ground shows through the paint layers. These layers appear to be applied in a very simple structure. The structure generally consists of one to four different layers on the slightly toned ground.

Staining of cross sections with fluorescein isothiocyanate and acid fuchine suggested that the medium of the calcite ground could be of proteinaceous nature. The binding medium of the lead white layer and of the actual paint layers was assumed, on the basis of staining with 2,7-dichlorofluorescein, and Rhodamine B, to be a drying oil. This was later confirmed through analysis by GCMS.

Blue

Blue colours were used in the sky, the sea and some clothes of the foreground figures. The blue areas were mostly painted in one layer of azurite. The azurite minerals were identified by PLM, as they generally showed pale blue, highly birefringent particles ($n > 1.66$) with an anomalous extinction. In addition, XRF-analyses on several blue areas on the painting, e.g. on a blue coat of a man and the blue of the sea, revealed the presence of copper and lead as well as small amounts of iron. The identification of the blue pigment as azurite was further confirmed by the perfect match of the XRD-pattern with that of azurite (JCPDS # 11-682).

The light-greyish sky, however, showed on XRF examination only a trace of copper. Cobalt and arsenic were found instead, suggesting the presence of smalt. In samples taken from two different parts of the sky, however, no smalt has yet been found by PLM. On the furthest background, just below the horizon, a pale bluish haze was painted over the landscape scene, in order to create the illusion of atmospheric depth. A sample taken from this landscape, near the church tower, showed the typical pale blue glassy particles with distinct conchoidal fracture, characteristic of smalt. The refractive index was below 1.66, and the particle showed a nice red under the Chelsea filter.

In one case a thin layer of natural ultramarine was detected on top of the azurite. This ultramarine was characterized by isotropic deep blue grains ($n < 1.66$). This pigment was only applied in the shaded areas of the blue coat of one of the figures.

Green

Green pigments were found in the background landscape and on some coats of the figures on the foreground. The structure of some of the green colours is more complex than that of the blue. The green pigment from the background bushes was identified by PLM as malachite, as it showed green very highly birefringent, pleochroic fragments with one of the refractive indices close to that of our mounting medium (1.66). XRF analyses of greenish areas consistently showed strong peaks for copper. Strong effervescence of green pigment sample, upon contact with dilute HCl, suggested the presence of the carbonate radical.

A cross section taken from the foliage in the background shows a green top layer, consisting of malachite, verdigris, organic yellow and an unidentified red pigment. PLS analysis resulted in an emission spectrum, which at an excitation wavelength of 415 nm showed maxima around 495 nm (Figure 5). Curve shape, maxima and position of shoulders gave a reasonable match with our weld (*Reseda luteola*) standard.[23] A staining test on the cross section of this sample revealed the presence of substantial amounts of lead-white in the yellowish green paint layer. Apparently the yellow paint was made by precipitation of a weld extract onto a lead white substrate. In the pigment dispersion of the sample, regular structures, obviously plant cells, were found, again alluding to the organic nature of the yellow pigment. Between the ground and the green paint a grey layer could be seen. This layer, consisting of lead white and lamp black, represents the meadow in the background.

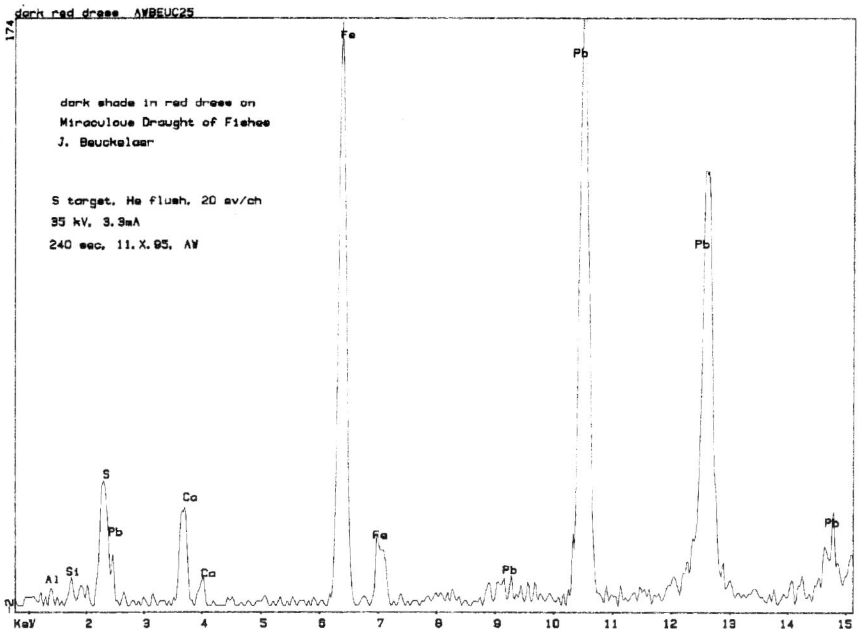

Figure 6. XRF spectrum showing strong peaks for iron and none for mercury

XRF analyses of the green meadow and green foliage in the background showed strong peaks for copper and lead, and smaller peaks for iron and tin.

XRD analyses of the yellow paint of the sleeve of the man in the foreground similarly showed the pattern for lead white (hydrocerussite JCPDS # 13-131). In the pattern there were also lines that strongly suggested the presence of a lead chloride (cotunnite, JCPDS # 26-1150). Cotunnite is known as the raw material in the manufacture of Pattison's white lead, Verona yellow and Turner's Patent Yellow. The presence of cotunnite in our sample must be interpreted as an unintentional corrosion product. The 1.766 and especially the 3.352 lines in our pattern probably relate to the 1.726 and 3.350 lines of the Doerner Institute's standard for lead tin yellow type I.[24] The 2.791 line in our pattern relates to the 2.79 line in the JCPDS file 11-233 for lead-tin yellow.

Red

Red colours were mainly used for the clothing of foreground figures and the two horses on the right of the painting. Furthermore, a purple-reddish lake has been used for the garments of the figures in the background scenes. The presence of organic red lakes was indicated by translucent bright red isotropic particles under the microscope. These non-birefringent particles appeared in many samples to be present with inorganic pigments. PLS spectra of a sample showed an excitation maximum at 338 nm at an emission maximum of 423 nm. With the emission monochromator set at 393 nm the sample showed quite a nice match with a second peak (l_{ex} = 338 nm, l_{em} = 393 nm) in our laboratory standard of kermes (*Kermococcus vermiglio* L.). The identification of the organic red as a kermes lake seemed confirmed by the chromatographic pattern, obtained by HPLC.

Surprisingly, no substantial amounts of vermilion were found in the red parts of the painting by XRF-analysis. XRF showed in all the examined reds strong peaks for iron, which leads to the conclusion that the red paint consists mainly of red ochre pigments rather than vermilion (Figure 6). The red iron oxide pigment was characterized by PLM as it sometimes showed very fine, deep red, highly birefringent crystals with indices distinctly higher than that of our mounting medium (n = 1.66). In all the red areas of the painting vermilion was conspicuously absent. Unfortunately, not enough investigations have been done into the nature of the red pigments in other paintings by Beuckelaer (or other paintings from the Antwerp group), to make it possible to state that this striking preference for the use of iron oxide reds rather than vermilion is exceptional.[25] Only in the red trousers of the rider on the right scenery were some trace amounts of mercury detected by XRF.

Conclusion

Visual inspection of the paint surface with the naked eye and a stereo microscope suggested the painting to have been made on a brownish coloured ground. Inspection of cross sections, however, invariably showed the calcium carbonate ground to be covered with a plain lead white layer. No admixture with other pigments could be detected in this lead white layer. The lead white paint appeared to be remarkably rich in tin.

The use of iron oxide reds rather than vermilion in this painting is quite conspicuous. This preference has not been found in other paintings by Beuckelaer where pigment identification has been done. The use of ultramarine was limited to the clothes of one background figure. In all other areas azurite and smalt were used.

The painting is characterized by a lavish use of organic lake pigments, based on extracts of *Reseda luteola*, and *Kermococcus vermiglio*.

Acknowledgements

The authors would like to express their thanks to Herant Khanjian, from the scientific department of the Getty Conservation Institute, who analysed the binding media of the painting. We thank Professor Dr J.R.J. van Asperen de Boer, Margreet Wolters and Dr Peter van der Brink of Groningen University for their support and information. We would also like to thank David Jaffe and Andrea Rothe of the J. Paul Getty Museum for their support on this project.

Notes and references

1. Curatorial records, Paintings Department, J. Paul Getty Museum.
2. The painting was included in *Masterpieces from Yorkshire Houses*, exhibition at York, 1951, no.3. Ellis Waterhouse discussed it briefly in a review of the exhibition in *The Burlington Magazine*, XCIII (1951): 262, Figure 15. It was later exhibited in the Royal Academy, *Flemish Art, 1300–1700*, (1953/54), no. 357. More recently, the painting appeared in K.P.F. Moxey, *Pieter Aertsen, Joachim Beuckelaer, and the Rise of Secular Painting in the Context of the Reformation* (New York: Garland Publishing, 1977), 91–94, Figure 48; in Paul Verbraeken, *Joachim Beuckelaer: Het markt- en keukenstuk in de Nederlanden, 1550–1650*, exhibition catalogue (Ghent: Museum voor Schone Kunsten, 1986/87), 120–121, Figure 1, note 4; and in R.L. Falkenburg, 'Iconographical connections between Antwerp landscapes, market scenes and kitchen pieces, 1500-1580', *Oud Holland*, 102 (1988): 122–123, Figure 14, 125 n. 20.
3. Moxey, *Pieter Aertsen*.
4. X-ray fluorescence analyses were done with a Kevex A 0750 spectrometer. X-ray fluorescence allows for non-destructive identification of most elements with atomic number $Z >$ aluminium. Use was made of barium/strontium, molybdenum, and zirconium secondary targets. The samples were mounted on sticky tape or on X-ray diffraction glass spindles. Excitation was at 50 kV and 3.3mA, for 240 s.
5. We used a Leitz Orthoplan polarized light microscope. Mounting medium for microscope slides was Aroclor meltmount ($n_D = 1.662$).
6. Debye–Scherrer powder diffraction patterns were made with Rigaku 114.6 mm Blake Industries Gandolfi cameras. The samples were mounted on glass spindles with mineral oil. Exposures in the Rigaku camera were for 6–10 h, with Cu *Ka* radiation at 40 kV, with the tube current at 30 mA.
7. Photo-luminescence spectrometry was done with an SLM-Aminco series 2 fluorescence spectrometer. Solvents used were reagent-grade concentrated sulphuric acid and spectroscopic grade methanol. Three-dimensional fluorescence spectra were made with excitation wavelength range set at 200 to 400 nm (stepsize 10 nm). Emission wavelength range was set at 320 to 620 nm.
8. Liquid chromatography was done with a Perkin Elmer Series 400 pump. The column was an Alltech Nucleosil C18 model, with a 5 m packing. A Perkin Elmer LC- 90 UV variable wavelength detector, was set at 254 nm. The chromatograms were recorded on a Perkin Elmer LCI-100 integrator.
9. A Hamamatsu N 214 vidicon, mounted with an Oriel (#58043) narrow-bandpass filter in a Hamamatsu C-1000-03 camera, was operated by Yvonne Szafran, paintings conservator at the J. Paul Getty Museum. The reflectograms were assembled on a Macintosh computer, with the use of the Adobe Photoshop 3.0 program.

10. R. Ehmke, 'Ein Tafelbild der Geburt Christi in der Ursulakirche zu Köln', in : *Jahrbuch der Rheinischen Denkmalpflege.* Band 27: *Berichte über die Tätigkeit der Restaurierungswerkstatt in den Jahren 1961-1965* (Kevelaer: Butzon & Bercker, 1967), 225.
11. R.E. Straub, 'Tafel- und Tüchleinmalerei des Mittelalters', in *Reclams Handbuch der Künstlerischen Techniken.* Band 1. *Farbmittel, Buchmalerei, Tafel- und Leinwandmalerei* (Stuttgart: Reclam, 1984), 167.
12. C. Périer-D'Ieteren, *Essays de l'Exposition de Hans Memling* (Bruges, 1994), 74–75.
13. H. Marq-Verouquestraete and R. van Schoute, 'Le Dessin de Peintre (Dessin sous-jacent) chez Pierre Brueghel. L'Adoration des Mages de la National Gallery à Londres', *Nederlands Kunsthistorisch Jaarboek* 26 (1975): 259–267.
14. M. Faries, 'Underdrawings in the Workshop Production of Jan van Scorel. A Study with Infrared Reflectography', *Nederlands Kunsthistorisch Jaarboek* 26 (1975): 89–228
15. P. Vanaise, 'Het veelluik van Vorst en de Benedictusluiken van Brussel', *Bulletin de l' Institut Royal du Patrimoine Artistique* 21 (1970): 112–176.
16. E. Hendriks and K. Levy-van Halm, 'Technical Developments in a 16th-Century Netherlandish Altarpiece by Maarten van Heemskerk and Cornelis Cornelisz. van Haarlem', (Paper deleivered at the Tenth Triennial Meeting of the International Council of Museums Committee for Conservation, Washington, DC, 22–27 August 1993), vol. I, 75–81.
17. P. van der Brink, 'Het Petrus en Paulus Altaarstuk van Pieter Pietersz', *Nederlands Kunsthistorisch Jaarboek* 40 (1989): 235–260 (see page 246).
18. J.P. Filedt Kok, 'Underdrawings and Other Technical Aspects in the Paintings of Lucas van Leyden', *Nederlands Kunsthistorisch Jaarboek* 29 (1978): 112–114, note 23.
19. M. Faries, 'Underdrawings in the Workshop Production of Jan van Scorel: A study with Infrared Reflectography', *Nederlands Kunsthistorisch Jaarboek* 26 (1975): 99. Figure 6.
20. J.M.C. Boreel and F.W.H. van Zon-Christoffels, 'Enkele Aspecten van de Schilderspractijk in het Atelier van Pieter Aertsen Natuurwetenschappelijk Bekeken', *Nederlands Kunsthistorisch Jaarboek* 40 (1989): 167–196, (see page 172, Figures 7–9).
21. Boreel and van Zon-Christoffels, 'Enkele Aspecten'.
22. M. Faries, 'Underdrawings'.
23. A. Wallert, 'Identification of Flavonoid Type Yellows in Small Paint Samples by Solution Absorption and Fluorescence Spectrometry', *Dyes in History and Archaeology* 13 (1995): 46–58.
24. H. Kühn, 'Lead-Tin Yellow', *Artists' Pigments; A Handbook of their History and Characteristics*, Vol. 2, ed. Ashok Roy (New York: Oxford University Press, 1993), 83–111 (see page 96).
25. Vermilion was found in Pieter Aertsen's 'van der Biest' retable; N. Goetghebeur and L. Kockaert, 'Le Retable van der Biest de Pieter Aertsen. Examen technologique et traitement', *Bulletin de l'Institut Royal du Patrimoine Artistique* 22 (1988/89):5–25. Vermilion was also found by J. R. J. van Asperen de Boer in Beuckelaer's 'Blessing of Jacob', which dates from 1568.

Les feuilles mixtes or-argent en peinture de chevalet

Myriam Eveno,* Elisabeth Martin
Laboratoire de Recherche des Musées de France
6, rue des Pyramides, 75041 Paris, France

Résumé

Une dizaine d'oeuvres italiennes, espagnoles et allemandes des XIVème et XVème siècles ainsi que deux icônes russes ont été étudiées. Sur les prélèvements issus de ces tableaux, le microscope électronique à balayage couplé à un systèmede microanalyse de rayons X permet de détecter conjointement de l'or et de l'argent. On a comparé des produits de référence, étalons en alliage et "Zwischgold" moderne, avec des échantillons anciens. La superposition des cartes de répartition élémentaires amène à des conclusions différentes suivant les cas: feuille d'or plaquée sur feuille d'argent ou alliage d'or et d'argent. La caractérisation des produits d'altération complète cette étude qui a pour objectif de mieux connaître et reconnaître "l'or-parti", souvent dégradé ou recouvert par une couche colorée.

Mots-clés
Or, argent, peinture de chevalet, microscope électronique à balayage, placage, alliage, Zwischgold, or-parti

Introduction

L'ornementation métallique a joué un rôle de premier plan dans les débuts de la peinture de chevalet, en particulier dans les pays méditerranéens. Le plus souvent en or, les décors peuvent aussi être exécutés en argent, tant pour des raisons analogiques afin de représenter les armures, les reflets de l'eau, les vitraux etc... que pour des raisons économiques à cause du prix moins élevé du métal blanc.

De plus, les artistes ont eu recours à divers procédés pour trouver des substituts à l'or. Ils recherchaient tout particulièrement les matériaux qui gardaient un aspect "doré", plus évocateur de la gloire divine que l'argent. Une des possibilités consistait à associer l'or et l'argent afin d'obtenir un métal d'une couleur jaune, moins onéreux que l'or pur. Dans certains cas, le choix, sur un même tableau, d'or, d'argent et de matériau intermédiaire contenant des proportions diverses d'or et d'argent, peut s'expliquer par la recherche d'effets décoratifs.

Le terme ancien "or parti" relevé dans le *Livre des métiers* d'Estienne Boileau,[1] datant du XIIIème siècle, semble correspondre à un composé d'or et d'argent. Il est cité au chapitre consacré aux peintres-selliers qui fabriquaient et ornaient des harnais; les règlements corporatistes parisiens interdisaient l'usage de ce type de materiau, jugé trop peu noble pour la confection des selles. Dans le *Libro dell Arte* à la fin du XIVème siècle, Cennino Cennini mentionne aussi un substitut sous le terme "oro di meta",[2] ce qui peut se traduire par "or de moitié". L'auteur décrit au chapitre XCV la manière d'orner sur mur avec de l'or, de l'argent et de l'étain doré et signale à ce propos l'"oro di meta" qu'il ne recommande pas et dont il ne fait pas mention pour la dorure sur panneau. Il ne décrit pas comment on obtient ce succédané de l'or, mais son texte suggère qu'il est prêt à l'emploi, car Cennini détaille, en général, la façon d'obtenir des matériaux composites comme l'étain doré.

Les références terminologiques évoquant ce type de dorure sont donc rares et ne permettent pas de comprendre la technique de mise en oeuvre et la manière d'obtenir ce matériau, fourni probablement par les orfèvres dont faisait partie la corporation des batteurs d'or et d'argent en feuilles. Les producteurs pouvaient avoir recours à plusieurs procédés. Le plus simple consiste à mélanger de l'or et de l'argent pour former un alliage qui porte le nom d'electrum quand il est d'origine naturelle. L'auteur de la *Mappae Clavicula*[3] signale l'utilisation de lingot en alliage or-argent avec des quantités égales de chacun des métaux, que l'on bat pour la fabrication de feuilles, sans que l'usage en soit précisé. Un autre procédé est évoqué par le moine Théophile,[4] lui même très probablement orfèvre au XIIème siècle,[5] au sujet de la fabrication de fils métalliques en argent doré, destinés à l'ornementation des textiles: à l'aide d'un fondant à partir de sels de cuivre, de cendres de bois et de saindoux, on pose une très fine couche d'or sur une feuille d'argent assez épaisse.[6] Enfin, le placage d'or sur argent sans soudure chimique, est la technique utilisée pour confectionner une feuille double face, dite "Zwischgold" en Allemagne, où cela se pratique encore actuellement. Ce matériau a été traditionnellement utilisé davantage, semble-t-il, pour la statuaire polychrome.[7] Il a perduré aussi en Russie pour l'ornementation des icônes sous le terme de "dvoinik".[8]

A notre connaissance, aucune publication scientifique faisant état d'analyses n'a encore abordé ce thème en ce qui concerne les peintures de chevalet.

* Auteur à qui la correspondance doit être adressée

Le Laboratoire de Recherche des Musées de France a eu la possibilité d'examiner une dizaine d'oeuvres présentant ce type de dorure, oeuvres sur bois d'origine italienne, espagnole ou allemande, datant des XIV et XVème siècles ainsi que deux icônes russes un peu plus tardives.[9] Il a pu aussi être employé en restauration comme c'est le cas pour certaines auréoles ornant des scènes du retable de la Passion, peint par le Maître à l'oeillet de Baden et conservé à Dijon au musée des Beaux-Arts.

Une étude systématique a été faite par microanalyse de rayons X couplée à un microscope électronique à balayage (M.E.B.) sur seize coupes stratigraphiques obtenues à partir de ces feuilles pour quantifier l'or et l'argent, pour préciser la mise en oeuvre du matériau et pour décrire l'état de dégradation.

Alliage ou placage

Les feuilles métalliques contenant à la fois de l'or et de l'argent présentent le plus souvent un reflet doré, lorsqu'on peut en juger à l'oeil nu (cf. annexe récapitulative). Comme pour les feuilles en or pur, elles reposent en général sur un bol rouge; elles peuvent aussi avoir été posées à mixtion pour constituer un décor plus restreint. Dans certains cas elles sont recouvertes par une couche colorée, soit opaque avec un décor "a sgraffito" soit posée en glacis, et la nuance du métal n'est pas toujours aisée à décrire. L'observation des coupes stratigraphiques sous le microscope optique ne permet pas d'individualiser l'or et l'argent, seule la brillance du métal est perceptible. L'épaisseur du matériau est trop faible pour être mesurable en microscopie optique, mais d'après les images au microscope électronique à balayage, elle est de l'ordre de grandeur du micromètre,[10] pouvant atteindre parfois trois micromètres comme pour l'icône de la Vierge géorgienne.

Les microanalyses de routine effectuées au M.E.B. permettent de déceler rapidement la présence conjointe d'or et d'argent. Cette étude ne prend pas en compte les cas où l'un des composants est très minoritaire (inférieur à 5 %); il s'agit alors d'une autre problématique qui pourra être étudiée ultérieurement. Ni le cuivre ni aucun autre métal supplémentaire n'a été détecté, même en faible quantité, dans les exemples retenus (cf. l'annexe récapitulative), les techniques utilisées ne permettant pas la détection de traces. Dans le but d'obtenir des résultats quantitatifs et de différencier les techniques de mise en oeuvre, on a commencé par analyser des échantillons de référence, d'une part sous forme d'étalons en alliage or/argent de différentes teneurs, d'autre part sous forme d'une feuille de "Zwischgold" moderne. Cette feuille, réalisée aux dires du fabricant[11] selon les techniques anciennes, est composée d'une feuille d'or 24 carats et d'une feuille d'argent pur, et après réalisation, on obtient une seule feuille double face avec un coté argenté et un coté doré.

L'analyse de la feuille sur sa surface donne les résultats suivants: du coté doré, il y a 75% d'argent et 25% d'or, tandis que du coté argenté on décèle 94% d'argent et 6% d'or. Compte tenu de la minceur du matériau composite (1 micromètre), on analyse à chaque fois toute son épaisseur et les résultats indiquent donc que la feuille d'argent est plus épaisse que la feuille d'or. Un fragment de cette feuille, non fixé sur une surface à orner, a été inclus dans de la résine et préparé sur sa tranche, comme le sont les prélèvements de matière picturale, afin de l'observer au microscope électronique à balayage et de l'analyser. On décèle une proportion d'argent très importante, assez variable cependant d'un point de mesure à l'autre.

Les analyses quantitatives ponctuelles effectuées sur les feuilles métalliques des oeuvres anciennes donnent des résultats très variables sur un même tableau, ce qui s'explique par l'état de conservation inégal du matériau; des moyennes significatives sont, de ce fait, très difficiles à établir (cf. annexe récapitulative). Les mesures indiquent cependant clairement que la quantité d'or est presque toujours inférieure à la quantité d'argent, même si localement on peut trouver jusqu'à 90% d'or comme pour le galon de la robe de l'Enfant Jésus peint par Niccolo di Tommaso.

Des profils de concentration ont été tentés sur la feuille en "Zwischgold" comme cela a été fait sur des fils dorés anciens par M. Jaro,[12] mais compte tenu de la minceur des matériaux utilisés en peinture de chevalet et de leurs altérations locales, les résultats ont été décevants et ne semblent pas représentatifs de l'échantillon. Nous avons donc choisi de mettre en évidence la distribution de l'or et de l'argent à l'aide de cartes de répartition élémentaire. La superposition des

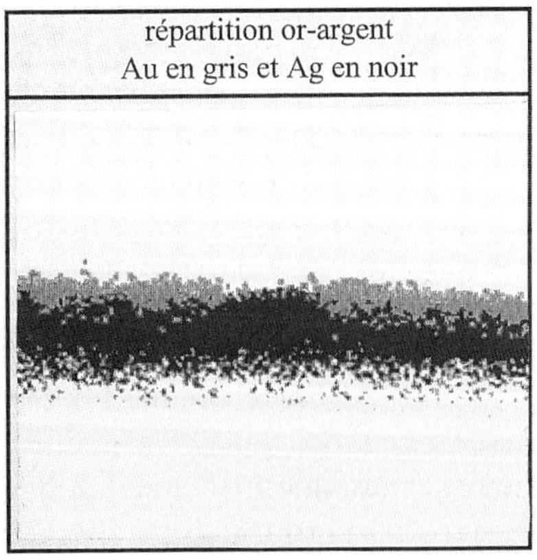

Figure 1. Distribution de l'or (en gris) et de l'argent (en noir) sur une feuille de "Zwischgold", par superposition des cartes de répartition de chaque élément.

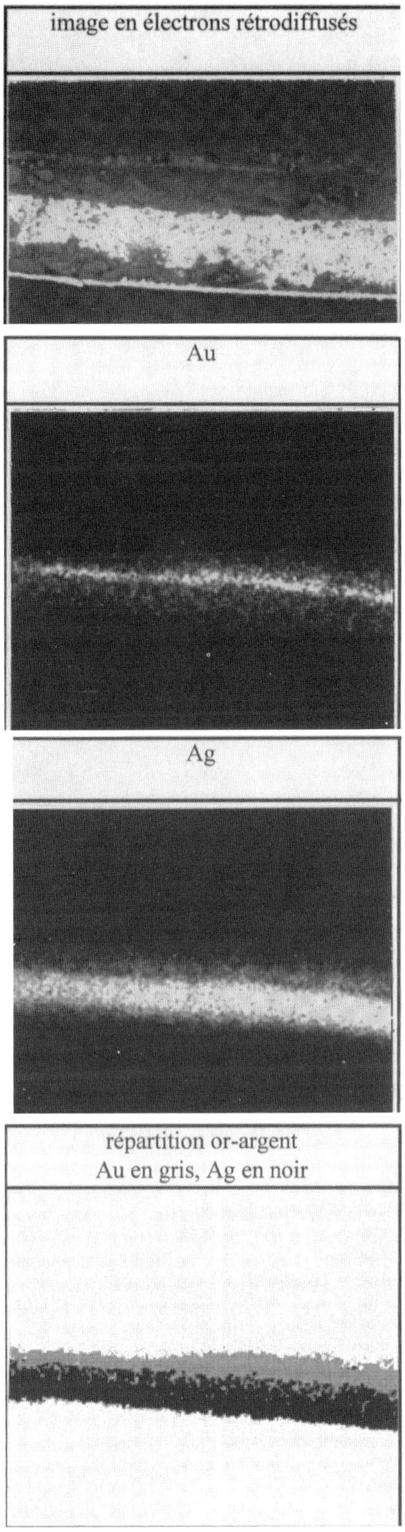

Figure 2. Bartolo di Fredi, Assomption. *Image en électrons rétrodiffusés du brocart de la robe de la Vierge exécuté "a sgraffito". Les couches profondes de l'échantillon sont absentes, on observe la feuille métallique, une fine couche bleue contenant du lapis lazuli, une couche de blanc de plomb surmontée d'un glacis de lapis lazuli. Répartition de l'or et de l'argent sur un détail de la feuille et superposition de ces cartes indiquant une technique de placage (or en gris et argent en noir).*

cartes des deux éléments en accroît considérablement l'intérêt (surtout en fausse-couleur!). Ainsi dans le cas de la feuille en matériau récent, on observe une répartition différenciée de l'argent et de l'or avec une zone d'interdiffusion, l'épaisseur de chaque feuille est de ce fait assez difficile à évaluer, la feuille d'argent étant environ trois fois plus épaisse que la feuille d'or (Figure 1).

Les coupes stratigraphiques des oeuvres ont été observées ensuite dans les mêmes conditions. Par comparaison avec les matériaux de référence, les images obtenues mettent en évidence deux techniques et les résultats sont regroupés en annexe:

- l'or et l'argent ont une répartition différenciée avec prédominance d'or dans la zone de surface ce qui suggère une technique de placage comme le "Zwischgold" récent. Les feuilles sont solidaires sans intervalle visible à l'échelle du document comme l'illustre l'échantillon issu de l'*Assomption* de Bartolo di Fredi (Figure 2).
- l'or et l'argent sont répartis uniformément sur toute l'épaisseur du matériau ce qui indique plutôt un alliage (Figure 3). C'est la conclusion à laquelle on aboutit pour la feuille utilisée à la mixtion par le Maître du Crucifix sur fond d'argent, actif en Ombrie au milieu du XIVème siècle, où la proportion d'or correspond à un tiers de l'ensemble. Sur certaines images, l'or et l'argent sont plus ou moins superposés par endroit avec des plages d'autant plus confuses que la feuille est mince; c'est pourquoi on a privilégié les zones les mieux conservées du prélèvement pour effectuer les cartes, mais la technique de mise en oeuvre ne peut pas être établie avec certitude sur chaque échantillon.

Altération

Ce matériau intermédiaire ne possède pas l'inaltérabilité de l'or et est sujet à des corrosions causées par les conditions atmosphériques. Les types d'altération peuvent être rapprochés de ceux qui ont été observés pour l'argent et décrits dans un précédent article.[13]

Cennino Cennini mentionne déjà le phénomène de dégradation entraînant un noircissement de "l'oro di meta".[14] En effet, lorsque la feuille mixte est à nu, des sulfures d'argent se forment à l'intérieur du matériau, ce qui entraîne un assombrissement avec parfois une désagrégation de celui-ci, comme on l'observe sur le galon de *Saint Ambroise* du Maître de Burgo de Osma. Pour *L'Assomption*, Bartolo di Fredi utilise un fond d'or très restreint et de larges plages avec une feuille mixte localement striée pour représenter les ailes des séraphins, ce qui a permis de juger des nuances respectives des zones au cours de la restauration de cette oeuvre exceptionnelle. La feuille mixte assez épaisse, bien conservée en apparence, présente un aspect doré très net, mais contrastant avec l'or pur par un certain grisaillement; de minuscules points noirs sont perceptibles sous le microscope dans le réseau de craquelures et dans les stries des ailes, confirmant que la technique résulte très probablement d'un placage d'or sur argent.

L'auteur ancien ne recommande pourtant pas la pose d'une couche protectrice qui aurait mis la feuille à l'abri de l'air. Il semble toutefois que dans deux des cas examinés, on observe la présence d'une couche de surface peu colorée ou jaunâtre qui a évité le noircissement du décor.[15] Le Maître du Crucifix sur fond d'argent a, semble-t-il, utilisé ce procédé pour protéger le décor à mixtion qui orne le vêtement de saint Thomas d'Aquin, ce qui a permis une bonne conservation de la feuille assez épaisse et a renforcé l'aspect doré de l'alliage assez pauvre en or[16] (Figure 3). Cela parait aussi le cas sous la couche partielle d'azurite représentant le brocard du vêtement de Zacharie dans *Les scènes de la vie de saint Jean Baptiste* par Borrassa, oeuvre qui possédait aussi d'autres décors en argent avec un glacis jaune.[17]

La feuille métallique peut être recouverte par une couche colorée opaque ou transparente. Le manteau de la Vierge de *L'Assomption* de Bartolo di Fredi est exemplaire puisqu'il comporte des motifs floraux se détachant "a sgraffito" sur un brocard blanc souligné de plis bleus en lapis-lazuli (Figure 2), avec des parements verts posés en glacis. Ces derniers sont très lacunaires et le bol rouge est très visible dans les motifs floraux poinçonnés à reflets dorés. On observe la formation très importante de sulfures d'argent sous le brocart blanc, et de chlorures d'argent sous le glacis vert. Il en va de même pour le revers vert du manteau de la Vierge peint par Ugolino di Nerio.[18] On détecte notamment un mélange de sulfures et de chlorures avec prédominance des sulfures à l'endroit des craquelures (*Le Calvaire*

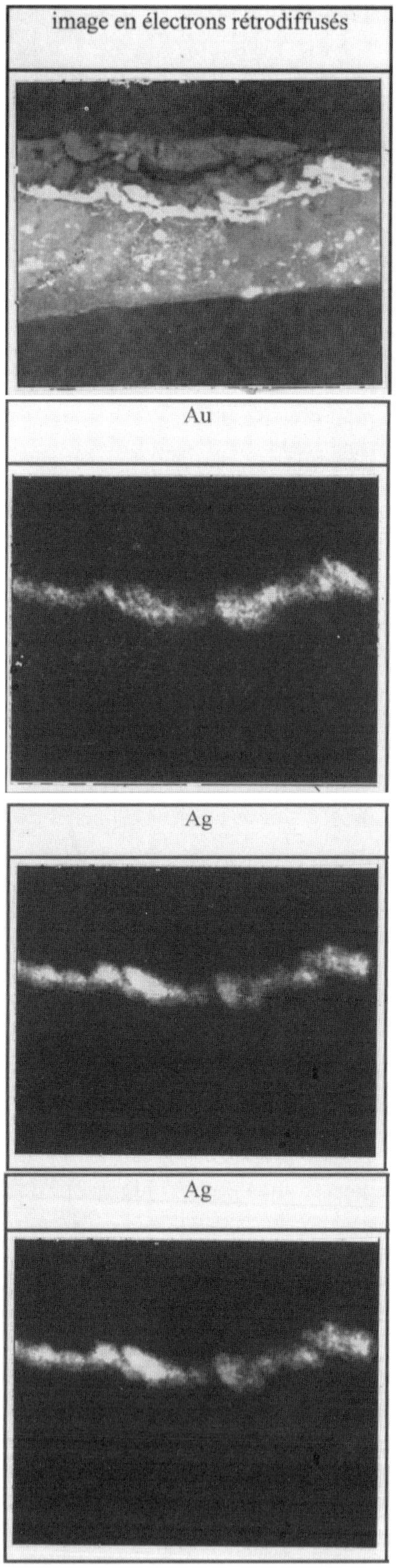

Figure 3. Maître du Crucifix sur fond d'argent, Douze Saints. *Image en électrons rétrodiffusés où on observe la mixtion, la feuille métallique épaisse (1à 3 ìm), avec des chevauchements, recouverte d'une couche superficielle. Répartition de l'or, de l'argent, et du chlore; les images de l'or et de l'argent se superposent parfaitement ce qui permet de conclure à un alliage.*

du Maître de la mort de saint Nicolas de Munster sous une laque rouge) (Figure 4). Le matériau, globalement en assez bon état de conservation, présente des hétérogénéités dans sa composition. En effet, on décèle parfois des amas où les concentrations en argent et en chlore sont très élevées (Figure 4). Une protubérance s'instaure perturbant l'arrangement initial, ce qui complique considérablement la mise en évidence du procédé utilisé par les artistes à l'origine.

Conclusion

Les différentes observations et analyses tendent à étayer la thèse selon laquelle la technique du placage sans soudure, encore vivace aujourd'hui dans certains pays, était déjà connue en Europe au XIVème siècle et peut-être avant, ce qui n'exclut pas d'autres possibilités, comme le recours aux alliages. Il n'a pas été possible de trouver des références sur les prix de revient respectifs de ces matériaux qui justifieraient leur emploi, des comparaisons chiffrées n'existant que pour l'or, l'argent et l'étain doré.[19] L'état de conservation n'est pas homogène, mais les exemples sont trop peu nombreux et trop divers pour que l'on puisse en tirer des conclusions générales. Il semble toutefois que le placage d'une feuille d'or sur une feuille d'argent n'ait pas complètement protégé celle-ci de la corrosion. L'état après vieillissement permettrait même parfois de reconnaître à l'oeil nu ce matériau composite, alors qu'à son origine, une fois mis en place, il ne se distingue pas, semble t-il, de l'or pur, ce qui justifiait les interdits des corporations médiévales.

Dégradé ou recouvert par une couche colorée qui privilégie les effets métalliques quelle que soit la couleur du métal, "l'or parti" n'a pas retenu l'attention qu'il méritait, en raison de surcroît du petit nombre d'indications dans les textes. Cette étude n'a pas pour objectif d'aborder les phénomènes métallurgiques liés au placage de feuilles très fines, elle souhaite susciter un rassemblement d'informations autour de ce sujet, encore trop peu exploré.

Notes et Références

1. Estienne Boileau, *Le livre des métiers*, publié par René de Lespinasse et François Bonnardot. Paris, imprimerie (1879). Titre LXXVIII, paragraphe 12, "Nus ne puet paindre de couleur a or sele derrière se elle n'est couverte de fin or c'est à dire d'or sans mesleure d'argent que en apele *or parti*", p. 169. Ce livre de règlements de corporation semble avoir été écrit en 1268.
2. Cennino Cennini, *Il libro dell Arte*, a cura di F. Tempesti, Milan, Longanesi (1975), traduction de C. Déroche, Paris, Berger-Levrault (1993).
3. Raub C., "How to coat objects with gold-Pliny, Leyden Papyrus X, *Mappae Clavicula and Theophilus seen with a modern chemist's eyes*", *Outils et ateliers d'orfèvres des temps anciens*, Saint Germain en Laye (1993), 101–110. Le recueil de la Mappae Clavicula comporte des textes qui vont du VIII au XIIIème siècle.
4. Moine Théophile, *Essai sur divers Arts*, traduction du Cte C. de L'Escapolier. Nogent-le-Roi (1977). Chapitre LXXVI, *De solidando auro et argento pariter.* "Manière de souder l'or et l'argent ensemble. On purifie de l'argent du poids de douze écus, on le bat étroit de la longueur de la moitié du petit doigt; ensuite on bat de l'or cuit du poids d'un écu, de même largeur et longueur, on réunit ces deux métaux avec la soudure d'or prescrite, jusqu'à ce qu'ils adhèrent tout à fait entre eux; on les battra ensemble jusqu'à ce que l'on obtienne une lame très mince. Ce produit ressemble à de l'argent doré d'un côté, et on ne pourrait avec deux ou trois écus d'or dorer d'une manière si brillante une lame aussi longue. De cette lame se font les bordures imprimées au fer..." Pour des précisions sur la soudure cf. ch. L *De solidatura auri.*
5. Theophilus, ou Roger von Hemarshausen, un moine bénédictin qui vivait vers 1100 dans le Nord de l'Allemagne. On lui attribue des objets d'orfèvrerie. Raub, *op. cit.* 106.
6. Rinuy A., "Fils d'or des textiles anciens: étude de leur mode de fabrication au cours du temps", catalogue de l'exposition *L'oeuvre d'art sous le regard des sciences*, du 17 mars au 15 mai 1994, Musée d'art et d'histoire de Genève (1994),123–133.
7. Colinart S., Eveno M., "La polychromie. Les études en laboratoire. Sculptures médiévales allemandes", *Actes du colloque conservation et restauration 1991.* Documentation française, Paris (1993), 159–175.
8. Mémoire de N. Delsaux "Etude sur la technique des icônes" à la demande de la Direction des Musées de France, non publié (1992).
9. La Vierge de Novgorod est généralement datée du début du XVIème siècle, mais le décor métallique posé sur la robe de l'Enfant recouvre des plis déjà peints; l'auréole de la Vierge et le décor des plis semblent contemporains, mais peut-être postérieurs au XVIème.

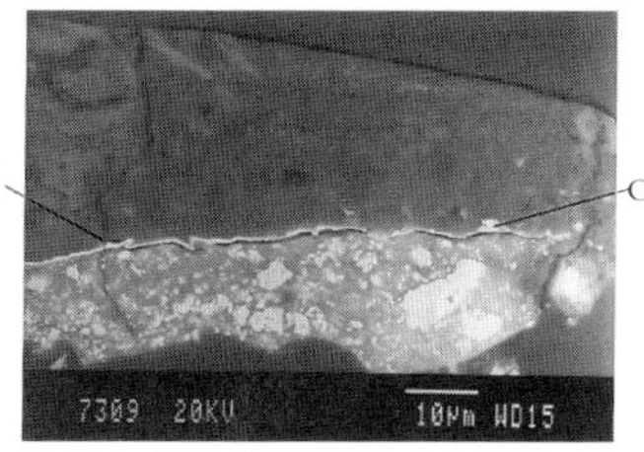

Figure 4. Maître de la mort de saint Nicolas de Münster, Le Calvaire. *Image en électrons rétrodiffusés où on observe la couche de mixtion contenant des pigments au plomb, la feuille métallique et une couche de laque épaisse. Au niveau de la feuille, des sulfures d'argent se sont formés dans la craquelure à gauche, alors que la protubérance de droite correspond à des chlorures d'argent.*

10. D'après les images au microscope électronique à balayage, l'épaisseur de la feuille d'or pur varie de façon assez importante suivant les tableaux et est, en général, plus fine pour les décors à mixtion que pour les feuilles ayant servi à dorer le fond du panneau, comme l'indique aussi Cennino Cennini, *op. cit.* ch. CXXXIX. D'après notre expérience, l'épaisseur de la feuille d'argent utilisée à l'époque pour les tableaux est de l'ordre de 1 micromètre. Des chevauchements s'observent avec en général un léger intervalle entre les deux feuilles, car l'adhésion se fait, d'après Cennino Cennini, simplement en soufflant sur le métal déjà posé, *op. cit.* ch. CXXXVIII. Des chevauchements de feuilles en alliage sont visibles sur les coupes stratigraphiques des *Douze saints* et de *La Vierge de Novgorod.*
11. Le fournisseur (Noris Blattgoldfabrik, Rennmühle 3. D. 8540. Schwabach, Allemagne) n'a pas souhaité nous communiquer la technique précise de fabrication.
12. Jaro M., Toth A., "Possibilities of reconstruction of metal coating techniques used for solid metal strips and wires in museum textiles", *4th International Conference on Non-Destructive Testing of Works of Art* (1994), 544–553.
13. Martin E., Eveno M., "Degradation of Silver Foils on Paintings", *4th International Conference on Non-Destructive Testing of Works of Art* (1994), 500–509.
14. "ancora ti guarda da oro di metà, ché di subito viene negro", *op. cit.*, 86.
15. Un glacis jaune parfois appelé "mecca" ou "doratura" est étendu sur l'argent en feuille pour lui conférer l'aspect de lor; ce glacis a aussi un rôle protecteur en favorisant la formation limitée de chlorures d'argent grisâtres (cf.13).
16. Ce tableau comporte de nombreux décors en argent sur bol, qui sont protégés aussi par une couche de surface du même type assez peu coloré en jaune, semble-t-il, d'après l'aspect du tableau (cf.13). Dans le cas de l'étoile à mixtion, on peut noter qu'un alliage avec deux-tiers d'argent devrait avoir une couleur plutôt argentée comme l'indiquent les étalons de référence; l'aspect "doré" est donc dû en partie à la "mecca". Le tableau dans son ensemble a bénéficié de conditions de conservation exceptionnelles.
17. La présence de couche organique jaunâtre entre la feuille métallique et une couche colorée de surface avait aussi été signalée dans le cas de l'argent (cf.13).
18. Delsaux N., Delteil-Ruffat F., Ausset P. "La restauration d'un primitif italien", *Science et technologie de Conservation et de la Restauration des oeuvres d'art et du patrimoine*, 1 (1988), 69–73. Par microsonde, seul lor avait été décelé.
19. Catalogue de l'exposition "Art in the Making Italian Painting Before 1400", London, National Gallery (1990), 201.

Examination of the Painting Technique of Nine Dutch Pictures of the First Half of the 18th Century

Karin Groen,* Matthijs de Keijzer
Central Research Laboratory for Objects of Art and Science,
Gabriël Metsustraat 8,
1071 EA Amsterdam, The Netherlands
Elisabeth Baadsgaard
Stichting Rijksmuseum, Twenthe
Lasondersingel 129–131, 7514 BP Enschede, The Netherlands

Abstract

Technical examination of the paint used in nine Dutch paintings of the first half of the 18th century is described. Some comparison is made with the practice of painting and the use of materials in the 17th century. The structure of a thin paint layer on a thick ground seems responsible for the smooth surfaces of the pictures from this period. Pigments used traditionally were found together with those that came into use at a later date. The early find of Prussian blue in a picture dated 1715 and the identification of lead antimonate yellow in a picture supposedly executed between 1718 and 1733 are of consequence for authentication studies. It is postulated that Dutch painters of the 17th and the early part of the 18th century did not use lead antimonate yellow, unless they had access to the pigment in a stay abroad, especially Rome, or they had a connection with the Elector Palatine at Düsseldorf.

Keywords

Dutch 18th century paintings, scientific examination, painting technique, identification of pigments, Prussian blue, lead antimonate yellow

Figure 1. Mathijs Naiveu, "Young woman feeding a parrot", signed and dated 1715, canvas 40.5 × 32.5 cm, Netherlands Office for Fine Arts, The Hague Cat. BR 330

Introduction

Unlike that of the 17th century, Dutch painting of the 18th century has so far received little attention. Art historical and technical literature on the 18th century, especially on its first half, is scarce.[1] The object of this study is to elucidate techniques and the use of materials in Dutch easel painting in the 18th century. Nine paintings from the collection of the Stichting Rijksmuseum Twenthe in Enschede were chosen for examination, all on canvas and executed in the first half of the century. This examination does not allow a reconstruction of all of the painting techniques used in the period concerned, but must be seen as the starting point for further study.

In the 17th century the Netherlands played a major role in the development of painting techniques. Painting culminated in a far-reaching equality between style and technique.[2] The idea and the execution of the picture tallied. Judging from stylistic elements, methods applied and the use of materials in the 18th century may differ from those in use in the 17th century: in the 18th century the paint is often lighter in colour than that used in the 17th century, the pictures on the whole have a smaller format, and the paint surface is smoother. By studying painting practices at the end of the 17th century and thereafter we have attempted to gather information that might be useful in art history. Information on the use of materials could provide terminal dates for certain pigments that could be of considerable value in authentication studies.

In order to obtain this information the following aspects were investigated:

- the fabric used as a support;
- the preparation of the canvasses;
- the colour of the ground
- the pigments and mixtures of pigments;
- pigments and binders used for the grounds and the paint layers;
- the layer structure and thickness of the layers;
- paint application; and
- any further technical information that could be obtained.[3]

The paintings studied are listed, as far as possible, in chronological order:

- Mathijs Naiveu (1647–1726), "*Jonge vrouw die een papagaai voert*" ("Young woman feeding a parrot"), signed and dated 1715, canvas 40.5 × 32.5 cm, inv. nr BR330 (Figure 1);
- Jan Huchtenburg (1647–1733), "*De slag bij Salankemen*" ("The battle at Salankemen"), between 1718 and 1733, canvas 65.5 × 79.5 cm, inv. nr BR354;
- Nicolaas Verkolje (1673–1746), "*Portret van een echtpaar en twee kinderen*" ("Portrait of a couple with two children"), canvas 91.5 × 71.0 cm, inv. nr 545;

* Author to whom correspondence should be addressed.

- Philip van Dijk (1680–1753), "*Portret van Samuel Rademacher en zijn kleinzoon*" ("Portrait of Samuel Rademacher and his grandson"), signed and dated 1750, canvas 116.2 × 91.8 cm, inv. nr BR302;
- Jacob de Wit (1695–1754), "*Venus, Bacchus en Ceres met slapende Amor*" ("Venus, Bacchus and Ceres with the sleeping Amor"), signed and dated 1720, canvas 122.3 × 136.5 cm, inv. nr BR301;
- Jacob de Wit (1695–1754), "*Apollo en Diana*", signed, canvas 119.5 × 94.5 cm, inv. nr BR300;
- Cornelis Troost (1697–1750), "*Portret van een onbekende Heer met zijn zoon*" ("Portrait of an unknown man with his son"), canvas 71.0 × 56.0 cm, inv. nr BR298,
- Cornelis Troost (1697–1750), "*Het Consult*" ("The Consultation"), canvas 81.5 × 104.0 cm, inv. nr BR382;
- Cornelis Troost (1697–1750), "*De ontdekte schijndeugd*" ("Pretence of virtue uncovered"), signed and dated 1734, canvas 104.5 × 82.0 cm, inv. nr BR326.[4]

Methods

In addition to the naked eye and ordinary photography, the following methods were applied in the examination of the nine paintings:

- X-radiography;
- ultraviolet fluorescence;
- examination in raking light.

Stereomicroscopy was used for assessing the condition of the paintings and for choosing suitable sample spots. Sometimes microphotographs were made. Paint samples were removed under examination through the stereomicroscope. Paint cross-sections were obtained by embedding a suitable part of the sample in a clear polyester resin and subsequent grinding and polishing. The cross-sections were studied in dark-field reflected light and ultraviolet fluorescence. In several cases dispersed pigment slides were made for examination in transmitted light. Chemical elements were identified in the cross-section using an electron microscope with energy-dispersive X-ray analysis (SEM-EDX) and, in some cases, electron microprobe analysis was used as well (the yellow pigments) at the Department of Earth Sciences of the Vrije Universiteit in Amsterdam. Some of the SEM-EDX was carried out at KSLA (Royal Dutch Shell Research Laboratory) in Amsterdam. One yellow sample was again analysed at DSM-Research, to confirm the presence of tin and antimony. Organic red pigments were analysed by thin layer chromatography (TLC) and high-pressure liquid chromatography (HPLC) at the Central Laboratory. Also at the Central Laboratory, Fourier transform infrared spectrometry (FTIR) was used for the identification of the blue pigments; the presence of Prussian blue was for instance clearly indicated by the absorption at 2092.1 cm^{-1}. Wet chemical analysis was used as an additional tool.

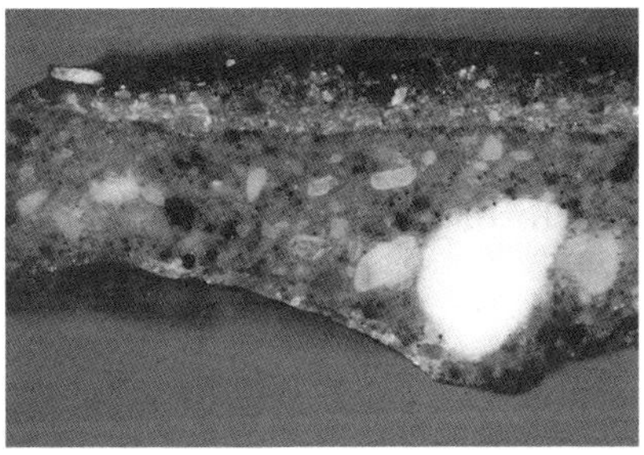

Figure 2. Paint cross-section of a sample from Jacob de Wit, "Venus, Bacchus and Ceres with the sleeping Amor", Venus's yellow drapery. From top to bottom: varnish; painted in two thin layers of orpiment, red ochre and a little black; thick ground layer containing coarse lead white, chalk, umber and a little yellow ochre

Paint-layer structure and composition

Ground layers

The paintings by Naiveu, de Wit, Huchtenburg and Verkolje were executed on a single ground of a brown colour, containing lead white, chalk and umber. The colour of this mixture was sometimes slightly modified: a little yellow ochre was added in both of de Wit's paintings and, in addition, a tiny amount of black and red in his "Venus". In Huchtenburg's painting the ground contains a relatively large proportion of chalk and has a warm orange hue because of the admixture of red, yellow and brown ochre. In all cases the ground was relatively thickly applied; thicknesses of up to c. 135 μm were measured. The pigment particles, or lumps of pigment, of lead white and umber are strikingly coarse. The lead white used is obviously still of the so-called "Dutch process" type (Figure 2).[5]

The ground in the three paintings by Troost differs in so far that in all three it is entirely composed of chalk, applied as one thick layer of c. 80–150 μm. The ground was given a greyish colour by the addition of a little charcoal black in a second application of the ground in "The Consultation" and "Pretence". The exact hue these chalk grounds originally possessed is now hard to judge, because of the presence of the – probably darkened – painting medium. All nine pictures in this study underwent wax-resin relining in the past, it is, therefore, difficult to establish the original medium used and the original colour. Proteins were identified in the chalk grounds, but oil seems present as well. In the paint cross-sections, the chalk grounds show a very strong fluorescence in ultraviolet light, a phenomenon we have come across in several other pictures of the 18th and the 19th centuries, where the cause of the fluorescence seemed to be the addition of a diterpenoid resin.[6] The study of the paint media will be the focus of attention at a later date.

The one ground that differs completely from the other eight is that used by Van Dijk. The dull greenish-appearing ground was built up from a thick chalk-glue layer with two thin light greyish-brown paint layers, containing lead white and chalk, on top. On top of this a final, thicker layer of lumpy lead white with a little yellow ochre and fine black was applied. This gives the unusual build-up of the ground with four applications of paint. It is difficult to give a valid explanation on the basis of one such finding; the purpose of the two thin layers of lead white (oil paint) is supposedly to make the chalk-glue ground less absorbent for the paint of the actual painting. The fourth and final layer of the ground would determine the colour of the ground.[7]

Local underpaint

In most of the paintings it was found that underpaint was applied to certain parts of the painting. For instance in Naiveu's picture, red, yellow and blue ornaments in the tablecloth are underlain with thin brown to brownish-black, red, and reddish-brown respectively. Pigments in the local underpaint are types of ochre and bone black. Jacob de Wit's "The Music" also has underpaint in different colours in different areas. There is a slightly brown tinted paint layer under a pinkish drapery, grey underneath the blue drapery and the landscape, while under the flesh colour the underpaint is off-white. The main component of these underlayers is lead white. In the other painting by De Wit, local underpaint consisting of a similar mixture to that used for the ground, only slightly lighter in tone, was found under the flesh colour of the two main figures, Venus and Bacchus. Since this phenomenon could only be observed in the samples deriving from the shadowy outline of the flesh, we suppose that it has to do with the sketching-in of the figures.[8] In Huchterburg's painting there is a thin grey underlayer under parts of the brown in a drapery and under the yellow of a bag. Under the flesh the underpaint is light grey. All these layers of underpaint contain lead white with varying proportions of ochre and umber. In the Verkolje picture a black paint, obviously used for sketching-in, underlies the light coloured drapery of the mother and light grey underlies the blue-green of the background. The yellow of the head dress is painted on top of the flesh.

In Troost's "Pretence" there is thin pink and grey underpaint under the blue draperies. In Troost's "Portrait" there is clearly a 5 μm brownish-black underpaint under the yellow cushion of the chair. In the Van Dijk, despite its complicated and already toned four-layer structure of the ground, areas to be painted were first laid down in different hues: brown under red, black under brownish-green, grey under blue.[9]

Blue and green

Three types of blue pigment were identified: smalt, indigo and Prussian blue. Smalt was found in both pictures by De Wit, in "Venus" it occurs in the background, while in "The Music" in the background and in the foliage, where it is mixed with yellow ochre and lead white. The putto's blue drapery in De Wit's "The Music" contains Prussian blue mixed with lead white. In Huchtenberg's "Battle scene" all three blue pigments occur. Smalt was used for grey areas in the sky, while indigo, mixed with lead white, was used in the bright blue of the sky. The blue drapery of the angel and the ornaments in the dress of the horse in the same picture have Prussian blue with lead white. Prussian blue was identified in all of the following cases, it was often mixed with lead white:

- In the Naiveu, blue ornamentation in the table cloth, two thin layers of each c. 7 μm;
- In the Verkolje, blue background, boy's blue drapery;
- In the Van Dijk, sash (identified with wet-chemical analysis only).

Prussian blue was also found in all three pictures by Troost: In "Portrait" in the blue coat lining; in "The Consultation" in the bed curtain; and in "Pretence" in the blue skirt of the maid. In all cases the blue was painted thinly, approximately 10 μm thick, in "Pretence" directly on the chalk ground.

Green only occurs in two pictures, namely in the Van Dijk, in the table cloth where it was made with a mixture of Prussian blue and finely ground orpiment, and in Troost's "The Consultation", in the green curtain, where it contained a mixture of Prussian blue, lead antimony yellow and lead white.

Yellow

Venus' yellow drapery in De Wit's "Venus" was painted in two thin paint layers (each c. 15 μm), from light to dark with mixtures of orpiment, red ochre and a little black. A highlight in the harp in De Wit's "The Music" is lead–tin yellow, mixed with chalk and lead white.[10]

Yellow in the ornamented pattern in the tablecloth in Naiveu's picture is lead–tin yellow mixed with a little orpiment and lead white (SEM-EDX), on top of red. Lead–tin yellow was found together with lead antimony yellow ("Naples yellow") in a brown mixture (with a little smalt, ochres and black) in the coat of the horseman in Huchtenburg's "Battle" as well as in his blue/red decorated yellow bag. The relatively thin yellow layers containing this mixture are situated on top of a black underpaint, which is also thin. From SEM-EDX analysis it appears that the mixture of yellow pigments is not a very intimate one; lead antimony yellow is situated towards the top of the yellow layer, lead–tin yellow towards the bottom.

The head-dress of the mother in Verkolje's "Portrait" contains a mixture of vermilion and yellow iron oxide.

In Troost's "The Consultation", the yellow in the table cloth is a mixture of yellow iron oxide with a little vermilion. The band along the yellow cushion in Troost's "Portrait" contains orpiment, mixed with very little fine red.

Red

The red in Naiveu's tablecloth is a mixture of red ochre and vermilion in the bright red areas and red ochre with Brasil wood (caesalpinia sappan) in the darker red shades. The reds were painted on a dark underlayer.

In the Huchtenburg painting, a red drapery consists of bright red iron oxide, in a 7 μm thin layer, while flesh paint has a mixture of lead white and vermilion. Vermilion was used in the flesh by Van Dijk as well.

De Wit's "Venus" has lead white and red ochre in the middle tone in Bacchus' right arm, with black added in the shadows. The red drapery has an organic red glaze on top of a mixture of red iron oxide and bone black.

The reddish flesh of a putto in De Wit's "The Music" was made with lead and vermilion, and the shadow has a build-up of layers, with a dark mixture of ochres applied last. The red drapery around the putties was built up from a light-coloured underpaint towards a darker deeper red by, quite traditionally, applying an organic red glaze over a layer of lead white mixed with organic red and a little red ochre. Alizarine was identified in the red glaze.[11] In Troost's "Pretence" vermilion was used in the flesh, mixed with white, and in the drapery, mixed with black. In the "Portrait" there is a bright, transparent glaze of cochineal, c. 35 μm thick, on a grey underpaint, on the cushion of the chair. In "The Consultation" the red of the tablecloth is a very bright, pure vermilion, evenly grained, suggesting that it was made by the 'wet process' which was discovered in 1687.[12]

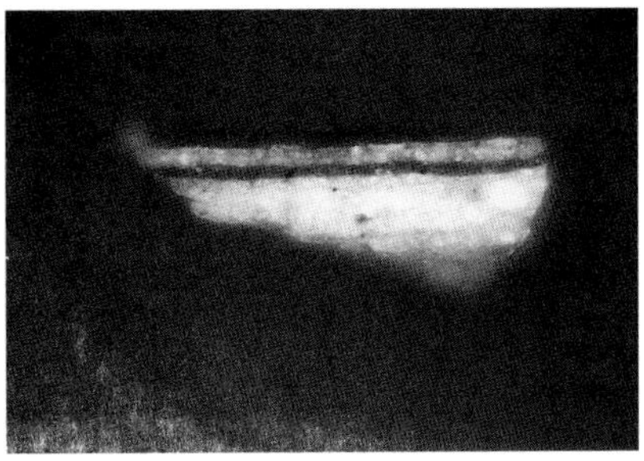

Figure 3. Paint cross-section of a sample from Philip van Dijk, "Portrait of Samuel Rademacher and his grandson", discoloured red curtain. From the bottom of the sample upwards, the light-coloured layers all constitute the ground. Above the ground, there is the even, 7 μm black underlayer for the curtain. Ared wood, now discoloured, is mixed with lead white

The curtain and the tablecloth in Van Dijk's "Portrait" are of a brownish, seemingly discoloured, hue. When the picture was taken out of its frame it was clear that both the table cloth and the drapery had badly discoloured. Under the frame there was a deep red translucent paint, which by analysis was identified as Brasil wood (*caesalpina sappan*) mixed with lead white. The red glaze of the tablecloth was painted rather thinly (c. 10 *m*m) directly on the complicated ground layer structure, while in the curtain, the red glaze is sitting on a thin blackish underpaint (Figure 3).

Discussion

The main points apparent from the study of nine pictures of the first half of the 18th century in Holland are:

- The painting technique is simple, one or two paint layers at most, sometimes applied in a traditional way with a glaze on top of an opaque paint.
- Ground layers were thickly applied, while the paint was thinly applied. The thick ground layers, together with the evenly applied thin paint layers, explain the smooth surfaces of the pictures. Impasto is lacking.
- Apart from the usual pigment mixtures, i.e. lead white, chalk and varieties of ochre and black added to a coloured pigment, pigment mixtures of two coloured pigments were found. The pigments in these mixtures sometimes differed only slightly in hue, e.g. two yellow pigments, or two red ones, were mixed together. The authors have not come across this phenomenon in 17th century pictures. In contrast, the use of a mixture of blue and yellow for making green is 17th century practice. In the 18th century azurite and smalt were replaced by Prussian blue in these mixtures. A few of the mixtures are as follows:

  - lead-tin yellow with orpiment
  - lead-tin yellow with Prussian blue
  - orpiment with Prussian blue
  - lead-tin yellow with lead antimony yellow (not an intimate mixture, lead antimony yellow on top of lead-tin yellow)
  - red iron oxide with vermilion
  - yellow iron oxide with vermilion.

  There is an obvious reason for mixing blue and yellow to make green: there was no good green pigment available in the 17th or 18th centuries – malachite had to be ground coarse, if finely ground it becomes too pale; copper resinate is too transparent for certain uses; green earth was found too dull. The reason for mixing two yellows is not so obvious, unless the reason is adjustment of the colour to obtain a larger range of tones.
- Pigments used traditionally were used together with those that came into use at a later date. For instance, lead-tin yellow was found together with lead antimony yellow, in one single yellow area in the picture by Jan Huchtenburg, painted between 1718 and 1733. The presence of lead antimony yellow in a picture of the first half of the 18th century at first does not strike one as unusual. The pigment has been identified in paintings dating from the 17th century and its occurrence gradually becomes more common until it reaches its peak at about the beginning of the 19th century.[13] However, it struck us as curious that some Dutch painters in both 17th and 18th centuries seemed to have access to the pigment while others did not. For authentication purposes it is quite important to have this matter clarified. Therefore, we would like to expand on this topic a bit further, even though lead antimonate yellow was only identified in one instance in our study.

  With the detection of lead antimony yellow in the picture by Huchtenburg, it became clear that the Dutch painters who did have access to the pigment had something in common: either they were working in Italy at the time the particular picture was executed (17th century) or they had some relationship with the Elector Palatine at Dusseldorf (in the last quarter of the 17th century and at the beginning of the 18th). Huchtenburg was in the service of the Elector Johann Wilhelm von der Pfalz in Düsseldorf from about 1710 and probably until 1719. Painters mentioned by Wainwright and others have this connection as well (see note 13): Eglon Hendrik van der Neer and Adriaen van der Werff were court painters for the Elector from 1690 and 1696 respectively and their pictures containing lead antimony yellow date from the third quarter of the 17th century and from 1703. Herman van der Mijn had the same function between about 1712 and 1716, exactly coinciding with his picture of 1715 which contains lead antimonate yellow. Although Van der Werff executed his work for the Elector in his own studio in Rotterdam, we presume that lead antimonate yellow was used mainly at the court. Van der Werff did visit the court to paint portraits. The pigment probably originated in Rome. The connection of the use of lead antimonate yellow and foreign painters working in Rome in the 17th century has been made earlier, in connection with Claude Lorrain, Caspar Dughet and Nicolas Poussin. For Dutch and German painters the same seems to be true (Matthias Stomer and Johann Heinrich Schönfeld – see note 13). Our thesis, therefore, is that lead antimony yellow was not generally available to artists in Holland in the 17th century or at the beginning of the 18th century except in the circumstances described.

- Smalt, indigo and Prussian blue were in use; sometimes all three in one picture. Azurite and ultramarine, in use in 17th century painting, were absent in these pictures. Prussian blue was the pigment used predominantly. A very important detection, because it represents a first occurrence, is that of Prussian blue in a painting by Naiveu, dated 1715. So far, the exact date of the first use of Prussian blue by artists is unknown. An even earlier occurrence – in 1712 but not on a painting – indicates that it was first used closest to the place of its discovery, Berlin. The earliest find recorded use in a painting is in "Récréation italienne", in Charlottenburg Castle in Berlin, dated 1715 or 1716.[14] Naiveu belongs to the tradition of "fine-painters" in Leiden. It is not clear how Navieu could have had access to this novel pigment.

In this study we hope to have demonstrated that it is necessary to consider detailed information about painters in interpreting the results of chemical analysis.

Acknowledgements

We want to thank Thea van Oosten and Riet Karreman at the Central Laboratory for the FTIR analysis, Wilma Roelofs and Raymond Heesters from the same Institution for the TLC and HPLC analysis, and the Royal Dutch Shell Research Laboratory (KSLA), DSM-Research and the Vrije Universiteit for carrying out SEM-EDX, electronmicroprobe and FTIR analyses.

Notes and references

1. J.W. Niemeijer, "Some aspects of Dutch Eighteenth Century Art" in Earl R. Mandle, *Dutch Masterpieces from the Eighteenth Century, Paintings and Drawings 1700–1800.* The Minneapolis Institute of Art, 1971; Wiepke Loos, Guido Janssen and Wouter Kloek, "Het Galante Tijdperk. Schilderijen uit de Collectie van het Rijksmuseum 1700–1800", *Catalogue Rijksmuseum*, (1995); *Kunstgeschiedenis der Nederlanden VIII, Achttiende eeuw*, H.E. van Gelder, J. Duvenger, C.J.A.C. Peeters and Ch. Wentinck, eds (Phoenix geillustreerde Standaardwerken, 1963–64); J.H. Plantenga, "De Kunst in de Noordelijke Nederlanden op den Overgang van de zeventiende naar de Achttiende Eeuw en het Ontstaan der Haagsche Academie (1682)," *De Gids* 101, no 9 (1937): 307–334. M. Kirby Talley and Karin Groen, "Thomas Bardwell and his Practice of Painting: A Comparative Investigation between Described and Actual Painting Technique," *Studies in Conservation* 220 (1975): 44–108.
2. H. Kühn, H. Roosen-Runge, R.E. Straub and M. Koller, Reclams *Handbuch der künstlerischen Techniken* (Stuttgart 1984), 377.
3. The Stichting Rijksmuseum Twenthe houses 30 18th century paintings, on a long-term loan basis, from the Netherlands Office for Fine Arts in The Hague. The paintings will be presented in a special exhibition in Enschede at the beginning of 1997. This report is part of a more extensive project by Elisabeth Baadsgaard at the Royal Academy of Fine Arts in Copenhagen concerning 18th century painting techniques. In particular, two 18th

century sources will be studied, namely G. de Lairesse's *Groot Schilderboek* and an unpublished manuscript by S. Eikelenberg, which could be of particular interest.

4. Mathijs Naiveu was born in Leiden, 1647, and died in 1726 in Amsterdam. He painted in the traditional style of the Leiden "fine-painters". Jan Huchtenburg was born in Haarlem in 1647 and died in Amsterdam in 1733. He was popular painter of battle scenes. Johannes Verkolje was baptized in Delft in 1683 and died in Amsterdam. Philip van Dijk was born in Amsterdam in 1680 and died in The Hague in 1753; he painted portraits and familygroups, became court painter to Prince William IV of Orange after 1747. Jacob de Wit was born in Amsterdam. He painted mainly decorative scenes, especially ceilings, also a few portraits of "little children". Cornelis Troost, a contempory of Hogarth is often called "the Dutch Hogarth" because of the similarity in the scenes he depicts. However, there is no good reason to look for similaraties in technique, other than a general comparison with 18th century practices. Troost was born in Amsterdam. He started his career painting traditional group portraits. Later he turned to small conversation pieces and vaguely moral genre scenes. For Hogarth see: Ashok Roy, "Hogarth's 'Marriage à la Mode' and contemporary painting practice," *National Gallery Technical Bulletin* 6 (1982): 59–67.
5. Ashok Roy, ed., *Artists' Pigments*, 2 (Washington, National Gallery of Art, 1993), 68.
6. DTMS analysis by Professor Dr J. Boon at the FOM Institute for Atomic and Molecular Physics in Amsterdam.
7. Whether the final paint layer of the ground was applied in the studio, on top of the ready-primed canvas, is a question that will be further studied by Elisabeth Baadsgaard as part of her larger project.
8. The practice of adjusting the tone of the ground with a material quite similar to that of the ground, with the purpose of laying-in the composition, was found, by the authors, to be have been used by Rembrandt in the painting of "The anatomical lesson of Dr Deyman" in the Historisch Museum in Amsterdam.
9. The authors found similar thin, dark layers of underpaint in pictures by Jan Steen and Johannes Vermeer.
10. SEM-EDX. There was not enough sample material available to determine by XRD whether lead-tin yellow type I or II had been used.
11. Thin-layer chromatography. Purpurine could not be identified and one reason for this could be that the sample was too small. More work on the identification of organic pigments is being done at the Central Laboratory and at the FOM Institute.
12. R. J. Gettens, R. L. Feller and W.T. Chase, "Vermilion and Cinnabar" in *Artists' Pigments*, ed. Ashok Roy, 2 (Washington, National Gallery of Art, 1993), 163.
13. I. M.N. Wainwright, J. M. Taylor and R. D. Harley, "Lead Antimonate Yellow" in *Artists Pigments*, ed. R. L. Feller, (Cambridge University Press, 1986), 225, 226. Occurrences of Naples yellow in Dutch pictures from the end of the 17th century and the beginning of the 18th century are mentioned in *Notable Occurrences*.
14. "On Prussian blue" *Bulletin of the American Group IIC* 5, no 1 (1964): 19–20; "On Prussian blue", *Bulletin of the American Group IIC* 5, no 2 (1965): 30; J. Kirby, "Fading and Colour Change of Prussian Blue: Occurrences and Early Reports," *National Gallery Technical Bulletin* 14 (1993): 63.

Expert Examination of Icons

Olga Lelekova
State Research Institute for Restoration,
44 Gastello st., Moscow, Russia 107014

Abstract

The paper contains results of laboratory analyses and restoration research conducted with the aim of determining which conditions of the paint surface of icons distinguish authentic icons from imitations and copies produced in the 19th and 20th centuries. The criteria are: the craquelure structure, damage caused by restoration, and the remains of overpaint removed during the cleaning process. The craquelure structure of 15th–16th century (and earlier) icons is different from both the natural craquelure of authentic 19th–20th century icons, imitations and copies painted at that time and artificially produced craquelure. Damage inflicted by restoration can be analyzed, recorded and classified. An authentic icon necessarily possesses typical restoration damage and remains of overpaint and varnish layers removed during restoration, while imitations and copies do not.

Keywords

Icon, expert examination, paint layer, craquelure, authenticity, restoration damage

In Russia, like anywhere around the world, the most popular aspect of icon research is attribution by art historians of icons, with the aim of establishing the date, style and authorship of an icon and its association with one of the historical icon-painting centers.

As a result of insufficient technical equipment in museums and the high cost of research, as well as through tradition, icon attribution in Russia, especially in provincial museums, is done according to general notions, descriptions and intuition, without any technical–technological studies. We believe, however, that there are other reasons for conducting icon research. These include, for example defining the authenticity of icons for inclusion in catalogues, exhibitions and articles, as well as before acquisition, when one needs a definite answer, based on facts. In this case one cannot do without technical–technological research.

The making of counterfeit icons in Russia came into being together with the appearance of a market for icons and the beginning of their being collected. After the nationalization of private collections, imitations could also have found their way into state museums; hence the problem of determining the authenticity of icons. Every museum has icons that are in doubt in this respect. Art-historian attribution often serves as a substitute for expert examination and is identified with it, which leads to errors having practical consequences. It often happens that icons are considered, without any further analysis, to be imitations only because there are unusual iconographical details.

It is important for experts to work out objective criteria. However, there are no ready methods of identifying icon imitations because the problem has never been discussed specifically. Each specialist has his own approach and criteria. A scientific conference held in 1995 was the first attempt to make the problem of expert examination the subject of discussion,[1] but it did not quite turn out that way: the papers dealt chiefly with particular cases of research and restoration of completely different icons.

The importance of establishing objective criteria for determining whether an icon is authentic or not is demonstrated by everyday situations in the life of museums. In 1995 the Tretyakov Gallery was offered an icon to purchase. The opinions on this icon varied greatly: the majority of art historians and restorers of the Gallery thought it to be an imitation done in the 19th century, while one or two specialists identified it as a genuine work of the 14th century. In spite of the difference of opinion, technical–technological studies were not carried out and the icon was not purchased.

Technical–technological research has not yet become the norm for icon analysis. The first catalogue of the icon collection of the Tretyakov Gallery was published in 1963 without any technical–technological research on the objects. More than 30 years later, in 1995, the first volume of the new catalogue of the Tretyakov Gallery icon collection still has no technical–technological data.[2]

Expert examination relies greatly on physical-chemical analysis of painting materials and various forms of photoanalysis, including modern methods of digital image processing.

However, we should emphasize from the beginning that all methods of research at the disposal of museums have their limits. For example, because of the lack of necessary equipment for materials analysis, it is practically impossible today to identify micro-admixtures in pigments.

Subjecting icons to X-radiography reveals the topography of heterogeneous areas in the panel, the canvas or the ground, but this method is ineffective when it comes to paint-layer analysis. Infrared and ultraviolet photographs need to be compared with the original and require deciphering based on microscopy and a laboratory analysis of the paint-layer components. A layer of varnish 50–100 years old completely disguises the image viewed under ultraviolet light. Not so long ago a high-sensitivity infrared film, which gave excellent results, was produced in Russia. At present, however, its production has been stopped.

All of these difficulties have also been encountered during studies conducted in the State Research Institute for Restoration. Nevertheless examination with the aim of determining the authenticity of icons has become one of the projects of the institute.[3] This is accounted for by a number of reasons. The institute has a great experience over the past 20 years of conducting technical–technological research on different medieval painting media. From the early 1970s icon restoration in the Institute has been carried out exclusively with the use of microscopes, which requires the condition of micro-areas of the paint surface to be analyzed and recorded. At the same time morphological properties of the paint surface on a microscopic level provide the most reliable data for icon examination.

There existed and can be found today two different methods of creating a counterfeit icon: they are reconstruction and imitation. While natural pigments and traditional painting techniques were used for reconstruction, imitation artists used contemporary factory-produced pigments, along with natural ones. If a laboratory analysis shows the presence of artificial pigments, the question of authenticity is resolved quite simply. However, when an icon under doubt has been painted with natural pigments, the methods available to museums do not bring the expected results. An analysis of the condition of the paint surface is more effective in this case.

The condition of the paint layer of authentic icons, especially its surface, depends on the age of the icon, the painting technique and materials used, the conditions in which it was kept and the quality of its restoration. As a result of technological peculiarities – the use of linseed oil as a protective covering, which inevitably darkens after 50 years – Russian icons were constantly painted over with new layers. That is why, in order to reveal the original paint layer of icons starting with the oldest ones and up till the 16th century, the restorer has to remove several later layers of paint. For over a 100 years, since the mid-19th century, when the restoration of icons in Russia began, and up until the 1970s the removal of overpaint from old icons was done with the use of a knife or a scalpel and a limited set of solvents, which caused inevitable damage to the original paint layer. During that period all of the most ancient and valuable icons have been cleaned in such manner.

The damage inflicted by restoration has the same character on all the cleaned icons: the elevated edges of the craquelure penetrating the whole surface of an icon are partly cut off, the final thick brushstrokes of white color (highlights) on the faces, arms, clothes and architecture are also partly cut off. This occurred because no optical devices were used during the cleaning process and the restorer could not see, and did not even guess, what was happening to the paint surface under his or her knife or scalpel.

While assessing the quality of restoration of icons carried out both 100 and 15–20 years ago, we find the same character of mechanical damage to the paint surface. Sometimes this can be seen only with the use of magnification and macro-photography. Together with traces of restoration, the layer of old painting also contains damage which is associated with the lengthy process of ageing of the painting media and various accidental injuries. However, the damage marks differ in shape from restoration damage, which has a "regular" character. Photography of the paint layer surface in raking light, as well as the employment of various filters, gives information about the direction in which the restorer's instrument was moved, its size and shape, its sharpness and so on.

The paint layer of icons has a more or less pronounced relief: white highlights raised above the level of the surrounding surface, furrows left by the brush, the relief of the ground itself. During the cleaning of the icon of overpaint and dark linseed oil (even when it is done under a microscope), there are always minute particles of the removed layers left in the indents of the original paint layer.

Figure 1. The Crucifixion. 15th–19th century. Micro-photograph of a detail of 19th century painting. Craquelure character. Magnification × 20

Figure 2. Baptism of Christ. Imitation of a 16th century icon. Micro-photograph of a detail of the face of St John the Baptist. Craquelure character. Magnification × 20

Figure 3. The Trinity. Imitation of a 16th century icon. Micro-photograph of a detail of the face of the central angel. Magnification × 6

The presence of two conditions, restoration damage and microscopic remains of removed later layers, is necessary for icons to be authentic and cannot be found on imitations and copies.

Another important condition for determining imitations can be the craquelure structure. The character of the craquelure is formed by many factors: the age of the icon, the properties of the wooden panel, the ground, the painting technology, the conditions in which it was kept. The variety of craquelure patterns is infinite and cannot be reduced to a system, but, however different may be the form of cracks on various icons, there can be noticed a general pattern in their development. There are two kinds of craquelure found on old icons, the larger, more prominent craquelure of the ground, which partly penetrates the paint surface, and the thinner cracks of the paint layer, which are also only partly associated with the ground.

The naked eye sees only the bigger cracks filled with dark linseed oil and surface grime. Under a microscope we can see, however, that the whole surface of an icon is penetrated with cracks, finer cracks spreading out from wider ones to resemble the branch system of a tree.

Some of the copies of icons painted in the late 19th and early 20th centuries which we have studied contain cracks either drawn or engraved by the artist, while no natural craquelure has yet been formed. Other copies of the same period, restoration fillings and imitations, contain a common type of craquelure. It represents a broken network with separate cracks not connected with one another; these often originate from a minute opening formed by the bursting of an air bubble (Figures 1 to 4). The latter are formed when the paint contains too much binding media and is applied in a thick layer. Such a broken network of cracks with holes left by bursting air bubbles is a feature of later painting. One time, however, we were puzzled by the appearance of the same kind of "later" craquelure on areas painted with a thick layer of vermilion on a 14th century icon. An interesting fact is that the character of the craquelure on these areas has not changed with time and the cracks have not formed a single network. However, this kind of craquelure appears only on vermilion areas of this icon, while the rest of its surface is covered with a fully developed single network of cracks, as it should be with old painting. As well as the craquelure of the paint layer, specific for each area containing different pigments, the face of the icon is penetrated by the craquelure of the ground, which is the same for all of the icon's surface, including the areas of vermilion.

We know that, when making an imitation, artists also tried to produce a craquelure system. There have survived notes describing this process in the village of Mstera, famous for its icon painting. An icon was painted on a canvas, which was then crumpled and after that glued onto a panel and covered with a layer of dirtied linseed oil. Nevertheless, any method of obtaining artificial craquelure is an abuse of the painting material and produces cracks that are different from the natural ones. Artificial craquelure is the same whether it is on the ground or on the paint layer and it is also filled with grime in the same fashion. We have not yet seen artificial craquelure on copies or imitations that resembles one occuring naturally.

At the request of different museums we have examined over 50 icons, the authenticity of which was in doubt, and we have found among them only three obvious imitations of the 16th century, painted on old panels. Two of the icons were painted in Moscow style with natural pigments and in traditional egg tempera technique. Neither icon had damage to the paint surface, nor remaining particles of overpaint caught in the indents of the paint surface, although an attempt had been made to imitate its removal. Areas of thick painting, containing ochre and white lead (the faces, hands and other exposed parts of the body), were covered with a broken network of cracks and a great number of openings left by bursting air bubbles (Figure 2). After removing the "oklad" from the border of one icon we discovered that there was no painting underneath, only a layer of unpainted ground.

In addition to the features mentioned above, the third icon had faces painted without a preliminary layer of "sankir" and the drawing was executed not on the ground, but stenciled over the finished painting (Figures 3 and 4).

The majority of icons that caused doubt had been previously restored for antique dealers. In the process of brutal restoration the original painting was partly destroyed, partly damaged. Besides that, there were large areas of complete ground loss. After restoration all damaged areas were painted in the style of the remaining

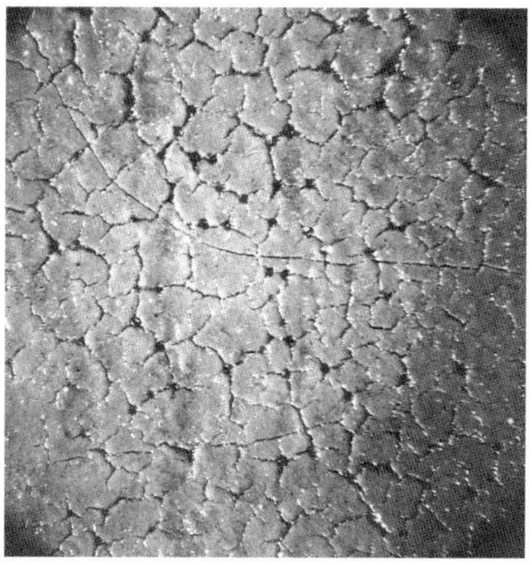

Figure 4. The Trinity. Imitation of a 16th century icon. Micro-photograph of a detail of the face of the central angel. Magnification × 25

fragments of the original with the use of both natural and artificial pigments, and with the imitation of craquelure. The additions on all the icons, instead of the blue pigments azurite and indigo, contain Prussian blue, as well as a red organic pigment that can be distinguished from the old one by the way it is prepared. The areas of the original, painted with a red organic pigment contain particles of various shapes, whereas the additions were painted with a modern red organic pigment, prepared in a lacquer form and containing no particles. Instead of a ground based on gypsum, the losses were filled with chalk ground. Red ochre was used to imitate vermilion and only one layer of paint was applied where the original would have had several. Finally, we found no verdigris, which is very common to original painting.

Thus restoration additions, imitating original painting, are different from the original painting on all icons examined, both in media and technique. Hence the additions are easily revealed with the help of a laboratory analysis of the paint layer, or examination under a microscope.

Our experience leads us to the conclusion that any additions to icons, restored up to the present day, however expertly executed they may seem, are different from the original painting.

Restoration additions imitate original painting; they are not and cannot be its technical–technological reconstruction. One must conduct first a detailed professional laboratory analysis of the paint layer in order to reconstruct the materials and technique of the original painting. Such analyses have only become possible recently and are conducted, as we have mentioned, in several restoration organizations. Theoretically speaking, there does exist today the technical basis for producing counterfeit icons that would be technologically closer to the originals, which means that there is a risk of the appearance of such imitations, although we have not seen such counterfeits yet. It is our opinion that there are not many imitations in museum collections, although the number of icons that are irreversibly damaged by restoration is rather great. In future, one of the aims of scientific restoration of Russian icons, both in Russia and in other countries, will possibly be the freeing of what remains of the original painting from the disfiguring additions of mediocre restoration. It is important to understand that, to a great extent, not all the icons that have restoration additions were deliberate imitations with the aim of deceiving the museum or the collector. One should keep in mind that during the first pre-scientific period of icon restoration in Russia, which lasted until the 1950–1960s, these were the principles and the technical level of restoration. The damage to the icon surface during the cleaning process was not recognized either by ordinary restorers or by their superiors to be a consequence of their restoration. The damage was considered to be normal, and so additions, no matter how extensive they may be, were thought to be a necessary and, indeed, the most important stage of restoration.

In our opinion any decision on whether an icon is authentic or not can be made today only if there is enough objective and properly recorded data, supplied by technical–technological research on the painting.

Conclusion

The suggested method of determining the authenticity of icons does not require vast expenditure and we hope that it will be of practical use to experts in the field of old Russian art.

Notes and references

1. State Tretyakov Gallery. Magnum ARS amalgamation. First scientific conference. Expert Examination of Objects of the Fine Arts. 31 May–2 June 1995.
2. *State Tretyakov Gallery. Catalogue.* Vol. 1. *Old Russian Art of the Xth- Early XVth Century.* (Moscow, 1995).
3. Together with the author, this project has been conducted by institute specialists, N.G. Bregman, M.M. Naumova and J.A. Ruzavin.

Technique picturale et problèmes de conservation des peintures mates d'Antoine Wiertz (1806-1865)

Françoise Rosier
rue H. Wafelaerts 10
1060 Bruxelles, Belgique

Résumé

Cette recherche concerne les peintures mates monumentales réalisées par Antoine Wiertz dans la dernière phase de son parcours artistique. Celles-ci ont été conçues à l'aide d'une technique personnelle qui a défavorablement engagé leur avenir. L'analyse des textes de l'artiste révèle la nature des matériaux constitutifs des peintures ainsi que certains aspects de leur élaboration. L'étude de la collection des peintures mates du musée Wiertz complète les données techniques.

Mots-clés

Mat, monumental, Antoine Wiertz, procédé de peinture, toile, térébenthine de Venise

Introduction

Dernière demeure du peintre belge Antoine Wiertz (1806-1865) léguée à l'état belge en 1865, le musée Wiertz offre au sein du quartier Léopold à Bruxelles un ensemble presque complet des réalisations de l'artiste intégrant ses peintures, ses sculptures et ses dessins. L'oeuvre peint du maître façonné par l'exigence de ses rêves démesurés dénote de la façon la plus évidente la coexistence de deux types de création d'aspect profondément différent. Un premier type de peinture présente une apparence brillante tandis qu'un second groupe, tout aussi remarquable en nombre, se distingue par un aspect de surface mat. C'est aux oeuvres mates que nous nous intéresserons de manière exclusive dans cette étude (Figure 1). Les commentaires relatifs à ces peintures ne donnent que des indications approximatives concernant la technique utilisée dans leur élaboration. Il y a là tout un domaine qui n'a pas encore été étudié.

Les peintures mates ont été conçues pendant la période qui va de 1853 à 1865, période pendant laquelle Wiertz, désespérant de ne pouvoir soumettre le langage de la peinture à l'huile vernie à sa volonté d'expression, se lance dans une série d'expérimentations techniques en vue d'établir une concordance plus grande entre ses conceptions picturales qui le poussent à rechercher la matité et les moyens d'y parvenir. Passionné par la peinture baroque de Pierre-Paul Rubens et en particulier son aisance technique, Wiertz désire peindre rapidement des compositions de grand format qui ne "miroitent" pas. Ni la technique traditionnelle de la peinture à l'huile ni les procédés mats déjà connus tels que la fresque ne lui permettaient de se libérer des contraintes de la matière. L'artiste choisit donc dans les dernières décennies de son existence une orientation technique neuve et personnelle. En 1859 le peintre rédige un texte traitant de ses travaux sur la matité. Ce texte est édité après sa mort en 1867 dans les *Oeuvres littéraires* sous le titre *"Peinture mate: le procédé"*. Ces écrits qui nous permettent de mieux supposer l'élaboration des oeuvres constituent pour nous un document fondamental.

Les peintures monumentales et mates de Wiertz sont aujourd'hui fortement altérées et nécessitent des travaux de sauvetage. La connaissance de la nature des matériaux et des procédés techniques utilisés par l'artiste est indispensable avant toute intervention sur les peintures ou sur leur environnement. Elle est également utile à la compréhension des causes de l'état actuel des peintures mates (fragilité des supports, aspect clair, terne et poudreux de la couche picturale). La confrontation des résultats apportés par l'observation des peintures mates[1] et des renseignements donnés par les écrits de l'artiste permettra de proposer une méthodologie d'approche de la connaissance de ces oeuvres.

Figure 1. Les choses du présent devant les hommes de l'avenir, *Antoine Wiertz, ensemble, Musée Wiertz, Bruxelles.*

Etude du procédé mat mis au point par Antoine Wiertz

Le texte *"Peinture mate: le procédé"* renseigne quatre techniques permettant d'obtenir un effet mat. L'auteur semble avoir l'expérience de chacun des procédés mais témoigne une préférence pour l'un d'eux: le procédé 1. La collection des peintures du musée comprend donc probablement une majorité d'oeuvres réalisées grâce à ce procédé mais des exemples d'application des trois autres techniques sont possibles dans le groupe de tableaux réalisés entre 1853 et 1859, période de recherches et d'hésitations.

Figure 2. Pensées et visions d'une tête coupée, *détail: partie centrale du triptyque. La toile laissée visible sur une grande partie de la composition constitue le ton moyen.*

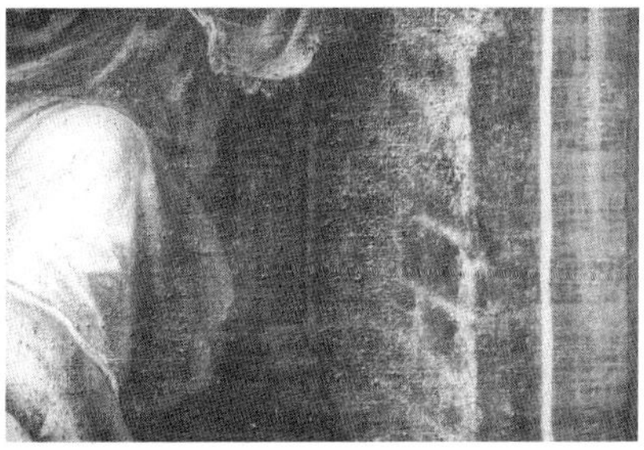

Figure 3. La civilisation du XIXème siècle, *détail. Le caractère pelucheux de la toile est particulièrement visible dans le mur de briques situé à l'extrême droite de l'image.*

La palette proposée par l'artiste pour l'ensemble des techniques se compose du blanc de zinc, du noir d'ivoire, de l'ocre jaune ou du jaune de Naples, de la terre de Sienne, du bleu de Prusse, du vermillon de Chine et des "laques ordinaires". La simplification de la gamme chromatique aux couleurs primaires étonne chez un artiste romantique qui connut la diversification des pigments et des colorants disponibles dans le commerce. Wiertz affirme ici sa filiation artistique avec Rubens mais utilise pour atteindre son but des pigments récents comme le blanc de zinc apparu en 1834. Le peintre s'impose l'obligation d'utiliser ces couleurs principales de manière à conserver autant que possible la vigueur et l'intensité des tons. La réalisation de formats monumentaux se passe de nuances intermédiaires qui ne résistent pas à la distance et introduisent une certaine monotonie dans la composition. Le choix restreint des teintes est motivé par l'exigence d'une exécution rapide et déterminée. Les mélanges sont simples. La systématisation des couleurs assure une unité harmonieuse à l'ensemble. Les pigments cités sont stables pour la plupart, du moins si on admet qu'ils correspondent à leur formulation habituelle ce qui n'était pas toujours le cas au XIXème siècle. Alors que le jaune de Naples véritable présente une bonne permanence, les jaunes de Naples à base de mélange de pigments (blanc de zinc et jaune de cadmium par exemple) courant vers le milieu du siècle témoignent d'une certaine instabilité à la lumière. Les "laques ordinaires", différentes de la laque de garance ou de la laque carminée (d'après les listes d'époque d'articles pour artistes) ont très certainement décoloré. Une perte de vigueur des tons rouges est donc envisageable. De même, un pâlissement des mélanges à base de blanc de zinc et de bleu de Prusse est prévisible quel que soit le liant. Ces quelques modifications d'aspect ne suffisent cependant pas à expliquer l'apparence terne et grisâtre des couleurs que montrent les peintures du musée. Nous verrons que les causes de cet état doivent être cherchées ailleurs.

Le procédé 1

Le liant de cette technique est formé d'une partie de térébenthine de Venise, résine extraite du tronc du mélèze, pour deux parties d'essence. Ce médium, mélangé à trois parties de pigments, produit une pâte dont la consistance est proche de celle de la peinture à l'huile.[2] La première étape du travail du peintre consiste à mêler les pigments en poudre au médium. Ces préparations sont ensuite conservées dans des pots hermétiquement fermés. L'idée d'associer à l'avance les pigments au liant facilite le travail de l'artiste pendant l'exécution. Le choix et l'application de la peinture devaient se faire rapidement.

Wiertz recherche la matité de ses peintures par le choix d'un support absorbant (la toile de lin) et d'un diluant maigre (l'essence de térébenthine). Les proportions de chaque constituant sont calculées de telle sorte qu'il n'y ait pas un excès de liant mais que celui-ci soit présent en quantité suffisante pour assurer au film de peinture une cohésion normale. Avec le temps, la térébenthine de Venise perd ses qualités mécaniques. Les particules de pigments moins liées qu'auparavant affleurent à la surface et diffusent davantage la lumière. L'aspect "délavé" des oeuvres mates n'est donc pas dû à une décoloration des pigments à la lumière mais à une diminution de la cohésion de la couche picturale superficielle. Le caractère poudreux du film de peinture n'est pas un trait propre aux oeuvres mates mais le résultat d'une altération du liant de ces peintures.

La toile de lin[3] occupe une place primordiale dans le procédé. En effet, la peinture y est directement appliquée de manière à ce que sa couleur soit le ton moyen sur lequel l'artiste va organiser sa composition (Figure 2). Cette manière de procéder le dispense de la préparation du support et de l'application de la couche d'impression telle que Rubens la concevait. Le résultat obtenu est toutefois très différent de la luminosité interne des peintures flamandes. La texture pelucheuse et veloutée du support contribue à la matité de la peinture ainsi qu'à la vibration des tons (Figure 3). Elle favorise cependant l'incrustation de poussières particulièrement nocives pour un support de nature végétale. La toile, apparente en de nombreux endroits est directement exposée aux dégradations photochimiques. Celles-ci se manifestent par une modification de la couleur de la toile et donc de ce qui correspondait au ton moyen. La volonté de conserver le caractère absorbant du subjectile a conduit l'artiste à négliger l'encollage. L'acidité du liant a par conséquent beaucoup affaibli le support végétal.

Si l'absorption du liant par la toile ne suffit pas à éliminer les brillances,[4] Wiertz conseille l'utilisation du *veloutoir*. Cet instrument qui s'apparente probablement à une brosse plate et large composée de poils raides permet d'entraîner par frottements l'excédent de matière picturale préalablement dissout à l'essence et de faire réapparaître le grain de la toile. Le veloutoir est donc un agent externe de matité.

L'artiste suggère enfin de vernir les zones de la peinture qui n'auraient pas été suffisament fixées à l'aide d'un mélange à base de résine mastic (une part) et d'essence de térébenthine (trois parts). Cette possibilité rompt avec l'assimilation automatique et réductrice du concept de peinture mate à celui de peinture non vernie. Ce vernis était vraisemblablement très discret car il n'est pas possible de distinguer à l'oeil nu les parties sur lesquelles il aurait été appliqué. Sa dégradation le rend probablement encore plus invisible.

Le procédé 2

La seconde technique repose sur les mêmes fondements que la première mais le liant utilisé est huileux. Le travail de la peinture à l'huile sur toile écrue non préparée permettait de jouir de l'agrément des pâtes sans que la mise en oeuvre soit ralentie par de longs temps de séchage. Cette méthode affaiblit le support. La composition exacte du médium n'est pas décrite mais il est permis de penser que l'huile était utilisée pure. L'introduction d'autres substances résineuses ou siccatives complique le travail et perd son sens: l'adjonction d'une résine augmente les risques de brillance et de jaunissement, l'addition d'un siccatif est superflue lorsqu'on applique la peinture en une seule couche sur un fond perméable. L'élimination des brillances éventuelles peut se faire à l'aide du veloutoir ou de la *houppe absorbante*. Il s'agissait sans doute d'un outil muni de poils doux de forme ronde, large et plate. En effet, il ne doit pas produire de frottements mais absorber le surplus de liant.

Le procédé 3

Cette technique qui consiste à peindre à l'huile sur un support rigide (carton, verre, marbre,etc.) et à produire la matité par l'introduction superficielle d'une charge inerte telle que la pierre ponce est secondaire. Wiertz reprend à son compte une technique usuelle au XIXème siècle dans la peinture en bâtiment. Ce procédé ne répondait pas véritablement à la volonté de l'artiste de réaliser des oeuvres monumentales légères et amovibles. L'usage d'un support rigide induit des limites au niveau du format.

Le procédé 4

La préparation des couleurs est ici différente puisque les pigments sont broyés à l'eau. Elles sont appliquées sur la toile non préparée. La composition est fixée par le revers de la toile à la fin du travail à l'aide d'un mélange de térébenthine de Venise (une part) et d'essence (trois parts). Remarquons d'emblée qu'il est difficile d'adapter la quantité de fixatif nécessaire aux besoins de chaque pigment par l'envers de la toile. Les oeuvres réalisées selon cette méthode développeront nécessairement des problèmes locaux de cohésion. Cette technique réduit les possibilités de varier les densités de la matière. Les oeuvres réalisées grâce à ce procédé présentent logiquement une couche picturale plus régulière et plus mince. Une fois de plus le support est affaibli par le caractère acide du fixatif. La décomposition de la térébenthine de Venise entraîne une perte de cohésion de la couche picturale.

Examen des peintures mates conservées au musée Wiertz

Les peintures mates sur toile ont été réalisées grâce aux procédés 1, 2 et 4. Il est cependant impossible de voir à l'oeil nu laquelle de ces trois techniques a été employée pour chacune des peintures. Nous les considérons donc dans leur ensemble. Les supports sont formés par une ou plusieurs toiles de lin assemblées par

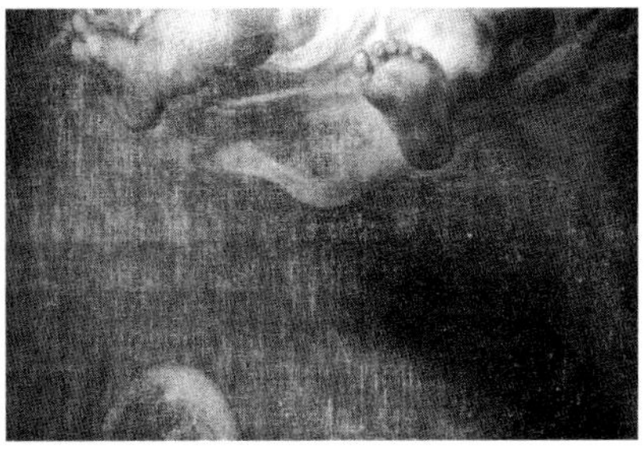

Figure 4. La puissance humaine n'a pas de limite, *détail. Une ligne horizontale est visible sur la toile laissée telle quelle en dessous des pieds de l'enfant.*

Figure 5. La lutte homérique, *détail. Le centre de tension de la peinture constitué ici par le personnage féminin et les deux guerriers est la partie la plus lumineuse et la plus détaillée de la composition.*

des coutures verticales. L'artiste utilise un tissu plus ou moins épais selon le format[5] et le sujet traité. On distingue des toiles fines qui comptent entre sept et neuf fils dans les deux sens et des toiles épaisses qui présentent dix à douze fils dans les deux sens. La texture affirmée de la toile est accentuée par la présence de noeuds. L'irrégularité de la surface contribue à la matité. Les toiles sont tendues sur châssis à l'aide de semences métalliques. La nature des châssis utilisés n'a pu être déterminée vu le nombre insuffisant de revers observés. Sur la toile non préparée, le peintre délimite le format de sa composition par un léger trait au pinceau[6] et dispose ce qui s'apparente probablement à un quadrillage de mise en place: des lignes horizontales et verticales ne correspondant à aucune figure de la composition sont visibles dans bon nombre d'oeuvres mates (Figure 4). L'artiste ébauche ensuite sommairement la scène par un dessin linéaire et ombré réalisé en camaïeu à l'aide d'un pinceau chargé d'une couleur brunâtre très diluée. Le point le plus lumineux est réservé au centre du tableau. Cette esquisse générale demeure en partie visible dans les parties ombrées de la peinture terminée. Viennent ensuite les cinq couleurs primitives qui sont distribuées en demi-pâtes à l'aide de larges brosses dans les différents points du tableau. Enfin les rehauts et les détails posés par empâtements achèvent les parties les plus lumineuses de la composition (Figure 5). La couleur est placée en une seule couche et les modelés sont réalisés dans le frais. Les traces de brosse visibles dans les empâtements animent la surface. L'aspect général est clair, mat et rugueux. Le nombre très limité de peintures mates sur support rigide actuellement étudié ne permet pas de commenter la technique de façon suffisamment complète.

Conclusion

L'étude des écrits de l'artiste a révélé l'existence de quatre procédés dont trois sur toile de lin. La prépondérance des peintures mates sur toiles souligne l'attrait manifesté par l'artiste à l'égard des qualités optiques et absorbantes de ce support. Les liants jouent dès lors un rôle secondaire. L'artiste ne recherche plus leurs qualités optiques particulières mais leur simple pouvoir agglutinant et leur rapidité de séchage. Il n'exploite pas pleinement les qualités des liants, ce qui rend difficile l'identification à l'oeil nu de la technique de chacune des peintures. Les procédés mats mises au point par Wiertz autorisaient l'artiste à peindre avec une étonnante rapidité et de manière impulsive sur l'ensemble de la composition mais entraînent une faiblesse structurelle des oeuvres liée à l'insuffisance de l'encollage des supports de toile. Aujourd'hui, les toiles monumentales altérées par l'acidité des liants et par la lumière menacent de se déchirer sous l'action de leur propre poids et lors de variations climatiques. Wiertz avait conçu des peintures aux couleurs vives et éclatantes, elles sont devenues uniformément claires et ternes en raison de la diminution du pouvoir liant de la térébenthine de Venise et de l'incrustation superficielle de poussières dans les irrégularités de la matière. Les techniques mates de Wiertz comportent des faiblesses qui ont irrémédiablement conditionné l'avenir des peintures ainsi réalisées. Le manque d'intérêt suscité par les peintures mates dans les années qui ont suivi la mort de l'artiste n'a pas contribué à améliorer le sort de ces grands tableaux devenus fragiles. Cette étude réunit l'ensemble des données relatives à la nature des matériaux et au caractère propre de la peinture mate que le restaurateur doit connaître avant d'envisager toute intervention de conservation.

Remerciements

Nos remerciements s'adressent particulièrement à C. Périer-D'Ieteren, professeur à la faculté d'Histoire de l'Art et Archéologie à l'Université Libre de Bruxelles et à A.A. Moerman, conservateur du Musée Wiertz à Bruxelles.

Notes

[1] Un regroupement d'oeuvres tel que celui que propose le musée Wiertz favorise l'émergence de données communes à ce genre si particulier de peintures.

[2] Wiertz indique que les proportions peuvent être plus ou mois élevées selon les pigments.

[3] Trois échantillons de toile ont été prélevés parmi les peintures mates conservées au musée. L'un sur une toile fine intitulée *Une scène de l'Enfer*. Les deux autres sur des toiles plus épaisses: *Une embuscade* et *La civilisation du XIXème siècle*. L'examen microscopique a révélé dans les trois cas l'utilisation du lin.
[4] Les reprises peuvent provoquer des brillances.
[5] Les formats des peintures mates sont compris entre 9,19 × 6,70 m pour la plus grande et O,55 × O,41 m pour la plus petite.
[6] Les bordures de la toiles qui ne serviront pas à la composition seront réservées au cadre peint en trompe-l'oeil.

Références

1. L. Libert, *Manuel des jeunes artistes ou traité élémentaire et pratique du dessin et de la peinture* (Liège: L. Libert, 1805).
2. A. A. Moerman, *Antoine Wiertz 1806-1865* (Paris-Bruxelles: Jacques Damase, 1974).
3. J.N.Paillot de Montabert, *Traité complet de la peinture* (Paris: Bossange, 1829).
4. Riffault, Vergnaud, *Nouveau manuel complet du peintre en bâtiments, vitier, doreur, argenteur et vernisseur* (Paris: Librairie encyclopédique Roret,1851).
5. Riffault, Vergnaud, Toussaint, *Nouveau manuel complet du fabricant de couleurs et de vernis* (Paris: Librairie encyclopédique Roret,1862).
6. P.F. Tingry, *Traité théorique et pratique sur l'art de faire et d'appliquer les vernis* (Genève: Manget,1803).
7. A. Wiertz, *Oeuvres littéraires* (Bruxelles: Parent, 1869).
8. A. Wiertz, *Peinture mate. Procédé nouveau* (Bruxelles: Parent, 1867).

Turner's 'Drawing Book', the *Liber Studorium*: Materials and Techniques

Joyce H. Townsend
Conservation Department
Tate Gallery, Millbank
London SW1P 4RG, UK

Abstract

Approximately ninety drawings, etchings and engravings, all monochrome, have been examined to elucidate and illustrate J.M.W. Turner's techniques of paint application for watercolours and his numerous means of creating highlights. Some of his techniques, e.g. scratching-out with a needle, derive from the etching and engraving processes. Samples were taken from drawings with rough, uncut edges and heavy washes, and analysed by EDX and FTIR microspectometry. The pigments in the drawings proved to be inorganic: burnt umber, burnt sienna and Indian red, with yellow ochre, vermilion and Prussian blue used less frequently. Umbers and ochres, ivory black and synthetic red ochres were used in varying mixtures in the printing inks. The medium was gum for the drawings, with possible additions or coatings of drying oil in many of the glossy areas, and drying oil for the printing inks.

Keywords

Turner, watercolour, etching, early 19th century, materials, techniques, brown pigments

Figure 1. Detail × 7 of Bridge and Goats, *pencil and watercolour on paper, 186mm by 260mm, c.1806, (Tate Gallery D08146, Turner Bequest CXVII R) showing the hard edges of a wet wash applied to dry paper.*

Introduction

J.M.W. Turner (1775–1851) planned a publication of 100 engravings in the early part of the 19th century, his *Liber Studiorum*. His subjects were divided into six categories of landscape: historical, pastoral, architectural, mountainous, 'EP' which is taken to mean 'elevated pastoral', and marine. The *Liber Studiorum* was published in several parts of five plates each, from 1807 over a period of more than a decade, but never completed. The drawings themselves date from c.1806–1824. Seventy plates and a frontispiece were issued and Turner produced a further twenty drawings as guides for his engravers, in brown monochrome for printing in brown inks. The majority of the plates were executed using a combination of hardground etching and mezzotint. Several incorporated aquatint, and softground etching was used instead of hardground in a few cases. As a rule, Turner etched the outlines onto the copper plates first and then passed them on to professional engravers after the etching had been proofed for the mezzotint and aquatint work. The *Liber* prints and drawings were first catalogued by Finberg.[1] The etchings, engravers' proofs, published states and the watercolour drawings (many examples of the last are in the Turner and Vaughan Bequests at the Tate Gallery) have recently been examined and discussed by Forrester and form the subject of an exhibition.[2] The author took the opportunity to examine all of the Tate Gallery watercolour drawings with a stereo microscope, to elucidate and compare the techniques which Turner used to apply watercolour wash and to create highlights. From the 1810s onwards, Turner would paint full-colour images in watercolour for engraving, then sale, and he would utilise all the techniques of paint handling which he had perfected earlier in monochrome.[3]

It was possible to select a limited number of *Liber* watercolour drawings with torn or unevenly cut edges and thick washes running out to the edges, for the removal of tiny paint samples. (The great majority have been trimmed for mounting). It would have been unrealistic to take many samples sufficiently large for full characterisation of the medium by chromatographic methods. Elemental analysis by energy dispersive X-ray (EDX) and Fourier-transform infrared (FTIR) microspectrometry were employed to characterise the materials, since these methods require even smaller samples than have to be taken for optical microscopy of watercolour paint. Such a study of materials is of use to conservators who may have to wash or locally treat these watercolours, since little has been published on the materials in use at this date. A parallel study was carried out on the paper supports by a specialist paper historian, but will not be discussed here.[4]

Methods of Examination

Examination at 7–20 times with a stereo microscope was sufficient for examining techniques of paint application. At 20–40 times, pigment mixtures can be recognised and washes of fine organic material (such as sepia or ink wash) can be distinguished from coarser inorganic pigments (such as ochres and umbers).

Small samples of paint were compressed in a diamond anvil cell for analysis with a Nicolet 510P FTIR bench and a Nicplan microscope, fitted with a 15 times reflachromat Cassegrain objective, and scanned from 4000 to 600 cm^{-1}. Areas of paper fibre or pigment could be avoided during data collection to give spectra of

Figure 2. Berry Pomeroy, *watercolour on paper, 204mm by 290mm, c.1812–15, (Tate Gallery D08159, TB CXVIII E).*

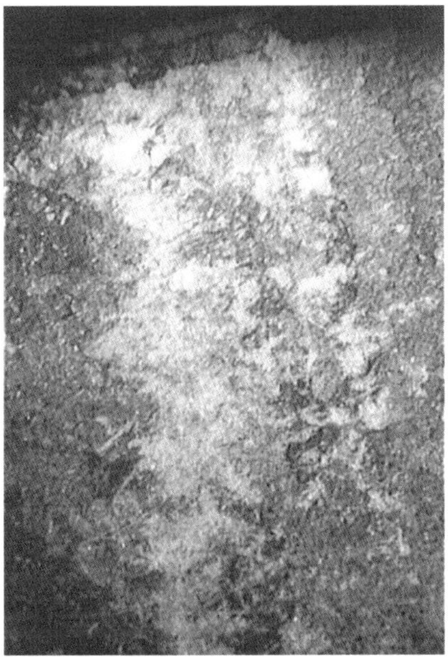

Figure 3. Detail × 7 of Temple of Minerva Medica, *watercolour on paper, 202mm by 273mm, c.1808, (Tate Gallery N08128, TB CXVII A), showing wash removed with a soft substance, perhaps bread.*

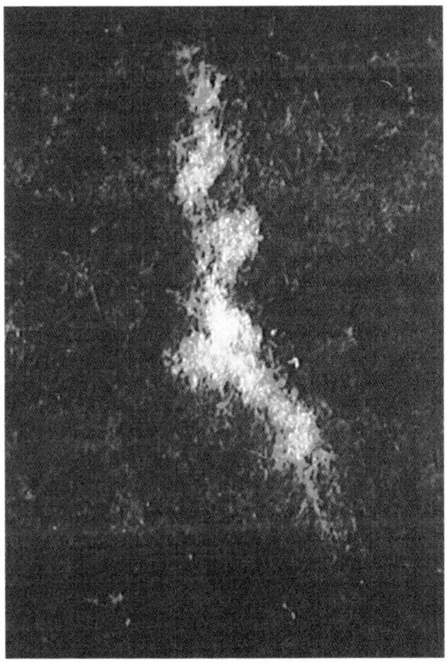

Figure 4. Detail × 7 of Isis, *watercolour on paper, 209mm by 300mm, c.1810–15, (Tate Gallery D08168, TB CXVIII N), showing a single scratch used to create a flying bird.*

the medium alone for samples of wash. The spectra were matched to those in the Getty Conservation Institute and Tate Gallery spectral libraries. Since much of the material in the reference spectra is fresh, while the samples are naturally aged, no attempt could be made to infer the specific type of gum or oil used.

Tiny fibres with pigment attached were coated with gold and examined at 20kV in a Hitachi S-2400 scanning electron microscope (SEM) fitted with Link ISIS software and an SEI detector.

Papers Used

All of the supports are wove paper, white or offwhite, medium weight with a fine-textured surface. Turner often used well-sized paper which could withstand scraping and rapid working even when very wet.[5] Many have J Whatman watermarks of 1794, 1801 or 1807. None are primed, but a few have a thin artist's wash of the brown pigment used for most of the composition.

Pigments Used

There are four shades of brown recognisable in the vast majority of the *Liber* watercolour drawings, though traditionally they have all been catalogued as 'pen and ink with sepia' (for example [6,7]). The shades match the colours of modern burnt umber, burnt sienna or else bistre, Indian red and sepia. EDX of at least six 'burnt umber' samples confirmed this identification, since all contained manganese (from the dioxide) as well as iron. The 'burnt sienna' and 'Indian red' samples (at least six of each colour) contained iron alone, which supports their identification too. The thinly-painted, fine-grained, greyer-toned 'sepia' gave very poor count-rates, suggestive of an organic material, but one sample included traces of iron, while the other samples had no metallic elements present. Genuine sepia is an organic material with no detectable metallic elements. FTIR spectra of 'sepia' samples included peaks attributable to the (gum) medium alone, so its identification is less certain.

In a minority of the late drawings, vermilion, yellow ochre and Prussian blue, used as small touches of colour, were identified by optical microscopy and confirmed by EDX or FTIR.

Printers' ink always included dark brown and black pigments, and sometimes a red pigment identified optically as Mars red. EDX showed Ca, P, Fe, and Mn to be the principal elements. These can be taken to indicate the presence of ivory or bone black, ochres and/or umbers. The ink formulations clearly varied from one print to another, depending on the shade of brown required. Turner sometimes specified the shade, or disputed it at the proof stage.[8]

In addition, elements from fillers in the paper or the glue size were detectable: Al, Si, K and Ca in every case, and Ba in a few cases. The first group can be attributed to china clay (kaolinite $Al_2O_3.2SiO_2.2H_2O$), pumice (Na,K,Al silicates) or chalk fillers ($CaCO_3$), and the last to barium sulphate or barytes ($BaSO_4$), whose presence was not obviously related to paper type. All the same trace elements were detectable in samples of printers' ink too. Mg was found in trace amounts in one case, attributable to talc ($3MgO.4SiO_2.H_2O$) filler. The glue size could have included papermakers' alum, potassium aluminium sulphate, but the minute quantities involved would not be detectable by EDX.

Paint and Printing Ink Media

Sulphur was detected by EDX in all the watercolour paint samples. It has also been found in a wider date range of Turner watercolour samples and can be attributed to glue size in the paper. The FTIR spectra indicated the presence of glue (size) in a few cases, presumed to be animal glue.

Turner applied localised washes of a glossy material with the appearance of gum, which was also sampled. It tends to crack and flake, since it was always applied relatively thickly, as Figure 1 shows. The major component is a gum, presumed to be gum arabic since the most common match was to this gum, though there seem to be additions of drying oil in more than half of the 10–12 washes analysed.

Figure 5. Near Blair Atholl, Scotland, *watercolour on paper, 183mm by 262mm, c.1808, (Tate Gallery D08134, TB CXVII G).*

Figure 6. Pembury Mill, Kent, *watercolour on paper, 183mm by 254mm, c.1806–7, (Tate Gallery D08116, TB CXVI O).*

Figure 7. Rivaux Abbey, *watercolour on paper, 183mm by 260mm, c.1806–7, (Tate Gallery D08154, TB CXVII Z).*

(Peaks were present at 1746, 2925, 2858cm^{-1}.) This seems too many to account for as contamination in Turner's or the engravers' studios, particularly as accidental oil stains are uncommon on the paper supports. It is possible that Turner added a thin layer of oil medium locally, to make these areas glossy and/or in an attempt to reduce cracking. The interpretation that he used a mixture of gum and drying oil seems unlikely; he would have had to add a surfactant such as ox gall to make them mix at all and there are no rings of oil stain around such areas. Samples of thinner, non-glossy wash contained gum arabic alone.

As expected, the ink samples were found to contain a drying oil, also with peaks at 1746, 2925, 2858cm^{-1}. Inks are always heavily loaded with pigments and peaks which matched to ochres and/or umbers were found to dominate most of the ink spectra. Pyrolysis-gas chromatography-mass spectrometry (Py-GC-MS) of one sample failed to detect resins or waxes.

Techniques for Watercolour Drawings

Most of the *Liber* watercolour drawings have been trimmed in the past, but a few retain wide margins of blank paper which may have helped Turner to envisage the effect of a finished engraving. Their large dimensions, and independent studies of the papers,[4] suggest he worked on loose sheets of paper, rather than in small notebooks. This allowed him to soak some or all of the sheet and then apply wet washes which had soft, nebulous outlines. On occasion he washed over the whole sheet by this means, in the brown pigment which he had selected for the overall tone. More usually, he used washing on wet paper for the initial, fairly uniform lay-in of the sky and the middle ground, without any preliminary drawing in pencil. Then clouds and distant scenery could be built up either by washing out some of this wash with a clean and wet brush or by adding darker washes of the same pigment to it, either soft-edged because applied on damp paper or harder-edged washes applied very wet to dried-out paper (Figure 1). Turner regularly used his fingers to manipulate washes too. This is very noticeable in *Berry Pomeroy* in Figure 2.

On occasion Turner drew in sketchy figures in pencil, or indicated the line of mountains or buildings with light pencil strokes, while the paper was drying sufficiently for the next stage. Whether he used pencil sketching or not, all the foreground details were applied as washes to dry paper, with differing amounts of water on the brush. Sometimes Turner reserved white paper to form highlights. In all these cases, here was virtually no line for the engravers to work from, but Turner may have thought this unnecessary, since he would himself have etched most of the plates.

Then Turner began to add finer brushstrokes, still in the same brown pigment, to give detail and to indicate where dense tone would be needed on the copper plate. In a very few of the *Liber* drawings he applied watercolour with a pen, presumably with a steel nib. This gave a scratchy, jagged outline compared to the fine brushes he used more often. Even the fine brushstrokes were applied in the watercolour pigment and medium used elsewhere in the drawing, and not in ink, with one exception, *Crowhurst* (Tate Gallery D08172). Turner expected a considerable degree of interpretation, skill and co-operation from his engravers, especially considering the hard bargains that he drove, and a considerable amount of his surviving correspondence relates to disputes with engravers.[9]

The next stage involved working from dark to light, by removing existing wash to reveal lighter washes, or the offwhite paper support, beneath. Earth pigments are relatively easy to wash off after recent application, but some pigment is usually left behind. The 'sepia', usually a minor component added late in painting, was generally applied and left, because its finer particles would have been difficult to remove from the paper once they had come to rest on the fibres. (Genuine bistre might have presented the same problem, which could account for its non-use by Turner. But a preference for the use of inorganic pigments or sepia post-1800 has been noted by Schwahn[10] too.) Turner frequently added localised washes of one of the other brown pigments mentioned above, either to reserved highlights or to newly-washed-out ones. Turner worked very freely as he created highlights, and did not always make use of his occasional initial sketching for human figures and animals. He created highlights by: reserving areas of paper; occasionally stopping

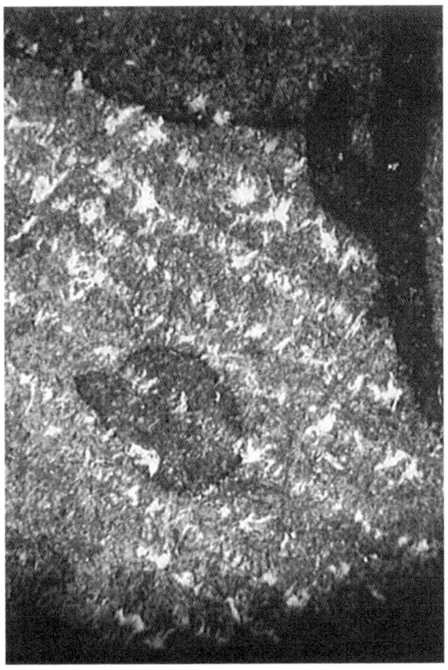

Figure 8. Detail × 7 of Figure 3, showing mezzotint rocker used to give character to a watercolour wash.

them out as well; washing out pigment with a wet brush; drawing the brush-end through a newly-applied and still-wet wash; re-wetting the wash and blotting some of it off; rubbing it off with a moderately soft material, as shown in Figure 3 (perhaps bread: Farington described Turner doing so,[11] and artists were advised to keep bread of differing age and hardness for this purpose); scratching into a dried wash with a fine needle (Figure 4); applying a localised medium-rich brushstroke over a dark wash to give a lighter tone by means of the turbid medium effect. Generally two or three of these techniques can be recognised in each drawing. Sometimes the scratching-out was used only for one crucial detail in the composition, where it gave the brightest highlight, for example in Figure 5 *Near Blair Atholl, Scotland* where only the fishing rod and line have been scratched out. On another occasion, Turner used very light and numerous scratches from a fine needle to depict the floury atmosphere of *Pembury Mill* shown in Figure 6. On occasion Turner made parallel scratches in wash with a mezzotint rocker, for example to indicate tooling marks on stone in *Rivaux Abbey* shown in Figure 7 and for fine details, as shown in Figure 8.

Forrester suggests[8] that the technique of the *Liber* drawings has many affinities with the engraving process, which Turner himself was learning and practising at the time. For example, the effect produced by washing onto wet paper replicates the effect of the aquatint ground which Turner used selectively for *Liber* plates, subsequent washing corresponds to strengthening it, the fine brushstrokes to adding definition and the application of highlights to burnishing and amending the plate at the proof stage. Engravers' tools gave him new means of creating lights on washed paper: it is very likely that he used etching needles of different sizes for scratching-out. The process of working from dark to light is analogous to the primary technique of mezzotint, where the plate is first completely grounded and lights are then created by burnishing and scraping the dark ground.

Techniques for Prints

Examination revealed many more examples of mezzotint than aquatint (as expected, since the *Liber* was advertised originally as being engraved in mezzotint). Aquatint grounds were found in some areas of sky and background. Turner's notes on engravers' proofs relating to the production of certain engravings makes it clear that he chose to specifiy when it was to be used.[8] Softground etching was used on some plates instead of hardground etching. Mezzotint was used additively at the proof stages to correct small areas in many cases and roulette rocker work can be seen in several of the prints examined. Mezzotint and aquatint were used together on some plates. The appearance of these techniques under magnification is shown in Figures 9 and 10. Etched lines varied considerably in width and depth, but were generally very deeply bitten-in: they were used expressively, as shown in Figure 11, which is an etching which Turner washed over in watercolour for the engraver.

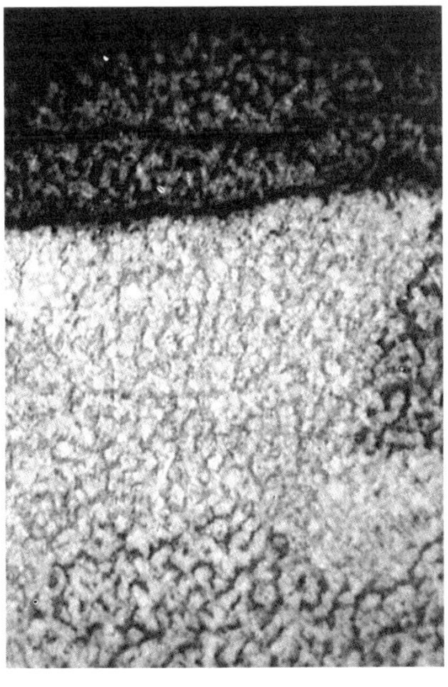

Figure 9. Detail × 7 of Bridge and Goats, *etching, aquatint and mezzotint on paper, image size 181mm by 252mm, 1812, (Tate Gallery A00997), showing different densities of aquatint.*

Conclusion

Turner used mainly inorganic pigments for the *Liber Studiorum* watercolour drawings: burnt umber, burnt sienna and Indian red. Sepia may well be present in small quantity, but could not be identified with certainty. His choice of brown pigment was not related to subject or date of painting. For a given drawing, he most commonly used one of these and added touches of another of them, or of sepia. The later drawings include touches of vermilion, yellow ochre or Prussian blue. The medium was generally gum for the drawings, though areas of glossy-looking gum medium appeared to include a drying oil component, possibly applied as a coating. The printing inks used for etching included burnt umber, ivory or bone black, a Mars red and/or brown, or reduced combinations of these, in a medium of drying oil.

Turner generally prepared *Liber* watercolour drawings by applying wash to wet paper, letting it dry, then applying watery washes as well as brushstrokes of denser watercolour, after which he created highlights by selectively removing areas of wash by a variety of means. Thus, he worked from dark to light. Turner used all

Figure 10. Detail × 7 of Entrance of Calais Harbour, *mezzotint, aquatint and etching on paper, image size 180mm by 267mm, 1816, (Tate Gallery A01116), showing different densities of mezzotint.*

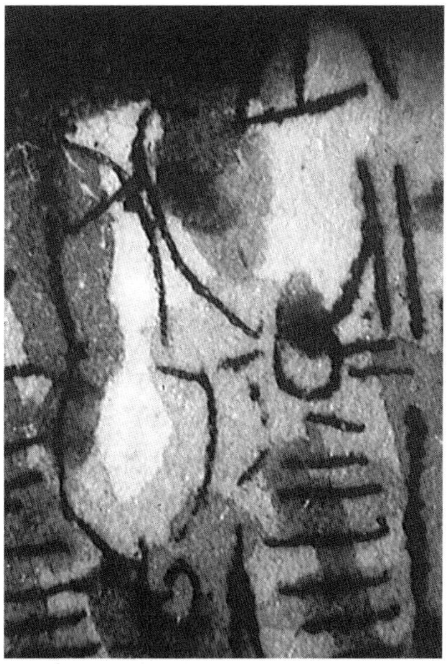

Figure 11. Detail × 7 of Basle, *etching and watercolour on paper, image size 182mm by 255mm, c1806–7, (Tate Gallery D08110, TB CXVI I), showing etched lines, washed with watercolour as a guide to the engraver.*

these techniques in later watercolours, but with less regard to this sequence of operations.

Acknowledgements

Gillian Forrester, Volkswagen Turner Scholar at the Tate Gallery 1993–5, has enthusiastically supported this study, examined the drawings with me, and commented on the text. She provided much information in the course of her own research into the *Liber Studiorum*. Kasia Szeleynski, Head of Paper Conservation, and Heather Norville-Day and Piers Townshend, paper conservators, all at the Tate Gallery, contributed advice, observations and reference materials, as well as studio space for the project, while Stephen Hackney, Head of Conservation Research, also discussed the text. Thanks are due to: Dr Anita Quye who made an FTIR microscope available at the National Museums of Scotland, and Tom Learner, conservation scientist at the Tate Gallery, who ran the software for spectral interpretation, made his spectral library available, and carried out Py-GC-MS. The Electron Microscope Unit of Royal Holloway, University of London, provided backup for the EDX work.

References

1. A.J. Finberg, *The History of Turner's* Liber Studiorum, *with a new catalogue raisonné*, (London: Ernest Benn, 1924).
2. G. Forrester, *Turner's 'Drawing Book': the* Liber Studiorum (London: Tate Gallery Publications, 1996).
3. J.H. Townsend, *Turner's Painting Techniques*, (London: Tate Gallery Publications, 1993).
4. P. Bower, unpublished research.
5. P. Bower, *Turner's Papers. A Study of the Manufacture, Selection and Use of his Drawing Papers 1787–1820*, (London: Tate Gallery Publications, 1990).
6. A. Lyles, and D. Perkins, *Colour into Line: Turner and the Art of Engraving*, (London: Tate Gallery Publications, 1989).
7. J. Gage, *J.M.W. Turner: Gravures/Engravings*, (Charleroi: Ville de Charleroi-Palais des Beaux-Arts, 1994).
8. Forrester, *Turner's 'Drawing Book': the* Liber Studiorum.
9. Lyles and Perkins, *Colour into Line: Turner and the Art of Engraving*, 8.
10. W. Schwahn, *"Bister oder sepia? Braune Tinten und ihre zeichnerische Anwendung"* ("Bistre or sepia? Brown inks and their application in drawing"), in *Zum* Thema Papier und Graphik, Restauratorenblatter, ed. M. Koller and R. Prendtstetten, 14 (1994): 25–30.
11. K. Garlick and A. MacIntyre (eds.), *The Diary of Joseph Farington* vol. VI (New Haven and London: Yale University Press, for Paul Mellon Centre for British Art, 1979), 2281.

A Proposal for the Classification of Painting Recipes

Margriet H. van Eikema Hommes
Kunsthistorisch Instituut,
Herengracht 286, 1016 BX Amsterdam, The Netherlands

Abstract

Since instructions on painting technique, provided by historical sources, are mostly fragmentary and unsystematic, this information is often difficult to interpret. In order to simplify the interpretation, it is proposed to categorize the instructions according to their function within the painting process. By doing so, it is possible to form groups of recipes which painters had at their disposal to obtain a specific aim with respect to painting techniques. In this way, fragmented instructions from divergent sources can be confronted and mutually explained. The present paper contains elements of the book the author is preparing on this subject[1].

Keywords

Painting technique, workshop practice, technical sources, interpretation of recipes

A great number of studies into 15th to 17th century oil paintings has revealed that painters at that time applied their paint in a methodical manner. Although many of such 'recipes' are already known, until now the question of the function of these recipes has received little attention. Workshop handbooks and treatises contain a great number of recipes regarding the build up of the paint layer and often mention the motive for a specific working method.

However, the information regarding painting techniques in historical texts is mostly fragmentary and unsystematic. Therefore, it is difficult to obtain a complete overview of the knowledge and techniques that painters formerly had at their disposal. By studying the instructions regarding painting techniques as to their function, a possibility is offered to structure this information. It also facilitates the interpretation of the divergent recipes. By assembling fragmented instructions with a similar function from divergent sources, the fragmentary information they contain can be connected, completed and explained. The *a priori* condition to be able to do this is that there would be a certain international uniformity in workshop practice as to oil painting. Given the high mobility of painters during their training and at the beginning of their careers, the presumption of a considerable degree of uniformity is justified. The painters' community then, could be compared to the international community of restorers today.

This article gives a survey of the various functions of painting by recipes. On the basis of 17th and early 18th century source material, the intention is to illustrate how focusing on the function can contribute to the interpretation of recipes. Although the reader may be familiar with some of the examples given, it appears from the literature that until now no attempt has been made to develop a system like the following with the above aim in mind.

Recipes with a view to the preservation of the original appearance of the painting

It is generally known, that a paint layer can change so much that in time it may deviate strongly from its original appearance. Discoloration of the paint can be the consequence of the discoloration of certain pigments or the yellowing and darkening of the oil medium; changes may occur as a result of bleeding, a too fast or too slow drying process of the paint and too much or too little sinking in of the medium. Furthermore, some paint layers seem to become more transparent over time.

From the sources examined it emerges that painters were conscious of such problems and took them into account when applying the pigments and media. An example is the handling of the pigment indigo. Owing to its limited light fastness and the fact that the pigment must be mixed with relatively much oil in order to be processed into paint, paint with indigo may discolor. It appears that painters were acquainted with the discoloration of indigo and they also knew that this discoloration especially occurred under the influence of light.[1] Because of its limited colour fastness, it was recommended that the use of indigo should be restricted to the under paint layer. In *The Art of Painting* [...] (1692), the English artlover Marshall Smith advises: "Indigo turns green in time and should be chiefly us'd in dead-colouring".[2]

The Dutch painter Wilhelm Beurs, whose book *De groote waereld in 't kleen geschildert* was published in the same year as Smith's, also advised painting a second layer on top of the indigo. Beurs, however, gives an explanation for this: discoloration of indigo is prevented by this second paint layer:

> [...] notice, that if one wants to make indigo and its colour permanent, it is necessary to glaze or paint a second layer of ultramarine, as it appears lighter or darker in nature.[3]

Beurs' advice could be based on the fact that a paint layer of colourfast ultramarine will function as a filter and reduce the intensity of the light transmitted and consequently protect the indigo from discoloration.

This is just one example of the numerous recipes which take into account the changing of appearance of the painting.

Recipes that take into account the limited compatibility of pigments

When mixed in paint, certain historical pigments can cause a chemical reaction. This could cause the paint to change colour. Sulphur-containing pigments can, for example, react with pigments consisting of lead or copper compounds. However, laboratory tests have proved that, in practice, these reactions almost exclusively occur in an aqueous medium and that problems rarely arise with oil paint.[4] Therefore, it is interesting to note that a great caution was also considered necessary in oil painting, according to the sources. Thus one source often warns about mixtures with verdigris or with orpiment,[5] whereas laboratory tests have proven that in mixtures with these pigments that are incompatible 'in theory' problems rarely occur in practice.[6] Another source cautions about mixtures of pigments concerning which currently – even in theory – no problems whatsoever are known, such as red lake with vermilion and pink and lead white.[7] Several recipes in sources are connected with the [supposed] incompatibility of pigments and the recommendations are to replace these pigments with compatible ones.[8] Furthermore, one often finds recipes which recommend applying the incompatible pigments in different paint layers, for example recipes regarding orpiment. In these recipes orpiment serves nearly exclusively for the last highlights, only applied when the other paint layers are completely dry. An instruction, which De Mayerne noted down from Anthoni van Dijck, is representative of this procedure:

> Painting yellow. One uses orpiment, which is the most beautiful yellow colour one can have [...] but mixed with any other colours it spoils them [...] And it must [only] be used unmixed, after the drapery (for which it is very suitable) has been made with other yellow colours. And on this [paint] when thoroughly dry, one must indicate the light [part of the drapery] with orpiment on the lit side. In this way the result will be very beautiful.[9]

Recipes that make use of differences in hiding power and tinting strength of the pigments

Pigments have different extents of hiding power, varying from opaque to transparent. Also, the tinting strength may vary considerably for any one pigment. Sources frequently recommend employing the various pigments such that their specific qualities are used completely. The advice is to apply pigments with little hiding power in the upper paint layer and to apply pigments with much hiding power and/or tinting strength in the underpainting. For example, the De Mayerne manuscript gives a recipe which recommends applying the pigment ivory black, about which it is mentioned that it possesses *point de corps*, as a translucent paintlayer, a glaze, over an opaque underpainting:

> The deepest black is made of ivory [...] This black does not have body [*n'a point de corps*] and serves to paint over another black, [such as] lamp black as a glaze and then it makes the darkest black.[10]

Written sources recommend glazes for various purposes. They advise glazing an opaque paint layer because of the beauty of the colour obtained[11] or so as to obtain a great number of different colours.[12] In addition, a glaze is recommended for obtaining unity in a specific part of the painting or for toning down a specific part when painted too distinctly. Wilhelm Beurs advises, for example, for the rendering of a red flower:

> [...] when it is painted in the described way and it is dry, glaze or paint it over lightly with only Florentine lake to tone down the strength of the lights and shadows.[13]

A glaze is also recommended for indicating locally the shadow of an object. In the workshop handbook of 'Le petit peintre de St. Jehan', the following recipe is mentioned for rendering a black drapery:

> Black draperie. Lamp black; a little umber, a bit of white. Shadow with ivory black mixed with a little verdigris. For the lights lamp black mixed with white and a little umber.[14]

Since the recipe quoted from the De Mayerne manuscript recommends the pigment ivory black for glazing, one may assume that in this recipe the ivory black has to be applied as a glaze.

Recipes to compensate for differences in drying time

The drying time of oil paint is influenced by the pigments employed. It is for example common knowledge that paint made of black pigments or red lake hardly dries, while lead-containing pigments can accelerate the drying process of oil paint considerably. If the painter takes into consideration the differences in drying time, he can work more efficiently. A great number of recipes are intended to prevent problems as a result of divergent drying times. Because of this, it is frequently advised that slow drying pigments are mixed with a siccative oil or that pigments which accelerate the drying process be added to the paint. Depending on the pigment used one could choose various siccatives. In the workshop handbook of 'Le petit peintre de St. Jehan' various siccatives are advised for various black pigments: "Ivory black [dries] with verdigris, smoke black with umber".[15] This remark explains why in the recipe quoted above verdigris had to be added to a glaze of ivory black.

Furthermore, it seems that the use of very slow drying paints should be restricted to the upper paint layer. De Mayerne recorded for example: "Asphaltum for the rendering of the darkest shadows of the flesh colour, when everything has dried".[16] In this recipe asphaltum will be applied as a glaze since this use is advised in a similar recipe *in Arte poetica e da pintura e symetria com principos da perspectiva* (1615) of the Spanish painter Nunes: "This [asphaltum] is to be used for shadowing the flesh colours in the manner of a glaze after the figure has dried".[17] It is interesting that De Mayerne and Nunes emphasize that the glaze may only be applied after complete drying of the other paint layers. Consequently the glaze can be applied more easily, but moreover more thinly, and will therefore dry more quickly.

Recipes with respect to fast and easy painting

The choice of a specific use of material or a specific painting technique may further depend on the fact that, as a result of this technique, one could paint faster and more easily. In the sources one regularly finds recipes in which a specific method is recommended for this very reason. In *El museo pictórico* (1724) the Spanish painter Palomino, for example, offers two different methods to finish a blue drapery, which is underpainted with smalt, white pigment and indigo. He mentions that the second method is the easier:

> When the *bosquexo* [underpainting] is dry, go over it with only fine smalt and white tempered only with walnut oil, and this may be improved by mixing a little turpentine spirit into the oil [...] . But the easiest way to work the finishing touches is to apply a glaze of smalt alone over the entire underpainting of the drapery, diluting it with the walnut oil and turpentine spirit. Then work over the glaze, and darken the darks with indigo alone.[18]

Note that only for the "easier" method does Palomino use indigo in the upper paint layer.

Recipes that take price differences into account

There used to be considerable differences in prices between the various pigments. Ocres and other earth pigments were rather inexpensive, but the price of bright yellow, red and blue pigments could often be considerable. Differences in price not only existed between various pigments, but also between the various qualities of a type of pigment. In the De Mayerne manuscript one finds, for example, a price list from which it appears that red lake of a good quality could be 25 times more expensive than the lesser types.[19] The painter would try to minimize the use of these costly pigments. By means of a systematic method of working he could, for example, only use the expensive pigments in the upper paint layer. The next recipe concerns an economical utilization of a relatively expensive pigment, vermilion. In *Der wohl anführende Mahler* (1719) the German painter Cröker advises:

> If you want to paint with vermilion, and employ it economically, ground first the '*Stüde*' [?] with red earth mixed with enough lead white, such that it becomes light red or skin colour, leave it to dry, and repaint this with vermilion. In this way the vermilion will be brighter, and one does not need so much of it.[20]

The Spanish painter Hidalgo recommends the same procedure in *Principos para estudiar el noblilisimo y real Arte de la Pintura* [...](1693), but without mentioning the function of this working method:

> If it is to be red, then the first coat is put on with almagra [= red earth] and red lead, and the last with vermilion and carmine.[21]

In the light of Cröker's advice, it is plausible that Hidalgo's recipe was also intended to reduce the costs.

Recipes for the indication of light and shadow and the rendering of objects

In the period examined, life-like reproduction was one of the most important ambitions in painting skills. In the course of time, various systems were developed to render these effects in the quickest, best and easiest way. Many of these procedures are described in recipes given in the sources examined, where it may be indicated which pigments and which medium one should use and in which sequence and in which way light and shadow have to be indicated. In *Het Schilderboeck* (1604) Karel van Mander, for example, warns that to render velvet, light and shadow have to be applied in a way which is different from that used to render other draperies:

> In constrast to [your] other textile, where you render with light paint all the relief in the folds, this is completely different with velvet [draperies], as you make these entirely dark and paint flat highlights only on the reflecting sides.[22]

It is interesting to compare this advice with an instruction regarding the painting of red velvet from the workshop handbook of 'Le petit peintre de St. Jehan':

> Red velvet. Red lake with couperose. Shadow with the same colour and a little lamp black. On the lit side [paint with] vermilion only by means of lines [without relief].[23]

The two recipes have several similarities. They both recommend applying a dark paint layer first. Moreover, they both suggest rendering the lights flat, without relief. Furthermore, the instructions appear to complement each other. The recipe of 'Le petit peintre de St. Jehan' provides information about the rendering of shadows and Van Mander mentions the exact place where the highlights should be painted.

By following these recipes, effects were not obtained by accident, but because the painter was certain of his results in advance. In this way, a painting could be built up accurately, which had several advantages. The painter could estimate the quantity of materials required for the painting so that the costs could be closely controlled.

Recipes to simplify the organization of the representation

Another advantage of working according to recipes was that one could divide the painting process into different phases. In the 17th century, for example, it was common practice to specify aspects such as composition, the main division of light and shadow and, according to some painting procedures, also the choice of the colours in the underpaint layer, the 'deadcolour'. After the 'deadcolouring', the painting process was divided into the following steps: first, the 'painting up' or 'finishing' and, second, the phase of 'retouching', in which the last details were painted. In the sources a large number of recipes refer to this working sequence. For example, in the *Groot Schilderboek* (1707) the Dutch painter Gerard de Lairesse mentions that during the 'deadcolouring' one should organize the following parts of the representation:

> Now, so as not to work in vain, one must bear in mind before all else that the overall harmony and illusion [= *houding*[24]] be well observed: that the tints and colours be arranged in such a way that, from the requirements of the recession and distance, when the eye glances at the painting, everything has an appearance of solidity [= *welstand*] and its appropriate qualities: then for the painting up [= *opmaken*] no much effort is required.[25]

Furthermore, it is important that De Lairesse goes into the function of the layered working sequence. He mentions that when the painter 'paints up' a well 'deadcoloured' painting, this has the advantage that he no longer needs to occupy himself with the organization of the representation as a whole, but can concentrate completely on the precise elaboration of the separate parts of the painting.[26] These pieces of advice may contribute to the interpretation of instructions regarding the layered working sequence from other sources. For example, in the light of De Lairesse's advice, it becomes apparent why the contemporary Dutch painter Beurs recommends 'painting up' the details of the representation only after "everything [of the representation] is reproduced with an appearance of solidity [= *in een goede welstand gevonden word*]".[27]

Recipes concerning the sequence of painting

Many recipes in sources refer to the working sequence the painter must keep to during the underpainting or 'deadcolouring' and 'painting up'. For example, during the underpainting, it is recommended that the painter proceeds, depending on the subject to be painted, from the foreground to the background or in the reverse sequence. Beurs advises, for example:

> The figures (to begin with) the painter must apply first. Both in a room, a landscape or in another meeting place of people. In a room it is not indelicate to paint the rear last. But in a landscape after the figures (if they are painted herein because of a history or [just] as ornament) [one has to paint] the sky, the mountains and the earth [= *gronden*] from the background to the foreground.[28]

Beurs does not mention the reason for the recommended sequence. However, some advice from De Lairesse, who recommends a comparable working sequence, may provide information about this. He advises:

> About deadcolouring and how one should do this surely and skilfully. It is my opinion that it is the best and surest way to begin from the background, especially when the landscape is most distinct. Since all objects should be subordinated to the brightness or gloominess of the sky and the tints of the objects must be found, the light on the foreground, and the strength of the figures, must be adapted to this; if begun otherwise, these aspects will be difficult to determine. However, when figures or other large objects are the most pronounced [in the painting], it is better to begin where one will see the greatest strength, on the first or second ground, and in this way proceed in the opposite direction.[29]

Recipes concerned with the division of labour within the workshop

By splitting up the painting process into different phases, division of labour became possible in the workshop, resulting in a quick and efficient production of paintings. Sometimes, sources go into this division of labour in the workshop, as in the treatise *Diálogos de la pintura* (1633) by the Spanish painter Carducho:

> The expert painter's tasks are to make sketches, to study every part of a composition separately, and then to join all the parts in a finished cartoon or drawing, arriving at the composition according to the precepts of good art. He gives this and the other drawings to the *oficial*, who transfers or draws them onto the canvas or wall by the squaring system; he then paints the *boquexo* [underpainting], and applies the colours, which is called finishing or impasting. The master is present to watch with care, to advise with words, and to correct with the brush when the *oficial* errs or when the work does not agree with the drawing (this is called corrupting the contours). When the *oficial* leaves the painting as finished, the master comes back to retouch and perfect it, which is the ultimate step [...].[30]

A similar procedure emerges, for example, from a notebook of the Flemish painter Pieter van Lint (1609–1693), in which he describes his duties as an apprentice in the workshop of the Antwerp painter Artus Wolffort, from 1624 to 1631.[31] Van Lint gives a detailed account of the paintings he did, and distinguishes in his work the phases: *dotverven* [= to deadcolour], *overdoen* or *vort te doen* [= to paint over] and *rectoceren* [= to retouch]. Several times, Van Lint mentions that he started to *overdoen* or *vort te doen* a painting, but he does not mention whether he painted the 'deadcolour'. For example: "and then, after the 17th of November, I begun to *overdoen* a Hercules, which I finished on 21 November". In the light of Carducho's description, it is plausible that these paintings were deadcoloured by another apprentice in the workshop.

Conclusion

By studying instructions concerning painting techniques in historical sources and starting from the idea of their function within the painting process, structure can be seen in this often divergent and fragmented information, such that the interpretation is simplified. A survey has been presented of the groups of functions that is most important to distinguish. On this basis it is possible to examine each recipe for its – one or several – technical painting aims. In this way various aspects of one recipe can be examined separately, and be compared with other recipes that refer to the same aspect of painting technique.

This categorization is only possible if one takes all European sources over a period of several (15th to 18th) centuries together. Once this is done, gradual changes and possible local variations emerge from the mass of data.

Acknowledgements

I am grateful to Prof. E. van de Wetering at the University of Amsterdam for reading and commenting on this text.

Notes and references

1. For example, M. Merrifield, *Original Treatises on the Arts of Painting* (2 parts) (New York, 1967), 817.
2. M. Smith, *The Art of painting* [...] (London, 1692), (Complete photocopy: Historical Department of the Central Research Laboratory for Objects of Art and Science in Amsterdam), 69.
3. W. Beurs, *De Groote Waereld in 't Kleen Geschildert* [...] (Amsterdam, 1692), (Complete photocopy: Historical Department of the Central Research Laboratory for Objects of Art and Science in Amsterdam), 40.
4. Chemical reactions mostly fail to occur because the pigment particles are separated by a layer of the oil medium. For example, in a oil medium, lead white, which can easily react with sulphur, appears to be compatible with sulphur-containing pigments, such as vermilion and ultramarine. In numerous paintings in which lead white is used mixed with

these pigments, no discoloration has been demonstrated. Concerning vermilion see: R. Gettens and R.. Feller, "Vermillion and cinnabar," in *Artists' Pigments. A Handbook of their History and Characteristics*, ed. A. Roy, (New York, 1993), 166. Concerning ultramarine see: J. Plesters, "Ultramarine Blue, Natural and Artificial," in Roy, *Artists' pigments*, 44.

5. Concerning verdigris see, for example: E. Berger, *Quellen für Maltechnik während der Renaissance und deren Folgezeit XVL.–XVIII. Jahrhundert* [...] (Walluf/Nendeln, 1973), 100. Concerning orpiment see, for example: Beurs, *De groote waereld*, 12.
6. Concerning verdigris see: H. Kühn, "Verdigris and Copper Resinate", in Roy, *Artists' pigments*, 136–137. Concerning auripigment see: A. Wallert, "Orpiment and Realgar," *Studies in Conservation* 39 (1984): 50.
7. For example: Berger, *Quellen für Maltechnik*, 250, 272. Recent publications about the qualities of pink, lead white, red lake and vermilion make no reference to any problem. See, respectively: A. Stoll, "Gelbe Planzenlacke, Schüttgelb und Saffran," *Maltechnik und Restauro* 78, (1981): 73–110; R. Gettens, H. Kühn and W.Chase, "Lead White," in Roy, *Artists' pigments*, 67– 81; K. Wehlte, *Werkstoffen und Techniken der Malerei* (Ravensburg 1981); R. Gettens and R. Feller, "Vermillion and cinnabar," in Roy, *Artists' pigments*, 159–182.
8. For example: Berger, *Quellen für Maltechnik*, 250.
9. Berger, *Quellen für Maltechnik*, 338.
10. Ibid., 104.
11. Johann Melchio Cröker, *Der wohl anführende Mahler, Herausgegeben und mit einen Einleitung, Bibliographie und Glossen versehen von Ulrich Schießl. Nachdruck der Ausgabe Jena 1736* (Mittenwald, 1982), 97.
12. Smith, *The art of painting*, 84.
13. Beurs, *De groote waereld*, 38.
14. Berger, *Quellen für Maltechnik*, 256.
15. Ibid., 254.
16. Ibid., 248.
17. Z.Veliz, *Artists, Techniques in Golden Age Spain* (Cambrich, 1986), 4. For the Spanish sources I made use of (edited) translations given by Z. Veliz.
18. Ibid., 166.
19. Berger, *Quellen für Maltechnik*, 248.
20. Cröker, *Der wohl anführende Mahler*, 97.
21. Veliz, *Artists, techniques*, 137. Red lead will probably be added to accelerate the drying process of the red earth.
22. H. Miedema, *Den Grondt der Edel Vry Schilder-const* [...], (Utrecht, 1973), 243.
23. Berger, *Quellen für Maltechnik*, 256: '*Sur le jour du vermillon seul par traits*': Larousse: *Designer au traits: ligne d'un design qui n'est pas ombré.*
24. P. Taylor, "The Concept of Houding in Dutch Art Theory, " *Journal of the Warburg and Courtauld Institutes* 55 (1992): 210–232.
25. G. de Lairesse, *Groot Schilderboeck* (Amsterdam, 1707), (Amsterdam: Facsimilé publication of the second edition 1740, 1969), 12.
26. Ibid., 13.
27. Beurs, *De groote waereld*, 53.
28. Ibid., 51–52.
29. De Lairesse, *Groot Schilderboeck*, 12.
30. Veliz, *Artists, techniques*.
31. Archive of the Institut Néerlandais, Paris. Inv. Nr. 433. A transcription of a part of the notebook is given by: H. Vlieghe, "De leerpraktijk van een jonge schilder. Het notitieboekje van Pieter van Lint in het instituut Néerlandais te Parijs," *Jaarboek van het Koninklijk Museum voor Schone Kunsten Antwerpen* (1979): 249–279.

Mongolian Thangka Paintings from the 18th and 19th Centuries. Techniques and Use of Materials in Thangka Paintings

Karin Vestergaard
The National Museum of Denmark, Department of Conservation,
Bevaringsafdelingen, Postboks 260, Brede,
DK-2800 Lyngby, Denmark

Abstract

Thangkas have been painted in Tibet since the 13th century and in Mongolia since the 17th century. This paper summarises previous investigations into the technology of thangka paintings and, on the basis of further research, describes the technology of 18th and 19th century Mongolian thangkas. Mongolian thangkas exhibit various characteristic details which demonstrate that variations in technique exist according to region and period.

Keywords

Thangka painting, Mongolian painting, Asian art, paint technology, painting materials, historical paint technology

The thangka comprises a painted motif on a scroll, which consists of a very thin grounded cotton canvas. This is sewn into a textile framing and a thin textile curtain covers the front of the painting. Hide glue is used as binding medium for the pigments.

Thangkas are sacred religious pictures used by Lamaist Buddhists in Tibet, Nepal, Mongolia and certain parts of China. Thangka paintings were known in Tibet in the 13th century, but they were first produced and used in Mongolia at the beginning of the 17th century.

Thangka paintings depict Buddhas, deities or narrative stories related to Buddhism. The sacred aspect and religious use of the thangka required that it should be painted in strict accordance to certain iconographic conventions that were passed from master to pupil through the centuries, thus ensuring a long and lasting tradition.

Throughout the 700-year history of the thangka the pictures have been executed with the same basic paint technology. Some earlier investigations and papers suggest that small variations exist in the technologies of thangkas from different periods and geographical locations. This paper summarises some of the technological investigations already published and it also present a wider investigation into Mongolian thangka paintings from the 18th and 19th centuries.[1] Mongolian paint technology is compared with that of Tibet. The investigation demonstrates that technical variations do exist in the thangka painting. The result of this research should be regarded as the first stage of what is ultimately intended to be a comprehensive review of historical paint technology employed in thangka paintings.

At the end of the 16th century Mongolia converted to Lamaist Buddhism, as practised in Tibet over the previous 500 years. The thangkas were introduced at the same time and from the beginning of the 17th century they were painted and used by the Buddhists in Mongolia. Thus Mongolia inherited a type of picture, which in style, iconography and paint technology had a history and tradition stretching back 500 years.

The thangka paintings of Mongolia can be characterised as "Late Style", a generic term which describes thangka painting throughout Central Asia in the 17th to 19th centuries. During the 18th century, Mongolian painters attained a very high standard in their own right, and over a period of time evolved their own variation on "Late Style" by incorporating Chinese elements into their pictures and using brighter and stronger colours.

"Late Style" is not well described in art history literature. Because of the mixture and uniformity of styles in paintings from this period, it is difficult to distinguish between pictures from different geographical regions. Descriptions of the Mongolian style or school, or for that matter Mongolian thangka paintings in general, are very sparse.

Until now there has been little tradition of research and collection of technical data with regard to the thangkas in the discussions of art historians, but there is no doubt that a technological history of thangka paintings will be most useful in the description and attribution of paintings in terms of period, geographical location and individual artist.

Mongolian painters

Throughout the 17th century painters' workshops were established at the larger monasteries in Mongolia. In the beginning the painter would have been Tibetan and, since some of the monasteries were funded by the Chinese Empire, the so-called Imperial monasteries, it is likely that there were Chinese artists employed in the workshops as well. As the monastery system became well established and the demand for thangkas in Mongolia increased, it can be assumed that, certainly from the start of the 18th century, indigenous artists, trained in the workshops, would have been producing thangkas.

The painters' workshops were probably organised in the same way as those in Tibet. The workshops would have been arranged in guilds and pupils would have undergone an apprenticeship lasting about eight years. Upon completion of their apprenticeship the Mongolian painters would most likely have gained further experience by travelling, as was also the custom in Tibet.[2]

Independent painters with their own small workshops were to be found in the larger cities and, Mongolian being a predominantly nomadic society, some painters wandered from market to market. These independent painters catered largely for the layman.

The Mongolian infrastructure was well developed and trade networks flourished in the cities and the seasonal markets as well as through the monasteries. Consequently the Mongolian painters had no difficulty obtaining the materials they required. Virtually all of this trade was in the hands of the Chinese.

Throughout the 300-year history of thangka painting in Mongolia the painters followed the traditional paint technology. Nevertheless they did develop small variations which characterise Mongolian paintings.

Material for investigation

The technical investigations presented in this paper were carried out on paintings from the thangka collection of the National Museum of Denmark. This collection contain thangkas from both Tibet and Mongolia from the 18th and 19th centuries. The thangkas from Mongolia number 150, which is unusual, both in terms of numbers and in the homogeneity of paintings. Many aspects are represented in the Mongolian paintings, not only with regard to iconography and style, but also in terms of various levels of skill and quality. These investigations centred on the Mongolian material with some reference investigations carried out on Tibetan thangkas.[3]

Technology and materials

Canvas

Thangkas from Tibet, Mongolia and Nepal are all painted on thin cotton canvas or cloth. The canvas was stretched on a working frame by means of a string system which allowed for further stretching during the working process. Information from available literature indicates that Tibetan painters used mostly Indian cotton but it is most likely that canvas for Mongolian paintings originated in China.

Previous investigations demonstrate variation in the quality of canvas according to period and region.[4] The investigations into Mongolian canvas confirm the existence of regional variations. Threadcounts are lower than those in Tibetan and Nepalese paintings from the same period. It is characteristic of Mongolian canvas from the 18th and 19th centuries that it is more coarse and open woven than other canvas from that time (Table 1).

Groundings

The canvas of the thangkas was grounded on both sides with a relatively thin layer of material. This material comprised a filler using hide glue as binder. In most cases the grounding was polished to obtain a smooth and elastic surface. Sometimes the painter sized the canvas before grounding.

Table 1. Thangka paintings: thread counts

Non-Mongolian from different centuries		Mongolian, 18th and 19th centuries National Museum of Denmark Reg. no.	
Nepal 12th	33 × 22	RXI 53	15 × 13
Nepal 14th	15 × 32	RXI 62	13 × 13
Tibet 15–16th	18 × 22	RXI 65	12 × 12
Tibet 14–15th	21 × 18	RXI 68	13 × 14
Nepal 16th	16 × 18	RXI 69	15 × 16
Central Tibet 16th	23 × 22	RVII 157	13 × 18
Tibet 16–17th	31 × 32	RVII 160	20 × 20
East Tibet 18–19th	35 × 30	RXIV 45	14 × 13
Central Tibet 19th	25 × 29	RXIV 58	15 × 13
Tibet 19th	28 × 35	RXVIII 25	14 × 16
Tibet 19–20th	18 × 19	RXVIII 73	14 × 14
East Tibet 19th	27 × 29	RXVIII 33	16 × 14
Nepal 19th	22 × 21	RXI 59	17 × 19
Buthan 19–20th	26 × 25	RXI 66	17 × 14
China/Tibet 18–19th	26 × 27	RXI 70	17 × 14
China/Tibet 18–19th	27 × 26		

Previous publications have pointed out differences in grounding technique according to period, region and from workshop to workshop. Differences can be seen, not only in the thickness of the grounding and the extent to which it penetrates the canvas, but also in the degree of polishing. There has been no thorough analysis of grounding techniques from different periods and regions characterising these variations, but an article written by Hungtington must be mentioned here.[5] He notes that the groundings of 18th- and 19th-century thangkas from Nepal and central and eastern Tibet have a superior uniformity with little penetration into the canvas. He further notes that the filler from central and eastern Tibet is very finely ground and the surface evenly polished, as opposite to western Tibetan groundings, which are very highly polished, and Nepalese groundings from the same period, which are coarsely polished.

Research indicates that Mongolian grounding is similar to 18th- and 19th-century groundings from central and eastern Tibet with regard to thickness and polishing, but with a significant difference: as a result of the tradition of having a more liquid consistency, the Mongolian grounding penetrated the canvas completely.

The analyses of the Mongolian thangkas show, moreover, that they contain kaolin as a filler. Previous investigations and reference analysis on Tibetan thangkas indicated the use primarily of chalk as filler, and only rarely kaolin. Thus the predominance of kaolin as filler would point decidedly to Mongolian origin.[6]

Binding media

Thangka painters used hide glue as a binding medium in both the grounding and pigment.

According to the literature, Tibetan painters in earlier times prepared their own hide glue from yak skin. The art of thangka painting is still practised today and we know that Tibetan and Nepalese painters, at least in our century, use hide glue from ox skin, ready-made in India.

The literature makes no mention as to how Mongolian painters in the 18th and 19th centuries obtained their binding media. It is quite likely that they manufactured the binder themselves, just as their Tibetan counterparts did, but it is by no means certain which skin material they used. Unlike Tibet, there are very few yaks in Mongolia.

Analysis of Mongolian binding media shows no variations in thangkas originating from that region. All the Mongolian thangkas have the same protein binding medium, which is slightly different to that used in many Tibetan reference thangkas from the same period. So far, analysis of binding medium has not yet revealed the precise identity of the protein used in the Mongolian thangkas or indeed whether other materials have been added to the protein. Further analysis will, in due course, lead to a precise description of the medium.

Pigments

The analysis of the Mongolian pigments shows that they are the same as the traditional inorganic pigments used in Tibetan thangkas, namely: azurite, malachite, vermillion, oripigment, minium and lampblack. In addition, the Mongolian thangkas have some variations in the use of pigments.

Ocre and kaolin, widely used in Tibetan paintings, are not found very often in Mongolian paintings.

The analysis also revealed the use of pigments in the Mongolian paintings that have not previously been associated with thangka paintings. For example Prussian blue and smalt were discovered, although the most common blue pigment used in Mongolia paintings remains azurite.

As well as malachite, it was discovered that copper chloride was widely used as a green pigment. In addition, examples were also found of copper phosphate and copper resinate. The 18th and 19th centuries saw the world-wide introduction of a great variety of green pigments and these were also used in Mongolian thangka paintings – green pigments that had not previously been used in this context.

White lead was shown to be the primary white pigment in Mongolian thangkas. The use of this pigment is a feature of Mongolian paintings from the 18th and 19th centuries. The use and mixing of pigments to obtain certain colours is often very characteristic of individual painters or workshops.

Previous literature on Tibetan thangka paintings describes various organic pigments: red lac-dye,[7] red sandalwood and yellow colours made of dye stuffs derived from various plants, for example Utpala, Saffron and Rosa Serica.

Mongolian thangkas were also painted with lac-dye, but, unlike the Tibetan paintings, very little use was made of yellow organic pigments. These were found in only a few paintings, where they were precipitated with aluminium.

A list of the pigments used in Tibetan and Mongolian thangka paintings is given in Table 2.

Painting technique

Figure 1. Mongolian thangka from the 18th–19th century

Thangkas painted after the 17th century can be characterised by a technique known as "shading". (Figures 1 and 2 show details from a thangka painted in this way.) The shading effect was achieved in various ways but was always used to obtain a graduation between different colours or a change of shade in the same colour. Shading was used to depict a degree of space, form and shadow within the motif without creating the three-dimensional appearance seen in European painting.

Shading was achieved by applying layers of paint on a dry ground colour. Tibetan thangkas from the 18th and 19th centuries are shaded from light to dark, that is dark shading colours were applied to a lighter ground.

Essentially, Mongolian thangkas are shaded in the same way as those from Tibet with one important variation: Mongolian paintings are generally shaded with lighter or white colours. The ground colour was usually a mid-tone and could be shaded lighter or darker.

There are many other technical variations to be found in Mongolian paintings, but they should be regarded as characteristic of individual painters or workshops rather than of Mongolian painting in general.

Motifs and outlining

Motifs in thangka paintings are generally outlined, sometimes in various colours, depending on the motif's main colour. It is characteristic of Mongolian paintings

Table 2. Inorganic pigments in thangka paintings

Blue	Green	Red	Orange	Yellow	Black	White
Azurite	Malachite	Vermillion	Minium	Oripigment	Lamp black	Kaolin
Ultramarine	Green earth			Yellow ocre		Chalk
Indigo	Verdigris					Zinc white
	Emerald green					Lead white
	Sceele's green					
		Mongolian, 18th and 19th centuries				
Azurite	Malachite	Vermillion	Minium	Oripigment	Lamp black	Kaolin
Prussian blue	Copper chloride			(ocre)		(kaolin)
Smalt	Copper phosphate					
Indigo	Copper resinate					

Figure 2. Detail from the thangka of Figure 1. Shading technique with a white shading

that the outlining is more pronounced with fewer nuances than the Tibetan paintings. Tibetan thangkas are usually outlined in indigo which the Mongolian rarely used, black being the preferred colour.

Many details of a thangka painting's motif were gilded. This was done by applying gold powder on a undercoat, which radiated through the gold. The gilded motif would be outlined with a colour. The undercoat used in Tibetan paintings would be either ocre or minium and the outlining would be carried out in red lac-dye. The gilding in Mongolian paintings would be applied in the same way but the primary undercoat would be either pink colour or minium, – the ocre undercoat is seldom found in Mongolian gilding. The Mongolian outlining would be either vermillion, minium or black. The choice of pigments for undercoat and outlining is quite characteristic of the thangka's region of origin.

Conclusion

Even though Mongolian thangka paintings from the 18th and 19th centuries are carried out in the same tradition and with the same paint technology as those from Tibet, there are significant technological differences in the grounding, binding media, and pigments, as well as minor variations in paint technique that are specific to the Mongolian paintings.

Further investigations and analysis of thangkas from different periods and regions will provide a comprehensive technological history of thangka paintings, and the knowledge of paint technology will be a vital part in the description and attributions of thangkas in terms of periods and region.

Acknowledgement

I would like to thank the Department of Conservation and Laboratory, The National Museum of Denmark, and The School of Conservation, The Danish Royal Academy of Fine Arts.

Notes and references

1. Of the literature already published the following require special mention:
   - O.P. Agrawal,"Study and Conservation of Thangkas" in ICC Preprint, Kyoto.
   - S.L. Daygab, *Tibetan Religious Art* (Weisbaden, 1977).
   - K.I Duffy and J.A. Elgar, "An Investigation of palette and Colour Notations Used to Create a Set of Tibetan Thangkas" in *Historical Painting techniques, Materials, and Studio Practice*, Preprint (University of Leiden, 1995)
   - J.C. Hungtington, "The Technique of Tibetan Paintings", *Studies in Conservation* 15 (1970).
   - D. Jackson and J. Jackson, *Tibetan Thangka Paintings, Methods and materials*, (London 1984).
   - V.R. Mehra, "Note on the Technique and Conservation of some Thangka paint ings", *Studies in Conservation* 15 (1970).
   - V. Ronge, "Das Tibetische Handwerktum vor 1959", *Beiträge zu Südasien Forschung*, 43 (1978).
   - A. Shaftel, "Notes on the Technique of Tibetan Thangkas" *Journal of the American Institute for Conservation* 30, no 1 (1991).
2. Ronge, "Das Tibetische".
3. The information presented in this paper represents only a part of the findings of a widespread investigation into the technology of Mongolian thangka paintings. Further information can be obtained from the author relating, amongst other things, to the technique and the style of painting characteristic of individual painters and workshops. Articles in *Zeischrift für Kunsttechnologie und Konservierung* and in an international publication on Asiatic art will be published in the future.
4. See note 3.
5. Hungtington, "The Technique".
6. The investigation of Mongolian groundings was comprehensive and the results can be considered as representative for Mongolian thangka paintings, but they cannot preclude the possibility that chalk was at some time used as a filler.
7. Lac-dye is the generic term of the Laccifer lac, which is produced as a by-product in the manufacture of Shellac.

A Preliminary Attempt to Identify Ruben's Studio Practice

Jørgen Wadum
Royal Cabinet of Paintings Mauritshuis,
P.O. Box 536, 2501 CM The Hague, The Netherlands

Abstract

Paintings in the style of P.P. Rubens have been examined with the aid of infrared reflectography. It is being proposed that certain phenomena along the contours of large scale Rubens-like figures in two mythological paintings could be ascribed as final corrections made by Rubens himself. Similar corrections have been observed in a painting by Rubens as well as in his drawings. Based on this it is being suggested that paintings in the 'Style of Rubens' showing these type of corrections may be re-attributed to "Studio of Rubens", adding to our understanding of the large output of paintings from this Antwerp master.

Keywords

Rubens, infrared reflectography, studio practice, under drawing, corrections

Figure 1. Studio of Rubens, "Venus and Adonis", panel, 59 × 81 cm. Mauritshuis inv. 254

Figure 2. Studio of Rubens and Jan Brueghel I, "Naiads Filling the Horn of Plenty", panel, 67 × 107 cm. Mauritshuis, inv. 234

That Peter Paul Rubens (1577–1640) had a large studio producing a vast number of paintings which could not all have been painted by the artist himself, was well known even in Rubens's own time. Paintings by the master are still the subject of study in order to clarify his painting technique in all its aspects from drawing, preparatory sketches to his finished paintings.[1] Two paintings showing large scale figures in the style of Rubens have been analyzed with infrared reflectography (IRR). Along the contours corrections seem to be present, possibly indicating that Rubens himself retouched the paintings before they left his studio.

Only a few of the hands of artists who worked in Rubens studio as pupils and assistants have been identified. On the other hand, a number of independent painters, such as Jan Brueghel I and II, Frans Snijders, Jan Wildens, and Paul de Vos, are well documented as regular collaborators with Rubens.[2]

There are a number of paintings, often neglected, which show strong affinities with Rubens's style, but are not of the same quality as those by the master himself. These paintings, referred to as "Manner of Rubens" or "Copy of Rubens", may, however, come from the master's assembly line for the production of paintings.

Two paintings in the Mauritshuis may provide evidence of this. One, formerly described as "Copy after Rubens", but presently as "Studio of Rubens", shows "Venus and Adonis" (Figure 1).[3] This painting is a free copy after Rubens's original in Düsseldorf,[4] and was further repeated in a number of versions now found in St Petersburg[5] and Dresden.[6]

The other painting, previously attributed to Hendrik van Balen, but recently attributed to Jan Brueghel I and "Studio of Rubens"[7] shows the "Naiads Filling the Horn of Plenty" (Figure 2).[8] Ten out of twelve figures in this painting derive from the oeuvre of Rubens, but they are all from different sources.[9] Both paintings contain figures executed by two different hands.

As the following will demonstrate, the two paintings mentioned above are examples of pictures done by artists, who knew well, not only Rubens's oeuvre, but also his style of painting. More important Rubens's hand may be discernible in the paintings, thus placing them in his studio.

"Naiads Filling the Horn of Plenty" was produced around 1612–1615,[10] as determined by the panel maker's mark on the reverse of the panel, a mark identical to that found on three other panels of almost identical size and out of the same tree trunk.[11] The "Venus & Adonis" panel can, both in terms of technique and materials and stylistically, be placed in the same period.

In studies with IRR, certain phenomena are visible which may lead to the conclusion that Rubens inspected the paintings and, before they left the studio, made a number of corrections.

It is apparent that in both paintings the outlines of the figures have been corrected before the panel was being passed on to the landscape painter. Along the thigh of Venus's right leg and along the right contour of Adonis's left leg in "Venus & Adonis" brush strokes of paint containing carbon black have been applied. Also the area between the faces of the two lovers shows similar corrections. The corrections show up dark with reflectography (Figure 3). In this context it is interesting to note that the entry on the almost identical "Venus and Adonis" in St Petersburg reads: "La radiographie fait constater des retouches à l'intersection des pieds de Vénus et d'Adonis, ainsi qu'au profil de Vénus".[12]

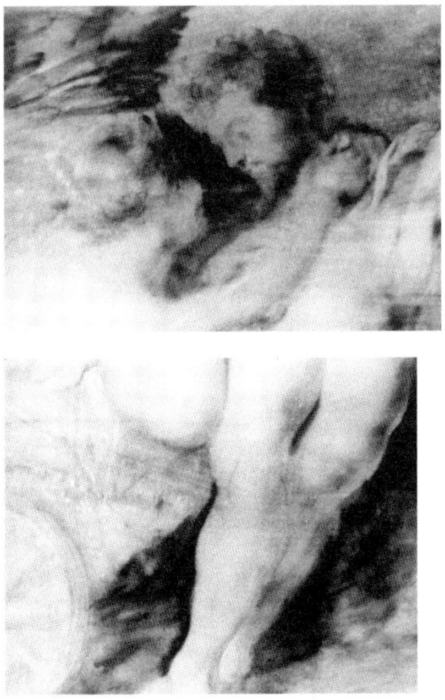

Figure 3. IRR details of "Venus and Adonis". Photo H. Geene/J. Wadum

Figure 4.. IRR detail of "Naiads Filling the Horn of Plenty". Photo H. Geene/J. Wadum

Figure 5. P.P. Rubens, "Kneeling Male Nude", drawing, 520 × 390 mm. Museum Boymans-van Beuningen, inv. V.52, Rotterdam

Equally the contours of the stomach and back of the seated "Naiad", right, adjusting the fruits in the "Cornucopia" (Figure 4) have been straightened up. The contour of her back is modelled in a curved line, but towards the right showing a loose, hatched outline typical of an area adjacent to an alteration.[13] In this painting the stomach and breast of another "Naiad", reaching for the fruit in a tree, have also been corrected to a more beneficial form.

The first of these corrections, of the outline of the woman's back, done with diagonal hatching, is comparable with similar corrections of drawn studies in Rubens's own hand, as observed in a "Kneeling Male Nude, seen from behind" (Figure 5).[14] In this drawing Rubens made corrections around the knee and angle of the leg in the lower left corner.[15]

Equally important is the comparison with the blocking in of contours in Rubens's oil sketches, a study that still has to be done. However, a first indication of the possible outcome of this investigation would be a comparison with "The Daughters of Cerops Discovering the Young Erichthonius",[16] where the woman on the left has been separated from the background by an almost total blocking in of her outline.

The underdrawing of the landscape in the "Naiad holding the Horn of Plenty" can be related to the kind of loose sketchy indications of a form or composition typical of Rubens's drawings.[17] This would probably indicate that Rubens would first have sketched the composition of the landscape on the ready-prepared panel. Then, Rubens or his pupil would arrange the figures, probably based on Rubens's sketches. In the third step, the figures would be painted and, fourth, the contours would be corrected by Rubens himself. Finally, Jan Brueghel I would have painted in the landscape according to the rough outline initially made by Rubens. Rubens's workshop would therefore be regarded as the atelier taking the initiative to produce this painting.

A similar schematic indication of the landscape can be observed with IRR in another a painting signed by both Rubens and Jan Brueghel I (Figure 6). The "Earthly Paradise"[18] with figures (and a few of the animals?) masterly executed by Rubens, shows in IRR comparable corrections along contours of the figures, such as along the hollow of the knee of Eve and around Adam's hands and feet and along his profile. The master obviously applied the same sort of scrutiny to his own paintings as he did to his pupils' work.

In the case of this painting we must also imagine the panel with its white ground, a sketchy outline of the landscape with an applied streaky isolating layer, called primuersel,[19] and "Adam & Eve" fully finished before Jan Brueghel was asked to take over the painting of the landscape and the numerous animals. Rubens would be regarded as the initiator of the creation of this painting and Jan Brueghel's role was that of applying the backdrop with his meticulous way of painting.[20]

As the above has shown, two differently skilled painters produced paintings in the manner of Rubens and both appear to show the same kind of final retouching. This may indicate that they were independent works of art, however, still being scrutinized by the master of the workshop, Rubens, before leaving the studio.

Examination of paintings characterized as "Style of Rubens" or "Copy after Rubens" may reveal that they were not productions of Antwerp ateliers, trying to imitate the artist, well known in the city, whose works were widely sought after, but that they were actually produced within Rubens's studio. It is evident that a painting ascribed as "Copy after Rubens" would benefit from the re-attribution to "Studio of Rubens". A thorough examination with IRR of paintings close to the style of Rubens will probably throw new light on Rubens's workshop or studio practice and thus result in a number of re-attributions.

In this way these, often overlooked, paintings by minor artists may help us understand, not only the practice of 17th century artists in general but also the way Rubens evaluated, and frequently modified, paintings by retouching. This would give us a far better understanding of the large output of pictures in Antwerp, so clearly influenced by the master's style and technique.

Acknowledgements

We are grateful for a stimulating discussion with and valuable suggestions from D. Tamis (University of Amsterdam), N. Van Hout (Rubenianum/UFSIA, Antwerp), and M. Jonker (Mauritshuis, The Hague).

Figure 6. P.P. Rubens and J. Brueghel I, "The Earthly Paradise", panel, 74.3 × 114.7 cm. Mauritshuis, inv. 253

Notes and references

1. Recently the Rubens-IRR-Project was initiated by A. Balis & N. Van Hout (Rubenianum/University of Antwerp [UFSIA], Antwerp); the results of the project are being awaited with great interest.
2. A. Balis, "'Fatto da un mio discepolo': Rubens's Studio Practices Reviewed", *Rubens and his Workshop. The Flight of Lot and his Family from Sodom* (Tokyo, 1994), 97–127; D. Tamis, "De hand van de meester", *kM* 16 (1995): 38–40.
3. Panel [thinned down to 4 mm], 59 × 81 cm. Mauritshuis inv. 254.
4. Canvas, 176 × 186 cm, Kunstmuseum, inv. 2300, Düsseldorf. Rubens's painting derives from Titian's painting of the same subject in the Prado, inv. 422, Madrid.
5. Panel, 83 × 90.5 cm. The Hermitage Museum, inv. 462, St Petersburg. This painting is regarded as the best of the known repetitions, all of which show the same slightly altered position of Adonis's spear, now pointing towards the right and placed against a group of trees.
6. Panel, 60.5 83 cm, Staatliche Kunstsammlungen, Gemäldegallerie, inv. 991, Dresden.
7. B. Broos, *Intrigues and Intimacies* (Gent, 1993), 380.
8. Panel [single plank], 67 × 107 cm. Mauritshuis, inv. 234.
9. A forthcoming article will focus on the sources for this painting.
10. Dendrochronological analysis by Dr P. Klein, Hamburg (1994 and 1995) confirms a felling date ±1610. One of the series of single-plank panels is signed and dated "A. Govaerts.1612" (Mauritshuis, inv. 45).
11. B. Broos and J. Wadum, "Vier panelen uit één boom/Four Panels from One Tree", *Mauritshuis in Focus*, 1 (1993): 13–16.
12. M.Y. Varchavskaya, *Pierre Paul Rubens: Tableaux dans les musées de l'Union Soviétique* (Leningrad 1989), 48–51.
13. An X-radiograph of the painting shows that the position of left foot of this "Naiad" was slightly altered to a more downward-pointing position.
14. Drawing, black chalk heightened with white, 520 × 390 mm. Museum Boymans-van Beuningen, inv. V.52, Rotterdam. The drawing is dated 1610–1615.
15. A number of drawings within Rubens oeuvre document this phenomenon. See "Francesco Gonzaga", drawing, 226 × 161 mm, black, red, and white chalk, Nationalmuseum, inv. 1917, Stockholm, which shows corrections at the jaw. (N. Van Hout drew my attention to this drawing.)
16. Collection of the late Count Seilern, Home House Trustees Collection, London. See J.S. Held, *Rubens and his Circle. Studies by Julius S. Held* (Princeton, 1982), 156–165, Figure XIV.3.
17. Compare with "Woodland Scene", drawing, black chalk with touches of red chalk and white body colour, 383 × 499 mm, The Ashmolean Museum, inv. 201, Oxford, which shows similarities, although this drawing is more finished than the underdrawing on a panel would be.
18. Panel [one plank], 74.3 × 114.7 cm. The panel has been incised with the mark of Guilliam Gabron (active 1609–1662). Probably painted around 1615. Mauritshuis, inv. 253. The most recent investigation with IRR was undertaken and stimulatingly discussed with Dorien Tamis (University of Amsterdam), Nico Van Hout (UFSIA, Rubenianum) and Christine Van Mulders (Rubenianum).
19. H. Miedema, *Karel van Mander. Den grondt der edel vry schilder-const* (Utrecht, 1973), 256, 257; B.K. Federspiel, *Observations on some technical innovations in the 16th century Netherlandish painting* (Dissertation, School of Conservation, Copenhagen, 1985); J. Wadum, "Primuersel of Imprimatura?", *kM* 15 (1995): 39–40.
20. Dorien Tamis (University of Amsterdam) will describe the complex production of this painting in her forthcoming dissertation on collaboration of artists in the 17th century.

Working Group B3

Polychrome sculpture

Résumé

Cette communication présente une analyse de vingt-deux sculptures en bois polychromé appartenant à la deuxième moitié du XVIIIe siècle à Minas Gerais, Brésil, au moyen d'études iconographiques, hagiographiques, formelles et stylistiques, et au moyen d'analyses macroscopiques, microscopiques, microchimiques et radiographiques. La *Cedrella aff. fissilis Vell.* est identifié comme support de presque toutes les pièces et la présence d'une couche complète ou de réserves[1] en feuilles d'or et d'argent est vérifiée, ainsi que poinçons, "pastiglia",[2] yeux en verre ou peints, polychromie à l'huile ou à détrempe huileuse sur les carnations, détrempe sur les "estofados", et dentelles dorées. Grâce à des analyses formelles et stylistiques, on arrive à une définition typologique des principales écoles de l'imagerie de Minas à cette période.

Mots-clés

Sculpture polychromée, bois polychromé, imagerie, analyse formelle, analyse stylistique, XVIIIe siècle, Brésil

Figure 1. Sainte-Anne la Maîtresse, Musée de l'Or, Sabará, Minas

La sculpture polychromée du XVIIIe siècle dans l'état de Minas Gerais, Brésil: quelques caractéristiques techniques, formelles et stylistiques

Beatriz Ramos de Vasconcelos Coelho,* Marcos César de Senna Hill
CECOR/EBA/UFMG, Avenida Antônio Carlos 6627
Belo Horizonte, Minas Gerais, Brésil

Introduction

Le Brésil a été découvert en 1500 par le navigateur portugais Pedro Alvares Cabral, étant pour cette raison le seul pays de langue portugaise de l'Amérique du Sud. Minas Gerais est un de ses plus vastes états, comprenant 587.172 Km^2. Il est situé loin de la côte, dans la région sud-est du pays et il n'a commencé à être habité par les colonisateurs que vers la fin du XVIIe siècle, quand, dans quelques-uns de ses fleuves, on a découvert de l'or pour la première fois au Brésil. Cette découverte a attiré vers la région un grand nombre de personnes, du Portugal et du litoral brésilien, avides d'enrichissement facile. Entre 1700 et 1770 le Brésil a produit près de la moitié du volume d'or obtenu dans le monde entier au cours de trois siècles (1500 à 1800).[3] Beaucoup d'artistes et d'artisans portugais et brésiliens ont vécu dans cette région et y ont développé une intense activité. Aujourd'hui à Minas Gerais il y a plusieurs villes qui ont surgi et qui se sont développées rapidement dans cette période (deux d'entre elles sont considérées par l'UNESCO "Patrimoine de l'Humanité": Ouro Preto et Congonhas). Il y a aussi un très riche patrimoine de biens immeubles et meubles. Les biens meubles sont constitués surtout par des oeuvres en bois polychromé: images et oeuvres en taille. L'imagerie en bois polychromé de la seconde moitié du XVIIIe siècle constitue le sujet de ce travail.

Dans la capitale de Minas Gerais fonctionne le Centre de conservation et de restauration des biens culturels meubles (CECOR), qui fait partie de l'Ecole de Beaux-Arts de l'Université fédérale de Minas Gerais. Depuis sa création en 1980, le CECOR réalise des études sur des oeuvres d'art de Minas et du Brésil, ayant comme objectif de connaître leur constitution pour pouvoir ainsi intervenir sur les procédés de conservation/restauration. A partir de 1990 nous avons commencé à développer de façon systématique, l'étude de l'imagerie en bois polychromé, assistés par une équipe de colaborateurs, parmi lesquels quelques restaurateurs, un botaniste - Dr. Pedro Luiz Braga Lisboa, du Musée de l'Etat de Pará Emilio Goeldi, et une spécialiste en chimie, Mme Claudina Maria Dutra Moresi. Récemment, Marcos César de Senna Hill professeur en Histoire de l'Art, est venu participer de cette équipe de travail. La participation de ce dernier a rendu possible l'approfondissement des l'analyses des caractéristiques formelles et stylistiques des oeuvres étudiées et l'élaboration d'une méthodologie propre à cette partie de la recherche. Parallèlement et postérieurement à ce groupe, d'autres chercheurs du CECOR ont développé des recherches sur l'imagerie de Minas.

Méthodologie

Nous avons selectionné et étudié vingt-deux sculptures de la deuxième moitié du XVIIIe siècle, qui appartiennent aux villes historiques de Sabará, Santa Luzia, Congonhas, Mariana, Itaverava et Ouro Preto. D'entre elles, neuf sont d'auteurs anonymes. Deux sont d'un auteur confirmé, Antônio Francisco Lisboa (1738-1814), surnommé Aleijadinho et appartiennent à la chapelle du Tiers Ordre de Notre-Dame du Carme de Sabará. Une autre sculpture lui est attribuée, Sainte-Anne Maîtresse du Musée de l'Or de la même ville (Figure 1). Quatre sculptures sont de la Basilique de Bom Jesus de Matosinhos à Congonhas, sur lesquelles

*Auteur à qui la correspondance doit être adressée.

existent des reçus de paiement donnés au tailleur portugais Francisco Vieira Servas (1720 -1811).[4,5] Six autres sculptures lui sont attribuées dont quatre appartiennent à la ville de Mariana et deux au Musée de l'Inconfidência à Ouro Preto. Il est important de souligner que les attributions citées sont toutes informelles, car on n'a trouvé aucune documentation publiée a ce sujet. Les sculptures qui sont attribuées à Francisco Vieira Servas font partie cependant, de l'inventaire de biens meubles de l'Institut du patrimoine historique et artistique national (IPHAN).

Les procédés suivants ont été adoptés dans cette recherche:

- choix des oeuvres dans quelques villes historiques de Minas Gerais,
- prélèvement de données biographiques existantes sur l'auteur s'il est connu, et sur la vie et l'iconographie du personnage représenté, faisant la comparaison entre l'iconographie traditionnelle et celle de la pièce analysée,
- examen de la sculpture à l'oeil nu et aussi au moyen des loupes monoculaires et binoculaires, en observant la structure de l'image, la direction des fibres du bois et tous les vestiges de fissures, pour que l'on puisse avoir une idée du nombre de blocs qui la composent et de la technique utilisée dans son élaboration; observation des traces des instruments utilisés, vérification de la présence des yeux en verre ou peints,
- examen de la préparation, bolus, feuilles métalliques, couche pictorique et éléments ornamentaux; types et formes de poinçons; présence de "pastiglia", de dentelles, de pierres et d'autres éléments décoratifs,
- prélèvement d'échantillons et analyses microscopiques et microchimiques des stratigraphies et des éléments constituants des polychromies; prélèvement d'échantillons minuscules du bois pour son identification,
- comparaison entre les résultats obtenus par les restaurateurs et ceux obtenus par les analyses de laboratoire,
- analyses formelle et stylistique de chaque sculpture, suivant un ordre pré-établi,
- radiographies, spécifiquement des têtes, mais aussi des autres parties d'intérêt, cherchant l'identifcation du type et du format des yeux, des vestiges de la section du visage et des possibles cavités dans la tête et dans le corps,
- constitution de documentation comprenant: des rapports écrits, des photographies en noir et blanc et des diapositifs, des décalques en grandeur nature et des schémas des détails d'intérêt.

Résultats obtenus: caractéristiques physiques

Nous avons prélevé des échantillons du support de quinze oeuvres d'entre les vingt-deux examinées. L'analyse a identifié sur le bois de toutes les sculptures la *Cedrella aff. fissilis Vell.*, sauf sur celui de l'image de Notre-Dame de la Conception à Sabará, qui possède trois differents types de bois: *Vismia aff. cayennensis (Jacq.) Pers/* famille *Guttiferae* qui constitue la plupart du support; *Aniba sp1/*famille *Lauraceae*, utilisé pour la tête, et *Aniba sp2/*famille *Lauraceae* formant une planche fixée sous la base de la sculpture.

Nous avons trouvé huit sculptures évidées, toutes en grandeur nature, et parmi lesquelles quatre ont une planche en bois fermant une ouverture sur la partie postérieure, et deux autres sont ouvertes. Nous avons trouvé aussi une image dont l'analyse et les processus de restauration révèlent une procédure de sculpture assez particulière: au départ il s'agit d'un seul morceau de bois qui à été divisé, inexplicablement, en deux dans le sens vertical. Les deux parties ont été, par la suite, collées l'une à l'autre et par après avoir été sculptées. Les autres sont massives et composées de blocs distincts qui varient entre deux (quand au moins une des mains a été faite séparément) et neuf blocs. Les blocs ne forment que la figure humaine et la base. Nous n'avons pas considéré les détails des attributs. Vingt ont des compléments en bois: auréoles, croix, palmes, cornes d'abondance, etc. Douze ont les yeux peints et dix, des yeux sphériques en verre et un pédoncule, caractéristique de pièces faites en verre soufflé.

Quant à la polychromie, effectuée généralement par un autre artiste que le tailleur, nous avons obtenu les résultats suivants:

Neuf ont la carnation faite à la détrempe huileuse et quatre à l'huile. La détrempe a été employée en tous les "estofados". Le "sgraffiato" (égratigné) a été utilisé en

Figure 2. Photo d'une décalque en grandeur nature de la polychromie de la sculpture de Saint Simon Stock, Eglise du Tiers Ordre de Notre-Dame du Carme, Sabará, Minas Gerais.

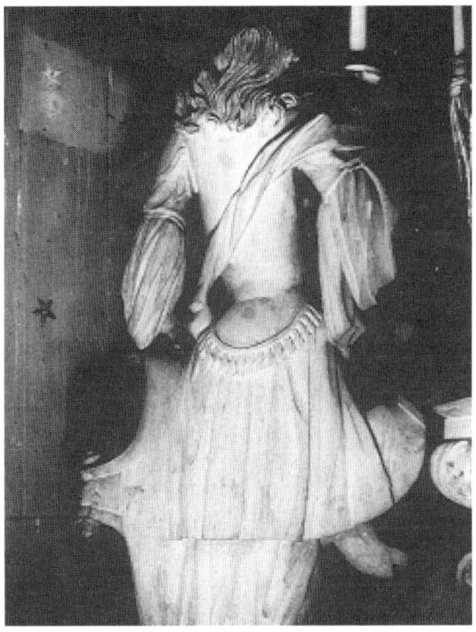

Figure 3. Partie postérieure, sans polychromie, d'un ange torchère attribué a Francisco Vieira Servas, Basilique de Bom Jesus do Matosinhos, Congonhas, Minas Gerais.

Figure 4. Notre-Dame de la Conception, partie postérieure, Eglise premier, Sabará, Minas Gerais.

quatorze sculptures, avec la mise en valeur de quelques parties, en petites touches de pinceau de couleur plus sombre. La technique connue comme peinture à pinceau[6] n'a été vérifiée qu'en cinq oeuvres. Nous avons observée en plusieurs oeuvres une fleur "sgraffiata" semblable à un chrysanthème (Figure 2).

Nous avons remarqué des feuilles d'or bruni en toutes les images. En quelques images, les feuilles d'or recouvrent toute la surface des "estofados". En d'autres, il y a un espace assez accentué entre les feuilles de la partie postérieure de l'image, comme c'est le cas de deux oeuvres de Aleijadinho.[7] En huit images dont six sont attribuées à Vieira Servas, on n'a trouvé que de réserves d'or ou des petits détails dorés. A notre surprise, des feuilles d'argent[8] ont été retrouvées en huit des vingt-deux sculptures examinées. On a aussi observé une simplification de l'"estofado" sur la partie postérieure de presque toutes les sculptures. En quatre anges torchères attribués à Francisco Vieira Servas (Figure 3), sur la partie postérieure, on n'a placé que la préparation. Ces parties inachevées deviennent très interessantes pour notre travail puisqu'elles font la mise à nu des procédés de l'artiste.

Trois sculptures présentent une riche polychromie aussi bien dans la partie postérieure que dans la partie frontale (Figure 4).

Nous avons observé la technique de la "pastiglia" en treize images, le plus souvent avec un relief assez accentué. En une seule sculpture on peut voir des reliefs avec un aspect de "pastiglia" obtenue cependant par l'exécution de l'entaille dans le bois même (Figures 5,6).

En onze oeuvres, nous avons noté des poinçons avec des formes et des grandeurs variées, qui enrichissent et donnent une texture différente à l'"estofado". En neuf pièces on a trouvé des vestiges ou des évidences sur le finissement des ourlets qui indiquent l'emploi de dentelles dorées en profusion (Figure 7).

Figure 5. L'Archange Saint Michel, Eglise premier, Santa Luzia, Minas Gerais.

Résultats obtenus: caractéristiques formelles et stylistiques

En étudiant la forme et le style de l'ensemble des images sculptées de l'art réligieux de Minas Gerais appartenant à la deuxième moitié du XVIIIe siècle, nous avons remarqué une série de caractéristiques qui nous aideront à comprendre le processus de leur évolution esthétique.

Tout d'abord nous vérifions que, dans la majorité des cas, les images ont un support de bois, détail technique qui confirme l'héritage d'une tradition portugaise et qui définit des particularités de la forme elle-même.

Ensuite, nous avons analysé les oeuvres du point de vue de leurs qualités sculpturelles. On peut les classer à trois niveaux dans l'ordre décroissant:

Figure 6. L'Archange Saint Michel, détail des reliefs sculptés, Santa Luzia, Minas Gerais.

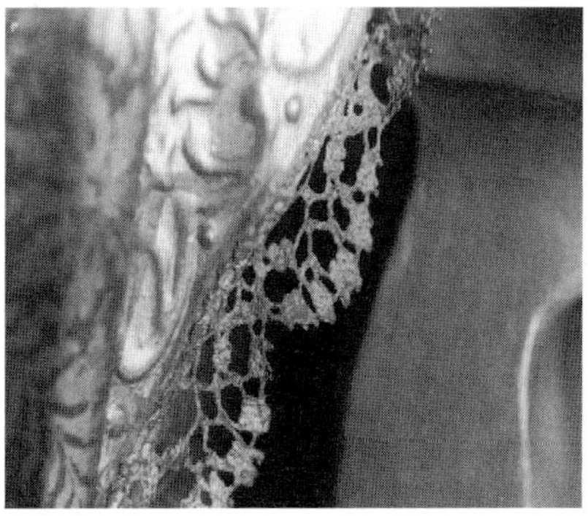

Figure 7. Sainte-Anne Maîtresse, détail du manteau de la jeune-fille avec des dentelles dorées, Musée de l'Or, Sabará, Minas Gerais.

Figure 8. Saint Benoit, Chapelle de Notre-Dame du Rosaire des Noirs, Santa Luzia, Minas Gerais.

1 **Le niveau érudit, qui détermine une qualité inhérente aux auteurs portugais.**

Premièrement, le niveau érudit doit être évalué selon le degré de perfection de l'anatomie humaine et de son rapport avec la draperie des vêtements. Sachant que, au Brésil, l'enseignement systématique de l'art n'a commencé qu'à partir de 1826 à Rio de Janeiro, nous pouvons affirmer que la perfection érudite de l'anatomie exprimée dans les sculptures était exclusivement assurée par des maîtres portugais.

Par conséquent, seulement deux hypothèses sont possibles: ou les images ont été importées du Portugal, ou elles ont été faites par un maître portugais qui avait fixé domicile au Brésil.

Dans l'ensemble des sculptures de Minas Gerais appartenant à la deuxième moitié du XVIIIe siècle, nous avons trouvé un grand nombre d'images érudites, dont l'un des maîtres le plus important est Francisco Vieira Servas.

2 **Le niveau de "frontière"[9] entre l'érudit et le populaire.**

Le niveau de "frontière" reflète l'histoire même de l'art colonial de Minas Gerais au cours de la deuxième moitié du XVIIIe siècle. A cette époque, on a vu surgir des maîtres brésiliens, formés dans la tradition artisanale portugaise, présente dans la région depuis plus de cinquante ans. Les techniques lusitaniennes assimilées se sont alors mélangées à un autre type de sensibilité: celle fortement influencée par la tradition culturelle africaine.

Un maître de "frontière" est donc celui qui, étant né et elevé au Brésil, a produit une oeuvre de talent qui s'approche de l'érudition sans s'éloigner complètement des tendances intrinsèquement populaires. Même s'il y avait l'intention de reproduire le plus fidèlement possible le modèle portugais, la sensibilité brésilienne a affleurée comme un fait qui s'est matérialisé dans l'oeuvre elle-même. C'est le cas d'Antônio Francisco Lisboa, surnommé Aleijadinho.

L'intensification de la production de l'art réligieux à partir de 1750 est due à l'émancipation des Confréries et à la création des Tiers Ordres, qui, dans le contexte de Minas, ont acquis une grande importance politique et réligieuse. Les maîtres brésiliens et portugais, reconnus par les communautés locales, ont crée des ateliers avec une dynamique de production en série pour satisfaire la demande. Pour cela, ils ont engagé des hommes libres et des esclaves qui ont appris le métier avec l'entraînement quotidien. Dans ces ateliers, on voit naître des oeuvres qui passent par les mains de plusieurs exécutants et par le mains du maître. On réalise ainsi un autre type de production de "frontière", où l'érudition est accompagnée d'une résolution technique de niveau inférieur. Les oeuvres creées dans l'atélier du maître portugais Francisco Vieira Servas, cité ci-dessus, reflètent cette organisation.

3 **Le niveau populaire.**

La disparition progressive de l'or, évidente à partir du troisième quart du siècle, a eu comme conséquence directe l'absence des maîtres portugais dans la région. Cependant, la production de l'art réligieux a gardé son importance de façon très vivante. Les maîtres brésiliens, qui cherchaient à saisir les paramètres artistiques alors en vigueur, ont commencé à compter de moins en moins sur l'orientation directe des maîtres portugais. Dans l'essai de combler cette lacune de leur formation, ils se sont tournés vers les modèles de l'imagerie érudite déjà existants dans les chapelles et les églises. Comptant sur les rudiments de la technique qui commençait à être oubliée, les sculpteurs d'images ont copié les modèles érudits avec l'intention consciente de les reproduire.

La première caractéristique remarquée dans cette production, est l'imperfection anatomique qui définit toutes les autres imperfections structurales. Maintes fois, au moyen d'un examen plus détaillé de la forme, nous découvrons la reproduction naïve des caractéristiques formelles du maître érudit. Chez les nouveaux maîtres brésiliens la volumétrie de l'art du vêtement accompagne difficilement la volumétrie de l'anatomie, créant des moments d'hésitation qu'ils essayent de surmonter grâce à leurs insistances à sculpter des surfaces. Comme résultat nous avons des formes redondantes (Figure 8). L'un des plus célèbres maîtres populaires de la région de Minas est un anonyme, à qui on a

Figure 9. Sainte Ephigénie, Chapelle de Notre-Dame du Rosaire des Noirs, Mariana, Minas Gerais.

donné le sobriquet de "Maître Piranga", car une bonne partie de son oeuvre se trouve concentrée dans la région de la ville de Minas du même nom.[10]

Une autre caractéristique qui définit cette période est la sensualité corporelle exprimée également à travers le rapport entre l'anatomie et le vêtement. Il est intéressant d'observer comment cette sensualité d'origine française, a influencé la création artistique et réligieuse européenne du XVIIIe siècle et comment son écho est arrivé au monde colonial portugais.

Minas Gerais est un important cellier de la manifestation du Rococo international de l'art réligieux. Par rapport à la période antérieure, définie comme Baroque plein, l'imagerie de Minas de la seconde moitié du siècle, présente une différence de base. Cette différence survit dans les formes corporelles qui commencent à disparaître sous les vêtements dont l'épaisseur est subtilisée.

Sur les images les plus érudites, les formes anatomiques sont entièrement visibles, même celles cachées par plusieurs couches d'étoffe sculptée. C'est ce que nous avons pu observer sur l'image de Sainte Ephigénie de la chapelle du Rosair à Mariana (Figure 9). Cette caractéristique rappelle l'effet du tissu mouillé du statuaire hellénistique. La priorité expressive de cette sensualité est donnée aux images féminines et plus spécifiquement aux représentations de Notre Dame. Nous trouvons surtout le souci d'expliciter la beauté de la silhouette féminine.

Dans les écoles les plus importantes de l'imagerie de Minas de la fin du XVIIIe siècle, à savoir celle de Antônio Francisco Lisboa et celle de Vieira Servas, on trouve certaines caractéristiques stylistiques communes qui définissent un modèle formel spécifique de cette région. Du point de vue structurel, il convient de remarquer que la forme circulaire sera constamment transformée en forme polygonale. Ce détail devient plus facile à observer sur l'ourlet des manches, des cols et des tuniques.

Ce besoin délibéré de formes angulaires traduit un souci de la conception structurelle de la sculpture. L'évolution vers des formes plus géométriques des volumes est une ressource qui reflète un degré accentué de raffinement esthétique.

En dehors de la tendence de subtilité et de géometrisation nous avons trouvé sur la draperie, des formes organiques animées par des courbes et des contre-courbes qui représentent les plis flottants. Ces formes organiques rappellent les éléments conchyliens qui constituent le vocabulaire ornamental Rococo et exemplifient les moments atéctoniques de la composition.

Figure 10. Ange torchère, Musée de l'Inconfidência, Ouro Preto, Minas Gerais.

Dans le contexte colonial brésilien, l'oeuvre artistique réligieuse de Minas Gerais représente, avec celle de Pernambuco (un état du nord-este brésilien), un ensemble important pour l'étude de l'esthétique Rococo manifeste dans l'Amérique Latine. Sur la peinture monumentale et sur le bois ornamental sculpté des retables, l'élément rocaille, ainsi que le recours à l'asymétrie, sont des évidences visuelles constantes, qui rendent plus facile l'identification stylistique. Nous présentons, ci-dessous, un tableau qui permet de localiser ces caractéristiques sur les vingt-deux sculptures analysées.

Conclusion

Après avoir recherché en détail les vingt-deux sculptures en bois doré et polychromé du XVIIIe siècle à Minas Gerais, nous considérons que d'importants résultats ont été atteints et nous croyons qu'ils pourront apporter une bonne contribution dans certains domaines de la conservation/restauration et de l'histoire de l'art au Brésil. Il a été important de constater l'emploi de *Cedrella aff. fissilis Vell.* en quatorze images dont le support a été analysé.

D'autres constatations ont été également importantes, telles que la présence de feuilles d'argent, l'emploi de la technique de la "pastiglia" et l'utilisation de dentelles dorées en grand nombre d'oeuvres. Ces observations ont été citées dans un article que nous avons publié récemment.[11]

Grâce aux études sur les sculptures de Francisco Vieira Servas, que nous allons bientôt finir, nous pouvons déjà affirmer que cet important sculpteur avait un groupe d'officiers et d'apprentis qui travaillaient avec lui. On constate même l'interférence de plus d'une main dans une même oeuvre. Francisco Vieira Servas a beaucoup employé des "réserves" d'or. Sur la partie postérieure de quatre images, plus précisement de deux grands anges torchères de la Basilique de Bom Jesus de Matosinhos à Congonhas et d'autres deux anges torchères du Musée l'Inconfidência à Ouro Preto, nous avons observé l'absence presque totale de polychromie (Figure 10). Une autre remarque intéressante: aucun des anges torchères de Vieira Servas n'a des yeux en verre. Tous sont des yeux peints.

Dans le cas spécifique de l'imagerie, la localisation de caractéristiques formelles qui définissent le style, est un travail qui exige un examen très attentif et exhaustif. Ce travail a le but d'expliciter, en ce qui concerne l'image sculptée, quelques-unes des caractéristiques correspondantes à l'esthétique Rococo trouvée sur des peintures et des retables de la même période dans la région de Minas. Il s'agit du résultat d'une recherche en cours qui, grâce à une étude approfondie des techniques et des formes, a l'intention de systématiser la connaissance de l'imagerie réalisée pour animer l'univers réligieux de Minas, dans la deuxième moitié du XVIIIe siècle.

Remerciements

Les auteurs remercient à la Fondation de soutien à la recherche dans l'Etat de Minas Gerais (FAPEMIG); au Conseil national de développement scientifique et technologique (CNPq); au Secteur de recherches de l'Université Fédérale de Minas Gerais; aux collaborateurs, spécialement au Docteur Pedro Luiz Braga Lisboa et aux boursiers, de l'appui et de l'intérêt témoignés, sans lesquels le développement de ce travail n'aurait pas été pas possible.

Notes et références

1. Terme utilisé au Brésil, pour définir l'emplacement ponctuel des feuilles d'or sur l'"estofado" des images sculptées en bois polychromé.
2. Mayer, *Materiales y técnicas del arte*, (Madrid: Hermann Blume, 1985), 250.
3. J. Bury, *Arquitetura e arte no Brasil colonial*, org. Myriam Ribeiro de Oliveira. (São Paulo: Nobel, 1991), 16.
4. Date de Baptême: Arquivo Distrital de Braga, Registro Paroquial de Eira Vedra (Vieira do Minho) Misto 5, fólio 36. Transcription faite par Eduardo Pires de Oliveira. Date de décès: Z. Vianna, Em torno da história de Sabará. A Ordem terceira do Carmo e a sua igreja, obras do Aleijadinho no templo. (Rio de Janeiro: Ministério da Educação e Saúde, 1940), 64.
5. J. Martins, *Dicionário de artistas e artífices dos séulos XVIII e XIX em Minas Gerais*, 2 volumes, (Rio de Janeiro: Ministério da Educação e Cultura, 1974), 216.
6. J. M. Echeveria, *Coleccionismo de escultura antigua*, (Madrid: Everest, 1979), 27.
7. B. Coelho, "A contribution to the study of Aleijadinho, the most important sculptor of colonial Brazil", in *Iberian and Latin America Cultural Heritage, IIC Preprints, Madrid*, (London: 1992), 27–30.
8. Au Brésil il n'y avait pas de mine d'argent, ce qui rendait ce minéral plus cher que l'or dans le XVIIIe siècle.
9. A. Bosi, *Dialética da colonização*, (São Paulo: Companhia das Letras, 1992), 41.
10. C.M.D. Moresi, M.S. Fantini, "Mestre Piranga - Study and Conservation of Brazilian Religious Sculptures from the Eighteenth Century", in *Iberian and Latin America Cultural Heritage, IIC Preprints, Madrid*, (London: 1992),94–98.
11. B. Coelho, "A escultura policromada do século XVIII em Minas gerais: uma abordagem interdisciplinar", in *Seminário da ABRACOR, 7, 1994, Petrópolis*, (Rio de Janeiro: ABRACOR - Associação Brasileira de Conservadores e Restauradores, 1994), 40–45.

Our Lady of Delivery: Restoration of a *tella encolada* Sculpture

Gilca Flores de Medeiros
Center for Conservation and Restoration of Movable Cultural Properties (CECOR), Federal University of Minas Gerais (UFMG),
Av. Antonio Carlos, 6627 – Belo Horizonte,
Minas Gerais, Brazil

Abstract

The paper reports the restoration of an image of Our Lady of Delivery from the 19th century, which presents a very peculiar construction technique: the artist made use of fabrics instead of wood as the support of the sculpture. Although this type of work is commonly found in some Latin American countries, it is very rare in Brazil. Moreover, this work differs from its Latin-American counterparts in that it is hollow, while the others are made from a solid support. In Our Lady of Delivery, we found a mixture of different techniques. This has made Our Lady of Delivery an unique image, so that, during the restoration process, creativeness was required to find the best solutions. The peculiarities of this technique are described and then the details given of the restoration process.

Keywords

Brazil, sculpture, image, Minas Gerais, fabric shaped, Our Lady of Delivery, restoration, support, fabrics, *tella encolada*

Figure 1. Our Lady of Delivery, image of "tela encolada", from the XIX century, before restoration

Figure 2. Back of image before restoration

Introduction

This work was carried out on an image of Our Lady of Delivery, from the early 19th century, owned by the church of Our Lady of Mercy (1769) at Tiradentes, a historic city of Minas Gerais, Brazil. The image is formed by the standing figure of the Virgin, carrying Jesus on the left arm. Its dimensions are: H 94 ´ W 37 ´ diameter 38 cm. When it first arrived at CECOR to be restored, the sculpture was in a terrible condition and attracted our attention because it was so different from the other pieces of art we normally work on (wooden polychrome sculptures and paintings on canvas). This piece used fabric, instead of wood, as the support (Figures 1 and 2).

In some Latin American countries, we find many images made with fabric, using a technique known as *tella encolada*. These pieces are created from a rigid structure, on which the fabric is glued and, sometimes, plastered. However, in Brazil, this type of sculpture is very rare. To our knowledge, there are only a dozen of them in the region of Tiradentes, Sào Joào Del Rey and Campanha, in Minas Gerais. The fact of the sculpture being hollow, differing from the other Latin American pieces we know, also drew our attention.

Besides being technically interesting, this work presents a fine aesthetic quality, being anatomically coherent, which indicates the artist's erudition.

The first step in our work was to understand the construction technique by observing and analysing the constitutive elements and materials. The following step, disassembling the piece, became necessary to allow treatment of each separate part. This enabled a better knowledge of the piece and we were then able to determine how it was made.

In order to give a clearer explanation of our work, first we will present the construction of the piece. Then, we will describe the conservation condition before treatment, the restoration carried out, the results obtained and, finally, the conclusions we arrived at.

Construction

As well as direct observation of the piece, a radiograph was taken in order to identify the type of internal structure. We also carried out the following tests: comparative optical microscopy, torsion test, IR (infrared) absorption spectrometry. On the agglutinant we made specific coloration tests of stratigraphic cuts, solubility tests and microchemical reactions. To investigate the pigments we used optical microscopy , with a JEOL 35C microscope coupled to an ORTEC EEDS X-ray energy-dispersive spectrometer. The protection layer was investigated with stratigraphic studies by plane-polarised light and fluorescent light.

All these tests helped us to understand how the piece was built: the Virgin and the Infant were made separately. From our studies, we concluded that, to make the Virgin, the author first shaped an image using clay, without baking. This interpretation is supported by our finding, during analysis of resin fragments, traces of clay between the fabric and the internal resin. The fabric was glued over this model, using irregular-shaped pieces.

In some areas, we found up to five fabric layers. Linen fabric of different thicknesses was used in the structure and drape, and thin cotton on the flesh of the Infant and the Virgin. We found mends on the neck and shoulders of the Virgin,

Figure 3. The Virgin's face with mend on the neck

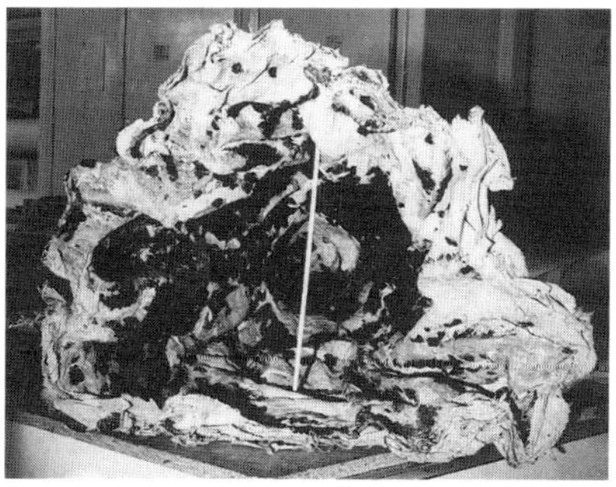

Figure 4. Internal area image with resin

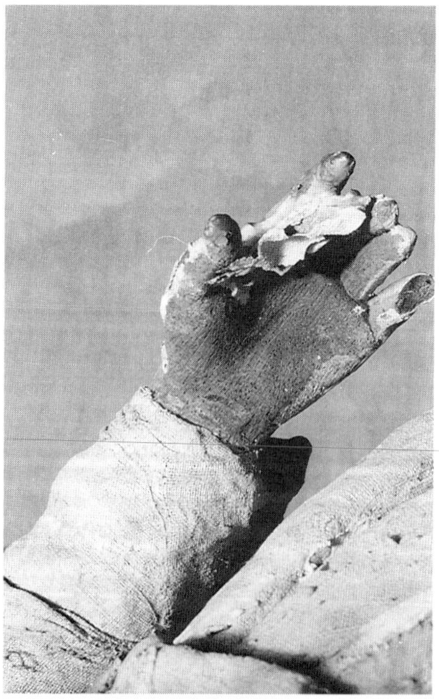

Figure 5. Detail of the wooden right hand and the arm with the fabric layers

indicating that head, arms and body were made separately and joined together after fabric glueing (Figure 3). In the next step, the artist applied resin over the entire internal area of the fabric, hardening it. Our tests showed that this resin is a diterpene resin (melting point: 60–61°C) with volatile compounds (monoterpenes and sesquiterpenes), probably a balsam of the region (Figure 4).

The Infant was made following the same technique. This piece is also hollow and completely closed. Curiously, we found the clay mould under the fabric on the Infant's hands and feet.

The Virgin was mounted on a wooden base and had wooden hands (Figure 5).

In order to mark the tunic border at the base, the artist used vegetable fibres and fabric pieces mixed with resin and plaster. This mixture provided the volume of the feet and determined the curves on the internal side of the border.

After this process, the image received the fabric forming the veil and the hair, made in vegetable fibres without treatment. The next step was the mantle assembly (linen lace). Finally, the Infant was attached to the left arm.

We observed a plaster preparation (gypsum and anhydrite) and animal glue in the polychromy. The original polychromy shows a tempera technique, the flesh tones being tempera/oil. The lace shows gilding on a white oily preparation and a flake white and ochre underpaint. For the Virgin's hair, a brown colour was painted on the vegetable fibres.

The original polychromy was: a white preparation layer; red vest with white cuffs; blue mantle with light blue lining; blue marbled base; flesh tones with protein water proofing and white and rose layers.

The polychromy showed repainting. In some cuts we observed two repaintings applied at different periods. A layer of varnish separates these repaintings in the mantle and the flesh. The repainting on the flesh area is of good quality in tempera/oil and flake white and seemed to be quite old. We also found flake white on the repainting of the draping.

After the repainting, the piece had these colours: yellow vest with flowers in orange, red and green, and green cuffs, dark blue mantle with red lining, red marbled base.

Conservation condition

The piece was in a terrible condition:

- General detachment of the polychromy, more accentuated on the lower area.
- A great amount of dirt (dust, insect excrement, candle sprinkles), interfering with a satisfactory interpretation of the work and damaging its materials.
- Loss of the fabric stiffness on the right arm and the lower area, causing a flattening of the piece, decreasing its original height by 9 cm.
- Large areas with lost polychromy, mainly on the mantle. These areas left both the original painting and the fabric exposed.
- Sinking on the faces of the Virgin and the Infant.
- A wooden post in the internal area of the Virgin, representing a bad quality intervention, made from wood scrap. This post had the same height as the flattened piece, indicating that it was not original (Figure 6).
- Small losses of fabric in many areas: on the right hand, complete loss of the fifth finger; on the left hand, separation of the fifth finger. There were many holes (of up to 1 cm) at the base.
- Repainting: the whole piece showed repainting. In some places this was of a good aesthetic quality (flesh tones, vest, base), but there was some very poor quality repainting applied directly to the fabric in the areas where the mantle was lost.
- Detachment of the lace in many areas.
- The tunic was almost detached from the base.

Conservation and restoration

Cleaning process

The cleaning was carried out with natural enzymes. Xylem was used on the areas where there were wax sprinkles. The cleaning process was carried out simultaneously with refixing the polychromy because of the great risk of detachments.

Figure 6. Wooden post found in the internal area of the Virgin – a poor quality intervention

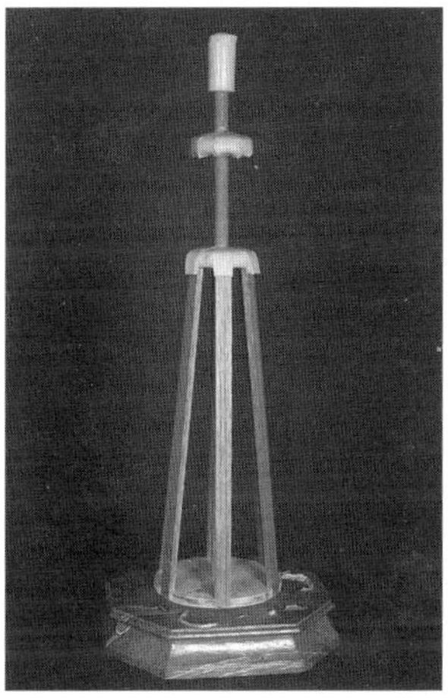

Figure 7. The new wooden frame

Figure 8. Treatment of sinking with the piece of polystyrene

Polychromy refixing

We tested both natural and synthetic adhesives, obtaining the best results with the natural adhesives. Eventually, we decided to use a 5% gelatine solution because it offered a non-strong adhesion and was easily retreatable with humidity, facilitating future movements and re-conservation of the piece.

Cleaning of each part

After disassembling the piece, we gained access to previously hidden areas, facilitating the cleaning process. In areas without polychromy, a vacuum cleaner was used to remove the dust. We removed the resin, fibres and plaster which were almost detached from the base because of the movement and loss of adhesion. At this time, we also removed the wooden post.

New internal structure

We decided that, for a safer future, we should fix a new internal wooden structure. We made a framework based on the internal structure of *de vestir* (to be dressed) images. The wooden structure received a layer of varnish (Osmocolor) for protection, and was then padded with synthetic foam on the areas that would support the image (head, shoulders and waist) (Figure 7). This new structure was placed inside the Virgin, providing a safer working condition.

Treatment of sinking

This phase of the work was carried out with the Virgin lying down on a table and without the wooden framework, in order that we could gain access to the internal area. Although it was complex, this problem was solved using simple resources.

We prepared two pieces of polystyrene and sculpted them following the curvature we wanted in the sunken areas. We then placed these pieces internally and used wires to pull the fabric outwards, returning it to its original position (Figure 8). In order to facilitate fabric movements and future fixing, while the wires were in place, we applied 10% rabbit glue internally with a brush.

On the Infant's face we used a bent wire with the desired curvature because it was not possible to gain access to the inside. We passed the wire through an orifice and carefully placed the fabric in its original position. We also applied 10% rabbit glue internally.

The Virgin's brace would be treated in a later part of the restoration process.

Because the Infant is a closed piece, we placed it with the face downwards and we applied the rabbit glue at 1:7 (strong glue) with a syringe into the inside of the piece. We then placed the Infant's face on a plaster mask, protected by transparent PVC film, to avoid any change in the face shape during the glue hardening. The Infant was left in this position for 24 hours, after which we considered the consolidation of this area to be complete.

Stiffening of the right arm

The arm was shapeless owing to internal detachment of the resin and it also showed loss of the polychromy and a small loss and detachment of the support. Using tweezers, we removed all loose resin fragments. We made a polystyrene column to fix the arm in its original position, after which we applied rabbit glue at 1:7 by aspersion through the aperture.

Support consolidation

FABRIC

There were small pieces of support lost in different areas. Where the fabric was used as support, we closed the holes using fabric (linen), using A 44 (neutral PVA) as adhesive. We also used this adhesive to repair some original mends.

Figure 9. Stiffening of the internal area. Removal of the wooden frame through the circular aperture

Wood

We did not replace the fifth finger on the right hand, while on the left hand, the detached finger was replaced using A 44 at 1:1 in water.

Stiffening of the internal area

In order to compensate for the resin lost at many points, we applied rabbit glue at 1:7 by spraying. This part of the work presented some difficulties because we needed to fix the image in the right position before applying the adhesive. We had the reference points of all curves of the tunic border on the base and we needed to keep the original shape. Therefore, we copied its design and applied it to an wood plate. Then a circle, slightly larger than the base of the internal wooden frame, was cut out of the plate.

The Virgin (with the framework) was placed over the plate and, using pins, we fixed the tunic border to the design in the correct position. We then prepared a place to put the image upside down. We inverted the image, now fixed to the plate and when we had achieved a stable position, we removed the wooden frame through the circular aperture (Figure 9).

At this point, we applied three layers of rabbit glue at 1:7 by spraying. In order to reduce the influence of humidity, we then applied Paraloid varnish at 10% in xylol + microcrystalline wax at 3% by spraying.

Fixing the internal frame to the base

While the fabric was stiffening, we fixed the frame to the base using three screws (Figure 7).

Consolidation of the Virgin to the base

The stiffened figure was replaced in its original position and its borders were fixed to the base using A 44.

Image assembly

The mantle, and then the Infant, were replaced on the Virgin. They were fixed with the same A 44.

Levelling of the holes

The levelling was carried out according to the needs of each area. On the Virgin's and Infant's flesh, the levelling was complete, with every hole closed. On the drape, small areas were completely levelled and, in large areas, we decided to use chamfer-shaped levelling, taking the polychromy onto the fabric, which helped consolidation of the painting (Figure 10).

Figure 10. Levelling of the holes

Polychromy retouching

The retouching process was also done according to the necessities of each area. On the flesh of both figures and the base, it was complete. On the drape, it followed levelling indications, completely closing small holes and making a chromatic passage onto the chamfer-shaped areas. We used Maimere pigment diluted in xylol and Dammar varnish at 10%.

Aesthetic preservation

There were large areas of exposed fabric on the mantle and these attracted too much attention. It was necessary to close some holes to give an aesthetic unity to the work. Therefore, where the fabric was exposed, it was isolated using two layers of Mowiol + water + alcohol at 4:25:50.

Figure 11. The image after the restoration

Protection varnish

We applied Paraloid at 10% in xylol + microcrystalin wax at 3% by aspersion (Figures 11 and 12).

Results

We obtained excellent results concerning the conservation aspect of the piece. Its initial condition not only precluded a proper study, but also increased the risk of further damage. The main problems were solved through polychromy reattachment, fabric stiffening, inserting an internal frame and polychromy retouching. We achieved a considerable aesthetic improvement, although the large parts of lost polychromy limited our work in this direction.

We believe that to a large extent we have recovered part of the lost aesthetic unity of the piece.

The conservation condition was remarkably improved. The original technology (use of resin as fabric stiffener) was preserved, since the rabbit glue leaves the adjacent resin visible. The rabbit glue had good penetration without large addition to the weight. Moreover, an internal frame will help in case of any future instability.

Conclusion

We encountered an excellent opportunity to improve our knowledge during this work because it differs from what we normally do. This demanded creativeness and discussion concerning materials and techniques. We achieved excellent results with simple solutions.

The research project work of my master's degree (MA) was developed from this work. These fabric images had never been studied before and they are not even mentioned in any bibliography about works of Minas Gerais, either from an aesthetic or a technical aspect. Therefore, research is continuing with the aim of locating similar works and studying their technical framework and aesthetic appearance, so that they can be compared with their Latin American counterparts.

We hope that once this work is complete, we shall be able to make known an almost unknown Brazilian piece of art.

Acknowledgements

I am grateful to everyone who helped me in this work, and especially to Professor Beatriz Coelho de Vasconcelos, who was the Restoration Co-ordinator; Gislaine Moura; Ive Madeira; Moema Queiroz (CECOR technicians) and Professor Regine Emery Quites for helpful discussions and collaboration in some parts of the restoration process. I would also like to thank Claudina Maria Dutra Moresi, who carried out the chemical and physical analysis, and Claudio Nadalin Vaz da Costa, who produced the photographic documentation.

Figure 12. Back of the image after the restoration

Materials

- Adhesive A 44 ED poly(vinyl acetate): Henkel do Brasil Indústria Química Ltda.
- Dammar: hydrocarbon, triterpenoid resin
- Maimeri restoring colour: F.lli Maimeri & C.s.r.l.
- Mowiol 18-88 polyvinyl alcohol: Hoechst do Brasil, Química e Farmacêutica S.A.
- Paraloid B 72 ethyl–methacrylat copolymer: Lascaux
- Rabbit glue protein: Restauració.Conservació.Materials/Barcelona
- Xilol PA – ACS aromatic hydrocarbon: Labsynth – Produtos para laboratórios Ltda.

Polychromed Sculpture and Textile Arts

Manfred Koller
Bundesdenkmalamt, Restaurierwerkstätten,
A 1030 Wien, Arsenal 15/4, Austria

Abstract

Since the late Gothic period various imitations of textile techniques have been observed in European sculpture. On the other hand, sculptors also influenced the textile arts, as, for example, in the development of textile relief between 1450 and 1600. In Austria these reliefs included precious pearl embroideries, which now undergoing conservation and examination in the laboratories of the Bundesdenkmalamt in Vienna. Historically and stylistically, some of these works are close to the works of famous artists of that time, such as Michael Pacher, Veit Stoss or Matthias Grünewald, painters and sculptors who were known to have in close contact with textile workers. During baroque times, religious manifestations meant that dressed sculptures again came into vogue, both medieval pieces, which were covered 'a la mode', or newly made figures, which often had articulated joints so that they could be moved into different positions. Several of the restored pieces of the 17th to 19th centuries were made of painted wood or had wax heads with natural hair, glass eyes and beautiful dresses from different periods. Examination of the construction, the polychromy and the textiles, together with the possible functions, has been part of the conservation process.

Keywords

Polychrome sculpture, textile arts conservation, embroidery, pearls, textile relieves, dressed sculptures

Introduction

During the last decade of research into the conservation of sculptures, we have learned much about the various elements of imitating different materials by means of polychromy on sculptures, which has been in use since medieval times, together with the techniques involved. The most important aspect was adornment with precious materials, either in the style of goldsmiths (jewels, crowns, brooches etc.) or with luxurious vestments having the look of textiles. In the romanesque period imitation was far from reality, but there was a general typology for gilded, silvered, purple or otherwise coloured details. During the 13th and 14th centuries the development of gothic polychromies enriched the increasingly realistic motifs with subtle relieved patterns. These included indented patterns, created with punches, elevated ones like pastiglia and patterns stamped from moulds; this was similar to the practice on paintings of the time (for example, the panels of master Theodoricus in the National Gallery, Prague, and screens like the Clarenaltar in Cologne Cathedral).[1]

Tracing, *tremolieren*, and punching, techniques coming from the practice of goldsmiths, were adopted for gilded and silvered surfaces. During the 14th century glazed lakes (such as madder or copper resinate) were used to create effects like that of enamel on bossed silverwork. With scratching into the still soft translucent paint layers (the so-called *sgraffitto* technique), the first steps towards the imitation of textile structures can be observed.[2] Between 1400 and about 1520/30 the most elaborate imitation of brocade textiles was introduced by means of developing the technique of brocade relief application. By this method weavings with metal threads and their patterns could be reproduced exactly, as examinations and reconstructions of the procedures since the late 1960s have shown.[3] However, in the creation of the polychromies of late gothic sculpture during the 15th century there existed even more co-operation between textileworkers, painters and sculptors, as we have already noted.

Textile reliefs and pearl embroideries

Around 1450 we can see in religious embroideries a slight tendency to create relieved surfaces by using underlying bundles of silk or strings of wool, which were then widely covered with pearls (for example, a chasuble in the Moravske Museum, Brno and an alb in the Treasury of Prague Cathedral, created for Bishop Johannes von Eych at Eichstätt).[4]

The next step towards closer co-operation between embroiders and sculptors can be seen in the chasuble at Mariazell (1470/80), showing in relief five figures of saints under late gothic baldachins (Figure 1(a) and (b)). Their elevation from the base level is 3 cm for figures and 4 cm for the baldachins. The style, composition and architecture show much detail taken over from the work of sculptors, combined with abundant embroidery on the surfaces, with coloured silk, gilded silver threads, silver spangles and pearls. The baldachin's three-dimensional shapes are composed by using different materials, such as glued canvas (for the spires) and rolled parchment covered with gold threads for the rings around the spires. The cores of the figures are formed only from threads (mixed with glue?) which were

a

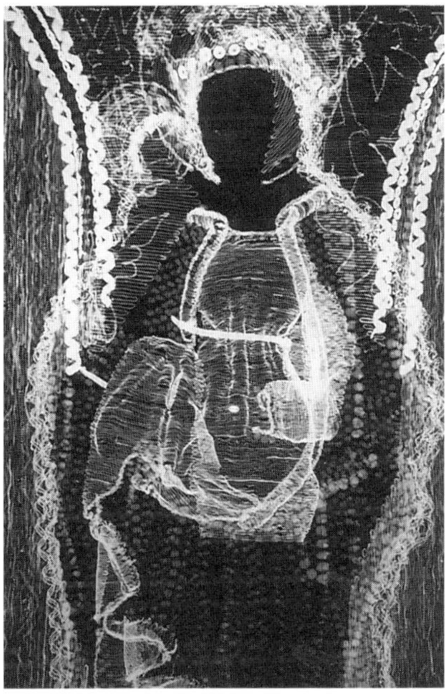

b

Figure 1. (a) Chasuble. c. 1470/80, Mariazell, Styria: detail of reverse of textile relief with embroidery of about 4,000 single pearls. (b) The same detail by X-ray examination

pressed into a negative mould. The moulded figure was then fixed onto a glued canvas ground and covered, layer by layer, with richer and richer details of vestments in the right sequence to create a spatial illusion. For one figure, 15 cm high, 13 separate pieces are evident. By close observation and X-ray-examination we were able to show that only for some attributes and spires were metal elements used (brass wires for hairs and spires, gilded silver for attributes). Most remarkable is the luxurious use of natural pearls, with 4,000 used on the figure of the madonna with child and about 15,000 pearls in total on the whole chasuble. The composition has been made with careful attention to the optical perspective, so as to enhance the effect of the relief for the viewer: larger pearls are placed on the top of folds, smaller down between them.[5]

Polishing and drilling of pearls was first described by Theophilus in the 12th century. A hole is made with a bow-drill, and then this pilot hole is enlarged by moving the pearl by hand along a stretched thread covered with fine sand.

Such flat applications of pearls with a diameter of 1 to 3 mm were realized by first using pearls of equal size to create chains and then sewing the chains close together. Attempts to reproduce this technique and sew pearls with modern needles failed. The only needles which worked were 0.1 to 0.2 mm needles used in eye surgery, but how could they have been manufactured in romanesque times?[6] The use of pearls was brought by Alexander the Great from the orient to Greece, where the technique was called 'margaritai' (from where the name Margaret is derived). Later in Rome the term 'unio' was usual, both names being based on the scientific name (*unio margaritifera* L. = riverpearlshell). Pliny the elder in his natural history from the first century AD describes how, in his time, pearls could be found at places on the Mediterranean Sea and those with ugly colours even in Britain. Pliny notes that pearls were then the costliest of all things and he criticised the luxury of using pearls for decorating hair, fingers, shoes and necklaces. Their owners both valued and bequeathed precious pearls.[7] In medieval times pearls became symbols for Christ and the reign of heaven, after the parables in the Bible and the stories in the *Physiologus* (agate and pearl).[8]

It is important to realise that prominent works of textile pearl reliefs between 1480 and 1520 are close to the polychrome works of known painters and sculptors of the time. So we find first exact imitations of pearl reliefs on liturgical vestments in the figures of Michael Pacher around 1470/80, made in his workshop in Southern Tyrol. The imitation has been done by using both pastiglia dots from glue-sized chalk with silvering, and by a painting technique on the figures of the patron saint and the panels of the St Wolfgang altarpieces and on the Kirchenväteraltar from Neustift in the Munich Gallery.[9] This proves textile reliefs with pearl embroidery to have been a fashionable luxury of the late 15th century, based on close co-operation between two different arts.

We know that Michael Pacher lived his last years (1495–1498) at Salzburg in the house of a silk embroiderer. Both in Salzburg and Munich painters, sculptors and embroiderers were sometimes members of the same guild.[10] Other examples are works in Crakow, Poland, influenced by the German sculptor Veit Stoss, who worked there from 1477 to 1496 (his works include the crucifixion at Wroclaw, 1497, a chasuble in the treasury of Wawel, Crakow, and a pluvial shield in the museum of Vienna cathedral, 1518).[11] A third artist to mention was the painter Matthias Grünewald. In 1521 he painted his panel with the saints Erasmus and Mauritius, now in the Munich Gallery, with the annunciation on the bishop's mitres imitating pearl embroidery. The original mitre was made by the silk embroiderer Plock, a close friend of Grünewald's from his stay at Halle.[12]

Sixteenth century works of relief embroidery show very detailed forms of faces and increased dimensions so that figures are 30 to 70 cm in height with 6–7 cm relief (e.g. the shrine of St Wolfgang of 1598 in the treasury at St Wolfgang, Upper Austria – Figure 2(a), (b) and (c)). Another later chasuble, in the treasury at Mariazell, showing the ascension of the Virgin, was donated in 1587.[13] An independent relief of a crucifixion from around 1600 with nearly 15 fully shaped figures, but without pearls, is in the castle of Weitra, Lower Austria (Figure 3(a) and (b)).

Several of these textile reliefs have been preserved and examined during the last two years in the laboratories of the Bundesdenkmalamt in Vienna in a close co-operation between textile restorers and conservators of polychrome sculptures.

a

b

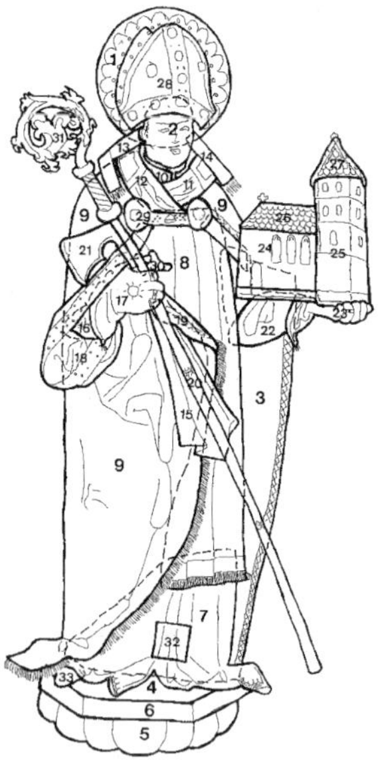

c

Figure 2. (a) Retable by Michael Pacher, 1471-1481, parish church, St. Wolfgang, Upper Austria: detail of polychromed wooden sculpture of bishop Wolfgang showing mitre with annunciation, made in imitation of textile-relief with pearl embroidery by means of a silvered pastiglia technique. (b) Shrine figure of St Wolfgang from 1598, St Wolfgang treasury: detail of textile relief after conservation. (c) The same figure as in (b), with the individual elements of the composition indicated

Examination took place by X-ray, cross section, scanning microscope analyses of metal threads, macrophotographs of patterns and close naked-eye observation of all elements of the fabric and the composition of the materials and the layers. Reconstruction of one of the Weitra figures by copying the original techniques confirmed the results obtained by examination (Figure 4). Cleaning and conservation were mainly done manually, following traditional methods of fixing with similar silk; glueing was used only for pearls it was impossible to sew on again.

To sum up, we can see a very close development of the two arts, polychrome sculpture and textile embroidery, between 1450 and the early 17th century, leading to a symbiosis of the highest efforts in representation and skilfulness. Although spatial qualities were originally not familiar in the textile arts and related techniques, we have to accept that there was a logical move towards the three-dimensional illusion and thus to competition between textile arts, painting and sculpture. To criticise this from the traditional viewpoint of textile history ignores the given facts.[14] It has to be acknowledged that this phenomenon reflects the concepts of the renaissance in moving towards increasing realism, as in many other areas of art at that time.

Dressed sculptures

A more or less parallel tradition was developing from the 14th century on. The custom in convents of draping figures of the child Jesus developed further, so that holy saints and the Virgin Mary with child were also draped. They were used for several liturgical functions. Made with different materials, such as polychromed wood, wax, terracotta or cartapesta used mainly for the flesh parts, and with different technologies, they often only have rough constructions made of wood or wires underneath the clothed parts.[15] For several sacred representations, gothic figures were constructed like 'mannequins' with adjustable joints so that head, arms, hands and feet can move; an example is the man of sorrows, c.1500, in the Augustinian church at Rattenberg. The gothic textiles used for clothing the figures have not been preserved in Austria.

Sculptures from the 17th to 19th centuries are preserved in various regions. These sculptures need systematic registration and conservation. Five clothed sculptures from 1687 to late 18th century rococo, coming from churches and chapels in Burgenland and Tyrol, have recently been shown in an exhibition at the Ethnographic Museum in Vienna after their restoration in the laboratories of the Bundesdenkmalamt, Wien.[16] Their realism is enhanced by the use of glass eyes, natural hair (or hair made from flax), adornments of metal or paper flowers etc.

Today there are still religious ceremonies and representations, mainly in catholic and Spanish-speaking countries, which use sculptures with rich textiles imitated in contemporary polychromies (so-called estofado).[17] In central Europe, mainly in the Tyrol, we find many beautiful dressed sculptures (Figure 5(a) and (b)). Some are protected in glassed shrines with curtains to hide them from the light. In comparison, we must never forget that during the same period it was usual to overpaint old figures, not only with new colouring, but even to style them with contemporary textile patterns, for example a 14th century stone madonna in the Marktkirche at St Florian, Upper-Austria, which bears its fourth polychromy, dating from around 1750 and imitating gold laces embroidery.

Conservation and possibly restoration of these artificial mixed compositions needs well organized co-operation, including a wide range of professions, such as restorers for polychromies and woodwork, textiles, wax sculpture and metals. We carried out a successful project with a series of figures by using the advantage of a multi-specialist workshop, a scientific laboratory and historical expertise. The main operations have been the consolidation of wooden and wax structures and the cleaning of polychromy and textiles. Drawings were made of all layers of the dresses. The necessary sewing and repair was followed by final re-assembly of all elements. Photographic documentation was made of every single step of composition. Lost glass eyes were replaced by new ones, because saints without eyes cannot be used for religious functions. However, we did not try to reconstruct hair when it was missing. We also refused to complete partial garments. We still know very little about the date and manufacture of the production and donation of clothing. Only in some well preserved cases, do we have figures with dated polychromy below the original clothing, so that it can be dated with the figure, for example, a madonna, dedicated 1687 by Paul Esterhazy, in the castle at Forchtenstein, Burgenland (Figure 6(a) and (b)).

During the enlightenment of the 18th century, we find increasing criticism about the abuse of these religious luxuries. In France many figures were destroyed during the revolution and in Austria they were systematically suppressed by laws of Emperor Joseph II. Especially for the 'exornment' of churches from 1784, he claimed that all sacred figures should look like the material they were made from.[18] Thus we now find many of the medieval polychrome sculptures overpainted. Some were later uncovered leaving damage around the neck because of the lost baroque textile vestments.

Conclusions

It is important to compare contemporary developments in different arts and techniques to understand their similarities and possible interactions. We find representation of volume and bodily realism (natural hairs, relieved black underpainted veins) both in polychrome sculpture between about 1480 and the early 17th century and in textile manufactures, made from negative moulds.

On the other hand, late gothic sculpture and painting started to reproduce precious brocade fabrics, by means of application techniques with pressed tinfoils, and used pastiglia-work to imitate pearl embroidery and even sometimes applied small gilded metal disks (spangles), as used in textiles. If we take into consideration the close rules of guilds, we can be sure that there was exchange and learning between workshops and crafts. Both crafts were trying to follow the latest fashions and styles in artistic and economic competition.

The final step of figurative representation 'effigies', that is true and lifelike depictions, were clothed figures in connection with both religious and secular functions. Their realism included moving parts of the body and changes of clothing for various events and fashions. From the few documents and studies existing until

a

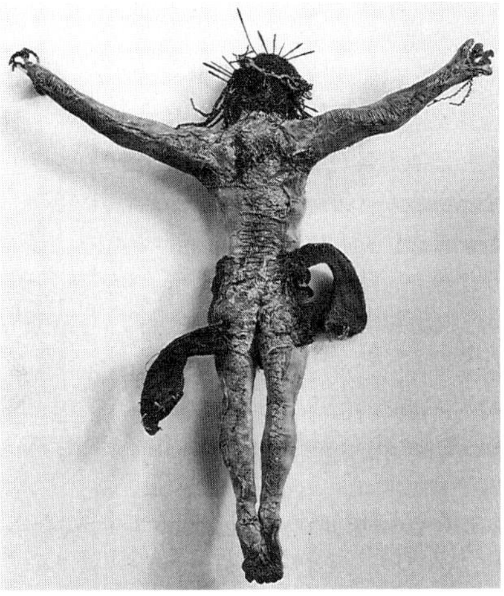

b

Figure 3. (a) Crucifixion, around 1600, castle, Weitra, Lower Austria: textile relief with silk embroideries mixed with silver and gold threads, hairs from brasswires, nails from horn etc. (b) Detail of figure from the back

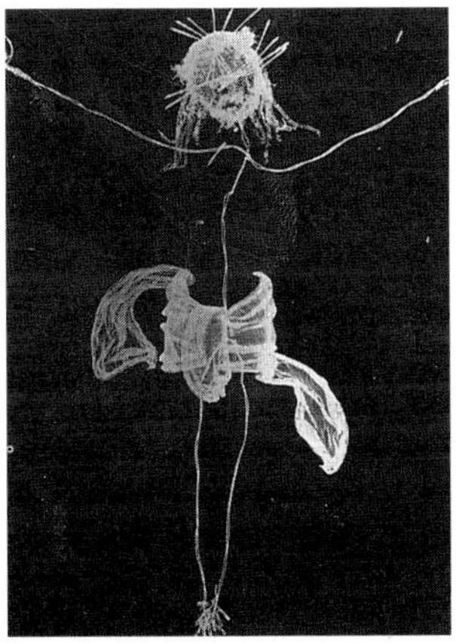

a

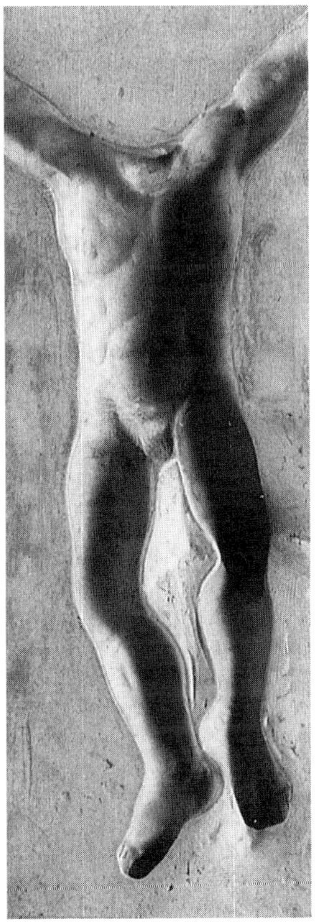

b

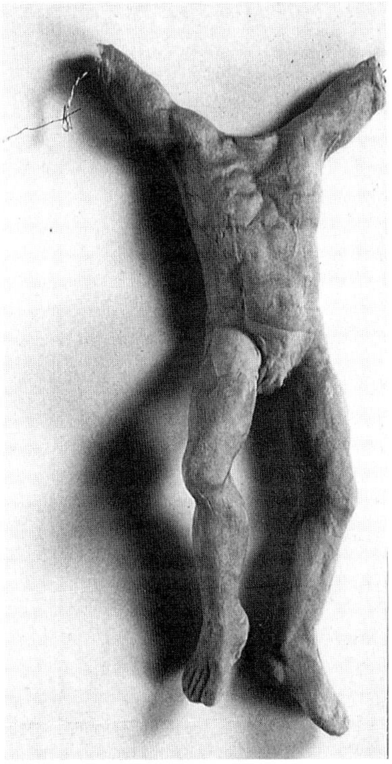

c

Figure 4.(a) X-ray of crucifix in Figure 3(b) showing the simple wire inside the textile figure. (b) Gesso negative of reconstructed textile figure. (c) Positive of reconstructed textile figure now, we may learn of the highly elaborate hierarchy of sculptural representation according to function and veneration through the ages. Gothic figures were overpainted or were clothed during the baroque period. We have to respect these later alterations and should not always just look for the, often small, traces of the first polychromy. Every piece of art bears traces of its whole history, suffered since its creation, and we have to evaluate them all together. Then we shall be able to know more about the true and many 'lives' of our sculptural heritage. Just as different artists communicated in the creation and subsequent metamorphosis of works of art before our time, restorers now have to exchange their experiences and become more than pure specialists.

a

b

Figure 5. (a) Madonna with child without clothing, c. 1350, church, Kaltenbrunn, Tyrol, after conservation of 18th century polychromy. (b) The same figure with her 18th century dress after conservation

Acknowledgements

The author wants to thank for their co-operation mainly Elisabeth-Macho-Biegler and Gabriele Klein, textile restorers, Rita Furrer, wax restorer, all Vienna Helmut Paschinger and Helmut Richard, anaytical laboratory, Johannes Nigisch, sculptor, all Bundesdenkmalamt Wien, and the restorers of polychrome sculpture working there for their contribution to the discussions and examinations. All relevant reports about examination and restoration are kept in the files of the department for art restoration, Bundesdenkmalamt Wien.

Notes and references

1. J.Taubert, 'Farbige Skulpturen', *Bedeutung, Fassung, Restaurierung* (Munich, 1978); T. Brachert and F. Kobler, 'Fassung von Skulpturen', in *Reallexikon zur deutschen Kunstgeschichte* 7, (Stuttgart, 1981), 743–826; M. Hamsik, 'Pastiglia and Technical History, and idem, Master Theodoric's Painting Technique', in *Technologia Artis* 2, (Prague 1992), 45–57.
2. R.E. Straub, 'Die Tafel- und Tüchleinmalerei des Mitelalters', *in Reclams Handbuch der künstlerischen Techniken* 1, (Stuttgart: Reclams, 1984), 168 ff; E. Brepohl, *Theophilus presbyter und die mittelalterliche Goldschmiedekunst* (Vienna, 1987); B. Klesse, *Seidenstoffe in der italienischen Malerei des 14. Jhs.* (Bern, 1967); J. Zander-Seidel, 'So wirt es gut und erhaben, gleich als der sammet. Textile Gewebeimitationen des späten Mittelalters und der frühen Neuzeit', in *Anzeiger des Germanischen Nationalmuseums* (Nuremberg, 1995), 216–227.
3. K.W. Bachmann et al., 'The conservation and technique of the Herlin altarpiece (1466)', *Studies in Conservation* 15, no.4 (1970): 327ff., 388ff; B. Hecht, 'Betrachtungen über Preßbrokate', *Maltechnik restauro*, no. 1 (1980): 22–49.
4. M. Schuette and S. Müller-Christensen, *Das Stickereiwerk* (Tübingen 1963); L.v.Wilckens, *Die textilen Künste von der Spätgotik bis um 1500* (Munich, 1991), 252ff; H. Herrmann, 'Die Restaurierung einer spätmittelalterlichen Perlenstickerei', *Maltechnik restauro*, no.3 (1975), 113–115.

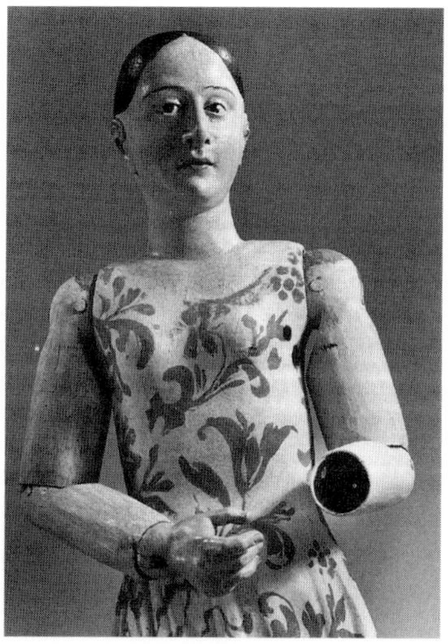

a

b

Figure 6. (a) Madonna with child, dated 1687, castle, Forchtenstein, Burgenland: polychromed woodcarving with movable arms. (b) The same figure with her dress from 1687 after conservation

5. M. Koller, 'Die beiden perlenbestickten Kaseln der Schatzkammer in Mariazell', in *Schatz und Schicksal* (Graz: Mariazell, 1996).
6. Brepohl *Seidenstoffe in der italienischen Malerei*, 303 (ch. XCIV. *De margaritis*); Herrmann, 'Die Restaurierung'.
7. 'Der kleine Pauly', *Lexikon der Antike*, vol.3 (Munich, 1979), 1020.
8. W. Braunfels (ed.), *Lexikon der christlichen Kunst*, vol.3. (Freibürg/Br., 1976), 393.
9. N. Rasmo, *Michael Pacher*, (Munich, 1969). M.Koller, N. Wibiral, 'Der Pacher-Altar in St. Wolfgang', *Untersuchung, Konservierung und Restaurierung 1969–1976*, (Vienna, 1981), 191ff, Fig. 42.
10. F. Wagner, 'Bemerkungen zu den sogenannten Pacher-Zeichnungen in Erlangen', *Alte und moderne Kunst* 160/161, (1978), 25ff; B. Degenhart and A. Schmitt, *Corpus der italienischen Zteichnungen 1300-1450* II (Berlin, 1980), cat. 652–663. Degenhart and Schmitt found designs on parchment from a Venetian silk embroiderer of the 14th century reused by Jacopo Bellini for his design.
11. A. Saliger, *Erzbischöfliches Dom- und Diözesanmuseum* (Vienna, 1987), cat. 25, fig.73.
12. B. Saran, 'Die Malausrüstung "Matthias Grünewalds"', *Maltechnik restauro*, no 3 (1973): 110ff.
13. Koller 'Die beiden perlenbestickten Kaseln'.
14. Wilckens *Die textilen Künste von der Spätgotik*, 253.
15. H. Wentzel, 'Bekleiden von Bildwerken', in *Reallexikon zur deutschen Kunstgeschichte* 1, (Stuttgart, 1937), 219–225; W. Brückner, 'Mannequins', in *Traumwelt der Puppen*, ed. B. Krafft, (Exhibition catalogue, Munich, 1992), 1–24; M. Koller, 'Kleider machen Heilige. Bekleidete Bildwerke in Österreich und ihre Restaurierung', *Österreichische Zeitschrift für Volkskunde* (1996),19–58.
16. Koller 'Kleider machen Heilige.'.
17. I. Gori and S. Barbieri, 'Tecnicas y caracteristicas esteticas, estilisticas e iconograficas de la imagineria de los siglos XVII–XX en el territorio Argentino', *Zeitschrift für Kunsttechnologie und Konservierung* 7 (1993): 1–72.
18. M. Koller, 'Zur Geschichte der Restaurierung in *Österreich' Internationaler Kongress Restauriergeschichte*, Interlaken, 1989. (Worms, 1991), 65ff., Fig.11.

The Processional Image in Minas Gerais, Brazil

Maria Regina Emery Quites
Center for Conservation and Restoration of Cultural Movable Properties (CECOR),
School of Fine Arts-Federal University of Minas Gerais (UFMG),
Av. Antônio Carlos, 6627, Pampulha, Belo Horizonte, Minas Gerais, Brazil

Abstract

This paper reports research on the processional image in Minas Gerais, Brazil, and specifically on images used during religious festivities during Holy Week. A classification is proposed in three distinct groups: *de vestir* ("to be dressed") images, *de roca* images and articulated images. This work aims to research their construction technique in relation to their social and religious functions, particularly as they have been used since the 18th century and are still in use today.

Keywords

Polychrome sculpture, *de vestir* (to be dressed) images, Holy Week, articulated images, Minas Gerais, Brazil

Introduction

The search for gold at the beginning of the 18th century was the main impulse for the formation of the Minas Gerais state, situated in inland Brazil. The development and the consolidation of the villages were directly linked to the artistic, cultural and religious life of the state. The large number of polychrome sculptures is evidence of this process. In this paper, we deal specifically with the processional images used during Holy Week and denominated *de vestir* (to be dressed), *de roca*[1] and articulated.

It was felt necessary to research this type of sculpture group, firstly because it is usually relegated to a lower level and considered as "bad taste" in comparison with the *talha inteira* (wholly carved) images. Another aspect that made us want to consider the importance of these images is that they have been in use since the 18th century and are still in use today. They continue to fulfil both social and religious functions, bringing together the majority of communities during the religious cortèges and ceremonies in Holy Week, and remaining amongst the most popular religious objects of the region.

Religious confraternities were founded in Minas Gerais. They, along with the manifestations of the baroque style and spirit in vogue during this period, helped the growth of personal devotions and public manifestations as part of religious cults and during religious festivals.

Work methodology

The iconographic representations selected for this study are those considered the most important in quality and quantity, as well as still being used at the present day during Holy Week: Our Lady of Sorrows, *Senhor dos Passos* (Christ, on one knee, carrying the cross) and the Dead Christ.
Holy Week is the apex of the religious festivals of the catholic church, when the martyrdom, death and resurrection of Christ are celebrated.

Cortèges (or processions), in which the images participate, are commonly found in the places studied and these are: Funeral Cortèges, Cortèges of the meeting of Jesus with his mother, and the Deposit Cortège. Traditionally important cities in Minas Gerais for their religious manifestations during Holy Week were selected for study: Santa Bárbara, Catas Altas, Santa Luzia and Sabará, which will be the next city to be studied.

We aim to study the technique of construction of the images, together with their accessories and attachments, and to classify them into categories associated with the functions for which they are used during the rituals of the martyrdom of Christ in Holy Week.

Individual studies of each image were carried out. Each image was analysed and documented photographically in black and white and on colour slides. Studies were also made of the preparation of the images for the ceremonies and the religious processions.

Through bibliographic research, we collected historic, iconographic and technological facts about these images and the places to which they belong. We made technical reports with the aim of setting up a database and propagating the knowledge we had acquired about the processional images of Minas Gerais.

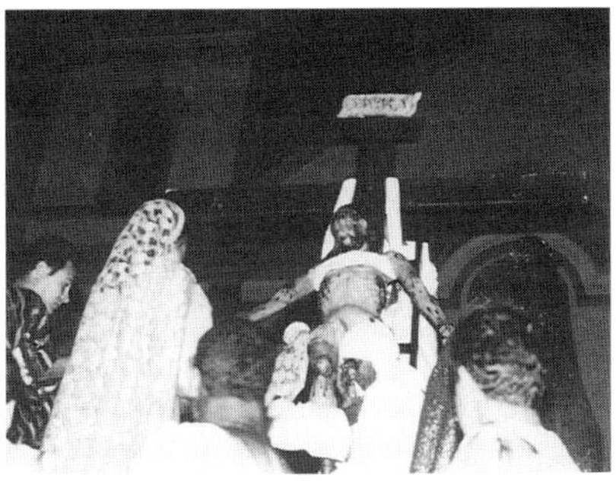

Figure 1. The Dead Christ of Santa Luzia – articulated image – descent ceremony

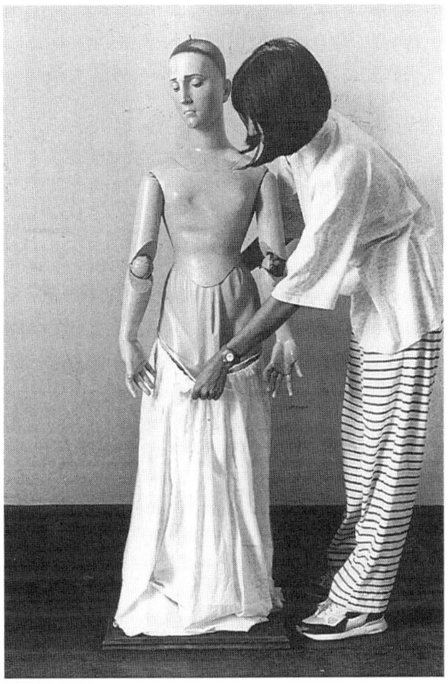

Figure 2. Our Lady of Sorrows of Santa Bárbara – de vestir *image – undressed*

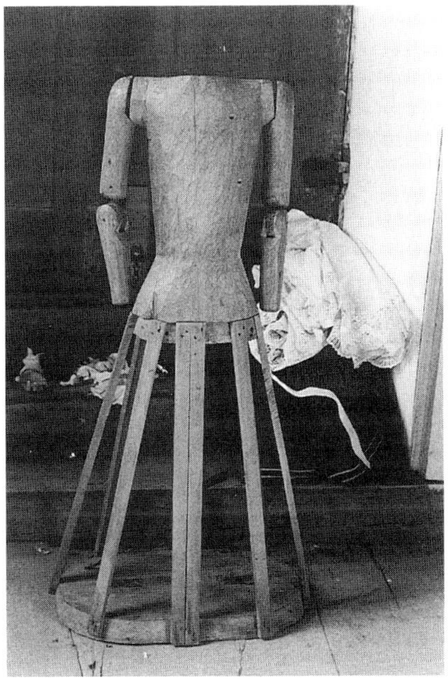

Figure 3. Our Lady of Sorrows of Catas Altas – roca *image – body, upper limbs and wooden framework*

Discussion of results

Polychrome sculptures in wood can be *talha inteira* – totally carved and polychromed – known for their technical quality and style. Defined in one single position, they do not have articulations that enable changes in position. They are also characterised for having drape areas represented with the use of polychromy adornment techniques such as *esgrafitos*, *pastiglio*, punctures and paintbrush painting, which aim to imitate the fabric with all its textures. The hair is also carved and polychromed.

The images we studied, in contrast, always have articulations, being able to be moved to different positions. They are clothed in natural fabrics and have, in most cases, natural hair. The polychromy and carving are finely done on the visible areas, but are much simpler on the hidden areas under the clothes. These images have eyes sculpted in wood or glass eyes.

In this work, in a more detailed analysis, we propose a classification into distinct groups, from the most complex to the simplest. We perceive that this simplification into groups has come about over time, as a result of the lack of resources that came from the decline of the gold cycle. Materials and resources for paying capable professionals were therefore saved.

Articulated images

These have a high level of carving elaboration and polychromy, as on the *talha inteira* images, although they have articulations hidden by polychrome leather. They are only draped with a few items of natural fabric, for example lace on the edges of the Christ's *perizônio* (the loincloth that covers Christ's pelvic area) or the fabric covering the *perizônio* articulation. In this group we can put the Dead Christ images, which have articulations on the shoulders, allowing participation in staging of the crucifixion (open arms fixed on the cross), in the descent (semi-open arms wrapped by the descent sheet) (Figure 1) and in the funeral cortège (arms extended along the body inside the coffin).

De vestir *images*

These sculptures were carved in a simple way, like a "mannequin", to be complemented with natural clothes. The hidden areas coincide with the body and limbs and these are usually presented monochromed or without polychromy (Figure 2). They have articulations on the shoulders and elbows and also natural hair. The visible parts, usually head, hands and feet, have detailed carving and polychromy.

Roca *images*

These sculptures have a simpler structure than the previous ones, having a wooden framework substituting the lower limbs (Figure 3). They have detailed carving and polychromy treatment only on the hands and head (Figure 4), although sometimes the feet are also carved and polychromed, and they have articulations on the shoulders and elbows.These images are, like the *de vestir* ones, complemented by clothes and natural hair.

Peculiarities

The construction of the carvings

The sculptures are composed of several wooden pieces, the number increasing in accordance with the compexity, as discussed above. We have found sculptures with up to 24 parts (Figure 5).

On the trunk area, the sculptures can be solid or hollow with a barrelhead on the back. The head can be either fixed or attached with a male/female linkage. Metal spikes, wooden pins and animal glue are utilised to join the parts.

The Our Lady of Sorrows sculptures always have a fixed base, while the *Senhor dos Passos* ones have a movable base, and do not need a litter to be carried, while the Dead Christ images never have a base.

Figure 4. Our Lady of Sorrows of Catas Altas – roca *image – head and hands*

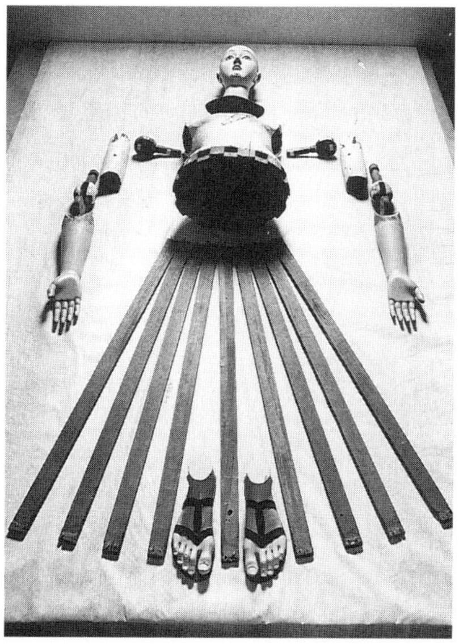

Figure 5. Our Lady of Sorrows of Santa Luzia – roca *image – disassembled for restoration, 24 wooden pieces*

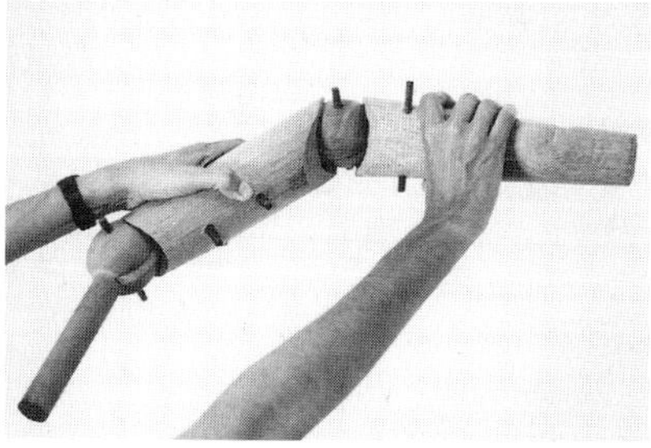

Figure 6. Facsimile of the most common articulation model found in our study

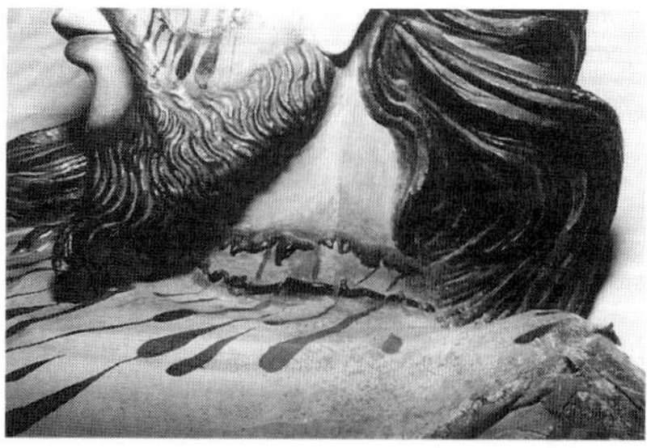

Figure 7. The Dead Christ of Santa Luzia – articulated image – polychrome leather on the healing representations

Articulations

The articulations have two defined functions: to allow the alteration of gestures by the sculpture and to facilitate handling during the dressing. The articulations are found on the shoulders and elbows, and occasionally on the knees, wrist and at the junction of the legs with the trunk. On the articulated sculptures, as the articulations are always visible, there is an original polychrome leather covering the gearing of the joint, in order to create a realistic effect.
The male/female sphere linkage is the most common in the articulation systems. The fixing of the articulated pieces is done with wooden pins. The most complex model is commonly found on the elbows and allows a 360° turn (Figure 6).

Polychromy

The flesh-tone is generally well reproduced on the articulated images of Christ, with representations of healing, bruises and blood drops[2] and even the use of polychrome leather in the healing representations (Figure 7).

Clothing

In general, the original clothing of the images was not found in the communities studied. There is a tradition of giving rich and new clothing to the images. However, it seems that there is no concern about conserving previous clothing.

The clothing of the *Senhor dos Passos* images consists of: underneath tunic, tunic and mantle. Our Lady of Sorrows is dressed with underneath tunic, tunic, petticoat, mantle and veil. White is used on the *Senhor dos Passos*'s underneath tunic, on Our Lady of Sorrow's petticoat, on the descent sheet and on the coffin sheet of the Dead Christ. Purple, which symbolises martyrdom, is used on the *Senhor dos Passos*'s and Our Lady of Sorrow's tunics and mantle. It is also used on the mantle that covers the Dead Christ in the coffin.

Hair

The hair is natural and usually long. Each image has more than one wig. The halo fixes the wig to the head. No original wig was found, since they are substituted by the believers.

Eyes

The eyes are usually made of glass (Figure 8). There is a cut between the top of the head and under the chin, which allows the eyes to be placed from behind. In some images, the eyes are sculpted from wood and polychromed. As well as the glass eyes, we also found glass tears on one Our Lady of Sorrows image.

Accessories

The accessories are: crown of thorns (made of liana) for the Dead Christ and *Senhor dos Passos*, haloes (made of silver) for *Senhor dos Passos* and Our Lady of Sorrows and a heart with swords or dagger for Our Lady of Sorrows.

Attachments

The attachments are an essential part of the participation of the images in the religious festivals. They are: two crosses, one where the Dead Christ is crucified and the other which *Senhor dos Passos* carries on its back; the litter, which the believers use to carry the images during the cortège; the litter handles (Figure 9); the *cirineu*;[3] and the coffin used to carry the Dead Christ. All of these are made of wood, with the exception of the *cirineu* and part of the litter handles, which are made of iron.

Figure 8. Senhor dos Passos *of Santa Bárbara – articulated image – glass eyes*

The religious festivals

Current study of the images in their religious context allowed an appraisal of the technique of their construction as it relates to their functions, as well as a review of their use over time. We were therefore able to verify that the *Senhor dos Passos* image originally represented three iconographic images: *Ecce Homo*, the Flagellation and the Cross on the back. However, today it is used only to represent the cross on the back and occasionally *Ecce Homo*.[4]

In all the communities studied, the sculptures are kept in the churches. They are placed in niches or coffins, under the altarpiece and even in cupboards throughout the year.

It is interesting that, traditionally, certain families are responsible for the preparation of the images for Holy Week, passing down this knowledge to the new generations. In the past, the religious confraternities of lay members were once responsible for this work. However, the families assumed this duty when the religious confraternities declined approximately 50 years ago.

In all the communities studied, we perceived a relationship of extreme respect between the believer and the image. The way that the image is preserved, with care and decency, from "curious eyes" during the preparations for the cortèges is an example of this respect. The funeral cortège has much prestige among the believers.

The herb basil[5] is always used to ornament both the coffin of the Dead Christ and the church on Good Friday. After the cortège, the believers take this blessed herb home.

Two processions from different churches join the cortège at the meeting of Christ with the cross and his mother. One of these processions carries Our Lady of Sorrows and the other one carries *Senhor dos Passos*. In one community, the women follow and carry the litter of Our Lady of Sorrows, which is a tradition that is kept up to the present day. Generally, however, this separation of sexes in the cortèges no longer occurs, and the men nearly always carry the litter.

Conservation/restoration

This group of images still has its social and religious functions defined today. Therefore, it is important to discuss its conservation. These sculptures were created with a particular function and they must retain this function. It is not the duty of the conservator to transform the images into museum pieces, taking away their main purpose. The conservator's role is to raise the level of awareness concerning preservation, conservation and restoration of this important cultural heritage. The images have been repainted several times because of the enormous devotion and utilisation in the religious ceremonies. The aim of this repainting is to give the images a new flesh-tone (Figure 10), as is done with the clothing.

Support problems found are: insect attacks, mainly termites; fractures; fissures (cleavage, crack) and support losses. These are due to the handling and to the lack of conservation.

The articulations were stuck, without movement, broken and, most of the time, without the original polychrome leather presented on the articulated images, or with inadequate interventions, where it was used other materials were used.

Figure 9. Our Lady of Sorrows of Catas Altas – roca *image – women carrying the litter and handles to join the cortège of the meeting of Christ and his mother*

Conclusion

With this research, we hope to contribute to the propagation and valorisation of this cultural heritage, so that the tradition which is still present in the cities studied can be handed on to future generations.

We emphasise that knowledge of the construction technique of a piece of art is essential to the conservator. In this way, a conscious and judicious intervention can be made.

Our role in these communities is the propagation of consciousness, orientation and, when possible, the conservation and restoration of this cultural heritage.

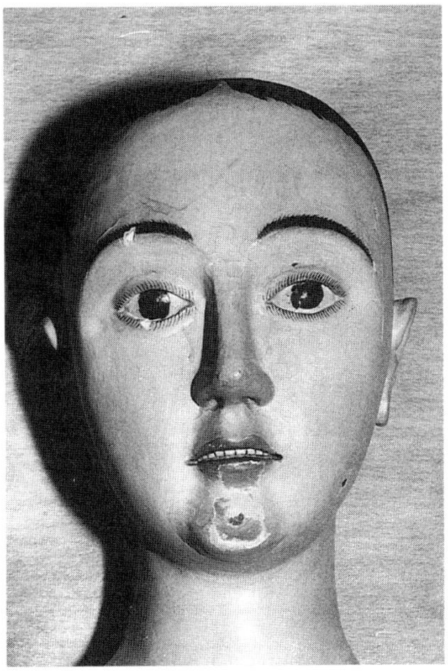

Figure 10. Our Lady of Sorrows of Santa Luzia – roca *image – Repainting in the flesh-tone has hidden the glass eyes which have been remodelled with gypsum over the original*

Acknowledgements

The author acknowledges financial support from the Federal University of Minas Gerais; and FAPEMIG for the concession of a research grant. The author is also grateful to student Tatiana Lúcia Costa Santos, for her dedication and responsibility; and to Beatriz Coelho and Ivê Madeira, for their collaboration.

Notes and references

1. "Some authors explain the naming of *Roca* images as referring to their first appearance in the 16th century. In this period, the tool used to produce fabric was the distaff. Therefore, saints dressed with fabric produced by this tool were called Roca Saints. It seems to us, however, that the nomenclature is more complex. The term "*Roca*" has been used to refer to a part of the sleeves, either feminine or masculine ones, since Medieval Ages. These sleeves were formed of strips, enabling the fabric underneath to be seen. The analogy with the wooden framework of these saint's body, made to support the articulated head and arms, is evident. Moreover, we note that in the majority of *Roca* images this kind of frame replaces the body, receiving clothing to camouflage it." in M. E. Paiva, "Imagens religiosas articuladas, o teatro místico e religioso do barroco", in *Mamulengo - Revista da Associação Brasileira de Teatro de Bonecos*, no 8 (Belo Horizonte: Associação Brasileira de Teatro de Bonecos, Dez/1994), 17–20.
2. "The blood drops, known as 'ruby', of all 8 pieces analysed were made of gold pigment (sulfide of arsenic III), natural mineral, according to descriptions in books of that epoch." in C. M. D. Moresi, "Estudo Científico de Policromias da imaginária Mineira do período colonial", *Seminário da ABRACOR*, 7 (1994), *Petrópolis* (Rio de Janeiro: ABRACOR – Associação Brasileira de Conservadores e Restauradores, 1994), 135.
3. The term "*Cirineu*" refers to the metal piece that holds the cross of *Senhor dos Passos* on its litter. This term is used in analogy to the biblical character Simon of Cyrene, who helped Jesus to carry the cross. We find this term referred to in the text: "When leaving the city they found a man from Cyrene, called Simon, who was obliged to carry Jesus' cross." in *Holy Bible* (São Paulo: Editora Ave Maria, 1992), Matthew 27: 33.
4. M.R.E. Quites, "Imaginaria processional: imagens de roca e articuladas em Minas Gerais", *Seminário da ABRACOR* ,7, 1994, *Petrópolis* (Rio de Janeiro: ABRACOR – Associação Brasileira de Conservadores e Restauradores, Nov. 1994), 178–183.
5. Basil is a herb, the leaves of which are said to have magical powers, and the flowers have a strong smell. Basil leaves are used in Central Congo to avoid bad luck and to protect from evil spirits. They are used to cure bruises and for healing; J. Chevalier and A. Gheerbrant, *Dicionário dos Símbolos* (Rio de Janeiro: José Olympio Editora, 1988).

Working Group B4

Mural paintings and rock art

Characterization of Pigments Used on Roman and Abbasid Frescoes in Jordan

Marie-Claude Corbeil*
Canadian Conservation Institute, Department of Canadian Heritage, 1030 Innes Road, Ottawa, Ontario, Canada K1A 0M5

John Peter Oleson
Department of Classics, University of Victoria, Victoria, British Columbia, Canada V8W 3P4

Rebecca Foote
Department of Fine Arts, Harvard University, Cambridge, MA 02138, USA

Abstract

Frescoes from a Roman fort and an Abbasid *qasr* (manor estate) were discovered in al-Humeima, Jordan. Ancient Hawar, now called al-Humeima or al-Humayma, was the major Nabataean, Roman, Byzantine, and early Islamic centre in the Hisma, Jordan's southern desert. The Roman fort was founded on unoccupied ground sometime in the first half of the second century AD. It seems to have been abandoned briefly in the later third century, then reoccupied for part of the fourth. The Abbasid *qasr* was erected in the early eighth century AD. The pigments used to paint the frescoes were analyzed using scanning electron microscopy/X-ray spectrometry (SEM/XES), X-ray diffraction (XRD) and polarized light microscopy (PLM). Fourier transform infrared (FTIR) spectroscopy was used to determine if any organic binding medium was present. The pigments were all traditional, mineral pigments, such as yellow ochre, red ochre, various iron earth pigments, and green earth. However, an unusual yellow pigment, lead silicate sulfate chloride, was found on fragments from the Abbasid *qasr* frescoes. It is a compound of the ellestadite group, which includes all of the apatite isotypes of composition $(Ca...)_5[(Si,S,P,C)O_4)]_3(OH,F,Cl))$.

Keywords

Apatite, ellestadite, mattheddleite, fresco, Roman, Abbasid, Humeima, Jordan, scanning electron microscopy/X-ray spectrometry, X ray diffraction, Fourier transform infrared spectroscopy, pigments

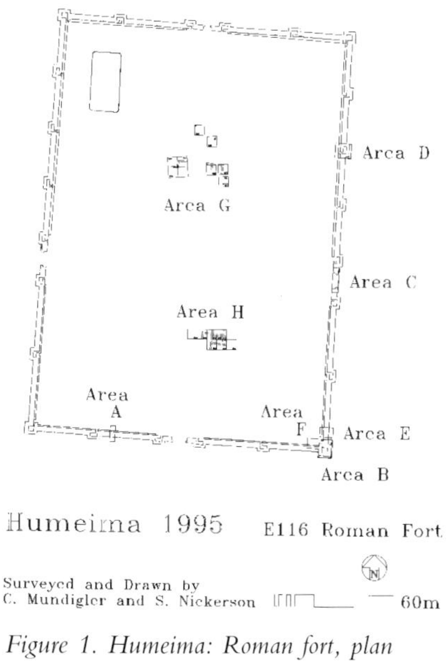

Figure 1. Humeima: Roman fort, plan

Introduction

Ancient Hawar, now called al-Humeima or al-Humayma, was the major Nabataean, Roman, Byzantine, and early Islamic centre in the Hisma, Jordan's southern desert.[1] The ruins of the settlement, approximately 10 ha in area, lie at an elevation of 955 m on the east slope of some rugged sandstone hills between the Jebel Qalkha and Jebel Humeima, 3 km east of the Wadi Araba. The site dominates the west edge of a rolling plane containing pockets of light, but fertile, loessal soil framed on the east and north by white sandstone hills. Precipitation in the lowland plain itself averages only 80 mm/year. The plain is watered by the winter rains that run off the al-Shara escarpment, which forms the dramatic north boundary of the roughly triangular catchment basin, 240 km^2 in area. The Wadi Qalkha carries run-off water past the site. Petra is 44 km to the north, the modern settlement of Ma'an 50 km to the northeast, and Aqaba (ancient Aila) is 55 km to the south.

According to Ouranios's *Arabika*, Hawar (in Greek spelled *Αυρα*/Auara) was founded by the Nabataean king Aretas III (87–62 BC) in response to an oracle.[2] Nothing is known of the early history of the settlement, but an extensive water-supply system was built in the first century BC, probably to attract settlers, caravans, and a market[3]. Early and Middle Nabataean ceramics are found at the site. Trajan's *Via Nova*, built along the course of a pre-existing Nabataean north/south road, passed through or very close to the settlement, and a large Roman fort was built soon after. Archaeological and literary evidence indicate that Hawar flourished in the Late Roman and Byzantine periods, and in the Umayyad and early Abbasid periods under the name Humeima or Humayma. Four Byzantine churches have been identified at the site. Soon after 687–688, 'Ali ibn 'Abd Allah ibn al-'Abbas purchased the town, which became a centre for the Abbasid family's revolt against the Umayyad dynasty. Historical sources report that the family built a manor estate (*qasr*) and adjoining mosque (*masjid*) at the site; these were identified by excavation in 1992. Ceramic evidence shows a marked decline in habitation after the mid-8th century, but there are traces of light, intermittent occupation through the Ottoman period.

This paper concerns the analysis of pigments from frescoes in the Roman fort and the Abbasid family *qasr*. The pigments used to paint the frescoes were all traditional, mineral pigments, but an unusual yellow pigment was found on fragments from the Abbasid *qasr* frescoes.

The Roman fort and Abbasid *qasr*

The Roman fort (206.32 × 148.32 m; ca. 700 × 500 Roman feet – henceforth abbreviated as RF) is set slightly apart from the habitation area, on a rise at the northeast edge of the site, close to a Nabataean reservoir and aqueduct. The fort has the typical rectangular plan (Figure 1), with a gate in each of the four walls, and 24 square towers (5.85 m wide; 20 RF) projecting (1.85 m; 6 RF) from the walls.

* Author to whom correspondence should be addressed

The walls are 3.00–3.06 m thick (c. 10 RF). The whole complex is oriented 10° east of north. Ceramics and coins found in the excavations of 1993 and 1995 have shown that the fort was founded on unoccupied ground sometime in the first half of the 2nd century AD, earlier than any other large Roman fort yet identified in Jordan.[4] The fort seems to have been abandoned briefly in the later 3rd century, then reoccupied for part of the 4th, with some rebuilding and rearrangement of the structures and rooms. There is no evidence for occupation after the 4th century.

The east and west gates are not located in the centre of their respective walls, but have been shifted to the south to accommodate a large headquarters building and parade ground, commander's residence, and possibly barracks or stables, in the northern half of the fort. The east wall extends 119 m north of the centre point of the east gate, and 87 m south of it (probably 400 and 300 RF, respectively). There are traces of walls, and mounds of structural debris throughout the interior of the fort, and the pattern of barracks blocks and ancillary structures can be seen in the aerial photographs taken in 1992.[5] In 1993, numerous fragments of painted wall plaster were found in Area A, a trench excavated against the inside of the south wall of the fort. The fragments were small (from 0.01–0.07 m maximum diameter; thickness 0.008–0.011 m), and consisted of a hard white backing heavily tempered with very fine sand, finished with a fine outer *intonaco*. No overall pattern of decoration could be discerned. Some fragments showed solid red, others solid golden yellow, green, or off white. Several fragments showed what may be green or red floral designs on white. The fresco fragments clearly had come from structures elsewhere on the site and had been dumped here, along with ceramics and coins datable as late as the early 4th century.

In 1995, some further fragments of similar manufacture and decoration were found in dumps associated with the *principia* building in Area G and the barracks in Area H. Although none of the fresco was found *in situ*, it seems likely that it originated in one or both of these areas, having fallen off the walls in some of the

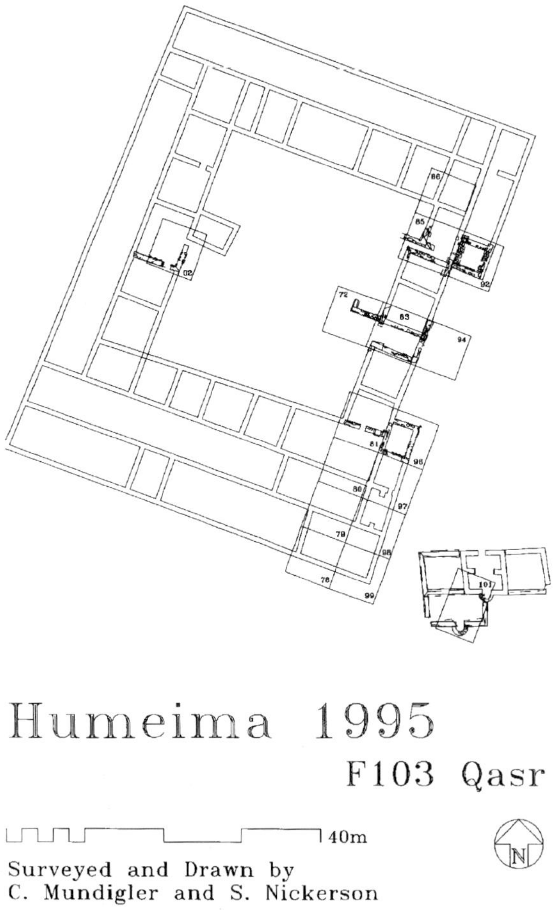

Figure 2. Humeima: Abbasid qasr, *plan*

rooms either before or during the 4th-century renovations. These structures may well be the source of the fresco fragments dumped in Area A.

Two structures have been under excavation in Field F103 at Humeima since 1992. One is a large rectangular building (61 × 50 m) centred around a trapezoidal court, with up to six courses of its masonry walls still intact and remains of a decorative wall fresco in one room. The other is a small rhomboidal structure with three extant courses of its original masonry walls and a projecting niche on the south side, located 15 m SE of the rectangular structure. No trace of any original ornamentation, for example fresco, was found in the rhomboidal structure. Ceramic evidence indicated that both were erected in the early 8th century AD and therefore probably in association with one another (Figure 2). The rectangular structure is called a *qasr*, the Arabic word for manor estate, and the rhomboidal one a mosque because of their typological similarity with other regional examples also dating to the early 8th century.[6] Historical texts relate that the Abbasid family (the second Islamic dynasty, ruling the Caliphate from 750–1250 AD) built a *qasr* and mosque at Humeima during the Umayyad period (first Islamic dynasty, ruling the Caliphate from 661–749 AD, whom the Abbasids overthrew), in the decades before their rise to power.[7] Given the absence of any other structures at Humeima fitting the descriptions, and the rich finds within the larger structure, the *qasr* and mosque have been identified as the Abbasid family complex.

Frescoes were discovered during the 1992 season in a central room (Figure 2, labelled 02) of the western wing of the manor estate. Excavation did not begin until the 1993 season when a conservator, Ms Judy Logan of the Canadian Conservation Institute in Ottawa, was present. The room measures 6.5 × 5.6 m. During the 1993 and 1995 seasons, remains of the fresco were systematically excavated along the entire extent of the room's southern wall measuring 5.6 m (except for a door break of 0.91 m), in an area extending 2.25 m out from the wall into the room. The findings indicate that the room was originally decorated with frescoes, executed probably as a solid red wash dado below an expanse of non-figural patterning. Some of the red-washed plaster remains affixed along the base of the exposed walls to a maximum height of 0.5 m along the base.

After a fire, probably in the 8th century, the patterned plaster collapsed into fragments onto the white plastered floor of the room. The fresco fragments are mixed into a thick layer of superstructure debris – mud-packing, burnt palm fronds, and burnt palm trunk sections of the fallen walls and roof. Artifacts made of ivory, ostrich eggshell, wood and iron have also been discovered among this collapsed layer. These luxury items, along with the fresco itself, are collateral evidence in identifying the building as the Abbasid *qasr*. Of 11 rooms in the *qasr* that have been excavated to floor level, this is the only room adorned with frescoes; the entry from the courtyard into it is slightly north of the axis of the only entrance to the *qasr*, on the east, and hence the room may have functioned as an audience hall or "throne room."

Though damaged by fire, several design patterns can be discerned, mostly floral, along with some vegetal and geometric, set within pearl-beaded rectangular bands. Reconstruction of their original deployment on the wall has also been undertaken. The original range of colours is still somewhat difficult to determine because of changes caused by the heat of the fire. With that consideration, black, grey, rust, orange, mauve, salmon, yellowish-green, yellow and white can be readily distinguished.

Experimental

Particulate samples were collected from fresco fragments. Some powdered samples were dispersed in a viscous mounting medium (Carmount-165 Medium, R.P. Cargille Laboratories, Inc.) and examined by polarized light microscopy. Cross sections were prepared using standard petrographic techniques and examined using incident light and fluorescence microscopy. Examinations by microscopy were performed using either a Leitz Orthoplan or Leitz DMR polarizing microscope. Particulate samples and cross sections were analyzed using a Hitachi S-530 scanning electron microscope equipped with an X-ray energy spectrometer (SEM/XES). A Noran Instruments Voyager microanalysis system and Si(Li) X-ray detector integrated with the SEM were used for X-ray analysis and digital imaging. The samples were subsequently analyzed by X-ray diffraction (XRD) to identify the major crystalline components in the support and pigment layers. X-ray diffraction patterns were obtained with a Rigaku RTP 300 RC generator equipped with a rotating anode and a cobalt target, using either a 115 mm Gandolfi camera and CEA Reflex 25 X-ray film, or a microdiffractometer.[8] The generator was operated at 45 kV and 160 mA. Exposure time varied from two-and-a-half to three hours. Fourier transform infrared (FTIR) spectroscopy was used to determine if any organic binding medium was present.

Pigment identification

In samples, both from the Roman fort and the Abbasid *qasr*, the fresco support was composed of calcite and gypsum, with large quartz inclusions. As no organic binding medium was detected in the paint layer of any of the samples, the frescoes are likely to be true frescoes in which the pigments were placed directly onto the wet support rather than *fresco secco* in which the pigments were applied to a dry support with an organic binding medium.

In the Roman fort, the colours white, beige, yellow, green, maroon, and three shades of red were used. Calcite was found in all samples, and most samples also contained quartz and kaolinite. The yellow pigment was identified as yellow ochre, the green as green earth (glauconite). The maroon paint contained red ochre and black particles, possibly bone black. The shades of red were obtained by using red ochre and calcite in various proportions.

In the Abbasid *qasr*, the colours white, beige, yellow, brown, grey, black, two shades of red, and two shades of orange were observed on the frescoes. Again, calcite was found in all samples, and most samples contained quartz and kaolinite. Some samples also contained gypsum; this may be associated with the support rather than with the paint layer, which was very thin and therefore difficult to sample without removing part of the support as well. The black and brown paints were mixtures of dark red and dark orange iron earth pigments, and a black pigment which was tentatively identified by polarized light microscopy as charcoal black. The shades of red were obtained by using red ochre and calcite in various proportions. The orange pigment was identified by polarized light microscopy as an orange iron earth pigment, similar to modern examples of burnt sienna.

The yellow pigment from the *qasr* was found to be a compound which has not previously been reported as being used as a pigment. The paint layer, although having a greenish tint at the surface, has a bright yellow colour when observed in cross section. It was found by SEM/XES to contain primarily lead. The paint layer, although very thin (approximately 2 μm), can easily be distinguished from the support in the SEM image because of the large difference in atomic number between lead and calcium. In addition to lead, minor amounts of calcium, chlorine, magnesium, silicon, and phosphorus, and traces of aluminum, potassium, and iron were also detected in the paint layer.

The X-ray pattern of the yellow paint (Table 1) closely matched published data on two very similar lead silicate sulfate chloride compounds from the apatite group (general formula $A_{10}(XO_4)_6Z_2$). The first, a yellow, synthetic compound, lead-ellestadite, has the formula $Pb_{10}(SiO_4)_3(SO_4)_3Cl_2$.[9] The second compound, the mineral mattheddleite, of formula $Pb_{20}(SiO_4)_7(SO_4)_4Cl_4$, is described as being colourless.[10] As shown in Table 1, the three patterns are almost identical, except for what appears to be an extra line at 2.20 Å in the pattern of the yellow paint from al-Humeima. This line corresponds to the mean of three very close lines (with d-spacings from about 2.28 to 2.15 Å) of intensity lower than 10, which are reported for both lead-ellestadite and mattheddleite. Similarly, two lines appear to be missing in the pattern of mattheddleite, but it is likely that two sets of lines were too close to be resolved: the line at 3.004 Å in the pattern of mattheddleite corresponds to the average of the 3.015 Å and 2.987 Å lines (3.001) in the lead-ellestadite pattern, and the one at 1.916 Å to the average of the 1.933 Å and 1.905 Å lines (1.919). It must be noted that the intensity of the line at 3.029 Å in the pattern of the yellow pigment is higher than expected. As calcium was detected by SEM/XES, it is likely that the sample contained calcite, which has its most intense line at 3.035 Å.[11]

According to Rouse and Dunn, apatites $A_{10}(XO_4)_6Z_2$ "... are notable for their ability to accommodate a great variety of atoms in their A, X, and Z sites by means of simple or coupled ionic substitutions".[12] This is exemplified by the ellestadites, which can be better described as solid solutions.[13] In the literature, ellestadites used to be described as having the general formula $Ca_5[(Si,S,P]O_4)_3(Cl,F,OH)$,[14] but Rouse and Dunn proposed that the name ellestadite be used as a group name for all of the apatite isotypes of composition $(Ca...)_5[(Si,S,P,C)O_4)]_3(OH,F,Cl))$,[15] in which calcium may also be replaced. Indeed, lead and strontium ellestadites were synthesized;[16] mattheddleite, found in nature, can be described as an ellestadite in which calcium has been replaced by lead, although it does not contain sulfur and silicon in the expected 1:1 ratio typical of ellestadites.[17]

It should be pointed out that sulfur was not readily detected by SEM/XES in the yellow paint from the Abbasid *qasr* because, in the presence of lead, it is impossible to confirm the presence of sulfur, the *M* line of lead overlapping with the *K* line of sulfur. However, phosphorus was detected, along with several other elements present in minor or trace amounts. Phosphorus could be present in other minerals associated with the main component of the yellow paint, ellestadite, but its presence may also indicate that the ellestadite in the yellow paint contains phosphate anions in addition to silicate and sulfate anions. This would not affect greatly the X-ray pattern of the mineral. Indeed, Rouse and Dunn state: "... the mean of the effective radii of SiO_4 and SO_4 is equal to the effective radius of PO_4. Thus changes in the (Si,S):P ratio should not affect the size of the unit cell".[18] No attempts were made to perform quantitative analysis to determine the exact chemical formula of the yellow compound, as it was known, based on the SEM/XES analysis, to be mixed with other minerals.

By polarized light microscopy, the yellow pigment was found to be a bright, lemon-coloured yellow. The particles are fairly small (5 to 10 μm) and spherical, with a globular appearance. They have a refractive index above 1.66 (strong contrast in Carmount-165 Medium) and are isotropic. The pigment, microscopically, resembles yellow ochre, except that the shade of yellow is different, yellow ochre, in general, being a darker, golden yellow.

Conclusion

All pigments from the Roman fort, built in the first half of the second century and occupied periodically until the fourth century, and most of those from the Abbasid *qasr*, dating from the eight century, were natural pigments which have been recommended and widely used for frescoes since Antiquity.[19] It is not possible to

Table 1. X-ray powder diffraction data for Pb-ellestadite, mattheddleite, and yellow pigment from Abbasid fresco. For simplification purposes, and with some exceptions, only lines above 1.5 Å with intensities above 10 were reported

Pb-ellestadite $Pb_{10}(SiO_4)_3(SO_4)_3Cl_2$ JCPDS 41-475		Mattheddleite $Pb_{20}(SiO_4)_7(SO_4)_4Cl_4$ JCPDS 41-610		Yellow pigment from Abbasid fresco	
d(Å)	*I*	*d*(Å)	*I*	*d*(Å)	*I*
4.367	26	4.31	40	4.372	7
4.168	31	4.16	40	4.166	19
3.705	28	3.71	5	3.665	12
3.411	28	3.44	20	3.368	16
3.300	30	3.26	30	3.311	20
3.015	86	3.004	100	3.029	100
2.987	100			2.975	77
2.911	15	2.88	40	2.931	46
2.2889	6	2.285	5		
2.2191	9	2.236	5	2.206	9
2.1826	7	2.154	5		
2.0841	17	2.076	20	2.087	23
2.0269	10	2.019	15	2.025	12
1.9770	15	1.977	15	1.968	25
1.9332	15	1.916	15	1.941	21
1.9046	12			1.913	19
1.8801	18	1.876	20	1.887	23
1.5558	5	1.570	15	1.553	14
1.5336	5	1.549	15	1.536	15

confirm if the pigments were from a local source or imported from another location.

The yellow pigment from the Abbasid *qasr* belongs to the ellestadite group. Such a pigment has never been identified on frescoes from other sites, suggesting that the mineral was found locally. However, we cannot exclude the possibility that this mineral may have been used elsewhere and was never identified or reported before. Indeed, ellestadites have been found in several regions including the USA, the former Soviet Union, Germany, Israel, and Japan;[20] mattheddleite has been found in Scotland.[21]

The lemon-coloured lead-ellestadite would have been an alternative to the golden yellow ochre, the only yellow pigment which was considered suitable for frescoes.[22] It is also interesting to note that, while most of the lead-containing pigments were not recommended for fresco because of their susceptibility to discoloration,[23] the lead-ellestadite was not affected. Only a slight change in colour was observed at the surface of the paint layer, which may have been caused by the fire that destroyed the *qasr*.

Acknowledgements

The authors would like to acknowledge the contribution of Judy Logan, Dr. Alison Murray, and Kate Helwig to this study.

Notes and references

1. The Project Director is J.P. Oleson, University of Victoria. Co-Directors are K. 'Amr, Department of Antiquities of Jordan, R. Schick, Albright Institute, and R. Foote, Harvard University. The project has been funded by the Social Sciences and Humanities Research Council of Canada, the Taggart Foundation, the Van Berchem Foundation, and the American Schools of Oriental Research. For recent reports and full bibliography, see J.P. Oleson, "The Water-Supply System of Ancient Auara: Preliminary Results of the Humeima Hydraulic Survey," in *Studies in the History and Archaeology of Jordan*, IV, ed. K. 'Amr (Ammam: Department of Antiquities, 1992), 269–275; J.P. Oleson, K. 'Amr, and R. Schick, "The Humeima Excavation Project, Jordan: Preliminary Report of the 1991-1992 Seasons," *Annual of the Department of Antiquities of Jordan* 37 (1993): 461–502; J.P. Oleson, K. 'Amr, R. Foote and R. Schick, "The Humeima Excavation Project, Jordan: Preliminary Report of the 1993 Season," *Classical Views/Échos du monde classique* 13 (1994): 141–179; J.P. Oleson, K. 'Amr and R. Schick, "Preliminary Report of the Humeima Excavation Project, 1993," *Annual of the Department of Antiquities of Jordan* 39 (1995): 00–00.
2. J.P. Oleson and J. Eadie, "The Water-Supply Systems of Nabataean and Roman Humayma," *Bulletin of the American Schools of Oriental Research* 262 (1986): 49–76.
3. J.P. Oleson. "Aqueducts, Cisterns, and the Strategy of Water Supply at Nabataean and Roman Auara (Jordan)," in *Future Currents in Aqueduct Studies*, ed. A. Trevor Hodge (Leeds: Francis Corns, 1991), 45–62.
4. Oleson, 'Amr, Foote, Schick, "Preliminary Report of the 1993 Season," 145–154.
5. Oleson, 'Amr, Foote, Schick, "Preliminary Report of the 1993 Season," 174.
6. 'Amra: A. Amagro Gorbea, *Tres monumentos islamicos restaurados por Espana en el mundo arabe* (Madrid: Instituto de Espana, 1981), 15–46; K.A.C. Creswell, revised and supplemented by J. Allan, *A Short Account of Early Muslim Architecture* (Cairo: American University in Cairo, 1989), 105–117. Qasr Burqu': Creswell, *A Short Account*, 91–93; H. Gaube, "An Examination of the Ruins of Qsar Burqu'," *Annual of the Department of Antiquities of Jordan* 19 (1974): 93–100. Qasr al-Hallabat: G. Bisheh, "The Second Season of Excavations at Hallabat," *Annual of the Department of Antiquities of Jordan* 26 (1982): 133–143; Creswell, *A Short Account*, 164–165. Qsar al-Hayr al-Gharbi: Creswell, *A Short Account*, 135–146; D. Schlumberger, *Qasr al Heir ai-Gharbi* (Paris: Librairie orientaliste Paul Geuthner, 1986). Qasr al-Hayr al Sharqi: Creswell, *A Short Account*, 149–164; O. Grabar et al. *City in the Desert* (Cambridge, MA: Harvard University, 1978). Jebel Seis: Creswell, *A Short Account*, 118–122. Qasr Kharana: Creswell, *A Short Account*, 96–105; S. Urice, *Qasr Kharana in the Transjordan* (Durham, NC: American Schools of Oriental Research, 1987). al-Mafjar: R.W. Hamilton, *Khirbat al-Mafjar: An Arabian Mansion in the Jordan Valley* (Oxford: Clarendon Press, 1959). al-Minya: Creswell, *A Short Account*, 93–95. Mshatta: Creswell, *A Short Account*, 201–208; L. Trumpelmann, *Mschatta: Ein Beitrag zur Bestimmung des Kunstkreises, zur Datierung und zum Stil der Ornamentik* (Tubingen: Max Niemeyer, 1962). Qastal: P. Carlier and F. Morin, *Qastal al-Balqa'* (Grignan: Philippe Devoghel, 1986); Creswell, *A Short Account*, 173–176. Ar-Risha: S. Helms, *Early Islamic Architecture of the Desert: A Bedouin Station in Eastern Jordan* (Edinburgh: Edinburgh University Press, 1990).

Qasr at-Tuba: Creswell, *A Short Account*, 208–212; J.A. Jaussen and R. Savignac, *Les Châteaux Arabes de Qeseir 'Amra, Haraneh et Tuba* (Paris: Librairie orientaliste Paul Geuthner, 1922). Umm al-Walid: J. Bujard, *Entre Byzance et l'Islam* (Geneva: Musée d'art et d'histoire, 1992). Zabib: G. King, C. Lenzen and G. Rollefson, "Survey of Byzantine and Islamic Sites in Jordan. Second Preliminary Season Report (1981)," *Annual of the Department of Antiquities of Jordan* 27 (1983): 399–405.

7. Anon., *Akhbar al-dawla al-abbasiya*, eds. A. Duri and A. al-Muttalibi (Beirut: Dar al-Tali'a, 1971), 107, 108, 149, 154; A. al-Bakri, *Mu'jam ma ista 'jama min asma' al-buidan wa al-mawadi'*, ed. M. al-Saqa (Cairo: Matba'at Lajnat al-Ta'lif wa al-Tarjama wa al-Nashr, 1945û51), 130.
8. For more information on the microdiffractometer, see: M.-C. Corbeil and P.J. Sirois, "Applications of Microdiffractometry to the Study of Artistic and Historic Objects," in: *Proceedings, 4th International Conference on Non-destructive Testing of Works of Art* (Berlin: Deutsche Gesellschaft für Zerstörungsfreie Prüfung e.V., 1994), 278–284.
9. J. Neubauer and E. Pöllmann, "Synthesis and Characterization of Chloride Bearing Silico-sulfate-apatites," *Neues Jahrbuch fuer Mineralogie. Monatshefte* 7 (1992): 295–310.
10. A. Livingstone, G. Ryback, E.E. Fejer and C.J. Stanley, "Mattheddleite, a New Mineral of the Apatite Group from Leadhills, Strathclyde Region," *Scottish Journal of Geology* 23, no. 1 (1987): 1–8.
11. JCPDS File 5-586, International Centre for Diffraction Data.
12. R. C. Rouse and P. J. Dunn, "A Contribution to the Crystal Chemistry of Ellestadite and the Silicate Sulfate Apatites," *American Mineralogist* 67 (1982): 90–96.
13. Ibid., 95; C. Palache, H. Berman, and C. Frondel, *The System of Mineralogy*, vol. II, 7th edn (New York: John Wiley and Sons, 1951), 877, 906.
14. Palache et al., *The System of Mineralogy*, 877, 906.
15. Rouse and Dunn, "A Contribution to the Crystal Chemistry," 95.
16. Neubauer and Pöllmann, "Synthesis and Characterization of Chloride Bearing Silico-sulfate-apatites."
17. Livingstone et al., "Mattheddleite, a New Mineral," 6.
18. Rouse and Dunn, "A Contribution to the Crystal Chemistry," 94.
19. P. Mora, L. Mora and P. Philippot, *La Conservation des Peintures Murales* (Bologne: ICCROM, 1977), 80.
20. Palache et al., *The System of Mineralogy*, 906; Rouse and Dunn, "A Contribution to the Crystal Chemistry," 91.
21. Livingstone et al., "Mattheddleite, a New Mineral," 1–2.
22. Mora et al., *La Conservation des Peintures Murales*, 80.
23. Ibid., 80.

Materials and Techniques of Thai Wall Paintings: A Comparative Study of Late 19th Century Murals and Early-period Murals

Chompunut Prasartset
Faculty of Archaeology, Silpakorn University,
Napralan Road, Bangkok 10200, Thailand

Abstract

This paper concerns the investigation of techniques and materials of late 19th century Thai murals and a comparison with those of earlier period murals from previous studies. It shows that the techniques of paintings are the same except in one case. However, there were changes in the use of pigments. From the early 19th century there was some western influence on the use of pigments and this increased significantly in the late 19th century. Materials found in Thai murals of various periods are summarized and reported. Lead dioxide is detected in this study as possible alternative to minium.

Keywords

Murals, 14th to 19th centuries, pigments, painting technique, scanning electron microscopy, energy-dispersive X-ray analysis, X-ray diffraction, CHN analyzer, Coomassie Blue R-250

Introduction

Thai traditional wall paintings depict life stories of the Lord Buddha, his past lives and subjects from Ramayana. They also depict social and cultural activities of the past. Most of them were painted on interior walls of ordination halls in temples, walls of pagodas and palaces. One of the very fine peculiarities of Thai traditional paintings is the primitive, parallel perspective, two-dimensional flat. The oldest Thai murals were painted around the end of the 13th century.[1]

In the traditional methods of producing Thai murals, there was a brief preparation of the wall before the painting was executed, as described by Bhirasri and Wenck as follows: [2,3] The lime wall was washed several times with aqueous extract of Keelek leaves (*cassia siamea leguminasae*) for days until, when tested with Kamin-chan root (*curcuma domestica*), they did not turn to red. Then the wall was washed with water. From a survey of the scientific literature, the preparation can possibly be explained in the following way.[4] Keelek leaves contain acidic compounds, i.e. p-coumaric acid, cassiamin and cassia chromone,[5] while the Kamin root turns red when it is in an alkaline medium.[6] Therefore, the washing of the wall was possibly intended to neutralize the alkaline residue in the plaster before the painting was executed.

Most of the traditional Thai murals of early periods have vanished, and many of the existing ones were conserved without scientific study and documentation on materials and techniques. However, as far as previous studies are concerned, the analysis of materials used in an early 19th century Thai mural was reported by Chanphosri,[7] while Thongyai et.al.[8] reported an analysis of materials of a mid-17th century mural. In addition, the present author has investigated the pigments and paint-layer structures of a mid-14th century mural,[9] an 18th century mural,[10] and two other early 19th century murals.[11]

As far as the stylistic change in Thai murals is concerned, Bhirasri, a highly regarded expert on traditional Thai arts has commented that after the third quarter of the 19th century, traditional Thai painting declined and was influenced by western ideas, which caused traditional Thai painting to lose its individuality, becoming a hybrid mixture of western and eastern characteristics.[12] It is therefore interesting to find evidence of western painting materials in Thai murals during the transition period. In earlier studies, Prussian Blue was the only new western pigment found in the three early 19th century paintings.

The present investigation of materials and techniques of three late 19th century murals is intended to provide more art-historical information about materials and techniques of Thai murals and about early western influence on Thai murals. A comparison of materials and techniques of Thai wall paintings at various periods will be made from the results of previous studies and the data from this work. In previous studies, only murals of royal temples were investigated. However, as it is also informative and interesting to know about local artists' technique and materials and because traditional art schools in western Thailand are nationally famous, samples for this study were taken from three late 19th century murals,[13–16] including one from a royal temple and two from local temples in western Thailand as follows:

'THE' Thewasungkaram temple, a royal monastery located in Kanchanaburi. The paintings are on the brick lime-plastered walls of Vihara (an edifice housing

Figure 1. Life story of Buddha. Scene on north-east wall of Thewasungkaram Temple

Figure 2. Buddha preaching to his disciples and walking Buddha. Scene on south wall of Ladhoi Temple

Figure 3. Buddhist disciples paying homage to the dead Buddha. Scene on west wall of Noi Temple

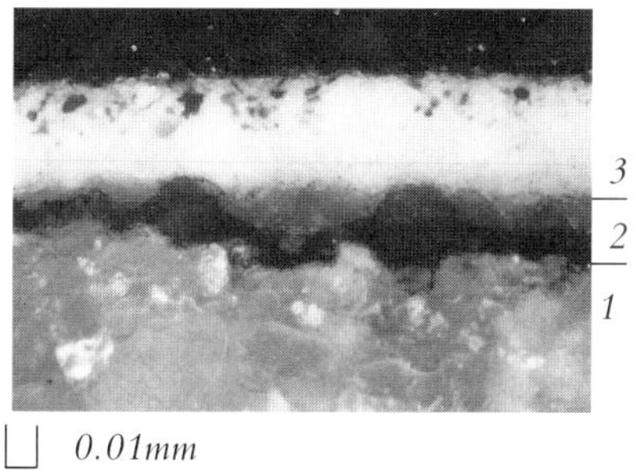

Figure 4. Cross section of green in leaf from Thewasungkaram mural: 1 preparative layer of divided calcite and clay; 2 layer of carbon black and emerald green; 3 layer of emerald green, hydrocerussite

a large image of Buddha) and are very finely executed. Most of the paintings are in Thai traditional style (two-dimensional), except that some parts of the landscape background are three dimensional (Figure 1).

'LAD' Ladhoi temple is a local Temple in Supanburi. The paintings are on wooden walls of the temple pavilion, painted by local artists. Most of the paintings are in Thai traditional style, except some landscape background, which is three dimensional (Figure 2).

'NOI' Noi temple is a local temple situated in Supanburi. The paintings are on brick lime-plastered walls of Mondob, painted by local artists. The style of paintings is traditional two-dimensional, flat. (Figure 3).

Techniques and materials of the murals

Microscopic examination of cross sections of the murals samples 'THE' and 'LAD' showed that there are preparative layers under the paint layers of both murals. The preparative layers contain greyish-white materials composed of clay (c, d) and very fine divided calcite (a, b, c). (The letters in parentheses indicate the identification methods: a microchemical tests, b X-ray diffraction, c microscopic examination, d scanning electron microscopy/ energy-dispersive X-ray analysis, e CHN analysis.) Materials in the preparative layers and paint layers disintegrated in water. However, from a staining test on cross sections, protein was not detected either in the preparative layer or in paint layer. No calcite was found in paint layers of either mural. The preparative layers and paint layers appeared very clearly separated from each other. This indicated that in the execution of the paintings, pigments were mixed in a binding medium and applied on a dry preparative layer. The binding medium in both layers is probably water soluble and of plant origin. This technique is the same as that found in all earlier period murals from previous studies, except a sample from Mahathat Temple.[17]

Of pigments in the 'THE' murals, hydrocerussitea (b), was found in the paint layer of white patterns or elements and in white background, as well as mixed with other pigments to produce various light colors. Cinnabar was found in red paint and in combination with other pigments to produce various tints. It was also painted under the layer of gold leaf (c,d). This technique of laying gold leaf was also found in earlier murals.[18] Pure cinnabar (a, b, c) was found in red paint of Buddha's robe. It was mixed with hydrocerussite at various ratios to produce the colors of flesh, pink stone, and pink background, as well as mixed with minium (a, b) together with carbon black (c) and the brown of hematite (a,b) to make the chocolate colour of the gate. Emerald green (a, b, d), $Cu(C_2H_3O_2)_2.3Cu(AsO_2)_2$, was mixed with hydrocerussite (b, d) to produce a green leaf paint over the dark paint of the bush background containing carbon black (c) and little emerald green (c, d) (Figure 4). The light-blue paint of the giant's flesh contains hydrocerrussite (a, b) with a smaller amount of ultramarine blue (a, b, d), $(Na,Ca)_8(AlSiO_4)_6(SO_4,S,Cl)_2$, which was painted over a white layer of hydrocerussite (b) laid on a green layer of emerald green (c, d) over black paint containing carbon black (c) and a little emerald green (c, d) (Figure 5). As well as in outlines, carbon black (c, e) was also found in some background.

Of the pigments in the murals of 'LAD', it was found that the preparative layer serves as a white background. However, pure hydrocerussite (a, b, c) was found in white paint of a divinity's flesh, a horse and a soldier's white jacket. These paint layers were on white preparative layers. Ultramarine blue (b, d) was mixed with barium sulphate (b, d) and hydrocerussite (b, d) in two different areas of the blue background. The intense blue layer of the roof tile contains ultramarine blue (a, b, c) with a little gypsum (b, c). One pink of Buddha's robe is composed of cinnabar (b, c> and barium sulphate (b) (Figure 6), whereas another pink contains cinnabar (b, c), hydrocerussite (a, b, c) and small amount of barium sulphate (b, c). No cinnabar or any red paint was found under gold leaf (c, d). Only some transparent binding medium (c), laid on a preparative layer, was observed underneath gold leaf. The paint layer of the brown tree trunk contains hematite (a, b), which was painted over a white background of hydrocerussite (b). In the black paint of a soldier's trousers, carbon black (c, e) was found painted over a white layer of hydrocerussite (b) tinted with a little ultramarine blue(c). Carbon black was also found mixed with

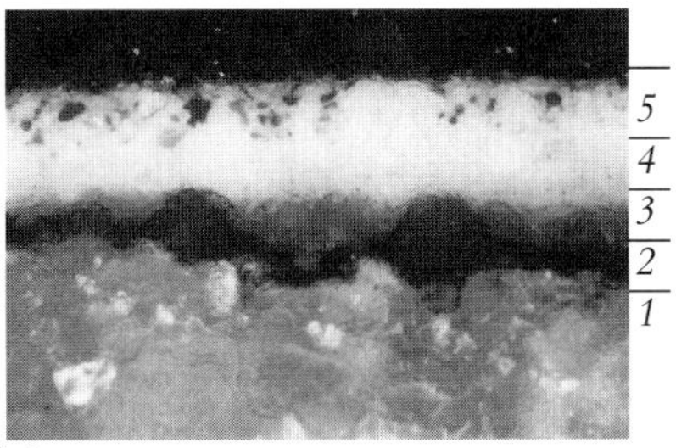

0.01mm

Figure 5. Cross-section of light blue in flesh of giant from Thewasungkaram mural: 1 preparative layer of divided calcite and clay; 2 layer of carbon black and emerald green; 3 layer of emerald green, hydrocerussite and carbon black; 4 layer of hydrocerussite; 5 layer of hydrocerussite and ultramarine blue

0.01mm

Figure 6. Cross-section of pink in Buddha's robe from the Ladhoi mural: 1 preparative layer of divided calcite and clay; 2 layer of cinnabar and barium sulphate

Figure 7. Cross-section of red background from the Noi mural: 1 preparative layer of carbonated lime; 2 layer of red ochre

ultramarine blue (c) in the dark background of the bush. Yellow lead pigment (a, d) was found mixed with barium sulphate (b, d) in the paint layer of a monk's robe.

The mural at NOI temple shows some different techniques. XRD analysis of materials and microscopic examination of cross sections showed that underneath the coloured paint layer, there is a white preparative layer of interlocking calcite crystals. This indicates that the calcite crystals are derived from lime that was carbonated and crystallized as calcite in the layer. Most patterns, elements and figures are the white color of the white lime preparative layer of about 0.5– 1.0 mm thickness and have a very smooth surface, as if they were polished. They are surrounded by a red background or outlines of red, grey and blue. The paint layer of the red background is very thin and contains red ochre (a, c) pigment and interlocking calcite (Figure 7). In addition, a sample of the blue roof tile pattern contains ultramarine blue (b, d), white pigment of hydrocerussite (b, d) and interlocking calcite in the paint layer. The pigments are strongly bound, which indicates that the pigments were mixed with whitewash as binder. Because the whitewash binder was used, many parts of the murals still exist, although the building has deteriorated very badly. However, in the paint layer of some decorative areas or elements with intense colour, such as the sample from a monk's robe, very little calcite was found with barium sulphate (b, d), orange red pigment (c), red ochre (a, c, d) and black pigment of lead dioxide (b, c, d). The pigments disintegrate in water. No protein was detected in the paint layer. In this case, the binding medium may be water soluble and of plant origin. Carbon black (c) was found in the outlines. As it is unusual for a Buddhist monk's robe to be painted in black, and because that painting area is near the broken roof and exposed to light and humidity , the presence of lead dioxide in the paint layer can be identified as decomposed minium within which traces of orange-red pigments (c) remain. Such pigment transformation has also been observed and explained previously.[19,20]

Table 1. Results of XRD analysis of selected paints containing some materials different from earlier murals (emerald green, lead dioxide, barium sulphate, lazurite or ultramarine blue). The analysis was carried out on Guinier- Hagg type focussing powder camera, Philips XDC-700 at 40 kV, 30 mA, Cu K radiation. Intensity of reflection lines was visually estimated: vs= very strong, s=strong, m=medium, w=weak, vw=very weak, vvw= very very weak

Green of bush d(Å) I/I	Standard emerald green d(Å) I/I	Hydro-cerussite JCPDS No.13-131 d(Å) I/I	Black on monk's robe d(Å) I/I	Lead dioxide JCPDS d(Å) I/I	Barium sulphate JCPDS No.8-185 d(Å) I/I	Blue back-ground No.5-448 d(Å) I/I	Lazurite JCPDS No.17 -749 d(Å) I/I	Hydro-cerussite JCPDS o.13-131 d(Å) I/I
9.77 vs	9.77 vs				4.44 17	7.93 vvw		
		7.80 5	4.38 vvw					7.80 5
7.06 w					4.34 36	6.45 vvw	6.43 40	
4.81 vvw			4.12 vvw			6.21 vvw		
			3.94 vw		3.90 57		4.86 6	
4.57 vvw	4.57 vw						4.54 18	
4.47 w		4.47 60	3.75 vvw		3.77 12	4.48 m		4.47 60
4.25 vw		4.25 60	3.62 vvw			4.25 m		4.25 60
	3.97 vw				3.576 31	3.71 vw	3.71 100	
3.60 s		3.61 90	3.53 vs	3.50 100		3.62 vs		3.61 90
3.50 vvw	3.49 vw						3.56 6	
3.38 vvw	3.38 vvw					3.49 vvw		
3.28 vs	3.31 vvw	3.29 90	3.47 w		3.442 100		3.43 6	
3.16 w			3.35 vw			3.35 vvw		
	3.11 vvw				3.317 67	3.29 vs		3.29 90
	3.08 vw		3.12 w		3.101 97		3.21 16	
2.75 vw	2.77 vvw		2.85 vvw			3.08 vvw		
2.72 vvw	2.72 vw	2.715 20	2.82 vs	2.80 100	2.834 53		3.03 6	
2.68 vw	2.68 w					2.88 vvw	2.87 45	
2.64 vvw	2.65 vvw		2.74 vw		2.734 16	2.72 vw		2.715 20
2.62 vw		2.623 100				2.726 47	2.63 vs	2.622 80
2.623 100								
2.57 vvw	2.56 vvw		2.50 m	2.48 70	2.481 14	2.53 vvw		
2.51 w	2.51 vvw	2.491 30	2.34 vvw				2.502 4	2.491 30
	2.41 vvw		2.22 vvw	2.21 10			2.427 16	
2.34 vvw	2.34 vvw		2.13 w			2.26 vvw	2.272 25	
			2.11 w					
			2.06 vvw					
			1.86 s	1.856 100				

Table 2. Materials found in Thai murals of various periods

Century Temple	Plaster type	Preparative layer	White	Red	Yellow	Black	Green	Blue
Mid 14th Mahrathat[9]	Mud, fibre	Clay + gypsum	Clay + gypsum	Cinnabar, minium	Gamboge	Carbon	–	–
Mid 17th Chongnonsi[8]	Lime	Clay + calcite	Clay + calcite	Cinnabar, minium, red ochre	–	Carbon	Malachite	Azurite
18th Maitepnimit[10]	Lime	Clay + calcite + fibre	White lead, gypsum, kaolinite	Cinnabar, minium, hematite	Gamboge, gold leaf	Carbon	Malachite	Indigo, cumengeite
Early 19th Suthat[7]	Lime	Calcium carbonate	White lead	Cinnabar, minium, red ochre	Yellow ochre, gold leaf	Carbon	Malachite	Prussian blue
Kruawan[11]	Lime	Clay + calcite	White lead, gypsum, kaolinite	Cinnabar, hematite	Yellow ochre, gamboge, gold leaf	Carbon	Malachite	Prussian blue
Napramain[11]	Lime	Clay + calcite	White lead, gypsum	cinnabar, minium, hematite	Gold leaf	Carbon	Malachite	Prussian blue
Late 19th Thewasungkaram	Lime	Clay + calcite	White lead	Cinnabar, minium, hematite	Gold leaf	Carbon	Emerald green	Ultramarine blue
Ladhoi	–	Clay + calcite	White lead, barium sulphate	Cinnabar, hematite	Gold leaf, lead pigment	Carbon	-	Ultramarine blue
Noi	Lime	Carbonated lime	White lead, lime, barium sulphate	Hematite, red lead (decomposed to lead dioxide)	–	lead dioxide(possibly as decomposed red lead)	–	Ultramariue blue

Experimental details

Microchemical tests were done on isolated loose materials from preparative layers and paint layers. Elemental analysis of materials was carried out by scanning electron microscopy/ energy-dispersive X-ray analysis (SEM/EDX) (JEOL JSM-35 CF Link EDS 860) on the cross sections prepared by embedding the samples in polyester resin (Eternal ER-7522 X 14 P). Most materials were identified by X-ray diffraction (XRD), as mentioned above, and some results are shown in Table 1.

In the cases where carbon black was identified with a CHN analyzer (Perkin Elmer 240 C), prior to using the analyzer, the pigments were washed with dilute hydrochloric acid, water, acetone, toluene and ethyl alcohol, respectively and dried at 105°C. for two hours. Attempts to find protein in the binding medium were done by staining cross sections with Coomassie Blue R-250, described as more sensitive than Amido Black 10 B when used as a general protein stain.[21]

Conclusion

For the execution of Thai murals, a preparative layer is laid on the wall before painting. The binding media in the preparative layer and paint layer are not lime, probably plant products. This technique is found in all Thai paintings that have been studied so far, except the mural at Noi Temple, in which the preparative layer is lime and the binding medium in some paint layers is whitewash. The materials used in Thai murals of various periods are shown in Table 2. Cinnabar, minium, carbon black and hematite have been used since earlier periods. There are changes in the use of white, green and blue pigments. Hydrocerussite has been found used in Thai murals since the 18th century (Table 2). This study has found that barium sulphate was used as a new material in late 19th century murals and in some cases it may not be an adulterant. Although Thailand has large baryte resources in many areas,[22] barium sulphate has never been found to have been used in mural paintings of earlier periods. However, barium sulphate has been used in connection with paints in Europe and the USA since about the beginning of 19th century.[23] Malachite, which was used in earlier period murals, is not found in the late 19th century murals, and emerald green has been used instead. This pigment was first produced in Germany in 1814.[24] As far as blue pigments are concerned, this study has found that ultramarine blue was introduced to replace Prussian blue, which was found to have been used in early 19th century Thai murals. Ultramarine blue was manufactured in France and Germany soon after 1830.[25] From previous studies[26,27] and the present study, it can be stated that western influence on Thai painting can be found not only in the style of painting, but also in the painting materials used since the early 19th century. This trend continued even more strongly in the late 19th century.

Acknowledgments

Thanks go to the Fine Arts Department, Thailand for permission for the study and also to the Department of Physics, King Mongkut Institute of Technology for facilitating the use of the XRD instrument. Professor Dr J. Riederer kindly provided standard emerald green for comparison. Professor Pongsak Pongprayoon kindly gave valuable comments on the microscopic examination. The author is grateful to the Research and Development Institute, Silpakorn University and the National Research Council of Thailand for support of this study.

References and notes

1. S. Bhirasri, *The Origin and Evolution of Thai Murals* (Bangkok: The Fine Arts Department, 1959), 23
2. Ibid., 24.
3. K. Wenck, *Mural Paintings in Thailand* (Zurich: Inigo Von Oppensdorff Verlag, 1975), LXXVII–LXXVIII.
4. C. Prasartset, 'Technique of Thai Murals and Causes of Deterioration', *Science*(Science Society of Thailand) 37, no.7 (1983), 412–418 (in Thai).
5. H. Wagner et.al. 'Chemical Constituents of *Cassia Siamea Lam.*', *Planta Medica*, 33, no.3 (1978): 258–261.
6. W. Aweruthnun, 'Indicators from Plants', *Science* (Science Society of Thailand), 36, no.9 (1982): 604 (in Thai).
7. K. Chanphosri, 'Materials used in the Mural Painting at Wat Suthat' in *Wat Suthat* (ein Beispiel Deutscher Kulturhilfe eine Dokumentation, 1985), 122–134 (in German and Thai).
8. T. Thongyai, et.al. ' The Methods of Mural Painting Conservation at Wat Chong Nonsi', (Research Report to the Toyota Foundation, Silpakorn University,1985), 241–245.
9. C. Prasartset, 'The Study of Pigments and Layer Structures of the Murals in Phra Prang of Wat Mahathat at Rajburi', *Science* (Science Society of Thailand), 40, no.12 (1986): 649–663.(in Thai with English Abstract).
10. C. Prasartset, 'The Investigation of Pigments and Paint Layer Structures of Mural Paintings at Maitepnimit Temple', *Journal of the National Research Council of Thaialnd* 22, no.1 (1990): 73–86.
11. C. Prasartset, and G. Satittada, 'Study of Pigments and Paint Layer Structures of the Wall Paintings at Kruawan Temple, Thonburi and at Napramain Temple, Ayudhaya', (Research Report to the National Research Council of Thailand, 1993), 6-10 (in Thai with English Abstract).
12. Bhirasri, *The Origin and Evoultion of Thai Murals*, 23–24
13. Interview with the abbot of Thewasungkaram Temple, 14 August 1993.
14. Interview with the abbot of Ladhoi Temple, 24 February 1993.
15. Interview with the abbot of Noi Temple, 24 February 1993.
16. *Traditional Thai Painting* 1 (Bangkok, Fine Arts Department, 1990), 138–139.
17. The black background in the mid-14th century mural at Mahathat Temple was painted directly on mud plaster.[9]
18. Gold leaf was laid on a red layer of cinnabar and a transparent binder in a Napramain mural of the early 19th century.[11] Cinnabar, as well as gamboge, was found under the gold leaf layer of an 18th century Maitepnimit mural.[10]
19. P. Bolling Toft and M.C. Christensen, 'Early Gothic Wall Paintings: An Investigation of Painting Techniques and Materials of 13th-Century Mural Paintings in a Danish Village Church' (Paper delivered at the Tenth Triennial Meeting of the International Council of Museums Committee for Conservation, Washington, DC, 1993), 531–535.
20. S. Giovannoni, M. Matteini and A. Moles, 'Studies and Developments Concerning the Problem of Altered Lead Pigments in Wall Painting', *Studies in Conservation* 35, no.1 (1990): 21–25.
21. B.D. Hames, 'Protein Staining with Organic Dyes and Quantitation', in *Gel Electrophoresis of Protiens*, eds B.D. Hammes and D. Rickwood (Oxford University Press, 1990), 52–54.
22. Kumarachan, P., 'Baryte', *Economic Geology Bulletin*, no.5(Department of Mineral Resources, Thailand, 1974), 1–22 (in Thai).
23. R.J. Gettens and G.L. Stout, *Paintings Materials, A Short Encyclopaedia* (New York: Dover Publications, 1966), 96.
24. Ibid., 113
25. Ibid., 163–164,
26. Chanphosri, 'Materials used', 132–134.
27. C. Prasartset and G. Satittada, 'Study of Pigments', 6–7.

Résumé

Ce qui, à première vue, peut sembler une finition scandaleusement négligée, apparaît après un examen plus approfondi et un peu de réflexion, comme le résultat d'une façon de faire admissible et cohérente. Ce mode d'exécution représente une conception des peintures monumentales qui est très répandue, chronologiquement et géographiquement, en Belgique. L'expression esthétique de ces peintures ne supporte pas n'importe quelle retouche d'autant plus que les dégradations accentuent leur structure assez informelle.

Mots-clés

Technique picturale, esthétique, degradation, restauration, retouche

Artiste et restaurateur face à la matière picturale et sa dégradation

Walter Schudel
Institut Royal du Patrimoine Artistique
Parc du Cinquantenaire 1
B-1040 Bruxelles, Belgique

Figure 1. Mur ouest de la chapelle Saint-Joseph (après dégagement).

La peinture murale

En 1592, le chanoine Gaspar van den Cruyce fit rénover l'ancienne salle du Chapitre de la cathédrale N.D. d'Anvers pour l'aménager en une chapelle dédiée à Sainte Ursule. Après sa mort (20 février 1593) la chapelle fut modifiée et agrandie par sa famille.[1] Au cours de l'étude préliminaire technico-matérielle qui précéda l'achèvement (en 1993) de la restauration du choeur et du transept, on découvrit une peinture murale dans l'ancienne chapelle Sainte-Ursule, actuellement chapelle Saint-Joseph. Elle portait des armoiries de la famille van den Cruyce et une date, 1602.[2] Elle fait très probablement partie des travaux d'après 1593 cités plus haut. Des sondages montrèrent que les peintures s'étendaient sur tous les murs de la chapelle et sur la travée correspondante du déambulatoire, à partir du niveau du plancher (actuellement environ 70cm plus élevé qu'alors) jusqu'à 300cm de haut. Elle n'est plus conservée en quantité suffisante pour une restauration que sur le mur ouest de la première travée de la chapelle et dans le déambulatoire.

Au cours de l'hiver 1994–95 la peinture a été dégagée.[3] Il s'agit d'une grisaille à caractère surtout décoratif. Des rinceaux en noir et blanc rehaussent un fond uniformément gris. Sur le mur ouest de la chapelle des anges musiciens à mis-corps "croissent" sur les branches. Deux petits chiens et des oiseaux complètent le décor (Figure 1). La peinture a été appliquée sur un support relativement héterogène: une maçonnerie en pierres naturelles et quelques couches de badigeon sur les piliers sud du déambulatoire; la même maçonnerie avec une couche de badigeon, une paire de couches de finition rouge uni, des restes d'une peinture très fragmentaire et une couche de badigeon sur les piliers nord; une maçonnerie en brique, un mortier de chaux, des restes ci-et-là d'une décoration noire et une couche de badigeon dans la chapelle. La peinture elle-même est composée d'une imprimatura orange-jaune (ocre et huile de lin) sur un fond gris (noir végétal, craie et jaune d'oeuf) puis un décor en noir (noir végétal dans un mélange huile de lin – résine de *Pinus*) et blanc (blanc de plomb et huile de lin).[4]

Les défauts

L'enlèvement des couches de badigeon mit au jour la peinture et ce qu'elle représente mais on découvrit en même temps tous ses "défauts". Ils sont étonnamment nombreux et importants. Nous avons essayé de les classer.

Un premier groupe de "défauts" se situe au niveau du support. Il s'agit surtout de trous. Ils sont plus ou moins ronds avec des diamètres allant jusqu'à environ 70mm et des profondeurs de 4 à 5 mm (Figure 2). Il y en a aussi des longs et étroits (jusqu'à 80 mm de long et 10 à 15 mm de large) et des petits et profonds (3 mm de diamètre et environ 4 mm de profondeur). On trouve également des pustules et des boursoufflures de toutes sortes et grandeurs (jusqu'à quelques cm de section et environ 5 mm d'épaisseur). Il y a, de plus, des bouchages d'originee dont la finitions ne répond en aucune façon aux règles de l'art (Figure 3). Cà et là une couche de badigeon manque et la peinture est appliquée directement sur une ancienne couche de finition rouge.

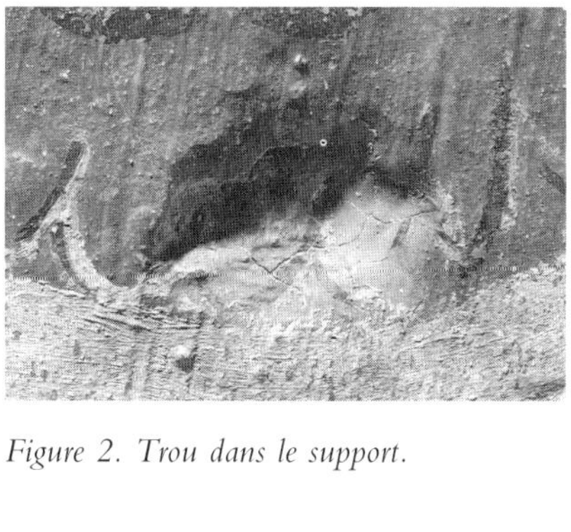

Figure 2. Trou dans le support.

Considérons ensuite la couche de badigeon en-dessous de l'imprimatura. Elle présente un grand nombre de coulées et surtout d'éclaboussures (Figure 4). De plus, comme en témoigne la quantité importante de grains, la masse ne devait pas

Figure 3. Support "animé".

Figure 4. Des éclaboussures dans le badigeon (lumière rasante).

Figure 5. Eclaboussure dans la peinture blanche.

être très homogêne. Le diamètre des grains và jusqu'à 3 mm env. Leur dispersion sur toute la surface de la peinture est assez irrégulière et ils forment des zônes plus concentrées (qui correspondent peut-être chaque fois au moment ou l'on atteignait le fond du récipient). Les éclaboussures ont environ 90 mm de long et 3 mm de large. Les coulées sont d'habitude plus courtes (20 à 30 mm) mais plus larges (jusqu'à 5 mm). La forme de ces dernières est moins nette que celle des éclaboussures ce qui est normal vu la différence de leur formation en durée et en force.

Dans une mesure plus limitée, qualitativement et quantitativement, on trouve aussi des coulées et des éclaboussures dans la couche picturale. Elles sont fortement liées aux matériaux. Ainsi les éclaboussures (jusqu'à 20 mm de long et 1 mm de large) se situent quasi exclusivement dans les blancs (huile de lin et blanc de plomb), tandis que les noirs (noir végétal dans un mélange d'huile de lin et de résine de *Pinus*) sont le domaine privilégié des coulées (jusqu'à 40 mm de long) (Figures 5, 6).

A certains endroits, pendant l'application du fond gris, la peinture a commencé tout à coup à glisser vers le bas, sans doute parce que le fond n'était pas assez absorbant ou trop mouillé ce qui, dans ce cas revient au même. Des coulées en négatif (comme des lits de rivière vides) se sont ainsi formées (Figure 7). Elles ont environ 2 à 5 mm de large et des dizaines à des centaines de mm de long. On ne constate ce phénomène qu'aux endroits où le badigeon, qui souffre du même mal aux mêmes endroits, se trouve directement sur un support en pierre. Dans les endroits où il y a plusieurs badigeons et/ou un mortier de chaux sous la peinture, cela ne se produit pas.

Des craquelures prématurées semblent avoir été formées dans les mêmes conditions. Elles apparaissent toujours sur des fonds (trop) peu absorbants et de même, aussi bien au travers du blanc que du noir.

Des poils de pinceau oubliés sont également des "animations" involontaires de la surface peinte. On trouve des fibres végétales raides (jusqu'à 60 mm de long) mais aussi des élégants poils animaux ondulés (jusqu'à 85 mm de long).

Pour être complet, signalons quelques dégâts, surtout des griffes, qui ont été produits pendant le travail dans la peinture encore mouillée.

En suivant le travail de l'artiste quelques observations sont encore à signaler. Il y a une série de repentirs difficiles à ne pas voir. Nous avons même découvert une faute que l'artiste a vue et notée mais qu'il a omis de corriger par la suite. De même une série d'ombres ont été oubliées. Bien que... le travail créatif etait peut-être ici plus important que l'exactitude des détails.

Enfin une série de contours sont ou trop larges ou trop minces (Figure 8). Mais, plus encore que pour les remarques précédentes sur les ombres oubliées, il faut relativer cette "faute" et la considérer sous l'angle de la contrainte, imposée à la sensibilité et à la créativité, que beaucoup d'entre nous éprouvent quand on les obligent à colorer "dans les lignes" (lignes qui d'ailleurs ont été ici dessinées par après).

Une mauvaise peinture?

Cette peinture est-elle "a bad painting" comme le prétendait un couple de touristes anglais? On pourrait le croire si l'on se rappelle tous les "défauts" décrits plus haut. L'artiste a peint librement sur les défauts du support. Il a vu les coulées et les éclaboussures, les poils de pinceau encollés, une série d'ombres oubliées (exprès?) et des contours délibérément (?) mal tracés. Les huit points décrits plus haut desservent tous l'obtention de formes nettes et précises. Ils concourrent à accentuer une puissante expression matérielle et donnent en même temps une idée sur la façon dont la peinture a été créée.

Il ne s'agit pas d'une exception. Citons (entre beaucoup d'autres) les peintures du XIe siècle à Ename, celles des XIIIe-XIVe à Vossem et du XVIe à Krewinkel. Elles présentent toutes des caractéristiques semblables à celles d'Anvers. Elles datent de périodes différentes, sont faites avec d'autres techniques et se trouvent de l'ouest à l'est, parfaitement dispersées dans tout le pays.

Les valeurs tactiles

Dans cette peinture, la matière, comme le dit Jean Dubuffet, "parle" aussi.[5] L'opinion assez négative que l'on pourrait se faire à première vue doit être, après

Figure 6. Coulée de la peinture noire.

Figure 7. Coulée en négatif.

Figure 8. Contour trop large.

examen plus approfondi, fort nuancée sinon totalement revue. Considérons en particulier les coups de pinceau rapides et souples dans le noir où les traces de coups de brosse sont en grande partie aplanies. Par contre dans la masse pâteuse du blanc qui n'autorisait pas d'égalisation, la structure est restée bien marquée (Figure 9). Tout cela se détache sur une surface mate, régulière bleu-gris qui se trouve à son tour sur un badigeon qui présente une facture caractéristique. Il en résulte que cette surface grise du fond est aussi très vivante.

Outre le contraste ombre-lumière propre aux grisailles, cette peinture présente aussi un contraste matériel mat-brillant des figures et du fond (cfr. les liants utilisés – le chaulage et les nettoyages successifs ont éliminé en grande partie le brillant). Il faut encore signaler une autre caractéristique vu son puissent ancrage dans la matière: c'est la façon de réaliser d'une part les rinceaux (extrèmement simple, un peu sèche et directe) et d'autre part les feuilles, les anges et les animaux (plus élaborée avec plusieurs formes d'ombrages) (Figures 10, 11). Il ne faut pas voir en cela une différence de qualité mais plutôt un désir de contraste.

Ces formes des rinceaux, des animaux et des anges ont-elles été arrachées à la matière après un dur combat?[6] On peut difficilement se représenter la genèse de cet ouvrage dans ces termes. A notre avis l'expression matérielle joue ici un rôle important et positif et implique aussi bien la facture de la couche picturale et du badigeon que les trous du support.

Est-ce qu'un coup de pinceau qui "est" la patte d'un oiseau ou la nervure d'une feuille, est plus important qu'une éclaboussure ou une coulée aussi grande? Ce sont tous deux plus que de la peinture. Les premiers sont des formes voulues subordonnées aux caprices de la volonté. Les seconds sont des sous-produits non directement intentionnels d'une façon de faire. Mais une peinture n'est-elle pas essentiellement le produit d'une action, realisée en étalant une pâte colorée avec une touffe de poils?[7] Les traces de cette action nous semble d'une importance fondamentale au moins autant que ce que les traces représentent et surtout, dans l'histoire de la peinture, plus permanent.

Retouche de la forme

Quand la peinture a été entièrement dégagée, la question de la retouche, ou présentation "esthétique" s'est posée. Nous étions confrontés à un difficile problème avec ce cas où la matière joue un rôle si important: est-il possible à l'aide d'une retouche d'améliorer la lisibilité d'une expression matérielle ou bien en augmentant la lisibilité de l'image, la retouche ne peut-elle que fausser l'expression de la matière? Le problème semble être que la matière ne peut s'exprimer que de deux manières:

- ou bien elle subit un traitement rapide et spontané et ainsi elle exprime sa nature propre un peu comme par hasard;
- ou bien la matière est soumise à une action lente et moins contraignante (p.ex. polissage) et elle montre sa nature comme un compromis avec le traitement subi.

La première manière est si on peut dire le modèle conflictuel, la seconde le modèle de négociation.

Dans le cas des peintures murales en Belgique, on rencontre surtout le premier modèle. Pour ce qui concerne l'expression matérielle ce modèle est impossible à retoucher. Toute imitation de traces du processus de création est vouée à l'échec vu les limitations imposées au geste du restaurateur. Le deuxième modèle est plus sujet à hésitation.

Il est à craindre que le principe, en partie justifié, de ne pas pousser la retouche jusqu'à l'arbitraire, soit inspiré par une surestimation de l'importance de la forme.[8] Pour toute peinture murale dont la facture est de quelque importance, toute retouche est nécessairement arbitraire.

Les dégradations

Comme si cela ne suffisait pas, nous devons constater que le processus de vieillissement ne contribue pas à une meilleure lisibilité des formes. Au contraire,

Figure 9. Les qualités rhéologiques différentes du noir et du blanc.

Figure 10. Technique picturale utilisée pour les rinceaux. (cfr. la facture de la fig. 11)

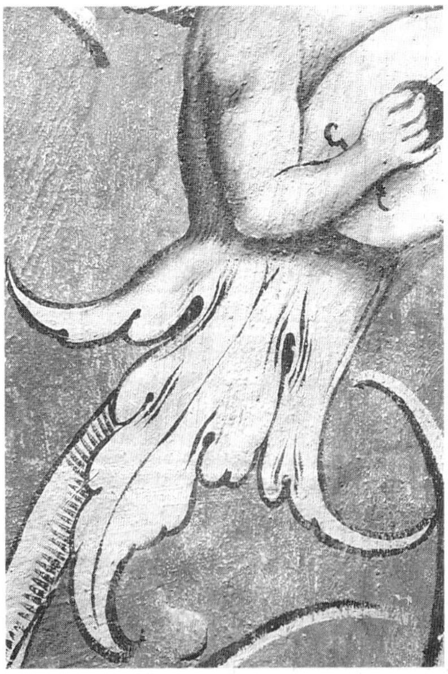

Figure 11. Technique picturale utilisée pour les feuilles, les animaux et les anges. (cfr. la facture de la Figure 10)

la matière retourne lentement à son état primitif naturel et impose de plus en plus sa propre vie à l'ensemble. L'identité de l'oeuvre change au profit de la matière et aux dépens de la forme. On ressent souvent les lacunes comme gênantes car elles rendent la lecture de l'image plus difficile alors que, en ce qui concerne l'expression matérielle elles possèdent un caractère propre qui ne peut pas impunément être supprimé. Elles déterminent dans une certaine mesure (changeante) l'identité actuelle de l'oeuvre d'art.[9] Cette identité, le restaurateur ne peut la connaître qu'en respectant l'authenticité de l'oeuvre degradée, quoi que cela puisse signifier (en tout cas l'accent doit être mis sur l'activité, "l'inter-activité" objet-restaurateur et non sur l'oeuvre comme un fait achevé).[10] La retouche devrait découler de cette étude aussi bien pour sa nature que pour son étendue. En conséquence il est difficile de proposer une méthode universelle clairement définie.[11]

Conclusion

Confrontés pendant le dégagement des peintures murales de la chapelle Saint-Joseph avec les multiples coulées et éclaboussures, les erreurs, les imperfections, les poils de pinceau oubliés, les trous et les bulles, sans oublier les coups de brosse caractéristiques et les démarches picturales qui en découlent, nous avons éprouvé beaucoup d'hésitation à combler les lacunes "gênantes" avec des petites lignes colorées pour préciser l'image. Que signifieraient ces petites lignes?

Les formes retouchées ne souffrent-elles pas en général des retouches? Ne sont-elles pas toujours moins sveltes et déliées que des formes intouchées justement parce que la matière ne peut pas "parler" selon sa nature? Il apparaît donc recommandable, quelle que soit la méthode utilisée, de limiter la retouche à ce que l'expression matérielle de la peinture concernée peut supporter sans inconvénient.[12] Cela signifie qu'il ne peut y avoir qu'une quantité fort limitée de retouche sans ancrage à la matière originale. Selon nous, elle ne peut constituer qu'une partie restreinte de la forme et doit être maintenue nettement en-dessous des valeurs de l'original dégradé, pour ce qui est de la texture ou de la texture simulée, de l'energie des couleurs et de l'expression matérielle. Et si cela ne suffit pas pour donner à l'ensemble un impact visuel satisfaisant alors, peut-être, est-il possible de rendre les formes dégradées plus attrayntes par la façon de les présenter c'est-à-dire en adaptant leur entourage.

Remerciements

Pour la traduction – L. Masschelein-Kleiner.
Pour les photographies – Jean-Luc Elias.

Notes et Références

1. L. Van Langendonck, "Onze-Lieve-Vrouwkathedraal te Antwerpen. Historisch onderzoek van Muur- en gewelfschilderingen in koor en kruisbeuk", (Antwerpen, 1988), 35.
2. L. De Clercq, W. Schudel, "Het materiëel-wetenschappelijk onderzoek" (in opdracht van *Algemene Ondernemingen E.G. Verstraete en Vanhecke N.V.*), (pré-étude non publiée, Antwerpen, 1990).
3. Dégagement réalisé par l'I.R.P.A. avec la collaboration de M- H. Ghisdal, G. Reyniers, J. Van den Eede et E. Pars.
4. Les analyses sont réalisées par M. Van Bos (liants) et L. Maes (pigments).
5. J. Dubuffet, "Prospectus et tous écrits suivants", (Paris, 1967), 56.
6. A. Riegl, "Spätrömische Kunstindustrie", (Wien, 1927), 9.
7. R.C. Kwant, "De stemmen van de stilte. Merleau-Ponty's analyse van de schilderkunst", (Hilversum/Antwerpen, 1966), 25, 36.
8. P. et L. Mora et P. Philippot, "Conservation des peintures murales", (Bologne, 1977), 349.
9. cfr. E. Burke, "A philosophical enquiry into the origin of our ideas of the sublime and the beautiful", (London, 1757).
10. cfr. H-G. Gadamer, "Die Aktualität des Schönen", (Stuttgart, 1977), 31–36.
11. D. Jakobs, "Restaurierung und Zeitgeschmack- Der Kruzifixus von Cimabue nach der restaurierung von Umberto Baldini", dans Zeitschrift für Kunsttechnologie und Konservierung, an.2, tôme1., (s.l., 1988), 53–67.
12. F.W.J. Schelling, "Texte zur Philosophie der Kunst", (Stuttgart, 1991), 81.

Les peintures de Saint-Savin-sur-Gartempe: étude 20 ans après leur restoration

M. Stefanaggi,* B. Callede, S. Demaily, P. Hugon, G. Orial, A. Brunet
Laboratoire de Recherche des Monument Historiques, Champs-sur-Marne, France
I. Dangas
restaurateur privé, France

Résumé

L'étude présentée ici concerne les peintures de la voûte de la nef de l'église de Saint Savin (France). Vingt ans après leur dernière restauration, dans le cadre d'un programme pluriannuel de conservation-restauration de l'édifice et du site de l'abbaye, ce travail interdisciplinaire, mené conjointement par le laboratoire et un restaurateur, permet d'établir un diagnostic commun, reposant sur l'observation *in situ* et les analyses de laboratoire, relatif à l'état général des peintures, les problèmes d'altération, leurs restaurations antérieures, les différentes techniques d'exécution selon les époques. Ce bilan permettra, le moment venu, d'être en possession des principaux éléments scientifiques et techniques nécessaires à une intervention cohérente de conservation-restauration de ces peintures exceptionnelles.

Mots clés

Stratigraphie, pigment, fixatif, altération, restauration, analyse, mortier, couche picturale, peinture murale, Saint-Savin-sur-Gartempe

Introduction

L'église abbatiale de Saint-Savin-sur-Gartempe est mondialement célèbre pour son ensemble de peintures murales romanes, ensemble qui concerne la totalité de l'édifice et dont une grande partie, révélée notamment par les publications de Mérimée en 1845, est d'origine, (fin 11ème à 12ème siècle). L'édifice a été classé patrimoine mondial par l'UNESCO en 1990.

Cet ensemble exceptionnel a nécessairement subi, au cours des siècles, de nombreuses interventions, liées à l'histoire et aux modifications de l'abbaye, aux travaux de réfection de l'édifice, à l'évolution du goût, etc. Exceptionnel, l'édifice l'est par plusieurs aspects: importance des surfaces peintes, dimensions, les plus grandes connues pour des peintures romanes (la voûte de la nef, située à plus de 20 m de haut, mesure 50 m de long), et bien sûr, qualité de la composition d'ensemble des peintures, du programme iconographique et de l'exécution artistique (encore que celle-ci soit variable selon les différentes parties de l'église – Figure 1).

Nous présentons ici une étude d'ensemble des peintures de la nef, réalisée à l'occasion de la mise en route d'un programme général de réhabilitation, conservation et restauration de l'église abbatiale et du décor peint.

Historique et origine de l'étude

Depuis de nombreuses années, les peintures de l'abbatiale de Saint-Savin ont fait l'objet d'interventions régulières, mais souvent disparates du point de vue de la conservation-restauration. On sait que des restaurations eurent lieu périodiquement sur les peintures depuis leur exécution, à différentes époques, et ce dès le 14ème siècle, et que des interventions ont eu lieu régulièrement depuis, notamment au 18ème siècle, puis au 19ème, et 20ème siècles.[1]

La dernière de ces interventions, mise en œuvre par le service des monuments historiques, date de 1974. Elle a concerné surtout les problèmes de refixage des couches picturales, de consolidation des mortiers, de réfection des lacunes.[2,3]

Cadre et objectifs de l'étude

Etant donné l'importance de cet édifice, il était logique d'envisager, non plus une série de campagnes ponctuelles d'intervention sur les peintures ou sur les différentes parties du bâtiment, mais un vaste programme pluriannuel. C'est ce qui a été décidé en 1994 par la conservation régionale des monuments historiques de Poitou-Charentes, à la suite d'un bilan des études menées depuis plusieurs années par le Laboratoire de Recherche des Monument Historiques (LRMH). Il s'agit d'un programme à long terme, intégrant l'ensemble de l'édifice et du site abbatial. Il a pour objectif l'assainissement général de l'édifice, avec notamment l'obtention d'un climat adéquat pour la conservation du décor peint dans des conditions optimales, et les interventions nécessaires à la conservation-restauration des parties peintes.

Pour parvenir à cet objectif, définir et cadrer les différentes interventions, il est prévu une étude préalable d'ensemble, devant déboucher (fin 1996) sur un projet global de travaux (contrat plan-état) qui seront menés à bien d'ici l'horizon 2000.

* Auteur à qui la correspondance doit être adressée

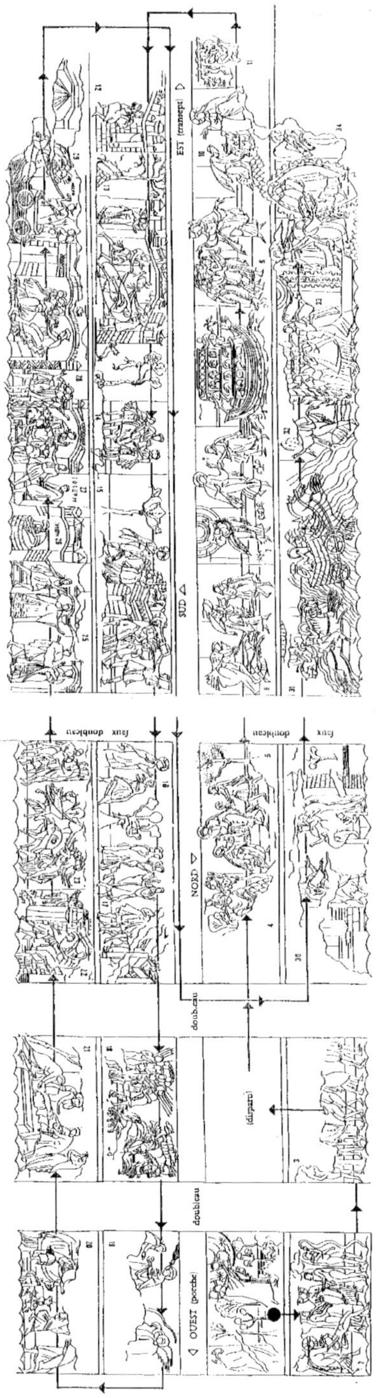

Figure 1. Schéma des différentes scènes de la voûte

C'est dans ce cadre[4] que se situe le travail présenté ici. Il s'agit donc d'une étude scientifique interdisciplinaire, menée conjointement par le LRMH et un restaurateur, ayant pour but la définition précise de l'état des peintures et des interventions de conservation-restauration éventuelles qu'elles nécessitent. Il a permis d'établir un diagnostic complet sur les peintures de la voûte (état de conservation, techniques de peinture, repeints, fixatifs, etc.), ceci environ 20 ans après la dernière intervention.

Méthodologie et organisation

Intervention in situ

Pour mener à bien ce travail, une équipe du LRMH a travaillé en collaboration avec un restaurateur à l'aide d'un échafaudage transportable, qui a permis, en quelques semaines, d'étudier l'ensemble de la voûte.[5] Le restaurateur a effectué des relevés systématiques qui ont permis d'établir une cartographie des états de surface, indiquant les types d'altérations observés, tant pour les enduits que pour les couches picturales, ainsi que la présence éventuelle de produits de restauration, anciens ou récents. Parallèlement à ce travail, le laboratoire a réalisé, en rapport avec les observations et les interrogations du restaurateur, un échantillonnage destiné à l'étude des stratigraphies, des types de matériaux d'origine ou rapportés (mortiers, fixatifs), et des diverses altérations. L'aspect microbiologique a également été examiné, et une couverture photographique (lumière visible et ultraviolet – UV) a été réalisée par le LRMH, ainsi que par l'Inventaire régional.[6]

Observations – échantillonnage

Les prélèvements analysés concernaient:

- les mortiers ou enduits, originaux ou de restauration;
- les enduits peints;
- les fixatifs et autres ajouts de surface;
- la présence éventuelle de micro-organismes.

Analyse des prélèvements – méthodologie

Cette étude rassemble un nombre important d'observations, puisque plus de 100 prélèvements ont été effectués pour analyse en laboratoire, indépendamment des observations et mesures effectuées sur place. Nous donnons ici une synthèse du dépouillement de ces observations, mené conjointement, comme on l'a dit, par l'équipe du laboratoire et le restaurateur.[7]

Ce dernier a établi des cartographies des altérations, permettant un diagnostic d'ensemble, zone par zone, de l'état des peintures. Certaines de ses observations ont été complétées par les analyses des échantillons.

Analyses de laboratoire

Les échantillons ont été analysés et observés au laboratoire selon les méthodes habituelles:

- observation au microscope optique pour les coupes stratigraphiques;
- analyse élémentaire par fluorescence X;
- observation au MEB (Microscope électronique à balayage) avec microanalyse (EDXRF – Energy dispersion X-ray fluorescence);
- analyse par IRTF (Infra-rouge à transformée de Fourier) (fixatifs, recherche de liants);
- analyse microbiologique (recherche et traitement de micro-organismes);
- analyse quantitative et caractérisation des mortiers[8] (hydraulicité, analyse de traces, etc.).

Tableau 1. Analyse des mortiers. On a synthétisé dans ce tableau les principales observations et analyses effectuées. Les analyses quantitatives indiquent la teneur en carbonate de calcium (chaux carbonatée) et la présence éventuelle de sulfates, ainsi que la perte au feu et le taux d'hydraulicité si celui-ci est notable

No.	Scène	Situation	Analyses LEM[a,b]	Analyses fluorescence	Observations	Présence de l'élément ou du caractère [c]indiqué				
						SO_4	Ti	Rb	Sr	H[a]
1-1	**Création des astres**	Restauration au dessus de la lune (rose + mortier)	**SO_4 16%** $CaCO_3$ 55% PF 33%	S Si K Fe Sr	Fluo UV blanche	x			x	
1-3		Sous le bras de Dieu	$CaCO_3$ 58% PF 10%	Si K S Fe Rb Sr				x	x	
2-1	**Création d'Eve**	Lacune ancienne entre les deux registres	$CaCO_3$ 59% PF 14%	Si K Fe Sr Rb				x	x	
3-2	**Arc doubleau 2** PF 14%	Côté N motif à disques	$CaCO_3$ 65%	Si K Fe Rb Sr	Aspect blanc mortier original?			x	x	
3-3	**Eve chassée du paradis**	Au dessus d'Eve	$CaCO_3$ 51% PF 13%	Si K Fe Sr Rb	Original			x	x	
4-1	**Eve filant**	Lacune grise (à g.)	$CaCO_3$ 76% PF 39%	Si S Sr Fe					x	
4-2		Zone mortier original	**SO_4 3%** $CaCO_3$ 73%	Si S K Al Fe Sr Rb Ti	Fluo UV blanche	x	x	x	x	
4-3			**H 1,39** $CaCO_3$ 54%	Si K S Al Fe Rb Sr Ti	Idem		x	x	x	x
15-2	**Tour de Babel**	Lacune mortier original	**H 1,67** $CaCO_3$ 27%	Si S K Al Fe Sr Rb Ti	Sels ?		x	x	x	x
20-1	**Abraham lègue ses troupeaux**	Mortier lacune MF	$CaCO_3$ 52%	Si S K Fe Sr	Fluo dorée				x	
21-1	**Arc doubleau 3**	Côté S-E mortier original	$CaCO_3$ 35% PF 9%	Si S K Al Fe Rb Sr Zr			x	x	x	x
21-2	**Ensevelissement d'Abraham**	Mortier original (lacune)	**H 1,21** $CaCO_3$ 23%	Si K Al Fe Rb Sr Zr Ti PF 13%4	Grains de chaux dans le mortier		x	x	x	
ADE1	**Arc doubleau 1**	Côté E	**SO_4 12%** $CaCO_3$ 74% PF 31%	S K Si Sr Fe	Mortier MF	x			x	
ADE2		Idem sous ADE1	$CaCO_3$3 52% PF 21%	Si S K Fe Sr Rb				x	x	
ADE3		Intrados coté S	$CaCO_3$ 56% PF 47%	Si K S Al Fe Sr Rb	Mortier roman ?			x	x	

[a] H Taux d'hydraulicité

[b] PF Perte au feu

[c] Eléménts identifiés par analyse en fluorescence X (dans l'ordre décroissant)

Résultats et synthèse

Etat de conservation des peintures

Les peintures et leur support présentent un état général très hétérogène, qu'il s'agisse de la couche picturale elle-même ou des enduits. L'importance des interventions antérieures accentue ce phénomène, comme le confirment les résultats des analyses de mortiers et de fixatifs de surface. Dans les deux cas, on observe la plupart des altérations habituellement rencontrées[9] sur les peintures murales.

ALTÉRATIONS DU SUPPORT

- Décollements d'enduit.
- Pertes de cohésion de l'enduit.
- Colmatages (voir Tableau 1).
- Fixatifs (voir Tableau 2).
- Accidents divers (impacts, fissures, ajouts métalliques).

Tableau 2. Analyse des fixatifs. Plusieurs remarques peuvent être dégagées de ce tableau: à l'inverse des mortiers, il est difficile ici de mettre en évidence des groupes de prélèvements bien caractérisés (par exemple, d'établir une corrélation nette entre fixatifs et fluorescence aux UV, même si ce phénomène a lieu dans une majorité de cas). Par ailleurs, la variété des produits trouvés est relativement importante par rapport au nombre d'échantillons étudiés pour fournir une statistique réellement significative. La possibilité de mélange ou d'additifs (tels que le dibutyl-phtalate, utilisé généralement comme plastifiant) rend l'analyse encore plus complexe

	Description et observations *in situ*			Résultats des analyses[a]						
No.	**Scènes**	**Situation**	**Observations faites sur place**	**Fluo. or**	**Fluo. mauve**	**B72**	**B67**	**Plexi -gum**	**PVA** ou vinylique	**Dibutyl-phtalate**
1-1	**Création des astres**	Restauration au-dessus de la lune	Fluo UV		x	*Prélèvement détruit pour analyse de mortier (pas d'analyse IR)(voir Tableau 1)*				
1-5	**Idem arbre**	Point rouge (grisatre)	Fluo dorée	x					x	
5-1	**Présents de Caïn et Abel**	Fond blanc	Fluo mauve		x				*Présence présumée*	
7-2	**Dieu et Noé**	Main de Dieu	Repeint (colmatage)						x	
7-3		Manteau de Dieu (épaule)	Repeint (14e ?) colmatage+ fixatif					x		
10-4	**Offrandes de Noé**	Fond blanc (derrière Dieu)	Brillance fixatif fluo UV				x			
12-1	**Noé goûtant le vin**	Jaune dans la porte du bâtiment arrière plan	Fluo UV		x	x	x			
17-1	**Loth emmené en prison**	Côté droit de la scène	Brillance fixatif	x			x			
17-2		Bande faitière; palmette rouge	Brillance fixatif			*Copolymère ou mélange acryl./vinyl.*				
20-1	**Abraham lègue ses troupeaux**	Mortier lacune 74	Fluo dorée	x	*Prélèvement détruit pour analyse de mortier (voir Tableau 1) (pas d'analyse IR)*					
20-2		Partie supérieure "fausse lacune"; rouge							x	
20-3		Idem 20-2 dans "fausse lacune"	Fluo mauve		x				x	
20-4		Arc (intérieur) vert (feuillage)	Fluo mauve		x				x	
23-2	**Joseph vendu par ses frères**	Partie g. de la scène: taches noires (microorganismes ?)	Imprégnation probable B72 (74 ?)			x				
28-2	**Joseph et Pharaon**	Fond du bonnet de Joseph: blanc rosé	Fluo dorée	x			x			
29-1	**Triomphe de Joseph**	Crinière du cheval de Joseph: rouge	Fixatifs probables				x			
31A-1	**Passage de la Mer rouge (est)**	Ventre du cheval au 1er plan	Soulèvement dû aux fixatifs			*Emulsion. acrylique*				
31A-2		Flots, sous le cheval	Tache jaunissement			x				
31B-2	**Passage de la Mer rouge (ouest)**	Sol sous les cavaliers	Coulure fixatif.				x			
32-2	**L'ange et la colonne de feu4**	Flammes noires (restauration possible) - zones grisâtres	Pigments ayant virés (minium probable)	x		x				

[a] Présence de l'élément ou du caractère indiqué (x)

ALTÉRATIONS DE LA COUCHE PICTURALE

- Ecaillages, imputables soit à une technique d'exécution défectueuse, soit à l'histoire matérielle de l'œuvre (infiltrations d'eau, condensation, ajouts).
- Etat de surface déséquilibré (couche picturale hétérogène, zones pulvérulentes ou saturées de fixatifs, brillance, assombrissement, jaunissement, blanchiment, craquelures, pelliculage).
- Usures, estompes, graffiti (par ex. une date "1839", une signature "T. CUE" (première travée).
- Altérations chromatiques (blanc de plomb, minium ayant viré au noir); certaines parties donnent une fluorescence jaune or qui n'est pas corrélée aux fixatifs, mais qui pourrait peut-être s'expliquer par la présence d'un liant blanc de Pb + tempera, si l'on en croit des cas analogues étudiés par ailleurs.[10]
- Repeints (ensemble remanié à diverses reprises, au moins depuis le 14ème s (cf. *Analyse des prélèvements*); les observations du restaurateur sont confirmées par les analyses.

Conditions climatiques, environnement

Des relevés thermo-hygrométriques effectués pendant la campagne ont permis d'étudier ponctuellement les conditions climatiques au niveau des peintures de la voûte; on a également mesuré l'humidité des enduits. Toutefois, ces études demeurent limitées et seront poursuivies dans le cadre de la mise en place du programme pluriannuel déjà cité.

Analyse des prélèvements

Les prélèvements effectués au total sont au nombre de 115. (cf. *Analyse des prélèvements – méthodologie*). 15 d'entre eux ont été sélectionnés pour les analyses de mortiers, 20 pour les analyses de fixatifs, 3 pour l'étude microbiologique. Les autres ont donné lieu à une étude systématique qui a permis de cerner les techniques de peinture en œuvre dans les peintures d'origine ainsi que dans les diverses restaurations.

Analyse des mortiers (Tableau 1)

Tous les prélèvements ont été analysés par fluorescence X, afin de caractériser qualitativement les différents éléments présents. De plus, un certain nombre d'échantillons a fait l'objet d'une analyse quantitative. Le tableau 1 montre l'ensemble des résultats.

Les indications caractéristiques sont:

- la présence notable de sulfates dans deux prélèvements, un peu moins importante dans un autre;
- l'utilisation de chaux hydraulique pour certains mortiers;
- des analogies entre certains mortiers en ce qui concerne la présence des éléments mineurs (Ti, Rb, Sr), correspondant vraisemblablement à des impuretés de la chaux.

Conclusions pour les mortiers. On peut observer quatre groupes principaux de prélèvements:

- *Premier groupe:* prélèvements (*création des astres, premier doubleau*) caractérisés par une teneur importante (12–16 %) de sulfates (accompagnée par une fluorescence UV blanche), ce qui semblerait indiquer l'utilisation d'un mortier de chaux-plâtre. Ils sont également caractérisés par la présence de strontium, à l'exclusion des autres éléments traces. Il y a donc lieu de penser que ces deux mortiers correspondent à une même restauration, peut-être ancienne.
- *Deuxième groupe:* prélèvements caractérisés uniquement par la présence d'éléments mineurs Rb et Sr. Ils correspondent aux scènes voisines 1 (*création des astres, création d'Eve, expulsion du paradis)* et du deuxième doubleau qui sépare cette dernière scène. Il peut donc s'agir de mortiers d'origine.
- *Troisième groupe:* prélèvements dans des mortiers de lacune, caractérisés par l'utilisation de chaux hydraulique, et les mêmes éléments mineurs (Ti, etc.). Ils sont vraisemblablement d'une fabrication commune, donc contemporains; l'utilisation de chaux hydraulique indique l'usage d'une pierre à chaux différente de celle utilisée pour les autres mortiers. Ils pourraient correspondre à une intervention ancienne.
- *Quatrième groupe:* prélèvements caractérisés par la présence d'un seul élément mineur (Sr) – comme le premier groupe, mais sans sulfates; ils correspondent tous deux à des lacunes répertoriées dans les interventions de restauration de 1974.

D'autres prélèvements sont plus difficiles à regrouper. Les conclusions sont donc beaucoup plus difficiles à établir pour ces derniers. Elles nécessiteront une étude d'ensemble plus étendue afin de pouvoir établir des statistiques sur un nombre d'échantillons plus représentatif.

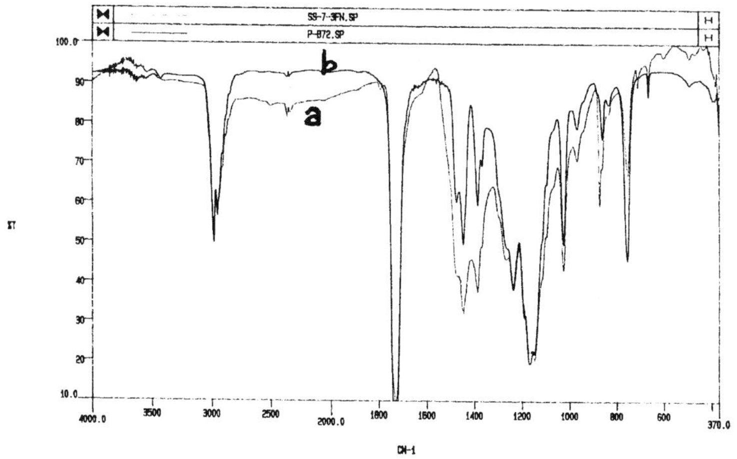

Figure 2. Spectre IRTF: identification du Paraloïd B72 (a: échantillon; b: référence)

Analyse des fixatifs (Tableau 2)

La présence de fixatifs, employés au cours des restaurations successives, est visible en de nombreux endroits (cf. *Altérations de la couche picturale*). On observe fréquemment des fluorescences aux UV, soit mauve, soit couleur or très brillant. On pourrait penser que les fixatifs sont responsables de ce phénomène; toutefois, comme on le verra, cette interprétation est loin d'être évidente.

Une vingtaine de prélèvements ont été sélectionnés pour l'étude de ces produits. Les spectres obtenus ont permis d'identifier de façon assez précise la nature des fixatifs, ou de les classer dans des familles de groupement chimique (acétate de polyvinyle, polyméthacrylate...). L'analyse a été faite par spectrométrie IRTF après extraction au chloroforme (spectres IRTF, cf. exemple, Figure 2). L'interprétation des résultats[11] a mis en évidence la présence de huit produits dont certains appartenant à la même famille chimique ou à des familles voisines (ex.: acétate de polyvinyle, polyméthacrylate, etc.).

Conclusions pour les fixatifs. Quoi qu'il en soit, on peut dire que la présence de fixatifs est quasi générale. Ces observations – résultant des analyses – sur la présence de fixatifs sont confirmées par les observations visuelles du restaurateur (voir plus haut).

Les produits identifiés sont les suivants:

- polymères acryliques (dix échantillons): polyméthacrylates
  - Plexigum N 80®,
  - Paraloïd B 67®,
  - Paraloïd B 72® (Figure 2),
  - émulsion acrylique;
- mélange ou copolymère acrylique/vinylique (un échantillon);
- polymères vinyliques (cinq échantillons):
  - poly(acétate de vinyle) (ou: acétate de polyvinyle);
- additifs (deux échantillons):
  - dibutyl-phtalate (plastifiant).

La diversité et le nombre de produits identifiés laisserait penser qu'il a été procédé à plusieurs essais ou tests dans différentes zones. Tous ces produits sont passés en concentration assez importante et semblent être restés en surface, ne pénétrant que très peu dans les pigments. D'autre part, tous ces fixatifs correspondent à des produits de fabrication assez récente et ne peuvent provenir que de la dernière restauration.

Analyse des couches picturales – techniques de peinture

Une centaine de prélèvements a donc été étudiée en laboratoire (*Analyse des prélèvements – méthodologie*); il serait fastidieux de donner ici le tableau complet des résultats, aussi présentons nous seulement les principaux résultats, tout en mentionnant les incertitudes qui subsistent ici ou là.

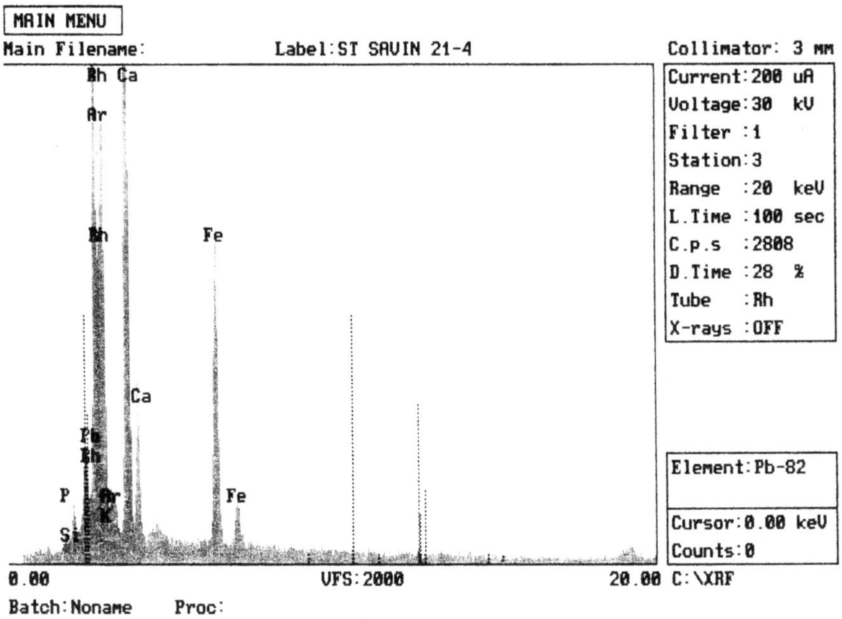

Figure 4. Mise en évidence des ocres (Fe) par fluorescence X

Ces résultats – recoupés avec les observations visuelles du restaurateur – permettent de dégager assez nettement un certain nombre d'observations concernant les techniques de peintures. Ils sont basés essentiellement sur la stratigraphie et l'analyse des pigments.

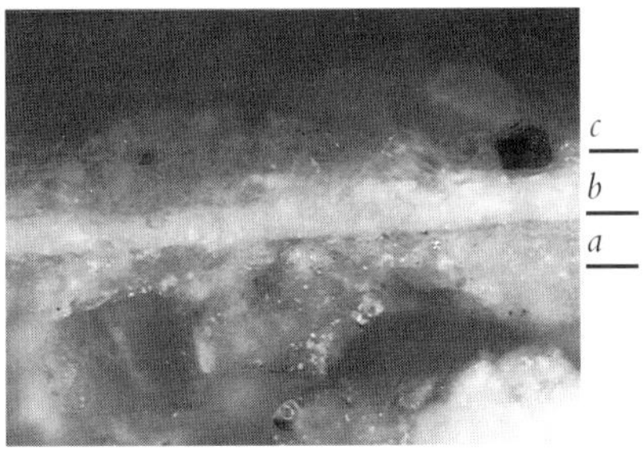

Figure 3. Stratigraphie de la technique originale: (a) mortier chaux + sable; (b) *intonaco; (c) couche picturale*

Technique originale (12ème siècle). Elle est caractérisée par des éléments relativement simples, à savoir:

- **Stratigraphie:** (Figure 3)
  – *mortier de chaux* (carbonatée: $CaCO_3$) + sable (arricio);
  – *intonaco* (couche de lait de chaux (idem) plus ou moins lissée); cette couche est présente dans plus de 90% des échantillons de peinture d'origine;
  – *couche(s) picturale(s)*: généralement une seule couche, parfois deux quand on a affaire à un rehaut (trait de vêtement, valeur sur un visage, etc.).
- **Pigments utilisés:** uniquement des terres (Figure 4): (rouges, jaunes, bruns). A noter que les verts ne sont pas présents dans les deux premières travées (avant le deuxième doubleau). On n'observe dans celles-ci que des ocres, ensuite apparaît la terre verte (troisième travée). Il semble donc que l'on ait commencé à peindre à partir de l'Ouest, travée par travée, et que la technique utilisée ait évolué (apparition de nouveaux pigments) au fur et à mesure que l'on avançait vers le chœur.
- **Dessin préparatoire** (Figure 5): dans certains prélèvements, on note la présence d'une couche d'ocre rouge située *sous* l'intonaco, ce qui correspond à un dessin préparatoire de mise en place (*sinopia*). Ceci s'observe en particulier dans les scènes proches du chœur (*Noé et la vigne*), où un repentir avait déjà été mis en évidence, ce qui tendrait à confirmer que l'ensemble des peintures a commencé à être mis en place à partir de l'Ouest, ce qui explique le décalage obtenu en arrivant près du chœur.
- **Liants**: en raison de la présence quasi générale de fixatifs en forte concentration, il est quasiment impossible de procéder à une analyse significative du liant d'origine. Néanmoins, les observations visuelles, comme l'observation des stratigraphies, ne permettent pas d'envisager une technique de vraie fresque, mais plutôt une peinture à la détrempe, ou une technique de *mezzo-fresco*, même si l'intention des artistes, comme le laisse supposer la stratigraphie relativement simple avec intonaco, était peut-être de se rapprocher de cette dernière technique.

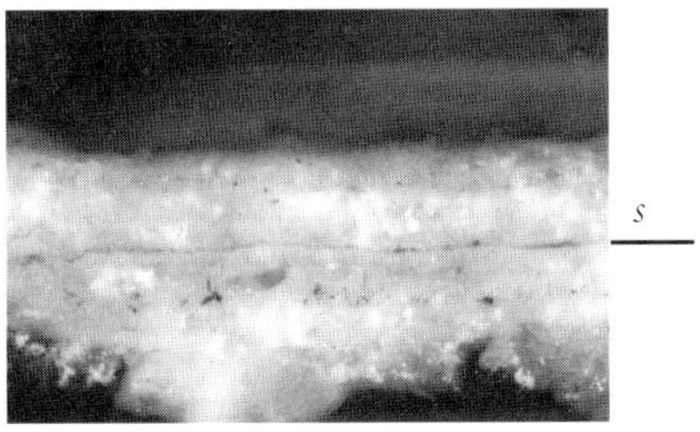

Figure 5. Technique originale, avec dessin préparatoire (sinopia) (s)

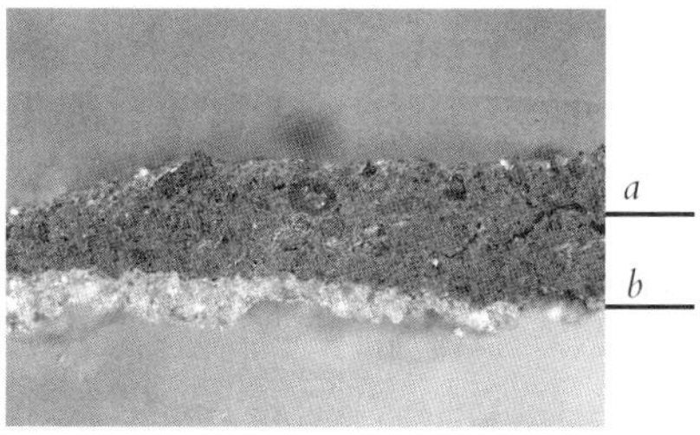

Figure 6. Surpeint: couche de minium (b) posée sur une couche d'ocre rouge (a)

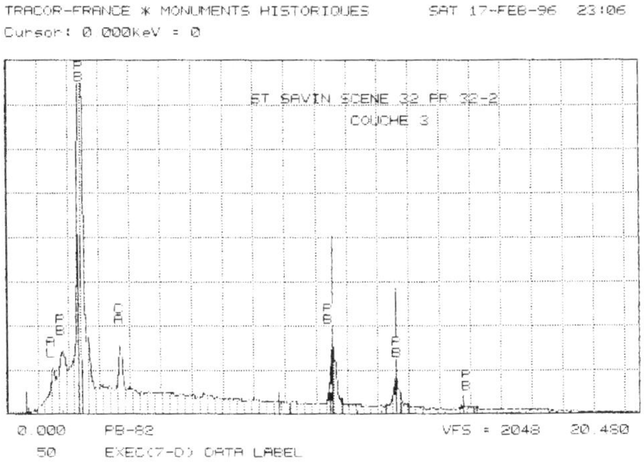

Figure 7. Mise en évidence du plomb (minium) par MEB/ microanalyse (EDS)

Restaurations. Comme on l'a dit plus haut, celles-ci ont été nombreuses au cours des siècles, du 14ème ou même 13ème jusqu'au 20ème siècle. L'évolution des techniques de peinture selon ces différentes époques ressort assez nettement des observations et analyses réalisées:

- **Repeints et surpeints:** en de nombreux endroits, on a affaire à des repeints (sans peinture d'origine) ou des surpeints (peinture d'origine, plus ou moins abondante, recouverte par une ou plusieurs couches postérieures. Celles-ci sont généralement de nature différente quant au pigments.
- **Restaurations 14ème–15ème siècles** (Figure 6)**:** en particulier, on peut noter en de nombreux endroits une couche de minium (ayant d'ailleurs viré au noir) superposée à une couche d'ocre rouge (*Moïse et la colonne de feu,* notamment). Il s'agit là de la restauration du 14ème siècle, pour laquelle il semble que l'on ait, un peu partout, recouvert l'ocre rouge d'origine, peut-être usé ou jugé insuffisamment coloré, par du minium (Figure 7).

  Par ailleurs, on trouve sur les arcs doubleaux (Figure 8) qui, on le sait, ont été repris au 14ème siècle, ainsi que sur des scènes voisines, une technique particulière comprenant un mortier avec couche picturale à base d'ocre, mais *sans intonaco.* En quelques endroits, cette technique semble être superposée à des restes de technique originale (12ème siècle).
- **Restaurations postérieures:** en d'autres endroits – deuxième travée *(Dieu et Abraham, meurtre d'Abel)* – on trouve des restaurations visiblement plus tardives d'un point de vue stylistique, caractérisées par l'emploi de pigments verts différents, contenant du cuivre, ainsi que des ions Cl^-, (verts au Cu, acétate de Cu etc.).
- Les **restaurations les plus récentes** enfin, outre le fait qu'elles sont connues par la documentation existante, sont caractérisées par la présence de certains

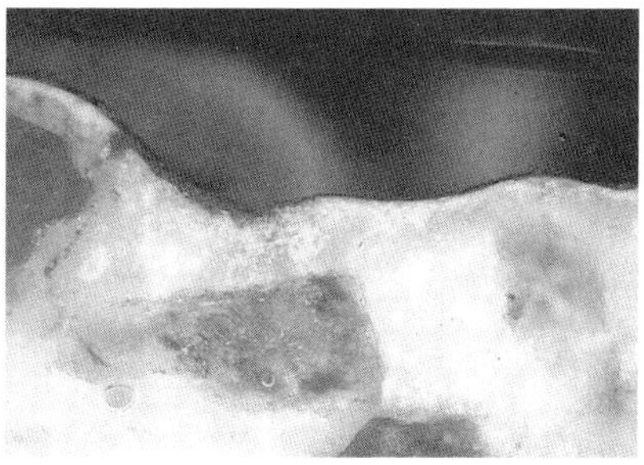

Figure 8. Technique des arcs doubleaux (pas d'intonaco) et des scènes de même époque

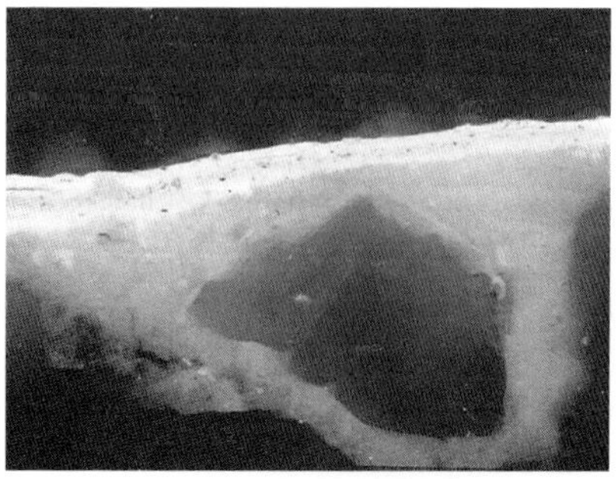

Figure 9. Restauration 20ème siécle: couche de blanc de titane

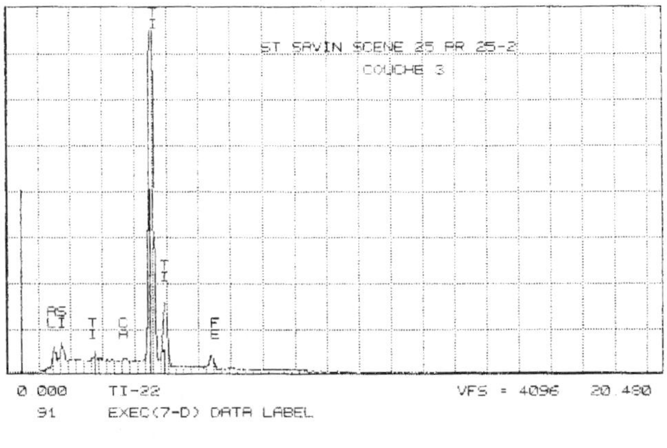

Figure 10. Mise en évidence du titane dans la restauration 20ème siécle par MEB/microanalyse (EDS)

pigments tels que le blanc de titane, pigment typiquement moderne (Figures 9 et 10).

- Quant à la **bande faîtière**, elle a subi énormément de remaniements, notamment aux 14ème et 15ème siècle, de sorte que sa technique est difficile à caractériser.
- **Points d'incertitudes**: un certain nombre d'interrogations demeurent, notamment, on l'a vu, pour la question des liants mais aussi pour des observations disparate; par exemple, nous avons trouvé, dans un des prélèvements, (bande faîtière), la présence d'étain, sans qu'il soit possible d'attribuer la présence de cet élément à une raison bien précise. Peut-être l'étain était-il utilisé pour les blasons fleurdelisés (14ème siècle) qui se trouvent dans cette zone, mais la technique employée reste incertaine. Autre interrogation: pour quelques prélèvements, peu nombreux il est vrai, on a affaire, très certainement, à une technique d'origine, mais l'intonaco n'apparaît pas nettement, sans qu'on puisse dire pour quelle raison.

Conclusion pour les techniques de peinture. Compte tenu de ces observations, on peut résumer l'histoire de ces peintures en se basant sur l'hypothèse suivante:

- *réalisation au 12ème siècle* avec une technique mortier de chaux/intonaco/couleur, en utilisant des ocres, puis des terres vertes à partir de la troisième travée;
- *au 14ème siècle (13ème ?) restauration des doubleaux* (reprise technique architecturale) et réfections ou superpositions sur différentes scènes, avec notamment l'usage du minium qui se superpose à l'ocre rouge ou qui le remplace;
- *vers le 18ème siècle*, reprise de certaines scènes avec principalement l'usage de verts au cuivre;
- *enfin, restaurations du 19ème et 20ème siècles.*

Bien entendu, il ne s'agit là que d'une hypothèse, qui nous paraît, au vu de toutes les observations et analyses connues à ce jour, la plus vraisemblable; elle pourra être confirmée ou infirmée par des observations ultérieures.

Analyses microbiologiques

Quelques prélèvements ont donné lieu à des analyses microbiologiques. De façon à caractériser l'activité des différents micro-organismes présents: on a ainsi pu procéder à la numération des espèces, et mettre en évidence une activité, fongique et bactérienne, et procéder à une identification des champignons, etc. Les résultats ont montré une activité localisée mais importante des champignons et surtout des bactéries sur les différents supports.

Il faut toutefois préciser que ces conclusions ne sont formulées que par rapport à quelques prélèvements. Il serait donc hasardeux d'extrapoler ces données à l'ensemble de la voûte. Comme pour d'autres questions, cette étude sera prolongé au fur et à mesure des interventions inscrites dans le programme prévu, déjà cité.

Conclusions générales

Bien que ce premier bilan ne soit pas exhaustif, il permet de mettre en évidence les points principaux relatifs à la conservation des peintures de la nef, et fait apparaître un état de conservation des peintures relativement précaire. Par ailleurs, il permet de préciser, même si des incertitudes demeurent, les techniques utilisées pour l'exécution des peintures ainsi que lors des restauration successives.

En ce qui concerne l'état de conservation, les conclusions mentionnées plus haut permettront de prendre un certain nombre de décisions quant aux interventions à mettre en œuvre, et à leur degré d'urgence (consolidation des mortiers, élimination des fixatifs et des divers produits de restauration, opération de désinfection de l'ensemble, etc.)

L'étude des stratigraphies et techniques de peinture d'origine et des restaurations vient compléter le diagnostic du restaurateur et pourra ainsi aider aux choix que le restaurateur aura à faire en vue d'une intervention éventuelle.

Il faut noter l'importance, dans ce travail, de son caractère interdisciplinaire, puisque les observations du restaurateur d'une part, du laboratoire d'autre part, sont complémentaires et convergent vers des conclusions communes. Ceci constitue la principale condition à une approche réellement scientifique pour l'établissement du diagnostic, sans perdre de vue, d'ailleurs, que ce diagnostic s'inscrit lui-même, comme on l'a dit au début de cette présentation, dans un cadre général d'étude, mettant en œuvre tous les acteurs de la conservation-restauration.

Notes et références

1. J. Taralon, "Observations techniques sur la voûte de la nef de Saint-Savin", *Bulletin de la Société nationale des antiquaires de France*, 4ème trimestre (1968): 247–256.
2. Le service ne disposait alors que de moyens scientifiques très restreints en personnel et en matériel, puisque le LRMH n'a été crée qu'au début des années 70, c'est pourquoi les études menées à l'époque ont une portée relativement limitée.
3. C. de Maupeou et M.F. de Christen, "Restauration des peintures murales de la voûte de la nef à Saint-Savin-sur-Gartempe" *Les Monuments historiques de la France*, no.3 (1976).
4. L'ensemble du programme est coordonné par M. Jeanneau, architecte en chef des Monument historiques; les principaux intervenants sont, outre l'architecte, M. Brochard, inspecteur général des Monument historiques, l'équipe du LRMH (29 rue de Paris, F-77420 Champs-sur-Marne, France, sections "peinture murale" et "microbiologie"), et I. Dangas, restaurateur (3 rue Edgard Quinet, F-92240 Malakoff, France).
5. L'échaffaudage en question couvrait à peu près la longueur d'une travée; il était déplacé d'une travée chaque semaine, et chaque étude, menée par des équipes se relayant, durait environ deux ou trois jours; la voûte comprenant sept travées peintes, l'intervention s'est donc étalée sur environ six semaines, en février–mars 1994.
6. A. Maulny, J.P. Joly et E. Dessert, *L'abbaye de Saint-Savin, Vienne* (F) (Poitiers: Inventaire général des monuments et des richesses artistiques de la France, Service régional de l'inventaire de Poitou-Charentes, 1992).
7. M. Stefanaggi et al., "Saint-Savin-sur-Gartempe (F - 86), église abbatiale: étude des peintures de la nef (première phase)" (Rapport LRMH no. 4 Q, diffusion restreinte, LRMH, F 77420 -Champs-sur-Marne, juin 1995).
8. Réalisée au LEM (Laboratoire d'essais des matériaux) de Strasbourg.
9. Les efflorescences salines sont dans l'ensemble peu décelables, sauf dans certains échantillons de mortiers (cf. Tableau 1). Il n'a pas été possible, dans le cadre de l'étude, de menser une analyse systématique des sels, mais cet objectif reste inscrit au programme des études suivantes.
10. *Un progetto per Piero della Francesca: indagini diagnostico-conoscitive per la conservazione della "leggenda della vera Croce"* (Firenze, Alinari: comiteo nazionale per il quinto centenario della morte di Piero della Francesca, 1989).
11. La lecture des résultats est parfois gênée par la présence de mélanges, ce qui rend plus difficile l'interprétation des spectres (extraction au chloroforme effectuée sur l'écaille entière).

Rock art on Lake Baikal: Research and Practice in Rock Art Preservation

Emma N.Ageeva, Natalia L.Rebrikova
State Research Institute for Restoration,
Department for the Conservation of Monuments and. Sculpture and
Biology Laboratory,
44 Gastello Street, 107014 Moscow, Russia

Abstract

This paper describes three examples of East Siberian rock art monuments: Shishkino petroglyphs on the River Lena, at Sagan-Zaba and at Orso on the shore of Lake Baikal. Their chemical and mineralogical composition, and the structural and physical characteristics of the stone support of the petroglyphs are given. The various kinds of damage to the monuments, both natural and anthropogenic, are characterized. Experimental and conservation work carried out in the location of the monuments is described.

Keywords

Petroglyphs, frost weathering, biodegradation, visitors' scribblings, protective overhang, cleaning, consolidation

Introduction

The paper is concerned with the urgent problem of the preservation of rock art monuments. Possible ways of resolving this problem are illustrated by consideration of three East Siberian monuments.

The Shishkino petroglyphs are stylized depictions of human beings, animals and hunting scenes. They are situated on a red sandstone rock massif on the bank of the River Lena and are about 2 km in length. The pictures have been executed with a range of techniques: engraving, polishing, surface chafing with a stone, and picture contouring with polished grooves (Figure 1). Academician A.P.Okladnikov dates the pictures to five periods, the earliest being the upper paleolithic and the latest the 11 to 18th centuries AD.

Figure 1. 'Shishkino petroglyphs'. Petroglyphs depicting horsemen

The Sagan-Zaba monument is situated on the shore of Lake Baikal. The petroglyphs, on three white marble outcrops from the shore, 12 to 15 m in height and about 25 m in length, were produced by a gouging technique. Pictures, dating from various periods from the Bronze Age to the Middle Ages, depict anthropomorphous figures, animals and birds, as well as glyphs (Figure 2).

The Orso monument is situated on a mountain range terrace high above Lake Baikal, at a distance of over 1.5 km from the shore. Petroglyphs depicting deer were produced by a contour gouging technique in a bracing style (Figure 3) on a 1.5 × 1.7 m marble block.

The monuments are situated in a continental climate zone characterized by sharp 24-hour and seasonal variations of temperature. They have been subject to such strong natural and anthropogenous effects that their further preservation may be in doubt.

Work to ensure the preservation of the monuments began in 1987 on the instruction of the Irkutsk Historical and Cultural Preservation Center and is still going on. Research is being done into the causes and character of the degradation of the monuments.

Conservation techniques have been developed on a specially allocated rock massif site outside the location of petroglyphs. Conservation materials are being used, which are distinguished for their high atmosphere resistance and which have shown themselves to advantage in restoration practice; these are mostly organosilicon compounds and compositions based thereon. The final selection of materials and techniques is being made with reference to the results of many years of observation of experimental sites. The assessment criteria are treatment efficiency and the absence of an adverse effect on the rock. In practical work on the monuments preference is given to preventive conservation techniques, such as the restoration of natural protective ledges, the making of artificial overhangs and changing the direction of water flows. Operations involving direct interference with a monument, such as the securing of exfoliating crusts, the consolidation of degraded rock, the stopping up of cavities and cracks and biocide treatment, have only been performed in extreme cases when loss of petroglyphs has been a possibility. This paper describes operations carried out on each of the three monuments given above.

Figure 2. 'Sagan-Zaba'. Pictures of birds

Cleaning off graffiti: the case of the Shishkino petroglyphs

The petroglyphs are found on nearly all vertical planes of the rock massif stretching down the river, which are both suitable and accessible enough for the petrogylphs

Figure 3. 'Orso'. Petroglyph depicting a deer

Figure 4. 'Shishkino petroglyphs'. The general view of the rock massif at one of its sites

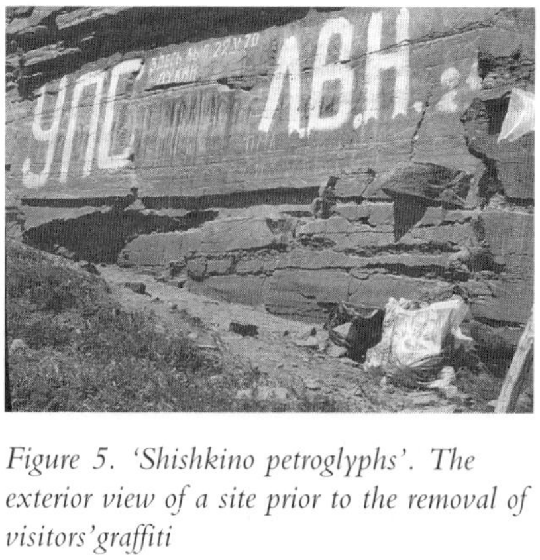

Figure 5. 'Shishkino petroglyphs'. The exterior view of a site prior to the removal of visitors'graffiti

to have been created. The general view of part of the rock massif is shown in Figure 4. The monument is made of a typical sandstone. It is composed of quartz and feldspar grains cemented with crystalline calcite and there are also small clay admixtures. In addition to the basic components, the rock also contains hematite., ferric hydroxide, manganese and mica compounds. Calcium oxalates have been discovered in the composition of the patinized surface layer. The petroglyph surfaces face south and often have a negative inclination. This, as well as natural ledges above, protect petroglyphs from the direct effect of precipitation. Only if there is heavy sideways rain, are the petroglyphs wetted. Wetting of the petroglyphs by water seeping through cracks occurs rarely and is of a local nature. There is reason to believe that another imperceptible source of moisture is condensation in capillaries of the surface layer as a result of daily temperature variations. The circumstantial evidence for this is the change in colour intensity of the sandstone in the morning. This is accounted for by physical weathering processes prevailing over chemical and biological ones requiring large quantities of water. The principal decay occurs in the thin surface layer and manifests itself by pulverizing of the sandstone and thin flakes peeling off. Crust decay can be seen on certain sites, seemingly caused by the insolation and non-uniform warming of rock layers in depth. The decay factor that is second in importance for this monument is anthropogenous. Most surfaces carrying petroglyphs have been 'superscribed' with contemporary visitors' scribblings, scratched and made with various paints, pencils, charcoal and chalk. Some petroglyphs have been damaged when copies have been made of them with a contact technique. Free access for visitors to monuments has resulted in partial damage to the rock massif as a result of paths collapsing. An earthen road along the outcrops has long been a source of much dust, which has settled on the petroglyphs.

The first step in ensuring preservation of the monument was the asphalting of the road in 1989 and the introduction of a 30 km per hour speed limit. Subsequently a rotation of watchmen was arranged to control visitors' conduct. A cottage was built for the watchmen in the nearest valley.

In 1990 one of the petroglyphed surfaces was cleaned of visitors' scribblings, which enabled the monument to appear natural again; it also allowed some new petroglyphs to be found on this site. A general view of the monument before and after the cleaning is given in Figures 5 and 6. In order to remove superimposed paintings, AFT-1 industrial wash was used, containing acetone, toluene, dioxane and paste made up on a base of an organic solvent mixture and containing the following components: methylene chloride (150 ml); white spirit (50 ml); acetone (100 ml); ammonia solution at 10% (50 ml); beeswax (20 g); and paraffin-wax (100 g). In order to remove coats of aged thick paint, an alkali composition was used: potassium hydroxyde (10 g); glycerin (13 g); carboxyl methyl cellulose (15 g); and water (100 g). Scribblings done with charcoal and chalk were removed with 0.05% solution of non-ionic surface active substance (syntanol DS-10).

Based on the positive results of a many years' monitoring, conservation was carried out in 1995 of a part of the rock surface with a zoomorphous petroglyph. A penciled outlining was removed mechanically with a soft eraser. Old white-paint remnants were finally removed from pores and cavities with an organic solvent mixture (toluene, pinene and isopropyl spirit), which enabled a whitish blot, superimposed on a part of the picture, to be weakened. Three deep cavities were stopped up and flaking crusts were consolidated with a mixture of a clayey paste (a sandstone weathering product, four parts) and MSN-7 organosilicon silazan resin (40% solution in toluene, one part). The 'KORABELNIKOV' graffiti, which appeared after the 1990 cleaning, was weakened by masticating and toning down the first five letters. In order to masticate deeply engraved letters, a compound was used containing four parts of the clayey paste and one part of the MSN-7 product (3% solution in toluene). Slightly engraved letters were toned down with a clayey paste suspension in water (particle size < 0.07 mm). The entire surface of the area received a double treatment with a 3% solution of the MSN-7 in toluene. Such a treatment consolidated the tonings and the pulverulent surface layer. In addition, it ensured the protection of the rock surface from any atmospheric effect resulting from its now having hydrophobic properties.

Figure 6. 'Shishkino petroglyphs'. The view of the site after cleaning

Figure 7. 'Sagan-Zaba'. The general view of the petroglyphed rock massif

Figure 8. 'Orso'. The upper part of an outcrop after had been rubble worked and defects had been stopped up with a lime cement mortar

Consolidation: the case of Sagan-Zaba

Outcrops with petroglyphs are situated in a cove next to the water; in one place they are separated from the water by a strip not more than one meter in width (Figure 7). Outcrops face south. The petroglyphs are on a vertical plane with a negative inclination angle. The rock making up the massif is crystalline, virtually pure, calcite with negligible admixtures, i.e. marble, which is built up of calcite grains, very often doubled, with grains 0.5 to 0.7 mm in size. The patina colour of the petroglyph spots has a broad spectrum of yellow–beige–brown shades and is made of recrystallized calcium carbonate and ferric hydroxide. The main causes of the decay of the monument are frost weathering and marble biodegradation. These processes have been contributed to by tectonic deformation and cracks in the rock, the rock's low petrostructural characteristics and excessive wetting of outcrops, resulting from rain and melted snow flowing down the slope, sprays and water dust during storms, as well as from water accumulating in two semi-closed karst fissures in the upper part of the outcrops. The alternate freezing and melting of water in cracks and pores has resulted in an intensive granulation and exfoliation of the marble to a depth of 10 cm or more. The porosity of these layers exceeds that of the rock by at least five times.

The loss of a considerable part of the petroglyphs is accounted for by the flaking of crusts. Various depths of exfoliation have been found, from thin surface crusts to layers several centimeters thick. The second most important decay factor is biological. In spite of the deep seasonal freezing of the rock and intensive solar radiation, virtually all the outcrops are infected with algae, which have developed in the subsurface layer down to several millimeters in depth. Algoflora consists of blue–green algae: *Gleocapsa sp.*, *Nostoc sp.*, *Stigonema sp.* and green unicellular algae of the *Protococcales sp.* These are similar to the algoflora of the marble of the 'St. Petersburg' monument in Canada, which is situated under similar climatic and hydrological conditions. Certain parts of rock surface are covered with lichen. These are most xerophilous and the species *Caloplaca* genus which prefers an alkaline substrate.

Local mechanical decay of the petroglyphed surfaces is taking place in certain parts of the outcrops as a result of rain water and melted snow flowing down the outcrops and carrying broken and falling abrasive material. The anthropogenous effect can be seen on the monument in the form of numerous graffiti.

Tests of the following technologies are being done on the monument: structural granulated marble consolidation; the securing of flaking crusts; and biocide treatment. A composition with hydrophilic effect, based on partially hydrolyzed tetraethoxisilan (ET-40 product), has been applied as a consolidator. In order to secure flaking crusts, finishing compositions based on organosilicon bindings of the siloxane type (Polysil-01) and silazans (MSN-7) were used. The two-year observation of the experimental sites has yielded a positive result. The stoppings are well preserved and no flaking and cracks have been noted. The strength and exterior appearance of the consolidated marble remain unchanged and the monitoring continues. A negative result has been obtained from the biocide treatment. The sealed surface patina has not only failed to prevent algae from developing, but it has also noticeably reduced the effectiveness of any biocide treatment because of the reduced transparency and vapour penetrability. At the same time, a high degree of algae inhibition was observed in the area treated with the consolidator, which may be accounted for by algae 'cementation' throughout the treated depth.

Plans have been made for priority conservation treatment:

- the construction of drainage systems to collect and divert rain water and melted snow flowing down the slope and thus the restoration of the lost natural shelter;
- monolithing of the karst fissures;
- the construction of catching devices to stop 'rock' flows.

Control of the natural decay process: the case of Orso

The rock composing the monument is white crystalline marble composed of double calcite with graphite inclusions. The outcrop surface carrying the petroglyphs

Figure 9. 'Orso'. The general view of the monument prior to the beginning of operations. Front view

Figure 10. 'Orso'. The general view of the monument after conservation. Front view

has a negative inclination angle, 12° on average, so that the pictures are very rarely wetted by direct precipitation, only when there is a strong oblique wind. At the same time rain water and melted snow, flowing down recesses and cracks, result periodically in intensive saturation of the rock with moisture, thus accelerating sharply weathering and biodecay processes. Rock decay by way of crust flaking and biogrowth has been detected in most wetted areas. The monument has been saved from anthropogenous interference by its remoteness and difficult access.

The following operations were performed on the monument in 1994 in order to slow down natural decay processes:

- Rain water and melted snow were diverted on the upper horizontal part of the outcrop. Water flow beds were moved away from the rock surface by using masonry and old water drains were filled with rubble and closed up with a lime cement mortar. The closures were toned down and treated with organosilicon water-repellant (Figure 8).
- Artificial kerbs were raised and a shelter and a stone water baffle were installed in the upper part of the monument. A plate of grey slate, toned into the colour of marble, was used as a shelter and the mechanical fastening of the shelter and the water baffle was reinforced by their being glued with an artificial paste based on a organosilicon binding (MSN-7 product). Artificial paste was also used to raise the kerbs.
- Flaking crusts were consolidated with a finishing paste based on lime and the MSN-7 product. Vertical cracks of tectonic origin crossing the petroglyphed surfaces were not stopped up so as not to disrupt the natural regime of the monument;
- Local biocide treatment was carried out. The upper part of the outcrop was cleaned of furry lichen and twice treated with the 30% H_2O_2 solution; an algicide treatment (with the 5% tin organocompound solution in toluene, specific application being 3 ml dm^{-2}) was applied on the lower part of the monument in areas with flaking crusts.

The general view of the monument before and after the operations is given in Figures 9 and 10. Observation of the monument is continuing. Up to now the complex anti-emergency conservation treatment that has been done has fully ensured the physical preservation of the monument.

Conclusion

The unique feature of rock art monuments lies in the fact that they are a natural system, directly depending on processes going on in the rock massif. Traditional conservation techniques, which have shown themselves to advantage on stone sculptural and architectural monuments, are quite often ineffective and at times unsafe when applied to rock art monuments, as is a mechanical transfer of conservation techniques from one rock art monument to another. For this reason the selection of conservation treatments must be based on the results of many years of monitoring.

Positive results have been obtained using traditional conservation techniques, such as:

- the removal of paint coats by using the AFT-1 industrial wash and paste made on a base of an organic solvents mixture (at Shishkino);
- protective treatment of stone by silazan MSN-7 (at Shishkino);
- the in-depth treatment of stone by using the consolidant-product ET-40 (at Sagan-Zaba);
- algicide treatment of stone with a tin organo-compound TBTO (at Orso).

The aim of petroglyph preservation is the maintenance and, whenever necessary, the restoration of the original conditions under which the monument existed for a long period of time. The first step in the practical application of conservation must be protective measures. It can be assumed that these methodologies will be appropriate for use in the practice of rock art preservation in future.

Acknowledgements

The authors express their deep gratitude, for contributions to research and for consultation, to the archeologists, M.Ya.Sklyarevski, O.I.Goryunova, L.I.Melnikova and T.F.Perzhakova, and also to the general manager of the Irkutsk Historical and Cultural Heritage Preservation Center, B.M.Bakharev, for operations funding. The photographs were taken by V.E.Netunayev of the State Research Institute for Restoration.

Abstract

The accurate documentation and interpretation of rock art continues to be a difficult challenge. The paper describes the recording undertaken as part of a rock art conservation project at the Cueva de El Ratón in Baja California, Mexico. Documentation and interpretation techniques of large format photography, hand measurement, land surveying, stereophotogrammetry and computer enhancement and manipulation were used to record the paintings. Successful restitution of the photogrammetric data was achieved only through the close collaboration of the plotting specialist with a rock art conservator and geologist already very familiar with the site.

Keywords

Recording, documentation, stereophotogrammetry, rock art, Mexico

Figure 1. Location of the Cueva de El Ratón (arrowed) (photo by J.-P. Jerome. Reprinted by permission of the J. Paul Getty Trust © 1994)

Figure 2. Detail of paintings in area B3 showing superimpositions (photo by J.-P. Jerome. Reprinted by permission of the J. Paul Getty Trust © 1994)

Stereophotogrammetric Recording of Rock Art at the Cueva de El Ratón, Baja California, Mexico

John Bell, Jean-Pierre Jerôme, Peter Sawyer
Heritage Recording and Technical Data Services,
Public Works and Government Services Canada,
10 Wellington, Hull, Quebec K1A 0M5, Canada

Valerie Magar
Coordinación de Restauración del patrimonio Cultural,
Ex-convento de Churubusco, Xicoténcatl y Gral. Anaya,
04120 México, D.F., México

Nicholas Stanley Price*
10754 Northgate Street, Culver City, CA 90230, USA

The Baja California rock art conservation project

The work reported here was carried out at a rockshelter in the Sierra de San Francisco in the central Baja California peninsula in northwest Mexico. Many rockshelter sites with paintings have been located in the Sierra de San Francisco.[1] Their dating is currently under investigation; the majority probably date to the late first and early second millennia AD. The sites were occupied and used by the prehistoric population of the peninsula and were first reported to the European world by missionaries arriving in the area in the 18th century. The extraordinarily impressive paintings, notable for their grand scale and vivid colours,[2,3] led to the inscription in 1993 of the Sierra de San Francisco on the World Heritage List of Unesco.

Concerned at the possible deterioration of the paintings, the Getty Conservation Institute launched a pilot conservation project in 1993 in association with the Instituto Nacional de Antropología e Historia of Mexico, the Governor of the State of Baja California Sur, and the non-profit Fundación Amigos de Sudcalifornia, A.C. The project has five principal objectives, including the systematic recording of the paintings at one site, the Cueva de El Ratón, the scientific study of deterioration factors and their possible control, the establishment of a management plan for all the archaeological sites of the Sierra de San Francisco, and the training of Latin American specialists in the conservation of rock art.[4]

The Cueva de El Ratón is located in the Arroyo San Pablo of the Sierra de San Francisco. It is approximately 66 m in length, 13 m in depth and 6 m in height at its highest point. When viewed from directly opposite, the rockshelter floor appears as a relatively flat plateau. It is situated on a hillside approximately 20 m above a streamcourse and the modern road level (Figure 1). Within the shelter, individual areas with paintings are of varying dimensions and textures and are multi-planed and faceted. The paintings surviving on varying rock planes, where protected from the elements, are found starting near the base of the rear shelter wall, and continuing above onto the ceiling, where they may be as much as 6 m above present ground level.

Painted in tones of red, black and yellow usually with a white outline, the paintings depict anthropomorphic, zoomorphic and abstract figures of large dimensions. They were executed on a substrate of volcanic conglomerate, presenting surfaces that are highly irregular and contorted in three dimensions. The task of recording the paintings is further complicated, not only by their inaccessibility unless scaffolding is used, but also by their apparent lack of composition and their frequently dense layers of superimpositions (Figure 2). Moreover, many of the paintings have lost their original distinct outlines, having been eroded by agents of weathering, and by the impact of animals and humans.

* Author to whom correspondence should be addressed

Recording techniques used at El Ratón

In the face of these difficulties, the campaign in 1994 to document and interpret the paintings of the Cueva de El Ratón had two main objectives:

- to produce baseline data, i.e. photographic (elevation mosaic, painted area delineation), graphic and digital (plan and elevation drawings of site, shelter and paintings) records;
- to instruct four trainees in the application of techniques for surveying, photogrammetry, photography, hand recording and low cost imaging/CAD overlay documentation.

Site elevation drawing and mosaic

Located as it is on a steep hillside, the Cueva de El Ratón required some kind of raised documentation platform for its elevation to be recorded. Solutions such as the use of small aircraft or helicopters were deemed impractical in this remote area; the modern road might have been viable but it did not pass below the site. This problem was solved by using a camera set-up on two rock outcrops, directly opposite the shelter, approximately 85 m distant from it. From these elevated vantage points a series of terrestrial stereograms (overlapping photographs) were taken with a Leica P31 metric camera. Additionally, panoramic photography with the aid of a 4 × 5 inch Technika view camera provided the required imagery to generate the site visualisation elevation mosaic at a scale of 1:100. To ensure the construction of a perfectly aligned mosaic, without introducing two different perspectives, the camera was centred and levelled to the site and the camera back shifted horizontally between exposures.

The terrestrial stereograms were restituted in a three-dimensional data capture mode using a Leica BC2 analytical plotter and ported to a 3D Cadd format using the AutoCad release 12 software. The process permitted the production of the site elevation drawing (scale 1:100, see Figure 3) along with a series of vertical profiles to define the accurate depth and shape of the shelter's individual subareas. With the assistance of Mr Alan Watchman, project field co-ordinator and geologist, it was

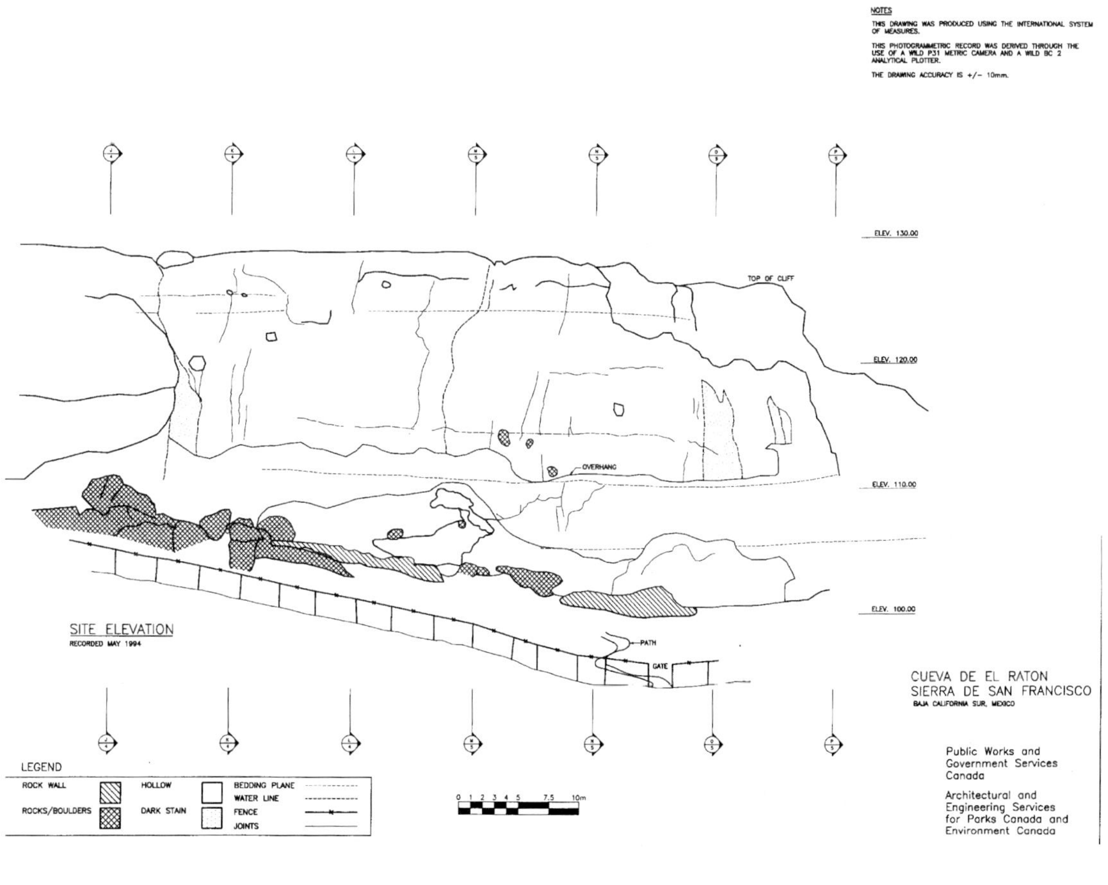

Figure 3. Cueva de El Ratón, site elevation with preliminary geological observations

possible to enhance the quality and quantity of information included on the elevation drawing. Looking through the plotter, Mr Watchman guided the plotter operator with his explanation and interpretation of bedding planes, water lines, rock fissures, stained areas, etc.

Photography and drawings of the paintings

Each shelter subarea with paintings was documented using colour (Kodachrome 64) and black and white (T-Max) film in 35 mm, 120 mm and 4 × 5 inch film formats. Nikon, Hasselblad, Linhof Technika and Leica P31 cameras with various lenses were used. To minimise distortions within the imagery, the camera was set perpendicular to the surface, or an approximation of the surface, to be recorded and the longest possible focal length lenses and time exposures (for greater depth of field) were utilised. A photographic tripod was used for all formats of photography to ensure stability under the low-light conditions characteristic of the study area. To illuminate the paintings for colour photography, the cross polarising technique was employed. This technique requires the use of a polarising filter on the flash oriented vertically and a second on the camera lens oriented horizontally. Executed properly, the technique ensures accurate light balance and colour rendition. For each photograph a Kodak color control patch, grey card and scale were inserted.

The limited projection (or rapid falloff) of the site's plateau (maximum depth 13 m) outwards from the shelter precluded the taking of overall photography. In a few situations, entire subareas with paintings could be documented as a whole. But in the majority of cases, a series of photographs and stereograms was needed, taken at varying angles of inclination and azimuth and at varying photo scales. This approach, apart from being more labour intensive, tends to make it difficult to reference details of rock art panels precisely, both to one another and within the overall site context. To address this problem, an extensive network of site control points were co-ordinated (*X*, *Y*, *Z*) using a Leica T1000 total survey station. For two main reasons, this proved to be not such a straightforward task: (a) no physical targets were permitted to be attached to the rock surface, hence only natural points could bc co-ordinated – the points always being in less than ideal locations and lacking precise definition; and (b) the magnification (30 ×) of the total station was too extreme *vis-à-vis* the close proximity of the total station to the object.

On an experimental basis, computer-assisted on-site analysis was evaluated. This component of the project consisted of a still and motion video data capture survey (Sony Hi-8 and Canon XZAP CCD), the assembly of a sample hypertext report, colour extractions, image enhancement, CAD overlay tracings and mosaicing.

The accurate interpretation of many of the paintings during the compilation stage proved to be rather difficult. This was in great measure due to the large photo scales, the multiple superimpositions of the figures and the less than ideal location and definition of the co-ordinated control points. Recalling the positive contribution by the geologist (see above) earlier in the compilation stage, it was decided that a rock art conservator familiar with the site could perhaps assist the plotter operator to interpret the complex nature of the paintings and add a more subjective interpretation to the results. As a result, one of us (VM), who had participated as conservator in the field recording campaign at El Ratón, collaborated with the specialist plotter (PS) in search of better results. This required mastering the operation of the plotting instrument and then applying her intimate knowledge of the site's motifs to recognize and restitute the majority of the paintings (details, contours and surface cracking).

As with the site elevation drawing, each painting, series of contours and cracks was converted into a 3D Cadd format. A separate Cadd layer and colour identification was assigned to each. By turning layers on and off, superimposed figures can now be separated and interpreted with greater ease.

Combining all the individual plotted components has allowed the creation of an orthographic elevation projection, at scale 1:50, of the entire interior shelter wall, inclusive of all painted surfaces. This elevation, although spatially correct, is

Figure 4. Cueva de El Ratón, area B3, stereophotogrammetric plot of painted motifs

not a true-to-scale graphic representation of the figures painted on the ceiling and walls of the shelter. This situation can be corrected, however, by rotating the 3D Cadd file in AutoCad until the viewer is perpendicular to the painting plane to be viewed (Figure 4). Of course, other viewing angles can be selected as the need arises.

Discussion

Recording of the paintings at El Ráton posed a number of problems arising from the remoteness of the area in which the site is located, and from the nature of their substrate, inaccessibility, large scale and superimpositions described earlier. They have been successfully recorded thanks to the variety of survey methods employed, and to close interdisciplinary collaboration. Computer-assisted analysis on site was used to a limited extent and proved useful as a quick means of generating site elevation drawings and individual images. These in turn aided in taking better field notes and arriving at more representative initial sketches of individual paintings for the purposes of preliminary analysis.

The use of stereophotogrammetry in combination with the total survey station has resulted in the production of a dimensionally accurate record of these complex paintings. This approach has required the intimate observation of the paintings to be recorded, the photogrammetric recording, the plotting, the refining of the records held in AutoCAD, and then fieldchecking of the photogrammetric plots for accuracy and completeness (carried out at El Ratón in 1995 with the aid of scaffolding). The resulting AutoCAD files can be manipulated as required, and additional information can be added to them following future on-site study of, for example, geological or hydrological data. Moreover, the information held in CAD files helps with future monitoring of the condition of the site since changes can be quickly visualized.

Conclusion

Recording of the paintings in the Cueva de El Ratón presented a number of difficulties because of their nature and their location. A variety of low- and high-end techniques have been used[5] to achieve a dimensionally-accurate record of the site itself and of its paintings. Stereophotogrammetry and the conversion of the results after restitution into a 3D Cadd format has proved a remarkably successful means of achieving this objective.

The restitution of the stereophotogrammetric data was much enhanced when the rock art conservator and the geologist familiar with the site collaborated with the specialist plotter in their interpretation. This experience suggests that a collaborative approach to the recording of rock art sites through photogrammetry has much to recommend it.[6]

Acknowledgements

Grateful acknowledgment is due to all project team members who assisted with the site's recording, to Kathleen McDonnell (documentation coordinator for the 1994 field campaign), and to the Special Projects staff of the Getty Conservation Institute.

References

1. Ma. de la Luz Gutiérrez, "Pintura rupestre en la Sierra de San Francisco, Baja California Sur," *Revista de Arqueología Mexicana* 1, no. 6 (1994): 57–63.
2. E. Hambleton, *La Pintura Rupestre de Baja California. Fotografías del Autor* (México: Fomento Cultural Banamex, 1979).
3. H. Crosby, *The Cave Paintings of Baja California: The Great Murals of an Unknown People*, revised edn (LaJolla, CA: Copley Books, 1984).
4. N.P. Stanley Price, *Conservation of Rock Art in Baja California, Mexico. Report on the First Two Field Campaigns, 1994–1995* (The Getty Conservation Institute, unpublished circulated report, 1995).
5. Ibid.
6. I.N.M. Wainwright, "Rock Painting and Petroglyph Recording Projects in Canada", *APT Bulletin* 22, no. 1/2 (1990): 55–84.

Intihuasi 5, Córdoba, Argentina: Back to the Original Ground Level

Erica Bolle
Cazadores de Coquimbo 3310,
1605 Munro – Buenos Aires, Argentina

Abstract

In order to preserve the rock art of the Casa Pintada (Painted House) site, which is one of the shelters of Cerro Intihuasi group, we reviewed in detail all the processes which affect the site. The earthen basis of the site has been excavated in the past and, as a result of the outward movement of the sediments, an artificial mound has been formed that channels rain water towards the interior. As the wall comes into contact with the collected water a significant increase in the support's humidity levels is observed. Flaking also affects small areas of the central part of the painted area. In order to protect the site from the constant attack to which it is exposed, the restoration of the floor to its original level is under discussion.

Keywords

Rock art, stone deterioration, rainwater flow, site protection, ground-level restoration

Introduction

The entire area of central Córdoba, Argentina, is rich in archaeological sites. Cerro Intihuasi lies some 50 km to the west of the city of Río Cuarto, in an area which is rich in rock art. A few meters from the top of the hill, on the southwest slope, we find a group of five deeply eroded boulders. Their inner walls have been decorated by Comechingonean Indians. According to a radiocarbon dating, performed on the remains of a fire found in the sediments at the site, the area was inhabitated during the 11th and 12th centuries. The paintings show abstract drawings, forming ornamental bands, together with scenes showing long lines of animals, mainly Ñandúes, american ostriches (*Rhea americana*), and Indians with bows and arrows. White pigments have been used, with only a few red strokes visible and all drawings have been carried out with extreme simplicity.

Site description

The site studied in this paper is named Intihuasi 5, Casa Pintada [Painted House], (IW5). It is located in a deep rock shelter on the western side of the group of boulders which host the Intihuasi Rock Art, and its access is through a wide corridor, located between the sites IW1 and IW2.[1]

Each of the sites is located in a boulder, separated from the adjacent one by narrow diaclases, filled with stones and debris.

The rock boulders are based on a rocky platform, with small depressions and some diaclases, filled with small quantities of humus, and some ferns and grasses growing therein. At the IW5 site the rocky platform presents a deep depression, which rises towards the West.

Cerro Intihuasi's rock paintings are exposed to deterioration, due to the constant and progressive alteration of the host rock boulders. This is mainly a result of the weakness of the rock, which, in spite of showing an apparent massive structure, has a high percentage of microfissures.

The rocky substrate is modified granite (granitoid), with less hardness than common granite, composed of medium sized and irregular quartz grains, potassium feldspars, plagioclases and biotites. Most of these minerals are altered by transformation processes (e.g. feldspars and plagioclases change into clayey minerals) which have weakened the inner structure of the rock as a result of intergranular cement loss.[2] This process is evident in the inner wall of the site, on which the paintings are to be found.

At the IW5 site, Casa Pintada (Painted House) we find a beautiful frieze representing a row of ostriches, running with open wings. The animals represented are depicted in different attitudes, giving exceptional dynamics to the whole frieze.[3] The few human figures represented are drawn in a very simple manner, with bows and arrows in their hands.

In general, the white and red pigments used are very well integrated with the support and the state of conservation of the paintings is satisfactory. Unfortunately, the support is suffering the effect of humidity caused by water stagnation on rainy days. We have found a wide area on the painted panel that shows flaking in small areas, 3–4 cm in diameter and 1–2 mm deep, which in some cases affect the painted

Figure 1. An indian with bow and arrow facing a row of "Ñandues." On the background we can see the flakings that affect the stone

motifs. In the main area of the frieze the motifs have been outlined with a fine white contour line (Figure 1).[4]

The base of the site is in a depression caused by an archeological excavation, dug by amateurs a long time ago. There is a slope outside the site, formed by the outward movement of the natural sediments. At present the inner basis of the site is almost 60 cm below the outer level. In front of the site there is a strip, about 10 m wide, covered by sediments and grass, bordering a rock exposure, which forms a secondary crest of the hill.

Intervention

An intervention program has been established, with the aim of implementing conservation of site IW5, in order to stop the natural processes continuing to destroy the weakened areas of the support, and to modify, as far as is possible, the adverse climatic conditions to which they are subject.

On both sides of the site we find diaclases which separate the blocks. The one on the right-hand side is located several meters away from the site, while on the left-hand side the rear wall of the rock shelter continues until it merges with the diaclase. The external walls of the boulder are almost vertical, and when it rains the water drains down these walls, channelling through the diaclases. We have been able to observe that in most cases the water runs through the diaclases, draining towards the slope of the hill. In the case of the IW5 site, however, the water flows along the left diaclase towards the excavation and, as it does not find natural drainage, it stagnates.

When this flooding takes place, the lower part of the support comes into contact with the stagnant water and, from that moment, the measured humidity levels of the support suffer a considerable increase, to a value which remains stable during the whole time of the contact, diminishing slowly two to three days after all the water has soaked into the earth.

During our first inspections of the sites, which took place in August 1991, during a period of rain, we observed, after a few hours of intense rain, that the moisture levels on the vault of shelter IW1 increased drastically, reaching levels of over 35 points, as measured on the scale of a Protimeter Minor IV. On the other hand, on the roof of shelter IW5 the increase of the values was not as significant as at site IW1. The difference between a normal sunny day and a rainy day may be 5 to 7 points, in spite of the normal average of 10 points measured on different zones of the inner wall of the site. To discover the percolation processes through the rock, the five sites where submitted to artificial rain.[5] After several measurement series, under different climatic conditions, we were able to confirm that percolation through the rock of site IW5 is much slower and of less volume than at the other sites.

On the other hand, on a day with heavy rain, we observed the flooding of the site and the wetting of the inner wall by the stagnant water. For a better comprehension of the influence of this on the inner wall of the site, we used a periodic control of the moisture. The wall was therefore divided into horizontal strips 30 cm wide, from the area in the contact with the water up to the vault of the roof. The moisture distribution along predefined control lines shows a high level, with a maximum value at the area in contact with the water and some 5 cm above it. Then the moisture content begins to fall gradually, until it reaches < 10 to 11.5 points, at a height of 0.90 m above the level of the water. This is the value that has been determined as the normal value for granite at Cerro Intihuasi. The height of the capillary rise coincides with the painted frieze, in such a way that the frieze is constantly undergoing a periodic wetting and drying process. The moisture levels we were able to record at that time remained almost constant during the full period of the flooding. Then, once the rain stopped, and the soil had absorbed all the water, the levels decreased gradually in the course of two or three days, until they reached the normal levels (between < 10 and 11.5), as determined by control measurements on sunny and dry days.

This increase in the hydration of the support, together with the percolation through the rock mass, means an increase in the activity of the disintegration processes of the already weakened rock.[6] We consider that these phenomena have caused the flaked areas we find on the background of the paintings (Figure 1).

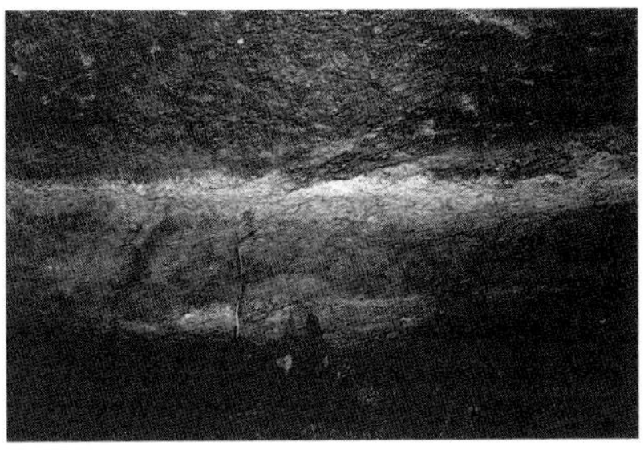

Figure 2. The back wall of the site showing the horizontal stripe which marks the original sedimentation height

Through a systematic monitoring of the painted inner wall, we have been able to observe that this damage is increasing slowly. Already several motifs have been damaged by these processes. For that reason, a pre-determined area was mapped periodically, over a three year period. The destroyed area was traced on a transparent plastic sheet and documented with photographs. Comparison of these documents revealed an increase in the size of some flakings, as well as the presence of some small new areas.

In the lower part of the painted panel there is a horizontal stripe, exhibiting a decoloration and a total lack of patina of the rock. This line marks the original sedimentation height (Figure 2).

To conserve the site, it would be beneficial to restore the base level, in order to prevent the rain water from accumulating in the interior and allow it to flow freely towards a pre-established drainage area.

Before starting the restoration work, an archaeological excavation of the sediments located within and in front of the site is to be performed, as these will be removed during the levelling, so that all possible information in it will be lost. It will also be necessary to eliminate part of the vegetation and grass, in order to make levelling easier.

In order to prevent humectation of the support through its contact with the soil, a containing wall is to be built. For this purpose, the wall will be made of stones bonded with clay and placed parallel to the decorated wall, at a distance of not more than 10 cm from it and protected by a geo-textile to diminish the water infiltration and accumulation in the free place under the rock. The left diaclase will be channelled by means of a drainage ditch made of natural stones. Another ditch will be installed along the drip line. It is important that both ditches have enough slope for the water flow to drain towards the slope of the hill. Finally, the interior of the site and the area in front of it will be filled with earth, restoring the original level,

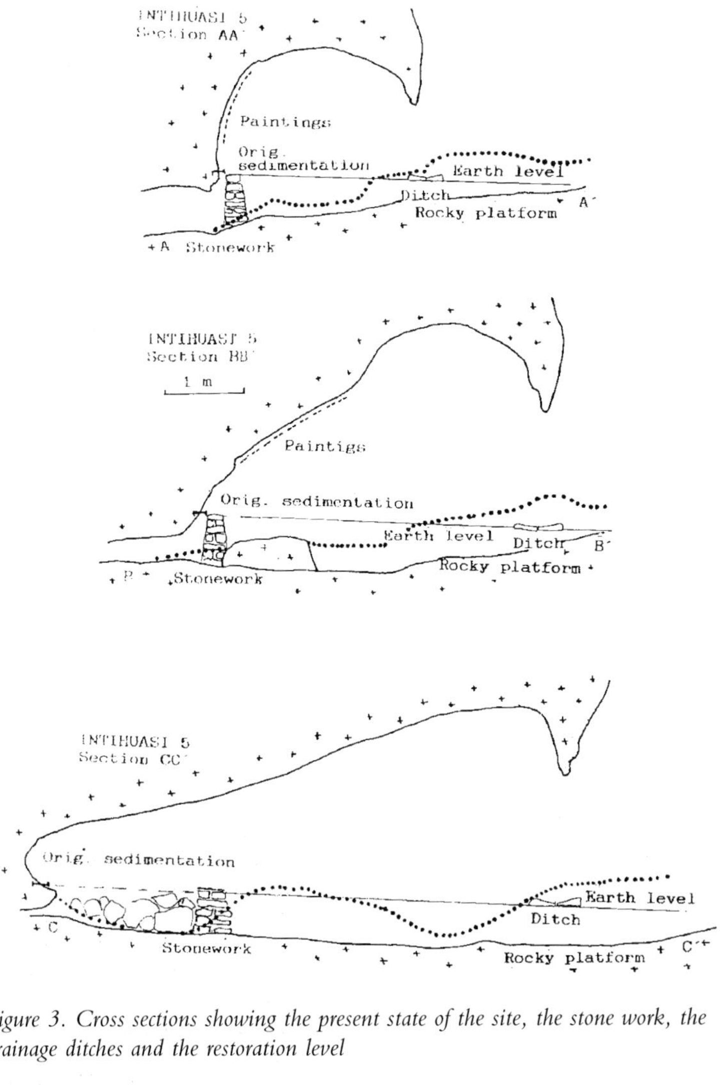

Figure 3. Cross sections showing the present state of the site, the stone work, the drainage ditches and the restoration level

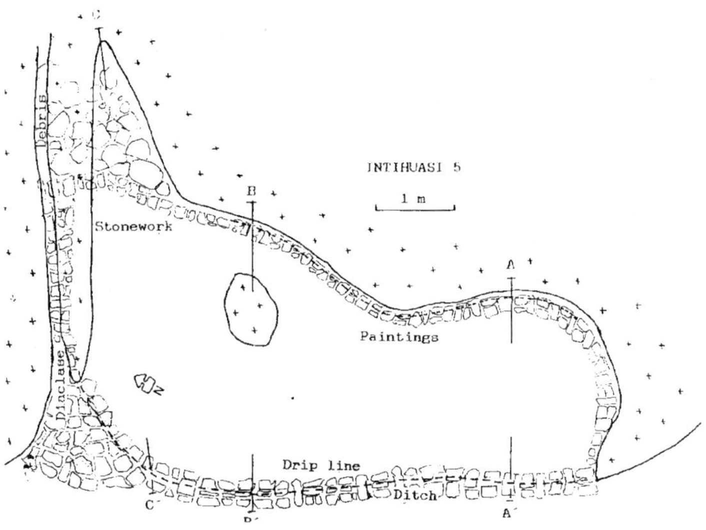

Figure 4. The restoration project for site Intihuasi 5

marked on the site's rear wall. The complete surface will have a slight slope towards north west and to the west. Once finished, replanting will take place to restore the area as it was before (Figures 3 and 4).

Conclusion

Through the levelling of the soil, the placement of the drainage ditches and the protection of the painted wall by means of a stone socle, we should achieve the following:

- solution of the water stagnation problem;
- drainage improvement towards the slope of the hill;
- reduction of accumulated humidity, at the level of the support, especially in the painted area;
- reduction of the destructive processes of the support;
- improvement of the site conditions, so that it can be used as a tourist center.

This project includes all aspects of the maintenance of the site, which is the main point as far as future conservation of the site is concerned.

Once the restoration of the floor has been concluded, a monitoring program will be required, in order to detect any changes that may appear in the course of time. This program should be carried out at regular intervals, and it should include photographic documentation of the support, in order to detect any change in or increase of the already existing damage, moisture controls at the level of the wall as well as on the floor, vegetation control inside and outside the site, and periodic cleaning of diaclases and drainage ditches, in order to avoid any overflow following a cloudburst.

We feel that the projected modifications to the IW5 site do not just apply to this case, but may well be adapted to other sites which may have similar problems.

References

1. E. Bolle, M. Faggiano and A.E. Charola, "The Rock Art at Cerro Intihuasi, Córdoba, Argentina. Deterioration of the Stone Support," (Paper delivered at the tenth Triennial Meeting of the International Council of Museums Committee for Conservation, Washington, DC, 1993), 821–824.
2. E. Bolle, "The Influence of Rain and Humidity on the Rock Paintings of Cerro Intihuasi, Córdoba, Argentina," (Paper delivered at the Second Australian Rock Art Research Association Congress, Cairns, 1992).
3. H. Gay, "Las Pictografias del Cerro Intihuasi" ("The pictographs of Cerro Intihuasi") *Notas del Museo Provincial de Ciencias Naturales «Bartolomé Mitre* (Córdoba, Argentina, 1958), 3–23.
4. E. Bolle, "The Influence of Rain."
5. Ibid.
6. Bolle, Faggiano and Charola, E. "The Rock Art at Cerro Intihuasi," 823.

Problèmatique liée à la conservation de la grotte ornée Henri Cosquer: l'accès artificiel est-il possible?

Philippe Malaurent et Jean Vouvé
CDGA - Groupe Hydrogéologie, Université de Bordeaux I
Avenue des Facultés, 33405 Talence Cedex, France

Jacques Brunet*
Laboratoire de Recherche des Monuments Historiques
29 rue de Paris, 77420 Champs-sur-Marne, France

Résumé

La découverte de tout nouveau site d'art pariétal pose les délicats problèmes de conservation, de protection et de sauvegarde d'un patrimoine toujours fragile. Ces finalités ne peuvent être acquises qu'après des études globales d'environnement des milieux géologiques, hydrochimiques, microbiologiques, végétatifs et climatiques. La démarche est rendu ici plus délicate en raison de l'imbrication karst/mer/eaux salées. Les résultats obtenus après quelques mois de recul montrent que le site sous-marin est soumis à une double dynamique continentale et marine, et le milieu karstique est actuellement clos et sous pression par rapport à l'ambiance aérienne actuelle. C'est une des conditions du maintien de l'état de conservation. L'ouverture en voûte d'un accès artificiel direct, quelles que soient les précautions prises, changerait d'une part l'équilibre de la grotte et d'autre part, provoquerait l'ennoyage irréversible des surfaces décorées proches du niveau actuel de l'eau dans la grotte.

Mots-clés

Karst orné, environnement continental et marin, milieux clos, mise en pression, climatologie souterraine

Introduction

Les peintures et gravures préhistoriques de la grotte H. Cosquer ont été découvertes durant l'été 1991 à quelques kilomètres du centre de la ville de Marseille (Figure 1). Il s'agit d'une cavité sous-marine en bordure du littoral, sans communication extérieure apparente. Elle s'ouvre au sud-ouest du lieu-dit "pointe de la voile" à 37 m de profondeur et à 30 m de la falaise calcaire du Cap Morgiou. De nombreuses cavités avaient été découvertes sous la mer dans cette région, mais celle-ci est la première à présenter des tracés préhistoriques peints et gravés.

Elle a déjà fait l'objet de plusieurs campagnes de prospection par des équipes de plongeurs spécialisés dans la reconnaissance de conduits noyés et de chercheurs aptes à ce type de plongée. La situation géologique associée à l'analyse géomorphologique d'une part, à la datation de charbons trouvés dans des foyers fossilisés d'autre part, a fait l'objet de publications.[1,2] De ce fait, nous ne rappellerons ici que l'essentiel. Ce réseau karstique orné est d'extension géographique limitée, dans la mesure où il est inscrit à la base noyée et dans la largeur d'un promontoire calcaire (faciès urgonien) dont l'extension maximale atteint 0,375 Km du Nord au Sud et 0,750 Km du N.N.O. - vers le S.S.E. La galerie d'accès remontante, orientée Nord-Sud, est longue de 175 m environ et la grotte qui lui fait suite mesure 60 m selon un axe N. 15° et 67 m selon un axe N. 65°.[1] A l'extrémité septentrionale du réseau, un puits-cheminée s'ouvre verticalement à travers la série urgonienne (crétacé inférieur). La tranche inférieure noyée mesure 24 m, alors que la partie libre n'a pas pu être mesurée avec précision en raison d'obstacles géomorphologiques (surplombs, encorbellements) proches de la partie sommitale oblique. Cette hauteur est estimée à une quarantaine de mètres. L'intense fracturation des roches peut laisser supposer l'existence d'un réseau complexe (renseignement oral J. Collina-Girard) de conduits assurant des communications avec l'extérieur, conduits de taille variable accessibles ou non à l'homme.

L'inventaire systématique des oeuvres pariétales n'est pas totalement terminé.[3] Des datations par la méthode du C_{14} faites sur des charbons de bois ramassés au sol et sur des tracés au fusain permettent de regrouper les oeuvres en deux séries chronologiques différentes, l'une correspond à une présence humaine il y a environ 27.000 ans BP et l'autre à 18.500 ans BP.[4] Les préhistoriens différencient d'innombrables tracés digitaux dessinés dans la pellicule de calcaire altéré des parois et des voûtes, des mains négatives obtenues au pochoir par projection de colorants noirs ou rouges et des représentations animales: chevaux, bouquetins, bisons, chamois, félin, phoques, pingouins et de nombreux signes peints ou gravés (Figures 2-5). Ce site est un jalon nouveau dans l'étude de la répartition européenne des grottes ornées; la qualité et l'originalité des tracés en font un apport majeur à la connaissance de cette partie de la préhistoire de l'Europe occidentale.

Etude du milieu souterrain

Depuis leur réalisation par les hommes préhistoriques, les tracés peints ou gravés ont subi de nombreux avatars. Aux écoulements d'eau, au concrétionnement, aux circulations d'air responsables les uns et les autres de dégradations, d'oblitérations

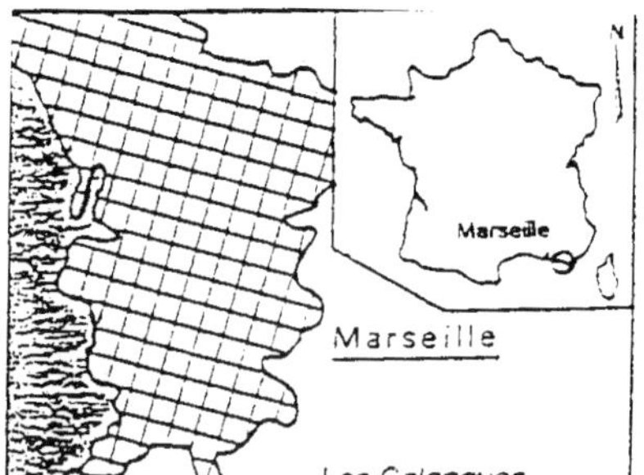

Figure 1. Carte de localisation du site

*Auteur à qui la correspondance doit être adressée

Figure 2. Ensemble dit du grand panneau des chevaux; il est actuellement situé au ras de l'eau dont le niveau présente des fluctuations non négligeables (marée, conditions climatiques locales...). Le support paraît en bon état et présente des concrétions teintées d'oxydes de fer dont l'évolution est mal connue. Toute modification du contexte souterrain entraînant la remontée du niveau de l'eau aura des conséquences néfastes pour la conservation de cet ensemble de chevaux. Cliché A. CHENE. CNRS. Ministère de la Culture.

Figure 3. Représentation de bouquetin peinte en noir, située sur une voûte basse; la moitié inférieure des pattes avant a disparu, témoin d'une érosion. Des plages de calcite recouvrent la tête et la corne de l'animal; elles sont le signe d'un processus évolutif que seule une longue étude permettra d'appréhender. Cliché. A. CHENE. CNRS. Ministère de la Culture.

Figure 4. Grand cerf peint en noir, tracé sur un support déjà en partie concrétionnée; cette figuration est recouverte d'une nappe de calcite au niveau de l'arrière train. Des concrétions tubulaires dites "fistuleuses" accidentent le support. Cliché. A. CHENE. CNRS. Ministère de la Culture.

du décor, il faut ajouter l'action de l'eau marine lors de la remontée générale du niveau de l'eau (Figure 6), phénomène dynamique actuel et futur.

De longue date, on sait qu'un tel ensemble doit être et est fragile,[5] d'autant plus que vient s'ajouter au confinement, un facteur environnemental actif nouveau qui est lié à la présence des eaux marines côtières qui jouxtent immédiatement les oeuvres pariétales. La conservation d'un tel chef-d'oeuvre est une priorité et un programme scientifique a été conçu au début de l'année 1994. Son démarrage réel ne fut effectif qu'en novembre 1994, suite à des retards répétés liés aux mauvaises conditions climatiques et marines. Les approches classiques rodées dans les milieux karstiques ornés[6,7] ne pouvaient s'appliquer à l'identique dans ce cas particulier. La fonction conservatoire du patrimoine pariétal ou "contenu", et l'évidement karstique ou "contenant", ne peuvent être analysés que dans la finalité d'une protection active des deux milieux en relation avec le suivi des dynamiques climatiques aériennes et marines.

L'interdépendance rapide ou différée entre les environnements aériens et souterrains est un élément acquis de longue date.[8] L'idée ancienne qui assimilait une grotte à un ensemble totalement ou presque totalement indépendant du contexte environnant a vécu et l'on doit retenir maintenant a priori que ces milieux évoluent sous l'impact direct ou retardé des flux entrants et des flux sortants (impact solaire, ondes thermiques, infiltration, évaporation, évapotranspiration...)[9] auxquels il faut ajouter les dynamiques aérologiques et biochimiques et dans le cas présent, la dynamique marine. Dans une finalité conservatoire, les interrogations initiales portent sur la nature des climats et microclimats aériens et souterrains d'une part et sur l'impact de la dynamique des marées d'autre part, replacées dans un contexte cyclique saisonnier, comme à moyen et plus long terme.

La réalisation du projet technique est basée sur la présence de deux centrales de mesures: une centrale principale est installée en surface et une centrale annexe, installée sur une plage calcifiée, sur le plancher de la salle Sud (Figure 7). Les signaux sont numérisés à l'intérieur de la cavité avant le transfert vers la surface, la distance entre les centrales ne perturbe pas la qualité des signaux transmis.

Confrontés à un site "pratiquement vierge" et indemne de toutes les modifications et de tous les changements déplorés dans les autres sites, nous ne devons pas oublier que la cavité est une source de données qu'il convient de ne pas détruire inconsidérément. Un premier bilan de santé fournira des informations sur l'évolution climatologique de la cavité et permettra de définir dans quelles conditions l'accès artificiel serait possible et quelles conditions du milieu souterrain il faudrait respecter pour en assurer la conservation. Les mesures effectuées dans la cavité concernent les variations du niveau d'un des plans d'eau souterrains, de la pression atmosphérique, de la température de l'air, de la roche et de l'eau, du taux de gaz carbonique de l'atmosphère souterraine. Celles effectuées à l'extérieur ont trait aux variations de la pression atmosphérique, de la température de l'air, de l'humidité relative de l'air, de la pluviométrie, du niveau de la Méditerranée au droit de la falaise.

Premiers résultats

Le dépouillement des données permet les commentaires suivants:

- la température de l'air est relativement élevée (température moyenne maxima enregistrée 19,73°C le 9.08.1995 et température moyenne minima enregistrée 17,90°C du 19 au 22.07.1995);
- le niveau dans la cavité fluctue en relation étroite avec le niveau de la Méditerranée (Figures 8, 9);
- l'air de la cavité reste toujours en surpression par rapport à la pression atmosphérique externe;
- le niveau de l'eau dans la cavité est très variable en fonction de la pression atmosphérique interne et l'état de la mer, il atteint la base des champs graphiques (Figure 10);
- la teneur en gaz carbonique, en l'absence de toute personne, fluctue en fonction du temps mais reste faible. A la fin de la mission d'octobre 1994 à janvier 1995, elle était de 0,3%. Après une décroissance régulière dans le temps, elle s'est plus ou moins stabilisée autour de 0,03%.

Figure 5. Représentations de pingouins tracés sur un support concrétionné; la desquamation de ce dépôt calcité superficiel a détruit une partie des animaux. Même s'il n'existe aucune écaille de calcite - tombée de la voûte - au sol, ce phénomène témoigne de la fragilité de tel support; toute modification des conditions actuelles risque d'entraîner la destruction de ce type de support. Cliché. A. CHENE. CNRS. Ministère de la Culture.

Conservation de ce patrimoine

A l'issue de la collecte et du dépouillement des données enregistrées, un certain nombre de questions peuvent être posées sur le site de la grotte concernant l'ouverture artificielle, le risque encouru pour la conservation des tracés préhistoriques et l'intérêt de maintenir la démarche scientifique.

Peut-on ouvrir la cavité par un accès direct sur l'extérieur?

La réponse est négative. La mise en communication de la cavité, d'une manière artificielle ou accidentelle, provoquerait une chute de la pression atmosphérique de la caverne et la ramènerait à la valeur de celle externe. La surpression actuelle contient en partie la remontée du niveau de l'eau; sa suppression aurait pour conséquence le relèvement du plan d'eau dans le site orné. A titre d'illustration, nous avons reporté sur la Figure 11, le niveau que pourrait atteindre l'eau de mer dans les salles si le réseau karstique semi-noyé était mis en relation directe avec la surface.

Quel serait l'importance du champ graphique qui serait affecté par l'ouverture?

Les relevés faits par les archéologues (J. Courtin, J. Collina-Girard, L. Long) et les plongeurs (G. Dauphin, J. Vicente, ...) ont souligné la présence de nombreux tracés juste au-dessus du plan d'eau. L'ensemble des petits chevaux illustre cette situation (Figures 2, 11). La mise en contact direct avec l'extérieur entraînerait l'ennoyage d'une partie importante des gravures et peintures de la grotte. Le relevé coté des champs graphiques étant en cours, il est trop tôt pour en donner l'inventaire exhaustif, d'autant plus que le niveau réel atteindrait sûrement une cote plus élevée que celle donnée par les premiers calculs, ceux-ci ayant été obtenus en statique et non en dynamique.

Quelles seraient les conséquences sur l'état des oeuvres noyées?

Le contact de l'eau de mer avec les surfaces ornées ne serait pas sans conséquences, d'autant plus que le plan d'eau serait évolutif avec le temps, les marées,... On peut a priori redouter la disparition lente ou rapide du décor peint selon que le support sera calcité ou non, selon l'imprégnation des pigments, la nature et la dureté du support (roche saine ou mondmilch).

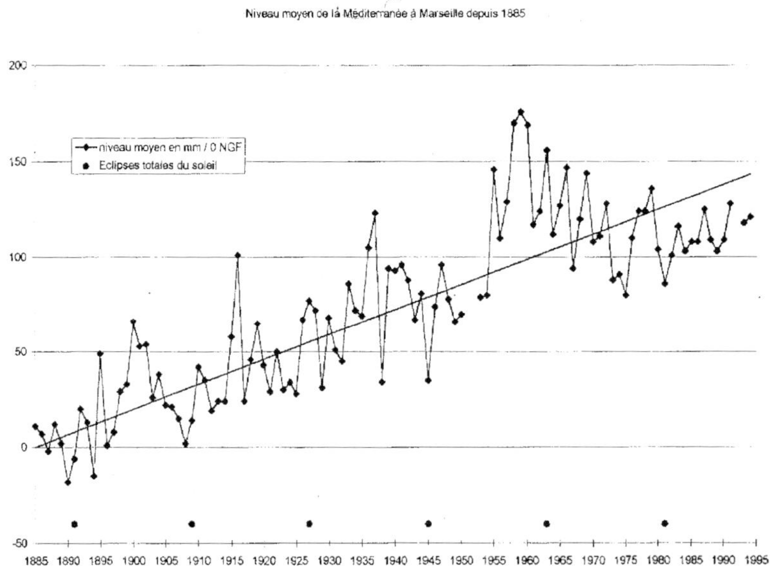

Figure 6. Niveau moyen de la Méditerranée à Marseille depuis 1885. Cette courbe illustre le fait bien connu que le niveau moyen de la Méditerranée augmente régulièrement. Nous noterons une hausse de 14 cm en 100 ans. Ces variations très lentes sont dues au stockage ou au destockage de l'eau par les glaces polaires en relations directes avec la température moyenne de l'air à la surface du globe.

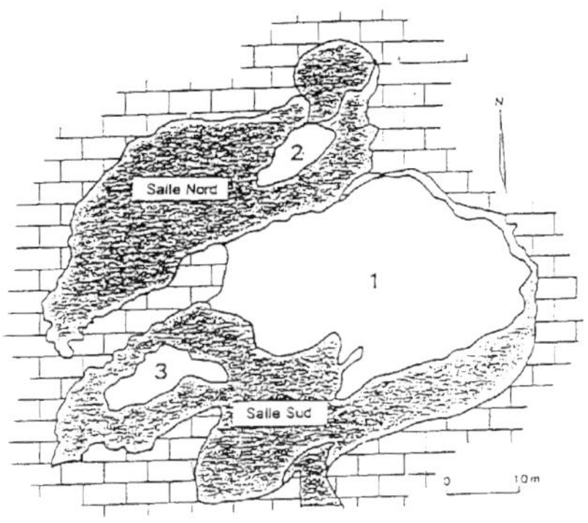

Figure 7. Plan de masse simplifié de la grotte ornée. En blanc les zones émergées (1–2), en grisé les zones noyées.

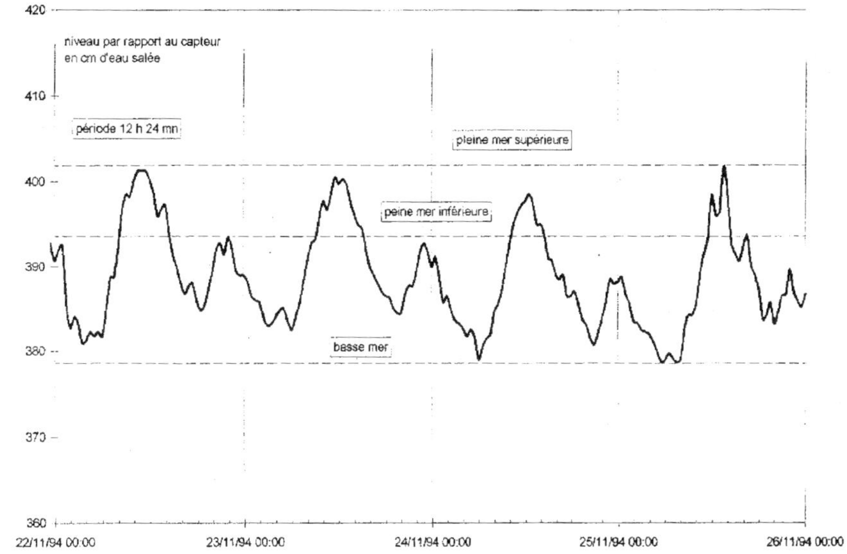

Figure 8. Courbe de marée semi-diurne à inégalité diurne. Mise en évidence de la marée. Ces différences de niveau moyen influencent le niveau des plans d'eau, en relation hydraulique, à l'intérieur de la cavité. Le marnage est d'environ 20 cm. Le niveau moyen, sans tenir compte des vagues, des houles, des composantes de marées inférieures à 25H, est en relation étroite avec la pression atmosphérique, et surtout au droit de la grotte H. Cosquer, avec la direction et la force du vent.

Conclusions

Que peut-on apprendre sur le plan de la démarche conservatoire, en maintenant le site orné sous-marin en l'état et sous surveillance scientifique?

La présente étude de terrain s'appuie sur deux objectifs précis. Il y a d'une part la connaissance de la dynamique marine externe et la caractérisation de son influence sur la dynamique marine interne. Il y a d'autre part l'analyse de la micro-climatologie interne en relation étroite avec la climatologie externe pour apprécier les échanges physico-chimiques aux interfaces air/parois, air/décors pariétaux.

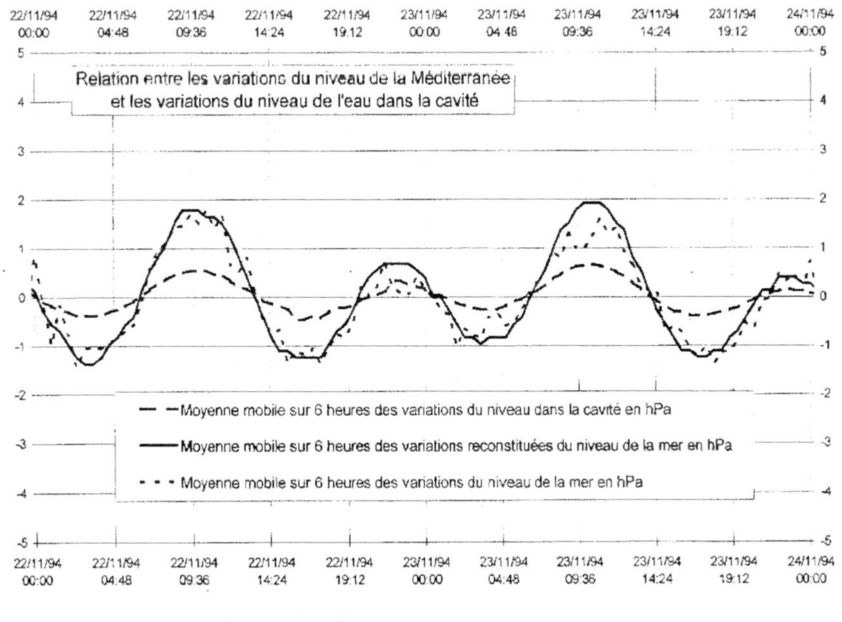

Figure 9. Relations entre le niveau de la mer et le niveau de l'eau dans la cavité. Le niveau de l'eau dans la cavité est soumis à au moins deux influences antagonistes bien visibles sur cet extrait de courbe d'évolution des niveaux d'eau en fonction du temps. En (1) l'élévation du niveau de la mer se traduit par une baisse du niveau dans la cavité. Nous devons rechercher la cause de ce phénomène particulier. En (2) les variations de niveau de la surface sont transmises conformément aux lois de la statique des fluides.

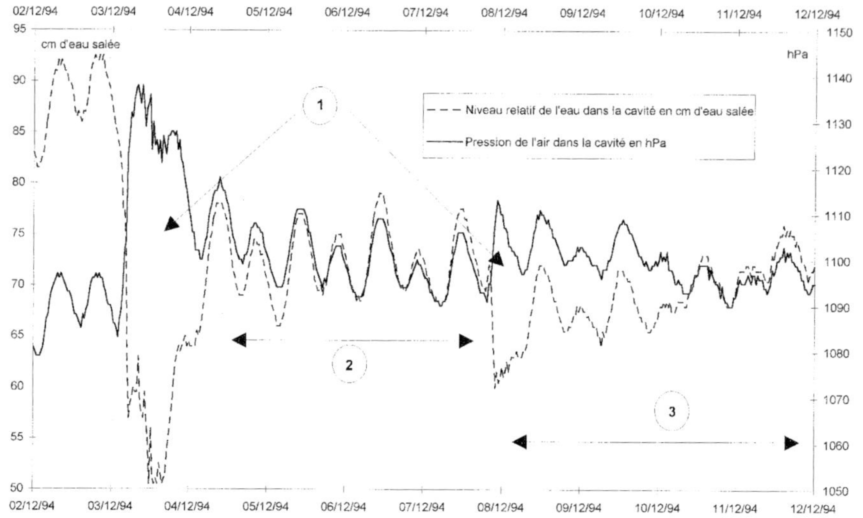

Figure 10. Exemples de relations entre le niveau de l'eau et la pression de l'air dans la cavité. Le niveau de l'eau dans la cavité est en relation étroite avec la pression de l'air de la cavité conformément à la loi de Mariotte. Le comportement dans le détail montre que la cavité est toujours en surpression par rapport à l·extérieur; en (1) que la pression de l'air de la cavité peut augmenter par apports extérieurs et repousser le niveau de l'eau dans la cavité; en (2) que les variations du niveau de l'eau dans la cavité entraînent des variations de pression de l'air dans la cavité. En (3) le réajustement progressif du niveau montre que la cavité n'est pas parfaitement étanche.

La caractérisation de l'influence de la dynamique externe sur la dynamique interne est prise en compte par les questions précédentes:

- Peut-on ouvrir la cavité par un accès direct sur l'extérieur?
- Quel serait l'importance du champ graphique qui serait affecté par l'ouverture?
- Quelles seraient les conséquences sur l'état des oeuvres noyées?

L'impact du climat extérieur sur le milieu souterrain se traduit par des écarts importants des valeurs mesurées en dépit de la coupure du câble de liaison en mars 1995 qui a momentanément interrompu la chronique des mesures (données sur l'air et l'eau de la grotte, variation du niveau du plan d'eau de la caverne,...). Ces écarts ne sont pas encore totalement expliqués, faute d'une chronique de mesures suffisamment longue.

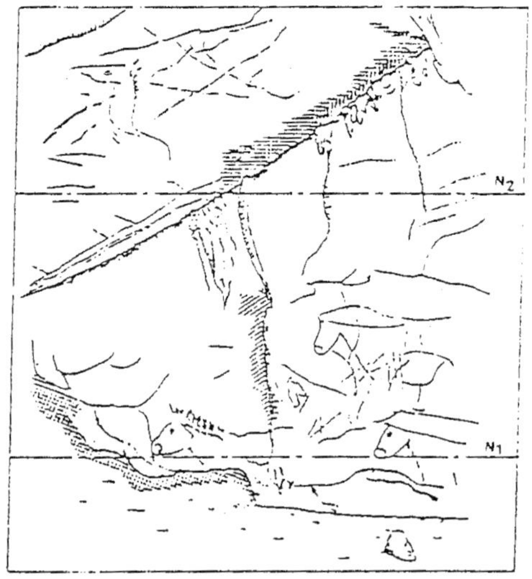

Figure 11. Relevé de la frise des chevaux sur la paroi S.O. de la salle Sud. Report des niveaux de la mer: (1) niveau d'eau le plus élevé mesuré le 17.01.1995, (2) niveau restitué en cas de mise en relation artificielle de la cavité avec l'extérieur.

Nous devons prendre en compte, à l'avenir, différentes observations et différents faits tels que:

- l'ignorance des états extrêmes de la mer (tempêtes, houles, vents,...), responsables de fortes variations momentanées du niveau de l'eau contre la falaise;
- l'existence d'un concrétionnement de calcite important lié à des infiltrations d'eau douce et à des variations de la teneur en gaz carbonique de l'air ambiant souterrain.

Remerciements

Cette étude a pu être réalisée grâce à l'aide financière apportée par le Ministère de la Culture (contrat de recherche du L.R.M.H.) et ses services (en ce qui concerne l'équipement en matériel) de la région Provence-Alpes-Côte-d'Azur (DRAC, SRA, CRMH et S.D.A). Nous tenons à remercier nos collègues J. Courtin, J. Collina-Girard, toute l'équipe du DRASM, plus particulièrement G. Dauphin et A. Vicente et Madame G. Tudéla du L.R.M.H.

Références

1. Collina-Girard J., "La Grotte Cosquer: cadre géologique d'un sanctuaire préhistorique submergé", *Bull. Soc. linn. Provence.* t. 45, 1994, 13–22.
2. Beltran A., J. Clottes, J. Courtin, H. Cosquer, "Une grotte paléolithique sur le littoral méditerranéen. La Grotte Cosquer à Marseille." *C.R.Acad. Sci. Paris*, t. 315, Série II (1992), 239–246.
3. Cosquer H., *La Grotte Cosquer - Plongée dans la Préhistoire*, Solar éditions, Paris 1993, 119 p.
4. Clottes J., J. Courtin, *La Grotte Cosquer, Peintures et Gravures de la Caverne engloutie.* Edition du Seuil, Paris 1994, 198 p.
5. Vouvé J., J. Brunet, "A propos de la protection de l'environnement des monuments rupestres ornés du patrimoine mondial. Mythe ou réalité?", in *ICOM Committee for Conservation 7th Triennial Meeting Preprints*, Copenhague 1984, 17–20.
6. Vouvé J., "Approche de la dynamique hétérothermique souterraine en milieu karstique: cas du modèle de Lascaux (France)", in *Actes (Supplément) des journées internationales d'études sur la conservation de l'art rupestre* (Périgord, 20–23 août 1990), 13–24.
7. Brunet J., P. Vidal, "Grotte de Gargas, Aventignan (Hautes-Pyrénées). Analyse des conditions climatiques actuelles. Conséquences pour la conservation", Extrait de *Altamira symposium: actas/del symposium internacional sobre Arte Prehistorico celebrado en conmemoracion del primer centenario del descubrimiento de las pinturas de Altamira (1879–1979)*; Ministerio de cultura, Direccion general de bellas artes, 1979, 643–660.
8. Vouvé J., *Etude en hydrogéologie et paléohydrogéologie karstiques*, Thèse de Doctorat, Université de Bordeaux I, 1975, Un ouvrage en 2 tomes.
9. Malaurent Ph., J. Vouvé, J. Brunet, "Les phénomènes d'évapocondensation et la conservation des milieux souterrains naturels et artificiels (décors et vestiges archéologiques). Approche théorique", in *ICOM Committee for Conservation 10th Triennial Meeting Preprints*, Washington 1993, 857–862.

Le parc national "Serra da Capivara, Piaui" Brésil: Essai de nettoyages des parois peintes

Maria Conceiçaõ Soares Meneses Lage
Departamento de Quimica, Centro de Ciêncas da Natureza
Campus universitário da Ininga, Universidade Federal do Piaui
64049-550 Teresina (Piaui) Brasil

Sonia Campello
Nucleo de Antropologia Pré-historica
PRPPG-UFPI, Campus da Ininga
64049-730 Teresina (Piaui) Brasil

Jacques Brunet*
Laboratoire de Recherche des Monuments Historiques
29 rue de Paris
77420 Champs sur Marne, France

Résumé

Les décors préhistoriques des parois des abris sous roche ne sont pas soustraits aux effets du vieillissement des intempéries, des phénomènes naturels et des actions humaines. Les parois sont des surfaces sensibles d'échanges régulièrement humidifiées, séchées, chauffées, refroidies, recouvertes d'eau de condensation ou soumises à l'évaporation, tapissées de particules minérales inertes ou actives ou d'éléments biologiques d'origine animale ou végétale. Cet aperçu des altéragènes révèle que la conservation comprend en matière d'art pariétal un ensemble d'actions permettant l'élimination des surcharges, des maculations, des dépôts, des structures construites par les insectes.

Mots-clés

Conservation, altéragènes, Brésil, intervention, art préhistorique

Introduction

Le Parc National de la Serra da Capivara se trouve au Nord-Est du Brésil dans l'état du Piaui et couvre une superficie de 130.000 hectares. L'érosion différentielle a creusé dans les falaises de grès de nombreux abris sous roche occupés par des populations autochtones. Dans cette région du Brésil, la richesse en sites archéologiques - plus de 300 - a justifié la création d'une structure de type parc national permettant la gestion et la protection de ces biens culturels. Les travaux des archéologues, sous l'autorité du Professeur Niède Guidon, ont permis de connaître cet art considéré comme très narratif et l'un des abris peints, la Toca do Boqueiraõ do Sitio da Pedra Furada est l'un des plus anciens sites connus d'Amérique.

L'art est riche et varié, avec une abondance de motifs figuratifs: représentations anthropomorphes, zoomorphes et phytomorphes et non figuratifs: points, lignes brisées, figures géométriques plus ou moins complexes. Les couleurs représentées sont le rouge (avec plusieurs tonalités), le jaune, le blanc, le noir et le gris.[1]

Une campagne de relevés de l'état de conservation des sites, effectuée à partir de 1991, a mis en évidence l'existence de nombreux agents responsables de détérioration des panneaux peints; les essais pour remédier à ces dégâts font l'objet de la présente communication.

Figure 1. Sitio do Vento, Saõ Raimundo Nonato, galeries de termites recouvrant indifféremment les parties non-ornées et ornées.

Les problèmes de conservation: les altéragènes

L'examen de 126 sites d'art rupestre a permis de reconnaître différents types d'états de parois caractérisés par la présence de:

- structures de boues (Figure 1) dues à l'activité d'insectes appartenant à la famille des Isoptères (termites) et à celles des Hyménoptères (fourmis, guêpes, mouches-maçonnes) (Figure 3); la construction de nids, de galeries sur les parois décorées, le passage répété d'insectes sur les mêmes pistes peuvent provoquer localement d'importants désordres;
- dépôts minéraux sous forme d'efflorescences en surface de la roche, dus par exemple au ruissellement ou à l'écoulement d'eau;
- accumulations de poussières sous forme de croûte;
- dépôts de noir de fumée;
- accumulation d'argile à la suite de projection;
- racines et branches de végétaux supérieurs, ces dernières en mouvement sous l'influence du vent peuvent être à l'origine de l'usure de surfaces décorées;

Figure 2. Même surface après nettoyage; l'essentiel de la matière constituant les galeries a pu être enlevé, cependant une légère trace persiste que l'application répétée de compresses ne peut éliminer.

*Auteur à qui la correspondance doit être adressée

Figure 3. Sitio do Vento, Saõ Raimundo Nonato, graffiti et nids d'insectes présents sur la paroi.

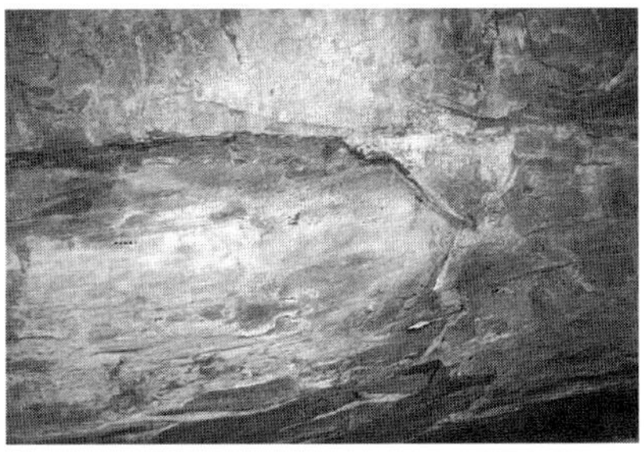

Figure 4. Même surface après nettoyage.

Figure 5. Sitio Baixaõ da Vaca, Saõ Raimundo Nonato, le contour des représentations animales a été souligné à la craie blanche.

Figure 6. Mêmes représentations après l'élimination des surcharges.

- micro-organismes végétaux développés à la faveur de zones d'humidité de la paroi ou d'écoulements d'eau; les cellules de ces micro-organismes (algues par exemple) en s'infiltrant dans les anfractuosités de la roche peuvent exercer des contraintes qui favoriseront la dégradation du support.

Les interventions

Mode opératoire

Des essais préliminaires, effectués en se basant sur les méthodes d'intervention utilisées pour la conservation des peintures murales d'édifices et de décors de cavités préhistoriques telles Baume Latrone, Niaux, Rouffignac en France,[2,3,4] il ressort que l'élimination des dépôts de surface peut se faire à l'aide d'agents mécaniques ou chimiques. Les interventions ont été menées dans les sites de Toca do Meio, Baixaõ das Mulheres, Toca do Paraguaio et Baixaiõ da Vaca, selon différentes étapes que l'on peut détailler ainsi:

- couverture photographique systématique en diapositives et en noir et blanc des surfaces où une intervention doit avoir lieu;
- élimination mécanique des dépôts superficiels à l'aide de spatules (en métal, en bois), de bistouris, de brosses de dureté différentes;
- applications de compresses imbibées de produits (solution d'ammoniaque, solution d'eau oxygénée) capables de faciliter la mise en suspension des dépôts résistant à l'enlèvement mécanique; - rinçage à l'eau déminéralisée des surfaces nettoyées;
- nouvelle couverture photographique après intervention.

Détails des interventions

A chaque type de dépôt décrit, a été adapté un traitement spécifique

DEPOTS	TRAITEMENTS
Accumulations d'argiles	Elimination d'abord mécanique, puis application de compresses humides pour les résidus
Nids d'insectes (Figures 1–2)	Elimination mécanique des éléments terreux, puis application de compresses d'eau oxygénée diluée (10 %) pour enlever le "fantôme" du dépôt
Taches de la roche liées aux galeries de termites	Elimination mécanique et application de compresses imbibées d'une solution aqueuse ammonicale à 1 %
Surcharges au charbon de bois (Figures 3–4)	Applications de compresses imbibées d'une solution d'ammoniaque à 1%
Surcharges à la craie (Figures 5–6)	Enlèvement mécanique et applications de compresses imbibées eau déminéralisée
Graffiti gravés	Les tracés sont masqués par de la poussière humidifiée

Résultats

Après ces différents traitements il est possible de porter un jugement sur leur efficacité. Les graffiti gravés ont été masqués par l'apport de poussières; lorsque le trait est profond et évasé, le résultat n'est pas parfait. Les matières placées dans l'incision ou dans le tracé incisé auraient besoin d'un liant pour adhérer et se maintenir en place. Des essais en ce sens seront poursuivis. La résistance à l'enlèvement des dépôts liés à l'activité d'insectes est variable; l'hydratation des nids est indispensable. Les traces de l'activité des termites sont plus difficiles à éliminer; quelquefois les galeries minent véritablement la surface de la roche et la rendent très friable. Lorsqu'elles se superposent aux traits peints, l'intervention risque de détériorer ces derniers. L'enlèvement des maculations argileuses d'origine anthropiques est aisé.

Conclusions

Les effets de nuisances naturelles (insectes, efflоscences), les résultats d'actes de vandalisme (graffiti, néogravures, surcharges diverses, projections d'argile,....) peuvent être éliminés quel que soit le type de support.

A côté de ces faits constatés qui expliquent un certain nombre de désordres morphologiques au niveau des parois décorées, il faut s'interroger sur l'effet éventuel de modifications aux abords mêmes des parois. Ainsi le passage d'une forêt à grandes frondaisons vivant dans un milieu humide, à des arbres de taille moyenne n'offre plus, par exemple, la même protection aux effets de l'ensoleillement. Les conséquences éventuelles sur la conservation des peintures seront à apprécier. La protection des parois décorées doit passer par une phase d'appréhension du site dans son cadre environnemental naturel.

Références

1. Soares Meneses Lage M.C., *Etude archéométrique de l'art rupestre du sud-est du Piaui, Brésil*, Thèse de doctorat, Université de Paris 1, 1990, p 402.
2. Brunet J., Dangas I., Vidal P., Vouvé J., *La conservation de l'art des cavernes et des abris*, Section française de l'Institut International de Conservation, 1990, 32 p.
3. Clarke J., "Conservation and Restoration of Painting and Engraving Sites in Western Australia", in *Conservation of Rock Art*, ed. C. Pearson, I.C.C.M. (1977), pp 89–94.
4. Brunet J., Guillamet E., Vidal P., Plassard J., "Elimination de surcharges de tracés préhistoriques: quelques exemples de la grotte du Cro de Granville à Rouffignac (France)", *ICOM Committee for Conservation 10th Triennial Meeting Preprints* (1993), p 842–847.

(Rogers 2).$7H_2O$

Andrew Thorn
Artcare,
2 McCabe Place, North Melbourne, 3051, Australia

Abstract

The Rogers 2 art site, located in the south eastern tip of Tasmania has been studied to assess the deterioration mechanisms and to resolve appropriate interventions. This paper discusses the Environmental Survey and links it to mineral formations that have led to advanced deterioration at the site. The paper highlights the benefits of conducting both investigations simultaneously.

Keywords

Epsomite, hexahydrite, environment, condition survey, data logging

Introduction

This paper describes the microclimatic and condition survey conducted for 17 months at the Rogers 2 painted site. The objectives of the study were to assess the causes of deterioration, particularly the impact of salts, and to draw up a preservation policy. Through discussions with the Tasmanian Aboriginal Land Council (TALC) site management strategies have been formulated to minimise the impact of visitation by livestock and people.

It can be stated unequivocally that any Aboriginal site in Tasmania is of great cultural significance. As a painted shelter, Rogers 2 is one of only five known at this time in Tasmania (Cosgrove, 1989) and the only site yet found within the Pangem : Mair : Re : Mener tribal area.[1] The Rogers 2 site is important for modern indigenous Tasmanians as a place with tangible links to pre-European tribal existence.

The Rogers 2 paintings consist of three hand stencils applied to an inclined laminar rock sheet with two further painted motifs on an exposed vertical wall adjacent to the hand stencils. The shelter faces almost due west and opens to the North offering direct afternoon sunshine in all seasons. The shelter is dry and reasonably deep and is ideally suited to occupation. The nearby creek appears to flow for most of the year.

The shelter is approximately 60 m long with the paintings confined to an area of about 3 m in length. Three hand stencils are located on the underside of a detaching stone slab with two infilled motifs found nearby on a more exposed and stable surface. All painting is in red, presumably haematite, and a number of other stains in the rock may also be remnant painting, but look more like natural mineralization patterns.

Condition survey

The shelter and its environment were assessed in detail to help understand the causes of deterioration. The assessment has been undertaken, not only to determine the causes, but to provide sufficient information to confirm or deny the suppositions inevitably generated when one is confronted with an eroded surface. Factors such as wind erosion and water percolation, mentioned at almost every site, have been assessed together with sun movement and rainfall distribution.

Shelter stability

The Rogers 2 shelter presents an interesting array of mineralisation and erosion features. Two different mineral formations have developed within close proximity to the paintings. One of these is water insoluble, while the other appears to be a highly soluble efflorescence. Both have formed in abundance, but it is only the soluble mineral that has an impact on the stability of the stone.

Preliminary salts concentration measurements have shown the stone above the paintings to be heavily laden with soluble salts, concentrated on the more horizontal surfaces. Rain has the potential to blow into the shelter and wash the vertical surfaces. Sunshine can also enter the shelter and the accumulation of salts can be represented in the following manner:

Moisture ingress ⇒ stone penetration ⇒ salt dissolution ⇒ percolation crystallization

This is a cyclic process and its magnitude is determined by the surface angle. For a more horizontal surface the following factors increase:

- greater water retention due to less runoff;
- greater depth of penetration into stone;
- greater heating due to increased perpendicularity with the sun;
- faster drying therefore more crystallisation cycles.

The greatest threat in the shelter is to the stone slab supporting the three stencils. The panel on which the stencils occur is an inclined bed that has become partially separated from the underlying rock. Water can gain access to the open bedding plane, activating salts and dissolving clay minerals.

The paint itself is, by contrast, considerably more stable. There is some evidence of lost pigment but generally the images appear fresh and complete. The more obscure infilled motifs appear less clear, but this is due to mineralization processes rather than pigment loss.

Analysis

Analysis at the site has been limited to samples that will help resolve the deterioration mechanisms. Thus no pigments have been removed from the painting or crusts that may provide archaeological data.

Analysis of the mineral formations has been carried out using X-ray diffraction (XRD) and X-ray fluorescence (XRF). This combined approach left some uncertainty about the exact nature of the soluble salt. Micro-refractometry using a polarizing light microscope (PLM) was used to support the findings of the X-ray techniques.

The results of the analysis are summarized as follows.

Salts

- silica (SiO_2) nodules forming on the low ceiling of the shelter;
- clinozoisite ($Ca_2Al_3Si_3O_{12}(OH)$) forming on the vertical rear wall;
- hexahydrite ($MgSO_4.6H_2O$) or Epsomite ($MgSO_4.7H_2O$) forming on the more horizontal ledges.

Sandstone

A thin section was taken from a fallen piece showing some case hardening, typical of that found at the west end of the painted area. As the sample was prepared it progressively lost details and was not taken to completion. The section revealed a well sorted transparent rounded quartz with colour coming from interstitial iron minerals.

Throughout the sample aggregates of up to 5 mm comprise quartz grains presumably with iron or manganese coatings. These dark coatings are opaque and give the stone a spotted appearance in polished section. This spotted appearance is less apparent in the natural rock.

A detached fragment gathered from the floor proved far more informative and critical to an understanding of the weathering process. What could be seen in the loose specimen, but not in thin section, were sparsely distributed biotite clusters that seem to be the origins of the hexahydrite. These clusters were difficult to locate, being spaced up to 40 mm apart and it is not surprising that a random thin section did not include these isolated clusters.

To confirm the presence of biotite the loose sample was scanned under a stereo microscope and clusters removed to provide a concentrated sample for PLM analysis. This proved to be a great revelation as the concentrated sample showed the presence of tinsleyite attached to the biotite. The weathering process that leads to the presence of hexahydrite can thus be fully understood when all the minerals in the matrix are considered. The minerals present are:

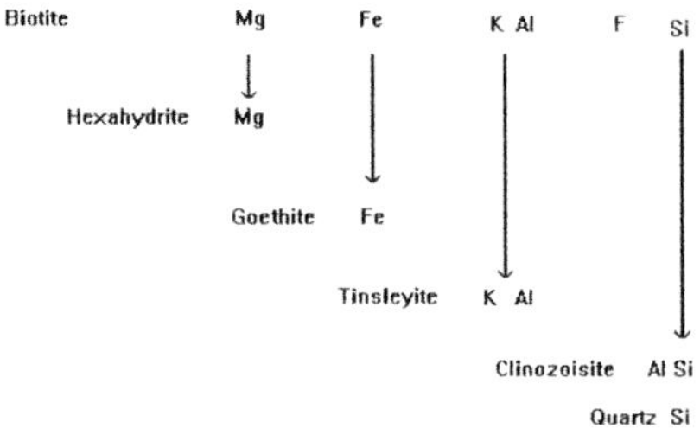

Figure 1. Weathering of biotite

- biotite $K(Mg,Fe)_3(Al,Fe)Si_3O_{10}(OH,F)_2$
- hexahydrite $MgSO_4.6H_2O$
- tinsleyite $KAl_2(PO_4)_2(OH).2H_2O$
- goethite $Fe^{+3}O(OH)$
- clinozoisite $(Ca_2Al_3Si_3O_{12}(OH))$

The weathering process has been summarized in Figure 1. The ions in the Biotite are listed with their occurrence in the resultant salts indicated by vertical arrows.

The minerals silica (Si) and fluorine (F) are significant in the weathering process. The extraordinary concentration of silica nodules on the underside of the low ceiling in the shelter may explained by the solubility that fluorine can have on silica. This has been outlined by Cortes and Martin on micaceous sandstone[2] and the influence of water on fluorine.[3] That research has shown, in summary, that fluorine in the presence of water will form hydrofluoric acid and dissolve silicon dioxide. If this information is considered in conjunction with Figure 3, showing evidence of flowing water through the stone it is reasonably clear that the Rogers 2 sandstone is prone to leaching by the combination of moisture and fluorine released during the breakdown of biotite. No evidence of fluorides has been found at the surface of the Rogers 2 shelter but these may be transformed during the migration to the surface or readily washed from the surface.

Hexahydrite has been studied in more detail as it is the salt causing deterioration of the surface supporting the paintings. The most important data is that pertaining to the moisture response of the salt and its water solubility: RH_{eq} (equilibrium relative humidity) = 86%; Water solubility = 600–800 g litre^{-1} (epsomite, 710 g litre^{-1}). These data indicate that hexahydrite is a moderately soluble salt being more soluble than halite. The Rogers 2 sample of hexahydrite ($MgSO_4.6H_2O$) was identified in the laboratory as epsomite ($MgSO_4.7H_2O$), a slightly more hydrated form, and presents a far more complex salts mechanism. Magnesium sulphate occurs in four different forms ranging from kieserite (monohydrate) through the two forms mentioned above to dodecahydrate ($12H_2O$). The RH_{eq}-dependent cycle of magnesium sulphate can be considered as follows:

$MgSO_4$ – 5% – kieserite – 23% – hexahydrite – 54% – epsomite – 87% – dodecahydrate

This can be superimposed over relative humidity readings at Rogers 2, as Figure 2 indicates. This figure shows that the relative humidity has fluctuated constantly through the RH_{eq} points of the three most hydrated forms. The excursion from epsomite to dodecahydrate occurred approximately 20 times every month while that from epsomite to hexahydrite was less frequent at half this number. It is interesting to note that the epsomite/dodecahydrate cycle was the only mecha-

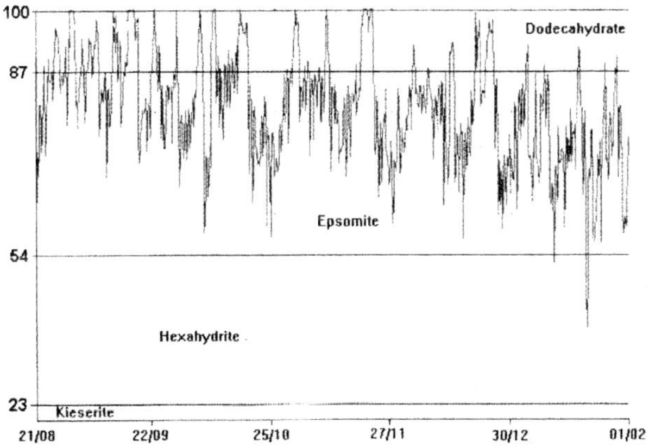

Figure 2. Relative humidity in summer

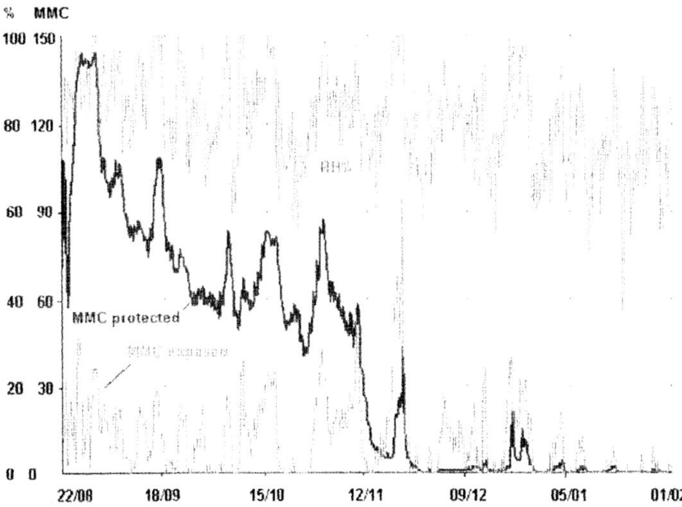

Figure 3. Moisture response

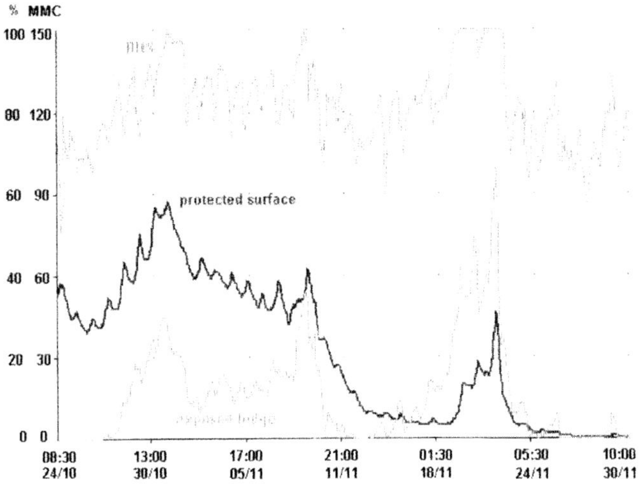

Figure 4. Detail view in November, from Figure 3

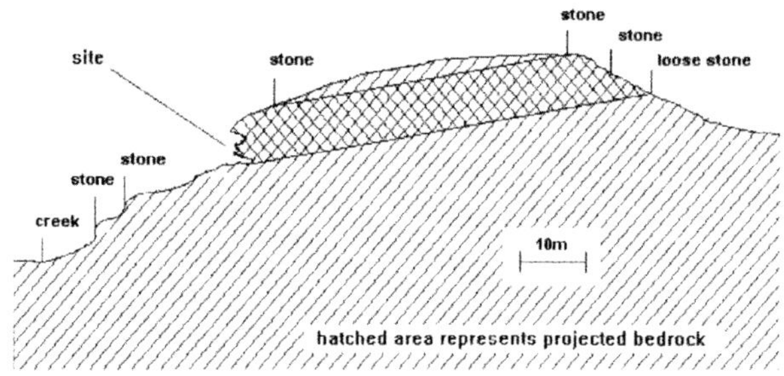

Figure 5. Section through the Hill

nism during spring with epsomite/hexahydrite cycles becoming more frequent into the summer.

Environmental study

Two data loggers were invisibly located at the site, comprising six data channels as follows:

channel
1 ambient temperature
2 ambient RH percentage
3 surface temperature, exposed position above paintings
4 surface temperature, protected position
5 surface moisture, exposed position
6 surface moisture, protected position

The probe pairs, i.e. surface temperature and surface moisture, are located in exposed and protected locations and referred to as such on all data logger graphs in this paper. Figure 8 shows the position of the protected and exposed moisture probes in relation to the moisture distribution across the surface, recorded on one day in February.

Figure 3 is among the most interesting data gathered from the site. It shows that both the exposed and protected surface respond to high relative humidity. The right-hand side of the graph shows a series of spikes that correspond almost exactly with air vapour saturation. The exposed surface has higher readings as a result of its exposure such that it could be wetted by rain.

Figure 4 shows a detail of the right-hand side of Figure 3, showing that the exposed surface dries out on several occasions. At every point where the 'exposed' curve rises from the base line the relative humidity is around 75 ± 2%. This hydration point is a common feature of sandstones studied by the author but is interestingly quite high.

Similar observations have been recorded at Manja Shelter, Grampians, but in that case the hydration point was much lower at 56 ± 3%.[4] The salt at Manja Shelter was halite, known to have an RH_{eq} of 75.3%. There is far less known about hexahydrite which has not been encountered at a rock art site before but found on buildings occasionally.[5–7] The RH_{eq} has been measured on a very small sample to be 86%. It can be expected that where a salt is abundant on the surface the rock moisture level will increase whenever the RH_{eq} is exceeded. In practice the actual point of deliquescence is lower than the RH_{eq}. Thus a halite-rich surface becomes moist at about 56% and it seems that at Rogers 2 the hexahydrite causes surface wetting at 75% RH.

The more interesting feature of Figure 3 is the left-hand side, showing the protected surface to be drying out from previously very high moisture levels. At the beginning of the monitoring in August the moisture level was much higher on the protected surface than on the exposed surface. The protected surface was in a

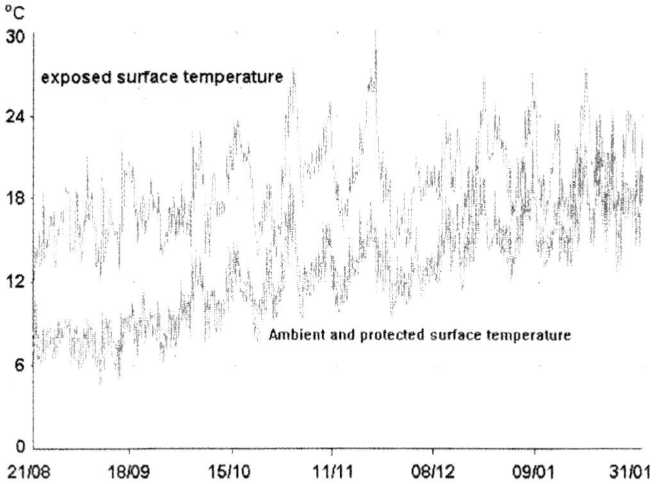

Figure 6. Temperature curves in spring

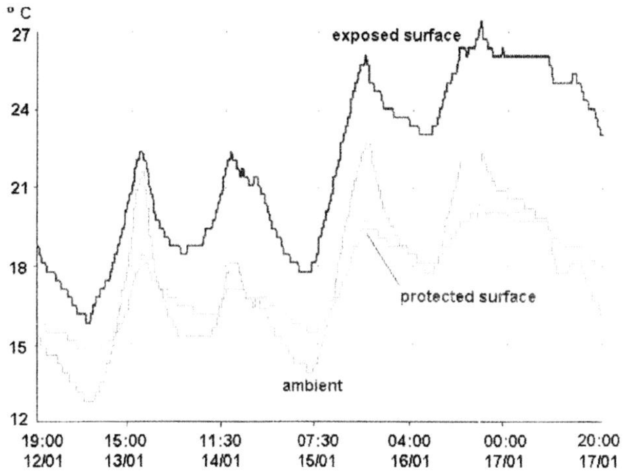

Figure 7. Condensation potential

drying phase, but did not reach the short-term fluctuation levels of the exposed surface until mid-November and dried out for the first time on 24 November.

It appears from the moisture pattern that there is considerable seepage through the hill arriving at the face some time in late winter to early summer. Figure 5 shows a section through the hill including six stone outcrops. A speculative rock band has been drawn (cross-hatched area) by connecting the first outcrop at the top of the hill with the outcrop above the shelter. A parallel line has been run from this to meet the bottom of the shelter which, coincidently, meets the lower outcrop on the hill.

Although this rock mass is purely speculative, it projects the probable water seepage path through the bedrock to the face of the shelter. Water falling on the hill would have a natural tendency to flow into the vicinity of the shelter. Discussion with the land holder[8] has determined that the slope above the site receives approximately 100 kg of super phosphate per hectare every year. This application rate deposits approximately 1.3 kg of fertiliser for every linear metre along the shelter. Not all of this is phosphate and much would be taken up by plants on the hill but is an obvious source of the anion in the tinsleyite alteration products.

Condensation

Figure 6 shows the general thermal trend from August through to the end of January 1993 and indicates the higher temperatures recorded on the exposed rock surface compared to both the protected surface and the air. It shows that the exposed temperatures are much higher than ambient in August and thus would guarantee that no condensation is possible during that period.

During August the exposed surface is generally 7–8°C warmer than the air at the coldest part of the night and up to 15°C warmer during the day. The protected surface on the other hand despite being slightly warmer during the night stays 1°C cooler during the peak of the day. There would therefore be a possibility of condensation on the protected surface during the day, but this is overshadowed on all surfaces by the deliquescent salt laden surface that absorbs moisture above 75% RH.

Figure 7 is a detail showing a few days in mid-January presenting the same pattern as the August figures. The sheltered surface falls 3–4°C below air temperature while the exposed surface is much warmer. When compared with the curves in Figure 3 it can be seen that during January both surfaces respond to moisture. The protected surface cannot receive rain, while the exposed surface cannot receive condensation and thus clearly salts play a large part in surface wetting. The wetting–drying cycles allow the salts to continually crystallize as discussed below.

Salts crystallization

Figure 3 shows that whereas the protected upper surface remains wet until late November the lower exposed surfaces dry out constantly. It is not possible to measure crystallization directly on the surface, but the drying as recorded by the

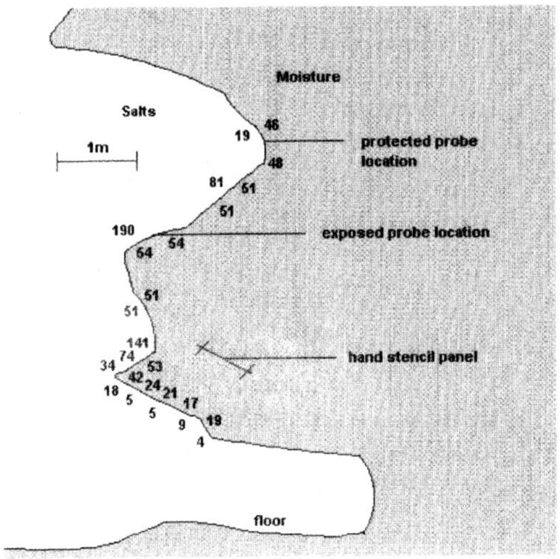

Figure 8. Salts and moisture distribution profile

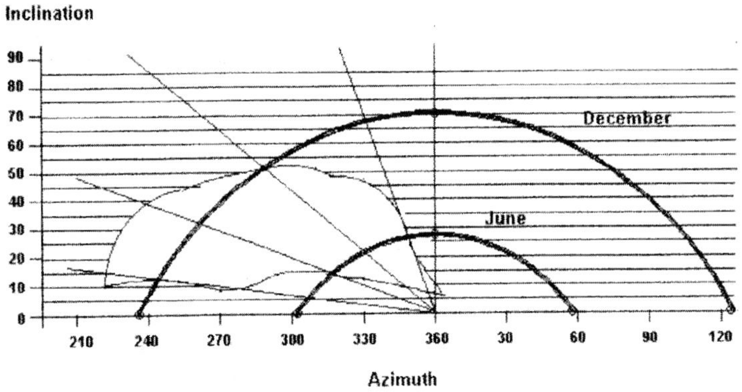

Figure 9. Solar window

data loggers gives a reasonable indication of this event. The loggers record saturation levels within the pores and thus when the curve reaches zero there is negligible moisture. If this is accepted as a reliable indication of crystallization, then it can be seen that for a large part of the year the upper surfaces will not permit salts crystallization while the exposed surface will undergo about 60 cycles per year. The sheltered surface would undergo about 20–30 cycles.

To support the logged data a survey of moisture and salts distribution was undertaken. The results have been summarised in Figure 8 showing that moisture is much higher in the upper shelter while salts accumulate on the more horizontal ledges. As explained from Figure 3 the protected surface receives moisture by infiltration from the slope above, the exposed section possibly from rain and both subject to salts hydration.

Only the underhangs of all surfaces do not have high levels of moisture. It is slightly fortuitous that the three hand stencils have been applied to such an overhang and have low moisture and salts levels. Although this is beneficial in the short term, the constant erosion to the surfaces above the paintings will eventually cause their loss. This is discussed further in later sections.

The salts distribution of Figure 8 is typical of that observed at different seasons. Of particular note are the high salts levels on the shelf immediately above the stencil panel. The salts levels were related very closely to the slope of the surface. The more horizontal surfaces had the highest readings while underhangs had very low readings.

High salts levels depend on two factors;

- Exposure to rain;
- Horizontal surfaces retained more moisture that penetrates more deeply into the stone. Subsequent evaporation produced more salts on the surface.

As a result of this synopsis protected surfaces have lower salts readings while the level on exposed surfaces increases depending on their horizontality.

Insolation

Insolation is an important contributory mechanism to a number of the processes discussed above. Figures 3, 4 and 6 all show the significant surface warming of exposed surfaces thus an understanding of the sun's movement throughout the year is essential.

The solar window diagram (Figure 9) shows the amount of sun entering the shelter throughout the year. The vertical axis marks the inclination of the sun (angle from the horizon) while the horizontal axis gives the azimuth (compass bearing). North is indicated by a vertical line at 360° and is taken as the position of the noon sun at its greatest inclination. The Shelter is shown as a thin unhatched closed shape in the centre left of the diagram. The shape of this solar window

Table 1. Insolation data

Solstice	Insolation arc		Azimuth		Time		Duration
	enter	exit	enter	exit	enter	exit	
December	36°	6°	288°	243°	3:30 p.m.	6:00 p.m.	2.8 h
June	67°	28°	348°	317°	1:00 p.m.	3:30 p.m.	2.3 h

represents the polar coordinates of the horizon and ceiling of the shelter. The outer azimuth bearings represent the opening and closing angles of the shelter ie 221° and 7°. The polar coordinates are determined by recording the inclination of the ceiling and horizon at 30° intervals along the azimuth.

The two heavy arcs represent the movement of the sun at the December and June solstices, specific for the site latitude, defining the outer extremities of its passage throughout the year. Where the sun's arc falls within the solar window, sunshine will fall onto the observation point in the shelter, in this case, the Stencil panel.

Although the diagram is complex and requires elaborate explanation, it enables the analyst to determine a number of important relationships between a surface and the sun. The following details have been extracted from the solar window diagram.

The hours of sunshine at the Rogers 2 latitude vary from 15.4 h in summer to 9 h in winter. The duration of sunshine in the shelter can be calculated as the entry angle minus the exit angle. The sun's travel per hour is calculated by dividing the azimuth travelled by the sunshine hours – 250/15.4 for summer and 120/9 for winter. In December it can be seen that the sun enters at 36° and exits at 6°. The azimuth position of the sun during the insolation period can be read off the x axis. Intermediate seasons fall within the solstice extremities for all dimensions. All of this information is presented in Table 1.

It can be seen from Table 1 that both the December and June insolation times are similar with December being 30 minutes longer. The main differences can be seen in the position of the sun during the insolation period. During summer the sun shines in the arc 288–243°, while in winter it comes in the arc 348–317°. This offers the opportunity to modify the thermal impact at the site by planting trees in the summer sector and leaving the winter arc as open as possible. This has the potential to reduce the drying cycles and thus minimize salts impact on the surface.

Conclusion

The deterioration of the Rogers 2 site is predominantly a result of the erosion of the sandstone caused by the interaction of the by-products of biotite weathering and the atmosphere. The pigment layer is relatively stable, as is typical of a haematite painting owing to its inherent physical and chemical stability.

As the biotite within the sandstone matrix deteriorates, it releases a range of ions including those forming the damaging salt magnesium sulphate. Other significant ions released from the biotite are fluorine that will combine with water to form an acid that dissolves silica. This fluorine-enriched water, which has been shown to flow through the stone has resulted in large nodules of amorphous silica forming in the shelter. While these are quite stable, hexahydrite accumulation over the surface is activated by moisture and the sun to provide a crystallization cycle leading to rapid deterioration.

The environmental study has shown that salts accumulate on the more horizontally inclined surfaces exposed to drying from the sun. The thermal study has shown that the zones of high salts concentration are warmed to levels considerably higher than either protected surfaces or the air, thus encouraging rapid phase changes with resultant erosion. Protected surfaces also contain salts at low levels but are more subject to water infiltration.

The salts action is serious because of its proximity to and noticeable impact on the painted areas of the site. The hand stencil panel, despite having very low levels of salts on the surface, has become almost completely detached from the parent rock through dissolution of bedding planes. This separation from the rock has prevented the migration of salts, but they will be accumulating in the fissures and accelerate the inevitable loss of the whole stencil panel. The surfaces above the stencil panel are also eroding quite rapidly and this erosion will reach a point where the parent rock has been completely removed from the stencil panel. This is a longer-term event, but one that needs to be controlled now.

The solid motif panel varies from the stencil panel in that it is exposed to direct sun and possibly rain but is formed on a case-hardened surface. This case hardened surface is approximately 2 cm thick but is beginning to be undermined by salts action in the softer stone beneath it.

Animals seem not to have had a major impact on the site, but one visit from a disinclined person could result in the loss of the hand stencils. Floor activity is confined to soft-footed animals with no evidence of cattle or goats entering the shelter during the research period.

Acknowledgements

The Rogers 2 Microclimatic Survey and Condition Report has been made possible through a grant from the Australian Institute of Aboriginal and Torres Strait Islander Studies through their Rock Art Protection Program. This grant has been administered by Parks Wildlife and Heritage in Hobart. The Tasmanian Aboriginal Land Council have approved and supported the project and have since acquired the land surrounding the paintings.

References

1. *Koorie Boogaja: A Map of Key Aboriginal Tribes* (Melbourne: Aboriginal Advancement League, 1971).
2. V. Cortes and A. Martin, 'The Effects of Atmospheric Pollution by Fluorides on Stone Alteration. I. Siliceous Materials. (Paper delivered at Deterioramento e Conservazione della Pietra: 3° Congresso Internazionale, Venezia, 1979), 1–12.
3. V. Cortes and A. Martin, 'The Effects of Atmospheric Pollution by Fluorides on Stone Alteration in Monuments. III. The Enhancing of the Deterioration Actions by water and Other Natural Agents. (Paper delivered at Deterioramento e conservazione della pietra: 3° Congresso Internazionale, Venezia, 1979), 23–24.
4. A. Thorn, 'The Control of Salts Damaging to Rock Art' (Second unpublished report to the Australian Institute of Aboriginal and Torres Strait Islander Studies, Canberra, 1992).
5. A. Arnold 'Nature and Reactions of Saline Minerals in Walls' (Paper delivered at The Conservation of Stone II, Bologna, 1981), 13–24.
6. R.R. Waller, 'The Prevention of Deliquescence, Efflorescence and Hydration in Mineral Specimens' (Paper delivered at Seventh Triennial Congress of the International Council of Museums Committee on Conservation, Copenhagen, 1984), 84.13.8.
7. A. Arnold, 'Determination of Mineral Salts from Monuments', *Studies in Conservation* 29, no. 3 (1984): 129–138.
8. D. Rogers, Titleholder to the land containing the Rogers 2 site, has farmed the land for the past 20 years and taken a close interest in the protection of the site.